G000138726

BRITANNICA
BOOK OF MUSIC

BRITANNICA BOOKS

editor	Frank Gibney
executive editor	Benjamin Hadley

ENCYCLOPAEDIA BRITANNICA, INC.

chairman of the board	Robert P. Gwinn
president	Charles E. Swanson

Britannica Books

BRITANNICA
BOOK OF MUSIC

edited by Benjamin Hadley

consulting editors
Michael Steinberg
George Gelles

DOUBLEDAY/BRITANNICA BOOKS
DOUBLEDAY & COMPANY, INC.
GARDEN CITY, NEW YORK

Library of Congress Cataloging in Publication Data

Main entry under title:

The Britannica book of music.

(Britannica books)
1. Music—Dictionaries. 2. Music—Bio-bibliog-
raphy. I. Hadley, Benjamin.
ML100.B848   780′.3

ISBN: 0-385-14191-2
Library of Congress Catalog Card Number 79-7195

copyright © 1980 by Encyclopaedia Britannica, Inc.
ALL RIGHTS RESERVED
PRINTED IN THE UNITED STATES OF AMERICA

Designed by Betsy Beach

9 8 7 6 5 4 3 2

staff for *The Britannica Book of Music*

editor	Benjamin Hadley
assistant editor	Susan S. Goodfellow
editorial assistant	Mary Hunt
production	Elizabeth Chastain
	Mary Berry

FOREWORD

"Musick is one of the seven sciences commonly called liberal; and is comprehended also among the mathematical, as having for its object discrete quantity or number, but not considering it in the abstract like arithmetick, but in relation to time and found, in order to make a delightful harmony: Or it is the art of disposing and conducting sounds considered as acute and grave; and proportioning them among themselves, and separating them by just intervals of pleasing to the sense."

So begins the article on music in Britannica's first edition, dated 1771. That was the year of Haydn's Six Quartets of his Opus 17 and his Symphony No. 42; Mozart was a 15-year-old prodigy, touring Italy and composing in Salzburg; Beethoven was only an infant. Over the decades since then, as the Britannica grew in scope and size, that original article expanded a thousandfold. The world's great experts on music discussed the intricacies of Renaissance polyphony, Japanese court music, and Schoenberg's 12-tone row. Some of these articles were monuments of their kind, such as Sir Donald Francis Tovey's memorable works on musical forms and his biographies of the great composers or Vaughan Wil-liams' article on folksong. Most yielded to revisions, as music felt the impact of modern musicological research.

From the wealth of material on music in its past editions, as well as newly-commissioned materials, our editors have produced this convenient Book of Music designed for the student who would like to learn more, the scholar interested in related fields, and, above all, the music lover who would like one volume that is compact and authoritative to tell him at a glance everything he needs to know about a particular musical subject. Our coverage, although comprehensive, has been carefully selected, with an aim not merely to give names and dates, but to answer the intelligent questioner on most musical subjects. As the Britannica authors in 1770 concluded, it is "the business of every searcher into nature to contemplate the things themselves, and to make the best use of such discoveries as offer themselves towards the further improvement of science."

FRANK GIBNEY, vice chairman
Board of Editors
Encyclopaedia Britannica

BRITANNICA
BOOK OF MUSIC

A

Abbado, Claudio (b. June 26, 1933) Educated at the Milan Conservatory and the Vienna Academy, the Italian conductor Claudio Abbado won the Koussevitzky Prize in conducting (1958) and the Mitropoulos Prize (1963). He was conductor at the Teatro alla Scala in Milan (1968–76; musical director from 1972), principal conductor of the Vienna Philharmonic (from 1973), and conductor of the London Symphony (from 1979). He divides his time almost equally between the opera and the concert hall; his repertoire is eclectic.

Abduction from the Seraglio, The: *see* CLASSICAL PERIOD (vocal music, 1750–1800); JANISSARY MUSIC; MOZART (later life); OPERA (developments in the 18th century); SINGSPIEL.

Abel, Karl Friedrich (December 22, 1723–June 20, 1787) The German composer and viola da gamba virtuoso Karl Friedrich Abel performed in Dresden (1748–58) before going to England, where he established his reputation even though the viola da gamba was by then nearly obsolete. Upon the arrival in England of Johann Christian Bach in 1762, the two musicians established the "Bach and Abel" concerts, at which were heard the first English performances of many of the symphonies of Haydn. Proficient on several instruments, he composed 40 symphonies, harpsichord concertos, and chamber music for strings. He played a six-string viola da gamba in the English style instead of the seven-string instrument preferred on the Continent.

Abravanel, Maurice (b. January 6, 1903) Greek born and Swiss reared, the conductor Maurice Abravanel began his career as choirmaster at the Municipal Theater in Zwickau. He conducted opera in Paris (debut 1932), Berlin, Rome, Mexico, Australia, and at the Metropolitan Opera (1936–38) in New York City, after which he led Broadway musicals for several seasons. In 1947 he became musical director and conductor of the Utah Symphony, retiring in 1979, and since 1954 has directed the Music Academy of the West in Santa Barbara, California. Abravanel has encouraged and premiered much contemporary music. Of his more than 60 recordings with the Utah Symphony, the cycles of Mahler and Brahms symphonies have been highly praised.

a cappella A designation for unaccompanied choral music, originally associated with church music (therefore, the Italian "in chapel style"), particularly that of Palestrina and his era. Recent scholarship shows that such music often included instruments either doubling or substituting for vocal parts.

accent An emphasis on certain notes or chords that clarifies rhythm and shape of phrase. Accents normally occur on the downbeat of each measure (actually it is the accent that determines where the measure begins) and are called metric accents. Accents may be placed elsewhere in the measure for harmonic or other structural emphasis or to make a rhetorical point. Accents on normally unaccented beats may produce syncopation. A tonic accent is one achieved by raising the pitch, an agogic accent by lengthening a note.

acciaccatura An ornamental note in late Baroque keyboard music, usually struck simultaneously with a chord and released immediately. It is notated as an ordinary note and is usually the lower second. More than one may occur in the same chord. The term is often used erroneously for a short APPOGGIATURA.

accidental A sign placed to the left of a note to show that the note must be changed in pitch. A sharp (♯) raises a note by a semitone; a flat (♭) lowers it a semitone; a natural (♮) restores it to the original pitch. Double sharps (×) and double flats (♭♭) indicate that the note is raised or lowered by two semitones. A single natural cancels a double sharp or flat; a natural next to a sharp or flat (as ♮♯) cancels half of a double sharp or flat. Sharps or flats placed at the beginning of a musical staff show the tonality, or key, of the music and are not considered accidentals. Other, but not yet standardized, signs indicate the raising or lowering of a pitch by an interval smaller than a semitone.

Accidentals were first applied to the note B by about the 10th century. To fulfill certain theoretical and aesthetic rules, B was sometimes flatted, and later F was sometimes sharped. At first there was no sign for a natural; a sharp (written ♯ or ♮) cancelled a flat, a flat cancelled a sharp. By the late Renaissance, E♭, A♭, and C♯ were fairly common. Accidentals applied to all notes became increasingly common in music of subsequent periods.

accompaniment A term signifying an auxiliary part or parts of a composition designed to support the principal part or to throw it into relief. In secular medieval music and early folk music, instrumental accompaniments for singers consisted of unison or octave reduplications, novel rhythmic features, or a primitive type of harmony in the form of a drone or sustained notes on wind or stringed instruments. In the 16th century solo songs were sung with simple harmonic or contrapuntal lute accompaniments, notably those of John Dowland and the French *airs de cour*. With the introduction of the FIGURED BASS at the beginning of the 17th century, the art was gradually developed of harmonic accompaniments improvised at the harpsichord or organ and based on chords that the composer indicated by figures. By the 18th century these improvised accompaniments—designed to support either a soloist (as in the sonatas and solo cantatas of Bach) or an instrumental ensemble (as in the operas of Alessandro Scarlatti)—demanded from the performer a high degree of ornamental and contrapuntal invention. The accompaniment thus assumed a role as important as that of the soloist.

The term obbligato accompaniment was applied to this form, as opposed to ad libitum accompaniment, a term used for the optional reduplication of a part or unessential ornamentation performed on another instrument. Obbligato accompaniments were sometimes written out, Bach being especially given to this practice. Eighteenth-century composers sometimes wrote sonatas for keyboard with accompaniment for violin, flute, etc., but this was often a convention of labeling more than an indicator of compositional practice.

The obbligato style persisted in both the solo and the concerted works of the Romantic composers where accompaniments became even more elaborate and expressive. The expressive resources of the piano allowed the accompaniments of Schubert to illustrate pictorial or psychological aspects of the texts of his lieder. His example was followed in the lieder of Schumann, Brahms, and Hugo Wolf. Piano accompaniments in works for stringed or wind instruments acquired the status of a concerted part. Orchestral accompaniment, which in the 18th century had hardly exceeded chamber-music proportions, was greatly developed in the Romantic concerto and in songs or song cycles with orchestra by numerous composers from Berlioz to Berg and Britten.

The art of the piano accompanist flourished chiefly in response to the demands in the 19th century of the German lied and the French *mélodie*. Qualities of poetic and musical insight and of ensemble playing distinguish the piano accompanist's art, which resembles the art of performance in chamber music. Accompanists such as Coenraad van Bos and Gerald Moore developed the art by their sensitive attitude to the soloist and by their power to interpret the composer's intention. Both Moore and van Bos have written valuable books on the art of the accompanist.

Acis and Galatea: *see* HANDEL; ORATORIO (Handel).

Adam, Adolphe-Charles (July 24, 1803–May 3, 1856) The French composer Adolphe-Charles Adam is remembered chiefly for his *Cantique de Noël* and music for the ballet *Giselle,* which, although not distinguished in its own right, is efficient and effective. He entered the Paris Conservatoire in 1817 as an amateur, but he became a pupil and close friend of François Adrien Boieldieu. A prolific composer and a victim of his own facility, he wrote more than 60 operas, of which the best are *Le Postillon de Longjumeau* (1836) and *Giralda* (1850). His ballets, subordinating music to choreographic demands, were written for production in London, Berlin, and St. Petersburg as well as Paris, where the success of *Giselle* (1841) led to its inclusion in the repertoires of most ballet companies ever since. Adam left two posthumous volumes of informative memoirs.

RECORDINGS: Ballets *Diable à quatre* and *Giselle.*

Adam de la Halle, called Adam le Bossu, or Adam the Hunchback (*c.* 1240–1285/88) The French trouvère and composer Adam de la Halle is most remembered for his dramatic pastoral *Le Jeu de Robin et de Marion* (*The Play of Robin and Marion,* Eng. trans. in Richard Axton and John Stevens, *Medieval French Plays,* 1971). It was written for the French court in Naples while he was in the service of Robert II d'Artois. A number of monodic pieces and polyphonic motets and rondeaux also survive.

RECORDINGS: *Le Jeu de Robin et de Marion.*

additional accompaniment   A 19th- and 20th-century practice of enlarging and revising the orchestration, particularly of 17th- and 18th-century works. The justification was that the increased size of performing groups and larger performing spaces required additional instrumentation, but most arrangers did more than just add parts. Handel was perhaps the chief victim, most famously in his *Messiah,* which for more than a century and a half was usually heard with layers of beautiful but wrong-headed "improvements" by Mozart and muddy ones by Ebenezer Prout. Mozart himself was the beneficiary of Grieg's additional accompaniments to several of his piano sonatas. Bach suffered as well, as did Gluck, at the hands of such "arrangers" as Mendelssohn, Robert Franz, and Wagner. Baroque style has been increasingly understood in the 20th century, and the practice has diminished. *See* ARRANGEMENT.

Admeto: *see* HANDEL (life).

Aeolian harp   A stringed musical instrument usually hung outdoors, where it can catch the wind, and so-called from Aeolus, god of the winds. It consists of a wooden sound box, usually about three feet long, five inches broad, and three inches deep (91 by 13 by 8 centimeters) with raised ends into which are fixed tuning- and hitch-pins and between which are loosely stretched 10 or 12 catgut strings, usually tuned in unison. These vary in thickness and therefore in elasticity, and the play of the wind causes them to vibrate in aliquot parts; *i.e.* (the fundamental note not being heard), the half or octave, the third or interval

of the twelfth, the second octave, and the third above it; in fact, the upper partials of the strings in regular succession.

The principle of the natural vibration of strings by the pressure of the wind has long been recognized. According to legend King David hung his *kinnor* (a kind of lyre) above his bed at night to catch the wind, and Dunstan of Canterbury was charged with sorcery for producing sounds from a harp by allowing the wind to blow through its strings. Athanasius Kircher constructed such an instrument and described it in his *Musurgia universalis* (1650). It became popular in Germany and England during the Romantic movement, and models were made by the poet Robert Blomfield, author of a pamphlet about them (*Nature's Music,* 1808). There have been attempts to construct keyboard instruments on this principle, using bellows-fed wind: J. J. Schnell's Anémocorde (Paris, 1789) and Isouard's Piano éolien (Paris, 1837) are among them.

Aeolian harp
The Mansell Collection, London

Aeolian mode   The first of the four additions by the 16th-century Swiss theorist Henricus Glareanus to the eight medieval church modes. Its general range comprises the eight natural notes from the A below middle C to the A above, a pattern identical to the minor scale. Melodies in Aeolian, or Mode IX, usually have A as the *finalis,* or final note, and C as the *tenor,* or reciting note.

In ancient Greek music Aeolian was one of several names for the scale pattern, or octave species, conventionally represented in modern writings as A-A.

aerophone A class of instruments in which a vibrating mass of air produces the initial sound, including woodwind, brass, and free-reed instruments and those that fall into none of these groups such as the bullroarer and siren. Aerophone replaces the term wind instruments in an acoustically based classification. *Compare* CHORDOPHONE; ELECTROPHONE; IDIOPHONE; MEMBRANOPHONE.

affections The doctrine of the affections, also known under the German term *Affektenlehre,* is the theory of musical aesthetics widely accepted by late Baroque theorists and composers, embracing the proposition that music is capable of arousing a variety of specific emotions within the listener from the use of the proper standard musical procedure or device. The devices and their affective counterparts were rigorously catalogued and described by such 17th- and 18th-century theorists as Athanasius Kircher, Andreas Werckmeister, Johann David Heinichen, and Johann Mattheson.

Mattheson is especially comprehensive in his treatment of the affections in music. In *Der vollkommene Capellmeister* (1739) he notes that joy is elicited by large intervals, sadness by small intervals; fury may be aroused by a roughness of harmony coupled with a rapid melody; obstinacy is evoked by the contrapuntal combination of highly independent (obstinate) melodies.

The contemplation of the emotional aspect of music is not limited to the Baroque era but may be found throughout the history of music. It is an essential part of ancient Greek musical theory (the doctrine of ethos), and it takes on a particular importance in the Romantic movement of the 19th century. It was in the Baroque era, however, that theorists, influenced by the Enlightenment's tendency toward the rigid, encyclopedic organization of all knowledge, attempted to delineate music into stereotyped affective categories.

Africaine, L': *see* MEYERBEER.

African music Africa falls musically into two main areas separated by an east-west line running south of the Sahara and Ethiopia.

North of this line the music is predominantly Arabic; south of it is found what is called African music—the music of the Negroid peoples. In spite of the different language families represented by the large number of tribes (more than 2,000), the music of this huge area is fundamentally homogeneous, and its chief characteristics are: (1) Spontaneous creation; while the tune and words of a song or the drumming for a dance will keep within the traditional pattern of melody or rhythm, they are not crystallized in a standard form but are modified at each rendering by the creative genius of the performers; this modification is not an embellishment but a fundamental principle of the system, which may be defined as "free creation around a traditional framework." (2) A melody tied to the rise and fall of speech in the tonal languages, where the meaning of words depends on the pitch at which each syllable is spoken; in such cases the course of a melody cannot be dictated solely by musical principles but must (to preserve the word sense) move generally up and down in conformity with the spoken word, a powerful inhibiting factor to development of musical form. (3) Limited harmonic development. (4) Exceedingly complex rhythmic structure.

rhythmic system The essence of the African rhythmic system is tension. In Western music the accents of a melody usually coincide with time beats (indicated by a baton or a handclap), but in African music they normally must not do so. The melodic accents are in free rhythm (yet in repetitions always falling in the same places), and although the melody itself is tied to the claps—which may be either a regular beat or an irregular short pattern constantly repeated—the claps do not determine the rhythm.

The principle of rhythm in drumming is different. Here tension is attained by a deliberate staggering of the main accented beats of the several drums. To state the matter at its simplest: if two drums were to beat in triple time, the main beats of the second drum would fall on the second or third beat of the first drum's bar—never on its first beat. In addition the various drums may be playing in different meters, thus further staggering the main beats (*e.g.,* 3 against 2; 4 against 3). But this is not necessarily the case; in practice, where three drums are used, the small drum beats a simple duple or triple pattern while the master drummer, playing the big drum, has in each different kind of dance five or six fairly long standard patterns in free rhythm, the accents of which lie athwart those of the small drum. Using one of the patterns as a basis, the master drummer plays spontaneous variations on it with great virtuosity, modifying them to suit the style of individual dancers. Meanwhile the middle drum gives standard replies to the master drum, the accents of which also cross those of the small drum. Thus a full dance, which is both the norm and the flower of African music, is a complex interweaving of melodic and rhythmic patterns with their inherent accents in a constant state of tension.

use of harmony Both vocal and instrumental forms of simple harmony or heterophony are found, though some tribes restrict themselves to unison. This heterophony is usually in the form of organum and is either in parallel thirds or in fourths or fifths. The groups favoring the one or the other are mutually exclusive, though there are a few borderline tribes that use both. There is reason to think that the thirds tradition is of Indonesian origin; it is met with in pockets in the Malay archipelago and notably on the island of Madagascar, while in Africa it seems to have started on both east and west coasts and to have spread inland.

instruments African musical instruments (a great variety of drums, xylophones, strings, horns, flutes, and idiophones), even if of primitive appearance, often exhibit a considerable musical precision, although it is necessary to distinguish between an instrument as it leaves the craftsman and as it is later modified by indifferent performers. Functionally instruments may be classified according to whether they are used for community occasions, for solo playing or solo accompaniment, or for the performer's own pleasure. In areas where Islamic influence is felt, such as the lake regions of Uganda, in the northeast part of Zaire, and in Nigeria, stringed instruments are prominent.

Among the Chopi in Mozambique, where the xylophone is paramount, drums play a minor role. The Venda of South Africa use a flute ensemble for some dances. All these instruments are used for communal dances, but usually the drums—with rattles and often iron clapperless bells—are the main communal instruments.

Of special interest are the *sansa* (known also as the *mbila,* or *mbira,* and the Kaffir, or thumb, piano) and the xylophone. The former consists of a calabash resonator with a small soundboard on which is mounted a tuned series of metal or bamboo prongs that are played by the thumbs, the instrument itself being supported by the fingers of both hands. The *sansa* has not been found in any other part of the world; yet its distribution in Africa is similar to that of the xylophone with which it sometimes shares the name *mbila* and to which it is similar in tuning. The African xylophone has two characteristic tunings: equitonal heptatonic and equitonal pentatonic.

Close parallels with the African xylophone in tuning and pitch are found in the xylophones of Thailand and Cambodia (for heptatonic) and in those of Java (for a modified heptatonic scale known as *pelog* and also for the pentatonic *slendro* system). Recent research suggests that Africa may owe a large musical debt to Indonesian colonization.

relation to tribal life Music is of the very fiber of African tribal life. It is an essential part—and not an adornment—of religious ceremonies. It is integrally associated with the events of the life cycle (birth, marriage, and death), with initiation (for which special music is learned), and with serious illness (when the patient must be induced to dance to the music). It is closely associated with royalty; the chiefs' own court orchestras, and their movements are accompanied by music. It is the universal spur to protracted work, and here the rhythms of work are deftly exploited: pounding grain, paddling canoes, hoeing the fields, and drilling rock in the copper mine are all accompanied by singing, while even the operation of a European sewing machine is turned into a rhythmic pattern. Communal recreation must have music: folk tales are interspersed with songs in which the chorus is sung by the audience; a "beer-drink" has singing and dancing; and the most common recreation for the whole village is to gather for drumming, singing, and dancing. But in addition to this communal aspect, music—instrumental or vocal—is a form of individual delectation. One sings or plays to oneself just for pleasure. Music thus plays a part in African life that is vital both to society and to the individual. African music proliferates without any conscious theoretical system, depending entirely on creative musicianship within traditional practice.

modern developments After about 1920 there developed all over this area a new type of music—part Western, part African—derived from the spread of popular U.S. dance music heard on phonograph records and from four-part Western harmony learned in schools and churches. Basically this music is Western in rhythm (usually in common time) and in harmony (the most usual chordal sequence being triads on tonic—subdominant—dominant—tonic constantly repeated), but as time passes the melody tends to become more and more African. It is played on Western dance band instruments, particularly the guitar and the accordion, though occasionally (*e.g.,* in Ghana) indigenous instruments or their substitutes are used (for instance, a wine bottle struck with a spoon in place of an African iron bell and wooden striker). This hybrid music, which has tended to replace the traditional forms at least in urban areas, has a great urge; new musical forms in this idiom and new modifications of it appear every few years.

BIBLIOGRAPHY: A. M. Jones, *African Music in Northern Rhodesia and Some Other Places,* rev. ed. (1958), *Studies in African Music,* 2 vols. (1959), *African Rhythm* (1961), and *Africa and Indonesia* (1964); Percival R. Kirby, *The Musical Instruments of the Native Races of South Africa* (1953); J. H. K. Nketia, *African Music in Ghana* (1962); Rose Brandel, *Music of Central Africa: An Ethnomusicological Study* (1969).

afterdance (German, *Nachtanz*) In European late-medieval and Renaissance dance, the second and livelier of two dances customarily performed together (*e.g.,* pavane and galliard; *basse danse* and saltarello). Its melody was often a variation in meter and tempo of the first dance melody.

Agazzari, Agostino (December 2, 1578–April 10, 1640) A prolific Italian composer, Agostino Agazzari is best known for his short treatise *Del sonare sopra al Basso con tutti li stromenti e dell'uso loro nel Conserto* (1607; facsimile edition 1933), one of the earliest instruction books for performing from figured bass. The treatise is particularly important because in it he distinguishes between melody and fundamental instruments and thus recognizes that, whereas usually in Renaissance music all voices of a composition had been equally important, in Baroque music a new and significant concept was being developed—the polarity of the upper and lower parts, with neutral improvised inner parts. He held various church appointments and wrote music in both the old and the new styles.

Agricola, Alexander (1446?–1506) One of the leading composers of the late Burgundian polyphonic school, Alexander Agricola was born in the Netherlands and was educated there. It is known that he was in the service of Charles VIII of France, leaving it for that of Lorenzo de' Medici. He was at the court in Milan by January 1472 until June 1474 and was *petit vicaire* at the cathedral of Cambrai in 1476. He was appointed chaplain and chanter to Philip I the Handsome of Burgundy, whom he accompanied to Spain. Of his masses and motets the *Missa in die pasce* and the motet *Regina coeli* are highly esteemed.

Agricola, Martin, real name, Martin Sore, or Sohr (January 6, 1486?–June 10, 1556) The German composer, teacher, and writer on music Martin Agricola was one of the first musicians to concern himself with the needs of the Reformed churches and to publish musical treatises in the vernacular. Much of the German musical vocabulary that he invented is still in use, and his books give a valuable picture of the musical life of his time, particularly his descriptions of early 16th-century instruments. He was self-taught, called to music "from the plough" as his chosen surname suggests. He worked in Magdeburg from about 1520 until his death. Most of his unpublished compositions are lost, but his printed volumes include a good deal of functional sacred music and many instrumental pieces that are transcriptions of vocal part-songs.

Aichinger, Gregor (1564–January 21, 1628) The German composer of church music Gregor Aichinger may have been a pupil of Orlando di Lasso before taking holy orders and becoming organist to the family of Jakob Fugger at Augsburg from 1584. He visited Italy in 1584–87 and Rome again in 1599–1600. His music is chiefly choral and ecclesiastical, to Latin words, and shows a conservative taste influenced by the Venetian school of composers, especially Giovanni Gabrieli. His motets were well known and frequently appeared in contemporary collections.

Aida: *see* OPERA (the 19th century); ROMANTIC PERIOD (non-German music of the 19th century); VERDI.

air A term that in general signifies a tune or song and hence a type of music in which the upper, or melody, line predominates.

The French *air de cour* ("court song") was a short strophic song for one or more voices with lute or harpsichord accompaniment developed in the late 16th and 17th centuries. The name became common after its use in a collection by Adrian Le Roy and Robert Ballard, *Livre d'airs de cour* (1571). The texts were usually love poems in stylized language.

In suites after about 1700 the air was an instrumental movement of melodic character, such as in Bach's orchestral Third Suite. *Compare* AYRE.

Alain, Marie-Claire (b. August 10, 1926) The French organist Marie-Claire Alain was educated at the Paris Conservatoire and began in 1955 appearing as a recitalist. She was associated with the summer organ institute at Haarlem, The Netherlands, from 1956. Her recordings have won the Grand Prix du Disque 10 times; she specializes in playing early French music, Bach, and the works of her brother, Jehan Alain (1911–40).

alba: *see* AUBADE.

Albéniz, Isaac (Manuel Francisco) (May 29, 1860–May 18, 1909) One of the leaders of the Spanish nationalist school of musicians,

Isaac Albéniz appeared as a piano prodigy at the age of four in Barcelona and at seven in Paris. Too young for admittance to the Paris Conservatoire, he went to Madrid to study, only to run away when he was nine. He embarked for Costa Rica, played throughout the United States, and returned via England to become a pupil at the Leipzig Conservatory at the age of 14. Returning to Spain without funds, he was fortunate in obtaining a royal grant enabling him to study in Brussels. In 1878 he fulfilled a long-held ambition by going to Budapest for lessons from Liszt, whose influence on his style was considerable. He toured extensively as a virtuoso, often playing small romantic pieces of his own, among them *Córdoba* and his well-known *Tango*. He then settled down to teach in Barcelona and Madrid.

Isaac Albéniz
courtesy, Biblioteca Nacional, Madrid

Not until 1890 did Albéniz take composition more seriously, when he came under the influence of Vincent d'Indy and Paul Dukas (and later Debussy). The following year the English banker Francis Burdett Money-Coutts offered Albéniz a handsome allowance if he would set to music some of Money-Coutts's poetical dramas. First, however, came the production in London of the comic opera *The Magic Opal* (1893; libretto by Arthur Law). The subjects of Money-Coutts's texts were not very congenial to Albéniz, but he wrote the three-act *Henry Clifford* (Barcelona, 1895), *Merlin,* the first of a projected Arthurian trilogy, and his first real stage success, *Pepita Jiménez* (Barcelona, 1896).

Albéniz developed Bright's disease (eventually to prove fatal) and after 1900 spent most of his time in Spain, where he worked at the Arthurian opera cycle and continued to write copiously for the piano. It is on his music for that instrument that his fame rests, particularly *Iberia,* a collection of 12 scenes of Spanish (mainly Andalusian) life, written during 1906–09, colored by the rhythms and harmonies of Spanish popular music but highly virtuosic and complex in texture.

RECORDINGS: *Cantos de España, Iberia, Navarra,* Suite *española* (all originally for piano but often transcribed for orchestra).

Albert, Eugène (Francis Charles) d' (April 10, 1864–March 3, 1932)   Known as the "little giant," the British-born German pianist and composer Eugène d'Albert was considered one of the great Beethoven interpreters of his day. Educated in England, he became a pupil of Liszt in the master's last days. Later d'Albert aggressively rejected all that was English and thought of himself as completely German. Liszt called him the "young Tausig" and described him as "an extraordinary pianist." Though thought of as a strong all-around pianist and proclaimed successor to Liszt, in the early 1900s he turned increasingly to composition, and his earlier prowess at the keyboard dimmed. He was a prolific composer, and his output included 21 operas, of which *Tiefland* (1903) still has some currency; also two piano concertos, a violin concerto, a symphony, chamber music, and piano solos. He was married briefly (1892–95) to another important pianist, Teresa Carreño.

RECORDING: Piano Concerto No. 2 in E Major.

Albert, Heinrich (July 8, 1604–October 6, 1651)   The composer of a famous and popular collection of songs, German-born Heinrich Albert was a cousin of Heinrich Schütz, with whom he studied composition at Dresden before taking a course in law at Leipzig, where his musical studies were encouraged by Johann Hermann Schein. In 1627 Albert moved to Königsberg (now Kaliningrad, U.S.S.R.), where he was appointed cathedral organist (1631) and published works from 1632. Albert composed numerous festival pieces for the Brandenburg princes but is best known for his *Arien,* published by himself between 1638 and 1651. These settings of sacred and secular texts form the most characteristically German song collection of the 17th century. He also has a place in the early history of German opera; the scores have not survived, but two pieces from *Cleomedes* occur among the *Arien.*

Alberti, Domenico (*c.* 1710–*c.* 1740)   The Venetian singer, harpsichordist, and composer Domenico Alberti is remembered primarily for the "Alberti bass," a familiar if little esteemed formula of keyboard accompaniment consisting of gently moving arpeggios in the left-hand part. It is unlikely that he actually invented the figuration, but his set of eight sonatas makes extensive use of it. A pupil of Antonio Lotti, he also wrote three operas.

Albinoni, Tommaso (June 8, 1671–January 17, 1750)   The Venetian composer Tommaso Albinoni is remembered chiefly for his instrumental music. The son of a wealthy paper merchant and of independent means, he described himself as a *dilettante veneto* ("Venetian amateur"), although he was a fully trained musician and at one time held a professional post as chamber musician to the Duke of Mantua. Little is known of his life except for the production (1694–1740, mainly at Venice) of his 48 operas.

As well as many vocal works, now forgotten, Albinoni published nine sets of instrumental works, which achieved wide popularity: two of his themes were used as subjects for fugues by Bach. Several have been republished during the 20th century. Especially notable are the *Sinfonie e concerti a 5* (Op. 2, 1707), the Concertos for solo violin (Op. 5, 1710), and the Concertos for one and two oboes in Op. 7 and Op. 9. His instrumental compositions, marked by intelligence and energy, are cousin to those of Vivaldi.

RECORDINGS: *Concerti a cinque* (Op. 5); Concerti grossi; Concertos for flute, oboe, and trumpet; *Sinfonie e concerti a 5* (Op. 2); Sonatas for flute and harpsichord and for violin and continuo.

Alboni, Marietta (March 6, 1823–June 23, 1894)   The only pupil of Rossini, the Italian contralto Marietta Alboni toured widely and achieved her greatest success in England between 1847 and 1858. Her voice had great beauty and precision and more predictability than that of many of her contemporaries. Possessed of a wide, even vocal range, she sang roles that included Amina in Bellini's *La Sonnambula* and on one occasion the baritone Don Carlo in Verdi's *Ernani.* She performed many Rossini roles (her Paris debut in 1847 was in *Semiramide*), and she premiered Daniel François Esprit Auber's *Zerlina,* which was written for her.

alborada: *see* AUBADE.

Albrechtsberger, Johann Georg (February 3, 1736–March 7, 1809)   The Austrian organist, composer, and theorist Johann Georg Albrechtsberger was the teacher of Beethoven. He studied organ and figured bass with Leopold Pittner and became one of the most learned and skillful contrapuntists of his time. From 1755 to 1766 he held various posts as organist, and in 1772 he was appointed deputy court organist in Vienna. From 1793 until his death he was Kapellmeister at the Stephansdom. His fame attracted many pupils, among them Beethoven, who recommended him to Czerny and Ferdinand Ries, Johann Nepomuk Hummel, Joseph Weigl, and others. Most of his compositions, which include many religious and chamber works, remain in manuscript. His main theoretical work was *Gründliche Anweisung zur Komposition* (1790). A collection of his theoretical writings was edited by his pupil, Ignaz Ritter von Seyfried (3 vols., 1826; Eng. trans. *Methods of Harmony, Figured Bass, and Composition,* 1834). A selection of his instrumental music was published in 1909.

RECORDINGS: Concertos for harpsichord, organ, five instruments, and harp.

Alceste: *see* CLASSICAL PERIOD (vocal music, 1750–1800); GLUCK; LULLY; OPERA (developments in the 18th century).

aleatory music or **chance music** (from Latin *alea,* "dice")   Music in which chance or indeterminate elements are left for the performer to realize. The term is a loose one, describing compositions with strictly demarcated areas for improvisation according to specific directions and also unstructured pieces consisting of vague directives, as "Play for five minutes."

Performers may be told to arrange the structure of the piece—*e.g.,* by reordering its sections or by playing sections simultaneously as they wish. The musical score may also indicate points where performers are to improvise or even to include quasi-theatrical gestures. Such requirements may give rise to inventive notation, including brackets enclosing a blacked-out space, suggesting pitch area and duration of the improvisation.

Among notable aleatory works are *Music of Changes* (1951) for piano and *Concert for Piano and Orchestra* (1958) by the U.S. composer John Cage and *Klavierstücke XI* (1956) by Stockhausen of West Germany.

"Dice music" was known in the 18th century, with a well-known example attributed to Mozart called *Musikalisches Würfelspiel* (1806). It contains first measures, second measures, etc., from which progressions are determined by a throw of dice. Johann Philipp Kirnberger wrote on the subject, and there are similar publications attributed to Carl Philipp Emanuel Bach and to Haydn.

Another kind of chance music is a technique of composition called STOCHASTIC MUSIC, originated by the 20th-century Greek composer Yannis Xenakis. In this technique large contours of the composition are worked out, but details are left to chance.

Alkan, real name, Charles Henri Valentin Morhange (November 30, 1813–March 29, 1888)   A child prodigy from a family of musicians, the French pianist and composer Alkan won first prize in piano at the Paris Conservatoire at the age of 10 and was an established virtuoso by age 17. Except for a brief stay in London (1833), he remained in Paris, teaching and living in seclusion. Although he wrote chamber music, he is best remembered for piano works on an extravagant scale as well as for études and for short, programmatic, dramatic, and sometimes macabre pieces that have been compared to the music of Berlioz.

RECORDINGS: Études (piano); Piano Trio in g minor.

allemande A 16th-century processional couple dance in duple time that became in the 17th century a standard first movement of the suite. By Bach's day it was usually in ¼ time with continuous movement of sixteenth notes. The word *allemande* is French for German. In the *Fitzwilliam Virginal Book* (*c.* 1620) English spellings are *alman* and *almayne*.

Allen, Hugh Percy (December 23, 1869–February 20, 1946) The English musician Hugh Allen Percy exerted a far-reaching influence upon the musical life of his time, especially in education. He received his early training at Chichester as an articled pupil of Frederick Read and at Cambridge, where in 1892 he became organ scholar at Christ's College. Appointments as organist at Ely Cathedral (1898) and New College, Oxford (1901), led to his appointment (1919) as director of the Royal College of Music in London. As conductor of the Bach choirs in Oxford (from 1901) and London (1907–20), he did much for English choral music, particularly by the performance of Bach's works and those of Hubert Parry and Vaughan Williams. In 1918 he became professor of music at Oxford, a position that enabled him to persuade a conservative university to admit music to its proper position in the curriculum and to make more adequate provision for research and teaching. These developments had wide influence elsewhere. Allen's studies in the music of Heinrich Schütz and Bach, though unpublished, stimulated musicians and scholars. He was knighted in 1920.

BIBLIOGRAPHY: Cyril Bailey, *Hugh Percy Allen* (1948).

Almenräder, Karl (October 3, 1786–September 14, 1843) The German bassoonist, instrument maker, and composer Karl Almenräder was principally self-taught. He served as a bandmaster in the Prussian militia from 1815 to 1817, when he became principal bassoonist in the theater at Mainz; there he made his major contribution to the development of the bassoon, the invention of an improved 15-key instrument. In 1820 he went to Cologne and established a workshop for the manufacture of flutes and clarinets. He wrote bassoon duets, works for bassoon and strings, and a *Pater noster* for chorus and orchestra. His bassoon method, still in use, was first published in 1841.

Alpine Symphony: *see* ROMANTIC PERIOD (20th-century transition); STRAUSS, RICHARD.

Also sprach Zarathustra: *see* PROGRAM MUSIC (problem of form); STRAUSS, RICHARD; SYMPHONIC POEM.

alto The female voice of low range often called contralto. The word is Italian for "high" and originally referred to the highest male voice, now usually called COUNTERTENOR. In standard four-part vocal writing, alto is the second highest part. Alto is also French for viola, a trap for translators; victims include C. K. Scott Moncrieff, who put Marcel Proust into English.

Amahl and the Night Visitors: *see* MENOTTI; OPERA (the 20th century).

Amati Celebrated Italian violin makers, the Amati family worked their craft in Cremona in the 16th and 17th centuries.

Andrea (*c.* 1520–*c.* 1578), the founder of the Cremona school of violin making, was perhaps originally influenced by the work of slightly earlier makers from Brescia. His earliest known violins are dated about 1564. In essentials they set the style for all the models made by later members of the family and, with the modifications introduced by ANTONIO STRADIVARI, for the modern violin. Andrea, like his descendants, made violins in two sizes, the larger of which later became known as the "grand Amati." He also introduced the characteristic amber varnish.

His two sons **Antonio** (*c.* 1550–1638) and **Girolamo (Hieronymus)** (1551–1635) worked together until the latter's death and are known as the brothers Amati.

Nicolo (September 3, 1596–August 12, 1684), the son of Girolamo, was the most famous of the family. He produced instruments notable for beauty of workmanship and tone and was the master from whom Stradivari and Andrea GUARNERI, among others, learned their craft. He was succeeded by his son **Girolamo** (February 26, 1649–February 27,

1740). Although the instruments made by him are as fine as those of his father and grandfather, they suffered in comparison with those made by Stradivari.

The great contribution of the Amatis was their evolution of the flat, shallow model, which, as improved by Stradivari, proved the fittest to survive in modern concert conditions because of the brilliant soprano tone.

Ambros, August Wilhelm (November 17, 1816–June 28, 1876)   The Austrian musicologist August Wilhelm Ambros is best known for his history of music. Of German-Bohemian parents, he was educated both in the law and in music, entering the Austrian civil service in 1840 and also establishing himself as a brilliant writer on music. His pamphlet *Die Grenzen der Poesie und der Musik* (1856; *The Boundaries of Music and Poetry,* 1893), answering Eduard Hanslick's *Vom musikalisch Schönen* (1854; *The Beautiful in Music,* 1891), was an important contribution to a heated aesthetic controversy. He was an early champion of Berlioz. In 1869 he became professor of music at Prague, and in 1872, with a post in the Ministry of Justice in Vienna, he was also made a professor at the Vienna Conservatory.

His main work is the comprehensively planned *Geschichte der Musik.* He published three volumes (1862–68); two more were compiled from his notes by C. F. Becker and G. Nottebohm (1878; revised by Hugo Leichtentritt, 1909) and by Otto Kade (1882), who also enlarged and revised the third volume (1893). Wilhelm Langhans produced a continuation up to the 19th century in two volumes (1883–86).

Ambrosian chant   The term for the kind of PLAINCHANT sung in the Diocese of Milan and the churches under its influence, which in the Middle Ages reached as far as Bavaria. It is still used in Milan and by some churches in Lugano and the Swiss canton of Ticino.

It was introduced probably by Auxentius, a Cappadocian who was Bishop of Milan (355–374) and came from Antioch. According to St. Augustine, Auxentius' successor St. Ambrose made use of the Syrian practice of singing in alternating choirs but adapted it in a special way. When he and his followers were besieged in their church by the armies of the Arian empress Justina, he raised their spirits by teaching them to sing psalms "in the oriental manner." From his own account it may be deduced that the whole congregation joined in the singing of strophic hymns and in responding to each verse of the psalm by a refrain taken from the first line. This way of singing soon spread to all the churches in the West. St. Ambrose was long considered to have introduced the chant that bears his name; though this is no longer thought to be so, he is still accepted as the author of some of the Latin metrical hymns known as Ambrosian hymns.

Adherence to Ambrosian chant and to the use of the Ambrosian liturgy by Milan churches was often challenged, notably by Charlemagne, who attempted to discourage, indeed to destroy, all music and ritual not in conformity with the Roman practice. Many of the chants were, however, gradually adapted to, or replaced by, Gregorian melodies. As no manuscripts containing Ambrosian chant earlier than the 12th century are extant, it is impossible to estimate how much of what survives has the character of the chant in its original form. It may be assumed that the *ambitus,* or range, of the Ambrosian melodies is smaller than that of Gregorian chant proper, that the texture is looser, and that a definite preference for the interval of the fourth (as opposed to the Gregorian fifth) is noticeable. There are, however, some melodia, obviously of a later date, consisting of a number of freely recurring melodic phrases, indicated by roman numerals (*e.g.,* I II III IIII V III IIII V III IIII). Such structure and numbering is a feature of Ambrosian chant. These melodies may represent forerunners of the sequence melodies or later imitations.

Ameling, Elly (b. February 8, 1938)   The Dutch soprano Elly Ameling studied voice in Rotterdam with Jo Bollenkamp and in Paris with Pierre Bernac, winning competitions in 's-Hertogenbosch (1956) and Geneva (1958). Though she made her opera debut in 1973 as Ilia in *Idomeneo,* she is known primarily as a concert singer, her singing of Bach, 19th-century lieder, and Fauré being especially esteemed. She is a prolific recording artist.

Amore dei tre re, L': *see* MONTEMEZZI.

ancient music The world's ancient civilizations fall approximately into seven regions, each of which has, despite internal differences and interconnections, certain distinctive musical traits. These regions are: (1) Egypt (Old, Middle, and New Kingdoms); (2) west Asia (Sumerian, Babylonian, Hebrew, Hittite, Phoenician, Iranian, Arabian); (3) Europe (Minoan, Hellenic, Etruscan, Latin, Orthodox Christian, Celtic Christian, pre-Christian Scandinavian); (4) India (Indo-Sumerian; Hindu); (5) northeast Asia (Chinese to the end of the Sung dynasty, A.D. 1297, Korean, Japanese); (6) southeast Asia (Khmer, Indo-Javanese); and (7) Central America and the Andes (Mayan, Aztec, Inca).

ancient attitudes High civilization has always brought with it an elevated concept of music as an art. This art has drawn upon a background of folk and tribal music for its raw materials, but the molding influence of ideas has been paramount. All early civilizations saw their ideal music as an image of cosmic order and its practice in temple ritual and court ceremonial as a means of helping to maintain or reflect universal harmony. From such a philosophy stem the age-old concepts of the efficacy of numerical proportions in musical sound; the ethos (magical effect) of particular modes; the music of the spheres; and the musical foundation of the state. Such ideas, steadfastly maintained throughout the ages, made for very conservative traditions of music whose fundamental patterns changed little over long periods of time and in certain cases persisted far into historical times.

ancient theories Alongside its music philosophy, to which it was related through a symbolism of numbers, each of the seven regions had a distinctive theory of music. The Mesopotamian, Egyptian, and Central American music theories are unfortunately no longer extant, although some features are open to inference, and southeast Asian theory is as yet little known. Extensive material survives, however, from northeast Asia (Chinese, Japa-

nese), India, west Asia (Arabian, Persian), and ancient Greece, which passed on so much to medieval Europe. The several known theories indicate distinct preferences for different aspects of the musical language. The Chinese (Chou dynasty, c. 1122–256 B.C.) and the Pythagorean Greeks, for instance, divided sound geometrically (the former constructing a cycle of fifths); on this basis the Chinese rationalized their principal or five-note scale (a scale known also in Central America) and the Pythagoreans their seven-note scale. India (taking the octave as the starting point) and west Asia and early Europe (taking the fourth) considered sound harmonically in accordance with the divisions of a stretched string and, in the main, favored a seven-note scale. The people of southeast Asia appear to have tended toward the principle of division by roots and the systems of equal temperament that this implies in both five-note and seven-note forms.

ancient forms Since the ancients made no use of harmony in the modern sense, their music sought a fine balance of melody, rhythm, and timbre. But in modern times the tracing of authentic ancient melody presents many problems. Traditions that, like those of China, claim a fabulous antiquity for certain surviving tunes must be treated with the greatest reserve, for the earliest actual surviving Chinese notation is as late as the T'ang dynasty (A.D. 618–906). True, some very ancient notations are still extant: *e.g.,* some chironomic signs on Egyptian tombs (Old Kingdom), a single hymn on a Sumerian tablet (*c.* 800 B.C.), fewer than 20 late Greek fragments (none earlier than the 2nd century B.C.), and a few signs in the Dead Sea scrolls having all the appearance of a musical notation. But most of the transcriptions are controversial. In fact scholars, since they are not able to hear the actual music of antiquity, were long confined to speculating about it until the Jewish cantor and ethnomusicologist Abraham Zevi Idelsohn (1882–1938) indicated a new possibility. This scholar proved the essential identity of various versions of Jewish chant surviving in different communities that had lived in isolation since Solomon's temple fell to Nebuchadrezzar in 586 B.C., and he further demonstrated a link with Christian Gregorian chant. Indeed in the second half of the 20th century, the growing use of the comparative method and the harvests gathered by the tape recorder brought a new perspective to the study of archaic survivals.

Ancient poetry also provides important clues, since ancient melody was usually designed to heighten the expression of words. Sanskrit poetry has always been metrical (patterns of long and short feet), and its meters underlie India's system of measures in music. The psalms sung in Solomon's temple, on the other hand, had a freely accentual basis, the poetic lines having a fixed number of stress accents and a varying number of syllables. This poetry, approximating prose, thus called for melody patterns that could be freely varied in length and stress. Chinese poetry, again different, is syllabic, its line comprising a chosen number of monosyllables whose meaning depends upon their total organization. The linguistic and poetic unit, the monosyllable without meter or dynamic accent, found its musical counterpart in the single note; although the result was naturally rather static rhythmically, the resulting tonal relationships encouraged the development of melody in song. Ancient Greek poetry combined both tonal and metrical elements and preserved a close relationship between music and words; though dating only from the 2nd century B.C., the first Delphic hymn, a poem in the cretic meter, is beautifully matched by a melody in ⅝ time.

The verse structures of the ancient Egyptians, Babylonians, and Hebrews lent themselves to antiphonal singing, a pattern found in Christian psalm singing in modern times. Their flexible nature called for an adaptable musical unit like the Oriental melody type— a musical idea with special melodic and rhythmic contours. Such it seems were the Sumerian *sir* and Greek *nomos* and the melody types of the Babylonians and Hebrews; the Indian *raga,* Persian *dastgah,* and Arabic *maqam* provide living examples. While these systems show many differences in material and mode, they normally use segments of seven-note scales, finely graduated intervals, melisma, rhythmic variety, simple heterophony, and sometimes (in India as in ancient Persia)

an accompanying drone. By contrast the Far East, demanding greater tonal clarity in speech, has always preferred larger intervals, five-note scales, some modulation, and a square rhythmic framework; the clarity was offset, however, by a complex system of polyphony, which was prevalent there much earlier than in Europe. From what can be inferred of the music of Central America, it is likely to have had affinities with the music of the Far East rather than that of Persia, the Arab countries, or India.

Whereas the solo voice was favored above instruments in India and west Asia, choral singing has seemed natural to Europe ever since its great popularity in ancient Greece and Crete. Solo instrumental performances have, on the other hand, always graced China and Japan, while the combination of large numbers of instruments in concert is characteristic of China and perhaps even more of the countries of southeast Asia, especially Indonesia.

ancient instruments   The knowledge of ancient instruments comes from literary and pictorial records and from archaeological finds. Certain instruments of Stone Age origin are shared by many civilizations, especially percussion (rattles, rasps, stampers, xylophone, Jew's harp, primitive drums) and wind instruments (bullroarer, primitive flutes, ribbon reeds, shell trumpets). The instruments of the Maya and Aztec cultures, which emerged directly from primitive societies, add little to this list, though the Incas knew the panpipe as well.

Stringed instruments, notably few in Stone Age societies (musical bow, ground harp, ground zither), emerge with the dawn of civilization especially in Egypt and west Asia from the 3rd millennium: arched harp, angle harp, lyre, long lute, short lute, and—in Phoenicia and China about 1100 B.C.—the zither. The ancients did not, however, know the use of the bow on the string; their techniques embraced plucking, rubbing, and numerous other methods.

Important early wind instruments include the shawm (west Asia), double reed-pipe (Egyptian Old Kingdom), reed mouth organ *sheng* (Chinese Chou dynasty and southeast

Asia), and, perhaps rather later, the cross flute (Etruria, China, and India).

Among percussion instruments drums assumed many new forms and became important particularly in India, while the bell was known early in China (early Chou dynasty), the cymbals in Egypt, India, and the Holy Land, and later the gong on the borders of Burma and Tibet. Stone chimes and bell chimes originated in China (Chou dynasty), and struck bamboo instruments were elaborated in southeast Asia.

Most modern instruments have ancestors in ancient civilizations, and it became apparent in the 20th century just how much Western musical tradition owes the civilizations that have gone before. *See also* BYZANTINE CHANT; CHINESE MUSIC; GREEK MUSIC, ANCIENT; INDIAN MUSIC; JAPANESE MUSIC.

BIBLIOGRAPHY: Carl Engel, *The Music of the Most Ancient Nations* (1864; reprint, 1909); John Stainer, *The Music of the Bible*, new ed. (1914; reprint, 1970); Francis W. Galpin, *The Music of the Sumerians . . . Babylonians and Assyrians* (1937); Curt Sachs, *The History of Musical Instruments* (1940) and *The Rise of Music in the Ancient World, East and West* (1943); Egon Wellesz, *Ancient and Oriental Music* (1957), Vol. 1 of *The New Oxford History of Music;* Eric Werner, *The Sacred Bridge* (1959); Peter Crossley-Holland, *The Pelican History of Music*, Vol. 1 (1960).

Anda, Géza (November 19, 1921–June 13, 1976)   A pupil of Ernst von Dohnányi at the Academy of Music in Budapest, the Hungarian-born pianist Géza Anda made his home in Switzerland after World War II. His repertoire featured works by Bartók and by Mozart.

Anderson, Marian (b. February 17, 1902)   A pioneer in overcoming racial discrimination, the U.S. contralto Marian Anderson began singing in a Baptist church in Philadelphia at the age of six. In 1925 she was selected from among 300 contestants to appear as soloist with the New York Philharmonic, after which she spent 10 years studying and singing in Europe. Prohibited from singing in Constitution Hall in Washington, D.C., because of her race, she performed instead on the steps of the Lincoln Memorial to an audience of more than 75,000, thereby increasing public

Marian Anderson
courtesy, ICM Artists, Ltd.

awareness of existing prejudice. Principally a recitalist, she was the first Black to sing at the Metropolitan Opera in New York City (1955), where she portrayed Ulrica in one performance of Verdi's *Un ballo in maschera,* the only operatic role she ever sang. Her voice was that rare thing, a genuine deep contralto, and her repertoire included oratorios and lieder, and especially the music of Bach, Handel, Mahler, Sibelius, and spirituals. Her autobiography, *My Lord, What a Morning,* appeared in 1957.

André, Maurice (b. May 21, 1933)   The French trumpeter Maurice André was educated at the Paris Conservatoire and was appointed a professor there in 1967. He made his debut in 1954 and has appeared as soloist with leading orchestras throughout the world, specializing in Baroque and 20th-century works. He has recorded most of the important trumpet concertos.

Andrea Chénier: *see* GIORDANO; VERISMO.

Anerio, Felice (*c.* 1560–September 27, 1614) A master of sacred polyphony, Felice Anerio (brother of Giovanni Francesco Anerio) was born in Rome and became one of the boy singers of Sta. Maria Maggiore (1568–75), later singing at St. Peter's under Palestrina. By 1584 he had become maestro di capella of the English College in Rome, from where he was called (1594) to succeed Palestrina as composer to the papal chapel. It is probable that he held that post until his death. A composer of many motets, psalms, masses, and other choral works, Anerio was a staunch follower of the school of polyphonic sacred music embodied most fully in Palestrina to the point that several of his compositions were attributed to that master.

Anerio, Giovanni Francesco (*c.* 1567–June 1630) One of the leading Roman composers of his day, Giovanni Francesco Anerio wrote both in the Palestrina style and the "new" style (especially in his secular works). He sang with his brother, Felice Anerio, as a boy soprano at St. Peter's in Rome (1575–79) and became *maestro di capella* at the Church of St. John Lateran in 1600. He held a succession of similar posts for the remainder of his life, broken only by a period (probably about 1606–07) as court musician to Sigismund II of Poland.

RECORDINGS: Oratorios *Conversione di S. Paolo* and *Vivean felici.*

Angeles, Victoria de los, real name, Victoria Gómez Cima (b. November 1, 1923) Known for the beauty of her voice and maturity of her interpretations, the Spanish soprano Victoria de los Angeles studied at the conservatory in Barcelona and made her stage debut there at the Teatro Liceo in 1946 as the Countess in *Le nozze di Figaro* (Mozart). Her eclecticism was foreshadowed in 1949–50, when she sang operas of Gounod in Paris, Puccini in London, and Richard Strauss in Italy, all with great success. She made her Metropolitan Opera debut in 1961 in Gounod's *Faust,* the same year that she sang Elisabeth (Wagner's *Tannhäuser*) at Bayreuth. Her wide range ac-

Victoria de los Angeles
courtesy, Herbert H. Breslin, Inc.
photograph, Christian Steiner

commodates the contralto coloratura roles of Rossini, and she is celebrated for her interpretations of Spanish songs.

Anglebert, Jean Henri d' (1628?–April 23, 1691) Probably the greatest of the 17th-century school of French harpsichord players and composers before François Couperin le Grand was Jean Henri d'Anglebert. A pupil of Jacques Champion de Chambonnières, he succeeded his master in 1664 as harpsichordist to Louis XIV. His *Pièces de clavecin avec la manière de les jouer* (1689) include arrangements of airs from Lully's operas, 22 variations on "La Folia," and original suites. He also wrote for the organ and a theoretical work, *Principes de l'accompagnement.* His son Jean Baptiste Henri succeeded his father in his court appointment and was, in turn, succeeded by Couperin le Grand.

RECORDINGS: *Pièces de clavecin.*

Anglican chant A simple harmonized setting of a melodic formula devised for singing prose versions of the psalms and canticles in churches of the Anglican Communion.

The formula is made up of a reciting tone

and middle and final cadences much like the PLAINCHANT psalm tones from which Anglican chant is derived. When John Marbeck published the *Booke of Common Praier Noted* (1550), he used the first seven psalm tones for the canticles and Tone VIII for the psalms. Like Marbeck various English composers used the psalm tones in their polyphonic psalm settings, placing them in the tenor part measured (*i.e.,* with a regular metrical pattern). The harmonic style of these polyphonic settings is probably derived from the continental *falsobordone* style, which also employed the plainchant psalm tones but in the topmost voice. *See* FAUX-BOURDON.

When the Restoration of the monarchy was effected in 1660 and choirs and organists returned to their posts, a great need was felt for cathedral choral service settings. Thus plainchant harmonizations again appeared as in James Clifford's *The Divine Services and Anthems Usually sung in Cathedral and Collegiate Churches of the Church of England* (1664). By the end of the 17th century, composers began to write their own melodies, using the recitation note and the cadences of the psalm tones as a framework but omitting the psalm tone's intonation. In the 18th century if a psalm tone melody was used, it was placed in the upper part.

After the Oxford Movement (promoting a reorientation toward Roman Catholic liturgy) began in 1833, parish churches expressed the desire to have choral services, formerly sung only in cathedrals. To facilitate congregational singing, about 1838 a method was developed called pointing, a system of signs that point out how a text is to be fitted to a given chant.

Animuccia, Giovanni (*c.* 1500–March 25, 1571) The Italian composer Giovanni Animuccia is remembered chiefly for his collaboration with St. Philip Neri, for whose popular services in the Roman oratory of S. Girolamo he wrote a number of *Laudi spirituali.* These performances probably had an influence on the later development of the oratorio.

Animuccia was one of the first to simplify the structure of early 16th-century church music. Though he was a prolific master of the traditional Flemish style, handling canon and cantus firmus with great fluency, his later taste

for short, clear-cut forms, syllabic melody, and homophonic declamation points toward Palestrina.

Like his brother Paolo (d. 1563), also a composer, Animuccia was born in Florence. In 1555 he became choirmaster of the Julian chapel at St. Peter's in Rome (succeeding Palestrina), where he remained until his death in 1571 (whereupon Palestrina resumed the post). He published three books of madrigals (1547, 1551, 1554) and a mixed volume with some motets (1548) in Venice, and in Rome books of masses (1567), Magnificat (1568), madrigals, motets, *Madrigali spirituali* (1565), and two *Laudi* (1563, 1570). Many sacred compositions remain unpublished.

Ansermet, Ernest (November 11, 1883–February 20, 1969) Founder and conductor of l'Orchestre de la Suisse Romande (1918–67), the Swiss conductor Ernest Ansermet was originally a mathematician. But he was also trained in music, studying with Ernest Bloch, Arthur Nikisch, and Felix Weingartner. A conductor of the French tradition, Ansermet

Ernest Ansermet   *Wide World Photos*

was engaged by Sergey Diaghilev for his Ballets Russes (1915–23), where he conducted premieres of ballets by Stravinsky, Ravel, and de Falla. He was an opponent of Stravinsky's late music and that of Schoenberg and his circle, publishing a book (1961) against serial composition and tonal disintegration.

Antes, John (March 24, 1740–December 17, 1811) Amateur composer and Moravian missionary, his father having been founder of the Moravian congregation in Bethlehem, Pennsylvania, U.S.-born John Antes was sent in 1769 as the first U.S. missionary to Egypt. Leaving Egypt in 1781, he went to England by way of Vienna, where an undocumented legend claims that he was befriended by Haydn. In 1801 he invented a device for turning pages of music by means of a pedal on a mechanical music stand, and a letter dated 1806 suggests improvements in the manufacture of violin pegs and bows and in piano hammers. An apprentice watchmaker, he constructed three violins prior to his departure for Egypt (one of which still exists). His known compositions consist of Three Trios for two violins and cello (written in Cairo and dedicated to the Swedish ambassador to Constantinople), 25 anthems, and 13 chorales. His autobiography, written in German, was published in English in 1811 as *Extract of the Narrative of Our Late Dear and Venerable Brother John Antes, Written by Himself.*

RECORDINGS: Three Chorales; Three Trios for two violins and cello.

Antheil, George (July 8, 1900–February 12, 1959) The U.S. composer George Antheil was known for the ultramodern music he wrote in the 1920s. He studied with Bloch in New York City, and in 1921 he went to Europe and played piano recitals. In Paris he became prominent in the literary and artistic circles of the avant-garde; Ezra Pound published a book about him, *Antheil and the Treatise on Harmony* (1924; with supplementary notes, 1927). His *Ballet mécanique,* scored for mechanical pianos, automobile horns, electric bells, and airplane propellers, was a sensation in Paris (1926) and in New York City's Carnegie Hall. His later works were less eventful; he wrote six symphonies; chamber music; the operas *Transatlantic* (1930), *Helen Retires*

(1934), *Volpone* (1953), *The Brothers* (1954), and *The Wish* (1955); several film scores; a murder mystery, a study of the role of glandular disorders in the etiology of criminality, and an inventive autobiography with the eloquent title *Bad Boy of Music* (1945).

RECORDINGS: Symphony No. 4; Violin Sonatas.

anthem A choral composition with English words, an optional part of the Anglican morning and evening services and of many other Protestant services that is analogous to the Roman Catholic MOTET. The term is derived from the Greek *antiphona,* through the Saxon *antefn,* a word that originally had the same meaning as antiphon. The anthem has been developed in England as a free type of musical composition since 1545. Its text is often biblical, but there are numerous examples of the use of other texts.

The musical resources needed for the performance of an anthem have never been standardized: at first unaccompanied choral writing (full anthem) was the norm, but the growth in the 16th century of the verse anthem (which made extensive use of a solo vocal part and eventually of many soloists) encouraged the use of instrumental accompaniment. The organ was clearly the first choice for this subsidiary though frequently important part, but there were many verse anthems provided with an elaborate accompaniment for an instrumental group such as viols or wind instruments. Shortly after the Restoration it was common, at least in the royal chapel, to perform anthems with orchestral accompaniment. In the 1700s the organ returned to favor, and the full anthem replaced to some extent the complex verse anthem, though solo passages were occasionally introduced for special effect.

Both full and verse anthems exploited the practice of antiphony between two sides of a choir, usually referred to as *decani* (the south, or dean's side) and *cantoris* (the north, or precentor's side). The alternation of these two sections of the choir, and those subsections specially designated in the more elaborate verse anthem, provided a subtle effect of fluctuating timbre and sonority that often reflected the mood or sense of the text. In the

19th and 20th centuries not only church music composers but those whose main activities lay in other spheres have written anthems for use (to quote *The Book of Common Prayer*) "in choirs and places where they sing." *See* CHURCH MUSIC.

BIBLIOGRAPHY: Myles B. Foster, *Anthems and Anthem Composers* (1901; reprinted 1970); Denis W. Stevens, *Tudor Church Music* (1955; reprinted 1973); Elwyn A. Wienandt, *Choral Music of the Church* (1965), and with Robert H. Young, *The Anthem in England and America* (1970); Edmund H. Fellowes, *English Cathedral Music*, rev. ed., Jack A. Westrup (1973).

antiphon A chant sung before and after a psalm verse, originally by alternating choirs. The term comes from the Greek *antiphonia* (literally, "countersound"), which means octave, and probably stems from one choir's (boys or women) singing an octave higher than the other.

Antiphonal psalm singing was adopted from Hebrew worship by the early Christian churches, notably that of Syria, and was introduced into the West in the 4th century by St. Ambrose. The two choirs sang the psalm text, or one choir sang a short refrain between verses (V) of the psalm (or pairs of verses) sung by the other choir. The refrain was called an antiphon (A). The resulting musical form was A V_1 A V_2 . . . A (or A V_1 V_2 A V_3 V_4 . . . A). The antiphon text normally referred to the meaning of the feast day or the psalm. Canticles from the New or Old Testament might also be sung in this way.

Antiphons are now found principally in the Canonical Hours, or Divine Office, in Roman Catholic liturgy. In the proper of the mass the introit, offertory, and communion originally consisted of antiphons and psalm verses. During the late Middle Ages the psalm verses were dropped from the offertory and the communion, which now consist only of an antiphon. The introit was shortened to one psalm verse and an antiphon (A V A). Musically the several thousand extant antiphons can be reduced to a small number of melodic types of simple structure. The old antiphonal method of performance was eventually abandoned, and antiphonal chants are now frequently sung responsorially; *i.e.,* by soloist(s) and choir. *See* RESPONSORY.

The four Marian antiphons are long hymns, not true antiphons but independent compositions especially noted for their beauty: the *Salve Regina, Ave Regina caelorum, Regina caeli, laetare,* and *Alma Redemptoris Mater.* They were frequently set polyphonically by composers from about 1400. There are other narrative antiphons that are usually associated with a particular feast and often sung in procession, such as *Occurrunt turbae* for Palm Sunday.

antiphonal singing Alternate singing by two choirs or singers. Antiphonal singing is of great antiquity and occurs in the folk and liturgical music of many cultures. Descriptions of it occur in the Old Testament. The antiphonal singing of psalms (*see* ANTIPHON) occurred both in ancient Hebrew and early Christian liturgies—*e.g.,* two choirs would sing alternate lines of psalms verses. Similar instances of antiphonal singing occur in the folk music of modern Yemenite Jews, in African and Afro-American folk music, and in Eastern European folk music. The principle is also used in large compositions for double choir by such composers as Bach. *Compare* RESPONSORIAL SINGING.

antique cymbals or **crotal** A pair of small cymbals at the ends of hinged sticks used in ancient Egypt, Greece, and Rome and probably also in the Middle Ages. Berlioz, Debussy, and Ravel were among the composers to reintroduce them.

Antony and Cleopatra: *see* BARBER, SAMUEL; MENOTTI; OPERA (the 20th century).

Appalachian Spring: *see* COPLAND; MODERN DANCE.

Appassionata: *see* BEETHOVEN (Beethoven and the theater); VARIATIONS.

appoggiatura An ornamental and frequently unwritten note of varying duration that temporarily displaces the main written note, subsequently resolving into it. The appoggiatura may stand at any interval to its main note but is most commonly adjacent; *i.e.,* at the distance of a tone or semitone according to the prevailing tonality (unless contradicted by accidentals or the performer's preference).

The Renaissance and early Baroque appoggiatura was of moderate length, averaging one-third of its subsequent main note, and was more in the nature of a melodic than of a harmonic ornament. By the time of Bach appoggiaturas became divided into two distinct species: the short (which takes an inconsiderable length from its subsequent main note and therefore has no substantial effect on the harmony) and the long (which takes upward of half the length from its subsequent main note and therefore has a substantial effect on the harmony). All true appoggiaturas are taken on the beat (not before) and with a degree (often a high degree) either of accentuation or of expressive emphasis. The name is derived from the Italian *appoggiare* ("to lean") and describes this aspect unmistakably: it is necessary to lean on the ornament and subside into the main note, above all with long appoggiaturas; and appoggiaturas are always slurred to their ensuing main notes.

The commonest Baroque signs for the appoggiatura came to be little notes showing the pitch of the ornament and apparently its duration, but this appearance is misleading and must normally be ignored. The duration is governed by the context, especially the harmonic context. The choice between a short and a long appoggiatura is not always obvious but can usually be made by responding to the natural implications of the music; in a few cases only one choice is compatible with the written harmony. Long appoggiaturas, however, are by far the most typical and should be given first preference in every suitable context. Certain rules existed for long appoggiaturas: standard lengths were half the duration of undotted notes; two-thirds of the duration of dotted notes; the whole duration of dotted notes in compound time if tied to a further note of the same pitch; and also the whole duration of notes followed by a rest if the main note can be forced forward into the time of that rest. These were described as minimum durations, which might be exceeded if the expression suggested so doing. There are, however, harmonic circumstances in which they must in fact be curtailed, and the decision is one that can ultimately be taken only by good musicianship.

Appoggiaturas are frequently implied in Baroque music without any sign or other written indication appearing in the notation. This is particularly the case in recitative, where to leave out an unwritten but implied appoggiatura is often tantamount to a wrong note.

In the 19th century the same rules and treatment remained current, but there was an increasing tendency to incorporate the long appoggiatura into the ordinary notated figuration instead of leaving it to the performer as an ornament shown only by signs or not at all. By the 20th century this tendency had reached its logical conclusions: all long appoggiaturas, and most short ones, were fully and accurately written out as part of the normal text. The short appoggiatura appeared as a small note with a slash through the stem and was called a GRACE NOTE or sometimes, incorrectly, ACCIACCATURA. The rules and treatment of ornamental appoggiaturas in earlier music fell into confusion, and many mistakes are made in performance through ignorance of the relevant conventions; but this ignorance is being increasingly corrected.

Apponyi Quartets: *see* HAYDN (London).

Apprenti sorcier, L': *see* SORCERER'S APPRENTICE, THE.

après-midi d'un faune, Prélude à l': *see* PRÉLUDE À L'APRÈS-MIDI D'UN FAUNE.

Arabella: *see* LIBRETTO (19th-century influences); STRAUSS, RICHARD.

arabesque A short fanciful piece, typically for the piano, with well-known examples by Schumann and Debussy. The term is also used in the ornamentation of a melody, an ornate figure derived from the ornament in Arab art and architecture. The word is French, meaning Arab, or Arabian.

Arab music This article is concerned principally with the art music of the Arabic-speaking peoples from the earliest written accounts to 20th-century practice.

The earliest extant Arabic texts on music date from the 9th century, and as the historical material they contain is not always trustworthy, there is little information on musical life in pre-Islamic Arabia. In terms of technical refinement, although hardly of idiom, it is likely that a distinction should be drawn between the music of the predominantly nomadic tribes of central Arabia and that of the settled population of Yemen and of the northern kingdoms of Hira and Ghassan. Philological evidence suggests certain parallels with other Semitic peoples and the early diffusion throughout the peninsula and beyond of certain musical instruments. Instrumental music was, however, subservient to vocal, which was intimately connected with poetry. Pre-Islamic poetry reflects Bedouin life, setting against the harsh environment the joys of love and wine, extolling the warlike deeds of the tribe and its heroes at the expense of the adversary, and lamenting the dead. Laments appear to have been sung exclusively by women, while singing girls are frequently mentioned in verses on the joys of the tavern and wine drinking. Music was no doubt also of importance to religious ceremonies, but as many pagan practices were repugnant to Islam, few traces remain.

There can be little doubt that music in pre-Islamic Arabia was primarily monophonic in nature; any accompanying instrument would be used either to support the vocal line or to beat out the rhythm, which at this period may have been subordinated to the poetic meter.

rise of Islam The advent of Islam affected the development of music in two main ways. Indirectly, as a result of the conquests of the 7th and 8th centuries, it brought the Arabs into immediate contact with the high cultures of Persia and Byzantium, and elements of Persian musical practice especially were adopted. Of greater importance was the effect on the social status of music and the musician. The legality of music was soon called into question, and the founders of the four orthodox law schools decided broadly against it. This did not check the popularity of music—especially at court—but it did confirm the widely held opinion that music was morally suspect and reinforced its association with other illicit activities and those who practiced them. The decision also ensured that music could never be used for religious purposes to the extent found in the Christian Church. The cantillation of the Koran exhibits obviously musical features, but by a legal fiction it was held to be quite distinct from secular music, and it acquired its own technical vocabulary.

With this attitude it is hardly surprising to find that most writers on music shied away from direct description and stressed the symbolic aspects. For the Sufis the emotional (primarily erotic) connotations were understood to represent divine love, so that music could be used as a means toward gnosis. Among the philosophers al-Kindi (d. *c.* 873), followed by many others, paid particular attention to the doctrine of *ta'thir* (ethos) (*see* GREEK MUSIC, ANCIENT), speculating on the cosmological affiliations of the four strings of the lute and of the rhythmic modes. Similar sets of associations were later propounded for the melodic modes. Al-Farabi (d. 950) and Avicenna (d. 1037), followed by a whole school of theorists, concentrated on the numerical analysis of intervals and the various tetrachord species compounded from them. The *Kitab al-Musiqi al-Kabir* of al-Farabi is in many respects a notable advance on its Greek models, while the detailed account of the main melody instruments—*'ud* and *tunbur* (short- and long-necked lutes); *rabāb* (fiddle); *mazamir* (woodwind); *ma'azif* (instrument with unstopped strings, such as the harp)—is a valuable guide to understanding the musical practice of the period.

Of nontechnical works by far the most important is the monumental 10th-century *Kitab al-Aghani*, the *Book of Songs*, which contains biographical information on poets and singers and reveals the role music played in court life. It also shows that with the growth of conscious virtuosity and the emergence of certain formal conventions the music of the court must have begun to differentiate itself from that of the common people. Folk material continued to be used by court singers but was probably altered and embellished. *See* FOLK MUSIC.

mode With the grafting of Byzantine and Persian elements onto the native tradition, a system of eight diatonic modes emerged in the Omayyad period (661–750). In intervallic structure they resembled the European ecclesiastical modes, although it is not known whether the similarity extended to melodic procedures. This system found its greatest exponent in Ishaq al-Mawsili (d. 850), singer, composer, and lute virtuoso, who was obliged to defend the system against the innovations (no doubt mainly of Persian origin) advocated by a rival school. His pupil Ziryab acquired equal renown in Spain and is credited with adding a fifth string to the 'ud, by this time the classical instrument par excellence.

Of the various innovations that made themselves felt during the 9th and 10th centuries—the efforts of Ishaq al-Mawsili and his followers notwithstanding—the most far-reaching in its consequences was the introduction into the hitherto purely diatonic modal system of a neutral (three-quarter-tone) interval. This led to the disruption of the old system and to the creation of many new modes. By the 13th century there were at least 30 modes in common use, and the vast majority contained the neutral interval, which has remained a characteristic feature of the art musics of the Middle East.

Theorists of the 13th to the 16th century (among the more important were Safi al-Din al-Urmawi, Qutb al-Din Shirazi, 'Abd al-Qadir, and al-Ladhiqi) tend to define these modes wherever possible in terms of octave scales. But it is evident from their methods of analysis, as well as from the surviving fragments of notation, that the modes should more properly be regarded as combinations of a limited number of smaller units—generally spanning a fourth and occasionally a third (neutral or major) or a fifth. The mode (called *shadd, awaz,* and later *maqam*) is thus not reducible to a simple succession of intervals but in most cases fuses together according to certain laws two or more such units, each of which is characterized by features of prominence and in certain instances by having a fixed melodic shape. Often, too, the position of initial and final notes is fixed for the mode as a whole: a frequent pattern is for the composition to begin on the upper octave note, to explore the melodic possibilities of the upper unit and then those of the lower unit, and to end with the tonic (lower octave note).

In the course of the exploration—especially in passages designed to test the performer's virtuosity—further units might be briefly introduced, the transitions effected with considerable subtlety. Certain treatises even discuss forms in which all notes of the theoretical gamut are included by this process or in which the performer passes through the whole repertoire of modal forms. *See* MODE (ancient and Oriental modal systems).

rhythm In definitions of rhythm most Arab writers postulate a fundamental time unit, indivisible by convention, from which the rhythmic cycles in theory derive. Each cycle consists of a fixed number of time units and is further characterized by the distribution of strong and weak beats and pauses within it. Thus the following cycles are quite distinct despite being the same length:

al-thaqil al-awwal

al-thaqil al-thani

(according to Safi al-Din)

In performance some of the pauses could be filled in, but the fundamental pattern had to be retained.

Parallel to the growth in the repertoire of melodic modes, the number of rhythmic modes increased from eight in the 9th century to more than 20 in the 16th. These latter include some of Persian and Turkish origin, while certain *aksak* dance rhythms that had evolved in the ceremonies of the Sufi fraternities were also adopted. The distinction between heavy and light rhythms, which has stylistic connotations, is strongest in the early period. Several of the rhythmic cycles are unusual in that they contain a large number of time-units (24 and more); mention is even made of one with 200. In general one rhythmic cycle would be used throughout a composition, although 'Abd al-Qadir (d. 1435) discusses forms in which several rhythms are introduced or in which two are used simultaneously. *See* RHYTHM.

form By the 9th century—and probably before—a number of formal procedures were recognized and certain genres distinguished as they had been in pre-Islamic times. Unfortunately the meaning of several of the technical terms employed is uncertain; some of them suggest that there may have subsisted a structural interrelationship between the verse (generally a couplet) and the song, but there is certainly no correlation between poetic meters and rhythmic cycles having the same names.

At a later period an informative account of the forms is provided by 'Abd al-Qadir. Among various features that distinguish one form from another, he mentions: with or without words; if the former, in Arabic or Persian; with an instrumental prelude or not; unmeasured or in one (or more) of the rhythmic cycles; and the presence or absence of a refrain. Among the more important forms he lists are the *basit,* a setting of Arabic verse in one of three given rhythms with an instrumental prelude; and the *nashid al'arab,* in which four Arabic couplets are sung, the first and third in free rhythm, the second and third separated by a vocalized section. Of greater complexity is the *nawba,* a suite of four movements ('Abd al-Qadir claims to have added a fifth). The first movement *(qawl)* and the fourth *(furudasht)* are stated to resemble the *basit;* the second *(ghazal)* is a setting of Persian verse; the third *(tarana)* is a setting of a quatrain *(ruba'i)* in Arabic or Persian with the same rhythmic limitations as the *basit.* The same melodic and rhythmic modes might be used in all four movements, each of which could be prefaced by an instrumental introduction.

There are indications that the precomposed part of a song may sometimes have consisted of a relatively simple melodic framework and that the soloist would demonstrate his artistry by adding various ornaments and melismas. These would naturally vary from performance to performance, and it is perhaps partly for this reason that there are so few examples of notated music despite the existence of an adequate system of notation. Another—and possibly more powerful—motive may have been the secretiveness of musicians unwilling to share their compositions with rivals.

distribution Of the theorists mentioned above 'Abd al-Qadir and Qutb al-Din wrote in Persian; and Persian as well as Arabic poetry was set to music. There is in fact a certain amount of evidence to suggest that the musical system of the 13th to the 16th century discussed above—the fruit of a considerable period of cultural interchange between Arabs and Persians—prevailed over an area extending from Palestine (and perhaps also Egypt) to eastern Persia. Whether or not the same system was common in North Africa and Spain is impossible to determine, as sources for this region are both scanty and uninformative. The *nawba* tradition preserved in North Africa may be a distant relative rather than a direct descendant of that described by 'Abd al-Qadir, and the differences that now distinguish the art music of North Africa from that of Egypt and the countries to the east can hardly be of recent origin.

The 16th to the 19th century, when a large part of the Arabic-speaking world was subject to the Ottomans, was for the Arabs a time of political and cultural decline. Art music, which relied to a great extent on the court for patronage, was inevitably influenced by Turkish classical music. As the latter was itself indebted to Arab and Persian traditions, no far-reaching changes were effected. Thus the same definitions of mode and rhythm are also applicable to 20th-century art music. The modern *maqam* may be somewhat more complex than its medieval ancestor in that it generally makes use of (in a fixed sequence) a greater number of basic units, but its structure is fundamentally the same.

The repertoire of modes varies somewhat in the area from Egypt to Iraq, but there is nevertheless a considerable degree of uniformity. More than 100 modes have been tabulated and as many rhythmic cycles, although the number in current use is in each case considerably smaller.

Among the most important instrumental forms in this area are the *taqsim* and the *bashraf.* The *taqsim* is an unmeasured improvisation in which instrumentalists usually alternate in developing the *maqam,* although solo performances are also frequent. A measured form of the *taqsim* is also found with the rhythmic cycle marked by an ostinato phrase on a melody instrument. The *bashraf* is a measured form consisting usually of four sections of equal length *(khana)* separated by a ritornello, which is also used to conclude the piece; the ritornello is played by the ensemble, while the sections are entrusted to various soloists.

The vocal equivalent of the *taqsim* is the *layali* in which the singer may accompany himself on the lute, using the instrument to give an intermittent drone. Both *taqsim* and *layali* provide a test of the performer's artistry in exploring the melodic potential of the mode and also constitute a vehicle for virtuoso display, which manifests itself in a profusion of melismas and ornaments. Melodic movement is predominantly stepwise, and sequential passages abound. Iraqi practice, which still remains close to Persian music in some respects, shares with it the vocal technique of *tahrir*— a glottal trill—together with an emphasis on the upper register and a preference for a delivery that is marked by tense articulation not generally found elsewhere in the Arab world.

Except in Mauritania, which has a separate system, the art music of North Africa *(ala, ma'luf)* is centered on the *nawba* tradition. Only 11 of the original 24 *nawba* survive (the set of 24, like the 12 *shadd* and 6 *awaz* in the 13th century, had a symbolic, cosmological significance, and it is particularly in North Africa that the doctrine of *ta'thir* persists with each *nawba* assigned in theory to a particular time of day). The number of vocal movements in each *nawba* varies from four to six according to the region. While the entire *nawba* is based on one mode, each movement has its own rhythmic cycle and is made up of a number of *san'a,* a setting of a strophic verse form. Continuity and climax are ensured by a gradual acceleration throughout the movement; by the end the tempo may have more than doubled. There are various instrumental forms that serve as preludes and interludes.

instruments The instruments used in a performance of a *nawba* are the *'ud* (short-necked lute); *rabāb* (two-stringed fiddle); *kamanja* (European violin or viola braced vertically against the thigh with the player seated cross-legged); *tar* (tambourine); and *darabukka* (a vase-shaped drum played with the fingers). In the Eastern countries the *rabāb* (often a spike-fiddle with one string) is more a folk-music instrument, often used by village bards to accompany the recitation of popular folk epics. Other important classical instru-

ments in the area are the *nay* (vertical flute) and *qanun* (psaltery), which is generally replaced in Iraq, as in Persia, by the *santur* (dulcimer). The *'ud,* which now usually has six strings, five of them double, remains the most favored solo instrument. The *tabl* (drum), *daff* (frame-drum), and the instruments of the shawm family, *zamr* and *ghayta,* are folk instruments used in outdoor ceremonies. In previous centuries they also formed part of the military band (*nawba,* but not to be confused with the suite form) to which belonged in addition the *naqqara* (kettle drum), *buq* (horn), and *nafir* (trumpet). Prior to and during the period of Ottoman domination, other instruments also found favor at court. These included the *tunbur* (long-necked lute), which was found in different sizes, and the *jank* (harp). Several other types of lute, fiddle, psaltery, and flute were also known, as well as various idiophones.

Western influence Art music has always been the preserve of the urban upper and middle classes and has relied heavily on court patronage. In the 20th century this virtually disappeared, and it is urban society that has been most exposed to Western influence. As a result the future of the classical tradition is by no means assured despite a recent increase in musicological activity. A number of musicians have attempted to evolve new forms combining features of Western classical music with the native tradition; the two remain uneasy bedfellows, however, and the results achieved in this direction are hardly encouraging. On the other hand the folk music of the rural population, has been little affected by westernization. Despite the leveling effect of mass media on other forms of music, folk music continues to flourish in all its regional varieties. *See* ANCIENT MUSIC; INDIAN MUSIC.

BIBLIOGRAPHY: Henry George Farmer, *A History of Arabian Music to the XIIIth Century* (1929; reprinted 1967), *Historical Facts for the Arabian Musical Influence* (1930), and "The Music of Islam" in *New Oxford History of Music,* Vol. 1 (1957); Curt Sachs, *The Rise of Music in the Ancient World, East and West* (1943); Peter Crossley-Holland, "The Arabic World" in the *Pelican History of Music,* Vol. 1 (1960).

Arcadelt, Jacob (c. 1500–c. 1570) An early master of the madrigal, Jacob Arcadelt was a native of Flanders. His first publication dates from 1532 (Lyons). He probably went to Italy about 1538 and became a singer and later choirmaster at the Sistine Chapel in Rome in 1539. In 1547 Arcadelt returned after a year's absence in France, leaving again before 1552. He was serving Charles, Duke of Guise, in 1555, and by 1557 he was a member of the French Chapel Royal. He vanished from the records about 1567 and died before 1572.

Arcadelt's fame rests on about 120 chansons and more than 200 Italian madrigals, as well as about 20 motets and three masses. His first book of madrigals (c. 1538) was the best-selling publication of its kind in the 16th century. With Costanzo Festa and Philippe Verdelot he set the style for a generation of madrigal composers. He favored four-voiced composition, and his secular music owes much to the simple declamation and tuneful treble of the frottola. Both Cipriano da Rore and Palestrina learned from Arcadelt's clarity.

RECORDING: *Missa Noe, Noe.*

Arensky, Anton (Stepanovich) (August 11 [July 30, old style], 1861–February 25 [February 12, old style], 1906) The Russian composer of instrumental music, operas, and songs, Anton Arensky, studied composition with Rimsky-Korsakov at the St. Petersburg Conservatory and from 1882 to 1895 taught harmony, and later composition, at the Moscow Conservatory. He was also active as a conductor in Moscow. From 1895 to 1901 he was director of the Imperial Chapel in St. Petersburg. The last years of his life—shortened by dissipation and ill-health—were devoted to composition.

Although a pupil of Rimsky-Korsakov, Arensky was more akin to Tchaikovsky; the predominant moods of his not very individual music are lyrical and elegiac. Of his three operas only the first, *A Dream on the Volga* (after a play by Aleksandr Nikolayevich Ostrovsky; Moscow, 1892), was successful; the one-act *Raphael* (Moscow, 1894) was stillborn, and *Nal and Damayanti* (composed 1899; performed Moscow, 1904) failed to keep the stage. Other stage music includes music to Pushkin's *Fountain of Bakhchisarai* and

Shakespeare's *Tempest* and a ballet, *Egyptian Night.* Arensky is best remembered for his Variations for string orchestra on a theme of Tchaikovsky, his Piano Trio in d minor, and, mainly because of a famous recording by Harold Bauer and Ossip Gabrilowitsch, the waltz from his Suite No. 1 for two pianos. He also wrote two symphonies, a violin concerto, an early piano concerto, and chamber music that includes the Piano Quintet in D Major and two quartets.

RECORDINGS: *Fountain of Bakhchisarai;* Piano Concerto; Trio in d minor; Variations on a Theme by Tchaikovsky.

Argento, Dominick (Joseph) (b. October 27, 1927) Best known for his operas and song cycles, the U.S. composer Dominick Argento studied at the Peabody Conservatory in Baltimore with Hugo Weisgall and Henry Cowell (composition) and Alexander Sklarewski (piano). He also studied with Luigi Dallapiccola at the Cherubini Conservatory in Florence (1951–52) and with Bernard Rogers, Howard Hanson, and Alan Hovhaness at the Eastman School of Music in Rochester, New York (1955–57), where he later worked as theory teacher and opera coach. Since 1958 he has taught at the University of Minnesota in Minneapolis, where he also composed (1965–69) incidental music for the stage productions of Sir Tyrone Guthrie. His principal operas are *The Boor* (1957), *Christopher Sly* (1963), *Colonel Jonathan the Saint* (1971), *Postcard from Morocco* (1971), *The Voyage of Edgar Allan Poe* (1976), and *Miss Havisham's Fire* (1979). In addition to music for voice and piano, he has written song cycles for chorus, *A Nation of Cowslips* (1968), and for tenor and guitar, *Letters from Composers* (1969), and the oratorio *Jonah and the Whale* (1974). He won the Pulitzer Prize for music in 1975 for the 12-tone song cycle *From the Diary of Virginia Woolf,* written for the English soprano Janet Baker. His *In Praise of Music* (1977) was commissioned by the Minnesota Orchestra in celebration of its 75th anniversary.

RECORDINGS: *Letters from Composers; Postcard from Morocco; To Be Sung upon the Water.*

aria A solo song, simple or elaborate, with

instrumental accompaniment. It is not only one of the most important ingredients of OPERA, especially up to the later 19th century, but is also found extensively outside opera in the 17th and 18th centuries, notably in the CANTATA and the ORATORIO. The term has also occasionally been used to denote instrumental pieces of a songlike nature (*e.g.*, the two middle movements of Stravinsky's Violin Concerto).

The aria originated in Italy in the 16th century and first gained currency with the publication of *Le Nuove Musiche* (1602), a collection of solo songs with continuo by Giulio Caccini, who called the strophic songs in his collection *arie*. The word can be seen as a counterpart to the contemporary English AYRE and French AIR; it was later adopted in Germany, where the songs of composers such as Heinrich Albert and Adam and Johann Philipp Krieger are called *Arien*. All the more serious strophic songs composed thereafter in Italy—and there were a great many of them—were called arias; the form soon made its way into opera (*e.g.*, Orpheus' "Vi ricord', o boschi ombrosi" in Monteverdi's *Orfeo*, 1607). Instead of using the same music for every verse, some composers varied a basic vocal line over a constant, steadily moving bass. Terms such as canzonetta and later arietta were used for arias of more popular or frivolous cast.

After about 1620 arias, still usually found as separate songs in published collections, were nearly always in triple time and became longer—notably at the hands of the Venetian organist Giovanni Pietro Berti. New structural schemes, often suggested by the texts, were devised to lend unity to what might otherwise have become a somewhat sprawling form. It was Berti who composed a song, "Dove sei gita" (1634), that is probably the earliest aria in *da capo* form, involving the organization of an aria as a whole and not merely that of a single verse repeated for subsequent verses. Berti achieved the new ABA form in a single verse by placing a triple-time refrain at the beginning as well as at the end; the main body of the text was set in a contrasting duple time between them.

For more than a century the da capo aria, now mainly found in Italian operas and cantatas, was one of the most popular musical forms of all time. Texts became much shorter; instead of having several verses sung to the same music, all that was required was a few lines heard twice in the outer A sections to the same music, which treated the words expansively with much repetition, and a few more lines for the central B section, which was usually much more terse, in a related key, and frequently contrasted in mood and tempo. Instrumental ritornellos (sometimes sharing the vocal material) framed the arias, and snatches of them often punctuated the vocal sections. While the story of an opera was advanced through recitative, the arias were dramatically static, affording opportunities for single characters to reflect on the preceding action, after which they left the stage. Arias might assume various moods and were codified as *Aria cantabile, Aria di bravura, Aria parlante,* and so on; these were supposed to be carefully distributed throughout an opera or single act, though in fact their finest composers—among them Alessandro Scarlatti and especially Handel—did not rigidly observe these conventions. The finest singers of these arias—particularly sopranos, both female and castrati—were the most popular international public entertainers of the age, and they decorated the reprise of the A section of an aria with brilliant improvised embellishments (sometimes in competition with an equally brilliant and agile obbligato instrument such as flute or trumpet), culminating in an unaccompanied cadenza at the final cadence. The da capo aria was also a staple constituent of chamber cantatas and to a lesser extent of sacred cantatas (many of Bach's, for example) and oratorios (the finest examples by Handel). Composers occasionally dispensed with the da capo form for dramatic effect.

By about the third quarter of the 18th century, influential voices—those of Rousseau, Francesco Algarotti, and Gluck, for instance—began to protest against the da capo aria, and it suffered a sharp decline. These writers protested against abuses such as excessive coloratura; the dramatic impropriety of a return to the mood of section A after this mood had been dispelled by the sense of section B; and the absurdity of a character who had sworn, say, "immediate vengeance" in a recitative having to wait before elaborating his point in the ensuing aria while the orchestra played a ritornello. It is tempting to attend to these admittedly reasonable complaints and to forget that in its long heyday the da capo aria gave immense pleasure. A reaction against it was inevitable. When Baroque opera began to return to the operatic stage about the middle of the 20th century, it was seen that in the hands of an imaginative producer and musical director, unshackled by virtuoso singers, long successions of recitative and aria need not lead to dramatic absurdity or stagnation.

After about 1770 the aria continued to play a prominent part in opera in many different, less stereotyped forms, ranging from simple strophic songs to long and elaborate *scenas*. Since Gluck was impatient of the da capo aria, and he was the greatest operatic composer between Handel and Mozart, it is not surprising that his operas are the first important ones to show this new diversity. In the late 18th century the aria enjoyed a vogue as a concert piece (Mozart). At this time too many arias were in two distinct parts—one dramatic, one lyrical (*e.g.,* Leporello's "Catalogue" Aria in Mozart's *Don Giovanni*). In Italian operas— those for instance of Donizetti and Verdi (up to *Aida* in 1871)—the aria was cultivated over a longer period than in German operas. Wagner cultivated a continuous texture and placed more of the burden of portrayal of character and situation into the orchestra; however, his opposition to the aria was more theoretical than actual, and his music dramas contain many examples of what one might term "closet" arias. In the 20th century arias occur mainly in operas by composers uninfluenced by, or hostile to, Wagner (*e.g.,* Stravinsky's *The Rake's Progress,* and the operas of Britten).

Ariadne: *see* HANDEL (life).

Ariadne auf Naxos: *see* BENDA; CLASSICAL PERIOD (vocal music, 1750–1800); LIBRETTO (19th-century influences); OPERA (the 20th century); STRAUSS, RICHARD.

Arianna: *see* BAROQUE ERA (beginnings); HANDEL (life); MONTEVERDI (early career).

Aristides Quintilianus (2nd or 3rd century A.D.) The Greek Neoplatonist Aristides Quintilianus was the author of a treatise on music, *Peri musikes,* that was regarded by Byzantine and Arab theorists as an important source for the study of Greek music, a judgment generally accepted by modern scholars. The treatise was first published in Marcus Meibohm's collection of writings by Greek musical theorists in 1652. A critical edition by A. Jahn appeared in 1882; and R. Schäfke published a German translation and commentary in 1937.

Arkhipova, Irina (Veloshkina) (b. January 2, 1925) The Soviet dramatic mezzo-soprano Irina Arkhipova made her debut in Rimsky-Korsakov's *Tsar's Bride* in 1954. A specialist in the Russian repertoire (Rimsky-Korsakov, Prokofiev, Mussorgsky), she has recorded *Carmen* and sung the Verdi mezzo roles of Amneris in *Aida,* Eboli in *Don Carlo,* and Ulrica in *Un ballo in maschera.* As a recitalist she has sung throughout Europe, Scandinavia, and in South America.

Armenian chant The vocal music of the Armenian Church and the religious prose and later poetry that serves as its texts.

Armenia was Christianized quite early by missionaries from Syria and Greek-speaking areas of the Eastern Mediterranean and accepted Christianity as the state religion by 302, probably the first nation to do so. The development of a distinctive Armenian liturgy was influenced by various factors. Toward the end of the 4th century, the Armenian Church proclaimed its independence from the Archbishopric of Caesarea in Cappadocia in Asia Minor. In 401 the Armenian scholar St. Mesrob (Mashtots) invented the Armenian alphabet and carried out many important translations of religious literature from Syrian and Greek. The introduction of the new alphabet stimulated a flourishing literature, an important and prominent part of which was religious poetry. The earliest preserved examples date from the 4th century.

In the 12th century the catholicos (patriarch) Nerses IV Shnorhali ("The Gracious") is credited with musical reforms of the chant. He is said to have simplified the texts of the religious poetry and the melodies of the chant, bringing it closer to the style of Armenian folk music. Nerses also wrote a number of *sharakan* (hymns). Armenian musical notation was also reformed in the 12th century. The final form of the collection of *Sharakan,* containing nearly 1200 hymns, was obtained *c.* 1300 and has apparently remained unchanged.

About 1820 an Armenian from Istanbul, Baba Hampartsoum Limondjian, proposed another reform and modernization of the musical notation along the lines of the contemporary notational reform in the Greek Church (which allowed more precise indications of pitch).

In its present-day performance Armenian chant consists of intricate melodies with great rhythmic variety, and the melodies use many intervals not found in European music.

According to a long-standing tradition the most reliable oral transmission of the chant ocurs in the religious capital of Armenia, Echmiadzin, and in a few isolated monasteries. An important center for Armenian musical studies is the Armenian Catholic monastery of San Lazzaro in Venice (founded 1717), where the traditional Armenian melodies are said to be fairly well preserved.

Armstrong, Louis: *see* JAZZ (origin and early development) and (orchestral style).

Arne, Thomas (Augustine) (March 12, 1710– March 5, 1778) The English composer Thomas Arne was known chiefly for his dramatic music and songs for London's theaters and pleasure gardens. Educated at Eton, he was intended for the law, but by secretly practicing he acquired such mastery of the violin and keyboard instruments that his father eventually withdrew objections to a musical career. Except for some lessons from Michael Festing, later leader of the Italian Opera orchestra, Arne was self-taught, and it was at the opera (which he attended in a footman's livery to obtain free admission) that his musical taste was largely formed. He taught both his sister, the actress Mrs. Theophilus (Susanna Maria) Cibber, and his young brother to sing, and they appeared in his first stage work, *Rosamond* (1733). Based on Joseph Addison's libretto of 1707, this opera was set "after the Italian manner," and its bravura air "Rise, Glory, Rise" was sung for the next 40 years.

Thomas Arne
engraving after Francesco Bartolozzi
(c. 1725–1815)
courtesy, National Portrait Gallery, London

Arne was soon engaged to write musical after-pieces and incidental music for the Drury Lane Theatre, and with *Comus* (1738), John Dalton's adaptation of Milton's masque, he became established as the leading English lyric composer. Charles Burney wrote, "He introduced a light, airy original and pleasing melody, wholly different from that of Purcell and Handel," and this individual melodic style can also be heard in *Alfred* (notable for "Rule, Britannia") and *The Judgment of Paris,* both produced at the Prince of Wales' residence at Cliveden in 1740. Arne's settings of Shakespeare's songs, written for revivals of *As You Like It, Twelfth Night,* and *The Merchant of Venice* in 1740–41, provide the culmination of this early melodious style. In 1737 Arne married Cecilia Young, who had already sung in Handel's operas and oratorios, and in 1742–44 the couple paid a highly successful visit to Dublin.

On his return Arne was engaged as composer to the Drury Lane Theatre and Vauxhall Gardens, and during the next decade he published song collections under such titles as *Lyric Harmony, Vocal Melody,* and *The Agreeable Musical Choice* that, as Dr. Burney wrote, were "the standard of all perfection at our theatres and public gardens." During the 1750s and '60s Arne composed prolifically for stage, concert room, and the home. In 1759 Oxford University made him a doctor of music.

In the final decade of his life Arne gave annual concerts of catches and glees together with musical pieces designed to display the talents of his singing pupils. He set Garrick's ode for the Stratford Shakespeare jubilee of 1769 and composed music for *The Fairy Prince* (1771) and Mason's *Elfrida* (1772) and *Caractacus* (1776).

Arne's early melodic style was natural and elegant, owing something to Scots, Irish, and Italian sources. His later music became more Italianate and ornamented, though in his final years there emerged an opera buffa style that anticipates Sir Arthur Sullivan. As the composer of such melodies as "Rule, Britannia," "Blow, Blow, Thou Winter Wind," and "Where the Bee Sucks," Arne, like Purcell, added substantially to the English heritage of song.

BIBLIOGRAPHY: Hubert Langley, *Doctor Arne* (1938).

RECORDINGS: Harpsichord Sonatas; Overtures.

Arnold, Samuel (August 10, 1740–October 22, 1802) The English composer and editor of the works of Handel, Samuel Arnold was educated at the Chapel Royal and became composer to the Covent Garden Theatre, where in 1765 he produced *The Maid of the Mill*. In 1777 he became music director of the Theatre Royal, Haymarket. Between 1765 and 1802 he composed music for nearly 100 successful musical productions—ballad operas, farces, and pantomimes—and also published sonatas, symphonies, and oratorios, the most important being *The Prodigal Son* (1773), and anthems for the Chapel Royal for which he became organist and composer in 1783. In 1793 he was appointed organist at Westminster Abbey.

Arnold's fame rests on his edition of the works of Handel (1787–97). Although defective in the light of later scholarship, it merits respect as the earliest attempt to publish an edition of a composer's complete works. His *Cathedral Music* (1790) was intended as a supplement to William Boyce's collection. His own music is facile, although one or two symphony overtures and several of his harpsichord lessons have charm.

arpeggio A chord whose notes are sounded successively rather than simultaneously. In the 19th and 20th centuries the motion is normally upward beginning on the beat. In the 17th and 18th centuries the sequence was often downward as well as upward—or even both— ad libitum. The French clavecinists often indicated *arpègement en montant* (ascending arpeggio) or *arpègement en descendant* (descending arpeggio) and the *arpègement figuré,* which introduced various unwritten notes foreign to the harmony that were sounded but not held.

arrangement The adaptation of a composition to fit a medium other than the original while retaining its character. The term is sometimes used interchangeably with transcription, although the second term frequently carries the connotation of elaboration of the original, as in the virtuoso piano transcriptions of Bach's organ works by Liszt, Busoni, and others.

In the 14th–16th centuries a vogue existed for arranging—for keyboard instruments or lutes—vocal music such as madrigals, motets, and parts of masses. The purpose of these early arrangements, sometimes called intabulations, was to permit a single player to perform music written for several singers.

During the Baroque period interest in arrangement declined, perhaps because of the increased importance of instrumental music and the waning significance of vocal writing. Bach, who arranged Vivaldi's violin concertos for harpsichord and for organ, was a notable exception to this loss of interest in transcribing music from one medium to another.

During the 19th century, with its stress on the piano, arrangements again became popular. Liszt transcribed Schubert's songs and scenes from Wagner's music dramas. Brahms arranged for orchestra his own Variations on a Theme by Haydn, originally for two pianos, and of Bach's Chaconne from the Partita in d minor for violin, which Brahms recast as a piano study for the left hand. In the 20th century many composers have arranged their own works for piano. A notable example is Stravinsky's piano arrangement of his *Petrushka* ballet music.

Arrangements of symphonic works, operas, and chamber music in piano score are usually used for rehearsal and study rather than for public performance. In recent years the transcriptions of Bach's organ works for piano and for orchestra, such as those by Respighi, Stokowski, and Eugene Ormandy, have fallen into disrepute as violating the true character of the original works.

Arrau, Claudio (b. February 6, 1903)   At the age of seven the Chilean pianist Claudio Arrau was sent by his government to Germany, where he studied with Martin Krause. Between 1925 and 1940 his work centered in Berlin, where he taught at Stern's Conservatory. He moved to the United States in 1941. Active well into his 70s, Arrau has been a major pianist of the 20th century, playing a wide variety of repertoire and renowned especially as an interpreter of Beethoven and Liszt.

Arriaga (y Balzola), Juan Crisóstomo (Jacobo Antonio) (January 27, 1806–January 17, 1826)   The Spanish composer Juan Crisóstomo Arriaga showed great promise that was cut short by his early death. He showed an extraordinary musical precocity; at the age of 13, without having received any lessons in harmony, he composed an opera, *Nada y mucho.* Its success when produced in Bilbao in 1820 led to his being sent to the Paris Conservatoire, where he studied violin with Pierre Baillot and harmony with François-Joseph Fétis. He matured with phenomenal rapidity and within two years had written an eight-part fugal *Et vitam venturi,* which Cherubini declared a masterpiece; by the age of 18 he was an assistant professor at the Conservatoire.

Among his compositions, remarkable for freshness, originality, abundant invention, and technical resource, are Three Quartets, which in style form a connective link between Haydn and Schubert (although the first contains one of Arriaga's rare suggestions of Spanish folk idiom), some French cantatas, a mass, *Salve Regina,* the opera *Los esclavos felices,* an octet for strings, trumpet, guitar, and piano, and a symphony, which, like most of his music, combines the classical tradition of Haydn and Mozart with the flavor of Rossini.

RECORDINGS: Overture to *Los esclavos felices;* Three Quartets; Symphony in D Major.

Arroyo, Martina (b. February 2, 193?)   Born and trained in the United States, the lyric spinto Martina Arroyo made her debut in 1958 at New York City's Carnegie Hall in the U.S. premiere of Ildebrando Pizzetti's *Murder in the Cathedral.* She then sang several seasons at the Berlin Deutsche Oper and the Vienna Statsoper and in 1965 returned to New York City to sing Aida at the Metropolitan. She has sung leading roles of Verdi, Mozart, Meyerbeer, and Mascagni, as well as Elsa in Wagner's *Lohengrin.* Her most acclaimed recordings include Verdi's *Aida* and Requiem, Rossini's *Stabat Mater,* and Stockhausen's *Momente.*

ars antiqua   A period of musical activity in 13th-century France characterized by increasingly sophisticated counterpoint that culminated in the innovations of the 14th-century ARS NOVA. The term ars antiqua originated with the ars nova theorists, some of whom

Claudio Arrau
courtesy, ICM Artists, Ltd.

spoke of the "ancient art" with praise, others with contempt. All of them, however, agreed upon a marked difference between the two styles, a difference rooted primarily in the profound rhythmic innovations of the ars nova. Those theorists limited the ars antiqua to the latter part of the 13th century, but modern music historians have broadened the term to encompass the entire century.

Most of the music of the ars antiqua is anonymous. Nevertheless, three important figures emerge from general obscurity: Pérotin (flourished late 12th century), who succeeded the famed Léonin at Notre-Dame in Paris and who composed the earliest known music for four voices; Franco of Cologne (flourished mid-13th century), a theorist whose *Ars cantus mensurabilis* served to organize and codify the newly formed mensural system (a more precise system of rhythmic notation); and Pierre de la Croix (flourished last half of 13th century), whose works anticipate the ars nova style by virtue of their greater rhythmic fluency.

The most important form to originate in the ars antiqua is the MOTET, which retained its popularity for centuries. The essence of this form is its simultaneous presentation of more than one text. It seems to have begun with the addition of a new text to the upper voice(s) of a sacred polyphonic composition, the slower moving lower voice retaining its original sacred text. The next text—in Latin like the original text—at first complemented or amplified the meaning of the original words. Later the language of the added text changed to French, while the sentiments became more worldly, resulting in compositions in which the sacred Latin text of the lower voice is accompanied by one or more secular French texts in the upper voice(s).

ars nova   The name given by modern historians to the music of the 14th century, particularly to that of France in the first half of the 14th century. The designation ars nova, as opposed to the ARS ANTIQUA of the late 13th century, was the title of a treatise written *c.* 1320 by the composer Philippe de Vitry.

Vitry, the most enthusiastic proponent of the "new art," demonstrates in his treatise the innovations in rhythmic notation that were characteristic of the new music. These innovations, anticipated to a degree in the music of Pierre de la Croix (last half of 13th century), are marked by the emancipation of music from the straitjacket of the rhythmic modes (dominated by triple meter) of the preceding age and by the increased use of smaller note values. An important opponent of Philippe de Vitry's progressive ideas was the theorist Jacques de Liège, whose *Speculum musicae* extols the virtues of the older masters of the ars antiqua.

Some of the earliest examples of works in the new style may be found in the *Roman de Fauvel* (*c.* 1315), a narrative manuscript that contains compositions from both the ars nova and the ars antiqua. In addition to Vitry the most important composer of the ars nova was Guillaume de Machaut, whose sizable output forms a substantial percentage of the surviving repertoire. Polyphonic secular music, represented by the ballade, virelai, and rondeau, increased decidedly in the 14th century.

The term ars nova, specifically applicable to the French music of the 14th century, has been used less discriminately by a number of writers who refer to "Italian ars nova." The most important theorist of this school is Marchettus of Padua, whose treatise *Pomerium* (early 14th century) outlines certain rhythmic innovations in the Italian notation of the time. The most important composers of 14th-century Italy are Jacopo da Bologna, Francesco Landini, and Ghirardello da Firenze.

BIBLIOGRAPHY: Gustave Reese, *Music in the Middle Ages* (1940); Dom Anselm Hughes and Gerald Abraham, eds., *Ars Nova and the Renaissance, 1300–1540* (1960), Vol. 3 of the *New Oxford History of Music.*

Art of the Fugue, The: *see* BACH, JOHANN SEBASTIAN (last years); BAROQUE ERA (Handel and Bach); CANON; COUNTERPOINT (Baroque era); FUGUE (Bach).

Ashkenazy, Vladimir (b. July 6, 1937)   A major pianist of his generation, the Russian Vladimir Ashkenazy studied with Lev Oborin at the Moscow Conservatory. He won first prizes at the Queen Elisabeth of Belgium Competition (1956) and at the International Tchaikov-

Vladimir Ashkenazy
courtesy, ICM Artists, Ltd.

sky Competition (1962). In 1963 he settled in the West. Ashkenazy's repertoire ranges from Mozart to 20th-century Russians. In the middle '70s he became increasingly and successfully active as a conductor.

Aston, Hugh (*c.* 1490–*c.* 1550) Hugh Aston was an English composer of church and keyboard music. Various spellings of his surname are found, and his identity has been long obscured by the fact that there was at the same period a prominent ecclesiastic of the same name, a canon of York and of St. Stephen's, Westminster. It has been established that the composer supplicated for the degree of B. Mus. at Oxford in 1510 and was master of the choristers at St. Mary's College, Leicester, from some time before 1525 until its dissolution in 1548. He was well enough known in 1525 for the Bishop of Lincoln to recommend him to Cardinal Wolsey for the latter's lavish new foundation at Oxford (Cardinal College, later Christ Church); he refused the offer, and the post went to John Taverner.

The style of Aston's music (most of it reprinted in *Tudor Church Music,* 1929), with its rich, largely nonimitative counterpoint, is very close to that of Taverner, though Aston lacks Taverner's melodic suppleness and control of large-scale design.

atonality The absence of TONALITY, or a concept of harmony with the impartial use of the 12 tones of the chromatic scale without reference to a key or tonal center.

Twentieth-century atonality was preceded by two developments. First there was a weakening of the system of keys that was an essential part of the tonality of the 17th to the 19th century. The nonchromatic relationships on which tonality had been based evolved into the chromaticism of 19th-century music, culminating in the works of Wagner and Mahler. From the seven-note major and minor scales and the chromatic tones used to color and transpose them, a scale of 12 equidistant tones evolved (the equally tempered chromatic scale) that by the late 19th century was recognized as a unique scale independent of the seven-note scales.

In practice the atonality of a composition is relative, for an atonal work may contain fragmentary passages in which tonal centers seem to exist. Schoenberg's *Pierrot Lunaire* (1912) and Berg's opera *Wozzeck* (1925) are typical examples of atonal works. Schoenberg, who pioneered in the language we commonly call atonal, disliked the word because of its negative prefix. Many theorists share his discomfort without, however, having yet been able to propose a universally accepted substitute. *See* CHROMATICISM, POLYTONALITY, SERIALISM.

BIBLIOGRAPHY: Rudolph Richard Reti, *Tonality, Atonality, Pantonality* (1958); George Perle, *Serial Composition and Atonality* (1962).

attacca A direction to a performer to begin the next movement of a composition without a break. It is also used in the direction *attacca subito*—"attack at once."

attack: *see* ENVELOPE.

Attaignant, Pierre (*c.* 1480–*c.* 1550) The early Parisian music printer and publisher Pierre Attaignant was among the first to use single-impression printing. He is first mentioned in 1515, and before 1527 he took over the movable music-type of Pierre Haultin, first using it in his *Chansons nouvelles . . .* (1528); there followed an ambitious series of publications. In 1538 he was music printer and bookseller to the king. After 1549 he disappeared from public life and died before July 1553.

Attaignant's prints comprise more than 30 masses, more than 300 motets, Magnificat, psalms, and passions; more than 2,000 chansons; five dance collections; 10 volumes for organ and two for lute. More than 150 composers are represented, including Josquin des Prés, Pierre de La Rue, Jean Mouton, Nicolas Gombert, Clément Janequin, Claude de Sermisy, Jacob Arcadelt, Adriaan Willaert, and Claude Le Jeune. His 111 surviving publications are a mine of information for early 16th-century music.

RECORDING: Dances.

aubade Music sung or played at dawn as opposed to SERENADE (evening music). The form originated with the troubadours in Provence, where it was known as the alba; the earliest known manuscript was an anonymous alba in Latin and Provençal. In the 12th and 13th centuries the Provençal alba was the warning song sung to lovers at dawn by a watchman (*see* TROUBADOUR). Examples are *Reis glorios* by Guiraut de Bornelh and the anonymous *Gaite de la tor.* The German minnesinger counterpart of the alba was the *Tagelied.* The Spanish term is *alborada,* a form of instrumental folk music played on a shawm or bagpipes and a *tamboril* (a small drum). In the 19th and 20th centuries the term aubade was used in a more general sense to describe morning music as in Édouard Lalo's opera *Le Roi d'Ys* and in Arthur Bliss's *Aubade for Coronation Morning.* In France the term is also used to describe music played at dawn in honor of distinguished people.

Auber, Daniel François (Esprit) (January 29, 1782–May 12, 1871) One of the principal figures in the development of the opéra comique in the first half of the 19th century, the French composer Daniel François Auber composed instinctively as a child and later became a pupil of Cherubini. His first publicly performed dramatic work was the one-act *Le Séjour militaire* (1813), followed by *Le Testament et les billets-doux* (1819); neither was remarkable. Auber's contribution to opéra comique derived partly from his association with the best librettist of the day, Eugène Scribe, and partly from the impact on French music by Rossini. Scribe's librettos, constructed with

an infallible sense of theater, offered an ideal framework for the romantic type of opéra comique to be cultivated by Auber, while the vivacious works of Rossini provided him with a musical style readily adaptable to French operatic taste. Between 1823 and 1864, 38 dramatic works of Auber on librettos of Scribe were produced in Paris. Most were opéras comiques, of which the most successful were *Le Maçon* (1825), *La Fiancée* (1829), *Fra Diavolo* (1830), *Le Domino noir* (1837), and *Les Diamants de la couronne* (1841). Rossini's tribute to their lively style, "petite musique mais d'un grand musicien," is still valid, and the tuneful, rambunctious overtures to some of these operas are still heard.

The Romantic vein explored by Auber and Scribe was also suited to grand opera, and several of their works, including *La Muette de Portici* (1828, also known as *Masaniello*), *Le Philtre* (1831), *Le Serment* (1832), and *Gustave III* (1833), anticipated the operas of Meyerbeer. Auber's religious music, consisting of motets and cantatas written between 1852 and 1855, is little known. He was elected a member of the Académie Française in 1829 and appointed director of the Paris Conservatoire in 1842 and chapel master to Napoleon III in 1857. Though few of his works were revived, his influence, recognized by both Wagner and Richard Strauss, was wide, extending to the early works of Gounod and Massenet.

RECORDINGS: Cello Concerto No. 1 in a minor; *Marco Spada* (ballet); overtures to various operas.

Auer, Leopold (June 7, 1845–July 15, 1930) A student of Joachim and the teacher of Mischa Elman, Heifetz, Efrem Zimbalist, and others, the Hungarian violinist Leopold Auer received his greatest musical impetus in Russia. In 1868 he went to St. Petersburg as soloist in the Imperial Orchestra and professor of violin at the Imperial Conservatory. According to tradition the violin soloist was expected to play a solo regularly in the ballets at the Imperial Opera, accounting for the excellent and challenging violin solos in the ballets of Tchaikovsky and other Russian composers. Tchaikovsky originally wrote his Violin Concerto for Auer but was so incensed at Auer's suggested revisions that he changed the dedication. However, the concerto became Auer's favorite work, and he taught it to all his students. Auer became a Russian subject in 1883, made his New York City debut in 1918, and then settled in the United States. He published violin manuals and methods as well as an autobiography, *My Long Life in Music* (1923).

Auric, Georges (b. February 15, 1899) One of the French composers known as LES SIX, Georges Auric studied in Paris with Vincent D'Indy and Albert Roussel, but he was influenced largely by Satie. In his early works he developed an ironic tone by mingling popular tunes with sophisticated harmony. His most notable compositions are the ballet *Les Matelots* (1925; "The Sailors") and his motion picture scores for René Clair's *A nous la liberté* (1931) and the biography of Toulouse-Lautrec, *Moulin Rouge* (1952). Other works include ballets produced by Sergey Diaghilev, Jean Louis Barrault, and Jean Cocteau, additional motion picture scores, an overture for orchestra (1938), songs, and chamber music. Auric wrote music criticism for *Marianne, Paris-Soir,* and *Nouvelles Littéraires* and was artistic director of the Paris Opéra and Opéra-Comique (1962–67).

RECORDING: Trio for oboe, clarinet, and bassoon.

Avison, Charles (baptized February 1709–May 10, 1770) The English composer Charles Avison was also an organist and a writer on musical aesthetics. Little is known of his early life; he may have gone to Italy, and he was perhaps a pupil of Francesco Geminiani, who was certainly a major influence. Avison was appointed organist at St. John's, Newcastle, in July 1736 and at St. Nicholas' in October. He taught harpsichord, violin, and flute and conducted the newly founded subscription concerts. He composed and published many concertos for stringed instruments, sonatas for harpsichord and strings, etc. His *Essay on Musical Expression* (1752) excited comment and evoked a pamphlet (published anonymously) from William Hayes, professor of music at Oxford (1753), to which

Avison replied with an enlarged edition of the *Essay.* A third edition appeared in 1770. Avison lived all his life at Newcastle, refusing appointments at York, Dublin, Edinburgh, and London. He was visited by Geminiani in 1760; among his many friends was the composer John Garth of Durham, whom he assisted in editing Marcello's *Psalms.*

As a composer Avison was a pleasing representative of the last phase of the late Baroque ancient style. It is difficult to enumerate his many concertos, for, like Geminiani, he was continually revising his earlier works. His trenchancy as a critic is shown in the famous *Essay* and in his explanatory or didactic prefaces to his own and his friends' works, which throw considerable light on 18th-century performance practices.

RECORDINGS: Concertos *à* 7 (26).

ayre A type of English solo song with lute accompaniment (or similar instrument, often with the bass line doubled by a viola da gamba) that flourished in the late 16th and early 17th centuries. The outstanding composers in the genre were the lutenist John Dowland, whose "Flow, my teares" ("Lachrimae") became so popular that a large number of continental and English instrumental pieces were based on its melody, and the poet and composer Thomas Campion. Other leading composers included John Danyel, Robert Jones, and Michael Cavendish.

Generally ayres were graceful, elegant, polished, often strophic songs, typically dealing with amorous subjects. Many, however, were lively and animated, full of rhythmic subtleties, and others were deeply emotional with bold, expressive harmonies and striking melodic lines.

The ayre developed from the French *air de cour* during a trend toward accompanied solo song in place of songs for several voices. Chansons, madrigals, and other polyphonic songs were frequently published in versions for voice and lute, and books of ayres often provided for optional performance by several singers by having, opposite the solo and lute version, the three additional voice parts printed so that they could be read from three sides of a table. *Compare* AIR.

B

Babbitt, Milton (b. May 10, 1916) The U.S. composer and theorist Milton Babbitt is known as a leading proponent of total serialism; *i.e.*, musical composition based on prior arrangements not only of all 12 pitches of the chromatic scale (as in 12-tone music) but also of dynamics, duration, timbre, and register.

Babbitt studied at the Universities of North Carolina and Pennsylvania, New York University, and Princeton; his teachers included Philip James, Marion Bauer, and Roger Sessions. He became a member of the music faculty at Princeton in 1938 and also taught mathematics, an interest evident both in his elaborate theories of composition and in his works themselves. He has taught also at the Berkshire Music Center and at the Darmstadt Internationale Ferienkurse. His interest in electronic music brought him to the committee of direction at the Columbia-Princeton Electronic Music Center. In 1959 he was elected to the National Institute of Arts and Letters.

Babbitt's *Composition for Synthesizer* (1961) displays his interest in establishing precise control over all elements of composition; the machine is used primarily to achieve such control rather than solely to generate novel sounds. *Philomel* (1964) combines synthesizer with the voices of live and recorded soprano. More traditional in medium is the *Partitions for Piano* (1957). Babbitt has written chamber music, including *Composition for Four Instruments* (1948) and three quartets (the latest in 1969), and motion picture sound tracks (*Into the Good Ground*, 1949), as well as songs, orchestral works, and compositions of electronically generated sound, with and without live singers and instrumentalists. He has published many articles on 12-tone and electronic music.

RECORDINGS: *All Set* (jazz ensemble), Quartet No. 2; ensembles for synthesizer.

Bach, Carl Philipp Emanuel (March 8, 1714– December 15, 1788) The second surviving son of Johann Sebastian and Maria Barbara Bach, Carl Philipp Emanuel was his father's true successor and a very important figure in his own generation. He writes: "For composition and keyboard-playing, I have never had any teacher other than my father." He studied law but probably never had any intention of a career other than music. In 1740 he was appointed harpsichordist to Frederick II of Prussia, himself a flutist and composer. The subservience grew irksome to Bach, but it was not until 1767 that he was able to resign and to take up an appointment as Kapellmeister at Hamburg. Meanwhile he had married (1744); published his *Versuch über die wahre Art das Klavier zu spielen* (1753 and 1762; *Essay on the True Art of Playing Keyboard Instruments,* 1949); and acquired an enviable reputation both as a composer and as a keyboard performer and teacher.

Unlike his brother Wilhelm Friedemann, C. P. E. Bach was successful in assimilating the powerful influence of their father and in making the transition into the new style. This represented a break with the past such as very few periods of musical development have equaled. The monumental character of Baroque music gave way to a mercurial romanticism for which the favorite contemporary description was sensibility *(Empfindsamkeit)*. C. P. E. Bach became a leader of this movement but retained the advantage of a solid craftsmanship and assurance for which he always gave full credit to his father's teaching and example.

C. P. E. Bach's compositions are numerous. Those of his Berlin period are comparatively old-fashioned in the main because of the conventional preferences of his royal employer. After his move to Hamburg he developed a more adventurous vein, and his work there did as much as any to open the future. His influence on Haydn, Mozart, and even Beethoven was freely acknowledged, and it is interesting that having influenced Haydn, C. P. E. Bach later allowed himself to be influenced just as Haydn allowed himself to be influenced by Mozart.

As a performer he was known for the precision of his playing, for the beauty of his touch, and for the intensity of his emotion. "He grew so animated and possessed," wrote Charles Burney, "that he looked like one inspired. His eyes were fixed, his underlip fell, and drops of effervescence distilled from his countenance."

The influence of C. P. E. Bach's *Essay* was unsurpassed for two generations. Haydn called it "the school of schools." Mozart said, "He is the father, we are the children." Beethoven, when undertaking to teach young Czerny, wrote "be sure of procuring Emanuel Bach's treatise." It is indeed one of the essential source books for understanding the style and interpretation of 18th-century music. It also had a particular bearing on the fingering of keyboard instruments, though it was less novel in this respect than has been claimed. It is comprehensive on thoroughbass and on ornaments and is an authentic guide to many other refinements of 18th-century performance.

BIBLIOGRAPHY: C. P. E. Bach, *Essay on the True Art of Playing Keyboard Instruments* (1949); Karl Geiringer, *The Bach Family* (1954).

RECORDINGS: Concertos; Magnificat; Sinfonias; Sonatas.

Bach, Johann Christian (September 5, 1735– January 1, 1782) The youngest son of Johann Sebastian and Anna Magdalena Bach, Johann Christian was called the "English Bach." He is likely to have received his early training from his father's cousin, Johann Elias Bach, but after his father's death in 1750 he enjoyed the advantage of working with his half brother, Carl Philipp Emanuel Bach, in Berlin. At the age of 20 he made his way to Italy and in 1756 became a pupil of Giovanni Battista Martini in Bologna. Having a grace and tactfulness of manner notably lacking in older generations of the Bach family, he found a generous patron. A convert to Roman Catholicism, he was appointed organist of the Milan Cathedral in 1760. His taste next turned to opera, and he was thought to have neglected his official duties.

In 1762 he became composer to the King's Theatre in London and wrote for it a number of successful Italian operas and produced much orchestral, chamber, and keyboard music and a few cantatas. In 1764 he started his fashionable series of concerts with Karl Friedrich Abel. He received a lucrative ap-

pointment as music master to Queen Charlotte and her children and became a social as well as musical success. In 1772 he was honored by an invitation to write an opera for the elector at Mannheim. In 1773 he married the Italian singer Cecilia Grassi.

J. C. Bach had no difficult transition to make into the post-Baroque style of music; he was born into it. Well-grounded by C. P. E. Bach, thoroughly trained by Martini, naturally receptive to the latest Italian music in Milan, Naples, and elsewhere, he early became a fashionable composer. Among those who learned from and greatly respected him was the young Mozart. Nevertheless, his early success apparently relieved him of any urgent pressure to continue developing, and, though always a sensitive and imaginative composer, he never grew to be a profound one.

BIBLIOGRAPHY: Charles Sanford Terry, *John Christian Bach* (1929); Karl Geiringer, *The Bach Family* (1954).

RECORDINGS: Concertos; Quartets; Quintets; Sinfonias; Sonatas.

Bach, Johann Sebastian (March 21, 1685– July 28, 1750) Now considered one of the greatest composers of all time, Johann Sebastian Bach was regarded by his contemporaries as an outstanding harpsichordist, organist, and expert on organ building but an out-of-date, excessively learned composer. He brought together the principal styles, forms, and national traditions of preceding generations and, by virtue of his synthesis, enriched them all.

He was a member of a remarkable family of musicians who were proud of their achievements, and about 1735 he drafted a genealogy, *Ursprung der musicalisch-Bachischen Familie* ("Origin of the Musical Bach Family"), in which he traced his ancestry back to his great-great grandfather Veit Bach, a Lutheran baker (or miller) who was driven from Hungary to Wechmar in Thuringia (a historic region now in East Germany) by religious persecution late in the 16th century. There were already Bachs in the area, and it may be that when Veit moved to Wechmar he was returning to his birthplace. He would take his cittern to the mill and play it while grinding was going on. Johann Sebastian remarked, "A pretty noise

Johann Sebastian Bach
lithograph by Rudolph Hoffmann
Bild-Archiv der Oesterreichischen
Nationalbibliothek, Wien

Georgenkirche, where Johann Christoph Bach was organist until 1703.

By 1695 both his parents were dead, and he was looked after by his eldest brother, also named Johann Christoph, organist at Ohrdruf. This Christoph had been a pupil of Johann Pachelbel, and he apparently gave Johann Sebastian his first formal keyboard lessons. The young Bach again did well at school, and in 1700 his voice secured him a place in a select choir of poor boys at the school of the Michaelskirche, Lüneburg (now in West Germany).

His voice must have broken soon after this, but he remained at Lüneburg for a long time, making himself generally useful. He probably studied in the school library, which had a large and up-to-date collection of church music and heard Georg Böhm, organist of the Johanneskirche, and he visited Hamburg to hear the renowned organist and composer Johann Adam Reinken at the Katharinenkirche, contriving also to hear the French orchestra maintained by the Duke of Celle.

He seems to have returned to Thuringia in the late summer of 1702; at some time between July and November, he applied for the post of organist at Sangerhausen (in modern East Germany). But for ducal interference he would have obtained it, and he must already have been a reasonably proficient organist. His experience at Lüneburg, if not at Ohrdruf, had turned him away from the secular string-playing tradition of his immediate ancestors; thenceforth he was chiefly, though not exclusively, a composer and performer of keyboard and sacred music. The next few months are wrapped in mystery, but by March 4, 1703, he was a member of the orchestra employed by Duke Johann Ernst of Weimar (brother of Wilhelm Ernst, whose service Bach entered in 1708). This post was a mere stopgap; he probably already had his eye on the organ then being built at the Neukirche in Arnstadt (on the northern edge of the Thuringian forest); when it was finished he helped to test it, and in August 1703 he was appointed organist—all this at the age of 18. Arnstadt documents imply that he had been court organist at Weimar; this is incredible, though it is likely enough that he had occasionally played there.

they must have made together! However, he learnt to keep time, and this apparently was the beginning of music in our family."

Until the birth of Johann Sebastian his was the least distinguished branch of the family; its members had been competent practical musicians but not composers such as Johann Christoph, Johann Michael, and Johann Ludwig. In later days the most important musicians in the family were Johann Sebastian's sons, Wilhelm Friedemann, Carl Philipp Emanuel, and Johann Christian (the "English Bach").

early years J. S. Bach was born at Eisenach, Thuringia, the youngest child of Johann Ambrosius and Elisabeth Lämmerhirt Bach. Ambrosius was a string player employed by the town council and the ducal court of Eisenach. Johann Sebastian started school in 1692 or 1693 and did well in spite of frequent absences. Of his musical education at this time, nothing definite is known; but he may have picked up the rudiments of string playing from his father, and he must have attended the

Arnstadt   At Arnstadt, where he remained until 1707, Bach devoted himself to keyboard music—the organ in particular. While at Lüneburg he apparently had no opportunity of becoming directly acquainted with the spectacular, flamboyant playing and compositions of Dietrich Buxtehude, the most significant exponent of the north German school of organ music. In October 1705 he rectified this gap in his knowledge by obtaining a month's leave and walking to Lübeck (more than 200 miles [300 kilometers]). His visit must have been profitable, for he did not return until about the middle of January 1706. In February his employers complained about his absence and about other things as well: he had harmonized the hymn tunes so freely that the congregation could not sing to his accompaniment, and he had produced no cantatas. Perhaps the real reasons for his neglect were that he was temporarily obsessed with the organ and was on bad terms with the local singers and instrumentalists, who were not under his control and did not come up to his standards. In the summer of 1705 he had made some offensive remark about a bassoon player that led to an unseemly scuffle in the street. His replies to these complaints were neither satisfactory nor even accommodating; the fact that he was not dismissed out of hand suggests that his employers were as well aware of his exceptional ability as he was himself and were reluctant to lose him.

During these early years Bach inherited the musical culture of the Thuringian area, a thorough familiarity with the traditional forms and chorales of the orthodox Lutheran service, and in keyboard music perhaps (through his brother, Johann Christoph) a bias toward the formalistic styles of the south. But he also learned eagerly from the northern rhapsodists—Buxtehude above all. By 1708 he had probably learned all that his German predecessors could teach him and arrived at a first synthesis of northern and southern German styles. He had also studied, on his own and during his presumed excursions to Celle, some French organ and instrumental music.

Among the few works that can be ascribed to these early years with anything more than a show of plausibility are the *Capriccio sopra la lontananza del suo fratello dilettissimo* (*Capriccio on the Departure of His Most Beloved Brother*, 1704, BWV 992); the chorale prelude on *Wie schön leuchtet* (*How Brightly Shines*, c. 1705, BWV 739); and the fragmentary early version of the organ Prelude and Fugue in g minor (before 1707, BWV 535a). (The BWV numbers provided are the standard catalog numbers of Bach's works as established in the Bach-Werke-Verzeichnis, prepared by the German musicologist Wolfgang Schmieder.)

Mühlhausen   In June 1707 Bach obtained a post at the Blasiuskirche in Mühlhausen in Thuringia. He moved there soon after and married his cousin Maria Barbara Bach at Dornheim on October 17. At Mühlhausen things seem to have gone more smoothly, at least for a while. He produced several church cantatas, all cast in a conservative mold, based on biblical and chorale texts, and displaying no influence of the modern Italian operatic forms that were to appear in his later cantatas. The popular organ Toccata in d minor (BWV 565), written in the rhapsodic northern style, and the Prelude and Fugue in D Major (BWV 532) may also have been composed during the Mühlhausen period, as well as the Passacaglia in c minor (BWV 582), an early example of Bach's skill in large-scale organization. Cantata No. 71, *Gott ist mein König (God Is My King)*, of February 4, 1708, was printed at the expense of the city council and was the first of Bach's compositions to be published. While at Mühlhausen Bach copied music to enlarge the choir library, tried to encourage music in the surrounding villages, and was in sufficient favor to interest his employers in a scheme for rebuilding the organ. His real reason for resigning on June 25, 1708, is not known. He said that his plans for a "well-regulated [concerted] church music" had been hindered by conditions in Mühlhausen and that his salary was inadequate. It is generally supposed that he had become involved in a theological controversy between his own Pastor Frohne and Archdeacon Eilmar of the Marienkirche. He was friendly with Eilmar, who provided him with librettos and became godfather to Bach's first child, and it is likely enough that he was not in sympathy with

Frohne, who as a Pietist would have frowned on elaborate church music. It is just as possible, however, that it was the dismal state of musical life in Mühlhausen that prompted Bach to seek employment elsewhere. His resignation was accepted, and he moved to Weimar, some miles west of Jena on the Ilm River. He continued to be on good terms with Mühlhausen personalities, for he supervised the rebuilding of the organ, is supposed to have inaugurated it on October 31, 1709, and composed a cantata for February 4, 1709, which was printed but has disappeared.

Weimar From the outset Bach was court organist at Weimar and a member of the orchestra. Encouraged by Wilhelm Ernst he concentrated on the organ during the first few years of his tenure. From Weimar Bach occasionally visited Weissenfels; in February 1713 he took part in a court celebration there that included a performance of his first secular cantata, *Was mir behagt,* or the *Hunt* Cantata (BWV 208).

Late in 1713 Bach had the opportunity of succeeding Friedrich Wilhelm Zachow at the Liebfrauenkirche, Halle; but the duke raised his salary, and he stayed on at Weimar, becoming concertmaster on March 2, 1714, with the duty of composing a cantata every month. He became friendly with a relative, Johann Gottfried Walther, a music lexicographer and composer who was organist of the town church, and, like Walther, Bach took part in the musical activities at the Yellow Castle, then occupied by Duke Wilhelm's two nephews, Ernst August and Johann Ernst, both of whom he taught. The latter was a talented composer who wrote concertos in the Italian manner, some of which Bach arranged for keyboard instruments.

Unfortunately Bach's development cannot be traced in detail during the vital years 1708–14, when his style underwent a profound change. There are too few datable works. From the series of cantatas written in 1714–16, it is obvious that he had been decisively influenced by the new styles and forms of the contemporary Italian opera and by the innovations of such Italian concerto composers as Vivaldi. The results of this encounter can be seen in such cantatas as numbers 182, 199,

and 61 in 1714; 31 and 161 in 1715; and 70 and 147 in 1716. His favorite forms appropriated from the Italians were those based on refrain (ritornello) or da capo schemes in which wholesale repetition—literal or with modifications—of entire sections of a piece permitted him to create coherent musical forms with much larger dimensions than had hitherto been possible. These newly acquired techniques henceforth governed a host of Bach's arias and concerto movements, as well as many of his larger fugues (especially the mature ones for organ), and profoundly affected his treatment of chorales.

Among other works almost certainly composed at Weimar are most of the *Orgelbüchlein (Little Organ Book),* all but the last of the so-called 18 *Great* Chorale Preludes, the earliest organ trios, and most of the organ preludes and fugues. The *Great* Prelude and Fugue in G Major for organ (BWV 541) was finally revised about 1715, and the Toccata and Fugue in F Major (BWV 540) may have been played at Weissenfels.

On December 1, 1716, the Kapellmeister at Weimar, Johann Samuel Drese, died. He was succeeded by his son, who was rather a nonentity. Bach presumably resented being passed over, and in due course he accepted an appointment as musical director to Prince Leopold of Köthen, which was confirmed in August 1717. Duke Wilhelm, however, refused to accept his resignation—partly, perhaps, because of Bach's friendship with the duke's nephews, with whom the duke was on the worst of terms. About September a contest between Bach and the well-known French organist Louis Marchand was arranged at Dresden. The exact circumstances are not known, but Marchand avoided the contest by leaving Dresden a few hours before it should have taken place. Bach won by default, and perhaps this emboldened him to renew his request for permission to leave Weimar. He did so but in such terms that the duke imprisoned him for a month (November 6–December 2). A few days after his release Bach moved to Köthen (in modern East Germany), some 30 miles (50 kilometers) north of Halle.

Köthen As Kapellmeister at Köthen he was concerned chiefly with chamber and orchestral music. Even though some of the works may have been composed earlier and revised later, it was at Köthen that the sonatas for violin and clavier, viola da gamba and clavier, and the works for unaccompanied violin and cello were put into something like their present form. The *Brandenburg* Concertos were finished by March 24, 1721; it has been suggested that in the Sixth Concerto Bach bore in mind the technical limitations of the prince, who played the gamba. Bach played the viola by choice as he liked to be "in the middle of the harmony." He also wrote a few cantatas for the prince's birthday and other such occasions; most seem to have survived only in later versions adapted to more generally useful words. And he found time to compile pedagogical keyboard works; the *Clavierbüchlein* for W. F. Bach (begun January 22, 1720); some of the *French* Suites; the Inventions (1720); and the first book (1722) of *Das Wohltemperierte Klavier* (*The Well-Tempered Clavier,* eventually consisting of two books, each of 24 preludes and fugues in all keys and known as the *Forty-eight*). This remarkable collection systematically explores both the potentials of a newly established tuning procedure, which for the first time in the history of keyboard music made all the keys equally usable, and the possibilities for musical organization afforded by the system of functional tonality, a kind of musical syntax consolidated in the music of the Italian concerto composers of the preceding generation and a system that was to prevail for the next 200 years. At the same time *The Well-Tempered Clavier* is a compendium of the most popular forms and styles of the era—dance types, arias, motets, concertos, etc.—presented within the unified aspect of a single compositional technique, the rigorously logical fugue.

Maria Barbara Bach died unexpectedly and was buried on July 7, 1720. About November Bach visited Hamburg; his wife's death may have unsettled him and led him to inquire after a vacant post at the Jacobikirche. Nothing came of this, but he played at the Katharinenkirche in the presence of Reinken. After hearing Bach improvise variations on a chorale, the old man said, "I thought this art was dead; but I see it still lives in you."

On December 3, 1721, Bach married Anna Magdalena Wilcken, daughter of a trumpeter at Weissenfels. Except for his first wife's death, the first four years at Köthen were probably the happiest of Bach's life. He was on the best of terms with the prince, who was genuinely musical, and in 1730 Bach said that he had expected to end his days there. But the prince married in December 1721, and conditions deteriorated. The princess—described by Bach as "an *amusa*" (that is to say, opposed to the muses)—required so much of her husband's attention that Bach began to feel neglected. He also had to think of the education of his elder sons, born in 1710 and 1714, and he probably began to think of moving to Leipzig as soon as the cantorate fell vacant with the death of Johann Kuhnau in June 1722. Bach applied in December, but the post—already turned down by Bach's friend, Georg Philipp Telemann—was offered to another prominent composer of the day, Christoph Graupner, Kapellmeister at Darmstadt. As the latter was not sure that he would be able to accept, Bach gave a trial performance (Cantata No. 22, *Jesu nahm zu sich die Zwölfe/Jesus called unto Him the Twelve/*) on February 7, 1723; when Graupner withdrew (April 9) Bach was so deeply committed to Leipzig that, although the anti-musical princess had died on April 4, he applied for permission to leave Köthen. This he obtained on April 13, and on May 13 he was sworn in at Leipzig.

He was appointed honorary Kapellmeister of Köthen, and both he and Anna Magdalena were employed there from time to time until the prince died in November 1728.

Leipzig As director of church music for the city of Leipzig, Bach supplied performers for four churches. At the Peterskirche the choir merely led the hymns. At the Neukirche, Nikolaikirche, and Thomaskirche part singing was required; but Bach himself conducted and his own church music was performed only at the last two. His first official performance was on May 30, 1723, the first Sunday after Trinity Sunday, with Cantata No. 75, *Die Elenden sollen essen*. New works produced during this year included many cantatas, the Magnificat in its first version, and the *St. John*

Passion, which was subsequently revised. The total number of cantatas produced during this ecclesiastical year was about 62, of which approximately 39 were new works.

On June 11, 1724, the first Sunday after Trinity, Bach began a fresh annual cycle of cantatas, and within the year he wrote 52 of the so-called chorale cantatas, formerly supposed to have been composed over the nine-year period 1735–44. The Sanctus of the Mass in b minor was produced at Christmas. During his first two or three years at Leipzig, Bach produced a large number of new cantatas, sometimes, as recent research has revealed, at the rate of one a week.

As a result of his intense activity in cantata production during his first three years in Leipzig, Bach had created a supply of church music to meet his future needs for the regular Sunday and feast-day services. After 1726, therefore, he turned his attention to other projects. He did, however, produce the *St. Matthew* Passion in 1729, a work that inaugurated a renewed interest in the mid 1730s for vocal works on a larger scale than the cantata; the now-lost *St. Mark* Passion (1731), the *Christmas* Oratorio, BWV 248 (1734), and the *Ascension* Oratorio (Cantata No. 11, *Lobet Gott in seinen Reichen,* 1735).

In addition to his responsibilities as musical director, Bach also had various nonmusical duties in his capacity as the cantor of the school at the Thomaskirche. Since he resented these latter obligations, Bach frequently absented himself without leave, playing or examining organs, taking his son Friedemann to hear the "pretty tunes," as he called them, at the Dresden opera, and fulfilling the duties of the honorary court posts that he contrived to hold all his life. To some extent, no doubt, he accepted engagements because he needed money; he complained in 1730 that his income was less than he had been led to expect (he remarked that because of a series of unseasonably mild winters there were not enough funerals); but obviously his routine work must have suffered. Friction between Bach and his employers thus developed almost at once. Bach's initial understanding of the fees and prerogatives accruing to his position—particularly regarding his responsibility for musical

activities in the University of Leipzig's Paulinerkirche—differed from that of the town council and the university organist, Johann Gottlieb Görner. Bach also remained in the eyes of his employers their third (and unenthusiastic) choice for the post—behind Telemann and Graupner. Furthermore the authorities insisted on admitting unmusical boys to the school, making it difficult for Bach to keep his churches supplied with competent singers, and they refused to spend enough money to keep a decent orchestra together. The resulting ill feeling had become serious by 1730. It was temporarily dispelled by the tact of the new rector, Johann Matthias Gesner, who admired Bach and had known him at Weimar; but Gesner stayed only until 1734 and was succeeded by Johann August Ernesti, a young man with up-to-date ideas on education, one of which was that music was not one of the humanities but a time-wasting sideline. Trouble flared again in July 1736 with a dispute over Bach's right to appoint prefects that became a public scandal. Fortunately for Bach he became court composer to the Elector of Saxony in November 1736. After some delay he was able to induce his friends at court to hold an official inquiry, and his dispute with Ernesti was settled in 1738. The exact terms of the settlement are not known, but thereafter Bach did as he liked.

In 1726, after he had completed the bulk of his cantatas, Bach began to publish the clavier partitas singly, with a collected edition in 1731, perhaps with the intention of attracting recognition beyond Leipzig and of securing a more amenable appointment elsewhere. The second part of the *Clavierübung,* containing the Concerto *in the Italian Taste* and the French Overture (Partita) in b minor, appeared in 1735. The third part, consisting of the Organ Mass with the Prelude and *(St. Anne)* Fugue in E-flat Major (BWV 552), appeared in 1739. From *c.* 1729–36 Bach was honorary musical director to Weissenfels, and from 1729 to 1737 and again from 1739 for a year or two, he directed the Leipzig Collegium Musicum. For these concerts he adapted some of his earlier concertos as harpsichord concertos, becoming one of the first composers in history—if not the first—of concertos for keyboard instrument and orchestra, just as he was one of the first to use the harpsichordist's right hand as a true melodic part in chamber music. These are just two of several respects in which the basically conservative and traditional Bach was a significant innovator.

About 1733 Bach began to produce cantatas in honor of the Elector of Saxony and his family, evidently with the court appointment he secured in 1736 in mind; many of these secular movements were adapted to sacred words and reused in the *Christmas* Oratorio. The Kyrie and Gloria of the Mass in b minor, written in 1733, were also dedicated to the elector, but the remainder of the mass was not put together until Bach's last years. On his visits to Dresden Bach had won the regard of Count Hermann Karl von Keyserlingk, the Russian envoy, who commissioned the so-called *Goldberg* Variations; these were published as part four of the *Clavierübung* about 1742, and book two of the *Forty-eight* seems to have been compiled about the same time. In addition he wrote a few cantatas, revised some of his Weimar organ works, and published the so-called *Schübler* Chorale Preludes in or after 1746.

last years   In May 1747 he visited his son Emanuel at Potsdam and played before Frederick II the Great of Prussia; in July his improvisations on a theme proposed by the king took shape as *The Musical Offering*. In June 1747 he joined the Society of the Musical Sciences that had been founded by his former pupil Lorenz Christoph Mizler; he presented the canonic variations on the chorale *Vom Himmel hoch da komm' ich her (From Heaven Above to Earth I Come)* to the society in manuscript and afterward published them.

Of Bach's last illness little is known except that it lasted several months and prevented him from finishing *The Art of the Fugue*. His constitution was undermined by two unsuccessful eye operations performed by John Taylor, the itinerant English quack who numbered Handel among his other failures, and he died on July 28, 1750, at Leipzig. His employers proceeded with relief to appoint a successor; Burgomaster Stieglitz remarked, "The school needs a cantor, not a musical director—

though certainly he ought to understand music." Anna Magdalena was left in a financially precarious state. For some reason her stepsons did nothing to help her, and her own sons were too young to do so. She died on February 27, 1760, and was given a pauper's funeral.

Unfinished as it was, *The Art of the Fugue* was published in 1751. It attracted little attention and was reissued in 1752 with a laudatory preface by Friedrich Wilhelm Marpurg, a well-known Berlin musician who later became director of the royal lottery. In spite of Marpurg and of some appreciative remarks by the influential Hamburg critic and composer Johann Mattheson, only about 30 copies had been sold by 1756 when Emanuel Bach offered the plates for sale. As far as is known they were sold for scrap.

Emanuel Bach and the organist-composer Johann Friedrich Agricola (a pupil of Sebastian's) wrote an obituary; Mizler added a few closing words and published the result in the journal of his society (1754). An English translation appears in *The Bach Reader*. Though incomplete and inaccurate, the obituary is of very great importance as a firsthand source of information.

Bach appears to have been a good husband and father. Indeed he was the father of 20 children, only 10 of whom survived to maturity. There is amusing evidence of a certain thriftiness—a necessary virtue—for he was never more than moderately well off, and he delighted in hospitality. Living as he did at a time when music was beginning to be regarded as no occupation for a gentleman, he occasionally had to stand up for his rights both as a man and as a musician; he was then obstinate in the extreme. But no sympathetic employer had any trouble with Bach, and with his professional brethren he was modest and friendly. He was also a good teacher and from his Mühlhausen days onward was never without pupils.

influence   For about 50 years after Bach's death, his music was neglected. This was only natural; in the days of Haydn and Mozart, no one could be expected to take much interest in a composer who had been considered old-fashioned even in his lifetime—especially since his music was not readily available, and half of it (the church cantatas) was fast becoming useless as a result of changes in religious thought.

At the same time musicians of the late 18th century were neither so ignorant of Bach's music nor so insensitive to its influence as some modern authors have suggested. Emanuel Bach's debt to his father was considerable, and Bach exercised a profound and acknowledged influence directly on Haydn, Mozart, and Beethoven.

After 1800 the revival of Bach's music gained momentum. The German writer Johann Nikolaus Forkel published a *Life, Genius and Works* in 1802 and acted as adviser to the publishers Hoffmeister and Kühnel, whose collected edition, begun in 1801, was cut short by the activities of Napoleon. By 1829 a representative selection of keyboard music was nonetheless available, although very few of the vocal works were published. But in that year the German musician Eduard Devrient and Mendelssohn took the next step with the centenary performance of the *St. Matthew* Passion. It and the *St. John* Passion were both published in 1830; the Mass in b minor followed (1832–45). The Leipzig publisher Peters began a collected edition of "piano" and instrumental works in 1837; the organ works followed in 1844–52.

Encouraged by Schumann, the Bach-Gesellschaft (BG) was founded in the centenary year 1850 with the purpose of publishing the complete works. By 1900 all the known works had been printed, and the BG was succeeded by the Neue Bach-Gesellschaft (NBG), which exists still, organizing festivals and publishing popular editions. Its chief publication is its research journal, the *Bach-Jahrbuch* (from 1904). By 1950 the deficiencies of the BG edition had become painfully obvious, and the Bach-Institut was founded with headquarters at Göttingen (West Germany) and Leipzig, to produce a new standard edition (the Neue Bach-Ausgabe or NBA) expected to comprise 84 volumes.

In retrospect the Bach revival, reaching back to 1800, can be recognized as the first conspicuous example of the deliberate exhumation of old music—accompanied by biographical and critical studies—and it served as an inspiration and a model for subsequent work of that kind.

Among the biographical and critical works on Bach, the most important was the monumental study *Johann Sebastian Bach* (2 vols., Leipzig, 1873–80) by the German musicologist Philipp Spitta, covering not only Bach's life and works but also much of the historical background. Although wrong in many details the book is still indispensable to the Bach student.

editions The word *Urtext* (original text) may lead the uninitiated to suppose that they are being offered an exact reproduction of what Bach wrote. It must be understood that the autographs of many important works no longer exist. Therefore Bach's intentions often have to be pieced together from anything up to 20 sources—all different. Even first editions and facsimiles of autograph manuscripts are not infallible guides to Bach's intentions. In fact they are often dangerously misleading, and practical musicians should take expert advice before consulting them. Editions published between 1752 and *c.* 1840 are little more than curiosities, chiefly interesting for the light they throw on the progress of the revival.

No comprehensive edition is trustworthy throughout: neither Peters nor the BG nor even the NBA. Nevertheless it is advisable to begin by finding out whether music desired has been published by the NBA.

BIBLIOGRAPHY: Philipp Spitta, *Johann Sebastian Bach,* 2 vols. (1873–80; Eng. trans., *Johann Sebastian Bach: His Work and Influence on the Music of Germany, 1685–1750,* 1883–85, reprinted 1951); Albert Schweitzer, *J. S. Bach,* 2 vols. (1905; Eng. trans., 1911; reprint, 1966); Charles Sanford Terry, *Bach: A Biography,* rev. ed. (1933; reprint, 1962); Hans David and Arthur Mendel, eds., *The Bach Reader,* rev. ed. (1966); Karl and Irene Geiringer, *Johann Sebastian Bach: The Culmination of an Era* (1966).

RECORDINGS: Numerous recordings of most works.

Bach, Wilhelm Friedemann (November 22, 1710–July 1, 1784) Perhaps most remembered from his father's *Clavierbüchlein vor Wilhelm Friedemann Bach,* written for his instruction when he was 10 (it includes the two- and three-part inventions), Wilhelm Friedemann was the eldest son of Johann Sebastian and Maria Barbara Bach and a composer during the transitional period between the Baroque and Rococo.

Already composing extensively in 1733, he was appointed organist of the Sophienkirche in Dresden. In 1746 he moved to the Liebfrauenkirche at Halle. At about this time, or perhaps after his father's death in 1750, he began to have personality difficulties, evidenced by excessive drinking and other lapses. After a late marriage in 1751 he became restless and applied unsuccessfully for a change of post in 1753 and again in 1758. In 1762 he won an appointment to the Darmstadt court but did not take it. Resigning his old post in Halle in 1764, he sought regular employment for 20 years. He became touchy and unreliable, and although his talents were never doubted, he imagined that they were. In 1774 he moved to Berlin, where he lived meagerly by giving recitals and teaching.

Of his compositions keyboard works and cantatas form the larger part; he also composed symphonies, chamber works, and an opera. His music vacillated between the Baroque style of his father and the newer *galant,* or Rococo, style. His compositions, few for his many years, are often impassioned and unpredictable in melody, harmony, and rhythm. His life has been the subject of more or less fictionalized treatment in novels, opera, and film.

BIBLIOGRAPHY: Karl Geiringer, *The Bach Family* (1954).

RECORDINGS: Concerto in c minor for two harpsichords and strings; Flute Duets; Trio in D Major for two flutes and cembalo.

Bachauer, Gina (May 21, 1913–August 22, 1976) The Greek pianist Gina Bachauer studied at the Athens Conservatory, with Alfred Cortot in Paris, and later with Sergei Rachmaninoff. A romantic pianist with a wide repertoire, she was considered best in large-scale virtuoso works.

Backhaus, Wilhelm (March 26, 1884–July 5, 1969) Educated at the Leipzig Conservatory, the German pianist Wilhelm Backhaus also studied with Eugène d'Albert. After World War II he made his home in Switzerland. He was known as an elegant technician and as a distinguished interpreter of Beethoven and Brahms.

Bacon, Ernst (b. May 26, 1898) A U.S. pianist, theorist, conductor, and composer, Ernst Bacon studied at Northwestern University (1915–18) and the University of California. In 1924 he went to Vienna, where he studied piano briefly with Franz Schmidt and theory with Karl Weigl. After a concert tour of Germany he returned to the United States in 1925 and was appointed professor of piano at the Eastman School of Music in Rochester, New York. He studied theory with Bloch (1928) and conducting with Eugene Goossens (1926), and from 1934 to 1937 he was supervisor of the Federal Music Project in San Francisco, also conducting several orchestras. Widely heard as a college lecturer, he has taught at Converse College in Spartanburg, South Carolina (1938–45), and at Syracuse (New York) University (1945–63). His works are primarily for voice and for orchestra, and the texts for his songs, cantatas, and oratorios draw heavily from U.S. poets: *My River* (1932; Emily Dickinson), *From Emily's Diary* (1945; Dickinson), *The Lord Star* (c. 1950; Walt Whitman), and *Six Songs* (1942; Dickinson, Whitman, Carl Sandburg). The two-act music play *A Tree on the Plains* (1940; revised 1962) has a libretto by Paul Horgan, and the third (1956) of Bacon's four symphonies is built around a poem by Horgan. Bacon's thoughts on music are elaborated in *Words on Music* (1960) and *Notes on the Piano* (1963).

Badings, Henk (b. January 17, 1907) The Indonesian-born Dutch composer Henk Badings studied mining engineering and geology in Delft, The Netherlands, and taught those subjects (1931–34) at the Technical Institute there before devoting himself exclusively to composition. Largely self-taught as a composer but briefly a student of the Dutch composer Willem Pijper, Badings was influenced by Hindemith, Honegger, and Milhaud. Badings combined experimental form and tonality with neoclassical and Baroque techniques, using new tunings and electronic sounds. He taught composition at the Rotterdam Conservatory (1934–37), following which he was co-director of the Music Lyceum in Amsterdam (1937–41) and director of the Royal Conservatory in The Hague (1941–44). Since 1961 he has taught acoustics at the University of Utrecht and since 1962 composition at the Hochschule für Musik in Stuttgart, West Germany.

RECORDINGS: *Cavatina* for flute and piano; Concerto for flute and wind orchestra; *Malinconia;* Octet for winds and strings; Passacaglia for timpani and organ.

Badura-Skoda, Paul (b. October 6, 1927) The Austrian pianist Paul Badura-Skoda studied in his native Vienna and with Edwin Fischer. Among his recordings are all of the Schubert and Beethoven piano sonatas. He played the first performance of Frank Martin's Second Piano Concerto (1970). He married the pianist Eva Halfer in 1951, and together they have written an important book, *Interpreting Mozart on the Keyboard* (1957). He is known as a duettist with his compatriot Jörg Demus and for his interest in performance on period instruments.

bagpipe A wind instrument consisting of two or more pipes with reeds to which wind is fed by arm pressure on a skin bag. The pipes are held in wooden sockets, or stocks, tied into the bag, which is inflated either by the mouth through a blowpipe provided with a leather nonreturn valve or by bellows strapped to the body and worked by the arm not applying the pressure. Melodies are played on the fingerholes of the melody pipe, or chanter, while one or more other pipes, or drones, sound single notes tuned against the chanter before performing by means of extendable joints. To articulate the melody and to reiterate notes, a piper employs the gracing technique, rapidly interpolating notes outside the melody to give a detached note effect.

Bagpipes probably originated in the Orient and existed in Europe by the 13th century; the instrument is alluded to in the 9th. Earlier evidence is scarce but includes four Greek and Latin references of *c.* A.D. 100 (*e.g.,* Suetonius' mention of Nero as *utricularius*) and without certainty an Alexandrian terra cotta of *c.* 100 B.C. (at Berlin).

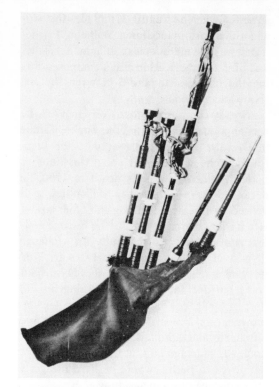

Highland bagpipe, Scottish, 19th century
courtesy, Metropolitan Museum of Art
The Crosby Brown Collection of Musical
Instruments, 1889

The typical west European bagpipe has a conically bored chanter sounded by a double reed; drones are cylindrical with single reeds. The Scottish highland bagpipe, now played widely over the world, has two tenor drones and a bass drone an octave below, and as with many bagpipes and other folk instruments its scale preserves traditional intervals foreign to learned musical systems. Once a pastoral and festive instrument, its military use with drums dates from the 18th century. The elaborate gracing technique is codified in tutors for the instrument.

National varieties exist under a number of different names: musette and cornemuse (France), *biniou* (Brittany), *piva* and *zampogna* (Italy), *gaita* (Spain), *gaida* (Bulgaria), *Dudelsack* and *Sackpfeife* (Germany), *dudy* (Czechoslovakia), and *koza* (Poland).

BIBLIOGRAPHY: William Grattan Flood, *The Story of the Bagpipe* (1911; reprint, 1976); Anthony Baines, *Bagpipes* (1960); Francis Collinson, *The Bagpipe: The History of a Musical Instrument* (1975).

Baker, Janet (b. August 21, 1933)   The English mezzo-soprano Janet Baker studied in London and in 1956 went to Salzburg as the recipient of the Kathleen Ferrier Award. A regular performer at the Edinburgh Festival, she was at first best known as an interpreter of oratorio and of English songs but won increasing renown for the force of her stage portrayals, notably as Didon in Berlioz' *Les Troyens.* She was created a dame of the Order of the British Empire in 1976.

Baker, Julius (b. September 23, 1915) Educated at the Eastman School and at the Curtis Institute, Julius Baker is perhaps the most prominent U.S. flutist of the mid-20th century. He has been first flutist with the Cleveland, Pittsburgh, CBS, and Chicago orchestras and with the New York Philharmonic since 1965. From 1947 to 1965 he was soloist with the New York City-based Bach Aria Group and has taught at the Juilliard School since 1954.

Balakirev, Mily (Alekseyevich)   (January 2, 1837 [December 21, 1836, old style]–May 29 [May 16, old style], 1910).   The leader of the group of Russian composers known as the *Kutchka* (the Mighty Five, including Borodin, César Cui, Mussorgsky, and Rimsky-Korsakov), Mily Balakirev is known mostly for his orchestral and piano works and for his songs.

After early study with his mother and John Field's pupil Aleksandr Dubuque, he continued with Karl Eisrich, who was music director for Aleksandr Dmitriyevich Ulybyshev, a wealthy landowner and author of books on Mozart and Beethoven. Balakirev had access to Ulybyshev's extensive music library (he later inherited it) and at 15 began to compose and was allowed to rehearse the local theater orchestra. From 1853 to 1855 he studied mathematics at the University of Kazan and wrote a piano concerto, among other things. In 1855 Ulybyshev took him to St. Petersburg and introduced him to Glinka and other leading musicians.

During 1857 to 1859 Balakirev made a number of appearances as a concert pianist, composed an Overture on Russian Themes, music to *King Lear,* and his earliest published songs. He became the mentor of two young officers who were amateur composers, Cui and Mussorgsky, and in 1861–62 his circle of disciples was joined by Rimsky-Korsakov and Borodin. In 1862 he threw himself into a new venture, the Free School of Music opened in opposition to the St. Petersburg Conservatory, and soon became principal conductor of its public concerts.

During the 1860s Balakirev was at the height of his influence and varied activity. He collected and published folk songs from the Volga area and introduced them in a Second Overture on Russian Themes, which ultimately became the symphonic poem *Russia;* he spent summer holidays in the Caucasus, gathering themes and inspiration for his piano fantasy *Islamey* (1869) and his symphonic poem *Tamara* (1867–82); he published the works of Glinka and visited Prague to produce them; and for a time (1867–69) he conducted the symphony concerts of the Russian Music Society.

His despotic nature and his tactlessness made innumerable enemies so that even his friends and disciples came to resent his tutelage, and a series of personal and artistic misfortunes led to his withdrawal from the world of music (1871–76) and his taking a humble post as a railway clerk. He had passed through a period of acute depression 10 years earlier; now he underwent a more severe crisis from which he emerged a totally changed man. He gradually returned to the musical world, resumed the directorship of the Free School, and from 1883 to 1894 was director of the imperial chapel. He also resumed composition, completing works—including a symphony—abandoned many years before and writing new ones, including his Piano Sonata (1905), Second Symphony (1908), and numerous piano pieces and songs. The last decade of his life was spent in almost complete retirement.

It has been said that it was Balakirev even more than Glinka who set the course for Russian orchestral music and lyrical song during the second half of the 19th century. He developed an idiom and technique that—though based on Glinka and Russian and Caucasian folk music on the one hand, and on Schumann, Berlioz, and Liszt on the other—were ultimately personal and idiosyncratic. They were imposed on his disciples—above all on Rimsky-Korsakov and Borodin and to some extent on Tchaikovsky—not only by example but by constant autocratic supervision of their early works. His music is colorful and imaginative, but his creative personality was arrested in its development after 1871, and his later work is couched in the idiom of his youth.

BIBLIOGRAPHY: Gerald E. H. Abraham, *Studies in Russian Music* (1935; reprint, 1976), and with Michel D. Calvocoressi, *Masters of Russian Music* (1936; reprint, 1971); Edward Garden, *Balakirev: A Critical Study of His Life and Music* (1967).

RECORDINGS: *Islamey;* Piano Concerto No. 2; Piano Sonata; Symphony No. 1; *Tamara.*

balalaika A stringed instrument of the guitar family. The modern instrument is a sophisticated version of a Russian folk instrument introduced by V. V. Andreyev of Bezhtsk, who made a first public appearance with a band of these improved instruments in 1888.

The balalaika is made in five sizes from treble to double bass, forming a complete, self-contained ensemble. Its characteristic shape is with a triangular table, or belly, widest at the bottom and tapering to the neck with a small round sound hole in the upper part. The body is vaulted and usually constructed in six sections or ribs, fanning out from the neck to the bottom of the body, which is flat. There are three gut strings hitched to the bottom and stretched over a pressure bridge. The neck is long and slender and carries up to 19 metal frets. The type-instrument is the *prima,* which is plucked by the fingers. To this group Andreyev added the oval-bodied domras, also three-stringed instruments strung with gut that differ from the balalaika in tuning and the use of a plectrum. This group also includes the diminutive piccolo domra.

ballad A genre of narrative song pepetuated by oral tradition and characterized by certain features of style and treatment; simple, concrete, and unimpassioned in diction; fairly uniform in meter and rhythm; compressed in narrative scope; objective and impersonal in presentation; usually dramatic in structure; and suggestive of the elemental and archetypal in its effect. The melody is repeated for each stanza, which is usually of four lines. This form of song is shared by most European peoples and has been carried to other areas such as the English-, French-, and Spanish-speaking parts of the New World. Since ballads exist as orally transmitted songs, they have been preserved only by fortuitous noting down and printing or in modern times by concerted efforts at collection. Much information about them has been irretrievably lost.

Since they are handed down by tradition, they are known only as anonymous compositions. But their anonymity extends beyond the mere loss of the authors' names, for in successive performances many singers have worked changes on any one ballad. The fluidity of musical and textual substance is at the heart of the nature of a ballad. This fluidity operates within traditional restraints, for the changes made by the tradition bearer are devoid of artful niceties and individualistic turns. Compare Browning's "The Glove," or the poems by Leigh Hunt and Schiller about the same incident, with the ballad "The Lady of Carlisle" for an illustration of the differences between traditional ballad and the poet's poem. Arnold's "Forsaken Merman" and Goethe's "Erlkönig" use themes from bal-

Russian tenor balalaika, 20th century
courtesy, Metropolitan Museum of Art
The Crosby Brown Collection of Musical
Instruments, 1889

lads—the poems owe their being to folk song—but they are unmistakably not ballads. The marks of the ballad are the structural, rhetorical, and stylistic necessities imposed by the process of oral transmission; although its origin may be obscure and it may tell a story, a song lacking the shaping effects of traditional rendering is not a true ballad.

Since the word *ballad* has at various times been applied to many kinds of popular verse, students of folk song frequently choose to qualify the term by the adjectives popular or traditional. Ballads are a variety of folk song, but they are sufficiently a group in themselves to be classed separately. The distinction was first argued by William Shenstone in 1761 in letters to Bishop Thomas Percy, where he suggested use of the term ballad to distinguish the narrative of action from songs that were expressions of sentiment. The word is derived from late Latin *ballare,* "to dance," which has helped to confuse the history of the ballad with dance song. Ballad was used indiscriminately after the 15th century to refer to any kind of simple or popular song; before that it had been used in English to describe a poem of complex structure that was French in origin (*see* BALLADE). Since the 18th century the word has been used increasingly in the particularized sense. Conversely what we now call a ballad went by many names—song, tale, ditty—during earlier centuries. In other languages various names are used: in German, *Volkslied;* in Danish, *Folkevise;* in French, *chanson populaire,* or *romance* after the Spanish usage; in Russian, *bylina.*

Critics hesitate to define the genre too narrowly, for by its very nature it is hard to circumscribe precisely. It differs in important respects from one linguistic area of Europe to another, and yet Spanish *romances,* Russian *byliny,* and Scottish ballads belong to the same genre in spite of differences. Even within a single language community such as the English-speaking one, there is considerable diversity in the body of narrative folk song comprehended by the term ballad.

characteristics Ballads all tell stories. The narratives are usually concentrated, episodic, leaping from one link to the next in the narrative chain, suggestive rather than explanatory, and they often proceed by dialogue interchange, which gives them a dramatic air. Usually the narrative is held back by the lyrical devices of repetition and refrain.

Certain themes appear frequently. By far the commonest subject is love, usually with tragic consequences—love requited, unrequited, stolen, betrayed, and complicated by family entanglements. Other favorite subjects are weird and monstrous changes in the appearance of a person under the spell of a supernatural being, ghosts, fights and forays, romance themes, riddles and tricks, broad and gross humor, religious legends, adventures at sea, or in the greenwood, and accounts of history and policy. The romantic and tragic ballads and the ballads of magic are among those with international analogues; the more strictly national ballads are those revealing a background of minstrelsy or that are based on historical events.

Ballads differ greatly in their geographical spread. Some are confined to an area like the Scottish border country; others are widely distributed throughout Europe and America. About a quarter of the ballads in Francis James Child's collection, it is estimated, are international. In these not only is the narrative shape maintained in versions of the same ballad from different countries, but the similarities of verbal phrasing underscore the relationships.

tunes Sir Walter Scott heard the tunes to the ballads that he recorded and later published in his *Minstrelsy of the Scottish Border* (1802–03), but he did not write them down. Attention to the melodic side of ballads came late. In Child's collection the "Airs" from manuscript sources number only 55 and are relegated to an appendix. The vast store of tunes that we now possess is the work in the 20th century of field collectors who have come to the understanding that ballads are half tune. The first collector to realize this fully was Cecil James Sharp, who collected about 5,000 oral records from singers in England and in the United States. Two others responsible for great collections of tunes were Gavin Greig in Scotland and Phillips Barry in New England. Sharp spurred collecting in other regions of America by his success in garnering melodies from the Southern Appalachians. The tunes of the British and the American ballad tradition have been painstakingly brought together, grouped, and edited by B. H. Bronson in *The Traditional Tunes of the Child Ballads,* 4 vols. (1959–71).

The analysis of tunes and of the families into which they may be grouped is a new direction in ballad study. Tunes in tradition undergo changes just as do texts. The modality of a tune may change, the melodic contour also; phrases may be transposed, repeated or replaced; one tune may influence another; the total range may be altered; and the rhythm shifted. The scales to which ballads are sung indicate a medieval musical heritage, for they correspond to the ecclesiastical modes named after Greek tribes by Glareanus in 1547. Ballad music is not, however, derived from ecclesiastical music, a frequent misconception; folk music and church music alike used the only scales, the modes, that were known in the Middle Ages. The modality of a tune depends on the position of semitones in a seven-toned scale; their absence makes for gapped six- and five-toned scales. The rhythm of ballad tunes is usually in double time, conforming with and dictating the dipodic verse rhythm.

Tunes and texts have a close interdependence—formal features such as line length, stanza length, and *abcb* rhyme all being held in check by the structure of the melody. Stressed tones in the melodic contour tend to coincide with the important words in the text, an aspect of the control that oral delivery has upon the ballad. The variants of a single ballad are by no means always sung to the same tune or tune family, and conversely a tune family will serve as the musical vehicle for many differing texts. One cannot speak of an original or right tune for any narrative. The tunes are not international in scope to the same degree as are the texts.

history Considerable debate has taken place as to the dating of ballads and their place in the history of literature. The matter of dating involves three separate questions: "When did ballads make their first appearance in western Europe?" "What are the dates of the manuscripts and early printings that provide documentary evidence of ballads?" and "In what period did the ballads flourish?"

Some scholars at the turn of the 19th century, among them Francis B. Gummere, used the then new anthropological evidence to demonstrate that primitive peoples sang and danced to impromptu narrative verses suggestive of ballads. This school of thought equated ballads and the ballad dance with the beginnings of poetic expression in any society, and consequently the ballad in European languages was viewed as a retention of a primitive form that had its roots in prehistory. A less hypothetical approach to the evidence was bound in time to displace such a theory, and the tendency in accounts about ballads has been to assign a later date to the beginning of the genre. The oldest ballad recorded in any language exists in English in a manuscript dating from the latter half of the 13th century. Some would deny that "Judas" in the Trinity College, Cambridge, manuscript is a true ballad; its way of treating a biblical story, its dialogue and repetitions, however, all suggest the ballad. The next record is two centuries younger, and by actual count fewer than 10 complete ballads are preserved in English in sources before 1600. The documentary evidence about balladry is then preponderantly from modern times. Early historians of poetry thought of the form as medieval, and in chronological surveys it became conventional to treat the ballads as if they belonged to the 15th century, the transition period between the Middle Ages and modern times. Such relegation of the ballads to a medieval limbo, treating them as "the literary debris of the Middle Ages," is not accepted by later scholars. Louise Pound demonstrated that the historical materials in English and Scottish balladry are largely from the 16th and 17th centuries, and American ballads reveal the emergence of an entire ballad tradition in relatively modern times. Like a number of American ballads "The Streets of Laredo" dates from the era of western expansion, but it derives from earlier British songs with antecedents that have been traced to the 18th century. The vigorous "Sam Hall" has its roots in even earlier British song. It would be foolhardy to say that any one age is a ballad age.

In later centuries it is clear that ballads have been a living tradition in rural and backwoods communities, but at times they have also been perpetuated by upper levels of society. The beginnings of the ballad as we know it cannot be pushed back beyond the emergence of rhyme in English about 1100. Since actual ballads cannot be cited from a period earlier than the 13th century, it would seem unreasonable to date the inception of the genre before then. The documentary evidence for British ballads increases the nearer one approaches modern times. Not until the late 18th century does the evidence become sizable, and not until the 19th does it become rich. In the 20th century the number of variants of ballads uncovered by assiduous collecting has increased tremendously; the collector does not find new ballads so much as add to the store of variants of known songs.

How many ballads are there in tradition? The question has been complicated by the shifting opinions about ballads and by the classifications different editors and critics have employed. From the mass of popular verse that his predecessors had collected and published, Francis James Child for his standard edition chose 305 ballads with their variants, though issue is taken at times with his procedures of inclusion and exclusion. Native U.S. balladry has greatly increased the number of ballads in the English language, although no one has chosen to establish a count.

Ballads have entered the area of more formal literature in two ways: as material for the broadside press and as models for the literary or imitation ballad written by the poet. Broadsides containing all forms of popular verse were issued by the commercial presses almost from the time of the earliest printers. From the 16th to the 19th century there is a horde of such ephemeral verse, much of it of interest only to the historian and student of popular taste. The printing of traditional ballads on such broadsides preserved copies of songs or variants of songs that might otherwise have been lost. The poetasters on occasion reworked the substance of ballads for printing, and their handiwork can be recognized. Comparison of a traditional version of "Riddles Wisely Expounded" (No. 1 C in the Child collection, taken down from recitation by William Motherwell early in the 19th century) with the 17th-century broadside copy in the collection made by Samuel Pepys (Child No. 1 A) reveals the false notes of supposed elegance and rectitude that the broadside poetaster is responsible for. The bathos of phrasing, the latinate vocabulary, the abstract terms, the moralizing conclusion, the intrusion of the maker into the song—all these are marks of an alien influence on traditional verse.

scholarship The main activity in ballad study since the beginning of the 19th century has been collecting and editing. Collecting may be a separate task as in field collecting (often with phonograph or tape recorder). The fruits of such collecting increase the holdings of such repositories as the Folk Song Archive of the Library of Congress, the libraries of the British Broadcasting Corporation and of Cecil Sharp House in London, Das Deutsche Volksliedarchiv in Freiburg, and Dansk Folkemindesamling in Copenhagen, to name only a few. The editor is also a collector; Svend Grundtvig and Child thought of themselves primarily as collectors, although the first great analytical contributions are also found in their editions. Collections are made in libraries as well as in the field. There have been three main phases in this era of collection. The first extends to the mid-19th century and is characterized by the cultured amateur preserving "reliques of antiquity" for a "polished age," atoning for rudeness of style, and taking liberties with the text. The second period is the age of emergence of scrupulous editing and scientific scholarship and is dominated by the work of Grundtvig and Child; in this period the significance of the variant is recognized. The third era results from Sharp's insistence on the music as of equal importance with the text. There has been a comparable scholarly development in other lands, although the Anglo-American, Danish, and German ballads are more adequately edited and presented for scrutiny than those from elsewhere.

During the early part of the 20th century, there was a fierce scholarly debate, now only of historical interest, on the origin of ballads. The case for a communal origin of ballad poetry, championed by Gummere, was based on the assumption that ballads represent that variety of spontaneously created poetry that a throng might produce in cooperative dance and ritual observance. His ideas were compounded of too narrow an interpretation of German romantic asseverations like Uhland's *die Völker dichten* (too literally read by Gummere as "the folk compose"), together with the application of the evolutionary principle to literature with the ballad regarded as the primal protoplasm. There were many attacks on the communalists, the most direct by Louise Pound in her *Poetic Origins and the Ballad* (1921). The ballad war proved of value primarily for its by-products: scholars came to understand ballad style and language better, they perceived differences in narrative structure, they documented such stylistic devices as incremental repetition, and they examined all the external historical evidence available.

Other major concerns of scholars include cataloguing and classifying of the material collected and the preparation of bibliographic aids for further study; study of individual ballads and their changes through time; analysis of international connections and the dissemination of ballads. But ballads are not of interest only to the scholar; since the 1930s the general public has been receptive to a growing avalanche of recorded ballad music that bespeaks a 20th-century ballad revival. *See also* FOLK MUSIC.

BIBLIOGRAPHY: Helen Child Sargent and George L. Kittredge, eds., *English and Scottish Popular Ballads* (1904, an abridgement of Child's 5 vols.); Cecil J. Sharp, *English Folk-Song: Some Conclusions* (1907; reprint, 1977); Arthur Quiller-Couch, ed., *The Oxford Book of Ballads* (1910; reprint 1955); Sigurd B. Hustvedt, *Ballad Books and Ballad Men* (1930; reprint, 1971); William J. Entwistle, *European Balladry* (1939; reprint, 1951); Matthew J. C. Hodgart, *The Ballads* (1950); MacEdward Leach, ed., *The Ballad Book* (1955); Albert B. Friedman, ed., *The Viking Book of Folk Ballads* (1956), and *The Ballad Revival* (1961); MacEdward Leach and Tristram P. Coffin, eds., *The Critics and the Ballad* (1961).

ballade One of the *formes fixes* in French lyric poetry and song that was cultivated particularly in the 14th and 15th centuries (*compare* RONDEAU; VIRELAI). Strictly the ballade consists of three stanzas and a shortened final dedicatory stanza. All stanzas have the same rhyme scheme and the same final line, which forms a refrain (R). Each of the three main stanzas is built in three sections, the first two having the same rhyme scheme. The total form can be expressed:

I	II	III	E
a a b R	a a b R	a a b R	b R

The final dedicatory stanza is called the *prince* (usually its first word), or envoi. The *chanson royale* is similar to the ballade but has five main stanzas.

The general shape of the ballade is present in the poetry of many ages. The odes of the Greek poet Pindar (5th century B.C.) have the same stanza form with their strophe, antistrophe, and epode. Much of the art song of the 16th century in Germany is cast in a similar form, though normally without the envoi, or the refrain line; when in Wagner's *Meistersinger* (1868) Fritz Kothner defines a *Bar* (a poetic form) as consisting of several *Gesetze* (stanzas), each made up of two *Stollen* (a a) and an *Abgesang* (b), he is accurately describing a historical reality. But in its purest form the ballade is found only in France and England.

The immediate precursors of the ballade can be found in the songs of the troubadours, which frequently employ the *a a b* stanza pattern with an envoi. They normally have more than three stanzas, however, and the refrain line, if there is one, is often not the last line of the stanza. In the later 13th century the standard form appears more and more frequently in the French songs of the trouvères (the northern counterparts of the troubadours).

The songs of the trouvères and troubadours are monophonic. The history of the polyphonic ballade begins with Guillaume de Machaut, the leading French poet and composer of the 14th century. He wrote more songs in this than in any other form. In his work can be seen the gradual emergence of a standard manner of setting a ballade and in particular the convention of closing the second *a* section with a musical epilogue that is repeated at the end of the stanza.

The ballade was the most expansive of the *formes fixes,* and Machaut used it to express the loftiest emotions. The texts more often contained elaborate symbolism and classical references than did those of the other *formes fixes.* Later in the 14th century the ballade was the form used for the most solemn and formal songs: the celebration of special patrons, the commemoration of magnificent occasions, the declarations of love in the highest style.

In the 15th century the form became less popular. The foremost Burgundian composer, Guillaume Dufay, wrote few ballades, almost all of which can be connected with specific occasions and all early in his life. Later in the century musical ballades are rare except in the work of English composers. The form gradually disappeared among the poets too, only to reappear spasmodically in the work of later writers as a conscious archaism.

Ballad of Baby Doe, The: *see* MOORE; OPERA (the 20th century).

ballad opera   A type of comic opera peculiar to England, where it originated in the 18th century. The plots were usually in the nature of a burlesque or extravaganza, and the music, confined mainly to songs or interludes interspersed in the spoken dialogue, was based on popular tunes—at first ballads or folk songs to which new words were adapted and later often tunes borrowed from the works of well-known composers. The best known and one of the earliest ballad operas was *The Beggar's Opera* (1728), a satire on contemporary politicians and Italian opera, on a text by John Gay with music adapted by John Christopher Pepusch. It had many imitators, and music for ballad operas was adapted or composed by Thomas Arne, Charles Dibdin, William Shield, Samuel Arnold, George and Thomas Linley, William Jackson, James Hook, and Stephen Storace, among others. The ballad opera also had an influence abroad and by its affinities with the French vaudeville led to the development of OPÉRA COMIQUE and of the German SINGSPIEL. In England it developed into the light opera of Gilbert and Sullivan and indirectly, through MUSICAL COMEDY, into the modern musical. In the 20th century there have been notable revivals of early ballad operas and attempts—closely connected with the revival of folk song—to revive the form itself, the most notable being Vaughan Williams' *Hugh the Drover* (1924).

BIBLIOGRAPHY: E. Walter White, *The Rise of English Opera* (1951).

Ballard   A family of printers, who from 1560 to 1750 had virtually a monopoly on music printing in France, was founded by Robert Ballard (d. 1588), a brother-in-law of Adrian le Roy, the celebrated lutenist and composer. Together they used movable type, cut in 1540 by Robert's father-in-law Guillaume le Bé (or du Gué), and printed much secular and sacred vocal music and volumes of lute tablature. Their first patent was granted in 1552 as sole music printers to Henry II. Robert's widow and son Pierre (d. 1639) continued the business, and further patents were obtained from Henry IV and Louis XIII. Robert's grandson Robert II ran the firm from 1640 to 1679, and it was taken over successively by Christophe (d. 1715), Jean Baptiste Christophe (d. 1750), Christophe Jean François (d. 1765), and Pierre Robert Christophe (d. 1812), who carried on management until 1788. Throughout the history of the family the women were often as active in the business as the men.

Ballard publications, both those with the early movable type and the later ones engraved on copper plates, were noted for their beauty and care of presentation. Their title pages were frequently superb examples of decorative engraving. The music published by the family represented almost all the French composers of the period, including lute tablatures by Adrian le Roy; organ music by Jean Titelouze; vocal works by Clément Janequin, Claude Goudimel, and Orlando di Lasso; Marin Mersenne's *Harmonie Universelle;* works by André Campra, François Couperin, Michel Richard de Lalande, Michel de Montéclair, François Philidor, and Rameau; and Lully's operas and ballets.

ballata   The most important Italian form of the 14th century that was almost identical to the VIRELAI, one of the *formes fixes.* It is usually assumed that the ballata (from the Latin *ballare,* "to dance") was originally a song accompanying a round dance, but there is no evidence to verify the assumption. Landini was a most prolific composer of ballate (91 survive for two voices and 49 for three voices).

ballet A form of theatrical performance in which classical dancing is employed, usually in conjunction with music, pantomime, and painting (in costumes and scenery), to tell a story or to express a theme. The term is also used to denote the technique of the classic dance, as when a child studies ballet. The word ballet derives from the Italian *ballare* ("to dance"). Originally a court spectacle in which performers as well as audiences were drawn exclusively from the nobility, ballet became popular with the general public as early as the 18th century, when itinerant troupes of dancers gave performances all over Europe and even in America. Until the 20th century, however, ballet developed most luxuriantly in the sheltered atmosphere of the court theater or state opera house. The extensive world tours of the great ballerina Anna Pavlova between 1910 and 1930, the widespread activities of organizations such as the Ballet Russe de Monte Carlo, Ballet Theatre (now the American Ballet Theatre), the New York City Ballet, the Royal Ballet, and the influence of motion pictures and television after 1950—all contributed to a tremendous growth of interest in ballet.

court ballet Ballet like opera is directly descended from the court festivals of the Italian Renaissance. In the days of the Medici it was customary to honor distinguished guests with elaborate banquets lasting five or six hours. The entertainment at these feasts often consisted of a series of entrees, or interludes of music, poetry, pantomime, and dancing, loosely linked together by a central theme. Costumes were lavish, and the scenery was often magnificent. One such fete in Tortona, Italy, in 1489 has been called the first actual ballet performance. Bergonzio di Botta, a wealthy gentleman addicted to extravagant entertaining, arranged a banquet in honor of Gian Galeazzo Sforza, Duke of Milan, and his bride, Isabella of Aragon. Between the courses the story of Jason and the Golden Fleece was enacted in music and dance. The participants were members of the nobility, and the dances they executed were based on the formal, elegant court dances of the period.

When Catherine de Médicis became Queen of France, she introduced the banquet entertainments of her native Italy. She made ballet history in 1581, when she presented the *Ballet comique de la reine,* celebrating the marriage of the duc de Joyeuse and Marguerite of Lorraine. It is the first ballet of which there is a complete printed account; its author and choreographer was Baldassarino de Belgiojoso (Balthazar de Beaujoyeulx), an Italian violinist whom Catherine had appointed official director of court festivals. The *Ballet comique* was a brilliant success, and Belgiojoso published a description of it in a sumptuous volume that might be called the first ballet libretto. His definition of ballet as "a geometrical arrangement of many persons dancing together under a diverse harmony of instruments" might still apply today.

In England the Italian custom of masquerading at balls, introduced in the reign of Henry VIII, grew in popularity and gradually evolved into the English masque, a form of spectacle similar to French court ballet. Ben Jonson, the author of delightful masques, owned a copy of the *Ballet comique de la reine.* Court dances in this period were of two general types: the *basse danse,* of which the stately and dignified pavane was an example; and the lively *danse haute,* typified by the merry galliard—the favorite dance of Queen Elizabeth I—with its quick running steps and jumps. Later French and Italian dancing was to polish and elaborate upon the simple steps of these popular dances until they became the foundation of the classical ballet technique.

ballet under Louis XIV In the reign of Louis XIV ballet developed into a serious art form. Fond of dancing in his youth, Louis participated in many performances at court. His name of *le Roi Soleil* ("the Sun King") originated when he took the part of the sun in *Ballet de la nuit* in 1653, when he was 15. Louis gave up performing at 30 but throughout his lifetime remained an enlightened patron of ballet. Artists of genius were attracted to the French court, and such men as Molière, Lully, the poet Isaac de Benserade, and the choreographer Charles Louis Beauchamp contributed to the development of the ballet. Their productions were conceived on a scale of unparalleled magnificence, but frequently they were hampered by a lack of trained performers.

This shortage of dancers and the inability of the noble amateurs to keep pace with the increasing technical demands of professional dancing masters inspired Louis XIV to establish the Académie Royale de Danse in 1661. The success of this academy, made up of the most experienced dancing masters of Paris, led Louis to found the Académie Royale de Musique in 1669 and to add in 1672 a school of dancing for the express purpose of training professional dancers. These united organizations became the Académie Royale de Musique et de Danse, or the Paris Opéra, which has remained for nearly three centuries a center of ballet production. It was Pierre Beauchamp, the first choreographer of the Paris Opéra, who defined the five positions of the feet on which classical ballet technique is based and who invented one of the earliest forms of dance notation.

rise of the virtuoso   With the professional dancer firmly established, ballet technique developed rapidly. Women were hampered by cumbersome costumes, but men were not so restricted and soon began to explore the possibilities of pas d'élévation, or jumping steps. Jean Balon, who appeared at the Opéra from 1691 to 1710, danced with such remarkable lightness that this quality in dancing is still called ballon.

Marie Camargo, who made her Paris debut in 1726, was one of the first important innovators in the technique of the classic dance. She excelled in entrechats, jetés battus, cabrioles, and other brilliant jumping steps formerly executed only by men. Her favorite vehicle, a plotless divertissement typical of the period, was *Les Caractères de la danse,* a series of solo dances in contrasting styles, including the minuet, courante, saraband, and gigue.

Camargo's rival Marie Sallé was noted for her extraordinary grace and expressive gesture, and she rebelled against the formal construction of the divertissements at the Paris Opéra. In London she created a ballet called *Pygmalion* (1734), which told the familiar story of the sculptor whose masterpiece came to life. As the statue Sallé discarded the usual ballet costume, with its stiff panniers, and ap-

peared in a simple muslin robe with her hair flowing. She attempted to unify the music, costume, and style of dancing, thus anticipating the reforms of Jean Georges Noverre by a quarter of a century.

dramatic ballet   Throughout ballet history there has been an unending struggle between the exponents of the pure dance of formal, decorative beauty and virtuosity and the advocates of dance as a means of dramatic expression. The most articulate and influential of the advocates of the ballet d'action, or drama in dance form, was Jean Georges Noverre, whose *Lettres sur la danse et sur les ballets* (1760) is still considered the authoritative work on the subject. Although the work of his predecessors and contemporaries should not be minimized, especially that of Gasparo Angiolini, who collaborated with Gluck, it was Noverre who forcefully called attention to the decadent state of ballet in Paris and brought about extensive reforms. When he wrote his revolutionary *Lettres,* he was only 33 and the ballet master of a provincial theater in Lyon. Nevertheless, he dared to challenge the potent authorities at the Paris Opéra. "A well-composed ballet . . . must be expressive in all its detail and speak to the soul through the eyes; . . . Dancing is possessed of all the advantages of a beautiful language, yet it is not sufficient to know the alphabet alone. When a man of genius arranges the letters to form words, and the words to form sentences, it will cease to be dumb; it will speak with both strength and energy; and then ballets will share with the best plays the merit of affecting and moving, and of making the tears flow, and, in their less serious styles, of being able to amuse, captivate and please."

Noverre's theories shocked dancers who had spent all their lives mastering mere technical feats. Although his ideas were not welcomed at the Paris Opéra, in Stuttgart, London, Vienna, and Milan he carried out his theories in nearly 100 ballets.

Drawn by curiosity Gaetan Vestris went to Stuttgart to observe Noverre's work and was so impressed that he returned each summer to dance in Noverre's ballets. In 1770 Vestris arranged for the production at the Paris Opéra of an abbreviated version of Noverre's *Medée et Jason.* In 1776 Noverre was finally called to the Paris Opéra. There in the ballerina Marie Madeleine Guimard he found the ideal interpreter of his ballets d'action. Her mime was as convincing as her technique was skillful. Two of his pupils, Jean Dauberval and Charles Le Picq, carried out his theories in the ballets they produced in Italy, England, France, and Russia. At the Grand Théâtre in Bordeaux in 1789, Dauberval staged *La Fille mal gardée*, which shares with Vincenzo Galeotti's *The Whims of Cupid and the Ballet Master* (in the repertoire of the Royal Danish Ballet continuously from 1786) the distinction of being the oldest ballet still performed in the late 20th century.

Noverre's theories were followed and amplified by the Italian choreographer Salvatore Viganò, a pupil of Dauberval. Long active in Vienna, he staged Beethoven's only ballet *Prometheus* in 1801. Whereas Noverre had been content to carry forward the dramatic action in long mimed scenes that alternated with formal dances, Viganò sought to achieve a synthesis of dancing and pantomime. In 1811 he became choreographer of La Scala in Milan, where during the next ten years he produced such heroic works as *La Vestale* and *Otello*.

Romantic ballet The spirit that infused the arts in the early years of the 19th century and that was expressed in the novels of Sir Walter Scott and Victor Hugo, in the music of Chopin and Berlioz, and in the painting of Eugène Delacroix found its perfect symbol in the fragile and delicate Marie Taglioni. The innovations of Auguste Vestris and Louis Antoine Duport, with their vigorous leaps and vertiginous pirouettes, had brought ballet technique to a high state of advancement by the time Taglioni began her training. Shortly after 1800—the exact date has never been established—women had begun to dance on the extreme tips, or points, of the toes. The possibilities of this new technical device had not yet been thoroughly explored, however, and it remained for Taglioni to make such imaginative use of points that their introduction has often been erroneously credited to her. Trained chiefly by her father, Filippo Taglioni, Marie made her debut in Vienna in 1822. With the creation of her father's ballet *La Sylphide*

at the Paris Opéra in 1832, she inaugurated a new era in the history of ballet that discarded ancient subjects for more romantic themes. "After *La Sylphide*," wrote Théophile Gautier, ". . . the Greek cothurnus was exchanged for satin shoes." The diaphanous dress worn by Taglioni in *La Sylphide*, with its fitted bodice and airy, bell-like skirt, was the prototype of the tutu, or full, light skirt that in various lengths has remained the accepted uniform of the classical ballerina for more than a century.

In the meantime a rival had appeared in Fanny Elssler, a Viennese dancer who epitomized the earthly aspects of Romanticism and was at her best in the fiery Spanish *Cachucha* and the spirited Polish *Cracovienne*. Elssler conquered Paris when she was 26 with the creation of the role of Florinda in *Le Diable boiteux* (1836). She followed in *La Gypsy* (1839) and *La Tarentule* (1839), both of which displayed to full advantage her warmth and vitality in pas de caractère, or theatricalized folk dances.

The spectacular interest added to women's dancing by their conquest of a new plane—dancing on the points of the toes—combined with the rare phenomenon of two contemporary but contrasted ballerinas of genius—Taglioni, daughter of the air, and Elssler, child of the earth—detracted from the importance of the male dancer and nearly caused the disappearance, in France at least, of male virtuosity in ballet. Jules Perrot, for one, turned his attention to choreography and achieved renown for his excellent ballets d'action, in which all the rich resources of the ethnic dance were brilliantly adapted for the theater. His finest works included *Ondine* (1843), *Esmeralda* (1844), and *Catarina* (1846)—all created in London, which he made an important ballet center.

While Elssler was touring America Taglioni was in Russia, and the post of leading ballerina at the Paris Opéra fell to a young Italian dancer, Carlotta Grisi, who combined the ethereal lightness of Taglioni with the appealing warmth of Elssler. For Grisi Gautier wrote the ballet *Giselle* (Paris Opéra, 1841). Combining as it does the two principal facets of the Romantic ballet through the colorful peasant scenes of the first act and the unearthly, haunting atmosphere of the second, *Giselle* not only has survived but has increased in popularity until it has become an indispensable feature of the repertoire of almost every ballet company. Its original choreography was by Jean Coralli, but the role of Giselle, still considered the touchstone of the ballerina's art, is said to have been staged by Grisi's husband, Perrot. The music was by Adolphe-Charles Adam.

Rich in great executants, the Romantic period also produced Fanny Cerrito, a vivacious Neapolitan, and Lucile Grahn, a Danish ballerina whose style resembled that of Taglioni. In 1845 Benjamin Lumley, an astute London theater manager, united Taglioni, Grisi, Cerrito, and Grahn in one pas de quatre. Expertly staged by Perrot, this divertissement marked the pinnacle of the Romantic ballet.

Italian school   The technique of the classic ballet, very much as it is practiced today, was codified by the Italian dancer Carlo Blasis in his *Traîté élémentaire, théorique et pratique de l'art de la danse* (1820). An experienced dancer and a prolific writer, Blasis issued several versions of this treatise as well as books on such allied subjects as music, history, drama, and pantomime. His indomitable energy found its principal expression, however, in his work as head of the ballet school at La Scala, a post he assumed in 1837. The teaching methods of Blasis and his wife Annunciata Ramaccini were strict and demanding. During his long directorship of the Scala school, it became the principal source of solo dancers for the entire theatrical world. Established stars like Cerrito and Grisi came to Milan to study with him, and his pupil Giovanni Lepri was the teacher of Enrico Cecchetti, one of the greatest dance pedagogues of the 20th century, who became in turn director of the Scala academy and who taught Anna Pavlova, Vaslav Nijinsky, and Ninette de Valois. The traditions of Blasis have been handed down directly and without interruption, including a number of discoveries and innovations. A statue of Mercury by Giovanni da Bologna inspired the attitude, which he invented. He probably discovered the snapping movement of the head that makes it possible

for dancers to turn indefinitely without dizziness. He enlarged the scope of dancing on the points. The invention of the reinforced, or blocked, toe-shoe—unknown to Taglioni and Elssler, who danced in soft satin slippers—enabled dancers to execute multiple pirouettes on the point instead of the demipoint as before. It was Pierina Legnani, a graduate of the Scala academy, who first executed 32 fouettés, the whipping turns on one toe featured in the third act of *Swan Lake.*

Late in the 19th century there emerged from La Scala an array of brilliant soloists whose dazzling techniques, combined with a prevailing laxity in the training of ensemble dancers, led choreographers to concentrate excessively on the prima ballerina. This led to the degeneration and ultimate stagnation of the ballet, which by 1900 had reached a low level in most of Europe and the United States. The exception was Russia, where the genius of Marius Petipa had fused the French and Italian schools into the form indelibly labeled Russian ballet.

Russia before 1900   Ballet was firmly established in Russia by 1801, when the French-Swedish dancer Charles Louis Didelot was appointed choreographer, principal dancer, and director of the ballet school. Before his retirement in 1829 he had produced dozens of ballets, reorganized the school, imported guest artists, and developed excellent Russian dancers. But the major force in the development of Russian ballet was Marius Petipa, who reached St. Petersburg in 1847 after a brief career that included appearances in his native France, Spain, and the United States. Petipa served as leading dancer until 1858, when he was allowed to produce his first ballet, *Un Mariage sous la régence,* at the Imperial Theater. *La Fille du Pharaon* (1862), a three-act spectacle, established him as an important choreographer. Although Perrot and Arthur Saint-Léon, who were frequent visitors to Russia, left their mark on its ballet, Petipa molded it into its distinctive national form. Appointed choreographer in 1862, he was the virtual dictator of the Russian ballet until his death in 1910.

Petipa collaborated extensively with Tchaikovsky and with his assistant, Lev Ivanov, shared the choreography for *Swan Lake*, still unsurpassed in the classic style. Following Petipa's preliminary notes Ivanov staged *The Nutcracker*. *The Sleeping Beauty*, probably Petipa's masterpiece, combined the smoothly flowing elegance of the French school with the virtuosity of the Italians. It is a perfect example of the elaborate, full-evening ballet in which set dances, emphasizing the spectacular art of the prima ballerina, alternate with static mimed scenes in which the story unfolds through stylized gestures.

Late in the century Petipa, always an admirer of virtuosity, began importing Italian stars to enhance his ballets with their glittering technique, among them Virginia Zucchi, Pierina Legnani, and Cecchetti. It was not long, however, before Mathilde Kchessinska and Olga Preobrajenska were emulating their most effective steps. Cecchetti remained to teach in Russia and helped to form Pavlova, Nijinsky, and the other artists who burst upon the Western world with such splendor in the first Paris season of the Diaghilev Ballet in 1909.

Diaghilev Ballet Sergey Diaghilev first stimulated Western interest in Russian art by presenting in Paris an exhibition of paintings and a series of concerts of Russian music. These attracted such wide attention that in 1909 he organized a troupe of dancers on vacation from the Maryinsky Theater and presented a season of ballet at the Théâtre du Châtelet.

As choreographer of the enterprise, Diaghilev chose Michel Fokine, a 29-year-old dancer who had demonstrated his reluctance to follow blindly the choreographic traditions of his predecessors. As early as 1904 he had declared his belief that ballets should no longer be broken into separate dances but should flow without interruption (as in Wagnerian opera); the whole story or theme should be expressed through dance movement and should not be exclusively classical but vary in style according to the theme expressed. This was, of course, simply a return to the forgotten principles of Noverre. The officials of the imperial theaters showed little sympathy for Fokine's revolutionary ideas, but he put them into practice in works including the miniature masterpiece immortalized by Pavlova, *The Dying*

Swan, and *Chopiniana* (1908), which we now know as *Les Sylphides* (to the music of Chopin).

For his first Paris season Diaghilev chose Fokine's ballets *Les Sylphides, Le Pavillon d'Armide,* and *Cléopâtre*—all of which had already been given in Russia. Fokine also put together a divertissement called *Le Festin,* which included dances by Petipa and other choreographers, and staged a new work of major importance, *Prince Igor* (to the *Polovtsian Dances* from Borodin's opera). This ballet departed from the pretty and innocuous trifles to which Parisian audiences were accustomed and was a triumph for Fokine and Diaghilev. The original Diaghilev company (eventually called the Ballets Russes) included Pavlova and Mikhail Mordkin (both of whom departed after the first season), Tamara Platonovna Karsavina, Nijinsky, Adolph Bolm, Vera Fokina, Alexandra Fedorova, Bronislava Nijinska, and other dancers who were to spread the fame of Russian ballet around the world.

The early Diaghilev seasons coincided with the richest period of Fokine's creative activity. In rapid succession he choreographed Rimsky-Korsakov's *Sheherazade* (1910), Stravinsky's *The Firebird* (1910) and *Petrushka* (1911), and Weber's *Le Spectre de la rose* (1911)—each work showing a new facet of his genius. Diaghilev had discovered Stravinsky and commissioned his first ballet scores. He had secured the collaboration of painters such as Aleksandr Benois and Léon Bakst, whose contribution to the initial impact of the Russian ballet on the world of art can scarcely be overestimated.

The dancing of Nijinsky came as a revelation to audiences in western Europe. At the Paris Opéra the custom of *travesti* then prevailed, and women frequently played men's roles. Nijinsky, the supreme male dancer of modern times, had a phenomenal elevation, made more spectacular by his seeming ability to remain suspended in air. Encouraged by Diaghilev to attempt choreography, he staged Debussy's *L'Aprés-midi d'un faune* (1912) and *Jeux* (1913) and Stravinsky's *Le Sacre du printemps* (1913). Each of these was marked by radical departures from accepted choreographic practice, utilizing angular, stylized movement far ahead of its time, and each precipitated a scandal; the furor attending the premiere of *Le Sacre* attained monumental proportions. Nijinsky created only one other ballet, *Till Eulenspiegel* (New York City, 1916; with music by Richard Strauss), before his tragic insanity cut short a phenomenal career.

Diaghilev also discovered the young Leonide Massine, whom he groomed to replace Nijinsky, presenting him first in Richard Strauss's *The Legend of Joseph* (1914). For Diaghilev he created such works as de Falla's *The Three-Cornered Hat* (1919), Respighi's *La Boutique fantasque* (1919) after Rossini, and Stravinsky's *Pulcinella* (1920), collaborating with painters Derain and Picasso.

By this time Diaghilev had broken his ties with Russia. His company toured constantly in Europe, South America, and the United States, where it appeared in 1916–17. At first Diaghilev worked only with Russians: Stravinsky, Bakst, Benois, and Fokine. Later his company became international. He commissioned scores from Satie, Georges Auric, Poulenc, de Falla, and Milhaud. Decors were designed by Maurice Utrillo, Georges Braque, Giorgio de Chirico, and André Bauchant. Russian dancers, including Lydia Lopokova (Lopoukhova), Felia Dubrovska, Vera Nemtchinova, Olga Spessivtzeva (Spessiva), Aleksandra Danilova, Pierre Vladimiroff, Anatole Vilzak, and Serge Lifar, were joined by Poles such as Leon Woicikowski and Stanislas Idzikowski and eventually by the English dancers Lydia Sokolova (Hilda Munnings), Anton Dolin, and the 14-year-old Alicia Markova (Alice Marks). In 1921 Diaghilev revived *The Sleeping Beauty* in London, but the Petipa classic became generally popular only a quarter of a century later.

Diaghilev's last choreographer was George Balanchine, an artist of marked originality as well as an ardent disciple of Petipa. Trained in the U.S.S.R., he left it in 1924 and joined Diaghilev, for whom he created about ten ballets, including Stravinsky's *Apollo* (1928) and Prokofiev's *L'Enfant prodigue* (1929). After Diaghilev's death in 1929 Balanchine was to exert a tremendous personal influence on the whole course of contemporary classic ballet.

Pavlova Anna Pavlova, trained in the Russian Imperial School in St. Petersburg, was already one of the finest dancers of the Maryinsky Theater when in 1907 she made her first foreign tour to Stockholm, Copenhagen, Prague, and Berlin. In 1909 she danced in Paris with the Diaghilev company, leaving it in 1910 to accept a contract at the Metropolitan Opera with her partner Mikhail Mordkin. Although she returned to Russia intermittently for limited engagements, she devoted herself more and more to the worldwide tours that absorbed the remainder of her life.

America, 1735–1932 Ballet was probably introduced to the American colonies by Henry Holt, a dancer from London who in 1735 presented *The Adventures of Harlequin and Scaramouch, with the Burgo'master Trick'd* in Charleston, South Carolina. Harlequinades and pantomimes were also often seen on colonial stages, and the hornpipe ranked high in popularity. However, ballets were not given in America with any frequency until after the French Revolution, which uprooted artists in great numbers. From the 1790s through the 1830s many of these European dancers toured the United States. Romantic ballet reached its peak in America with the visit of Fanny Elssler in 1840–42. The great Austrian dancer created a furor comparable only to that greeting the singer Jenny Lind a decade later. When Elssler danced in Washington, D.C., Congress was obliged to recess because it could not obtain a quorum. In Baltimore young admirers unhitched the horses from her carriage and pulled her from the theater to her hotel, then serenaded her until early morning.

With the opening of the Metropolitan Opera House in 1883, one might have expected the encouragement of U.S. dancers and choreographers, but such was not the case. The Metropolitan imported its dancers until 1909, when Malvina Cavalazzi, who had been its first ballerina, returned to open the company's first ballet school. Its first U.S.-born choreographer, Zachary Solov, was not engaged until 1951. It was the depressing sterility of the ballet around 1900 that caused creative artists like Isadora Duncan, Loie Fuller, and Ruth St. Denis to turn to other forms of dance expression (*see* MODERN DANCE). A glimpse of hope for the traditional art came with the debut of the Danish dancer Adeline Genée. In the musical comedy *The Soul Kiss* (1908) and later as guest artist at the Metropolitan, Genée—with her precise technique and delicate charm—did much to reawaken U.S. interest in ballet. Cia Fornaroli, the Metropolitan's ballerina from 1910 to 1913, also rose far above the prevalent level of mediocrity.

The Russian renaissance of the dance was announced in the United States by the debut of Pavlova and Mordkin in *Coppélia* at the Metropolitan Opera early in 1910. Their success was followed by the appearance of several more or less Russian ballet companies and in 1916 by the arrival of the full Diaghilev Ballet. American artists and critics were profoundly impressed by Fokine's masterpieces in their original settings by Bakst and Benois, but the general public was not yet ready to give wholehearted support. Not even the belated appearance of Nijinsky, delayed by wartime internment in Hungary, was able to save the tour from financial collapse. In 1918 Adolph Bolm staged Fokine's version of Rimsky-Korsakov's opera-ballet *Le Coq d'or* for the Metropolitan with Rosina Galli as the Queen of Shemakha. In 1919 he staged and danced Stravinsky's *Petrushka.* Two U.S. works, Henry Gilbert's *The Dance in the Place Congo* (1917) and John Alden Carpenter's *Skyscrapers* (1926), completed the list of independent ballets given at the Metropolitan until Balanchine's appointment as choreographer in 1935.

England The British Isles have produced good dancers since Shakespeare's day, and an Irishman named Simon Slingsby appeared as a soloist in Noverre's London company of 1781. British dancers competed successfully with imported stars in the London of 1800, and England might have claimed one of the great ballerinas of the Romantic period if the promising young Clara Webster had not been burned to death in 1844.

In the last years of the 19th century, when ballet was on the decline elsewhere, it was solidly established on an entertainment level in two of London's most popular theaters, the Alhambra and the Empire. Cavalazzi, Legnani, and Cecchetti all danced at the Alham-

bra. Prima ballerina of the Empire Theatre (1897–1907) was Adeline Genée, who starred in the theater's productions of the Léo Delibes classics *Coppélia* and *Sylvia*. Genée was succeeded by Lydia Kyasht of the Russian Imperial Ballet and then by Phyllis Bedells, the first English woman in nearly a century to attain recognition as a classic ballerina.

Two women, the Irish-born Ninette de Valois (Edris Stannus) and the Polish Marie Rambert (Miriam Rambach), were chiefly responsible for the high status attained by British ballet in the 20th century. Rambert was a student of Émile Jaques-Dalcroze when Diaghilev invited her to teach eurythmics to his company. Her lessons influenced Nijinsky's choreography for *L'Aprés-midi d'un faune* and *Sacre du printemps*. Rambert in turn learned the value of classic ballet technique. She studied under Cecchetti, following his methods when she opened her own school in London in 1920. She had a decided flair for discovering choreographic talent and encouraged Frederick Ashton in the creation in 1926 of his first ballet, *A Tragedy of Fashion*. Among her other protégés were Antony Tudor, Walter Gore, Norman Morrice, Frank Staff, and Andrée Howard. In 1930 she founded the Ballet Club, devoted to developing English choreographers and dancers. Later known as the Ballet Rambert, this enterprising and progressive company has remained active. Dancers who worked intensively under Rambert include Agnes de Mille, Maude Lloyd, Peggy van Praagh, Celia Franca (founder and director of the National Ballet of Canada, 1951–74), Sally Gilmour, Hugh Laing, Harold Turner, and John Gilpin. Tudor's first works, *Cross Gartered* (1931), *Lysistrata* (1932), *Dark Elegies* (1937), and *Lilac Garden* (1936), were created for the Ballet Club under Rambert's supervision.

By 1933 the Vic-Wells Ballet, later to become England's Royal Ballet, was firmly established. De Valois, its director and guiding spirit, had danced in pantomime, Italian opera, and in the Diaghilev's Ballets Russes before establishing a school in London in 1926. When the Sadler's Wells Theatre was reopened in 1931, the Vic-Wells Ballet was officially organized with six dancers. Soon Markova, Dolin, Lopokova, and Idzikowski made guest appearances. The company was gradually enlarged, and in 1933 Markova became its ballerina. *Giselle, The Nutcracker,* and *Swan Lake* were produced for her. In the years that followed, de Valois's ballets *Job, The Rake's Progress,* and *Checkmate* were added to the repertoire. Through such works as *Façade, Les Patineurs,* and *A Wedding Bouquet,* Ashton was recognized as a major choreographer. Robert Helpmann, who joined the company in 1933, soon became its principal male dancer, preeminent in dramatic roles. When Markova left the Vic-Wells in 1935, many of her roles were inherited by 16-year-old Margot Fonteyn, who later matured into one of the great ballerinas of the century.

After World War II the Sadler's Wells Ballet, as it was then known, was invited to reopen the Royal Opera House at Covent Garden. *The Sleeping Beauty* was revived for the occasion, and in that same year Massine revived *The Three-Cornered Hat* and *La Boutique fantasque* especially for the company, dancing in these ballets himself. Ashton choreographed Prokofiev's *Cinderella* (1948), Delibes' *Sylvia* (1952), Hans Werner Henze's *Ondine* (1958), and a new version of one of the oldest ballets extant, Dauberval's creation of 1789, *La Fille mal gardée* (1960). Despite Ashton's retirement as artistic director in 1970 and competition from the younger Festival Ballet, the Royal remains the preeminent British company.

France after 1920   The somnolence of the Paris Opéra Ballet, stagnant since the death of Saint-Léon in 1870, was interrupted in 1924 by the revival of *Giselle* for the great Russian ballerina Spessivtzeva and in 1930 with the appointment of Serge Lifar, Diaghilev's last premier danseur, as ballet master.

Lifar cleared the Opéra Ballet of deadwood, raised its technical standards, and greatly enlarged its repertoire. His ballets included *Promethée, Icare* (danced to a percussion accompaniment of his own devising), and dozens of others. Except for an interlude following World War II, he continued as director of the Opéra Ballet until 1958, when he was replaced by George Skibine. Yvette Chauviré, noted for her feminine elegance, Nina Vyrou-

bova, trained by Russian teachers outside the Opéra, and the U.S. ballerina Marjorie Tallchief achieved distinction among its stars. Harald Lander choreographed several successful works for the company, and in 1960 Gene Kelly became the first American to produce a ballet for the Opéra when he staged *Pas des dieux* to music by Gershwin. Many gifted dancers educated at the Opéra, such as Janine Charrat, Renée Jeanmaire, Colette Marchand, Jean Babilée, and Roland Petit, revolted against its rigid hierarchy and left to form their own companies or to dance in revues and films. Petit formed Les Ballets des Champs Élysées in 1945 and later headed Les Ballets de Paris. Most hopeful for the future of the Opéra Ballet was the appointment in 1977 of Violette Verdy, a former star of the New York City Ballet, as artistic director.

Denmark   The Royal Danish Ballet has enjoyed an uninterrupted existence since the mid-18th century. The principal architect of the Danish ballet was August Bournonville, born in Copenhagen in 1805. He studied under Auguste Vestris, danced at the Paris Opéra, and returned to Copenhagen in 1829 to guide its ballet for nearly half a century. The Danish style, with its emphasis on masculine virtuosity and expressive mime, is actually the pre-Romantic style of Vestris and Duport that Bournonville brought from Paris and meticulously preserved. The Bournonville ballets *La Sylphide, Napoli,* and *Konservatoriet,* with Galeotti's *The Whims of Cupid and the Ballet Master* (the oldest ballet still performed in its original choreography, dating from 1786), still maintained a key position in the Danish repertoire late in the 20th century.

Soviet Union   Ballet in the U.S.S.R. has followed the traditions established by Marius Petipa in the 19th century. Many Petipa classics remain in the repertoire, although they are sometimes restaged. Ballet technique was developed to an extraordinarily high level of proficiency, sometimes approaching the acrobatic, through the work of such fine teachers as Vasili Tikhomirov (1876–1956) in Moscow and Agrippina Vaganova (1879–1951) in Leningrad. Vaganova's textbook, *Fundamentals of the Classic Dance* (1934), was translated into many languages.

Soviet choreography in general tended to conventionality, although much imagination was shown in devising unusual lifts and in the careful delineation of each ballet's story. Principal centers of ballet production were the Bolshoi Theater in Moscow and the Kirov Theater in Leningrad, although ballet companies functioned even in remote sections of the Soviet Union. The chief glory of Soviet ballet in the early 1960s was its ballerina Galina Ulanova, a lyrical dancer with a phenomenal ability to sustain a role. Her contemporaries Olga Lepeshinskaya and Natalia Dudinskaya remained popular favorites, while among her younger colleagues Maya Plisetskaya, Raissa Struchkova, Yuri Zhdanov, and Nikolai Fadeyechev earned high praise.

Beginning in 1958 foreign ballet companies and guest stars were invited to the U.S.S.R. for the first time in many years. The Paris Opéra Ballet with Marjorie Tallchief was one of the earliest visitors. In 1960 the American Ballet Theatre with Marjorie's sister, Maria Tallchief, and Erik Bruhn was the first U.S. dance company to appear in the Soviet Union.

United States after 1932   After the death of Diaghilev a number of his associates formed the Ballet Russe de Monte Carlo with Col. Wassily de Basil as its head. Balanchine and Massine were the principal choreographers, with Aleksandra Danilova, Irina Baronova, Tamara Toumanova, Tatiana Riabouchinska, and David Lichine as leading dancers. The company made its U.S. debut late in 1933, and as well as many works originally produced by Diaghilev, the repertoire included new ballets by Balanchine (*Cotillon, La Concurrence*) and Massine (*Jeux d'enfants, Scuola di Ballo*). During the 1930s Massine's controversial experiments in the use of symphonic music produced several important productions. *Les Présages* used Tchaikovsky's Fifth Symphony; *Choreartium,* Brahms' Fourth; and *Seventh Symphony,* Beethoven's score. Discord within the company caused a split in its ranks in 1938, after which time de Basil led a group called the Original Ballet Russe and Massine reorganized the Ballet Russe de Monte Carlo, bringing it back to the United States with new ballets (*Gaîté Parisienne, St. Francis,* a revival of *Giselle*) and a galaxy of dancers new to this country, including Alicia Markova, Mia Slavenska, Frederic Franklin, and Igor Youskevitch.

During the war years the Ballet Russe became, in everything but name, a U.S. company. European dancers dropped out and were replaced by Americans (Maria Tallchief, Mary Ellen Moylan, Leon Danielian). The company presented American ballets, Ruth Page and Bentley Stone's *Frankie and Johnny* (1938) and Agnes de Mille's *Rodeo* (1942; Copland). After Massine's departure Balanchine was for a time the principal choreographer, creating *Night Shadow* and *Le Bourgeois gentilhomme.* After he left in 1946 no firm hand guided artistic policies, and its productions became haphazard, although it frequently offered excellent dancing from its stars, including Danilova and Franklin.

American Ballet Theatre (after 1957; established by Lucia Chase in 1940 as Ballet Theatre) united some of the most distinguished dance artists of England and America: Tudor, de Mille, Dolin, Laing, Bolm, and Fokine, who prepared *Les Sylphides* for the opening performance. The dancers, almost exclusively American, demonstrated conclusively that permanent schools with good teachers had produced technicians able to compete with the best of the Europeans. From the ranks of American Ballet Theatre came Nora Kaye, acknowledged the finest dramatic dancer of her time, Alicia Alonso, Melissa Hayden, Diana Adams, Janet Reed, Rosella Hightower, Jerome Robbins, Michael Kidd, John Kriza, Ivan Nagy, Cynthia Gregory, and a score of others who helped raise the standards of U.S. ballet. American Ballet Theatre's first program included Tudor's *Lilac Garden,* and a major contribution was the production of his memorable *Pillar of Fire* (1942; Schoenberg), which first revealed Kaye's capacities as a dance actress. The company also encouraged U.S. choreographers and composers and the use of American themes, producing Robbins' *Fancy Free* (1944; Bernstein) and de Mille's *Fall River Legend* (1948; Morton Gould). Before leaving the company to become Balanchine's associate at the New York City Ballet, Robbins choreographed a completely new production of Stravinsky's *Les Noces* (1965), and new ground was broken with Alvin Ailey's *The River* (1970; Duke Ellington) and with the controversial Twyla Tharp's *Push Comes to Shove* (1976; Haydn and Joseph Lamb).

In a sense the oldest of the major U.S. companies is the New York City Ballet. At the invitation of Lincoln Kirstein, Balanchine came to the United States in 1933 to found the School of American Ballet. The first company to grow out of the school was the American Ballet, which made its debut in Hartford, Connecticut, in 1934, and had a brief New York City season early in 1935, becoming the official ballet of the Metropolitan Opera that autumn. The repertoire, entirely by Balanchine, included *Serenade* (1934; Tchaikovsky) and the college satire *Alma Mater* (1935; Kay Swift and Morton Gould). Balanchine's progressive classicism did not mix with the Metropolitan's old-fashioned operatic traditions, and the American Ballet disbanded after three years, but not before it had presented three works to music by Stravinsky, *Apollo, The Card Party,* and *Le Baiser de la fée.*

Meanwhile, several of the dancers had banded together under Kirstein's leadership to form the Ballet Caravan, which rapidly became the incubator for a generation of U.S. choreographers: Eugene Loring, who created *Yankee Clipper* (1937) and *Billy the Kid* (1938; Copland); Lew Christensen with *Pocahontas* (1936; Elliott Carter) and *Filling Station* (1938; Virgil Thomson); and William Dollar with *Le Combat* (1949). Here, especially in the work of Loring, the influence of the modern dance on American ballet choreography first became strongly apparent. The reaction against stilted ballet convention, which had motivated dance revolutionaries like Isadora Duncan, Martha Graham, and Doris Humphrey, had borne fruit in a new vocabulary of movement that ballet choreographers began to absorb, adapt, and incorporate into their own works.

Although the American Ballet was reactivated for a goodwill tour of South America in 1941, it was not until 1946 that Kirstein and Balanchine again joined forces in the creation of a company. This was the Ballet Society, a subscription organization dedicated to the production of works for the lyric theater, including both ballet and opera. Attracting dancers of the caliber of Maria Tallchief, Tanaquil LeClercq, Nicolas Magallanes, Todd Bolender, and Francisco Moncion, the Ballet Society during its two years of existence produced nine new works by Balanchine and ballets by six young Americans: Bolender, Dollar, John Taras, Lew Christensen, Merce Cunningham, and Fred Danieli. In 1948 the New York City Center of Music and Drama invited the young company to join it with the title of the New York City Ballet. It thus achieved the unique advantage of a permanent home theater, something no American ballet company had previously enjoyed. In its first decade of existence the New York City Ballet gave nearly 75 ballets, most of them original works by Balanchine or his associate artistic director, Robbins.

Working for his own company Balanchine reached the full flowering of his genius. He has been largely responsible for the American classic style (splendidly exemplified in his *Symphony in C,* 1946; Bizet), based on the pure classic technique as transmitted through the Russians, but incorporating certain American qualities of clean, cool, buoyant athleticism. Balanchine explored new paths in his provocative and fascinating *Agon* (1957; Stravinsky) and pursued them still further in the equally unorthodox *Episodes* (1959), in which he collaborated with Martha Graham, using music by Webern. The unusual gifts of Robbins provided the company with a wealth of works ranging from the thoughtful *Age of Anxiety* (1950; Bernstein) and exhilarating *Pied Piper* (1951; Copland) to the enigmatic *Watermill* (1972; Teiji Ito).

The New York City Ballet in the 1960s and '70s has included stars such as Melissa Hayden, Patricia Wilde, Violette Verdy, Jacques d'Amboise, Allegra Kent, Edward Villella, Patricia McBride, Suzanne Farrell, and Gelsey Kirkland, who left for American Ballet Theatre in 1974.

The youngest of the three major U.S. companies is the City Center Joffrey Ballet. Established in 1956 and named for its founder, choreographer Robert Joffrey, the troupe is less biased toward traditions than either the New

York City Ballet or the American Ballet Theatre. Rather than extending the classical syntax, as George Balanchine has done, or presenting recensions of the great 19th-century favorites, which is Ballet Theatre's forte, the Joffrey favors works that are highly reflective of 20th-century popular culture. In the mid-1970s it was most active among U.S. companies in restaging the works of Sir Frederick Ashton—*Façade* (1931; William Walton), *Les Patineurs* (1937; Meyerbeer), *The Dream* (1964; Mendelssohn), and *Monotones* (1965; Satie) were all in its repertoire—and it also presented revivals of notable pieces first presented by Diaghilev's Ballets Russes, including *Petrushka* (1911; Stravinsky), *Parade* (1917; Satie), and *Pulcinella* (1920; Stravinsky). More visible perhaps were the ballets by Joffrey's long-time associate and resident choreographer, Gerald Arpino. In a series of ballets set to popular music—*Trinity* (1970) to rock music and *Confetti* (1970) to Rossini are typical of his work—Arpino proved to be facile and workmanlike but a choreographer of little substance.

Ballet activity in the United States has not been confined to the major companies. In the 1930s Catherine and Dorothie Littlefield built the Philadelphia Ballet into an admirable ensemble, the first U.S. company to visit Europe (in 1937). Ruth Page, Bentley Stone, and Walter Camryn in Chicago made valuable experiments with U.S. thematic material. The San Francisco Ballet, developed by Willam Christensen and directed after 1952 by his brother Lew Christensen, consistently produced fresh and original works in addition to staging classics like *The Nutcracker, Swan Lake,* and *Coppélia.* It undertook government-sponsored tours of South America, the Orient, and the Near East with notable success.

In the early 1960s a tendency toward the establishment of regional ballet companies was increasingly evident. As teaching standards were gradually raised all over the country, professional and semiprofessional groups were established in such widely scattered centers as Atlanta, Detroit, Houston, Miami, New Orleans, Seattle, and Salt Lake City. A young company of solid accomplishment and exceptional promise was the National Ballet (1962–74), directed by Frederic Franklin and Ben Stevenson in the U.S. capital.

Enlivening the dance world in 1961 was the defection to the West of Rudolf Nureyev. A product of the once Imperial Academy in Leningrad and a star performer with the Kirov Ballet, Nureyev claimed that his artistic growth was being stunted under an inflexible and regressive Soviet regime. Rather than commit himself to any single company in the United States or Europe, Nureyev chose to appear as guest artist with numerous troupes, although his closest association was with England's Royal Ballet, where for more than a decade he forged a fabled partnership with Dame Margot Fonteyn. In the 1970s Nureyev broadened his stylistic base and worked with several modern dance choreographers, the most notable among them Martha Graham and Paul Taylor.

Nureyev's complaint about the restricted creative scope under the Soviet regime was echoed in 1970 when Natalia Makarova defected from the Kirov Ballet, and again in 1974, when Mikhail Baryshnikov, perhaps the most celebrated of the Kirov's younger stars, quit the company to make the United States his home. Both Makarova and Baryshnikov joined the American Ballet Theatre, which took advantage of their expertise in the 19th-century repertoire and offered them new avenues of growth by working with choreographers as diverse as Antony Tudor and Twyla Tharp. Baryshnikov, however, stunned the dance world in 1978 when he announced that he would leave Ballet Theatre for the New York City Ballet, where he would be able to work under George Balanchine, who himself left Leningrad for the West in 1924. The following year, though, he was appointed director of the American Ballet Theatre beginning in 1980.

BIBLIOGRAPHY: Léon Bakst, *The Decorative Art of Léon Bakst* (1913; reprint, 1969) and *The Designs of Léon Bakst for the Sleeping Princess* (1923; reprint, 1969); Walter Archibald Propert, *Russian Ballet in Western Europe, 1909–1920* (1921); Lincoln Kirstein, *Dance: A Short History of Classic Theatrical Dancing* (1935; reprint, 1969), *The Classic Ballet* (1952), *What Ballet Is About: An Ameri-*

can Glossary (1959), *Movement and Metaphor; Four Centuries of Ballet* (1970), *The New York City Ballet* (1973), and *Nijinsky Dancing* (1975); Prince Peter Lieven, *The Birth of the Ballets-Russes* (1936; reprint, 1973); Juri Slonimsky, *Soviet Ballet* (1947; reprint, 1970); Ivor Guest, *Alhambra Ballet* (1959), *The Romantic Ballet in England,* 2nd ed. (1972), and *The Ballet of the Second Empire* (1974); Selma J. Cohen, *Stravinsky and the Dance: A Survey of Ballet Productions 1910–1962* (1962); Edwin Denby, *Dancers, Buildings and People in the Streets* (1965) and *Looking at the Dance* (1976); UNESCO, *Ten Years of Films on Ballet and Classical Dance, 1955–1965* (1968); Nancy Goldner, *The Stravinsky Festival* (1973); Joseph H. Mazo, *Dance Is a Contact Sport* (1974); Valerian Svetloff, *Anna Pavlova* (1974); Bernard Taper, *Balanchine* (1974); Mary Clarke and David Vaughn, eds., *The Encyclopedia of Dance and Ballet* (1977); Margot Fonteyn, *Margot Fonteyn* (1977); Arnold Haskell, *Balletomania: Then and Now* (1977); Lillian Moore, *Echoes of American Ballet* (1977).

balletto (English and German spelling, *ballett*) A vocal composition distinguished by homophonic texture, strongly marked dance-like rhythms, and refrains in which the voices sing such syllables as "fa la la." The earliest examples are found in Giovanni Giacomo Gastoldi's *Balletti a cinque voci* (1591). Thomas Morley published his *First Booke of Balletts to Five Voyces* (1595) in both English and Italian editions, which suggests that Italian pieces of this kind had already achieved popularity in England; an edition with German words was printed at Nürnberg in 1609. Morley, the most Italianate composer of his generation, did not return to the genre, but Thomas Weelkes published a collection of *Balletts and Madrigals,* again for five voices, in 1598. Though it would have been possible to dance to a *balletto,* it should be regarded as idealized dance music that has been translated into the sphere of the madrigal.

ballo in maschera, Un: *see* VERDI.

Banchieri, Adriano (1567–1634) The Italian composer Adriano Banchieri was best known for his madrigal-comedies, but he was also an organist, musical theorist, and poet. Born at Bologna, he spent most of his life at the monastery of S. Michele in Bosco near Bologna, becoming abbot in 1620. He was also prominent in Bolognese academies. His numerous madrigal-comedies are second in importance only to those of Orazio Vecchi. *Il festino nella sera del giovedì grasso avanti cena* (1608; *The Animals Improvise Counterpoint,* 1937) contains some delightful characterization. Although he used the basso continuo, the style of his music on the whole looks back toward the 16th century.

band A term used to describe a group of instruments played together. The instruments are generally of one family or type, and in the United States the term has been restricted more specifically to groups of wind instruments. Colloquially it may be synonymous with orchestra.

Derived from the French *bande* ("group"), the term was first applied in England to the "king's band" of 24 violins at the court of Charles II. This was modeled on Louis XIV's group of violins, a development of the practice of employing musicians at court and in noble households that was widespread throughout Europe in the 16th and 17th centuries. The string band remained popular, and composers from Bach and Handel to Britten wrote music for small groups of stringed instruments.

The wind, brass, and percussion ensemble that is called a band originated in 15th-century Germany, where ensembles consisting chiefly of oboes and bassoons formed part of the paraphernalia of military life. German musicians joined foreign groups, and wind bands spread eventually through France and England and to the New World. Toward the end of the 18th century in Europe, a style of band music identified as Turkish, or Janissary (after the elite troops who guarded the Turkish sultans *c.* 1400–1826), music became popular in Europe. Its characteristically strident sound, produced in the original by shrill flutes and large drums, jangling triangles, cymbals, and Turkish crescents (jingling Johnnies), and its emphatic duple accent appealed to a taste for exoticism that led also to the employment of black drummers, who marched brandishing their drumsticks in the manner of the later drum major. JANISSARY MUSIC inspired imitation by some of the greatest composers, including Haydn in the second movement of his *Military* Symphony; Mozart in the "Rondo alla Turca" movement of his Piano Sonata in A Major; and Beethoven in his orchestral suite *The Ruins of Athens.*

By the end of the 19th century the number of wind instruments had increased greatly; Haydn's marches written for the Derbyshire yeomanry were scored for trumpet, two horns, two clarinets, two bassoons, and serpent. In Berlin in 1838, 1,000 wind instruments and 200 drummers were assembled by the organizer of Prussian military music to perform in honor of the Russian tsar.

In England the brass band began to replace the earlier bands of the town waits (public musicians) and of village churches at the end of the 18th century. The formation of such bands was encouraged by employers in industrial areas, and the development of the cornopean, a predecessor of the cornet, and of a family of brass instruments with similar fingering invented by the French instrument builder Adolphe Sax facilitated the adoption of brass instruments by amateur players. Composers such as Elgar, Arthur Sullivan, Gustav Holst, and Britten contributed to band literature. Such works were usually scored for cornets, flugelhorns, horns, B-flat baritones, euphoniums and basses.

In the United States professional bands such as the celebrated band of Patrick Sarsfield Gilmore (1829–92) competed in attracting virtuoso soloists. Gilmore, whose musical skill was matched by a flair for showmanship, was particularly influential in promoting technical skill and repertoire of high quality. His true successor was John Philip Sousa (1854–1932), bandmaster of the U.S. Marine Band and composer of such marches as *Semper Fidelis,* the *Washington Post* March, and *The Stars and Stripes Forever.* The accomplishments of Gilmore and Sousa were to raise the art of the band to a distinguished level, making band music in a sense a very American musical genre. It remains a staple in parades and in the extravaganzas that form an important part of the entertainment incidental to sports events, though late in the 20th century bands began to play more show tunes and even modified rock.

Wind band is the name given to a small group of brass and woodwind instruments used by composers in works destined for concert performance. Works for wind band were written by Mozart and in the 20th century by Hindemith and Schoenberg. The Italian word *banda* signifies the brass band on the stage or, in opera, behind the scenes, notably in Berlioz' *Requiem* and in Verdi's *Rigoletto* and *La Traviata.*

In schools the percussion band is a term used for a children's orchestra of percussion instruments, its purpose being to develop a sense of rhythm. Britten introduced a children's percussion band in his setting of the Chester miracle play *Noye's Fludde.* Dance bands or jazz bands originated in the United States at the end of the 19th century and assumed a large variety of forms (*see* JAZZ).

BIBLIOGRAPHY: Henry George Farmer, *The Rise and Development of Military Music* (1912; reprint, 1970); John F. Russell and John H. Elliott, *The Brass Band Movement* (1936).

bar: *see* MEASURE.

Barber of Seville, The: *see* BARBIERE DI SIVIGLIA, IL.

Barber, Samuel (b. March 9, 1910) One of the most frequently performed of U.S. composers, Samuel Barber is generally regarded as in the mainstream of musical tradition—a representative of 20th-century lyricism and post-Romanticism.

Barber began piano lessons at the age of six and soon began to compose. After graduation from the Curtis Institute in Philadelphia (1934), Barber devoted himself entirely to composition. He developed a distinctive style, absorbing some technical procedures of modern music but without indulging in experimentation for its own sake. His Overture to *The School for Scandal* (1933), based on Sheridan's comedy and composed while he was still a student, and *Music for a Scene from Shelley* (1935), inspired by *Prometheus Unbound,* established his reputation. Although literary allusions occur in many of Barber's works, his music is not programmatic in the literal sense. Significant in this respect are the two *Essays* for orchestra (1938 and 1942), which are intended as musical counterparts of the literary form. Structural considerations govern Barber's instrumental writing; there is great astringency in harmony, but the basic tonality remains secure; the rhythmic lines are very strong without loss of coherence.

In 1936 Barber composed a Quartet, the slow movement of which was arranged for string orchestra, performed under the title *Adagio for Strings* by the NBC Symphony Orchestra under Toscanini in New York City on November 5, 1938, and acquired extraordinary popularity both in America and in Europe. Barber's First Symphony (1936; revised 1942) is in the romantic tradition; in the Second Symphony (1944; revised 1947), commissioned by the U.S. Army Air Forces (which Barber had joined in 1943), he introduced a special electronic instrument imitating radio signals for air navigation, replaced in the revised version by an E-flat clarinet.

Barber wrote concertos for violin (1939), cello (1945), and piano (1962), for which he was awarded a Pulitzer Prize in 1963. His Piano Sonata (1948) is one of the most ambitious works in this form by a 20th-century composer. Other compositions are *Dover Beach* for voice and string quartet (1931); four vocal works with orchestra, *Knoxville, Summer of 1915* (1948), *Prayers of Kierkegaard* (1954), *Andromache's Farewell* (1963), and *The Lovers* (1971), with a text by Pablo Neruda; a ballet *Medea* (originally *The Serpent Heart,* 1946); Toccata *Festiva* (1960), composed for the opening of the Philadelphia Orchestra's new organ in the Academy of Music; and three operas, *Vanessa,* for which he received a Pulitzer Prize in 1958, *A Hand of Bridge* (1959), with a libretto by Gian Carlo Menotti, and *Antony and Cleopatra,* commissioned for the opening (1966) of the new Metropolitan Opera House at Lincoln Center in New York City. *Fadograph of a Yestern Scene* (for orchestra) after James Joyce's *Finnegans Wake* was first performed in 1971.

BIBLIOGRAPHY: W. Broder, *Samuel Barber* (1954).

RECORDINGS: *Adagio for Strings* (from Quartet): *Dover Beach; Knoxville, Summer of 1915;* Piano Concerto; Quartet; Symphony No. 1; Toccata *Festiva; Vanessa;* Violin Concerto.

barbiere di Siviglia, Il: *see* CLASSICAL PERIOD (vocal music, 1750–1800); PAISIELLO; PROGRAM MUSIC (imagery); ROSSINI.

Barbirolli, John (December 2, 1899–July 28, 1970)   Beginning his musical career as a cellist, the English conductor John Barbirolli was educated at Trinity College and the Royal Academy of Music. He was chosen to succeed Toscanini at the New York Philharmonic (1937–43) and then to lead the Hallé Orchestra in Manchester (1943–68). He also was conductor of the Houston Symphony (1961–67). Barbirolli was knighted in 1949. A traditionalist, he was conservative in repertoire, and his interpretations were noted for their rhetorical expansiveness and warmth of sound.

barcarole (French spelling, *barcarolle*)   A boat song derived from the songs sung by the *barcaruoli,* the old Italian word for boatmen, particularly the gondoliers of Venice. It is characterized by a gentle rhythm associated with the motion of the boat and the lapping of the waves. Usually in $\frac{6}{8}$ time, the entire composition is pervaded by alternating strong and light beats with a moderate triplet figure.

Nineteenth-century barcaroles are stylized examples of this model. Louis Joseph Ferdinand Hérold, Daniel François Esprit Auber, Donizetti, and Offenbach are among the composers who introduced the barcarole into opera. Schubert used the barcarole rhythm in his song "Auf dem Wasser zu singen" and Mendelssohn in his *Songs without Words.* Barcaroles for the piano are by Chopin and a series of 13 pieces by Fauré.

Bardi, Giovanni, Count (of Vernio) (February 5, 1534–1612)   Founder of the Florentine camerata, Giovanni Bardi was an Italian nobleman, patron of the arts, and composer. The camerata, founded about 1580, sought to revive ancient Greek music and drama, and its participants composed the earliest operas. Among members were the poet Ottavio Rinuccini, the theorist Vincenzo Galilei (father of Galileo), and the composers Giulio Caccini,

Jacopo Peri, and Emilio del Cavaliere, with most of whom Bardi collaborated in court entertainments from 1579 to 1608.

Bardi's *Discorso mandato a Cuccini sopra la Musica Antica* (1580; "Discourse to Caccini on Ancient Music") develops ideas similar to those of Caccini and Galilei: counterpoint obscures the words in musical settings and should be abandoned; music should consist of a single vocal line, lightly accompanied, exactly reflecting the rhythm and intonation of speech. These theories underlie the musical style of the early Florentine operas. Ironically Bardi's only surviving compositions are two highly contrapuntal madrigals. Bardi also belonged to the Crusca Academy, a literary association, and in 1592 became a chamberlain to Pope Clement VIII.

Barenboim, Daniel (b. November 15, 1942) With a career divided almost equally between pianist and conductor, the Argentina-born Israeli Daniel Barenboim studied piano in Salzburg with Edwin Fischer and conducting with Igor Markevitch. He later worked with Boulanger and at the Santa Cecilia Conservatory in Rome. As a pianist he has recorded all of the Beethoven sonatas and concertos, but his repertoire in both of his roles covers a broad range.

baritone A valved brass instrument pitched in B-flat or C that has been a popular band instrument from the 19th century and is derived from the cornet and flugelhorn (valved bugle). It resembles the euphonium but has a narrower bore and three, rather than four or five, valves. Its range extends three octaves from the E below the bass staff; the notes in the treble clef are written a ninth above the actual sound. The term baritone sometimes causes confusion; in Germany and often in the United States the instrument is called both the tenor horn and the EUPHONIUM. All three terms may also refer to saxhorn of similar pitch.

Baritone also refers to the male singing voice between tenor and bass, ranging from about the second A below middle C to the F above.

Barnby, Joseph (August 12, 1838–January 28, 1896) The English composer, organist, and conductor Joseph Barnby did much to promote an interest in choral music. He studied at the Royal Academy and subsequently became organist at a succession of London churches. He gave Bach's *St. Matthew* Passion at Westminster Abbey in 1871, and, appointed to St. Anne's, Soho, in the same year, he conducted annual performances of the *St. John* Passion. His choir was amalgamated in 1871 with the Royal Albert Hall Choral Society, later the Royal Choral Society. Barnby gave the first performances in England of Dvořák's *Stabat Mater* (1883) and of a concert version of Wagner's *Parsifal* (1884). He became precentor of music at Eton in 1875 and principal of the Guildhall School of Music in 1892, the same year he was knighted. His compositions consist chiefly of services, anthems, hymns, and part songs, of which the most popular was his setting of *Sweet and Low* (1863).

Baroque era Although the term Baroque came into music history in the 18th century, alongside its use in the visual arts, its appropriateness as a catchall label for music between 1600 and 1750 has long been questioned. In the 18th century the term had pejorative connotations—the strained, effusive, eccentric age that lay between the lean clarity of the cinquecento (*see* RENAISSANCE) and the proportioned lucidity of the Enlightenment. While later ages have removed this negative tinge, we might still ask whether works as diverse as the madrigals of Monteverdi, the *ordres* of François Couperin, the operas of Alessandro Scarlatti, and the passions of Bach manifest a single aesthetic concept. Some scholars have tried to sidestep the issue entirely by referring to the "thoroughbass period," thus delimiting the era on the basis of an objective compositional technique; yet abstract, imitative works defy such a description. Others have tried to unite the period by focusing on a single expressive principle: music's ability to depict an affection, to illustrate and convey the emotion of a literary text; yet pure instrumental music does not respect such a scheme.

The temporal boundaries of the Baroque era have fluctuated with different generations of scholars, and the dates 1600 and 1750 are indeed quite arbitrary. The first represents Jacopo Peri's setting of Ottavio Rinuccini's *Euridice*, the first complete extant opera and one of the first published works to employ the basso continuo; the latter is the death of Bach. And yet both of these dates might be altered radically according to the above criteria. As early as the 1550s northern Italian madrigalists were experimenting with new means to depict intensely the emotional import of a text. In the preface to his *Quinto libro de Madrigali* (1605), Monteverdi cited Cipriano da Rore, Giaches de Wert, and Luca Marenzio among others to give historical justification for his *seconda prattica*, the principle that stylistic eccentricities were admissible if they were suggested by the text. Similarly, well before Bach's death, a lighter, more genial style can be detected in the works of Italian symphonists and opera composers. Not only do figures such as Sammartini and Pergolesi breathe this new air, but so do the late works of such Baroque heavyweights as Vivaldi, Alessandro Scarlatti, and (according to a recent theory) certain late works of Bach himself. And yet the basso continuo—as a performing tradition if not a structural device of composition—hangs on well past 1750 (*see* FIGURED BASS). The mid-18th century is still very much a hornet's nest for musical scholars, and the paths of stylistic change that led from the fugues and cantatas of Bach to the Viennese Classical style a half century later are still not fully understood. *See* CLASSICAL PERIOD.

beginnings The beginnings of Baroque style are manifest on several fronts during the first years of the seicento. Most fundamental is the birth of MONODY, or solo song, as a musical medium. While a single voice had often sung to instrumental accompaniment during the previous century, lute songs or consort songs were inherently polyphonic. Even the elaborate solo songs from the *intermedi* to Bargagli's "La Pellegrina" (Florence, 1589) were conceived as a contrapuntal web with an elaborate top voice. Thus Giulio Caccini's *Nuove Musiche* (Florence, 1602) was new music in the truest sense; for in these delightfully ornamental *madrigali* and simple, dancelike *arie*, Caccini displayed a revolutionary two-voice texture, vertical rather than horizontal in orientation, which allowed the solo voice

complete freedom of declamation as well as a new floridity. Caccini's detailed preface, which describes the new vocal nuances and ornaments, is the best contemporary description of this new art of solo song that flourished in the early years of the 17th century.

Monody not only arose as an independent medium, it also ruptured the chief secular genre of the previous century, the five-voice polyphonic MADRIGAL. The stylistic progression in Monteverdi's eight madrigal books shows the disastrous effect that monody wreaked on the carefully wrought contrapuntal texture. While many of the works in his first four books (1587–1603) are traditional in harmony and sport a conventional equal-voiced texture, a number pit the upper two voices against the bass, prefiguring the trio texture that will dominate Baroque music. Moreover madrigals such as *Si ch'io vorrei morire* (Book IV) and the famous *Cruda Amarilli* (Book V) contain pungent dissonances that cannot easily be explained according to the theorist Gioseffo Zarlino's principles regarding the classic, horizontal web of counterpoint but only in terms of a vertically oriented chord structure. Indeed at the end of Book V Monteverdi burst the polyphonic web irrevocably by his addition of an obligatory basso continuo part to the last six works, a phenomenon that would form part of all of his remaining madrigals. One might in fact wonder just what Monteverdi's later madrigals have to do with the 16th-century tradition other than their being vocal works on secular texts, for by the final book, the *Madrigali Guerrieri e Amorosi* (1638), they have become vast tone pictures for singers and instruments in which the new solo idiom has completely supplanted older polyphony. It is no accident that 18 years earlier Monteverdi's younger colleague Alessandro Grandi had already published a vocal collection under the new title *Cantade ed Arie* (1620), suggesting that the madrigal had already burst its strictures and would soon develop into a more expansive genre, the secular cantata.

Monody did not arise in an intellectual vacuum but stemmed from research by a Roman philologist, Girolami Mei, into the nature of ancient Greek music. Mei surmised that ancient music was monophonic and that Greek drama had been sung throughout. His ideas were taken up by a Florentine academy, the CAMERATA, and used as a manifesto by Vincenzo Galilei, whose *Dialogo della musica antica e della moderna* (1581) attacked polyphony and asserted that the only true tonal representation of a literary text would be a single line of music, one that echoed the inflections of normal speech. The application of this principle finally led to complete musical settings of pastoral dramatic texts and with them the birth of opera. If Peri and Caccini did not realize the full potential of the medium in their settings of *Euridice* (1600), Monteverdi had the invention to combine disparate musical elements in *L'Orfeo* (Mantua, 1607)— new monody, older madrigalian choruses, affective instrumental sinfonie, and sprightly dances—forming a unique fusion of old and new musical idioms. And the great lament from his lost *Arianna* (Mantua, 1608) shows the heights that pure monody could attain in the depiction of grief.

Monody also worked its way into sacred music. The small motets of Viadana's *Cento Concerti Ecclesiastici* (1602) used the new basso continuo to create modest compositions for provincial churches. Monody also found a place in isolated sections of large choral works, and this intrusion brought the ripe CONCERTATO STYLE into sacred music. The concerted style is predicated upon the opposition of forces and can be seen in a number of guises in a large sacred work like Monteverdi's *Vespers* of 1610: works pitting solo singers against chorus and instruments (Magnificat); two choruses against one another *(Nisi Dominus)*; instrumental choirs against singers *(Domine ad adiuvandum)*; and even several solo singers against one another *(Duo seraphim)*. The style is found in the madrigal as well. And yet early Baroque sacred music differed from its secular counterparts in one important respect. Whereas the older polyphonic style fell into disuse in secular music, it coexisted with the newer idioms in sacred music as the *stile antico,* a sanctified sacred style that lasted in Italy right through the 18th century. Thus Baroque church music manifests a duality unparalleled in the history of music, in which an archaic and a modern style survived side by side for nearly two centuries. Moreover they could often be found in different parts of the same composition; Bach's b minor Mass retains a number of movements in the learned *stile antico.*

The advent of monody, the transfiguration of the Italian madrigal, the birth of opera, and the changed face of sacred music made the musical world of 1620 a transformed environment from that of 1580. In the area of instrumental music, however, the change was much slower and more gradual. Keyboard composers adopted the forms of the previous century with few drastic changes; indeed the works of Frescobaldi could be looked upon more as a summary of 16th-century forms than as a harbinger of the future: toccate, ricercari, canzone, capricci, partite, organ masses, dance sets. Yet here too there is a forcefulness, a sense of display and extravagance that quite outstrips his predecessors.

Change was also slow in the music for instrumental ensemble. The transformation of the CANZONA into the Baroque instrumental SONATA is one that spans a full half century. Here, however, the influence of monody and madrigal is more in evidence, for the archetypal texture of two high voices and basso continuo dominates the violin sonata for the entire 17th century. The stylistic change in instrumental music results to an extent from the sudden discovery of the technical capabilities of the violin, and it is amazing that the first sonatas for violin per se (published from 1610 onward) are such completely finished and idiomatic products. The sonatas of Salamone Rossi Dario Castello, Tarquinio Merula, Biagio Marini, and a host of others are often quite fanciful works whose aesthetic basis seems little more than a reveling in the sheer glory of the sound of the instrument. The point is an important one; for such delight in pure sonority created for the first time in Western music a large body of instrumental works that were idiomatically conceived and totally independent of vocal music.

The period from 1600 to *c.* 1640 was thus one of fast change and almost reckless experimentation. New idioms and styles were forged, and composers worked almost playfully with the new possibilities of vertical harmony. Indeed many musicians today find the music of the early Italian Baroque some of the most attractive of the entire period precisely for its sense of improvisation, its unpredictability, its refusal to adhere to rigid rules, its Janus-like fluctuation between older modal harmony and nascent tonal harmony based on modern major and minor keys.

The remainder of the Baroque period is often seen as an assimilation and development of the principles established in early seicento Italy. In many ways a certain standardization takes place during the second half of the century, as the rampant experimentation of the early years gives way to a formalism and to the establishment of archetypal formulas in every genre.

This new formalism is perhaps best seen in the OPERA. From the earliest works musical organization had clearly differentiated pure RECITATIVE from more structured arioso and more rigid ARIA. The use of these three styles fluctuated with the needs of the text, and as late as the Venetian works of the 1640s and '50s the interplay of the musical idioms is delightfully unfettered and irregular, following the nuances of the drama with complete freedom. In a work like Monteverdi's *L'Incoronazione di Poppea* (Venice, 1642), only a few scenes are based on large repetitive patterns that organize an entire scenic complex. Most scenes are musical mosaics of recitative and arioso, though they are unified from a dramatic standpoint. The arias and duets of the score are open structures and are not yet the autonomous units they will become in later opera. By the end of the century, however, the basic elements of 18th-century OPERA SERIA have been established. Recitative and aria are segregated into mutually exclusive camps, the operas eventually consisting of little more than a string of da capo arias presenting the emotional lives of the characters as a series of varying affections. A look at the *oeuvre* of Alessandro Scarlatti, from his early *Gli Equivoci nel sembiante* (Rome, 1679) through his masterpiece *La Griselda* (Rome, 1721), confirms the extraordinary variety and subtlety that can be wrought from an essentially static, stereotyped form.

The new formalism is easily seen in one other area: instrumental ensemble music. The effusive, experimental pieces of the early sonata composers are gradually tamed and systematized until they become the rigid church and chamber sonatas of Corelli, with their predictable formal structures and sequences of movements. While his solo violin sonatas recall the flamboyance of earlier string writing, the trio sonatas progress in tight, invariable formulas. And while his concerti grossi might be freer in form, the same genre taken up by Giuseppe Torelli and Vivaldi is cast from a recognizable mold and has an eternally familiar contour. This is not to say that a collection like Vivaldi's *L'Estro Armonico* lacks individuality; but the basic materials and techniques are repeated from work to work. *See* CONCERTO GROSSO.

Until now we have been speaking of Italian music alone, for the Baroque era has its roots in the final humanistic upheaval of the Italian Renaissance, and for nearly a century the essential thrust of the Baroque is Italian. It was Italy that set the pace, created the styles, and established the media of the age. The diffusion of this language throughout Europe and its encounter with indigenous styles and forms constitutes the other side of music history in these years.

Germany The first recipient of the new Italian style is Germany. As early as the first decade of the 17th century, Heinrich Schütz was in Venice, studying with Giovanni Gabrieli and assimilating the new sounds of the concertato style. After his second trip to Venice, where he encountered the music of Monteverdi and his circle, Schütz's contact with the most progressive musical voices of Italy was complete, and his works display the varied facets of the new style. The *Psalmen Davids* (1619) are a tribute to the dying polychoral art of Gabrieli; the *Symphoniae Sacrae,* to the large concertato sacred works of Monteverdi as well as the more intimate sacred concerti of his younger colleagues at San Marco; and the motets from the *Geistliche Chormusik* are Schütz's belated tribute to the *stile antico,* though they are infused with chromatic intensity and expressive subjectivity that betray their 17th-century origins.

German keyboard music assimilates Italian innovations in stages. The Italian keyboard *partitura* replaces old German tablature as early as Samuel Scheidt's *Tabulatura Nova* (1624), though the contents of the collection are mainly strict Germanic workings of Lutheran chorales. The Italian style enters the Germanic orbit more completely in the compositions of Johann Jakob Froberger. A pupil of Frescobaldi, Froberger assimilated the Italian imitative forms of the ricercar, canzona, and capriccio, as well as the toccata; he also entered French territory and was one of the first to standardize the movements of the Baroque dance SUITE.

The invasion of northern Europe by Italian opera is a more complex affair. During the late 17th century a number of Italian composers worked in German and Austrian courts, transplanting the Italian idiom and gradually creating an international style of opera. Pietro Andrea Ziani worked in Vienna, Carlo Pallavicino in Dresden, and Agostino Steffani in Hanover and Munich. Gradually there developed a school of native German composers who followed the international Italian style, culminating in the prodigious creativity of Johann Adolph Hasse in the mid-18th century. Although a fledgling German opera did develop, it could not withstand the popularity of the Italian idiom.

France The story of Italian opera in France is entirely different. Francesco Sacrati's *La Finta pazza,* Francesco Cavalli's *L'Egisto,* and Luigi Rossi's *Orfeo* all had been performed in Paris by 1650 but were met with indifference by the French public. And yet French national opera made little headway in the face of the cultural prominence of the French classic theater. Lully's success with his *tragédies lyriques* stemmed from his uniting the spectacle of the old *ballet de cour* with the dramatic power of his own invention, French recitative. Studying dramatic declamation as a prelude to composition, Lully tried to depict the natural flow of a speech with exact rhythmic notation (he changed meter often to accommodate the irregular accents of French speech) and to represent speech levels by precisely chosen pitches. In this sense his recitative was very much a throwback to

the principles of Florentine monody and contrasted dramatically with the rapid recitativo secco then current in Italian opera. Lully is easily the most neglected of the major composers of the 17th century—partially because his operas were conceived for the rarefied social milieu of the court at Versailles, partially because of the difficulties in training a large body of musicians in the extraordinary subtleties of French Baroque performance practices. Yet a glance at one of his major works, *L'Armide* (1686), shows the grandeur of his conception and subtlety of his means: the stately, carefully wrought overture; Armide's impassioned monologue over the sleeping Renaud, which was cited by Rameau as representing the epitome of the powers of French recitative; Renaud's affective slumber scene, accompanied expressively by muted strings; and the grandiose, hypnotic chaconne that ends the opera.

The establishment of a French operatic language fed the fire of international controversy over the supremacy of the French and Italian musical styles, a polemic that lasted into the late 18th century. François Raguenet's *Parallel des Italiens et des Français* (1702) and Le Cerf de la Viéville's *Comparaison de la musique italienne et de la musique française* (1704–06) are but the two most famous examples of countless tracts that argued the relative musical merits of the two countries. Though predominantly concerned with opera, the controversy spread into other areas as well, with François Couperin's *Apothéoses* of Corelli and Lully forming the ultimate statement on instrumental music, setting the impassioned style of the Italian trio sonata against the stately, courtly dances of France.

All Lully's operas contain elaborate dance sequences; indeed the dance was such a national institution that its forms and rhythms dominated almost all French music in the 17th and early 18th centuries. The development of dance music—both for actual dancing and as stylized movements in purely abstract works—occurred not only in the opera and ballet but in a subtler, more exacting manner in the works of the French *clavecinistes,* lutenists, and composers for the viola da gamba. Denys Gaultier's *La Rhétorique des dieux,* a collection of 12 sets of dances, is the culmination of the lute school. The *clavecinistes* form an impressive array of miniaturists, from Jacques Champion Chambonnières, Louis Couperin, and Jean Henri d'Anglebert to the vast *ordres* of François Couperin and the keyboard suites of Rameau. The composers for the viola da gamba are more obscure today because the viol family is only now being revived as a performing instrument; but the five books of *Pièces de viole* of Marin Marais, as well as the works of Caix d'Hervelois and the Sieur de Saint-Colombe are as varied realizations of stylized dance types as the works of the *clavecin* composers.

England   France was not the only country of Europe to balk at the conquering Italian style. Because of her very isolation, England had always led a musical life somewhat removed from that of the Continent, and the insular nature of English music history is seen to best advantage in the 17th century. While monody and the concertato style were dominating Italy, England was still enjoying the Indian summer of the madrigal, recently imported from Italy and quickly assimilated. The 17th-century lutenist songwriters and composers of music for viol consort were working in mediums that originated in the previous century on the Continent and now enjoyed a new lease on life. While Italian and French idioms did find a place in the music for the English court masque, neither style was adopted wholesale, and both were so transformed and combined with elements of native English song that the essentially English cast of the musical language was retained.

The figure of Purcell must be seen not only as a summation of 17th-century England but also as the recipient of amalgamated elements of the Italian and French musical languages. Portions of his works are quite clearly patterned after foreign models; the great chaconne "How happy the lover," from the music to Dryden's *King Arthur,* is based on the similar chaconne that ends Lully's *Armide.* The trio sonatas pay tribute to Corelli. *Dido and Aeneas* is eclectic: the overture is based on French models; recitative and arioso sections occasionally recall Caccini's affective monodies; and Dido's basso ostinato laments recall Cavalli and the Venetians. While a number

of the choruses use French dance rhythms, others recall the more serious side of the English madrigal tradition. *Dido's* unique place as a through-composed English opera is perhaps less significant than its role as an arena where national styles are fused as well as juxtaposed.

Handel and Bach   It is in the light of such a union of national styles—and of their summation of the musical accomplishments of the Baroque era—that Handel and Bach may be seen. Handel's position is perhaps the less complex. Born into a Germany dominated by Italian opera seria, he was necessarily drawn to Italian music, particularly to the operas of Agostino Steffani, the reigning operatic composer in the German orbit. After a formative period in Germany Handel journeyed to Italy, where he met with the most celebrated figures of the day: Alessandro and Domenico Scarlatti, Corelli, Bernardo Pasquini, and Benedetto Marcello, among others. Handel's musical production became effusive, and he dedicated himself to the chief Italian genres of the day: the cantata, church music, the oratorio, and of course opera seria. Handel's Italian period is one of gushing productivity, and many of his compositions from these years were reused later as parts of other works. A decisive turn in his life came when Handel traveled to England for a production of his *Rinaldo* (1711), the first of about 40 operas he composed for the London stage. All are in the strict opera seria mold, though Handel's Germanic training makes them contrapuntally richer than many Italian creations of the era. He also takes occasional liberties with the form of opera seria for the sake of the drama, and his best works, such as *Alcina* (1735) and *Giulio Cesare* (1724), are infused with a true sense of theater.

Handel's turn to ORATORIO in mid-life resulted from the economic conditions surrounding opera in London rather than artistic considerations. The oratorios combine a number of conflicting styles. The choral writing, developed by Handel through the composition of his *Chandos* Anthems, is of the utmost variety and subtlety; it pays homage not only to the English choral tradition but also to the Lutheran church cantata and to the Italian *oratorio latino* of the previous century. The solo pieces, however, are purely operatic and not far in style from the arias in Handel's stage works. A survey of his choral idioms would include the old *prima prattica* of learned 16th-century counterpoint, massive homophonic double choruses, light choruses harking back to the early Baroque air and madrigal, and broad vocal chaconnes in the Lullian manner. The idioms of the concerto grosso are often present.

The music of Bach can also be viewed as a compendium of the forms, genres, and styles that had been developed since 1600. Of course Germany had developed its own idioms alongside its incorporation of those from Italy and France—the Lullian overture and orchestral technique, the refined keyboard writing of the *clavecinistes,* the trio sonata of Corelli, and the concerto of Vivaldi. Specific German idioms are varied. In a general sense German writing of the high Baroque is more contrapuntally complex, more highly colored harmonically than most French writing and even much Italian music. The Germans also developed certain genres of their own, based on the needs of the Lutheran liturgy and on the rich heritage of the Lutheran CHORALE. The most distinctive genre of keyboard music was the CHORALE PRELUDE, developed by the host of German organists from the early 17th century onward. The chorale prelude must be viewed as a general type rather than a specific means of working a chorale tune, for the chorales were treated in a number of ways: as decorated melodies, as long-note canti firmi, as a series of imitative points, and as fugue subjects. The most important vocal genre was the church cantata, which was in the tradition of the sacred concerti of Schütz and the chorale motet. In addition to its German heritage, however, the church cantata relied on Italian operatic style, a secular intrusion that was a source of controversy throughout the high Baroque.

Bach assimilated and reconciled virtually all indigenous and foreign musical currents with one exception; while he absorbed the styles of Italian opera, he composed no operas per se. We have records of the composers whose works he copied out by hand during his formative years, and they are a cross section of the most influential figures of the Baroque; Frescobaldi, Tommaso Albinoni, Corelli, Vivaldi, Couperin, Froberger, Buxtehude, Johann Pachelbel, Handel, and Telemann are only the most prominent of a larger group.

It is in the area of the CANTATA that Bach departs the furthest from tradition; while he forms the end of the long Germanic tradition of the Lutheran cantata, only his early works are in the mold established in the 17th century. When he embarks upon his chorale cantatas in Leipzig, he is perfecting a form that is quite his own with no prototypes. There is no forerunner to Cantata 4, *Christ lag in Todesbanden,* set as a tight series of chorale variations, nor for the more loosely structured *Ein feste Burg* (Cantata 80) or *Jesu, der du meine Seele* (Cantata 78). Indeed the opening movement of Cantata 78, a chaconne in the rhythm of a sarabande that forms the cradle for a cantus firmus, is a new and unique compilation and fusion of Baroque constructive devices.

Bach's instrumental works are more clearly the culmination of more than a century of tradition. The chorale preludes are extensions of the forms used by German composers for several generations; yet a comparison of one of Bach's settings with an earlier setting of the same chorale invariably points out his keener technique and broader sense of invention. The same might be said for the organ toccate, fantasies, and fugues. The concerti of his Köthen period are in the Vivaldi mold, illuminated by Bach's luxuriant counterpoint; the *Brandenburg* Concerti form the final statement on the problem of the concerto grosso. The keyboard works have clear roots: the *Italian* Concerto, the Overture *in the French Style,* the partitas. Most impressive are the learned works, which recapitulate virtually all that the era had to say about contrapuntal devices: the two books of the *Well-Tempered Clavier,* the Canonic Variations on *Vom Himmel hoch,* the *Musical Offering,* the newly discovered canons connected with the *Goldberg* Variations, and the *Art of the Fugue.*

While it has been suggested recently that stylistic features of a number of Bach's late works show his assimilation of the more progressive trends of the mid-18th century, we must essentially consider him a conservative who inherited the genres, styles, and forms of the Baroque era and expanded every one in new ways. If one were to summarize his works in a word, the proper one might well be balance—not balance in the sense of late 18th-century Classicism, but a balance between form and content, between harmony and counterpoint, between fixed forms and infinite vision. While the Baroque era may not circumscribe a completely unified body of music, we cannot deny that Bach does synthesize its diverse technical devices and national idioms. The existence of Bach's *oeuvre* is perhaps the best argument one could put forth for the validity of a single term to cover the years 1600 to 1750 and the existence of a true Baroque era, which, though heterogeneous in many respects, does attain homogeneity in the body of works that form its culmination.

James H. Moore

BIBLIOGRAPHY: Arnold Dolmetsch, *The Interpretation of the Music of the XVII and XVIII Centuries* (1915; reprint, 1969); Manfred F. Bukofzer, *Music in the Baroque Era* (1947); Oliver Strunk, *Source Readings in Music History* (1950; reprint, 1965); Johann Joachim Quantz, *On Playing the Flute* (1966); Friedrich Blume, *Renaissance and Baroque Music* (1967); Thurston Dart, *The Interpretation of Music,* 4th ed. (1967); William S. Newman, *The Sonata in the Baroque Era,* 3rd ed. (1972); Robert Donington, *A Performer's Guide to Baroque Music* (1973), *The Interpretation of Early Music,* rev. ed. (1974), and *String Playing in Baroque Music* (1977).

barrel organ The term is popularly understood to mean an instrument of street music in which a simple piano action is worked by a pinned barrel turned by a handle. This is more correctly a barrel piano.

In a true barrel organ the barrel causes one or more ranks of organ pipes to play the tunes, the handle simultaneously actuating the bellows. The pinned barrel was known in the 16th century, generally in conjunction with a clock mechanism. The handle-operated organ reached its greatest popularity during the late 18th and early 19th centuries, when such

barrel organ
courtesy, Smithsonian Institution

instruments were in regular demand and ranged from miniature bird organs used to encourage songbirds to large versions that played the psalms in village churches. Some of the latter remained in use until well into the 20th century. Modern musicians find barrel organs of particular interest because they preserve evidence of old styles of musical execution and ornamentation.

Intermediate in size and reaching a peak of popularity about 1830 were the cabinet-sized domestic barrel organs, commonly supplied with one barrel for religious music and two for entertainment. Each wooden barrel is pinned with brass staples of varying length according to the lengths of the notes to be sounded. As the handle is turned the staples raise levers that admit wind to the pipes as required. The levers are opposite their respective pipes and therefore well separated, leaving space for 10 or more tunes to be set on a single barrel. For instance, the staples that serve the note G in the second tune are placed just to the left of those for G in the first tune, and so on, the tune being selected by shifting the barrel in its wooden carrier sideways and holding it in correct alignment by a catch on the outside. The usual disposition was one or two ranks of stopped wooden pipes and a rank of open metal at the octave. Domestic models often included a drum and cymbal actuated by additional pins. *See also* MECHANICAL INSTRUMENTS.

BIBLIOGRAPHY: Arthur Ord-Hume, *The Barrel Organ* (1977).

Barrère, Georges (October 31, 1876–June 14, 1944)   A student of Joseph-Henri Altès and Paul Taffanel at the Paris Conservatoire, the French-born flutist Georges Barrère first obtained professional orchestral experience at the Paris Opéra. In 1905 he came to the United States where he played with the New York Symphony (1905–28) and taught at the Institute of Musical Art (later the Juilliard School). He formed the Barrère Little Symphony, which played concerts of little-known chamber music for 30 years, and composed and edited solos and collections of studies for the flute.

Bartered Bride, The: *see* SMETANA.

Bartók, Béla (March 25, 1881–September 26, 1945)   One of the dominant and most original figures in the first half of the 20th century, the Hungarian composer Béla Bartók was distinguished as a pianist, teacher, and ethnomusicologist.

Béla Bartók
courtesy, Mrs. Fritz Reiner

Born in Nagyszentmiklós, Hungary (now in Romania), he showed early musical talent and was taught by his mother. He entered the Royal Hungarian Academy in Budapest in 1899, progressing rapidly as a pianist but less so as a composer. After discovering the music of Richard Strauss, he resumed composing and in 1903 wrote a symphonic poem, *Kossuth,* that glorified the leader of the Hungarian revolution of 1848–49.

Shortly after Bartók completed his studies in 1903, he and his lifelong friend Kodály discovered genuine Hungarian peasant music (then almost unknown to musicians). A vast reservoir was subsequently unearthed by the research of the two composers. Their original intention was the revitalization of Hungarian music, and they not only transcribed folk tunes for the piano and other media but incorporated the melodic, rhythmic, and textural elements of peasant music into their original works, ultimately absorbing the folk spirit into their own styles.

Bartók was appointed to the faculty of the academy in 1907, remaining in the post until 1934, when he was released to work at the Academy of Sciences in the preparation for publication of great quantities of Hungarian folk music that he and others had collected. Concurrently Bartók was composing works for piano, for orchestra, and for string quartet; his six quartets ultimately came to constitute one of his major achievements. The First Quartet (1908–09) reveals little folk influence, but in the others it is ever present. The quartets parallel and illuminate Bartók's stylistic development; in the second (1915–17) Arab elements reflect his collecting trip to North Africa; in the third (1927) and fourth (1928) there is a more intensive use of dissonance; and in the fifth (1934) and sixth (1939) there is a reaffirmation of traditional tonality.

In 1911 Bartók wrote his only opera, *Duke Bluebeard's Castle* (Budapest, 1918), an allegorical treatment of the legendary wife murderer, whose score includes many characteristics of old Hungarian folk song—especially in the speechlike rhythms. The technique is reminiscent of Debussy. A ballet, *The Wooden Prince* (1914–16; Budapest, 1917), and a pantomime, *The Miraculous Mandarin* (1918–19;

Cologne, 1926), were his last works for the stage.

After World War I his international reputation grew rapidly, and his musical language was completely and expressively formulated. He had assimilated many disparate influences—Richard Strauss, Debussy, Liszt, Stravinsky, and Schoenberg—arriving at a vital and varied style, rhythmically animated, in which diatonic and chromatic elements are homogeneously juxtaposed. During this period he produced his first two piano concertos (1926 and 1930–31); Cantata *Profana* (1930), his only major choral work; Second Violin Concerto (1937–38); and a number of chamber scores, including Music for strings, percussion, and celesta (1936) and Sonata for two pianos and percussion (1937; transcribed as Concerto for two pianos and orchestra, 1940). He also toured many parts of the world as a concert pianist.

By the late 1930s Hungary appeared to be in the path of expanding Nazi Germany, and Bartók chose to emigrate to the United States. In 1941–42 he worked at Columbia University on transcriptions and editions of Serbo-Croatian songs, part of a recorded collection of Yugoslav folk material. With his wife, the pianist Ditta Pásztory, he concertized, but his declining health with advancing leukemia increasingly curtailed his teaching, lecturing, and performing. Nevertheless he composed Concerto for orchestra (1943), Sonata for solo violin (1944), and all but the final bars of the Third Piano Concerto (1945). At his death in New York City his final Viola Concerto was only an array of incomplete sketches.

Immediately after Bartók's death his music won wide acclaim, and he is generally acknowledged with Schoenberg and Stravinsky as one of the three great masters of his time. With Kodály he created the first genuinely Hungarian music of universal and enduring interest.

BIBLIOGRAPHY: Gyorgy Kepes, ed., *Module, Proportion, Symmetry, Rhythm* (1966); Halsey Stevens, *The Life and Music of Béla Bartók*, rev. ed. (1967); Agatha Fassett, *Bela Bartók—the American Years* (1970; original title, *The Naked Face of Genius*); Ernö Lendvai, *Béla Bartók: An Analysis of His Mu-*sic (1971); Jozsef Ujfalussy, *Béla Bartók* (1972); Lajos Lesznai, *Bartók* (1973); György Kroó, *A Guide to Bartók* (1974); John McCabe, *Bartók Orchestral Music* (1974); Serge Moreux, *Béla Bartók* (1974); Béla Bartók, *Béla Bartók: Essays* (1976).

RECORDINGS: *(Duke) Bluebeard's Castle;* Concerto for orchestra; *Mikrokosmos; The Miraculous Mandarin;* Music for strings, percussion, and celesta; Piano Concertos (3); Piano Sonata; Sonata for solo violin; Quartets (6); Violin Concertos (2); Violin Sonatas (2); numerous Hungarian and other folk songs.

Bartoletti, Bruno (b. June 10, 1926)   One of the leading Italian opera conductors of his generation, Bruno Bartoletti studied at the Florence Conservatory and made his debut as a conductor in 1953. He was in charge of Italian opera in Copenhagen (1957–60) and has been the principal conductor of the Chicago Lyric Opera since 1964 and a regular conductor at the Rome Opera since 1965. He has promoted 20th-century repertoire in Italy.

baryton   An 18th-century bowed stringed instrument related to the viol family and about

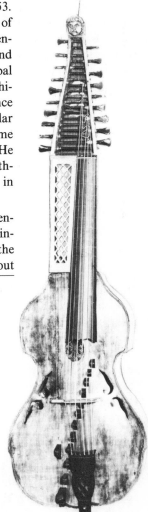

German baryton
*Leslie Lindsey Mason
Collection of
Musical Instruments
(formerly the
Galpin Collection)
Museum of Fine Arts,
Boston*

the size of a cello; it had six melody strings and a fretted fingerboard. Up to 40 sympathetically vibrating strings ran behind the wide neck, some of which were plucked with the left-hand thumb. Haydn wrote 175 baryton compositions for his patron, Prince Miklós Esterházy, a skilled baryton player.

Baryton also refers to an oboe pitched an octave below the ordinary oboe *(hautbois baryton)*.

bass The lowest male voice with a normal range from the second E below middle C to the F♯ above; the lowest pitched member of a family of musical instruments such as the bass recorder, bass viol, double bass, or tuba; and the lowest part of a composition in several parts, or voices.

In singing a basso profundo is a low, rich bass voice (almost nonexistent); basso cantante ("singing bass") is a lighter, more lyric voice. Basso continuo is a written bass line over which a chordal accompaniment is improvised. *See* FIGURED BASS.

Bassariden, Die: *see* HENZE.

bass drum The largest and deepest sounding military and orchestral drum. The military bass has two heads, tensioned by rope lacings or metal rods, and is struck on both heads; the orchestral bass often has only one head, rod tensioned, but even when two-headed is normally struck on one head only. Both are usually played with a pair of large felt-headed sticks, although in jazz bands the drum is commonly struck by one stick operated by a pedal. In maximum size bass drums may reach 40 inches (100 centimeters) in diameter and 20 inches (50 centimeters) in height. A larger form of one-headed bass drum is the gong drum, often used in British orchestras.

The bass drum was introduced into Europe in the 18th century as part of the vogue for Turkish music, an imitation of the music of the Turkish Janissary bands, and typically appeared in combination with cymbals and triangle. It was at first known as the Turkish drum or, with deep-shelled instruments, the long drum, which resembled the *davul* of modern Turkey and the Balkans. Originally it was beaten with a stick in the right hand and a switch in the left; similarly in modern regi-

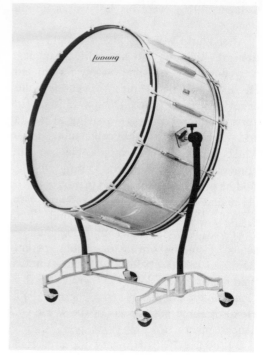

bass drum   *courtesy, Ludwig Industries*

mental bands the right hand beats time with a larger stick than that used for the accompanying rhythms played by the left. The bass drum entered the symphony orchestra in the 18th century, at first for special effects as in Haydn's *Military* Symphony (1794).

basse danse A courtly dance for couples that originated in 14th-century Italy and was fashionable in many varieties for two centuries. Its French name ("low dance") is attributed both to its possible origin as a peasant, or "low," dance and to its style of small gliding steps in which the feet remain close to the ground. Danced by hand-holding couples in a column, it was performed with various combinations of small bows and a series of forward walking steps completed by drawing the back foot up to the leading foot. The music was in the modern equivalent of $\frac{12}{8}$ time. The *basse danse* was typically followed by its afterdance, the SALTARELLO.

basset horn A clarinet pitched a fourth lower than the ordinary B-flat clarinet. It was probably invented *c.* 1770 by A. and M. Mayrhofer. The name is derived from its basset ("small bass") pitch and its original curved-horn shape

Bohemian basset horn,
boxwood and brass, 18th century
*courtesy, Metropolitan Museum of Art
gift of the University Museum,
University of Pennsylvania, 1953*

(later supplanted by an angular form). Its bore is narrower than that of the E-flat alto clarinet, and it has a downward extension of compass to the low F of the bass voice (written as C). It is usually built to order in straight form with upturned bell.

Although employed notably by Mozart, it had almost vanished by 1850 but was revived by Richard Strauss (*Elektra,* first performed 1909) and has on occasion been used since.

Bassett, Leslie (Raymond) (b. January 22, 1923)   A student of Ross Lee Finney, Honegger, and Boulanger, the U.S. composer Leslie Bassett began investigating advanced techniques in 1964 while studying with Mario Davidovsky. He has written liturgical music for voices and tape (*Collect,* 1969), as well as music for string quartet, solo voice, and orchestra. His *Notes in the Silence* (1966) is set to poems by Dag Hammarskjöld. Since 1952 he has taught at the University of Michigan. His *Variations for orchestra* won the Pulitzer Prize in 1966.

RECORDINGS: Music for cello and piano; Music for saxophone and piano; Sextet for piano and strings; *Sounds Remembered* for violin and piano; Suite for unaccompanied trombone; Variations for orchestra.

basso continuo: *see* FIGURED BASS.

bassoon (German, *Fagott;* Italian, *fagotto*) The normal tenor and bass instrument of the orchestral woodwinds. Its narrow conical bore leads from the curved metal crook, on to which the double reed is placed, downward through the wing joint (with the left-hand fingerholes) to the butt joint (with the right-hand holes). The bore then doubles back, ascending through the butt to the long joint and bell, where the holes are controlled by keywork for the left thumb. The bassoon is held on a sling that slants across the body, and thus—with the doubled-back bore—the tubing (which is eight feet, two and one-half meters long, too long to be controlled if in a straight line) is comfortably manageable. Its classical compass is three octaves from the B-flat below the bass staff, the most-used melodic range coinciding with that of the tenor voice. Higher notes up to treble E have come into use since the mid-19th century, adding to the difficulty of what is in any case an exceptionally difficult instrument to play. The traditional placing of the fingerholes is scientifically irrational yet essential to the production of a tone that has been one of the primary colors of the composer's orchestral palette from Handel's time. The reed, made by bending double a shaped strip of matured cane, is placed between the lips retracted over the teeth.

The bassoon is a 17th-century development of the earlier *fagotto* or *Dulzian,* the English form of which was known as the curtal. It was first mentioned *c.* 1540 in Italy with the descending and ascending bores contained in a single place of wood. Many examples survive in museums at Brussels, Berlin, Vienna, etc. The present construction in four separate joints is thought to have been developed in France after 1650, closely following the reconstruction of the shawm that produced the OBOE, to which the bassoon serves as bass. During the 18th century the individuality of the bassoon became recognized not only in the orchestra (in which two are normally employed) but also as a solo instrument for concertos; yet well into Mozart's time no mechanism was required beyond four keys, most of the semitones outside the natural scale of C having been well obtained by cross-fingerings. The leisurely addition of keys from *c.* 1780 led to J. N. Savary's Paris models of *c.* 1840, which with further improvements in bore and mechanism have become the 20-keyed French bassoon made by the famous firm of Buffet-Crampon. Of rosewood, it is used in France, Italy, and Spain, and some British players still play it or other similar models.

While it has preserved and developed the sympathetic vocal sonority of the classical instrument, the French bassoon remains a difficult instrument to control because of inherent unevenness in the quality and steadiness of many notes. A good player can overcome these defects, but alterations to minimize them were initiated in Germany in 1825 by Karl Almenräder. A reformed model was developed by the firm of J. A. Heckel and perfected in the German bassoon now standard everywhere except in the Latin countries named above. It is of European maple and has its own positions and sizes of the holes to give a more even and positive response throughout the compass. It is quicker to learn, easier to choose reeds for, and in many respects more telling in a large orchestra. Research on old bassoons suggests that its tone quality, different from the French and by some considered to

bassoon
courtesy,
C. G. Conn, Ltd.

have sacrificed eloquence for expediency, may not represent as gross a deviation from classical tone as was hitherto believed.

The first useful contrabassoon, or double bassoon, sounding an octave lower than the bassoon and much employed in large scores, was developed in Vienna and used occasionally by the Classical composers. The modern contrabassoon follows Heckel's design of *c.* 1870, with the tubing doubled back four times and often with a metal bell that points downward.

BIBLIOGRAPHY: Adam Carse, *Musical Wind Instruments* (1939; reprint, 1965); Anthony Baines, *Woodwind Instruments and Their History,* rev. ed. (1963); Lyndesay G. Langwill, *The Bassoon and Contrabassoon* (1965).

Bastien und Bastienne: *see* MOZART (early life); OPÉRA COMIQUE.

Bataille, Gabriel (1574/75–December 17, 1630) The French lutenist and composer Gabriel Bataille was master of the queen's music at the court of Louis XIII. On his marriage in 1600 he stated his occupation as clerk to a nobleman, but he later devoted himself to music and in 1617 acquired the court position he held until his death. He shared with Pierre Guédron, Jacques Mauduit, and Antoine Boësset the responsibility for the composition of the *ballets de cour.* His music appeared in contemporary collections, and the first of six volumes of *Airs de différents autheurs mis en tablature de luth par Gabriel Bataille,* in which Bataille provided lute accompaniments for songs by other composers, was published by Ballard in 1608.

Bauer, Harold (April 28, 1873–March 12, 1951) An English pianist who eventually settled in the United States, Harold Bauer began a career as a concert violinist, changing to piano when he was 19. Although he had a few lessons with Paderewski, he was largely self-taught. Bauer had an intense interest in chamber music, performing trios with Fritz Kreisler and Casals and appearing with the violinist Jacques Thibaud. He was a founder of the Beethoven Association (1919–40), an important chamber music society in New York City. His playing combined elements both of 19th-century Romanticism and 20th-century restraint.

Bax, Arnold (Edward Trevor) (November 8, 1883–October 3, 1953) The English composer Arnold Bax, whose work represents romantic musical tendencies between World Wars I and II, contributed considerably to the revival of English music. In 1900 he entered the Royal Academy, where he studied piano with Tobias Matthay and composition with Frederick Corder. Influenced by the Celtic revival and Irish poetry, he wrote the symphonic poem *In the Faery Hills* (1909). Bax spent the year 1910 in Russia, where he composed piano pieces in a pseudo-Russian style. Under the pseudonym Dermot O'Byrne he published short stories and poems in Ireland, where he spent much time. In 1916 and 1917 he wrote three symphonic poems, *The Garden of Fand, Tintagel,* and *November Woods,* which established his reputation. In 1920 Sergey Diaghilev produced his ballet, *The Truth About the Russian Dancers,* on a scenario by James Barrie. Between 1921 and 1939 he wrote seven symphonies dedicated to the musicians he admired, among them John Ireland and Sibelius. He also wrote numerous piano and chamber works, including Sonata for viola and harp (1928) and Nonet (1930). Living for long periods on the coasts of Ireland and Scotland, he wrote music that was romantically evocative and richly orchestrated though sometimes turgid in texture. He was knighted in 1937 and in 1942 was appointed master of the king's music.

RECORDINGS: Clarinet Sonata; *Elegiac Trio;* Symphony No. 7; *Tintagel.*

Bay Psalm Book: *see* RENAISSANCE (Reformation); PSALMODY.

Beach, Mrs. H. H. A., before her marriage, Amy Marcy Cheney (September 5, 1867–December 27, 1944) The U.S. composer and pianist Mrs. H. H. A. Beach is known for her *Gaelic* Symphony (1896), the first symphony to be composed by a U.S. woman. Her early musical training was mostly in Boston, where she made her debut as a pianist when she was 16. Largely self-taught as a composer, she was the only woman member of the "Boston group" of U.S. composers who were

heavily influenced by the German Romantic style. Her first important work was a Mass in E-flat Major (performed by Boston's Handel and Haydn Society in February 1892), and she appeared as soloist with the Boston Symphony in her Piano Concerto (1900). Other works include cantatas, church music, a one-act opera, chamber music, piano pieces, and songs.

RECORDINGS: Piano Concerto in c-sharp minor; Piano Quintet in f-sharp minor; Violin Sonata in a minor; piano pieces.

Beardslee, Bethany (b. December 25, 1927) Educated at Michigan State University and the Juilliard School, the U.S. soprano Bethany Beardslee is known for her work with the New York Pro Musica and especially for her recordings and concerts of 20th-century avant-garde music. She won the Laurel Leaf award from the American Composers Alliance (1962) and an honorary doctorate from Princeton University (1977).

beat The unit division of musical time, or the pulse underlying a musical work. Music may be organized by grouping a regular succession of beats into measures often of two, three, or four beats with periodic accentuation, usually of the first beat of the grouping. *See also* RHYTHM.

Beaumarchais, Pierre Augustin Caron de: *see* ROSSINI.

Becker, John J(oseph) (January 22, 1886–January 21, 1961) One of the "American five" (with Henry Cowell, Wallingford Riegger, Ives, and Carl Ruggles), the U.S. composer John J. Becker studied composition and conducting with Alexander von Fielitz (1907–08), Carl Busch (1908), and Wilhelm Middelschulte (1923). His doctoral dissertation (Wisconsin Conservatory, 1923) concerned German literature and music and was the beginning of his preoccupation with mixed media, fusing music, poetry, mime, dance, and visual art. He also investigated the polyphonic style of 16th-century Dutch choral literature, which is reflected in his large output of church music. After 1930 his stage works contain a message of social protest. His later works utilize percussive effects, dissonance, overtones, and the combination of widely disparate timbres. In addition to symphonies and songs are his "soundpieces" (seven of them written between 1935 and 1959) for various chamber music groups in unconventional forms; *Abongo* (1933) for percussion orchestra, two solo dancers, and dance ensemble; and *A Marriage with Space* (1933–35) for solo and mass recitation, solo dancer, dance ensemble, and orchestra. His films and incidental music include *Julius Caesar* (1949) and *Madeleine et Judas* (1958). He taught at North Texas College (1906–14), University of Notre Dame (1918–28), College of St. Thomas in St. Paul, Minnesota (1928–33), and Barat College in Illinois (1943–57). From 1935 to 1941 he was director of the Federal Music Project in Minnesota, and from 1936 to 1940 he was associate editor of *New Music Quarterly*. He has written many articles on American music and on his influential compatriots Cowell, Riegger, and Ives.

RECORDING: Symphony No. 3.

Beecham, Thomas (April 29, 1879–March 8, 1961)   The leading English conductor of his time and the main figure in the revival of opera in England, Thomas Beecham was also a master of language who endeared himself to the public by his witty speeches and tirades against the insufficiencies of British musical standards—often made from the rostrum.

Educated at Oxford, Beecham conducted

Sir Thomas Beecham   *EB Inc.*

his first concert in London in 1905 and the following year began a series of concerts with his own New Symphony. He was appointed artistic director at Covent Garden in 1933 and founded the Royal Philharmonic in 1947. Beecham championed the music of Frederick Delius, but he was also known for his interpretations of Mozart and Haydn, with special attention to Sibelius. He wrote his autobiography, *A Mingled Chime* (1943), and the biography *Frederick Delius* (1959).

BIOGRAPHY: Neville Cardus, *Sir Thomas Beecham, a Memoir* (1961); Charles Reid, *Thomas Beecham: An Independent Biography* (1961); Harold Atkins and Archie Newman, eds., *Anecdotes, Sayings, and Impressions by Sir Thomas Beecham* (1979).

Beeson, Jack (Hamilton) (b. July 15, 1921)   The U.S. composer and theorist Jack Beeson studied with Bernard Rogers and Howard Hanson at the Eastman School in Rochester, New York (1939–44); and for the next two years was one of the few U.S. students of Bartók. An early desire to become an opera composer led him at the age of 12 to begin a scenario for a verse libretto based on Shelley's *The Cenci*. As a student of musicology at Columbia University (1945–46), he conducted and accompanied the opera workshop there, continuing until 1948, when he was appointed professor and later chairman of the music department. Although he has written works for band and orchestra, he is best known for his operas, which include *Jonah* (1950), *Hello Out There* (1953), and *My Heart's in the Highlands* (1969), all with libretti by the composer, and his most performed work, *Lizzie Borden* (1965).

RECORDINGS: Operas *Captain Jinks of the Horse Marines, Hello Out There, Lizzie Borden,* and *The Sweet Bye and Bye;* Symphony No. 1 in A Major; Three Rounds.

Beethoven, Ludwig van (baptized December 17, 1770–March 26, 1827)   One of the great musical geniuses of all times, the German composer Ludwig van Beethoven represents the culmination of the Viennese Classical school. But it was as a virtuoso pianist that he first made his reputation, probably the first major pianist who played in the grand orchestral manner with fire and expression. Even so, he was a musician first and a pianist second, and his writing for piano clearly reflects this.

early years Born in Bonn, northwest Germany, Beethoven was the eldest surviving child of Johann and Maria Magdalena van Beethoven. The family was Flemish in origin and can be traced back to Mechelen (Malines). It was Beethoven's grandfather who first settled in Bonn, when he became a singer in the choir of the Elector of Cologne and eventually rose to become Kapellmeister—an unusual feat for one who was not a composer. His son Johann was also a singer in the electoral choir; thus, like most 18th-century musicians, Beethoven was born into the profession. At first his family was quite prosperous, but with the death of his grandfather in 1773 and with the decline of his father into alcoholism the family became steadily poorer. Of the five children born after Beethoven, only two survived. By the age of 13 Beethoven had to leave school; at 16 he was the breadwinner of the family.

Having observed in him signs of a talent for the piano, Johann had tried to make of his son a child prodigy like Mozart but with-

Ludwig van Beethoven,
oil painting by Ferdinand Schimon, 1819
permission, Beethoven-Haus, Bonn, West Germany

out success. It was not until his adolescence that Beethoven began to attract mild attention.

When Joseph II became the sole ruler of the Holy Roman Empire in 1780, he appointed his brother Maximilian Francis as adjutant and successor designate to the Archbishop-Elector of Cologne. Under Maximilian's rule Bonn became transformed from a minor provincial town into a thriving and cultured capital city. A liberal Roman Catholic, he endowed Bonn with a university, limited the power of his own clergy, and opened the city to the full tide of the German literary renaissance associated with Lessing, Klopstock, and the young Goethe and Schiller. A sign of the times was the nomination as court organist of Christian Gottlob Neefe, a Protestant from Saxony, who became Beethoven's teacher. Although somewhat limited as a musician, Neefe was nonetheless a man of high ideals and wide culture, a *littérateur* as well as a composer of songs and light theatrical pieces. It was through Neefe that in 1783 Beethoven had his first composition, Variations on a March by Dressler, published at Mannheim. By June 1782 Beethoven had become Neefe's assistant as court organist, an appointment that was officially confirmed two years later.

In 1783 Beethoven was appointed continuo player at the Bonn opera. By 1787 he had made such progress that Maximilian Francis, archbishop-elector since 1784, was persuaded to send him to Vienna to study with Mozart; but the visit was cut short when after only two months Beethoven received the news of his mother's death. There is a tradition that Mozart was highly impressed with Beethoven's powers of improvisation and told some friends that "this young man will make a great name for himself in the world." For the next five years Beethoven remained at Bonn; to his other court duties was now added that of playing viola in the theater orchestra. Although the archbishop for the time being showed him no further mark of special favor, he was beginning to make valuable acquaintances. Sometime previously he had come to know the widow of the chancellor, Joseph von Breuning, and she engaged him as music teacher to two of her four children. From then on the Breunings' house became for him a second and far more congenial home. Through Mme von Breuning Beethoven acquired a number of wealthy pupils. His most useful social contact came in 1787 with the arrival in Bonn of Count Ferdinand Waldstein, a member of the highest Viennese aristocracy and an enthusiastic music lover. Waldstein became a member of the Breuning circle, where he heard Beethoven play and at once became his devoted admirer. At a fancy dress ball in 1700 the ballet music was said in the *Almanach de Gotha* to have been written by Count Waldstein, but it was generally known that it had been ghosted by Beethoven. In the same year Emperor Joseph II died—a blow to the liberal cause throughout Europe. Through Waldstein again Beethoven was invited to compose a funeral ode for soloists, chorus, and orchestra, but as was often to happen later he failed to meet his deadline. He then added to it a complementary cantata celebrating the accession of Joseph's brother Leopold II; but there is no record that either was ever performed until the end of the 19th century, when the critic Eduard Hanslick rediscovered the manuscripts in Vienna and showed them to Brahms, who affirmed their authenticity. But in 1790 another great composer had already seen and admired them: that year Haydn passed through Bonn on his way to London; he was shown Beethoven's score and was sufficiently impressed by it to offer to take Beethoven as a pupil when he returned. Any further hopes of study with Mozart were not to be realized, for by the time Haydn returned Mozart was dead. Beethoven therefore accepted Haydn's offer and in the autumn of 1792, while the armies of the French Revolution stormed into the Rhineland provinces, Beethoven left Bonn, never to return. The album that he took with him (preserved in the Beethoven-Haus in Bonn) indicates the wide circle of his acquaintances and friends in Bonn, and the most prophetic of the entries runs: "The spirit of Mozart is mourning and weeping over the death of her beloved. With the inexhaustible Haydn she found repose but no occupation. With the help of unremitting labor you shall receive Mozart's spirit from Haydn's hands. Count Waldstein."

The compositions belonging to the years at Bonn—excluding those probably begun at Bonn but revised and completed in Vienna—are of more interest to the Beethoven student than to the ordinary music lover. They show influences in which his art was rooted as well as the natural difficulties that he had to overcome and that his early training was inadequate to remedy. Three piano sonatas written in 1783 remind us that musically Bonn was an outpost of Mannheim, the cradle of the modern orchestra in Germany and the nursery of a style that was to make a vital contribution to the Classical symphony. But at the time of Beethoven's childhood, the Mannheim school was already in decline. The once famous orchestra was in effect dissolved after the war of 1778 between Austria and Prussia. The Mannheim preoccupation with extremes of *piano* and *forte* (often in contradiction to the musical phrasing) is found in Beethoven's early sonatas and in much else written by him at that time—which is not surprising as the symphonies of later Mannheim composers formed the staple fare of the Bonn court orchestra. This was, moreover, to remain a fundamental element in Beethoven's style. The sudden *pianos,* the unexpected outbursts, the wide leaping arpeggio figures known as "Mannheim rockets"—all these are central to his musical personality, and they helped him toward the liberation of instrumental music from its dependence on vocal style.

Like other composers of his generation Beethoven was subject to the influence of popular music and of folk music, influences particularly strong in the Waldstein ballet music of 1790 and in several of his early songs and unison choruses. Heavy Rhineland dance rhythms can be found in many of his mature compositions, but he could assimilate other local idioms as well—Italian, French, Slavic, and even Celtic. Although never a nationalist or folk composer in the 20th-century sense, he often allowed the unusual contours of folk melody to lead him away from traditional harmonic procedure.

French music impinged on him from two main directions: from Mannheim, whose artistic links with Paris had always been strong; and from the Bonn Nationaltheater, which relied mainly for its repertoire on comic operas translated from the French. In fashionable Bonn society sympathy with the French Revolution was strong, and the flavor of the French revolutionary march is present in many of Beethoven's symphonic allegros. The jigging six-eight rhythms to be found in several of his scherzos are also of French provenance.

Like all pianists of the late 18th century, Beethoven was brought up on the sonatas of Carl Philipp Emanuel Bach, the chief exponent of expressive music at a time when music was rated, according to the current aesthetic, as "the art of pleasing sounds." These sonatas, with their quirks of rhythms and harmony and their occasional wordless recitative, were equally familiar to Haydn and Mozart; but in Beethoven they evoked a much readier response, not only for reasons of temperament but also because of the intellectual climate in which he himself was reared. The favorite literary fare of the Breunings and their friends was associated with the *Sturm und Drang.* A reaction against the rationalism of the early 18th century, it exalted feeling and instinct over reason. Its gospel was enshrined in Goethe's early novel, *Die Leiden des jungen Werthers (The Sorrows of Young Werther),* whose language finds an echo in certain of Beethoven's letters and especially in the "Heiligenstadt Testament." In such a movement music took on a new importance as an art of feeling. The sharp conflicts of mood that characterize the sonatas of C. P. E. Bach appear much more powerfully again in Beethoven, to whom feeling was as important in practice as it was in theory to his master Neefe, who proclaimed it the only condition of artistic value. All this, however, does not make Beethoven a Romantic, although Romantics attempted to claim him as one of themselves. His literary world—he read widely and voraciously despite a formal education that in arithmetic had not carried him as far as the multiplication table—was rooted in the German classics, above all Goethe and Schiller. Like them he was to achieve in music a balance of form and emotion that can only be called Classical.

The Bonn compositions of most enduring interest date, as might be expected, from the last years: a Rondino and an Octet for wind instruments, composed in 1792 probably for the elector's wind band; a Trio in G for flute, bassoon, and piano (1790); and the two cantatas. The songs—written doubtless under Neefe's inspiration—show little specific feeling for the solo voice. This is strange in one whose father and grandfather had been singers, but it remained a limitation that pursued Beethoven throughout his career. Of particular interest are the 24 Variations on a Theme of Vincenzo Righini (for keyboard), which, like the String Trio in E-flat (1792), Beethoven revised and published at a much later date. These variations represented a compendium of Beethoven's piano technique, and for a long time they were to serve as his specialty in the salons of Vienna.

Vienna Before Beethoven left Bonn he had acquired a considerable reputation in northwest Germany as a piano virtuoso with a particular talent for extemporization. Mozart had been one of the finest improvisers of his age, but by all accounts Beethoven surpassed him. In the age of sensibility he could move an audience to tears more easily than any other pianist of the time. He was taken up by the Viennese aristocracy almost from the moment he set foot in Vienna. Count Waldstein had, of course, prepared the way with his talk of a successor to Mozart, and it is significant that Beethoven's earliest patrons in Vienna were Baron van Swieten and Prince Karl Lichnowsky, who alone among the aristocracy had remained Mozart's supporters until his death. In the Vienna of the 1790s music had become more and more the favorite pastime of a cultured aristocracy for whom politics were now discreditable and dangerous and who had never shown a like appreciation of any of the other fine arts. Many played instruments well enough to be able to take their places beside professionals in the popular Augarten Morning Concerts directed by the violinist Ignaz Schuppanzigh.

As a composer, however, Beethoven still had many technical problems to overcome, and it soon became clear that Haydn was not the best person to help him. Outwardly their relations remained cordial, but Beethoven soon began taking extra lessons in secret, first from Johann Schenk and then from the organist of St. Stephen's Cathedral, Johann Albrechtsberger, a learned contrapuntist of the old school who equipped him with the comprehensive technique he needed. He also studied vocal composition with Antonio Salieri, the imperial Kapellmeister. When Haydn left for his second visit to London in 1794, there was no longer any question of Beethoven's returning to Bonn, which was now in French hands. The elector himself had left, and consequently Beethoven's subsidy came to an end. But he had no need to worry, for apart from what he earned by teaching and playing he received free board and lodging from Prince Lichnowsky. The year 1795 marked Beethoven's first public appearance in Vienna as a pianist. He played "a concerto" of his own (probably No. 2) and one by Mozart in Vienna's only regular public concert series, the four annual "academies" of the Society of Composers in aid of the widows and orphans of musicians. He also took part in a benefit concert for Haydn. More important still, his Three Piano Trios, Op. 1, were published with a long list of aristocratic subscribers. In the next three years he undertook concert tours in Berlin and Prague and might have traveled more widely had the international situation permitted. In 1800 he launched a public concert on a grand scale in which his own more recent piano concerto, the Septet (Op. 20), and the First Symphony were given together with works by Haydn and Mozart. Fully attended and widely reported in the foreign press, the event did much to spread Beethoven's fame abroad.

The turn of the century concluded what is generally referred to as Beethoven's first period, a period during which his art kept closely within the bounds of 18th-century technique and ideas. Most of his published works during that time are for the piano, alone or with other instruments, important exceptions being the String Trios, Op. 3 and Op. 9, the String Quartets, Op. 18, and the First Symphony. Beethoven extended his range slowly and methodically, but he was still a piano composer par excellence.

approaching deafness The change in direction occurred with Beethoven's gradual realization that he was becoming deaf. First symptoms had appeared even before 1800; yet for a few years Beethoven's life continued unchanged: he still played in the houses of the nobility in rivalry with other pianists and performed in public with such visiting virtuosos as violinist George Bridgetower (for whom the *Kreutzer* Sonata was composed). But by 1802 he could no longer be in doubt that his malady was both permanent and progressive. During a summer spent at the (then) country village of Heiligenstadt, he wrote the "Heiligenstadt Testament." Ostensibly intended for his two brothers but never sent to them, this document begins: "O ye men who think or say that I am malevolent, stubborn or misanthropic, how greatly do you wrong me. You do not know the causes of my seeming so. From childhood my heart and mind were disposed to the gentle feeling of good will. I was ever eager to accomplish great deeds, but reflect now that for six years I have been in a hopeless case, made worse by ignorant doctors, yearly betrayed in the hope of getting better, finally forced to face the prospect of a permanent malady whose cure will take years or even prove impossible." He was tempted to take his own life—"But only Art held back; for, ah, it seemed unthinkable for me to leave the world forever before I had produced all that I felt called upon to produce . . ." There is a Werther-like postscript: "As the leaves of autumn wither and fall, so has my own life become barren: almost as I came, so I go hence. Even that high courage that inspired me in the fair days of summer has now vanished." More significant, perhaps, are his words in a letter to his friend Franz Wegeler: "I will seize fate by the throat. . . ." Elsewhere he remarks, "If only I were rid of my affliction I would embrace the whole world." He was to do both, though the condition he hoped for was not fulfilled.

From now on his days as a virtuoso were numbered. Although it was not until about 1819 that his deafness became total, making necessary the use of those conversation books in which friends wrote down their questions and he sometimes replied as well, his playing degenerated as he became able to hear less and less. As a technician he was easily surpassed by Johann Nepomuk Hummel, though Beethoven's improvisations showed more power of imagination than those of his rival. He continued to appear in public from time to time, but most of his energies were absorbed in composing. He would spend the summer months from May to October in one of the little villages near Vienna—Mödling, Baden, Hetzendorf, Grinzing, and others. Many of his musical ideas came to him on long country walks; he noted them in a sketch book.

These sketch books, many of which have been preserved, shed a revealing light on Beethoven's methods of work. The man who could improvise the most intricate fantasies on the spur of the moment took infinite pains in the shaping of a considered composition. We can see such melodies as the adagio of the *Emperor* Concerto or the andante of the *Kreutzer* Sonata emerging from a trivial and characterless beginning into the form in which we know them. It seems too that Beethoven worked on more than one composition at a time and that he was rarely in a hurry to finish anything that he had on hand. Early sketches for the Fifth Symphony, for instance, date originally from 1800, although the finished work did not appear till 1807. Sometimes the sketches are accompanied by verbal comments as a kind of *aide-mémoire*. But once he had the continuity of a piece before him, Beethoven was able to write it out in full without the need of further jottings, which explains why the sketches rarely contain more than a melody and a bass. Sometimes, as in the sketching of the Third *(Eroica)* Symphony, he would leave several bars blank, making it clear that the rhythmic scheme had preceded the melodic in his mind. No other composer allows us such a fascinating glimpse into his workshop.

Beethoven and the theater   In the next few years Beethoven had a short-lived connection with the theater. In 1801 he provided the score for Salvatore Vigano's ballet *Die Geschöpfe des Prometheus (The Creatures of Prometheus).* Two years later he was offered a contract for an opera on a classical subject by Emanuel Schikaneder, then impresario of the Theater an der Wien. Two or three completed numbers show that Beethoven had begun

work on it before Schikaneder was ousted from the management and the contract annulled—somewhat to Beethoven's relief, as he had found Schikaneder's verses "such as could only have proceeded from the mouths of our Viennese applewomen." When the new management reengaged Beethoven the following year, it was largely on the strength of his now almost forgotten oratorio, *Christus am Ölberg (Christ on the Mount of Olives),* which had been given in an all-Beethoven benefit concert with the first two symphonies and the Third Piano Concerto. Completion of the *Eroica* Symphony, regarded by most biographers as a landmark in Beethoven's development, was in 1804. It is the answer to the "Heiligenstadt Testament," a symphony on an unprecedented scale and at the same time a prodigious assertion in art of the human will. The work was to have been dedicated to Napoleon, one of Beethoven's heroes, but Beethoven struck out the dedication on hearing that Napoleon had taken the title of emperor. Outraged in his republican principles, Beethoven substituted the words "for the memory of a great man," though with characteristic ambivalence Beethoven insisted to his publisher only a few months later that the symphony was "really Bonaparte," and some years after that he proposed dedicating the C Major Mass to Napoleon. From then on the masterworks followed rapidly: the Sonata in f minor, Op. 57, known as the *Appassionata;* the Fourth Piano Concerto in G Major, Op. 58; the three *Razumovsky* Quartets, Op. 59; the Fourth Symphony, Op. 60; and the Violin Concerto, Op. 61. To this period also belongs his one opera, *Fidelio,* commissioned for the winter season of 1805. The plot concerns a wife who disguises herself as a boy in order to rescue her imprisoned husband, and in setting this to music Beethoven was influenced by Cherubini, the composer of similar "rescue" operas and a musician whom Beethoven greatly admired. *Fidelio* enjoyed no great success at first, partly because the presence of French troops occupying Vienna after the Battle of Austerlitz kept most of the Viennese away. With great difficulty Beethoven was persuaded to make certain changes for a revival in the following spring with a libretto modified by Stephen von

Breuning. This time the opera survived two performances and would have run longer but for a quarrel between Beethoven and the management, after which the composer in a fury withdrew his score. It was not until eight years later that *Fidelio,* heavily revised by Beethoven himself and a new librettist, returned to the Vienna stage to become one of the classics of the German theater. Beethoven later turned over many operatic projects in his mind but without bringing any to fruition.

establishment During all this time Beethoven, like Mozart, had maintained himself without the benefit of an official position— but with far greater success insofar as he had no family to support. His reputation as a composer was steadily soaring both in Austria and abroad. The critics of the Leipzig *Allgemeine musikalische Zeitung,* the most authoritative music journal in Europe, had long since passed from carping impertinence to unqualified praise so that, although there were as yet no copyright laws to ensure a system of royalties, Beethoven was able to drive far more favorable bargains with the publishing firms than Haydn and Mozart before him or Schubert after him. Despite the restrictions on Viennese musical life imposed by the war with France, Beethoven had no difficulty in getting his most ambitious works performed, largely because of the generosity of such patrons as Prince Lichnowsky, who at one point made him a regular allowance of 600 florins a year. Others would pay handsomely for a dedication. And Beethoven's pupils included Archduke Rudolf, youngest brother of the emperor. Consequently, poverty never became a serious threat. But because of increasing deafness, combined with a habitual readiness to take offense, Beethoven's relations with the Viennese musicians on whose cooperation he depended became steadily worse. In 1808 at a benefit concert where the Fifth and Sixth *(Pastoral)* Symphonies were first performed, together with the *Choral* Fantasia, Op. 80, there occurred a quarrel so serious that Beethoven thought of leaving Vienna altogether. The threat of his departure was sufficient to stir Beethoven's patrons into action. Archduke Rudolf, Prince Lobkowitz, and Count

Kinsky banded together to provide him with an annuity of 4,000 florins, requiring only that he should remain in Vienna and compose. The agreement remained in force until Beethoven's death, though it was to be affected by circumstances, one of which was the *Finanzpatent* of 1811 that devalued all paper money by four-fifths. The archduke increased his contribution accordingly, but it was some time before his partners could do the same. Nevertheless, from 1809 Beethoven remained adequately provided for, although his habits of life often gave visitors the impression that he was miserably poor. Inevitably his public appearances became less and less frequent.

Beethoven and women In this period he considered more seriously than before the idea of marriage. As early as 1801 letters to his friend Wegeler refer to "a dear sweet girl who loves me and whom I love." This is thought to have been Countess Giulietta Guicciardi, his piano pupil and the cousin of two other pupils, Therese and Josephine, daughters of Count von Brunsvik. It was to Countess Giulietta that he dedicated the *Moonlight* Sonata. But Giulietta married Count Gallenberg in 1803, and in later years Beethoven seems to have remembered her only with mild contempt. It seems clear that he did propose marriage to her cousin Josephine, whose elderly husband Count von Deym died in 1804, and the understanding appears to have continued for about three years until it was brought to an end partly by Beethoven's own indecisiveness and partly by pressure from Josephine's family. The prospective bride of 1810 is thought to have been Therese Malfatti, daughter of one of Beethoven's doctors, but like the other marriage projects this too lapsed, and Beethoven remained a bachelor. A curious item was found among his effects at the time of his death: three letters, written but never sent, to "the immortal beloved." The content, which varies from high-flown poetic sentiments to banal complaints about his health and discomfort, make it clear that this is no literary exercise but was intended for a real person whom Beethoven was on his way to meet. The month and day of the week are given but not the year. Date and addressee were identified by Maynard Solomon as 1812 and Antonie Brentano, the dedicatee years later of the *Diabelli* Variations.

wider recognition In 1810 the Berlin critic E. T. A. Hoffmann wrote an appreciation of the Fifth Symphony that undoubtedly did much to launch that work on its triumphant career throughout the world and above all to interest the Romantics in its composer. The same year Beethoven made the acquaintance of Bettina Brentano, the sister of Clemens Brentano and later the wife of Count Achim von Arnim, the two compilers of the well-known collection of German folk poetry, *Des Knaben Wunderhorn*. Of the letters that Bettina gave out as written to her by Beethoven, only one can be accepted as genuine; at least one of the others, in which the composer is made to philosophize on music in the most uncharacteristically romantic terms, must be dismissed as spurious. Bettina also performed the questionable service of bringing together Beethoven and Goethe at Teplice in 1812. The admiration had been all on Beethoven's side; to Goethe Beethoven was little more than a famous name, and the meeting was not a success. "Goethe is too fond of the atmosphere of the courts," Beethoven wrote to the music publishers Breitkopf and Härtel, "more so than is becoming to a poet. . . ." Goethe considered Beethoven to be "an utterly untamed personality, who is not altogether in the wrong in holding the world to be detestable, but surely does not make it any the more enjoyable either for himself or for others by his attitude." He showed no interest in the incidental music written in 1810 for *Egmont* "out of pure love for the subject."

The chief compositions of 1812–13 were the Seventh and Eighth Symphonies, the first of which had its premiere in 1813 at a concert given in aid of those wounded at the Battle of Hanau. Another novelty at the same concert was the so-called *Battle* Symphony written to celebrate Wellington's victory at Vitoria. Composed originally for a mechanical musical instrument, the Panharmonicon, invented by Johannes Nepomuk Maelzel, Beethoven later scored the work for orchestra. He frankly admitted it was program music of the worst kind, so different from the ideals of "more as an expression of feeling than painting" expressed in his own *Pastoral* Symphony; but in view of its success he was ready enough to score it for orchestra and even to send a copy of the score to the English prince regent, who, much to Beethoven's annoyance, made no acknowledgment. The concert, profitable as it was for the composer, led to a bitter quarrel with Maelzel, from which Beethoven emerges with little credit. By 1817, when Maelzel had returned to Vienna, peace was restored and sealed by a little humorous canon on a theme from his Eighth Symphony.

Despite the difficulties over the annuity, the years 1813–14 were profitable ones for Beethoven. The first performance of the Seventh Symphony was a huge success, and the audience insisted on having the allegretto repeated. When the Congress of Vienna assembled in 1814, Beethoven's music was universally known, and he himself was courted by the crowned heads of Europe. *Fidelio* was revived with tumultuous success, and the fall of France was celebrated with a grand patriotic cantata, *Der glorreiche Augenblick (The Glorious Moment)*, with words by Alois Weissenbach and music by Beethoven. In 1814, after years of war, Vienna was to enjoy a brief hour of glory before the Austrian economy collapsed and the city sank into a state of dowdy provincialism that lasted for nearly 40 years.

last years With the start of the so-called Vormärz ("pre-March," referring to the uprising in March 1848), the long reign of Metternich, and the middle-class Vienna of Biedermeier (and of Schubert), Beethoven's creative life entered its third and final phase. Inevitably he became more of a recluse than ever, and his rate of composition began to decrease. The works written between 1815 and 1827 comprise a mere fraction of his output after 1792, but they have a density of musical thought far surpassing anything that he had composed before. Though he now went less into society, he concerned himself more and more with business matters and not always with happy results.

It was about this time that he entered into relations with the Philharmonic Society of

London. Contact with Britain had begun in 1803, when he had been approached by the Edinburgh publisher George Thomson with a proposal that he write sonatas based on Scottish folk tunes as Ignaz Pleyel and Leopold Koželuch had done. Although nothing came of this Thomson somewhat later succeeded in contracting him to arrange national folk melodies for violin, cello, and piano—each with an introduction and coda. These remained an easy and profitable source of income to Beethoven for many years.

In 1813 the Philharmonic Society's first season of eight concerts included a Beethoven work at each, and the following year Sir George Smart, a founding member of the society and its chief conductor for many years, introduced the *Mount of Olives* oratorio to English audiences. Another society member, the pianist Charles Neate, visited Beethoven in Vienna in 1815 and brought about the commission of three new overtures to be performed by the society and published by Birchall. The overtures *König Stephan, Namensfeier,* and *Die Ruinen von Athen* were late in arriving, and the discovery that they were not new caused considerable bad feeling; for a time relations became strained on both sides. Beethoven's pupil Ferdinand Ries did much to effect a reconciliation, but a planned visit to London never materialized, though Beethoven continued to hope that it would. The Philharmonic Society never ceased to interest itself in Beethoven's music, and it undoubtedly played an important part in the genesis of the Ninth Symphony, which in a sense it commissioned. The society's archives contain an autograph of the first movement with a dedication by the composer. The first performance of the work was not, however, given in London but in Vienna, and in the printed edition it was dedicated to Frederick William III, King of Prussia. On his deathbed Beethoven received from the society a gift of £100, which moved him profoundly.

In 1815 all prospects of foreign travel were cut short for Beethoven by the death of his brother Caspar Anton Karl, who left a widow and a nine-year-old son, Karl. The will, which appointed Beethoven and the widow as joint guardians, was contested by Beethoven on the grounds of the widow's immorality, and after five years of litigation he won his case. Despite all the affection that he lavished on young Karl, Beethoven was far from being an ideal guardian. Quarrels between uncle and nephew were frequent and bitter and came to a head in 1826 when, just before sitting for his university examination, Karl attempted suicide. He recovered in a hospital, and Beethoven, on the advice of friends, agreed reluctantly that the boy should be launched on an army career. Once away from his uncle Karl seems to have led a successful, law-abiding life, but the events of 1826 upset Beethoven profoundly and almost certainly hastened his death.

The important compositions of the final period begin with the Two Cello Sonatas, Op. 102, and the Piano Sonatas, Op. 101 and 106, the latter known as the *Hammerklavier.* Beethoven then reverted to sketches he had begun for the Ninth Symphony. This was broken off when the news came that Archduke Rudolf was to be appointed Archbishop of Olmutz, and Beethoven decided to write a large-scale solemn mass for the installation ceremony. Work on this progressed slowly, and, like the early cantata for Joseph II, it was not completed in time for the intended occasion. Only in 1823, three years after the enthronement, was Beethoven able to send to the new archbishop the completed manuscript of the *Missa solemnis.*

In the meantime Beethoven had written the last three piano sonatas in 1820 and had worked desultorily on the symphonic sketches. The mass was followed by his last important piano work, variations on a theme that Diabelli had sent to a number of composers, Beethoven included. Most of them, including Schubert and Archduke Rudolf himself, obliged; Beethoven, however, at first declined, then changed his mind and decided to write a complete set of 33 variations.

The Ninth Symphony had begun to take shape; by the following year it was finished and performed, together with movements from the *Missa solemnis* and the Overture from Opus 124, with great success at the Kärntnertor Theater. The composer, following with the score, remained unaware of the applause until one of the soloists made him turn to face the audience. The Ninth Symphony was Beethoven's last work for large-scale forces. His final commission came in 1823 from Prince Nikolas Galitzin, who offered 50 ducats each for three string quartets. Beethoven accepted with alacrity, though only in 1825 was the first of the three, the Quartet in E-flat, Op. 127, completed. Not two but four more followed, including an extra movement that was substituted for the original fugal finale *(Grosse Fuge)* of the Quartet in B-flat, Op. 130. The last quartet was finished in 1826, about the time of Karl's attempted suicide. Beethoven spent that summer on the estate belonging to his surviving brother, Nikolaus Johann, at Gneixendorf near Krems. On his return to Vienna he contracted pneumonia, from which he never fully recovered. He remained bedridden and died from cirrhosis of the liver in Vienna in March of the next year. The funeral three days later was attended by 20,000 people. Pallbearers included Hummel; Schubert was among the torchbearers; Franz Grillparzer, Austria's greatest living dramatist, wrote the funeral oration.

achievement Beethoven's greatest achievement was to raise instrumental music, hitherto considered inferior to vocal, to the highest plane. During the 18th century music, being a nonimitative art, was ranked below literature and painting. Its highest manifestations were held to be those in which it had the aid of a text—that is, cantata, opera, and oratorio—the sonata and the suite being relegated to a lower plane. A number of factors combined to bring about a gradual change of outlook: the instrumental prowess of the Mannheim Orchestra, which made possible the development of the symphony; the reaction on the part of writers against pure rationalism in favor of feeling; and the works of Haydn and Mozart. But above all it was the example of Beethoven that made possible the late-Romantic dictum of Walter Pater: "All arts aspire to the condition of music."

After Beethoven it was no longer possible to speak of music merely as "the art of pleasing sounds." His instrumental works combine a forceful intensity of feeling with a striking originality, force, and perfection of design. He carried to a further point of development than

his predecessors all the inherited forms of music (with the exception of opera and song) but particularly the symphony, the solo sonata, and the quartet. He was more the heir of Haydn than of Mozart, whose outstanding achievements lie more in opera and concerto.

It was the biographer Wilhelm von Lenz who first divided Beethoven's output into three periods, omitting the years of his apprenticeship in Bonn. The first period begins with the completion of the Three Piano Trios, Op. 1, in 1794 and ends about 1800, the year of the first public performance of the First Symphony and the Septet. The second period extends from 1801 to 1814, from the *Moonlight* Sonata to the Piano Sonata in e minor, Op. 90. The last period runs from 1814 to 1827, the year of his death. Though the division is a useful one, it cannot be applied rigidly. A composition begun in one period was often completed in another. Hence the existence of such transitional works as the Third Piano Concerto and the Second Symphony, which belong partly to the first period and partly to the second. Again the tide of Beethoven's maturity advanced at a rate that varied according to his familiarity with the medium in which he happened to be writing. The piano was his home ground; therefore it is in the piano sonatas that middle- and late-period characteristics first make their appearance.

Apart from the First Symphony and the first two piano concertos, the works of the first period consist entirely of chamber music, most of it based on Beethoven's own instrument, the piano. All show a preoccupation with craftsmanship in the 18th-century manner. The material for the most part has a family likeness to that of Haydn and Mozart, but in keeping with the contemporary style it is slightly coarser and more blunt. Beethoven's treatment of the forms in current use is usually expansive. The expositions are long and polythematic; the developments are relatively short. Slow movements are long and lyrical with copious decoration. The third movement, though sometimes called a scherzo, remains true to its minuet origins, though its surface is often disturbed by unminuet-like accents. Finales are models of high-spirited elegance. Two characteristics, however, mark Beethoven from other composers of the time: one is an individual use of contrasted dynamics and especially the device of *crescendo* leading to a sudden *piano;* the other, most noticeable in the piano sonatas, is the gradual infiltration of techniques derived from improvisation—unexpected accents, rhythmic ambiguities designed to keep the audience guessing, and especially the use of apparently trivial, almost senseless, material from which to generate a cogent musical argument.

The second period may be said to begin in the piano music with the Two Sonatas *quasi una fantasia,* Op. 27, of 1801 (the second is the *Moonlight*), but in the symphony and concerto it is not fully apparent before the *Eroica* (1804) and the Fourth Piano Concerto (1806). Here the use of improvisatory material is more and more marked; in the earlier period Beethoven was more concerned to show how it could fit naturally to a traditional 18th-century framework; here he explores in greater detail the logical implication of every departure from the norm. His harmony remains basically simple—less chromatic, certainly, than much of Mozart's; what is new is the way it is used in relation to the basic pulse. From this Beethoven creates in his main themes an infinite variety of stress and accent out of which the form of each movement is generated. The result is that, of all composers, Beethoven is the least inclined to repeat himself; all his works, but especially those of the middle and late periods, inhabit their own individual formal world. Other characteristics of the middle period include sometimes shorter expositions and almost always longer developments and codas; slow movements too become much shorter, sometimes being turned into transitions or introductions, or in effect vanishing altogether. The third movement is now always a scherzo, not a minuet, with frequent use of unexpected accents and syncopation. Finales tend to take on much more weight than before and in certain cases become the principal movement. Decoration begins to disappear as each note becomes more functional melodically and harmonically. Another feature of these works is their immediate accessibility. Here Beethoven's power is most

evident, and the majority of the repertoire works belong to this period.

The third period is marked by a growing concentration of musical thought combined with an increasingly wider range of harmony and texture. Beethoven's enthusiasm for Handel began to bear fruit in a much more thoroughgoing use of counterpoint. But he never lost touch with the simplicity of his earliest manner, so that the range of expression and mood in these last works is something that has never been surpassed. A form to which he gave more and more attention at this time was that of the variation. As an improviser he had always found it congenial; though some of the sets he had published in earlier years are merely decorative, he created such outstanding examples of the genre as the finale of the *Eroica* and the *Prometheus* variations, both on the same theme. It is the type of variation that Beethoven began to pursue in his final period. A unique feature of such sets as he produced in his last quartets and sonatas is the sense of cumulative growth—not merely from variation to variation but within each variation itself. In the astonishing quartets written for Prince Galitzin, everything in the composer's musical equipment is deployed—fugue, variation, dance, sonata movement, march, even modal and pentatonic melody.

structural innovations   Beethoven remains the supreme exponent of what may be called the architectonic use of tonality. Of his innovations in the symphony and quartet, the most notable is the replacement of the minuet by the more dynamic scherzo; he enriched both the orchestra and the quartet with a new range of sonority and a variety of texture.

The same is true of the concerto, where strictly speaking he introduced no formal innovations, the entry of solo instrument before the orchestral ritornello in the Fourth and Fifth Piano Concertos having in some respects been already anticipated by Mozart. Although in the finale of the Ninth Symphony and in the *Missa solemnis* Beethoven shows himself a master of choral effects, he always wrote for the solo voice in a problematic manner. His many songs form, perhaps, the least important part of his output. His one opera,

Fidelio, owes its preeminence to the excellence of the music rather than to any real understanding of the operatic medium. But even this lack of vocal sense could be made to bear fruit in that it set his mind free in other directions. A composer such as Mozart—or even Haydn, whose conception of melody was rooted in what could be sung, could never have written the opening of the *Eroica,* where the melody takes shape from three instrumental strands—each giving way to the other. Wagner was perceptive in hailing Beethoven as the discoverer of instrumental melody.

Beethoven holds an important place in the history of the piano. In his day the piano sonata was the most intimate form of chamber music that existed—far more so than the quartet, which was often performed in public. For Beethoven the piano sonata was the vehicle for his most bold and inward thoughts. He did not anticipate the technical devices of such later composers as Chopin and Liszt, which were designed to counteract the percussiveness of the piano, partly because he himself had a *cantabile* touch that could make the most simply laid-out melody sing and partly because he himself valued its percussive quality and could turn this to good account. Piano tone cannot move forward, as can that of the violin, although careful phrasing on the player's part can make it seem to do so. Beethoven, however, is almost alone in writing melodies that accept this limitation; melodies of utter stillness in which each chord is like a stone dropped into a calm pool. But it is above all in the piano sonata that we find the most striking use of improvisatory techniques as an element of construction. Here too we first meet with the procedure—so frequent in the late-period works—whereby the main structural weight is transferred from the first movement to the finale so that the whole work gathers significance as it goes along. These ideals and principles make Beethoven an ever-present model, as stimulating as he was scary and dangerous to his successors through the duration of the 19th century.

BIBLIOGRAPHY: Alexander Wheelock Thayer, *Thayer's Life of Beethoven,* 2 vols., rev. ed. (1967); George R. Marek, *Beethoven:* *Biography of a Genius* (1969); H. C. Robbins Landon, *Beethoven* (1970); Paul Henry Lang, *The Creative World of Beethoven* (1971); Charles Rosen, *The Classical Style* (1971); Anton F. Schindler, *Beethoven as I Knew Him* (1972); Maynard Solomon, *Beethoven* (1977); Ates Orga, *Beethoven* (1978).

RECORDINGS: Numerous recordings of many works.

Beggar's Opera, The: *see* BALLAD OPERA; CLASSICAL PERIOD (vocal music, 1720–50); HANDEL (life); OPERA (developments in the 18th century); POPULAR MUSIC (Renaissance).

Beinum, Eduard (Alexander) van (September 3, 1901–April 13, 1959) Long associated with the Concertgebouw Orchestra in Amsterdam (second conductor 1931–38; co-conductor to 1945; principal conductor until his death), the Dutch conductor Eduard van Beinum was educated at the Amsterdam Conservatory and began his musical career as violinist, violist, and pianist. He maintained the high standards of the Concertgebouw and was also appointed to the Los Angeles Philharmonic in 1956.

bel canto A style of singing (literally "beautiful song") that has its origin in a style associated with the polyphony of 16th-century Italy. Since this music was remarkable for its symbolism expressing the significance or the moods of the text, a great range of expression was required from the singers, who assumed something of the function of a vocal orchestra. The art of bel canto singing accordingly evolved to allow the singers the maximum power and variety of expression. The style depended on the technique of intensity; that is, tone was varied by increasing or decreasing the air pressure on the glottal lips and not by enlarging the oral chamber, which merely resulted in a larger tonal volume. The bel canto style was also based on the principle that the voice has two tones, a diapason tone produced when the larynx is in a relatively low position and a flute tone when the larynx assumes a higher position. Both singers and composers were aware of these distinctions, which were largely obliterated when a broader style of singing was introduced by Wagner and later composers.

Among the different genres of the bel canto style was the *canto spianato,* with a great variety of coloring as in the arias of Alessandro Scarlatti and his contemporaries; and the *canto fiorito,* or florid song, using the flute tone in agile arias and the diapason tone in dramatic arias. There was also the *canto declamato,* or declamatory chant, of which the subdivisions were the *serioso,* using the diapason tone, and the *buffo,* usually sung in the flute tone. In the 18th-century opera buffa accompanied recitative was sung in the full tone and recitativo secco in the lighter tone.

Among the masters of bel canto were the male soprano Farinelli (1705–82), the tenor Manuel del Popolo García (1775–1832), his daughter, the contralto Maria Malibran (1808–36), and the soprano Jenny Lind (1820–87). The technique of bel canto had died out by the beginning of the 20th century, partly as a result of the demand for louder singing as orchestras became larger. It then experienced a notable revival in the 1950s, thanks in the first place to the soprano María Callas and also to the work of Joan Sutherland. With the rediscovery of this vocal technique, much of the early 19th-century operatic repertoire that posited such a technique was reconquered.

bell A percussion instrument, usually of metal, made to vibrate by the action of a clapper within the bell or by a hammer striking the bell from outside.

bell founding The identifying characteristic of the bell is the campaniform. The earliest bells were probably beaten out of flat plates until the advent of the metal age, when small bells began to be cast. Later the art of casting was either lost or failed to spread as fast as civilization did, resulting in riveted plate bells. About the 8th century casting was resumed, and from that time on all bells with worthwhile musical tones have been cast of bronze.

A bronze alloy of 77 percent copper and 23 percent tin is now generally used. The bells excavated at Nimrud were 10 parts copper to one of tin; other mixtures have been found in bells from widely different locations. While other metals such as iron, steel, gold, silver, zinc, and lead have been used, in combinations and alone, none has been found that can compare in tone value with a clean bronze alloy.

Resumption of bronze casting led to the primitive bell form, a type of the tintinnabulum (the onomatopoeic Latin word for anything tinkling) whose height was greater than its diameter. Constant striking by the clapper caused early bells to crack, since their walls were about the same thickness from the top ring to the edge of the lip. Later a ring of metal was added to the lip of the bell to strengthen it at the point of clapper impact. Curiously this thickening of the lip improved the tone of the bell. It is now known that the strike tone, the main tone of the bell, is dependent upon the thickness of the lip. The primitive bell, invariably convex from top to lip, resembled a beehive in shape and later became even more like one when rings were cast around the sides.

Early in the 13th century the shape of the bell made a definite break with all primitive forms. The hallmark of the new form was a change in the waist from convex to concave, scarcely noticed at first as the waist became almost straight and potlike. As the superior tone of the new shape was noted, the bell took on the gradually inward-sloping sides that are now used. Known as the archaic bell, this type evolved through flattening of the crown, squaring of the shoulders, flaring of the sides down to the mouth or the sound bow, and variations in its wall thickness into the modern bell.

Originally bells were often founded with considerable ceremony; many were beautifully inscribed, often with prayer or verse. Prayers were said while the metal was poured into the molds. The bells were then blessed by a church official, often by anointing, followed by thanksgiving and rejoicing.

The chief English centers of the art of bell founding in medieval times were London, York, Gloucester, and Nottingham. Bells by John of York (14th century), Miles Graye (1605), Samuel Smith, father and son of York (1680–1730), Abraham Rudhall and his descendants of Gloucester (1648–1774), Robert Mot (16th century), Lester and Pack (1750),

Christopher Hodson of London (who cast "Great Tom" of Oxford, 1681), Richard Phelps (1716), and H. Bagley (18th century) are still held in high repute. The Whitechapel bell foundry was established by Robert Mot in the early part of the reign of Elizabeth I. It incorporated the business of the Gloucester foundry (Rudhall's), the Hertford foundry (John Briant), the Aldbourne foundry (the Wells), the Downham foundry, Norfolk (Dobson), and, as Mears and Stainbank, became one of the leading bell founders. Many of Mot's bells are still in existence, among them the fifth and seventh at Westminster Abbey cast in 1583 and 1598. Later the firm cast the original American Liberty bell, Big Ben, and the famous Bow bells. The latter, originally cast in 1738 and 1762, were recast (with others) following their destruction during World War II. John Taylor and Company, Loughborough, were the founders of "Great Paul," weighing 17 tons, for St. Paul's Cathedral, London, and of "Great George," 15 tons, for the Anglican cathedral in Liverpool. The carillon in the Bok Singing Tower, Lake Wales, Florida, with its 71 bells covering a range of four and one-half octaves chromatic, is a product of the Loughborough foundry. Gillett & Johnston, formerly of Croydon, built the carillons in New York City's Riverside Church and at the University of Chicago.

On the Continent of Europe famous founders were Pieter van den Gheyn of Mechelen and Louvain (1554); Frans and Pieter Hemony, members of a Lorrainese family, who founded bells in Zutphen and Amsterdam (1641–77); Pieter, Matthias, and Andreas Josef van den Gheyn of Louvain and St. Trond (1717–91); Joris Dumery of Bruges (1738–1834); four members of the van Aerschodt family of Louvain (1830–1926); and Ernest, Amadee, and A. Jr. Bollee of Orleans (1860–1929). Other founders include Petit & Fritsen, Aarle-Rixtel (1868), and Paccard of Annecy-le-Vieux (1895–1929).

early bells The oldest bell in the world, found near Babylon, is reputed to be more than 3,000 years old. China, Japan, Burma, India, Egypt, and other ancient civilizations made use of bells in different forms so long ago that to trace their history is almost impossible. Bells for horses are mentioned in Zechariah, and in Greek literature bells are spoken of by Euripides, Aristophanes, and Phaedrus.

The development of the bell from its most primitive forms took two distinct directions— Eastern and Western. The pot and bowl were favored in the Orient, while the West later developed its bells on the cup. The pot as used here means a hollow object with straight sides and a height exceeding its diameter; bowl describes an absolutely convex object with diameter far exceeding its height. A cup is an object of nearly equal height and diameter with convex sides. The bowl became the gong—a distinctly Oriental instrument. The pot evolved into the Chinese and Japanese barrel-formed bells with walls of equal thickness throughout and of impressive tone though of no particular note.

Western civilizations, using the cup as the form, developed the technique of ringing bells with a clapper striking from the inside. The bells found in Nimrud, others of cast bronze in Hyderabad, India, and still later ones in Rome —all with small finger loops on top—are those to which tintinnabulum was first applied.

change ringing The evolution of the bell from its archaic form to the forms in use in the 20th century split in two directions in the West because of differences in bell-music tastes between the English and the people of the Low Countries.

In England bell music has always been most appreciated when the bells are clocked; *i.e.,* rung in single note sequences as chimes and in mathematically precise change ringing, or ringing rounds. The people of the Low Countries found that bell music was most satisfying to them when full harmony was played from their towers. The chiming bell thus developed in England, while on the Continent the Flemish carillon-type bell was favored.

Clocking the bell consists of causing it to sound by letting it hang motionless and by pulling the clapper against the side of the bell with a rope. An alternate method was to place a striking hammer outside the bell, causing the strike to be made against the sound bow. This practice was disliked because it cracked and destroyed many of the early bells. Chiming the bells is achieved by swinging the bell

bell ringers at Westminster Abbey, London
The Times, London—Pictorial Parade

just enough to permit the clapper to strike the sound bow, a method that provides little sound volume but permits one ringer to cause as many as three bells to ring gently. For ringing the bell is swung through slightly more than a complete circle, the clapper striking with its full weight against the sound bow at each change of direction or turn. The sound is thus louder and more far-reaching.

The art of scientific change ringing originated in England and is used there and in Scotland, Canada, South Africa, Australia, and the United States. Change ringing is a method for producing changes in the note sequences in sets of bells numbering from four to 12, all tuned to notes of a major scale, with the tenor bell (largest in size and smallest in number) being the tonic, or keynote, while the smallest in size (largest in number) is the treble. With one ringer assigned to the rope on each bell, the rules governing change ringing are: (1) alter the sequence of the bells at each successive blow of the clappers; (2) each bell must move up or down ("hunt") in sequence only one place at a time (*see* Table 1); (3) the first sequence is "rounds," *i.e.*, ringing down the sequence of the bell group from the treble to the tenor bell; and (4) the

full composition of the changes, the "peal," is not completed until the sequence of rounds is reached again. Proper change ringing is not possible on less than four or more than 12 bells (*see* Table 2). Changes are rung on seven, nine, and 11 bells, but in each case eight, 10, and 12 bells are used—the tenor bell remaining the last note of each sequence throughout

TABLE 1
First 20 changes of a "Plain Course"
of "Grand-sire Triples" (changes on seven bells)

Rounds

```
1 2 3 4 5 6 7
2 1 3 5 4 7 6 (1st change)
2 3 1 4 5 6 7
3 2 4 1 6 5 7
3 4 2 6 1 7 5
4 3 6 2 7 1 5 (5th change)
4 6 3 7 2 5 1
6 4 7 3 5 2 1
6 7 4 5 3 1 2
7 6 5 4 1 3 2
7 5 6 1 4 2 3 (10th change)
5 7 1 6 2 4 3
5 1 7 2 6 3 4
1 5 2 7 3 6 4
1 2 5 3 7 4 6
2 1 5 7 3 6 4 (15th change)
2 5 1 3 7 4 6
2 5 1 3 7 4 6
5 2 3 1 4 7 6
5 3 2 4 1 6 7
3 5 4 2 6 1 7
3 4 5 6 2 7 1 (20th change)
```

TABLE 2
Changes possible on various numbers of bells *

No. of bells	Name	No. of changes	Time needed			
			Years	Days	Hrs.	Mins.
4	Singles	24	—	—	—	1
5	Doubles	120	—	—	—	5
6	Minor	720	—	—	—	30
7	Triples	5,040	—	—	3	30
8	Major	40,320	—	1	4	—
9	Caters (quaters)	362,880	—	10	12	—
10	Royal	3,628,800	—	105	—	—
11	Cinques	39,916,800	3	60	—	—
12	Maximus	479,001,600	37	355	—	—

*The number of possible changes on *any* series of bells may be determined, using the mathematical formula of permutations, by multiplying the number of bells together. On three bells only six changes, or variations, in the order 1 x 2 x 3 can be produced; on five bells, 1 x 2 x 3 x 4 x 5 = 120; and so on up to the astronomical total of 479,001,600 changes on 12 bells.

the composition. The principal methods of change ringing, each of which has its special rules and advocates, are "Grandsire" (see Table 1); "Plain Bob"; and "Stedman," named for its inventor Fabian Stedman of Cambridge, c. 1670.

A relay of ringers rang 40,320 changes in 27 hours at Leeds in Kent, England, in 1761. Because a relay of ringers was used, this is not accepted as a true record, although it is not known to have been exceeded. In 1950 a single group of ringers at Winsford in Cheshire rang 21,600 changes in 12 hours 58 minutes, an accepted record.

Because ringing the bell, as the English prefer to do, demands that it be rotated slightly more than a complete circle on each change of direction (a stay pawl on a slider stops the bell at the top of its inverted swing just as it passes the vertical center line of motion), it was found necessary to make the height of the bell somewhat less than its major diameter. Mounting the bell higher between its gudgeons, the pivot points around which it rotates, permitted a nearly perfect balance of the bell and reduced the muscular effort needed to swing it the many hundreds of times required for a complete set of changes.

The original English tone pattern was based on five main partial tones as follows: the strike, or fundamental, tone (the pitch note of the bell); a minor third and perfect fifth above the strike tone; the nominal, heard as an octave above the strike tone; and the hum tone (now a full tone), a major sixth or seventh below the strike tone on the octave of the minor third. Above the nominal in larger bells a major third and perfect fifth can be heard; in smaller bells they are too weak to be noted. Actually English founders tuned only the fundamental, or strike note, depending on careful design of their casting molds to cause the other partials to fall into position.

Tuning of a cast bell is achieved by placing the rough casting of the bell as it comes out of the mold on a lathe suitable for shaving off metal from the inside surface of the casting. Small bells are turned on a horizontal lathe, while large ones are usually machined on a vertical lathe. Bell metal is removed by cutting tools as the bell revolves in the lathe at the

points inside the bell surface where the various partial tones are produced. Extreme care must be used in machining the bell, because the removal of even a few thousandths of an inch of metal at the wrong place can ruin the tone of a partial produced by a previously machined section. If too much metal is removed from one area, the bell will have a false tone, and the only remedy is to melt it down and recast it for tuning again. In the United States most church bells, both singly and in peals, were cast in England or cast in the United States by English methods.

handbells Sets of handbells tuned diatonically first appeared in England in the 17th century for practicing the mathematical permutations of change ringing. By the 18th century groups of ringers had branched out into tune playing, with the bells' range expanded to several chromatic octaves.

In 1847 the U.S. showman P. T. Barnum brought to the United States the Lancashire Bell Ringers under the pseudonym Swiss Bell Ringers, a label retained by all subsequent professional handbell groups. Most bands in the United States consist of eight to 12 players, each of whom may control from two to 12 bells spread out on a table. Handbell ringing has remained a popular form of amateur music making.

carillon The people of Flanders have worked for several centuries to make sure that their tower bells are used as true musical instruments; these bells are capable of playing intricate trills, arpeggios, runs, and full harmony that are familiar to lovers of carillon music.

Originally four small bells in a row (hence the medieval Latin form *quadrilionem*) were struck by hand with a hammer. From the 13th century they were operated mechanically by means of a barrel set with pegs or studs and revolving in connection with the machinery of a clock. The introduction of a keyboard mechanism to the carillon in Antwerp about 1480 led to a great increase in the instrument's range and expression, and both these methods of playing continued in use. In hand playing a clavier of levers and pedals is connected mechanically to the bell clappers; this arrangement allows a great range of dynamics. Older

Wendell Westcott at the clavier of the
47-bell carillon in Beaumont Tower,
Michigan State University, East Lansing
courtesy, Michigan State University

The oldest carillon is that of 24 bells in the Rijksmuseum, Amsterdam, cast in 1554 by Pieter van den Gheyn. The carillons of Utrecht, Delft, and Amersfoort (cast *c.* 1660) are among the most musically expressive. In Flanders the outstanding instruments are those at Bruges (cast by Joris Dumery), Antwerp, Ghent, and Mechelen (cast by Frans and Pieter Hemony). Mechelen's bells became sadly inferior to those of other carillons after centuries of mechanical playing and the practicing of students. Louvain is the best endowed of the older carillon cities, possessing three large instruments.

The largest modern carillons are those at the Riverside Church, New York City, and the Rockefeller Chapel, University of Chicago—each with 72 bells. In the United States the carillon has not been confined to cast bells alone. Electronics permitted a new type of instrument to be produced, and electropneumatic or all-electric systems can be used for playing the carillon.

automatic systems employ a drum similar to a Swiss music box, where pegs control hammers that strike the outside of the bell.

As early as the 13th century continental founders considered it necessary for every good bell to produce three prominent notes. Frans Hemony declared in the 17th century that each true carillon bell must be designed and finished to include in the arrangement of its partials three octaves, a minor third, a major third, and two fifths. An analysis of the great bell of Erfurt, Germany, however, proves that Hemony's theory was carried out almost two centuries before his time, inasmuch as this nearly perfect bell was cast in 1497.

Flemish carillon bells, based on the research and experiments of nearly seven centuries, possess a group of partials as follows: the strike, or fundamental tone; a minor third and perfect fifth above the strike tone of the bell; the nominal, heard as an octave above the strike tone; and the hum tone, a full octave below the strike tone (compared with the original English tuning of the hum tone, a major sixth or seventh below the strike tone). The major third and perfect fifth above the nominal can be heard in Flemish bells of large size but are too weak to be noticed in smaller bells.

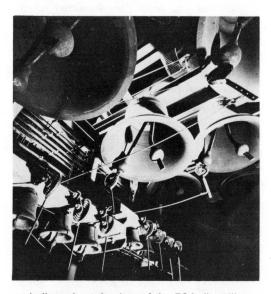

bells and mechanism of the 72-bell carillon
in the tower of Rockefeller Memorial Chapel
University of Chicago
courtesy, University of Chicago

Mechelen has been the focal point of the carillon since the 16th century, the first post of municipal carillonneur being established there in 1557. The distinguished Jef Denyn, who played there from 1881 to 1941, led in the restoration of the art, establishing in 1922 the first carillon school and a publishing enterprise. Repertoire for the instrument includes a set of carillon preludes by the Flemish composer Matthias van den Gheyn (1721–85) and works by such 20th-century composers as Poulenc, Samuel Barber, Easley Blackwood, John Cage, and Daniel Pinkham. However, the largest proportion of the repertoire consists of arrangements of works for other mediums—most frequently keyboard pieces—usually by a carillonneur to fit a specific instrument.

BIBLIOGRAPHY: William Gorham Rice, *Carillons of Belgium and Holland* (1914), *The Carillon in Literature* (1916), and *Carillon Music and Singing Towers of the Old World and the New,* rev. ed. (1930); Satis N. Coleman, *Bells, Their History, Legends, Making, and Uses* (1928; reprinted 1971); F. Percival Price, *The Carillon* (1953) and *Campanology, Europe 1945–47* (1948).

Belle Hélène, La: *see* OFFENBACH; OPERETTA.

Bellini, Vincenzo (November 3, 1801–September 23, 1835) An Italian opera composer who was the supreme master of melodic style, Vincenzo Bellini was a major influence not only on Italian opera but even early Wagner and on the instrumental music of Chopin and Liszt.

Born at Catania, Sicily, Bellini came of a family of musicians. With financial help from a Sicilian nobleman, he went in 1819 to study at the Naples Conservatory with Nicola Zingarelli. While a student he attracted the notice of Domenico Barbaia, director of the San Carlo Theater in Naples and La Scala in Milan, who commissioned an opera for Naples. When that proved successful Bellini graduated to La Scala, where his first important opera, *Il Pirata,* was enthusiastically received in 1827. He was fortunate in having as librettist the best Italian theater poet of the day, Felice Romani, with whom he collaborated in his next six operas. Of these the most important are *I Capuleti e i Montecchi,* based on Shakespeare's *Romeo and Juliet* (Venice, 1830), *La Sonnambula,* an opera semi-seria given at one of the smaller Milanese theaters in 1831, and *Norma,* his masterpiece, which was performed

at La Scala on December 26, 1831, with Giuditta Pasta in the title role. In 1833 Bellini spent some time in London, where *Beatrice di Tenda* (produced in Venice earlier in the year) was given without much success. In the same year he moved to Paris, where Rossini's influence secured him a commission to compose an opera for the Théâtre Italien. This was *I Puritani,* produced in 1835 with Giulia Grisi, Giovanni Battista Rubini, Antonio Tamburini, and Luigi Lablache in the cast. Unfortunately an inept libretto handicapped Bellini's most ambitious and beautiful work. Soon after its production he visited an English friend at Puteaux outside Paris. Never robust in health, he fell ill and died there.

Bellini's fame was so closely bound up with the bel canto style of the great singers of his day that it was inevitably eclipsed by the music of the later 19th century with its greater resources of dramatic power and orchestral color. Bellini was no forceful reformer, but with gentle perseverance he did correct some of the grosser abuses of opera in his day. While he subordinates the orchestral accompaniment to the singers and places upon their voices the responsibility for dramatic expression, his harmony is more enterprising than Donizetti's, and his handling of the orchestra in introductions and interludes is far from perfunctory. It is, however, for the individual charm and elegance of his luminous vocal melody that Bellini is treasured.

BIBLIOGRAPHY: Herbert Weinstock, *Vincenzo Bellini; His Life and His Operas* (1971).

RECORDINGS: *Beatrice di Tenda; I Capuleti e i Montecchi; Norma;* Oboe Concerto in E-flat; *Il Pirata; I Puritani; La Sonnambula.*

Bell Song: *see* DELIBES; GLOCKENSPIEL

Belshazzar's Feast: *see* ORATORIO (late 19th century); WALTON.

Benda, Georg, original name, Jiří Antonín Benda (June 30, 1722–November 6, 1795) A Bohemian-born composer widely admired during his lifetime for his stage works, Georg Benda was the third son (his older brother was Franz Benda, a celebrated violinist) of Jan Jiří Benda and his wife, Dorota Brixi, both musicians. He accompanied his family to Berlin in 1742 and secured a position in the royal orchestra, playing violin until 1749. The following year he was appointed Kapellmeister to the Duke of Gotha, staying until 1778. He toured Italy in 1765–66 and composed Italian operas and intermezzi, but the works that won him renown throughout Europe were his melodramas *Ariadne auf Naxos, Medea* (both 1775), and *Pygmalion* (1779) and several singspiele, of which the best known was *Der Dorfjahrmarkt* (1775).

His son Friedrich Ludwig Benda was a composer of theatrical music, cantatas, and instrumental works.

RECORDINGS: Harpsichord Concerto in f minor; Piano Sonata in a minor.

Bennet, John (*c.* 1575–?)   The English composer John Bennet wrote chiefly madrigals. Scarcely anything is known of Bennet's life, but the dedication of his *Madrigalls to Foure Voyces* (1599) suggests that he may have come from the border of Lancashire and Cheshire. As the title page also describes this collection as "his first works," it may be presumed that he was born *c.* 1575. He contributed a madrigal, the well-known "All creatures now are merry minded," to Morley's *The Triumphes of Oriana* (1601) and five four-part settings of traditional tunes to the undated psalter printed by William Barley. As Barley was one of those to whom Morley had assigned his patent to print music and Morley also contributed to this psalter, he and Bennet probably knew one another. This is also suggested by the style of Bennet's madrigals, which is light but highly finished in Morley's Italianate manner. Bennet's music was also valued by the composer and compiler Thomas Ravenscroft, who reprinted two of the psalm-settings in his psalter of 1621 and included six new compositions by Bennet in his *Briefe Discourse* (1614).

Bennett, Richard Rodney (b. March 29, 1936)   Educated at the Royal Academy (with Lennox Berkeley) and subsequently on the faculty there (1963–65), the English composer Richard Rodney Bennett also studied with Pierre Boulez. He was composer in residence at the Peabody Conservatory (Baltimore) in 1970–72. He has written in a variety of musical forms as well as for films *(Murder on the Orient Express)* and television. Works include five operas (best known are *The Mines of Sulphur,* 1963, and *Victory,* 1968–69, based on a novel by Joseph Conrad); a ballet, *Jazz Calendar* (1964); two symphonies; concertos for piano (1968), oboe (1970), and guitar (1970); Sonatina (1954) for flute; vocal works; chamber music; and compositions for voice and jazz ensemble.

RECORDINGS: *Calendar* for chamber ensemble; *Capriccio* for piano duet; *Comedia IV* for brass; Five Studies for piano; Guitar Concerto.

Bennett, William Sterndale (April 13, 1816–February 1, 1875)   The English pianist, conductor, and composer William Sterndale Bennett was a notable figure in the musical life of his time. Born at Sheffield, he became a chorister at King's College, Cambridge, and in 1826 entered the Royal Academy, where he studied composition with William Crotch and Cipriani Potter. While there he wrote several symphonies and piano concertos. In 1833 his First Piano Concerto greatly impressed Mendelssohn, who became a close friend. In 1836 he played his Third Piano Concerto and conducted his overture *The Naiads* at the Gewandhaus concerts in Leipzig, where he was enthusiastically received by Schumann.

In 1842 he was appointed one of the directors of the Philharmonic Society in London, and in 1849 he founded the London Bach Society, at which in 1854 he gave the first performance in England of Bach's *St. Matthew Passion,* beginning the movement for the performance of Bach's choral music in England. He was appointed conductor of the Philharmonic Society and professor of music at Cambridge in 1856. Ten years later he became principal of the Royal Academy of Music, and he was knighted in 1871.

Bennett's work, consisting chiefly of concertos and solo pieces for the piano, enjoyed a wide popularity in England and Germany, and his cantata *The May Queen,* written, like so many of his works, for a festival (Leeds, 1858), and the quartet "God Is a Spirit," from the oratorio *The Woman of Samaria* (1867), were sung by village and church choirs well into the 20th century.

RECORDING: Piano Sonata in f minor.

Benoit, Peter (Léonard Léopold) (August 17, 1834–March 8, 1901) The Belgian composer Peter Benoit was the chief promoter of the Flemish musical revival. He entered the Brussels Conservatory in 1851 and studied composition with François-Joseph Fétis. Winning the Grand Prix de Rome in 1857, he traveled throughout Germany on a government grant instead of going to Rome. He went to Paris in 1861 to produce an opera at the Théâtre-Lyrique but served as a conductor at the Théâtre des Bouffes-Parisiens. Returning to Belgium, he produced at Antwerp in 1864 a *Quadrilogie religieuse,* consisting of four earlier compositions, his *Cantate de Noël* (1860), *Messe solennelle* (1861), Te Deum (1863), and Requiem (1863). Two years later the first of his oratorios, *Lucifer,* was given in Brussels to great acclaim; this is usually considered his masterwork.

Benvenuto Cellini: *see* BERLIOZ.

Berberian, Cathy (b. ?) The U.S. soprano Cathy Berberian is best known as an interpreter of avant-garde music. Educated at Columbia University and at the G. Verdi Conservatory in Milan, she made her debut in Naples in 1957. She has sung at the opera houses of La Scala, Covent Garden, Hamburg, and Stockholm and at contemporary music festivals throughout the world. Her recordings include Monteverdi's *Orfeo* and *L'Incoronazione di Poppea* as well as songs by Stravinsky, Berio, and the Beatles.

berceuse The French word for "lullaby" is used as the title of a character piece, usually for piano. Berceuse does not imply a set musical form. The most famous example is Chopin's Opus 57, which takes the form of lacy figurations played by the right hand against a sequence of chords continuously repeated in the bass.

Berg, Alban (February 9, 1885–December 24, 1935) The Austrian composer Alban Berg shared the leadership of the revolutionary second Viennese school with his teacher Schoenberg and his fellow pupil Webern, translating

Schoenberg's style of free dissonance into a more conventional harmonic idiom.

Born in Vienna of middle-class parents, Berg began to compose music in his teens and became a pupil of Schoenberg in 1904. He gave the first public performance of his works in 1907 and continued his studies with Schoenberg until 1910. Berg's musical style is more immediately accessible than that of Schoenberg and Webern—he owed much to his youthful idols Mahler and Wagner. His music is expressive and capable of conveying deep

Alban Berg
*oil painting by Arnold Schoenberg, c. 1900
courtesy, Historisches Museum der Stadt Wien*

emotion, with strong dramatic and lyric qualities.

Berg was a perfectionist. He worked slowly, although his compositions are few and thoroughly thought out. His first opera *Wozzeck* (Berlin, December 14, 1925) is a powerful expressionist work, whose flow is channeled by Berg's use of highly organized classical forms. Founded on Georg Büchner's play *Woyzeck,* the opera is the story of a poor soldier who murders his unfaithful common-law wife. Written during World War I and completed in 1921, it is somber and gripping—an unforgettable theatrical as well as musical experience.

The *Lyric* Suite for quartet (1925–26; Vienna, January 8, 1927) was Berg's first work to use the 12-tone technique, the composer's command of this new way of composing being so complete that the work became one of the most intensely emotional of the century. His unfinished second opera *Lulu* (Zurich, June 2, 1937) and the expressive Violin Concerto (Barcelona, April 19, 1936) revealed the great possibilities of associating the 12-tone technique with traditional harmonic and melodic elements and demonstrated the true classical lineage of 12-tone music. Other compositions include Five Orchestral Songs (1912); Three Pieces for orchestra (1914–15); Chamber Concerto (1923–25); and *Der Wein* ("Wine"), for soprano and orchestra (1929).

Berg seldom left Vienna. His wife Helene Nahowski was also Viennese and of distinguished lineage—she was generally believed to be the natural daughter of Emperor Franz Joseph. Berg was a respected, if rather aloof, figure in his native city and was celebrated throughout the world as *the* representative Austrian composer, though his works were never popular in Austria—then as always artistically conservative. After the Nazis came to power in Germany, he was increasingly under attack for his degenerate art, which offended the simplistic orthodoxy of Hitler's cultural arbiters. He taught and composed until his death, but his last years were less than happy. He had a frail constitution and suffered from asthma for many years. He died of blood poisoning in Vienna.

BIBLIOGRAPHY: Hans F. Redlich,

Alban Berg: The Man and His Music (1957); Willi Reich, *The Life and Work of Alban Berg* (1965); Alban Berg, *Letters to His Wife* (1971); Mosco Carner, *Alban Berg: The Man and the Work* (1975).

RECORDINGS: *Altenberg* Lieder; Chamber Concerto; *Lulu; Lyric* Suite; Piano Sonata; String Quartet; Three Pieces for orchestra; Violin Concerto; *Wozzeck.*

bergamasca A lusty 16th-century dance depicting the reputedly awkward manners of the natives of Bergamo in northern Italy. It never became a court dance but had some popularity as an instrumental composition built on a ground base in lively $\frac{2}{2}$ time. The pastoral *bergamasque* of 19th-century France bears no likeness to the true bergamasca. Debussy's Suite *bergamasque* and Fauré's *Masques et bergamasques* were inspired by Verlaine's poem *Clair de lune.*

Berganza, Teresa (b. March 16, 1936) A first-prize winner in 1954 at the Madrid Conservatory, the Spanish mezzo-soprano Teresa Berganza made her opera debut in Madrid the following year and two years later sang Dorabella in Mozart's *Così fan tutte* at Aix-en-Provence. She has sung annually at the festivals at Aix and at Glyndebourne (since 1958) and at the Metropolitan Opera since 1968, with guest appearances at opera houses throughout the world. The dark but agile quality of her voice enables her to sing coloratura contralto as well as soprano roles. A specialist in Mozart and Rossini, she is also celebrated as an interpreter of oratorio and of Spanish songs.

Berger, Arthur (Victor) (b. May 15, 1912) A student of Walter Piston, the U.S. composer and critic Arthur Berger also worked with Milhaud and Boulanger in Paris. He has taught at Mills College in California, North Texas College, the Juilliard School, and Brandeis University. His writings include criticism for the *Boston Transcript* and the *New York Herald Tribune,* a biography of Copland, and essays on theory and esthetics. Berger's early music was influenced by Stravinsky; with *Chamber Music for 13 Players* (1956), he returned to the serial procedures he had not used since 1933. His music is characterized by spareness of texture. Additional chamber music includes the neoclassical Woodwind Quartet in C Major (1941), *Ideas of Order* (1952), Quartet (1958), Chamber Concerto (1960), Three Pieces for two pianos (1961), Septet (1966), Five Pieces for piano (1969), and Music for piano duet (1977); he has also written works for orchestra, voice, and chorus (*92nd Psalm,* 1946), and a ballet (*Entertainment Piece,* 1940).

RECORDINGS: *Chamber Music for 13 Players;* Three Pieces for two pianos; Woodwind Quartet in C Major.

Berio, Luciano (b. October 24, 1925) A successful theorist, conductor, composer, and teacher, Luciano Berio is among the leading representatives of the musical avant-garde. His style is notable for combining lyric and expressive qualities with the most advanced techniques of electronic and aleatory music.

Born in Oniglia, Italy, Berio studied composition and conducting at the Conservatorio di Musica Giuseppe Verdi in Milan, and in 1952 he received a Koussevitzky Foundation scholarship at Tanglewood, Massachusetts, where he studied with Luigi Dallapiccola. With another Italian composer, Bruno Maderna, he founded (1954) the Studio di Fonologia Musicale at the Milan Radio. Under Berio's direction until 1959, it became one of the leading electronic music studios in Europe. There he attacked the problem of reconciling electronic music with *musique concrète (i.e.,* composition using as raw material recorded sounds). Berio and Maderna also founded the journal *Incontri Musicali,* a review of avant-garde music. He has taught extensively in Europe and the United States.

Berio has composed in a variety of idioms for conventional instruments, voice, and especially for electronic media and tape. In all his work his logical and clear constructions are considered highly imaginative and poetic, drawing elements of style from such composers as Stravinsky and Webern. Works include *Serenade I* for solo flute and 14 instruments (1957), dedicated to Pierre Boulez; *Esposizione* for voice, orchestral instruments, and tape; *Différences* (1958–60) for five instruments and multi-channel tape; and a series of virtuoso

Sequenze for solo performers. Berio has also written for the ballet (*Mimusic #2,* 1953) and opera stage (*Allez, hop!,* 1959).

He was married for a time to the U.S. singer Cathy Berberian, who inspired many highly original vocal works, the most important of which are *Circles* (1960), *Sequenza III* (1965), and *Passaggio* (1961–62).

His *Sinfonia* (1968) is described as a "surrealist musicorama in four parts," combining texts from Brazilian mythology, Martin Luther King, Samuel Beckett, James Joyce, and French graffiti with disoriented bits of Mahler, Berlioz, Debussy, and Stravinsky in a "totality of discordance." This was followed by *Cela veut dire que . . .* (1969–70), which in its revised version included choreographic and visual elements as well. *Coro* (1976) is scored for 40 individual singers and 44 solo players and interweaves folk texts in native languages and native styles with fragments of Pablo Neruda's poetry.

RECORDINGS: *Circles;* Concerto for two pianos and orchestra; *Différences; Laborintus II; Sequenza* for solo flute; *Sequenza III; Sincronie; Sinfonia.*

Bériot, Charles (-Auguste) de (February 20, 1802–April 8, 1870) Founder of the modern Franco-Belgian school of playing, the Belgian violinist Charles de Bériot taught from 1843 to 1852 at the Brussels Conservatory, where his students included Henri Vieuxtemps. In his youth he was influenced by Giovanni Battista Viotti, whose concerto he performed at the age of nine. He married the opera star Maria Malibran. Bériot's style included elaborate harmonics, arpeggios, and pizzicati.

Berlin, Irving: *see* MUSICAL COMEDY; POPULAR MUSIC (20th century).

Berlioz (Louis) Hector (December 11, 1803–March 8, 1869) With Chopin, Schumann, Liszt, and Mendelssohn, Berlioz shaped the musical style of the generation that fell heir to Beethoven and Schubert. One of the first composers to recognize the vast compositional implications of Beethoven's Sixth and Ninth Symphonies, he developed a convincing answer to the growing demand for a dramatic music capable of expressing the subject matter of Romantic literature, drama, and painting.

He was the only Frenchman of his era to win an international following and thereby to exert substantial influence on composition and performance for the remainder of the century.

life Berlioz was born in La Côte–St.-André (Isère) in the foothills of the Alps. His father, a prosperous physician, took the lead in inviting a succession of music masters to settle in the town. From them Berlioz learned flute, guitar, and the rudiments of composition; otherwise his education was based largely on the reading of classical texts with his father, and to these he remained attached for the rest of his life. As there was no piano in La Côte, his first compositional ventures were primarily for orchestral instruments. They were read (and admired) by amateur players at chamber music sessions organized by the composer. In retrospect it seems clear that his confident musicality stems at least in part from the comparatively rich musical life of family and town.

In the autumn of 1821 Berlioz departed for Paris to enroll in the College of Medicine. He began to attend performances at the Opéra and discovered that he could study orchestral scores in the library of the Conservatoire. He became a private pupil of Jean François Lesueur and subsequently enrolled at the Conservatoire in Lesueur's composition course and in Anton Reicha's counterpoint class. It was Lesueur's artistic and moral support that led Berlioz to abandon medicine for composition. This decision occasioned a violent rupture with his family, which in turn precipitated a series of financial crises as parental support was withdrawn; the composer would not be fully reconciled with his parents until after his marriage and the birth of a son in 1834.

Berlioz composed passionately and seriously during his student years, completing dozens of works—among them at least one opera, *Les Francs-Juges* (1826)—from which he later drew the best material for reuse in many of his masterpieces. It was a time of prodigious industry, of dozens of plans made and forgotten, of first concerts and publications, and of growing attention from the public and press. In July 1830, on his fifth attempt, he won the Prix de Rome for composition. Shortly thereafter he completed and performed the first version of his *Symphonie fantastique* (December 5, 1830). The first published edition, in a transcription for piano by Liszt, received enthusiastic praise from Schumann in his *Neue Zeitschrift für Musik*.

The composer's Prix de Rome sojourn and his travels there and back occupied the period from December 1830 to May 1832. In Rome, Florence, Naples, and the Abruzzi Mountains, Berlioz absorbed a life-style and subject matter that he would never tire of depicting in his music. Indeed nearly every one of his major works is related in some way to the Italian experience.

When he returned to Paris in 1832, Berlioz set about establishing himself as a free-lance professional composer. At approximately the same time he was drawn into two related careers in which he would become equally celebrated: journalism, which assured him a regular income, and conducting, through which he hoped to insure that his own compositions would be satisfactorily performed. Reinforc-

Hector Berlioz
The Bettmann Archive, Inc.

ing each other, the three professions kept Berlioz continually in the public view, and within a short time he had become one of the most influential—if often misunderstood—musical forces in France. He was exceptionally articulate, gifted with a marked sense of humor, and widely read. He devoured the principal manifestos of Romanticism and the works of Shakespeare, Thomas Moore, Goethe, and Hugo, drawing from them material for compositions and essays. He was capable of administering musical projects on a vast scale, and he would supervise the details of concert giving with the shrewdness of a professional diplomat. His aggressive, original views on artistic responsibility inflamed the stagnant musical life of Paris under Louis-Philippe.

On October 3, 1833, after a long and tempestuous courtship, Berlioz married the Irish actress Harriet Smithson, whom he had first seen in a performance of *Hamlet* in September 1827. Their son Louis was born the following year. The marriage was doomed from the beginning: neither ever learned to speak the other's language fluently, and Smithson's career was declining at the same time the composer's was on the rise. They lived apart from 1844, although as early as 1841–42 Berlioz had become involved in an affair with a soprano named Marie Recio, whom he married shortly after Harriet's death in 1854.

The years from 1832 to 1842 produced an uninterrupted series of masterworks, the most consistently strong of the composer's career: *Harold en Italie* (1834), the Requiem (1837), *Benvenuto Cellini* (1838), *Roméo et Juliette* (1839), *Les Nuits d'été* (1840), and the *Symphonie funèbre et triomphale* (1840). Paganini was so moved on hearing *Harold en Italie* (which he had first suggested to Berlioz but then later declined to play) that he sent the composer a draft for 20,000 francs. This money afforded Berlioz the leisure to complete *Roméo et Juliette,* a work that in many ways represents his arrival at artistic maturity. As government commissions the Requiem and *Symphonie funèbre* constituted formal recognition of Berlioz' national prominence. His only failure with the public was *Benvenuto Cellini,* which closed after only four complete performances at the Opéra.

In 1842 Berlioz made the first of eighteen concert tours outside France, during which he conducted his works in Belgium, Germany, Austria, Hungary, Bohemia, Russia, and England. His foreign audiences were unfailingly receptive to his works. These trips yielded a variety of musical and intellectual experiences that find expression in the compositions of the 1840s and '50s. The German tours of 1843–45 led Berlioz to expand his early *Huit Scènes de Faust* (1829) into the largest of his concert works, *La Damnation de Faust* (1846). The Te Deum (1849; performed 1855) incorporates performing forces and textural ideas discovered during the 1847 tour of Russia and a concert at St. Paul's Cathedral in London (June 1851). The success of *La Fuite en Egypte* (1852) during his tour of Germany in 1853 prompted him to incorporate it in an oratorio, *L'Enfance du Christ* (1854), which became one of his most popular compositions. Sojourns in Weimar with Liszt and Carolyne Sayn-Wittgenstein in 1855 and 1856 apparently stimulated him to undertake *Les Troyens,* now recognized as one of the major operas of the century.

Berlioz refined the art of concert giving with techniques that have since become common practice. His system of sectional rehearsals is now universally followed together with his use of rehearsal letters in scores and parts. He traveled with 500 pounds of carefully prepared copies of his performing materials. His scores are full of instructions (still likely to be ignored) to conductors and instrumentalists as to how passages must be played; he frequently suggests the manner of placement for the performing forces. He had announced his theories of orchestration in a *Grand Traité d'instrumentation et d'orchestration modernes* (1843); this fundamental work was studied for the remainder of the century and later imitated by Richard Strauss and Rimsky-Korsakov. To the second edition he added in 1855 an essay on the art of conducting.

Meanwhile he was widely recognized and copiously rewarded by his followers. His awards include the orders of the Red Eagle of Prussia, the White Falcon of Saxe-Weimar, membership in academies of music in Berlin, Stockholm, Rotterdam, Leipzig, and Rome, and in the philharmonic societies of Vienna, Stuttgart, and St. Petersburg. In 1856, on his fourth nomination, he was elected a member of the Académie des Beaux-Arts of the Institut de France, a post that guaranteed a lifetime annual stipend. The only permanent positions he ever held were with the library of the Conservatoire and as music critic of the daily *Journal des Débats.*

After his return from Weimar in 1855, Berlioz partially retired from concert life in order to complete *Les Troyens* (1856–58), an opera in five acts. *Béatrice et Bénédict,* a comic opera in two acts based on Shakespeare's *Much Ado about Nothing,* followed in 1862. *Les Troyens* was not produced in full until 1967; rather a version of the second half, *Les Troyens à Carthage,* had 21 performances at the Théâtre-Lyrique in 1863.

His last years were marred by ill health and an increasing frustration over his inability to secure a complete performance of *Les Troyens.* In 1863 he donated much of his music to the Société des Concerts du Conservatoire; this effectively marked his retirement from public life. He resigned his position as critic in 1864. His son Louis, who had become a captain in the merchant marine, died in 1867 of yellow fever while his ship was at anchor in the Havana harbor. News of Louis' death came as a shock to the already melancholy composer, and thereafter his physical condition declined radically. Descriptions of Berlioz in his last months paint the sad portrait of a decrepit figure who spoke in cadaverous tones, failed to recognize even his closest friends, and burst into tears upon hearing his own music. He died in March 1869 of an intestinal disorder and was buried in the cemetery in Montmartre, close to where he had lived during the most productive period of his life.

works Asked by a biographer to summarize his style, Berlioz wrote that the principal features of his music were "passionate expression, inward intensity, rhythmic impetus, and a quality of unexpectedness." The rhythmic drive of which he speaks is perhaps the most obvious of these features; it clearly propels works like the "Roman Carnival" overture and the "Queen Mab" scherzo from *Roméo et Juliette* but more subtly animates his ex-

traordinary slow movements, the "Scène aux champs" from the *Symphonie fantastique* and the exquisite love scene in *Roméo et Juliette.* His experiments with exotic meters produced the earliest successful movements in irregular patterns, including a cabalistic dance in $\frac{7}{4}$ from *L'Enfance du Christ* and ballet music in $\frac{5}{8}$ in *Les Troyens.* More sophisticated still are the metrical modulations in *Harold en Italie* and the purposeful ambiguities of the first few bars of the *Benvenuto Cellini* overture and *Le Corsaire* (1852).

He achieved the quality of unexpectedness largely through suppressing four-square phrases and periods in favor of sweeping, lyrical melodic lines that extend and reweave themselves as they unfold, delighting the listener in their irregularity. He generated the same surprises in harmonic structure, mutating conventional chord progressions into more bizarre ones through subtle voice-leading and often returning to his home key through dazzling excursions into foreign regions. The multiple tonal implications of his more complex melodic passages—notably at the opening of the second movement of *Roméo et Juliette*—often suggest Wagner's harmonic rhetoric in *Tristan und Isolde.*

When Berlioz wrote of passionate expression and inward intensity and talked of the ability of music to express feelings and poetic ideals, he was articulating the premises of a search for a style in which dramatic notions could be expressed musically with only passing reference to text or setting. He applies his theory of drama to all musical genres in which he wrote. The most provocative result of his musings was the dramatic symphony, a genre widely imitated and developed, notably in the symphonic poem of the second half of the century.

In the *Symphonie fantastique* and *Harold en Italie,* Berlioz investigates the new possibilities of symphonic form suggested by Beethoven, adding a fifth movement to the *Fantastique* and experimenting in both with thematic recall and programmatic scaffolding. Both works introduce a melodic passage, or *idée fixe* in the composer's own term, that recurs in each movement in a different guise. It was perhaps to be expected that he should add a chorus for *Roméo et Juliette,* a work that loosens still further the grip of four-movement symphonic form, shading it with recitatives, arias with orchestra, and a choral finale. The *Symphonie funèbre et triomphale* confirms the new freedom of symphonic style with its funeral dirge for marching band, movement for trombone solo, and orchestral and choral apotheosis at the end. In his most radical symphonic work, *La Damnation de Faust* (called a *légende dramatique* by its composer), Berlioz encompasses in a single work the many constituent parts of a 19th-century musical evening and uses soloists, chorus, and orchestra to suggest elements of opera and ballet as well as symphony.

His fondness in the operas for tableau and spectacle often leaves the audience to fill in bits of the plot, a practice that vexed critics schooled in the old style; yet he captures the best of grand opera in the tradition of Spontini and Meyerbeer. After the failure of *Benvenuto Cellini* he always wrote his own libretti, carefully crafted to the demands of singers and musical setting.

Among the hallmarks of the Berlioz style is the *réunion des thèmes,* in which movements culminate with their two contrastive melodies superimposed. Concert audiences of the era were particularly fond of his marches, especially the "Marche des pèlerins" from *Harold* and the "Rakoczy" March in *La Damnation de Faust.* Generally, however, Berlioz shows a marked predilection for movements in triple and compound meters, perhaps another reflection of his fondness for the Italianate. Movements based on the Viennese sonata principle decline during the composer's life in favor of strophic forms animated by progressively complex musical decoration. The four brass bands in the Requiem and the antiphonal organ of the Te Deum are the more obvious manifestations of what writers of the era called Berlioz' architectural style; a subtler interest in textural and spatial possibilities in the placement of the performers pervades his works.

As early as the *Symphonie fantastique,* in fact, Berlioz' mastery of performing force is manifest. Whether he writes for the six-part chorus of French tradition, new wind instruments, or harp and strings in harmonics, it is with the conviction of one who has subjected instruments and voices to careful scrutiny. He deploys massive orchestral forces with consummate grace, reserving their full effect for two or three climactic spots. More impressive than all the percussion summoned for the "Dies irae" of the Requiem are the single bass drum strokes in its "Lacrymosa" and in the "Rakoczy" March from *Faust;* these are the work of a master of musical suspense.

For various specific occasions Berlioz orchestrated piano works of other composers, which he accomplished (unlike others) with scrupulous regard for the integrity of the original. Likewise he orchestrated many of his own songs, chief among them the melancholy *La Captive* (composed 1832 to a text of Hugo; orchestrated 1834) and the collection of songs to texts of Théophile Gautier, *Les Nuits d'été* (composed 1840; orchestrated 1843–56).

Berlioz discovered in his songs a lyricism that he applied to all his works. In a sense they serve as studies for the symphonies and operas, and several of the early songs actually reappear in later works. The most moving of his arias—perhaps "Premiers transports" of *Roméo et Juliette,* Méphistophélès's "Voici des roses" in *Faust,* or Iopas's song in the fourth act of *Les Troyens*—proceed from the same premises as his simplest songs. Not the least of his contributions is to the technique of song writing, for it transformed the musically insignificant romance of the late 18th and early 19th centuries into the *mélodie* favored by Fauré, Ravel, and Debussy.

summary Berlioz could scarcely have been unaware of the many political dangers of being at once critic, conductor, and composer; yet these he chose to ignore, fulfilling his obligations with an unflagging sense of high purpose. The inevitable result was indignation aroused in some quarters and antipathy in others, both of which contributed to the failure of a greater number of projects than he deserved. Yet the triumphs of his career were many, and the affection in which he was held by those who recognized the unique and original nature of his genius was a source of satisfaction that usually compensated for the setbacks. His credo of "genuine and devoted love for art" raised the standards of musical life in his own generation and set the precedents for future generations.

BIBLIOGRAPHY: Hector Berlioz, *New Letters of Berlioz, 1830–68,* trans. and ed. by Jacques Barzun (1954; reprint, 1974), *Evenings With the Orchestra,* trans. by Jacques Barzun (1956; reprint, 1973), *The Memoirs of Hector Berlioz,* trans. and ed. by David Cairns, rev. ed. (1975); Jacques Barzun, *Berlioz and the Romantic Century,* 2 vols. (1950; reprint, 1969), condensed in 1 vol. as *Berlioz and His Century* (1956); Hugh Macdonald, *Berlioz's Orchestral Music* (1969).

RECORDINGS: Numerous recordings of most works.

D. Kern Holoman

Berman, Lazar (b. February 2, 1930) The Soviet pianist Lazar Berman began studying piano with his mother in his native Leningrad and then with Aleksandr Goldenweiser, first at the Central Music School in Moscow and then at the Moscow Conservatory (1948–57). He made his debut with the Moscow Symphony when he was 10, but his international reputation did not begin until his first tour of Italy in 1970 and his U.S. debut in 1976. A pianist of the romantic virtuoso school, Berman specializes in Tchaikovsky, Rachmaninoff, Scriabin, and Liszt (his recording of the *Transcendental* Études won the Liszt Prize in Budapest, 1977).

Bernstein, Leonard (b. August 25, 1918) One of the most influential musicians in the cultural life of the United States in the mid-20th century has been Leonard Bernstein— conductor, pianist, lecturer, and composer. As music director of the New York Philharmonic, he was known for wide-ranging programs, showing special fondness for Stravinsky and the disciples of Boulanger; as a pianist he occasionally played concertos while conducting from the keyboard; his illustrated lectures on television made his name a household word; as a composer he was a true eclectic, producing both serious symphonic works and Broadway musical shows.

Born in Lawrence, Massachusetts, Bernstein grew up in Boston and studied composition with Walter Piston at Harvard Univer-

sity, graduating in 1939. At the Curtis Institute in Philadelphia he studied conducting with Fritz Reiner, orchestration with Randall Thompson, and piano with Isabelle Vengerova, winning a scholarship in conducting at the Berkshire Music Center at Tanglewood, where he became a pupil and protégé of Serge Koussevitzky.

Bernstein was appointed assistant conductor of the New York Philharmonic in 1943 and made a spectacular debut, substituting for the ailing Bruno Walter on short notice and without a rehearsal. This marked the beginning of a brilliant career. He was subsequently musical director of the New York City Center orchestra (1945–47) and made many guest appearances around the world. He was the first U.S. conductor to direct a regular performance at La Scala in Milan (1953). In 1958 Bernstein was appointed director of the Philharmonic, a post he held until 1969, making extensive tours of the United States, South America, Europe, the Soviet Union, and the Orient.

Although his fame as a performer has tended to overshadow his work as a composer, Bernstein has been no less successful in the latter role. His *Jeremiah* Symphony (Pittsburgh, January 28, 1944) was the first of a number of works to embody elements of Hebrew music. Only a few weeks later Bernstein conducted his ballet *Fancy Free* (Metropolitan Opera, April 18, 1944), with Jerome Robbins' first choreography, acclaimed (by someone who had forgotten Bernstein's model, Copland) as "the first substantial ballet . . . in . . . genuine American style." The scenario of three sailors looking for girls while on shore leave was expanded into a full-scale musical comedy *On the Town* (opened on Broadway, December 28, 1944), the first in a series of successful shows that culminated in *West Side Story* (opened September 26, 1957). Rhythmic energy is one of the most striking characteristics of Bernstein's style—whether in his serious music or for the Broadway stage. His orchestration often features solo piano, virtuoso percussion, and brass with a high tessitura; stage works are unusually well organized; *e.g.,* the one-act opera *Trouble in Tahiti* (Brandeis University, Waltham, Massachusetts, June 12,

Leonard Bernstein   *courtesy, Amberson*

1952), a satire on suburban family life. Bernstein made important contributions to choral repertoire in his *Chichester Psalms* (1965) and *Mass*, written for the opening of the John F. Kennedy Center for the Performing Arts in Washington, D.C., in September 1971. At the beginning (1977) of Mstislav Rostropovich's first season as conductor of the National Symphony at the center, Bernstein premiered three works: *Slava! (A Political Overture)*, three *Meditations* for cello (with Rostropovich as soloist) and orchestra on themes from *Mass*, and *Songfest*, "a cycle of American poems for six singers and orchestra."

Bernstein's pedagogical gifts found fruition in several series of television appearances, beginning in 1955 on the "Omnibus" program (published as *The Joy of Music*, 1959), and including Philharmonic concerts for young people (published as *Leonard Bernstein's Young People's Concerts, for Reading and Listening*, 1962), a series for adults ending in 1962 (published as *Infinite Variety of Music*, 1966), and *The Unanswered Question*, delivered as

the Charles Eliot Norton lectures at Harvard in 1973 and subsequently published in printed and recorded form.

BIBLIOGRAPHY: David Ewen, *Leonard Bernstein* (1960); John Briggs, *Leonard Bernstein; the Man, His Work, and His World* (1961); John Gruen, *The Private World of Leonard Bernstein* (1968).

RECORDINGS: Ballets *The Dybbuk* and *Facsimile; Candide; Chichester Psalms;* Clarinet Sonata; *Fancy Free; Mass; On the Town; On the Waterfront* (Symphonic Suite); Prelude, Fugue, and *Riffs;* Serenade for violin, strings, and percussion; *Songfest;* Symphonies (3); *Trouble in Tahiti; West Side Story.*

Berwald, Franz (Adolf) (July 23, 1796–April 3, 1868)   The most important Swedish composer of the 19th century was Franz Adolf Berwald. Born at Stockholm of a renowned family of musicians, he studied violin with his father and composition with Édouard Du Puy. After writing numerous concertos and orchestral and chamber works between 1818

107

and 1828, he lived in Berlin (1829–41) and Vienna (1842), where, as in Sweden, his music was received with respect rather then enthusiasm. His works include six symphonies (1820–45), the opera *Estrella de Soria* (Stockholm; 1862, revived 1946), and many choral and chamber works. Harmonically resourceful and original in construction. Berwald's music has a northern character, the severity of which is often relieved by a light and capricious sense of rhythm.

RECORDINGS: *Estrella de Soria* (selections); Piano Concerto; Piano Quintets (2); Quartets (3); Symphonies (6).

Best, W(illiam) T(homas) (August 13, 1826–May 10, 1897)   The first English organ recitalist to explore the secular possibilities of the instrument, William Best began his career with an appointment at the Pembroke Road Church in his native Liverpool in 1840, and eight years later he became organist of the Philharmonic Society there. In 1854 he was appointed organist at London's Church of St. Martin's in the Fields, but the following year he was back in Liverpool at St. George's Hall. He was associated with the Handel Festival from 1871 to 1891 and in 1871 opened the organ of the Albert Hall. He wrote *The Modern School for the Organ* (1853) and *The Art of Organ Playing* (begun 1869) and arranged for organ much orchestral music to play in his weekly recitals.

Biber, Heinrich (Ignaz Franz) von (August 12, 1644–May 3, 1704)   The first notable central European violinist and composer, the Bohemian-born Heinrich von Biber spent most of his life at the court of the Archbishop of Salzburg, rising from a humble position to that of high steward and musical director (from 1676). He traveled widely as a virtuoso and he died at Salzburg.

Biber composed mainly for his own instrument. His sonatas for violin and clavier and his solo sonatas with continuo are of well-defined form and some technical difficulty. They show development of the resources of the violin, especially the use of the *scordatura* (abnormal tuning to produce special effects). His best known works are five sonatas on the 15 mysteries in the life of Mary. He also composed

a few stage works of which only the librettos, and the score of *Chi la dura la vince* (1687), have survived.

RECORDINGS: Cantatas; Passacaglia (violin solo); Serenade; Sonatas for two trumpets and strings (6), Trumpet Concerto in C Major; Violin Sonatas (15).

Biggs, E(dward George) Power (March 29, 1906–March 10, 1977)   The noted U.S. organist of English birth E. Power Biggs did perhaps more than any other performer to promote organ literature through his extensive recordings, recitals, and radio broadcasts. He also championed the neoclassical organ and a revival of interest in extant instruments of the Baroque era. Educated at the Royal Academy of Music in London (1929), he emigrated to the United States and established his reputation with a series of recitals of the complete organ works of Bach at Harvard and Columbia Universities. He appeared as soloist with most of the major symphony orchestras in the United States at a time when the performance of organ concertos was highly unusual.

E. Power Biggs   *courtesy, CBS Records*

Billings, William (October 7, 1746–Sept. 26, 1800) The foremost composer of the early American primitive style, whose works have become an integral part of the American folk tradition, William Billings was a tanner by trade and self-taught in music, early declaring his independence from all rules of composition. Among his friends were many prominent figures of the American Revolution, including Samuel Adams and Paul Revere.

Billings' compositions include hymns, psalms, anthems, and fuging tunes. His music is noted for its rhythmic vitality, freshness, and straightforward harmonies. His fuging tunes, he announced, were "twenty times more powerful than the old slow tunes" and were marked by "each part striving for mastery and victory." The emotions embodied in his music range from the exuberant glory of the anthem "The Lord is Risen Indeed" and the profound grief of the anthem "David's Lamentation" to the buoyant humor of the secular song "Modern Music" and the austerity of the canon "When Jesus Wept."

Once criticized for never including dissonance in his music, he composed "Jargon," a choral piece consisting entirely of dissonances, prefaced by a tongue-in-check dedication and hilarious performance directions. His patriotic hymn "Chester," to his own inflammatory text, became the unofficial hymn of the American Revolution, and his lyric hymn "The Rose of Sharon," one of the most popular of early American hymns.

Billings was active as an itinerant singing master and was influential in furthering the singing school tradition of American folk culture. Many of his hymns and fuging tunes continue to be printed in the shape-note hymnals of the singing schools. His six publications include *The New-England Psalm-Singer* (1770; engraved by Revere and the first collection entirely by an American composer); *The Singing Master's Assistant* (1778; known as "Billings' Best"); and *The Continental Harmony* (1794).

BIBLIOGRAPHY: David P. McKay and Richard Crawford, *William Billings of Boston: Eighteenth-Century Composer* (1975).

RECORDINGS: Anthems; Hymns.

Billy Budd: *see* BRITTEN; OPERA (the 20th century).

Billy the Kid: *see* BALLET (United States after 1932); COPLAND.

binary form A two-part form that is the basis for many short pieces and movements of the 17th–19th centuries. Also called two-part song form, binary form is perhaps the simplest and most basic form cultivated by a great number of composers. It may be represented schematically as AB, although it should be understood that the music in section B is almost invariably derived from and related to material in section A. The form is essentially monothematic with much of the music consisting of either development of the opening subject or passagework of little melodic individuality. Each of the two sections, which are separated by a double bar, is repeated, thus creating an actual form of AABB. The first section characteristically effects a modulation to the dominant key. The second section begins in the dominant key, but by the end of the section the tonic key is re-established. Numerous examples of binary form are provided by the various dances in the instrumental suites of Bach.

In many examples of binary form the closing measures of the second section repeat material that formed the closing measures of the first section; the repeat may be at the same or different pitch level. Whenever this repeat is of considerable length (a repeat of perhaps half the first section), the piece may be said to be in rounded binary form. Many keyboard sonatas of Domenico Scarlatti are representative of this type, which many scholars believe to be the immediate forerunner of sonata form.

Binchois, Gilles (Egidius), also known as Gilles de Binche (*c.* 1400–September 20, 1460) A Burgundian composer of secular chansons and church music, Gilles Binchois was born at Mons in Hainaut. In 1424 he was in the service of William de la Pole, Earl of Suffolk, in Paris and must have been in contact with English musicians. He went with Suffolk to Hainaut in 1425 and joined the chapel of Philip of Burgundy in 1430, where he remained until his death, eventually becoming second chaplain and cantor. The text of

Jean d'Ockeghem's *Déploration* on his death affirms that he was a soldier in his youth, calls him *"le pere de joyeuseté,"* and suggests that he wrote some of the verses he set.

In the manuscript of Martin le Franc's poem *Le Champion des dames* (1440), Guillaume Dufay is depicted next to a small organ, symbolizing church music, while Binchois holds a harp, symbolizing secular music. Le Franc's comment that both took John Dunstable as their model applies equally to the sacred and secular music of Binchois. In both he cultivated the gently subtle rhythm, the suavely graceful melody, and the smooth treatment of dissonance characteristic of his English contemporaries. Some of his church music is related to English liturgical use, and his techniques in these have English affiliations. While his sacred music has historical importance at a time of interchange between English and French traditions, his secular chansons are among the finest examples of their genre.

Birtwistle, Harrison (b. July 15, 1934) A student of Richard Hall at the Royal Manchester College of Music (and with Peter Maxwell Davies and Alexander Goehr, one of the "Manchester school"), the British composer Harrison Birtwistle began his music study as a clarinetist, and many of his major works use combinations of instruments found in the traditional wind quintet. He was director of music at the Cranborne Chase School near Salisbury from 1962 to 1965 and in 1964 directed the first summer school for music there. After two years (1966–68) as a visiting fellow at Princeton University, he returned to London, where he and Maxwell Davies formed the Pierrot Players, performing new chamber music and mixed-media theatrical productions. Birtwistle's music is characterized by unison and octave sonorities and homophonic rhythmic and melodic material, repeated notes, and ostinato. Much of this is already seen in his early *Refrains and Choruses* (1957) for wind quintet. He has written a number of songs, often to Greek or medieval texts; principal examples are *Monody for Corpus Christi* (1959; medieval), *Prologue* (1971; Greek), and Cantata (1969; Greek). Other works include Three Movements with Fanfares (1964; chamber orchestra), *Tragoedia* (1965; wind quintet, harp, string quartet), *The Mark of the Goat* (1965–66; school cantata for variable orchestration), *The Visions of Francesco Petrarca* (1966; baritone, chamber ensemble, and school orchestra), and four musical landscapes for orchestra, *An Imaginary Landscape* (1971), *The Triumph of Time* (1972), *Melencolia I* (1976), and *Silbury Air* (1977).

RECORDINGS: *Chronometer; The Fields of Sorrow; Nenia on the Death of Orpheus; Ring a Dumb Carillon; Tragoedia; The Triumph of Time;* Verses for ensemble.

Bishop, Henry Rowley (November 18, 1786– April 30, 1855) The English composer and conductor Henry Rowley Bishop is remembered for the songs "Home, Sweet Home" and "Lo, Here the Gentle Lark." He began writing theatrical music in 1804 and for many years was closely connected with the theater, composing the music for many light operatic pieces, productions of Shakespeare's plays and adaptations of Sir Walter Scott's novels, and arranging operas by well-known composers. He held appointments at Covent Garden (1810), the King's Theatre, Haymarket (1816–17), Drury Lane (from 1825), and Vauxhall (1830). For Drury Lane he wrote his ambitious and unsuccessful *Aladdin* (1826), his only opera without spoken dialogue, as a rival to Weber's *Oberon* at Covent Garden. He was a founder of the Philharmonic Society (1813) and was professor of music successively at Edinburgh (1841) and at Oxford (1848). He was knighted in 1842. His works included oratorios, part songs, and glees. His slender talent is seen at its best in the tuneful songs that remain popular; "Home, Sweet Home," an early example of the theme song, from *Clari* (1823) became world-famous.

Bizet, Georges (October 25, 1838–June 3, 1875) After Berlioz the most gifted and original French composer of the mid-19th century, Georges Bizet combined a graceful and fluent style in the tradition of Mozart and Rossini with a realism that influenced the *verismo* school of opera.

Born in Paris and baptized Georges, Bizet's registered names were Alexandre-César-Léopold. He showed precocious musical gifts and entered the Paris Conservatoire in 1848, receiving instruction from Gounod, whose music greatly influenced him. He won many prizes, culminating in the Prix de Rome in 1857 for his cantata *Clovis et Clotilde*. His delightfully fresh Symphony in C Major, discovered and first performed in 1935, was written in 1855 within a month of his 17th birthday. His first stage work was the one-act operetta *Le Docteur miracle,* produced at the Théâtre des Bouffes-Parisiens in 1857.

During his years in Rome (1857–60) Bizet composed *Don Procopio* (Monte Carlo, 1906), a lively opera buffa, and the ode-symphony *Vasco de Gama* and planned a number of other works, including the symphony known as *Roma* (performed 1869). On his return to Paris he supported himself by teaching, scoring dance music, and making piano transcriptions, etc. He was a superb pianist who won the admiration of Liszt but shrank from the career of a virtuoso.

In 1862–63 he composed the grand opera *Ivan IV,* probably for the theater at Baden-Baden, but put it aside when Léon Carvalho, director of the Théâtre-Lyrique in Paris, offered him the libretto of *Les Pêcheurs de perles* (*The Pearl Fishers,* first performed 1863). This opera shows the influence of Gounod, Meyerbeer, and Verdi but contains much charming and original music. *La Jolie Fille de Perth* (*The Fair Maid of Perth,* Théâtre-Lyrique, 1867) shows an advance in dramatic skill and orchestration but is hampered by a feeble libretto. During the years 1865–68 Bizet wrote many songs, a few with the vitality of his best dramatic music, and some piano pieces, of which the best is the experimental *Variations chromatiques de concert.*

Bizet's discouragement during the 1860s is reflected in the numerous operas he left unfinished and in the constant self-doubts and suspicions, expressed in his letters. When in 1868 the Opéra offered a prize for a setting of *La Coupe de Roi de Thulé,* a libretto with a remarkable likeness to that of *Carmen,* he submitted an entry but on failing to win the prize strove to conceal the fact. His score, which survives only in fragments, shows high promise.

On June 3, 1869, he married Geneviève Halévy, the daughter of his composition teacher Fromental Halévy. Between his engagement in 1867 and his marriage, Bizet was aware of undergoing "an extraordinary change . . . both as artist and man. I am purifying myself and becoming better." In addition to the happiness of his marriage, which produced a son in 1872, his letters show that he was moved by the events of the Franco-Prussian War, and he served in the national guard during the siege of Paris.

The compositions of Bizet's last four years are nearly all masterpieces. The suite for piano duet, *Jeux d'enfants* (1871), shows a rare mastery of miniature forms and an insight into the child's mind; the one-act *Djamileh* (1872), though again marred by a weak libretto, contains some of his most seductive music in an Oriental idiom; and the incidental music to Alphonse Daudet's *L'Arlésienne* (1872), in which he collaborated closely with the dramatist, is marked by a new delicacy and tenderness. Two further orchestral works were the *Petite* Suite (1873), adapted from *Jeux d'enfants,* and the *Patrie* Overture (1874).

Bizet's last and finest work, *Carmen,* with a libretto by Henri Meilhac and Ludovic Halévy based on a tale by Prosper Mérimée, was produced at the Opéra-Comique on March 3, 1875. It was received with indifference by the public and with hostility by much of the press; only after a worldwide triumph did it come into its own in Paris. Here for the first time Bizet set an excellent libretto (the subject was his own choice, and he helped shape the words), and the music reveals all his qualities as a musician—vitality, rich color, abundant and varied melody, masterly orchestration, and rare insight into the dramatic manipulation of character. In opera he penetrated to the deeper emotions that govern human behavior, especially jealousy. He revitalized opéra comique but did not live to exploit his success. Soon after the production of *Carmen* he was taken ill with an infection of the throat, from which he had suffered chronically since childhood, and died suddenly at Bougival near Paris.

BIBLIOGRAPHY: Winton B. Dean, *Bizet* (1948); Mina K. Curtiss, *Bizet and His World*

(1959; reprint, 1977); Martin Cooper, *Georges Bizet* (1971); Harvey E. Phillips, *The Carmen Chronicle; the Making of an Opera* (1973).

RECORDINGS: *L'Arlésienne:* Suites 1 and 2; *Carmen; Jeux d'enfants; Patrie* Overture; *Les Pêcheurs de perles;* Symphony in C Major; Variations *chromatiques de concert.*

Björling, Jussi (Johan Jonathan) (February 2, 1911–September 9, 1960) The Swedish lyric tenor Jussi Björling sang and toured with a family quartet from the age of six. In 1930 he made his debut as Don Ottavio in Mozart's *Don Giovanni,* and eight years later he first sang at the Metropolitan Opera as Rodolfo in Puccini's *La Bohème.* A member of the Stockholm Royal Opera, he specialized in the Italian and French repertoires, though he never recorded a complete French opera. His autobiography, in Swedish and not translated, appeared in 1945. He was noted for the silvery brilliance of his voice and for a clean musicianship rarely found among "Italian" tenors.

Jussi Björling   *courtesy, RCA Victor*

Blacher, Boris (January 6, 1903–January 30, 1975) Born in China to Baltic parents, composer and educator Boris Blacher began his musical study on piano and violin. As a boy he went to Russia and studied in Irkutsk

(1914–17), and in 1924 he began studying composition in Berlin with Friedrich Ernst Koch. Remaining in Berlin, he made a living by copying music and composing for films until 1945, when he became professor of composition at the Hochschule für Musik and, from 1953 to 1970, its director. Characteristic of his style are alternations of tonality and polytonality, small intervals, short rhythmic motives, and variable meters, in which systematically changing meters alternate in a pattern introduced in *Ornamente* (1950) for piano. He uses 12-tone techniques in the ballet *Lysistrata* (1950) and in the opera *Rosamunde Floris* (1960). Jazz is important in the early *Jazzkoloraturen* (1929) and in *Two Poems* for jazz quartet (1958). Experiments and lectures at the Technische Hochschule in Berlin resulted in compositions for electronic sounds, exemplified by the opera *Zwischenfälle bei einer Notlandung* (1966; "Incidents at an Emergency Landing"). In addition to music for films and radio, Blacher wrote three piano concertos, orchestra pieces, the best known of which is the Variations on a Theme of Paganini (1947), and chamber music.

RECORDINGS: Divertimento for trumpet, trombone, and piano; Orchestral Fantasy; *Ornaments* for orchestra.

Blackwood, Easley (b. April 21, 1933) A piano prodigy, composer Easley Blackwood studied composition with Messiaen, Hindemith (at Yale University, where Blackwood received a master's degree in 1954), and Boulanger. He has taught at the University of Chicago since 1958. Blackwood has written four symphonies (the second was commissioned in 1960 by G. Schirmer to commemorate the publishing company's 100th anniversary); concertos for clarinet (1964), oboe (1966), violin (1967), and flute (1968); *Un Voyage à Cythère* for piano and 10 instruments; and chamber music. Much of his later music uses serial techniques (though not exclusively) and unorthodox treatment of conventional instruments. As a pianist, Blackwood is known as an interpreter of Berg, Ives, and Webern.

RECORDINGS: Sonata for flute and harpsichord; Violin Concerto.

Bliss, Arthur (Edward Drummond) (August 2, 1891–March 27, 1975) One of the leading

English composers of the first half of the 20th century, Arthur Bliss was noted both for his early, experimental works and for his later, more subjective compositions. He studied with Charles Wood at Cambridge and later with Vaughan Williams and Gustav Holst. Until the early 1920s his music was frequently experimental; *e.g., Rhapsody* (1919) for solo voices and chamber ensemble, in which the voice plays an instrumental role singing vocalises, and *A Colour Symphony* (1922, revised 1932), whose four movements were intended to suggest the colors purple, red, blue, and green. Later, although he never abandoned experimentation, he began composing in classical forms: the Quintet for oboe and strings, Quintet for clarinet and strings, the Piano Concerto, and the *Conversations* for chamber orchestra. He composed scores for three motion pictures, including *Things to Come* (1935; after H. G. Wells). Other works included the television opera *Tobias and the Angel* (1960) and his choral symphony *Morning Heroes* (1930). His ballets were *Checkmate* (1937; choreographed by Ninette de Valois), *Miracle in the Gorbals* (1944; choreographed by Robert Helpmann), and *Adam Zero* (1946; Helpmann). His last composition, a choral work called *Shield of Faith,* was performed for the first time a few weeks after his death at the 500th anniversary celebration of St. George's Chapel, Windsor. Bliss was knighted in 1950 and in 1953 became Master of the Queen's Musick. He published his autobiography, *As I Remember,* in 1970.

RECORDINGS: Introduction and Allegro for full orchestra; Quintet (clarinet); Quintet (oboe); *Things to Come* (suite).

Blitzstein, Marc (March 2, 1905–January 22, 1964)   The U.S. composer, activist, and musical satirist Marc Blitzstein studied at the Curtis Institute in Philadelphia (1923–26) and then in Paris (1926) with Boulanger and in Berlin (1927) with Schoenberg. Exasperated with U.S. politics during the Depression, he embraced the political left, which influenced his opera *The Cradle Will Rock* (1936; from an idea by Bertolt Brecht) and the radio songplay *I've Got the Tune* (1937)—he wrote the librettos for both. His early chamber music was influenced by Stravinsky and the neoclas-

sical Parisian composers, but his later music used jazz and pop idioms as well as polyrhythms and polytonality. Banality in his music often consciously parodies commonplaces and clichés, especially those associated with the wealthy classes (the environment in which he was reared). Conversely he uses sophisticated techniques to set off a simple tune, a practice that influenced Bernstein and the rock musicians of the 1960s. Blitzstein collaborated with Virgil Thomson on the motion picture score for *The Spanish Earth* (1938) and 10 years later with Jerome Robbins on the ballet *The Guests.* His operas *No for an Answer* (1941) and *Regina* (1948–49; after Lillian Hellman's *The Little Foxes*) and the cantata *This Is the Garden* (1957) all had texts by the composer. At his death he was working on two operas: one based on a story of Bernard Malamud and the other concerning the trial of Sacco and Vanzetti. It was his English version of the Brecht-Weill *Three-Penny Opera* that finally gave that work its foothold in the United States in the 1950s.

RECORDINGS: *Airborne* Symphony; *The Cradle Will Rock.*

Bloch, Ernest (July 24, 1880–July 15, 1959) A composer of music with a strong Jewish personality, Ernest Bloch was influenced by post-Romanticism in his early years but turned increasingly to classicism in his maturity. In the words of Olin Downes his style contains "the principles of sound workmanship, and the increasing devotion . . . to form, balance of parts and classic relations of tonality and movements. Polytonality is there. Oriental imagery is there, and intense feeling and drama. But the overall design is as classic as Brahms or Beethoven of the middle period."

Born at Geneva, Switzerland, Bloch studied harmony under Émile Jaques-Dalcroze, violin with Eugène Ysaÿe, and composition with Iwan Knorr. The performance of his opera *Macbeth* at the Paris Opéra-Comique (1910) brought Bloch to the attention of the musical world. In 1916 he went to the United States, where he became a citizen (1923), director of the Cleveland Institute of Music (1921–25) and of the San Francisco Conservatory (1925–30), and in 1939 professor at the University of California. As a teacher Bloch exerted a vital influence on musical development in the United States; his students included Roger Sessions and Randall Thompson.

Of Bloch's early works *Macbeth* best reveals the gradual emergence of a strong individuality, which flowered fully in the works of the "Jewish cycle," in which Bloch aimed not to reconstruct Jewish music but to embody the aspirations of the Jewish people. *Trois Poèmes juifs, Israel* Symphony, and his rhapsody *Schelòmo* (Solomon) for cello and orchestra date from 1913 to 1917. The Sacred Service *Avodath Hakodesh* (1933) brings this phase to a monumental climax.

But Bloch was not content to remain a purely Jewish composer. The First Violin Sonata (1921) and Piano Quintet (1923) reveal a highly personal style and strong feeling for classic form. Noteworthy are five quartets, a violin concerto, a piano concerto, three suites for solo cello, and *Last Poems* for flute and orchestra.

BIBLIOGRAPHY: Maria Tebaldi-Chiesa, *Ernest Bloch* (1933).

RECORDINGS: *Israel* Symphony; Piano Quintet; Piano Sonata; Sacred Service *Avodath Hakodesh; Schelòmo;* Quartets (Nos. 3 and 5); Violin Concerto; Violin Sonata No. 1.

Blomdahl, Karl-Birger (October 19, 1916–June 14, 1968)   A student of Hilding Rosenberg and Møgens Wöldike and an admirer of Hindemith, the Swedish composer Karl-Birger Blomdahl was important in the growth of modern music in Sweden through his participation in the Monday Group and in reorganizing the chamber music society Fylkingen into a forum for contemporary music. As music director for the Swedish Radio, he instituted an electronic music studio, and he was professor of composition at the Royal Academy in Stockholm from 1960 to 1964. His early work is tonal and rhythmically energetic until 1949, when, in collaboration with choreographer Birgit Åkesson and poet Erik Lindegren, he created a ballet and a song cycle (completed 1951) using serial techniques. His music has been compared to that of Bartók, György Ligeti, and Krzysztof Penderecki. Perhaps his most radical piece is the orchestral *Forma Ferritonans* (1961), written for the opening of the iron works at Oxelösund; it depicts processes

in the iron industry and is composed from chemical number and letter symbols. In *Altisonans* (1966) Blomdahl combined sounds of nature, such as bird calls, with electronic processes. Also notable are the operas *Aniara* (1959) and *Herr von Hancken* (1962–64) and two choreographic suites, *Sisyphos* (1954) and *Spel för 8* (1962).

RECORDING: Third Symphony, *Facetter.*

Bloom, Robert (b. May 3, 1908)   Beginning as a major in cello, the U.S. oboist Robert Bloom soon turned to oboe and studied with Marcel Tabuteau at the Curtis Institute in Philadelphia. He played assistant first oboe to Tabuteau in the Philadelphia Orchestra, first oboe with the Rochester (New York) Philharmonic, six years as solo oboist in Toscanini's NBC Symphony, and since 1947 with the Bach Aria Group. Bloom taught at the Eastman School, Yale University (emeritus, 1976), and since 1973 at the Juilliard School in New York City.

Bloomfield Zeisler, Fannie (July 16, 1863–August 20, 1927)   One of the great performers of her day, Fannie Bloomfield Zeisler was sometimes called the "Sarah Bernhardt of the piano." Born in Austria, she was brought to the United States as a child but returned to study with Leschetizky in Vienna. She was known as a powerful technician, and her repertoire was enormous—she once played eight recitals in less than three weeks without repeating the same piece.

Blow, John (baptized February 23, 1649–October 1, 1708)   One of the most important English composers of the Restoration period, John Blow was selected as a chorister in the Chapel Royal and received his musical training from Henry Cooke and Christopher Gibbons. At the age of 19 he was appointed organist of Westminster Abbey, and from that time he held a great number of official positions, which included king's composer, musician for the virginals, organist and Master of the Children at the Chapel Royal, and Almoner and Master of the Children at St. Paul's Cathedral. In 1677 the dean of Canterbury conferred on him the title Doctor of Music. He died in London and was buried in Westminster Abbey.

As Master of the Children, Blow taught many important composers of the next generation, among them Jeremiah Clarke, William Croft, and Henry Purcell. To his contemporaries Blow was the leading composer of his time, equaled only, though not surpassed, by Purcell. Soon after his death his music was neglected as a result of the vogue for Italian and Italianate music that had already started in England during his lifetime; by the late 18th century, when Sir John Hawkins and Charles Burney were writing their histories of music, his reputation as a composer was at its lowest. Some of his compositions for the church, however, remained in constant use, and since the 1930s a revival of his music has been in progress that allows a fairer and enthusiastic assessment of his works.

Blow's output was considerable; there are extant more than 120 works for the church, two dozen secular odes, an opera *(Venus and Adonis),* a collection of songs (*Amphion Anglicus,* 1700), organ and harpsichord pieces, and a number of smaller instrumental and vocal works. Such anthems as "Salvator mundi," the Service in G, and the evening canticles in G belong to the best liturgical music of the Restoration period, but many of his secular works are of no less importance. The "Marriage Ode" is one of the most felicitous pieces in 17th-century music; and the "Ode on the Death of Mr. Henry Purcell" is one of the finest memorials written by one composer for another.

The basis of Blow's music is English with the influence of Matthew Locke, Christopher Gibbons, and to a lesser degree Henry William Lawes quite evident. The intense interest in the middle parts in his orchestral and choral writing, as opposed to the preference for the top part, is also retrospective and typically English. He was led occasionally to harmonic experimentation, resulting in rather harsh diatonic (not chromatic) progressions for which he was condemned in the late 18th century, particularly by Burney, but which were again appreciated in the 20th century. He tried to assimilate new ideas with his own style by writing anthems with string accompaniments for the French-influenced Charles II, dance movements in the Italian and French manner,

and highly ornamented recitatives (in the ode on Purcell's death). Blow's strength lay less in gaiety and brilliance than in restraint and profundity.

BIBLIOGRAPHY: Harold Watkins Shaw, *John Blow, Doctor of Music* (1937).

RECORDINGS: *Amphion Anglicus* (selections); Anthems; "Ode on the Death of Mr. Henry Purcell."

Bluebeard's Castle: *see* DUKE BLUEBEARD'S CASTLE.

Boccherini, Luigi (Rodolfo) (February 19, 1743–May 28, 1805) An Italian composer and cellist who helped to develop the quartet and string and piano quintets, Luigi Boccherini wrote about 500 works, including more than 150 quintets, 100 quartets, and 50 trios. He also composed sacred music, symphonies, and concertos, particularly for his own instrument.

Born in Lucca, the son of a double-bass player, he was put under the care of the musical director of the local cathedral at an early age. At 13 he was sent to Rome to study with the cellist Giovanni Battista Costanzi, musical director at St. Peter's. In Rome he was influenced by the polyphonic tradition that stemmed from the works of Palestrina and the instrumental music of Corelli.

In 1757 Boccherini and his father were invited to play in the Imperial Theater orchestra in Vienna, where young Boccherini had the opportunity to absorb the musical Classicism dominated by Gluck. On his second journey to Vienna (1760), Boccherini, at 17, made his debut as a composer with his Six String Trios, which were appreciated by the renowned Gluck. During his third stay in that city (1764), a public concert by Boccherini was enthusiastically received.

In spite of his success Boccherini grew homesick for Lucca, to which he returned (August 1764), having obtained a permanent position with the local church and theater orchestras. As a composer he took part in the religious celebrations in the Church of Sta. Croce and other festivities, composing oratorios around 1765. Boccherini was also in Lombardy in 1765 in the orchestra of Giovanni Battista Sammartini. Through his association with this Milanese composer, the 22-year-old Boccherini strengthened the new conversational style of the quartet: the cello's line was now as important as those of the violins and viola. Boccherini could put into practice this conquest with an extraordinary quartet of outstanding Tuscan virtuosos.

After his father's death (1766) he left Lucca with one of the Tuscan virtuosos, Filippo Manfredi, for Paris—a happy choice since France welcomed Italian musicians. The French publishers Grangé, Venier, and Chevardière published Boccherini's compositions of the previous years (Six Quartets and Six Duets for two violins) and the new ones (Six String Trios and Symphony in D Major), and musical Paris competed for the young man from Lucca. From his contact with the harpsichordist Mme Brillon de Jouy were born Six Sonatas for *clavecin* and violin. Boccherini's style spread throughout Europe, and his Cello Concerto No. 6 in D Major (*c.* 1768?) became the model for Mozart's Violin Concerto in D Major, K.218 (1775).

Such contact and enthusiasm were interrupted when the Spanish ambassador to Paris persuaded Boccherini to move to Madrid. Attracted by this hopeful and flattering offer, he began his long segregation at the intrigue-ridden court of Charles III. The king's brother, Infante Don Luis, provided a yearly endowment of 30,000 reals as a cellist and composer and kept Boccherini with him even when he retired to the Las Arenas castle several miles from Madrid. Far from the intrigues of the scornful Prince of the Asturias (afterward Charles IV) and from jealous court musicians, Boccherini worked in tranquillity and performed in a quartet formed by members of the aristocracy. During this period he wrote his well-known Six Quartets (Boccherini's Opus 15, Opus 11 in some editions, composed 1772) and the first of many sets of string quintets with virtuoso parts for the two cellos. Here he also composed the 12 quintets for flute and string quartet.

Madrid became Boccherini's second home. There he married Clementina Pelicho, who bore him five children. At the infante's death (1785), the king granted him a pension of 12,000 reals. He received another pension from Frederick William II of Prussia, who was an amateur cellist. Boccherini had a long, friendly relationship with Frederick and dedicated to him a symphony and dozens of trios, quartets, and quintets. The Duchess of Osuna appointed him conductor of her private orchestra at the Puerta de la Vega Palace in Madrid. To his prodigious instrumental production Boccherini added vocal compositions: *Stabat Mater* (1781), the zarzuela *La Clementina,* (composed 1786), and the Christmas *Villancicos* (1783). Though faithful to traditional forms, Boccherini was also receptive to Spanish popular music. In fact he became the musical representative of the Goya epoch, the age of the Spanish painter Francisco Goya, who was one of Boccherini's friends.

After his wife's death, Boccherini married Joaquina Porreti (1787). From 1787 to 1797 he was probably in Berlin at a post provided by Frederick William II, but historical evidence for his stay there is lacking. In 1798 the new King of Prussia withdrew Boccherini's pension, the Duchess of Osuna moved to Paris, and Boccherini's financial stress was aggravated by poor health. His trusting nature was shaken by the greed of the Parisian publisher Pleyel, and his life was saddened by the death of his second wife and two daughters in an epidemic. After living for some years in straitened circumstances, his situation was improved briefly by the patronage of Lucien Bonaparte, who had been appointed in 1800 as ambassador of the French Republic in Madrid and to whom Boccherini dedicated a set of quintets with two violas (1801–02). After 1801 he fell into greater poverty, and in 1804 he was forced to live in one room with his three surviving children. His last complete work, Quartet No. 90 in F Major, was composed that year. He died in Madrid and was buried in the Church of San Justo. In 1927 Boccherini's remains were moved to the Church of S. Francesco in Lucca.

BIBLIOGRAPHY: Germaine de Rothschild, *Luigi Boccherini; His Life and Work* (1965).

RECORDINGS: Cello Concertos; Cello Sonatas; Quintets; Symphonies.

Bochsa, Robert (Nicolas Charles) (August 9, 1789–January 6, 1856)   Educated at the Paris Conservatoire, the French harpist and composer Robert Bochsa before the age of 20 had composed an opera *(Trajan)* that was performed for the emperor and written a ballet and an oratorio. In 1813 he became harpist to Napoleon and then to Louis XVIII. In 1817 he went to London, where he served as professor of harp at the Royal Academy of Music (1822–27) and gave annual concerts that included transcriptions for harp of the symphonic repertoire. Until the end of his life he toured throughout the United States and Europe except for France and England, from which he was forced to flee because of scandal. He revolutionized the technique of his instrument and developed many new effects, which were described in a harp method.

Boehm, Theobald (April 9, 1794–November 25, 1881)   The German flutist and innovator Theobald Boehm initially learned mechanics as a goldsmith in his father's business. After studying flute with Capeller he became court musician at Munich in 1818 and established a flute factory there 10 years later. A trip to England and acquaintanceship with the playing of the English flutist Charles Nicholson inspired Boehm to rework the mechanics of the flute; his first new model had larger tone holes and a modified bore for a fuller tone. The finger holes were placed for proper intonation rather than for convenience, and the fingered keys were joined to other keys to cover holes that were impossible to reach. In 1847 Boehm refined the cylindrical flute with a parabolic head joint, the form of the modern flute. Boehm also experimented in the theory of acoustics and invented a piano stringing design; he published *Über den Flötenbau* (1847; *An Essay on the Construction of Flutes,* trans. by W. S. Broadwood, 1882) and *Die Flöte und das Flötenspiel* (1871; *The Flute and Flute-playing,* 1922).

Bohème, La: *see* OPERA (the 19th century); PUCCINI.

Böhm, Georg (September 2, 1661–May 18, 1733)   A German composer known for his keyboard music, Georg Böhm was born at Hohenkirchen near Ohrdruf, Thuringia, the son of an organist-schoolmaster. After an early education at Goldbach and Gotha, he went to Jena University in 1684 and left probably in 1690. In 1698 he became organist of the Johanneskirche in Lüneburg, where he remained until his death.

Bach may possibly have studied with Böhm; he was certainly influenced by his work. Though Böhm wrote many cantatas and sacred songs, he is chiefly remembered for his keyboard works in which he deploys differing styles for harpsichord and organ. The harpsichord suites are in the manner of Johann Jakob Froberger. Böhm is at his most original in his impressive toccatas, preludes, and fugues for organ and above all in his organ partitas on chorales, where he shows an independence and freedom much in the spirit, though not in technique, of earlier harpsichord suites. His collected works were edited by Johannes Wolgast in two volumes (1927–33).

RECORDINGS: Harpsichord Suites; organ pieces.

Böhm, Karl (b. August 28, 1894)   A leading authority on the operas of Richard Strauss —he conducted the first performances of *Die schweigsame Frau* (1935) and *Daphne* (1938)—the Austrian conductor Karl Böhm began a career in the law but soon was conducting in his native Graz and working his way through the opera houses at Munich (1921), Darmstadt (1927), Hamburg (1931), Dresden (1934), and finally Vienna (1943–45 and 1954–56). A regular conductor at Bayreuth and Salzburg, he is equally at home in the German-Austrian symphonic repertoire.

Boieldieu, François Adrien (December 16, 1775–October 8, 1834)   A French composer who developed the farcical opéra comique into a more serious form of early Romantic opera, François Adrien Boieldieu was born at Rouen and studied with the cathedral organist, Charles Broche. His first operas were produced in 1793 and 1795. At Rouen he also composed and performed numerous piano sonatas, remarkable for their form, which constitute the first important body of works written for the piano by a French composer. In 1796 he settled in Paris, where he met Joseph Méhul and Cherubini, and in the following year produced three one-act comic operas, *La Famille Swisse, L'Heureuse nouvelle,* and *Le Pari,* that established his reputation. Appointed professor of piano at the Conservatoire in 1798, he continued to write for the theater, his main successes being *Le Calife de Bagdad* (1800) and *Ma Tante Aurore* (1803). From 1804 to 1810 he directed opera at St. Petersburg and composed a score for Jean Racine's *Athalie.* Appointed director of music to Louis XVIII in 1816, he was elected a member of the French Institute in 1817 and professor of composition at the Conservatoire in 1820. His main operas of this period were *Jean de Paris* (1812), *Le Petit Chaperon rouge* (1818), and *La Dame blanche* (1825), on a libretto of Eugène Scribe derived from Sir Walter Scott's *The Lady of the Lake, The Monastery,* and *Guy Mannering.* Proclaimed his masterpiece, it remained a standard work in the repertoire of French opera. His last opera, *Les Deux Nuits* (1829), contains some fine music but has a poor libretto. Ruined by the revolution of 1830, he died at Jarcy.

Boieldieu's work illustrates the evolution of French operatic and instrumental music in the generation following the French Revolution. His operatic style in its lighter aspects has been compared to that of Rossini. In scenes of mystery and romance that suggest Weber, particularly in *La Dame blanche,* he brought the comic opera to the borders of Romantic grand opera. In addition to operas and piano works he wrote numerous romances for voice accompanied by harp or piano, some showing his original melodic gifts.

RECORDINGS: Harp Concerto in C Major; Piano Concerto in F Major; Overtures.

Boismortier, Joseph Bodin de (1691–1755)   The prolific French composer Joseph Bodin de Boismortier (whose works comprise more than 100 opus numbers, mostly published by himself) spent most of his life in Paris, where he was professor of singing at the Royal Academy. He wrote chamber music for strings and winds, including the musette and *vielle* (popular instruments of his time), as well as seven cantatas, four opera-ballets

in the style of Lully, and numerous motets, the best known of which is *Fugit Nox.* His theoretical work, *Quinque sur l'Octave, ou Espèce de dictionnaire harmonique* (1734), was widely studied in his time.

RECORDINGS: Bassoon Concerto in D Major; Concertos (6) for five flutes; Concerto in e minor for flute, violin, oboe, and bassoon; *Diane et Acteon* (cantata).

Boito, Arrigo, originally Enrico (February 24, 1842–June 10, 1918)   The fame of the Italian poet and composer Arrigo Boito rests on his opera *Mefistofele* and the librettos based on Shakespeare's *Othello* and *The Merry Wives of Windsor* that he wrote for Verdi.

The son of an Italian miniature painter and a Polish countess, Boito was born at Padua and from 1853 to 1861 received his musical education at the Milan Conservatory, where he also studied Italian literature. A traveling scholarship took him to Paris, where he met Verdi, for whom he wrote the text of the "Hymn of the Nations" in 1862. When war broke out in 1866 he joined Garibaldi's volunteers. While working on *Mefistofele,* for which he derived his text from Goethe's *Faust,* he occupied himself with musical journalism, championing German and attacking Italian music and musicians with more vigor than discretion. Verdi was deeply offended by one of Boito's remarks, which seemed to reflect on his artistic integrity. By 1868, when *Mefistofele* was produced at Milan, Boito's polemics had provoked such hostility that the opera was withdrawn after two performances. A much-revised version was successfully produced at Bologna in 1875 and has remained in the Italian repertoire. Boito's second opera, *Nerone,* occupied him for nearly 50 years and was still not quite finished when he died. Completed by Vincenzo Tommasini and Toscanini, it was produced at La Scala in 1924, but despite its grand design and spectacle it was found to be lacking in the musical character that distinguished *Mefistofele.*

A reconciliation between Boito and Verdi was effected in 1873, and Boito undertook the revision of the libretto of Verdi's *Simon Boccanegra.* His masterly versions of *Othello* and of *The Merry Wives* (the libretto for *Falstaff*) stimulated the imagination of the aged composer to its greatest feats. In addition to the librettos for Verdi and for himself, Boito wrote texts for several other composers, the only survivor in the modern repertoire being Amilcare Ponchielli's *La Gioconda.*

RECORDINGS: *Mefistofele.*

Bolcom, William (Elden) (b. May 26, 1928) A student of Milhaud, Messiaen, and Jean Rivier, U.S. composer William Bolcom studied at Mills College in California (1958–59; 1961), the Paris Conservatoire (1959–61), and Stanford University (1961–64). He has taught at the University of Washington (1965–66) and at Queens College in New York (1966–68). After a year as visiting critic in musical theater at the Yale drama school, he was composer in residence at the New York University school of the arts (1969–70) and the University of Michigan (from 1973). Greatly influenced by Pierre Boulez' lectures in Darmstadt in 1960, Bolcom's music uses a variety of techniques from serial and pop idioms to microtones and improvisation. Primarily a composer of chamber music, Bolcom has also written *Dynamite Tonite* (1960–66), a pop opera for actors and 11 instruments, and *Greatshot* (1967–69), an actors' opera. As a pianist Bolcom teams with his wife, mezzo-soprano Joan Morris, in concerts of ragtime and classical popular songs.

RECORDS: *Black Host* for organ, percussion, and tape; *Commedia* for chamber orchestra; Études (12) for piano; *Frescoes* for two pianists; *Open House* (song cycle); *Whisper Moon* for chamber ensemble.

bolero A lively Spanish dance in ¾ time with a strongly marked rhythm. Not of folk origin, its creation about 1780 is attributed to Sebastián Cerezo, a celebrated dancer of Cádiz. In the bolero (probably from *volar,* "to fly") the dancers, either singly or by couples, display virtuosic skill in brilliant and intricately difficult steps to a constant rattle of their castanets. Distinctive features are the *paseo* ("walk"), *bien prado* ("sudden stop"), *cuatra (entrechats-quatre),* and various beating steps *(battements).* Outstanding among musical examples is Ravel's popular *Bolero* (1928) for large orchestra.

Bolet, Jorge (b. November 15, 1914) The Cuban-born pianist Jorge Bolet studied at the Curtis Institute (1935), later teaching there (1938–42) and heading the piano department from 1977. He won the Naumburg competition in 1937 and taught at Indiana University (1968–77). His recordings range from Chopin and Liszt to Rachmaninoff and Prokofiev.

bongos Small Afro-Cuban drums played with the fingers, used principally in Latin-American dance music (in which they are usually tuned a fifth apart, as C–G). They are yoked in pairs, and the two heads (about five inches [13 centimeters] and about seven inches [18 centimeters] across) are nailed or rod tensioned. The shells are wooden and open at one end. In Cuban folk music several other drums are also called bongos.

Bonnet, Joseph (Élie Georges Marie) (March 17, 1884–August 2, 1944) The French organist Joseph Bonnet was a pupil of Alexandre Guilmant at the Paris Conservatoire. He won the post of organist at Saint-Eustache in Paris in 1906 and soon established himself as a leading recitalist. After World War II he made his home in the United States and in Canada. He wrote original organ compositions and edited several volumes of historical works.

Bononcini, Giovanni (July 18, 1670–July 9, 1747) The Italian composer Giovanni Bononcini is remembered chiefly as Handel's rival in England. He was born at Modena and studied with his father, the composer and theoretician Giovanni Maria Bononcini, and later under Giovanni Paolo Colonna at Bologna. He showed precocious musical gifts, obtaining his first appointment (as a cellist) in 1687, and soon becoming maestro di cappella of San Giovanni in Monte. By 1691 he had published eight sets of works, mainly instrumental music, but it was chiefly as an operatic composer that he was to be known. He moved to Rome about 1692 and in 1699, after a brief period in Venice, settled in Vienna with his brother, the composer Antonio Maria Bononcini. He was appointed court composer the next year and remained at Vienna until 1711, when he probably returned to Italy.

In 1720 he was invited to London by the new operatic organization, the Royal Academy of Music. The stories of his rivalry with Handel, and their backing by opposing political and social factions, are well known. Eight of his operas were produced in London, the most successful being *Astarto, Crispo,* and *Griselda.* Other compositions of this period include an anthem on the death (1722) of the Duke of Marlborough (whose family favored Bononcini) as well as harpsichord and chamber music. He left England in disgrace in the early 1730s and went to Paris, after submitting to the Academy of Ancient Music as his own composition a madrigal actually written by Antonio Lotti. His last known work, a Te Deum, was written in Vienna in the 1740s, and he died there in obscurity.

Though he was a prolific and gifted composer, Bononcini's abilities are dwarfed by comparison with Handel's (in spite of the contemporary rhyme that likened them to Tweedledum and Tweedledee). Only in opera, where both used the same highly conventionalized idiom, are the two men comparable. Bononcini may not have possessed Handel's orchestral or contrapuntal techniques nor his gifts of musical characterization, but his simple and fluent melodic style and his ability to write well for his singers partly compensated. In other fields he was a competent and typical composer of the period of Vivaldi and Tommaso Albinoni.

RECORDING: Divertimenti da camera (recorder and continuo).

Bordes, Charles (May 12, 1863–November 8, 1909) The French composer, choirmaster, and musicologist Charles Bordes played an important part in reviving Renaissance polyphonic choral music. Born at La Roche-Corbon, near Vouvray (Indre-et-Loire), he was a pupil of Franck. In 1890 he became chapelmaster of St. Gervais in Paris and made it the center of the study and practice of 15th-, 16th-, and 17th-century vocal music. With the organist Alexandre Guilmant and the composer d'Indy, he founded (1894) the Schola Cantorum, a society that in 1896 became a school for church music with Bordes as professor. Its publication, *La Tribune de St. Gervais* (1895), became the main organ of French musicology. He also began publication of the *Anthologie des maîtres religieux primitifs,*

which provided choral societies with invaluable material. By 1905 he had moved to Montpellier, where he started a provincial branch of the Schola Cantorum.

Also interested in folk song, Bordes toured the Basque country in 1889 to collect traditional melodies, 100 of which were published in *Archives de la tradition basque* (1889–90). As a composer he achieved particular success with his songs. He also wrote piano music, sacred and secular choral works, a Suite *basque* for flute and strings, *Danses béarnaises,* and a symphonic poem for orchestra.

Bordoni (Hasse), Faustina (*c.* 1700–November 4, 1781) A student of the composer Francesco Gasparini and then of his student Benedetto Marcello, the Venetian dramatic mezzo-soprano Faustina Bordoni became a member of the court theater in Dresden and then in Vienna. There she was heard by Handel, who engaged her for his London opera productions (her debut was in *Alessandro* in 1726). After two seasons she returned to Venice. Her singing was noted for accurate pitch and intricate ornamentation.

Boris Godunov: *see* MUSSORGSKY; OPERA (the 19th century); RIMSKY-KORSAKOV; ROMANTIC PERIOD (non-German music of the 19th century).

Borodin, Aleksandr (Porfiryevich) (November 12 [October 31, old style], 1833–February 27 [15, old style], 1887) A Russian composer of symphonies and opera in an epic-heroic style, Aleksandr Borodin was also a scientist notable for research on aldehydes and amarine. He was born in St. Petersburg, the illegitimate son of an Imeretian prince by the wife of an army doctor.

Borodin showed marked gifts for languages and music, learned to play the piano, flute, and cello, and composed even as a schoolboy. From 1850 to 1856 he studied at the Medico-Surgical Academy, where he specialized in chemistry; in 1858 he was granted a doctorate for his thesis on the analogy of arsenic acid with phosphoric acid. From 1859 to 1862 he studied in Western Europe, mostly at Heidelberg and in Italy, and met a young Russian pianist, whom he married on his return to Russia.

He was at once made adjunct professor of chemistry at the Medico-Surgical Academy and became full professor in 1864; yet from the same period dates his first important composition, a Symphony in E-flat Major, written between 1862 and 1867 as a result of his acquaintance with Mily Balakirev and his circle, known as the *Kutchka* (the Mighty Five that also included César Cui, Mussorgsky, and Rimsky-Korsakov). The success of this symphony when performed in 1869 led to the composition of a second in b minor. From the same year until the end of his life, Borodin was engaged desultorily on an opera, *Prince Igor;* he also found time to write two string quartets and a dozen remarkable songs.

But Borodin's musical work was never more than a relaxation from his professional work of research, teaching, and administration. He was active not only in the academy but in the medical courses for women that he helped to found in 1872, and during the 1880s pressure of work and ill health left little leisure for composition. He died suddenly at a ball in St. Petersburg.

Few though they are, Borodin's compositions are outstanding. His two completed symphonies, with the torso of a third (in a minor), and his quartets place him in the front rank of Russian instrumental composers; *Prince Igor,* completed by Rimsky-Korsakov, is a classic of Russian opera. Borodin had a strong lyrical vein that gave him a posthumous success as the involuntary composer of a Broadway musical called *Kismet,* but he was also outstanding in both the epic-heroic and the epigrammatic manner.

BIBLIOGRAPHY: Gerald E. H. Abraham, *Borodin, the Composer and His Music* (1927; reprint, 1976), *Studies in Russian Music* (1935, reprint, 1976), *On Russian Music* (1939; reprint, 1976), and with Michel D. Calvocoressi, *Masters of Russian Music* (1936; reprint, 1971); Donald Brook, *Six Great Russian Composers* (1946); Sergei A. Dianin, *Borodin* (1963).

RECORDINGS: *In the Steppes of Central Asia; Prince Igor;* Piano Quintet; Quartets (2); Symphonies (3).

Bottesini, Giovanni (December 24, 1821–July 7, 1889) A student at the conservatory in Milan, the Italian double bassist, composer, and conductor Giovanni Bottesini played in the orchestra in Havana, Cuba, then at the Italian Opera in Paris (1855–57) and opera houses in Palermo (Italy), Barcelona, and Cairo. He wrote several operas that were produced at the theater with which he was currently associated and was most popular as a bassist and conductor in England, where he conducted Italian opera at the Lyceum. He played a three-string bass, which he favored for its sonority, and used a bow resembling that for a cello. His compositions for double bass include a fantasia of airs from Bellini's *La Sonnambula* and variations on the *Carnival of Venice.*

RECORDINGS: *Grand Duo* for violin, double bass, and orchestra.

Boulanger, Nadia (b. September 16, 1887) With Schoenberg, and in opposition to him, Nadia Boulanger has probably been the most influential teacher of composition in the 20th century. Her family had been associated for two generations with the Paris Conservatoire, in which her father, Ernest Boulanger—her own first instructor—was a teacher of singing. She received her formal training there (1897–1904), studying composition with Fauré and organ with Charles-Marie Widor, later teaching composition there and privately. She also published a few short works and in 1908 won second place in the Prix de Rome competition with her cantata *Sirène.* She ceased composing, rating her works "useless," after the death in 1918 of her talented sister Lili, also a composer.

In 1921 Mlle Boulanger began her long association with the Conservatoire Américain, founded at Fontainebleu by Walter Damrosch after World War I for U.S. musicians. She was organist for the premiere of her first U.S. student Aaron Copland's *Organ* Symphony in 1925 and appeared as the first woman conductor of the Boston, New York Philharmonic, and Philadelphia orchestras in 1938; she had already (1937) become the first woman to conduct an entire program of London's Royal Philharmonic. In the late 1930s Mlle Boulanger made recordings of the then-unknown Monteverdi, also championing such rarely performed works as the Heinrich

Schütz Passions and the Fauré Requiem, now considered standards; she also promoted early French music. She spent the period of World War II in the United States, mainly as a teacher at the Washington (D.C.) College of Music and the Peabody Conservatory in Baltimore. After returning to France she taught again at the Paris and American conservatories, becoming director of the latter—her special academic home—in 1949.

Mlle Boulanger's pupils have included composers Arthur Berger, Lennox Berkeley, Easley Blackwood, Marc Blitzstein, Elliott Carter, Copland, David Diamond, Jean Françaix, Roy Harris, Milhaud, Walter Piston, and Virgil Thomson. Her influence as a teacher was always personal rather than pedantic: she refused to write a textbook of theory. Her aim was to enlarge the student's aesthetic comprehensions while developing his individual gifts.

Boulez, Pierre (b. March 26, 1925) The most significant French composer of his generation, Pierre Boulez is also a noted conductor and pianist. The son of a steel manufacturer, he majored in mathematics at the Collège de Saint-Étienne, where he also studied music, later studying mathematics, engineering, and music in Lyons. In 1944–45 he studied with Messiaen at the Paris Conservatoire and counterpoint privately with Andrée Vaurabourg, the wife of Honegger. Subsequently (1945–46) he studied 12-tone technique with René Leibowitz, its leading French exponent and a pupil of its originator, Schoenberg. At 22 he became music director of the Marigny, a theatrical company newly formed by Jean-Louis Barrault and Madeleine Renaud, where he remained for 10 years. In 1954 he founded a series of avant-garde concerts, the Concerts Marigny, later called Domaine Musical. In 1966, protesting the appointment by the novelist André Malraux (then minister of cultural affairs) of the neoromantic composer Marcel Landowski as musical director to the ministry, Boulez severed all ties with the French musical establishment. By the 1960s he had gained an international reputation not only as a composer but also as a conductor of both 20th-century and Classical repertoires. In 1971 he was named musical director of the New York Philharmonic, replacing the retiring Bernstein. After a controversial tenure at the Philharmonic, Boulez left New York City in 1977 to head the Institut de Recherche et de Coordination Acoustique/Musique, the massively subsidized experimental music center in the

Pierre Boulez

courtesy, Festspielleitung Bayreuth

French government's Centre National D'Art et de Culture Georges Pompidou (popularly known as Beaubourg) in Paris.

Boulez' music is characterized by a rigorous control of every element in an extremely dense arrangement that includes the serialization not only of pitch but of other elements such as rhythm. Yet it is also marked by a sensitivity to the nuances of instrumental texture and color, a concern he also shows as a conductor. His earlier compositions combine the influence of 12-tone composers with that of Messiaen and through him of certain Oriental music. Boulez was also influenced by the work of poets Stéphane Mallarmé and René Char. In his *Sonatine* (1946) for flute and piano, the 12-tone imitations and canons fly so fast as to leave an impression merely of movement and texture. In *Structures,* Book I (1952), for two pianos, the actual 12-tone series is simply taken from a work of Messiaen's; but Boulez elaborates it to a remarkable degree in strict permutations of pitch, duration, dynamics, and even attack (total serialization), and it is these densities and speed of movement that become the dominant feature rather than the series itself. In *Le Marteau sans maître (The Hammer Without a Master,* 1954) for voice and six instruments, florid decorative textures flow into one another, voice and instruments rise and fall with the utmost apparent spontaneity, punctuated by pairs of bongos, snare drums, or gongs. In each movement of the work the instrumentation is varied, and a number of processes—hockets, imitations, etc.—are set in motion. The serialized rhythmic and motivic cells yield an impression not of structure but of movement, texture, and timbre. Boulez' concern with the physical activity of singing or playing was taken in *Pli selon pli (Fold According to Fold;* first performed 1960) to the point of temporarily providing no absolute pulse. Performers must orient themselves by maintaining a constant awareness of the structure of the work. In his Third Piano Sonata, as in *Pli selon pli,* he introduced elements of aleatory music.

Boulez' other works include *Le Visage nuptial* (composed 1946–50) for two voices, women's chorus, and orchestra; *Poésie pour pouvoir* (first performed 1958) for tape and three orchestras; *Structures II* (completed 1961) for two pianos; *Figures-Doubles-Prismes* (completed 1968) and *Eclat-Multiples* (completed 1971) for orchestra; *Domaines* (1968) for clarinet and several instruments; and *Cummings ist der Dichter* (1970) for 16 solo voices and instruments. English translations of his two books are *Notes of an Apprenticeship* (1968) and *Boulez on Music Today* (1971).

BIBLIOGRAPHY: Joan Peyser, *Boulez* (1976).

RECORDINGS: Livre pour cordes; Livre pour quatuor; *Le Marteau sans maître;* Piano Sonata No. 2; *Pli selon pli; Le Soleil des eaux.*

Boult, Adrian (Cedric) (b. April 8, 1889) One of the foremost English conductors in the 20th century, Adrian Boult was educated at Oxford and was a student of Arthur Nikisch and Max Reger in Leipzig. Knighted in 1937, his major posts were as conductor of the BBC Symphony (1930–50) and of the London Philharmonic (1950–57). His repertoire is catholic with an emphasis on British composers, especially Vaughan Williams and Elgar.

bourrée   A French folk dance with many varieties but characteristically danced with quick, skipping steps. Dancers occasionally wear wooden clogs to emphasize the sounds made by their feet. Notably associated with Auvergne, bourreés are also danced elsewhere in France and in Biscay, Spain. Praetorius mentions the bourrée in his musical compendium *Syntagma musicum* in 1615.

Stylized bourrées in $\frac{2}{4}$ or $\frac{4}{4}$ time (folk bourrées also occur in $\frac{3}{8}$ time) have been composed as abstract musical pieces since the mid-16th century. In such 18th-century suites as those of Bach and Handel, the bourrée often appears as one of the *galanteries,* or optional movements. The bourrée was among the dances from which ballet derived its early steps.

bow   A strong, light, flexible wooden stick, sprung so that a ribbon of horsehairs can be stretched between its ends and used to play stringed instruments of the violin family and related instruments. The hair is drawn across a solid cake of resin and rubs off a small quantity in powder form; this supplies the frictional element that is necessary to make the string vibrate. Proper design is as important in a

123

violin bow, Tourte pattern, modern; and treble viol bow, late 17th century

photographs, Eric Halfpenny

violin bow as in the violin itself, for it must give the player complete control over the tone and must respond to every nuance of pressure and attack imposed upon it.

The modern bow, which is really the culmination of a long line of evolution, was perfected late in the 18th century by François Tourte of Paris. The light tapering stick now is made of Pernambuco wood (brazilwood) with a hatchet-shaped head formed at the thinner end. At the other end is a movable frog, which has a threaded eye projecting into a mortise, or groove, cut in the stick and runs on a screw that can be turned at the lower end of the stick. The hank of hair is stretched between the head and frog, and its tension is adjusted by the screw. When the screw is slackened off, the stick curves toward the hair. When the hair is tightened, the stick straightens out, or rather the curve flattens somewhat. It is the correct setting of this curve, which is put into the stick by bending under dry heat, and the exact shaping of the tapering section of the stick that give a good bow its desired qualities.

The earlier bow, which was used almost everywhere from the beginning of the 17th century until the end of the 18th, was shorter and had a lighter head and a narrower ribbon of hair. Its chief characteristic, however, was the shape of the stick, which bent outward from the hair under working tension. This design would not stand up to modern ideas of bowing technique, where on occasion optimum sonority must be developed from the instrument, but it was suited to the smaller scale and neat articulations of Baroque and early Classical violin music.

The larger instruments have followed the violin in bow design, adapting it to their special purposes by adjustments of dimension and weight. For a long time the double bass lagged behind, and during the first half of the 19th century this instrument was still being played with a broad, heavy version of the earlier out-curved bow. This was supplanted in France and in other countries under French influence by the violin-type bow and in Austria and German-speaking countries generally by the Simandl bow, named after a contemporary professor at the Vienna Academy.

Boyce, William (1710– February 7, 1779) One of the foremost English composers of church music, William Boyce was also notable for his symphonies and as an organist and music editor. He was probably born in London and was a chorister under Charles King at St. Paul's Cathedral, later becoming a student of Maurice Greene, the cathedral organist. He became organist of the Oxford Chapel, Vere Street, London, in 1734. Other appointments included that of conductor of the Three Choirs Festival (1737).

Boyce's career as a composer was closely related to his many official positions. He became composer to the Chapel Royal in 1736, and many of his anthems and church services were written for use there and at the London churches of which he was organist—St. Michael's, Cornhill, 1736–68, and All Hallows, Thames Street, 1749–69. On Greene's death in 1755 Boyce succeeded him as master of the King's Band of Music and thereafter composed the music for the annual new year and birthday odes by the poet laureate. In 1758 he became one of the organists at the Chapel Royal. Boyce had been long afflicted by deafness, and in 1769 he gave up all appointments except that at the Chapel Royal. He was still able to teach, however, and his pupils included the child prodigies, Charles and Samuel Wesley. He died in London and was honored with burial under the dome of St. Paul's Cathedral.

Boyce's magnum opus is his three-volume collection of *Cathedral Music* (1760–73). Based in part on materials collected by Greene, it was a landmark in the history of church music, the first collection since the Restoration and the first to be printed in score. Boyce performed his work well by the standards of his time, and his collection, which covered three centuries of British church music, was only superseded in the mid-19th century.

His own songs and cantatas were published in several volumes called *Lyra Britannica* from 1745 to 1755, with later collections of anthems published posthumously in 1780 and 1790. Instrumental works include Twelve Overtures (1720), Twelve Sonatas (1745) for two violins and bass, Eight Symphonies (1750) in eight parts, and Ten Voluntaries (1785) for organ or harpsichord. They enjoyed some success but were considered out of fashion in the latter part of Boyce's life when the symphonies of the Mannheim school were in vogue. The vigor and spontaneous invention of his non-keyboard instrumental works has recently been recognized and the music revived.

Though his fame has long rested in his church music, Boyce wrote rather extensively for the stage as well, including *Pileus and Thetis* (1747), *The Chaplet* (1749), *The Shepherd's Lottery* (1751), and *Harlequin's Invasion* (1759), which includes his best known song "Heart of Oak."

RECORDINGS: Eight Symphonies; Twelve Overtures; Twelve Sonatas.

Brahms, Johannes (May 7, 1833–April 3, 1897) The German composer Johannes Brahms was the great master of symphonic and sonata style in the second half of the 19th century and the protagonist of the Classical tradition of Haydn, Mozart, and Beethoven in a period when the standards of this tradition were generally questioned or overturned by the Romantics.

life The son of Jakob Brahms, an impecunious double-bass player, he was born in Hamburg. Showing early promise as a pianist, he had his first music instruction from his father and at the age of seven was sent for piano lessons to Otto Cossel, who three years later passed him to his own teacher, Eduard Marx-

Johannes Brahms,
*lithograph by Rudolf Fenzl, 1897
Bild-Archiv der Oesterreichischen
Nationalbibliothek, Wien*

sen. This distinguished teacher wisely recommended against the suggestion of Brahms *père* that the boy should undertake a tour of the United States, and Johannes remained with him for several years. Between the ages of 14 and 16 Brahms earned money to help his family by playing in rough inns in the dock area of Hamburg and in the meantime composing and sometimes giving recitals. In 1850 he met Eduard Reményi, a Jewish-Hungarian violinist with whom he gave concerts and from whom he learned something of gypsy music—an influence that remained with him all his life.

The first turning point came in 1853, when he met Joachim who instantly realized the talent of Brahms. Joachim recommended him to Schumann, and an immediate friendship between the two composers resulted. Schumann wrote enthusiastically about him in the *Neue Zeitschrift für Musik:* "It seemed to me . . . that . . . a musician would inevitably appear to whom it was vouchsafed to give the highest and most ideal expression to the tendencies of our time, one who would not show his mastery in a gradual development, but, like Athena, would spring fully armed from the head of Zeus. And he has come, a

young man over whose cradle Graces and Heroes stood watch. His name is Johannes
Brahms." From this moment Brahms was a
force in the world of music, though there were
always factors that made difficulties for him.

The chief of these was the nature of Schumann's panegyric itself. There was already
conflict between the neo-German school, dominated by Liszt and Wagner, and the more
conservative elements, whose main spokesman
was Schumann. His praise of Brahms dis-
pleased the enemy; Brahms himself, though
kindly received (as was almost everyone) by
Liszt, did not conceal his lack of sympathy
with the self-conscious modernists. He was
therefore drawn into controversy, and many
of the disturbances later in his otherwise uneventful personal life arose from this situation.
For example, his close friendship with the conductor Hermann Levi was broken off because
of Levi's increasing admiration for Wagner's
music; whereas Hans von Bülow, once an ardent Wagnerian, came over to Brahms's side
as a consequence of his wife's elopement with
Wagner. Gradually Brahms came to be on
close terms with the Schumann household,
and when Schumann was first taken mentally
ill in 1854, Brahms assisted Clara Schumann
in managing her family. He fell in love with
her, and the feeling appears to have been re-
ciprocated, but though they remained deep
friends after Schumann's death in 1856, their
relationship did not, it seems, go further.

Between 1857 and 1860 Brahms moved between the court of Detmold—where he taught
piano and conducted a choral society—and
Göttingen, while in 1859 he was appointed
conductor of a women's choir in Hamburg.
By 1861 he was back in Hamburg, and in
the following year he made his first visit to
Vienna with some success. Having failed to
secure the post of conductor of the Hamburg
Philharmonic concerts, he settled in Vienna
in 1863. His life there was on the whole regular
and quiet, disturbed only by the ups and
downs of his musical success, by altercations
occasioned by his own quick temper and by
the often virulent rivalry between his supporters and those of Wagner and Bruckner, and
by one or two inconclusive love affairs. His
music, despite a few failures such as that of

the First Piano Concerto (Leipzig, 1859) and
constant attacks by the Wagnerites, was established, and his reputation grew steadily. By
1872 he was principal conductor of the
Gesellschaft der Musikfreunde and for three
seasons directed the Vienna Philharmonic. His
choice of music was not as conservative as
might have been expected (Berlioz' *Harold en
Italie* was one of the works he conducted),
and though the "Brahmins" continued their
war against Wagner, Brahms himself always
spoke of his rival with respect. He showed
no such regard for Bruckner, whose symphonies he described with characteristic sarcasm
as "boa constrictors." Brahms had no difficulty in understanding Wagner but did not
sympathize with his aims. Yet he was able
at length to find something in Bruckner—near
the end of his life he was seen to applaud
the Austrian's Mass in f minor, and he
persuaded Richard von Perger to conduct
Bruckner's Te Deum. Brahms is sometimes
portrayed as unsympathetic toward his contemporaries. His kindness to Dvořák is always
acknowledged, but his encouragement even of
such a composer as the young Mahler is not
always realized, while his enthusiasm for Carl
Nielsen's First Symphony is not generally
known.

Once settled in Vienna Brahms traveled
only occasionally. Like Beethoven he disliked
traveling and feared the sea; he was invited
to England to receive an honorary degree at
Cambridge but declined to make the journey
(1877). Italy attracted him—the country, decidedly not its music—and he visited it several
times. He made tours of Germany, the Netherlands, Hungary, and ventured as far north as
Copenhagen. His lack of tact and his general
dislike of women frequently led him into difficult situations; yet so far as women were concerned it is a fact that—apart from Joachim—
the two musical friends whose criticism he
most valued were Clara Schumann and Elisabeth von Herzogenberg. The latter, the daughter of a diplomat, came first to him as a pupil
but remained a lifelong friend and brilliantly
intelligent correspondent. The nearest Brahms
ever came to marriage was in his affair with
Agathe von Siebold in 1858; from this he re-
coiled suddenly, and he was never thereafter

seriously involved in the prospect. The reasons for this are unclear, but it is probable that his immense reserve and his inability to express emotion in any way but musically were responsible. He probably was aware also that his natural irascibility and resentment of sympathy would have made him an impossible husband. He wrote in a letter, "I couldn't bear to have in the house a woman who has the right to be kind to me, to comfort me when things go wrong." All this, together with his intense love of children and animals, goes some way to explain certain aspects of his music—its concentrated inner reserve that hides and sometimes dams powerful currents of feeling.

Brahms's last tour of Germany in 1895 was made with Richard Mühlfeld, a fine clarinetist for whom he had written a trio, a quintet, and two sonatas. Brahms's health was already precarious, and he was unwilling to discuss the matter with anyone. By the middle of 1896 he was definitely ill; in May of that year Clara Schumann died, and Brahms, in a desperate journey to Frankfurt to attend her funeral service, missed a night train, was too late, and had to go to Bonn, where she had been taken to be buried beside her husband. After this he was compelled to seek medical treatment, and his liver was discovered to be seriously diseased. He appeared for the last time at a concert in March 1897, and the next month he died in Vienna of cancer.

works Since the feud between the Wagnerians and the Brahmsians is now a matter of history, it can be seen that Brahms supplied to the art what was needed to complement and counteract the rapid growth of Romantic individualism. He was a traditionalist in the sense that he revered above all things the subtlety and power of movement displayed by Haydn, Mozart, and Beethoven with an added influence from Schubert. The Romantic preoccupation with the emotional moment had created new harmonic vistas, but it had also two inescapable consequences. First it had produced a tendency toward rhapsody that often resulted in want of structure. Second it had slowed down the processes of music, so that Wagner had been able to discover a means of writing music that moved as slowly as his

often argumentative stage action. Many composers were decreasingly concerned to preserve the skill of taut, brilliant, and dramatic symphonic development that had so eminently distinguished the masters at the turn of the 18th and 19th centuries, culminating in Beethoven's chamber music and symphonies.

Brahms was acutely conscious of this loss, repudiated it, and set himself to compensate for it in order to keep alive a force he felt strongly was far from spent. Both during his lifetime and long after his death he was dubbed a "conservative," though Schoenberg balanced the books with an essay entitled "Brahms the Progressive" that pointed out the forward-looking features of Brahms's style. But he was desirous not of reproducing old styles but of infusing the language of his own time with constructive power. Brahms's musical language bears little resemblance to Beethoven's or even Schubert's; harmonically it was much influenced by Schumann and even to some extent by Wagner—if we examine his early f-sharp minor Piano Sonata, we can also find a trace of the influence of Liszt. Indeed in this work of his late adolescence it is clear that for a brief time he fancied himself as something of an avant-gardist, abandoning for experiment the more rigorous methods of the e-flat minor Scherzo that slightly preceded it and returning to them in the C Major Sonata soon afterward in 1853. In that year he also composed a Third Piano Sonata in f minor, in which he is often more harmonically adventurous than any of his contemporaries.

Schumann was perceptive in referring to Brahms's being "fully armed"; he may well have foreseen that Brahms's essential musical nature was to remain decisively constant throughout his life. Critics who blame Brahms for not developing the character of his art fail to see that Brahms developed inwardly rather than outwardly, that it was concentration of thought that deepened a personality whose maturity was reached earlier than is usual. One of the best ways of discovering this is to study his late revision of the early Trio in B Major for piano, violin, and cello. The first version was written in 1854 when he was 21; he afterward regretted its publication and would have destroyed it if he could have, as

he did fully three-quarters of what he composed. But the accident of publication made
sure that Brahms would leave the world one
of the most remarkable lessons in composition
by a great composer: unable to endure any
longer the existence of a published work that
failed to satisfy him, in 1889 the 56-year-old
master reworked the entire trio, of which only
the scherzo escaped drastic treatment. A
study of these two scores reveals that Brahms
is able to take his youthful subject matter as
a starting point without a trace of incongruity,
now creating a new sense of breadth while
at the same time composing a considerably
shorter work. His inner concentration had developed to give him a mastery of movement
that the earlier score merely hinted at; it is
this sense and supple control of movement
that largely distinguishes his later from his
earlier music.

It is often supposed that because Brahms
frequently indicates moderate tempi, his sense
of movement was generally slower than that
of his most admired predecessor Beethoven.
But tempo and pace of thought are two different things; when Brahms begins a movement
in apparent leisure (as in the openings of the
Second and Fourth Symphonies or that of the
Clarinet Quintet), he is always able to vary
the rate of his thought in a startling manner,
often tightening and speeding it without a
change of tempo. It is a question of subtlety
in command of tonality, harmony, and
rhythm, and no 19th-century composer after
Beethoven is able to surpass him in this respect. At all periods in Brahms's work we
find a great variety of expression—from the
subtly humorous to the tragic—but his larger
works show an increasing mastery of movement and an ever greater economy and concentration.

The Four Symphonies, Four Concertos,
Two Serenades, and Two Overtures, together
with his larger sonatas and chamber works,
reveal Brahms a supreme master of extended
composition with an intensely characteristic
kind of melody and harmony in which the
organic nature of each conception is its paramount quality. To find his sense of color deficient is to hear only the sounds and not what
happens to them, to miss the individuality of

each separate composition. There is an unmistakable and highly distinctive Brahmsian way
of deploying color—his use of woodwind and
brass instruments is completely different from
Wagner's, and the sound of his string writing
is so personal that it became dangerously imitable by minor composers—but the important
thing about it is that color is deployed, not
laid on for its own sake. Brahms was less interested in what he called *Effekt* than in organic
growth, and Julius Harrison in *Brahms and
His Four Symphonies* has shown how fascinat-
ingly close is the relationship between orchestration and architecture in the symphonies.
The First Symphony, for instance, shows a
gradual brightening during its course from the
dark strife of its opening movement to the
warm brilliance of its last, and it is demonstra-
ble that the orchestration contributes as much
to this impression as do the harmony and tonality and the changing nature of the themes.
In the woodwinds the clarinet gradually assumes leadership, usurping the more plangent
oboe—except in the profoundly gloomy and
mysterious introduction to the finale, where
the oboe momentarily regains its sway.
Brahms also uses the brass with notably strate-
gic intent and success; in this same work, as
also in the Fourth Symphony, we do not hear
the trombones until the last movement. Harrison points out that in the First the trombones
play only 83 bars out of 1,262, while the first
horn is given no principal theme until the finale. In the *Tragic* Overture the trombones
are used with sparing but telling power, only
emphasized by their omission from the final
emphatic passage, which is thereby imbued
with a sense of Classical objectivity that is
deeply impressive. This kind of artistry dominates Brahms's orchestral music, which must
therefore seem uninteresting to anyone seeking nothing but surface color; but it is the
deepest, most demanding, and most rewarding
type of artistry.

As in the concertos of Beethoven and Mozart, such an attitude to orchestration proves
in Brahms to be peculiarly adapted to the
more subtle aspects of the relation between
orchestra and soloist. The Classical concerto
had achieved in Mozart's mature works for
piano and orchestra an unsurpassable degree

of organization; Beethoven had transcended them in scale of design and range of expression. The higher subtleties of such works inevitably escaped many subsequent composers; Mendelssohn had "abolished" the opening orchestral tutti, or ritornello, and if he did not believe it to be superfluous many another lesser composer certainly did. Brahms saw that this easy avoidance of a magnificent artistic challenge was essentially debilitating and set himself to recover the depth and grandeur of the concerto idea. Like Mozart and Beethoven he realized that the long introductory passage of the orchestra, far from being superfluous, was the means of sharpening and deepening the whole complex relationship of orchestra to solo, especially when the time came for recapitulation, where an entirely new and often revelatory distribution of themes, keys, instrumentation, and tensions was possible. Many of Brahms's contemporaries thought him reactionary on this account, but the result is that Brahms's concertos have withstood far greater wear and tear than many works thought in their day to outshine them.

At the other end of the scale, Brahms was a masterly miniaturist, not only in many of his fine and varied songs but also in his terse, cunningly wrought, intensely personal late piano works. As a song composer he ranged from the complex and highly organized to the extremely simple, strophic type; his melodic invention is always original and direct, while the accompaniments are deeply illustrative without ever being merely picturesque. The late piano music, usually of small dimension but wide implication, is (as Schoenberg was to recognize) among the most concentrated attainments of its kind. It is generally expressive of a profound isolation of mind and heart and is therefore not readily approachable, while its apparent overall tone and mood may seem to the superficial ear monotonous. But each individual piece has a quiet and intense quality of its own that renders the occasional outburst of angry passion the more potent; the internal economy and subtlety of these works is extraordinary.

The range of Brahms is finally attested by his choral music. His strong melodic gift made him a natural vocal composer, and his choral writing combines the commonsense solidity of Handel's with a contrapuntal skill worthy of Bach—yet it achieves total independence. The *Deutsches* Requiem, one of the choral masterpieces of its period, shows all his characteristics in this field together with an ability to integrate solo and tutti with the same kind of subtlety as in the concertos. The spaciousness and grandeur of its lines and the power of its construction place his underlying melancholy within the scope of a large, objective, nonreligious humane vision. Thus he is distinct from the self-regarding Romantic; his essential quality is perhaps stoicism.

BIBLIOGRAPHY: Edwin Evans, *Historical, Descriptive and Analytical Account of the Entire Works of Johannes Brahms,* 4 vols. (1912–36); Karl Geiringer, *Brahms: His Life and Work* (1936; rev. and enl. ed., 1961); Julius Harrison, *Brahms and His Four Symphonies* (1939; reprint, 1971); Peter Latham, *Brahms* (1948; rev. ed., 1966); Hans Gál, *Johannes Brahms: His Work and Personality* (1963); Burnett James, *Brahms: A Critical Study* (1972); Bernard Jacobson, *The Music of Johannes Brahms* (1977).

RECORDINGS: Numerous recordings of most works.

Brailowsky, Alexander (February 16, 1896–April 25, 1976) The Russian-born pianist Alexander Brailowsky was noted primarily for his interpretation of Chopin, playing a complete cycle of his works in Paris in 1924 and in New York City in 1937–38. He had been a pupil of Leschetizky.

Brain, Dennis (May 17, 1921–September 1, 1957) A student of his father, Aubrey Brain (Royal College of Music), the English virtuoso on the French horn Dennis Brain played with the Royal Philharmonic and later with the Philharmonia. He made numerous appearances as soloist with orchestras and at music festivals, where he was extremely popular. Britten and Hindemith wrote works for him.

BIBLIOGRAPHY: Stephen Pettitt, *Dennis Brain* (1976).

Brandenburg Concertos: *see* BACH, JOHANN SEBASTIAN (Köthen); BAROQUE ERA (Handel and Bach); CHAMBER ORCHESTRA; CON-

CERTO (concerto grosso); COUNTERPOINT (Baroque era).

Brant, Henry (Dreyfus) (b. September 15, 1913) Composer, conductor, instrumentalist, and orchestrator, Canadian-born Henry Brant was making homemade instruments on which to play his own music at the age of eight. In 1929 he moved to New York City, where he studied composition with Leonard Mannes at the Institute of Musical Art and with Rubin Goldmark at the Juilliard School. He later studied privately with Wallingford Riegger (1930–31) and George Antheil (1934–35). During this time he arranged music for André Kostelanetz and Benny Goodman and wrote his own scores for radio and film. He taught composition and orchestration at Columbia University (1945–52), Juilliard (1947–54), and Bennington College (since 1957), where his students collaborate on the production of one large work. An early proponent of Ives, Brant adopted the Ivesian technique of using several spaced orchestras, often with different timbres and styles, each with its own conductor, in a single composition. After 1953 he used this antiphonal effect in all his major compositions in the belief that it portrayed the "layered insanities and multi-directional assaults of contemporary life on the spirit." These ideas are elaborated in the essay "Space as an Essential Aspect of Musical Composition" (1967).

Brant wrote for orchestra, chorus, soloists, and theater. An accomplished flutist, his *Angels and Devils* (1931) is a flute concerto with an orchestra of ten piccolos, flutes, and alto flutes. *Music for a Five and Dime Store* (1931) uses the sounds of kitchen implements; *Origins* (1952) calls for an orchestra of pitched and unpitched percussion instruments; and the antiphonal pieces are best represented by *Millennium 2* (1954), *The Grand Universal Circus* (1956), and *Windjammer* (1969), in which the players walk through the hall while performing. His knowledge of non-Western instruments is seen in his *Machinations* (1970) for E-flat flute, ceramic flute, double flageolet, double ocarina, organ, harp, and percussion. He inaugurated the concept of controlled improvisation, in which the players select the pitches within a given framework of range, dynamics, and rhythmic character.

RECORDINGS: *Crossroads* for four violins; *Hieroglyphics* for violin; *Hieroglyphics 3* for viola, mezzo-soprano, and chamber ensemble; *Millennium 4* for brass; *Music 1970;* Trumpet Concerto (with nine instruments).

brass instruments Wind instruments—usually of brass or other metal but formerly of wood or horn—in which the vibration of the player's lips against a cup- or funnel-shaped mouthpiece causes the initial vibration of an air column; a more precise term is lip-vibrated instruments. Ethnologists frequently refer to any instrument of this class as a trumpet, but when they are made of or derived from animal horns they are also often known as horns.

A lip-vibrated instrument consisting of a cylindrical or conical tube produces only a fundamental note and, when vigorously overblown, its natural harmonics (as, for the fundamental note C: c-g-c'-e'-g'-bb' [approximately] -c''-d''-e'', etc.). Most modern brass instruments are provided with valves or slides that alter the length of the tube. This gives the player several fundamentals, each with its own harmonic series, making available a full chromatic (12-note) scale. Brass instruments, like all wind instruments, are classified as aerophones.

See BARITONE; BUGLE; CORNET; CORNETT; EUPHONIUM; FLUGELHORN; FRENCH HORN; HORN; OPHICLEIDE; SACKBUT; SERPENT; TROMBONE; TRUMPET; TUBA.

Bream, Julian (b. July 15, 1933) Educated at the Royal College of Music in England and then a protégé of Spanish guitarist Andrés Segovia, the English guitarist and lutenist Julian Bream has revived much Elizabethan lute music from the original tablature. He has also promoted contemporary English guitar works. Since his debut at the age of 12, he has toured extensively and performed at festivals in the United Kingdom, The Netherlands, and Canada. He has collaborated in recording with the English tenor Peter Pears, performing Elizabethan and contemporary songs.

Brendel, Alfred (b. January 5, 1931) The Austrian-born pianist Alfred Brendel was educated in Vienna and studied piano with Edwin

Alfred Brendel
courtesy, Colbert Artists Management, Inc.

Fischer. He has recorded the complete piano works of Beethoven and of Schubert as well as extensive repertoire by Mozart, Liszt, Brahms, and 20th-century composers. His book *Musical Thoughts and Afterthoughts* (1977) discusses Beethoven, Schubert, Liszt, Busoni, and Edwin Fischer.

Bridge, Frank (February 26, 1879–January 10, 1941)   The English composer, violist, and conductor Frank Bridge attended the Royal College of Music, where he began as a violinist but changed to viola, becoming a virtuoso performer. He studied composition with Charles Villiers Stanford. Bridge played viola in the Joachim and English String Quartets (1906–15) and conducted the Marie Brema Opera at the Savoy Theatre in London (1910–11), later conducting at Covent Garden and the Promenade Concerts and touring the United States. He composed for orchestra, chamber music, and songs; until about 1920 his style was conventional Romantic, but thereafter he turned to polytonality with swiftly changing

moods and intensity. He was highly regarded as a teacher and was especially influential on his student Britten.

RECORDINGS: Cello Sonata; *Phantasm* for piano and orchestra; *Sir Roger de Coverley* for quartet.

brindisi   A drinking song in 19th-century Italian opera from *brindisi,* "a toast." Typical examples are the ensemble "Libiamo" ("let's drink") in Verdi's *La traviata* and "Viva il vino" in Mascagni's *Cavalleria rusticana.* The genre reached its height in the dramatic drinking song by Iago, accompanied by Cassio, Roderigo, and the chorus, in Verdi's *Otello.*

Britten, (Edward) Benjamin (November 22, 1913–December 4, 1976)   The leading British composer of the mid-20th century, Benjamin Britten was considered the finest English opera composer since Purcell; he was also an outstanding pianist and conductor.

Britten composed as a child and at age 12 began study with Frank Bridge, whose tutelage can be seen in Britten's works. He later studied at the Royal College of Music in London with Arthur Benjamin and John Ireland and while there composed a set of choral variations, *A Boy Was Born* (1933; revised, 1958). He worked as a composer for radio, theater, and cinema, coming into close contact with the poet W. H. Auden. In 1937 his Variations on a Theme of Frank Bridge for string orchestra won him international acclaim.

From 1939 to 1942 he was in the United States, where his first stage work, the operetta *Paul Bunyan* (1941; libretto by W. H. Auden), was performed. A commission by the Koussevitzky Foundation led to the composition of his opera *Peter Grimes* (1945; libretto by M. Slater after George Crabbe's poem "The Borough"), which placed Britten in the forefront of 20th-century opera composers. Later operas included *The Rape of Lucretia* (1946); *Albert Herring* (1947), a comic opera; *Billy Budd* (1951; after Herman Melville); *Gloriana* (1953; written for the coronation of Queen Elizabeth II); *The Turn of the Screw* (1954; after Henry James); *A Midsummer Night's Dream* (1960); *The Little Sweep,* or *Let's Make an Opera* (1949), in which both the audience and the cast—mostly children—participate;

Benjamin Britten, 1960   *Camera Press*

his ballet *The Prince of the Pagodas* (1957).

The Rape of Lucretia marked the inception of the English Opera Group with Britten as artistic director, composer, and conductor. This undertaking gave rise to the Aldeburgh Festival (founded 1947), which became one of the most important English music festivals and the center of Britten's musical activities.

Preeminent among Britten's nontheatrical music are his song cycles. Among those that established his stature as a songwriter are (for voice and piano) *Seven Sonnets of Michelangelo* (1940; written for the tenor Peter Pears, his lifelong friend and artistic partner); *The Holy Sonnets of John Donne* (1945); *Winter Words* (1953); *Hölderlin Fragment* (1958); *Songs and Proverbs of William Blake* (1965); and *The Poet's Echo* (1965); and (for voice and orchestra) *Our Hunting Fathers* (1936; text by Auden); *Les Illuminations* (1939); *Serenade* (1943); and *Nocturne* (1958). His three canticles were solo chamber cantatas.

Britten's most notable choral work is the *War* Requiem (1962), a massive work for choir and orchestra based on the Latin requiem mass text and poems of Wilfred Owen, who was killed in World War I. Other choral works include the *Hymn to St. Cecilia* (1942; text by Auden), *Ceremony of Carols* (1942), *Rejoice in the Lamb* (1943), *Festival* Te Deum (1945), *St. Nicolas* (1948), *Spring* Symphony (1949), *Missa Brevis* (1959), Cantata *Misericordium* (1963), *Voices for Today* (1965), written for the 20th anniversary of the United Nations, and *Sacred and Profane* (1975).

Among his principal instrumental works are the *Simple* Symphony for strings (1925); three Quartets (1941, 1945, and 1976); Piano Concerto (1938; revised 1945); Violin Concerto (1939; revised 1950); *Diversions on a Theme* for piano, left hand alone, and orchestra (1940; revised 1950); *The Young Person's Guide to the Orchestra* (1945); and the *Sinfonia da Requiem* (1940). The Symphony for cello and orchestra (1963) was written for the Russian cellist Mstislav Rostropovich, as were two suites for cello solo.

Britten was created Companion of Honour in 1953, was awarded the Order of Merit in 1965, and was made a life peer in 1976.

BIBLIOGRAPHY: Imogen Holst, *Britten*

The Golden Vanity (1967), for boys' voices and piano; and *Death in Venice* (1973; after Thomas Mann). A leading role in *The Turn of the Screw* also calls for a boy's voice. *Owen Wingrave* (1971), another opera based on Henry James, was written especially for television.

In 1964, with the performance of his first church parable *Curlew River,* his conception of musical theater took a new direction. Intended for church performance, *Curlew River* combined influences from the Japanese Nō theater and English medieval religious drama. Two other church parables followed: *The Burning Fiery Furnace* (1966) and *The Prodigal Son* (1968). Their predecessor, the church pageant opera *Noye's Fludde* (1958), made use of one of the medieval Chester miracle plays.

Britten's operas are admired for skillful setting of English words, orchestral interludes, dramatic aptness, and depth of psychological characterization. In chamber operas, such as *The Rape of Lucretia* and the church parables, he proved that serious music theater could flourish outside the opera house.

The influence of Oriental music is prominent in the church parables. Britten's early interest in the Balinese music was increased by a visit to Bali in 1956; it was apparent in

(1965); Michael Hurd, *Benjamin Britten* (1966); Patricia Howard, *The Operas of Benjamin Britten; an Introduction* (1969); Eric Walter White, *Benjamin Britten, His Life and Operas* (1970).

RECORDINGS: Numerous recordings of most works.

Broschi, Carlo: *see* FARINELLI.

Brown, Earle (b. December 26, 1926) Initially a student of engineering and mathematics, the U.S. composer Earle Brown began his career in association with John Cage in the early 1950s. He was editor and recording engineer for Capital Records before becoming director (1960) of Contemporary Sound, a series presenting new music from the United States, Europe, and the Far East. He joined the faculty of the conservatory at Cologne in 1966 and taught at the Peabody Conservatory (1968–70) in Baltimore. Brown considers the influence of artists Alexander Calder and Jackson Pollock to be more important to his development than that of any musician, and he rejects form in favor of spontaneity. Representative works include *Available Forms I* (1961) and *II* (1962), the latter using two conductors and 98 musicians; *Four Systems* for "any number of instruments for indefinite time"; *Folio* (1952) for keyboard—individual pieces in different notations; chamber music; and works for multiple magnetic tapes.

RECORDINGS: *Corroboree* for two or three pianos; *December 1952* (from *Folio); Four systems; Hodograph* for flute, piano, and percussion; Music for violin, cello, and piano; Music for cello and piano; *Novara* for flute, bass clarinet, trumpet, piano, and string quartet; Quartet; *Times Five.*

Browning, John (b. May 22, 1933) A pupil of Lee Pattison and of Rosina Lhévinne, the U.S. pianist John Browning won first prizes in the Leventritt competition (1955) and the Queen Elisabeth of Belgium competition (1956). Browning became well known from the first performance of Samuel Barber's Piano Concerto (1962), but his repertoire is eclectic.

Bruch, Max (January 6, 1838–October 2, 1920) The German composer Max Bruch is remembered chiefly for his violin concertos. Born at Cologne, he was a precocious child;

at 14 he wrote a symphony and won a scholarship from the Mozart Foundation at Frankfurt that enabled him to study under Ferdinand Hiller and Carl Reinecke at Cologne. His first opera, *Scherz, List und Rache,* was performed there in 1858. Bruch was a conductor of choral and orchestral societies at Koblenz (1865), Sondershausen (1867), Berlin (of the Sternscher Gesangverein, 1878), Liverpool (the Philharmonic, 1880–83), and Breslau (1883–90). From 1891 until his retirement in 1910, he was in charge of a master class at the Berlin Academy of Arts.

Bruch was an unusually productive and ambitious composer. His greatest successes in his own lifetime were massive works for choir and orchestra; *Schön Ellen* (1867), *Odysseus* (1872), *Das Lied von der Glocke* (1878), and *Gustav Adolf* (1898) were favorites with German choral societies during the late 19th century. The only works to outlive him were his first two brilliant violin concertos, the first of which in g minor has a permanent place in the violin repertoire, the *Scottish* Fantasy for violin and orchestra, and his *Kol Nidre* fantasy for cello and orchestra.

RECORDINGS: *Kol Nidre; Scottish* Fantasy; Symphony No. 2 in f minor; Trios (8) for clarinet, viola, and piano; Violin Concertos (g minor and d minor).

Bruckner, (Josef) Anton (September 4, 1824– October 11, 1896) The Austrian composer of strikingly original symphonic works, Anton Bruckner is less well known for his sacred music in which the great tradition of Austrian church music perhaps reached its final and most perfect consummation.

Bruckner was born in Ansfelden, a small village near Linz in Upper Austria. His musical talent was soon recognized, and in the spring of 1835 he was sent to Hörsching to study organ with his godfather. His father's illness brought this interlude to a sudden end, and Bruckner returned to Ansfelden to assist his father as village schoolmaster and organist. After his father's death in June 1837, Bruckner was accepted as a choirboy at St. Florian Abbey near Linz. Here he spent the next three years, receiving a broad general education with emphasis on music. Following in his fa-

Anton Bruckner
portrait by Ferry Bératon, 1889
Bild-Archiv der Oesterreichischen
Nationalbibliothek, Wien

ther's footsteps, he became a teacher with various appointments, eventually receiving one back at St. Florian.

Bruckner's second stay at St. Florian (1845–55) was a critical period in his artistic life. The turning point in the transition from the life of a teacher to that of a musician and composer was probably his appointment—provisionally in 1848, officially in 1851—as organist of St. Florian Abbey. In 1856 he secured the position of cathedral organist in Linz. A few months earlier Bruckner had been accepted as a pupil by Simon Sechter in Vienna. Between 1855 and 1861 he pursued an intensive course of counterpoint, undertaken partly by correspondence and partly during his visits during holidays.

Bruckner's 12 years in Linz were filled with both happiness and disappointment. His happiness lay in his numerous friendships and in his association with the Frohsinn Choir, which he conducted in 1860–61 and 1868. He was aware also of an increasing facility in composition, particularly after 1861, when as part of a course in musical form and orchestration he undertook a thorough study of Wagner's *Tannhäuser*. This was Bruckner's first acquaintance with the music of the composer whom he came to esteem. The Wagnerian example provided a foil to Sechter's contrapuntal training and led to the composition of his first major works—the three great Masses, the Overture in g minor, Symphony No. 0 in d minor, and Symphony No. 1 in c minor. Bruckner's disappointments in the Linz years stemmed largely from his failure to find a suitable marriage partner. His many proposals were rejected without exception, and his strong religious convictions made it impossible for him to enter into any physical relationship outside marriage.

In 1867 Sechter died, and Bruckner applied for the vacant position of organist at the Hofkapelle in Vienna. His application was rejected, but he was offered a professorship of harmony and counterpoint at the Vienna Conservatory and an unpaid provisional appointment as court organist. Ten more years were to elapse before Bruckner was made a full member of the Hofkapelle, and his attempts to secure a lectureship at the University of Vienna were to be unsuccessful until 1875. The delay was caused largely by the hostility of the powerful Viennese critic and dean of the music faculty, Eduard Hanslick, who was a champion of Brahms and antipathetic toward Wagner. For years Bruckner was erroneously branded as a disciple of the latter.

The last 28 years of Bruckner's life were spent in Vienna devoted to the composition of Symphonies 2 to 9 (the last of which remained unfinished), the String Quintet in F Major, the Te Deum, Psalm CL, *Helgoland,* and several smaller sacred and secular choral works. He rarely moved far from the capital, except for visits to France in 1869 and to England in 1871 as an organ virtuoso. In the 1880s and early 1890s he traveled to various German towns to hear performances of his symphonies and major sacred works. During these years he battled against the apathy of the public and the hostility of many critics in addition to Hanslick. His pupils and others sympathetic to his cause stood by him, however, and he gradually gained recognition. They also did him the disservice of rewriting, specifically Wagnerizing, his music, so that many of his works were not performed in correct texts until the 1930s. In 1891 the University of Vienna conferred on him the honorary degree of doctor of philosophy, but the universal acceptance of his monumental nine symphonies dates only from the years beginning after World War I.

BIBLIOGRAPHY: Hans Ferdinand Redlich, *Bruckner and Mahler* (1955; rev. ed. 1963); Robert W. L. Simpson, *The Essence of Bruckner* (1967); Hans Hubert Schonzeler, *Bruckner* (1970); Derek Watson, *Bruckner* (1975).

RECORDINGS: Numerous recordings of most works.

Brudieu, Jean, or **Joan Brudieu** (*c.* 1520–1591)   The French composer Jean Brudieu was probably born near Limoges and arrived at Seo de Urgel in Catalonia in 1538–39 with four other French singers. He seems to have remained there as choirmaster of the cathedral almost continuously until his death. His only known works—a *Missa defunctorum* and a set of 16 Madrigals (some in Castilian, some in Catalan) dedicated to the Duke of Savoy (1585)—are stylistically rather old-fashioned, but the melodic and rhythmic influence of Catalan folk song gives the madrigals a particular interest.

Brüggen, Frans (b. October 30, 1934)   The Dutch recorder virtuoso, flutist, and musicologist Frans Brüggen taught at the Royal Conservatory in The Hague until he came to the United States to teach, first at Harvard University (1972–73) and then at the University of California at Berkeley (since 1974). Recordings feature his performing and conducting Renaissance and early Baroque music in the original instrumentation.

Brumel, Antoine (*c.* 1460–*c.* 1525)   A leading church composer of his time, Antoine Brumel was probably born in Flanders. He may have been in Chartres in 1483, certainly worked in Laon in 1497, and was choirmaster of Notre Dame de Paris in 1498–1500. In 1505 he went to Lyons; he was in Rome in 1513 and in Ferrara in 1520. No further record is known. His music, highly regarded by contemporary writers, consists mainly of four-voiced masses and motets, but of his 16 complete masses that survive, the *Missa Et ecce terraemotus* is for 12 voices. He was the first to apply the style of the chanson to the mass (*e.g., Missa L'Homme armé*).

Bruneau, (Louis-Charles-Bonaventure-) Alfred (March 3, 1857–June 15, 1934)   A composer influential in the movement toward realism in French opera, Alfred Bruneau was a pupil of Massenet at the Paris Conservatoire and was later employed as a copyist to the publisher Georges Hartmann. His earliest works included three choral symphonies and an opera *Kérim* (1887). In 1888 he met Émile Zola, who became a close friend and whose works provided the librettos for eight operas. The first, *Le Rêve* (1891) was considered too Wagnerian, but *Messidor* (1897) and *L'Ouragon* (1901) displayed Bruneau's original dramatic gifts. In *L'Attaque du moulin* (1893; after Zola's *Soirées de Médan*) and in the incidental music for Zola's *Faute de l'abbé Mouret* (1907), he achieved his goal that music "should be both realistic and symbolical." After the failure of *L'Enfant-roi* (1905) and *Naïs Micoulin* (1907), Bruneau composed the ballets *Les Bacchantes* (1922) and *L'Amoureuse Leçon* (1913) and the operas *Angelo* (1928) and *Virginie* (1931). He also wrote music criticism for *Gil Blas, Le Figaro,* and *Le Matin* and published books on contemporary French and Russian music. His works were widely performed during his lifetime; his music is noted for its dramatic aptness, and he frequently used unconventional dissonances for dramatic effect. Bruneau's works also include a Requiem (1896) and songs.

bugle   A wind instrument sounded by the vibration of the lips against a cup mouthpiece. As a modern military signaling instrument it dates from *c.* 1750, when Hanoverian jäger (light infantry) battalions adopted the semicircular copper horn with widely expanding bore used by the *Flügelmeister,* an official of the hunt. English light infantry did the same, the German flugelhorn, or horn, taking the name bugle horn (from Old French *bugle,* derived from the Latin *buculus,* meaning "bullock"). This early semicircular bugle was pitched in C or D, often lowered to B by a coiled crook. From *c.* 1800 it was once-looped in trumpet shape; the British design, twice-coiled with narrow bell, became official in 1858.

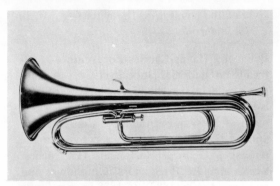

single-valved bugle   *courtesy, C. G. Conn, Ltd.*

Bugle calls require only the second to sixth notes of the natural harmonic series, written c′ -g′ -c″ -e″ -g″ but sounding a tone lower.

The popularity of the bugle horn at the end of the 18th century is reflected both in the publication of many bugle marches with military band and in the featuring of the instrument in light opera. In 1810 Joseph Halliday patented the key, or Royal Kent, bugle with six brass keys (five closed, one open-standing) fitted to the once-coiled bugle to give it a complete diatonic scale. It became a leading solo instrument in military bands until replaced by the cornet. In France it inspired the OPHICLEIDE, its bass version.

Valves were fitted to the same once-coiled bugle during the 1820s, the new instrument keeping the old name FLUGELHORN. Pitched in B-flat, it remains the principal treble brass instrument of continental military and brass bands; soprano and alto versions in E-flat are sometimes used with it. Modern instruments are considerably narrower in bore than earlier ones.

The valved bugle also gave rise to related instruments in the tenor, baritone, and bass ranges. Their names vary from country to country and often apply to more than one instrument. They include the baritone, euphonium, and the saxhorns (some of which are also referred to as flugelhorns). These instruments also vary in the degree to which they retain the bugle's characteristic wide bore.

Bull, John (1562/63–March 12/13, 1628) An English composer of outstanding technical ability and a keyboard virtuoso, John Bull was educated as a chorister of the Chapel Royal,

probably by its organist William Blitheman. In the surviving fragment of his Gresham lecture, delivered in 1597, Bull appears to make oblique reference to Byrd also as "my master," but this may refer to a later period. From December 1582 to January 1585 Bull was organist at the Hereford Cathedral but then returned to the Chapel Royal, where in 1591 he succeeded Blitheman as organist. He became a doctor of music of both Oxford and Cambridge Universities, though he was opposed in Oxford, according to Anthony Wood's *Fasti*, by "clowns and rigid puritans who could not endure church music."

Elizabeth I had already contributed to the cost of Bull's studies, and in 1596 she appointed him to the professorship of music in the college newly founded in London by Sir Thomas Gresham. In 1601 he traveled in France, Germany, and the Netherlands, where his virtuosity as a keyboard player was much admired. On his return to England he continued in the royal service, and although he resigned his professorship in 1607 in order to marry, he was evidently highly esteemed at court, being named "doctor of music to the king" in 1612. In 1613 he left England without permission and entered the service of Archduke Albert in Brussels; the British ambassador claimed that he was a fugitive from the just punishment of numerous misdeeds, but this has not been otherwise confirmed. Bull remained in the Netherlands, becoming in 1617 organist at the cathedral of Antwerp, where he died.

Little of Bull's vocal music survives, and his reputation rests on his extensive compositions for virginals and organ (some 150 extant pieces) published in *Musica Britannica* (1951–   ). It is distinguished less by emotional depth or freshness of invention than by an unfailing resourcefulness in devising keyboard figuration—a characteristic that helps to explain the great length of some of his sets of variations. Bull combined with an essentially conservative outlook a taste for technical experiment and the solution of unusual problems—enharmonic modulations, for example, and asymmetrical rhythmic patterns. His command of the English virginalists' technique undoubtedly had an influence on his friend and contemporary, Jan Pieter-szoon Sweelinck, the Amsterdam organist, and through him on Samuel Scheidt and the north German school.

Bull, Ole (Bornemann) (February 5, 1810–August 17, 1880)   Primarily self-taught, the colorful Norwegian violinist and patriot Ole Bull played in the musical society orchestra of his native Bergen at the age of nine. His maturity as an artist came in 1831, when he went to Paris and heard Paganini; a year later he made a successful debut there. He traveled widely, in 1836–37 giving 274 concerts in 16 months in the British Isles alone. In 1843 he made his first of five successful U.S. tours. He used a larger-than-standard bow and a nearly flat bridge, the latter facilitating the playing of passages in four parts. His recital programs rarely featured standard repertoire, consisting rather of extemporizations, Norwegian folk music, and his own compositions, which include two violin concertos and programmatic solo pieces.

Bülow, Hans (Guido) von (January 8, 1830–February 12, 1894)   The German pianist and conductor Hans von Bülow was esteemed for his performances of Beethoven and as the in-

Hans von Bülow
courtesy, New York Public Library

terpreter of the music of Liszt and Wagner. Born at Dresden, he studied piano with Friedrich Wieck and Liszt and conducting with Wagner and Karl Ritter. In 1857 he married Liszt's daughter Cosima. In 1864 he was appointed director of music to Ludwig II at Munich, where he conducted the first performances of Wagner's *Tristan und Isolde* (1865) and *Die Meistersinger* (1868). Abandoned by Cosima, who married Wagner in 1870, Bülow continued to propagate Wagner's work both in performance and in his critical writings. He conducted at Hanover (1877–80) and at Meiningen (1880–85), where his orchestra became one of the finest in Europe. Bülow was among the earliest interpreters of Brahms and Richard Strauss and the first to play Tchaikovsky's Concerto in b-flat minor. He was admired for his performances of the Beethoven piano sonatas, though his edition of them was criticized. He died in Cairo, Egypt.

Burgundian school   The dominant musical style of Europe during most of the 15th century. In the 14th and 15th centuries, when the dukes of Burgundy expanded their domain to include most of present-day Netherlands, Belgium, Luxembourg, and Lorraine (now part of France), the prosperous and powerful dukes, particularly Philip the Good (reigned 1419–67) and Charles the Bold (reigned 1467–77), were devoted patrons of the arts who maintained large chapels of musicians, including composers, singers, and instrumentalists. Among the chapel members in the 15th century were Nicolas Grenon, Jacques Vide, Gilles Binchois, Pierre Fontaine, Robert Morton, Hayne van Ghizeghem, and Antoine Busnois. Although GUILLAUME DUFAY (c. 1400–74), the most illustrious Burgundian composer, was probably never a regular member of the chapel, he was associated with the ducal court at Dijon as a musician and chaplain.

Dufay composed masses, motets, hymns, and chansons—musical forms inherited from medieval music. His three earliest masses are in the old soprano-dominated style, in which the melodic interest is concentrated in the highest of the three parts. His five later masses, however, are of the progressive cantus firmus type, in which a preexistent melody is set out

137

in long notes in the tenor. The reappearance of this melody throughout movements of the ordinary (Kyrie, Gloria, etc.) creates a cyclic form that unifies the mass. The development of the cantus firmus mass is one of the great innovations of the 15th century and one for which Dufay is primarily responsible. The late Dufay masses also employ a head motif, or recognizable phrase, that appears at the beginning of each section as a unifying device. In these masses Dufay created a state of harmonious equilibrium between the parts. In his last mass, the *Missa Ave Regina coelorum,* he anticipated the technique of the 16th-century parody mass, in which all voices of a preexistent polyphonic work—in this case the motet *Ave Regina coelorum*—are freely used as a basis for the composer's elaboration and invention.

Despite these developments in the mass as a musical genre, however, the polyphonic chanson, or secular song, is the most characteristic expression of the Burgundian school. Its clear musical structure is based on the stanza patterns of the ballade, rondeau, and virelai, written in the traditional *formes fixes* of French poetry. Early in the 15th century composers shifted their attention from the intricate and lengthy ballade to the simpler and more concise rondeau. This shift reflects the general tendency toward greater simplicity, brevity, and naturalness in the Burgundian chanson. Typically the chanson is dominated by the vocal top part in which the melodic interest is greatest. Of the two lower parts the instrumental tenor is the most important, for it provides the main harmonic support for the soprano. In several Dufay chansons the tenor also has a text and a share of the melodic interest. Gilles Binchois (*c.* 1400–60) was the consummate master of the chanson; he composed more than 50 examples, most of them rondeaux. By organizing the chanson around a series of tonally related cadences, Binchois established a hierarchy of structure and new unity within a small form.

The Burgundian composers synthesized French form and polyphony with the English predilection for full sonority, which was brought to their awareness largely through the music of English composers (such as John

Dunstable), several of whom spent time on the Continent. With this synthesis the Burgundians created a refined, courtly art in the early Renaissance.

Burleigh, Henry (Thacker) (December 2, 1866–September 12, 1949) Influenced as a student by Dvořák, the U.S. singer and composer Henry Burleigh pioneered in bringing attention to Negro spirituals as an art form. He is best remembered for a version of the popular spiritual "Deep River." A choir director and organist in several New York City churches, he received the Spingarn medal from the National Association for the Advancement of Colored People in 1916.

Burney, Charles (April 7, 1726–April 12, 1814) The foremost music historian of his time in England, Charles Burney was also an organist and composer. He attended Chester Free School (1739–42) and returned to his birthplace Shrewsbury, where he assisted his half-brother, a church organist, and learned violin and French from Nicola Matteis. In 1744 he began a musical apprenticeship with Arne at Drury Lane in London, where he later collaborated with David Garrick. After two years he was engaged as domestic maestro and companion by Fulke Greville. He married Esther Sleepe (their daughter was the novelist Fanny Burney) in June 1749, became organist at St. Dionis' Backchurch in October, and that winter succeeded John Stanley as organist and harpsichordist of the concerts at the King's Arms, Cornhill. During 1749 Burney became a Freeman of the Musicians' Company. Because of serious illness Burney left London in 1751 and settled in King's Lynn, where he served as organist at St. Margaret's Church. But his activities demanded the larger arena of London, and he returned there early in 1760. In 1762 Burney's wife died; five years later he secretly married Mrs. Stephen Allen, widow of a wealthy merchant. He was elected to the Society of Arts in 1764, was appointed to positions in the king's musical establishment in 1767 and 1774, obtained a doctorate at Oxford in 1769, and became a fellow of the Royal Society in 1774.

In 1770 Burney toured France and Italy, collecting materials for a projected history of music. A similar visit to the Netherlands, Germany, and Austria followed in 1772. On his return he devoted to his *General History of Music* every moment he could spare from teaching. His final appointment was as organist at Chelsea Hospital from 1783. Burney virtually retired in 1805 and returned to his *Memoirs,* begun in 1782. He was granted a king's pension in 1806 and in 1810 became a correspondent of the Institut de France. He died at Chelsea, Middlesex.

Burney was a practicing musician, but his ambition was for success as a writer. Most of his publications between 1748 and 1770 were musical compositions—chamber music for various instrumental combinations and music for the theater. During the 1750s in Norfolk he became increasingly interested in the history and theory of music, and his general intellectual curiosity was intensified by extensive reading—poetry, history, travel, and science. He was stimulated in particular by the writings of D'Alembert and Rousseau among his contemporaries.

Burney was also an amateur astronomer, and his first literary publication was *An Essay Towards a History of the Principal Comets that Have Appeared Since the Year 1742* (1769). But his first success as a writer came with the publication of his travel journals, *The Present State of Music in France and Italy* (1771) and *The Present State of Music in Germany, the Netherlands and the United Provinces* (1773). Material from these was incorporated into Burney's major work, *A General History of Music,* published between 1776 and 1789 in four volumes. Progress was interrupted between volumes two and three; under the king's supervision Burney wrote an account of the 1784 Handel centenary celebrations. A three-volume *Memoirs of the Life and Writings of the Abate Metastasio* appeared in 1796. Between 1801 and 1805 Burney wrote the music articles for Abraham Rees's *Cyclopedia* and was handsomely rewarded with a fee of £1,000.

Burney's *General History of Music* established him as the foremost writer on music in the country. It was not an antiquarian's history but a readable account, catering to amateurs as well as professionals and embodying the author's firsthand experience of music in England and Europe. What most interested Burney—and his subscribers—was contemporary music; he was an enthusiastic champion of Haydn and devoted a long chapter to Italian opera in England. Burney warmed also to early music: that he could write on the Renaissance at greater length and far more sympathetically than he had originally envisaged is evidence of his musicality and responsiveness. Nevertheless it is principally for its insight into fashionable musical taste in 18th-century London that Burney's *History* is indispensable.

BIBLIOGRAPHY: Percy A. Scholes, *The Great Dr. Burney,* 2 vols. (1948; reprint, 1971); Roger H. Lonsdale, *Dr. Charles Burney; a Literary Biography* (1965).

Burning Fiery Furnace, The: *see* BRITTEN; OPERA (the 20th century).

Busch, Adolf (Georg Wilhelm) (August 8, 1891–June 9, 1952) The German violinist Adolf Busch studied in Cologne and Bonn and then taught at the Hochschule für Musik in Berlin (1918). The following year he organized the Busch Quartet, which ranked as one of the finest chamber groups of its day. He appeared in numerous joint recitals with his son-in-law, the pianist Rudolf Serkin, specializing in cycles of Beethoven sonatas. His performances with his Busch Chamber Players (both live and recorded) of Bach's Suites and *Brandenburg* Concertos were significant steps in the retrieving of an authentic Baroque style.

Busch, Fritz (March 13, 1890–September 14, 1951) Educated at the conservatory in Cologne, the German conductor and pianist Fritz Busch began his career as conductor at the municipal theater in Riga (Latvia) for a season in 1909 and in 1912 became music director at Aachen. An admirer of Max Reger, he conducted the Berlin Philharmonic at the Reger Festival in Jena in 1918, when he also became conductor and then musical director of the Stuttgart Opera. Four years later he succeeded Fritz Reiner as musical director of the Dresden State Opera. In 1933 he conducted a season of German opera in Buenos Aires. From 1934 until his death he conducted opera at the Glyndebourne Festival, where his first complete recordings of Mozart operas were made and greatly admired. His autobiography, published in German in 1949, was translated as *Pages from a Musician's Life* (1953).

Busnois, Antoine (d. November 6, 1492) Much remains unknown of the life of the franco-Flemish composer Antoine Busnois. He claimed to be a student of Jean d'Ockeghem, and he was a member of the Burgundian court chapel in 1467, where he remained at least until 1481 and nominally until 1487. During those 20 years he held non-residential posts at Fournes (near Lille, France), as chapelmaster at Mons, at Lièrre, and in the chapters of Condé and of Tholne in Holland. He was highly regarded by contemporaneous theorists, and his name often figures in the dedications of their works. Extant are more than 40 songs, six motets, three masses, and various secular pieces.

RECORDINGS: Chansons.

Busoni, Ferruccio (Benvenuto) (April 1, 1866–July 27, 1924)   An Italian musician who attained fame as a pianist of brilliance and intellectual power, Ferruccio Busoni was also an important composer. The son of an Italian clarinetist and a pianist of German descent, Busoni was born at Empoli, Tuscany. Taught

Ferruccio Busoni
drawing by Edmond X. Kapp, 1921
Edmond X. Kapp

by his mother, he appeared as a child prodigy and later completed his studies in Vienna and Leipzig. In 1888 he became professor of piano at Helsingfors (Helsinki), and from there he moved to Moscow and later to the United States. From 1894 to 1914 he lived in Berlin, conducting a series of orchestral concerts containing music by his contemporaries and making recital tours devoted mainly to Bach, Beethoven, and Liszt. During World War I he retired to Zürich, conscious of the pull between his Italian nationality and his affinity with German music. This dichotomy affected him also as a composer, his music being compounded of romantic fervor controlled by an austere intellect and Latin brilliance and clarity. His most ambitious work was the unfinished opera *Doktor Faust,* based not on Goethe but on earlier versions of the Faust legend. It was completed by his pupil Philipp Jarnach and performed in Dresden (1925). Two other short operas, *Arlecchino* and *Turandot,* composed at Zürich, attempted to revive the commedia dell' arte in modern form. Busoni's piano works include an immense concerto with choral finale, six sonatinas, which contain the essence of his musical thought, and the great Fantasia *contrappuntistica* on an unfinished fugue by Bach (two versions, 1910; one version, 1912; fourth version for two pianos, 1921), which sums up his lifelong experience of Bach's music. In 1920 he returned to Berlin.

BIBLIOGRAPHY: Ferruccio Busoni, *Sketch of a New Esthetic of Music* (1911; reprint, 1962) and *Letters to His Wife* (1938); Edward Joseph Dent, *Ferruccio Busoni* (1933; reprint, 1966).

RECORDINGS: Piano Concerto; Piano Sonatinas; Violin Sonatas; various piano pieces.

Buxtehude, Dietrich (*c.* 1637 May 9, 1707) The Danish-born organist and composer of church music Dietrich Buxtehude was probably the greatest musical influence for northern Europe in his day. His exact place of birth is uncertain, and nothing is known of his early youth. It is usually assumed that he began his musical education with his father, who was organist at Helsingbor (*c.* 1638–41) and at Helsingor (Elsinor; *c.* 1642–71). He settled at Lübeck in 1688 as organist of the Marienkirche. There he developed as a composer and gained such fame that the city became the mecca for musicians of northern Germany. The young Handel visited him in 1703, and in 1705 young Bach walked more than 200 miles to see him. Both young men hoped to succeed the master at Lübeck, but marriage to one of Buxtehude's daughters was a condition and each found it unacceptable.

Buxtehude's duties as church organist included composing works for public festivals and for the marriages and funerals of the great merchant families of the city. He left a considerable amount of vocal and instrumental music, much of which was not recovered until the 20th century; much more certainly remains lost.

His instrumental music is simple and pleasing; though well constructed, it seldom aims at technical virtuosities. His most important and influential works are considered to be those for organ, which include toccatas, preludes, fugues, chaconnes, pieces based on chorales, and a passacaglia to which Bach's Passacaglia in c minor is indebted. The preludes are usually brief, and, with one exception, they are unlike Bach's in having no thematic connection with the fugues that follow them. Most of the harpsichord music has been lost.

The vocal music consists chiefly of church cantatas in a variety of forms, more than 100 of which are extant. Their texts are rarely liturgical; the Bible, the hymnbook, and sacred verse of the time are their main sources. All are imbued with a devout simplicity that contrasts strongly with the elaboration of their Bachian successors. It is possible that some were written for the famous Abendmusiken, concerts of mixed vocal and instrumental music held in the Marienkirche in the late afternoons the five Sundays before Christmas. These performances, instituted by Buxtehude in 1673, became the pride of Lübeck, and their tradition was continued into the 19th century.

RECORDINGS: Cantatas; Clavier Suites (19); Magnificat; organ music; Sonata in F Major for four viols and continuo; Sonatas for violin and gamba.

Byrd, William (1543–July 4, 1623) The greatest English composer of the age of Shakespeare, William Byrd excelled in music that was religious in character but that possessed a power and originality transcending the purely liturgical.

Of Byrd's origins and early life virtually nothing is known; he may have been born in Lincolnshire, and he was a pupil and protégé of Tallis. Byrd's first authenticated appointment was as organist at Lincoln Cathedral in 1563. In 1572 he moved to London to assume his post as a gentleman of the Chapel Royal, in which he shared the duties of organist with Tallis.

The close personal and professional relationship between the two men had important musical consequences. In 1575 Elizabeth I granted them a monopoly for the printing, publishing, importing, and sale of music and the printing of music paper. The first work under their imprint appeared in that year—a collection of *Cantiones Sacrae* dedicated to the queen; of the 34 motets it contained Tallis contributed 16 and Byrd 18.

In 1577 Byrd moved to Harlington, Middlesex, where he and his family lived for the next 15 years. As a devout and lifelong Roman Catholic, he probably preferred the greater privacy of living outside London. Yet in spite

William Byrd
*engraving by Nicola Francesco Haym,
after a portrait by Gerard van der Gucht
courtesy, trustees of the British Museum
photograph, J. R. Freeman & Co., Ltd.*

of his close social contact with many other Catholics, some of whom were certainly implicated in treasonable activities, his own loyalty to the government was never questioned.

Tallis died in 1585, and so in the following year did Byrd's first wife, Juliana. These sad events may have prompted him to set his musical house in order, for in the next three years he published four collections of his own music: *Psalmes, Sonets, and songs of Sadness and pietie* (1588), *Songs of sundrie natures* (1589), and two additional books of *Cantiones Sacrae* (1589 and 1591). The two secular volumes were dedicated, respectively, to Sir Christopher Hatton, the lord chancellor, and to Lord Hunsdon, the lord chamberlain and first cousin to the queen. Both volumes of motets were dedicated to prominent Catholics: the Earl of Worcester, a friend and patron of Byrd's whose loyalty to the crown was unimpeachable, and Lord Lumley, who was then again in favor after being deeply implicated in the Ridolfi plot (1571). Also in 1591 a manuscript volume of Byrd's keyboard music was prepared for "my Ladye Nevell" (probably Rachel, wife of Sir Edward Nevill), while many more keyboard pieces found their way into the volume known as the *Fitzwilliam Virginal Book,* copied by another well-known Catholic, Francis Tregian, during his imprisonment in the Fleet.

In 1592 or 1593 Byrd moved with his family to Stondon Massey, Essex, and despite prolonged litigation he lived there for the remainder of his life. At the accession of James I the Catholics' prospects temporarily brightened, and this probably prompted Byrd's next three publications. In his three masses and two books of *Gradualia* (1605 and 1607) he attempted to provide a basic liturgical repertoire, consisting of music for the ordinary of the mass and for the proper of all main feasts. It is significant that the dedicatees of both books of *Gradualia* were prominent Catholics ennobled within the first years of James's reign: the Earl of Northampton and Lord Petre of Writtle, another close friend of Byrd's. One further publication came from Byrd, the *Psalmes, Songs and Sonnets* of 1611, containing sacred and secular music in English.

Byrd's musical stature can hardly be over-rated. He wrote extensively for every medium then available except, it seems, the lute. His virginal and organ music brought the English keyboard style to new heights and pointed the way to the achievements of John Bull, Giles Farnaby, Gibbons, and Thomas Tomkins. In music for viol consort he also played an extremely important role, pioneering the development of the freely composed fantasia, which was to become the most important form for Jacobean and later composers. Although he admired Italian madrigals and as a publisher helped introduce them to England, Byrd's own secular vocal music is distinctly conservative; much of it is conceived for the old-fashioned medium of solo voice accompanied by viol consort, later abandoned by the English madrigalists with Morley (Byrd's pupil) at their head. Byrd sometimes added texts to the polyphonic accompaniments of these songs, in effect making them madrigals.

Byrd's religious beliefs did not prevent him from composing a great deal of church music to English words, most of which has survived only in manuscript. Although this is of generally high quality, it cannot be denied that Byrd maintained his highest consistent level in his Latin sacred music. Of this the 1589 and 1591 sets of *Cantiones Sacrae* (mostly designed for the private education of the Catholic circles Byrd moved in and therefore unrestricted by liturgical considerations) have an intensity unrivaled in England and a breadth of scale unknown on the Continent. Although the *Gradualia* are necessarily more concise and superficially more similar to the work of Palestrina and Victoria, with which Byrd was well acquainted, closer examination reveals their real individuality as well as an astonishingly consistent level of inspiration.

BIBLIOGRAPHY: Edmund H. Fellowes, *William Byrd,* 2nd ed. (1948).

RECORDINGS: *Ave Verum Corpus; Cantiones Sacrae* in 5 and 6 voices; *Magnificat; Masses* (3); selections of keyboard music, madrigals, and motets.

Byzantine chant   The liturgical chant of the Byzantine (Eastern Orthodox) Church down to the 16th century; it has survived in some monasteries to the present day. It has been preserved in a great number of manuscripts from the 8th to the 19th century; the most interesting is that written before the end of the 14th century. Before the deciphering of the notation and the transcription of the main body of Byzantine liturgical chant in the second quarter of the 20th century, Byzantine music was believed to derive from ancient Greek music. This misapprehension was furthered by the fact that Byzantine theorists applied the speculations of Greek and Hellenistic mathematicians to their own chant, though according to Nicolas Mesarites (*c.* 1200) in his description of the Church of the Holy Apostles at Constantinople the teaching of singing was in practice independent of Greek theory.

In fact Byzantine chant, like Western chant, is derived in the main from that of the Syro-Palestinian liturgy, which had inherited the practice of the Jewish synagogue, and is in no way connected with classical Greek music. The earliest example in style of Byzantine music is the famous Oxyrhynchus hymn to the Trinity (late 3rd century) that formerly was considered as the last document of Greek music. It is written on a strip of papyrus in the letter notation ascribed to Alypius.

melodic structure The 20th-century deciphering of the notation and transcription of the chants led to the discovery of the principle of Byzantine musical composition. It is now seen that each melody consists of a number of melodic formulas. They are the archetypes from which the musician worked. His creative activity consisted in adapting the formulas to the text and in composing connecting passages. The formulas were divided into eight groups, each of which represented a certain mode *(Echos)*. This principle of melodic construction was taken over from the Syrian Church. There it was the custom to sing in cycles of eight weeks a repertoire of hymns in all eight modes, each week being assigned to a single mode. This custom derived from Gnostic calendaric speculations and can be traced back to Babylonian cosmology; it caused late Neoplatonic theorists to identify the Byzantine modes with the ancient Greek *echoi* and to attribute to each of the scales a certain quality of mood. These theorists over-

looked the fact that in Greek scales the division into tones and semitones runs downward, whereas in Byzantine scales, as in medieval modes, it runs upward. The *Echos* theory of the Greek philosophers cannot therefore be applied to the Byzantine modes. At the beginning of the melody the mode was indicated by the Greek numerals one to four and their plagal correspondents.

notation Like Western musical notation Byzantine notation is a system of neumes based in the main on the prosodic signs of the Greek grammarians. Its first phase is the ekphonetic notation, designed to indicate the correct cantillation (chanting) of the lessons without giving any pitch; it occurs fully developed in 8th-century manuscripts and has remained unchanged. The earliest musical manuscripts date from the 9th century. In these the notation is primarily intended to guide the singers in performing correctly chants they have memorized. The signs indicated the rise and fall of the melody but not the exact intervals. They fixed the rhythmic nuances and showed the signs to be accentuated, prolonged, and shortened. In the 11th century, when many of the old hymns were replaced by new ones, it became necessary to give clearer indications. Some signs were added and others interpreted in a different way in order to mark the intervals. The third stage, beginning about 1200, was the adaptation of the approximate interval values into exact ones. Finally, at the beginning of the 14th century, supplementary signs were added in red ink to indicate the correct execution of groups of notes. Thus the system of Byzantine neumes was from the earliest times more precise than that of the Gregorian chant in indicating the rhythmic nuances of the melodies, and in its later stages as precise as Western staff notation in giving the size of the intervals.

However, the system was a complex one. In the 17th and 18th centuries, when the art of Byzantine chanting gradually decayed, the signs were no longer understood, and the neo-Hellenic notation introduced by Chrysanthus of Madytus in his *Theoretikon mega* (1832) is an artificially simplified version for the modern printed hymnbooks.

Literal transcriptions can be made only

from manuscripts written after 1200, because in these the exact pitch is clearly indicated. Yet it is obvious from the similarity between the later, more elaborate and the earlier, simpler notation that the shape of the syllabic melodies remained almost unaltered from the 10th to the 15th century, whereas from the 13th century on the melismatic chants increased their coloraturas so abundantly that the words became incomprehensible, and the original shape of the melodies could hardly be recognized. Some 18th-century *stichera* (*sticheron* is a short hymn following a verse from the Psalms), however, preserved the 13th-century shape of the melodies.

types of hymn The earliest form of Byzantine hymn was the *troparion,* a short stanza inserted after each of the last six, or three, verses of a psalm. Composition of *troparia* independent of a psalm originated in the time of Emperor Leo I (457–474). Anthimus and Timocles are mentioned as the first hymn writers, soon to be followed by a great number of poet-musicians who were the authors of innumerable *troparia.* In the 6th century Sophronius, Patriarch of Jerusalem (634–638), wrote cycles for Christmas and for Good Friday, each consisting of 12 *troparia.*

In the same century a composite form appeared, the kontakion, a poetical homily that in its content, poetical form, and dramatic character is derived from Syriac poetry. The greatest master of the kontakion was Romanos, a Syrian who went to Constantinople during the reign of Anastasius I (491–518) and composed several hundred kontakia in Greek. He is possibly the poet-composer of the most famous hymn of the Greek Church, the Akathistos hymn for the feast of the Annunciation. None of the surviving kontakia is earlier than the late 13th century, and the melodies are of a richly melismatic type. It is doubtful if they are the original melodies, for the words of the hymns, mostly by Romanos, are of such quality that they were certainly chanted originally in a simple way, as were the lessons. It is possible that there is a liturgical reason for the increase in ornamentation. After the Trullan Council (691–692) preaching became an obligatory part of the service, and the kontakion, the sung homily, became superfluous

and fell out of use. This is why only the proemium and first stanza are included in the later collections but have more extended melodies. The Akathistos, however, has an exceptional position; all 25 stanzas are still sung.

Toward the end of the 7th century a new form, the *kanōn,* came into being. Though poetically inferior to the kontakion, it was in its form and content such a perfect expression of Byzantine piety that *kanōn* singing holds an important place in the liturgy to the present day. The first *kanōn* writers, Andrew of Crete, John of Damascus, and Cosmas of Jerusalem, came from the monasteries at Jerusalem; a second group, writing in the 8th and 9th centuries, belonged to the Studios monastery in Constantinople during the worst days of iconoclasm. There was also the nun Kasia (b. *c.* 810), a gifted poetess known for her monostrophic poems. In the 11th century St. Nilus founded the monastery of Grottaferrata near Rome, and south Italian and Sicilian *kanōn* writing flourished for another century.

In the heyday of the Byzantine Empire the office was so rich in hymns that a great orientalist speaks of the "ivy of poetry" that overgrew the liturgy. Now that so great a part of Byzantine chant has been transcribed, it has become clear that it is in no way inferior to Western chant and that it is no less impressive than Byzantine visual art.

secular Byzantine music Music also played a great part in the ceremonial life of the emperor. Wherever he went he was greeted by the acclamations of the two factions, the Blues and the Greens. Acclamations were chanted when he appeared at the hippodrome and when he and the patriarch went to church. Portable organs were carried in processions; they were played during meals and in the hippodrome, but they were never taken into the church. In 1880 S. Lambros discovered a collection of folk songs in an Iviron manuscript on Mount Athos written by Athanasios Kapetanos between 1650 and 1670. The melodies, written in late Byzantine (Koukouzelian) notation, the only document from these days, are of the same type as neo-Greek folk songs.

BIBLIOGRAPHY: S. G. Hatherly, *A Treatise on Byzantine Music* (1892; reprint, 1977); Henry J. Tillyard, *Byzantine Music and Hym-*

nography (1923; reprint, 1976); Egon Wellesz, *A History of Byzantine Music and Hymnography,* 2nd ed. (1961), and, with Milos Velimirovic, eds., *Studies in Eastern Chant,* 3 vols. (1966–73); Oliver Strunk, *Essays on Music in the Byzantine World* (1977).

C

cabaletta   Originally an operatic aria based on a simple animated rhythm and later the concluding section of an operatic aria, usually at the end of an act. The term is derived from the diminutive of the Italian *cobola,* "a couplet." An early example is "Le belle immagini" in Gluck's *Paride ed Elena* (1770). In 19th-century Italian opera it signifies either a short aria in quick tempo with repeats, of which there are examples in the operas of Rossini, or a brilliant conclusion to an aria such as Violetta's "Sempre libera degg'io" in Verdi'a *La Traviata.*

Caballé, Montserrat (b. April 12, 1933)   Reputed for both bel canto and dramatic roles, the Spanish soprano Montserrat Caballé studied at the conservatory in Barcelona and made her debut at the Municipal Theater in Basel, Switzerland, in 1957, where she sang Mimi in Puccini's *La Bohème.* Arriving in the Americas in 1964, she sang in Mexico City and the following year made her New York Metropolitan Opera debut as Marguérite in Gounod's *Faust.* Possessed of an exceptionally clear voice, she also sings recitals and appears as soloist with orchestras. She claims that her favorite role is Richard Strauss's *Salome.*

Cabanilles, Juan Bautista (José) (baptized September 6, 1644–April 20, 1712)   The last notable representative of the 16th- and 17th-century Spanish school of organ composers, Juan Bautista Cabanilles spent his adult life as organist of the Valencia Cathedral. He was appointed on May 15, 1665, following the death of his predecessor and teacher, Jerónimo de la Torre, and, as his position required, was ordained a priest in 1668. He appears to have traveled little, although his reputation spread as far as France, where he is known to have played. His surviving works include a huge number of pieces for organ and other keyboard instruments: *tientos, tocatas, versos, pasacalles, gallardas.* These contain many interesting features, for example the brilliant figuration of the *tocatas* and the dissonances of the *tientos de falsas,* but Cabanilles was content to extend Renaissance techniques without wholeheartedly accepting the new Baroque style.

Cabezón, Antonio de, last name also spelled Cabeçon (*c.* 1508–March 26, 1566)   The first important Spanish keyboard composer and one of the earliest of the great keyboard virtuoso-composers, Antonio de Cabezón became blind in infancy. In 1526 he became organist to the Empress Isabel and in January 1548 was appointed organist to Philip II. From 1548 to 1551 Cabezón accompanied Philip's court to Italy, Germany, and the Low Countries, going to England in 1554 for Philip's marriage to Queen Mary and remaining there until 1556, when he returned to Spain.

The bulk of Cabezón's surviving music was published in two books, the *Libro de cifra nueva* (1557) of Luys Venegas de Henestrosa and the *Obras de música para tecla, arpa, y vihuela de Antonio Cabeçon* (1578). Both books are printed in *cifra nueva* ("new tablature") and specify the keyboard, harp, or vihuela (the Spanish form of the lute) although clearly designed for organ or harpsichord. The first volume consists of about 40 pieces, including *tientos,* hymn verses, and a number of dances. The *Obras de música* includes *tientos,* hymn verses, verses of each of the psalm tones and their *fabordones,* Magnificat verses, Kyrie verses, variations and divisions, and nearly 50 sets of divisions on chansons and motets by leading continental composers. A few vocal pieces have survived.

An influential figure in the history of keyboard music, Cabezón's work represents a bridge between the forms of the 15th and 16th centuries as well as between the somewhat stereotyped German keyboard style of the early 1500s and the smoother, more international style of writing that was emerging toward the middle of the 16th century.

RECORDINGS: *Obras de música para tecla, arpa, y vihuela.*

caccia   A setting of a text realistically describing a hunt or similar event. The musical

145

form originated in France about 1300 under the name *chace* and later was adopted in Italy. The French *chace* was a three-part vocal canon; the Italian *caccia* ("hunt") was a canon for two voices accompanied by an independent instrumental tenor. Polyphonic compositions with similar texts occur in Italy and France up to the late 16th century, but these lack the canonic and other formal features of the 14th-century caccia. The English word CATCH, a type of round, may be derived from caccia.

Caccini, Giulio, sometimes called Giulio Roman (*c.* 1550–December 1618) An Italian singer and composer, Giulio Caccini was a member of the Florentine society of musicians and poets, the camerata. His songs helped to establish and disseminate the new monodic music introduced in Italy about 1600. Little is known of his early years. He was born in Rome, but Florence, where he lived from at least 1579, was the scene of his triumphs. During the last 20 years of the 16th century, while playing and singing in court masques (for some of which he composed music), he perfected the new conception of song that he revealed to the world in *Le Nuove Musiche* (1602). This consists mainly of solo madrigals and arias, preceded by an important explanatory preface (Eng. trans. in O. Strunk, *Source Readings in Music History,* 1952). The madrigals show his new manner most clearly: an elegant and pliable vocal line, scrupulously following the inflections of the words and heightened by affective embellishments, stands out against a subdued chordal accompaniment in diatonic harmony improvised from the newly invented basso continuo. During the next 30 years many other Italian composers took up the fashion for monodies, and Caccini himself produced two more collections. He also produced an opera in 1600 (performed Florence, 1602) on the same libretto as Jacopo Peri's *Euridice,* to which it is markedly inferior. Caccini's was essentially a lyrical, undramatic talent. He died in Florence and was buried there on December 10, 1618.

cadence The approach to the end of a phrase, section, or end of a composition. Passing cadences have about the same value as commas or semicolons in prose; half cadences as colons or full stops; full cadences as paragraph endings. The word cadence means "fall" (Latin, *cadere*), and its use in this connection is derived from the fall of a tone in the tenor part that defined a formal cadence in medieval music. In later music a cadence is defined mainly by the harmony, of which the momentum is more or less momentarily checked. Important cadences generally need to be acknowledged by a corresponding slackening of the tempo.

The authentic cadence progresses from the dominant (V) to the tonic (I); plagal cadence from the subdominant (IV) to the tonic; deceptive cadence from V (sometimes IV) to a chord other than the tonic, most often the submediant (VI).

cadenza A bravura passage introduced at or near the close of a movement (hence the Italian word for cadence) as a brilliant climax, particularly in solo concertos of a virtuoso character. Until well into the 19th century these interpolated passages were often improvised by the performer at suitable openings left for the purpose by the composer. They were displays not only of executive powers but also of more or less spontaneous imagination and invention. They also have a structural, in fact cadential, function in that they help to tie the movement together. Beethoven, in his so-called *Emperor* Piano Concerto, was the first to write out a cadenza, leaving the soloist no option to play another, and most composers followed his example. Beethoven also wrote separate cadenzas for his other concertos, as did Mozart for some of his. The violin concertos of Elgar and Schoenberg offer notable examples of elaborately accompanied cadenzas. A tradition of writing cadenzas for other composers' works was also well established, often in a greatly differing style from the work being embellished.

Cadman, Charles Wakefield (December 24, 1881–December 30, 1946) One of the first U.S. composers to become interested in the music and folklore of the American Indian, Charles Wakefield Cadman was born at Johnstown, Pennsylvania. His songs "At Dawning" (1906) and "The Land of the Sky Blue Water" (1908) became U.S. classics. Among his operas are *Shanewis (The Robin Woman),* produced at the Metropolitan Opera in 1918 and repeated in 1919, the first U.S. opera to be carried over into a second season; *The Garden of Mystery* (1925); *The Sunset Trail* (1925); and *A Witch of Salem* (1926). Other compositions include a cantata, *The Vision of Sir Launfal; American* Suite for strings; *Thunderbird* Suite for piano; *Huckleberry Finn* Overture; and *The Willow Tree* (1931), the first U.S. opera written for radio. Cadman was one of the founders of the Hollywood Bowl.

Cage, John (b. September 5, 1912) A U.S. composer whose work and revolutionary ideas profoundly influenced mid-20th century music, John Cage studied with three of the leading innovative composers of the century, Schoenberg, Henry Cowell, and Edgard Varèse. While teaching in Seattle (1936–38) he experimented with works for percussion ensemble and for the dance (in collaboration with the choreographer Merce Cunningham). His music gained an early adherent in David Tudor, a pianist with whom Cage toured extensively and who performed Cage's pieces for prepared piano (the piano was prepared by having objects placed on its strings to produce novel sound effects). Cage also experimented with tape recorders, record players, and radios in his effort to step outside the bounds of Western music and of individual self-expression.

Cage turned to Zen and other non-European philosophies for enlightenment and concluded that all activities that make up music must be seen as part of a single natural process. His aim was to encourage audiences to use their ears as funnels rather than as filters, to take note of all sonic phenomena rather than just the pitches selected by a composer. To this end he cultivated the principle of indeterminism. He uses a number of devices to ensure randomness and thus to eliminate any element of personal taste on the part of the performer: unspecified instruments and numbers of performers, freedom of duration of sounds and

entire pieces, inexact notation, and sequences of events determined by random means such as by consultation with the Chinese *I Ching,* or "Classic of Changes." In his later works he has extended these freedoms over other media so that a performance of *HPSCHD* for 1–7 harpsichordists, 1–51 tape recorders (completed in 1968 with Lejaren Hiller) might include a light show, slide projections, and costumed performers, with the audience free to wander among the instruments.

Among his best known works are Sonatas and Interludes (1946–48) for prepared piano; *Imaginary Landscape* No. 4 (1951) for 12 randomly tuned radios, 24 performers, and conductor; *4'33"* (1954), a silent piece for any instrument or combination; and *Fontana Mix* (1958), based on a series of programmed transparent cards that, when superimposed, give a graph for the random selection of electronic sounds. Later works include *Bird Cage* (1972) for 12 tapes; *Études Australes* (1975), piano pieces based on star maps; *Empty Words* (1976), a text–sound piece on fragments from Thoreau passed through chance operations; *Renga with Apartment House 1776* (1976) for orchestra with singers, commissioned for the U.S. bicentennial and based on drawings of Thoreau and on various types of indigenous music; and *Branches* and *Child of Tree* (both 1977), based on amplified sounds from plucking, stroking, or striking parts of plants.

Cage has written several books, including *Silence* (1961), *A Year from Monday* (1967), and *Notations* (1969), and is an accomplished amateur mycologist. He has taught at a number of universities and has collaborated in the production of multimedia theater works. His influence extends to such established composers as Earle Brown, Lejaren Hiller, Morton Feldman, and Christian Wolff and to numerous younger composers who find his philosophy of indeterminism compatible with the urge to create.

BIBLIOGRAPHY: Richard Kostelanetz, ed., *John Cage* (1970).

RECORDINGS: For prepared piano, *Amores* (with percussion), Concerto, *Perilous Night,* Three Dances (two amplified prepared pianos); *Cartridge Music; Dream* (viola);

Fontana Mix; HPSCHD; String Quartet; *26'
1.1499" for a String Player; 27' 10.554" for
a Percussionist; Winter Music* (four pianos).
A *25-year Retrospective Concert of the Music
of John Cage* on three disks includes informative notes.

Callas, Maria, real name, Maria Kalogero-
poulos (December 2, 1923–September 16,
1977)   After study in Athens and a debut
with the Athens Opera as Beatrice in Franz
von Suppé's *Boccaccio,* the U.S.-born dramatic
coloratura soprano Maria Callas won acclaim
in Verona for her performance (1947) in the
title role of Amilcare Ponchielli's *La Gioconda.* Her U.S. debut (Chicago, 1954) was
the title role in Bellini's *Norma.* A convincing
actress, she became a leading soprano at La
Scala in 1950 and subsequently sang coloratura, bel canto, and dramatic roles around the
world. She recorded much Italian repertoire
(Puccini, Verdi, and Bellini) and Bizet's
Carmen, one of her most popular roles. She
had a voice of instantly recognizable timbre
(not pleasing to all tastes), and she was a musician of impeccable taste. In being the first
singer in 100 years to realize the expressive

Maria Callas
*courtesy, Angel Records
photograph, Christian Steiner*

powers of Romantic vocal embellishment, she
became the prime force in the late 20th-cen-
tury revival of Bellini, Rossini, and Donizetti.

BIBLIOGRAPHY: John Ardoin, *The Callas Legacy* (1977).

Calvé, Emma, real name, Rosa Emma Calvet
(August 15, 1858–January 6, 1942)   A student of Mathildé Marchesi, the French dramatic soprano Emma Calvé sang throughout
France and Italy following her debut as Marguérite in Gounod's *Faust* (Brussels, 1882).
In 1891 she performed her first Carmen, a
role for which she became famous. She sang
at the Opéra-Comique (1891–92), Covent
Garden (1892 season, with annual return engagements), and the Metropolitan Opera
(1893–1904). Acclaimed for her acting, which
was influenced by the observation of Eleanore
Duse, she created roles in operas by Massenet
and Ambroise Thomas. Her autobiography,
Sous tous les ciels j'ai chanté ("I have sung
under all skies") was published in 1940.

Calzabigi, Ranieri: *see* GLUCK; LIBRETTO
(emergence of historical subjects); OPERA (developments in the 18th century).

Cambert, Robert (*c.* 1628–1677)   Considered
the first French composer of opera, Robert
Cambert was born in Paris and became a pupil
of the harpsichord composer Jacques Champion de Chambonnières. His first stage work,
the *Pastorale d'Issy* with text by the poet
Pierre Perrin, was performed in 1659. The
greatest success of these two men came in 1669
when Louis XIV granted them the exclusive
right to produce operatic performances. They
founded the first Académie Royale de Musique and opened with a performance in 1671
of their masterpiece, the five-act pastoral opera
Pomone. In 1672 Lully gained the royal "opera privilege," and Cambert left France for
England. He arrived in London in 1673 and
is said to have become superintendent of music
at the court of Charles II. On the French
model he founded a short-lived Royall Academy of Musick in Covent Garden. He died
in London, supposedly poisoned by a servant.

camerata   An Italian name for small academies that became associated with a Florentine
society of poets and musicians whose theories
and musical experiments led in 1597 to the

composition of the first opera, *Dafne,* by Jacopo Peri and the poet Ottavio Rinuccini. The camerata fell into three groups, the earliest of which met *c.* 1576–82 under the patronage of Count Giovanni Bardi. Although they were more conservative than the later camerata, their efforts to revive ancient Greek music were an important factor in the evolution of MONODY. The two subsequent, somewhat rival groups were composed largely of members of Bardi's camerata and were led by the composers Jacopo Corsi and Emilio del Cavaliere. Other members were the theorists Girolamo Mei and Vincenzo Galilei (father of the astronomer Galileo) and the composer Giulio Caccini.

Campra, André (December 4, 1660–June 29, 1744) The most important French opera composer between Lully and Rameau, André Campra was born of Italian descent at Aix-en-Provence. He is supposed to have been maître de musique at the Toulon Cathedral at the age of 19 and certainly held similar posts at Arles in 1681 and Toulouse in 1683. In 1694 he went to Paris as director of music at Nôtre Dame, where he was the first to introduce instrumental music into the services. Already well-known for his motets, he turned to secular music and produced his first dramatic work, *L'Europe galante,* in 1697 under an assumed name. In 1700 he gave up his church appointment and for 40 years enjoyed a wide reputation for his stage works. The opera-ballet in his hands became a charming vehicle for danced and sung divertissements uncomplicated by any great dramatic unity. His religious music does not compare with that by Louis Nicholas Clérambault or Michel Richard de Lalande but is nevertheless of power and beauty.

RECORDINGS: *Ages* (opera-ballet); Suite from *L'Europe galante.*

cancan A lively dance of French origin, usually for four women. Known for its high kicks that exposed petticoat and leg, the cancan was popular in Parisian dance halls in the 1830s and appeared in variety shows and revues in the 1840s. Its predecessor was the somewhat milder *chahut* (*c.* 1800). The cancan is in $\frac{4}{4}$ time and was at first danced to QUADRILLE

music. Specific cancans were composed by Offenbach and other composers after about 1840.

canon A musical device in COUNTERPOINT, from the Greek *kanōn,* a "law" or "rule," consisting of a theme played or sung as a single part but imitated by other parts either at a specified distance in time or at a specified interval in pitch. The opening part of a canon is called *dux* ("leader") and the following parts *comes* ("companion").

Different forms of canon include exact repetition of the theme after a given time interval (as in the round); a canon at the unison or at an interval of the second, third, or fourth, etc.; a canon in augmentation or diminution (the note values being lengthened or shortened); a canon mirror in which the ascending intervals become descending in the imitating parts, and vice versa; a retrograde, or crab, canon in which the theme is played backwards by the imitating part; and a mensuration canon with a single written part that is read simultaneously in differing mensurations, or proportions.

The principle of the canon underlies the form of the round: the medieval English six-part round "Sumer is icumen in" is in the form of a canon for four voices accompanied by a double canon. Many intellectual devices of canon were practiced by Jakob Obrecht, Jean d'Ockeghem, and other composers of the 15th-century Flemish school. In the 18th century devices of canon were incorporated in the FUGUE, notably in Bach's *The Art of Fugue* and *Goldberg* Variations. Similar devices were revived in the 20th century by Schoenberg and his followers, who made a wide use of the canon in 12-tone music.

cantata A musical term derived from the Italian *cantare,* "to sing"; a composition intended to be sung, in contradistinction to a sonata, which is one to be played instrumentally. The term is now loosely used to describe any work for voices and instruments; it may take almost any form, as is seen in application of the title to works by Bartók, Stravinsky, and Schoenberg, who have adapted new techniques to the old form.

In its earliest form the word appears in Alessandro Grandi's *Cantade et arie a voce sola* (1620), in which the individual items are constructed on much the same pattern as the strophic arias of Giulio Caccini and Jacopo Peri (*see* ARIA). The *Lettera amorosa* and *Partenza amorosa* of Monteverdi (1567–1643) are also regarded as forerunners of the cantata. The true chamber cantata *(cantata da camera),* which became one of the most important forms of the late 17th and early 18th centuries, consisted of a sequence of movements following a recitative-aria-recitative-aria pattern, sometimes with only a figured bass accompaniment, sometimes with an orchestral one. The pattern could be extended to include an overture, duets, trios, and even choruses, though the apparently choral items were often sung by the soloists. Early composers of chamber cantatas were Francesco Rasi, Giovanni Berti, Giovanni Sances, and Benedetto Ferrari; and, more famous, Luigi Rossi, Carissimi, and Pietro Antonio Cesti. Later the cantata form was taken over by the great Neapolitans, Alessandro Stradella and Alessandro Scarlatti; the latter is credited with more than 600 cantatas, and in his hands the form became one of the most thoughtful and expressive of musical mediums. Handel, Leonardo Leo, Leonardo Vinci, and Johann Adolph Hasse later contributed to the enormous repertoire of chamber cantatas; Handel wrote a large number, of which *Apollo e Dafne*—almost a miniature opera—is perhaps his best known. Although the chamber cantata died out among Italian composers of the later 18th century, an amusing late example is *Il Maestro di Cappella* by Cimarosa (1749–1801), in which the basic cantata pattern is still apparent, the whole forming a sparkling satire on contemporary operatic rehearsal methods.

In England the cantata appeared in the late 17th century as a forerunner of the strong Italian influence of the 18th century; the extended songs of Purcell are claimed as early examples. Many cantatas were composed and published in England during the 18th century by both English and foreign musicians, some as satires on the prevailing Italian operatic fashions; *e.g.,* James Oswald's *Dustcart* Cantata (1753) and James Hook's *Musical Courtship* (*c.* 1787).

Italian influence was also strong in 18th-century France, where the Italian type of cantata with French texts was introduced about 1700. Lully's rival, Marc-Antoine Charpentier (1634–1704), was one of the first to enter the field, but the next generation with André Campra, Nicolas Bernier, Michel Monteclair, Jean Baptiste Morin, Jean Joseph Mouret, and the especially distinguished Louis Nicolas Clérambault and Rameau represented the greatest period of cantata composition.

In the German Protestant states the development of the cantata took a religious turn, and the most noteworthy contributions to the form were the church cantatas, which were serious in style and purpose. Franz Tunder, Matthias Weckmann, Buxtehude, and members of the Bach family all composed numerous church cantatas, especially chorale cantatas in which a well-known chorale-melody was used as the basis for at least part of the composition. Johann Philipp Krieger, Philipp Erlebach, Telemann, and above all J. S. Bach are the most celebrated names in the history of the German church cantata; their texts frequently were provided by the highly dramatic religious poems of Erdmann Neumeister (1671–1756). A typical Bach church cantata opens with a more or less extended chorus, followed by a group of recitatives and arias, and ends with a chorale for chorus and orchestra in which the congregation may have joined. Cantata and service were closely interwoven. Some German composers, Telemann in particular, wrote large numbers of church cantatas for solo voice with varying instrumental accompaniment.

North German composers also produced many secular cantatas as birthday or congratulatory odes; J. S. Bach composed several, including the *Coffee* Cantata (*c.* 1732) and the *Peasant* Cantata (1742)—titles conferred by a later generation. Telemann's *Schoolmaster* Cantata is another example of the secular type, of which there were both comic and serious versions. In the Roman Catholic provinces of south Germany and Austria, cantatas were more often secular than sacred, for church music consisted mainly of settings of Latin texts, but in Bohemia strong local patriotism produced a thriving religious music that used vernacular texts; the charming Bohemian

Christmas pastorales form a special type of church cantata. The great Viennese composers also wrote occasional secular cantatas to German words; *e.g.,* Haydn's *Esterhazy Festkantate* (1763–64) and Mozart's Masonic cantata *Die Maurerfreude* (1785).

From about 1800 the style of the cantata became increasingly free, and the term was generally applied to any fairly large work for solo voice or voices, chorus, and orchestra from Beethoven's *Der glorreiche Augenblick* (1814) onward, though the word cantata may not appear in the title. Mendelssohn's *Die erste Walpurgisnacht* (final version, 1843) and Brahms's *Rinaldo* (1869) are two 19th-century examples. Mendelssohn combined the cantata with the symphony in the so-called symphony-cantata *Lobgesang* (1840; "Hymn of Praise"). Numerous and diverse 20th-century examples are provided in works by Samuel Barber, Britten, Hindemith, Honegger, Milhaud, William Schuman, Vaughan Williams, and Webern.

Cantelli, Guido (April 27, 1920–November 24, 1956)   The Italian conductor and protégé of Toscanini, Guido Cantelli studied in Milan and began conducting at the Teatro Coccia in his native Novara; his predecessor there had been Toscanini. After internment in a prison camp during World War II, he conducted at La Scala and made his U.S. debut in 1949 with the NBC Symphony. He appeared at the Edinburgh Festival in 1950 and conducted the Philharmonia (London, 1951) and the New York Philharmonic (1952). His conducting style was intense and precise, and he inherited Toscanini's purity of taste. He was killed in a plane crash near Paris.

Canteloube (de Malaret), (Marie-) Joseph (October 21, 1879–November 4, 1957)   A student of d'Indy, the French composer and lecturer Joseph Canteloube contributed extensively to the knowledge of French folk music, particularly songs of the Auvergne district, of which he published several collections between 1923 and 1955. He also wrote concert songs and music for piano and violin with orchestra. His larger works include *Le Mas* (1926; first performed 1929), a lyric drama with libretto by the composer; *Laurier* (1931) for orchestra; and *Vercingétorix* (1933), a lyric

drama from Gallic history. He wrote a biography of d'Indy (1949).

RECORDINGS: Songs of the Auvergne.

Canticum sacrum: *see* MODERN PERIOD (rediscovery of serialism); STRAVINSKY.

Canti di prigionia: *see* CANTUS FIRMUS; DALLAPICCOLA.

cantiga   A 13th-century Spanish monophonic song often honoring the Virgin Mary. The most famous collection is the *Cantigas de Santa Maria,* compiled for King Alfonso X the Wise of Castile and Leon in the second half of the century and preserved in copies at the library of El Escorial, the Biblioteca Nacional, Madrid, and the Biblioteca Nazionale Centrale, Florence. The collection contains the words and music of more than 400 songs in the Galician language, celebrating the miracles of the Virgin. Most of the songs are in virelai form and show an affinity with the songs of the contemporary troubadours. The Escorial copy contains miniatures of medieval musicians playing instruments and is therefore valuable in determining performance practices of the time.

cantilena   A term applied to both vocal and instrumental passages of a lyrical, melodious nature as opposed to a dramatic or brilliant one; it is sometimes substituted for the similar term cantabile.

In the late Middle Ages and early Renaissance it referred to certain vocal forms and also a musical texture. Cantilena, or ballade, style (now more generally termed treble-dominated style) is characterized by a predominant vocal top line supported by less complex, usually instrumental tenor and countertenor lines both in homophonic and in polyphonic music. Cantilena was defined by the Flemish theorist Johannes Tinctoris (1436–1511) as one of the smaller forms that usually treated love, although any subject was suitable. In England homophonic carols of the period were called *cantilenae* if the texts were entirely Latin. Rondeaux and virelais as well as ballades were set to music with this texture, as were some masses and motets. Guillaume de Machaut (*c.* 1300–1377) and Guillaume Dufay (*c.* 1400–

1474) were the most important composers who wrote in this style. It was thus primarily a French idiom in the early 1400s, though it soon surfaced in Italy in works by such composers as Corrado da Pistoia and Ludovico da Rimini.

Cantique de Noël: *see* ADAM, ADOLPHE-CHARLES.

cantor In Western Catholic liturgy, the cantor (usually in pairs) sings the intonations and solo parts of the chant, antiphonating with the schola, or choir. In the Middle Ages the cantor, or precentor, was the ecclesiastical official in charge of music at a cathedral. His duty, later undertaken by the organist, was to supervise the singing of the choir, particularly in the psalms and canticles. The term was also used for the head of a college of church music, such as the Roman Schola Cantorum of the early Middle Ages, and the singing schools founded by Charlemagne. In Germany in the 17th and 18th centuries the cantor (or *Kantor*) was the choirmaster and organist of a school or college subordinate to the rector; Bach held this post at the Thomasschule in Leipzig. The duties of the German cantor corresponded to those of the French maître de chapelle and of the Italian maestro di cappella. In the synagogue the cantor *(chazzan)* chants the service, accompanied by the choir, and leads the congregation in prayer.

cantus firmus An existing melody, such as a plainchant excerpt or a chorale, used as the basis for a polyphonic composition.

In the organum of the 11th and 12th centuries, a second melody was composed to be sung above an existing plainchant melody as a means of ornamention. By the late 12th century the plainchant notes were frequently elongated, a florid melody in quick notes being sung above the plainchant cantus firmus. In the 13th century organum gave rise to another polyphonic form, the motet, which also used a plainchant cantus firmus in the tenor, a word deriving from Latin *tenere,* "to hold" (*i.e.,* the voice part holding the plainchant).

From the 14th to the 16th century, masses and motets were composed on plainchant canti firmi, usually appearing in the tenor but sometimes appearing in the top voice in orna-

mented or paraphrased form. The plainchant melody, familiar to most worshippers, served as a means of religious symbolism as well as a musical technique. But Renaissance composers also used secular canti firmi, such as a folk song or a tenor or top line of a chanson. The folk song "L'Homme armé" ("The Armed Man") appears as a cantus firmus in more than 30 masses by composers such as Guillaume Dufay (*c.* 1400–74), Josquin des Prés (*c.* 1445–1521), and Palestrina (*c.* 1525–94).

Another cantus firmus was the notes of the hexachord (the note-name syllables *ut, re, mi, fa, sol, la*) in a *soggetto cavato* ("carved-out subject")—as Josquin did in his mass honoring Ercole I, the Duke of Ferrara (*Missa Hercules Dux Ferrariae,* the vowel sounds of which were matched to the vowels of hexachord syllables *re ut re ut re fa mi re*).

Lutheran composers of the Baroque era such as Bach utilized chorale melodies as canti firmi in their cantatas and organ preludes. Secular popular and folk songs appear as canti firmi in the keyboard variations of composers such as Byrd (1543–1623) and Cabezón (1510–66).

In the 20th century organists often improvise preludes and variations on a chorale cantus firmus. The practice occasionally appears in written compositions, as in one section of the *Canti di prigionia (Songs of Imprisonment),* by Luigi Dallapiccola.

A non-Western practice resembling cantus firmus is the use of a "nuclear melody" in the music of the gamelan, or Indonesian orchestra.

canzona or **canzone** A term derived from the Provençal *canso* (French *chanson*) and used at different times to describe various musical forms, both vocal and instrumental. It was applied in the early 16th century in Italy to an important song form preceding the madrigal and later in the century to secular pieces in a lighter vein than the madrigal (*e.g., canzoni villanesche,* first published in 1537), though works in this style were more commonly called by the diminutive form canzonetta. In the 18th and 19th centuries the term was used occasionally for lyrical songs (sometimes in opera) and for instrumental pieces of a songlike nature.

In the above cases the word is loosely used in its original meaning to denote a type of song. A more precise, specialized, and important use occurs in reference to instrumental music of the 16th and 17th centuries, though here too the form of the canzona derives from the French chanson for voices, known in Italy as *canzon(a) francese*. Instrumental canzonas are usually fairly light and lively pieces in common time beginning, like chansons, with three repeated notes in dactylic rhythm and consisting of alternating polyphonic and homophonic sections. At first they were composed mainly by Italians, who did not distinguish initially between those for the keyboard and those for instrumental ensemble. Gradually the form spread to Germany and to other countries, though Italy remained its principal home; with the emergence in the later 16th century of idiosyncratic instrumental styles, canzonas written for the two different media began to grow apart. Keyboard canzonas became more polyphonic and prepared the way for the fugue, though more than one subject was often still treated in succession, while those for an instrumental group led to the TRIO SONATA of the 17th century. Of the former the important composers are Girolamo Cavazzoni (*c.* 1540) and later his fellow countrymen Claudio Merulo (1533–1604), Andrea Gabrieli (*c.* 1520–86), Giovanni Maria Trabaci (d. 1647), and Frescobaldi (1583–1643), with Johann Jakob Froberger (1600–67) in Germany, where quite early in the 17th century the term fugue was used synonymously with canzona. Some canzonas for instrumental ensemble continued to resemble those for keyboard, but the most distinctive are those that, unlike keyboard canzonas, emphasized diversity rather than unity of texture. From the clearly defined sections of the canzonas of Giovanni Gabrieli (1557–1612) and Frescobaldi, with their contrasting tempi, meters, and rhythms, the movements of the trio sonata emerged. Toward the middle of the 17th century, when the movements were reduced to four and became longer, the terms trio sonata (more especially *sonata da chiesa*) and canzona became synonymous. Italian composers such as Biagio Marini (d. 1665) and Giovanni Legrenzi (1626–90) clearly illustrate the new tendencies. By the time sonatas were habitually called sonatas, the word canzona was still sometimes applied (*e.g.,* by Purcell) to a fugal movement in a sonata.

BIBLIOGRAPHY: Gerald S. Bedbrook, *Keyboard Music From the Middle Ages to the Beginnings of the Baroque* (1949); Gustave Reese, *Music in the Renaissance,* rev. ed. (1959).

canzonetta   A form of 16th-century (*c.* 1565 and later) Italian vocal music, the most popular of the lighter secular forms in Italy and England and perhaps in Germany as well. The canzonetta follows the poetic form of the same name; it is strophic and in an AABCC pattern. It is considered a refinement of the villanella but bears some resemblance to the more serious madrigal. It is light in mood, with a clear four- to six-voice texture, and is characterized by dancelike rhythms, some word painting, and much use of simple melodic imitation. Although Monteverdi, Morley, and Hassler wrote in the form, Orazio Vecchi is perhaps the most outstanding canzonetta composer. Though primarily secular, examples with religious text were also composed. Instrumental accompaniment and even entirely instrumental writing were frequent in the later *canzonette.*

capriccio (French, *caprice*)   A title given to various types of composition, usually implying a vivacity of rhythm and a freedom of construction. In the 16th century the term was synonymous with the vocal canzona and the instrumental fantasia and ricercare. In the 17th century Frescobaldi wrote fugal capriccios on themes of arias or to illustrate devices of counterpoint, and Domenico Scarlatti gave the title to one of his one-movement sonatas. The term was widely applied in German 18th-century keyboard music, notably by Bach. Nineteenth-century examples include a set of 24 for violin solo by Paganini and the brilliantly scored *Capriccio italien* by Tchaikovsky and the *Capriccio espagnol* by Rimsky-Korsakov. The term *capriccioso* was used by Weber and Mendelssohn to convey a fleeting sense of fantasy.

153

carillon: *see* BELL (carillon).

Carissimi, Giacomo (baptized April 18, 1605–January 12, 1674)   One of the finest Italian composers of the 17th century, Giacomo Carissimi was chiefly notable for his oratorios and secular cantatas. Following brief appointments at Tivoli and Assisi, he settled in Rome in the late 1620s as director of music at the Church of S. Apollinare and retained this post until he died.

Although not an operatic composer, Carissimi helped to satisfy the Italians' inordinate enthusiasm for opera, which was performed in few centers and only at certain times of the year. He made its pastoral or dramatic content and idiom available through his numerous chamber cantatas and his 16 oratorios, short "substitute operas" on Old Testament subjects performed during Lent when operas were forbidden. In his cantatas he consolidated the pioneer work of Luigi Rossi, but in oratorio he was himself a pioneer. Carissimi's genius is well displayed in his finest oratorio, *Jephtha,* where both solo narrator and chorus act as commentators and the latter also take the roles of opposing groups in the story. Handel expanded this basic scheme, and Carissimi also exercised influence on later music not only through his music but through his numerous pupils such as Alessandro Scarlatti, Johann Kaspar Kerll, and Marc-Antoine Charpentier.

Carmen: *see* BIZET; LIBRETTO (modern status); OPERA. (developments in the 18th century) and (the 19th century); OPÉRA COMIQUE.

Carmina Burana: *see* GOLIARD SONG; MIDDLE AGES (secular monophony); ORFF.

Carnaval: *see* SCHUMANN, ROBERT (early career) and (assessment).

carol   In general usage, a song of religious joy associated with a particular season, especially Christmas. In the Middle Ages the words *carol* and *carole* (French and Anglo-Norman) could mean a popular dance-song with pagan associations, a courtly dance or dance-song, a song of popular piety, a polyphonic song in a certain style, or a popular religious procession.

In the golden age of the English carol (*c.* 1350–*c.* 1550), the second definition covers the majority of those songs that may properly be called carol—burden (refrain), verse [1], burden, verse [2] . . . burden—but it seems to have crystallized in the early 14th century essentially as a popular religious song, a member of a European family of popular religious songs such as the Spanish *Cantigas de Santa Maria,* the German *Geisslerlieder,* the Italian *laude spirituali,* and the French *noëls.* Each of these is originally monophonic with words in a popular, direct, vernacular style; the tunes tend toward balance, brevity, and catchiness; in many cases the alternating burden-verse form of the carol is used. More than 500 carol texts survive from this period. Their main theme is praise of the Virgin Mary, the Infant Christ, the saints whose feast days are celebrated in the week after Christmas—SS. Stephen, John, and Thomas of Canterbury—and the Innocents. The close connection between carol and mystery play is shown by the two carols in the Coventry Corpus Christi plays and by the survival in folk song (as in the "Cherry-Tree Carol," not written in the set burden-verse form) of scenes treated in the plays.

During the 15th century the carol developed as the most important English *forme fixe,* comparable to the French rondeau, virelai, and ballade. The repertoire is one of the most substantial monuments of English medieval music. As in other music of the period—the Burgundian chanson, for example—the chief musical interest is not harmonic but melodic and rhythmic. At the end of the 15th century elaborate carols, mostly on themes connected with the passion, were written for three or four voices in a flexible, sophisticated style based on duple rhythm in which the dramatic nature of the words often decisively determines the musical effects. In this period (roughly during the reign of Henry VII) the composers are often named—William Cornish, Robert Fayrfax, John Browne. A decade or two later the only surviving examples of what may be called the court carol were light songs of apparently popular origin in simple versions by court composers—for example, Henry VIII's own "Green groweth the holly."

The existence of some kind of close connection between the medieval carol and the liturgy of the medieval church would help to explain the swift, almost complete, disappearance of the carol at the Reformation. In Elizabethan times there is a paucity of both polyphonic and popular-song carols, and the rift between the two extends also to the words. It is at this period, too, that the essential definition of the carol by form ceases to be valid. Significantly it was Byrd, a devout Catholic, who wrote two of the best carols of the period, "An earthly tree an heavenly fruit doth bear" (burden: "Cast off all doubtful care") and the "Lullaby Carol"; both are in the traditional carol form. During the 17th century the carol, or Christmas song as it had become, is indistinguishable from other compositions in fashionable styles. The popular carol, on the other hand, becomes merged with the street-ballad and the metrical psalm.

The carol revival began in the second half of the 18th century, when the original traditions of both popular and art carol had reached their nadir. The best Christmas hymns of the period came from the poets and musicians of Methodism (*e.g.,* Charles Wesley's "Hark, the herald angels sing"), but these lack the distinctive carol touch. The revival gathered slowly and was later enriched by a harvest of folk song (Vaughan Williams, Cecil James Sharp), by still wider borrowings from foreign repertoires, by new music to medieval words, and by the rediscovery of the rich musical tradition of the English medieval carol.

BIBLIOGRAPHY: William J. Phillips, *Carols; Their Origin, Music, and Connection with Mystery-Plays* (1921; reprint, 1970); Percy Dearmer, Ralph Vaughan Williams, and Martin Shaw, eds., *The Oxford Book of Carols* (1928; reprint, 1964); Richard L. Greene, ed., *The Early English Carols* (1935; reprint, 1977); Manfred F. Bukofzer, *Studies in Medieval and Renaissance Music* (1950); Frank L. Harrison, *Music in Medieval Britain* (1958; reprint, 1967); Erik Routley, *The English Carol* (1958; reprint, 1973).

Carpenter, John Alden (February 28, 1876– April 26, 1951)   A U.S. composer who was primarily a businessman, John Alden Carpenter studied music in Chicago and at Harvard University. He became vice-president of his father's railway and shipping business but maintained his interest in music and in 1906 studied for a short time with Elgar in Rome, continuing his studies from 1908 to 1912 with Bernhard Ziehn in Chicago. His orchestral suite *Adventures in a Perambulator* (1915), inspired by a child's view of city life, shows his gift for musical humor and effective orchestration. The piano Concertino (1917) was similarly successful. His ballets include *Krazy Kat* (1922), using jazz idioms, and his powerful *Skyscrapers* (1926), written at the suggestion of Sergey Diaghilev. Carpenter's output was small but of a generally high quality. It includes settings of poems of Rabindranath Tagore and chamber works.

RECORDINGS: *Adventures in a Perambulator;* Concertino; Violin Sonata in g minor.

Carreño, (Maria) Teresa (December 22, 1853– June 12, 1917)   Called the "Walküre of the piano," the Venezuelan Teresa Carreño was an overpowering pianist. She was also a mezzo-soprano and made a number of appearances in opera. A pupil of Louis Moreau Gottschalk and of Anton Rubinstein, she specialized in playing big works with a heavy-handed virtuosity. After her marriage to the pianist Eugène d'Albert (1892–95), her playing was said to have become more controlled. One of her most successful pupils was MacDowell.

Carte, Richard D'Oyly (May 3, 1844–April 3, 1901)   The English impresario who successfully managed the first productions of the operas of W. S. Gilbert and Arthur Sullivan, Richard D'Oyly Carte was born in London. After some experience in his father's musical instrument business, Carte opened a concert and lecture agency and became manager of the Royalty Theatre, London (1870). In 1875 he presented *Trial by Jury,* a dramatic cantata in which Gilbert and Sullivan had successfully collaborated at Carte's instigation. Carte then formed the Comedy Opera Company (1876) to produce other operettas at the Opéra Comique in the Strand. The success of *H.M.S. Pinafore* (1878) ended the necessity for this syndicate, but Carte, Sullivan, and Gilbert continued as partners. Carte later opened the new Savoy Theatre (1881), the first London theater to have electric lighting, where for many years the Gilbert and Sullivan operettas enjoyed immense popularity.

A less successful venture was the building of a Royal English Opera house, for which Sullivan wrote *Ivanhoe* as the opening attraction (1891). This attempt to establish serious English opera on a permanent basis collapsed, and Carte sold the house to Sir Augustus Harris, who turned it into the Palace Theatre. After Carte's death his touring companies, which had secured copyright of the Gilbert and Sullivan operettas, were continued in Britain and the United States by his heirs.

BIBLIOGRAPHY: François A. Cellier and Cunningham Bridgeman, *Gilbert, Sullivan and D'Oyly Carte* (1914; reprint, 1970).

Carter, Elliott (Cook) (b. December 11, 1908) The U.S. composer Elliott Carter is known for an erudite style and novel principles of polyrhythm, called metrical modulation (in which changes of tempo and meter become part of the structural design), and for a manner of composing in which the scores are perceived as "auditory scenarios" played out dramatically by the performers.

Carter was born of a wealthy family and received his M.A. degree from Harvard University, where he earlier majored in English but studied music under Walter Piston and Gustav Holst. His interest in music dated from his teens and was fostered by Ives, who was Carter's neighbor in 1924–25.

Carter began composing seriously in 1933 while studying in Paris with Boulanger. His early works were in a diatonic style that was influenced by Copland. Among his early works were choral and instrumental pieces and a ballet. His First Symphony dates from 1941, as does an especially representative work of this period, *The Defense of Corinth* for narrator, men's chorus, and two pianos. Based on a text of the 16th-century French writer François Rabelais, it was written while Carter was teaching Greek, mathematics, music, philosophy, and physics at St. John's College, Annapolis, Maryland. While with the Office of War Information in World War II, Carter composed some refined and sensitive songs.

His virtuoso Piano Sonata (1945–46) marked a turning point in Carter's stylistic development; in it he used a complex texture of irregularly cross-accented counterpoint within a large-scale framework. The Cello Sonata (1948) found the principles of metric modulation well established. The technique culminated in his First String Quartet (1951), characterized by the densely woven counterpoint that has become a hallmark of Carter's style. Both that quartet and the Second String Quartet (1959), which won the Pulitzer Prize of 1960, became part of the standard repertoire. The Double Concerto for harpsichord, piano, and two chamber orchestras (1961), which won rare praise from Stravinsky, displayed Carter's interest in unusual instrumentation and canonic texture. The conflict generated between the two orchestral groups and the great difficulty of the concerto were mirrored in the Piano Concerto (1967). Concerto for orchestra was first performed in 1970.

Probably unsurpassed as a composer of chamber music in the late 20th century, Carter continued in the medium with Canon for 3 (1972) in memory of Stravinsky; Third String Quartet (1972), which won another Pulitzer Prize in 1973; Duo for violin and piano (1974); Brass Quintet (1974); and a song cycle on poems by Elizabeth Bishop, *A Mirror on Which to Dwell* (1975).

His Symphony of Three Orchestras (1977), inspired by Hart Crane's poem *The Bridge,* was commissioned by the New York Philharmonic for the U.S. bicentennial.

BIBLIOGRAPHY: Allen Edwards, *Flawed Words and Stubborn Sounds; a Conversation with Elliott Carter* (1972); Elliott Carter, *The Writings of Elliott Carter,* ed. by Else and Kurt Stone (1977).

RECORDINGS: Brass Quintet; Canon for 3; Cello Sonata; Concerto for orchestra; Double Concerto for harpsichord, piano, and two chamber orchestras; Duo for violin and piano; Eight pieces for four timpani; Quartets (3); Sonata for flute, oboe, cello, and harpsichord; Variations for orchestra.

Caruso, Enrico (February 25, 1873–August 2, 1921) Although he made an inauspicious debut in 1894 in Gounod's *Faust,* the Italian

Enrico Caruso
self-portrait in ink, 1906
The Andre Meyer Collection—J. P. Ziolo

lyric tenor Enrico Caruso won major recognition in Milan in 1896 and at Covent Garden in 1902. He sang at the latter from 1904 to 1907 and again in 1913. His Metropolitan Opera debut (1903) was in Verdi's *Rigoletto* as the duke, and he was also noted there for Rodolfo (Puccini's *La Bohème*), Canio (Leoncavallo's *Pagliacci*), and Rhadames (Verdi's *Aida*). He created the leading tenor roles in Francesco Cilea's *Adriana Lecouvreur* and Puccini's *La fanciulla del west*. The first singer to make phonograph records and to recognize the potential of this invention, he helped create a wider public for opera. His voice had great range of pitch and dynamics, a rich low register, and an exceptional mezza-voce.

Carver, Robert (b. 1487) An outstanding Scottish composer of the 16th century, Robert Carver is known only by his five masses and two motets, including one for 19 voices, found in a large choir book compiled in the first half of the 16th century at Scone Abbey, Perthshire, and now in the National Library of Scotland. The book also contains works by Robert Fayrfax and Guillaume Dufay. From information in this volume it appears that Carver took orders at the age of 16 and

remained at the Augustinian abbey until at least 1546; after that date no more is known of him. In style his compositions are similar to those of the earlier Eton choir book.

Casadesus, Robert (Marcel) (April 7, 1899–September 19, 1972) The best known of a distinguished French family of musicians, Robert Casadesus studied piano with Louis Diémer at the Paris Conservatoire. Although his repertoire included all the basic French literature, he also played much Mozart, Beethoven, and Schumann. He composed a number of symphonies, chamber music, piano concertos, and miscellaneous pieces. His wife Gaby is a respected pianist, and his son Jean (1927–72) had established a concert career before his premature death in an automobile accident.

Robert Casadesus   *courtesy, CBS, Inc.*

Casals, Pablo, in Catalan, Pau Casals (December 29, 1876–October 22, 1973) The Spanish cellist, pianist, conductor, and composer Pablo Casals was one of the most influential musicians of the 20th century. After study at the Royal Conservatory in Madrid and a

Pablo Casals, 1971
*courtesy, Casals Festival
Organization of Puerto Rico*

ing for a session of the United Nations General Assembly, which was broadcast to 48 countries. After the mid-1950s he rarely played outside Puerto Rico or his summer festivals.

Casals set new technical standards for cello playing and was a performer of singular intensity, the latter aspect becoming exaggerated at the expense of coherence in the last two decades of his career. He was the first musician since the 18th century to play Bach's Cello Suites and did much to rescue Bach from his 19th-century reputation as a purveyor of "dry mathematics." His own compositions include cello pieces and choral works.

BIBLIOGRAPHY: Lillian Littlehales, *Pablo Casals,* rev. ed. (1948); Pablo Casals, *Joys and Sorrows* (1970); H. L. Kirk, *Pablo Casals* (1974).

Casella, Alfredo (July 25, 1883–March 5, 1947) An Italian composer, pianist, conductor, and teacher whose cosmopolitan outlook permeated 20th-century Italian music-making, Alfred Casella was born in Turin and studied piano under Louis Diémer in Paris, where he stayed until 1914. His early symphonies (1905–09) show the influence of Richard Strauss and Mahler and his later chamber and orchestral works that of Ravel and Stravinsky, but he established a more personal style in the ballet *La Giara* (1924) and in the orchestral works *Scarlattiana* (1926) and *Paganiniana* (1942). In 1917 he founded the Società Nazionale di Musica and helped to revive interest in early Italian music. He published editions of the keyboard works of Bach, Mozart, Beethoven, and Chopin. As a conductor he was Arthur Fiedler's predecessor (1927–30) at the Boston Pops. His memoirs were translated as *Music in My Time* (1955).

RECORDINGS: Harp Sonata; *La Giara; Paganiniana.*

faculty position at the conservatory in Barcelona, he was highly acclaimed for a performance of the Lalo Cello Concerto at the Lamoureux concerts in 1899; his performance career is said to date from that year. In 1901 he made his U.S. debut. He founded his own orchestra in Barcelona in 1919 to introduce classical music to the working classes of his native Catalonia, and he played in a trio with Alfred Cortot and Jacques Thibaud. A Loyalist supporter during the Spanish Civil War, he felt exiled at the defeat of the Loyalists and went to Prades in the French Pyrenees, where in the year (1950) of the Bach bicentennial he established an annual summer music festival. In 1956 he organized a similar festival in Puerto Rico, where many of the greatest living musicians assembled to play and teach. Following World War II Casals refused to play in England or in the United States because both governments tolerated Franco's government in Spain, and he also would not play in Fascist Italy, Nazi Germany, or the Soviet Union. In 1958 he was honored by play-

cassation An 18th-century work of orchestral or chamber music in several short movements similar to a serenade or a suite. Among suggested origins of the term are the Italian *cassa,* "drum" (Mozart's Cassations, K.63 and 99, open with marchlike movements), and the Austrian dialect expression *gassatim gehen,* "to go courting," which would explain the serenadelike nature of the cassation. Other contributors to the form are Haydn and Karl Ditters von Dittersdorf.

castanets Percussion instruments, perhaps Phoenician in origin, introduced into Spain by the Moors. They were used by the ancient Greeks, Egyptians, and Romans. Originally shaped like a small boot, they later resembled a chestnut *(castaña),* from which wood they were made and from which they took their name. As *castañuelas* they became the characteristic instrument of the Spanish peasantry, and their use remains a feature of Spanish dancing.

Each pair of castanets consists of two hollowed-out, pear-shaped pieces of hardwood (now ebony, rosewood, or other similar wood), sometimes ivory or even plastic, hinged together and sprung by a cord that is secured firmly to the thumb. The two halves are struck together by the fingers. The fingers of the left hand perform a simple rhythm on a larger pair *(macho,* male), while the right-hand fingers manipulate a more complicated dance rhythm on a smaller pair *(hembra,* female). In the orchestra the two bowls are attached to one or more handles and played either singly or with a handle in each hand. Another method is to secure the bowls to a block of wood by spring steel or elastic and manipulate them with the fingers or with drumsticks.

castanets
courtesy,
Ludwig Industries

Castelnuovo-Tedesco, Mario (April 3, 1895–March 15, 1968) A neoromantic composer, Mario Castelnuovo-Tedesco was born in Florence and studied composition there with Ildebrando Pizzetti. In 1939 Mussolini's anti-Semitic policies caused him to emigrate to the United States, where he settled in Beverly Hills, California, and composed motion picture scores. For many years he taught a whole generation of young composers to write for the screen. Castelnuovo-Tedesco appeared as soloist in his Second Piano Concerto in 1939 and wrote concertos for violin, cello, and guitar (1939; arranged from his earlier *Capriccio diabolico,* 1935). His orchestral works include a series of overtures to 12 plays by Shakespeare, whose sonnets and poems he frequently set to music. He also composed two Shakespearean operas, *All's Well That Ends Well* (1956) and *The Merchant of Venice* (1958). His chamber music is scored for a variety of combinations; his piano pieces are conceived as miniature symphonic poems; his songs retain the melodiousness of the Italian school; and his harmonies are opulent and often complex.

RECORDINGS: Bassoon Sonatina; Concerto for two guitars; Guitar Concerto; Guitar Sonata; Harp Concertino; Sonata for cello and harp.

castrato A male soprano or contralto voice of great range, flexibility, and force produced as a result of castration before puberty. The castrato voice was introduced while women were banned from church choirs and the stage. The extraordinary power resulted from great lung capacity and a greater physical bulk. The unique quality of the voice, coupled with the ability to execute extremely difficult and florid vocal passages, made the castrati the rage of opera audiences of the day and contributed to the growth and spread of Italian opera. In 18th-century Italian opera the majority of male singers were castrati, and more than 200 of them sang in churches in Rome. The most famous of them all was FARINELLI; the last at the Sistine Chapel was Alessandro Moreschi, who retired in 1913.

BIBLIOGRAPHY: Angus Heriot, *The Castrati in Opera* (1956; reprint, 1974).

catch A specifically English name for round, or perpetual canon, designed to be sung by three or more voices. It may possibly derive from the 14th-century Italian CACCIA but is in any case appropriate in that each singer must take up, or catch, the tune in turn. Literary evidence shows that catch singing was popular in the 16th century, but the first published collection, Thomas Ravenscroft's *Pammelia,* dates from 1609. Its success encouraged him to bring out two further publications, also containing some catches: *Deuteromelia* (1609) and *Melismata* (1611). John Hilton's *Catch That Catch Can* (1652) is probably the best known of catch collections, but the zenith of the catch came with the Restoration, when the finest composers vied with one another in lavishing ingenuity and indecence on this originally humble form; Purcell ranks supreme on the first account and very high on the second. During the 18th century, when the Noblemen and Gentlemen's Catch Club was founded (1761), catches became textually more polite and musically more insipid, although they retained their popularity among convivial musicians. Many of the best examples, however, remain in manuscript for obvious reasons.

Cavaliere, Emilio del, also spelled Emilio de' Cavalieri (*c.* 1550–March 11, 1602)   One of the earliest composers of dramatic music, Emilio del Cavaliere was a nobleman, and he became supervisor of fine arts and entertainments at the court of Grand Duke Ferdinand I of Tuscany. He was a member of the camerata in Florence, a group whose theories gave rise to the first operas. He composed intermezzi and pastorals, which stood midway between the masquelike intermezzi and true operas. Historically his most significant work is *La rappresentazione de anima e di corpo (Representation of Soul and Body),* an allegorical morality play. Important as a precursor of opera and of oratorio, it had characteristics of both. It was set to music throughout and was acted with scenery. It included texts characteristic of oratorios and, like the early oratorios, was written to stimulate popular piety. Published in 1600, it contained the earliest printed examples of figured bass. Although it was surpassed in musical and dramatic intensity by the first true operas (those of Jacopo Peri and Giulio Caccini), it was one of the earliest examples of the monodic recitative style that blossomed in early opera.

Cavalleria Rusticana: *see* INTERMEZZO; MASCAGNI; VERISMO.

Cavalli, (Pietro) Francesco (February 14, 1602–January 14, 1676)   The most important Italian opera composer of the mid-17th century, Francesco Cavalli was born at Crema, the son of Gian Battista Caletti-Bruni; he assumed the name of his Venetian patron, Federigo Cavalli. In 1617 he became a singer in the choir of St. Mark's, Venice, directed by Monteverdi and subsequently held various posts there, becoming maestro di cappella in 1668.

During his lifetime Cavalli had a considerable influence on European taste. *La Didone* (1641) is perhaps his most interesting work, but it was his *Egisto,* given in Paris in 1646, that initiated the rivalry between French and Italian styles. As a dramatic composer Cavalli ranks with Lully as a true successor of Monteverdi. His music is intended for a small string orchestra, and his operas require no trained chorus. He wrote few concerted numbers for soloists, but his works have signs of the beginnings of the formal recitative aria technique, sometimes even with a da capo section. Compensation for the level character of his music was provided by the brilliant costumes and lavish sets, devised by Jacopo Torelli and others, without which, in spite of their dramatic power and grotesque humor, Cavalli's works are incomplete. Although performed throughout Italy, his more than 40 operas were generally written for the public opera houses that flourished in 17th-century Venice.

Cavalli also composed church music that was published in two collections, *Musiche Sacre* (1656) and *Vesperi* (1675). Modern editions have been made of the eight-part *Messa Concertata* and the motets *Laetatus sum* and *Salve Regina.* These, together with several of the operas, have been part of a late 20th-century revival, though most often in tarted up editions.

BIBLIOGRAPHY: Jane Glover, *Cavalli* (1978).

RECORDINGS: *Messa Concertata;* operas *La Calisto* and *L'Ormindo;* Sonata *a* 3; arias.

cavatina   A form, the diminutive of *cavata* (from the Italian *cavare,* "to dig out"), which in early 18th-century cantatas, notably those of Bach, was a short, epigrammatic vocal piece following the recitative and preceding the arioso. In opera, with examples by Haydn, Mozart, Weber, Rossini, and Gounod, the cavatina is a song (often the one that introduces a new character) generally of a brilliant nature and in one or two sections but without repetition. The term was also used as a title of songlike instrumental works, such as one movement of Beethoven's Quartet, Op. 130.

celesta A percussion instrument resembling in shape a small piano, usually heard in a large orchestra. Patented about 1886 by Auguste Mustel, it consists of a series of small metal bars that are set in vibration by hammers operated by a piano action and keyboard. Each metal bar is resonated by a wooden box or similar chamber, the fundamental thus being reinforced. The bars are sustained and controlled by a foot pedal. Pressure on the pedal lifts a felt pad from the bars, permitting the use of short or sustained notes. It normally has a chromatic range of four octaves. The celesta is frequently used in the standard repertoire of the modern orchestra; Tchaikovsky, in his *Nutcracker* Suite (1891–92), was one of the first composers to write for it.

cello, front view and side view   *EB Inc.*

celesta   *courtesy, Mustel, Paris*

cello The bass instrument of the violin family with four strings pitched C G d a (from two octaves below middle C), an octave and

a fifth below the violin and, standing approximately four feet tall, about twice its length. In build it differs somewhat, the ribs being proportionately much deeper and the much higher bridge standing on legs rather than feet. The neck is raked back at a sharper angle to allow for the height of the bridge. The instrument is held between the knees while it rests on an end pin, which is telescoped through the tailpin and can be clamped in any position to adjust the height of the instrument above the floor. This playing position leaves both arms exceptionally free; the left-hand technique is more fluid and covers a wider range than in any other stringed instrument, shown by the ease with which a good cellist commands the brilliant solo register of the top (a) string, high above the normal tessitura of the instrument.

The name cello is actually an abbreviation for violoncello. The earliest instruments extant are two by Andrea Amati from 1560–70. The cello served primarily as a continuo instrument until the 18th century. One of the first to write for cello as a solo instrument was Domenico Gabrieli (*Ricercari per violoncello solo,* 1689), and the concerto repertoire began with Giuseppe M. Jacchini (1701), continuing with works by Vivaldi, Leonardo Leo, Carl Philipp Emanuel Bach, and Haydn. J. S.

Bach's Six Suites for unaccompanied cello date from *c.* 1720. Perhaps the most enthusiastic 18th-century exponent was Boccherini, who was a virtuoso performer on the instrument and composed four concertos and 113 quintets with two cello parts. Important methods were published by Michel Corrette (1741) and by Jean-Louis Duport (1749–1819), considered the foundation of present-day technique. Concertos, sonatas, and solo pieces for the cello have been written in the 19th and 20th centuries by many of the major composers.

BIBLIOGRAPHY: W. J. von Wasielewski, *The Violoncello and Its History* (1894; reprint, 1968); Edmund van der Straeten, *History of the Violoncello, the Viol da Gamba, Their Precursors and Collateral Instruments,* 2 vols. (1915; reprint, 1976); Elizabeth Cowling, *The Cello* (1975).

cembalo The Italian word for HARPSI-CHORD, actually an abbreviation of *clavicembalo,* derived from the Latin *clavis* ("key") and *cymbalum* (a psaltery or dulcimer): hence *clavicymbalum,* a psaltery with keys. Cembalo is used also in Germany synonymously with *Kielflügel,* the German word for harpsichord.

Cenerentola, La: *see* ROSSINI.

Ceremony of Carols: *see* BRITTEN.

Cesti, Pietro Antonio (August 5, 1623–October 14, 1669)   One of the leading Italian composers of the 17th century, Pietro Antonio Cesti was born at Arezzo and studied in Rome. He moved to Venice, where the first of his 15 known operas, *Orontea,* was produced (1649). In 1652 he became maestro di cappella to Archduke Ferdinand of Austria at Innsbruck, a post he combined for a time with membership in the papal choir. From 1666 until 1669 he was vice-Kapellmeister to the imperial court in Vienna. He died in Florence.

After Francesco Cavalli, Cesti was probably the best-known composer of his generation. Throughout the 17th century his operas were frequently performed in Italy and elsewhere. He wrote sacred and secular music, the former influenced by the Roman school, the latter by the Venetian. Though his works are too

rare for the tracing of any development of style, they show an originality uncommon at that time. Christ Church, Oxford, possesses an important manuscript collection of 18 secular and three sacred cantatas. His most sumptuous opera, *Il Pomo d'oro,* was produced to celebrate the marriage of Leopold I to the Infanta Margherita of Spain in 1667.

RECORDINGS: Solo cantata *Languia già alba.*

Chabrier, (Alexis) Emmanuel (January 18, 1841–September 13, 1894)   A French composer whose best works reflect the verve and wit of the Paris scene of the 1880s, Emmanuel Chabrier was attracted in his youth both to music and to painting. He studied law in Paris from 1858 to 1862, piano with Edouard Wolf, and harmony and counterpoint with Théophile Semet and Aristide Hignard. His technical training was, however, limited, and as a composer he was self-taught. From 1862 to 1880 he was employed at the ministry of the interior, producing during this period the operas *L'Étoile* (1877) and *L'Éducation manquée* (first performed with piano accompaniment, 1879; with orchestra, 1913). Two unfinished operettas were sketched between 1863 and 1865 in cooperation with Paul Verlaine. He was closely associated with the Impressionist painters, particularly with Edouard Manet from whom he purchased the painting "Le Bar aux Folies-Bergère."

After hearing Wagner's *Tristan und Isolde* at Munich in 1879, Chabrier left the ministry to devote himself exclusively to music. As chorusmaster at the Concerts Lamoureux, he helped to produce a concert performance of *Tristan* and became associated with d'Indy, Henri Duparc, and Fauré as one of a group known as "Le Petit Bayreuth." Chabrier's best music was written between 1881 and 1891, when he had been inspired by Spanish folk music and had settled at La Membrolle (Touraine). It includes the piano works *Dix Pièces pittoresques* (1881), *Trois Valses romantiques* (1883) for two pianos, and *Bourrée fantasque* (1891); orchestral works *España* (1883) and *Joyeuse Marche* (1888); the opera *Le Roi malgré lui* (1887); and six songs (1890). Less successful was his opera *Gwendoline* (1886).

The last three years of his life were marked by mental and physical collapse, and he died in Paris. One act of his unfinished opera, *Briséis,* was posthumously produced in concert form (1897).

With his vigorous melodic style, frequently irregular rhythms, humor, and original ear for orchestral sound, Chabrier was a musical personality of singularly sharp profile.

RECORDINGS: *Bourrée fantasque; España;* "Fête polonaise" from *Le Roi malgré lui;* Overture from *Gwendoline; Joyeuse Marche; Trois Valses romantiques;* piano music; songs.

chaconne   An exotic, sensual dance of Spain but of doubtful ancestry and etymology. At the French court of the 17th and 18th centuries it was transformed into a solemn dance in $\frac{3}{4}$ time, becoming the concluding dance of court balls. Later it appeared in the theater as an extended finale, especially in the operas of Gluck, Rameau, and Lully.

As a musical form the chaconne attained great stature. Consisting of divisions over a GROUND BASS, it and its musical twin, the passacaglia, developed along identical lines into three of the important forms of musical literature—rondo, theme and VARIATIONS, and PASSACAGLIA. A famous example of the chaconne appears in the last movement of Bach's Second Partita for solo violin.

Chadwick, George Whitefield (November 13, 1854–April 4, 1931)   A U.S. composer of the so-called New England group, George Whitefield Chadwick worked in the traditions of European Romanticism. He studied organ and theory in Boston and in 1877 went to Germany to study under Carl Reinecke and Salomon Jadassohn in Leipzig and Joseph Rheinberger in Munich. Returning to the United States in 1880, he was engaged as a theory instructor at the New England Conservatory in Boston; in 1897 he became its director and held this post until his death. As an educator he played an important role in U.S. music; among his pupils were Horatio Parker, Henry Hadley, and Frederick Shepherd Converse. He also conducted orchestral and choral concerts.

Chadwick was a firm believer in the representational meaning of music; most of his orchestral works bear programmatic titles. In his harmonic writing he followed the procedures of German Romantic music with some Wagnerian characteristics.

The list of Chadwick's works is considerable and includes Three Symphonies (1882, 1885, and 1894); concert overtures *Rip van Winkle* (1879), *Thalia* (1883), *Melpomene* (1887), *Adonais* (1898), *Euterpe* (1903); symphonic poems *Aphrodite* (1912), *Tam o'Shanter* (1915), and *The Angel of Death* (1917); cantatas *Phoenix expirans* (1892) and *The Lily Nymph* (1893); burlesque opera *Tabasco* (1894); lyric drama *Judith* (1901); numerous choruses; Five String Quartets; Piano Quintet; and many songs and organ pieces. Chadwick also published a textbook, *Harmony* (1897; revised 1922).

Chaliapin, Feodor (February 11, 1873–April 12, 1938)   The Russian bass Feodor Chaliapin studied in Tiflis (Tbilisi) and made his debut there in 1893 as Mephistophélès in Gounod's *Faust.* His success came after a private appearance in Moscow in 1897 and two years later at the Moscow Imperial Opera.

Feodor Chaliapin
drawing by Edmond X. Kapp, 1924
Edmond X. Kapp

Renowned for the title role in Mussorgsky's *Boris Godunov,* he became the first to perform the role in western Europe. His world premieres include the title role in Massenet's *Don Quichotte* and Dositheus in Mussorgsky's *Khovanshchina.* Although he was named an "Artist of the People" by the Soviet government, he left his country permanently in 1920. He was a member of the Metropolitan Opera (1921–28), where he had great success, although he had been dismissed by the critics after performing there in 1907. His voice was notable for its lyricism and also for a developed parlando style. For his vocal power and for characterization, Chaliapin is considered second only to Enrico Caruso. And, in addition to his fine voice, he was a skilled and colorful actor. His memoirs, *Pages From My Life* (1926) and *Man and Music* (1932), were published in New York City.

chamber music A term usually applied to music written for from two to nine or ten solo instruments, each playing an independent part equal in importance to the others, and generally though by no means invariably planned on the lines of the four-movement SONATA. The Classical age of chamber music began in the late 18th century with the quartets of Haydn, and the string quartet (two violins, viola, and cello) has been the favorite and most important combination ever since. But intimate music for small instrumental ensembles had flourished for centuries before Haydn.

pre-Classical chamber music The phrase *musica da camera* seems to have appeared first in Italy in the latter part of the 16th century to indicate any kind of music not intended for use in church or for a dramatic or festive purpose; it was not limited to instrumental music, and the first publication to which the English term was applied—Martin Peerson's *Mottects or Grave Chamber Musique* (1630)—consisted of "Songs of five parts. . .fit for Voyces and Vials, with an Organ Part." There was at this period still no sharp differentiation between vocal and instrumental music (other than that written for lutes or keyboard instruments), and vocal ensemble music was commonly performed partly or wholly on instruments. Yet even the Middle Ages had been

acquainted with purely instrumental compositions other than those written for dancing; a 13th-century manuscript at Bamberg contains three-part instrumental motets *(In seculum viellatoris),* and the 15th-century Trent codices have preserved at least one indisputably instrumental trio. In the collections printed from the 1530s by continental and (later) English publishers as "suitable to sing and play on any sort of instrument" or "apt for the Viols and voices," unmistakably instrumental pieces appear. The style of the ricercare, canzona, and fantasia is based on vocal motets or polyphonic chansons but was modified more and more by considerations of instrumental technique. Such are the two "Fantazias" for four (No. 15) and six viols (No. 26) of the *Psalmes, Songs, and Sonnets* (1611) by Byrd.

The favorite combination was the homogeneous consort of viols, though mixed ensembles (broken consorts) were also common. No particular instruments were specified by composers until the last years of the 16th century: by Giovanni Gabrieli in some of the *canzoni da sonar* of his *Sacrae symphoniae* (Venice, 1597) and Thomas Morley in his *First Booke of Consort Lessons, made by divers exquisite Authors for sixe Instruments* (1599).

Although the viols were gradually superseded by the violin family, and the polyphonic style was succeeded by one in which one or two melodic lines were accompanied by a bass (basso continuo) over which a keyboard player or lutenist filled out the harmony in accordance with a shorthand of figures, the sonatas of the early 17th century were still modeled to some extent on vocal prototypes. However, the development of violin technique brought complete emancipation. Just as the vocal monody was paralleled by the solo sonata, the then-favorite form of the vocal duet with continuo suggested a type of instrumental canzona, or sonata, in which two instruments duetted in the same way; indeed the duet sonata appeared (in Salomone Rossi's *Varie sonate,* 1613) before the solo (in Biagio Marini's *Affetti musicali,* 1617). The duet sonata has become universally known as the TRIO SONATA from the circumstances that it was conceived in three "real" parts and that in the course of time the bass exchanged its merely supporting function for a more active role in the thematic interplay; it became the most important type of Baroque chamber music. But while the instrumental combination remained constant, the structure underwent various changes. The connected sections of the canzona, with their contrasts of pace and rhythm, had become by the 1660s four or five separate, self-contained movements—as in the *Sonate,* Op. 2 (1667), of the Bolognese violinist-composer, Giovanni Battista Vitali. Generally consisting of two slow movements alternating with two quick ones and commonly used in Italy, like the earlier canzoni for preludes and interludes in church services, such sonatas were known as *sonate da chiesa* ("church sonatas"). Simultaneously another type of sonata derived from the dance suite was known as *sonata da camera* ("chamber sonata"). The two types reached classical perfection in the *sonate da chiesa* (1681 and 1689) and *da camera* (1685 and 1694) of Corelli, the last and greatest of the Bolognese school. But there had always been some interchange between the two types; even Vitali's *sonate da chiesa* sometimes have gigue-like last movements, and after Corelli they became so assimilated that the distinction disappeared. The trio sonatas of Handel and his generation represent the final maturity of the form.

The trio sonata was originally and essentially an Italian form. Purcell's two sets of sonatas (1683; 1697) were confessedly written in "imitation of the most fam'd Italian Masters" (in particular, Vitali); and although trio sonatas had been published in Germany (*e.g.,* by Johann Pachelbel and Buxtehude in the 1690s) the classic form seems to have been introduced there by the Veronese Evaristo Felice dall'Abaco, whose Opus 3 (Paris, *c.* 1712) is outstanding. The much earlier *Sonate da camera* of Johann Rosenmüller (Venice, 1667) were five-part works. In France even François Couperin fell victim to the fashionable "fureur de composer des sonates à la manière italienne," and, despite characteristic picturesque, even programmatic elements (as in *Le Parnasse, ou L'Apothéose de Corelli,* 1725), his chamber works are the most Italianate of all his compositions.

Trio sonatas and other instrumental compositions of the Baroque period were normally performed by one player to each part other than the bass, which was played on a stringed instrument (or bassoon) and filled out on the organ or harpsichord. But there was no distinction between chamber music in the modern sense and orchestral music. A number of movements in Handel's trio sonatas figure, with or without additional viola parts, in his overtures and concertos, and as late as the middle of the 18th century passages in trio sonatas were sometimes marked tutti, indicating that trios could be converted into concertos by employing additional players for the passages so marked. Nor was there any differentiation between chamber and orchestral in the instrumental works—divertimenti, *quadri, quartetti,* and the rest—in the new style that was replacing the Baroque and was to lead to Viennese Classicism. Johann Stamitz' Opus 1 (Paris, *c.* 1755) consisted of *Sonates. . .ou a trois ou avec toutes* [sic] *l'orchestre.* Haydn's earliest "string quartets," Opp. 1 and 2 (composed in the 1750s), were not originally so called; they certainly need a double bass in addition to the cello; parts for oboes and horns exist for Opus 1, No. 5, and horn parts for Opus 2, Nos. 3 and 5.

Classical chamber music It was principally in Haydn's hands that the quartet for solo strings established itself as a favorite form of instrumental music during the latter part of the 18th century among the innumerable combinations of strings and winds (with or without continuo) that flourished during the age of rococo. In his Opus 17 set (composed in 1771) the virtuoso first-violin parts are unmistakably for a solo player; henceforth there was a real chamber style as distinct from an orchestral one. In Opus 20 (1772) the other instruments in the quartet began to assert their individual voices, if not yet to claim equality with the leader, and in Opus 33 (1781), "written," as he pointed out, "in an entirely new manner," Haydn employed that fragmentation of thematic material and distribution of it among all four instruments that was to give the Classical string-quartet style its character of a conversation among equals.

The keyboard continuo disappeared from

the string quartet but lingered on in other combinations long after it was redundant; characteristically Johann Christian Bach's Quintets, Op. 11, for flute, oboe, violin, viola, and bass were originally published about 1777 with the bass figured while another contemporary edition omitted the figuring. On the other hand, fully written-out keyboard parts now became more common. Johann Christian's father, Johann Sebastian, had written six sonatas for violin and cembalo concertante: that is, true duets for violin and harpsichord, not accompanied violin solos. Very typical of the midcentury are Franz Xaver Richter's *Sonate da camera* for flute (or violin), cello, and harpsichord obbligato. But such works are not the true ancestors of the Viennese Classical violin sonata (piano and violin duet) and piano trio (piano, violin, and cello). These sprang from the keyboard sonatas, popular from the 1760s onward, which were provided with ad libitum parts for violin or violin and cello. Even Haydn seldom liberated the strings from this unaccustomed subordinate role; the process of gradual emancipation can be traced in Mozart but was really completed only with Beethoven.

Mozart took over the developed form of string quartet from Haydn, imbued it with his own personal qualities, above all in the sets dedicated to Haydn (1785) and to Frederick William II of Prussia (1791), and in turn influenced the last and greatest of Haydn's quartets, most of which (from Opus 71 onward) were written after the younger composer's death. Beethoven's first Six Quartets, Op. 18 (published 1801), already showed a strongly marked creative personality without adding anything remarkable to the medium as such, but in the Three Quartets, Op. 59 (published 1808), dedicated to Count Razumovsky, the dimensions are enormously extended; in architecture, though not in texture, the *Razumovsky* Quartets are really symphonic. Two quartets, Opp. 74 and 95 (written 1809 and 1810), return to more normal dimensions, though they are adventurous in style, and in the last five—six if the *Grosse Fuge* originally composed as the finale of Opus 130 is included—the so-called "posthumous quartets" Opp. 127, 130, 131, 132, and 135 (composed 1824–26), Beethoven advanced into a world of sound that even he had never entered before and where the most sympathetic of his contemporaries were unable to follow him. Ellipsis, deliberate sketchiness of texture, and disregard of euphony combined to puzzle the musicians of the next generation as well; it was not until 1853 that the c-sharp minor Quartet, Op. 131, was "made clear" to Wagner "for the first time."

While the quartet was Beethoven's favorite chamber-music medium, he also embodied some of his finest music in duet sonatas for violin or cello with piano and in the piano trio. On the other hand, his only string quintet, though fine, is an early work, whereas Mozart's string quintets are among the finest of his mature chamber compositions. They are scored with two violas, whereas Schubert, in his great C Major Quintet, Op. 163, followed Boccherini in using two cellos. Schubert's chamber music is mostly for quartet or piano trio, but he also wrote a superb string and wind Octet, Op. 166, deliberately as a companion piece to Beethoven's early Septet, Op. 20, and the popular *Trout* Quintet, Op. 114, for an ad hoc combination of violin, viola, cello, bass, and piano.

The piano quartet (piano, violin, viola, and cello) was taken over by Mozart from Johann Christian Bach and other composers of that generation, but it never seriously attracted Beethoven; despite the popular Schumann specimen of Opus 47, it was really left to Brahms, Dvořák, and Fauré in the late 19th century to exploit its possibilities. As for the combination of piano with string quartet (piano quintet), which one might have expected to be popular, this was long left to minor masters such as Prince Louis Ferdinand of Prussia; the earliest example by a well-known composer is that by Schumann (Opus 44, 1842), by whose time the piano had developed more power; next came Opus 34 of Brahms (1864) and after that a small but distinguished series of successors by Franck, Fauré, Dvořák, Max Reger, Florent Schmitt, and others. As for the clarinet quintet (clarinet and string quartet), the challenge of Mozart's great exemplar was never seriously taken up until Brahms ventured at the very end of his life (Opus 115).

Chamber-music composers tend to be conservative in their choice of media—in which they are wise, as it is more difficult to find ensembles to play unusual combinations. Innovations, such as Louis Spohr's double quartets (employing two string quartets antiphonally), have completely failed to establish themselves.

post-Classical chamber music The chamber music of the middle and later 19th century has certain marked characteristics—notably domination by the piano, even in the nature of the string writing. This is very marked in Schumann and Mendelssohn and is also perceptible in Brahms. Shorter and lighter forms were introduced, from Schumann's *Phantasiestücke,* Op. 88, for piano trio to Glazunov's *Novelletten* for quartet, Op. 15. The true nature of chamber music was sometimes lost sight of as composers became conscious that their quartets and trios would be performed not only in intimate circles but also in fairly large concert halls; the fine workmanship of the Classical quartet texture was too often forgotten and quasi-orchestral effects introduced, as in Tchaikovsky's Piano Trio, Op. 50 (composed in 1882 in memory of Nicholas Rubinstein). The Tchaikovsky Trio has as its second and last movement a gigantic set of variations, each of which is associated with an (unspecified) episode of Rubinstein's life; it is therefore program music with an enigmatic program. But on the whole the 19th-century vogue for program music left chamber composition untouched; the only really successful example is Smetana's autobiographical Quartet in e minor, *From my Life* (1876), which is also marred by passages of quasi-orchestral writing. The true tradition of Classical chamber music was preserved during the latter part of the century by Brahms and Dvořák in central Europe, Borodin and Sergey Taneyev in Russia, and Franck, d'Indy, and Fauré in France.

The 20th century has seen the employment of ad hoc combinations such as Debussy's Sonata for flute, viola, and harp (1916) and Webern's Quartet for violin, clarinet, saxophone, and piano (1930), the co-option of the human voice to the string quartet as in Schoenberg's Opus 10 (1908), as distinct from the use of chamber-music combinations to accompany the human voice, as in Vaughan Williams' song cycle *On Wenlock Edge,* 1909, and the introduction of new technical devices of string writing in the quartet itself by Bartók, Stravinsky, and others. It has seen a vogue—perhaps suggested by Wagner's *Siegfried Idyll* (1870)—for the CHAMBER ORCHESTRA, which has been used not only in chamber symphonies—such as Schoenberg's two (1906 and 1939)—but also in opera—*e.g.,* Britten's *The Rape of Lucretia* (1946) and *Albert Herring* (1947). Yet such innovations have proved no more than sidetracks leading to no very important consequences. Most of the important chamber music of the 20th century has been conceived for the established Classical combinations—above all for the string quartet—which has proved the most adaptable of media and as suited to Impressionism, neoclassicism, polytonality, and serialism as to the idioms of Viennese Classicism or 19th-century Romanticism. Such profoundly different 20th-century masters as Bartók, Milhaud, and Shostakovich have put much of the best of themselves into their quartets, and hardly any instrumental composer of any significance has failed to contribute at least one work to the literature. The duet sonata for piano and some other instrument (usually the violin) has remained almost equally popular—the various examples by Debussy, Hindemith, Janáček, Bartók, and Copland (to take names almost at random) are among the established masterpieces of 20th-century music—and the other conventional combinations hardly less so: the piano quintet, piano trio, and string trio have inspired outstanding works by musicians as diverse as Florent Schmitt and Shostakovich, Ravel, Albert Roussel, and Webern.

BIBLIOGRAPHY: Nicholas Kilburn, *The Story of Chamber Music* (1904; reprint, 1977); Thomas F. Dunhill, *Chamber Music* (1913; reprint, 1972); Daniel G. Mason, *The Chamber Music of Brahms* (1933); Ernst Meyer, *English Chamber Music* (1946; reprint, 1970); Ruth H. Rowen, *Early Chamber Music* (1949; reprint, 1969); Walter W. Cobbett, ed., *Cyclopedic Survey of Chamber Music,* 3 vols., 2nd ed. (1963); Donald N. Ferguson, *Image and Structure in Chamber Music* (1964; reprint, 1977); Homer Ulrich, *Chamber Music,*

2nd ed. (1966); Jack A. Westrup, *Schubert Chamber Music* (1969); James Joyce, *Chamber Music* (1971).

chamber orchestra Called an "orchestra of soloists" and generally numbering from 10 to 35 members, the chamber orchestra had its roots in Baroque performance practice, especially in two aspects in which this practice differed from that of Renaissance music. By the end of the 16th century composers were rejecting the concept of homogeneous consorts—in which all instruments of an ensemble were of the same family and type—and were instead grouping instruments of different timbres and ranges (broken consorts). In addition the emancipation of solo instruments from the basso continuo and the discontinuance of the keyboard led to the development of the string trio, string quartet, and small orchestra of several independent parts.

Early orchestras used by Jacopo Peri and Emilio del Cavaliere consisted of harpsichord, lutes and lyres, and several flutes. This orchestra was not used independently but rather to provide chordal accompaniment for dramatic recitative. Cavaliere also recommended that the violin double the voice throughout.

The first documented use of a chamber orchestra of the approximate size and diversity of the modern concept was by the Florentine composers Alessandro Striggio and Francesco Corteccia for Giovanni Battista Cini's *intermedio Psiche ed Amore* (1565), written for the marriage of Francesco de' Medici to Joanna of Austria. It was scored for two gravicembali, four violins, six various sizes of lutes and lyres, six flutes and flageolets, three violas, four cornets, four trombones, and several minor instruments.

Important in the development of the musically independent chamber orchestra was the group of 37 diverse players assembled by Monteverdi for the premiere (1607) of his opera *Orfeo*. There was a preponderance of brass, and it has been inferred that much of the playing was improvised. Monteverdi used the orchestra as an instrument of independent expressiveness in his *Il Combattimento di Tancredi e Clorinda* (1624), which called for tremolo, pizzicato, and descriptive accompa-

niment to recitative. Throughout the century there were generally equal numbers of strings and winds.

Lully, without increasing the number of players, added timpani, German flutes, horns, guitars, and bagpipes to the orchestra for his operas, and Alessandro Scarlatti made the violas independent of the basses, assigning treble, alto, tenor, and bass after the manner of the modern quartet. In the latter half of the 17th century, Alessandro Stradella wrote for two solo violins and solo cello with accompaniment of violins, violas, and basses—an arrangement that would culminate in the concerti grossi of Corelli and Handel.

The philosophy of the chamber orchestra advanced with Bach, whose polyphonic textures treated each instrument as an independent voice and required virtuosity of each player. Examples of polyphonic writing for soloists and small orchestra are the six *Brandenburg* Concertos (1721). Bach's orchestra was usually comprised of 18 musicians, including strings and paired winds, plus an organ; Handel's numbered approximately 30 players.

These orchestras were often appended to the royal courts, and the number of players was dependent on the extent of the royal treasury. Composers wrote for available instrumentation rather than for an idealized ensemble. Thus, for example, many works for flute and chamber orchestra came from the Berlin and Potsdam courts of Frederick II the Great of Prussia, who played flute concerts nearly every evening and whose musical entourage included Quantz and Carl Philipp Emanuel Bach.

Music from Haydn through the middle period of Beethoven was performed with a relatively small force of musicians. However, this music does not belong to the history of the chamber orchestra, as the music was adaptable to a larger group once the tradition had been established. That tradition was becoming evident in the 18th century. When Franz Benda was available to conduct opera at the Berlin court, the performance took place in an elaborate opera house with 50 to 60 instrumentalists. Rousseau's *Dictionnaire de la musique* shows the placement for an orchestra of 44 at Dresden in the service of the King of Poland. As the number of winds increased (flutes and oboes instead of flutes replacing oboes; and, with Gluck, the introduction of the harp, modern trombone, and clarinet) and independent melodies were given to bassoons, the number of strings had to be increased. Thus by 1790 there was an orchestra of 70 in Paris and the 50-piece Mannheim orchestra was said to have a forte "like thunder." But in 1787 Mozart went to Prague to produce *Don Giovanni* with an orchestra of 25.

It was not until the 20th century that composers again began to write extensively for chamber orchestra (as opposed to a string orchestra, used with such advantage by Tchaikovsky and others a century earlier). Sometimes the instrumentation was for a conventional small orchestra, such as Stravinsky's *Dumbarton Oaks* Concerto (1938) and *Danses Concertantes* (1942), while other works would explore new sonorities, such as Charles Wuorinen's Composition (1964) for violin and 10 instruments and his Chamber Concerto (1970) for tuba, 12 winds, and 12 drums. Composers often specify the exact number of players, although the exact instrumentation may be variable. The music may be very complex; Ives's *The Unanswered Question* for trumpet, four flutes, and a "distant choir" of strings is often performed—of necessity—with two conductors.

The repertoire of modern chamber orchestras consists principally of Baroque and 20th-century music, and most groups specialize in one or the other. One of the first conductors to distinguish himself and his group in Baroque repertoire was Karl Münchinger, founder and conductor of the Stuttgart Chamber Orchestra. The St. Paul Chamber Orchestra, conducted by Dennis Russell Davies, features 20th-century music as well as traditional repertoire. Antonio Janigro, first a distinguished cellist and then founder (1953) and conductor of the 12-member I Solisti di Zagreb, plays Baroque and Classical works. Neville Marriner's London orchestra of the Academy of St. Martin-in-the-Fields plays everything, with a range of performances and recordings from Monteverdi to Britten; as conductor of the Los Angeles Chamber Or-

chestra, Marriner featured 20th-century works. The Jean-François Paillard Chamber Orchestra, also founded in 1953, excells in Baroque music as does the conductorless I Musici. The English Chamber Orchestra has an extensive and eclectic repertoire. Some European chamber orchestras are known in the United States for their recordings rather than for live appearances: the Concentus Musicus of Vienna and the Chamber Orchestra of the Saar in Germany. Specialized chamber orchestras include Karl Richter's Munich Bach Orchestra; Boston's Musica Viva for contemporary music; the Columbia Chamber Ensemble with whom Stravinsky recorded many of his works; Arthur Weisberg's New York-based Contemporary Chamber Ensemble with a rotating group of musicians; the London Sinfonietta with whom numerous avant-garde composers have recorded their music; the Mainz (Germany) Chamber Orchestra, conducted by Gunter Kehr and concentrating on the music of Bach and Mozart; the similar repertoire of the Württemberg Chamber Orchestra under Jörg Faerber; and ensembles specializing in Renaissance music (Musica Antiqua; Musica Reservata).

Susan S. Goodfellow

Chambonnières, Jacques Champion de (*c.* 1602–1672) The first of the great 17th-century school of French harpsichord players and composers *(clavecinistes),* Jacques Champion de Chambonnières came from an old and distinguished family of musicians and succeeded his father as a musician to Louis XIII, a position he retained under Louis XIV. He also was employed at the courts of Sweden and Brandenburg and became one of the most widely known players of his time.

His *Pièces de clavecin* (1670) reflect in style and texture the compositions of the noted lutenist-composer Denys Gaultier (*c.* 1603–72) and thus emphasize the roots of the early harpsichord style in lute music. Chambonnières was one of the first to attach tables of ornaments to his works, indicating the manner of performance of the many embellishments so vital to his free-voiced style. He was a noted teacher and included among his students many of the outstanding *clavecinistes* of the next generation, notably Louis Couperin, Nicolas Lebègue, and Jean Henri d'Anglebert.

Chaminade, Cécile (August 8, 1857–April 18, 1944)   Concert pianist and composer of lyrical salon pieces, French musician Cécile Chaminade studied with Félix Le Couppey and Benjamin Godard. She regularly toured Europe and later England, where, after first appearing in 1892, she became popular as a performer of her own music. Although she is remembered for her songs and piano pieces, particularly the *Scarf Dance,* she also wrote two orchestral suites, a ballet (*Callirhoë;* 1888), and a comic opera (*La Sévillane;* unpublished).

RECORDINGS: Concertino for flute; piano music.

chance music: *see* ALEATORY MUSIC

Chandos Anthems: *see* BAROQUE ERA (Handel and Bach); HANDEL (life) and (works).

change ringing: *see* BELL (change ringing).

chanson   The French word for song, but in English it normally refers to the medieval or Renaissance art song cultivated in France and using French texts. The Latin theorists of the Middle Ages called it *carmen* or cantilena, while the Provençal writers spoke of the canso. The troubadours were the first canso poets and composers, and the author of a 13th-century Provençal treatise considers the canso to be a love song that cannot be set to an existing melody but must have a new one. A 14th-century treatise, *Las leys d'amor,* is more precise and points out that the canso has from five to seven strophes. Such details prove mainly that the troubadour definitions referred to the content rather than the form of a song, for the *vers* also had five or more strophes, but its text was concerned with philosophical and intellectual matters.

The heyday of the southern French troubadours was the 12th century, that of the northern French trouvères the 13th. The latter imitated the troubadours to a great extent, but they have left some 1,500 pieces as against the troubadours' 300. The *chansons de geste* are, of course, one type of northern French

chanson, but unfortunately only two melodies exist that can be associated with the long epic poems that flourished in the 11th and 12th centuries. Undoubtedly a single melodic phrase was used in these pieces for every line of the strophe, or *laisse,* except that a variant might be used for a concluding line in the manner of a coda. Johannes de Grocheo, writing in Paris about 1300, includes the rondeau among the cantilenae; *i.e.,* the type of dance song popular in the 13th century, which had the form *A B a A a b A B* (the capitals represent refrain lines with identical text; the music consists throughout of the two phrases *A* and *B*). The typical 13th-century chanson derives from certain troubadour songs such as "Be ma'an perdut" by Bernard de Ventadour with the verse from *a b a b c d b.* The identity of the two parts of the first half of the composition persisted in northern France, although the length of the strophe might vary, for instance in works by Thibaut IV, King of Navarre. In the 14th century this type developed into the popular ballade form, which was usually polyphonic. In fact this was the most important 14th-century development in the history of song. The music of the troubadours and trouvères had been monodic, and instrumental accompaniments were never written down.

The rondeau continued to be fairly popular but attained its greatest favor as a polyphonic form in the early 15th century. Most of the other forms of early song disappeared, and the so-called *formes fixes*—ballade, rondeau, and virelai—reigned supreme. The virelai, which had a basic form *A b b a A,* was much less frequently composed than the other two song types. These pieces were solos with an accompaniment of one, two, or three instruments. The three-part work was standard until the end of the 15th century. However, four-part writing had become the norm in church music by the middle of the 15th century, so that it was only natural that about 1500 the style of mass and motet began to transfer itself to the chanson. At first the transference was very literal, and such men as Josquin des Prés and his Flemish contemporaries wrote chansons of a serious cast with learned counterpoint in four or five completely vocal parts. Antoine de Févin seems to have been the leader of a school of simpler chanson composition, often with folklike texts and in only three parts. From about 1530, however, it was the Parisian school that triumphed with a light-textured four-part type of chanson that employed two sorts of texts, the first fairly conventional love poems and the second definitely obscene verses. The two leading composers in the first half of the 16th century were Clément Janequin and Claude de Sermisy. Janequin is best known for his so-called program chansons, which can be paralleled by 14th-century virelais and works in canon called chaces. Such compositions, which imitate the sounds of battles ("La bataille de Marignan") and nature ("L'alouette"), are not typical of either the 14th or the 16th century but must be taken into account in the history of song.

The second half of the 16th century revealed three new trends. One was the imitation of the ancients that led to the *chanson mesurée à l'antique*. Modern measures such as duple and triple time were abandoned, and the quantitative prosody of longs and shorts produced music that alternated quarter and half notes without the feeling of a bar line. The finest composer in this style was Claude Le Jeune, who also wrote in a more contrapuntal style than Janequin or Sermisy, sometimes in five or more parts and on a large scale. Orlando di Lasso was one of the greatest chanson composers, though his genius expressed itself in Italian madrigals, German lieder, and even Latin secular works as well. The last important chanson composer seems to have been Eustache du Caurroy (1549–1609). By the first years of the 17th century, polyphonic secular music for unaccompanied voices was outmoded, and the new age demanded solo airs with lute accompaniment.

BIBLIOGRAPHY: Denis Stevens, ed., *A History of Song,* rev. ed. (1970); Howard Mayer Brown, *Theatrical Chansons of the Fifteenth and Early Sixteenth Centuries* (1963).

chant: *see* AMBROSIAN CHANT; ANGLICAN CHANT; BYZANTINE CHANT; CHURCH MUSIC; MIDDLE AGES (chant); MOZARABIC CHANT; PLAINCHANT.

Chappell, William (November 20, 1809–August 20, 1888)   A pioneer in English musical research, William Chappell was the eldest son of Samuel Chappell, founder of a music business that William and his two brothers continued. William's interest, however, was in old music, and he helped to establish the Musical Antiquarian Society (1840), which issued valuable works by forgotten English composers. His *Collection of National English Airs* (1838–40), revised as *Popular Music of the Olden Time* (1855–59), was a lively guide to traditional songs.

Chapuis, Michel (b. January 15, 1930)   The French organist and musicologist Michel Chapuis was a pupil of Marcel Dupré at the Paris Conservatoire, winning first prizes in organ and improvisation in 1951. He soon became involved in the classic organ revival and specialized in playing Baroque music. His recordings include the complete organ works of Bach. Chapuis has been a professor at the Strasbourg Conservatory since 1956, titular organist of Saint-Séverin in Paris since 1964, and founder and professor of the summer academy of Saint-Maximin (Provence).

Charpentier, Gustave (June 25, 1860–February 18, 1956)   A French composer whose fame rests on his opera *Louise,* Gustave Charpentier studied at the Lille Conservatory and later under Massenet at the Paris Conservatoire, where he won the Prix de Rome (1887). The popularity of *Louise,* first produced in Paris at the Opéra-Comique in 1900 and performed there more than 1,000 times in the following 60 years, is probably because of the plot's sentimental realism, the picturesque setting (Montmartre), the businesslike vocal writing in the Massenet tradition, and the mildly Wagnerian scoring. Its sequel *Julien* (1913) achieved less success. Earlier works included *Les Impressions fausses* for voice and orchestra (1895) and *Chant d'Apothéose,* written in 1902 for the Victor Hugo centenary. In 1902 Charpentier founded the Conservatoire Populaire de Mimi Pinson, which provided free music lessons for working people.

RECORDINGS: *Impressions d'Italie* (suite); *Louise.*

Charpentier, Marc-Antoine (1634–February 24, 1704)   One of the leading composers of church music in 17th-century France, Marc-Antoine Charpentier introduced the oratorio to his fellow countrymen after a discipleship with Giacomo Carissimi in Italy. He also contributed substantially to music for the stage but was overshadowed by Lully, who ruled French music with an iron hand until his death in 1687.

Born in Paris, Charpentier went to Italy to study painting but turned to music under the influence of Carissimi. He collaborated with Molière at the Théâtre Français in 1672–73, writing the music for a revival of *Le Mariage forcé* and for Molière's last play *Le Malade imaginaire.* After Molière's death Charpentier continued his association with the theater until 1685; his greatest stage work, *Médée,* to Thomas Corneille's text, was produced in 1693 at the Opéra.

Though never holding a direct appointment at court, Charpentier composed music for the Jesuit Church of Saint-Louis (the dauphin's private chapel) from 1679, was employed as a composer in residence (1680–88) by the king's cousin, the Princesse de Guise, and about 1692 taught the king's nephew Philippe II, duc d'Orleans; in 1698 he was appointed maître de musique at the Sainte-Chapelle.

Charpentier's Latin and French oratorios (he called them *Histoires sacrées*) were modeled on those of his master Carissimi, but he consistently used a larger orchestra and incorporated dissonance for expressive purposes; *Le Reniement de Saint-Pierre (The Denial of St. Peter)* is considered to be his masterpiece. His *grands motets,* like those of Lully, were expansive cantatas not unlike the English anthem. He was one of the few French composers of the day to contribute a significant number of masses, totaling 12 and including a unique instrumental substitute for the traditional organ mass, *Messe pour plusieurs instruments au lieu des orgues,* and the earliest example of one based on noels, *Messe de minuit pour Noël,* a work that has become popular in the 20th century.

RECORDINGS: *Epithalamium;* Magnificat; *Médée* (excerpts); *Messe de minuit pour Noël; Messe pour plusieurs instruments au lieu des orgues;* Te Deum.

Chausson, Ernest (Amédée) (January 21, 1855–June 10, 1899)   The French composer Ernest Chausson was a disciple of Franck. He studied with Massenet at the Paris Conservatoire and from 1880 to 1883 was a private pupil of Franck. His early works include songs on poems by Leconte de Lisle, notably "Le Colibri." Later he set poems by Paul Verlaine and cycles of poems by Maurice Bouchor *(Poème de l'amour et de la mer),* Jean Cros (Chanson *perpétuelle*), and Maurice Maeterlinck *(Serres chaudes).* Orchestral works include the Symphony in B-flat Major (*c.* 1890) and the *Poème* for violin and orchestra (1896). His principal chamber works are the *Concert* for violin, piano, and string quartet (1890–91) and the Piano Quartet (published 1917). Well-to-do and generous, Chausson was secretary of the Société Nationale de Musique and did much to encourage contemporary French music. His opera *Le Roi Arthus* was produced posthumously at Brussels (1903), and his last work, a string quartet, was completed by d'Indy. Though harmonically indebted to Franck and Wagner, much of Chausson's music is nostalgic and melancholy in mood. The more powerful aspects of his work are displayed in his symphony and in the *Serres chaudes* song cycle.

RECORDINGS: Chanson *perpétuelle;* Concert for violin, piano and quartet; Piano Quartet; *Poème de l'amour et de la mer; Poème* for violin and orchestra; Symphony in B-flat Major.

Chávez, Carlos (June 13, 1899–August 2, 1978)   The foremost Mexican conductor and composer of the 20th century, Carlos Chávez skillfully combined elements of folk songs and modern techniques. At the age of 19 he completed his first symphony. In 1921 he wrote his first significant work in a Mexican style, the ballet *El fuego nuevo.* After traveling in Europe and in the United States, he became conductor of the Orquesta Sinfónica de México (1928–48) and director of the National Conservatory in Mexico City (1928–34), later heading a composers' workshop there (1960–65). He also appeared as guest conductor with major U.S. orchestras. Chávez published numerous essays on Mexican music and a book, *Toward a New Music* (1937); his Charles Eliot Norton lectures (1958–59) at Harvard University were collected in *Musical Thought* (1960). The music of Chávez is unmistakably Mexican in its melodic patterns and rhythmic inflections; from Mexican Indian music he utilized elements of percussion, primitive rhythms, archaisms of harmony and melody, and violence in dynamic range. To these he added influences of modern European and American music, especially that of Stravinsky and Schoenberg.

His output includes Three Quartets (1921, 1932, and 1943); ballets *El fuego nuevo* (1928) and *Los cuatros soles* (1930); an opera, *The Visitors* (1953); and six symphonies: the first two, Sinfonía de *Antigona* (1933) and Sinfonía *India* (1936), are one-movement works utilizing Indian themes, in the former combined with Greek modes. The Fourth, Sinfonía *Romántica* (1953), is a traditional work, the Fifth (1953) for string orchestra is neoclassic, and the Sixth (1964) is written "within classic limitations." The Piano Concerto (1942) is highly percussive and austere with native Indian rhythms and archaic idioms; Toccata for percussion (1947) is scored for 11 types of percussion instruments played by six performers. The Violin Concerto (1952) was revised and reorchestrated for a new premiere in 1965, and *Xochipilli Macuilxochitl* (1940) is for percussion orchestra with native instruments. Later works include *Resonancias* (1964), *Clio* (1969), and *Discovery* (1969), all for orchestra; and *Tambuco* (1964) for six percussion.

RECORDINGS: *Los cuatros soles;* Piano Concerto; Piano Sonata No. 6; *Soli I* for oboe, clarinet, bassoon, and trumpet; *Soli II* for wind quintet; *Soli IV* for horn, trumpet and trombone; Symphonies (6); Toccata for percussion.

Cherubini, (Maria) Luigi (Carlo Zenobio Salvatore) (September 14, 1760–March 15, 1842)   A leading Italian composer during the transition period from Classicism to Romanticism, Luigi Cherubini contributed to the de-velopment of French opera and was also a master of sacred music. For long eclipsed by Beethoven and stigmatized as an exceedingly stuffy reactionary force by Berlioz, he became the focus of renewed interest with modern revivals of such works as his opera *Médée* and his Requiem in d minor. His mature operas are characterized by the way they use some of the new techniques and subject matter of the Romantics but derive their dramatic force from a Classical dignity and restraint.

The son of a musician, Cherubini studied under Giuseppe Sarti. The bulk of Cherubini's early work consists of sacred music, but he later turned most of his attention to the musical stage, writing 15 Italian and 14 French operas. He was composer to King George III in England in 1785. The next year he settled in France, and in 1795 he became an inspector of the newly established Paris Conservatoire. He found little favor with Napoleon, but with the restoration of the French monarchy in 1814 he became music director of the royal chapel of Louis XVIII. In 1822 he was made director of the Conservatoire, a position that gave him great influence over the younger generation of composers.

Cherubini presents the paradox of an innate conservative compelled to function in an era politically and musically revolutionary. He was trained in the traditions of the opera seria, the aristocratic style of 18th-century opera, and his earlier works retain that style's heroic and aristocratic grandeur. But his later works, especially those in French, follow the operatic reforms of Gluck in seeking subjects relevant to a changing world. Even in operas that dealt with subjects from classical antiquity, such as *Médée* (1797), he reveals a concern for human traits. The opera that inaugurated his new style was *Lodoïska* (1791). It moved away from the emphasis on the solo voice found in opera seria to give new scope to ensembles and choruses and a fresh dramatic importance to the orchestra. He thus forged a link between the older style and the grand opera of 19th-century France.

In his harmonies, rhythms, and form he remained in the Classical idiom and did not attempt the incipient Romantic style. But Romantics who did, like Schumann, were influ-

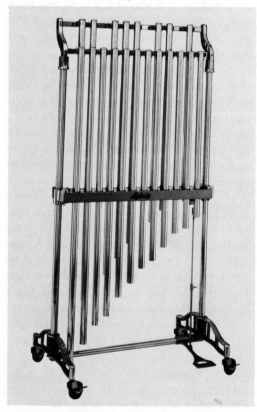

enced by his operas. Before writing *Fidelio* Beethoven studied the score of a Cherubini opera with a similar "rescue" theme: *Les Deux Journées* (1800; *The Two Days,* also known as *The Water Carrier* from its German title, *Der Wasserträger*). This opera is considered by many to be Cherubini's masterpiece.

In later life he turned to church music. Works such as his Mass in F Major (1809) and his two Requiems, especially that in d minor for male voices (1836), are characterized instead by a Classical lucidity combined with a sense of religious grandeur.

He wrote several treatises, including the celebrated and conservative *Cours de contrepoint et de fugue* (1835; "Course in Counterpoint and Fugue").

BIBLIOGRAPHY: Basil Deane, *Cherubini* (1965).

RECORDINGS: *Médée; Missa solemnis;* Quartets (6); Requiem in d minor.

chime   A percussion instrument in the modern orchestra consisting of a set of tuned brass

chime
courtesy, Ludwig Industries

(originally bronze) tubes of graded length, struck with wooden hammers. Greater rhythmic precision is possible than with true bells, and the tone is clearer (fewer higher harmonics). The compass normally extends one and one-half octaves from the C above middle C. Exemplary use is made of the instrument in Tchaikovsky's *1812* Overture, Mahler's Second Symphony, and Sibelius' Fourth Symphony.

The term is also used to refer to the bell chime, a set of tuned bells, usually from two to 20 in number in church or civic towers, played by an automatic clock mechanism; or for playing unharmonized hymn tunes, usually attached to a mechanical or electric keyboard.

Chinese music   Though Chinese scholars have written about the history and theory of their music since the 2nd century B.C., only in the mid-20th century have they begun to explore living Chinese music and to analyze the music itself, whether folk, popular, or art music. The types of music practiced in a multinational state, such as China, will differ widely from one region to another, and this account is confined chiefly to the music of the *Hanjen*—the Chinese in a limited, ethnic sense.

Certain surviving specimens of Chinese musical instruments are at least 4,000 years old, and the earliest texts (engraved on bone fragments) mentioning musical instruments and their ritual use date from *c.* 1000 B.C. The oldest lyrics (in the *Sung* section of the *Book of Songs: Shih Ching*) date from between 1100 and 1000 B.C. and contain references to lithophones, bells (both wooden and metal) and scrapers, drums (including rattle drums), flutes, and panpipes. These continued to be used in the Confucian ritual orchestra up to the founding of the Republic of China in 1912. It may be significant that stringed instruments are first mentioned in the next oldest group of lyrics, the *Ta Ya,* dating from between 1000 and 900 B.C.

melody   It is not easy to define Chinese melody in such a way that melodies from all periods and styles fall within the limits of the definition. (1) It may be agreed that it is predominantly five-note melody, provided that the frequency with which it makes use of seven notes is acknowledged. (2) The melodic line tends to break into units of a fourth; while chains of fourths (d, g, c', for example) are not uncommon, broken triads are rare. (3) The fourths are spanned by three notes, spaced as a minor third and a major second D FG or DE G. (4) Its rhythms are for the most part binary or quaternary, rarely ternary; though often momentarily irregular, they are never continuously so, as are the irregular, (aksak) rhythms of India, the Middle East, or the Balkans. (5) Chinese tunes do not show sequential structure and are often nonsymmetrical in spite of their binary rhythmic structure. All these properties are exhibited in example 1, taken from a folk dance tune from south of the Yangtze River in Kiangsu and Anhwei provinces and called "The golden snake's wild dance."

is the answer at the fifth. This is exemplified by tunes consisting of two phrases, A A', where A' is a slightly varied statement of A at the fifth below.

The impression of unusual intonation that a Western listener sometimes receives may arise from (1) the gracing of notes by microtonal on- or off-glides, or by the deliberate sharpening of sustained notes (by flute players, for example), thereby heightening tension; (2) the fact that the major thirds are sharper than just major thirds (in a modulatory passage such as $c\ d\ e\ g/a\ d\ c\ B/A\ G$, the e and the B may both be about five cents sharper than their equal-tempered values and about 16 cents sharper than their just values; *see* TUNING AND TEMPERAMENT); (3) in some types of local Chinese music (in Ch'ao-chou opera, for example), a distinction between "major" and "minor" tones is to be heard, as in the sequence $b/a^{+c}\ b\ a^{+c}\ c\sharp/b\ a^{+c}\ g\sharp\ f\sharp/e$, where $b\ a^{+c}$ is a "minor" tone of about 180 cents (the a being about one comma sharp), while the tones between $g\sharp$ and $f\sharp$ and $f\sharp$ and e are "major" tones of about 204 cents. Fourths, fifths, and octaves are usually perfect. Though semitone steps are chiefly used in modulating from one five-note mode to another in folk and popular music, they also occur as passing notes in tunes of this kind (*see* Example 1), and in art song their use is frequent in heptatonic tunes with a pentatonic skeleton, as in Example 2.

musical practice Of great importance for the practicing musician is the art of gracing. A fiddler or flutist accompanying a singer decorates a cadence.

E D, for example, becomes E G D, E GE D, or EAGE D. A lutenist not only graces but fills out sustained notes of the tune with a pattern of repeated notes. In a small band of, say, flute, fiddle, and lute, all play the same tune in unison or at the

Example 1

Example 2
Chiang Pai-shih. Stanza 1 of Song 8 (printed 1202)

One structural feature common to Western folk song and some Chinese tunes (though much less frequent in China than in the West)

octave with graces and in a manner appropriate to the properties of each instrument against a rhythmic framework of percussion—drums and clappers and single gongs or cymbals, for example. If this ensemble is compared with similar groups from India or the Middle East, conspicuous differences are apparent not only in the specific timbre of instruments and in the predominantly five-note melody but also in the rhythmic framework. The elaboration of rhythmic modes, so striking in Indian and Middle Eastern music, is much less conspicuous in China, where rhythmic patterns are simpler and less numerous.

One feature of the instrumental ensemble of the theater, for which there is no parallel in India or the Middle East, is the use of the *sheng,* or mouth organ, doubling the melody at the fifth above or at the fourth below, adding the octave of the melody-note or of the fourth or fifth, where it is available among the 13 notes of the *sheng.* This diaphony is subservient to the purely melodic interest of the tune, but it serves as a reminder that the common view of Chinese music as purely linear does not take into account the practices of folk music. In folk and popular music the *sheng* is used not only to play tunes in fourths or fifths (as far as its structure permits) but also to provide ostinato accompaniments—two chords played in alternation, for example. An analogous use of the *sheng* is found among certain national minorities, such as the Miao and Yao, as well as south of the border in Vietnam, and there can be little doubt that these harmonic features belong to an ancient musical tradition, modified by contact with ideas and practices coming from Central Asia.

Reduced to staff notation and played on an equal-tempered instrument, Chinese music strikes Westerners as Scottish because of its five-note character. Heard on Chinese instruments, however, it is strange still because of the peculiarities of intonation and the distinctive timbres of the instruments. The muted tone of the two-stringed fiddle, *erh-hu,* is due to the snakeskin diaphragm on which the bridge rests; the edge to the sound of the side-blown flute, *ti,* is due to the vibration of a thin membrane closing a supernumerary hole; the shrillness of the shawm, *suo-na,* derives

from the smallness of the double reed; the dry sound of the pear-shaped lute, *p'i-p'a,* depends on the special qualities of the closed resonator; and among percussion instruments the flat, circular drum, *pang-ku,* provides an essentially Chinese element with its unique and indescribable sound.

opera and classical music In addition to the wealth of local folk music related to all aspects of daily life—including such characteristic features as storytelling in rhythmized prose to the accompaniment of a long-necked lute, the *san-hsien*—two major kinds of Chinese music must be considered: opera and classical music. The term opera is commonly applied to the music dramas, sung throughout except for brief passages in highly stylized speech where the tonal accent of the syllables is so emphasized that the result sounds like the *Sprechstimme* of Schoenberg.

A large number of different Chinese operatic traditions are to be distinguished. They may be grouped into five main classes: (1) Peking opera, or *ching-hsi,* a 19th-century development with a fiddle as the chief accompanying instrument. It exists in a number of variants (*erh-huang, hsi-p'i,* etc.), and is sometimes referred to as the "classical Chinese theater." (2) The category of provincial opera, of which many different traditions may survive in a single province, as in Canton or Fukien. These southeastern traditions include what is probably the oldest surviving Chinese opera tradition, *Nan-kuan.* This has almost vanished as a stage performance but is still cultivated by amateurs. Song texts in 17th-century editions survive in this tradition. (3) Pieces from the 16th-century tradition, *k'un-ch'u,* in which the chief accompanying instrument is a flute. Though the origins of the style are to be sought in the 16th century, the tradition as it survives probably reflects 17th- and 18th-century developments. Its melodies are frequently more highly melismatic than those of *Nan-kuan.* (4) Folk opera is of great interest and has been inadequately recorded and documented. (5) Modern opera. An important component of provincial opera may properly be described as religious drama. It includes pieces performed as a part of funeral rites, partly Buddhist and partly Taoist in character. In listening to Chinese opera the foreigner has first to accept the use of the voice in high falsetto before the richness of melodic invention, the dramatic appropriateness of the music, and the artistry of the performers can be appreciated.

The term classical is often applied to the solo music for lute *(p'i-p'a),* flute (both side blown and end blown), and zither that is preserved as a repertoire of scores. The zithers—*ku-ch'in,* or *ch'i-hsien-ch'in,* and *cheng*—are the oldest Chinese stringed instruments with a documented history from before the 5th century B.C. The repertoire of the former *(ku-ch'in)* includes pieces already printed in tablature in the early 15th century and is beyond question the greatest musical treasure of the Chinese tradition. Its music is the equal of Chinese painting and ceramics in universal appeal. The sounds of this instrument are intrinsically beautiful and evocative, even for foreign ears at a first hearing, and the musical structure of the suitelike pieces from the classical repertoire is of the greatest interest.

Glancing briefly at the music of certain groups other than the *Han-jen,* it may be said that while the music of Mongolia often resembles that of north China, there is a striking difference in the abundance of unmeasured song in Mongolia in contrast to China. In Tibet, Lamaist music and the music of the historical music dramas differ profoundly from Chinese music in the characteristics of the melodic line. Finally, in Sinkiang province, and among the Turkic peoples—such as the Wei-wu-erh and Khazaks—seven-note melody is the rule rather than the exception.

history Excavation of graves of the Yin dynasty *(c.* 1523–*c.* 1027 B.C.) has revealed lithophones (slabs of sonorous stone), bronze bells, and earthenware vessel flutes, all yielding notes at the same or related pitches, so that there is reason to believe that the Shang people observed a standard pitch. At least by the 3rd century B.C. (and, from the tuning of sets of bells of the Shang period, probably much earlier) an arithmetical procedure for generating the note series was known. Starting with a bamboo tube of length x, if other tubes are cut to lengths of $\frac{2}{3} x$, $\frac{4}{3} (\frac{2}{3} x)$, $\frac{2}{3} [\frac{4}{3} (\frac{2}{3} x)]$, etc., the first five tubes when blown will yield

five notes of relative pitches C G D A E, that is, the five-note series, C D E G A. It is possible that both Greece and China derived from Babylonia their knowledge of the $1:\frac{2}{3}$ ratio between fundamental and fifth. There are reasons for believing that the Shang people, like some of the national minorities in modern China, may have practiced a three-note ritual music at times.

A majority of the musical instruments in use in modern China came from Central Asia. Of those originating in East Asia, only the zithers *ku-ch'in* and *cheng,* the notched vertical flute *hsiao,* and the mouth organ *sheng* continue in modern use, and of these *ku-ch'in* and *hsiao* are predominantly solo instruments. The use both of *cheng* and *sheng* has been encouraged in the mid-20th century. Iconographical evidence establishes that a pear-shaped lute with a short straight neck, coming from the West, was known in the later eastern Han dynasty (before A.D. 200?), and a circular, straight-necked lute is attested by contemporary documents and a figure on a pottery vessel from A.D. 260. The date of entry of the fiddle is still uncertain, but rubbed half-tube zithers were known in the T'ang dynasty (A.D. 618–906). The Persian dulcimer, called in China *yang-ch'in,* associated with popular Cantonese music, entered during the Ming period (1368–1644).

Beginning with the Sui dynasty (A.D. 605–618) and continuing during the T'ang period, there was an astonishing influx of instruments, music, musicians, and dancers coming from Central Asia to the imperial court. This influx was perhaps stimulated by the raised status of Buddhism at court and the ensuing tolerance toward the entire cultural complex of which Buddhism was a part. Much of this imported music was popular, if not folk, in character; it included drinking songs and dance tunes and was a cause for scandal among good Confucians. Some of the pieces have been preserved virtually unchanged in the mouth-organ partbooks of the musicians of the Japanese imperial court. The title of one such tune (transcribed as Example 3) refers to a puppet, representing a Western foreigner, blue-eyed, bearded, and with a prominent nose. This was played with in drinking houses. When the puppet fell over, the drinker at whom it pointed had to empty his wine cup.

Example 3
Chiu Hu-tzu, The Wine-Puppet (Vinous Sogdian; before A.D. 800) (transcribed from a mouth organ part book in the Japanese *tōgaku* repertoire)

The simplest tunes preserved in these part-books are suitable for singing T'ang lyric verse in stanzas of 4 or 8 lines of 7 syllables. They are tunes in measures of 8 beats, each measure being composed of 6 quarter notes followed by a half, and they consist of from 4 to 8 such measures. Secular tunes of the Sung dynasty (960–1279), on the other hand, exhibit more complex rhythmic structures and make use of notes of three different durations—halves, quarters, and eighths, for example (Example 2). It seems likely that this latter type of tune, in which the detailed rhythmic structure of each musical line is varied while the metrical framework remains unchanged, originated to the west of China. Furthermore, it was perhaps the attempt to write lyrics (one syllable to one note) for such tunes that led to the development of heterometric verse in T'ang times and to the rise of the *tz'u* as the predominant lyric form, reaching its climax during the Sung period.

Most of the surviving T'ang or Sung tunes are hexatonic or heptatonic, as were the so-called Northern Songs of Yüan and Ming times; but the fundamentally five-note character of Chinese melody always shows through the seven-note structure. It is evident from the secular songs included in the works of Chiang Pai-shih (1155–1229) that Chinese songs were still essentially syllabic rather than melismatic at that time. At what date Chinese art song became melismatic cannot as yet be stated with certainty.

modern music In the mid-20th century Chinese composers were experimenting with Western instruments and with harmonic and contrapuntal devices adapted to the national idiom. Among many modern works mention may be made of the *Yellow River* Cantata (for soloists, chorus, and an orchestra of Chinese instruments) by Hsien Hsing-hai and of the impressive opera *The White-Haired Girl* (1945) by a group of composers and writers perhaps better regarded as a collective work than a work composed in the usual sense. Many of its tunes, indeed, are folk and popular songs. The orchestral texture marks a new departure in Chinese music, and there are passages of striking originality and affecting pathos. *See also* GONG.

BIBLIOGRAPHY: Egon Wellesz, ed., *Ancient and Oriental Music* (1957), Vol. 1 of *The New Oxford History of Music;* Rulan Chao Pian, *Song Dynasty Musical Sources and Their Interpretation* (1967); Mei-Pa Chao, *The Yellow Bell: A Brief Sketch of the History of Chinese Music* (1974); Robert W. Clack, *Celestial Symphonies: A History of Chinese Music* (1975); J. I. Crump and William P. Malm, *Chinese and Japanese Music-Dramas* (1975).

chitarrone: *see* LUTE.

choir A body of singers with more than one voice to a part formed for the purpose of singing either sacred or secular music, or both. A mixed choir normally consists of women and men, but the term is sometimes used to include children with women and men. A boys' and men's choir (the boys usually sing the soprano part(s) and the men alto, tenor, and bass) was long a tradition in churches and cathedrals in England and on the Continent and is still maintained in some places, including the United States. A boy choir usually refers to a choir of boys with treble voices but sometimes boys with changed voices as well, or even men. The male choir can be boys alone, men alone, or boys and men. A female choir includes girls, women, or both.

The growth of the secular choir coincided to a large extent with the beginnings of opera, in which choruses have always taken some part. In most operas crowd scenes provide the opportunity for the composition of parts for a choir. It has usually been the custom to employ professional singers in opera-house choruses. An oratorio choir, on the other hand, is part of a different tradition, which stems from the augmented church choirs used to provide the choral portions of a given work, whether sung in or out of church. The oratorio choir is the home of the amateur singer, and although there are notable exceptions, its almost universal application is made a virtual necessity by the sheer weight of numbers customarily employed.

Handel was in the habit of presenting his oratorios and operas with a choir of medium size, but the Handel commemoration of 1784, which took place in Westminster Abbey and in the Pantheon in London, called for as large a body of singers as could be conveniently found; the choir numbered 274. This choir was, however, dwarfed by the 2,000 singers who took part in the first Handel festival at the Crystal Palace, London, in 1857, while subsequent years of this same festival saw the number creep up to well over 3,000. Even the *concerts monstres* of Berlioz rarely made use of a choir numbering more than 500, although he claims that he once heard, in St. Paul's Cathedral in London, a choir of 6,500 at the anniversary meeting of the Charity Children in 1851. It was from such meetings as these, beginning with the meetings of the Three Choirs of Gloucester, Worcester, and Hereford (1724 or perhaps earlier), that local choral festivals, widely popular in the 20th century, sprang. In modern times professional recording choirs often number about 30.

Choirs have taken part in church services from the earliest times, but for many centuries their role was confined to singing plainsong in unison. This kind of choir varied considerably in size and style. In a well-endowed abbey, cathedral, collegiate church, or royal chapel,

the choir might consist of as many as 50 or 60 trained voices. In England the medieval system whereby a canon could appoint a substitute led to the formation of self-governing colleges of vicars choral, who were usually in deacon's or subdeacon's orders. Below them in rank were clerks of the choir, also in minor orders, who were sometimes referred to as altarists or secondaries.

Boys in choirs of secular cathedrals were trained by the precentor to take part not only in the singing but also in the liturgy. A boy with intelligence and a good voice could progress via thurifer, subdeacon, and deacon to vicar choral; and as time went on boys enjoyed lodgings and privileges of their own as well as tuition in subjects other than music.

Apart from plainsong there was no choral singing in the early church, for when harmony first came into use its relative complexity demanded soloists as interpreters. Italian manuscripts begin, however, to hint about 1430 at the use of a choir for straightforward polyphony, with the direction that sections of the liturgy in three-part harmony are to be sung by the chorus (*i.e.*, by all voices) in contrast to the sections in two-part harmony, marked either *unus* (to indicate one voice to a part) or *duo* (to describe such sections as duets for solo voices). This alternation of soloists and chorus eventually led to the use of two choirs, one on each side of the church, or placed (as at St. Mark's, Venice) in galleries so that psalms, canticles, and even masses could be sung antiphonally. Music for divided choirs *(cori spezzati)* was developed in the early 16th century and brought to a splendid peak of excellence in the early 17th by Giovanni Gabrieli. *See also* CHURCH MUSIC.

Chopin, Frédéric (François), originally Fryderyk Franciszek (March 1, 1810–October 17, 1849) Creator of an original piano style—both in playing and in composition—Frédéric Chopin ranks as one of music's greatest tone poets—the first of the Romantic pianists but never removed from Classic purity.

life Born at Zelazowa Wola, near Warsaw, Poland, Chopin was of pure French stock on his paternal side, his father Nicholas Chopin having been born at Marainville in the

Frédéric Chopin
portrait by Eugène Delacroix (1798–1863)
Giraudon

Vosges. Nicholas traveled to Warsaw at age 16, identified himself with his new country, and in 1806 married Tekla Justyna Krzyza-nowska, a relative of the Skarbek family with whom he had found employment as a tutor.

Frédéric was the second of four children. He was brought up in a refined and cultivated, if modest, home, and the characteristics of elegance and aristocratic distinction that soon marked his personality and later gave a unique stamp to his compositions derived from this home atmosphere and from the high social circles of Warsaw to which the young prodigy was admitted from his earliest years. The boy's remarkable musical gifts were directed by Adalbert Zywny, a Czech established in War-saw, but his simple instruction in piano play-ing was soon left behind by his pupil, who discovered for himself an original approach to the piano and was allowed to develop un-hindered by academic rules and formal disci-pline. Chopin's parents were wise enough to insist on their son's receiving a thorough gen-eral education, and it was only on the comple-

tion of his high school studies that he was placed in 1826 under the able guidance of Jo-seph Elsner, director of the Warsaw Conserva-tory. Even before he came under Elsner's eye, Chopin had shown interest in the folk music of the Polish countryside and had received those impressions that later gave an unmistak-able national coloring to his work. At the con-servatory he was put through a solid course of instruction in harmony and composition; it was only in piano playing itself that he was practically self-taught.

After a preliminary expedition to Berlin in 1828, Chopin made his first real contact with the outside world when he visited Vienna and made his debut there in 1829. A second con-cert confirmed his success, and on his return home he prepared himself for further achieve-ments abroad by writing his two piano concer-tos in f minor (1829) and e minor (1830) and other works for piano and orchestra designed to exploit his brilliantly original piano style. His first études were also written at this time (1829–32) to enable him and others to master the technical difficulties in his new conception of piano playing. In March and October 1830 he presented his new works to the Warsaw public and then left Poland with the intention of visiting Germany and Italy for further study. He had gone no farther than Vienna when news reached him of the Polish revolt against the Russians; this added to the dis-turbed state of Europe, causing him to remain profitlessly in Vienna until the following July, when he decided to make his way to Paris. Soon after his arrival in what was then the center of European culture and a focal point of the Romantic movement Chopin realized that he had found the exact milieu in which his genius could flourish. The circles to which his talents and distinction admitted him quickly acknowledged that they had found the artist whom the moment required, and after a brief period of uncertainty Chopin settled down to the main business of his life—teaching and composing. His high income from these sources set him free from the strain of concert giving to which he had an innate repugnance. Nevertheless his reputation as a pianist did not suffer from this quasi-retirement, and a legend grew around his name even during his lifetime, thanks to the rapturous accounts of the few who heard him privately and to the steady flow of new compositions that began with the publication of his early mazurkas in 1832 and continued without interruption until 1847.

Chopin's youthful love affairs with Constantia Gladkowska in Warsaw (1830) and Maria Wodzinska in Dresden (1835–36) came to nothing, although he actually became engaged to the latter. In 1836 he met for the first time Aurore Dudevant, better known as George Sand, and their liaison began in the summer of 1838. In the autumn of that year the pair made their celebrated excursion to Majorca during which Chopin completed his Preludes, Op. 28, but in most other respects the trip was disastrous, and the privations that Chopin endured brought on the slow decline in his health that ended with his death from tuberculosis 10 years later. However, the period following the return from Majorca was the happiest and most productive of his life, and the long summers spent at Nohant, George Sand's country estate, bore fruit in a succession of masterpieces. Family dissensions caused by the marriage of George Sand's daughter Solange brought the liaison to an end in 1847, and thereafter Chopin seems to have given up his struggle with ill-health. The revolution of February 1848 produced a temporary dissolution of the society upon which he depended for his living, and he sought escape in a visit to England and Scotland during the summer of 1848. His reception was enthusiastic, but he did not have the strength to profit by it. His last public appearance on a concert platform was made at the Guildhall in London on November 16, 1848, when, in a final patriotic gesture, he played for the benefit of Polish refugees. He returned to Paris, where he died the following year; he was buried at the cemetery of Père Lachaise.

evaluation As a pianist Chopin was unique in acquiring a reputation of the highest order on the basis of a minimum of public appearances—few more than 30 in the course of his lifetime. His original and uninhibited approach to the keyboard allowed him to exploit all the resources of the piano of his day. He was inexhaustible in discovering colorful new passage work and technical figures; he understood as no one before him the true nature of the piano as an expressive instrument, and he had the secret of writing music that is bound with the instrument for which it was conceived and which cannot be imagined apart from it. His innovations in fingering, his use of the pedals, and general treatment of the keyboard form a milestone in the history of the piano, and his works set a standard that is recognized as unsurpassable.

Chopin as a composer has acquired increased stature after a period (the later years of the 19th century) during which his work was judged by academic standards that were in fact inapplicable to its individual character. In keyboard style, harmony, and form, he was innovative according to the demands of each specific compositional situation. He had the rare gift of a very personal melody, expressive of heartfelt emotion, and his music is penetrated by a poetic feeling with almost universal appeal. Although "romantic" in its essence, Chopin's music has none of the expected trappings of romanticism—there is a classic purity and discretion in everything he wrote and not a sign of romantic exhibitionism. That Bach was one of his gods is no surprise. He found within himself and in the tragic story of Poland the chief sources of his inspiration. The theme of Poland's glories and sufferings was constantly before him, and in his polonaises and numerous mazurkas he transmuted the primitive rhythms and melodies of his youth into enduring art forms. From the great Italian singers of the age he learned the art of "singing" on the piano, and his nocturnes reveal the perfection of his cantabile style and delicate charm of ornamentation, while his ballades and scherzos have a dramatic turbulence and passion such as to dispel the notion that Chopin was merely a drawing-room composer. His total output was small and mostly limited to solo piano; yet within its limited framework its range is seen to be vast, comprehending every variety of intensely experienced emotion.

works Chopin's works are available in many collected editions, the best of which are the Polish National editions published in Warsaw from 1949 onward and based on original manuscripts. His work consists of two piano concertos; 21 nocturnes; 27 studies; nearly 60 mazurkas, of which 42 were published by Chopin himself; 21 waltzes; four scherzos; four ballades; 26 preludes; four impromptus; 16 polonaises; three piano sonatas; and many individual pieces such as *Barcarolle,* Op. 60, Fantasia, Op. 49, Berceuse, Op. 57, and 19 Polish songs.

BIBLIOGRAPHY: Ignacy Paderewski, *Chopin; a Discourse* (1911; reprint, 1978); William Murdoch, *Chopin: His Life* (1935; reprint, 1971); André Gide, *Notes on Chopin* (1949; reprint, 1978); Alan Walker, ed., *The Chopin Companion; Profiles of the Man and the Musician* (1973); Arthur Hedley, *Chopin,* rev. ed. (1974); Bernard Gavoty, *Chopin* (1977); George R. Marek and Maria Gordon-Smith, *Chopin* (1978); Ates Orga, *Chopin: His Life and Times* (1978).

RECORDINGS: Numerous recordings of most works.

chorale (German spelling, *Choral*) A metrical hymn tune associated with the Protestant Church in Germany. Martin Luther himself composed, or caused to be composed, many hymn tunes that were known as chorales because they were designed for congregational singing. That they were called chorales does not imply that they were designed for singing in harmony; unison singing was the rule of the Reformed churches, both in Germany and in other countries. It was only gradually, however, that the melody shifted from the tenor to the treble line and that the organ was established as the harmonic base for congregational singing.

The earliest large collection of such melodies was the *Encheiridion* (1524), edited by Luther and Johann Walther (1496–1570). From that time the technique of chorale writing expanded, and many collections were published. Luther himself is credited with the composition of several, including *Ein' feste Burg* and *Vom Himmel hoch,* of which he certainly wrote the words and almost certainly wrote or adapted the music.

Landmarks in the history of chorale development are the names of Michael Weisse (*c.* 1484–1534), Nikolaus Herman (1480–1561), Nikolaus Selnecker (1530–92), Philipp Nicolai

(1556–1608), composer of the celebrated *Wachet auf,* Melchior Vulpius (*c.* 1560–1615), Johann Hermann Schein (1586–1630), and, greatest of all, Johann Crüger (1598–1662). Crüger edited the first editions of *Praxis pietatis melica,* a collection of tunes first published in 1644 and continuing in successive editions.

More complex chorales come from Johannes Eccard (1553–1611), Praetorius (1571–1621), and Heinrich Schütz (1585–1672). Eccard's chorales are virtually brief motets; Praetorius was one of the first systematic arrangers in polyphonic style of tunes from earlier sources (*Musae Zionae,* 1609); Schütz's contributions are in his *Psalmen Davids* (1628), in many of which is foreshadowed the more sophisticated and lyrical style adopted by the later pietist composers. For these and for later German hymnody, *see* HYMN.

In Bach's passions and cantatas the chorale appears as a richly harmonized hymn tune in which the audience is expected to join with the choir. Bach's chorales (some of which are sung as English hymn tunes) are strictly chorale arrangements not unlike those of Samuel Scheidt (1587–1654). It was Bach's practice to take a well-known hymn tune, remove (as the convention of his day required) its irregular rhythm, and adorn it with elaborate harmony. Bach's own compositions in this field were devotional songs; it is fair to say that he never composed a chorale. But in later works that imitate the passions of Bach, a congregational hymn is not infrequently inserted, and sometimes this is by analogy known as a chorale.

The CHORALE PRELUDE is a polyphonic form, usually for organ, using a chorale melody as a basis.

BIBLIOGRAPHY: Erik Routley, *The Music of Christian Hymnody* (1957); Johannes Riedel, *The Lutheran Chorale; Its Basic Traditions* (1967).

chorale prelude A form most closely associated with the organ, in which a chorale is made the basis of a (usually) short piece that decorates or varies the chorale. The organist in German Protestant churches traditionally introduced congregational hymns by extemporizing briefly on the tune (hence the term prelude), and these extemporizations became chorale preludes.

Early examples of the form are to be found in E. Nicolaus Ammerbach's collection *Orgel oder Instrument Tabulatur* (1571) and Augustus Nörmiger's *Tabulaturbuch auff dem Instrumente* (1598). Notable advances were made by the 16th-century Dutch composer Jan Pieterszoon Sweelinck and his pupil Samuel Scheidt, who developed the chorale variations. The form approached its zenith in the works of Buxtehude (17th century) and arrived in the masterpieces of Bach. Brahms and Max Reger made contributions in the 19th century, and such composers as Marcel Dupré, Heinrich Kaminsky, Sigfrid Karg-Elert, Hermann Schroeder, Alan Stout, and Helmut Walcha in the 20th.

BIBLIOGRAPHY: Stainton de B. Taylor, *The Chorale Preludes of J. S. Bach* (1942); Robert L. Tusler, *The Style of J. S. Bach's Chorale Preludes* (1956; reprint, 1968).

Choral Symphony (Ninth): *see* BEETHOVEN (last years) and (structural innovations; SYMPHONY (Haydn, Mozart, and Beethoven); VARIATIONS.

chord   The combination of three or more tones sounded at once. In the analysis of harmony chords may be consonant, implying repose, or dissonant, demanding movement to another chord. The triad, which underlies the Western system of harmony, is a chord composed of three tones that form two intervals of a third and one of a fifth; for example: e-g (a third) superimposed on c-e (another third) becomes the triad c-e-g (which includes the fifth c-g). Superimposing an additional third upon a triad forms a seventh chord (for example, c-e-g-b or c-e-g-bb; c-b and c-bb are sevenths); still another superimposed third forms a ninth chord (c-e-g-b-d'; c-d' is a ninth). Seventh and ninth chords are essentially expressive expansions of the triads on which they are built and are particularly characteristic of 19th-century music.

Late 19th- and 20th-century composers frequently used chords of superimposed fourths, for example, c-f♯-bb-e'-a'-d", the mystic chord of the Russian composer Aleksandr Scriabin, and tone clusters, chords composed of super-

imposed seconds (as c-d-e-f♯-g♯). Theorists of 20th-century music have often preferred the term "simultaneity."

chordophone   A class of instruments in which a stretched, vibrating string produces the initial sound. Chordophone replaces the term stringed instruments in an acoustically based designation. *Compare* AEROPHONE; ELECTROPHONE; IDIOPHONE; MEMBRANOPHONE.

chorus   A term that applies to the organized body of singers in opera, oratorio, cantata, and church music (*see* CHOIR); to compositions sung by such bodies; and to the refrain of a song sung by a group of singers between verses for solo voice.

Christmas Oratorio: *see* BACH, JOHANN SEBASTIAN (Leipzig); ORATORIO (Schütz) and (Bach); SCHÜTZ.

Christoff, Boris (b. May 19, 1918)   Known for Italian and Russian operatic roles, the Bulgarian bass Boris Christoff initially prepared for a law career. After being discovered as opera material while singing with a men's chorus, he studied with Riccardo Stracciari in Italy, where he made his debut in 1946 as Colline in Puccini's *La Bohème*. The following year he sang the title role of Mussorgsky's *Boris Godunov*, for which he is best known, at La Scala. In the United States he has sung with the San Francisco Opera (U.S. debut, 1956, in *Boris*), the Chicago Lyric Opera, and the Opera Company of Boston. His great vocal and dramatic intensity are well suited to opera, but he is also a fine singer of Russian art songs. He has recorded *Boris*, Gounod's *Faust*, Verdi's *Don Carlo*, and songs by Mussorgsky.

chromatic: *see* SCALE.

chromaticism   A term signifying the use of notes extraneous to the mode or scale in which a piece is written and introduced to intensify melodic design or harmonic texture. The term is derived from the Greek *chroma* ("color"), the chromatic tetrachord in Greek music consisting of four notes—A, F-sharp, F, E—marked by two semitone intervals. Possibly under the influence of Oriental melodies, the intervals of the Greek tetrachords were modified or colored by fractions of a tone; such inflections were known as the *chroai*.

In medieval music chromaticism was associated with the theory of musica ficta that provided for the introduction of notes foreign to the modes. In the 16th and 17th centuries chromaticism was widely used to illustrate or underline literary associations, notably in the English and Italian madrigals. An early English example is John Danyel's "Chromatic tunes most like my passions sound" (1606). With the establishment of the major and minor scales of tonality, chromaticism was integrated into contrapuntal technique. Chromatic themes were used as subjects for fugues. At the same period chromatic harmony was used in cantatas, oratorios, and operas for dramatic or pictorial purposes, notably to convey a sense of inchoate in "The Representation of Chaos" in Haydn's *Creation*. The expressive resources of chromaticism were progressively explored by Mozart, Beethoven, and the Romantic composers.

At the end of the 19th century, a much wider use was made of chromaticism, and this was soon to present a dilemma. From the technical viewpoint chromatic features in Classical or Romantic harmony had been mainly used for the purpose of modulation to another key. In the works of Franck and Aleksandr Scriabin, chromaticism and modulation were almost constant. In the works of Wagner chromatic inflections were increased to a point that frequently obscured or undermined the sense of tonality. As a result the function of chromaticism as a means of intensifying expression was correspondingly reduced. Later composers either rejected the tonal scale in favor of a chromatic scale in which none of the 12 notes in the octave is allowed to predominate (12-tone music, a form of serialism), or established harmonic systems based on personal conceptions of chromaticism.

Chrysander, Karl Franz Friedrich (July 8, 1826–September 3, 1901) A German musical scholar, Karl Franz Friedrich Chrysander was a founder of modern musicology. Born at Lübtheen, Mecklenburg, he studied at Rostock until 1855. He devoted most of his life to research on Handel, whose complete works he published single-handedly and at his own expense in 93 volumes (1858–94); the *Deutsche Handelsgesellschaft,* founded in 1856 to promote the edition, existed only nominally. His biography on Handel (three volumes, 1858–67), though unfinished, remains a classic, despite errors of judgment and the additional findings of later scholars. He also edited the works of other 17th- and 18th-century composers and inaugurated the German *Denkmäler* movement, which published library editions of the music of earlier periods.

church music Christian church services, like the Jewish temple rites from which they derived, have always used music as a means of enhancing verbal communication and heightening the emotional effect of the liturgy. Words when sung or chanted enjoy greater carrying power both physically, as in the vast interior of an abbey or cathedral, and psychologically, as a melody may call to mind texts otherwise in danger of being forgotten. In chant there is a division between what is sung by the officiant (and the choir, originally made up of clergy) and what is sung by the congregation. In the former elements of virtuosity hinting at professional execution are often found, whereas the latter must be relatively simple. Hence the difference between the chant for a gradual, alleluia, or offertory and that for a hymn, psalm, or canticle. These characteristics are generally true of the music of Eastern churches as well as of the Roman Catholic Church, whose music underwent continual revision with a view to standardization during the Middle Ages. Because of the widespread acceptance of Roman chant in its basic form and the prevailing differences in pronunciation and performance between one nation and another, this vast body of music was in fact prone to local deviations until a fairly late date.

Two branches of the Roman Church have maintained non-Roman types of chant that were originally connected with the localities concerned: Milan, the source of the Ambrosian chant, and Toledo, the home of Mozarabic chant. Ambrosian chant was formerly held to be of earlier origin than Roman, but it is possible that part of it may be a later and more ornate form of certain common antecedents. Mozarabic chant was evolved by Christian communities in the parts of Spain under Arab domination before the 11th century. Only the plainchant of the Roman Church has influenced polyphonic music to any degree, the first written signs of the movement toward polyphony being almost contemporary with the vast extensions made to the chant of mass and office by means of trope, sequence, and liturgical drama. From the 10th century there emerged also a vast number of hymns, of which only a small proportion are still sung, since the mortality rate of texts is greater than that of melodies.

The use of polyphony was from the earliest times restricted to major feasts, often including the patron saint of a cathedral or its dedication festival. Elaborate ecclesiastical rules determined the portions of the mass or office that might be set polyphonically, but these were often disregarded because of the sensuous appeal of the new art. Professional singers delighted in solo or duet virtuoso performances, accompanied by the organ or possibly by a group of instruments. By the end of the 12th century, the art of harmony had matured, especially in France where the early polyphonic tropes of Limoges had stimulated the later and more spectacular organa of Léonin and Pérotin, both associated with the Parisian school of composers. Musicians of other nations studied in Paris and brought to Spain, Italy, Germany, and England some of the secrets of vocal polyphony, which were in due course modified.

The 14th century saw a proliferation of locally produced verbal tropes, and these were set to music by more or less trained practitioners of the art, often in a relatively simply homophonic manner. This may have been part of a trend away from the overdecorative compositions of the former age, although subtlety of an unusual kind persisted in French circles, where the old *ordo* or reiterated note group was expanded to form the new and complex isorhythm, a structural feature sometimes pervading all voice parts. Isorhythmic technique was applied to the motet as well as to sections of the mass and is present in certain movements of the Mass by Guillaume de Machaut, one of several cyclic masses written during the second half of the 14th century.

Church music during the later Middle Ages became progressively more direct in its method and expression, the former subtlety of rhythm being replaced by a strong feeling for tonality and a penchant for order and symmetry. Guillaume Dufay and his followers in France and the Netherlands (*see* BURGUNDIAN SCHOOL), John Dunstable and Leonel Power in England, and many anonymous imitators throughout Europe brought a new freshness and force to liturgical music, written for princely chapels and court ceremonies rather than for abbey and cathedral services. Music had reached a pitch of perfection, and it could be properly interpreted only by the finest singers and players. Manuscripts containing liturgical polyphony used in monasteries frequently do not mention composers by name, for the *Opus Dei* was a matter for communal concern and not a vehicle for display. But in spite of attacks on its manner and content, church music survived to play a considerable part in the arts of the Renaissance. The techniques of the Netherlanders Jakob Obrecht and Jean d'Ockeghem (*see* FLEMISH SCHOOL) were taken over by the Henrician composers in England and to some extent by Josquin des Prés, who brought clarity and lyricism to an art that had sometimes leaned toward the sombre. Cristóbal de Morales in Spain; his countryman Tomás Luis de Victoria, who lived for many years in Rome; Orlando di Lasso, the international and prolific writer of church music in all forms; and later in the 16th century Byrd and Palestrina—all helped to develop Renaissance church music to a high peak of expression.

This same period also saw the growth of liturgical organ music, used originally when there was no choir capable of singing polyphony. It was the organist who played harmonized settings of plainchant hymns, canticles, and masses, alternating his verses with the plainchant of choir or congregation, and in due course the organ was used to accompany singing as well as to alternate with it. The rise of the verse anthem in England and the Baroque motet in Italy made demands on the organist's ability to improvise accompaniments. In Venice a splendid new concept of church music resulted from Andrea and Giovanni Gabrieli and their followers, chief among them Monteverdi and Alessandro Grandi, who made dramatic use of spatial contrasts and opposing forces of strings, winds, and voices. Eventually an anthem without an orchestra was unthinkable, and the music of Lully, Alessandro Scarlatti, Purcell, and John Blow continued to stress instrumental participation.

From the time of the Reformation, church music in Germany had followed a clear-cut path. The chorale, or hymn melody, was an all-important ingredient of motet and organ solo, and later in the 17th century it pervaded the cantata also. The music of Heinrich Schütz, Franz Tunder, and Buxtehude possessed a sweetness and gravity that slowly led music into a position of the greatest importance in church services. Bach's morning service at Leipzig went on for several hours, and music was used to accompany almost every part of the service except the sermon. This genuinely liturgical music marked a high point in Protestant church music and in the history of church music as a whole. Anthems, motets, and masses continued to be written in all Christian countries of Europe and the New World, but with few exceptions they were routine works. The great composers of the day wrote music set to liturgical texts but often with the concert hall rather than the church in mind. The resounding masses of the early Viennese masters, especially Haydn, who cheerfully used trumpets and drums in his scores, remained a local product that other countries and other churches could hardly hope to use.

The masses of Beethoven, Schubert, and Bruckner, the motets of Rossini and Brahms, the organ music of Franck and Max Reger, the requiems of Verdi and Berlioz—all belong to the extremely varied development of church music during the 19th century. One result of this revival was a series of attempts to write music in 16th-century style, and though much of this was no more than elegant pastiche it did serve to draw composers of church music away from the earlier Romantic flamboyance.

The 20th century has been a strange mixture of extreme conservatism at one end and the avant-garde at the other—with all degrees represented between. Among names of composers that stand out are, in Britain, Gustav Holst, Vaughan Williams, William Walton, and later Britten, Peter Maxwell Davies, Richard Rodney Bennett, and Kenneth Leighton; in the United States, Ives, Randall Thompson, Ulysses Kay, Daniel Pinkham, George Rochberg, Ned Rorem, Roger Sessions, and Alan Stout; in France, Maurice Duruflé, Jean Langlais, Messiaen, and Poulenc; in Hungary, Kodály and György Ligeti; in Germany-Austria, Hugo Distler, Anton Heiller, Johann Nepomuk David, and Ernst Pepping; and from Russia via the United States, Rachmaninoff and Stravinsky. Though well beyond the resources of most churches, the choral works of the Polish Krzysztof Penderecki use sacred texts and may point in a new direction.

Though anathema to some musicians and serious listeners, the introduction of jazz and folk music to the church service in the mid-20th century has established itself as a continuing tradition in some places. Geoffrey Beaumont's *20th-Century Folk Mass* (1957) and Frank Tirro's *American Jazz Mass* (1960) were pioneers in the idiom. Such eminent jazz figures as Dave Brubeck and Duke Ellington have contributed to the movement, and the German composer Heinz Werner Zimmermann combined jazz elements with the chorale in *Psalmkonzert* (1957) and in motets. All this may well have prepared the way for the introduction of *Sprechstimme* by such composers as the Norwegian Knut Nystedt and electronic music as exemplified in the works of Leslie Bassett and Richard Felciano. *See also* AMBROSIAN CHANT; ANTHEM; CANTATA; CHORALE; HYMN; ISORHYTHM; MASS; MOTET; MOZARABIC CHANT; PLAINCHANT.

BIBLIOGRAPHY: Archibald T. Davison, *Church Music; Illusion and Reality* (1952); Leonard Ellinwood, *The History of American Church Music* (1953); Denis W. Stevens, *Tudor Church Music* (1955; reprint, 1973); Frank L. Harrison, *Music in Medieval Britain* (1958); Karl Gustav Fellerer, *The History of Catholic Church Music* (1961); Winfred Douglas, *Church Music in History and Practice,* rev. ed. (1962); Erik Routley, *Twentieth Century Church Music* (1964); Elwyn A. Wienandt, *Choral Music of the Church* (1965), and with Robert H. Young, *The Anthem in England and America* (1970); Robert Stevenson, *Protestant Church Music in America* (1970); Edmund H. Fellowes, *English Cathedral Music,* rev. ed. (1973); James Robert Davidson, *A Dictionary of Protestant Church Music* (1975).

Ciccolini, Aldo (b. August 15, 1925)   Trained at the Naples Conservatory, the Italian pianist Aldo Ciccolini won the Santa Cecilia Prize (1948) in Rome. His recordings feature French music, especially that of Satie.

Cilea, Francesco (July 26, 1866–November 20, 1950)   An Italian composer of verismo operas, Francesco Cilea produced his first opera *Gina* in 1889 while still a student at the Naples Conservatory. His first major work was *L'Arlesiana* (1877), based on Alphonse Daudet's drama, followed by *Adriana Lecouvreur* (1902) with a libretto by Arturo Colautti from Scribe's well-known play. Cilea held several teaching positions, among them the directorship of the Naples Conservatory (1916–35). He also composed chamber music.

RECORDINGS: *Adriana Lecouvreur.*

Cimarosa, Domenico (December 17, 1749–January 11, 1801)   One of the principal Italian composers of comic operas, Domenico Cimarosa was born of a poor family at Aversa in the kingdom of Naples. Beginning in 1761 he studied for 11 years at Naples' Conservatory of Sta. Maria di Loreto, where his masters included Antonio Sacchini and probably Niccolò Piccinni.

He began his career by writing the comic opera *Le stravaganze del conte,* performed at the Teatro de' Fiorentini at Naples in 1772. Its success was followed by *L'Italiana in Londra* (Rome, 1779), a work that is still performed in Italy. From 1784 to 1787 Cimarosa lived in various Italian cities, composing both serious and comic operas that were produced in Rome, Naples, Florence, Vicenza, Milan, and Turin. At the invitation of Catherine II, he went to St. Petersburg as court musician,

replacing Giovanni Paisiello. There he produced two operas in 1788 and 1789. In 1791 he proceeded to Vienna at the invitation of Leopold II and produced his masterpiece, *Il matrimonio segreto* (1792; "The Secret Marriage"), one of the highest achievements in comic opera. In 1793 he returned to Italy, where *Il matrimonio segreto* and many of his other works were enthusiastically received. New works of this period included *Le astuzie femminili* (Naples, 1794) and his tragic masterpiece, *Gli Orazi ed i Curiazi* (Venice, 1796).

His chief residence was now in Naples, and during the occupation of the city by the French Republican troops in 1799, Cimarosa openly showed his republican sympathies so that on the return of the Bourbons he was imprisoned. After being released he left Naples broken in health and died in Venice.

Cimarosa was a prolific composer whose music abounds in fresh and never-failing melody. His more than 60 operas are remarkable for their characterizations and abundant comic life; his main fault is his repetitiveness. Among his instrumental works, which, like his operas, have been successfully revived, are many sparkling harpsichord sonatas and a concerto for two flutes; he also composed church music.

RECORDINGS: Concerto in G Major for two flutes; Harpsichord Sonatas (32); *Il matrimonio segreto;* Oboe Concerto; Quartets (2) for flute and strings.

cimbalom   The Magyar name for an elaborate form of DULCIMER. Used in small instrumental ensembles in Hungary for the performance of light music, it has a chromatic compass of four octaves and, unlike the earlier dulcimer, a foot mechanism for damping the strings. The strings are set in vibration by two small, spoon-shaped hammers. The number of strings to each note varies from three to five, some of which are bridged into two or three parts. The hammer heads are covered on each side with hard and soft leather to produce two distinct tone qualities. Hungarian players of the cimbalom perform mainly by ear and add to the effect of a small orchestra with florid extemporization. The cimbalom

man playing cimbalom
courtesy, John Leach
photograph, C. Brunel

was used in a large orchestra by Kodály in *Háry János* and in smaller combinations by Stravinsky in his *Ragtime* and *Renard*.

Cinderella: *see* CENERENJOLA, LA.

cittern A plucked stringed instrument popular in the 16th-18th centuries with a shallow, pear-shaped body and asymmetrical neck that was thicker under the treble strings. Derived from the citole, a 14th- and 15th-century instrument with gut strings, the cittern had four unison courses of wire strings; diapasons, additional courses to reinforce the basses of chords, were common. The strings were fastened to the instrument end and passed over a violin-type, or pressure, bridge. Tuning of the principal strings was b-g-d-e (Italian) or a-g-d-e (French) in the octave below middle C. Two bass variants of the cittern, the orpharion and the pandora, or bandore, appeared in the 17th century. The English guitar of the 18th and 19th centuries was a cittern with six courses of strings, the upper two double.

Civil, Alan (b. June 13, 1929) A student of Aubrey Brain, the English French horn player and composer Alan Civil played principal horn with the Royal Philharmonic (1952–55), the Philharmonia (1955) and New Philharmonia, and the BBC Symphony since 1966. He is a professor at the Royal College of Music

XLIX *Pandura*

man playing cittern
from Filippo Bonanni's Gabinetto armonico,
18th century courtesy, Dover Publications, Inc.

and is a member of several chamber music ensembles based in London. He has composed music for horn and for wind and brass ensembles and a symphony for brass and percussion (1951). In addition to the Mozart Horn Concertos one would expect, he has recorded with the Beatles.

clarinet A single-reed woodwind instrument employed in the orchestra and in brass and dance bands with a distinguished solo repertoire.

Usually made of African blackwood, it has a cylindrical bore of about 0.6 inch terminating in a flared bell. All-metal instruments are made but are little used in the best work. The mouthpiece, usually of ebonite, has a slotlike opening in one side over which a single reed, made from natural cane, is secured by a screw clip, or ligature, or (in earlier times and still often in Germany) by string lapping. The player grips the mouthpiece, reed down, between his lips or lower lip and upper teeth.

The ordinary clarinet is in B-flat and is

about 26 inches (66 centimeters) long; its notes, made with the finger holes and key mechanism, sound a step lower than written. The cyclindrical pipe, coupled to a reed mouthpiece, acts acoustically as a stopped pipe (closed at one end). This arrangement accounts for (1) the deep-pitched fundamental register; (2) the characteristic tone color caused largely by the virtual absence of even-numbered overtones; and (3) the overblowing (effected by a thumb key) to an upper register at the 12th (third harmonic) above the fundamental instead of at the octave (second harmonic), as in other woodwind instruments. A high register, using fifth and seventh harmonics, extends the compass to more than three and one-half octaves from the D (written E) below middle C.

The invention of the clarinet in the early 18th century is ascribed to Johann Christoph

Boehm clarinet, 1844; and modern bass clarinet
courtesy, C. G. Conn, Ltd.

Denner, a well-known flute maker in Nürnberg. Previously single reeds were used only in organs and in folk instruments. The clarinet's immediate predecessor was the small mock trumpet, or chalumeau, an adaptation of a folk reed pipe that Denner is credited with improving. His *clarinette* was longer and intended for playing mainly in the upper register with the fundamentals (to which the chalumeau was confined) as an adjunct. It thus provided a complete trumpet *(clarino)* compass with steadier, clearer notes.

The earliest known music for it are tune books published by Estienne Roger of Amsterdam (2nd edition 1716, extant). It was played with the reed up (playing with the reed down is described only after 1800 in Germany) and had two keys with F below middle C as the lowest note. A short bell was added by 1720, and the important extension of the tube to carry the low E key (also providing the upper B, formerly imperfectly available) followed *c.* 1740–50. By the late 18th century it had five or six keys and was built in various pitches, the written music being transposed to preserve the same finger rings. Clarinets were used in most large orchestras from *c.* 1780.

The modern clarinet developed between 1800 and 1850. Further keys were added to improve certain notes. Bores and mouthpieces were enlarged following general trends toward greater tonal power. Technological advances, including keywork mounted on pillars, the ring keys introduced by the flute maker Theobald Boehm, and Auguste Buffet's needle springs, led in the 1840s to the appearance in their main essentials of the two principal modern systems.

The simple, or Albert, system, named for the Brussels maker Eugène Albert, is a modernization of the earlier 13-key system of the clarinetist-builder Iwan Müller. It is used in German-speaking countries and has a complex accretion of auxiliary keywork but with conservative features in bore, mouthpiece, and reed (the last being smaller and harder than elsewhere) that give a deeper tone quality. The Boehm system, patented by Hyacinthe E. Klosé and Buffet (Paris, 1844) and still standard in most countries, incorporates much of Boehm's 1832 flute fingering system, bringing many technical advantages. It is distinguished from the other system by the ring at the back for the thumb and by the four or five keys for the right little finger. A more elaborate full Boehm model is used mainly in Italy, where orchestral players transpose A clarinet parts on the B-flat instruments.

Clarinets in sizes other than B-flat and its sharp-key equivalent in A include the C clarinet, much used in the Classical period and often preserved in German orchestration; octave clarinets in A-flat, used in large European bands; and sopranino clarinets in F and later E-flat, the second often used with its sharp-key equivalent in D (popular in the earlier days). Alto (or tenor) clarinets that followed the late-18th-century *clarinette d' amour* in A-flat, G, or F and the more successful BASSET HORN in F include the wider bore alto clarinet in F and later E-flat, made with upturned metal bell and a curved metal crook holding the mouthpiece. Bass clarinets in B-flat were at first built experimentally but after 1810 were built in many designs. The modern version with twice-curved crook was influenced by the 1838 design of the Belgian instrument maker Adolphe Sax, to which the upturned bell was later added. Contrabass clarinets are made in E-flat or in B-flat.

BIBLIOGRAPHY: Robert Willaman, *The Clarinet and Clarinet Playing*, rev. ed. (1954); Francis Geoffrey Rendall, *The Clarinet; Some Notes upon Its History and Construction*, rev. ed. (1957); Anthony Baines, *Woodwind Instruments and Their History*, rev. ed. (1963); Frederick Thurston, *Clarinet Technique*, 2nd ed. (1964).

Clarke, Jeremiah (c. 1674–December 1, 1707) An English organist and composer of church and sacred music, Jeremiah Clarke became a boy chorister at the Chapel Royal under John Blow, whom he succeeded as master of the choristers at St. Paul's Cathedral (1703). In 1700 with William Croft he became a gentleman extraordinary at the Chapel Royal and in 1704 was joint organist there with Croft. He committed suicide after a hopeless love affair.

Clarke's sacred music is sometimes in the dramatic style of Purcell and sometimes in an archaic style. His occasional anthems include "Praise the Lord O Jerusalem," written for the coronation of Queen Anne in 1702, and "The Lord is my strength" for the victory of Ramillies in 1706. His secular odes include the original setting of John Dryden's "Alexander's Feast" (1697). He is the composer of the famous Trumpet Voluntary, once wrongly ascribed to Purcell, and it was originally either a harpsichord piece, *The Prince of Denmark's March*, or an orchestral rondeau. He also wrote incidental music for plays, solo songs, and harpsichord music.

RECORDINGS: Trumpet Voluntary.

Classical period As currently defined by most music historians, the Classical period encompasses most of Western art music from the operatic reforms associated with the poet Pietro Metastasio in the 1720s (overlapping the BAROQUE ERA) to the expansive works Beethoven began writing at Vienna in the first decade of the 19th century. No one seriously contends that a single "classical style" adequately describes the principal musical achievements of this time-span; many, however, use this term for what is more properly called the Viennese Classical style, in particular the instrumental works of Haydn, Mozart, and Beethoven up to the *Eroica* Symphony. Some subsume Beethoven's later works and even much of Schubert under the rubric Classical, and Friedrich Blume goes so far as to posit a single Classic-Romantic period. *See* ROMANTIC PERIOD.

The internal periodization of the Classical era has occasioned much disagreement, particularly in the use of the terms galant, rococo, *Empfindsamkeit* (sensibility), *Sturm und Drang* (storm and stress), and the revolting pre-Classical. The stylistic diversity responsible for this terminological proliferation argues for a broad view of the period as overlapping "waves piling toward the same shore."

The Classical period assumes greatest coherence in relation to general European intellectual and cultural history in the 18th century. The Enlightenment is clearly echoed in such new musical values as clarity, simplicity, and naturalness, as well as in the emerging interest in folk music, the clear preeminence of secular genres over sacred ones, the rise of paying middle-class audiences and public concerts, the gradual emancipation of the composer and performer from the more onerous artistic and social restrictions of the prevailing system of servitude and patronage, and the first stirrings of music historiography.

Throughout the era melody commanded supreme importance, with ideals derived from the best vocal writing and singing lying behind even many instrumental works (*e.g.*, the slow movements of Haydn's symphonies, Mozart's concertos, Carl Philipp Emanuel Bach's sonatas and fantasies). Before 1770 texture and harmonic vocabulary were often drastically simplified to serve the end of concentrated melodic expression. Greater variety and subtlety of rhythmic patterns arose as a natural concomitant, as did a clarified sense of periodic phrases (antecedent-consequent), although the four-bar phrase was far from inviolate as a natural ideal. Around 1770 counterpoint returned to enrich this clear, strong frame.

Tonal language concentrated on the most basic areas—I, IV, and V (as well as III in minor-mode pieces, now become relatively less common)—which achieve in consequence far greater structural significance. Most importantly patterns of harmonic rhythm became emancipated from the bass line (despite the survival of the basso continuo throughout the period) in keeping with the new melodic-periodic conception. While V and III (in the minor) remained unchallenged as principal tonal goals in articulating the internal shape of a piece or movement, variety of key areas was preferred between movements and numbers.

vocal music, 1720–1750 A new and uniquely 18th-century chapter in Italian opera began with the reforms of the poets Apostolo Zeno and more especially Pietro Metastasio. The tone of Baroque opera was elevated with the *tragédies classiques* of Racine clearly in mind as models. Comic characters and ballet were excluded; plot was simplified to intrigues involving a few central characters; the *lieto fine* became standard (though exceptions occur) as a frequent and seldom very compelling conclusion extolling the hero's magnanimity. Arias were carefully apportioned to set off the skills and soothe the professional jealousy of the leading singers.

A generation of composers, almost all trained at Naples and active there, brought international attention to this new kind of opera in the 1720s and '30s. Many of their musical practices are drawn from the master operas of Alessandro Scarlatti; some of his arias adopt such "modern" procedures as prominent, periodic melodies supported by simplified and decelerated harmonic movement and are very often in da capo form. The luminaries of this new generation—Leonardo Vinci, Leonardo Leo, and Pergolesi—crystallized the musical means that, together with Metastasian dramatic practices, constitute opera seria. Observers of the day credited especially Vinci with a new, periodic, and beguiling melodic style; they also praised his puissant obbligato recitatives such as those in the last act of his *Didone abbandonata* (1725).

The next generation of opera seria composers (many scarcely younger than this triumvirate) began carrying these operatic innovations to the rest of Europe. What was (and remained) a popular art in Italy became associated with court audiences and tastes abroad. The period's most admired master of opera seria and Metastasio's own ideal composer was Johann Adolph Hasse, active chiefly at Dresden (1734–64). Niccolò Jommelli and Baldassare Galuppi attained nearly commensurate prominence and went beyond Hasse in matters of fuller texture and sonority even before leaving Italy.

Comic opera was strictly a local affair before 1750. Italy saw the development of dialect comedies as well as the intermezzi (played between the acts of serious operas) familiar from Pergolesi's *Serva padrona* (1733). The modest and often uncouth ballad opera in England (*e.g., The Beggar's Opera*, 1728) follows the *comédie en vaudeville* given at Parisian fairs in trading on familiar tunes set to new words and in using spoken dialogue. All genres of comic opera call for contemporary settings and characters; and from the beginning the musical style was more motivic and modulatory, the atmosphere more realistic.

The Italian oratorio, which Zeno and Metastasio also elevated and purified, absorbed something of the new Neapolitan operatic language. Pergolesi's famous setting of *Stabat mater* and his *Salve regina* juxtapose up-to-date arias and duets with imitative numbers in the older style. A pseudo-Palestrina idiom also continued to be cultivated. Mass settings show operatic inroads as early as Scarlatti (*c.* 1720); later Catholic composers cultivated an ever less severe style, but the chorus retained a considerable role.

instrumental music, 1720–1750 Of all the varied instrumental forms cultivated in the 18th century, the symphony underwent the most profound and spectacular development. The Italian opera overture was at first little more than a call to order for notoriously unruly Italian audiences. The Vinci–Leo–Pergolesi generation and later Galuppi and Jommelli explored the dramatic possibilities of crescendos, clear thematic differentiation, simplified chordal texture, and vigorous rhythmic drive. The chamber symphony, at first scarcely distinguishable from the ripieno concerto (*i.e.,* without solo parts), received a fruitful infusion of the opera overture's new effects at the hands of Giovanni Battista Sammartini of Milan.

German-speaking lands, where the symphony as a concert piece really came into its own, found their first great symphonic master in the Czech-born Johann Stamitz, concertmaster at Mannheim (*see* MANNHEIM SCHOOL). Stamitz gave new structural weight to earlier dynamic innovations, deepened the exposition's sense of thematic contrast, and standardized the four-movement plan. Next to him the northerners Hasse and the brothers Graun seem conservative. The Viennese masters Georg Matthias Monn and Georg Christoph Wagenseil, also active around mid-century, explored some of the techniques Haydn was to integrate into his symphonic style—major-minor contrast, motivic insistence, and striking rhythmic effects.

While Naples assumed leadership in operatic developments, northern Italy produced a corps of composer-performers who contributed vitally to the emergence of the Classical solo concerto, particularly for the violin. Vivaldi was one of the first to expand the solo concerto (which already preferred a fast–slow–fast pattern) and to cultivate a brilliant, idiomatic violin style. He is vigorous and often folklike in outer movements, and his slow ones

speak with directness of expression cast in limpid formal clarity. Younger Italian violinists such as Pietro Locatelli and Giuseppe Tartini astonished European audiences with unexampled technical feats in their cadenzas, but in general their solo parts strove to be songful—particularly in Tartini's slow movements, some of which carry text incipits that point to their source of inspiration in the new bel canto style.

The violin sonata followed a parallel course. Already in the second decade of the century, Francesco Veracini began writing clearly phrased rounded binary movements, a potent scheme that was expanded and adapted in the concerto as well as the symphony. By and large the trio sonata remained under the spell of Corelli's models until mid-century.

Domenico Scarlatti is today the best known of Italian keyboardists of this period for his highly original one-movement sonatas (often paired). Scarlatti employs a spare two-voice texture in a parallel rather than symmetric binary frame that supports idiomatic keyboard writing of often considerable technical difficulty. His works, however, were scarcely known in Europe outside of the Iberian peninsula, where he worked, and London. Other Italians more attuned to the needs of the perfumed, galant drawing room fared better, notably Giovanni Battista Pescetti and the enigmatic Domenico Alberti. All these keyboard composer–performers relied on foreign aristocratic patrons and pupils for support, and they often resorted to foreign music publishers as well.

vocal music, 1750–1800 The story of opera seria in Italy after mid-century is one of a cautious and damped assimilation of elements and ideas from other nations; abroad this process was much more rapid, and the consequences more dramatic. By 1780 Paris was the European capital of serious opera, and the other centers that contributed most vitally to the transformation of the genre in these years were all strongholds of French cultural influence—Stuttgart, Vienna, Parma, and Mannheim.

Jommelli moved to Karl Eugen's court at Stuttgart in 1753, where he was Kapellmeister until 1769. With a free hand and an excellent band, he intensified his scores with powerful orchestral effects and imposing choruses, all for clearly dramatic ends. French influence is stronger still in the operas of Tommaso Traetta, whose pictorial numbers and dances derive from the *tragédies lyriques* of Rameau. His freedom from the galant, Arcadian mannerisms of Hasse, his tragic choruses, and bold obbligato recitatives remind one of the contemporaneous rediscovery of a more genuine antiquity based on archaeological research, heralded in Johann Winckelmann's *Reflections on the Painting and Sculpture of the Greeks* (1755).

Galuppi's works written for Venice around mid-century earned admiration all over the Continent but in dramatic power and expression stand far behind what he himself dared to write in setting *Artaserse* for Vienna in 1749. Metastasio, by then imperial poet at Vienna, inveighed against Galuppi's arrogation of dramatic control in this score. "He thinks as much about the words as you think of becoming Pope," he wrote to the castrato Farinelli.

Gluck aroused the poet's displeasure at this time for similar transgressions, but these antedate the so-called reforms of *Orfeo* (1762) and *Alceste* (1767). The preface to the latter presents more a critique of the excesses of operatic practice in the 1760s than an attack on Metastasio's art, and the opera itself is scarcely a faithful execution of the preface's astringent prescription. The tonal and expressive control in Orfeo's confrontation with the Furies and his entry into Elysium, combined with the simple grandeur and emotive directness of Gluck's aria style, spoke far more compellingly to his auditors and emulators. Gluck's activities as arranger, then composer of *opéras comiques* for Vienna (1754–65) are not to be overlooked in considering his reforms. That Gluck went to Paris in the 1770s bespeaks a sort of stylistic logic. Here almost single-handedly he revivified the *tragédie lyrique*—and not by importing "German" virtues; in setting *Armide* in 1777 Gluck was striving to beat Lully at his own game. Gluck was represented to be the French as against the Italian side in the idle skirmishes of the Gluckists and

Piccinnists, while he himself went on in sovereign indifference to his masterpiece, *Iphigénie en Tauride* (1779), perhaps the most severely and purely "classical" of all operas of the era.

As had Lully before him, Gluck dominated French serious opera even after departing. The prolific Niccolò Piccinni, however, arrived at a similar style largely on his own. His *Didon* (1783) can stand comparison to Gluck's best operas, as can works more obviously under the impress of Gluck's achievements—*Oedipe à Colone* (1786) of Antonio Sacchini and the powerful *Danaïdes* (1784) of Antonio Salieri.

Artaxerxes (1762), set by Thomas Arne, is the one worthy attempt at English serious opera. In a city totally dominated by opera seria, it could not help being Italianate. Only slightly less so are three German serious operas—*Alceste* (1773) and *Rosamunde* (1777) by the poet Christoph Martin Wieland, music by Anton Schweitzer; and *Günther von Schwarzburg* (1777), set by Ignaz Holzbauer on a German subject. Of greater artistic and historic significance are the two melodramas of Georg Benda, *Ariadne auf Naxos* and *Medea* (both 1775), which in form and style profoundly impressed Mozart, Beethoven, and Weber.

Opera buffa as an independent genre gained clear artistic definition and international currency around mid-century largely through the combined achievements of the dramatist Carlo Goldoni and Galuppi, notably in the action, or "chain," finale, cast as a miniature drama of contrasting sections and ever-increasing confusion. Sentimental attitudes were adopted only sporadically by the opera buffa (Piccinni's *Buona figliuola,* 1760), whose finales depend for their lifeblood on the time-tested intrigues and character types of Molière and the commedia dell' arte.

The French opéra comique, which incorporates spoken dialogue, responded more profoundly to the *comédie larmoyante* and largely avoided the complications, musical and dramatic, of its Italian sister. The traces of the vaudeville are still clear in many of the contributions of Egidio Romoaldo Duni and François Philidor; so are the mixture of French melodic disingenuousness with Italian motivic and constructive virtues, present already in Rousseau's celebrated intermezzo *Le Devin du village* (1752). This mixture, which fueled the *guerre des bouffons* at Paris in the 1750s, made of opéra comique a potent new force on the international scene. An expansion of means and dimension and an elevation of tone appeared with the opera *Le Déserteur* (1769) of Pierre Alexandre Monsigny, tendencies pursued by André-Modeste Grétry, notably in *Zémire et Azor* (1771), which also illustrates a growing fondness for exotic settings and themes. Grétry was the genre's foremost exponent until the Revolution.

In Germany one school of singspiel composers clung to the modest dimensions of the early opéra comique as adapted to a more Italian melodic style by Johann Adam Hiller and his librettist Christian Felix Weisse. Attempts at expansion were scattered, although Benda's *Romeo und Julie* (1776) was an ambitious experiment in serious opera with spoken dialogue.

A mutual exchange of forms and features characterizes nearly all serious and comic opera genres after 1770. The tendency is discernible as early as Giuseppe Sarti's *Giulio Sabino* (1781) and Giovanni Paisiello's *Barbiere di Siviglia* (1782) and clearly evident in Cimarosa's best opera seria *Gli Orazi ed i Curiazi* (1796), no less than in his master opera buffa *Il matrimonio segreto* (1792). In France Salieri's setting of Beaumarchais's *Tarare* (1787) provides a dramatic example.

Mozart's operatic gifts came to maturity during this propitious period. Of all composers of the century Mozart was the most universal and cosmopolitan; yet he was also one of the most individual, for he absorbed every conceivable style (even that of Bach) without a trace of eclecticism. *Idomeneo* (1781) amalgamates *tragédie lyrique,* opera ballet, and opera seria into a spectacle *sui generis. The Abduction from the Seraglio* (1782) is at once singspiel, opéra comique, and opera buffa in a city where all three genres crossed paths. Mozart's last five operas are saturated with this multivariate, transfigured heritage, and in their unprecedented depth of psychological characterization they constitute as well the *ne plus ultra* of Mozart's own view of music's dramatic primacy in Classical opera. Without

detracting from the other four, *The Magic Flute* (1791) may be proposed as a compendium of all toward which opera strove during the Enlightenment—optimistic humanism; ethical instruction pleasingly imparted; variety, clarity, and directness of expression.

In areas dominated by Italian opera its influence on oratorio and mass remained strong. But increasingly composers turned to the sounds and shapes of the symphony, perceptible in Johann Ernst Eberlin and especially Michael Haydn, whose best masses rank with his brother's in substance and skill. This rapprochement was facilitated by textural and expressive developments in instrumental music after 1770, which in some ways parallel the vocal heritage of Neapolitan mellifluousness and Fuxian contrapuntal severity in Austrian sacred music.

Joseph Haydn's masses are uneven, but the late ones (after his return from London in 1795) contain some of his greatest movements in any genre—the *Missa in tempore belli* (1796) and especially the so-called *Nelson* Mass (*Missa in angustiis,* 1798). Mozart's *Coronation* Mass in C Major (K.331, 1779) is well known for the operatic cast of its arias as well as moments of solemn grandeur. His greatest mass, the incomplete c minor (K.427, 1782–83), parallels his mature operas in embracing the century's traditions in all their variety. Mozart's Requiem, K. 626, completed by Franz Xaver Süssmayr, begins to explore a dark, personal region in many ways closer to the masses of Cherubini and Beethoven than to those of its own century.

Haydn's *The Creation* (1798, based on an English adaptation of Milton) recurs to the Handelian oratorio derived from the Old Testament, and *The Seasons* (1801, van Swieten, after Thomson) to the secular oratorio, both forms relatively uncommon in the second half of the 18th century. Though replete with pictorialisms and handsome arias and duets, their greatest glories are the choruses, luminously humanistic and surely not without their effect on Beethoven.

Little in the remainder of Europe can stand comparison to Austrian achievements in sacred music. France showed an almost total unconcern. North Germans mostly pursued the sentimental, meditative oratorio, epitomized by the then much admired *Tod Jesu* of Karl Heinrich Graun (1755, Ramler). The sacred dramas of the Magdeburger Johann Heinrich Rolle are exceptional in drawing inspiration from Handel and Gluck. The oratorios of C. P. E. Bach lie somewhere between. More characteristic of both Bach and the north in general are his sacred odes and songs in their direct and expressive earnestness.

In secular song northern Germany also figured prominently. The French-derived and artificial simplicity of the first Berlin song school of mid-century yielded to, on the one hand, a more Herderesque search for primeval simplicity, best represented by Johann Abraham Peter Schulz in his *Lieder im Volkston* (1782) and, on the other hand, to more ambitious works looking toward Schubert, among them Johann André's setting of Bürger's "Lenore," the first through-composed ballade.

Haydn and Mozart both contributed to the lied, and mention should be made as well of Haydn's fine English songs of 1794–95 and settings of Scottish folk songs. More characteristic of Mozart are his concert arias—expressive, virtuoso works for voice, orchestra, and often a concertizing solo instrument.

instrumental music, 1750–1800 The last decades of the Classical period constitute the first great era of instrumental music. In this sphere attention has been largely concentrated on the Viennese Classical masters—and not without reason. We must think of the symphonies and chamber works of Hayden and Mozart and the latter's concertos as a quintessential corpus in any definition of "classical." The instrumental heritage these men found is as yet imperfectly known, although agreement is growing that the unique and unprecedented curve of development along which both carried these genres has refracted what investigators have seen, or sought, in earlier works.

By the time Haydn began writing his first symphony in the late 1750s, the expansion of rounded binary form to dimensions capable of sustaining real tension and drama between two strongly articulated key areas was an accomplished fact. Still the concept of sonata form as a preexisting compositional construct, and in particular the notion of thematic dualism, remained altogether foreign to Haydn, Mozart, and the 18th century generally though valid in the 19th century when these ideas were first formulated.

Instrumental fare was rich and varied at Vienna when Haydn was learning his craft there in the 1750s; yet there is great truth to his subsequent remark, "I was forced to become original," describing his situation at Esterházy in the Hungarian marshes. Haydn's first symphonies for his new employer, the programmatic Nos. 6–8, signal the wealth of possibilities the genre offered—H. C. Robbins Landon calls them "an astonishing combination of concerto grosso, divertimento, concerto, suite, and symphony," to which may be added recitative and aria. At the same time one detects Haydn's unique and never-failing instinct for economical use of material, evident in his compact motivic work, bright orchestral sonorities, formal proportioning, and contrapuntal touches. Haydn's so-called *Sturm und Drang* symphonies of the late 1760s and early '70s actually have little in common with the German literary movement; they do not shock, horrify, or fly in the face of formal discipline but instead demonstrate the expressive and spiritual weight Haydn's strong, wonderfully adaptive frames could carry. No clearer example can be adduced than No. 44, the *Trauersymphonie* in e minor.

At this stage Haydn's symphonies found their way into print almost as soon as they were written. Their international popularity generated the commissions that produced his greatest symphonies, the Paris set (Nos. 82–87, 1785–86) and the two hexads for London (Nos. 93–98, 1791–92, and Nos. 99–104, 1794–95). It was his departure for England in 1790 that occasioned Haydn's remark to Mozart that his language was "understood the world over." Indeed few masterpieces can claim the immediate success these symphonies found in London. Nor can any assert as compelling a case for the epithet "classical" by virtue of a perfect equipoise of the personal and the universal, of unity and variety, of form matched to content, of profundity and accessibility.

Mozart's few mature symphonies, while clearly owing a great deal to Haydn's example, pursue somewhat different ends. They repose on formal structures no less perfect but less vital than Haydn's; thematic contrast and integrity is greater, and as always with Mozart the writing is rich yet clear, particularly in the use of chromaticism. Nowhere are Mozart's virtues and ambitions clearer than in the great g minor Symphony, K.550, which for many is the greatest symphony ever written.

Other symphonists of the era have been harshly judged in light of Haydn and Mozart; yet the number of attractive movements in the works of Carlos d'Ordoñez, Leopold Hofmann, Leopold Koželuch, Jan Vanhal, and Karl Ditters von Dittersdorf is impressive. At Mannheim, on the other hand, the generation of symphonists after Stamitz (including his son Carl) offer relatively little of interest.

In France, where the hegemony of vocal music was almost a cultural necessity, the symphony played a subordinate though by no means negligible role. The long-lived François-Joseph Gossec kept abreast of Italian, German, and Austrian innovations in his symphonic *oeuvre,* not a very difficult feat in as active a publishing center as Paris. Other important French symphonists include Henri Jean Rigel and Ignaz Pleyel.

After mid-century northern Germany's symphonic production was the primary concern of almost no one, although Johann Wilhelm Hertel and Johann Christoph Friedrich Bach betray a far from provincial feel for the genre. The symphonies of C. P. E. Bach, original and eloquent, are among his best works, particularly those for van Swieten (1773) and the masterful Four Symphonies for twelve obbligato instruments (1775–76). Bach's eager quest for originality and expressive weight earned him universal admiration among his contemporaries, including Haydn and Mozart. Yet his disquieting formal and stylistic vagaries disturb some critics and at all events argue for a cautious interpretation of his role in the musical world from which he kept his undeniable genius so curiously detached.

In England only Arne showed any real gift for the new symphony. Those of William Boyce are old-fashioned. True leadership, artistic as well as entrepreneurial, was exercised by the Germans Johann Christian Bach—whose formal and thematic procedures profoundly affected young Mozart—and Carl Friedrich Abel.

The solo concerto after mid-century turned more to the keyboard and away from the violin; and many composers, particularly in Germany, began organizing its tutti and solo sections into the familiar pattern often called double-exposition form, derived from sonata form. The violin concerto, so akin to the opera aria, remained strong among Italian composers, including Tartini's pupils but more especially Giovanni Battista Viotti. Like most Italian instrumentalists he worked mostly abroad, adapting his heritage to French concert traditions in the 1780s, which included the *symphonie concertant* (with two or more soloists). Native French genius in this as well as the solo concerto is best represented by the flutist François Devienne. The best concerto composers in England are again foreigners, notably J. C. Bach and the virtuoso oboist Johann Christian Fischer, whose concertos and playing were all the rage at London's outdoor summer concerts.

Many of the concertos, players, and models found in France and England at this time migrated from Mannheim, whose record here is scarcely less distinguished than in symphonic production. Stamitz and Anton Filtz led the first generation, and the prolific Carl Stamitz led the next. In far more conservative shapes the concerto found ready pens in northern Germany as well. Almost all composers there, from Frederick the Great and his flute teacher Johann Joachim Quantz to Hertel and the brothers Graun and Benda, regarded Baroque concepts of thematic structure, rhythmic continuity, and carousel-like tonal planning as a necessity in the concerto. Only C. P. E. Bach made a virtue of them.

Mozart's concertos have long been admired as one of the loftiest eminences of Classical art, and their kinship to the other great peak in his *oeuvre,* the operas, has often been noticed. Indeed neither Mozart's symphonies nor his chamber music can equal the vital dramatic interplay of soloist and orchestra, the astonishing compass of the expressive regions explored, and the constructive variety in his concertos. As with his operas their special character derives from his cosmopolitan, assimilative nature, which works to set his concertos apart from the rather indifferent specimens of other Austrian composers, not excepting Dittersdorf and even Haydn. Maturity in the concerto actually antedates Mozart's operatic coming of age with the E-flat Concerto, K.271 of 1777, although his greatest concertos, all for the keyboard, date from 1784–86, culminating in the majestic C Major Concerto, K.503.

A variety of new chamber genres emerged during the Classical period. For several their exact nature and interrelationship cannot be precisely defined. Neither the divertimento (usually a chamber work), nor the serenade (more often an orchestral genre), nor the nocturne (which apparently can be either) has a fixed structure of movements. These and similar works were popular in much of Europe, finding an especially congenial reception at Vienna and uncongenial one in the dour north.

The string quartet is of course the chamber genre par excellence of the second half of the 18th century. As such it is effectively the creation of Haydn, and significantly attempts at finding antecedents ("the first string quartet") have borne no fruit, due largely to the very real difficulty of proposing a conception of the genre independent of Haydn's models. Haydn effected a final emancipation of the cello from figured-bass thinking only in his Opus 20 set (1772), which also boasts three final fugues and a studied effort to achieve individuality in every movement. The revelation came with Opus 33 (1781) and a fluid collegiality of obbligato parts that give enrichment to and draw coherence from the homophonic, periodic frame. No greater tribute has been paid to Haydn's unique gift as a composer of quartets than Mozart's unwontedly heavy laboring from 1782 to 1785 on his Six Quartets, Op. 10, dedicated to Haydn. They contain some of the imperishable glories of quartet literature and are unthinkable without the genius of both composer and dedicatee.

The quintet proved an especially happy medium for the cellist Boccherini, who wrote nearly 200 of them, about half for strings. Michael Haydn and J. C. Bach also contributed to the genre, but nothing in their works prepares for the great quintets Mozart composed in 1787 and 1790–91; the g minor (K.516, 1787) goes far beyond his quartets in matching hitherto unknown expressive pessimism with perfectly controlled formal flexibility.

Chamber music for keyboard and other instruments included some of the most attractive genres for amateurs and consequently music publishers. Technically demanding works for violin and keyboard (rarely for solo violin) continued to appear, notably those of Jean Joseph Cassanéa de Mondonville and Tartini's pupil Pietro Nardini. But when such duets carry written-out keyboard parts, they are almost always keyboard sonatas with violin accompaniment. To this combination a cello and occasionally a second violin were sometimes added. The Paris-based German Johann Schobert wrote some impressive works for such combinations, unusual in recalling the darkling spirit of C. P. E. Bach. Another new chamber—indeed domestic—genre of the period comprises literature for keyboard four hands, to which J. C. Bach and the historian Charles Burney were early contributors and which Mozart subsequently elevated. In the more familiar categories of piano trio, quartet, and quintet (showing a more or less equal partnership among the participants), it was again Mozart who created the first real masterpieces, namely the Trio, K.498; Quintet, K.452, for piano and winds; and the two Quartets, K.478 and 493, for piano and strings. Charles Rosen pleads as well, and not without justice, for Haydn's piano trios.

The literature for solo keyboard in the second half of the 18th century served virtuoso and rank amateur alike; the instrument intended (harpsichord, clavichord, or fortepiano) is not always specified. The terms style galant and *empfindsamer Stil* are most often invoked with reference to these keyboard works. The former is best seen in Italian examples of 1740–70, such as Galuppi's spare but elegant sonatas. The latter term is very much associated with C. P. E. Bach's expressive, intense sonatas, rondos, and fantasies. Their impact on Haydn, Mozart, and young Beethoven is attested by these composers themselves, and their unbridled emotive character has also occasioned attempts at contriving direct connections with 19th-century Romanticism. An older, contrapuntal keyboard idiom in Germany is well represented by Wilhelm Friedemann Bach; his works also illustrate the expressive sources of much of what his brother Carl Philipp Emanuel transplanted.

At Paris Schobert plied the salons with fiery works that Burney saw as imitations of orchestral style. From 1782 Clementi wrote and published some of his most impressive sonatas at London. They are as much German as Italian and bear witness to the abiding influence of J. S. Bach's *Well-Tempered Clavier* on all important keyboard composers throughout the 18th century.

The keyboard sonatas of Haydn, though generally acknowledged to be of lesser significance than his quartets and symphonies, show at their best no less inspiration and craftsmanship. Mozart's keyboard sonatas reflect the many facets of his musical personality no less than other genres, and when performed on the fortepiano—where most of them belong—they take on a sensuous transparency that should disabuse those who labor under the misapprehension that they are too thin. Particularly the six sonatas he wrote in 1774–75 represent a landmark in the de-amateurizing of the genre and anticipate something of the perfect artistic maturity permeating K.330–333.

The end of the Classical period appears at different times in different places, depending largely on the involvement of composers with the legacy of Haydn and Mozart. Not surprisingly a breakthrough to a new aesthetic occurred first in opera, notably French post-Revolutionary works such as Cherubini's *Lodoïska* (1790), less spectacularly in the Italian operas of the Bavarian Johann Simon Mayr. In instrumental genres the transition can best be studied in Beethoven, who was more vitally involved with his great Viennese predecessors than anyone else. In his works of 1803 and onward he embraces grander dimensions, attempts precarious feats of formal and rhetorical derring-do that spare no musical element, interjects discursive vagaries and acts of pure willfulness, and effects a heroic-pathetic confrontation of the personal and cos-

mic—all of which belongs to a new era. The nature of this new era is perceptible already in Beethoven's Opus 18 Quartets, brought out in 1801—inconceivable apart from Haydn and Mozart, yet inconceivable as theirs. The new paths presaged in this set must have been very much on Beethoven's mind, when, on hearing Mozart's c minor Concerto, K.491, in the last year of the old century, he is said to have turned suddenly and remarked to his companion, "We shall never be able to do anything like that!"

Thomas A. Bauman

BIBLIOGRAPHY: William Henry Hadow, *The Viennese Period* (1931; reprint, 1973); Oliver Strunk, *Source Readings in Music History* (1950); Karl Geiringer, ed., *Music of the Bach Family* (1955); Friedrich Blume, *Classic and Romantic Music* (1970); H. C. Robbins Landon, *Essays on the Viennese Classical Style* (1970); Charles Rosen, *The Classical Style* (1971); William S. Newman, *The Sonata in the Classic Era,* 2nd ed. (1972); Reinhard G. Pauly, *Music in the Classic Period,* 2nd ed. (1973); Egon Wellesz and Frederick Sternfeld, eds., *The Age of Enlightenment 1745–1790* (1973), Vol. 7 of *The New Oxford History of Music.*

Classical Symphony: *see* NEOCLASSICISM; PROKOFIEV.

clausula In the music of the NOTRE DAME SCHOOL (late 12th, early 13th centuries), the clausula was an animated and more nearly homophonic section within an ORGANUM, a larger polyphonic setting of a plainchant melody. In organum the plainchant typically is placed in the lowest of the two to four voices and is sung in notes held an extremely long time beneath the faster moving upper parts. In the clausula sections, which correspond to the melismas of the chant (sections prolonging one syllable over many notes), the lower voice accelerates in order to accommodate the syllable's extra notes; and there are fewer upper voice notes for each lower voice note. Although clausulae were employed in the organa of Léonin, one of the two Notre Dame composers known by name, their greatest exponent was his successor Pérotin, who composed numerous "substitute-clausulae," suitable for insertion within older organa, allowing the entire plainchant setting to be performed in much less time. Clausulae were also performed as separate compositions and were important in the development of the MOTET.

In 16th-century polyphony, the clausula is a cadential formula defined by Johannes Tinctoris *c.* 1475 as a "particle at the end of which there is a general pause or a perfection."

clavichord Developing from the medieval monochord, the clavichord is a stringed keyboard instrument that flourished from about 1400 to 1800 and was revived in the 20th century.

By the 16th century the words clavichord, monochord, virginal, and clavicymbalum were freely used to describe any of the forerunners of the piano, but a more precise use of those words was adopted in the second half of the following century. In Germany, however, the word clavier became generic and was applied to any domestic keyboard instrument, including the piano. This untidy nomenclature makes it difficult and often impossible to identify the particular instrument, clavichord or harpsichord, when reading the directions of early composers or historians.

The clavichord usually has a compass of from three and one-half to five octaves. The right-hand, or treble, part of the instrument, which is oblong in shape, contains the soundboard, the bridge, and the wrest, or tuning pins. The strings run horizontally from the tuning pins over the bridge and are secured to the hitch pins in the left-hand, or bass, part of the instrument, where strips of felt are woven through the strings to act as dampers. A small blade of brass, the tangent, stands on each key just below the string that the individual key controls. When the key is depressed the tangent rises and strikes the string, dividing it into two parts. The right-hand part between the tangent and the bridge vibrates and produces the appropriate pitch; the left-hand part between the tangent and the hitch pin is damped by the felt and is silent. The tangent has done two things: it has determined the vibrating length of the string, as does the finger of a string player, and it has caused the string to sound, as does a piano's hammer. When the key is released the tangent falls away from the string, which is immediately silenced by the felt dampers. The clavichord is usually built with two strings for a pitch, but it does not always have an independent pair of strings for each key on the keyboard. Thus the tangents of two or three adjacent keys, involving pitches that are unlikely to be required together, are sometimes made to share a single pair of strings, each tangent marking the proper speaking length for the pitch in question. Such clavichords are fretted, or, in German, *gebunden,* while those with independent strings for each key are unfretted, or *bundfrei;* the nomenclature is reminiscent of the fretted fingerboards of lutes and viols.

The tone of the clavichord is very soft, and the instrument is essentially suited to domestic use. It possesses two musical qualities that are unique among the forerunners of the piano: a capacity for dynamic variation—including piano, forte, crescendo, and diminuendo—all of which are obtained by touch

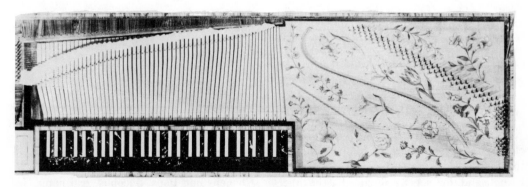

German clavichord by Johann Adolph Hass, Hamburg, 1764   *Raymond Russell*

alone; and the ability to vary a pitch that is sounding with a vibrato, or *Bebung,* the rapid sequence of a normal and a slightly sharpened pitch obtained by a corresponding variation of finger pressure on the key and thus of the tension of the string—a technique familiar to all string players.

Music expressly written for the clavichord is not easily identified with certainty; the simultaneous presence of three or four types of domestic keyboard instruments resulted in the use of the instrument at hand, a practice that is therefore sound today. Some idea of the type of music that will sound well on the clavichord can, however, be obtained by considering some of the works for which Bach particularly specified the harpsichord and not the clavichord: his *Italian* Concerto, Partita in b minor, *Goldberg* Variations, *Chromatic* Fantasy and Fugue, and Toccata in D Major.

Thus it can be seen that the clavichord is not the best medium for brilliant or virtuoso music, extended works, or compositions calling for two manuals. The instrument is best suited to contrapuntal music in two or three parts and to other works of the smaller and more intimate sort contained within a four-octave compass such as the Six Sonatas (1753) of Carl Philipp Emanuel Bach.

With the increased use of the piano, the clavichord fell into disuse. It has been revived in the 20th century, however, and finds favor in the home, for broadcasting, and occasionally with electronic amplification in larger spaces.

BIBLIOGRAPHY: Donald H. Boalch, *Makers of the Harpsichord and Clavichord, 1440–1840* (1956; 2nd ed., 1974); Raymond Russell, *The Harpsichord and Clavichord; An Introductory Study* (1959); Hanns Neupert, *The Clavichord* (1965).

clavier (German spelling, *Klavier*) A keyboard of a musical instrument. In Germany from the 17th century it has meant any keyboard instrument with strings such as the harpsichord, clavichord, or, later, piano.

clef The symbol placed at the beginning of the staff that determines the pitch of a particular note and thus sets a reference for the other notes of the staff. Clef is the French word

for key. Three clef symbols are in current use: the treble, bass, and C clefs; they are conventionalized forms of the letters G, F, and C.

Music for instruments and voices is written in the clef corresponding most closely to the range of the part. The treble, or G, clef fixes the position of the G above middle C. In modern notation this is invariably the second line from the bottom of the staff:

In the former French violin clef, however, the G was set as the bottom line of the staff:

Music for the tenor voice is usually written in an octave transposing treble clef; a small 8 under the clef indicates that the music is to be sung an octave lower than written:

The bass, or F, clef sets the position of the F below middle C. In modern notation this is fixed at the second line from the top of the staff:

In the baritone clef, never very common, F was set as the middle line:

The movable C clef determines the position of middle C. It is found in two principal positions: the alto clef. in which middle C is the middle line:

and the tenor clef, in which middle C is the second line from the top:

Formerly common forms of the C clef are the soprano clef, with middle C as the bottom line, and the mezzo-soprano clef, with middle C as the second line from the bottom of the staff.

Clemens non Papa, Jacobus, real name, Jacques Clément (*c.* 1510–*c.* 1558) One of the

Muzio Clementi
*engraving by an unknown artist, published 1803
courtesy, trustees of the British Museum
photograph, J. R. Freeman & Co., Ltd.*

most distinguished Flemish composers of his day, Jacobus Clemens was born in Ypres and from 1546 called himself Clemens non Papa to avoid confusion with a priest and poet of the same name there. In 1544 he was in Bruges as probationary choirmaster of St. Donatien, leaving before 1545; in 1550 he was a singer and composer at 's Hertogenbosch. His outstanding *Souter Liedekens* (1556), an almost complete series of Flemish metrical psalms, were probably interrupted by illness or death; an elegy of 1558 suggests that he died violently. His works include 15 masses (10 published 1557–59); many motets (six published 1546; 11, 1556; 92, 1559); and 90 chansons. He composed in all the current styles, using simple themes, melodious lines, and skillful imitation that foreshadows Orlando di Lasso.

BIBLIOGRAPHY: Edward E. Lowinsky, *Secret Chromatic Art in the Netherlands Motet* (1946).

Clementi, Muzio (January 24, 1752–March 10, 1832) The first of the great piano virtuosos and a composer whose studies and sonatas formed the basis for the modern art of piano playing, Muzio Clementi was born in Italy but spent most of his life in England.

A youthful prodigy, he was appointed an organist at 9 and at 12 had composed an oratorio. In 1766 Peter Beckford, a cousin of William Beckford, the author of *Vathek,* prevailed upon Clementi's father to allow him to take the talented boy to England, where he lived quietly in Wiltshire pursuing a rigid course of studies. In 1773 he went to London and met with immediate and lasting success as a composer and as a pianist. The piano had become more popular in England than anywhere else, and Clementi, in studying its special features, made brilliant use of the new instrument and its capabilities. From 1777 to 1780 he was employed as harpsichordist at the Italian Opera in London. In 1780 he went on tour to Paris, Strasbourg, Munich, and Vienna, where he became engaged in a friendly musical duel with Mozart at the instigation of Emperor Joseph II.

In 1782 Clementi returned to London, where for the next 20 years he continued his lucrative occupations of fashionable teacher, composer, and performer. He took shares in the music publishing firm of Longman and Broderip and lost a good deal of money when they went bankrupt, but he was a shrewd businessman and in 1799 founded in partnership with Longman a firm for both music publishing and the manufacture of pianos. Among his numerous pupils were John Baptist Cramer, Meyerbeer, and John Field. Clementi visited the Continent again in 1820 and 1821. In his later years he devoted himself to composition, and to this period belonged several symphonies, the scores of which were either lost or incomplete. During the later part of his life he had a country residence at Evesham in Worcestershire, where he died. He was buried in Westminster Abbey.

Clementi composed 60 sonatas for piano alone and 46 for piano with violin, cello, or flute. His 100 studies in the *Gradus ad Parnassum* (1817) covered every aspect of piano technique; nothing significant was added until Chopin's études nearly 25 years later. Late 20th-century research has increased Clementi's stature both as a pianist and as a composer.

BIBLIOGRAPHY: Leon Plantinga, *Clementi: His Life and Music* (1977).

RECORDINGS: *Gradus ad Parnassum;* Piano Concerto in C Major; Piano Sonatas; Piano Sonatinas (6); Sonatas (2) for two pianos.

clemenza di Tito, La: *see* GLUCK; LIBRETTO (emergence of historical subjects); MOZART (later life).

Clérambault, Louis Nicholas (December 19, 1676–October 26, 1749) The Parisian composer and organist Louis Nicholas Clérambault is known for his chamber cantatas and his book of organ music. A pupil of André Raison, he succeeded his master as organist at the Church of Saint-Jacques and held later appointments at Saint-Louis, Saint-Cyr, and Saint-Sulpice. He was also music superintendent to Mme de Maintenon and, perhaps through her and his position at Saint-Cyr, wrote the music for the wedding of the Dauphin with the Infanta of Spain in 1745.

Clérambault's cantatas, often on subjects from classical mythology, were published in five volumes (from 1710) and are probably the most significant French contribution to the medium. The recitatives are in French style, but the arias are in the prevailing Italian tradition. In *Orphée, Héro et Léandre,* and *Pigmalion,* the instrumental introductions, or *simphonies,* show a mastery of the concerto style. Works for the stage include one of his best compositions, *Le Soleil vainqueur des nuages,* a thanksgiving for Louis XV's recovery from illness (1721). His church music includes a large Te Deum. His organ music ranks with that of Couperin le Grand, his *clavecin* pieces are less interesting.

RECORDINGS: Organ pieces.

Cleva, Fausto (May 17, 1902–August 6, 1971) The Italian born and educated conductor Fausto Cleva went to New York City at age 18 to become assistant chorus master at the Metropolitan Opera. He left in 1942, having risen to assistant conductor, and returned as resident conductor in 1950. During the intervening years he was staff conductor of the San Francisco Opera (1942–44) and general manager of the Chicago Civic Opera (1944–46). At the 50th anniversary of his joining the Metropolitan, he had conducted 27 operas and a total of 657 performances. He died while conducting Gluck's *Orfeo ed Euri-*

dice in Athens. Available recordings of complete operas include Gounod's *Faust,* Donizetti's *Lucia di Lammermoor,* Verdi's *Luisa Miller,* and Leoncavallo's *Pagliacci.*

Cliburn, Van (Harvey Lavan, Jr.) (b. July 12, 1934) The U.S. pianist Van Cliburn studied with Rosina Lhévinne at the Juilliard School in New York City. He won the Leventritt competition (1954) and was the first American to win the Tchaikovsky competition in Moscow (1958). The Van Cliburn competition in Fort Worth, Texas, was first held in 1962 and has become a major contest for pianists. A pianist of the romantic school, Cliburn made his debut as a conductor in 1964.

Cluytens, André (March 26, 1905–June 3, 1967) The Belgian-born conductor André Cluytens began his career as choral coach at the Royal Theater in Antwerp and later conducted opera there (1927–32), in Toulouse (1932–35), Lyon (1935), and Paris after 1941. From a position as conductor of the Opéra-Comique (1947), he became principal conductor of the French National Radio Orchestra (with whom he recorded the Shostakovich Piano Concertos Nos. 1 and 2 with the composer as soloist) and conducted at Bayreuth. He was a frequent guest conductor of the Vienna Philharmonic, in which capacity he made his U.S. debut in 1956. Available recordings of complete operas include Gounod's *Faust* and Mussorgsky's *Boris Godunov.*

Coates, Albert (April 23, 1882–December 11, 1953) A student of Arthur Nikisch at the Leipzig Conservatory, the Russian-born English conductor Albert Coates began his career conducting German opera in Elberfeld (1906–08), then at the Dresden Opera, and for five years in St. Petersburg. In 1913 he conducted Wagner at Covent Garden. After the Russian Revolution he settled permanently in England, where he was responsible for the British National Opera Company and was a regular conductor of the London Symphony. Coates conducted the Philharmonic Society of New York (1920) and the Rochester (New York) Philharmonic (1923–25). He introduced many Russian scores to the West, especially those of Rimsky-Korsakov and Aleksandr Scriabin. Also a composer, he wrote a symphonic poem

(*The Eagle,* 1925, dedicated to Nikisch) and two operas (*Samuel Pepys,* 1929; and *Pickwick,* 1936). He was a pioneer in sound reproduction during the age of acoustic recordings. Highly acclaimed were his recordings of Wagner with Lauritz Melchior and Frida Leider.

coda The concluding passage of a composition or movement; the word is Italian for tail. The growth of the coda from mere emphasis and rhetoric to matter of structural importance can be seen most clearly in the works of Haydn and Beethoven. In the latter's sonatas, symphonies, and similar works, the codas frequently assume an independent weight that balances the energy of a given movement's development section. Later composers followed Beethoven's tendency to save some musical invention for the end of the movement, a practice that may be seen as a parallel to the shift of emphasis from the first movement (Mozart, Haydn) to the last (Brahms, Mahler) in symphonies and sonatas.

A codetta, or short coda, can often be found in the middle of a movement, especially at the end of the exposition section of a sonata form or between entries of the subject in a fugue exposition.

Coleman, Ornette: *see* JAZZ (recent developments).

Coleridge-Taylor, Samuel (August 15, 1875–September 1, 1912) A British composer who enjoyed considerable acclaim in the early years of the 20th century, Samuel Coleridge-Taylor was born in London of an African black father and an English mother. He entered the Royal College of Music in 1890 to study violin, but he came under the influence of Charles Villiers Stanford, who urged him to devote himself to composition. While still a student he composed anthems and chamber works that were performed (the Joachim Quartet played his Clarinet Quintet in Berlin in 1897), and it was at the RCM that his major work, *Hiawatha's Wedding Feast,* was performed in 1898 and received national attention. The two remaining parts of his Longfellow trilogy followed: *The Death of Minnehaha* (1899) and *Hiawatha's Departure* (1900). He continued to compose in many forms, includ-ing incidental music, choral works, and a violin concerto (1911), but no later works achieved the popularity of his first Hiawatha piece. An admirer of Dvořák, Coleridge-Taylor shows influences from that composer.

RECORDINGS: Movements from *Hiawatha's Wedding Feast.*

Colonne, Édouard, real name, Judas Colonne (July 23, 1838–March 28, 1910) One of the important French conductors of the 19th century, Édouard Colonne was a product of the Paris Conservatoire, and he began his musical career as a violinist in the Opéra orchestra (1858–67). His first conducting was not very successful, but in 1874 he formed the Concerts du Châtelet (later called the Concerts Colonne). In competition with Jules Pasdeloup's established Concerts Populaires, Colonne specialized in the works of the young French composers—Massenet, Édouard Lalo, Théodore Dubois, Franck, and Saint-Saëns—and later those of Berlioz. Colonne's conducting technique was considered somewhat limited, but he was full of fire and warmth and did much for the French Romantic repertoire.

combination tone or **resultant tone** A faint tone produced by the ear's distortion of sound waves and heard above, between, or below two simultaneously sounded musical tones. Because such tones are caused by the ear rather than by an external source of sound, they are sometimes also called subjective tones. The two varieties are difference tone, with a pitch below or between the original tones; and summation tone, with a pitch lying above the original. The more common is the difference tone; discovered by the celebrated 18th-century violinist and composer Giuseppe Tartini, it is also called Tartini tone.

comic opera A general designation for musical plays with light or sentimental subject matter, comic elements, and happy endings. Until the middle of the 19th century, the dialogue was usually spoken rather than sung (except for opera buffa). The term applies to English BALLAD OPERA, MUSICAL COMEDY, Italian OPERA BUFFA, OPERETTA, German SINGSPIEL, and Spanish TONADILLA and ZARZUELA. The French OPÉRA COMIQUE originated as comic opera but later dealt with serious subject matter.

Comissiona, Sergiu (b. June 16, 1928) Educated at the Bucharest Conservatory (1947), the Romanian conductor Sergiu Comissiona was conductor at the Romanian State Opera (1955–59), the Haifa (Israel) Symphony (1959–66), the Göteborg (Sweden) Symphony (1967), and the Baltimore Symphony (from 1969). He was named music advisor to the American Symphony in 1978.

Compère, Loyset, real name, Louis Compère (*c.* 1450–August 16, 1518) An important composer of the Flemish school, Loyset Compère was apparently a pupil of Jean d'Ockeghem; in 1486 he was a singer with the master in the service of Charles VIII of France. In 1509 he was made a canon of St. Quentin. Compère was a transitional figure, uniting the elegance of Guillaume Dufay with the humanism of Josquin des Prés. His numerous works include motets, masses, and chansons.

BIBLIOGRAPHY: Lutz Finscher, *Loyset Compère* (1964).

computer music The use of the computer as a technique of composition or of actual sound synthesis is normally what is understood to be computer music. However, data processing and information retrieval in a music library; processing of music notation and printing; and musicological, theoretical, and acoustical research are all widespread uses of the computer in relation to music.

Composition and sound synthesis are complementary processes because the first may lead to the second. A composer may elect to use a set of compositional programs to produce a composition; then stop using a computer and print the results for transcription to instrumental performance. Alternatively the results may be transferred directly into electronic sounds by means of a second set of programs for sound synthesis. Finally an already composed score may be converted into sound by translating the score into a form that can be entered into a computer, say, by data cards, and using the computer essentially as a data translator.

In principle any kind of music, from traditional to completely novel, can be written by these machines. For a composer, however, the main appeal consists not in duplicating known styles of music but in seeking new modes of musical expression.

The earliest example of computer-composed music is *Illiac* Suite for string quartet (1957) by two Americans, the composer Lejaren Hiller and the mathematician Leonard Isaacson. It was a set of four experiments in which the computer was programmed to generate random integers representing various musical elements such as pitches, rhythms, and dynamics, that were subsequently screened through programmed rules of composition. Several basic styles of composition—from traditional to experimental—were tested in an exploratory way, and the results were transcribed for instrumental performance.

Two very different compositions, *ST/10-1,080262* (1962) by Iannis Xenakis and *HPSCHD* (1969) by John Cage and Hiller, are illustrative of two typical approaches. *ST/10-1,080262* is one of a number of works realized by Xenakis from a Fortran program he wrote in 1961 for an IBM 7090 computer. Xenakis had composed a work called *Achorripsis* (1958) by employing statistical calculations and a Poisson distribution to assign pitches, durations, and playing instructions to the various instruments so that a uniform distribution occurs. He redid the work with a computer, retitled it, and also produced a number of other, similar compositions. *HPSCHD,* by contrast, is a work of indeterminate length for one to seven harpsichords and one to 51 tape recorders. When first performed it was put on as a multimedia work and was allowed to run nearly five hours. The composers wrote three sets of computer programs. The first, for the harpsichord solos, solved Mozart's *Musical Dice Game* (K.294d), an early chance composition in which successive measures are selected by rolling dice, and modified it with other compositions chosen with a program based on the Chinese oracle *I Ching (Book of Changes).* The second set of programs generated the 51 sound tracks on tape. These contained monophonic lines in microtone tunings based on speculations regarding Mozart's melodic writing. The third program generated sheets of instructions to the purchasers of a record of the composition.

The three basic techniques for producing sounds with a computer are sign-bit extraction, digital-to-analog conversion, and hybrid digital-analog systems. Of these, the first is inexpensive but limited, the second is the most sophisticated and expensive; the third, the most recent, permits synthesis in real time.

Sign-bit extraction has occasionally been used for compositions of serious intent—for example in *Computer* Cantata (1963) by Hiller and Robert A. Baker and in *Sonoriferous loops* (1965) by Herbert Brün—but more often it is an amusement indulged in around computer laboratories for playing Christmas carols and things of that sort.

Digital-to-analog conversion is the ideal technique for computer sound synthesis. This process was developed in the United States by Max V. Mathews and his colleagues at the Bell Telephone Laboratories in the early 1960s and depends on the sampling theorem. It is more than simply a hardware system; it embodies an orchestration program that simulates many of the processes employed in the classical electronic-music studio. It specifies unit generators for the standard wave forms, adders, modulators, filters, reverberators, and so on and is sufficiently generalized that a user can freely define his own generators. *See* ELECTRONIC MUSIC.

BIBLIOGRAPHY: Lejaren Hiller and Leonard Isaacson, *Experimental Music* (1959); Gerald Lefkopp, ed., *Computer Applications in Music* (1967); Heinz von Foerster and James W. Beauchamp, eds., *Music by Computers* (1969); Max V. Mathews *et al., The Technology of Computer Music* (1969); Harry B. Lincoln, ed., *The Computer and Music* (1970); Hubert S. Howe, Jr., *Electronic Music Synthesis* (1975).

concert The concert is a social institution for the performance of absolute, as distinct from religious or dramatic, music that developed to its present form from the informal music making of the 17th century. The social influences affecting the concert also affected the music conceived for it, and the evolution in music from Mozart to Beethoven has a counterpart in the aristocratic, as opposed to the democratic, patronage of the concert. Similarly, cosmopolitan aspects of music in the second half of the 20th century are associated with the increasingly international outlook of concert audiences.

Early forms of the concert were associated with university activities. In the first half of the 18th century many German universities maintained a Collegium Musicum for the performance of chamber music, and "music meetings" were regularly held at Oxford and Cambridge. Gatherings of amateurs to hear music had been a feature of the Italian academies of the Renaissance, notably those at Bologna and Milan founded in the 15th century. Like the French academies that succeeded them, they fostered music as one of the humanities and anticipated in this respect the function of 18th-century concert patrons. The more important Italian and French academies, however, were principally concerned with exploring the borderlands of music and poetry, and these opened a way to the opera rather than to the concert.

The first public concerts for which admission was charged were given in London by the violinist John Banister at his home in Whitefriars in 1672. In 1678 Thomas Britton, a charcoal seller, established weekly concerts in a loft in Clerkenwell at the subscription rate of 10s. a year. Handel and John Christopher Pepusch were among the performers at these humble but historic concerts that were the forerunners of several other London series, particularly in the neighborhood of Covent Garden.

Concerts of instrumental and vocal music were frequently given at the homes of the nobility in France in the 17th century. The first public concerts in France were the Concerts Spirituels, organized by the composer Anne Danican Philidor on days of religious festivals when the Opéra was closed. These flourished in Paris from 1725 to 1791. Closely associated with the development of the symphony and bringing the 18th-century repertoire to a wide public, the Concert Spirituel served as a model for similar concert societies in other countries.

In the second half of the 18th century the symphonies of Haydn and Mozart were introduced in England at the professional concerts, and Haydn wrote a famous set of 12 symphonies for performance in London at the Salomon concerts. Earlier concerts reflecting the social elegance of 18th-century London were given in elaborate settings at the gardens of Vauxhall, Ranelagh, and Marylebone. An English equivalent of a *fête galante* was suggested by the masquerades and Handelian opera singers at these pleasure gardens, where the programs ranged from works by the seven-year old Mozart to popular songs of the day. Something of the spirit of the London garden concerts was revived at the end of the 19th century at the Crystal Palace concerts in London. Among the numerous 18th-century concert societies in Germany and Austria, the Gewandhaus concerts at Leipzig (from 1781) and the Tonkünstlersocietät (Musicians' Society, founded 1771) in Vienna were later to be associated with the great figures of Romantic music. The court concerts by the orchestra of the elector palatine between 1743 and 1778 at Mannheim, described by Charles Burney as "an orchestra of generals," reached the highest standard of orchestral playing in Europe at that time.

A change came at the beginning of the 19th century when concerts attracted audiences drawn from a wider social range. New concert societies were formed to meet the demands of a growing democratic spirit. Many societies, formed when the symphonies of Beethoven and the Romantic works of Berlioz were first heard, exist to the present day, notably the Philharmonic Society (1813; later the Royal Philharmonic Society) in London, the Concerts du Conservatoire (1828) in Paris, and the Gesellschaft der Musikfreunde (1813) in Vienna.

So far concert giving had been mainly confined to England, France, Germany, and Italy. With the growth of nationalism concert societies were formed for the promotion of national music in many European countries, notably the Russian Music Society founded in 1859. In the United States concerts had been given in the 18th century in New York City, Philadelphia, and Boston and also at Charleston, South Carolina, where a St. Cecilia Society was founded in 1762 and where concerts were inaugurated (1767) under the title New Vaux-

hall on the model of the London garden concerts. But the main U.S. contribution to concert activity came with the foundation in the 19th century of symphony orchestras in New York City (1842), Boston (1881), Chicago (1891), and Cincinnati, Ohio (1895). Philadelphia was close behind in 1900.

In the 20th century concert activity was greatly stimulated by the radio and the phonograph. Larger concert halls were built, and orchestral and chamber-music concerts became one of the main attractions at music festivals. Concert societies were established in countries of the British Commonwealth and South America. Others sprang up in India and Japan. With the worldwide popularization of music, concert repertoires were marked by new trends, but well-established works of the Classical and Romantic periods were generally more favored than contemporary works.

By mid-century, however, musicological research had begun to influence actual performance practices, and an increasing interest in Baroque music and even Renaissance and medieval works evolved. The revival of old instruments and modern reproductions (the harpsichord, viola da gamba, recorder, and lute, for example) added a new dimension to the enjoyment of these works, and more authentic approaches to music of the Classical period and early Romantic era were in evidence. The chamber orchestra became a new medium of concert life, and societies (both performers and audience) specializing in particular styles came into existence.

General resistance to new music continued as in any age, but enthusiastic organizations such as the International Society for Contemporary Music (founded 1922) made its mark. The medium of electronic music opened new horizons with multimedia events sometimes more happenings than concerts.

In general, performance standards have become higher and higher—probably more so than in any previous age. Though professional organizations are largely confined to metropolitan areas, some efforts have been made for such institutions to make appearances in smaller centers.

Many medium-sized cities have founded semi-professional orchestras, and such organizations as Community Concerts, Inc., have promoted solo artists and small as well as large ensembles in even the most remote corners. In the late 20th century radio and recordings began to offer the concert hall serious competition as the principal distribution point for music.

concertante An adjective related to the word concerto that is usually used in the form sinfonia concertante (or the French form *symphonie concertant*) in the Classical period for an orchestral work with parts for one or more solo instruments as in the Baroque CONCERTO GROSSO. Haydn and Mozart, among others, used the title, and it has been used in later periods (*e.g.*, Karol Szymanowski, 1932). The word is also used synonymously with concertato (*see* CONCERTATO STYLE) and with CONCERTINO, the group of soloists in a sinfonia concertante.

concertato style A style characterized by two often unequal groups of instruments or voices in opposition. The term is derived from the Latin *concertare*, "to compete," the competition between different performing groups.

The advent of the concertato style occurred in Venice in the late 16th and early 17th centuries. The polychoral music of Andrea and Giovanni Gabrieli at St. Mark's made frequent use of the alternation between various combinations of singers and instrumentalists, producing novel antiphonal effects. These compositions (occasionally entitled concerti) demonstrate those traits—simple homophonic texture, strong declamatory rhythm, varied alternation and combination of blocks of sound—that became prominent in Baroque instrumental and choral music. The concertato style continued throughout the early 17th century and is exemplified by the choral works of the Italians Lodovico Viadana, Adriano Banchieri, and Orazio Benevoli, the German Heinrich Schütz, and others. The aesthetic of this style was taken over in the purely instrumental mid-Baroque CONCERTO GROSSO, in which a large body of players (ripieno, or tutti) alternates with a small group of soloists (concertino).

concertina An instrument of the free-reed class patented in 1829 by Sir Charles Wheat-

Wheatstone concertina, 1829
courtesy, C. Wheatstone & Company

stone in London. Hexagonal hand bellows are fastened between two sets of boards that carry the reeds in fraised sockets and the pallet valves and finger buttons by which air is selectively admitted to the reeds. The reed tongues, of steel or brass, are attached to their individual brass frames by screwed plates. The concertina employs double action with a pair of reeds for each note—one to sound on the press of the bellows, the other on the draw. In the original and subsequently the most usual model, the chromatic scale is divided between the two hands; in some later models a chromatic scale is provided for each hand. Tchaikovsky calls for its use in his Orchestral Suite No. 2 (1884). After the days of the concertina virtuoso in the 19th century, from Giulio Regondi to Alexander Prince, the instrument gradually became superseded from *c.* 1910 by the accordion.

concertino In the Baroque era, the group of soloists in the CONCERTO GROSSO. In the 19th and 20th centuries the term has come to mean a short concerto, usually in one movement. A German equivalent for this is *Konzertstück*. Examples are by Weber (for horn, 1806; clarinet, 1811; piano, 1821), Schumann (piano, 1849), Anton Rubinstein (piano, Op. 113), Ernst von Dohnányi (cello, Op. 12), Max Bruch (violin, 1911), John Alden Carpenter (piano, 1916), Janáček (piano, 1925), Jean

Françaix (piano, 1934), and Walter Piston (piano, 1937).

concerto   Since about 1750 the term concerto has been most often used as the title for compositions in which the skill of a single virtuoso instrumentalist (or sometimes two or more) is set into relief against an orchestra background. The word has two, apparently contradictory, meanings: first, it describes music played in consort; *i.e.,* together; second, it describes music characterized by a conflict between separate groups of instruments with differences in sound, weight, and presence.

early concerto   The early history of the concerto is not easy to trace because of the confusion in meaning and because of the inexact application of the term—a difficulty that is also encountered with the sonata and the symphony. The word concerto first makes its appearance in late 16th-century Italian sources: in anthologies of music by Andrea and Giovanni Gabrieli (1587), Christofano Malvezzi and Luca Marenzio (1591), and Adriano Banchieri (1596); and in the title of a treatise on instrumentation by Ercole Bottrigari, *Il desiderio, overo de' concerti di varii strumenti musicali* (1594). In these books, as in dozens of others published during the first 40 years of the 17th century, the Italian term concerto is exactly synonymous with the Latin *concentus,* the English consort, or the French ensemble. A concerto of this time was a comparatively short piece of polyphonic music for a relatively small number of singers and players, or players alone, each performing an individual part of no particular technical difficulty. The ensemble was usually welded together by the accompaniment of an organ, harpsichord, or lute, and the performers were expected to improvise their own embellishments to their written parts. Such a style could only arise in cities such as Venice, where there was a long tradition for elaborate ensemble music on great church and state occasions, or at the courts of wealthy art-loving despots (*e.g.,* the Medici of Florence); all of the early concertos are associated with such surroundings. In many early concertos the players were arrayed in two or more groups so that the

music formed an antiphonal dialogue. In others—notably the influential *Concerti ecclesiastici* of Ludovico Viadana (1602)—the music is what now would be termed a motet or, more rarely, a madrigal for one or more solo voices, accompanied by the organ and sometimes by other instruments as well.

Throughout the first 40 years of the 17th century the concerto remained an Italian form, practiced almost exclusively by Italian composers, and it retained its connotations of ceremony, the church and court, and improvised embellishment. Between *c.* 1640 and 1680 the word disappeared for reasons that are far from clear in favor of sonata or sinfonia (for instruments) and cantata (for voices). When it reappeared (Giovanni Bononcini's *Concerti da camera,* 1685; Giuseppe Torelli's *Sinfonia e concerti,* 1692; Giulio Taglietti's *Concerti e sinfonie,* 1696) its meaning had become restricted to instrumental music, and it has remained so ever since. Concertos of this date are distinguishable from the TRIO SONATA (for two violins, cello, and keyboard) only in that the composers appear to have envisaged several players to a part. An attempt also seems to have been made at distinguishing between the church concerto—solemn, pompous, contrapuntal—and the chamber concerto, which was more lighthearted and less intricate. *See* CHAMBER MUSIC.

concerto grosso   By 1700 or so the viola had become an integral part of the ensemble, and each violin part had forked into two, one for an accomplished soloist and the other for his less proficient colleagues. This orchestral ensemble of strings and keyboards was usually handled by composers as a double body: a concertino ("little concerto") consisting of the old trio-sonata combination of two violins, cello, and keyboard; and a ripieno ("filling out") of strings in four or five parts with a second keyboard. Music for such an ensemble was called a CONCERTO GROSSO (a term first encountered in 1698), and the style was perfected by Torelli (1698), Tommaso Albinoni (1700), Corelli (published posthumously in 1714), and Vivaldi (1710–20). Most of this music was composed in Rome, Bologna, or Venice during the years from 1680 to 1720;

it was widely disseminated, above all by the enterprising though piratical music publishers Estienne Roger of Amsterdam and his rival John Walsh of London; and it was widely imitated, by Handel and Bach among others.

Soon the concerto grosso broke into two diverging forms; the solo concerto for a single soloist and the orchestral concerto for an ensemble of strings, woodwinds, and accompanying keyboard. Vivaldi took the lead in the development of both forms, and he also established the pattern of an animated rhythmic first movement, an expressively singing slow movement, and a high-spirited brilliant finale. His hundreds of concertos include 71 (printed) for violin, 27 for cello, 37 for bassoon, and three for oboe as well as many orchestral concertos for highly diversified ensembles. Bach and Handel were the first to write concertos for a solo keyboard instrument—they were renowned as virtuosos on the harpsichord and organ just as Vivaldi was on the violin—and they also carried the development of the orchestral concerto a stage further, notably in Bach's set of six *Brandenburg* Concertos composed between 1716 and 1721. Each of the *Brandenburg* Concertos displays a different combination of soloists, but at least three of them belong to the repertoire of chamber music rather than to that of the symphony orchestra since all the parts are for single players.

By 1730 Vivaldi's three-movement form (quick, slow, quick) had become standard throughout Europe. Its dramatic elements of contrast and display appealed instantly to an age that was mad about opera; Bach's *Italian* Concerto for unaccompanied two-manual harpsichord is not only a perfect example of the genre but also demonstrates how it could be transferred intact to a single instrument. Such a work as this is very close to the Classical sonata, concerto, or symphony of the next generation, lacking only the minuet and trio and the new structure of sonata form. With the concertos of Bach's sons Carl Philipp Emanuel and Johann Christian, the bridge between the two styles is crossed into the familiar territory of Mozart, Haydn, and Beethoven. In their music the violin at last yielded its supremacy as a solo instrument, and the newly

perfected piano took over instead. Mozart composed six concertos for violin but 27 for piano; Haydn nine for violin, 20 for piano; Beethoven one for violin, five for piano.

Classical concerto During the Classical period the concerto steadily increased in length, brilliance, and emotional content; the listener found it ever easier to identify himself with the soloist's problems and triumphs, as an analogue with his own attempts to make his way in the world, and the concerto soon became the favorite among all forms of concert music. The piano's increasing power permitted an ever richer and louder orchestral accompaniment; its keyboard was extended to higher and lower notes until its range exceeded that of all other orchestral instruments put together, and the piano concerto became more and more an adventure in contest and endurance rather than an essay in contrast and elegance. Small wonder that the great Romantic composers of the 19th century chose it with such unanimity: two piano concertos each by Weber, Mendelssohn, Chopin, Liszt, and Brahms; one each by Schumann and Grieg; three by Tchaikovsky. The array of violin concertos by the same composers makes a striking comparison: one each by Mendelssohn, Schumann, Brahms, and Tchaikovsky.

Some special developments in the concerto during the Classical and Romantic periods are worth noting: (1) the appearance of concertos for almost every instrument of the symphony orchestra (*e.g.,* Haydn's for trumpet and for cello; Mozart's for horn, bassoon, clarinet, oboe, flute, and harp; Domenico Dragonetti's for double bass; Rimsky-Korsakov's for trombone); (2) the growth of the accompanied cadenza, finally reducing the soloist's improvisatory freedom to nil; (3) the cyclic form adopted by Liszt for his concertos in which the three movements become welded together into one fantasia; (4) the single-movement concerto or *Konzertstück;* (5) the introduction of new concerto forms (*e.g.,* Franck's *Symphonic* Variations for piano and orchestra; (6) the return of the multiple concerto (concertos for two or three soloists are usually known as double or triple concertos; *e.g.,* those by Beethoven, Schumann, and Brahms, rather than sinfonia concertante as in the 18th century; (7) the ever-increasing technical difficulty of the solo parts.

20th century By 1900, as the result of more than a century of change, the concerto had often lost contact with the form perfected by Mozart: 20th-century composers have worked new veins. Some composers have tried to revive the ideals in style or sound of the early 18th-century concerto, occasionally by using single instruments for every part of the texture (Bloch, Gustav Holst, d'Indy, Henk Badings, Goffredo Petrassi, Hindemith, Stravinsky, de Falla, and Poulenc). Others have sought to even out the disparity in technique between soloist and accompaniment by writing concertos for virtuoso orchestra (Hindemith and Bartók). A third group has continued to ride the tiger of virtuosity in solo concertos, not for its own sake but as a means of personal expression (Rachmaninoff, Elgar, Prokofiev, Shostakovich, Schoenberg, Berg, Michael Tippett, and William Walton). A fourth group has endeavored to cure the elephantiasis afflicting the late 19th-century concerto by writing much shorter works, reviving for this purpose the diminutive term concertino, which first appeared on a title page of 1687 and already had been adopted by Weber for his *Clarinet* Concertino, Op. 26; among them are John Alden Carpenter (1916), Jean Françaix (1934), and Walter Piston (1937), all for piano.

Such new developments as these show that the concept of the concerto is far from outworn. Audiences will always enjoy a contest provided its rules are comprehensible; they will always enjoy a musical debate; and they will always enjoy observing a virtuoso in action, for it is the most exciting of all musical experiences.

BIBLIOGRAPHY: Benjamin Franklin Swalin, *The Violin Concerto; a Study in German Romanticism* (1941); Cuthbert Morton Girdlestone, *Mozart's Piano Concertos* (1948; U.S. ed., *Mozart and His Piano Concertos,* 1952); Arthur Hutchings, *A Companion to Mozart's Piano Concertos* (1948); John Culshaw, *The Concerto* (1949); Ralph Hill, ed., *The Concerto* (1961); Abraham Veinus, *The Concerto*, rev. ed. (1964); Paul Henry Lang, *The Concerto, 1800–1900* (1970).

concerto grosso The most important orchestral form of the Baroque era (*c.* 1600–*c.* 1750), characterized by a small group of soloists (concertino or *principale*) in contrast to a full orchestra (tutti, concerto grosso, ripieno).

The titles of early concerti grossi often reflected their performance locales, as in *concerto da chiesa* (church concerto) and *concerto da camera* (chamber concerto, played at court), titles also applied to works not strictly concerti grossi. Ultimately the concerto grosso flourished as secular court music.

The typical instrumentation for the concertino was that of the trio sonata, the prevalent genre of chamber music: two violins and continuo; wind instruments also were common. The ripieno normally consisted of a string orchestra with continuo, often augmented by woodwinds or brass instruments.

In early examples, such as those of Corelli, the number of movements varied. Later composers, such as Giuseppe Torelli and Vivaldi, adopted a standard three movements in the pattern fast-slow-fast. Fast movements often used a ritornello structure in which a recurrent section, or ritornello, alternates with episodes played by the soloists.

Around 1750 the concerto grosso was eclipsed by the solo CONCERTO. In the 20th century the form was revived by such composers as Ernst Krenek (1921), Bloch (1925), Hindemith (1925), Walter Piston (1933), Stravinsky (1938), Bartók (1943), Samuel Barber (1944), and Henry Cowell (1963).

BIBLIOGRAPHY: Marc Pincherle, *Vivaldi: Genius of the Baroque* (1957); Arthur Hutchings, *The Baroque Concerto* (1961); Norman Carrell, *Bach's Brandenburg Concertos* (1963).

concord: *see* DISCORD/CONCORD.

Concord Sonata: *see* IVES; MODERN PERIOD (music in the United States).

conducting The art of controlling a group of performers in the execution and interpretation of a composition, principally by means of silent and partially codified gestures. These gestures indicate the rhythm and phrasing of the music, the direction making immediately apparent to the musicians the number of beats to the measure. These beats are normally given by a slender baton held in the conductor's right hand; the left is reserved largely for expression, nuances, entries of different parts, and other subtleties of interpretation. Some conductors have developed a technique that dispenses with a baton. This has long been the more usual style in unaccompanied choral conducting, where the number of different parts is limited and each singer usually has a full score of the music.

origins The art of conducting has been pursued in a highly specialized form only since the early 19th century, though its origins are undoubtedly of great antiquity. The earliest positive records of such external control are of the 15th-century custom within the Sistine Chapel choir in Rome of beating the pulse of the music with a roll of paper. This practice, whether with paper or with a lengthy pole or baton, seems to have continued and even to have been much abused to the point of becoming grossly audible during actual performance. By the time of Bach and Handel it had become established tradition, especially in Germany, that a composer was appointed to court or chapel not only to write the music required but to be in charge of all performances. The act of presiding would generally be carried out by the Kapellmeister seated at the organ or harpsichord. This custom was also widely accepted in other countries, and it was from the keyboard that Haydn directed the performances of his symphonies at the Salomon concerts in London in 1791 and 1794.

In Paris, with its particular requirements for the Opéra, the evolution of the conductor passed from the time thumpers to the concertmaster (or leader, as he has always been called in Great Britain), who controlled the proceedings as best he could from the first violin desk. This custom was also adopted in opera houses in Germany and Italy, though the leader might be responsible only for the orchestra, the singers coming under the jurisdiction of the *maestro al cembalo,* who would probably be seated in the midst of the orchestral musi-

cians. Such divided control led on many occasions to confusion and doubtless precipitated the rise of the conductor, who alone among performers makes no sound whatever and whose direction is necessary for the more complicated scores since the middle of the 19th century.

the modern conductor From 1745, when Johann Stamitz became concertmaster at Mannheim, there were distinct improvements in the standard of performance, further advanced by Spontini's years at the Berlin Opera (1820–41). With the composer-conductors Berlioz, Weber, Louis Spohr, Mendelssohn, and Wagner following closely on their heels, the musical scene was quickly transformed. If Berlioz may be regarded as the father figure of modern conducting, it is Wagner and the dominating personalities who followed his inspired example of imaginative gesture and control who are the first important conductors in the 20th-century sense of the term. Hans von Bülow, Hermann Levi, Hans Richter, Felix Mottl, Karl Muck, and Felix Weingartner were the pioneers of a new tradition in the art of orchestral training and comprehensive direction to a degree of finesse and sensitivity hitherto undreamed of.

As the conductor found his power and prestige rising, so his opportunities grew for influencing the musical taste of the time and even of changing the course of musical history. Mendelssohn's position of undisputed authority at the Gewandhaus in Leipzig enabled him to inaugurate a revival of the music of Bach, and conductors were also able to play an important part in the promotion and commissioning of contemporary compositions. In his earlier days as a resident conductor, Richard Strauss did admirable work in the championing of music by his younger contemporaries such as Engelbert Humperdinck and Mahler. The concerts in Berlin promoted and conducted by Busoni at the beginning of the 20th century were of paramount importance in their presentation for the first time of works by Debussy, Bartók, Sibelius, Elgar, Frederick Delius, and Carl Nielsen. The name of Serge Koussevitzky stands as an example of enlightened autocracy in this respect during his term as conductor of the Boston Symphony, his patronage extending at one time to the creation of a publishing house bearing his name. Hermann Scherchen similarly inaugurated an edition devoted to the publication of contemporary music.

As the new standards set and made possible by the baton-wielding conductors influenced the course of musical composition, so in its turn the new music made the tasks of the conductor enormously more varied and specialized. Apart from the already wide difference of organization and control required in the opera house and the concert hall (the latter now entailing expert flexibility in following the freedom of the modern virtuoso soloist), new factors arose born of the changes in musical life all over the world. Recording, radio, ballet, television, fitting music to films, and above all the wide variety of styles in modern composition on the one hand and music of earlier periods on the other (the latter often entailing much scholarly research)—all these and other tasks of musical direction may enter the conductor's province, requiring specialized knowledge, a thorough understanding of the music and of those who are playing under him, and a highly developed baton technique.

During the years immediately preceding and between World Wars I and II, the figure of the international conductor was exalted to a remarkable extent. This in some measure resulted from the dynamic personalities of many who rose to unprecedented heights in this most far-reaching and demanding of musical careers. Mahler and Toscanini, for example, became legends for their tyrannical demands in the relentless search for the highest artistic standards. It was Toscanini who initiated the vogue for conducting from memory, an accomplishment that poor eyesight led him to develop. The undeniably impressive feat of handling a large body of performers in an intricate work entirely without a score has since been exploited for its own sake, part of a tendency to throw a spotlight on the conductor as a glamorous figure per se. Rehearsing is one of the most important facets of the conductor's job and the one in which he is most likely to reveal his true potential. It has been said that the truly great conductors have been men of wide learning and culture; yet these qualities may not suffice to command a tough body of orchestral players unless they are accompanied by a powerful personality that arouses respect and maintains discipline. This strikes at the root of the conductor's position.

BIBLIOGRAPHY: Hector Berlioz, *The Conductor, the Theory of His Art* (1902); Richard Wagner, *On Conducting* (1919; reprint, 1977); Archibald T. Davison, *Choral Conducting* (1940); Adrian C. Boult, *A Handbook on the Technique of Conducting,* rev. ed. (1951); Harold C. Schonberg, *The Great Conductors* (1967); Wilhelm Ehmann, *Choral Directing* (1968); Max Rudolph, *The Grammar of Conducting,* rev. ed. (1969); Bernard Shore, *The Orchestra Speaks* (1972); Bernard Jacobson, *Conductors on Conducting: The Interpretation and Performance of Music* (1978).

conductus   A term employed in the 12th and 13th centuries for a setting of a Latin metrical poem for one, two, or three voices. It is applied (in the form *conductum* in the *Codex Calixtinus, c.* 1130) to pieces that accompanied the reader of a lesson as he walked to the lectern and to pieces accompanying processions in liturgical plays at Sens (*Conductus ad tabulam* for the Carnival of the Ass) and Beauvais *(e.g., Conductus Danielis venientis ad Regem).* In church use the term was soon transferred to the tropes of and substitutes for the *Benedicamus Domino* at the end of the offices, a genre of composition that flourished in the NOTRE DAME SCHOOL of the late 12th and early 13th centuries. Unlike the medieval motet, which arose about 1225, the polyphonic conductus was an original composition not based on a preexisting tenor and was composed with uniform rhythm in the parts, all of which sang the same text.

conservatory   A public institution for instruction in music. The word comes from the Italian *conservatorio,* "workhouse," which in the Renaissance period was used to describe a type of orphanage sometimes attached to a hospital or hostel. The foundlings *(conservati)* were given instruction in music, and the *conservatori* were thus the first secular institutions equipped for musical tuition. Sixteenth-century schools of this kind were De' Poveri di Gesù Cristo and Della Pietà dei Turchini at Naples where Nicola Antonio Porpora and Leonardo Leo were pupils respectively, and Sant' Onofrio at Venice where Don Angelo Duranté was a teacher.

The first secular school of music for the public at large was established in Paris by the Convention Nationale in 1795 through efforts of the bandmaster Bernard Sarrette. This was originally to have been called the Institut National de Musique, but the name Conservatoire de Musique, borrowed from the Italian, was decided upon to avoid confusion with the Institut des Sciences et Arts. The purpose of the Paris Conservatoire was, however, radically different from that of the Italian schools. Formed during the Terror, its aim was to train musicians to take part in public concerts, fêtes, and celebrations organized by the republic. A state subsidy was granted, admission was by competitive examination, and tuition was free. Later the curriculum was enlarged to include all branches of composition as well as all forms of instrumental and vocal technique. Classes were held in acting, thus enabling students to train for the Opéra, the Opéra-Comique, and the Comédie Française. Similar institutions were founded in the French provinces, and important prizes, scholarships, and publications were sponsored, including the great *Encyclopédie de la Musique et Dictionnaire du Conservatoire* founded by Albert Lavignac and edited after his death in 1916 by Lionel de La Laurencie. Though many famous pupils of the Conservatoire revolted against its academic severities, it became the acknowledged center of musical practice and erudition.

Throughout the 19th century the French model was copied with modifications in most European countries and in the United States. Conservatoires were founded in Milan (1807) and Naples (1808) and later in other Italian towns. Prague followed in 1811, Vienna in 1817, and in 1843 Mendelssohn and Schumann founded the Leipizig Konservatorium. Not all the German schools, however, followed the principles of the Conservatoire, and this was also true of similar institutes for musical education in Great Britain, of which the most notable were the Royal Academy of Music (1822; royal charter, 1830) and the Royal College of Music (first called the National Training-School of Music, founded 1882; royal charter, 1883). The Royal Irish Academy of Music was founded in 1848 and the Royal Scottish Academy of Music and Drama in 1890.

Such institutions began to appear in the United States in the 1860s. Two of the first were those at Oberlin, Ohio (1865), and the Peabody Conservatory of Music, Baltimore, founded 1857 (first classes held in 1868). In Boston the New England Conservatory of Music and the Boston Conservatory of Music followed in 1867 and the National Conservatory of Music in New York City in 1885. Other important institutions of music in the United States are the Eastman School of Music at Rochester, New York (1919), the Curtis Institute of Music, Philadelphia (1924), and the Juilliard School, New York City (1926; a merger of the Institute of Musical Art, 1905, and the Juilliard Graduate School, 1924).

consonance / dissonance Repose (consonance) in relation to tension (dissonance) experienced by a listener when certain combinations of tones are sounded together. In a composition movement to and from consonance and dissonance gives shape and a sense of direction, for example, by reinforcing the contour of the melody or by helping build a climax.

The conception of what constitutes consonance and dissonance has changed in the course of history. Around 900 the fourth was considered the most consonant interval, to be replaced by the fifth *c.* 1100. Guido of Arezzo (d. 1050) ruled out the fifth and the semitone, admitting only the fourth, whole tone, and major and minor thirds as consonant. In the 13th century only the unison and octave were perfect consonances, major and minor thirds imperfect, and the fourth and fifth intermediate, with major and minor sixths dissonances. Johannes Tinctoris (*c.* 1475) regarded the unison and upper and lower fifth as *concordantia perfecta,* major and minor thirds and sixths as *concordantia imperfecta,* and the fourth as consonant only with a third or fifth below it.

In the 20th century atonality, polytonality, and serial techniques have made the differences more or less obsolete, although Hindemith has classified the 12 tones of the chromatic scale in order of consonance (*The Craft of Musical Composition,* 2 vols., 1941–45).

Consul, The: *see* LIBRETTO (modern status); MENOTTI; OPERA (the 20th century).

continuo: *see* FIGURED BASS.

contralto: *see* ALTO.

contrapuntal: *see* COUNTERPOINT.

contredanse   A dance derived from the English country dance from which it takes its name. It enjoyed much popularity both in France and Germany during the 18th century and later. Although the derivation of the name has been disputed, it is confirmed by the character of the dance itself, which had obvious features in common with those of its English original. Music for such dances includes examples by Mozart and Beethoven.

Cooke, Henry (*c.* 1616–July 13, 1672)   An English bass singer, choirmaster, and composer noted for building the choir of the Chapel Royal after the Restoration, Henry Cooke was probably born at Lichfield and brought up as a chorister in the Chapel Royal. He fought for Charles I in the Civil War, which explains his title of "Captain" Cooke. During the Commonwealth he taught music and may have studied in Italy. Appointed a bass in the Chapel Royal and Master of the Children at the Restoration, he built a great choir within three years although he began with only five former members and the order of service forgotten by most organists. His military discipline, combined with an ability to choose the right boys (William Turner, John Blow, Pelham Humfrey, and Thomas Tudway were among his earliest choristers) and to teach them well, made his work known. The boys not only learned sight-singing and composition but also to play the violin, organ, lute, and harpsichord.

Probably on Charles II's suggestion Cooke introduced instrumental music into the services; he also used sackbuts in processions to enable the singers to keep pitch. He frequently sang solos at the services, and both Pepys and Evelyn recorded their praise of him. As a composer he contributed to Sir William Davenant's *Siege of Rhodes* (1656) but was mainly concerned with anthems and music for court functions, including coronation music.

Copland, Aaron (b. November 14, 1900)   A U.S. composer whose name has become almost synonymous with American music, Aaron Copland is indeed a significant 20th-century composer, but he is also notable as an active promoter of U.S. composers and a distinguished conductor, pianist, and author.

The son of Lithuanian Jewish immigrants, Copland was born in Brooklyn, New York. An older sister taught him piano, and by the time he was 15 he had decided to become a composer. As a first step Copland tried to learn harmony through a correspondence course. Haltingly and in an environment not particularly conducive to art, he struggled toward his goal.

In the summer of 1921 Copland attended the newly founded school for Americans at Fontainebleau, where he came under the influence of Boulanger. He stayed on in Paris,

Aaron Copland
courtesy, Boston Symphony Orchestra

where he became Boulanger's first U.S. student in composition. During his three years in Paris Copland's music became more and more experimental. He returned to New York in 1924 with an important commission: Boulanger had asked him to write an organ concerto for her U.S. appearances. Copland composed the piece while working as the pianist of a hotel trio at a summer resort in Pennsylvania. That season the Symphony for organ and orchestra had its premiere in Carnegie Hall with the New York Symphony under the direction of Walter Damrosch with Boulanger as soloist. (It was repeated the next month by the Boston Symphony under Serge Koussevitzky.)

In his growth as a composer Copland mirrored the important trends of his time. After his return from Paris he worked with jazz rhythms in *Music for the Theater* (1925) and the Piano Concerto (1926). There followed a period during which he was strongly influenced by Stravinsky's neoclassicism, turning toward an abstract style he described as "more spare in sonority, more lean in texture." This outlook prevailed in the Piano Variations (1930), *Short* Symphony (1933), and *Statements* for orchestra (1933–35). After this last work there occurred a change of direction that was to usher in the most productive phase of Copland's career. He summed up the new orientation: "During these years I began to feel an increasing dissatisfaction with the relations of the music-loving public and the living composer. It seemed to me that we composers were in danger of working in a vacuum." Furthermore, he realized that a new public for modern music was being created by the new media of radio, phonograph, and film scores: "It made no sense to ignore them and to continue writing as if they did not exist. I felt that it was worth the effort to see if I couldn't say what I had to say in the simplest possible terms." Copland therefore was led to what became a most significant development after the 1930s: the attempt to simplify the new music in order that it would have meaning for a large public.

In the decade that followed Copland produced scores that spread his fame throughout the world. The most important of these were three ballets based on American folk material, *Billy the Kid* (1938), *Rodeo* (1942), and *Appalachian Spring* (1944); *El Salón México* (1936), an orchestral piece based on Mexican melodies and rhythms; two works for high-school students—the "play opera" *The Second Hurricane* (1937) and *An Outdoor Overture* (1938); and a series of film scores, of which the best known are *Of Mice and Men* (1939), *Our Town* (1940), *The Red Pony* (1948), and *The Heiress* (1949). Typical too of the Copland style are two major works that were written in time of war, *Lincoln Portrait* (1942) for speaker and chorus on a text drawn from Lincoln's speeches and *Letter from Home* (1944), as well as the melodious Third Symphony (1946).

In his later years Copland refined his treatment of Americana. "I no longer feel the need of seeking out conscious Americanism. Because we live here and work here, we can be certain that when our music is mature it will also be American in quality." His later works include an opera, *The Tender Land* (1954); *Twelve Poems of Emily Dickinson* for voice and piano (1950); and the delightful *Nonet* of 1960. During these years Copland also produced a number of works in which he showed himself increasingly receptive to the serial techniques of the so-called twelve-tone school of composer Schoenberg, although, like Stravinsky's, his approach was highly individual. Notable among such works are the *Piano Fantasy* (1957), *Connotations* for orchestra (1962), commissioned for the opening of the Lincoln Center for the Performing Arts in New York City, and *Inscape* (1967). By the 1970s Copland had ceased to compose, but he still made appearances as conductor as well as fulfilling his responsibilities as senior musician with dignity and verve.

Copland has written a number of books on music: *What to Listen for in Music* (1939), *Our New Music* (1941; rev. ed., *The New Music,* 1968), *Music and Imagination* (1952), *The Pleasures of Music* (1959), and *Copland on Music* (1960). As composer, teacher, writer, organizer of musical events, and conductor, Copland has succeeded in expressing "the deepest reactions of the American consciousness to the American scene."

BIBLIOGRAPHY: Arthur Berger, *Aaron Copland* (1953); Julia Smith, *Aaron Copland* (1955).

RECORDINGS: Numerous recordings of most works.

Coppélia: *see* BALLET (America, 1735–1932) and (England); DELIBES; HOFFMANN.

Coq d'or, Le: *see* BALLET (America, 1735–1932); RIMSKY-KORSAKOV.

cor anglais: *see* ENGLISH HORN.

Corelli, Arcangelo (February 17, 1653–January 8, 1713)   One of the leading Italian violinist-composers of his day, Arcangelo Corelli studied principally at Bologna, then a center of instrumental music. By 1675 he had settled in Rome, which remained his home for the remainder of his life. He won a reputation as a performer and composer and made extended visits to other Italian cities and possibly abroad. His music was published in Italy and abroad, and he attracted several pupils who later became eminent, among them Francesco Geminiani.

His published chamber works consist of five sets of 12 sonatas, two of *sonate da chiesa* and two of *sonate da camera,* all for two violins, violoncello, and continuo (respectively for organ and harpsichord), and one of solo violin sonatas with harpsichord continuo. He also wrote a set of concerti grossi. Corelli seems not to have been a virtuoso violinist—the technical demands of his surviving violin music never go beyond the third position—but rather one who cultivated a pure, graceful, yet lively style. His slow movements are on the whole his finest, his fast movements tending to become somewhat mechanical. He used only the simplest harmonies within the then-new tonal system.

BIBLIOGRAPHY: Marc Pincherle, *Corelli: His Life, His Work* (1956).

RECORDINGS: Concerti Grossi (12); Sonatas (12) for two violins and continuo; Sonatas (12) for violin and continuo.

Corelli, Franco (b. April 8, 1923)   After study at the conservatories in Pesaro and Milan, the Italian lyric tenor Franco Corelli made his debut in 1952. Guest appearances throughout Europe and the United States followed a successful La Scala performance in 1954. He first sang at the Metropolitan Opera in 1960 as Manrico in Verdi's *Il Trovatore.* He uses his forceful voice especially in Italian and French repertoire. Recordings include operas of Verdi, Puccini, Bellini, Bizet, Gounod, and Umberto Giordano.

Cornelius, Peter (December 24, 1824–October 26, 1874)   A German composer and author, Peter Cornelius began a career as an actor. In 1844 he studied composition with Siegfried Dehn and was later music critic for two Berlin journals. From 1853 to 1858 he lived at Weimar in the circle of Liszt and translated articles by Berlioz and Liszt for the *Neue Zeitschrift für Musik.* In 1857 he began his elegant and inventive comic opera *Der Barbier von Bagdad* on a libretto of his own based on *A Thousand and One Nights,* which was conducted by Liszt at Weimar the following year. Though it is the work on which Cornelius' reputation now rests, it was a failure and led to Liszt's resignation from the Weimar Opera. It was successfully revived in a reorchestrated version by Felix Mottl after the composer's death. From 1859 to 1864 Cornelius lived in Vienna, where he became a friend of Wagner.

Arcangelo Corelli
portrait by Hugh Howard (1675–1737)
courtesy, National Gallery of Ireland, Dublin

His opera *Der Cid,* on a libretto adapted by Cornelius from the play by Corneille, was successfully produced at Weimar in 1865. In the same year he accompanied Wagner to Munich, where he was reader to Ludwig II and professor at the Royal School of Music. His last opera *Gunlöd* (libretto adapted from the *Edda*) was completed by C. Hoffbauer and E. Lassen and produced at Weimar in 1891.

A versatile and sensitive musician, Cornelius hardly fulfilled his original gifts, among them a gift for writing lyric poetry. He wrote many settings of his own poems, notably the *Weihnachtslieder,* which includes the well-known "Three Kings From Persian Lands Afar."

cornet (French, *cornet-à-pistons,* or *piston*) A valved brass instrument evolved in the 1820s from the continental post horn (*cornet-de-poste,* which is circular in shape like a small French horn). One of the first makers was the Parisian Halary (Jean Asté) in 1828. The tube is conical except through the three valves, tapering gently to a narrow detachable shank into which the brass mouthpiece is placed. The taper, coupled with a fairly deep mouthpiece, imparts a mellowness to the tone and a flexibility to the technique that quickly established the cornet in a leading position in brass and military bands, especially in England and the United States. It is built in B-flat, its music written a tone above the actual sound. Brass bands also employ an E-flat soprano cornet, a fourth higher than the B-flat instrument. Some older B-flat cornets built for use in the-

aters can be changed to the key of A by turning a rotary valve.

The cornet became a popular solo instrument. Many of the earliest virtuosi were horn players and employed different crooks for different tonalities or musical moods, the longer crooks, down to E-flat, giving a darker tone-quality. In English and U.S. symphony orchestras cornets were frequently used for all trumpet parts as well as for genuine cornet parts (common in French orchestration from Berlioz onward). In the 20th century, however, the trumpet has replaced the cornet in the orchestra (except for parts specifically intended for it), as well as in dance and jazz bands, leaving the cornet in general use only in brass bands.

BIBLIOGRAPHY: Adam Carse, *Musical Wind Instruments* (1939; reprint, 1965).

cornett or **cornetto** (German, *Zink*) A leading wind instrument of the period 1500–1670. A leather-covered conical wooden pipe about 24 inches (60 centimeters) long, it is octagonal in cross section and has finger holes and a small mouthpiece of horn or ivory. Its compass extends two octaves from the G below the treble staff. Other sizes of cornett included the descant, the S-shaped tenor, and straight forms such as the mute cornett with the mouthpiece cut in the head of the pipe itself.

With the trombones, to which it supplied the treble voice, it was one of the first wind instruments specifically scored for (by the Italian composer Giovanni Gabrieli, 1557–1612). Although obsolescent by 1700, the cornett

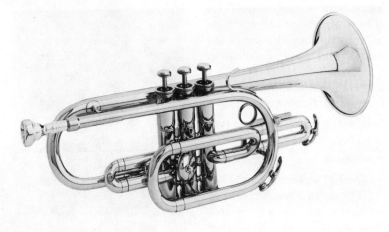

B-flat cornet   *courtesy, C. G. Conn, Ltd.*

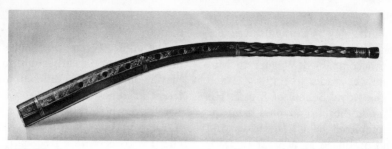

cornett   *courtesy, Kunsthistorisches Museum, Vienna*

continued to be played locally in Germany to support treble voices in choirs until about 1750 as well as with trombones in tower music until the 1830s. Its clear tone quality, essential for the works of Monteverdi and others, is essentially unmatched by any other instrument, and it began to be revived in the mid-20th century. *See* SERPENT.

Cornyshe, William (d. October 1523) The English composer and actor William Cornyshe was the favorite court musician of Henry VIII. He came from a family closely connected with the Chapel Royal; an older William Cornyshe (d. 1502), possibly his father, was the first master of the choristers at Westminster Abbey (1479–91). Cornyshe was connected with the Chapel Royal from 1496, taking over as master in 1509. He took the Chapel Royal to France with the king in 1513 and also again in 1520 to the Field of Cloth of Gold, meeting with the King of France. He devised and performed in plays, masques, and pageants, being a principal actor at the court from 1508 to 1516. He wrote both secular and sacred music. Thirty-eight of the king's songs were bound with a collection of his songs. A poem he wrote while in Fleet Prison for slander was printed in a collection of the poet John Skelton's works and is sometimes attributed to that poet.

BIBLIOGRAPHY: John Stevens, *Music and Poetry in the Early Tudor Court* (1961).

Coronation Mass: *see* CLASSICAL PERIOD (vocal music, 1750–1800); MOZART (early life).

corrente: *see* COURANTE.

Cortot, Alfred (-Denis) (September 26, 1877–June 15, 1962) The major French pianist of his time, Alfred Cortot was also a conductor of note, championing the works of Wagner and of young French composers. He was a

pupil of Louis Diémer at the Paris Conservatoire, winning a *premier prix* (1896). With Jacques Thibaud and Pablo Casals he formed a trio in 1905 that gained an international reputation. He became professor of piano at the Conservatoire in 1907, remaining as titular department head until 1920. His playing was known for its intellectual authority, fantasy, and some want in marksmanship. Cortot published works on piano technique and a historical survey of French piano music, and he edited the works of Schumann and of Chopin.

Alfred Cortot   *courtesy, Steinway & Sons*

Così fan tutte: *see* COUNTERPOINT (Classical period); MOZART (later life); OPERA (the 19th century).

Costa, Michael (Andrew Agnus), originally Michele Andrea Agniello (February 4, 1808–April 29, 1884)   The first conductor of importance in England, Michael Costa was educated in his native Naples. He settled in London in 1830 as maestro al cembalo at the King's Theatre, Haymarket (after 1837 called Her Majesty's Theatre), taking over the orchestra in 1833 and shaping it into the first disciplined ensemble to be heard in the country. With most of his players he moved in 1847 to the new Royal Italian Opera at the rebuilt Covent Garden. Costa was also conductor of the Philharmonic (1846–54), the Sacred Harmonic Society (1848–82), the Birmingham Festival (1849–82), and the Handel Festival (1857–80). Primarily a craftsman rather than artist, Costa nevertheless felt free to embellish and rescore his musical texts in the fashion of the day. He was also a prolific composer, but none of his output endured.

counterpoint   The art of combining melodies, counterpoint is the most characteristic element in Western music and a major distinguishing feature between the music of the West and that of the Orient and of primitive peoples. Both historically and aesthetically counterpoint and HARMONY are inextricably blended, for nearly every harmonic fact is in its origin a phenomenon of counterpoint. What is always important is the peculiar life breathed into harmony by contrapuntal organization.

Middle Ages   The earliest examples of actual written counterpoint appear in the late-9th-century treatise *Musica enchiriadis.* Here a plainchant melody, or principal voice *(vox principalis),* is combined with another part, organal voice *(vox organalis),* singing the same melody in parallel motion a perfect fourth or fifth below *(e.g.,* G or F below C). Such music was called organum, probably because it resembled the sound of contemporary organs. In the early 11th century the teacher and theorist Guido of Arezzo in his *Micrologus* described a variety of organum in which the accompanying or organal voice had become

more individualized. In addition to moving parallel to the main voice, it included oblique (diverging or converging) motion and contrary (opposite) motion. In this period the organal voice remains melodically awkward and subservient to the chant voice as though it were composed one note at a time simply to color or ornament each note of the chant. Early organum is thus not far removed from heterophony. Until the end of the 11th century, organum was written entirely in note-against-note style, described in 1336 as *punctus contra punctum* ("point against point"; *i.e.,* note against note), hence the name counterpoint.

Te   hu — mi — les   fa — mu — li

mo — du — lis   ve — ne — ran — do   oi — is

early organum from *Musica enchiriadis, c.* 859

In the 12th century true polyphony comes into being; the melodic lines become individualized mostly by being given different rhythms. There emerges a hierarchy between the voice parts. The emphasis is upon the chant voice, which now becomes the lower part. Its notes are prolonged, or held, and this part is now called the tenor, from the Latin *tenere,* "to hold." The contrapuntal genius of the Middle Ages realizes itself mostly through the use of rhythmic contrasts between the different voice parts, and such contrasts gradually increase in complexity from *c.* 1100 to *c.* 1400. Around 1200 Pérotin, a composer of the Notre Dame school in Paris who wrote some of the earliest music in three and four parts, superimposed different RHYTHMIC MODES in the voice parts. In his three-part

(Al-)le-   (luia)

from Pérotin, *Alleluia nativitas*

Alleluia nativitas the voices are in different rhythmic modes, and they are also distinguished by different phrase lengths, consisting of more or fewer repetitions of the rhythmic pattern. In the 13th century such contrasts were carried still further in the motet, a musical form usually in three voice parts, each in a different rhythmic mode. The theorist Franco of Cologne advocated the use of consonance at the beginning of each measure; such consonances (usually a chord made up of the unison, fifth, and octave, such as C–G–C′) served as fixed pillars in terms of which the horizontal extensions of different rhythmic lengths were like soaring arches of sound. The tenor voice part in the motets of the 14th and early 15th centuries was organized by huge rhythmic recurrences known as ISORHYTHM (*i.e.,* the return throughout the piece of a complex rhythmic pattern, not necessarily in conjunction with the same pitches of the melody). In the 14th century, particularly in the works of Guillaume de Machaut, the upper voice part was sometimes displaced by a beat or more in respect to the other parts, giving it further rhythmic independence. In the late 14th century complicated syncopations and the simultaneous use of different meters characterized some of the most complex counterpoint in history. *See also* MIDDLE AGES.

Renaissance   If the medieval composer explored mostly the possibilities of rhythmic counterpoint, the Renaissance composer was concerned primarily with melodic relationships between the voice parts. The predominant technique used was that of imitation; *i.e.,* the successive statement of the same or similar melody in each of the voice parts so that one voice imitates another.

Imitation had appeared earlier in the Italian caccia and French *chace,* roundlike vocal forms of the 14th century, and in England in the 13th-century round *Sumer is icumen in.* These compositions anticipate the Renaissance and also emphasize the rhythmic relationships typical of medieval counterpoint.

During the Renaissance the technique of imitation contributed to a new unity between the voices as opposed to the hierarchy found in medieval counterpoint. Renaissance composers strove also for clear melodic relation-

ships between voices; consequently imitations usually began on the same beat of a measure and were separated in pitch by simple intervals such as the fifth or octave. Renaissance theorists, among them Johannes Tinctoris and Gioseffo Zarlino, categorized dissonances according to type and governed each type by definite rhythmic and melodic restrictions.

What is often proclaimed as the golden age of counterpoint—meaning melodic counterpoint—stretches from the late 15th to the late 16th century, from the Flemish–French master Jean d'Ockeghem to the Spanish Victoria and the Elizabethan Byrd. Its leading masters were Josquin des Prés, Palestrina, and Orlando di Lasso. The northern composers in particular showed a penchant for complex melodic relationships. Ockeghem's *Missa prolationum,* for example, involves the simultaneous use of canon in two pairs of voices. The most versatile craftsman of the Renaissance was Josquin, whose music displays a continual variety of contrapuntal ingenuities, including melodic imitation. His use of successive imitation in several voices, as in his *Missa Da pacem,* is coupled with melodic smoothness and rhythmic vitality. The imitative style came to

from Josquin, *Missa Da pacem*

its fullest flowering in the late 16th century, not only in the masses and motets of di Lasso and Palestrina but also in secular songs such as the French chanson and Italian madrigal. It also flourished in instrumental music in such contrapuntal forms as the fantasia, canzona, and ricercare. *See also* RENAISSANCE.

Baroque era   In the 17th and early 18th centuries the pure linear—*i.e.,* melodic—counterpoint of the Renaissance, now called the first practice, was retained alongside the newer type of counterpoint known as the second practice. This latter type was characterized by a freer treatment of dissonance and a richer employment of tone color. The new liberties with dissonance disturbed the conservative theorists of the time, but they were justified by their proponents on the ground that they allowed a more expressive treatment of the text. Still more distinct was a new use of tone color. Although the individual melodic lines often resembled those of the Renaissance, they were intensified and made to stand out through differences of scoring or instrumentation. In figured bass compositions the counterpoint was between the upper melody and the bass line. These stood out clearly from one another because of their differences of instrumental or vocal tone color. Also significant at this time was the development of concerto-like scoring. Concerto style emphasized contrasts between the numbers of performers, the high and low registers, and the tone colors of two or more performing groups. This was anticipated in some of the madrigals of the late Renaissance, especially those of Luca Marenzio and Carlo Gesualdo, in which two or three voice parts in a high or low register were immediately answered by parts in a contrasting register. Giovanni Gabrieli of Venice expanded this principle in his *Symphoniae sacrae* by setting off choirs of voices or instruments, thus achieving a counterpoint of contrasting sonorities. Such concerto-like effects became an essential part of the later madrigals and operas of Monteverdi. In his madrigal *Lament of the Nymph,* a single soprano voice is pitted against three male voices and both in turn against an instrumental continuo. This type of counterpoint was ideal for emphasizing

from Monteverdi, *Lament of the Nymph*

dramatic contrasts in the new forms of the opera and the oratorio. In these forms soloists, ensembles, and instrumental parts were opposed and combined in a great variety of ways by composers like Heinrich Schütz, Carissimi, and Purcell. In the late Baroque Corelli and

Vivaldi added this style of dramatic contrasts to the purely instrumental contrasts of the concerto. The Baroque concerto culminated in Bach's *Brandenburg* Concertos, which are characterized by a remarkable fusion of contrapuntal lines and instrumental colors.

from Bach, *Brandenburg* Concerto No. 5

Bach's counterpoint has a retrospective side, which uses a mainly melodic approach. The fugue, a composition using the technique of melodic imitation, became highly developed in Bach's hands—*e.g.,* the fugues of the *Well-Tempered Clavier,* and his final compendium of contrapuntal devices, *The Art of the Fugue.* A similar melodic, rather than tone-color, approach occurs in works such as the Inventions and in the canons of the *Musical Offering.* These works are akin to the first practice, the melodic counterpoint of the Renaissance, although in their use of dissonance and harmony they go considerably beyond Renaissance convention. *See also* BAROQUE ERA.

Classical period The turn from the Baroque to the Classical period was marked by the change from a luxuriant polyphonic to a relatively simple homophonic texture—*i.e.,* a texture of a single melodic line plus chordal accompaniment. Composers of the early Classical period (*c.* 1730–70) largely eschewed counterpoint altogether, drawing on it only when preparing church music in the "learned style," as the Renaissance style was then called. Many of the keyboard sonatas of Domenico Scarlatti and Carl Philipp Emanuel Bach, despite a basically homophonic approach, reveal a skillful interplay between the main melody and accompaniment. In the late Classical period (*c.* 1770–1820), especially in the music of the Viennese school of Haydn,

Mozart, and Beethoven, there was an ever-increasing penetration of counterpoint into forms based on this homophonic style and its contrasts of tonality, or key. This counterpoint in turn was tempered by the Classical style and musical forms. For example, although combined melodic lines are heard as counterpoint, together they can also be heard as a series of harmonies. In this way they form unified phrases in the homophonic style. This satisfied demands for symmetrical phrase lengths and clear-cut cadences necessary to mark the sections of Classical forms such as the sonata.

Haydn underwent his contrapuntal crisis, or movement toward counterpoint, during the 1770s, the period of *Sturm und Drang* in German literature, which had a deepening effect on other arts as well. Three of his *Sun* Quartets (1772) had fugues as final movements, and in the *Russian* Quartets (1781) Haydn proclaimed "an entirely new manner" in which the thematic material was to be more equally shared by all of the stringed instruments instead of being given to a single principal melody instrument. Haydn heard Handel's oratorios in London, which inspired him to write his own richly contrapuntal late oratorios, *The Creation* and *The Seasons.*

Mozart's discovery of the contrapuntal art of Bach and Handel impressed him so deeply that almost all of his later works were affected. The ensembles of the operas—*e.g., Don Giovanni* and *Così fan tutte*—with their clear delineation of several characters through their vocal lines, only became possible because of his new feeling for counterpoint. And at one point in his *Jupiter* Symphony, five different themes are stated simultaneously, singly, or in combination. Nevertheless the counterpoint is kept entirely subservient to the harmonies of the symphony's tonal design, or its use of keys. Each voice is also governed by an underlying phrase structure applied to all of them so that the combined parts form unified musical phrases.

Beethoven began his career in Vienna under the tutelage of the noted contrapuntal theorist Johann Georg Albrechtsberger; this, coupled with his admiration for Handel, probably accounts for his lifetime interest in counterpoint.

from Mozart, Quartet, K.490

He drew upon counterpoint to create intensity, especially in the development section of sonata form (the first movement of the *Razumovsky* Quartet, Op. 59, No. 1, for example). In his late sonatas and quartets, except for obvious fugal works such as the first movement of Opus 131 or the *Grosse Fuge,* Op. 133, almost every movement shows the interpenetration of the principles of counterpoint—which deals with melodic lines, and tonality—which deals with harmonies.

Romantic period   Counterpoint in the 19th century had a retrospective side in addition to a characteristically Romantic style. Wagner admired the counterpoint of Palestrina, and Brahms revered the Baroque masters. Mendelssohn revived Bach's *St. Matthew* Passion in 1829, and this led to numerous Bach-like works such as Mendelssohn's organ sonatas and numerous organ works by Max Reger as well as arrangements of Bach's works by Liszt. Yet the true bent of Romantic composers was toward combinations of motifs, motivic accompaniments against themes, and later of the combination of leitmotivs with significance beyond the music itself. The lieder of Schubert were highly innovative because of their motivic accompaniments, which balance in interest the vocal part itself and contrapuntally interact with it. This technique is still more pronounced in the songs of Schumann and Hugo Wolf. It is also the tendency in 19th-century opera. In the later operas of Verdi the voices often have a *parlante* character (imitating speech through music) while the orchestra defines the dramatic substance. This too is the principle of the Wagner music dramas, with their *Sprechgesang,* or "speech-song," in the voice balanced contrapuntally by the leitmotivs of the accompaniment. In *Tristan und Isolde* Wagner set the leitmotivs in counterpoint against one another. Similarly in the Prelude to Act III of *Siegfried,* a motif known as the "Need of the Gods" is cast against one associated with the Valkyries. This results in

from Wagner, *Siegfried* (Act III)

a "counterpoint" of connotations and of emotions as well as in a musical counterpoint. In purely instrumental music a similar joining of motifs previously heard separately is encountered in the finale of Berlioz' *Symphonie fantastique* when the plainchant melody "Dies Irae" is heard together with the theme called "Round of Sabbath." Richard Strauss in his tone poem *Ein Heldenleben,* skillfully combines several themes taken from his earlier tone poems. And in the late symphonies of Mahler there is sometimes a complex of interwoven motifs, each of which stands out contrapuntally through its presentation by a solo instrument.

modern period In the 20th century Schoenberg carried this technique further, especially in his works based on a 12-tone row arranged in such a way as to avoid a sense of tonality. In some 12-tone operas—*e.g., Moses und Aron* by Schoenberg and *Lulu* by Berg—there is but one tone row used in the entire work; nonetheless, several hours of music are spun out of it through a continual variety of thematic shapes and contrapuntal combinations.

The 20th century, like the 19th, has had its counterpoint inspired by earlier music. Webern, for example, advocated a return to the forms of counterpoint used by Renaissance composers such as Heinrich Isaac, and in numerous of his own works *(e.g., Symphonie)* he makes use of Renaissance contrapuntal devices such as simultaneous canons and retrograde movement between the voice parts. Out of a similar return to Baroque forms came works such as the double fugue that forms the second movement of the *Symphony of Psalms* by Stravinsky.

But the use of older musical forms is no more of the essence of 20th-century counterpoint than it was of the 19th. A basic characteristic of 20th-century counterpoint is the separation of the voice parts into isolated entities of sound that are of themselves rather static. This may take the form of polytonality, using as static entities the notes of each key. It may also take the form of contrast of individual tone color effects rather than of melodies that is found in much electronic music. (This use extends beyond the original definition of counterpoint simply as the combination of melodies.)

Richard Strauss's *Elektra* (1909) was one of the earliest works to make use of polytonality; in certain passages the instruments and voice parts are grouped into layers, each of which defines a different tonality, or key, although in this case all of the keys can also be interpreted as complicated aspects of the basic key. Stravinsky's Three Pieces for string quartet suggests four keys at the same time: G, B, D, and A-flat. In this particular work each instrument is limited throughout the piece to a few notes assigned to it. Thus each part is absolutely individual and, except for the viola, consists of an ostinato melodic and rhythmic pattern. The coming together of these ostinato patterns at different times and

from Stravinsky, Three Pieces for string quartet (No. 1)

in continually shifting arrangements suggests the effect of a mobile.

Bartók carried out a similar procedure in many of the short piano pieces of his *Mikrokosmos* (1926–39), and in his Fourth Quartet (1928) he set apart tone clusters (chords built up in seconds, as C–D–E–F–G) in this way.

Turning now to a counterpoint purely of tone colors, *Intégrales* (1925) by Edgard Varèse presents 11-note "sound-clouds" in the wind instruments in opposition to the sounds of a large battery of percussion instruments. This approach probably grew directly out of earlier experiments with polytonality, but here tone colors rather than keys or tones are differentiated. Elliott Carter in his Double Concerto (1961) set apart two groups of instruments—one around a piano, another around a harpsichord—each with its distinctive tone colors and its own distinctive harmonic intervals or note combinations. In György Ligeti's *Atmospheres* (1961) every instrument in a symphony orchestra, including every string part, plays its own unique melodic pattern; all of these parts coalesce into gigantic bands or spectra of tone color that contrast with one another. In later experiments the sound-producing groups are further set off by visual or spatial contrasts in the physical placement of performers; *e.g.,* Ramon Zupko's *Third Planet from the Sun* (1970).

BIBLIOGRAPHY: Johann Joseph Fux, *Gradus ad Parnassum* (1725; Eng. trans. by Alfred Mann and John Edmunds, *Steps to Parnassus,* 1943; reprint, *Study of Counterpoint,* 1965); Knud Jeppesen, *Counterpoint, the Polyphonic Vocal Style of the Sixteenth Century* (1939; reprint, 1960); William Oliver Strunk, *Source Readings in Music History* (1950); Gustave Reese, *Fourscore Classics of Music Literature* (1957); Hugo Riemann, *History of Music Theory* (1962).

countertenor The adult male alto voice, either natural or falsetto. In England the word generally refers to a falsetto alto rather than a high tenor. Some writers reserve the term countertenor for a naturally produced voice, terming the falsetto voice a male alto.

Derived from the Renaissance *contratenor*

altus, abbreviated to *contratenor* (countertenor) or *altus* (alto), the term countertenor was originally applied to an alto part as well as to the voice or the instrument taking this part (*see* TENOR). Although the falsetto voice lost favor on the Continent in the 18th century, the tradition was preserved in England in cathedral choirs. In the 20th century the solo countertenor voice was successfully revived and, although it remains associated principally with the performance of Renaissance and Baroque music, several modern composers—notably Britten and Krzysztof Penderecki—have written for it.

Couperin A French family that produced a succession of musicians from the early 17th to the mid-19th century, the Couperins achieved their greatest fame through two composers of genius who were court musicians to Louis XIV.

Louis Couperin (*c.* 1626–August 29, 1661) was born at Chaumes in the province of Brie, the first of the many Couperins to become organist at the Church of St. Gervais in Paris; he also played the viol and violin in the ballet music of the court. He was a brilliant harpsichordist, and contemporary accounts suggest that his vigorous style of playing revealed the same qualities as his harpsichord compositions, which are distinguished by an almost aggressive use of dissonance and of Baroque ornamentation. He had command of a sturdy contrapuntal technique that recalls the French organ school of the 16th century, but at times his tonal architecture, built on Italian models, and his bel canto melodies suggest Handel. It is significant that his finest compositions were conceived in the transitional convention of the chaconne or passacaglia, for as a composer he is both reactionary and progressive.

François Couperin (November 10, 1668–September 12, 1733), Louis' nephew known as "Le Grand," was born in Paris. His father, Charles Couperin, who had succeeded Louis as organist at St. Gervais, died in 1679; François inherited the post, although he did not assume it until 1685 or early 1686. Meanwhile he was educated in music by an uncle, also François Couperin (1631–1701), and by Jacques Thomelin, who gave him a thorough

François Couperin le Grand
*portrait by an unknown French artist,
18th century Giraudon*

grounding in counterpoint. Like his uncle Louis, François is remembered mainly for his keyboard pieces, though the Oiseau Lyre edition of his works (1933) reveals that his chamber music and church music are also important. His first published works were two organ masses, composed *c.* 1690, and long erroneously ascribed to his uncle François. In 1693 he succeeded Thomelin as one of the organists of the royal chapel and in 1694 was appointed to teach the royal children. He was ennobled in 1696 and from about 1701 performed the functions of director of music at the court although not officially succeeding to the appointment until 1717. He kept his position as organist at St. Gervais until 1723 and his offices at court till 1730, being succeeded in both by other members of his family.

The personal voice beneath the traditionalism of Couperin's masses becomes unmistakable in the succession of harpsichord pieces, *Livre de clavecin,* that he published in four exquisitely engraved volumes between 1713 and 1730. Although the plan of Couperin's movements is conceived harmonically, his music marks a transitional stage between polyphony and homophony with frequent dialogues between treble and bass. Implied polyphony exists together with the ripest de-

velopment of tonal harmony, and Couperin is thus, among the late Baroque composers, the nearest to Bach. This is evident in his fine trio sonatas (especially "L'Impériale" from *Les Nations* and *Le Parnasse, ou L'Apothéose de Corelli*) and in many of the movements from the *Concerts Royaux* (*c.* 1714–15), which he composed for the king's Sunday evening entertainments. In his church music, as in his chamber pieces, Couperin achieves a fusion of the French and Italian styles, as illustrated in the early Motet *de Ste. Suzanne* (1698), which is voluptuous in its brilliant Italian cantilena and virginal in its harmony, rhythms, and textures. Couperin's last and greatest liturgical work, the *Leçons des Ténèbres* (1715), brings to the linear subtlety of the French vocal style and the pathos of Italian harmony a quality of mysticism that has no parallel in French or Italian music of the period. Bach's well-attested admiration for Couperin was not fortuitous. Couperin also wrote an important, if somewhat ambiguous and obscure, theoretical work, *L'Art de toucher le clavecin* (1717), which also includes eight preludes and an allemande in the appendix.

BIBLIOGRAPHY: Wilfred Mellers, *François Couperin and the French Classical Tradition* (1950).

RECORDINGS: Louis Couperin—Organ Pieces; *Pièces de clavecin.* François Couperin "le Grand"—*L'Art de toucher le clavecin* (eight preludes); *Concerts royaux* (4); *Les Goûts-réunis* (selections); *Leçons des Ténèbres* (3); Organ Masses (2); *La Sultane;* Trio Sonatas *Apothéose de Lulli, Les Nations* (4), *Le Parnasse, ou L'Apothéose de Corelli, La Steinquerque;* numerous pieces from *Livre de clavecin.*

courante A court dance for couples that was prominent in the late 16th century and fashionable in aristocratic European ballrooms, especially in France and England, for the next 200 years. It reputedly originated as an Italian folk dance with running steps (from the Latin *currere,* "to run"). As a court dance it was performed with small, back and forth, springing steps, later subdued to stately glides. Each couple held hands to move forward and backward or dropped hands to face each other or turn. In its early courtly form the dance was preceded by a wooing pantomime for three couples.

As a musical form the dance appears as the French courante in modern $\frac{3}{2}$ time with some contrasting measures in $\frac{6}{4}$ (HEMIOLA) and as the Italian corrente in rapid $\frac{3}{4}$ or $\frac{3}{8}$ time with running passages of eighth notes. Telemann, Handel, Bach, and other Baroque composers used both types in their orchestral and keyboard suites. In these suites the courante follows the allemande as it did in the ballroom.

Cowell, Henry (Dixon) (March 11, 1887–December 10, 1965)   One of the most innovative U.S. composers of the 20th century, Henry Cowell grew up in poverty in San Francisco and on family farms in Kansas, Iowa, and Oklahoma. At 14 he acquired a piano and at 15 in San Francisco gave a recital of his highly experimental piano compositions. At 17 he studied at the University of California with Charles Seeger, who persuaded him to undertake systematic study of traditional European musical techniques. He also urged Cowell to formulate a theoretical framework for his innovations, which he did in his book *New Musical Resources* (1919; published 1930). He later studied comparative musicology with Erich von Hornbostel. This experience stimulated and deepened his interest in the music of non-Western cultures; he later did original study of Oriental and Middle Eastern music, and non-Western elements appear in many of his compositions. He taught at the New School for Social Research, New York City (1932–52), and from 1949 at Columbia University.

In addition to his innovations Cowell's music reflects three main interests: a rural American hymnology, an interest in Irish lore and music, and non-Western music.

His innovations appear particularly in the piano pieces written between 1912 and 1930. Seeking new sonorities, he developed tone clusters, chords that on the piano are produced by simultaneously depressing several adjacent keys (*e.g.,* with the forearm). Later he called these sonorities secondal harmonies—*i.e.,* harmonies based on the interval of a second in contrast to the traditional basis

of a third. Secondal harmonies appear in his Piano Concerto (1930), in his early piano pieces such as *The Tides of Manaunaun* (1912), and in his *Synchrony* (1931) for orchestra and trumpet solo. Other piano compositions are played directly on the piano strings, which are rubbed, plucked, struck, or otherwise sounded by the hands or by an object. In *Aeolian Harp* (1923) the effect is quiet and mysterious; in *The Banshee* (1925) it is that of the eerie wailing of the Irish death spirit. Cowell's *Mosaic* Quartet (1934) was an experiment with musical form; the performers are given blocks of music to arrange in any desired order. With the Russian engineer Leon Theremin, Cowell built the rhythmicon, an electronic instrument that could produce 16 different simultaneous rhythms (he used it in *Rhythmicana,* 1931).

Cowell's *Gaelic* Symphony (1942) and his tone-cluster piece *The Lilt of Reel* (1925), echoing an Irish dance, reflect his Irish heritage. Non-Western influences appear in the Koto Concerto (1964), the *Persian Set* (1957) for 12 instruments, and the *Madras* Symphony (1959), which utilizes modes and rhythms of Indian music.

Cowell founded *New Music* (1927; editor until 1936), a quarterly devoted to the publication of new works, particularly American. It was here that Ives was first brought to the attention of the musical world, and Cowell served as the chief link to him in his emergence as a major composer. Cowell also edited *American Composers on American Music* (1933) and, with his wife Sidney Robertson Cowell, wrote *Charles Ives and His Music* (1955).

RECORDINGS: *Hymn and Fuguing Tunes; Ostinato Pianissimo* for percussion; Quartet *Euphometric;* Sinfonietta; *Six Casual Developments* for clarinet and piano; *Synchrony;* piano pieces.

Craft, Robert (b. October 20, 1923)   Best known for his association with Stravinsky, the U.S. conductor and musicologist Robert Craft studied at the Juilliard School in New York City and at the Berkshire Music Center as well as with Pierre Monteux. He conducted the New York Chamber Art Society (1947–

50) and the Los Angeles Monday Evening Concerts before collaborating with Stravinsky in a six-volume set of memoirs, *Conversations with Stravinsky* (1959–68). His *Stravinsky: Chronicle of a Friendship* (1972) was challenged by other musicologists on its interpretation of Stravinsky and his music. In addition to his recordings of Stravinsky's works, Craft has recorded the complete works of Webern and much of the music of Berg, Schoenberg, and Edgard Varèse. He is an erudite critic on a wide range of musical, literary, and other humanistic subjects.

Cramer, John (Johann) Baptist (February 24, 1771–April 16, 1858)   Pianist, composer, and publisher, the German-born John Baptist Cramer grew up in London, where he studied with Clementi and became known to his English audiences as "glorious John." To generations of piano students he is known for the studies published in many editions from his *Grosse praktische Pianoforte-Schule* (1815). Admired by Beethoven, Cramer was the most classic of the Classicists, preferring to play Bach and Mozart. His touch was famous for its singing legato, but he outlived the style of his era and was not admired by his younger contemporaries (such as Liszt). In 1824 he established a music publishing firm bearing his name (in various combinations with others to the late 20th century, later manufacturing pianos as well). He was a prolific composer, but only his studies have endured.

Crawford Seeger, Ruth (Porter): *see* SEEGER, RUTH (PORTER) CRAWFORD.

Creation, The: *see* CLASSICAL PERIOD (vocal music, 1750–1800); COUNTERPOINT (Classical period); HAYDN (late oratorios); ORATORIO (late 18th century).

Créquillon, Thomas (d. 1557)   An early master of polyphony in the style of Palestrina, the Flemish composer Thomas Créquillon served as choirmaster at the imperial chapel of Charles V in the Netherlands between 1544 and 1550. Highly praised in its time for harmonic and expressive excellence, Créquillon's music includes chansons, motets, and masses. Representative examples are found in all the great 16th-century collections of sacred music.
   RECORDINGS: Motets (116).

Creston, Paul, real name, Joseph Guttoveggio (b. October 10, 1906)   A U.S. composer noted for the rhythmic vitality and full harmonies of his music, Paul Creston writes in a conservative style but uses modern dissonances and polyrhythms. He grew up in a poor family, studied organ with Pietro Yon, became a theater organist (1926–29), and in 1934 became organist at St. Malachy's Church in New York City. He taught himself composition by studying musical scores and reading. He was president of the National Association for American Composers and Conductors (1956–60) and in 1960 traveled in Israel and Turkey on a U.S. Department of State grant. He was active as a conductor and lecturer, and he taught at Swarthmore College (1956), New York College of Music (1963–67), and Central Washington State College (from 1968).

   He gained prominence with his *Threnody* (1938) and *Two Choric Dances* (1938), both for orchestra. He wrote five symphonies, some with programmatic connotations (*e.g.,* the Third Symphony [1950], *Three Mysteries*). His *Corinthians XIII* (1963), like the Third Symphony, utilizes themes from Gregorian chant. His belief that song and dance are the basis of music is reflected in the *Invocation and Dance* for orchestra (1954), in the two-part *Janus* for strings, piano, and percussion (1959), and in the two-movement Second Symphony (1945). In *Janus* and in the Toccata for orchestra (1957) he used polyrhythms. His *Pavane* Variations (1966) utilizes the dance rhythms of the 16th-century pavane and, although not written in serial technique, comprises variations on four 12-tone rows. His other works include the symphonic poem *Walt Whitman* (1951); Concertino for marimba (1940); concertos for saxophone, for piano, and for violin; solo piano pieces; and sacred vocal works.

   RECORDINGS: Concertino for marimba and orchestra; Concerto for alto saxophone and band; *Corinthians XIII;* Prelude and Dance for band; *A Rumor* (symphonic sketch); Sonata for saxophone and piano; Suite for violin and piano.

criticism   In his *Essays in Musical Analysis,* Donald Francis Tovey treats the question of criticism with handsome dispatch. Checking the index to this winning collection, one finds the following cross-references: Critics: *see* Experts; Experts, *see* Critics. This circular insularity is an apt approximation of the present state of the art. Criticism to many seems to be rooted in soil that is intellectually sere and reflective of confused sensibilities. Whatever the merits of contemporary commentators, it is likely that earlier writers faced a simpler challenge.

development The criticism of music first gained serious hold in the 17th and 18th centuries; generally speaking, the criticism of the time was characterized by an obsessive interest in the rules of music, and it tended to judge practice in the light of theory. Among the first writer-musicians to make systematic contributions to criticism were Jean-Jacques Rousseau in France, Johann Mattheson in Germany, and Charles Avison and Charles Burney in England. Their work coincided with the emergence of periodicals and newspapers all over Europe. The first journal devoted entirely to music criticism was *Critica Musica,* founded by Mattheson in 1722. Mattheson had a number of successors, notably the Leipzig composer Johann Adolph Scheibe, who brought out his weekly *Der critische Musicus* between the years 1737 and 1740 and whose chief claim to notoriety was his scurrilous attack on Bach.

At the turn of the century the age of academicism dissolved into the age of description. Schumann, Liszt, and Berlioz, the leaders of the Romantic era, frequently saw in music the embodiment of some poetic or literary idea. They composed program symphonies, symphonic poems, and lesser pieces bearing such titles as "novellette," "ballade," and "romance." Their literary outlook naturally influenced criticism, the more so as they themselves frequently wrote it. In his pamphlet *On John Field's Nocturnes* (1859), Liszt wrote in the purple prose of the time of their "balmy freshness, seeming to exhale copious perfumes; soothing as the slow, measured rocking of a boat or the swinging of a hammock, amid whose smoothly placid oscillations we seem to hear the dying murmur of melting caresses." Most of the Romantics were guilty

of this type of descriptive criticism. Its weakness is that unless the music is already known, the criticism is meaningless; and once the music is known, the criticism is redundant, as the music itself says it all far more effectively.

The most influential critic of the age was Schumann. In 1834 he founded the periodical *Neue Zeitschrift für Musik* and remained its editor in chief for ten years. Its pages are full of the most perceptive insights into music and music makers. The first major article Schumann wrote was a laudatory essay on the young Chopin, "Hats off, gentlemen, a genius" (1834), and the last, called "New Paths" (1853), introduced to the world the young Brahms.

During the second half of the 19th century, the critical scene was dominated by the Viennese critic Eduard Hanslick, who is rightly regarded as the father of modern musical criticism. He was a prolific writer, and his book *Vom Musikalisch-Schönen* (1854; *The Beautiful in Music*) is a milestone in the history of criticism. It took an anti-Romantic stand, stressing the autonomy of music and its basic independence of the other arts, and it encouraged a more analytical, less descriptive approach toward criticism. The book was continually reprinted until 1895, appearing in many languages.

Inspired by Hanslick's example critics in the 20th century rejected the age of description for the age of analysis. Scientific materialism created a climate of rationalism from which music did not remain immune. Critics spoke of structure, thematicism, tonality—a far cry from Liszt's "dying murmur of melting caresses." A group of musician-thinkers arose who questioned the very basis of musical aesthetics. They included Hugo Riemann, Heinrich Schenker, Henry Hadow, Tovey, Ernest Newman, and above all Schoenberg, whose theoretical writings show him to be one of the most radical thinkers of the age. Criticism itself was criticized, its basic weakness clearly diagnosed. The search was on to discover the criteria for the evaluation of music. This quest has dominated the work of serious critics ever since. What will become of it is difficult to say, as the language of music itself is now rapidly changing. Under the leadership of such composers as John Cage and Stockhausen, aleatory techniques have been introduced in which nothing can be predicted, nothing can be repeated, everything is random, and every possible link with the past has been broken. This is a challenge to the theory of criticism that thus far has not been met successfully.

theory If the practice of criticism can be reduced to one thing—expressing value judgments—the theory of criticism is essentially one thing too—explaining them. It is not enough for critics to assert that one work is a masterpiece, another a mediocrity. An attempt must be made to explain why, and this may lead to a central discovery. A masterpiece is not a matter of chance, nor is a mediocrity. Both are symptomatic of deep, far-reaching principles.

When the Viennese critic Rudolph Reti was a young man studying music at the Vienna Conservatory, he once stood up in the middle of a composition class and put the following question to his professor: "Why can't we take the themes of one work and substitute the themes of another?" Reti did not receive a very convincing reply and was therefore stimulated to think about the problem for himself. Forty years later he worked out an answer in his book *The Thematic Process in Music* (1951). Briefly it was that masterpieces diversify a unity. They grow from an all-embracing idea. Their contrasting themes hang together because each of them represents a different aspect of a single basic thought. This observation was not new. Schoenberg had made it years earlier. So too had Heinrich Schenker, who used it as the basis for a major theory of aesthetics in his monumental *Das Meisterwerk in der Musik,* three volumes (1926–29). Reti sharpened the concept. He made the critics think again about what, precisely, they mean when they talk about the integrity of a musical structure.

Reti's thesis can be vividly demonstrated by taking an existing masterpiece and substituting random themes from another. Even if such themes preserve a semblance of continuity (matching the key, meter, and mood of the themes they displace), they lose the deep sense of unity communicated by the original.

Not all musicians accept this theory. They argue that many composers, notably Bach, have put together works by borrowing materials from other sources. They fail to realize, however, that the act of borrowing is so highly selected that it too must be regarded as part of the creative process. The question then becomes: Why was that particular theme or movement borrowed?

Another question is why a composition expresses itself through its particular medium. Why that medium rather than another?

If a masterpiece is transferred from the instrumental medium for which it was conceived to some alien medium, it undergoes a curious distortion. Such distortion offers the clearest proof that a musical law is operating in the original—an identity of the idea with its medium. A master's inner inspiration adapts to outer terms of reference. Individual instruments lay down individual limitations. If a composer ignores this fact, there can be no certainty that creative aims will coincide with musical results.

Occasionally a great composer deliberately engineers a collision between the idea and the medium for a special musical purpose. The fugue in Beethoven's *Hammerklavier* Sonata, for example, is one of the most physically awkward works to play in the entire piano repertoire. It has been composed against, rather than for, the instrument. Some measures are unplayable, and Beethoven knew it; they contribute to the sense of struggle that is an essential part of musical communication—present even in the greatest performance. The orchestration of this fugue by Felix Weingartner does a major service to musical aesthetics by providing an alternative musical experience of the same work; but by rendering the difficult easy, his orchestral version robs the music of its basic characteristics. It is a splendid illustration of the way in which, in Beethoven's original, a creative aim has been identified with a physical limitation.

A further question is why the chronology of the themes of a masterpiece cannot be changed. Why does one thematic chronology sound good, another bad? If the movements of a great sonata or a symphony are switched around, the result will be musically inferior.

If the themes of one movement are mixed with those from the same work's companion movements, the result may even be an artistic disaster.

An illuminating exercise in criticism is to reconstruct a masterpiece so that its thematic running order is altered; that is, to transfer the first movement's second subject to the position occupied by the finale's second subject and vice versa. Any musician can carry out this simple experiment. Nothing is better calculated to reveal the presence of a creative principle of contrast distribution in the original. Given the thousands of different directions in which the material of a work could be unfolded, a master chooses the "right" one, the one that maintains structural tension—and hence musical interest. The themes of a masterpiece cannot assume one another's functions. They are born to fulfill specific roles. They develop out of each other because they create a musical need for each other.

Composers through the ages have hinted at a law of economy toward which all great music strives. Brahms once said of composing in a characteristic piece of understatement that "the essential thing is that every note should be in its place." Beethoven expressed the same truth another way. After he had heard the "Funeral March" from the opera *Achille* by Ferdinando Paër, he observed: "I must compose that!" To fix the idea, to define it, to pin it down—both composers felt that this was of the essence. Notes are redundant that do not stand for precisely those musical thoughts they are supposed to express. To have more notes, or less, than are actually required to communicate musical meaning must render such meaning correspondingly obscure. This law may be divided into three subsidiary principles.

First is the principle of identity between the idea and its utterance. There is a concrete musical difference between what a composer intends (the idea) and what is actually said (the utterance). Some musicians contend that the distinction is merely theoretical, that in practice it cannot be made. Fortunately composers have left ample evidence to the contrary. Consider the act of revision. Revision is an acknowledgment by the composer that

what was actually written was not, on reflection, what was meant. Revision is self-criticism. The very word implies that a composer has a *re*-vision of the work, that a return to the utterance and modification of it is necessary to be truer to the idea. Revision can sometimes result in criticism on a grand, creative level. Composers occasionally revise the work of other composers with such effective results that the original composition may be eclipsed by the new version, the "criticism" often succeeding where the original work failed. Bach's arrangement for four harpsichords (in a minor) of Vivaldi's Violin Concerto in b minor, for example, is more than an adaptation from one medium to another. It is an act of musical criticism *par excellence*. Vivaldi created the idea. But it was left to Bach to give it complete utterance.

Why does music unfold a particular structure? Why that kind of structure rather than another? The textbooks on form remain silent; yet this is a profound question. It is surely of paramount interest to know why music unrolls in one direction rather than another. Inspired music appears to carry within itself its own blueprint, according to which it propels itself across precise distances and in precise directions. If it is prematurely halted, diverted, or too long continued—all hallmarks of creative immaturity—it loses the sense of punctuality, the feeling of arriving on time, the knowledge of being in the right place at the right moment, which characterizes each stage of an emerging structure masterfully handled.

Some musicians have observed that the distinction between form and content is a false one. They rightly argue that no one hears one without the other, that the one is an organic result of the other. Therefore why not abolish the distinction? They are right in regard to good forms, forms that arise inevitably from the musical material, in which case there is indeed no distinction to abolish. But bad forms—those that are not true to their content—produce a symptomatic division between the inner direction the music was born to follow and the outer direction in was made to follow.

The objective of all compositions is to make a total aural impact. There have been some famous miscalculations—intrinsically inaudible passages—which even the most illustrious performance could not render audible. A striking case of inaudibility occurs toward the end of Grieg's Piano Concerto in a minor, in which the big tune of the finale returns in full orchestral splendor and obliterates the part of the solo pianist. In the concert hall it is an extraordinary sight to see the soloist racing up and down the keyboard fortissimo without producing any sound. The observation is beyond all question and may be checked every time the work is played in public.

In 1937 Schoenberg completed an orchestration of Brahms's Piano Quartet in g minor, Op. 25. As a young man he had regularly participated in performances of the Quartet. Time and again he was bothered by its intermittent inaudibility: the piano tended to swamp the strings. Schoenberg's orchestration, as he himself claimed, attempted to put matters right. It remains an exercise in musical audibility—one master helping another to communicate. It constitutes an act of criticism on the highest creative level.

Other principles could be formulated to show that a theory of criticism is also a theory of composition. A search for these principles is really a search for the ultimate justification of the feelings of value inspired by great music.

practice Since music does not exist until it is brought to life by the player, two basic requirements are demanded of the critic: a knowledge of the work and a knowledge of the instrument. Many critics talk loosely about "the work" and "the performance" as though they were separate aspects of musical experience. They are in fact different aspects of a total musical experience, and it can be misleading to split them. Much bad criticism results from trying to do so. Leopold Godowsky would survey his audience before beginning a recital in an effort to discover how many detectives there were in the house. Being such a superb pianist he attracted all those critics interested exclusively in keyboard gymnastics. On the other hand, those interested exclusively in the composition may be equally biased. In this age of authenticity when the *ur*-text is the thing, many a promising career has been blighted through what in the profession is called a "departure from the text." It is not always appreciated that at least a part of the total musical experience is created by the performer, who has a two-fold artistic duty: first, to the fundamental character of the work interpreted; and second, to a personal artistic conscience, which tells how the work should unfold. The two are not necessarily mutually exclusive.

The criticism of performance is the most public—and publicized—aspect of a critic's function. It is also the least important. Unfortunately what particular critics think of particular artists accounts for most contemporary music criticism. This is determined by arbitrary factors rather than the critics' sense of priority. Most newspapers insist that a musical event be reported the following day. Immediately after a concert, therefore, the critic must write a review and limit it to a strictly prescribed number of words. Under these conditions it is not surprising that most criticism consists of predictable accounts of what was played, who played it, and how it was played. Nevertheless, musical journalism in newspapers and periodicals has on occasion reached inspired heights. Among the finest critics have been men of letters such as George Bernard Shaw and Paul Rosenfeld and composers such as Virgil Thomson and Copland. Though they did not deal overtly with the aesthetics of criticism, they left lively and perceptive records of the musical life of their times.

BIBLIOGRAPHY: George Bernard Shaw, *Music in London,* 3 vols. (1932; reprint, 1956), and *London Music* (1937); Donald Francis Tovey, *Essays in Musical Analysis,* 6 vols. (1935–39); David W. Prall, *Aesthetic Analysis* (1936; reprint, 1967); Max Graf, *Composer and Critic: Two Hundred Years of Music Criticism* (1946; reprint, 1971); Virgil Thomson, *The Art of Judging Music* (1948; reprint, 1969) and *Music Reviewed, 1940–54* (1967); Victor Zuckerkandl, *Sound and Symbol,* 2 vols. (1956, 1973); Aaron Copland, *Copland on Music* (1963); Alan Walker, *An Anatomy of Musical Criticism* (1966); Paul Rosenfeld, *Musical Impressions: Selections from Paul Rosenfeld's Criticism* (1969); Arnold Schoenberg, "Criteria for the Evaluation of Music" in *Style and Idea* (1975).

Croce, Giovanni (*c.* 1557–May 15, 1609) The leading Venetian composer of his day, Giovanni Croce was a pupil of Gioseffo Zarlino, who secured for him a place in the choir of St. Mark's, Venice. By 1585 he was a priest; in 1595 he became assistant choirmaster at St. Mark's and in 1603 won the competition for the choirmastership.

Croce's madrigals and canzonets (published in seven books, 1585–1607), though conservative, were widely admired for their light touch and alert rhythms. Croce's sacred music (published 1591–1610), including masses, motets, Magnificats, psalms, etc., shows a development from the manner of Palestrina to the polychoral style associated with Monteverdi, using solo voices, instrumental rhythms, and basso continuo.

Croft, William (1678–August 14, 1727) An English organist and composer chiefly of church music, William Croft was born at Nether Ettington, Warwickshire, and received a musical education at the Chapel Royal under John Blow. He was organist of St. Anne's, Soho, from 1700 till 1712, of the Chapel Royal from 1707, on the death of Jeremiah Clarke, and of Westminster Abbey from 1708. In 1700 he collaborated with Clarke, Francis Piggott, and John Barrett in a *Choice Collection of Ayres for the Harpsichord or Spinnet.* In 1724 appeared his *Musica sacra, or Select Anthems in Score* containing a setting of the burial service of the Church of England that remains in use in the 20th century. Croft's occasional anthems, such as "I will give thanks," for the victory at Blenheim (1704), contain some of his best writing. He also wrote incidental music and works for violin, voice, and harpsichord. His hymn-tune "St. Anne," usually sung to the words "O God our help in ages past," is widely known.

RECORDINGS: Vocal and instrumental pieces.

cross rhythm Rhythmic conflict or ambiguity in contradiction to the regular metrical patterns in a composition. *See* POLYRHYTHM.

crotal: *see* ANTIQUE CYMBALS.

Crüger, Johann (April 9, 1598–February 23, 1662) The German composer and organist Johann Crüger received his education at the Jesuit college of Olmütz, the School of Poetry at Regensburg, and the University of Wittenberg. Appointed cantor and organist at the church of St. Nicholas in Berlin in 1622, he remained there until his death. The best known of Crüger's works were published in 1644 in a volume titled *Praxis pietatis melica* and include the well-known chorales "Nun danket alle Gott," "Schmücke dich, o liebe Seele," and "Jesu meine Freude." A few of the many motets, concertos, and hymns that he wrote are extant. He also published several works on musical theory, including *Synopsis musices* (1624), a method for thoroughbass; *Perceptae musicae practicae figuralis* (1625; published in German as *Rechter Weg zur Singekunst,* 1660), and *Questiones musicae practicae* (1650).

Crumb, George (Henry) (b. October 24, 1929) A student of Ross Lee Finney and Boris Blacher, U.S. composer George Crumb is one of very few avant-garde musicians to achieve spontaneous success with the public and has become known to a wider audience through the use of his music for choreography (*Ancient Voices of Children,* composed 1970, choreographed 1976). His music shows the influence of Debussy and Webern; it is delicate in sound, often nearly static, with alternating aleatory and composed sections in varied densities and instrumental combinations and involving a highly theatrical mode of presentation. Most characteristic is the use of exotic percussion sounds (such as water gongs to produce glissandi, cowbells, antique cymbals, and extended piano harmonics that vibrate from an amplified soprano voice). Crumb's mature music dates from *Variazioni* (1959; orchestra), but most of his later music is for a small chamber group with percussion, and almost all of it uses words by Federico García Lorca. In several works instrumentalists double as vocalists. Much of his work explores the interrelation of sound and silence. In 1968 Crumb won the Pulitzer Prize for *Echoes of Time and the River* (composed 1967; orchestra). His *Star-Child* was scored for soprano, chorus, more than 70 pieces of percussion, brass, and strings—the forces required two conductors for its first performance in 1977.

Formerly on the faculty of the University of Colorado and the Berkshire (Massachusetts) Music Center, in 1965 Crumb joined the faculty of the University of Pennsylvania.

RECORDINGS: *Ancient Voices of Children; Black Angels* for electric string quartet; *Cello Sonata; Echoes of Time and the River; Madrigals* (4 books); *Makrokosmos* (3 books); *Songs, Drones, and Refrains of Death; Voice of the Whale.*

crumhorn (French, *cromorne, tournebout;* German, *Krummhorn*) A double-reed wind instrument that flourished between 1500 and 1630 (from Middle English *crump,* "crooked"). It consists of a small wooden pipe of cylindrical bore, curved upward at the lower end and pierced with finger holes like those of a recorder. Its reed is enclosed in a wooden cap with a blowing orifice in the top. The tone is reedy and nasal. Crumhorns were built in families, from great bass to sopranino, each instrument having a compass of a ninth. Their manufacture was resumed in the 20th century.

Cubana, La: *see* HENZE; OPERA (the 20th century).

Curlew River: *see* BRITTEN; OPERA (the 20th century).

crwth A Welsh stringed instrument that became extinct early in the 19th century; it was also known in medieval England (the *crouth* or *crowd*). Basically it is a LYRE, but it was played with a bow as early as the 11th century, one of the first uses of the bow in northern Europe. Late in the 13th century it was given a fingerboard, one or more strings lying off the fingerboard for drone use.

Cuénod, Hugues (b. June 26, 1902) Educated at the Basel Conservatory and then in Vienna, the Swiss tenor Hugues Cuénod performs lieder, early music, opera, and oratorio. He has toured extensively in Europe and the United States and was on the faculty of the conservatory in Geneva (1940–46). He sang in the premiere of Stravinsky's *The Rake's Progress* and in recordings of that composer's *Oedipus Rex,* Ravel's *L'Enfant et les Sortilèges,* and Richard Strauss's *Ariadne auf Naxos.* He is admired as an interpreter of Bach, especially in his recording of the role of the evangelist in the *St. Matthew* Passion.

Cui, César (Antonovich) (January 18 [January 6, old style], 1835–March 24, 1918) One of the group of Russian composers known as the *Kutchka* (the Mighty Five, including Mily Ba-

crwth
*Leslie Lindsey Mason Collection of Musical Instruments
(formerly the Galpin Collection)
Museum of Fine Arts, Boston*

French crumhorns, boxwood, late 16th century
*courtesy, Musée Instrumental, Brussels
photograph, © A.C.L., Brussels*

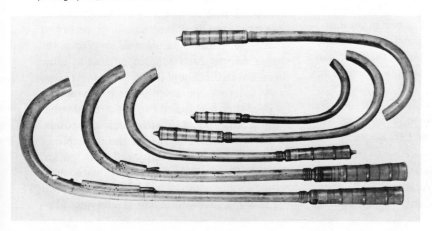

233

lakirev, Borodin, Mussorgsky, and Rimsky-Korsakov), César Cui was also a music critic and a military engineer. His father was a French officer who remained in Russia after Napoleon's invasion of 1812, and his mother was Lithuanian. Cui began to compose as a boy, imitating Chopin, and received lessons in composition from Stanislaw Moniuszko, but in 1851 he was sent to St. Petersburg, where he entered the school of engineering, and in 1855 the academy of military engineering, becoming a lecturer there in 1857. In 1878 he became professor of fortification—his pupils included Gen. M. D. Skobelev and Tsar Nicholas II—and he retired with the rank of lieutenant general.

Friendship with Balakirev and Aleksandr Dargomyzhsky developed his musical interests; he began to compose copiously and, although he had no Russian blood, became a pugnacious journalistic champion of the Russian nationalist school. From 1864 to 1877 he was music critic of the *St. Peterburgskiye vedomosti,* and later he became a successful propagandist of Russian music in Belgium and France, notably with his *La musique en Russie* (1881). Cui's own music has little Russian flavor; of his 10 operas only the first, *The Prisoner of the Caucasus* (begun 1857, produced 1883), the last, *The Captain's Daughter* (St. Petersburg, 1911), and the one-act *Feast in the Time of the Plague* (Moscow, 1901) are on Russian subjects—all by Pushkin. He turned more readily to French sources: Hugo, Jean Richepin, Dumas *père,* Maupassant, and Mérimée, and his only moderately successful operas are based on Heine's *William Ratcliff* (St. Petersburg, 1869) and Maupassant's *Mam'selle Fifi* (Moscow, 1903). Cui is at his best in the miniature forms, notably his short piano compositions ranging in manner from the Schumannesque to the tasteful salon-piece and in his songs.

BIBLIOGRAPHY: Michel D. Calvocoressi and Gerald E. H. Abraham, *Masters of Russian Music* (1936; reprint, 1971).

Curzon, Clifford (Michael) (b. May 18, 1907) Educated at the Royal Academy in London, the English pianist Clifford Curzon studied with Artur Schnabel, Landowska, and Boulanger. He was professor of piano at the academy (1926–32). An immaculate pianist, he plays a catholic repertoire based on the classics. He was knighted in 1976.

Cuzzoni, Francesca (*c.* 1700–1770) The Italian soprano Francesca Cuzzoni sang throughout Italy before going to England in 1722. Acclaimed for her interpretations of Handel, she appeared with all the leading singers of her time and was involved in several well-publicized rivalries, most notably with Faustina Bordoni.

cyclic form A method of composition involving the repetition of motives, themes, or whole sections from an earlier movement; the intention of the composer is usually unification of the work. The need for such a device became particularly strong during the last third of the 19th century, when the traditional Classical balance of Mozart and Haydn had been disturbed by the ever more varied and extreme states of feeling or moods.

The frequent use of recurrent material in large-scale works begins with Beethoven's Fifth Symphony, in which the movements are bound together by a recurring motive as well as by literal repetition of a sizable section of music.

There are many examples of cyclic technique in the works of the generation following Beethoven. Many are in the form of the free, improvisatory fantasia, notably the *Wanderer Fantasie* of Schubert and the Fourth Symphony of Schumann. In these works the cyclic material is increasingly more melodic rather than motivic. This tendency culminates in the *idée fixe* (literally, "fixed idea"), or recurrent theme, of Berlioz. In *Harold en Italie* the theme returns each time in much the same form, but in the *Symphonie fantastique* it takes on a different character in each movement.

The latter method of thematic transformation became popular with later composers. Liszt based whole works on the principle of a single theme in vastly different guises: Second Piano Concerto and Sonata in b minor. Some composers of the period, such as Brahms, avoided cyclic technique altogether; others, such as Dvořák and Franck, made use of it in completely different ways.

A kind of cyclic school developed around Franck that was well publicized by his disciple d'Indy. The great composers of the following generations, however, used the technique as only one, and often not the most important, means of unifying a piece. Such composers as Mahler and Richard Strauss, despite their frequent use of thematic repetition and even *idées fixes* (Strauss's *Till Eulenspiegel*), can no longer be considered practitioners of the cyclic technique.

cymbals A percussion instrument consisting of two circular metal plates struck separately or together. The use of cymbals is recorded in many ancient civilizations; they appeared in Israel about 1100 B.C. and are mentioned in the Bible. In China and elsewhere in Asia there were two kinds, the broad-rimmed cymbal held horizontally, and the small-rimmed cymbal held vertically. In the Middle Ages the term *cymbala* signified the small bells used to accompany a liturgical chant.

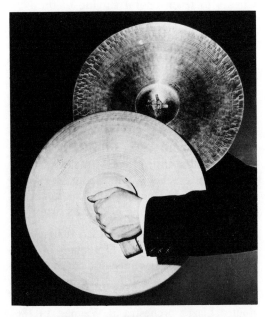

orchestral cymbals
courtesy Avedis Zildjian Company

Modern orchestral cymbals are derived from those used in Turkish military bands. In the 18th century Turkish military music enjoyed a vogue in central Europe, and cymbals were introduced in works by Haydn (notably his *Military* Symphony, 1794), Mozart, and Beethoven. Of indefinite pitch, modern cymbals consist of a pair of thin circular plates from 14 to 18 inches (36 to 46 centimeters) in diameter, made from an alloy of copper and tin. The plates are domed for the inclusion of the knot of the holding strap and are slightly tapered to secure contact at the edges only.

Cymbals are played (1) by clashing the plates together; (2) by striking a single plate with a soft or hard-ended drumstick; (3) by producing a sustained note in the form of a tremolo on one suspended cymbal; and (4) by rubbing the plates together. The sounds produced cover a wide range of dynamics. In Romantic music, *e.g.*, Wagner's *Tannhauser,* they are frequently used to mark a dramatic climax. Berlioz, Debussy, and Ravel specified the use in their scores of small cymbals producing high notes of a definite pitch. Twentieth-century composers introduced the pianissimo tremolo on a suspended cymbal. Jazz musicians employ several different ways of playing cymbals, including a method of striking them at elbow height with the help of a pedal mechanism.

Czerny, Karl (February 20, 1791–July 15, 1857) An Austrian pianist, teacher, and composer best known for his pedagogical works for the piano, Karl Czerny was born in Vienna and studied piano with his father and later with Beethoven. He was a teacher in Vienna at the age of 15, his pupils including Beethoven's nephew and Liszt. His published works of all kinds number nearly 1,000. He made ingenious arrangements of orchestral works, including versions for eight pianos— four hands at each—of two overtures by Rossini. He is known, however, for his studies, greatly esteemed by later teachers, which include the *School of Velocity,* the *School of Virtuosity,* and the *School of the Left Hand.* He also left a valuable essay on the performance of Beethoven's piano sonatas.

RECORDINGS: Concerto in C Major for piano 4-hands; Fantasie Variations (piano); Piano Sonata No. 1 in A-flat Major.

D

d'Albert, Eugène: *see* ALBERT, EUGÈNE D'.

Dallapiccola, Luigi (February 3, 1904–February 19, 1975)   The first and the most significant Italian composer to use the 12-tone technique, Luigi Dallapiccola was born in Pisino, Istria (now in Yugoslavia), but spent much of his childhood in Trieste. He was interned with his family in Graz, Austria, during World War I, where he became acquainted with the music of Verdi and Wagner. In 1921 Dallapiccola entered the Conservatorio Luigi Cherubini in Florence and was named to its faculty in 1934.

Known before World War II as a teacher and pianist, Dallapiccola had an early interest in the music of Busoni, Schoenberg, and Webern. He began experiments in the 12-tone idiom around 1934. His triptych *Canti di prigionia* (1938–41; *Songs of Prison*) marked him as a mature composer; this work, for chorus with an orchestra of percussion, harps, and pianos, was a protest against Fascist doctrine and was based in part on the chant "Dies Irae" ("Day of Wrath") from the mass for the dead. In it he used an original version of 12-tone technique.

Dallapiccola's love of Renaissance and Baroque vocal music and the music of the French Impressionists led him to base musical forms on the literary models of James Joyce and Marcel Proust. Dallapiccola's vocal music is considered among his most effective. Using impassioned texts and a variety of imaginative effects of articulation, his choral writing is Latin in its warmth although technically complex. The rhythmic intricacies of the *Quaderno musicale di Annalibera* (1952; *Musical Notebook of Annalibera*), a piano book written for his daughter, serve as the basis for much of his *Canti di liberazione* (1955; *Songs of Liberation*), a triptych for chorus and orchestra celebrating the liberation of Italy from Fascist control. Operas include *Volo di notte* (1940; *Night Flight*), *Il Prigioniero* (1949; *The Prisoner*), and *Ulisse* (1968).

Dallapiccola taught composition in the United States in the 1950s and '60s at Tanglewood and other centers and was a great influence on the younger Italian composers; among his students was Berio, a leading composer of electronic music.

BIBLIOGRAPHY: Roman Vlad, *Luigi Dallapiccola* (1957).

RECORDINGS: Chorus and orchestra—*Canti di prigionia, Cori di Michelangelo, Tempus destruendi/Tempus aedificandi;* Solo voice with orchestra—*Concerto per la notte di natale dell'anno 1956, Parole di San Paolo, Preghiere, Sex carmina Alcaei, Sicut Umbra;* Due studi for violin and piano; *Il Prigioniero; Piccola musica notturna* (orchestra).

Damnation de Faust, La: *see* BERLIOZ.

Damrosch, Frank (June 22, 1859–October 22, 1937)   Son of Leopold and brother of Walter Damrosch, the choral conductor and music educator Frank Damrosch began his career teaching in the public schools in Denver until going to New York City to become chorus master at the Metropolitan Opera (1885–91). In 1892 he organized the People's Singing Classes to teach choral singing to the New York work force, which evolved into the People's Choral Union. He helped to found the Musical Art Society for a cappella singing, which he conducted until it was discontinued in 1920. In 1897 he became supervisor of music for the New York public schools and the following year succeeded his brother Walter as conductor of the Oratorio Society, which he retained until 1912. In 1904 he became director of the Institute of Musical Art (later the Juilliard School). He wrote *A Popular Method of Sight-Singing* (1894) and *Some Essentials in the Teaching of Music* (1916).

Damrosch, Leopold (October 22, 1832–February 15, 1885)   Patriarch of a family of musicians, the German violinist and conductor Leopold Damrosch studied at the university in Berlin. He performed with Liszt and conducted Liszt's orchestra at Weimar. In 1867 he founded the Orchesterverein at Breslau, which he conducted until 1871, when he went to the United States. He founded the Oratorio Society of New York (1874) and the New York Symphony Society (1878), conducting both until his death. He led the Philharmonic

Society in the 1876–77 season and in 1881 conducted the first New York music festival, which included a 250-piece orchestra and a chorus of 1200. During the 1884–85 season he established German repertoire at the Metropolitan Opera and conducted every performance of German opera there until five days before his death.

Damrosch, Walter (Johannes) (January 30, 1862–December 22, 1950) The German-born U.S. conductor and composer Walter Damrosch was the son of the German violinist and conductor Leopold Damrosch, who settled in New York City in 1871, and brother of the choral conductor and music educator Frank Damrosch. Walter Damrosch studied with his father, and at the latter's death he assumed the conductorship of the New York Symphony Society and the New York Oratorio Society founded by his father and also conducted at the Metropolitan Opera (1885–91). Later he organized the Damrosch Opera Company (1895–1900), specializing in German operas. In 1903 Damrosch reorganized the New York Symphony Society and conducted it until 1927, when it was combined with the Philharmonic Society.

Like his father Damrosch was an avowed propagandist of Wagner; as early as 1886 he gave a concert performance of *Parsifal* in New York. He also presented first U.S. performances of symphonies by Brahms and Tchaikovsky. Although not in sympathy with new music, he introduced several works by contemporary European and U.S. composers. He was a pioneer of symphonic broadcasting and established a weekly series of radio lectures on music appreciation for schools (1928–42). A competent composer, Damrosch wrote several operas that lacked distinction: *The Scarlet Letter* (1896), *Cyrano de Bergerac* (1913), *The Man Without a Country* (1937), and *The Opera Cloak* (1942). He also composed incidental music to plays and published an autobiography, *My Musical Life* (1923).

d'Anglebert, Jean Henri: *see* ANGLEBERT, JEAN HENRI D'.

Daniel, Play of: *see* GREENBERG; MIDDLE AGES (chant); OPERA (beginnings).

Danse Macabre: *see* SAINT-SAËNS.

Dante Symphony: *see* LISZT.

Danzi, Franz (May 15, 1763–April 13, 1826) The German composer and cellist Franz Danzi wrote 11 operas, church music, 50 works of chamber music for strings and winds, and vocal exercises. A student of Abbé Vogler, he played in the court orchestra in Mannheim and then in Munich. He was court Kapellmeister in Stuttgart (1807–12) and held that same position at Karlsruhe until the end of his life. His operas foreshadow those of German Romanticism and especially of Weber, whose mentor Danzi became.

RECORDINGS: Cello Concerto in e minor; Flute Concerto No. 2 in d minor; Horn Concerto in E Major; Quartets (2) for bassoon and strings; Sonata in E-flat Major for horn and piano; Woodwind Quintets (6).

Daphnis et Chloe: *see* RAVEL.

Daquin, Louis Claude (July 4, 1694–June 15, 1772) The Parisian organist, harpsichordist, and composer Louis Claude Daquin was a godson of the harpsichordist and composer Élisabeth Claude Jacquet de La Guerre, whose husband Marin de La Guerre probably taught him to play the organ. The boy was a prodigy, playing before Louis XIV at the age of six. His first appointment came when he was 12, with successive appointments culminating in that of organist to the Chapel Royal in 1739. He studied organ with Louis Marchand, succeeding his master at the Convent of the Cordeliers in 1732. He was known as a virtuoso performer and great improviser.

His published works include *Premier Livre de pièces pour le clavecin* (1735), which contains the well-known "Le Coucou," *Noëls pour l'orgue et le clavecin,* and a cantata *La Rose.* A great many manuscripts of church music and instrumental works also survive.

RECORDINGS: *Noëls pour l'orgue* (12).

Dargomyzhsky, Aleksandr (Sergeyevich) (February 14 [February 2, old style], 1813–January 17 [January 5, old style], 1869) A Russian composer of songs and opera, Aleksandr Dargomyzhsky grew up in St. Petersburg as a talented amateur musician, playing the violin and piano and dabbling in compo-

237

sition. Acquaintance with Glinka (1833) turned his thoughts more seriously toward composition, and in 1839 he completed his first opera, *Esmeralda* (after Victor Hugo), though it waited eight years for performance. The next, *The Triumph of Bacchus,* was not performed until 1867, but his third opera, *Rusalka* (after Pushkin), was successfully produced in 1856. Some of Dargomyzhsky's best songs date from the late 1850s; in these he developed an individual vein of humor and satire. A little later came three orchestral pieces notable for their harmonic experiments.

After 1866 Dargomyzhsky was occupied with a more striking experiment: a setting of Pushkin's play *The Stone Guest,* just as it stood, to a species of declamatory musical prose with entire passages composed in the whole-tone mode. This work aroused the interest of Balakirev and his circle, particularly Mussorgsky, who was deeply impressed by Dargomyzhsky's slogan of "the note as the direct expression of the word"; when Dargomyzhsky died the score was completed by César Cui and orchestrated by Rimsky-Korsakov. *The Stone Guest* is no more than an important historical landmark, a stimulating experiment, but some of Dargomyzhsky's songs are of lasting value.

BIBLIOGRAPHY: Gerald E. H. Abraham, *Studies in Russian Music* (1935; reprint, 1976) and *On Russian Music* (1939; reprint, 1976).

Dart, (Robert) Thurston (September 3, 1921–March 6, 1971)   A noted musicologist who specialized in early English music, Thurston Dart was also known as harpsichordist and conductor. He studied at the Royal College of Music, London, and at Cambridge University, where he also served on the faculty (1947–62). From 1964 he was King Edward Professor of Music at King's College, University of London. His book, *The Interpretation of Music,* was published in 1954.

David, Félicien (César) (April 13, 1810–August 29, 1876)   A French composer who introduced Oriental elements into French music, Félicien David received his early musical education at the Jesuit college at Aix-en-Provence, where he was appointed chapelmaster

at the Cathedral of St. Sauveur in 1829. In 1830 he studied at the Paris Conservatoire with Henri Réber and François-Joseph Fétis. In 1831 he joined the socialist brotherhood of the Saint-Simonians. David became their main artistic figure and in 1830 published a series of religious chants, *Menilmontant,* that were sung at their ceremonies. When the sect was dispersed David spent two years (1833–35) preaching their doctrines in the Middle East. Recollections of music heard in Jerusalem, Cairo, and Syria were incorporated in the works he wrote on his return. In 1844 he produced *Le Désert,* a descriptive choral and orchestral work in three sections on words by Auguste Colin that embodied Arabian melodies. Described as a symphonic ode, *Le Désert* was more properly an oratorio bordering on the style of opera and resembling the *opéra de concert* of Berlioz. David's later works in this style, *Moïse au Sinaï* (1846), *Christophe Colomb* (1847), and *Éden* (1848), were less well received. Of his five operas *Lalla Roukh* (1862), based on the tales of Thomas Moore, was the most original. Neglected in the 20th century, David's work was admired by Berlioz and Saint-Saëns, and it also foreshadowed Oriental influences in later Romantic opera, notably in Bizet's *Djamileh,* Léo Delibes' *Lakmé,* and Verdi's *Aida.*

David, Ferdinand (January 19, 1810–July 14, 1873)   After study with Louis Spohr and Moritz Hauptmann at Kassel, the German violinist Ferdinand David went to Russia (1829–35), where he was acclaimed both for solo and for chamber playing. In 1836 he returned to Germany to play in the Gewandhaus Orchestra at Leipzig under Mendelssohn. He gave the first performance (1845) of Mendelssohn's Violin Concerto. While a professor at the Leipzig Conservatory, his students included Joachim and August Wilhelmj. David's playing combined the discipline of Spohr's style with the technical facility of a later school of playing. He wrote manuals of violin exercises that are still used.

Davidovsky, Mario (b. March 4, 1934)   The Argentine composer and teacher Mario Davidovsky has lived in the United States since 1960. He joined the faculty of Columbia University two years later and in 1964 became associate director of the Columbia-Princeton Electronic Music Center. Since 1966 he has been an associate professor at City College in New York City. The recipient of numerous grants from the Guggenheim (1961–63), Koussevitzky (1964), and Rockefeller (1965) foundations, he is a member of the American Academy of Arts and Letters. He has written for orchestra, chamber groups, and electronic combinations: Three Electronic Studies (1961–65); *Contrastes* No. 1 (1962) for strings and electronic sounds; *Synchronisms* (1963–70) for various instruments and electronic sounds (No. 6 received a Pulitzer Prize); and *Inflexions* (1967) for 14 instruments, commissioned for the 75th anniversary of the University of Chicago.

RECORDINGS: *Chacona* for violin, cello, and piano; *Inflexions; Synchronisms* Nos. 1, 2, 3, 5, 6, and 8.

Davies, Dennis Russell (b. April 16, 1944)   The U.S. conductor and pianist Dennis Russell Davies was educated at the Juilliard School, studying conducting with Jorge Mester and Jean Morel, and taught there (1968–71). The following year he became music director of the Saint Paul (Minnesota) Chamber Orchestra. He first conducted at Bayreuth in 1978 and the same year became a regular guest conductor at the Stuttgart Opera, where he has been named general music director beginning in 1980. In Stuttgart he is conducting the complete stage works of Hans Werner Henze in collaboration with the composer.

Davies, Peter Maxwell: *see* MAXWELL DAVIES, PETER.

Davies, (Henry) Walford (September 6, 1869–March 11, 1941)   An English organist and composer who exerted a wide influence on musical education, Walford Davies became a chorister at St. George's Chapel, Windsor, in 1882 and three years later assistant organist to Sir Walter Parratt there. During 1890–94 he was a pupil and scholar at the Royal College of Music, where in 1895 he became a teacher of counterpoint. He was organist of the Temple Church, London (1898–1923), conductor of the London Bach Choir (1903–

07), and professor of music in the University College of Wales at Aberystwith (1919–26). During World War I, with the rank of major, Davies worked for the organization of music among the troops and in 1917 was made director of music to the Royal Air Force. He was appointed director of music and chairman of the National Council of Music, University of Wales, in 1919 and Gresham professor of music in 1924. He was organist of St. George's Chapel, Windsor, from 1927 to 1932. Along with his work as a composer, Davies was a stimulating force (not least by means of his popular radio talks) in musical education in England. He wrote *Music and Worship* (1935) with Harvey Grace, *The Pursuit of Music* (1935), and edited several songbooks. He was knighted in 1922 and was Master of the King's Music (1934–41).

Davis, Andrew (Frank) (b. February 2, 1944)   Educated at Cambridge University and at the Sta. Cecilia Conservatory in Rome, the English conductor Andrew Davis was assistant conductor of the BBC Scottish Symphony (1970–72), becoming associate conductor of the New Philharmonia in 1973 and musical director of the Toronto (Canada) Symphony in 1975. His recordings have featured 19th-century music.

Davis, Colin (Rex) (b. September 25, 1927)   Educated as a clarinetist at the Royal College of Music in his native London and largely self-taught as a conductor, Colin Davis began his conducting career with the BBC Scottish Symphony (1957–59). He was appointed a conductor at the Sadler's Wells (London) Opera in 1959 and attracted critical acclaim when he replaced Otto Klemperer in a concert performance of Mozart's *Don Giovanni.* He became principal conductor at Sadler's Wells in 1960 and was musical director there from 1961 to 1965. In 1960 he conducted at the Glyndebourne Festival and the following year made his U.S. debut with the Minneapolis Symphony. Davis first conducted at the Metropolitan Opera in New York City in a 1967 performance of Britten's *Peter Grimes,* and the same year he became principal conductor of the BBC Symphony. In 1971 he became co-director (with Peter Hall) and later director of the Royal Opera at Covent Garden. In 1972 he became principal guest conductor of the Boston Symphony. His recordings are prodigious, the most important being a complete cycle of the works of Berlioz (near completion in 1978); Handel's *Messiah;* and several Mozart operas.

Death and Transfiguration: *see* STRAUSS, RICHARD; SYMPHONIC POEM.

Debost, Michel (b. January 20, 1934) Having exhibited an affinity for the flute since the age of 10, Paris-born Michel Debost entered medical school to please his father but after one month transferred to the Paris Conservatoire, where he received first prize for flute and chamber music. In 1957 he won first prize at the Concours International in Moscow and appeared as soloist with the Office de Radiodiffusion et Télévision Française (ORTF). From 1957 to 1964 he was first flutist with the orchestra of the Société des Concerts du Conservatoire, and in the following year he founded the Secolo Barocco ensemble to promote the study and performance of Baroque chamber music. His eclectic repertoire ranges from Bach to Bruno Maderna.

Debussy, (Achille) Claude (August 22, 1862– March 25, 1918) The most important French composer around the turn of the century, Claude Debussy was a principal figure in the evolution of music between Wagner and the present day. Born at St. Germain-en-Laye, near Paris, he was the son of a former soldier in the marines who intended that he should become a sailor. The works of his mature years, *Sirènes, La Mer,* and the sea music in *Pelléas et Mélisande* show his nostalgia for the sea, which he evoked with great imagination and poetry. Debussy's family had shown no musical talent, and his own musical gifts were not discovered (by Antoinette Flore Mauté, mother-in-law of the poet Verlaine) until he was 10 years old. He entered the Paris Conservatoire in 1872; there he studied with Antoine Marmontel (piano), Ernest Guiraud (composition), and with Albert Lavignac, Massenet, and Émile Durand.

Though he lived in poverty, Debussy cherished an innate sense of luxury, which he was

Claude Debussy
painting by Marcel-André Baschet, 1884
Giraudon
© SPADEM, 1979

able to satisfy between 1879 and 1882 by engagements as chamber pianist at the Château de Chenonceaux and at the palatial residences in Switzerland, Italy, and Russia of Nadezhda von Meck, the patroness of Tchaikovsky. In 1884 he won the Prix de Rome with the cantata *L'Enfant prodigue* and spent the following two years at the Villa Medici in Rome, where new horizons were opened by *Lohengrin* and the works of Orlando di Lasso and Palestrina as revealed to him by Liszt.

To fulfill the condition of the Prix de Rome that entails the periodic submission of compositions to the judges, Debussy sent to them his symphonic suite *Printemps,* to which the judges took exception on the ground of its formlessness. After *Printemps* came *La Damoiselle élue* for female voices and orchestra— a setting of a French version of Dante Gabriel Rossetti's "The Blessed Damozel"—which in the eyes of the judges was even more unorthodox than its predecessor. Both works were denied the customary public performance.

The Rome period over, Debussy returned to Paris and shortly after left for Russia. There he absorbed Russian music, especially that of Mussorgsky. From 1888 to 1892 Debussy developed under influences that ranged from

Tristan, Meistersinger, and *Parsifal,* all heard at Bayreuth, to Gregorian chant and the Javanese gamelan orchestra, introduced at the Paris Exhibition of 1889. He was also attracted to the paintings of the Nabis, a group of Impressionists, and the many English associations of the art nouveau movement. Other early works were inspired by Edgar Allan Poe's "Fall of the House of Usher," left unfinished; Baudelaire's *Fleurs du mal;* and Henri de Regnier's *Scènes au crépuscule,* later developed into the Nocturnes for orchestra (1892–99).

The first concert of his works was given in Brussels on March 1, 1894, at the gallery of La Libre Esthétique, which was hung with the freshly painted canvases of Renoir, Gauguin, Sisley, and other Impressionists. With the exception of the string quartet (1893) and the late sonatas and piano studies, the whole of Debussy's work was enriched by pictorial or poetic themes. With his illustration of Mallarmé's *L'Après-midi d'un faune* (1894), he approached the realization of the ideal, common to the poets of Mallarmé's circle, of the fusion of the arts.

In 1893 he was present with Mallarmé at the first performance of Maeterlinck's *Pelléas et Mélisande,* an allegory of innocence and guilt plunging far into the dream world. Over the following nine years, when the psychological theories of the dream as expounded by Wagner, Poe, and Freud were increasingly taking root in the arts, Debussy gradually evolved an original musical style that enhanced the symbolism of Maurice Maeterlinck's allegory and established opera as an imaginary theater of the mind. The first performance of Debussy's *Pelléas et Mélisande* (Opéra-Comique, April 30, 1902) met with hostility, but the adverse feeling was soon overcome, though by its nature this entirely poetic conception of opera was to remain unique.

The composition of *Pelléas* liberated Debussy's imagination on another plane, and he further developed his style in the orchestral triptych *La Mer* (1905), followed by the largest of his orchestral works, *Images* (1906–09). These and other works of this period, which are largely parallel expressions of the aesthetics of Marcel Proust, consist of finely drawn musical images that arouse innumerable sensations and half-forgotten memories.

In 1904 he abandoned his first wife, Rosalie Texier, for Emma Bardac, to whom his daughter Claude Emma was born in 1905 and whom he married in 1908. In the same year he dedicated to his daughter a group of piano pieces called *Children's Corner.* Afflicted with cancer and unable to meet his debts, he undertook concert tours throughout Europe and Russia from 1909 until 1913; his works of this period include the 24 Preludes for piano, incidental music for the mystery play *Le Martyre de Saint-Sébastien* by Gabriele d'Annunzio, and the ballet *Jeux* (1913). During World War I he wrote some of his finest works, the twelve Études for piano and three sonatas for various instruments.

In form, harmony, and instrumentation Debussy greatly enriched the musical language. His free structures are in the form of sophisticated improvisations since his ideal was music "that should seem not to have been written down." In his orchestral works he explored little-used registers of instruments, sought novel combinations, and gave to each instrument—even the divided strings—a role of its own in the manner of a vast chamber orchestra. In his piano works he created the most original style since Chopin by experimenting with new sonorities, contrasts of register, and effects obtained by a subtle use of the pedals. His vocal music is in the form of a supple recitative alive to the inflections of French speech.

The significance of his work is twofold: by his use of the pentatonic and Gregorian modes and his development of the whole-tone scale, he enlarged the musical horizon to embrace the musical civilizations of the Middle Ages and of the Orient; and the distinctions that he challenged between consonance and dissonance became the basis of many new harmonic developments. Also texture assumed new prominence as primary building material, an idea that proved especially fruitful to later composers. He expressed the quintessential sensibility of the generation before World War I and also was a Janus-headed figure who faced both the remote musical past, which he was able to revive, and the stylistic eclecticism of later generations.

BIBLIOGRAPHY: Leon Vallas, *Claude Debussy: His Life and Works* (1933; reprint, 1973); Edward Lockspeiser, *Debussy: His Life and Mind,* 2 vols. (1962–65); Percy M. Young, *Debussy* (1968); Roger Nichols, *Debussy* (1973); Claude Debussy, *Debussy on Music* (1977).

RECORDINGS: Numerous recordings of most works.

decay: *see* ENVELOPE.

De Koven, Reginald: *see* OPERETTA.

Delalande, Michel Richard: *see* LALANDE, MI-CHEL RICHARD DE.

Delibes, (Clément-Philibert-) Léo (February 21, 1836–January 16, 1891)   The opera and ballet composer Léo Delibes was the first to write music of high quality for the ballet. His pioneering symphonic work for the ballet opened a field for serious composers, and his influence can be traced in the work of Tchaikovsky and others who wrote for the dance. His own music—light, graceful, elegant, with a tendency toward exoticism—reflects the spirit of the Second Empire in France.

Delibes studied at the Paris Conservatoire with Adolphe Charles Adam and in 1853 was appointed accompanist at the Théâtre-Lyrique. He became accompanist at the Paris Opéra in 1863, professor of composition at the Conservatoire in 1881, and a member of the French Institute in 1884. His first produced works were a series of amusing operettas, parodies, and farces in which Delibes was associated with Offenbach and other light-opera composers. He collaborated with Ludwig Minkus in the ballet *La Source* (1866), and its success led to commissions to write his large-scale ballets, *Coppélia* (1870), based on a story of E. T. A. Hoffmann, and *Sylvia* (1876), based on a mythological theme. In the meantime he developed his gifts for opera. The opéra comique *Le Roi l'a dit* (1873; *The King Said So*) was followed by the serious operas *Jean de Nivelle* (1880) and *Lakmé* (1883), his masterpiece known for its coloratura aria "Bell Song." An organist, Delibes also wrote church music and some picturesque songs, among which is "Les Filles de Cadiz" ("The Girls of Cadiz").

RECORDINGS: *Coppélia; Lakmé; La Source; Sylvia.*

Delius, Frederick (January 29, 1862–June 10, 1934)   One of the most distinctive figures in the revival of English music at the end of the 19th century, the composer Frederick Delius was educated at International College, Isleworth, London.

After a period as a traveler for his father's firm, he went in 1884 to Florida as an orange planter but devoted his spare time to musical study with a friend, Thomas Ward, an organist. In 1886 he left Florida for Leipzig and there underwent a more or less regular training from Salomon Jadassohn and became a friend of Grieg. Two years later he moved to Paris and after his marriage in 1901 to the painter Delka Rosen made his home at Grez-sur-Loing (Seine-et-Marne). Some songs, an orchestral suite *Florida,* and an opera *Irmelin* were all written before he had a work published; the first published work was *Legend* (1893) for violin and orchestra. More ambitious works followed, arousing considerable interest during the first decade of the 20th century, especially in Germany. Three of his six operas, *Koanga* (1895–97), *A Village Romeo and Juliet* (1900–01), and *Fennimore and Gerda* (1908–10), and several of his larger choral and orchestral works, *Appalachia* (1902), *Sea Drift* (1903), and *Paris: the Song of a Great City* (1899), were first heard in Germany. Later his reputation spread to England, mainly through the persuasive advocacy of Sir Thomas Beecham, who was his finest interpreter.

Even after he was stricken blind and paralyzed in his early 60s, Delius continued to compose, working with an amanuensis, Eric Fenby. His other major works included *A Mass of Life* (1904–05) and a *Requiem* (1914–16), both to texts by Nietzsche; *Brigg Fair* (1907) for orchestra; four concertos for various instruments; three sonatas for violin and piano; and many smaller orchestral pieces and songs. He was created a Companion of Honour in 1929.

In distinction and originality of idiom Delius' music is comparable to that of his contemporary Elgar, and for a time he was considered by many to be a composer of equal stature. But his expressive range was more limited and his invention less vigorous than Elgar's. His miniatures, such as the orchestral tone poems *Over the Hills and Far Away* (1895) and *On Hearing the First Cuckoo in Spring* (1912), are the works that have held their place best.

BIBLIOGRAPHY: Eric Fenby, *Delius as I Knew Him* (1948; reprint, 1976); Arthur Hutchings, *Delius* (1949; reprint, 1970); Thomas Beecham, *Delius* (1959; reprint, 1973); Alan Jefferson, *Delius* (1972); Christopher Palmer, *Delius: Portrait of a Cosmopolitan* (1976); Christopher Redwood, ed., *A Delius Companion* (1977).

RECORDINGS: Numerous recordings of many works.

Deller, Alfred (George) (May 30, 1912–July 16, 1979)   The English countertenor and conductor Alfred Deller studied voice with his father and sang as a boy soprano. He sang alto at Canterbury Cathedral (1940–47) and then at St. Paul's Cathedral in London. He founded the Deller Consort in 1948 and with it has been a major influence in the revival of Renaissance music, especially late 17th-century English repertoire. Britten created the role of Oberon in his *A Midsummer Night's Dream* for him.

BIBLIOGRAPHY: Michael and Mollie Hardwick, *Alfred Deller, a Singularity of Voice* (1968).

Dello Joio, Norman (b. January 24, 1913) One of the most successful exponents of neoclassicism in the United States, the composer and educator Norman Dello Joio was born in New York City of a musical Italo-American family. He studied organ with his father and with Pietro Yon and attended the Institute of Musical Art and the Juilliard Graduate School; his composition teachers were Bernard Wagenaar and Hindemith. He served on the faculty at Sarah Lawrence College (1944–50), was professor at the Mannes College of Music (1956–72), and was dean of the School of Fine and Applied Arts at Boston University (from 1972).

As a composer Dello Joio frequently combines old forms (*e.g.*, ricercari, variations, sonata, chaconne) with contemporary musical techniques. His music is harmonically conservative but has melodic appeal (showing the influence of Gregorian chant) and a rhythmic liveliness. He is particularly noted for his choral music, such as *A Psalm of David* (1950), Mass and *To St. Cecilia* (1968), *Evocations* (1970), and *Psalm of Peace* (1971). In 1957 he received the Pulitzer Prize in music for *Meditation on Ecclesiastes* for string orchestra. Other compositions include the operas *The Trial at Rouen* (1955; rev. 1959 and retitled *The Triumph of St. Joan*) and *Blood Moon* (1961); *Antiphonal* Fantasy on a Theme by Vincenzo Albrici (1965) for organ, brass, and strings; *Homage to Haydn* (1969) for orchestra; *Choreography* (1972) for strings; chamber music; ballets; and songs.

RECORDINGS: *The Developing Flutist* for flute and piano; *Homage to Haydn; New York Profiles* for orchestra; Two Nocturnes for piano.

de los Angeles, Victoria: *see* ANGELES, VICTORIA DE LOS.

Del Tredici, David (Walter) (b. March 16, 1937)   A member of the Harvard University music faculty (1967–72) and at Boston University since 1973, U.S. composer David Del Tredici studied with Arnold Elston, Seymour J. Shifrin, Roger Huntington Sessions, and Milhaud. He taught piano at the Berkshire (Massachusetts) Music Center in 1964–65 and was composer in residence at the Marlboro (Vermont) Festival in 1966 and 1967. His works include songs for voice and string quartet to texts by James Joyce, *I Hear an Army* (1964); music for piano and for piano four hands, Scherzo (1960); and, beginning with *Pop-pourri* (1968), a series of works based on texts by Lewis Carroll, among which *Final Alice* (1976) enjoyed particular public success.

RECORDINGS: Fantasy Pieces for piano; *I Hear an Army; Night Conjure-Verse* for two solo voices and instruments; Scherzo for piano four hands.

Demantius, (Johann) Christoph (1567–1643) A German composer of much vocal and some instrumental music, both sacred and secular, Christoph Demantius served as cantor at Zittau (1597–1604) and Freiberg (1604–43). His numerous works include a six-part *Deutsche Passion nach Johannes* (1631; *St. John* Passion, 1934) and *Tympanum Militare* ("Military Drum"), a collection of 21 songs for from 5 to 10 voices. Demantius was also the author of several treatises on music and singing, including *Isagoge Artis Musicae* (1605; "Introduction to the Art of Music").

RECORDINGS: *Prophecy of the Suffering and Death of Jesus Christ; St. John* Passion.

Demessieux, Jeanne (February 14, 1921–November 11, 1968) The French organist Jeanne Demessieux was one of the leading pupils of Marcel Dupré at the Paris Conservatoire. She was a popular recitalist in Europe and in North America and was known for her recordings of French literature and for her improvisations. She was appointed to the Conservatoire at Liège, Belgium, in 1952.

Demus, Jörg (b. December 2, 1928) A student of Walter Gieseking and Edwin Fischer in piano and of Josef Krips in conducting, Jörg Demus made his piano debut in his native Vienna in 1943. After 1948 he toured extensively in Europe, Africa, and the Far East. He made his U.S. debut in 1955, and the following year won the Busoni Prize at the International Pianists Competition in Bolzano, Italy. He has recorded music of Mozart, Schubert, and Beethoven, much of it on period instruments.

De Peyer, Gervase (Alan) (b. April 11, 1926) A founding member of the Melos Ensemble of London, the English clarinetist Gervase De Peyer studied at the Royal College of Music. He played principal clarinet with the London Symphony (1955–71). In addition to recitals he has appeared in television documentaries and broadcasts in Europe, the United States, and Japan and has recorded with the Melos Ensemble and the New York City-based Chamber Music Society of Lincoln Center.

De Reszke, Édouard (December 22, 1853–May 25, 1917) Brother of tenor Jean and soprano Josephine De Reszke, the Polish bass Edouard De Reszke made his debut as the king in Verdi's *Aida*, with the composer conducting, at the Paris Opéra in 1876. After appearances throughout Italy he sang in London, where his most popular role was Daland in Wagner's *The Flying Dutchman*. He sang many operas with his brother in Paris and in the United States, where he made his debut in Chicago in 1891 as the king in Wagner's *Lohengrin*. The same year he made his Metropolitan Opera debut as Frère Laurent in Gounod's *Roméo et Juliette;* he was to sing there until 1903. He sang his first German role, that of King Marke (Wagner's *Tristan und Isolde*) in 1895, reinforcing a precedent for learning German as an operatic language. His favorite roles included Hans Sachs (Wagner's *Die Meistersinger*), Méphistophélès (Gounod's *Faust*), and comedy roles of Leporello (Mozart's *Don Giovanni*) and Plunkett (Friedrich Flotow's *Martha*). His voice was exceptional in its volume, richness, and flexibility.

De Reszke, Jean, real name, Jan Mieczislav de Reszke (January 14, 1850–April 3, 1925) A stage performer who never appeared in the concert hall, the Polish tenor Jean de Reszke is considered one of the great personalities in the art of singing. The brother of the renowned bass Édouard De Reszke, Jean studied in Warsaw and then in Venice, where he made his debut as Alfonso (a baritone role) in Donizetti's *La Favorita* in 1874. His debut as a tenor came in the role of Robert le Diable (Meyerbeer) in Paris in 1879. He was esteemed as the greatest tenor of his time during his career at the Paris Opéra beginning in 1884 and at the Metropolitan Opera (1891–1901), where he sang the Wagnerian heldentenor roles. In 1902 he retired to Paris to teach. The sound of his voice is preserved on transfers from early acoustic recordings.

Dering, Richard, or **Richard Deering** (*c.* 1580–buried March 22, 1630) The English organist and composer Richard Dering is remembered chiefly for his vocal music. He supplicated for the Oxford B.Mus. in 1610, stating that he had studied music for 10 years. In 1612 he may have journeyed to Italy, but by

1617 he was organist to the convent of English nuns in Brussels, having become a Roman Catholic. In 1625 he was appointed organist to Henrietta Maria, and in the same year he was "musician for the lute and voice" to Charles I. He died in London.

Collections of his music, all vocal and with basso continuo, were published at Antwerp between 1617 and 1620. His works remained popular after his death—Cromwell admired them and John Playford published some—and include motets, instrumental music, madrigals, English church music, and two pieces based on London and country cries.

des Prés, Josquin: *see* JOSQUIN DES PRÉS.

Dessau, Paul (December 19, 1894–June 28, 1979)   German-born Paul Dessau studied violin, piano, conducting, and composition at the Klindworth-Scharwenka Conservatory in Berlin (1910–12); his professional career has centered around music for the theater. In the 1913–14 season he was a coach at the Hamburg State Theater, followed by conducting posts at the Cologne Opera (1918–23) and the Berlin State Opera (1926). He admired the work of conductors Otto Klemperer and Arthur Nikisch, and his compositions were influenced by Schoenberg. A disciple of Bertolt Brecht, he wrote incidental music for many of Brecht's plays, and the latter's works figure in Dessau's *Deutsches miserere* (1944–47) and the operas *Die Verurteilung des Lukullus* (1949; revised 1951, 1960) and *Puntila* (1957–59). *In Memoriam Bertolt Brecht* appeared in 1957. Dessau has written a melodrama for Sprechstimme, *Lilo Hermann* (1953); an oratorio, *Appell der Arbeiterklasse* (1961); *Requiem for Lumumba* (1965); *Three Vietnamese Melodramas;* and conventionally instrumented chamber music.

RECORDING: *Die Verurteilung des Lukullus.*

Destinn, Emmy, real name, Ema Kittl (February 26, 1878–January 28, 1930)   Possessed of a voice with exceptional richness, power, and control, the Czech dramatic soprano and actress Emmy Destinn made her debut as Santuzza in Mascagni's *Cavalleria Rusticana* (Berlin, 1898). She sang with the Berlin Hofoper from 1898 to 1908. In 1901 she sang the role of Senta in the first Bayreuth production of Wagner's *Der Fliegende Holländer* and in 1906 was chosen by the composer to create the title role in Richard Strauss's *Salome.* In 1904 Destinn made her debut at Covent Garden as Donna Anna in Mozart's *Don Giovanni* and remained very popular in England. Her U.S. debut was at the Metropolitan Opera in 1908 as Verdi's Aida, and it was there that she created the role of Minnie in Puccini's *La fanciulla del West.* She sang French and Italian opera, and Wagner rarely, although she was heard as Eva *(Die Meistersinger),* Elsa *(Lohengrin),* and Elisabeth *(Tannhäuser).* She retired in 1921.

Destouches, André Cardinal (baptized April 6, 1672–February 7, 1749)   The French opera composer André Cardinal Destouches was a pupil at the College des Jésuites in Paris and was one of the few Europeans to visit Siam in the 17th century. Later he became a "mousquetaire du Roy" before finally leaving military service to study with André Campra, to whose opera-ballet, *L'Europe Galante,* he contributed three airs. Destouches' first opera, *Issé,* was produced in 1697. He wrote nine more operas (one in collaboration with Michel Richard de Lalande) and in 1713 was appointed inspector-general of the Paris Opéra. Fifteen years later he became director and in the same year "surintendant de la musique du roy," remaining in that post until his death. His works also include drinking songs, cantatas, motets, and a Te Deum.

RECORDINGS: Suite from *Issé.*

deutsches Requiem, Ein: *see* BRAHMS (works); MASS (requiem); ORATORIO (late 19th century).

development   The expansion or exploration of given musical material (*e.g.,* themes, rhythms). Development is also the second section in sonata form, in which the musical material stated in the exposition, or initial section, is so treated. *See* SONATA (sonata form).

Devil and Daniel Webster, The: *see* MOORE.

Diabelli, Anton (September 6, 1781–April 7, 1858)   The Austrian publisher and composer Anton Diabelli is remembered for his waltz, or Ländler, on which Beethoven wrote his 33

Variations for piano (Op. 120). He was intended for the priesthood and was educated at the monastery of Raitenhaslach, where his studies were supervised by Michael Haydn. On the secularization of the Bavarian monasteries in 1803, Diabelli went to Vienna; his piano pieces were widely played, and he became known as a teacher of the piano and the guitar. In 1818 he founded a publishing firm with Peter Cappi, six years later taking it over entirely. He published works by Schubert, Czerny, and Beethoven and in 1851 issued the first thematic catalogue of the works of Schubert. Known for his sure instinct in publishing matters, he was called by Beethoven "Diabolus Diabelli." His own works include operettas, church music, piano works, and numerous light pieces for the flute, guitar, and other instruments.

RECORDING: Guitar Sonata in A Major.

Diabelli Variations: see BEETHOVEN (last years); VARIATIONS.

Diaghilev, Sergey: BALLET (Diaghilev Ballet); LAMBERT; MODERN PERIOD (new paths); STRAVINSKY.

Dialogues des Carmélites: see POULENC.

Diamond, David (Leo) (b. July 9, 1915) A student of Bernard Rogers, Roger Sessions, and Boulanger, U.S. composer David Diamond wrote his first important compositions while in Paris. There he was influenced by the music of Stravinsky and of Ravel, in whose memory he wrote an Elegy for brass, harps, and percussion (1938). After spending 13 years in Italy he was chairman of the composition department at the Manhattan (New York City) School of Music from 1965 to 1967. His music is classical in form, rhythmically vital, with a preponderance of counterpoint and variations. Early works, such as the *Psalm* for orchestra (1936), are tonal, whereas his later works tend toward greater chromaticism. His String Quartet No. 3 received the New York Music Critics' Circle Award in 1947, and eight symphonies were written between 1940 and 1961. His songs, numerous and widely sung, include *The Midnight Meditation* (1950; text by Elder Olson) and *Hebrew Melodies* (1967; text by Byron).

A violinist, Diamond is known for his concertos, sonatas, and solo pieces for strings.

RECORDINGS: Nonet for three violins, three violas, and three cellos; Quartet No. 9; Quintet for clarinet, two violas, and two cellos; Quintet in b minor for flute, string trio, and piano; *Romeo and Juliet.*

diapason In medieval music, the interval that encompasses all degrees of the scale; *i.e.,* the octave. The word is derived from the Greek, *dia pasōn chordōn,* "through all the strings." In French diapason indicates the range of a voice and is also the word for a tuning fork and for pitch. On the organ the open diapason, or principal, is the foundation stop of the instrument.

diatonic: see SCALE.

Dido and Aeneas: see BAROQUE ERA (England); OPERA (beginnings); PURCELL.

Diémer, Louis (February 14, 1843–December 21, 1919) A pupil of Antoine-François Marmontel and his successor (1887) at the Paris Conservatoire, the French pianist Louis Diémer taught such outstanding French musicians as Édouard Risler, Alfred Cortot, Marcel Dupré, and Robert Casadesus. A series of historical recitals (1889) was so successful that he specialized in the performance of early music. But he also played the first performances of many French works, including Franck's Variations *Symphoniques* (1885).

d'Indy, Vincent: see INDY (PAUL MARIE THÉODORE), VINCENT D'.

discord/concord A combination of tones that includes at least one dissonance (discord) in relation to a combination of tones that is pleasing to the ear (concord). In popular use the terms are subjective words for unpleasant versus pleasant sounds. See CONSONANCE/ DISSONANCE.

dissonance: see CONSONANCE/DISSONANCE.

Di Stefano, Giuseppe (b. July 24, 1921) The Sicilian lyric tenor Giuseppe Di Stefano studied in Milan with Luigi Montesanto. He made his debut in 1946 as Des Grieux in Puccini's *Manon Lescaut* and had great success at the Metropolitan Opera (1948–50). He has sung throughout the Americas, Europe, and South

Africa. Available recordings include operas of Puccini *(La Bohème, Madama Butterfly, Tosca),* Verdi *(Rigoletto, Il Trovatore),* Donizetti *(Lucia di Lammermoor,* recorded twice), and Bellini *(I Puritani)* as well as Neapolitan songs.

Dittersdorf, Karl Ditters von (November 2, 1739–October 24, 1799) One of the earliest composers of the Viennese Classical school, Karl Ditters von Dittersdorf is remembered primarily for his light operas that established the form of the singspiel.

Born Karl Ditters (he was ennobled in 1773), he was a child prodigy on the violin and was engaged at the age of 12 in the orchestra of Prince von Sachsen-Hildburghausen. Later he played in the orchestra of the Vienna Opera and became a friend of Gluck, whom he accompanied in 1763 to Bologna. In 1765 he became Kapellmeister to the Bishop of Grosswardein (Oradea) in Hungary, where he set up a private stage in the episcopal palace and wrote for it his first opera, *Amore in musica.* His first oratorio, *Isacco,* was also from this period.

The following year Ditters was again in the service of an ecclesiastical patron, Count Schaffgotsch, Prince-Bishop of Breslau, at Johannisberg, Silesia. There he composed 11 comic operas, among them *Il Viaggiatore americano* (1770), and an oratorio, *Davidde penitente* (1770). In 1773 he produced the oratorio *Esther* in Vienna.

He formed a close friendship with Haydn, who introduced his operas to Esterházy, and from 1783 he played in string quartets with Mozart. From this period onward his output was enormous. He produced the oratorio *Giobbe* (1786) and several operas, three of which, *Doktor und Apotheker* (1786), *Hieronymus Knicker* (1787) and *Das rote Käppchen* (1788), had great success. *Doktor und Apotheker,* in particular, became one of the classic examples of the German singspiel. He also wrote a large quantity of instrumental music. In 1796, following the bishop's death, he was dismissed with a small pension. Poor and broken in health, he accepted a post with Baron Ignaz von Stillfried at Schloss Rothlhotta, Neuhof, Bohemia. On his deathbed he dictated his autobiography (English transla-

tion 1896; reprinted 1970) that, although naive in concept, is of great interest to students of 18th-century music.

Dittersdorf's symphonies, although overshadowed by those of Haydn, are sometimes of interest, especially those of a programmatic nature such as the six surviving symphonies on Ovid's *Metamorphoses.* His violin concertos are worthy of study, and several of his quartets have their own personality. His partitas for wind instruments are notable for the formidable nature of the horn parts.

RECORDINGS: Double Bass Concerto in E Major; Harp Concertos in A Major; Harpsichord Concerto in A Major; Quartet in D Major; Quartet in E-flat Major; Sinfonia Concertante for double bass and viola.

divertimento A term in fashion in the second half of the 18th century for an instrumental work of a light or entertaining nature (from the Italian word meaning diversion; French form, divertissement). It was especially popular with Haydn and Mozart and consisted of several movements for strings or winds, with or without harpsichord, or for both combined. The movements were in sonata or variation form or followed the style of dance movements in the suite. Among the numerous divertimenti of Haydn are a sextet in the form of a double string trio to be played by two groups simultaneously in different rooms and his Quintet in G Major *(Cassatio)* for two violins, two violas, and cello. The divertimenti of Mozart resemble his works having the name serenade or cassation, though the genre can embrace a work so serious and ambitious as his Divertimento in E-flat for string trio, K.563. The style of the divertimento was to some extent maintained in the Septet, Op. 20, by Beethoven and the Octet, Op. 166, by Schubert, both for winds and strings. The term was also applied in the 20th century to compositions by Bartók and others.

Dohnányi, Christoph von (b. September 8, 1929) The German conductor Christoph von Dohnányi is the grandson of the composer Ernst von Dohnányi. Educated in Munich and the United States, he has held conducting posts in Lübeck (1957–64), Kassel (1964–66), the WDR (Westdeutscher Rundfunk) Sym-

247

phony (1964–69), the Museum Society Orchestra in Frankfurt (1968–77), and the Hamburg State Opera and Philharmonic (since 1977). Dohnányi has championed 20th-century music and conducted the premiere of Hans Werner Henze's opera, *The Bassarids* (1966).

Dohnányi, Ernst von (July 27, 1877–February 11, 1960) The Hungarian composer Ernst von Dohnányi was also a noted pianist, conductor, and teacher. His style was so influenced by Brahms that his First Piano Quintet (1895) has sometimes been called "Brahms's Second Piano Quintet."

Dohnányi studied at the Budapest Royal Academy with István Thomán and Hans Koessler and later with Eugène d'Albert. His First Symphony and the *Zrinyi* Overture jointly won the Hungarian Millennium Prize in 1896. His career as a concert pianist began the following year, and by 1905 he was acclaimed as one of the great virtuosos of the day. Appointments included the Berlin Hochschule (1905–15; professor of piano from 1908), conductor of the Budapest Philharmonic (1919–44), and associate director of the Budapest Academy (1919; full director from 1933). After World War II he taught in Argentina and from 1949 was composer-in-residence at Florida State College in Tallahassee.

Dohnányi was an active musician until the end of his life, but his output as a composer was sporadic after 1930. His best-known work is Variations on a Nursery Song (1914; first performance 1916), but he also composed two piano concertos, two violin concertos, a harp concertino, three operas, three symphonies, three quartets, other chamber music, and songs. His *Ruralia Hungarica* was one of the rare exceptions from his Brahmsian style to win success. It was originally for piano but was arranged by the composer for orchestra and for violin and piano.

RECORDINGS: Piano Concertos (2); *Ruralia Hungarica;* Suite in f-sharp minor for orchestra; Variations on a Nursery Song; Violin Sonata; piano music.

Dolmetsch, Arnold (February 24, 1858–February 28, 1940) One of the pioneers in the modern search for authenticity in the performance and instrumentation of early music, French-born Arnold Dolmetsch learned piano and organ building from his father and grandfather but was trained as a violinist at the Brussels Conservatory (a pupil of Henri Vieuxtemps) and at the Royal College of Music in London. He was appointed an instructor of violin at Dulwich College and was soon an established teacher.

Always interested in the music of Bach and the old masters, Dolmetsch came into the possession of a well preserved viola d'amore. In learning to play the instrument he discovered manuscripts in the British Museum of viol music by early English composers, began investigating how to perform their music in authentic style, and in 1890 gave his first viol concert.

With his wife and Kathleen Salmon he formed a trio for the performance of early music on authentic instruments. A concert tour of the United States in 1902 prompted the Chickering Company in Boston to extend its facilities to him. There he supervised the building of harpsichords, lutes, and viols (1905–09). From 1911 to 1914 he was at the Gaveau factory in Paris. After World War I he built the first successful modern recorders.

Like George Bernard Shaw, who reviewed his concerts with enthusiasm, Dolmetsch was a rebel whose reforms aroused a response both of alarm and fascination. His work slowly gained acceptance after 1914, when he settled permanently in England. He published several editions of early music, and his book, *The Interpretation of the Music of the XVII and XVIII Centuries* (1915 and 1944), became a basic work in its field. In 1916 Dolmetsch established a center for the study of early music in Haslemere, and in 1925 the annual Haslemere Festival was begun. The Dolmetsch Foundation was organized (1928) to support him and his work.

BIBLIOGRAPHY: Robert Donington, *The Work and Ideas of Arnold Dolmetsch* (1932); Mabel Dolmetsch, *Personal Recollections of Arnold Dolmetsch* (1958); Margaret Campbell, *Dolmetsch: The Man and His Work* (1975).

dominant The fifth tone of the diatonic scale.

In Western music of the 17th to 19th century, the dominant was a particularly important tone, for it stood in strongest relation to the tonic, or keynote. Chords based on the dominant had a strong tendency to move to the tonic chord, and the key built upon the dominant was most strongly related to the tonic key.

Don Carlos: *see* VERDI.

Don Giovanni: *see* ARIA; COUNTERPOINT (Classical period); MOZART (later life); OPERA (the 19th century).

Donizetti, (Domenico) Gaetano (Maria) (November 29, 1797–April 8, 1848) One of the most prolific 19th-century composers of Italian opera, Gaetano Donizetti represents a transitional stage between Rossini and Verdi.

Donizetti began his musical studies with Simon Mayr, organist of the Bergamo Cathedral and a composer of operas, and completed them at the Liceo Filarmonico at Bologna with Stanislao Mattei. Donizetti's father intended him to become a church musician, but the young man's tastes lay in the theater. His first success was at one of the Venetian opera houses in 1818, and during the next 12 years he composed no fewer than 31 operas, most of them produced in Naples and now forgotten. In 1830 his *Anna Bolena,* produced in Milan, carried his fame abroad to all the Euro-

Gaetano Donizetti
attributed to Giovanni Carnevali (1806–73)
courtesy, Museo Donizettiano, Bergamo, Italy

pean capitals and across the Atlantic. Two years later he had another lasting success with *L'Elisir d'amore,* a comedy full of charm and character with a text by Felice Romani. *Lucrezia Borgia,* also with a libretto by Romani, achieved considerable success in 1833 at La Scala in Milan and elsewhere. Like Rossini and Bellini before him, Donizetti now gravitated to Paris. His *Marino Faliero,* produced in Paris, suffered from comparison with Bellini's *I Puritani,* and he returned to Naples for the production of his tragic masterpiece, *Lucia di Lammermoor* (1835). He continued working in Naples (where his young wife died in 1837) until in 1838 the censor refused to allow the production of *Poliuto* on religious grounds. He returned to Paris, where the field had been cleared for him by the death of Bellini and Rossini's retirement. There he revived some of his best operas, including *Lucrezia Borgia,* which was withdrawn because of the opposition of Victor Hugo, on whose drama the libretto was based. *Poliuto* was produced as *Les Martyrs* in 1840, preceded a few months earlier by the opéra comique, *La Fille du régiment,* which gained enormous popularity through the performances of Jenny Lind, Adelina Patti, Emma Albani, and others throughout the 19th century. Later in the same year the Paris Opéra produced *La Favorite,* Donizetti's first essay in French grand opera, for which he himself wrote the text of the last (and best) act. The piano arrangement of the score was made by the as yet unknown Wagner, who was in Paris at the time. Apart from *Linda di Chamounix,* produced in Vienna in 1842, the only other work of note is the opera buffa, *Don Pasquale,* produced at the Théâtre Italien in Paris in 1843. For this delightful and witty farce Donizetti wrote his own text. *Dom Sébastien,* his second work for the Opéra, was a complete failure. Melancholia, presaging the final stages of general paralysis, had already begun to quench the spirit of the gay and debonair composer. The remaining years are a sad story of degeneration to helpless insanity, first in an asylum near Paris and then at his native Bergamo, where he died.

As the list of his numerous operas shows, Donizetti was a most facile composer. He acquired from his masters, Mayr and Mattei, the right amount of technical proficiency to serve his purpose and no more. His theatrical flair enabled him to give musical emphasis to the dramatic situations on the stage without probing deeply below their surface, while his abundant fund of melodic invention never failed to provide lyrical expression to the emotions of the characters. Apart from opera and songs he composed quartets and other chamber works and also sacred music.

BIBLIOGRAPHY: Herbert Weinstock, *Donizetti and the World of Opera in Italy, Paris and Vienna in the First Half of the Nineteenth Century* (1963); William Ashbrook, *Donizetti* (1965); John Allitt, ed., *Donizetti and the Tradition of Romantic Love* (1975).

RECORDINGS: Concertino in G Major for English horn and orchestra; Flute Sonata; operas *Anna Bolena, Don Pasquale, L'Elisir d'amore, La Favorite, La Fille du régiment, Gemma di Vergy, Lucia di Lammermoor, Lucrezia Borgia, Maria Stuarda, Roberto Devereux;* Quartets (12).

Don Juan: *see* GLUCK; STRAUSS, RICHARD; SYMPHONIC POEM.

Donna del lago, La: *see* OPERA (the 19th century).

Don Pasquale: *see* DONIZETTI.

Don Quixote: *see* STRAUSS, RICHARD; SYMPHONIC POEM.

Dorati, Antal (b. April 9, 1906) Educated at the Budapest Academy and the University of Vienna, the Hungarian-U.S. conductor Antal Dorati established his reputation conducting ballet in Europe and later in the United States. He was conductor of the Dallas (Texas) Symphony (1945–49), Minneapolis Symphony (1949–60), principal conductor of the BBC Symphony (1962–66) and the Stockholm Philharmonic (from 1966), and conductor of the National Symphony in Washington, D.C., where he had made his U.S. debut in 1937 (1970–77), and the Detroit Symphony from 1977. His recordings of the three Tchaikovsky ballets (*Nutcracker, Swan Lake,* and *Sleeping Beauty*) have been highly praised as have his recordings with the Philharmonia Hungarica of the complete symphonies of Haydn. He spends his summers composing and has pro-

duced chamber music, a cantata, mass, symphony, ballet, a Piano Concerto (1975) for his wife, the pianist Ilse von Alpenheim, and a Cello Concerto (1976) for Janos Starker.

Dorian mode The first of the eight medieval church modes. Its general range comprises the eight natural notes from the D below middle C to the D above. Melodies in Dorian, or Mode I, usually have D as the *finalis,* or final note, and A as the *tenor,* or reciting note.

In ancient Greek music Dorian referred to the scale pattern, or octave species, conventionally represented in modern writings as E-E.

double bass The contrabass of the violin family, normally about six feet (1.8 meters) high and strung with four heavy strings pitched E-A-D-G that are notated from the second E below middle C but sounding an octave lower.

Because of its great size the double bass has always shown less regularity of form, stringing, tuning, and technique than other members of the violin family. Double basses have been in use for as long as the parent instrument, but they are not yet completely standardized in number of strings, tuning, shape, or body size. The bass is sometimes made with the blunt corners and flat back of the viol and therefore has been called a hybrid instrument. But true double bass violins, with arched back and outturned corners, have existed since the early 17th century and are still in the majority. It is immaterial whether the back is flat or arched, except that the flat back is both more convenient for the player and more economical to make. It is the fitting and adjustment of the bass, which follows that of the cello, that makes it what it is—a double bass violin. The tuning in fourths, which is almost universal, has been adopted on the bass because of the great length of the strings ($42\frac{1}{2}$ in. [slightly more than one meter]), which makes the whole-tone interval in the fingering so large that it can be covered only by the span of the first and fourth fingers. The closer tuning brings the technique of fingering more into line with what is possible on the smaller instruments, namely a scalewise (diatonic) fingering that reduces hand move-

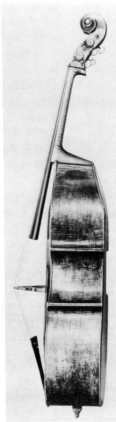

double bass, front and side views
EB Inc.

are replaced by a machine head, such as is commonly used on guitars and other plucked instruments; each tuning peg, of solid brass, is fitted with a worm-and-wheel screw adjuster. The "tail-gut" of the smaller instruments is also replaced by metal, usually a thick copper wire but preferably a stranded steel cable. An extending end pin, similar to the pin used on the cello, is now in universal use. On most basses the ribs are not of equal depth but are cut away at the top so that the back slants toward the shoulder of the neck in its upper part. This enables the player to bring the neck and upper portion of the body closer to him and makes for ease of handling. Beethoven and later composers gave the bass increased importance in the symphony orchestra. Beethoven's friend Domenico Dragonetti and the conductor Serge Koussevitzky, both skilled bassists, composed concertos for the instrument as did Gunther Schuller (1968). In the 1960s Gary Karr began a career as a solo bassist.

ments to a minimum. The normal tuning means that the bass cannot descend an octave below the cello's bottom string, and it is for this reason that the low fifth string is sometimes added, tuned to 16-ft. C. The note commonly occurs in symphonic works from the Classical period onward and is being more specifically demanded by modern composers. Coversely the high fifth C string, tuned a fourth above the normal top string, is occasionally used in dance bands, where it simplifies the fingering of high pizzicato notes.

Another method of obtaining 16-ft. C is to fit an attachment that lengthens the existing E string, which is carried up to the top of the head on an extension bar, when these low notes are wanted. This has the advantage of preserving the normal four strings and their normal tuning for all ordinary purposes and imposing no extra load on the bridge, as does the fifth string. On the double bass the pegs

Dowland, John (1562/63–buried March 2 [February 20, old style], 1626)   The English composer and lutenist John Dowland was one of the most famous musicians of his time and one of the few English musicians who enjoyed as great a reputation on the Continent as he did at home. In the second half of the 17th century his music dropped out of fashion, but early in the 19th century he was rediscovered and appreciation of his work grew steadily until his full stature was again recognized.

On his own testimony he was born in 1562 or 1563, but where he was born is unknown. There is no satisfactory evidence to confirm the story that he was born at Dalkey near Dublin, and the statement made by Thomas Fuller in *The Worthies of England* (1662), that he believed him to have been a native of Westminster, may well be true. Nothing is known of his childhood, but in 1580 he accompanied Sir Henry Cobham to Paris as "servant" when

Cobham was appointed ambassador to the French court. In 1588 he received the degree of Mus. Bac. from the University of Oxford and from Cambridge before 1597. During his stay in France he was converted to the Roman Catholic faith, a fact that he believed to have been responsible for the rejection of his application to fill a vacant post as one of the court lutenists in 1594. After this disappointment he determined to leave England for a time and to travel on the Continent. He first visited the Duke of Brunswick at Wolfenbüttel and then the Landgrave of Hesse at Kassel, being received at both courts with exceptional marks of friendship and esteem.

After leaving Kassel he continued his journey toward Rome, where he intended to visit his friend the madrigalist Luca Marenzio, but at Florence he became involved with a group of English Roman Catholics who were plotting against the life of Queen Elizabeth. He took fright on learning their plans and fled to Nürnberg, where he wrote a letter to Sir Robert Cecil informing him of the activities of his coreligionists. He returned to the court of Hesse and appears to have remained there until early in 1597, when he left for England.

In 1598 he became lutenist to Christian IV of Denmark with the exceptionally generous salary of 500 daler a year. He seems to have found the appointment uncongenial, and in 1606 he was dismissed for unsatisfactory conduct.

Between 1609 and 1612 Dowland entered the service of Theophilus, Lord Howard de Walden, but before October 28, 1612, he was appointed one of the "musicians for the lutes" to James I. He remained in royal employment until shortly before his death; he was succeeded in his post at court by his son Robert.

Working at a time of musical transition, Dowland absorbed many of the new ideas he encountered on his continental travels, and his 88 lute songs (printed between 1597 and 1612) reflect these developments. Of about 90 works for solo lute, the majority exist only in widely scattered manuscript collections. Dance forms are used extensively, often with highly elaborate divisions to the repeats. His pavan *Lachrimae* became one of the most widely known compositions of the time. In

his chromatic fantasies, the finest of which are "Forlorne Hope fancye" and "Farwell," he developed this particular form to a height of intensity unequaled by any other writer for the Renaissance lute.

In addition to the songs and lute music his compositions include six harmonizations in Thomas East's *The Whole Booke of Psalmes* (1592); *Mr. Henry Noel his funerall psalmes* (1597); *Lachrimae, or Seaven Teares . . .* (1604); two sacred songs in Sir William Leighton's *Teares or Lamentations of a Sorrowfull Soule* (1614). A pavan *à* 5, and volta and pavan *à* 4, that are not arrangements of other known works, are included in Thomas Simpson's collections, *Opusculum* (Frankfurt, 1610) and *Taffel-Consort* (Hamburg, 1621).

BIBLIOGRAPHY: Diana Poulton, *John Dowland* (1972).

RECORDINGS: *First Booke of Songes* (1597); *Lachrimae, or Seaven Teares;* various ayres, dances for lute, and lute songs.

D'Oyly Carte, Richard: *see* CARTE, RICHARD D'OYLY.

Dragonetti, Domenico (April 7, 1763–April 16, 1846)   Principally self-taught, the Venetian prodigy bass player Domenico Dragonetti was performing in the opera orchestra of San Benedetto at age 13 and at St. Mark's Cathedral five years later. He had a successful career in England beginning in 1794 and made three visits to Vienna, where he made the friendships of Beethoven and Haydn. In 1845 he played principal bass in the Beethoven festival at Bonn, where reportedly his vigor belied his age. His extensive collection of instruments and scores is in the British Museum.

Dream of Gerontius, The: *see* ELGAR; GLOCKENSPIEL; ORATORIO (late 19th century).

Dreigroschenoper, Die: *see* WEILL.

Dreyschock, Alexander (October 15, 1818–April 1, 1869)   The rival of Liszt in technical prowess, the Bohemian piano virtuoso Alexander Dreyschock was known primarily for that technique and particularly for his brilliant display of octaves. He studied with Johann Wenzel Tomaschek at Prague and was popular with the general public if not with his colleagues and the critics. Named professor of piano at the new St. Petersburg Conservatory in 1862, he also composed a number of works, mostly piano pieces.

drone A sustained tone, usually relatively low in pitch, against which a melody is heard; on a musical instrument, a pipe or string that produces a drone—*e.g.,* the drone strings on a hurdy-gurdy, sometimes called bourdons, or the three drone pipes on a bagpipe.

Drones occur widely both in vocal and in instrumental folk music, particularly European. Balkan singers frequently sustain a drone against a sung melody. Various instruments have drones built into them, contributing to the characteristic sound of the instrument—*e.g.,* the *launeddas,* a Sardinian triple clarinet; the Appalachian dulcimer; the five-string banjo; and the *vielle,* the medieval troubadours' fiddle. Twentieth-century folk fiddlers often bow open strings to drone beneath the melody played on a neighboring string.

In the art music of India the drone played on the tambura sounds the two predominant notes of the raga (the melodic pattern developed by the soloist), producing a framework in which the raga is heard.

A PEDAL POINT is a drone used in the context of European harmony of the 17th to 19th century.

Drucker, Stanley (b. February 4, 1929) Educated at the Curtis Institute, the U.S. clarinetist Stanley Drucker studied with Leon Russianoff. He has played solo clarinet with the Indianapolis Symphony, Busch Chamber Players, Buffalo Philharmonic, and New York Philharmonic (member since 1948 and principal since 1960) and has taught at the Juilliard School since 1968. Known primarily for playing 20th-century music, he has recorded Debussy and Carl Nielsen to Mario Davidovsky.

Druckman, Jacob (b. June 6, 1928) U.S. composer Jacob Druckman studied at the Juilliard School in New York City with Bernard Wagenaar, Vincent Persichetti, and Peter Mennin and in 1957 joined the faculty there. During his student years he also studied briefly with Tony Aubin in Paris and with Copland. In 1965–66 he studied at the Columbia-Princeton Electronic Music Center in New York City, of which he became an associate in 1967. In 1971–72 he was director of the electronic music studio at the Yale University School of Music, and in 1977 he was appointed a professor there. In addition to vocal and chamber music, his principal compositions are *Animus I* (1966) for trombone and tape; *Animus II* (1969) for voice, percussion, and tape; and *Animus III* (1969) for clarinet and tape. *Windows* for orchestra won the Pulitzer Prize in 1972. Druckman wrote *Chiaroscuro* (first performance 1977) for large orchestra with a huge percussion section on a joint commission by the orchestras of Boston, Chicago, Cleveland, Los Angeles, New York, and Philadelphia. His Viola Concerto (1978) was commissioned by the New York Philharmonic. Much of his music has been choreographed.

RECORDINGS: *Animus II; Animus III; Delizie Contente Che l'Alme Beate* for wind quintet and tape; *Incenters* for 13 players; Quartet No. 2.

drum A percussion instrument common to most nations and ages. Unlike most musical instruments that have their origins in the practice of ritual magic, the drum has never completely lost these associations. In its form the drum is basically either a cylinder or a bowl of wood, metal, or earthenware; the shell is covered at one or both ends with a membrane called the head that is set in vibration by direct percussion of hand or stick. Western drums may be divided into three groups according to the nature of their construction: a single head on a shell open at one end as the tambourine; a single head on a closed shell as the kettledrum; two heads, one at each end of the shell, as the snare, or side, drum and tabor. Of the several drums used in the modern orchestra only the kettledrums are designed to produce a note of a definite musical pitch. In Oriental and African countries drums are often played by striking them with the hand; in these countries this technique is developed to an astonishing degree of rhythmic intricacy and virtuosity. In Western music the drum—generally played with one or two sticks—is traditionally a less sophisticated instrument that fulfills the relatively simple purpose of marking the rhythm for dancing or marching.

Very little is known about European drums and drumming in the Middle Ages, the only evidence being that of representations in paintings and sculpture and a certain amount of not very helpful information from literary sources. No medieval drums have survived, and it is not until the 16th century that written percussion parts appear, and even then only in instruction books. Before the middle of the 17th century the composer did not feel obliged to notate any percussion parts, knowing that the player's training would have made him thoroughly conversant with what was then a traditional technique. By the 13th century three types of drum were established: nakers, tabor (in several forms), and tambourine.

Nakers, a 13th-century importation derived from the Arab *naqqara,* were a pair of hemispherical drums like very small kettledrums and were played by one drummer. The shells were made of metal or wood, the head was tensioned by ropes or thongs, and sometimes the instrument was equipped with a snare; *i.e.,* a string of gut or silk stretched across the head to cause a rattling sound. They were suspended from the waist and played with two sticks. Pairs of nakers were tuned to a high and a low rather indefinite pitch and were used to accompany bands of loud instruments—trumpets, shawms, bagpipes, etc.—in ceremonial music.

The tabor was a small cylindrical drum of variable depth with a wooden shell and a drumhead at each end. It was rope-tensioned and usually had a snare on both heads. The tabor was always used in conjunction with the tabor pipe, a long three-holed whistle-flute; both instruments were played by one musician. The pipe was played with the left hand while the tabor, generally suspended from the left wrist, was struck with a stick held in the right hand. The pipe-and-tabor combination

English pipe (18th century) and tabor (19th century)
courtesy, Metropolitan Museum of Art
The Crosby Brown Collection of Musical Instruments, 1889

dates from at least the 13th century and despite early pastoral associations provided court dance music until as late as the 16th century. It is still used in the popular music of Provence.

The tambourine, a shallow wooden hoop with a single head and metal jingles set in the sides, is struck with the hand, rubbed with the thumb, or shaken. The tambourine (a similar instrument was the ancient Greek *tympanon*) was a medieval adaptation of an instrument used by the Arabs. Like its Arabic prototype the tambourine in the Middle Ages often had a snare. By the end of the 15th century its use seems to have declined except where it survived as a folk instrument. Early in the 19th century the tambourine was introduced to the orchestra via the opera (the usual route to respectability for percussion instruments) for special Spanish or gypsy effects. *See also* TAMBOURINE. For drums of the modern orchestra, *see* BASS DRUM; SNARE DRUM; TENOR DRUM; TIMPANI.

BIBLIOGRAPHY: Curt Sachs, *The History of Musical Instruments* (1940); Sibyl Marcuse, *Musical Instruments: A Comprehensive Dictionary* (1964), and *A Survey of Musical Instruments* (1975); James Blades, *Percussion Instruments and Their History,* rev. ed. (1978).

Dubois, (François Clément) Théodore (August 24, 1837–June 11, 1924)   The French composer, organist, and teacher Théodore Dubois was known for his technical treatises on harmony, counterpoint, and sight reading. He studied at Reims under the cathedral organist and at the Paris Conservatoire with Antoine-François Marmontel and Ambroise Thomas. After winning the Prix de Rome in 1861 for his cantata *Atala,* he succeeded Franck as organist at Sainte-Clotilde. In 1868 he was choirmaster at the Madeleine and later succeeded Saint-Saëns as organist there (1877). Dubois was professor of harmony at the Paris Conservatoire (1871–90), elected to the French Institute (1894), and followed Thomas as director of the Conservatoire (1896–1905). He wrote music of all types, including operas and choral and orchestral works.

Ducasse, Roger Jean Jules Aimable: *see* ROGER-DUCASSE, JEAN JULES AIMABLE.

Dufay, Guillaume (*c.* 1400–November 27, 1474)   The most illustrious composer of the Burgundian school, Guillaume Dufay was a chorister at the Cambrai Cathedral (1409), entered the service of Carlo Malatesta of Rimini *c.* 1420, and in 1428 joined the papal singers. In 1426 he became a canon of Cambrai. After seven years with the Duke of Savoy, he lived at Cambrai from about 1440 and supervised the music of the cathedral. He took a degree in canon law about 1445 and in 1446 became a canon of Mons. Dufay's surviving works include 87 motets, 59 French chansons, 7 Italian chansons, 7 complete masses, and 35 mass sections. He often used and may have originated the technique of faux-bourdon.

During his Italian period Dufay composed a number of ceremonial motets for public celebrations, among them the election of Pope Eugenius IV (1431), the Treaty of Viterbo (1433), and the dedication of Brunelleschi's dome for Sta. Maria del Fiore in Florence (1436). For the brilliant "Feast of the Pheasant," held in 1454 by Philip the Good of Burgundy and intended to initiate a crusade to recapture Jerusalem, Dufay composed a lamentation for the Church in Constantinople.

Dufay's chansons, normally in three voices, deal with subjects such as springtime, love, and melancholy. Most use the poetic-musical forms of the ballade, rondeau, and virelai; a few are written in freer form.

Dufay's masses laid the foundation for the rapid musical development of the mass in the second half of the 15th century. His complete mass settings are in four voices and use a cantus firmus placed in the tenor line. His canti firmi include secular songs, such as *L'Homme armé* (used by many composers up to Palestrina) and his own ballade *Se la face ay pale,* and plainchant melodies, such as *Ave Regina.*

In these and other works of his Cambrai period, Dufay perfected a graceful and expressive style that incorporated into continental music the sweet harmonies of the *contenance angloise,* or "English manner," that according to Martin le Franc's *Le Champion des Dames* (*c.* 1440) he had adopted from John Dunstable. In his music he created the characteristic style of the Burgundian composers that links late medieval music with the style of later

Franco-Flemish composers of the Renaissance.

RECORDINGS: Masses *Ave Regina, Caput, L'Homme armé, Sine nomine, Se la face ay pale;* various motets, hymns, choruses, and songs.

Dukas, Paul (Abraham) (October 1, 1865–May 17, 1935) The fame of the Parisian composer Paul Dukas rests on a single orchestral work, *L'Apprenti sorcier* (1897; *The Sorcerer's Apprentice*), though his musicianship was of a considerably wider range than this brilliant period piece attests.

Dukas studied at the Paris Conservatoire with Théodore Dubois, Georges Mathias, and Ernest Guiraud. After winning a second Grand Prix de Rome with his cantata *Velléda* (1888), he established his position among the younger composers with an overture to Corneille's *Polyeucte,* first performed in 1892, and the Symphony in C Major (1896). The remainder of his output (never large because of his own strict censorship of his works) consisted mainly of dramatic and program music and compositions for piano. Dukas was a master of orchestration and was professor of the orchestral class (1910–13) at the Conservatoire and professor of composition (1913–35). He contributed musical criticism to several Paris papers, and his collected writings, *Les Écrits de Paul Dukas* (1948), include some of the best essays ever published on Rameau, Gluck, and Berlioz.

Dukas's *L'Apprenti sorcier,* based on Goethe's *Der Zauberlehrling,* was a piece of descriptive music written at the same time and in much the same style as Richard Strauss's *Till Eulenspiegel.* His Piano Sonata (1901) is one of the last great works in the tradition of Beethoven, Schumann, and Liszt; his *Variations, Interlude et Finale pour piano sur un thème de Rameau* (1903) represents a translation into French musical idiom and style of Beethoven's *Diabelli* Variations. The ballet *La Péri* (1912), on the other hand, displays the mastery of impressionist scoring; and in the opera *Ariane et Barbe-Bleue* (1907) on the play of Maurice Maeterlinck, poetic atmosphere and the perfection of musical texture make up for a lack of dramatic impact.

After 1912 Dukas ceased publishing his compositions—except for a piano piece in memory of Debussy, *La Plainte au loin du Faune* (1920), and a song, *Sonnet de Ronsard* (1924)—and a few weeks before his death he destroyed all his musical manuscripts. Dukas collaborated with the Paris publishing firm of Durand in preparing modern editions of some of the works of Rameau, Couperin, and Domenico Scarlatti and of the piano works of Beethoven.

An admirable pedagogue (de Falla was among his disciples and Messiaen was one of his pupils), a shrewd observer of the musical scene, a tireless reader of every score ancient and modern and of every literary work he could lay hands on, Dukas was that rare man among modern musicians: a 20th-century humanist.

RECORDINGS: *La Péri;* Piano Sonata; *The Sorcerer's Apprentice;* Symphony in C Major; Variations, Interlude, and Finale on a Theme by Rameau.

Duke Bluebeard's Castle: *see* BARTÓK; OPERA (the 20th century).

dulcimer An instrument with strings stretched over a flat, shallow soundbox. In Britain the word denotes the beaten form of the instrument, known in European folk music as the Alpine *Hackbrett,* the Hungarian CIMBALOM, the Romanian *tsambal,* and the Greek *santouri.* These have a trapeze-shaped soundbox and two or more metal strings for each note; the notes are sounded by striking the strings with a pair of light beaters often made of cane. There are two long bridges, which are perforated so that the strings bearing on one bridge can pass freely under the other—they do so on alternate sides. Thus the strings slope alternately to right and left and are struck where they rise toward their respective bridges. This greatly facilitates rapid technique. Tunings vary regionally. The elaborate concert *cimbalom* of Hungarian gypsy orchestras is fully chromatic, is built on legs, and is fitted with a damper pedal. The simpler varieties are placed on a table or carried on a sling and are used chiefly to accompany the violin or other instruments. Historically these dulcimers appear to be beaten versions of the

woman with dulcimer
from Filippo Bonanni's Gabinetto armonico,
18th century courtesy, Dover Publications, Inc.

plucked psaltery and to have entered central Europe from Persia about the 15th century A.D.

The Appalachian, or mountain, dulcimer of the United States is different, being a true ZITHER with stopped melody strings running over a fretted fingerboard.

Dunstable, John (*c.* 1385–December 24, 1453)   One of the few English composers to have an influence on the development of European music was John Dunstable. This was recognized by his contemporaries, including the French poet Martin le Franc, who wrote in his *Champion des Dames* (*c.* 1440) that the two leading composers of the day, Guillaume Dufay and Gilles de Binchois, owed their superiority to what they had learned from Dunstable's "English manner."

Information about Dunstable's life is scanty. In 1419 he was made a secular canon of Hereford Cathedral, but there was no obligation of residence—probably a financial gift by the Duke of Bedford, in whose service he

was for some time. The mass sections on the plainsong *Da gaudiorum premia* and the well-known motet *Veni sancte spiritus—Veni creator spiritus* were almost certainly written in 1431 for Henry VI's French coronation; Dunstable may well have spent the years 1423–35 in France, where the Duke of Bedford held his court as regent, although there is no documentary evidence for this. About his later life nothing is known beyond the fact that he died in London and was buried at St. Stephen's, Walbrook. His epitaph, recorded before its destruction in the Great Fire, referred to him as skilled in mathematics and astronomy as well as in music, and this is confirmed by the existence of manuscript treatises on astronomy that belonged to him and are now preserved at libraries in Oxford and Cambridge.

Although Dunstable's influence on French music was widely admitted by musical historians, its nature remained obscure and misunderstood until it was elucidated by Manfred Bukofzer, the editor of his complete works (*Musica Britannica,* vol. viii, 1953). It is to be seen above all in the relaxation of harmony (by a new regulation of dissonance) and of rhythm (by the cultivation of a flowing, gently asymmetrical triple meter). These characteristics of the English school Dunstable combined with a thorough understanding of the French structural principles of isorhythm, displayed in many of his larger motets and mass sections. His surviving compositions are almost entirely ecclesiastical, but both this and the fact that scarcely any of them are preserved in English manuscripts are probably mere accidents. It is unfortunate that his only recorded five-part composition has been torn out of the Eton College choirbook, written in the last decade of the 15th century. Three of his compositions are to be found in elaborated keyboard settings in a 15th-century German manuscript, the Buxheim Organ Book.

BIBLIOGRAPHY: Frank Llewellyn Harrison, *Music in Medieval Britain* (1958; reprint, 1967).

RECORDINGS: Motets.

Duparc, (Marie Eugène) Henri, originally Fouques-Duparc (January 21, 1848–February

13, 1933) The French composer Henri Duparc was known for his songs on poems of Baudelaire, Leconte de Lisle, Théophile Gautier, and others. He studied with Franck at the Jesuit College of Vaugirard. In 1869 he met Liszt and Wagner at Weimar and in 1870 published *Cinq Mélodies,* including "Soupir" and "Chanson triste," later incorporated in his collection of 15 songs, written between 1869 and 1884. In these, of which eight are with orchestral accompaniment, Duparc enlarged the French song into an operatic *scena* ("Au pays où se fait la guerre"), brought to it a poetic sense of musical prosody ("La Vie antérieure"), and, in "Phydilé" and "L'Invitation au voyage," a symphonic conception of form. In his youth Duparc wrote two orchestral works, *Aux Étoiles* and *Lénore,* and a motet. He was also keenly interested in Russian literature, planning an opera, *Roussalka,* based on Pushkin, and in the plays of Ibsen. Later he worked at painting, chiefly in watercolors, sepias, and pastels. About 1890 his creative faculties began to be undermined by doubts, and he thereafter produced little. In a spirit of severe self-criticism, he destroyed nearly all his subsequent works and sketches, together with his earlier unpublished manuscripts and the correspondence addressed to him by Wagner and contemporary poets. During the latter part of his life he was associated with Francis Jammes and Paul Claudel and wrote a long religious prayer in prose (*Testament,* 1906–13).

BIBLIOGRAPHY: Sydney Northcote, *The Songs of Henri Duparc* (1949).

Duport, Jean-Louis (October 4, 1749–September 7, 1819) A member of a well-known musical family and the brother of another cellist, Jean-Pierre for whom Beethoven wrote his Sonatas, Op. 5, French cellist Jean-Louis Duport played with the Imperial (later Royal) Orchestra in Paris and was musician to ex-King Charles IV of Spain at Marseilles. He is best remembered for his *Essai sur le doigté du violoncelle et la conduite de l'archet, avec une suite d'exercices* ("Study of Cello Fingering and Bowing Technique, with Exercises"), which is considered to be the foundation of modern cello virtuosity.

DuPré, Jacqueline (b. January 26, 1945–) After making her first public appearance at the age of seven, the English cellist Jacqueline DuPré studied with Casals and with Mstislav Rostropovich at the Moscow Conservatory. She toured Europe, the British Isles, and North America, making her U.S. debut in 1965. In 1967 she married the conductor and pianist Daniel Barenboim, with whom she has appeared in the major works of the Classical and Romantic repertoire. A prolonged illness virtually ended her performance career after 1973.

Dupré, Marcel (May 3, 1886–May 30, 1971) The French organist and composer Marcel Dupré was noted especially for his improvisations. A child prodigy, he was named titular organist of Saint-Vivien, Rouen, when he was only 12. He entered the Paris Conservatoire, winning first prizes in piano (1905, with Louis Diémer), organ (1907, with Alexandre Guilmant), and fugue (1909, with Charles-Marie Widor). He won the Grand Prix de Rome (1914) for his cantata *Psyché.* Dupré was named assistant to Widor at Saint-Sulpice (1906) and served as interim organist of Notre Dame (1916–22 during Louis Vierne's illness), finally succeeding Widor at Saint-Sulpice (1934). He succeeded Eugène Gigout as professor of organ at the Conservatoire (1926) and was director of the American Conservatory at Fountainebleau (1947–54) and the Paris Conservatoire (1954–56).

Dupré's playing came into prominence in 1920, when he played the complete organ works of Bach in a series of 10 recitals at the Conservatoire (repeated in 1921 at the Trocadero, now the Palais de Chaillot).

Though he composed some church music, orchestral works, piano pieces, and songs, he is known primarily for his organ works, including a concerto and two *Symphonies* (the first with orchestra). Many of his published compositions began as improvisations in recital and were later written down, such as *Symphonie-Passion* (1921–24) and *Le Chemin de la croix* (1931–32; "The Way of the Cross"). Other works that have become staples of late-20th-century organ repertoire are his first set of Three Preludes and Fugues (Op.

7), *Vêpres du commun,* and Variations *sur un vieux noël.* Dupré was the author of several instruction books, including *Traité d'improvisation a l'orgue* (1925) and a widely used organ method.

RECORDINGS: Preludes and Fugues (6); *Symphonie-Passion;* Variations *sur un vieux noël; Vêpres du commun.*

Duprez, Gilbert Louis (December 6, 1806–September 23, 1896)   Educated at the Paris Conservatoire and a professor there from 1842 to 1850, the French tenor Gilbert Louis Duprez created roles in Berlioz' *Benvenuto Cellini* (1838) and Donizetti's *La Favorita* (1840) while a member of the Paris Opéra. He wrote eight operas, an oratorio, and chamber music and in 1853 founded a singing school. His philosophy of vocal production and style is preserved in *L'Art du chant* (1845) and *La Mélodie* (1873).

Durante, Francesco (March 31, 1684–August 13, 1755)   An Italian composer of religious and instrumental music, Francesco Durante was known chiefly as a teacher. The details of his early life and musical education are obscure, but he probably received his training at one of the Naples conservatories and later may also have studied in Rome. All that is known for certain is that he taught at the San Onofrio Conservatory for a short time in 1710. From 1728 to 1739 he was maestro di cappella at the Conservatorio dei Poveri in Naples, from 1742 he taught at the Santa Maria di Loreto Conservatory, and in 1745 he succeeded Leonardo Leo as principal teacher at the San Onofrio Conservatory. There was much rivalry between his pupils and those of Leo; they included Niccolò Jommelli, Giovanni Paisiello, Pergolesi, Niccolò Piccinni, and Leonardo Vinci.

Many motets, several masses, at least three oratorios, a *Pastoral* Mass for four voices, and the Lamentations of the Prophet Jeremiah are among his more important settings. He also composed harpsichord pieces and eight concertante quartets for strings.

Durey, Louis: *see* SIX, LES.

Duruflé, Maurice (b. January 11, 1902)   The French organist and composer Maurice Duru-

flé was educated at the Paris Conservatoire, studying organ with Charles Tournemire, Louis Vierne, and Eugène Gigout (first prize 1922) and composition with Paul Dukas. He served as assistant to Tournemire at Sainte-Clotilde (1919–29), at Notre Dame (1929–31 substituting for Vierne), and as organist of Saint-Etienne-du-Mont since 1930. He was professor of harmony at the Conservatoire (1943–75).

Duruflé and his wife, Marie-Madeleine Chevalier-Duruflé, are both virtuoso recitalists and have toured extensively—often playing joint recitals. An extremely careful and conscientious composer, Duruflé has published relatively little over a long period. His best-known work is a Requiem (1947); other choral works are Four Motets (1960) and Mass *Cum Jubilo* (1966). His organ pieces, all standards in late-20th-century organ repertoire, are Scherzo (1926; arranged for orchestra, 1940); Prelude, Adagio, and Chorale Variations on *Veni creator spiritus* (1930); Suite (1934); and Prelude and Fugue on the name *Alain* (1942). Other works are *Triptyque* (1927) for piano; Prelude, Recitative, and Variations (1928) for flute, viola, and piano; and Three Dances (1936) for orchestra.

RECORDINGS: Four Motets; Prelude, Adagio, and Chorale Variations on *Veni creator spiritus;* Prelude and Fugue on the name *Alain;* Requiem.

Dussek, Jan Ladislav (February 12, 1760–March 20, 1812)   The first important virtuoso pianist who toured regularly and the first to make systematic use of the sustaining pedal, the Bohemian pianist and composer Jan Ladislav Dussek established the custom of sitting at the piano with his right side to the audience—which has prevailed ever since. He studied in Hamburg with Carl Philipp Emanuel Bach (*c.* 1783) and secured several wealthy patrons (Polish Prince Radziwill, Queen Marie-Antoinette in France, and Prince Louis Ferdinand of Prussia) in whose households he lived and worked. Ten years after a successful London debut (1790) he fled his English creditors and remained until his death at the home of his patron Charles-Maurice de Talleyrand. He wrote numerous piano concertos, sonatas, and chamber music, most of which were forgotten until a late-20th-century revival.

RECORDINGS: *La Consolation* for piano; Harp Sonatinas (6); Piano Sonatas; Piano Trios (14); Trio Sonata in B-flat for violin, cello, and harp.

Dvořák, Antonín (September 8, 1841–May 1, 1904) The first Bohemian composer to achieve worldwide recognition, Antonín Dvořák became one of the leading figures in the movements that injected traditional native folk materials into the general framework of musical Romanticism that was characteristic of the 19th century. His fellow Bohemian Smetana, 17 years his senior, already had laid the foundations of the Bohemian nationalist movement in music. His Symphony No. 9 (1893; "From the New World") remains his best-known work, probably because it was thought to be based on Negro spirituals and other influences gained during Dvořák's years in the United States. Although this may be partially true, the music is characteristically Bohemian in its themes, possibly revealing the composer's nostalgia for his homeland.

Dvořák was born in Nelahozeves, a Bohemian village (now in Czechoslovakia) on the Vltava River north of Prague. He came to know music in and about his father's inn, becoming an accomplished violinist and contributing to the amateur music making that accompanied the dances of the local couples. In 1857 a perceptive music teacher persuaded the elder Dvořák to enroll his son in an organ school in Prague. Dvořák completed a two-year course and played the viola in inns and with theater bands, augmenting his small salary with a few private pupils.

The 1860s were trying years for Dvořák, who was hard pressed both for time and the means, even paper and a piano, to compose. In later years he said he had little recollection of what he wrote in those days, but around 1864 two symphonies, an opera, chamber music, and numerous songs lay unheard in his desk. The varied works of this period show, however, that his earlier leanings toward Beethoven and Schubert were becoming increasingly influenced by Wagner and Liszt. In November 1873, at a time when a few successful

Antonín Dvořák
portrait by Max Švabinský, c. 1900
courtesy, Museum Antonín Dvořák, Prague

concerts of his works had begun to make his name known in Prague, he married Anna Čermáková and began an unusually happy family life.

In 1875 Dvořák was awarded a grant by the Austrian government that brought him into contact with Brahms, with whom he formed a close and beneficial friendship. Brahms gave him valuable technical advice and found him an influential publisher in Fritz Simrock; it was with his firm's publication of the Moravian Duets (composed 1876) for soprano and contralto and the Slavonic Dances (1878) for piano duet that Dvořák first attracted worldwide attention. The admiration of the leading critics, instrumentalists, and conductors of the day spread his fame abroad, leading to even greater triumphs in his own country. In 1884 he made the first of 10 visits to England, where the success of his works, especially choral, was a source of constant pride to him, although only the Stabat Mater (1877) and Te Deum (1892) continue to hold a position among the finer works of their kind. In 1890 he enjoyed a triumph in Moscow, where two concerts were arranged for him by his friend Tchaikovsky, and the following year he was made an honorary doctor of music by Cambridge University.

Dvořák accepted the post of director of the newly established National Conservatory of Music in New York City in 1892, and, during his years in the United States, he traveled as far west as Iowa. Though he found much to interest and stimulate him in the New World environment, he missed his own country and returned to Bohemia in 1895. In the final years of his life he composed several string quartets and symphonic poems and his last three operas.

The appeal of Dvořák's music lies chiefly in melodic invention and heart-warming simplicity. His extensive works include nine symphonies, six overtures, five symphonic poems, four concertos, much chamber music, and numerous songs and duets and piano solos and duets. Only his nine operas have failed to enjoy lasting success.

BIBLIOGRAPHY: Alec Robertson, *Dvořák* (1945; reprint, 1949); Otakar Sourek, *Antonín Dvořák: His Life and Works* (1954); John Clapham, *Antonín Dvořák: Musician and Craftsman* (1966); Gervase Hughes, *Dvořák: His Life and Music* (1967); Viktor Fischl, ed., *Antonin Dvořák, His Achievement* (1970); Karel Hoffmeister, *Antonín Dvořák* (1970); Percy M. Young, *Dvořák* (1971).

RECORDINGS: Numerous recordings of most works.

E

Eames, Emma (August 13, 1865–June 13, 1952) Born in China but reared in the United States, the dramatic soprano Emma Eames studied in Boston and with Mathilde Marchesi in Paris, where she made her debut opposite Jean de Reszke in Gounod's *Romeo et Juliette* in 1889. After two years at the Opéra she went to New York City and was prima donna at the Metropolitan Opera for 18 years. She specialized in French opera, although she sang Wagner's Elisabeth (*Tannhäuser*) in London in 1897 with much acclaim.

Eccard, Johannes (1553–1611) A German composer known for his setting of the year's cycle of Lutheran chorales, Johannes Eccard

was born at Mühlhausen. After serving Jacob Fugger in Augsburg (1577–78), he joined the Königsberg chapel of Prince Georg Friedrich of Preussen-Ansbach in 1579, becoming Kapellmeister in 1604. From 1608 until his death in Berlin, he was Kapellmeister to the electors of Brandenburg. Eccard wrote in a narrow range of forms, his songs and early masses recalling Orlando di Lasso. He favored short sacred pieces, vocal and instrumental, culminating in the cycle of chorale settings, *Geistliche Lieder auf den Choral* for five voices (1597). These represent a fusion of choral song and polyphonic motet and avoid the stark economy advocated by some Lutheran extremists.

Eccles, John (*c.* 1650–January 12, 1735) A member of an English family of musicians, violinist and composer John Eccles succeeded Nicholas Staggins in 1700 as master of the King's Band of Music and in the same year was second in a competition for the best setting of William Congreve's masque *The Judgement of Paris*. He published three volumes of theater music and a collection of about 100 songs and wrote the music for Queen Anne's coronation in 1702.

Éclair, L': *see* HALÉVY.

écossaise A dance in quick ² ⁄ ₄ time, similar to a contredanse and first known in France in the early 18th century, where its popularity rivaled that of the anglaise and the minuet. The Scottish origin of the French écossaise is unproved, though Scottish tunes are believed to have accompanied the dancing of écossaises in England toward the end of the 18th century. In the early 19th century the écossaise flourished in Germany, where it was succeeded by the schottische, a round dance similar to the polka. The vogue of the écossaise inspired compositions for piano bearing this name by Schubert, Chopin, and Beethoven, who also wrote écossaises for military band and small orchestra.

Egk, Werner (b. May 17, 1901) Primarily self-taught, but influenced by Stravinsky and briefly a student of Carl Orff in Munich, Bavarian composer and conductor Werner Egk writes for the theater. His music, scenarios, and libretti show sarcasm, irony, and political philosophy. From 1937 to 1941 he was Kapell-meister at the Berlin State Opera, and he was director of the Berlin Hochschule für Musik from 1950 to 1953. Since 1968 he has been president of the German Music Council. He chooses his subjects from history and legend, as in *Columbus* (radio opera, 1932; stage opera, 1942), *Peer Gynt* (1938; opera after Ibsen), *Irische Legende* (1955; opera after Yeats), and *Der Revisor* (1956; opera after Gogol). His early oratorio *Furchtlosigkeit und Wohlwollen* (1931) was a pacifist work denounced for its philosophy. Egk's ballets include *Joan von Zarissa* (1939, performed 1940), based on the story of Don Juan, and *Casanova in London* (1969). He also wrote the libretto for Boris Blacher's opera *Abstrakte Oper* (1953), where the emotion was conveyed through the free juxtaposition of syllables for the effect of their sounds. Egk's music is carefully crafted, polytonal, and polyrhythmic.

Ehmann, Wilhelm (b. December 5, 1904) The German musicologist and choral conductor Wilhelm Ehmann taught at Freiburg University, where he had been a student, from 1938 to 1940, when he joined the faculty of the University of Innsbruck. In 1948 he founded the Westphalian Church Music School in Herford, West Germany, and until 1954 taught at the University of Münster. He has written texts on church music and *Die Chorführung,* 2 vols. (1949; *Choral Directing,* 1968). Ehmann has recorded 17th-century brass music on reproductions of period instruments and with his Westphalian groups music of Bach and especially of Heinrich Schütz.

Ehrling, (Evert) Sixten (b. April 3, 1918) The Swedish conductor and pianist Sixten Ehrling studied at the Royal Academy in Stockholm and in Paris. Advancing from coach to conductor at the Royal Opera in Stockholm, he was its music director from 1953 to 1960. He was conductor and music director of the Detroit Symphony from 1963 to 1973, when he joined the conducting faculty of the Juilliard School in New York City. Ehrling conducted at the Metropolitan Opera (1972–75) and in 1978 became music adviser and principal guest conductor of the Denver Symphony. In the early part of his career Ehrling toured widely

as a pianist and did much to promote 20th-century music. Elected to the Swedish Royal Music Academy in 1956, he was knighted by the Finnish government in 1970. His most important recordings as a conductor include the music of his countrymen Franz Berwald and Karl-Birger Blomdahl and the first complete recorded cycle of the seven symphonies of Sibelius.

1812 Overture: *see* CHIME; TCHAIKOVSKY (later life and works).

electronic music Music produced or modified by electrical, and mainly electronic, means. A more accurate term, electrophonic music, is preferred by some authorities as being inclusive of those methods of sound production that are electrical but not technically electronic; *i.e.,* not dependent on devices utilizing the emission of electrons. However, in conformity with popular usage the term electronic music is used here as being fully synonymous with the more precise term.

Electronic music embraces a great variety of 20th-century music, ranging from popular song settings and film or television sound tracks to serious concert works. It can be produced by diverse means, ranging from the use of relatively simple, conventional instruments with electronic amplification (*e.g.,* the electric guitar) to complex music synthesizers and computers that can be programmed to produce sound. A common characteristic of this music, arising from the design of electronic instruments, is the requirement that it be heard through loudspeakers or, on occasion, earphones. In the more complex instruments the musical output is usually recorded on magnetic tape before the listener can have access to it.

From a historical standpoint electronic music can be regarded as part of a larger development in modern music: the search for new modes of expression, both compositional and instrumental. Modern composers have been particularly interested in the expansion of instrumental resources to include new timbres and temperaments, and many have sought precise personal control over every aspect of music, including frequency, intensity, timbre, rhythm, and spatial arrangement. These requirements have been met by concurrent advances in electronic science, leading to the development of highly sophisticated electronic instruments.

beginnings Electricity was applied to the mechanism of musical instruments as early as 1761, when J.B. Delaborde of Paris invented an electric harpsichord. Experimental instruments continued to be invented throughout the 19th century. The earliest instrument to generate sound electrically, however, was Thaddeus Cahill's Telharmonium, introduced in Mount Holyoke, Massachusetts, in 1906. This machine employed rotary generators and telephone receivers to convert electrical impulses into sound. Complex, bulky, and impractical, it was nevertheless the forerunner of the Hammond electronic organ and the more recent music synthesizers. The invention of the three-electrode tube by Lee de Forest (also in 1906) was significant for electronic music insofar as the tube made possible the later invention of smaller, more practical machines.

The first major stage of development occurred from about 1920 until the beginning of World War II. This period was marked by the invention of a number of electronic instruments designed for performance in the conventional sense. These may be classified as follows:

1. Instruments that produce vibrations in familiar mechanical ways—the striking of strings with hammers, the bowing or plucking of strings, the activation of reeds—but with the conventional resonating agent, such as a sounding board, replaced by a pickup system, an amplifier, and a loudspeaker, which enable the performer to modify both the quality and the intensity of the tone. These instruments include electric pianos (Superpiano, 1927; Neo-Bechstein, 1931; Elektrochord, 1933); electronic organs that employ vibrating reeds (Rangertone, 1931; Orgatron, 1935); electric violins, violas, cellos, and basses; and electric guitars, banjos, and mandolins.

2. Instruments that produce vibrations by means of oscillating electric circuits at set frequencies. The oscillations are amplified and heard through a loudspeaker. This group of instruments, which is a large one, can be fur-

ther subdivided into those designed to simulate existing timbres, notably the electronic organs, and—of particular interest to composers—those designed to produce new timbres. Among the latter Leon Theremin's Thereminvox (Theremin), or Etherophone (1920), Maurice Martenot's ondes Martenot (1928), Friedrich Trautwein's Trautonium (1930), and the later Mixturtrautonium of Oskar Sala (1952) have been widely used; composers of the stature of Richard Strauss, Hindemith, Honegger, Milhaud, Messiaen, André Jolivet, Edgard Varèse, and Bohuslav Martinů have written for one or more of these instruments. Others of this type include Jörg Mager's Sphärophon (1926), Bruno Helberger's and Peter Lertes' Hellertion (1928), and N. Langer's and J. Halmagyi's Emicon (1930). Among the electronic organs three basic systems of tone-generation are noteworthy: the use of rotating electromagnetic generators as in the Hammond organ (1935), the use of rotating electrostatic generators as in the Compton electrone (1932), and the transformation of light into sound by a photoelectric cell as in the Organova.

tape music The next stage dates from the discovery of magnetic tape recording techniques and their refinement, especially during and after World War II (*see* RECORDING). These techniques enable the composer to record any sounds whatever on tape and then to manipulate the tape to achieve desired effects (tape music). Recorded sounds can be superimposed upon each other (mixed), altered in timbre by means of filters, or reverberated. Dynamic levels can be changed. Repeated sound-patterns can be created by means of circular strands of tape (loops). By changing the speed of the tape, extreme variations in register can be effected, and with certain equipment tape speed can be changed without altering pitch. Attack-and-decay patterns (*see* ENVELOPE) of recorded sounds can likewise be altered. By playing the tape backward attack-and-decay patterns can be reversed. Splicing can also be employed to alter these patterns (*e.g.,* by reducing attack to zero) as well as to achieve striking juxtapositions of sounds. Thus the composer can exercise precise control over every aspect of his original sound material.

Although Hindemith, Ernst Toch, and others had experimented with it previously, the development of tape music began in earnest in 1948 with the work of Pierre Schaeffer and his associates at the Club d'Essai in Paris under the auspices of Radiodiffusion Française. They called their creations MUSIQUE CONCRÈTE—a term emphasizing their choice of a variety of natural sounds as raw material. These sounds were put together (or "composed"), altered, or distorted to form a unified artistic whole. The *Symphonie pour un homme seul* by Schaeffer and his collaborator Pierre Henry in 1949–50 is one of the landmarks of *musique concrète,* for it laid the technical and aesthetic foundations for much of the later tape music.

In 1951 a studio for *elektronische Musik* was founded at Cologne by Herbert Eimert, Werner Meyer-Eppler, and others under the auspices of the Nordwest Deutsche Rundfunk. While the composers associated with this studio used many of the same techniques of tape manipulation as did the French group, they favored synthetic rather than natural sound sources. In particular they utilized simple sine-wave signals, or pure tones (*i.e.,* tones without overtones), as raw material for the formation of complex sounds. Certain compositions of Stockhausen, such as the *Gesang der Jünglinge,* are illustrative of the resources available in the Cologne studio. The notation of electronic music is not standardized and is seldom published, as the magnetic tape upon which the music is recorded and stored constitutes a relatively permanent record.

Subsequently studios for the production of electronic music were established throughout the world. Among the earliest were those in Milan (1953), Tokyo (1955), Rome, Warsaw, Brussels, Delft, and Tel Aviv (all in 1957), and Toronto (1959). Other studios were established in the 1950s and '60s in Baden-Baden, Berlin, Copenhagen, Darmstadt, Geneva, Helsinki, London, Munich, Stockholm, Utrecht, and many other places, including certain universities in the United States—notably Columbia-Princeton (in partnership), Yale, Illinois, Michigan, and Pennsylvania.

music synthesizer   The third stage of development was marked by the construction of the RCA Electronic Music Synthesizer by Harry Olson and Herbert Belar at the Radio Corporation of America laboratories at Princeton, New Jersey. This machine was introduced in 1955; an enlarged and modified version (Mark II) was constructed and installed in the Columbia-Princeton Electronic Music Center in New York City in 1959. The Mark II, which outwardly resembles a large computer, has panel controls grouped as follows: (1) transposers, decibel meter, oscilloscope, and frequency counter; (2) tone and noise generators and mixer for additive synthesis; (3) programming input (two panels); (4) other mixing equipment; (5) timbre control: filters, resonators, and compensators (three panels); and (6) tape recording.

The synthesizer is capable of producing by electronic means tones of any desired frequency, intensity, duration, rate of attack and decay, timbre, or degree of vibrato. Such tones can be played by the machine at any rate of speed or in any desired rhythmic patterns, including those that would be physically impossible for a human performer. In addition to "additive synthesis"—the method employed earlier at Cologne and elsewhere wherein complex tones are built up by the superimposition of sine-wave signals—the synthesizer is also capable of subtractive synthesis wherein sawtooth-wave signals (containing fundamentals and all their related overtones) are generated and modified by resonation or attenuation to achieve the desired tone-spectrum. Noise or aperiodic sounds of any kind can also be produced by the generation and modification of WHITE NOISE. Furthermore prerecorded sounds can be fed into the machine and modified as in *musique concrète.* The composer specifies the properties of the desired sounds through programming input in the form of binary code instructions punched on paper tape. At any time during the programming process, the composer may aurally test any sound before permanently coding it by calling for production of the sound and then listening to it over a loudspeaker. When programmed the machine then plays the specified sounds by recording them directly on magnetic tape for future performance through amplifiers.

The music synthesizer is capable of producing virtually any sound or combination of sounds; it is limited only by the composer's ability to specify such sounds in terms of the coded input and by the thresholds of aural perception. Theoretically it could duplicate with perfect precision the sounds of conventional instruments, but in practice it has been employed chiefly for new effects not possible of achievement by any other means. The works composed on this machine by Milton Babbitt and several others are among the important contributions to the expanding repertoire of electronic music.

computers as musical instruments The most recent stage of development involves the use of computers for both the composition and synthesis of music and for musical research. An early example of COMPUTER MUSIC is the *Illiac* Suite for string quartet, done by the Illiac high-speed digital computer at the University of Illinois in 1957. The computer was programmed to generate random integers representing pitches and note-values. These integers were screened by programming instructions based on traditional rules of composition; *i.e.,* the computer was told to compose in certain prescribed styles. The computer output was then transcribed into conventional musical notation. Subsequent and continuing experiments of this type have thrown light on the nature of the compositional process itself.

Of greater importance for the future of music, however, is the direct synthesis of sound by computers first described in 1963 by Max V. Mathews and co-workers at the Bell Telephone Laboratories (BTL). The BTL system employs an IBM 7094 computer; the program (score) consists of a deck of punched cards.

Following the development of the BTL process, further progress in computer-generated music was made at Princeton University, the University of Illinois, the Massachusetts Institute of Technology, and elsewhere.

problems and prospects It can be seen that electronic science has brought about a tremendous expansion of musical resources. It has made available to the composer a spectrum of sounds ranging from pure tones at one extreme to the most complex noises at the other. It has made possible the rhythmic organiza-

tion of music to a degree of subtlety and complexity hitherto unattainable. One consequence has been the wide acceptance of a new definition of music as organized sound—a concept that has important implications for the future. Of equal import is the direct control the composer of electronic music now has over his own work. Except for certain compositions by Henk Badings, Berio, Karl-Birger Blomdahl, and others, which are composed for performers with an electronic accompaniment, most electronic works eliminate the need for the performer as an interpreter and intermediary between the composer and his audience. The performance is accomplished by loudspeakers carefully distributed throughout the hall for optimum stereophonic effect: for example, Edgard Varèse' *Poème électronique,* commissioned for performance at the 1958 Brussels World's Fair, utilized 400 loudspeakers. The absence of performers places the audience in a new and unaccustomed relationship to the composer and his music. Moreover the usual absence of any form of notation places the critical listener in a problematic situation, as his analysis of what he hears must be carried out solely by ear.

Some composers, however, have used the new electronic technology to add an extra dimension to the conventional performance format. In his set of *Synchronisms* (1963–70), for example, Mario Davidovsky weds one or more "live" instrumental performers with a prerecorded score on tape. Milton Babbitt, as well, has demonstrated with telling effect how poetically the human voice and a synthesized score can be melded in his setting of Dylan Thomas' *Vision and Prayer* (1961).

Some observers have felt that the elimination of the performer as interpreter, while it may enable the composer to realize perfectly his intentions, is nevertheless a serious loss. Performance, it is argued, is a creative discipline complementary to that of composition itself, and varieties of interpretation add richness to the musical experience; moreover the physical presence of the performer infuses drama into what would be otherwise a purely aural, intellectual, and, by implication, somewhat lifeless event. But in fact certain developments in 20th-century music, such as JAZZ and ALEATORY MUSIC, have given the performer a role of freedom and responsibility unprecedented in Western musical tradition.

The most urgent problems arising from recent advances in electronic music lie in the field of psychoacoustics. These have to do with determining the limits of aural perception. With virtually limitless musical resources at his command, the composer is confronted with the necessity of choosing those that are aurally meaningful and rejecting those that are not. In order to do so much more must be learned about hearing in general and about the perception of music in particular than is known at the present time. Cooperative experimentation by musicians, acoustical engineers, psychologists, and other scientists is crucial—not only within the domain of electronic music but outside it as well.

BIBLIOGRAPHY: Music—John Cage, *Silence* (1961); Lowell Cross, *Bibliography of Electronic Music* (1967); Iannis Xenakis, *Formalized Music: Thought and Mathematics in Music* (1971); Herbert Russcol, *The Liberation of Sound: An Introduction to Electronic Music* (1972); Gilbert Trythall, *Principles and Practice of Electronic Music* (1973); Jon Appleton and Ronald C. Perera, eds., *The Development and Practice of Electronic Music*

(1975); Hubert S. Howe, Jr., *Electronic Music Synthesis* (1975); Elliott Schwartz, ed., *Electronic Music: A Listener's Guide* (1975); Herbert Deutsch, *Synthesis: An Introduction to the History, Theory, and Practice of Electronic Music* (1976). Instruments—Alan L. Douglas, *The Electrical Production of Music* (1957) and *The Electronic Musical Instrument Manual: A Guide to Theory and Design,* 4th ed. (1961); Richard H. Dorf, *Electronic Musical Instruments,* 3rd ed. (1968).

electronic organ A keyboard instrument that produces its sound by means of electricity. Meant to serve as an economical and compact substitute for the pipe organ, the electronic organ in size and general shape resembles a spinet, or upright, piano. Most instruments rely upon electronic oscillators (circuits carrying an alternating current at a specific frequency) to produce their sound. One of the earliest (1935) and best known, however, is the Hammond organ, which originally produced its sound through rotary, motor-driven generators that produced alternating current at frequencies matching tones of the tempered chromatic scale. By means of a series of controls, a variety of timbres could be reproduced that to some degree imitated the sounds of

model of Hammond electronic organ, 1937–75
courtesy, Hammond Organ Company

other instruments. *See* ELECTRONIC MUSIC.

electrophone A class of instruments in which the initial sound is produced by electronic means or is conventionally produced (as by a vibrating string) and electronically amplified. Electronically amplified instruments include guitars, pianos, violins, etc. Instruments using electronic means of generating sound include the theremin, ondes Martenot, electronic organ, and music synthesizer. *Compare* AEROPHONE; CHORDOPHONE; IDIOPHONE; MEMBRANOPHONE.

Elegy for Young Lovers: *see* HENZE; OPERA (the 20th century).

Elektra: *see* BASSET HORN; COUNTERPOINT (modern period); LIBRETTO (19th-century influences); OPERA (the 20th century); ROMANTIC PERIOD (20th-century transition); STRAUSS, RICHARD.

Elgar, Edward (William) (June 2, 1857–February 23, 1934) The foremost English composer at the beginning of the 20th century, Edward Elgar was born at Broadheath near Worcester, the son of a music dealer and organist. Leaving school at the age of 15, Elgar worked for a few months in a lawyer's office, but his talent clearly lay in music; he played the violin, bassoon, and organ and made an early start as a composer. Local conducting appointments and a position as organist of St. George's Roman Catholic Church afforded opportunities to hear his own works. An indefatigable student, Elgar invested his early savings in a visit to Leipzig (1883) and in violin lessons in London. In 1883 his Intermezzo *Mauresque* was well received in Birmingham.

After his marriage to Caroline Alice Roberts in 1889, he moved to London in the hope of gaining notice, but, although he published minor pieces such as *Salut d'Amour,* the move was unproductive, and in 1891 the Elgars returned to Worcestershire. Almost immediately larger works began to make an impression, at least in the Midlands, where choral societies were eager for new scores. Among these works were *The Black Knight* (Worcester, 1893), *Lux Christi* (Worcester, 1896), and *King Olaf* (Hanley, 1896). *King Olaf* was performed at the Crystal Palace in 1897, and in the same year the *Imperial* March gave evidence that a new and distinctive talent had arrived. In 1898 *Caractacus,* dedicated to Queen Victoria, was warmly received, and Elgar commented that an article in *The Musical Standard* had given "me the place I've fought for."

Caractacus was followed by the *Enigma* Variations (1899); *Sea Pictures* (1899); *The Dream of Gerontius* (1900); the overture *Cockaigne* (1901); and the first two *Pomp and Circumstance* marches (1901). In 1902 a performance in Düsseldorf of *Gerontius*—unsuccessful at its first Birmingham performance—drew praise from Richard Strauss, who said that "with that work England for the first time became one of the modern musical states."

Elgar was the favorite composer of King Edward VII, and acknowledgment of his national standing came in the form of honorary degrees and a knighthood in 1904. Among other compositions of this period were the oratorio *The Apostles* (1903), the overture *In the South* (1904), and the third *Pomp and Circumstance* march (1905). In spite of the success of his works—which he conducted both in England and abroad—and the prolificacy of his pen, Elgar was relatively poor. Thus, against his inclinations, he accepted a new chair of music in Birmingham University in 1904. The professorship brought many difficulties, and Elgar, whose health was rarely good, relinquished to Granville Bantock in 1908.

In 1906 *The Kingdom,* sequel to *The Apostles* and the second part of an unfinished trilogy, was performed in Birmingham; in 1908 the Symphony in A-flat Major was given in Manchester, and in 1910 the Violin Concerto was first performed by Fritz Kreisler. The Second Symphony (1911) was a tribute to Edward VII, and the same year Elgar wrote the music for the coronation of George V. Before the outbreak of World War I the symphonic study *Falstaff* was produced at Leeds (1913).

During the war Elgar wrote some occasional pieces, of which *The Spirit of England* (1916–17) contains the best music. After the war came a violin sonata and string quartet (1918) and a piano quintet and cello concerto (1919). The death of Lady Elgar in 1920 was a blow from which Sir Edward never fully recovered. As Master of the King's Musick (from 1924) he wrote further occasional pieces, but he preferred a quiet, semiretired life in Worcestershire. Friendship with George Bernard Shaw, however, stimulated in Elgar a late desire to compose, and at his death he left unfinished a third symphony, a piano concerto, and an opera based on Ben Jonson's *The Devil Is an Ass.* A memorial window in Worcester Cathedral recalls Elgar's long association with the city and the Three Choirs Festival.

One of the last of the Romantic composers, Elgar's fame rests on bold tunes—some have the force of folk music—striking color effects, and a massive sense of structure. But like Schumann, whom he admired, he reveals an acute sensitivity, which may also be found in his prose writings.

BIBLIOGRAPHY: William H. Reed, *Elgar* (1939; reprint, 1949); Michael Kennedy, *Portrait of Elgar* (1968) and *Elgar Orchestral Music* (1971); Ian Parrott, *Elgar* (1971); Jerrold Moore, *Elgar, a Life in Photographs* (1972) and *Elgar on Record: The Composer and the Gramophone* (1975); Ernest Newman, *Elgar* (1976).

RECORDINGS: Numerous recordings of many works.

Elijah: *see* MENDELSSOHN; ORATORIO (late 19th century).

Elisir d'amore, L': *see* DONIZETTI.

Ellington, Edward "Duke": *see* CHURCH MUSIC; JAZZ (origin and early development) and (orchestral style); POPULAR MUSIC (the 20th century).

Ellis, Osian (Gwynn) (b. February 8, 1928)   Educated at the Royal College of Music and the Royal Academy of Music in London, the Welsh harpist Osian Ellis plays principal harp with the London Symphony and is a member of the London-based Melos Ensemble. A popular recitalist, he has premiered and recorded many works by Britten (Britten composed Harp Suite in C Major for Ellis in 1969). He has done extensive radio and television broadcasting and won the Grand Prix du Disque for his recordings of the harp concertos of Handel. His film, *The Harp,* won

the Paris prize. Ellis was made a Commander of the British Empire in 1971.

Elman, Mischa (January 20, 1891–April 5, 1967)   An exponent of the Romantic tradition, Russian violinist Mischa Elman studied with Leopold Auer at the Imperial Conservatory in St. Petersburg. He came to the United States in 1908, made annual tours, and became a U.S. citizen in 1923. He was known for his especially resonant tone, and he played a Stradivarius that once belonged to Joachim. He arranged Romantic works, primarily of Schumann and Beethoven, for violin and piano.

embellishment: *see* ORNAMENTATION.

Emperor Concerto (Fifth); *see* BEETHOVEN (approaching deafness); CADENZA; MENDELSSOHN.

empfindsamer Stil   An important movement in North German instrumental music in the second half of the 18th century characterized by an emphasis on deeply felt emotions (from the German for sensitive style). This aesthetic, somewhat opposed to the polished style galant (*see* GALLANT STYLE) of the contemporary French music, is typical of an age much given to the open expression of sentiment not only in art but in everyday life.

Closely allied with sensitivity was the desire for simplicity and naturalness, qualities highly prized in the philosophical outlook of the Enlightenment. Composers wanted to increase the effect of their music by imbuing each theme with a well-defined, even exaggerated, expressive character. Because the effect seemed to be considerably intensified by rapid changes of mood, phrases and sections of highly contrasting moods were placed in close juxtaposition. This changeability of mood marked the main difference between the Baroque "doctrine of affects" and the Classical *empfindsamer Stil:* in the Baroque a single mood, or affection, ruled and unified an entire piece of movement.

The most significant representatives of the *empfindsamer Stil* were Carl Philipp Emanuel Bach, Johann Joachim Quantz, Wilhelm Friedemann Bach, and Georg Benda.

Enesco (Enescu), Georges (August 19, 1881–May 4, 1955)   The Romanian violinist, composer, and conductor Georges Enesco was known for his interpretations of Bach and his works in a Romanian national style. At age seven he entered the Vienna Conservatory, where he studied violin with Joseph Hellmesberger, Jr. In 1894 he became acquainted with Brahms, whose formal symphonic developments he later took as a model, and in 1895 he went to Paris, where he studied composition with Massenet and Fauré and violin with Martin Marsick. His *Poème roumain* was played in Paris (1897), and in 1899 he won the first prize for violin at the Conservatoire; he then began his career as a virtuoso violinist.

Though Enesco spent most of his life in France, his music shows little French influence. His chamber works include three violin sonatas, the last "in the popular Romanian style," three piano sonatas, and two string quartets. Among his orchestral works are three symphonies, two *Romanian* Rhapsodies and an overture on Romanian folk themes. National themes are also used in his opera *Oedipe* on a libretto by Edmond Fleg adapted from Sophocles (Paris Opéra, 1936). In his later years he became the leader of the Romanian school of composers. He was also respected as a violin teacher; Yehudi Menuhin was one of his outstanding pupils.

RECORDINGS: Cantabile e presto for flute and piano; *Romanian* Rhapsodies (2); Violin Sonata No. 3; songs.

Enfance du Christ, L': *see* BERLIOZ; ORATORIO (late 19th century).

Enfant prodigue, L': *see* BALLET (Diaghiler Ballet); DEBUSSY; PROKOFIEV.

English horn or **cor anglais** A woodwind instrument of the

English horn
(shown without mouthpiece)
courtesy, T. W. Howarth & Co.,
London

oboe family pitched a fifth below the ordinary OBOE. It has a bulbous bell and at the top end a bent metal crook on which the double reed is placed. It is pitched in F, being written a fifth higher than it sounds, and its compass is from the E below middle C to the second E above. The name first appeared in Vienna about 1760; cor refers to the curved or hornlike shape it then had, but anglais remains a mystery. The curved form, which survived locally to 1900, was nearly identical to the 18th-century *oboe da caccia* and is now sometimes used for Bach's parts for that instrument. The English horn was also built in angular form. The modern straight form was first exhibited in 1839 by Henri Brod of Paris. The English horn appears in many Romantic works, notably those of Berlioz, Franck, Wagner, and Dvořák.

English Suites: *see* FUGUE (Bach); SUITE.

enharmonic In the system of equally tempered tuning used on keyboard instruments, two tones or intervals that sound the same but are notated differently; for example, C♯ or D♭ (enharmonic tones) or C-F♯ and C-G♭ (enharmonic intervals). The different notations indicate the key to which the tone or interval belongs. Enharmonic tones and intervals often serve as pivots in modulation. In the example the same chord of the diminished seventh belongs respectively to the keys of C, A, F♯ and D♯:

In earlier systems of tuning such as just intonation and meantone tuning, the pitch of enharmonic tones was not identical; C♯ then sounded slightly lower than D♭ by about one-fifth of a tone. While the piano, harpsichord, and other fixed-pitch, equally tempered instruments cannot maintain this distinction, singers and violinists frequently do. Enharmonic in ancient Greek music referred to the tetrachord, or four-note series, containing intervals of less than a semitone.

Enigma Variations: *see* ELGAR; VARIATIONS.

Entführung aus dem Serail, Die: *see* ABDUCTION FROM THE SERAGLIO, THE.

envelope The growth, duration, and decay of a sound. Growth consists of the attack, or onset, of a sound and its rate of growth to steady-state intensity. Duration is the steady state of a sound at its maximum intensity, and decay is the rate at which it fades to silence. Envelope is an important element of timbre, the distinctive quality, or tone color, of a sound. Every musical instrument has its characteristic attack, duration, and decay pattern.

equal temperament: *see* TUNING AND TEMPERAMENT.

Erdödy Quartets: *see* HAYDN (achievement).

Erlkönig: *see* BALLAD; SCHUBERT (years of promise) and (maturity).

Ernani: *see* VERDI.

Ernst, Heinrich Wilhelm (May 6, 1814–October 8, 1865) Educated in violin and composition at the Vienna Conservatory, the Moravian violinist Heinrich Ernst made his first concert tour at age 16. He continued to tour the Continent and England until retirement in London in 1855. He patterned his style after the technical brilliance and emotional depth of Paganini.

Eroica Symphony (Third): *see* BEETHOVEN (approaching deafness), (achievement), and (structural innovations); HARMONY (classical key relationships); PROGRAM MUSIC (problem of form); ROMANTIC PERIOD (Wagnerian development); SYMPHONY (Haydn, Mozart, and Beethoven); VARIATIONS.

Erwartung: *see* MODERN PERIOD (disintegration of tonality); OPERA (the 20th century); SCHOENBERG.

Eschenbach, Christoph (b. February 20, 1940) Educated also as a violinist and conductor, the German pianist Christoph Eschenbach studied at the German conservatories of Cologne and Hamburg. After touring Europe, he made his U.S. debut as soloist with the Cleveland Orchestra in 1969. Recordings include the complete sonatas of Mozart, sonatas and chamber music of Schubert, Chopin, and Hans Werner Henze.

Essipoff, Annette, originally Anna Nikolayevna Essipova (February 13, 1851–August 18, 1914) A pupil and wife (1880–92) of Leschetizky, the Russian pianist and teacher Annette Essipoff was world renowned and known for her singing tone and, in the words of the critic George Bernard Shaw, her "terrible precision . . . , miraculous speed . . . , [and] grace and finesse . . . ," the antithesis of her contemporary Teresa Carreño. She was professor of piano at the St. Petersburg Conservatory from 1893, teaching such musicians as Prokofiev.

estampie (Provençal, *estampida*) A courtly dance of the 12th-14th centuries. Mentioned in trouvère poetry, it was probably danced with sliding steps by couples to the music of *vielles* (medieval fiddles); its afterdance was the saltarello. In musical form the estampie derives from the sequence, a medieval genre of Latin hymn. Like the sequence it has a series of repeated melodic phrases (*aa, bb, cc,* etc.); phrase endings in the repetitions are often varied.

Estampies are among the earliest surviving examples of written instrumental music. The famous troubadour song "Kalenda maya" (probably by Raimbaut de Vaqueiras, died 1207) is a poem set to an existing estampie. Whether the estampie was identical with, or merely related to, the *stantipes,* a dance mentioned in the 13th century, is debated by scholars.

Esther: *see* HANDEL (life) and (works); ORATORIO (Handel).

ethnomusicology The scientific study of music in terms of its sounds and performance practice in relation to a specific culture and in comparison with other cultures. The field was originally called comparative MUSICOLOGY by scholars concerned with the measurement of pitches, anthropological data, museum archiving, or the study of exotic music. Jaap Kunst, a Dutch expert in Indonesian music, created the term ethnomusicology in the 1930s; in 1956 an ethnomusicology society was founded, consisting of musicians and anthropologists interested in world music. The field has expanded so that such topics as Japanese art music, New Guinean tribal music,

African court music, English folk songs, jazz, and the social and financial structure of European-American popular music can be found in its studies.

BIBLIOGRAPHY: Curt Sachs, *The Wellsprings of Music* (1962; reprint, 1977); Alan P. Merriam, *The Anthropology of Music* (1964); Bruno Nettl, *Theory and Method in Ethnomusicology* (1964) and with Charles E. Hamm and Ronald Byrnside, *Contemporary Music and Music Cultures* (1975); Mantle Hood, *Ethnomusicologist* (1971); John Blacking, *How Musical Is Man?* (1973); Jaap Kunst, *Ethnomusicology,* rev. ed. (1974); John Greenway, *Ethnomusicology* (1976).

étude   The French term in common use for a musical study. The étude was primarily designed to exercise the player, usually of a keyboard instrument, in a technical problem. Works of this kind are also known as lessons (notably those of Purcell and Handel), *Essercizi* (the original name of the harpsichord sonatas of Domenico Scarlatti), or *studien* (e.g., the *Charakteristische Studien* of Ignaz Moscheles). Études fall into two main classes. They may either serve as technical exercises, such as the studies of Czerny, Clementi, John Baptist Cramer, and Brahms for piano and Rodolphe Kreutzer, Pierre Rode, and Paganini for violin; or they may far transcend this function, as in the Études of Chopin, Études *d'exécution transcendantes* of Liszt, Études *symphoniques* of Schumann, and Twelve Études of Debussy, in which a technical problem itself provides a composer's inspiration.

Études symphoniques: *see* ÉTUDE; SCHUMANN, ROBERT (early career); VARIATIONS.

Eugene Onegin: *see* OPERA (the 19th century); TCHAIKOVSKY (later life and works).

euphonium   A valved brass wind instrument pitched in B-flat an octave below the cornet and trumpet with a wide tubalike bore and often in the United States with the bell turned forward. It is similar to the BARITONE but with a wider bore and consequently a broader sound. In military and brass bands it is the leading instrument in the tenor-bass range with a role corresponding to that of the cello in the orchestra. It normally carries a fourth

euphonium   *courtesy, C. G. Conn, Ltd.*

valve in addition to the essential three in order to take the compass continuously down to the fundamental pitches below the bass staff, from which the total compass rises to the middle of the treble staff. Its notation is in the bass clef at actual pitch in military bands and in the treble clef a ninth above actual sounds in brass bands. In duplex models an alternative bell is fitted; it is switched in by a valve to supply a lighter, tenor-horn tone quality. French composers sometimes use it in place of the tuba, as in Ravel's orchestration of Mussorgsky's *Pictures at an Exhibition.*

Euridice, L': *see* BAROQUE ERA; CACCINI; OPERA (beginnings); PERI.

Euryanthe: *see* LEITMOTIV; LIBRETTO (19th-century influences); OPERA (the 19th century); WEBER.

Evans, Geraint (b. February 16, 1922)   After study in Cardiff (Wales) and Hamburg (Germany), the Welsh baritone Geraint Evans made his debut in 1948 at Covent Garden as the night watchman in Wagner's *Die Meistersinger.* He sang regularly at Covent Garden and at the Glyndebourne Festival and annually at the Metropolitan Opera from 1963, when he made his debut there as Verdi's Falstaff. Evans is particularly admired for his interpretations of Mozart and Britten operas. Recordings of complete operas include Mozart's *Don Giovanni,* Verdi's *Falstaff* and *La Forza del Destino,* and Wagner's *Die Meistersinger.* He was knighted in 1969.

exposition In SONATA form, the first section with modulation to a new key and statement of the main themes. The new key is often the dominant or, in works in minor keys, the relative major, and most often new and contrasted themes are associated with the new key.

In a fugue the exposition is the statement of the subject in each of the voices.

expression The part of a musical performance that is something more than mere notes. Western music is notated on a system designed to specify the pitch and relative length of the notes to be performed. Factors such as tempo and dynamics can be indicated only by words or commonly accepted abbreviations of them; technical directions to the performer, often with very particular musical consequences, are mostly expressible only by words. The finer musical points are even more difficult to indicate and must eventually stem from the performer or from a familiar performance tradition.

In European music before the 19th century, as in Oriental music and mid-20th-century jazz, the performer's share of the responsibility included not only the nuances but often the notes themselves. In much music of the 17th and early 18th centuries, it was usual for the composer to notate the main structural notes of the solo part and leave it to the performer to improvise the ornamental figuration. In all movements the performer was expected to introduce specific ornaments such as trills, appoggiaturas, etc., and in many cases to modify the notated rhythms. Similarly the accompanist, provided with a FIGURED BASS line with few specific indications of what to play, was expected to provide the correct style of accompaniment for the piece being performed. Clues to this correct style were provided in many ways, ranging from the title to the tempo indication and kind of note values employed.

Instructions for the speed (tempo) of a performance have the longest history. As early as the 9th century the signs "c" *(celeriter,* "quick") and "t" *(trahere,* "slow") are to be found in plainchant manuscripts. Such indications were exceptional as the repertoire was limited and well known to the performers; the written source was used purely for reference purposes. Not until the 16th century were there frequent directions for tempo and these mostly in collections containing a wide variety of musical forms and styles, such as the vihuela (guitar-shaped lute) publications of Luis Milán (1536) and Luis de Narvaez (1538) or the lute books of Hans Newsidler. These directions were often long-winded and elaborate but led to the initiation of more methodical tempo indications, first of all by means of defining the type of piece to be performed. Thus pavane indicated a type of dance and also that it was to be played in a stately and subdued fashion. In the 18th century allemande, gavotte, or courante, all gave precise information as to the speed and style of performance. In the 17th century began the use of Italian terms that have been used ever since. Again their meaning for the musician is oblique; any Italian dictionary can give the literal meanings, but for musical purposes allegro means "gay" and therefore "fast," allegretto, etymologically its diminutive, is a direction for a slightly slower speed. The whole list of these terms is to some extent imprecise, but a rough hierarchical list starting from the slowest would run: adagissimo, adagio, lento, andante, andantino, allegretto, allegro, presto, prestissimo.

Dynamics are expressed more simply and directly. Giovanni Gabrieli (1557–1612) is renowned for having written piano and forte in some of his scores. The words became the basis of a system that runs: pianissimo (pp), piano (p), mezzo-piano (mp), mezzo-forte (mf), forte (f), fortissimo (ff), with extensions at either end *(e.g.,* piano-pianissimo, ppp).

Sforzato (sfz) means a sudden sharp accent, and sforzando (sf) is a slight modification of this. Increases and decreases are indicated in graphic manner as < and > but also written as crescendo and diminuendo.

The more technical indications to the performer, though often in Italian, frequently appear in some other language. These include the insertion or removal of mutes (con sordino; senza sordino), the retuning of a string (scordatura), raising the bell of a wind instrument into the air (mostly in German music, thus *Schalltrichter auf!),* and many others whose meanings are usually clear and precise.

Musical expression proper is difficult to indicate directly. *Mit Empfindung, espressivo, expressif* are to be found in abundance in late 19th-century scores, and similar indications are mostly self-explanatory though few so inventive as Elgar's *Moglio* (in the Violin Concerto), which is in fact the name of an Italian town that had caught his fancy.

Although many composers, particularly in the 20th century, have preferred to put indications of expression into their scores in their own language, Italian is the predominant language for all indications to the performer if only because this vocabulary is known throughout the world and taught to every musician with the basic principles of notation.

BIBLIOGRAPHY: Rosamund E. M. Harding, *Origins of Musical Time and Expression* (1938); Frederick Dorian, *History of Music in Performance* (1942; reprint, 1966); Thurston Dart, *The Interpretation of Music* (1954; reprint, 1969); Edward T. Cone, *Musical Form and Musical Performance* (1968); Robert Donnington, *The Interpretation of Early Music,* rev. ed. (1974).

expressionism A movement in painting, sculpture, and literature (roughly 1905–30) with its parallel in music that has been defined as the opposite of Impressionism. It has come to refer primarily to the group of painters who exhibited in Germany just before World War I, with Wassily Kandinsky and Paul Klee as the greatest exponents to emerge from the group, and their literary counterparts, the playwrights August Strindberg and Frank Wedekind. Schoenberg contributed painting and poetry as well as music to the movement, and the term as applied to music now usually refers to Schoenberg and Berg and to some extent Webern.

F

faburden: *see* FAUX-BOURDON.

Fairy Queen, The: *see* OPERA (beginnings); PURCELL.

Falla, Manuel de (November 23, 1876–November 14, 1946)   The most distinguished Spanish composer of the early 20th century, Manuel de Falla achieved a fusion of poetry, asceticism, and ardor that represents the spirit of Spain at its purest.

Falla took piano lessons from his mother and later went to Madrid to continue piano and to study composition with Felipe Pedrell, who inspired him with his own enthusiasm for 16th-century Spanish church music, folk music, and native opera. In 1905 Falla won two prizes, one for piano playing and the other for a national opera, *La vida breve* ("The Short Life").

In 1907 he moved to Paris, where he met Debussy, Paul Dukas, and Ravel (whose orchestration influenced his own) and published his first piano pieces and songs. In 1914 he returned to Madrid, where he wrote the music for a ballet, *El amor brujo* (Madrid, 1915; "Love, the Magician"), remarkable for its distillation of Andalusian folk music. Falla followed this with *El corregidor y la molinera* (Madrid, 1917; "The Governor and the Miller"), which Sergey Diaghilev persuaded him to rescore for a ballet by Léonide Massine called *El sombrero de tres picos* (London, 1919; *The Three-Cornered Hat). Noches en los jardines de España* (Madrid, 1916; *Nights in the Gardens of Spain*), a suite of three impressions for piano and orchestra, evoked the Andalusian atmosphere through erotic and suggestive orchestration. All these works established Falla internationally as the leading Spanish composer.

Falla then retired to Granada, where in 1922 he organized a *cante hondo* festival and composed a puppet opera, *El retablo de Maese Pedro* ("Master Peter's Puppet Show"). Like the subsequent Harpsichord Concerto (1926), containing echoes of Domenico Scarlatti, the *Retablo* shows Falla much influenced by Stravinsky. Falla's style had become neoclassical instead of Romantic—still essentially Spanish but Castilian rather than Andalusian. After 1926 he wrote little, living first in Mallorca and from 1939 in Argentina, where he worked fitfully on a cantata, *L'Atlántida* (completed after his death by a pupil). Falla's writings on music were published as *Escritos sobre música y músicos* (1950; *On Music and Musicians,* 1979).

BIBLIOGRAPHY: John B. Trend, *Manuel de Falla and Spanish Music* (1929; reprint, 1934); Jaime Pahissa, *Manuel de Falla: His Life and Works* (1954).

RECORDINGS: *El amor brujo;* Concerto for harpsichord, flute, oboe, clarinet, violin, and cello; Harpsichord Concerto; *Nights in the Gardens of Spain; Psyché* for voice, flute, harp, and string trio; *El retablo de Maese Pedro; Soneto a Córdoba* for voice and harp; *The Three-Cornered Hat; La vida breve;* piano pieces; songs.

falsobordone: *see* FAUX-BOURDON.

Falstaff: *see* BOITO; ELGAR; FUGUE (after Bach and Handel); LIBRETTO (19th-century influences); OPERA (the 19th century); PROGRAM MUSIC (problem of form); ROMANTIC PERIOD (non-German music of the 19th century); VERDI.

Fanciulla del West, La: *see* PUCCINI.

fandango An exuberant Spanish courtship dance and a genre of Spanish folk song. Probably of Moorish origin, the dance was popular in Europe in the 18th century and survives in the 20th century as a folk dance in Spain, Portugal, southern France, and Latin America. Danced by couples, it begins slowly with the rhythm marked by castanets, snapping fingers, and the stamping of feet; the speed gradually increases. The music is in $\frac{3}{4}$ or $\frac{6}{8}$ time.

As song the fandango consists of *coplas,* improvised satirical, religious, or romantic verses, sung to melodies improvised according

to set rules. Fandangos can be sung to accompany the dance or as solos.

Composers such as Gluck (ballet *Don Juan*), Mozart (*Le nozze di Figaro*), Rimsky-Korsakov *(Capriccio espagnol),* and Granados (*Goyescas* No. 3) have used the form.

fanfare A short instrumental work, usually for trumpets and timpani, employed for ceremonial purposes. The word is probably derived from the Arabic *anfár* ("trumpets"), which became altered in Spanish to *fanfarronada.* The usual association of fanfares with the military is suggested in J. H. Zedler's *Grosses Vollständiges Universal Lexicon,* which adds that "such pieces are played by trumpets and timpani, fifes and drums, and generally have little artistic merit."

Fanfares are essentially functional music and were often improvised by trumpeters with their ancillary kettledrummers. Court and military fanfares were intended to serve as signals, specifically for the purpose of attracting attention or communicating a basic command. Royal households, as well as military organizations, frequently had their own distinctive fanfares and could be identified by a particular flourish. The earliest surviving notated fanfares are the late 16th-century manuscript collections of trumpet music of Hendrick Lübeck and Magnus Thomsen, court trumpeters to Christian IV of Denmark. The traditional association of the fanfare with court and military ceremony led to its abundant use in Western art music and in the drama. Referred to by several names, such as sennet *(sonnada, Siegnate),* tucket (toccata), or *Aufzug,* fanfares occur whenever a composer or playwright needed a short distinctive composition of a ceremonial character.

In addition to the many Renaissance and Baroque compositions called "Battaglia," with their programmatic use of trumpet calls, there are numerous works with fanfare figures by composers from the 15th century on. The following works include distinctive fanfare subjects: Josquin des Prés, "Vive le Roy"; Monteverdi, Toccata from *L'Orfeo* (an expanded version is employed in the opening bars of the 1610 Vespers); Bach, *Christmas Oratorio* (initial chorus); Beethoven, *Leonore*

Overtures Nos. 2 and 3; Wagner, many brass fanfares in his operas, especially the guild fanfares from *Die Meistersinger;* Mahler, Fifth Symphony; Copland, *Fanfare for the Common Man;* William Walton, music for the film productions of Shakespeare's *Henry V, Hamlet,* and *Richard III.*

fantasia or **fantasy** (French, *fantaisie;* German, *Fantasie* or *Phantasie*) A piece of instrumental music in a form governed entirely by the composer's wishes. In the 16th and 17th centuries the term described a fugal type of composition for a consort of string or wind instruments or for solo keyboard instruments, lute, or guitar. From the earliest times fantasias have been used as vehicles for the elaboration of popular songs.

The one-movement fantasia, the earliest form, appeared at the beginning of the 16th century. It consisted of short sections expertly knit together and was based on one or more motives. In England the fantasia (also called fantasy or fancy) had a late flowering. Many of the English composers from Byrd to Purcell wrote fantasias for lute, keyboard instrument, or viols. The term *Fantasie* was used by 18th-century German organists to describe a keyboard piece of a free improvisatory character that provided the maximum possible contrast with the fugue that often followed.

This idea of freedom in form and the additional ingredient of extempore feeling persisted in the fantasias of Carl Philipp Emanuel Bach as well as in the works of certain composers of the Romantic period. Brahms in his *Fantasien,* Op. 116, and Schumann in his *Fantasiestücke* maintain the tradition of single, self-contained movements, although more modern works such as Schoenberg's Fantasia for violin and piano have something in common with the sectionalized forms of the Renaissance. Complex and contrapuntal fantasias inspired by J. S. Bach's name or his music have been written by Liszt, Max Reger, and Busoni. Some fantasias are in several movements and take on the aspect of free sonata form, as in Beethoven's two Sonatas, *quasi una fantasia,* Op. 27, and Schumann's Fantasy, Op. 17. Others have the character of program music, ranging from the fantasia on

the weather by John Munday (d. 1630) to Tchaikovsky's *Francesca da Rimini.*

From the earliest times fantasias have been used as musical vehicles for the elaboration of popular songs; *e.g.,* in the 16th century, Giles Farnaby's fantasia on one of his own madrigals, and later Schubert's *Wanderer Fantasie* and the potpourris on songs and arias by Liszt, Johann Nepomuk Hummel, and Ignaz Moscheles. Yet another aspect is apparent in the fantasias based on given themes, such as the popular hexachord fantasias of the 16th and 17th centuries; the consort music of Eustache du Courroy (1549–1609), drawing on both sacred and secular melodies; the *Choralfantasien* of Bach and his contemporaries; and Beethoven's *Choral* Fantasia, which uses the melody of one of the composer's songs as the theme for an elaborate set of variations. The early years of the 20th century saw an artificial revival of the English fancy in the so-called phantasy quartets of William Hurlstone, Frank Bridge, John Ireland, Thomas Dunhill, and Vaughan Williams.

farandole A Provençal and Catalan chain dance mentioned as early as the 14th century. According to tradition it was taken to Marseilles from Greece by Phoenician sailors. Performed on feast days, the farandole is danced by men and women who hold hands in a chain and follow the leader in a variety of steps to music in $\frac{6}{8}$ time on the pipe and tabor.

The dance of the French Revolution, the carmagnole, was a variety of farandole.

Farewell Symphony (No. 45): *see* HAYDN (Esterházy service); PROGRAM MUSIC (program symphony).

Farinelli, real name, Carlo Broschi (January 24, 1705–July 15, 1782) Perhaps the best known of the Baroque castrati, the Italian male soprano Farinelli studied in Naples and in 1724 began a series of successful engagements throughout Italy. His style was initially one of bravura but was later modified to one of simplicity, supposedly suggested during a tour of Vienna and a conversation with the Emperor Charles VI. In 1737 he went to Spain, where he remained for nearly 25 years under royal patronage, advised the king on affairs of state, and established an Italian opera theater. After the ascent of Charles III he returned to Italy for political reasons and spent the remainder of his life near Bologna, composing for harpsichord and viola d'amore.

Farnaby, Giles (*c.* 1565–1640) Giles Farnaby was an English composer of virginal music and madrigals. Sir John Hawkins (d. 1789) says that Farnaby came of the same family, originally of Truro, Cornwall, as the schoolmaster and scholar Thomas Farnaby, but it is not known whether he was born before or after they moved to London. Like his father he was a citizen of London and a member of the Joiner's Company; the fact that a cousin, Nicholas, was a virginal maker suggests that Giles's activity as a musician may have had the same beginning. This would also explain why the composer of one set of fresh but rather unimportant canzonets (1598) and a number of psalm settings should rank with the greatest keyboard composers of his day. Not that Farnaby was without academic training—he graduated as bachelor of music at Oxford university in 1592; but his marked disregard for the current conventions of written counterpoint points to the virginal player rather than the church-trained organist. Of the 54 pieces by him in the Fitzwilliam Virginal Book, the most individual are such short and intimate ones as "His Dream" and "His Rest," but his larger sets of variations exploit a vein of brilliant virtuosity scarcely inferior to that of John Bull.

His son Richard (born *c.* 1590) is represented by four pieces in the same collection.
RECORDINGS: Virginal pieces.

Farnam, (W.) Lynnwood (January 13, 1885–November 23, 1930) The Canadian-born organist Lynnwood Farnam won a scholarship to the Royal College of Music in London (1900–04), returning to Montreal, where he established his reputation. He served Emmanuel Church, Boston (1913–18), and the Church of the Holy Communion, New York City, where his renowned series of recitals set a new U.S. standard. He also taught at the Curtis Institute from 1927.

Farrant, Richard (*c.* 1530–1581) The earliest and most distinguished member of an English

musical family, Richard Farrant was a gentleman of the Chapel Royal from 1552 until his appointment in 1564 as master of the choristers at St. George's, Windsor. This post entailed the annual presentation of a play before the queen, and some of his music for these survives as well as anthems and a service. In 1569 he was reappointed to the Chapel Royal, retaining both posts until his death.

Farrar, Geraldine (February 28, 1882–March 11, 1967) A student of Lilli Lehmann in Berlin, the U.S. soprano Geraldine Farrar sang at the Imperial Opera there from 1901 to 1906, when she went to the Metropolitan Opera (New York City) as Juliette in Gounod's opera. She was prima donna there, where she regularly sang opposite Caruso, until 1922, when she retired except for occasional tours and recitals. Possessed of a broad repertoire, she was best known for Carmen and for the Puccini heroines. She wrote two autobiographical books, *Geraldine Farrar by Herself* (1916) and *Such Sweet Compulsion* (1938) and was one of the first opera stars to appear in films, of which she made 14.

Farrell, Eileen (b. February 13, 1920) A member of a traveling vaudeville family, the U.S. dramatic soprano Eileen Farrell sang on her own radio program, "Eileen Farrell Presents," from 1942 to 1946. She first appeared on the concert stage the following year and became known for concert performances of Maria in Berg's *Wozzeck* and for Cherubini's Medea. Her operatic debut (1956) in San Francisco as Leonora in Verdi's *Il Trovatore* was followed by appearances at the Chicago Lyric Opera and the Metropolitan Opera, where she made her debut in Gluck's *Alceste*. She was a member of the New York City-based Bach Aria Group, has included popular music in her repertoire (one of very few classical singers to do so without embarrassment to her listeners), and was an outstanding Wagnerian soprano.

Fauré, Gabriel-(Urbain) (May 12, 1845–November 4, 1924) A French composer and teacher who influenced the course of French music, Gabriel Fauré was born at Pamiers (Ariège). His musical gifts were early in evidence; when the Swiss composer and teacher Louis Niedermeyer heard the boy, he immediately accepted him as a pupil, foregoing the customary fees. He studied piano with Saint-Saëns, who introduced him to the music of Liszt and Wagner. While still a student Fauré published his first composition, *Trois Romances sans paroles* for piano. In 1896 Fauré was appointed organist at La Madeleine and professor of composition at the Paris Conservatoire, and in 1905 he succeeded Théodore Dubois as director of the Conservatoire, remaining in office until ill health and deafness obliged him to resign in 1920.

Fauré excelled as a songwriter of refinement and sensitivity and as a composer in every branch of chamber music. He wrote more than 100 songs, including the well-known "Après un rêve" (*c.* 1865) and "Les roses d'Ispahan" (1884), and the two song cycles *La Bonne Chanson* (1891–92) and *L'Horizon chimérique* (1922). Above all he enriched the literature of the piano with a number of highly original works, of which his 13 nocturnes, 13 barcarolles, and 5 impromptus are perhaps the most representative and best known. His contributions to chamber music occupied almost all the years of his creative life. He was not instinctively attracted to the theater as were so many of his contemporaries in France, but he wrote incidental music for several plays, including Maeterlinck's *Pélleas et Mélisande* (1898), as well as two so-called lyric dramas, *Prométhée* (1900) and *Pénélope* (1913). He wrote little for the orchestra, but a notable exception is the Requiem (1888) for solo voices, chorus, orchestra, and organ. Although it did not gain immediate popularity, it has since become one of the works for which Fauré is best remembered.

As a teacher Fauré had a great influence, and his composition classes were attended by almost every notable French composer of the next generation; Florent Schmitt, Ravel, Jean Jules Aimable Roger-Ducasse, Charles Koechlin, Boulanger, and Georges Enesco were among his students. His teaching was anything but academic, and he had little sympathy with the upholders of tradition for tradition's sake; under Fauré's direction the Conservatoire took on a new direction.

BIBLIOGRAPHY: Charles Koechlin, *Gabriel Fauré, 1845–1924,* (1945; reprint, 1976).

RECORDINGS: Numerous recordings of many works.

Faust: *see* GOUNOD; OPERA (the 19th century); PROGRAM MUSIC (problem of form); ROMANTIC PERIOD (non-German music of the 19th century); SPOHR.

Faust Symphony: *see* LISZT.

faux-bourdon A 15th-century French technique of adding two or three parts to a plain-chant melody. It was probably invented by Guillaume Dufay about 1428 in the communion of his *Missa Sancti Jacobi*. In this technique the upper parts moved in parallel fourths following the melodic line of the plainsong, while the lowest part, the faux-bourdon, sang an octave below the treble (a fifth below the middle part) at the beginning and end of each phrase and occasionally at other points, and elsewhere sang a series of sixths below the treble (thirds below the middle part):

It was customary to write only the outer parts of the faux-bourdon; the middle part was sung at sight in fourths below the treble.

The term in England was faburden. It occurs *c.* 1430, but there are many English pieces of the 14th century that use the parallel movement characteristic of the technique. From about 1460 English composers used the faburden not only for simple polyphonic treatment of such chants as hymns, processional psalms, and litanies but also as the basis for composition in more elaborate ways. The faburdens of the Magnificat tones, for example, were paraphrased and extended by ornamentation to serve as the tenor of large-scale settings for four or more voices. Similarly in the 16th century settings for organ of hymns and the Te Deum were often composed by writing contrapuntal figuration on the faburden, which could be put in any part of the texture.

In Italy and Spain a different method, called *falsobordone,* was adopted; it consisted of applying chordal polyphony for four or more voices to simple chants. Examples of this, which consisted essentially of chords in root position over a functional bass, may be found in the work of Tomás Luis de Victoria, Lodovico Viadana, and many other church composers of the 16th and early 17th centuries. Though some printed sets of *falsibordoni* were rather elaborate, the simpler style continued in use. It is well exemplified in the *Improperia* ("Reproaches" for Good Friday) by Palestrina and Victoria.

BIBLIOGRAPHY: Ernest Lorenz Trumble, *Fauxbourdon, an Historical Survey* (1959).

Fayrfax, Robert (April 23, 1464–October 24, 1521)   The English Tudor composer Robert Fayrfax was called by Anthony à Wood "the prime musician of the nation." Nothing is known of his career until 1497, when he was granted the first of a series of benefices for his services as a singer and composer. He is referred to as one of the "Gentlemen of the King's Chapel," a position he held until the year of his death. Since Chapel Royal duties were of an occasional nature, Fayrfax settled at St. Albans, Hertfordshire, where he directed the choir and played the organ at the abbey from 1498. He gained the degrees of bachelor and doctor of music at Cambridge and wrote the five-part motet *Aeterne laudis lilium* for Elizabeth of York, who visited St. Albans in 1502. The work submitted for his Cambridge doctorate was the Mass *O quam glorifica.*

Fayrfax was made a "poor knight" of Wind-sor in 1514 and so received an extra pension; his position was such that frequent requests were made for the provision of music destined for court entertainments. His greatest hour came in June 1520, when he was put in charge of the Chapel Royal musicians when they accompanied Henry VIII to his meeting with Francis I of France at the Field of Cloth of Gold.

The masses by Fayrfax are based on antiphons such as *Regali ex progenie, Tecum principium,* and *Allequio dulcis,* the first word of whose fifth line—"Albanus Domini laudans mirabile nomen"—gives the mass its title and shows it to be in honor of St. Alban. The music of Fayrfax, which was published by the American Institute of Musicology (1960), proves him eminently worthy of the praise bestowed on, him during his lifetime.

Feldman, Morton (b. January 12, 1926)   A student of Wallingford Riegger and Stefan Wolpe, the U.S. composer and lecturer Morton Feldman developed his principles of aesthetics in association with John Cage, Earle Brown, David Tudor, and Christian Wolff in the early 1950s. They experimented with alternative methods of musical notation and new sound relationships. *Projections* (1950–51; several pieces for diverse instruments) explores musical indeterminacy by giving each instrument freedom to select pitches within a given register and expresses duration by horizontal rectangles placed spatially over short lines marking the steady beat. The predominance of sound relationships over form is shown in *Marginal Intersection* (1951), with a soloist playing against an ensemble of indeterminate pitches and two electric oscillators generating very low and high frequencies. *The Swallows of Salangan* (1960) for chorus and 16 instruments has notated pitches but leaves the durations to the discretion of the performers. Since each block of pitch changes never occurs simultaneously, there are no rhythmic articulations. The effect is similar, though the method different, in *First Principles* (1966–67); definite changes in sonorities are concealed by irregular spacing, and cross-rhythms are blurred by the extreme length of the durations. Feldman favors low dynamic levels and chamber-size ensembles, giving prime importance to sound rather than to drama and conventional movement.

RECORDINGS: *Chorus and Instruments; Christian Wolff in Cambridge; Durations; False Relationships and Extended Ending* for two chamber groups; *For Frank O'Hara* for flute, clarinet, violin, cello, piano, and percussion; *King of Denmark* (electronic); *Rothko Chapel* for chorus, viola, and percussion; *Structures* for quartet; *Viola in My Life* for viola and six instruments.

Ferrabosco, Alfonso (baptized January 18, 1543–August 12, 1588) The Italian composer Alfonso Ferrabosco was a member of a musical family from Bologna. He composed madrigals, motets, and music for the lute. By 1562 he had settled in England, but he traveled abroad on several occasions, acting as a spy for the English government. He was granted a life pension by Elizabeth I but in 1578 returned to Italy and entered the service of the Duke of Savoy. Two sets of his madrigals were printed in 1587, and several other madrigals were included in English collections. Two fine pieces for the lute were printed in Robert Dowland's *Varietie of Lute Lessons* (1610).

Ferrabosco's son Alfonso (*c.* 1575–1628) was a composer, violist, and lutenist. He collaborated with Ben Jonson and Inigo Jones in the extravagant masques produced at the court of James I.

Ferrier, Kathleen (Mary) (April 22, 1912–October 8, 1953) Originally intending a career as a pianist, the English contralto Kathleen Ferrier was encouraged to become a singer by the conductor Malcolm Sargent. She was known for only two opera roles: Gluck's *Orfeo ed Euridice* and Britten's *Rape of Lucretia.* A fine oratorio and lieder singer, she specialized in the music of Mahler and in English songs; both areas are documented on recordings. She also recorded albums of opera arias. Britten and Arthur Bliss wrote music for her. She died of cancer at the height of her career.

BIBLIOGRAPHY: Neville Cardus, ed., *Kathleen Ferrier—A Memoir* (1955; reprint, 1969).

Feuermann, Emanuel (November 22, 1902–May 25, 1942) After studying in Vienna and Leipzig the Polish-born Austrian cellist Emanuel Feuermann taught at the Cologne Conservatory at the age of 16. Five years earlier he had made his debut with the Vienna Philharmonic. In 1930 he became a professor at the Hochschule für Musik in Berlin, where he also played in a trio with Artur Schnabel and Bronislaw Huberman. He settled permanently in the United States in 1938, three years after a successful U.S. debut; his trio partners now were Artur Rubinstein and Heifetz. He played a cello believed to be the last one made by Antonio Stradivari.

fiddle (French, *vielle*) A medieval European bowed stringed instrument and a generic term for similar instruments.

A forerunner of the violin, the medieval fiddle appeared in 10th-century Europe, possibly deriving from the LIRA, a Byzantine version of the Arab *rabāb*. Medieval fiddles varied in size and shape but characteristically had front or back tuning pegs set in a flat and round or heart-shaped peg disk with three to five strings tuned in fifths. The body was often waisted.

Fiddle also refers generically to any bowed stringed instrument with a neck (bowed lute),

figure playing fiddle
from M. Severinus Boetius,
De Arythmetica, de musica, *14th century*
courtesy, Biblioteca Nazionale, Naples
photograph, Antonio Beuf

especially the violin. If the neck appears to skewer the body, the instrument is called a spike fiddle.

Fidelio: *see* BEETHOVEN (Beethoven and the theater) and (structural innovations); LIBRETTO (emergence of historical subjects); OPERA (developments in the 18th century) and (the 19th century).

Fiedler, Arthur (December 17, 1894–July 10, 1979) Educated at the Royal Academy of Music in Berlin, the U.S. conductor and violinist Arthur Fiedler joined the Boston Symphony, in which his father had been a violinist, in 1915. From the personnel of that orchestra he formed the Boston Sinfonietta (1924) and conducted it on tours of the United States. A participant in the early Boston Pops concerts, he became their permanent conductor in 1930, a year after organizing the Boston Esplanade Concerts. During his long tenure with the Pops, he established its reputation and popularity through tours and recordings. The latter include albums of marches, children's songs, show tunes, and popular standards as well as the music of Tchaikovsky, Copland, and Gershwin.

Field, John (July 26, 1782–January 23, 1837) An apprentice and student of Clementi, the Irish pianist and composer John Field settled in St. Petersburg, Russia, in 1804 to teach and perform. After 1832 he played throughout England and Europe, where he was considered to be one of the finest pianists of the 19th century. He composed seven piano concertos, four sonatas, chamber music, and numerous piano pieces, including 12 nocturnes that influenced Chopin.

BIBLIOGRAPHY: Patrick Piggott, *The Life and Music of John Field, 1782–1837, Creator of the Nocturne* (1973).

figured bass, thoroughbass, or **basso continuo** A system of accompaniment in the 17th and 18th centuries for a keyboard (harpsichord) or plucked (lute) instrument; the bass line, played on a bass melody instrument (viola da gamba, cello, or bassoon), is written out all "thorough" (*i.e.,* through) the composition, but its harmonization is left to the accompanist to provide more or less impromptu. Usually, though not invariably, the accompanist

is kept generally informed as to the harmony resulting from the melodic part or parts being accompanied so as not to conflict with it. This information is conveyed by figures added to the bass line, which is then more specifically described as figured bass.

The accompanist is said to realize the bass. This may be done impromptu; *i.e.,* reading it strictly at sight in the course of performance—a very skilled achievement. But it was always customary to look through the music in advance if opportunity occurred. This allows the performer to improve first thoughts and is normally the best course in music suited to an elaborate accompaniment. It hardly matters whether preparations are memorized or written out in whole or in part, but it does matter that the result shall sound free, flexible, and spontaneous as if it had been improvised. Modern editors who provide printed realizations usually bear this in mind, keeping their parts on the light side.

The information conveyed by the figures is never complete and is often so sketchy that the performer, when no preparation has been possible, must rely on a grasp of where the music is going. This came more easily to a contemporary performer than it does to present-day musicians, but the faculty can be cultivated. According to J.F. Daube's *General-Bass* (1756), the style of improvised accompaniment was brought to its height by Bach: "He knew how to introduce a point of imitation so ingeniously in either right or left hand and how to bring in so unexpected a countertheme, that the listener would have sworn that it had all been composed in that form with the most careful preparation . . ." The true reason for figured bass is the freshness of the invention. It was thus not merely a convenient shorthand for saving the composer's time but a means of giving zest to the accompaniment by inviting the performer to draw on the capacity for spontaneous enjoyment.

The figures themselves are numerals set one above the other to indicate the intervals of the harmonies required as counted up from the bass note. In realizing these intervals the performer can invert them in any order of notes; *i.e.,* manipulate the spacing of the chord, though normally not above the solo part for long at a time if at all. The figures are kept to the minimum necessary for determining the harmony by indicating its most characteristic intervals; the remainder of the chord is understood. Necessary accidentals are indicated. Only the main harmonies—and not the passing harmonies—are normally shown. There is great scope for varying and enriching the indicated harmony by introducing passing notes and for contriving an interesting melodic outline to the accompaniment.

The elaboration given to the realization will vary from the simplest harmonization to an exploitation of all the harmonic and contrapuntal possibilities. Four-part harmony is standard, though the nature of the music to be accompanied sometimes requires only three or even two parts, and occasionally the unharmonized bass line. Alternatively a full accompaniment requires as many notes to each hand as the fingers can accommodate, and in such realizations rules forbidding consecutive fifths, etc., may be waived except as between the two outside (bottom and top) parts.

Good figured-bass accompaniment takes into account not only the character of the piece but the performers, the auditorium, and the audience, thus making a heavy demand on the performer's judgment and imagination.

BIBLIOGRAPHY: Frank Thomas Arnold, *The Art of Accompaniment from a Thorough-Bass as Practised in the XVIIth and XVIIIth Centuries* (1931); Carl Philipp Emanuel Bach, Eng. trans. by William J. Mitchell, *Essay on the True Art of Playing Keyboard Instruments* (1959).

finale   The last movement of an instrumental composition or a concluding scene in each act of an opera. In the symphony, sonata, quartet, trio, and other multi-movement forms of the Classical era (*c.* 1750–*c.* 1820), the finale is most often in RONDO form, although SONATA form became increasingly common toward the end of the 18th century. The tempo is usually rapid. Although the great majority of finales from works of the mature Classical period adhere to these rules, there are a number of striking exceptions; for example, Mozart's Piano Sonata in D Major, K.284, and Beethoven's Third Symphony end with theme and varia-

tion movements. Beginning especially with Beethoven and continuing through the 19th century, the finale assumed an increasing importance to the composition as a whole. In many works, such as Franck's Symphony in d minor (1888), material that appeared earlier in the work is repeated in the finale.

The operatic finale is often more dynamic than what has preceded it. Frequently complex ensembles or rousing choruses are used to create an exhilarating close. Alessandro Scarlatti is credited with originating the dramatic finale and Niccolò Piccinni with developing its form.

Finlandia: *see* SIBELIUS; SYMPHONIC POEM.

Finney, Ross Lee (b. December 23, 1906) The U.S. composer and lecturer Ross Lee Finney played cello and piano before turning to composition. His principal mentors in the latter field were Boulanger, Berg, and Roger Huntington Sessions, with whom Finney studied intermittently for more than 20 years. On the faculty of the University of Michigan at Ann Arbor from 1948 to 1974, Finney established the electronic music studio there. He also founded the Valley (now New Valley) Music Press. After 1950 Finney's works combined tonal with serial and dodecaphonic writing. He has written four symphonies (1942, 1959, 1960, 1972); Concerto for strings (1977); sonatas for piano (No. 4, 1945), cello (No. 2, 1950), viola (No. 2, 1953), and violin (No. 3, 1955); eight quartets; two piano quintets; works for chorus and orchestra; and songs.

RECORDINGS: Cello Sonata No. 2; Concerto for saxophone and winds; Third Symphony.

Firebird, The: *see* BALLET (Diaghilev Ballet); STRAVINSKY.

Fireworks: *see* STRAVINSKY; SYMPHONIC POEM.

Fireworks Music: *see* HANDEL (life) and (works).

Firkušný, Rudolf (b. February 11, 1912) Educated at the conservatories in Prague and Brno, the Czech pianist Rudolf Firkušný studied with such illustrious figures as Janáček and Artur Schnabel. His repertoire has centered on the works of Mozart, Beethoven,

Brahms, and his compatriots Dvořák, Janáček, and Bohuslav Martinů.

Fischer, Edwin (October 6, 1886–January 24, 1960) The Swiss pianist and conductor Edwin Fischer was a pupil of Hans Huber in Basel and of Martin Krause in Berlin, where Fischer taught for many years. He was known particularly for his playing of Bach, Mozart, Beethoven, and Schubert, and he published books on Bach and Beethoven.

BIBLIOGRAPHY: Alfred Brendel, *Musical Thoughts and Afterthoughts* (1977).

Fischer, Ludwig (August 18, 1745–July 10, 1825) A friend of Mozart who created the role of Osmin in *Entführung aus dem Serail*, the German bass Ludwig Fischer was popular throughout European opera houses. He had an exceptional vocal range of two and one-half octaves.

Fischer-Dieskau, Dietrich (b. May 28, 1925) Educated in Berlin under Georg Walter and Hermann Weissenborn, the German baritone Dietrich Fischer-Dieskau made his stage debut in 1948 at the Berlin German Opera, with which he has remained affiliated. He first sang in England in 1951 and has had great success at the festivals at Salzburg, Glyndebourne, Edinburgh, and since 1954 Bayreuth. He has a

very wide repertoire of German and Italian opera and is considered unsurpassed in the interpretation of lieder; he was the first singer to record the more than 500 extant songs of Schubert. He has recorded music from Bach to Berg, numerous operas of Verdi, and is featured in two complete cycles of Wagner's *Der Ring des Nibelungen*. For a time in the early 1970s, he was also active as a conductor. His lieder recitals have often involved the collaboration of such concert pianists as Daniel Barenboim, Alfred Brendel, Sviatoslav Richter, and Jörg Demus.

Fitzwilliam Virginal Book: *see* ALLEMANDE; BYRD; FARNABY; PHILIPS.

flageolet A wind instrument of the fipple, or whistle, flute class related to the RECORDER; the name is a diminutive of Old French *flageol*, a pipe or tabor pipe. Its principal French form, described from the 16th century, has a contracting bore, an elongated, bone-tipped mouthpiece, and four fingerholes on the front and two thumbholes at the back. With keywork added this became the popular "quadrille flageolet" of the mid-19th century that was made famous by the virtuoso Collinet. A variant is the Catalan *fluviol,* played as a tabor pipe with one hand only. An English adaptation from the 18th century has six holes on the front and sometimes keywork; the double flageolets patented by Bainbridge and oth-

Dietrich Fischer-Dieskau
courtesy, Colbert Artists Management, Inc.

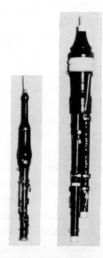

single and double flageolets
Leslie Lindsey Mason Collection of Musical Instruments (formerly the Galpin Collection) Museum of Fine Arts, Boston

ers shortly after 1800 had two parallel pipes arranged for playing in harmony. There also exist many folk instruments of the same class.

Flagstad, Kirsten (July 12, 1895–December 7, 1962)   Called the greatest Wagnerian soprano of the mid-20th century, the Norwegian soprano Kirsten Flagstad studied in Oslo, where she made her debut in 1913. Originally performing light opera and operetta roles, she began singing Wagner in 1932 with the role of Isolde and made her New York Metropolitan Opera debut three years later as Sieglinde in *Die Walküre*. Although she also sang roles of Gluck (Alceste), Beethoven (Leonore), and Purcell (Dido), her greatest triumphs were as Isolde and as Brünnhilde in the *Ring* operas. She recorded a complete *Ring* cycle from La Scala as well as many scenes from Wagner (with tenor Lauritz Melchior) and a complete *Tristan und Isolde*. She continued to make records after her retirement from the stage in 1953. From 1958 to 1960 she was the first director of the Royal Norwegian Opera. For a time she was under a cloud because of her insistence for family reasons on spending the war years in Nazi-occupied Norway.

Kirsten Flagstad
Suddeutscher Verlag

flat   The sign ♭ placed immediately to the left of a note that lowers its pitch a semitone (half step). The word is also used to denote incorrect intonation (under the correct pitch).

Fledermaus, Die: *see* OPERETTA; STRAUSS, JOHANN THE YOUNGER.

Fleisher, Leon (b. July 23, 1928)   A pupil of Artur Schnabel, the pianist Leon Fleisher was the first American to win the Queen Elisabeth of Belgium Competition (1952). He recorded all of the Beethoven piano concertos and since the mid 1960s, as the result of a form of writer's cramp in the right hand, has performed and recorded works for one hand alone. Fleisher has taught at the Peabody Conservatory in Baltimore since 1959 and has been active as a conductor since the '60s, serving as associate conductor of the Baltimore Symphony.

Flemish school   The major style of composition (*c.* 1450–*c.* 1550) that dominated the Renaissance following the BURGUNDIAN SCHOOL. It was so named because most of its leading musicians were born or trained in Flanders, the Netherlands, and northern France, though many of them lived abroad for most of their professional lives. It thus became a truly international style.

Beginning with JEAN D'OCKEGHEM and climaxing with JOSQUIN DES PRÉS, the style established a new polyphony with an equality of parts characterized (particularly in Josquin) by a consistent use of imitation. It was based solidly in sacred music, the mass and the motet, and the chanson continued in its Burgundian tradition until about 1500, when it too began to take on the characteristics of the new polyphonic style.

The most significant early feature was the change from three-part to four-part writing. Ockeghem moved from sophisticated subtleties to a "noble simplicity," and a texture of continuous, spun-out counterpoint was cultivated, varied at times by short chordal sections. The mass received the more conservative treatment, with the motet providing a greater outlet for expressiveness.

By the mid-16th century national styles were evolving. The Flemish tradition remained viable but was often given distinct national qualities. Composers such as Orlando di Lasso were adept practitioners of several national styles as well as of the international Flemish style. Flemish techniques were applied to Italian and German secular song, the madrigal and the lied, genres that developed far from the Flemish style toward the oncoming Baroque era.

Flesch, Carl (October 9, 1873–November 14, 1944) A student of Martin-Pierre-Joseph Marsick, the Hungarian violinist Carl Flesch taught at the conservatories at Bucharest (1897–1902) and Amsterdam (1903–08), during which time he made numerous tours of Europe and the United States. He performed chamber music with Artur Schnabel and in 1909 gave three recitals in Berlin tracing the history of the violin repertoire. Known principally as a teacher, he taught at the Berlin Hochschule für Musik (1921–22) and from 1924 to 1928 was chairman of the violin department at the Curtis Institute in Philadelphia. He wrote violin methods, *Urstudien* (1910) and *Die Kunst des Violinspiels* (1923, 1928), and edited violin works by Mozart, Beethoven, Rodolphe Kreutzer, and Paganini.

Floss der Medusa, Das: *see* HENZE; OPERA (the 20th century).

Flotow, Friedrich von (April 26, 1812–January 24, 1883) The German composer Friedrich von Flotow is known primarily for his opera *Martha*. Flotow was the son of a landed nobleman who planned a diplomatic career for his son. But his exposure to the Parisian life of art and music, coupled with his own awareness of his musical talents, led him to study music with Anton Reicha.

In 1837 he produced the first and very brief version of the opera *Alessandro Stradella,* which later in its complete form enjoyed great success. His reputation was established with *Le Naufrage de la Méduse* (1839), written in collaboration with Albert Grisar and Auguste Pilati. Between 1840 and 1878 he produced 19 light operas in France, Italy, and Germany of which the best known is *Martha* (Vienna, 1847; in its original form a ballet given at the Paris Opéra in 1844). Introducing the Irish song, "The Last Rose of Summer," and appealing by its melodic charm, *Martha* won a

place in the operatic repertoire. Flotow also wrote ballets produced at Schwerin, where he was director of the court theater, and incidental music for Shakespeare's *A Winter's Tale.*
RECORDING: *Martha.*

Floyd, Carlisle (b. June 11, 1926) A student of Ernst Bacon at Converse College (Spartanburg, South Carolina) and then at Syracuse (New York) University, the U.S. composer Carlisle Floyd is best known for his operas. Concerned with violent confrontations between individuals, his operas include *Susannah* (1955), *Wuthering Heights* (1958; revised 1959), *The Passion of Jonathan Wade* (1962), *Of Mice and Men* (1970), and *Bilby's Doll* (1976). He began teaching at Florida State University in 1947.

RECORDINGS: *In Celebration* (overture); *Pilgrimage* (song cycle).

flugelhorn A valved bugle with a wide conical bore and a medium-sized bell used in European military bands. The name comes from the small German bugle used in the hunt by a *Flügelmeister.* The bore has been increasingly narrowed until the instrument became similar to the cornet. The soprano size in B-flat is the most popular, and there are normally three valves. The name is sometimes also applied to the saxhorn.

flute A wind instrument with sound produced by a stream of air directed against a sharp edge, upon which the air breaks up into eddies that alternate regularly above and below the edge, setting into vibration the air enclosed in the flute. In vertical, end-vibrated flutes, such as the Balkan *kaval,* the Arabic *nāy,* and panpipes, the player holds the pipe end to his mouth, directing his breath against the opposite edge. In China, South America, Africa, and elsewhere, a notch may be cut in the edge to facilitate sound generation (notched flutes). Vertical flutes such as the recorder, in which an internal flue or duct directs the air against a hole cut in the side of the instrument, are known as fipple, duct, or whistle flutes. Vertical nose flutes are also found, especially in Oceania. In transverse, or cross, flutes (*i.e.,* horizontally held and side blown), the stream of breath strikes the opposite rim of a lateral mouth hole.

Flutes are typically tubular but may also be globular, as with the ocarina and primitive gourd flutes. If a tubular flute is stopped at the lower end, its pitch is an octave lower than that of a comparable open flute.

The characteristic flute of Western music is the transverse flute held sideways to the right of the player. Known in Greece and Etruria by the 2nd century B.C., it is next recorded in India, then China and Japan, where it remains a leading wind instrument. It is first depicted in Europe *c.* A.D. 1100. In the 16th century the tenor flute, pitched in G, was played in consort with descant and bass sizes (pitched in D and C respectively). All were typically of boxwood with six finger holes and no keys, semitones being made by cross fingering (uncovering the holes out of sequence), and retained the cylindrical bore of their Asiatic bamboo relatives. These 16th-century flutes were superseded late in the 17th century by the one-keyed conical flute, probably conceived by the celebrated Hotteterre family of makers and players in Paris; it was for this instrument that the solo flute works of Mozart were written. A conical flute is made in separate joints, the head joint being cylindrical, the others contracting toward the foot. Two joints were usual in the 18th century, the upper being supplied in alternate lengths for tuning purposes. The instrument was known then as the *flauto traverso, traversa,* or German flute, as distinct from the common flute, or recorder.

From 1760, in order to improve the sound and pitch of various semitones, three chromatic keys in addition to the original E-flat key began to be used. By 1800 the typical orchestral flute had these keys plus a lengthened foot joint to middle C, making six keys altogether. Two more keys produced the eight-keyed flute, which preceded the modern instrument. The finest players of the eight-keyed system drew from it a voluminous tone—especially with Charles Nicholson's 19th-century model with enlarged finger holes—and demonstrated a fluent technique in tonalities previously denied to the flute. This type of flute was found with various auxiliary keys in some German orchestras in the 20th century.

Theobald Boehm, the Munich flute player and inventor, set out to rationalize the instrument, creating his new conical model in 1832. He replaced the traditional hole layout with an acoustically based one and improved the venting by replacing closed chromatic keys with open-standing keys, devising for their manipulation a system of ring keys on longitudinal axles (rings allow a player to close an out-of-reach key in the same motion as covering a finger hole).

This flute was superseded in 1847 by Boehm's second design with its experimentally evolved cylindrical bore (with contracting or parabolic head)—the flute since used. Its principal modification has been the standardization of the closed G-sharp key. The loss of a certain depth and intimacy of tone of the old conical flute has been offset by gains in evenness of notes, complete expressive control throughout the compass at all dynamic levels, and almost limitless technical flexibility.

A modern Boehm system flute (pitched in C with the range c'–c'''') is made of wood (cocuswood or blackwood) or metal (silver or a substitute). It is $26\frac{1}{2}$ inches (67 centimeters) long, with a bore of about $\frac{3}{4}$ inch, built in three sections. The body, or middle joint, and the foot joint (sometimes made in one piece) have the note holes (13 at least), which are controlled by an interlocking mechanism of padded key plates hinged on a longitudinal axis. The bore narrows in the head joint, which contains the mouth hole, and is closed just above the hole by a cork or fiber stopper; it is open at the foot end. In the mid-20th century an English flutist and acoustician reset some of the tone holes to correct intonation

modern transverse flute   *courtesy, Conn Corporation*

problems on the traditional Boehm flute (*e.g.,* sharp C-sharp, flat low E-flat). In the late 20th century flutists remain divided as to the long-term benefits of this model.

Other flute sizes include the PICCOLO, the alto flute (in England, bass flute) in G, the bass (or contrabass) flute an octave below the flute, and the sizes used in military flute bands, generally pitched in D-flat and A-flat.

Flute repertoire really begins in the 18th century with such notable composers as Bach and Handel (seven sonatas each), Telemann (12 fantasias), Quantz (two concertos), Carl Philipp Emanuel Bach (more than 100 sonatas), and Mozart (two concertos, one for flute and harp, and three flute quartets). In the 19th century Schubert, Weber, and Beethoven included the flute in chamber music, and François Devienne wrote numerous concertos. French composers have been particularly attracted to the instrument in the 20th century, including Debussy, Ravel, Fauré, Ibert, Edgard Varèse, Poulenc, Messiaen, and André Jolivet. Flute concertos have been written by Carl Nielsen, Ibert, Henk Badings, and Andrew Welsh Imbrie; sonatas by Prokofiev, Hindemith, Bohuslav Martinů, Poulenc, and Walter Piston.

BIBLIOGRAPHY: Theobald Boehm, *An Essay on the Construction of Flutes Giving a History and Description* . . . (1882; reprint, 1976) and *Flute and Flute-Playing in Acoustical, Technical and Artistic Aspects* (1922, rev. ed., 1964); Philip Bate, *The Flute: A Study of Its History, Development and Construction* (1969); John C. Krell, *Kincaidiana; a Flute Player's Notebook* (1973); Johann Joachim Quantz, *On Playing the Flute* (1975).

Flying Dutchman, The: *see* PROGRAM MUSIC (imagery); ROMANTIC PERIOD (Wagnerian development); SPOHR; WAGNER (life) and (development).

folia (Italian spelling, *follia*) A Portuguese dance mentioned as early as the 15th century, probably a "fool's dance." By the 17th century it had become a stylized form called *folies d'Espagne* that has been used frequently by composers as a theme for variations. Examples are by Jean Henri d'Anglebert and Alessandro

Scarlatti for harpsichord, Marin Marais for viola da gamba, Corelli for violin, Bach in his *Peasant* Cantata, Carl Philipp Emanuel Bach, Liszt, and Rachmaninoff for piano, and Cherubini and Carl Nielsen in operas.

folk music A definition of folk music as serviceable as any is the one accepted in 1954 by the International Folk Music Council: "Folk music is the product of a musical tradition that has been evolved through the process of oral transmission. The factors that shape the tradition are: (i) continuity which links the present with the past; (ii) variation which springs from the creative impulse of the individual or the group; and (iii) selection by the community, which determines the form or forms in which the music survives. The term can be applied to music that has been evolved from rudimentary beginnings by a community uninfluenced by popular and art music, and it can likewise be applied to music which has originated with an individual composer and has subsequently been absorbed into the unwritten living tradition of a community. The term does not cover composed popular music that has been taken over ready-made by a community and remains unchanged, for it is the refashioning and re-creation of the music by the community that gives it its folk character."

The council's definition (based on a formulation by Cecil Sharp in 1907) may be employed as a rough guide to indicate what is and what is not a folk song, but not all scholars accept its implications. With the advent of the tape recorder and more candid contact between collector and informant, the quantity of folk song study data has increased enormously and its quality much improved.

origins The knottiest problems are those relating to the creation of folk music. In the 19th century lively dispute raged over the question: Is folk music communal in origin and created by a community or group rather than by an individual? Cases are attested in which a company of North American lumberjacks or Romanian frontier guards may have whiled away a winter evening around the stove by the collective creation of a song text and even a tune. However, this method of composition seems rather the exception than the rule. The modern state of studies indicates that a more usual role for the collective is not so much one of creation as of re-creation.

Hypothetically the process might be illustrated thus: Under stress of emotion or as a diversion from a dull task, a person begins to fashion a song. A ready-made tune may be used, or a tune adapted, or a new melody created. Words are set to this tune. Perhaps that evening in the kitchen or the tavern the song is tried out among congenial company. Someone in the group likes the song and strives to repeat it, but some passages are remembered imperfectly, and gaps in text and tune must somehow be filled. The performer may feel that certain details can be improved, and so individual fancy is brought to the task. The result is different from the original. A third singer may learn the song from the re-creator and submit it to a similar process. In the course of time and transmission, many variants will come into being, some remaining close to the original while others differ from it to such a degree that they may be considered as quite separate songs. Inevitably in this process of communal re-creation, some variants are improved while others are marred and "sung to tatters."

The foregoing may serve as hypothesis, but scientific information on the way in which folk music is created is weak and deficient, for the folklorists' experience with authentic song makers, though increasing, still is not extensive. So obscure is the process that Bartók wrote: "Whether peasants are individually capable of inventing absolutely new tunes is open to doubt. We have no data to go on. And the way in which the peasant's musical instinct asserts itself encourages no such view." For folklorists of this school variation is the key to the mystery, and Bartók's compatriot László Lajtha puts the matter in these terms: "Folk music is *par excellence* an art of variation. The feeling for variation assures the strength, the capacity for evolution, the life of folk song, and it manifests itself as long as the folk song keeps its malleable and ductile qualities."

Some German scholars, notably Hans Naumann, have offered the theory that song, like every form of art, evolves among the educated classes and filters downward through the layers of society until it comes to rest among the lower classes; there it dwindles on as folk song, which is but the vague and sometimes distorted echo of a once-fashionable musical and poetic culture.

This theory of *abgesunkenes Kulturgut*, of a come-down cultural heritage, is fortified by the facts that songs written by troubadours of Provence 800 years ago still survive among Catalan peasants, that German scholars have been able to trace the bookish origins of hundreds of folk songs, and that French traditional song is known to have been affected for centuries by the music and poetry of the courts and of the *bourgeoisie*, to say nothing of the influence of songbooks of urban origin, popular theaters, cabarets, and the like. Indeed the process is so marked in France that Patrice Coirault and other French folklorists hold the view that song may become folk song but is not so in the first place.

Similarly urban influences have worked on folk song in Britain and the United States, notably on the texts. Printed ballad sheets were appearing by the 1540s in England and were taken through the country districts by peddlers, while street singers and stall stationers distributed them in the towns. In North America ballad sheets containing either native compositions or copies of British texts were being printed in the 17th century, and as in Britain the production of these broadsides and garlands, or songsters, continued vigorously through the 18th and 19th centuries before dwindling away during the early years of the 20th century. The extent to which town culture and print have worked on the predominantly rural and oral folk traditions of Britain and the United States has not been fully evaluated, but its general effect is doubtless considerable.

The traffic, however, has not flowed only in one direction. The troubadours themselves imitated folk music forms, the polyphonists of Tudor times employed in their works not only traditional song tunes but also street cries, and 20th-century composers—including some of the most advanced—have freely made use of what Bartók paradoxically called the novelties of the rural repertoire.

From speculation about folk music origins other considerations arise concerning such factors as illiteracy and anonymity. Is illiteracy a necessary factor for the creation and survival of folk music? Whatever the case in the past, modern experience seems to show that education does not necessarily diminish the life of traditional song. Indeed some U.S. collectors have found that illiteracy is a negative factor, particularly where ballad singing is concerned. As to anonymity Sharp considered it essential that the author be unknown. Others deem this to be a mere accident. To those who maintain that folk songs are refashioned by so many generations that the original is lost in a forest of variants, the answer is made that not all songs change to a great extent, nor are they necessarily of such antiquity; moreover in some traditions—in Gaelic Ireland, for instance, and the northeastern woods of the United States—the names of the original creators are often known and are long remembered by the bearers of the songs. Two names that spring to mind are those of Blind Raftery of Mayo and the shanty boy song maker, Larry Gorman of Miramichi, New Brunswick. Nevertheless, whether or not anonymity is *sine qua non,* it is a usual condition of folk song.

In attempting to reach an objective view of the nature of folk music, theorists have been hampered by generalizations based on experience in western and central Europe, where the traditional repertoire has shrunk through the loss of many of its ancient genres and has for centuries been hovering between two levels of art and between two societies—educated and unlettered, urban and rural. Furthermore, over much of this area the practice of folk music has diminished and its creation ceased; thus theory is sometimes based rather on speculation than on full evidence.

The folk traditions of southern and eastern Europe offer firmer ground for theorists; while these traditions have not remained unaffected by urban-educated influence, they are at once more complete in range of genres and more vigorously alive than their counterparts in the north and west. From a view offered by the Balkans, for instance, the scholar may plausibly reconstruct, at least in rough outline, the condition of folk music as it may have prevailed over most of Europe in the past. In countries such as Yugoslavia, Romania, Bulgaria, and to a lesser extent Greece, a large number of peasant rituals—magical or not—rural ceremonies, and calendar feasts are occasions for folk music. Critical periods of the year and decisive moments in life—the winter and summer solstices, seedtime and harvest, funerals and weddings, etc.—have their prescribed musical repertoire, often of great amplitude and importance. In addition to ceremonial songs other ritual pieces are still performed, such as musical charms to induce rain or to make a girl's hair grow beautifully. The shepherds' repertoire also contains survivals evoking an ancient pastoral civilization, including alphorn signals to celebrate the coming of spring and extended flute or bagpipe solos—doubtless once of magical intent—that are nothing less than folk tone poems describing the losing and refinding of beloved sheep. The range of functional music—of songs-for-a-purpose—extends far beyond field work, churning, cheese making, and such. Pairing off (courtship) is also urged along by song, and many apparently gratuitous lyrical pieces are associated with working bees and are designed to lighten such communal tasks as corn shucking, apple paring, sewing, and embroidering. The rich treasury of dance music has its vital function too, for the weekend dances are of peculiar importance to many villages, providing prime opportunity for exchange of news with neighbors from outlying districts, for the enlistment of help with a job on hand, and notably for courtship.

A folk music repertoire of this kind, comprising a wide range of ceremonial and functional types and only a relatively small proportion of purely diversionary songs and instrumental tunes "for listening to," may be considered as "classical" and probably represents the general situation in Europe in past times. Along the Mediterranean, particularly in southern Italy and Spain, ritual and occasional items still make up an important part of the rural musical fund, but elsewhere in western Europe the functional songs exist only as vestigial relics. In the United States, apart from Christmas carols, there is an almost total absence of ritual songs; the impressive work chants of black labor gangs are now rarely heard. As in western Europe by far the greater part of folk music is now of diversionary and more or less gratuitous kind.

If functional songs are plentiful in southeastern Europe, it should not be thought that the traditions there consist only of reflections of the past. On the contrary 20th-century variations abound, and particularly since the end of World War II there has been a vivacious flowering of creation that was already in bud during the inter-war years. Specialists working in such fertile terrain are privileged, since fruits of knowledge that elsewhere are objects of speculation or legend grow there before the scholar's eyes and within grasp. From local experience the Eastern folklorist is able to confirm what many in the West had suspected: that in fact folk song may be created either by individual composition on the part of a member of the folk-singing community, it may arise as a product of variation, or it may be received from an urban-educated source and digested into the tradition. All these processes are common. Variation is still the most familiar method by which the inventiveness of the folk shows itself; but in traditions where new songs are constantly arising, the process of variation may show itself in ways other than the oral transmission of a song over a considerable period of time. A Bulgarian peasant singer and song maker interviewed in 1954 said in effect: "I have about 500 songs in my head. I take a bit from here, a bit from there, and so my new tune is made."

Some of the ancient stock of European music shows itself to be remarkably tough and durable, but with social advance the forms of folk song draw ever closer to art song. The process has been going on for centuries but is more noticeable in the 20th century as its pace accelerates. It seems that anonymity and perhaps orality too become less and less important as song makers living within the orbit of traditional music prepare written (perhaps even typewritten) copies of their texts and as literacy, sometimes even musical literacy,

spreads in areas where folk song is still the dominant musical activity. Such developments, most noticeable in eastern Europe but affecting other parts of the Continent and the United States, indicate that the test of a folk song may lie neither in its origin as was thought in the 19th century, nor in its evolution as maintained by most 20th-century folklorists, but in the positive function it fulfills in a society. It is still more closely bound to the material life than art music; it is still capable of acting on the prime conditions of existence as in its ancient magical days; and over a large part of the world common people still employ it as solace in dark times or as cheer to accomplish a hard task or as release for pent-up joys.

An extension of this social function is seen in the development of industrial folklore—the self-made songs of miners, textile workers, railway men, etc.—both in Europe and North America. Some of these have an epic quality that has served to encourage workers to almost superhuman effort as in the Negro ballad of the railway tunneler John Henry, who is often called the black Paul Bunyan. Industrial folk songs that convey an expression of protest have been used effectively in many countries, notably in the United States during the 1930s, for purposes of labor organization. The study of folk song began with the literary scholars; they yielded to the musicologists; in the mid-20th century, with living folk music running with outstretched arms toward art music and shedding its folkish appearance while retaining its folkish function, it would seem that the musicologists in turn must give way increasingly to the specialists in social studies.

After about 1945 an urban folk music revival manifested itself in the United States and Britain, affecting particularly the middle-class youth of large cities. Charles Seeger, noting that this coincides with the tendency of many rural singers toward urban musical habits, describes the current development metaphorically as two alternate highways—one leading from the comparatively authentic folk idiom to the comparatively authentic fine art idiom, the other following the contrary course. Thus some city performers of folk music, in their move toward rural habits of music making, pass country performers traveling in the opposite direction. The urban performers of revived folk music are only of marginal interest to the folklorist, as they are but visitors to that area of traditional culture in which the authentic folk singers (so long as they remain authentic folk singers) are the permanent residents.

Folklorists' attention centers on Europe and America; the tendency has been to leave Africa to the ethnographers and Asia to the students of Eastern classical music. In Europe migrations, conquests, and a diversity of material and social conditions have produced variegated markings on the map of musical folklore. In the southeast folk song lives most vigorously and in its widest range from the oldest to the newest forms. Distinctive rural musics still flourish in parts of central Europe (Slovakia, Hungary, Croatia, Slovenia) and in the Mediterranean countries; but in Switzerland, France, Germany, and Scandinavia the authentic performance of folk song is more rare, and the repertoires have long been influenced by town culture, though impressive relics of ancient music may still be heard here and there. In the British Isles traditional music, though much shrunken, has remained distinct from art music to a greater degree than usual in western Europe and by no means only in those outlying Gaelic areas where singers sometimes seem separated from the world of conventional music by 1,000 years or more. In America too the folk song map shows differentiations of style and wealth. Both in Canada and the United States traditional music flourishes mainly in the east and diminishes sharply toward the west. Notable style areas are those of the northern seamen and woodsmen, the southern mountain farmers (among whom Sharp made his impressive collection of U.S. ballads of British descent), the Negro plantation workers (whose song belt extends from east of the Appalachian Mountains in Virginia to Louisiana), and the western cowboys. The prevalent occupations in those areas have deeply influenced the songs and not only with regard to the texts.

The influence of the Negro tradition was most strongly felt in the southern states, though that influence pervades almost all of U.S. folk song. Three well-known groups of songs were produced by the U.S. black population. From work gangs in southern prisons and from laborers building the railroads come the rhythmic work songs. From the days of slavery come the famous spirituals in which the enslaved Negroes identified themselves with the Jews in bondage in Egypt. Some of the spirituals were used as signals and messages in the underground movement of escape from slavery; all of them are characterized by powerful emotion and deceptively simple structure. From the sharecrop farms and from the cities along the Mississippi River come the blues, also deceptively simple, which in turn were part of the origin of jazz.

Even when smaller areas are under survey, the condition of folk music is far from homogeneous. In a single region some villages may display a large amount of fine music, while others in the same neighborhood know only a few poor pieces. Nor are folk songs evenly spread inside the village itself as Kodály found in Hungary. The more prosperous villagers are likely to distinguish themselves from the poor even in their songs (often leaving the oldest and most beautiful items to the lowest classes), while farmers above a certain level of property ownership may feel that any kind of folk singing is unfitted to their dignity. Considerations of age and sex are of some weight too. Game songs usually remain the property of children, though they may once have been impressive items in the adult repertoire. Funeral laments (where they still occur) and lullabies are sung exclusively by women; epic ballads are often deemed proper only to men, and the female epic singer is looked on as abnormal, a "crowing hen." Rapid waves of social change involving, say, the advent of a bus service or the establishment of a cultural center in a remote and backward settlement may result in the old people not knowing the middle-aged people's songs nor the middle-aged the songs of the young, with each age group having its own distinctive style of performance.

performance The idea that folk music is natural, spontaneous, and produced as a bird sings on the bough does not bear close consideration. In many parts the folk singer's voice is produced with an artifice that may differ from that of the bel canto singer but is quite as considerable. The more experience the folklorist gains with traditions in flower, the better realized is the part played by individual skill, taste, fantasy, and diligence. The vast amount of data that has accumulated since the tape recorder came into general use has helped the specialist to understand that every Slovak shepherd or Congo canoe paddler does not necessarily have the same ability to display the musical treasures of a community. In the world of folk music, as of art music, there are performers with talent and others with no gifts; some have inventive imagination while others are passive imitators; some are great virtuosos, others are novices. Where the folk arts predominate the average member of the community will join in music making to a much greater extent than the city dweller, but outstanding performers are acknowledged and prized.

The qualities that make a performer important are assessed differently in different places. Regional variations in ways of producing the voice are admired. English folk singers like to pitch their voices as high as possible, whereas in Sardinia a guttural growl is practiced that in chorus sounds like the roaring of musical lions; in southern Spain a squeezed, agonized voice is esteemed, while in the northwest region of that country a round rich voice is preferred. In the United States the song style of the whites—rigidly pitched, solo voiced, of limited color, simple rhythm, and with well-developed text—seems the antithesis of the relaxed, mainly choral song of the blacks with its varied vocal color, ingenious rhythms, and fragmentary rambling texts.

Generally speaking a deliberately melodious tone is seldom sought by folk singers and instrumentalists, and once started each piece of music is produced impassively with little variation of volume, timbre, or tempo (beyond a steady speeding up in some dance tunes). The expressive devices of folk song consist rather of tiny details of intonation, rhythm, and ornament that may be far from obvious, yet eminently flavorsome. In some folk music areas—for example, in the Balkans, Hungary, and Spain—a measure of professionalism is found, especially among instrumentalists, and these

performers—many of them gypsies—may resort to pathos and exaggerated dynamism.

The increase of rural professionalism has also greatly affected U.S. folk music, both white and black. The melodies have tended to gain impetus at the expense of their contour, and experimentation with the tonal and rhythmic possibilities of the fiddle, the five-string banjo, and the guitar has often led to brilliant virtuosity but a lessening of musical expressiveness.

The educated ear is struck by many features of folk singing that do not correspond to the conventions of European music. Until recently most published folk music was based on skeletal notations taken down by hand directly from the informant, although as early as 1897 E. Lineva in Russia was demonstrating the importance of recording folk song by phonograph; by 1906 both Percy Grainger in England and Bartók in Hungary had accepted this idea almost as a *sine qua non*. In the United States their example was followed a few years later by John A. Lomax, though he was not concerned as the Europeans were with the painstakingly accurate transcription of the recordings. Today the tape recorder provides a simple means of reproducing folk performance in all its nuances, though problems of transcription still remain, since staff notation that is reasonably adequate for art music is not able to describe clearly the deviant intonations and rhythms of folk song, much less its timbre, etc. The folklorist looks forward to an easily read and supple graphic notation, possibly produced with electronic aid.

melodic and rhythmic patterns The melodies of the oldest type of folk song are generally restricted in range. Songs on a single note have been reported from Bulgaria, while the compass of two or three notes abounds, particularly among songs attached to calendar and funeral customs (*e.g.,* the English "Souling song," connected with a ritual for the dead, consists essentially of the series *re mi fa*). Likewise songs consisting of four or five stepwise notes are found not only in the Slav countries but also in the West in such well-known songs as "The Keys of Canterbury." George Herzog stressed the importance of realizing that these restricted note series form the scales of the tunes and are not to be considered as incomplete fragments of octave scales. "The scale of a folk tune is no more nor less than the series of notes used."

Scales of five notes within the compass of a fifth are called pentachordal. Those of five notes within the compass of an octave are pentatonic. Formerly these were considered to be characteristically Chinese, though it was early recognized that they also abounded in, for instance, Irish and Scottish music. Research shows the virtual universality of pentatonism, which is found with or without semitones not only in the British Isles and the Far East but also in the oldest layer of Hungarian music and among the Russians, south Bulgarians, south Italians, Spaniards, and Turks, to say nothing of its wide diffusion in black Africa and Andean America. The United States received this scale system from two sources—British settlers and Negro slaves—and it occurs in many familiar Negro spirituals as well as in white folk songs, as shown by Sharp's great Appalachian collection where nearly 20 percent of the 969 tunes are pentatonic and a still greater proportion in the hexatonic (six-note) system. Both pentatonic and hexatonic scales are sometimes called gapped scales, and it is commonly assumed that the normal heptatonic (seven-note) scales have evolved from these more fundamental forms by the process of filling in the gaps. Pentatonism is not necessarily a sign of antiquity, however, and many seven-note tunes are older than many in the gapped scales.

Among the heptatonic scales or modes (*see* MODE) common in folk music are a number known to medieval church theorists. In addition to the so-called church modes—a misleading appellation—are others unknown to medieval theory. One is C D E F G A♭ B♭ C, occurring in Moravia and Hungary and less commonly in England and France. Another is a Romanian scale found attractive by Bartók, combining the augmented fourth of the Lydian with the flat seventh of the Mixolydian, as C D E F♯ G A B♭ C. These are but a few specimens of the tonal riches of traditional music.

The rhythms of this music also show great resources. Apart from the huge corpus of melody performed in free tempo rubato that hardly permits the tune to be confined within bar lines, a wide range of tempo *giusto* rhythms are also heard, either binary or ternary or in compound. Chopin and Tchaikovsky are among 19th-century composers who derived unusual rhythms from their native folk music, and 20th-century composers such as Stravinsky, Bartók, and their successors have profited particularly from the discovery of the peculiar system sometimes miscalled Bulgarian rhythm. This system—which folklorists, borrowing a term from Turkish theory, now prefer to call *aksak*—was first noticed in Bulgaria but later was found to exist also in Turkey, Greece, Romania, Yugoslavia, and Albania, to name only the main European areas of diffusion. *Aksak* rhythms differ from classical ones in that the short and long units of duration, instead of being one-half or twice the value of each other, are two-thirds or one and one-half times the value. Thus the bar is not made up of the play of, say, quarter note and half note but of quarter and dotted quarter. In this system the eight eighth notes of a $\frac{4}{4}$ bar do not fall into two groups of four as with standard Western music; the folk musician may subdivide them as 3+3+2, or 3+2+3, or 2+3+3. Similarly a $\frac{9}{8}$ bar would not consist of three threes but of 2+2+2+3 or some other combination determined by placing the beat of three elsewhere in the bar. With this kind of rhythm unconventional time signatures such as $\frac{11}{16}$ or $\frac{13}{16}$ are often encountered. The resources of the system are large, and Constantin Brăiloiu has tabulated 1,884 theoretical forms of *aksak* measure without claiming to have exhausted the possibilities.

Most folk music is monophonic, either solo or in unison, but polyphony is found to be more common and varied than once imagined. In southern Albania alone 32 different forms of part singing have been reported, ranging from simple drone-based diaphony to complex four-part styles that yet owe nothing to classical European theory. In several parts of the Continent ritual songs are performed antiphonally, and when the second group begins its response a little before the first group has finished its statement, an overlap occurs by which a more or less involuntary polyphonic effect may be momentarily achieved (much as in the traditional method of antiphonating plainchant).

Two distinct kinds of polyphonic folk music are found in Europe, one based on a drone, the other not. Vocal drones are found in Switzerland (in the canton of Appenzell) and in northern Italy, but principally they occur in isolated spots scattered across the map from Sardinia through southern Albania, Yugoslavia, and Macedonia and across to the Caucasus. In the center of this area—in southwestern Bulgaria and northern Greece—the form has generally shrunk to consist of a solo melody sung to the monotone bass of a group, but at either extremity—in Sardinia and particularly in the Caucasus—more complex part singing survives. A peculiar feature of drone-based polyphony is the frequent and much-admired clash of major seconds; indeed in some parts of western Yugoslavia singing in parallel seconds without a drone is also practiced.

The spread of "correct" harmony among folk singers is even more scattered, occurring in northwestern Spain, abounding in Germany, Austria, northern Italy, and Slovenia, missing in Hungary but reappearing strongly among the Moravians, Slovaks, Ukrainians, and particularly the Great Russians.

Instrumental polyphony shows itself in similar fashion. In its rudimentary forms the accompanying instruments provide a fixed or moving drone, but in more advanced forms greater enterprise is shown—particularly in the case of the relatively recent string bands in the south of the United States made up of fiddles, banjos, guitars, and bass.

folk instruments Among the more rudimentary "sonorous engines" in use among European folk musicians are leaves (Ireland), slips of birch bark (southern Germany), and along the eastern Danube fish scales inserted in the mouth and blown as a free reed. From any of these pseudo instruments the rustic virtuoso is capable of producing brilliant music. At the other end of the evolutionary scale, a number of modern factory-made instruments such as the violin, guitar, mandolin, cimbalom, and (in western Romania) saxophone are found in the hands of country players; folklorists are forced to the opinion that any instrument may be classed as a folk instrument, depending on the way it is played.

Many instruments familiar in their evolved concert hall form are found among folk musicians in primitive condition: the shepherd pipe with or without fipple or finger holes; the rustic oboe (shawm) that is known in Yugoslavia as the *zurla,* in Persia as the *zurna,* and in China as the *sona;* the rebec with or without sympathetically vibrating strings (*gusle, gudulka,* etc.); and many others. A folk instrument that has never graduated into the world of symphonic music is the widespread bagpipe, either bellows-blown or mouth-blown, which extends from Spanish Galicia to Russia and from Scotland to southern Italy. Another is the giant alphorn, sometimes 12 feet long, whose mournful bellow is still heard in the Alps and the Carpathians.

Over much of Europe the violin has been the dominant folk instrument for several centuries, though of recent years its supremacy has been threatened by the accordion. Similarly in the United States the fiddle has been popular for rural dance music. Many U.S. folk fiddlers still retain the old custom of bracing the instrument against their chests when playing; it is said that any fiddler worth his salt knows at least the eight tunings and perhaps a half dozen more. But in the United States also the fiddle has been yielding ground. Since the mid-19th century the five-string banjo has become enormously popular among white musicians in the south and east, and since the beginning of the 20th century prestige has attached to the guitar, an instrument that began to produce specifically North American sounds in the hands of black players at a time when jazz still resided in the orbit of folk rather than popular music.

See also BALLAD; JAZZ; SONG.

BIBLIOGRAPHY: Irwin Stambler and Grelun Landon, *Encyclopedia of Folk, Country, and Western Music* (1969); Zoltán Kodály, *Folk Music of Hungary,* rev. ed. (1971); Pete Seeger, *The Incompleat Folksinger* (1972);

Béla Bartók, *Turkish Folk Music from Asia Minor* (1976), *Rumanian Folk Music,* 5 vols. (1978), and *Yugoslav Folk Music,* 4 vols. (1978).

Foote, Arthur (William) (March 5, 1853– April 8, 1937)   The U.S. organist and composer Arthur Foote received in 1875 the first graduate degree in music awarded from Harvard University. He served as organist of the First Unitarian Church in Boston (1878–1910) and was co-founder and then president of the American Guild of Organists. He wrote three works for chorus and orchestra that show the influence of Wagner, chamber music, songs, and about 35 compositions for piano. He is the author of *Modern Harmony* (1905) and *Modulation and Related Harmonic Questions* (1912). His autobiography appeared in 1946.

RECORDINGS: *Francesca da Rimini* for orchestra; Piano Quintet; Piano Trio in c minor; Quartets (3); Violin Sonata.

Forkel, Johann Nikolaus (February 22, 1749– March 20, 1818)   A German musicologist known for his biography of J. S. Bach, Johann Nikolaus Forkel studied at Göttingen University and in 1770 became organist of the university church. In 1779 he was made musical director of the university.

Forkel's most important work is probably his *Allgemeine Literatur der Musik* (1792); his *Über J. S. Bachs Leben, Kunst und Kunstwerke* (1802), the first biography of that master, remains valuable (Eng. trans. by C. S. Terry, 1920). Though the claim that he was the founder of musicology ignores the existence of such men as John Christopher Pepusch, Sir John Hawkins, Charles Burney, and Giovanni Battista Martini, Forkel was undoubtedly one of the first great musicologists. His library forms part of the Berlin State Library.

Forrester, Maureen (b. July 25, 1930)   The Canadian contralto Maureen Forrester made her concert debut in Toronto in 1953 and three years later was acclaimed in New York City for her part in the *Resurrection* Symphony of Mahler, in whose music she has specialized. Rarely seen on the opera stage, she has sung with the major U.S. orchestras and has toured Europe. Notable recordings include the song

cycles *Kindertotenlieder* and *Lieder eines fahrenden Gesellen* of Mahler, Italian operas of Handel *(Julius Caesar, Rodelinda, Theodora, Serse),* and Gluck's *Orfeo ed Euridice.*

Förster, Josef Bohuslav (December 30, 1859– May 29, 1951)   The Czech composer Josef Bohuslav Förster belonged to the school of Dvořák and Smetana. Born at Prague, he was the son of Josef Förster (1833–1907), a composer of organ music. After studying at the Prague Conservatory, he was organist at several Prague churches and music critic of *Narodny Listy.* In 1888 he married the Wagnerian soprano Berta Lauterer and from 1893 to 1903 lived in Hamburg, where he became a friend of Mahler and taught at the conservatory. He was music critic (1903–18) of *Die Zeit* in Vienna, and he taught composition (1919) at the Prague Conservatory and was later appointed director.

Förster's music was largely inspired by personal memories and associations. His second and fifth symphonies, the cantata *Mortuis fratribus,* and the Trio in a minor were tributes to his near relatives. He was a devout man, and his fourth symphony *(Easter Eve)* and his operas *Nepromozeni* (1918), *Srdce* (1923), and *Bloud* (1936) were inspired by religious subjects. He also wrote four masses, two violin concertos, a cello concerto, and chamber and vocal works. Though his romantic and religious outlook suggests Mahler, his simpler, lyrical works, notably the song-cycle *Liebe,* show his allegiance to the heritage of Dvořák and Smetana.

fortepiano   As commonly used today, the term fortepiano denotes the type of harpsichord-shaped grand piano (as opposed to the clavichord-shaped square piano) played in the 18th and early 19th centuries and revived in the mid-20th century chiefly for the performance of the music of Mozart, Haydn, and their contemporaries. During the 19th century the fortepiano was transformed into the familiar modern grand piano as a result of Romanticism's demand for greater emotional expansiveness, requiring of the piano a wider compass of notes and a louder, lusher, more uniform tone capable of filling large concert halls and competing in concertos with powerful orchestras. These musical objectives were met through structural changes, chiefly a sturdier mechanism and frame and heavier, tenser strings that changed the character of the piano radically.

Though the fortepiano, essentially a chamber instrument, is technologically less complicated than its descendant and is relatively restricted in loudness and range (normally five to six octaves), it is a fully developed instrument in its own right, capable of beguiling subtlety of expression through dynamic variety and articulation. Typically its clear, intimate timbre changes quality throughout the compass from a warm, reedy bass through a more vocal tenor to a dry, incisive, yet short-sustaining treble. This inherent tonal richness, present even in the first instruments of Bartolommeo Cristofori, is one of the fortepiano's most appealing features.

The fortepiano's small, hard, leather-covered hammers, controlled by a simple but responsive English or German action, impart a sharp but light blow to its thin, loosely-stretched strings. In contrast the modern piano's fat felt-covered hammers strike with greater force and damp out certain harmonics of its stiffer strings. Having fewer strings than the modern piano, and being tuned to lower pitch, the fortepiano does not require a massive case and internal metal plate to withstand the strings' tension; instead its resonant framework is built entirely of wood. Pianos with metal reinforcing members or partial plates may be considered transitional between the fortepiano and modern types. Like the harpsichord, the fortepiano has an enclosed bottom beneath the soundboard so that the soundboard forms the top of an amplifying chamber or box with sound radiating mainly upward; the modern grand piano is open on the bottom with its heavier soundboard communicating directly with the outside air on both sides. Thus the fortepiano can be classified as a box-zither, whereas the modern piano more closely resembles a board-zither. These acoustical and structural factors, which are subject to regional and individual variation, account for the fortepiano's elegant form and charming sound.

The fortepiano became obsolete not long after the harpsichord did, and its revival in the 20th century came about correspondingly later as an outgrowth of renewed interest in the harpsichord. Harpsichords returned to popularity in modernized form under the hands of Landowska; she and other pioneers kindled interest in performing Baroque music with historical fidelity to the composers' intentions. Concern for authentic performance on period instruments led instrument makers to study antique instruments preserved in collections so that the surviving old instruments could be reproduced for wider use. Initially builders sought to improve upon the original technology to overcome supposed defects and take advantage of modern methods of production. Such was the case with the harpsichord under Pleyel and Arnold Dolmetsch around the turn of the century, and with the fortepiano in mid-century under John Challis (1907–74), a pupil of Dolmetsch who worked in Michigan and later in New York City. Challis, an innovative harpsichord maker, introduced cast aluminum frames and honeycombed metal soundboards to his novel instruments to render them stable. As a sideline to his harpsichord production, Challis designed several lightly-strung "Mozart" pianos, which like his other instruments are modern reinterpretations of classic forms rather than copies. Originally the Challis Mozart piano had a curious four-and-three-quarters-octave range, and later he adopted the anachronistic, standard seven-and-one-third-octave compass using a modified commercial grand piano action. Thus the well-known Challis piano is classical in name only, and though its tone differs substantially from the modern piano's it falls outside the mainstream of the fortepiano revival.

Reacting against the philosophy of improvement, most contemporary fortepiano makers seek to copy—more or less exactly—particular examples by fine old builders, mainly of the German and Austrian schools. British and Germanic fortepianos differ considerably in structure and playing characteristics, and the present revival has favored the latter style for several reasons: original English-action instruments are still available on the market for less than the cost of a reproduction, though they tend to be of later date; German-action pianos are widely considered superior in mechanism and tone; and Viennese instruments in particular are more closely associated with major Classical composers. Further the English fortepianos appear not to have been so well-designed internally as their continental rivals. Johann Andreas Stein, Anton Walter, and Louis Dulcken are among the famous builders whose productions provide the chief models for today's craftsmen. Most recently interest has turned toward reproducing Beethoven-era instruments by Streicher and Graf. The 1720 Cristofori piano has also been reproduced (1976), so it appears that builders are looking farther afield for models as the revival proceeds.

Though the Rück Piano Company in Nürnberg began reproducing Walter fortepianos at least as far back as the 1940s, the major locus of authentic construction has been the United States, following the Boston school's rediscovery of classic harpsichord design. The most active U.S. maker (18 fortepianos by 1978) has been Philip Belt, who first became interested in these instruments in 1959 and who made a copy of the Smithsonian Institution's Dulcken at the Boston harpsichord shop of Frank Hubbard before becoming an independent builder in 1967. He has since reproduced models by Stein and Walter. Belt has provided fortepianos for Malcolm Bilson, the leading American exponent of these instruments, who has been a highly influential performer and teacher. Maribel Meisel, a scholar whose extensive research since the late 1960s has documented many previously obscure areas of fortepiano production in the 18th century, has worked closely with Belt in exploring Viennese-style instruments in particular.

In England Margaret Cranmer has devoted much attention to studying English-action pianos, while Derek Adlam has built a number of copies. Hugh Gough, better known as a

modern fortepiano by Hugh Gough
replica of Viennese instrument, c. 1780
courtesy, Hugh Gough

clavichord and harpsichord maker in the United States and England and a pioneer in the recovery of classic designs and techniques, has made five fortepianos and remains a leading figure in the movement toward authenticity. Martin Scholz, formerly associated with the Rück collection, has built fortepianos under the aegis of Hug & Co. in Basel. Robert Smith, Carl Fudge, and Tom Wolf are among a generation of younger builders in the United States.

The fortepiano's revival depends on performers for its vitality. In addition to Bilson, Jörg Demus and Paul Badura-Skoda have done much to give the instrument exposure; Eva Badura-Skoda and Arthur Loesser have also focused attention on the fortepiano through their publications. Malcolm Frager has recorded on original instruments at the Colt Clavier Collection; Stanley Hoogland is one of the performers who has recorded at the Germanisches Nationalmuseum in Nürnberg; Fritz Neumeyer and Rolf Junghanns have made the restored instruments of the Neumeyer collection known through recordings; and Mieczyslaw Horszowski has performed Lodovico Giustini's seminal sonatas on the Metropolitan Museum's Cristofori. Through such performances and recordings the fortepiano is quickly becoming widely appreciated, and its revival now seems permanently assured. No more evidence of this is needed than to remark on the sale of fortepiano kits intended for assembly by amateurs.

Laurence Libin

forza del Destino, La: *see* VERDI.

Foss, Lukas, originally, Lukas Fuchs (b. August 15, 1922)   The German-born U.S. composer, conductor, and pianist Lukas Foss is widely recognized for his experiments with improvisation and chance music. He studied in Berlin and Paris and, after moving to the United States in 1937, with the composers Randall Thompson and Hindemith and the conductors Fritz Reiner and Serge Koussevitzky; he graduated from the Curtis Institute (1940) in Philadelphia. Foss published his first work at age 15, and in 1945 he became the youngest composer to win a Guggenheim Fellowship. In 1957, while professor of composition and orchestra director at the University of California at Los Angeles, he founded the Improvisation Chamber Ensemble, the vehicle of many of his experiments in aleatory and stochastic music. He was conductor of the Buffalo Philharmonic (1963–70), the Brooklyn Philharmonia (from 1971), and was composer-in-residence at the Cincinnati (Ohio) College-Conservatory (from 1975).

Foss's early works are neoclassical: tonal and well-organized in harmony and counterpoint. Among these works are symphonic music (*Ode,* first performed 1945), ballet (*Gift of the Magi,* 1945), concerti (Second Piano Concerto, 1951; rev. 1953; Music Critics' Award, 1954), opera (*Griffelkin,* commissioned by and first performed on NBC-TV, 1955), cantatas, and chamber music. His later chamber pieces (*Echoi,* 1963; *Elytres,* 1964) are avant-garde in their treatment of the ordering of musical events by means of chance operations and in the variety of controls over musical form—controls determined to a large extent by the performers during the performance. Later large-scale works include *Fragments of Archilochos* (1965) for countertenor, speakers, choruses, mandolin, guitar, and percussion; Cello Concert (1966) for cello, orchestra, and tape; and *Baroque* Variations (1967) for orchestra.

RECORDINGS: *Baroque* Variations; *Cave of the Winds* for wind quintet; *Elytres* for flute, violins, piano, harp, and percussion; Oboe Concerto; *Paradigm* for percussion, guitar, and three selected instruments; *The Prairie; Psalms* for chorus; *Time Cycle* (four songs).

Fountains of Rome: *see* PROGRAM MUSIC (problem of form); RESPIGHI.

Fournier, Pierre (Léon) (b. June 24, 1906)   A student and later professor (1941–49) at the Paris Conservatoire, the French cellist Pierre Fournier took up the cello at age 13 after poliomyelitis affected his legs enough for him to abandon serious study of the piano. His repertoire is prodigious; in 1939 he made 32 appearances in Berlin, and in 1947, with Joseph Szigeti, Artur Schnabel, and William Primrose, he performed in two cycles nearly all the chamber music for strings of Schubert and Brahms. With Schnabel he recorded all of the Beethoven sonatas, and he has also recorded the six unaccompanied suites by Bach. Since 1950 he has been a regular performer at the Edinburgh Festival. His U.S. debut was in 1948, and in 1953 he was made a chevalier of the Legion of Honor, being elevated to the rank of officier 10 years later.

Four Saints in Three Acts: *see* OPERA (the 20th century); THOMSON.

Four Seasons, The: *see* VIVALDI.

Fox, Virgil (Keel) (b. May 3, 1912) The U.S. organist Virgil Fox studied in Chicago with Wilhelm Middelschulte and in Paris with Marcel Dupré. He served as organist of the Riverside Church in New York City (1946–64). Though his reputation was established in serious organ music, he also performs lighter repertoire. Opposing the Baroque revival in organ design and performance style, he has promoted the large eclectic organ, and he also plays electronic instruments as well as turning recitals into theatrical events.

Frager, Malcolm (b. January 15, 1935) Educated at Columbia University with a major in Russian (1957), the U.S. pianist Malcolm Frager studied piano with Carl Friedberg (1949–55). Winning both the Leventritt Competition (1959) and the Queen Elisabeth of Belgium Competition (1960), his career was at first especially successful in the Soviet Union.

Françaix, Jean (b. May 23, 1912) A student of Boulanger at the Paris Conservatoire, the French composer Jean Françaix achieved great success with his music for the theater and has worked in almost all traditional forms. His early works are among his best: Concertino (1932) for piano and orchestra, a string trio (1933), and a piano concerto (1936). Stage works include eight ballets (the most successful is *Les Demoiselles de la nuit,* 1948); an unpublished four-act opera, *La Main de gloire;* and a musical comedy, *L'Apostrophe* (1940). An extensive choral work is the oratorio *L'Apocalypse de Saint Jean* (1939) for soloists, chorus, and two orchestras, the second of which is augmented with unusual instruments

and represents hell. Françaix's music is characterized by restraint, clarity, technical proficiency, and wit.

RECORDINGS: Divertissement for bassoon and quartet; Divertissement for oboe, clarinet, and bassoon; Piano Concerto; Rhapsody for viola and small orchestra; *Sonatine* for violin and piano; String Trio; Suite for violin and orchestra; Woodwind Quintet.

Francesca da Rimini: *see* FANTASIA; GÖTZ; RACHMANINOFF; SYMPHONIC POEM; TCHAIKOVSKY.

Francescatti, Zino (b. August 9, 1905) A child prodigy who gave his first performance at the age of five, the French violinist Zino Francescatti has toured throughout the world in recitals and as soloist with orchestras. He was reputed for his intense tone and accurate technique. He played the standard repertoire, and current recordings include concertos of Mozart, Beethoven, Saint-Saëns, and Paganini and the Double Concerto of Brahms.

Franck, César (Auguste Jean Guillaume Hubert) (December 10, 1822–November 8, 1890) The Belgian-born French composer and organist César Franck was one of the most important post-Wagnerian figures, greatly influencing the composers of his time.

Franck studied at the Liège Conservatory in his youth and in 1835 went to Paris, where he studied composition with Anton Reicha, entering the Paris Conservatoire in 1837. His first compositions, *Trois Trios Concertants* (1841–42), were followed by the cantata *Ruth* (1845). He was appointed organist in 1851 at St. Jean–St. François in Paris and in 1858 at Ste. Clotilde, holding this post until his death. While professor of organ at the Conservatoire (1872), he became a greatly admired *chef d'école,* his pupils including d'Indy, Chausson, Charles Bordes, Henri Duparc, and Augusta Holmès, the French-born composer of Irish extraction.

Basing his style on the contrapuntal technique of Bach and the chromatic harmony of Wagner's *Tristan,* he established the cyclic form in composition in which a cell-like theme is repeated throughout the movements of a sonata or symphony in different guises. This principle became the basis of the teaching of

César Franck
portrait by J. Rongier, 19th century
C. Caroly—J. P. Ziolo

d'Indy, who enlarged upon it at the Schola Cantorum, founded in 1894.

In 1879 Franck completed *Les Béatitudes* and in 1888 his Symphony in d minor (first performed in Paris, 1889). Franck's best works were written in the latter part of his life and include, in addition to the symphony, the Piano Quintet (1879), the String Quartet (1889), *Les Djinns* (1884), and the Variations *symphoniques* (1885) for piano and orchestra, the Sonata (1886) for piano and violin, and the symphonic poems *Les Éolides* (1876) and *Le Chasseur Maudit* (1882). Among his organ works are *Six Pièces* (1862), *Trois Pièces* (1878), and *Trois Chorals* (1890). The finest of his works for solo piano are the *Prélude, choral et fugue* (1884) and the *Prélude, aria et finale* (1887). Though his strong, romantic style deeply affected his pupils, his influence faded with the first decade of the 20th century. The best of his own works have continued, however, to be widely performed.

BIBLIOGRAPHY: Vincent d'Indy, *César Franck* (1909; reprinted 1965); Leon Vallas, *César Franck* (1951; reprint, 1973); Laurence Davies, *Cesar Franck and His Circle* (1970; reprint, 1977) and *Franck* (1973).

RECORDINGS: Numerous recordings of most works.

Frank, Claude (b. December 24, 1925) A student of Artur Schnabel, the German pianist Claude Frank made his U.S. debut in 1950. He has performed widely as soloist with orchestras in the Americas, Europe, and Asia and has played chamber music at festivals throughout the world. In 1972 he joined the faculty of Yale University. Recordings include the complete Piano Sonatas of Beethoven and chamber music of Mozart, Schubert, and Brahms.

Franz, Robert (June 28, 1815–October 24, 1892) A German composer of songs in the tradition of Schubert and Schumann, Robert Franz was born at Halle and studied organ with Friedrich Schneider at Dessau (1835–37). On return to Halle he became a friend of Wilhelm Osterwald, many of whose poems he later set to music. In 1841 he was appointed organist at the Ulrichskirche at Halle and in 1842 became director of the Singakademie. In 1843 he published his *Twelve Songs;* their intimate character was admired by Schumann and also by Liszt, who later transcribed a series of Franz's songs for the piano. In the same year his hearing became affected and he was later afflicted with nervous disorders. Obliged to relinquish his post at the Singakademie in 1868, he was supported for the remainder of his life by a singer, Arnold von Pilsach. Franz devoted his later years to arranging works by Bach, Handel, Mozart, and Schubert.

Franz wrote about 350 songs, remarkable for their sensitive musical prosody. "My music does not pretend to be much in itself," he told Liszt, by which he meant not to undervalue his work but to indicate the subservience of his settings to the poetic texts. Heine's poems form nearly a quarter of his texts. Most of his songs are in strophic form and were written for mezzo-soprano of limited range. Among his most expressive songs are "Gewitternacht," "Die Heide ist braun," and "Es hat die Rose sich beklagt." He also wrote a series of choral and religious works.

Frau ohne Schatten, Die: *see* GLASS HARMONICA; LIBRETTO (19th-century influences);

ROMANTIC PERIOD (20th-century transition);
STRAUSS, RICHARD.

Frederick II the Great, King of Prussia (January 24, 1712–August 17, 1786) As crown prince, Frederick of Prussia learned keyboard, figured bass, and harmony from the age of seven. In 1728 he began to study flute with Quantz, whom he invited to a permanent residence at court upon his accession as king in 1740. There Frederick continued his study of the flute, wrote 121 flute sonatas, and performed at hour-long concerts every evening. He was a generous patron of musicians; J. S. Bach presented his *Musical Offering* to Frederick after being invited to Potsdam in 1747. Frederick established a court band (C. P. E. Bach was cembalist until 1767) and decreed that there should be singing lessons three times a week in the public schools. Although many music historians deprecate his technique as a flutist, the 18th-century English chronicler Charles Burney wrote that "The king plays with great precision and neatness of execution."

Freischütz, Der: *see* LEITMOTIV; LIBRETTO (19th-century influences); OPERA (the 19th century); WEBER.

Fremstad, Olive (March 14, 1871–April 21, 1951) After early study of the piano, the Swedish-born U.S. soprano Olive Fremstad first sang in Gilbert and Sullivan operettas as a contralto. She then went to Berlin to study with Lilli Lehmann, who trained her as a soprano. Fremstad sang three seasons with the Cologne Opera (1895–98), minor roles at Bayreuth (1896), and the role of Venus in *Tannhäuser* (London, 1897). She performed 70 contralto and mezzo-soprano roles with the Munich Opera from 1900 to 1903 and in the latter year made her Metropolitan Opera debut as Sieglinde *(Die Walküre).* After her Metropolitan farewell (1914) Fremstad appeared with Boston and Chicago opera companies. Her early acoustical recordings included arias from *Tannhäuser, Die Walküre, Tosca,* and Ambroise Thomas' *Mignon.*

French horn A brass instrument with a narrow conical bore wound into a coil and ending

modern double horn   *A. C. Baines*

in a flared bell, used both in the modern orchestra and in the military band. It has a funnel-shaped mouthpiece and is built in F or a fourth higher in B-flat, or more commonly as a double horn (introduced shortly before 1900 by Fritz Kruspe), which provides for the instantaneous choice by means of a thumb valve of two tonalities, usually F and B-flat, or B-flat and A, thereby bringing various technical benefits such as greater certainty on the higher notes. Muting is effected by two methods: either by insertion of a separate mute of closed conical form or by fully stopping the bell throat with the right hand. By the latter method (often indicated in music by a cross) the pitch is raised roughly a semitone, for which the player compensates either by fingering a semitone lower or by depressing a special muting valve that lowers the instrument by the requisite amount.

A symphony orchestra normally includes four horn players. Orchestral use of the horn, as opposed to its mere appearance in operatic hunting scenes (as employed by Lully), began in Germany *c.* 1700 after Count Franz von Spörck had introduced the French *trompe* into neighboring Bohemia. In England the *trompe* was imported after the Restoration for hunting but was not used orchestrally before Handel. Through most of the 18th century orchestral horns were still held up in the open-air manner, the notes being limited to those of the natural series; crooks were used in various forms and combinations to alter the instrument's tonality as required by the music. About 1750 A. J. Hampel, a well-known Dresden player, rationalized a hand horn chromatic technique of placing the right hand in the bell for the partial stopping needed to flatten a harmonic by a semitone or more and also for whole stopping to raise it a semitone. Works written for this technique, which depended on skillful matching of the open and stopped notes, include Haydn's, Mozart's, and Beethoven's solo and chamber works for horn. Though this technique was gradually superseded by the valved horn from about 1825, it is the legacy of the hand horn that the player still places one hand in the bell, where its musical function is now to control the tone and intonation and to mute as already described.

Later works for the instrument include Adagio and Allegro for horn and piano and *Konzertstück* for four horns and orchestra (both 1849) by Schumann; a Horn Trio (1865) by Brahms; Two Concertos (1885 and 1943) by Richard Strauss; Serenade for tenor, horn, and strings (1943) by Britten; and a Concerto (1971), *Music for Horn and Piano* (1967), and *Night Music* for two horns and orchestra (1969) by Thea Musgrave. *See also* HORN.

BIBLIOGRAPHY: R. Morley-Pegge, *The French Horn* (1960; 2nd ed., 1973); Gunther Schuller, *Horn Technique* (1962); J. Murray Barbour, *Trumpets, Horns, and Music* (1964).

French Suites (Bach): *see* SUITE.

Freni, Mirella (b. February 27, 1935) The Italian lyric coloratura soprano Mirella Freni made her debut in 1955 in Modena, Italy, as Micaëla in *Carmen,* a role with which she remained closely associated. After receiving first prize in the Concorso Viotti (1958), she sang with most of the major Italian opera companies and at the Holland (1959) and Glyndebourne (1960) festivals. In 1961 she first sang at London's Covent Garden with subsequent appearances in Germany and Austria. Her New York Metropolitan Opera debut (1965) was as Mimi in *La Bohème,* a role that she recreated on film and in recording. Other recordings of complete operas include *Carmen* (as Micaëla), *Manon, Don Giovanni* (Zerlina), and *Otello.*

Frescobaldi, Girolamo (baptized September 9, 1583–March 1, 1643) The Italian organist and composer Girolamo Frescobaldi was perhaps the first great master of organ composition. His predecessors, to name only Antonio de Cabezón, Girolamo Cavazzoni, Andrea Gabrieli, and the composers in Germany represented in the Buxheim Organ Book (*c.* 1460–70), had developed a keyboard style based largely on transcriptions or imitations of vocal pieces. Frescobaldi, noted from his early years for his skill as a performer, produced in his numerous compositions a model that, through his pupil Johann Jakob Froberger, was to reach supreme heights in the German Baroque school of J. S. Bach. His influence here was equaled only by that of Jan Pieterszoon Sweelinck.

A pupil of Luzzasco Luzzaschi, Frescobaldi began his public career as organist at the Church of Sta. Maria in Trastevere in Rome in 1607; he soon left Italy for the Netherlands and published in Antwerp a book of madrigals. Within a year or so he was back in Rome, where he played in St. Peter's (1608) to a vast audience. Twenty years later Frescobaldi left Rome for Florence, where he remained until he returned to his former position at St. Peter's in 1634. He retained this post until his death.

Unlike Sweelinck and the Gabrielis, Frescobaldi wrote no vocal music of great significance, and his fame as one of the great masters of the early Baroque rests on his instrumental works. Among them keyboard compositions greatly predominate, though the canzone for unspecified instruments with basso continuo are of outstanding historical significance in the development of the trio sonata.

In 1608 Frescobaldi published his first collection under the title *Il primo libro delle fantasie a quattro di Geronimo Frescobaldi Ferrarense, organista*. These fantasias, 12 in number, are notable for variety and for contrapuntal mastery of the highest order. The textures are idiomatic in a way rarely found in earlier examples of the form. Chromaticism is not favored by Frescobaldi (the latter part of No. 2 is exceptional), though modulation is used in many pieces. In 1624 he published a collection of 10 ricercari, 5 canzone, and 11 capricci. The composer's preface contains valuable information about performance.

Much of Frescobaldi's keyboard music was

intended for the harpsichord, made clear in the title of *Toccate d'intavolature di cimbalo e organo* (1637). The volume also includes partitas on various melodies and pieces on ground basses. These show Frescobaldi's free inventiveness in genuine keyboard textures and figuration. A collection first published in 1627 and reprinted in 1637 contains, in addition to toccatas, canzone, verse d'hinni, Magnificat, gagliarde, correnti ed altre partite. The preface here again gives information of great value to the interpretation of Baroque instrumental music. Frescobaldi's remaining publication, the *Fiori Musicali* of 1635, consists of organ music intended for liturgical use. Quite apart from its historical importance Frescobaldi's music deserves to take its place among the most imaginative and vital products of the early 17th century.

RECORDINGS: *Arie musicale a più voci; Canzoni per sonar* (5); Harpsichord Toccatas (Books 1 and 2); various keyboard pieces.

Friedman, Ignaz (February 14, 1882–January 26, 1948) One of the most brilliant pupils of Leschetizky, the Polish pianist Ignaz Friedman also studied with Guido Adler (history) and Hugo Riemann (composition). A very individual, indeed eccentric, pianist of the Romantic school (Chopin was a specialty), he prepared editions of Chopin, Liszt, and Schumann and composed more than 90 works, mostly for piano.

Friml, Rudolf: *see* OPERETTA; POPULAR MUSIC (the 20th century).

Froberger, Johann Jakob (May 19, 1616–May 7, 1667) The German organist and composer Johann Jakob Froberger was born in Stuttgart and probably received his musical education from his father, who was a cantor. Froberger became court organist in Vienna in 1637 but later in the same year went to Italy, where he studied with Girolamo Frescobaldi until 1641. From the evidence of two pieces inscribed *fait à Bruxelles 1650* and *à Paris 1656,* it appears that he visited those two cities. The composer Johann Mattheson states that he also visited Dresden, where he engaged in a friendly trial of skill with the organist and harpsichordist Matthias Weckmann. Froberger left the imperial service in 1657. He trav-

eled to London in 1662 and was twice robbed on the way. Mattheson says he arrived in such a state of destitution that he was glad to accept the post of organ-blower offered him by Christopher Gibbons, then organist at Westminster Abbey and the Chapel Royal. On the occasion of the marriage of Charles II (1661), when Gibbons was playing before the court, Froberger overblew the organ. In the pause brought about by the mishap, Froberger seized the opportunity to play something himself. A foreign woman who had been his pupil recognized his style, and Froberger was presented to the king and asked to play the harpsichord.

Froberger's compositions are for keyboard and are among the richest and most attractive productions of the early Baroque era. Most were published posthumously. The pieces for organ include powerful and imaginative toccatas and fantasias whose forms show the influence of his master Frescobaldi; they were highly regarded by J. S. Bach. In some other works, such as the partitas, it is more difficult to say for which of the two instruments (organ or harpsichord) the music was intended. In his ricercari and capriccios Froberger provided two versions, one for each instrument. The suites, however, are clearly for harpsichord or clavichord, and Froberger is the first German master in this form. His suites owe something to the French suites for lute and for harpsichord but show well his individual and cosmopolitan character.

RECORDINGS: Suites, toccatas, and fantasias.

frottola A type of Italian secular song popular in the late 15th and early 16th centuries. In three or four parts in simple chordal style, the frottola had a text only in the upper part, so it is probable that it was performed as a solo song with instrumental accompaniment (viols, lute, harpsichord, etc.), though it is also possible that all parts were sung. The primary source is 11 books printed by Ottaviano dei Petrucci in Venice between 1504 and 1514. The typical frottola consists of several six-line verses, each followed by a four-line refrain, both verse and refrain using the same music. As it developed by 1530, the frottola was the direct antecedent of the 16th-century MADRIGAL.

Under the patronage of Isabella d'Este the frottola developed at the court at Mantua and was popular at other courts of northern Italy, particularly at Ferrara and Urbino. Serafino dall' Aquila (d. 1500) was an important frottola poet. The most important composers were Bartolomeo Tromboncino (died *c.* 1535) and Marchetto Cara (died *c.* 1530).

Frühbeck de Burgos, Rafael (b. September 15, 1933) Educated at the music academy in Madrid and at the University of Munich, the Spanish conductor Rafael Frühbeck de Burgos led the Municipal Orchestra of Bilbao (1958–62), the Spanish National Orchestra (since 1962), and the Düsseldorf Symphony (since 1966). Notable recordings, many with the New Philharmonia, are those of Mendelssohn's oratorios *Elijah* and *St. Paul,* Carl Orff's *Carmina Burana,* and music of Spanish composers, including de Falla and Joaquín Turina.

fuging tune A form of hymnody developed in New England during the American Revolution (1775–83). A typical fuging tune places the tune in the tenor voice and harmonizes it with block chords. The term is a shortened form of the English fuging psalm fune, a type of hymn setting popular in England in the 17th and early 18th centuries. A freer style and the placement of the fuging section in the next-to-last instead of last line distinguish the American fuging tune from its British parent.

James Lyon's collection *Urania* (1762) contains the first fuging psalm tune published in America. The first fuging tunes appeared in William Billings' *Singing Master's Assistant* of 1778. Other American composers such as Daniel Read, Timothy Swan, Jacob French, and Justin Morgan wrote in the form until around 1800, and it remained popular outside New England for at least another 50 years.

fugue A musical texture and a method of composition. A fugal texture consists of a melodic phrase repeated in various keys and at various intervals and is also known as fugato. The name fugue is given to a piece of music built out of fugal texture.

During the 19th century, when fugal writing was scarcely part of the normal musical language, certain pedagogues such as Cherubini devised rules for the writing of academic fugues as exercises that they considered to be an indispensable part of a student's training; what had been a procedure in periods of contrapuntal style was designated a form. This artificial designation has led to a great misunderstanding of the application of fugue in true composition.

The early history of fugue is the early history of CANON. The distinction between the two procedures does not become clear for some centuries. During the great canonic era of the Flemish school culminating in Josquin des Prés, a new chanson and motet style developed, consisting of imitative treatment of successive phrases of text. In some of these pieces imitative entries between voices occur at intervals other than the unison and octave, though no rigid system is apparent. From the early part of the 16th century, imitation at intervals other than the unison and octave increased; as the modal system inclined toward what later became the diatonic system, a tendency for answering voices at the fourth or fifth developed; the opening of the Christe Eleison of the *Audi filia* mass (1558) by the French composer Claude Goudimel resembles later fugal writing in this respect.

Claude Goudimel, *Missa Audi filia*

A common feature in Palestrina, commoner still in Byrd, is the simultaneous introduction of two-part counterpoint in the exposition, the voices entering in pairs, as in the following example, *Benedicta et venerabilis* from Byrd's *Gradualia* (1605). Note the alteration of the initial interval in the fourth voice (third entry) for modal reasons.

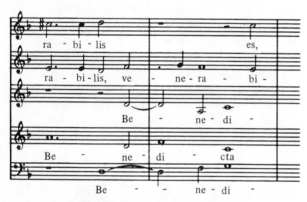

William Byrd, *Benedicta et venerabilis*
(Gradualia)

During the 16th century the terms ricercare, fantasia, and canzona were often applied to instrumental fugal pieces. Among the earliest fugal ricercari are those for organ by Marco Antonio Cavazzoni (b. *c.* 1490) in imitation of the current motet style adapted to the instrumental medium. Canzoni and ricercari consisted of series of little fugal sections, each using a different theme for imitation. Further developments in the 17th century included the use of opening subjects in closing sections (Thomas Tomkins' keyboard fantasias) and rhythmic alteration of existing subjects for different sections (works by Dietrich Buxtehude and Jan Pieterszoon Sweelinck).

By this time the diatonic system had almost completely replaced the modal system, resulting in the answer to the subject usually at the interval of a fifth above (or fourth below). It should not be thought that such an answer is in the dominant; it is in the plagal form of the tonic key, or if the subject itself is plagal the answer is in the authentic form (*see* MODE [medieval modes]). Thus the natural answer to C G (in C Major) is not G D but G C. When this principle is understood the 19th-century theorists' complicated rules for the behavior of the real answer (an exact transposition of the subject) and the tonal answer (a modification of the subject for tonal reasons) become unnecessary. The adoption of the diatonic system also offered opportunities of modulation from one key to another. Harmonic contrast supplemented thematic contrast, and this reduced the thematic material necessary.

Bach   For the average musician in the 20th century, the word fugue is almost synonymous with the name of Bach. Yet the conception of the fugue as a form has produced much misapprehension concerning Bach's fugal output; his *Well-Tempered Clavier, The Art of Fugue,* his organ and other keyboard fugues, together with one or two well-known vocal fugues, are regarded as the bulk of his fugal writing. Fugue, however, can scarcely be discussed without reference to those other movements that are fugal in style though their forms may belong to the categories of concerto, chorale, prelude, and movements in binary form. Many of the gigues in the keyboard suites, though of binary structure, are also fugues as are several preludes that are cast in concerto form (*e.g.,* the *English* Suite in e minor); less obviously the Prelude to the first *English* Suite is fugal, and so are the Fantasia of the Partita in a minor and at least three preludes of "The Forty-eight." Similar fugal methods abound in the inventions, the trio sonatas, and the sonatas for violin and harpsichord.

The keyboard works contain a higher percentage of pure fugues (those that have no other definable structure) than do other works of Bach. Among the vocal music, the Mass in b minor and Magnificat contain an unusually high proportion of pure fugues. However, the first Kyrie Eleison of the Mass, for example, is not a pure fugue; though it contains a five-part fugue, it is also a vast concerto movement in structure. Before the choral fugal exposition (a fugal exposition is said to end when all voices have entered with the subject) there is a long ritornello, which no more than suggests that its opening melody will be treated exhaustively as a fugue. The ritornello is perhaps more orchestral than fugal in conception, and orchestral material is later used in fugal episodes (*i.e.,* passages not containing the subject). The fugue is incidental to the main ritornello structure, and the structure of the fugue in shape and key is dependent on that of the ritornello structure.

A less familiar but clearer example is the opening movement of Cantata 65, "Sie werden aus Saba kommen." Its structure may be summarized as follows: measures 1–8, ritornello in orchestra; 9–19, chorus and orchestra being ritornello in tonic and recommence in dominant; leading to measures 19–44, four-part vocal fugue on new material accompanied only by continuo, orchestra entering at measure 34. Stretto (the overlapping of entries of the subject) is used, and there are two recurring countersubjects. (A regular countersubject is recurrent matter accompanying the subject and usually invertible with it so that the voices may be interchanged; *see* COUNTERPOINT.) Measures 45–53, orchestra and chorus join in the original ritornello. In this movement, therefore, the fugue is a large solo episode in the main concerto structure. Bach uses fugue similarly in chorale preludes (*e.g.,* the first movement of Cantata 80).

Handel   Consideration of Handel's fugues is more difficult because his style is less systematic than Bach's. His are rarely discussed by modern books on fugue. Theorists who have replaced Cherubini's fugal rules with a new set based on Bach's pure fugues fall into the same fundamental error as Cherubini in assuming that there should be a recognized method; such people are often shocked by Handel's propensity to change or ignore his fugue subject. Paradoxically Handel's fugues

are more commonly pure fugues than Bach's, but at the same time they are more diverse in their detail.

A study of the vocal fugues in Handel's *Messiah* and *Israel in Egypt* (referred to as "M" and "I" respectively) will give some idea of the enormous variety of method. Apart from more straightforward fugues like "They Loathed to Drink" (I), "And With His Stripes," "He Trusted in God," and "Amen" (M), typical Handelian features in these works include: (1) continuation of fugal material in the orchestral part with block harmony in the chorus; *e.g.,* "He Smote" (I); (2) sharing of subject between voices; *e.g.,* "And He Shall Purify" (M); (3) successive entries in the same key in the exposition; *e.g.,* "His Yoke Is Easy" (M); (4) homophonic presentation of subject as a tune (rare in the German school); *e.g.,* "He Smote" (I), "And He Shall Purify," "His Yoke Is Easy" (M); (5) combination of fugue and descriptive choral writing; *e.g.,* "And With the Blast of Thy Nostrils" (I); (6) fugue succeeding a homophonic opening; *e.g.,* "But as for His People" (I).

Stretto, invertible counterpoint, and other contrapuntal devices are used constantly by both Bach and Handel but rarely systematically by Handel.

after Bach and Handel   A great simplification in the details of harmony and counterpoint is one of the features of late 18th-century style. Fugue, though occasionally used with great success by Haydn and Mozart, became associated with an archaic and severe style. Quasi-fugal development of motives is common in works by these composers, though predominantly fugal movements were confined generally to choral music with some notable exceptions. The rediscovery of some of Bach's works stimulated Mozart's interest in fugue, and it was natural that the more deliberately serious Beethoven should show an increasing preoccupation with fugal writing. His later works contain some important fugues: the Piano Sonatas, Opp. 101, 106, and 110 (Opp. 109 and 111 contain fugal matter); the Quartets, Opp. 131 and 133 *(Grosse Fuge);* the overture *The Consecration of the House;* and the Mass in D Major. Of these, that in Opus 101 occupies the development section of a sonata movement, while that in Opus 110 alternates with an aria. In one way or another Beethoven's fugues usually combine with some kind of sonata structure; consequently his fugues are more dramatic in conception than those of the Baroque period since the sonata style concerns itself with new tonics as well as transitory modulation. Many of Beethoven's fugues also show a preoccupation with the more artificial fugal devices such as diminution and augmentation, melodic inversion, and double fugue. In the latter, Beethoven favors the Italian type (commoner also in Handel) where subject and invertible countersubject (or second subject) are stated together at the outset. In the German type (used more frequently by Bach) each subject has a separate exposition, though they are usually later combined in invertible counterpoint. There are many types of double and triple fugue. Fugue 4, Book 1, from Bach's "Forty-eight," for example, has two countersubjects; only the subject itself has an exposition, the countersubjects being added later. The final chorus of *Israel in Egypt* by Handel has two main subjects in alternation, one of them with countersubject, and subsequently used in a remarkable stretto with diminution.

Later in the 19th century fugue either became a deliberate archaism following the dissemination of Bach's music or underwent deliberately romantic treatment on a large scale. Brahms, the one important 19th-century composer whose style was deliberately Classical in concept, left only a handful of fugues. Keyboard fugues were written by Mendelssohn, Schumann, and Liszt, and fugues occur in Berlioz' choral works and in Verdi's Requiem and his opera *Falstaff.*

In the 20th century many composers adopted a more contrapuntal style, and fugal writing came into its own again. Fugal writing is found in Shostakovich's 24 Preludes and Fugues; Hindemith's *Ludus Tonalis,* quartets, and *Mathis der Maler;* Stravinsky's *Symphony of Psalms,* Mass, Piano Concerto, and Sonata for two pianos; Bartók's quartets and Concerto for orchestra; Vaughan Williams' Fourth and Sixth Symphonies; and Michael Tippett's Second Quartet.

BIBLIOGRAPHY: Ebenezer Prout, *Fugue* (1891; reprint, 1969); André Gedalge, *Treatise on the Fugue* (1901; Eng. trans., 1965); Donald F. Tovey, *A Companion to the Art of Fugue of J. S. Bach* (1931); George Oldroyd, *The Technique and Spirit of Fugue; An Historical Study* (1948); Alfred Mann, *The Study of Fugue* (1958; reprint, 1965); John W. Verrall, *Fugue and Invention in Theory and Practice* (1966); Roger Bullivant, *Fugue* (1971).

Fuller, Albert (b. July 21, 1926) The U.S. harpsichordist Albert Fuller was educated at Johns Hopkins and Yale Universities, studying with Ralph Kirkpatrick and Hindemith. He has taught at Catholic University in Washington, D.C., Yale, and since 1964 at the Juilliard School. Fuller is also artistic director of the Aston Magna Foundation. His special interest is the French Baroque; he has edited the keyboard works of Gaspard Le Roux and has recorded Rameau and the Couperins as well as Bach and Domenico Scarlatti.

fundamental: *see* OVERTONE.

Furtwängler, (Gustav Heinrich Ernst Martin) Wilhelm (January 25, 1886–November 30, 1954) One of the major German Romantic conductors of the 20th century, Wilhelm Furtwängler was the logical heir (appointed in 1922 to the Berlin Philharmonic and the Gewandhaus Orchestra in Leipzig) to Arthur Nikisch, whose influence on his successor had been profound. Despite a most elusive baton technique, Furtwängler had the ability to implant a hugeness of concept and a spaciousness of line in any ensemble that could become accustomed to his unorthodox beat. Unorthodox, sometimes erratic in tempo and unmusicological in approach, he nevertheless had a sense of structure and proportion that produced a unified and artistic result in Romantic literature.

Furtwängler's musical training was in Munich with Joseph Rheinberger and Felix Mottl, and his first big success as a conductor was at Mannheim (1915–19). Though widely experienced in both opera and symphonic repertoire, he is best known for his work with the Berlin Philharmonic and the Vienna Philharmonic (1928–53).

Furtwängler's relations with the Nazi re-

Wilhelm Furtwängler   *Suddeutscher Verlag*

and instrumental music, composing no fewer than 18 operas, 10 oratorios, and 50 masses. His celebrated *Missa Canonica* (1708) is written in canon throughout. The *Gradus ad Parnassum* was long the standard textbook on the subject of counterpoint and was studied by 18th-century composers that included Mozart and Haydn. It is published in English in an abridged form, *Steps to Parnassus* (1943).

BIBLIOGRAPHY: Egon Wellesz, *Fux* (1965).

RECORDINGS: *Concentus musico-instrumentalis;* Harpsichord Suite in G Major; *Parthie* in A Major; Partita *à* 3 in g minor; Sinfonia in F Major for flute, oboe, and continuo.

G

Gabrieli, Andrea (*c.* 1520–1586)   A musician who, with his nephew Giovanni Gabrieli, form the apex of the Venetian school of composers that flourished toward the end of the 16th century.

Nothing is known of Gabrieli's early life, though he began to publish music in the 1550s. In the first years of the following decade he was in the service of the Duke of Bavaria at a time when Orlando di Lasso was in charge of the musical establishment at Munich. He returned to Venice to become one of the organists at St. Mark's in 1564 and remained in this post until his death. Among his pupils were his nephew and Hans Leo Hassler.

Gabrieli changed the music of the doge's chapel from something quite modest into one of the wonders of the artistic world. His experience at Munich, where one of the largest and most distinguished groups of musicians flourished, together with the material opportunities afforded by Venetian peace and prosperity after the Battle of Lepanto, made him the ideal composer for the great state festivals. Although he wrote small-scale music for the lesser churches, his finest work was composed for the resources of St. Mark's. He was one of the earliest composers to realize that sonority in itself is impressive, and his grand motets and masses exploit the tonal variety possible

gime in Germany were not entirely clear. In Germany he was generally considered anti-Nazi, and in the remainder of the world he was branded as a conspirator. Except for brief periods in 1934–35 and 1945–46, he continued his association with the Berlin orchestra. Near appointments to the New York Philharmonic (1936) and the Chicago Symphony (1949) were prevented by public hostility to his alleged Nazi collaboration.

He was a prolific composer, but his works, many on an exceedingly large scale, have been perceived as essentially derivative.

Fux, Johann Joseph (1660–February 13, 1741)   The Austrian composer Johann Joseph Fux is known for his theoretical work on counterpoint, *Gradus ad Parnassum* (1725). He became organist of the Schottenkirche in Vienna in 1696 and was appointed court composer to Emperor Leopold I in 1698. He remained at the imperial court for the remainder of his life, also holding the post of Kapellmeister at St. Stephen's Cathedral in Vienna from 1705 to 1715.

Fux was a prolific composer both of vocal

when instruments are added to a choir. He was also the first composer to exploit the architecture of St. Mark's fully, placing musicians in the several galleries high above the floor of the church to produce the dialogue effects that were to become popular in the Baroque era.

Many of his madrigals were written for secular state occasions, and he was a master of the grand style for wedding music. But his most influential works in this sphere were the less serious madrigals and canzonettas in which he displays an astonishingly light touch, using themes with attractively memorable rhythms, and a clarity of diatonic harmony that made him the model for all later Venetian composers and, through them, a strong influence on the English madrigalists. There are signs in his late music that the greater emotionalism produced by the Counter Reformation and the onset of the Mannerist madrigal were beginning to affect him; but he died before any radical change took place, and he remains the master composer of Venice's grandeur.

RECORDINGS: Aria *della battaglia;* Canzoni, Motets, Ricercare.

Gabrieli, Giovanni (c. 1557–August 12, 1612) The most important Venetian composer after his uncle Andrea Gabrieli, Giovanni Gabrieli spent time in Munich with Orlando di Lasso, returning to Venice to become organist at St. Mark's in 1585. At the same time he occupied the part-time post of organist at the Scuola Grande di S. Rocco.

The grandeur of his church music was encouraged by a particularly opulent era in Venetian public life when Marino Grimani was doge (1595–1605). During this time the musical establishment at St. Mark's was increased, with a great number of players employed and some fine castrato singers hired from Spain and elsewhere. Starting from the standpoint of his uncle, Gabrieli was to increase the splendor of sound of ceremonial music, first by composing with the timbre of contrasting groups of instruments in mind, and then by exploiting the virtuosity of both singers and players. Some of his instrumental music (notably the famed *Sonata pian'e forte*) in his *Sacrae*

Symphoniae (1597) has the names of the required instruments marked in the parts, while one canzona established the principle of the later concerto by having two highly decorated parts for cornetti contrasted with the unornamented lines given to the rest of the ensemble. If much of his church music follows his uncle quite closely in using the dialogue technique suggested by the choir galleries of St. Mark's, a number of motets expand this technique, sharpening the contrasts with sections for solo voices accompanied by organ placed adjacent to massive chordal writing for the full choir. The instrumental ensemble both accompanies the voices and plays separate interludes usually marked "sinfonia."

In his later years Gabrieli suffered from ill health, and after the doge's death the calm of Venetian life was interrupted by the break with Rome over theological disagreements. These things and the trends toward Mannerism evident in the madrigals of Monteverdi and Carlo Gesualdo caused a change of style toward the end of Gabrieli's life, and a greater intensity dominates some of his last motets. His pupils followed him in this modernism, and he was one of the most influential figures in early 17th-century German music. Never a revolutionary, he remained content to enrich the splendid colors of his uncle's work with some darker tinges reflecting a new and more troubled age.

BIBLIOGRAPHY: E. F. Kenton, *The Life and Works of Giovanni Gabrieli* (1967).

RECORDINGS: Canzoni; Intonazioni d'organo (11); Motets; Sonatas; *Sacrae Symphoniae.*

Gabrilowitsch, Ossip (February 7, 1878–September 14, 1936) Often called "the poet of the piano," the Russian-born pianist and conductor Ossip Gabrilowitsch was educated at the St. Petersburg Conservatory, studying with Anton Rubinstein (he won the Rubinstein Prize in 1894) and later with Leschetizky in Vienna. At 18 he toured in Germany, Austria, and England, and in 1900 he first toured the United States. He married the singer Clara Clemens, Mark Twain's daughter, in 1906. After conducting in Munich and Vienna he settled in the United States in 1918 and became conductor of the Detroit Symphony, alternating between conducting and concertizing. Gabrilowitsch composed an *Ouverture Rhapsodie* for orchestra, an elegy for cello, and piano pieces.

BIBLIOGRAPHY: Clara Clemens, *My Husband, Gabrilowitsch* (1938).

Gade, Niels (Vilhelm) (February 22, 1817–December 21, 1890)   A Danish conductor and composer inspired by folk music, Niels Gade studied violin with F. T. Wexschall and composition with A. P. Berggreen, who introduced him to Danish poetry and folk music. His overture *Echoes from Ossian* won the Copenhagen Musical Society's prize in 1840. Both Mendelssohn and Schumann, who wrote of him in the *Neue Zeitschrift für Musik,* were attracted by the Scandinavian character of his music, and in 1843 Mendelssohn conducted his First Symphony in Leipzig. In the following year and also in 1847 the Gewandhaus concerts in Leipzig were conducted by Gade. He was conductor of the Copenhagen Musical Society in 1850 and in 1866 was appointed one of the directors of the Copenhagen Conservatory. In 1876 he conducted his cantatas *Zion* and *The Crusaders* at the Birmingham Festival, for which he also wrote the cantata *Psyche* (1882). His works include eight symphonies, three ballets, a violin concerto, and chamber works. Gade's early works, spontaneously reflecting the spirit of Danish folk tunes, were among the first 19th-century examples of national music. Under the influence of Mendelssohn his later works show greater technical command but often at the expense of the ingenious style that had made his earlier works attractive.

RECORDINGS: *Aquarelles* for piano; cantata *Elverskud.*

Gagliano, Marco da (*c.* 1575–February 24, 1642)   The Italian composer Marco da Gagliano is remembered chiefly for his operas. He worked in Florence from about 1608 to 1625 as organist to Cosimo II de' Medici. In 1607 he visited Duke Ferdinando Gonzaga of Mantua, staging his opera *Dafne* at Mantua in 1608. *Il Medoro,* composed with Jacopo Peri in 1619, is lost; *La Flora* was produced in Florence in 1628. Gagliano kept to the simple

pastoral idiom of the Florentine camerata, though his recitative is musically richer than Peri's or Giulio Caccini's, and he provides a greater variety of set numbers. His work seems pale, however, beside the dramatic and musical grasp of Monteverdi's *Orfeo* (Mantua, 1607). He also published sacred music and madrigals between 1594 and 1630.

RECORDINGS: *Dafne.*

gallant style (French, *style galant*)   An 18th-century movement that emphasized the light and sophisticated as opposed to the stylistic complexity of the preceding Baroque era. The gallant style was most closely associated with France, although its influence was felt throughout Europe.

As applied to music the term appeared as early as 1708 in Johann Gottfried Walther's *Praecepta der musikalischen Composition.* Music in the gallant style was characterized by a studied simplicity of texture and form, a tendency toward excessive ornamentation, and a witty, nonserious emotional stance—an aristocratic music for aristocratic listeners who were receptive to its refined, highly mannered tone. It represented a reaction against the weighty Baroque style as exemplified by the ponderous operas of Lully and the complex polyphony of Bach. It found its most characteristic manifestation in the elegant keyboard music of such French composers as François Couperin, Jean-François Dandrieu, Louis Marchand, and Louis Claude Daquin. Their graceful miniatures for harpsichord charmed and eventually influenced a number of German and Italian musicians. In dramatic music the opera-ballets of André Campra and Rameau marked a definite departure from the stilted, courtly operas of Lully and led the way to such gallant comic works as *La serva padrona* (1733) by Pergolesi and *Le Devin du village* (1752) by Rousseau.

Throughout the first half of the 18th century, gallant style music became increasingly popular, but during the second half of the century such men as Carl Philipp Emanuel Bach were attempting to inject a new sensivity to emotion, leading to the more expressive idiom known as the EMPFINDSAMER STIL.

Visual practitioners of the gallant style include such 18th-century French painters as Antoine Watteau, Nicolas Lancet, and Jean-Baptiste Pater, whose aesthetic ideal was sophisticated lightness and ornamentation, intimacy and smallness of scale, technical and formal refinement, and prettiness.

galliard (French, *gaillard;* Italian, *gagliarda;* Spanish, *gallarda*) A 16th-century court dance from the French for "lively" but originating in 15th-century Italy. Coupled with the pavane, it became the earliest of court dances. Although the music was in $\frac{3}{4}$ time, the dance was performed, often without holding hands, to counts of six (two measures) with various kicking and jumping steps on 1, 2, 3, 4, a high jump on 5, and a cadence posture on 6. Hence it acquired the name of *cinqpas,* or the English cincopace. Musicians usually wrote pavanes and galliards in pairs, the galliard tune becoming a rhythmic adaptation of the pavane that it followed. Early examples are to be found in a collection printed by Pierre Attaingnant in 1529.

Gallican chant The music of the ancient liturgies used in France for about 400 years from the beginning of the 5th century. The problem of tracing its origin and development to its suppression under Charlemagne at the end of the 8th century can only be solved in relation to the origin of the Gallican liturgy. Scholars tend to assume that a virtually uniform liturgical chant existed in the West to the end of the 5th century and that only in the 6th and 7th centuries did the Gallican Church develop its peculiar rite by introducing a number of feasts and customs from the East together with their melodies. One of the main differences between the celebration of the mass in the Roman and the Gallican rites was the Gallican adoption of the Eastern Orthodox *Trisagion* in place of the Gloria in the Roman mass. Gallican chant differs from the so-called Gregorian chant in that it is richly ornamented and contains traits that are common in Eastern chant. When Pepin III came to power in 751, he tried to unify the Western rites, a tendency pursued even more vigorously by his son Charlemagne. Their intention of making the Roman rite the only legal one was widely opposed by the clergy and was hampered by

the small number of books of Roman chant available. In fact the opposite of what was intended occurred: the richness and beauty of some of the Gallican customs and their music impressed the liturgists of Rome so that a number of Gallican chants were introduced into the Roman repertoire. Thus from the 9th century the chant of the Roman Church became a mixture of Roman and Gallican elements and has descended in that form.

BIBLIOGRAPHY: Egon Wellesz, *Eastern Elements in Western Chant* (1947).

Galli-Curci, Amelita (November 18, 1882–November 26, 1963) Self-taught as a singer, the coloratura soprano Amelita Galli-Curci studied composition and piano in her native Milan. After her Italian debut as Gilda in Verdi's *Rigoletto,* she toured in Egypt, South America, Spain, and Russia. A U.S. debut in Chicago in 1916, again as Gilda, was followed

Amelita Galli-Curci as Lakmé, c. 1925
The Bettmann Archive, Inc.

by acclaimed performances in New York City, and from 1921 to 1930 she sang at the Metropolitan Opera. Her repertoire included 28 operas from Rossini to Richard Strauss, and she was especially celebrated as Meyerbeer's Dinorah. She retired in 1936.

Gallus, Jacobus: *see* HANDL, JAKOB.

galop A lively social dance in $\frac{2}{4}$ time of German origin but popular in England and France during the 19th century. Its spirited rhythm occurs in Amilcare Ponchielli's "Dance of the Hours" from *La Gioconda* (1876) and in many ballets. Liszt used the form in the piano pieces *Grand Galop Chromatique, Galop de Bal,* and *Galop* in a minor (all 1838 to *c.* 1841). Its basic step (slide, close, and slide) is considerably elaborated for theatrical usage.

Galuppi, Baldassare (October 18, 1706–January 3, 1785) An Italian composer known chiefly for his comic operas, Baldassare Galuppi was born on the island of Burano near Venice—hence his nickname Il Buranello. His father, a barber and a violinist at the local theater, was his first teacher, and later he studied at Venice with Antonio Lotti. After producing two operas in collaboration with Giovanni Battista Pescetti, Galuppi began to compose operas for the Venetian theater, writing sometimes as many as five a year. In 1741 he visited London and arranged a pasticcio, *Alexander in Persia,* for the Haymarket Theatre; several of his own operas were produced in England, including *Enrico* (1743), and Charles Burney considered his influence on English composers to have been powerful. In 1748 he was appointed maestro di cappella at St. Mark's in Venice and in 1762 director of the Conservatorio degli Incurabili. Catherine II invited him to Russia, where in 1768 he composed the opera seria, *Ifigenia in Tauride.* He returned to Venice later that year.

Galuppi's best works are his comic operas, of which *Il Filosofo di Campagna* (Venice, 1754) was the most popular. His melodies are vivacious and attractive and his harmonic and orchestral technique often superior to that of his contemporaries. He also wrote religious works and some instrumental pieces, especially sonatas for harpsichord and concertante quartets for strings.

RECORDINGS: Harpsichord Sonatas (12); Trio in G Major.

gamba: *see* VIOLA DA GAMBA.

gamelan The indigenous orchestra of Java and Bali consisting mostly of several varieties of gongs and of instruments of the xylophone type. The gongs are suspended vertically or, as with the kettle-shaped *bonang,* are placed flat. The xylophone type includes instruments with metal plates, or keys, freely suspended (the *saron*) or placed on top of resonance tubes (the *gendèr*) and xylophones proper, viz., with wooden keys (the *gamban kayu*). Sustaining a melody falls to the bamboo flute *(suling),* to a bowed stringed instrument *(rebab),* or to the human voice—in theatrical performances known as *wayang*—the voice being part of the orchestral texture. Dominating these two groups is the drum (the *kendang*), uniting them and acting as leader.

The highly developed polyphony or heterophony of the gamelan has a rhythmic origin. A nuclear theme extends over a number of measures (almost invariably in $\frac{4}{4}$ time), against which other instruments play a largely independent countermelody. Another group plays rhythmical paraphrases of this theme, and a fourth group fills out the texture with delicate rhythmical improvisations. Highly important are the punctuating, or colotomic, instruments that divide the musical sentence, marking, as it were, the commas, semicolons, and full stops. This last-named function is entrusted to the big gong. Over this scintillating pattern of hammered sound floats the uninterrupted melodic line of the voice, flute, or *rebab.*

This type of music with its peculiar tonal system is not confined to the Indonesian archipelago but has close relatives in other parts of southeast Asia, particularly in Burma and Thailand. Nowhere else, however, has it attained such refinement. In view of undeniable kinship with prehistoric lithophones (stone chimes) discovered in Indochina, it seems likely that the music of the gamelan was brought to the Indonesian archipelago by migrant tribes from the mainland. Some scholars believe that the scales of Java and Bali are of Chinese origin, possibly from the pre-emigration period. The main outside influences

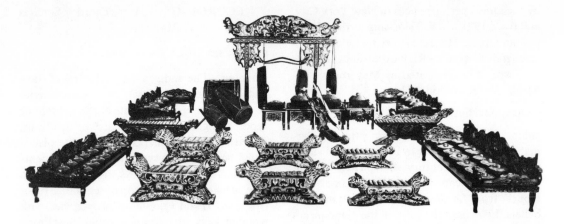

Javanese gamelan   *courtesy, Field Museum of Natural History, Chicago*

certainly came from China and—until about
A.D. 900—from India. Following the conversion (*c.* 1300) of the archipelago (except Bali)
to the Islamic relgion, Persian-Arabic influences made themselves felt. In view of the
basically different scale systems of India and
Indonesia, Indian influence is not immediately
apparent, but it is possible that the Indonesian
modal character and the connection of its
modal patterns *(patet)* with special episodes
of dramatic performances are derived from
Indian conceptions. The name of one of the
two scales in use, the pentatonic *sléndro,* is
sometimes thought to have been derived from
Shailendra, the name of an Indian dynasty
during the latter half of the first millennium.
Certainly the *sléndro* scale, if it is of Indian
origin, has completely coalesced with the indigenous system and flourishes side by side
with the heptatonic *pélog.* Many of the Indian
instruments, however, that are depicted on ancient Hindu-Javanese temples have disappeared. The melody-carrying *rebab* is of Persian-Arabic origin.

Although the gamelan styles of Java and
Bali are closely related, they are strongly differentiated individually, perhaps because the
finest of the Javanese gamelans were developed
at the highly formalized courts of middle Java,
whereas in Bali art belongs to people of all
strata of society and is an expression of their
natural exuberance.

BIBLIOGRAPHY: Mantle Hood, *The Nuclear Theme as Determinant of Patet in Javanese Music* (1954; reprint, 1977); Donald A.
Lentz, *The Gamelan Music of Java and Bali*
(1965); Jaap Kunst, *Music in Java,* 2 vols.,
rev. ed. (1973).

Ganz, Rudolph (February 24, 1877–August
2, 1972)   Educated in Zürich and later a pupil
of Busoni, the Swiss-American Rudolph Ganz
had a career balanced almost equally among
those of pianist, conductor, composer, and
educator. A pioneer recording artist (before
1910), he also championed works by the avant-
garde, introducing pieces by Busoni, Debussy,
Ravel, Bartók, Honegger, and Copland.
Among a number of conducting posts he held
was that of the St. Louis Symphony (1921–
27). As an educator he was associated with
Chicago Musical College (1901–05 and from
1927; later part of Roosevelt University),
where he taught into his 90s. His compositions
cover a wide spectrum.

García, Manuel (del Popolo Vicente) (January
22, 1775–June 2, 1832)   The first of a family
of renowned singers (including daughters Maria Malibran and Pauline Viardot), the Spanish tenor and composer Manuel García made
his debut in Paris in 1808 in Ferdinando Paër's
La Griselda. He was acclaimed also in England, where he founded a singing school, and
in the United States, where he established an
Italian opera company that gave nine new operas in the 1825–26 season. Rossini wrote the
role of Count Almaviva *(Il barbiero di Siviglia)*
for him. Catalogues of the music historian

François Joseph Fétis list 97 operas (71 Spanish, 19 Italian, and seven French) among his compositions. His son, Manuel Patricio Rodriguez García, was the most celebrated singing teacher of his century.

Garden, Mary (February 20, 1877–January 3, 1967)   The Scottish-born soprano and actress Mary Garden was educated in Chicago and then in Paris with Mathilde Marchesi. She made her Paris debut in 1900 as a last-minute replacement in the role of Gustave Charpentier's Louise; with Verdi's Violetta *(La Traviata),* Richard Strauss's Salome, and Debussy's Mélisande, this remained one of her most popular roles. Her U.S. debut was as Massenet's Thaïs in 1907. She was chosen (over the objection of playwright Maurice Maeterlinck) by Debussy to create the role of Mélisande in *Pelléas et Mélisande.* In 1910 she joined the Chicago Opera and was director of the opera association there in 1921–22. Her influence helped retain French opera in the

Mary Garden as Mélisande
The Bettmann Archive, Inc.

company's repertoire. In 1935 she taught master classes at Chicago Musical College and then went to Hollywood as technical adviser for operatic sequences in films. Her autobiography, *Mary Garden's Story,* written with Louis Biancolli, appeared in 1951. She made some acoustic recordings of French opera arias and Scottish and Irish songs.

Gaultier, Denys, or **Gaultier le Jeune** (1597 or 1603–January 1672)   The last great exponent of the group of lutenists called the École de Paris, Denys Gaultier came from a renowned family of lutenists that also included Jacques and Ennemond Gaultier. He was also a composer whose chief contribution to the music literature of the period is the Hamilton codex of 69 compositions called *La Rhétorique des Dieux* (1664–72), a collection of short pieces, mainly dances, in tablature for lute, arranged in groups of suites. The characteristic way in which Gaultier labeled his pieces with fanciful and descriptive titles is a feature later to be found in the music of the clavecinists. His style explores the full range of the French style ornamentation and broken chords *(style brisé)* are to be found in all his work, again a facet of the lute style later to be transferred to the keyboard. Gaultier was enormously popular in his own time, and toward the end of his life much of his music was transcribed in staff notation so that it might reach the wider public of keyboard players. He was the originator of the *tombeau,* a small piece written to the memory of a great personage.

Gautier, Théophile: *see* BALLET (Romantic ballet).

gavotte   Originally a sturdy peasants' dance that became fashionable at the 17th- and 18th-century courts of France and England. Supposedly originated by the natives of Gap (Gavots) in the French province of Dauphiné, the gavotte was danced in royal ballrooms as a round with skipping steps adapted from the branle. Couples concluded improvised duet performances by kissing their partners. Later the dance developed more formal figures, and flowers were exchanged instead of kisses. At the French court in the 18th century, the gavotte was at first stately and later more ornate; its slow walking steps were in $\frac{4}{4}$ time with upbeats on beats 3 and 4.

Lully introduced the form into his operas and ballets, and it began to appear in the suites of Jean Henri d'Anglebert, François Couperin, Johann Pachelbel, and Bach. Its three-part composition is written in its early lusty $\frac{2}{2}$ rhythm but retains the later two upbeats; its second section is a musette (French for bagpipe), a pastoral air in which a drone bass runs throughout.

Gay, John: *see* BALLAD OPERA; HANDEL (life); POPULAR MUSIC (Baroque).

Gebrauchsmusik A 20th-century term for music written specifically for performance by the talented amateur instead of the virtuoso. The word is German meaning "music for use." Associated with neoclassicism, Gebrauchsmusik can be traced back to the simple keyboard and lute pieces of the Renaissance and to the chamber music of the Baroque and Classical eras. The leading exponent of Gebrauchsmusik and the inventor of the word was Hindemith, whose numerous sonatas for a wide variety of instruments have attracted musicians of all types.

Gedda, Nicolai (b. July 11, 1925) A student of his father (one of the Don Cossack chorus) and later at the Stockholm Academy, the Swedish-Russian lyric *spinto* tenor Nicolai Gedda made his debut in Stockholm (1952) as Chapelou in Adolphe Adam's *Le Postillon de Longjumeau*. In 1957 he made his New York Metropolitan debut as Gounod's Faust. He has toured Europe and the United States and is esteemed in opera, oratorio, and recital. His repertoire ranges from Handel to Carl Orff, and he premiered the role of Anatol in Samuel Barber's *Vanessa* in 1958 at the Metropolitan. He is heard in two recordings of Mussorgsky's *Boris Godunov,* in the highly regarded Colin Davis recordings of Berlioz' *Damnation of Faust* and *Benvenuto Cellini,* in four Mozart operas, Bizet's *Carmen,* and Albert Lortzing's *Zar und Zimmermann* and *Undine.*

Geminiani, Francesco (baptized December 5, 1687–September 17, 1762) The Italian composer and violinist Francesco Geminiani was a writer on musical performance and a leading figure in early 18th-century music. Born at Lucca, he held posts in his native city and in Naples before going to England in 1714. In London he established himself as an exceptionally brilliant performer. His Opus 1 Sonatas for violin and continuo were published in 1716 and were widely regarded as equal to those of Corelli, under whom Geminiani may have studied. They were, however, considered to be almost unplayable because of their technical difficulty. He advanced violin technique by using and teaching double stops and changes of position. Geminiani published further solo and trio sonatas but was chiefly noted for his concerti grossi, of which his Opus 2 and Opus 3 sets became extremely popular in England and held a place in the concert repertoire until early in the 19th century. Later in his life Geminiani spent periods in Paris and Dublin. His theoretical works, of which *The Art of Playing on the Violin* (1731) is the most important, had considerable influence in 18th-century England and remain an important source of information on the performance of late Baroque music.

RECORDINGS: Cello Sonatas (6); Concerti Grossi, Opp. 2, 3, and 4; Flute Sonata in D Major.

Genevan Psalter: *see* HYMN (Genevan psalmody); LE JEUNE; PSALMODY; RENAISSANCE (Reformation).

Gerhard, Roberto (September 25, 1896–January 5, 1970) A naturalized English citizen, the Spanish-born composer Roberto Gerhard studied with Enrique Granados and with Schoenberg. Early works show the influence of Debussy and Ravel (Piano Trio, 1918). By 1928 his music reflected Schoenberg's tutelage (Wind Quintet), although Gerhard's treatment of the series was not dodecaphonic. His opera *The Duenna* (1949), although Spanish in idiom, summarized the styles and techniques of his previous work. The Piano Concerto (1950) was consistently 12-tone, combined with the traditions of early polyphonic Spanish keyboard music, and the Harpsichord Concerto (1955–56) is based on a Spanish folk tune. Conventional formal and thematic writing was abandoned in the Symphonies Nos.

1, 2, and 4 (1953, 1959, 1967); the Third and Fourth Symphonies call for electronic tape. Although his music has some echoes of Bartók, it is never imitative; innovative techniques are the reconciliation of dodecaphony with a harmonic basis (Violin Concerto, 1942–49) and the use of time proportions derived from pitch by measuring distances of semitones (Quartet, 1955). He wrote chamber music, five ballets (*Ariel,* 1934; *Soirées de Barcelone,* 1936–38; *Don Quixote,* 1941; *Alegrias,* 1942; *Pandora,* 1944), an oratorio after Albert Camus (*La Peste,* 1963), and a chamber symphony (1969). His aesthetics are found in his essays *Tonality in Twelve-tone Music and Developments in Twelve-tone Technique* (1952). He has also edited the works of several 18th-century Spanish composers.

RECORDINGS: *Alegrias* (suite); Concerto for orchestra; *Don Quixote* (suite); *The Plague* (cantata); Symphonies Nos. 1 and 4; Violin Concerto; Wind Quintet.

Gerhardt, Elena (November 11, 1883–January 11, 1961) A noted lieder recitalist and a pioneer in promoting the songs of Hugo Wolf, the German mezzo-soprano Elena Gerhardt studied at the Leipzig Conservatory and coached with Arthur Nikisch. In 1933 she went to London and devoted her time to teaching. Her autobiography *Recital* appeared in 1953.

Germani, Fernando (b. April 5, 1906) Primarily self-taught, the Italian organist Fernando Germani taught at the Accademia di Santa Cecilia in Rome before his appointment as head of the organ department of the Curtis Institute (1931–33) and professor of organ at the Accademia Chigiana of Siena (1939). He has made extensive tours as an organ virtuoso in Europe and the United States and has recorded music of Bach and of 19th-century French composers. He published an organ method in 1942.

Gershwin, George (September 26, 1898–July 11, 1937) A U.S. composer whose songs and orchestral and stage works derived from jazz created a new type of urban American music, George Gershwin was born in Brooklyn of Jewish-Russian immigrant parents. He took music lessons in New York City and was employed as a pianist in a music publishing house. In 1919 Gershwin achieved his first popular success with the song *Swanee,* its nervous energy already characteristic of his style. He subsequently collaborated with his brother Ira Gershwin, a gifted writer of lyrics, and together they produced popular and elegantly composed musical comedies on Broadway, among them *Lady Be Good* (1924), *Strike Up the Band* (1927), and *Of Thee I Sing* (1931), the last a political satire that was awarded the Pulitzer Prize.

In his *Rhapsody in Blue,* commissioned by Paul Whiteman and orchestrated by Ferde Grofé, Gershwin originated a novel type of symphonic jazz in which popular American rhythms and melodic patterns provide thematic material for works in traditional forms. Gershwin was the soloist at its first performance in 1924. The next year a sequel was produced with the Piano Concerto in F Major, following the traditional piano concerto form. In 1928 Gershwin wrote the symphonic poem *An American in Paris,* in which quotations from popular French music alternate with original dance tunes, the score including parts to be played by Paris taxi horns. The Second Rhapsody for piano and orchestra, which Gershwin played with the Boston Symphony in 1932, fell below the spontaneous inspiration of the *Rhapsody in Blue* and remained unsuccessful.

Gershwin's last and finest work was the opera *Porgy and Bess* with a libretto based on Negro life by DuBose Heyward and written for black singers. It was first staged in Boston in 1935 and subsequently in New York City, Europe, and the U.S.S.R. Although its initial reception was not enthusiastic, the opera grew in popularity and became especially known for its songs, "Summertime," "I Got Plenty o'Nuttin" and "It Ain't Necessarily So."

BIBLIOGRAPHY: Isaac Goldberg, *George Gershwin, a Study in American Music* (1931); Merle Armitage, ed., *George Gershwin* (1938; reprinted as *George Gershwin, Man and Legend,* 1958); David Ewen, *A Journey to Greatness; the Life and Music of George Gershwin* (1956); Edward Jablonski and Lawrence D. Stewart, *The Gershwin Years* (1973); Robert

Kimball and Alfred Simon, *The Gershwins* (1973).

RECORDINGS: Numerous recordings of most works.

Gesang der Jünglinge: *see* ELECTRONIC MUSIC (tape music); MODERN PERIOD (electronic music); STOCKHAUSEN.

Gesualdo, Carlo (*c.* 1560–September 8, 1613) An Italian composer and lutenist whose musical fame rests on his six sets of five-part madrigals, Carlo Gesualdo was born in Naples and was Prince of Venosa from 1591. He won notoriety by ordering the murder of his first wife for her unfaithfulness. His madrigals were published between 1594 and 1611 in the usual partbooks and in 1613 were printed in score—one of the first publications of its kind. The madrigals in the first four books are conventional pieces of competent workmanship, typical of their age. The astonishing madrigals in the last two books, with their dramatic exclamations, discontinuous texture, and harmonic license, are not "progressive" as has often been said. They are, rather, the work of a highly individual composer and as such lacked any successors in this vein.

BIBLIOGRAPHY: Cecil Gray and Philip Heseltine, *Carlo Gesualdo, Prince of Venosa, Musician and Murderer* (1926); Glenn Watkins, *Gesualdo; the Man and His Music* (1973).

RECORDINGS: Madrigals and responsories.

Ghiglia, Oscar (b. August 13, 1938) The Italian guitarist Oscar Ghiglia graduated from the Conservatorio di Santa Cecilia in Rome (1961) and then studied guitar with Andrés Segovia and Alirio Diaz. He made his debut at Spoleto (1962) and the following year won first prize at the international competition at Santiago de Compostela in Spain. He has been artist-in-residence at the Aspen (Colorado) Festival since 1969 and has taught summers since 1976 at the Accademia Chigiana in Siena, Italy. His repertoire is eclectic, and his recordings range from the Baroque masters to *Dark Angels* (1976) by Peter Maxwell Davies, in which he appears with soprano Jan de Gaetani.

Giacosa, Giuseppe: *see* PUCCINI.

Gianni Schicchi: *see* OPERA (the 19th century); PUCCINI.

Giannini, Vittorio (October 19, 1903–November 28, 1966) A U.S. composer of Italian extraction known for his operas, Vittorio Giannini was born in Philadelphia and studied in Milan and in New York City with Rubin Goldmark and Hans Letz. In 1932 he won the music prize of the American Academy in Rome and in 1939 was appointed teacher of composition at the Juilliard School in New York. Two of his early operas were first performed in Germany: *Lucedia* (Munich, 1934) and *The Scarlet Letter* (Hamburg, 1938), based on the novel by Nathaniel Hawthorne and with Giannini's sister Dusolina in the principal part. He wrote two operas for radio production, *Beauty and the Beast* (1938) and *Blennerhasset* (1939), and his opera *The Taming of the Shrew* was the first produced for color television (1954). His last two operas were *Rehearsal Call* (1962), an opera buffa, and *The Servant of Two Masters* (produced posthumously in 1967), after the play by Carlo Goldoni. Between 1936 and 1959 he also wrote symphonies, a requiem (1937), chamber music, songs, and concertos for piano, violin, and organ.

RECORDINGS: Symphony No. 3; *The Taming of the Shrew.*

Giardini, Felice (April 12, 1716–June 8, 1796) A celebrated Italian violinist and composer who influenced musical development in England, Felice Giardini was a chorister at the Milan Cathedral and studied singing, composition, and harpsichord with Paladini. He returned to Turin to study violin with Giovanni Battista Somis, a well-known violinist of the period. As a youth Giardini played in the opera orchestras in Rome and Naples. In 1748 he toured Germany and made his way to London, where he arrived about 1750. His brilliant style of playing won him a great reputation in England, and he spent the greater part of his life in London as a composer, violinist, concert director, leader at the opera, and sometimes even impresario. With his younger colleagues Johann Christian Bach,

Karl Friedrich Abel, and Johann Christian Fischer, he was one of the acknowledged leaders of the new gallant style, which they introduced and established in Britain. Giardini was long accepted as the greatest violinist in England, a position he held without dispute until the arrival of Wilhelm Cramer and Johann Peter Salomon in the latter part of the century. In 1784 Giardini left England to retire to his native Italy, but he returned again to London and about 1790 was directing operas at the Haymarket. He then went to St. Petersburg (c. 1793), and he died in Moscow. Giardini was a prolific composer, but his music lacks the spontaneity and warmth of Bach and Abel.

Gibbons, Orlando (1583–June 5, 1625) One of the last great figures of the English polyphonic school, Orlando Gibbons was the most illustrious of a large family of musicians.

At the age of 12 Gibbons became a chorister at King's College, Cambridge, where he took the degree of bachelor of music in 1606. At the age of 21 he was made organist of the Chapel Royal, a post he retained for the remainder of his life. In 1619 he was appointed one of the "musicians for the virginalles to attend in his highnes privie chamber," and in 1622 he was made an honorary doctor of music at Oxford University. The following year he became organist of Westminster Abbey, where in April 1625 he conducted the music for the funeral service of James I. Gibbons was part of the retinue attending Charles I when the king traveled to Dover to meet his bride, Henrietta Maria, on her arrival from France. On the journey back Gibbons succumbed to apoplexy at Canterbury and was buried in the cathedral there.

Of the considerable amount of church music written by Gibbons, only two anthems were published in his lifetime. After his death J. Barnard in his *First Book of Selected Church Musick* (1641) included both of Gibbons' services for the English rite, his first preces and psalms and five anthems. The first service and three of the anthems were reprinted in William Boyce's *Cathedral Music* (1760–73), and these works remained for a long time in the English cathedral repertoire. Of the 40 or so anthems

that survive, only 15 are purely polyphonic; the remainder are verse anthems in which the solo voice, accompanied by organ or viols, alternates with the chorus. Gibbons' full anthems are among the most distinguished works of any British composer of any age, as are the "little" anthems of four parts.

His *Madrigals and Motetts of 5 parts . . .* was published in 1612. This collection contains deeply felt and very personal settings of texts that are, for the most part, of a moral or philosophical nature. It shows Gibbons' mastery of the polyphonic idiom of his day and contains many undisputed masterpieces of late madrigalist style, among them the well-known "The Silver Swan" and "What Is Our Life?" Two years previously there appeared *Fantasies in Three Parts Compos'd for viols* (c. 1610), said to be the first music printed in England from engraved copperplates. This, together with a quantity of viol music preserved in manuscript, shows Gibbons to be one of the foremost composers at a time when English viol music was in its prime.

Gibbons was famous as a keyboard player, and toward the end of his life he was said to be without rival in England as an organist and virginalist. Several of his virginal pieces were published in *Parthenia* (c. 1612), and more than 40 others survive in manuscript. Gibbons lived at a time when the polyphonic and basically vocal styles of the 16th century were becoming modified by a more markedly instrumental and harmonically conceived idiom. These changes left him almost untouched; rather his music sums up the achievement of the past generation.

Gibbons had seven children, one of whom, his son Christopher (1615–76), was a distinguished composer of keyboard music as well as a notable contributor to the stage music of his time.

BIBLIOGRAPHY: Edmund H. Fellowes, *Orlando Gibbons; a Short Account of His Life and Work* (1925; reprinted as *Orlando Gibbons and His Family; the Last of the Tudor School of Musicians,* 1951).

RECORDINGS: First Set of Madrigals and Motets in 5 Parts; *Veni Creator;* various pieces for keyboard.

Gieseking, Walter (Wilhelm) (November 5, 1895–October 26, 1956)   Perhaps the greatest interpreter of the French Impressionists, the German pianist Walter Gieseking studied with Karl Leimer at the Hanover Conservatory. Although his repertoire was widely varied (he played all of the Beethoven piano sonatas in a series of recitals when he was 15), his control of tone and color and his use of the pedal brought him acclaim in the works of Debussy and Ravel. Gieseking also composed, mostly chamber music involving the piano.

Walter Gieseking   *courtesy, Angel Records*

Gigli, Beniamino (March 20, 1890–November 30, 1957)   A student at the Conservatorio di Santa Cecilia, the Italian lyric-dramatic tenor Beniamino Gigli made his debut as Enzo in Amilcare Ponchielli's *La Gioconda* in 1914. Tours of European opera houses culminated in success at La Scala in 1918 as Faust in

Arrigo Boito's *Mefistofele,* in which role he made his New York Metropolitan debut two years later. Recognized as one of the finest tenors of his time, his roles included standard Italian and French opera as well as Wagner's Lohengrin. He was one of the most recorded tenors of his day, noted for a Verdi Requiem and roles in Umberto Giordano's *Andrea Chenier,* Mascagni's *Cavalleria Rusticana,* and Leoncavallo's *Pagliacci.* He recorded several Verdi and Puccini operas complete on 78s, an unusual practice at that time.

Gigout, Eugène (March 23, 1844–December 9, 1925)   A student of Saint-Saëns at the Niedermeyer École de Musique Religieuse in Paris, the French organist and composer Eugène Gigout taught there (1863–85 and 1900–05). He became organist at the church of Saint-Augustin in 1863 and in 1885 established a state subsidized organ school. He succeeded Alexandre Guilmant as organ professor at the Paris Conservatoire in 1911. A prominent recitalist in Europe, he was noted for his improvisations. His songs, anthems, and instrumental works are forgotten except for his organ music, which comprises approximately 50 large works and 400 smaller pieces.

gigue   The courtly version of the English jig from which it derived its name when entering the court circles of continental Europe in the 17th century. Scottish and Irish jigs were quick and wild and of indefinite form and rhythm, but gigues were danced by couples in formal ballet style generally in $\frac{6}{8}$ or $\frac{12}{8}$ time with melodic lines fashioned of rapidly moving groups of three eighth-notes. In the instrumental suite the gigue attained importance as the final movement, invariably written in fugal style and retaining the rapid groups of three eighth-notes. The Italian *giga* was quicker and not fugal.

Gilbert, W. S.: *see* CARTE; OPERETTA; SULLIVAN.

Gilels, Emil (Grigoryevich) (b. October 19, 1916)   The Soviet pianist Emil Gilels was educated at the conservatories in Odessa and in Moscow, and he has taught at the latter since 1936 (professor since 1954). Among his numerous prizes were the Stalin (1946) and the Lenin (1962). A strong, objective player of the Russian Romantic school, Gilels was one of the first to emerge past the Iron Curtain. He has since toured and recorded extensively.

Gillet, Georges (1854–?)   The French oboist Georges Gillet was trained at the Paris Conservatoire, winning the first prize in oboe when he was only 15. He was solo oboist at the Théâtre-Italien, Colonne concerts, Société des Concerts, Opéra-Comique, and Paris Opéra (1878–1904). Gillet was appointed professor at the Conservatoire in 1881, where one of his pupils was Marcel Tabuteau. He published a set of very difficult studies in 1909.

Gilmore, Patrick Sarsfield: *see* BAND.

Ginastera, Alberto (Evaristo) (b. April 11, 1916)   A leading 20th-century Latin-American composer, Alberto Ginastera is known for his use of local and national musical idioms. He studied in Buenos Aires at the Conservatorio Williams and the National Conservatory; he received a Guggenheim award and lived in the United States in 1946–47. Ginastera returned to Argentina and organized the Center for Advanced Musical Studies at the Instituto Torcuato di Tella in Buenos Aires, serving as its director (1963–71). He later made his home in Geneva, Switzerland.

Ginastera considers himself a traditionalist despite his advanced musical vocabulary, which owes much to the great musical figures of the early 20th century. In synthesis of techniques he makes use of microtones, serial procedures, *Sprechstimme,* and aleatory, or chance, music as well as older established forms and manners. Ginastera's First Piano Concerto and Cantata *para América mágica* won great acclaim at the 1961 Inter-American Music Festival. Other works include two ballets (*Panumbi* and *Estancia*), a violin concerto, a second piano concerto, orchestral pieces, songs, and chamber music.

His first opera *Don Rodrigo* (1964), unsuccessful in its premiere in Buenos Aires, was hailed as a triumph in New York City in 1966. Ginastera's chamber opera *Bomarzo* (1967) also attracted considerable attention. A third opera, *Beatrix Cenci,* was commissioned for the opening of the John F. Kennedy Center for the Performing Arts in Washington, D.C.,

in 1971; it further exemplified Ginastera's statement that "sex, violence and hallucination are three of the basic elements from which grand opera can be constructed."

RECORDINGS: *American* Preludes (12) for piano; Cantata *para América mágica;* Concerto for Strings; suites from *Estancia* and *Panambi;* Piano Concertos (2); Piano Quintet; Piano Sonata; Quartet No. 2; Variaciones Concertantes for orchestra.

Gioconda, La: *see* BOITO; GALOP; PONCHIELLI.

gioielli della Madonna, I: *see* OPERA (the 20th century); WOLF-FERRARI.

Giordano, Umberto (August 27, 1867–November 12, 1948)   An Italian opera composer in the verismo tradition, Umberto Giordano is known primarily for his *Andrea Chénier.* The son of an artisan, he studied music first in his native town of Foggia and then at the Naples Conservatory. He reached manhood when Mascagni was startling the world with the realism of *Cavalleria Rusticana* (1890); Giordano's early operas, among them *Mala vita* (1892), were written in the same forceful, melodramatic style. In *Andrea Chénier* (1896), based on the life of the French revolutionary poet, he tempered violence with gentler characteristics and scored a lasting success. Neither *Fedora* (1898), based on Victorien Sardou's play, nor its chief successors, *Siberia* (1903) and *Madame Sans-Gêne* (1915), achieved a similar popularity. In *La Cena delle Beffe* (1924) Giordano reverted to a sensational manner with a story set in medieval Florence.

RECORDINGS: *Andrea Chénier; Fedora.*

Girl of the Golden West: *see* PUCCINI.

Giselle: *see* ADAM, ADOLPHE-CHARLES; BALLET (Romantic ballet).

Giuliani, Mauro (1781–May 8, 1828)   Entirely self-taught, the Italian guitar virtuoso Mauro Giuliani toured Europe when he was 19 and in 1807 settled in Vienna, where he became acquainted with Johann Nepomuk Hummel, Ignaz Moscheles, and Diabelli; Beethoven wrote guitar music especially for him. He composed a concerto with band accompaniment for the *chitarra di terza,* a short-necked guitar tuned a third higher than normal that he helped perfect.

Giulini, Carlo Maria (b. May 9, 1914) A student of Alfredo Casella and Bernardino Molinari, the Italian conductor Carlo Maria Giulini made his opera debut at La Scala in 1951, one year after he became conductor of the orchestra of Radio Milan. In 1955 he conducted Verdi's *Falstaff* at Glyndebourne and since then has appeared as guest conductor at Covent Garden, the Edinburgh Festival, and with the New Philharmonia. His U.S. debut (also 1955) with the Chicago Symphony led to an appointment as principal guest conductor there, where he remained until 1978 when he succeeded Zubin Mehta as music director of the Los Angeles Philharmonic. His best recordings include a Verdi Requiem, two Mozart operas (*Don Giovanni* and *The Marriage of Figaro*), and the First and Ninth Symphonies of Mahler, acclaimed as Best Recording of the Year in 1977. In 1977 he began a cycle of Bruckner symphonies.

Giulio Cesare: *see* BAROQUE ERA (Handel and Bach); HANDEL (life) and (works).

glass harmonica An instrument consisting of a set of graduated, tuned glass bowls on a revolving horizontal spindle sounded by the friction of fingers on their moistened rims. Invented by Benjamin Franklin, it was derived from the *vérillon* (musical glasses): a set of glasses each holding a different amount of water and thus sounding a different note, placed on a soundboard and rubbed by the fingers or, rarely, struck with rods. Gluck performed his concerto for this instrument in London in 1746. In 1761 Franklin, impressed by the playing of the Irish virtuoso Richard Pockrich, produced his armonica, or harmonica, in which hemispherical glasses were suspended on a treadle-operated spindle, overlapping so that only their rims were visible. A trough of water beneath the glasses moistened them as they rotated through it. The diatonic notes were progressively colored the hues of the spectrum, the sharps being black, as on a piano. The compass was ultimately extended to four octaves from the C below middle C. Long in vogue in Europe, it was an expressive instrument and attracted many composers. Among these were Mozart (Adagio in C Major, K.356, and Adagio and Rondo, K.617), Beethoven (melodrama *Leonora Prohaska*, 1814), and Richard Strauss (*Die Frau ohne Schatten*, 1919).

glass harmonica, 18th century
courtesy, Metropolitan Museum of Art
The Crosby Brown Collection of Musical Instruments, 1889

Glazunov, Aleksandr (Konstantinovich) (August 10, 1865–March 21, 1936)   The leading Russian symphonic composer of the generation after Tchaikovsky, Aleksandr Glazunov was born at St. Petersburg. His mother, a piano pupil of Balakirev, took her obviously talented son to her teacher who nicknamed him "the little Glinka" and advised a course of study with Rimsky-Korsakov. This began in 1880, and the following year the boy wrote his First Symphony, which was publicly performed by Balakirev early in 1882. It was revised several times before the timber merchant M. P. Belyaev printed it in 1886. By that time Glazunov had also written two quartets, two overtures on Greek folk tunes, and the symphonic poem *Stenka Razin.* In 1886 he finished his Second Symphony. He was now the recognized heir of the nationalist group and composed in their styles, but he also absorbed the influence of Liszt, whom he visited at Weimar in 1884. Other influences, notably those of Wagner and Tchaikovsky, later made themselves felt, and Glazunov's music gradually deteriorated into a weak, though pleasant, eclecticism. Most of his best works—the Fourth, Fifth, and Sixth Symphonies and his ballets, *Raymonda, Ruses d'amour,* and *Les Saisons*—date from the 1890s. He finished his last complete symphony, the Eighth, in 1906 just after he had become director of the St. Petersburg Conservatory, where he had been professor of orchestration since 1899. Glazunov, who became more and more involved in teaching and administration, wrote few large-scale works after 1906: two piano concertos (1911 and 1917), two string quartets (1920 and 1930), and a Concerto-Ballata for cello and orchestra (1931). After the Revolution Glazunov remained at his post until the summer of 1928, when, feeling completely isolated, he left Russia. After an unsuccessful U.S. concert tour in the winter of 1929–30, he made his home in Paris.

BIBLIOGRAPHY: Michel D. Calvocoressi and Gerald E. H. Abraham, *Masters of Russian Music* (1936; reprint, 1971); Gerald E. H. Abraham, *On Russian Music* (1939; reprint, 1976).

RECORDINGS: Piano Concerto No. 2; Piano Sonatas (2); suite from *Raymonda; Stenka Razin;* Symphony No. 5; Theme and Variations for piano; Violin Concerto No. 2; numerous orchestral works.

glee   An 18th-century English choral form for three or more unaccompanied solo male voices, including a countertenor. The term comes from Old English *gléo,* "entertainment." It is homophonic and consists of several short sections of contrasting character, each ending in a full close. The glee flourished from about 1740 to about 1830. The term is also loosely applied to various vocal compositions of the 17th–19th centuries that do not conform to these characteristics; *e.g.,* the instrumentally accompanied part-songs by Henry Rowley Bishop.

The glee is a purely English form and with the catch, or round, it made up the greater part of the repertoire of the glee clubs once prominent in English musical life. The most famous was the Glee Club (London, 1783–1857). Others include the Noblemen and Gentlemen's Catch Club (founded 1761) and the City Glee Club (founded 1853). Glee clubs in U.S. universities are generally simply male choral societies.

Among the finest examples of glees are "Glorious Apollo" by Samuel Webbe the Elder (1740–1816), "Music All-Powerful" by Thomas Forbes Walmisley (1783–1866), and "Great Bacchus" by Charles Evans (1778–1849).

Glière, Reinhold (Moritsevich) (January 11, 1875–June 23, 1956)   A Russian composer who became prominent in Soviet music, Reinhold Glière was noted for his works incorporating elements of the folk music of Russia, the Ukraine, and surrounding republics.

Of Belgian descent, Glière was the son of a Kiev musician and instrument maker. In 1900 he graduated from the Moscow Conservatory, where he studied violin with Adalbert Hřimaly, theory with Anton Arensky, and composition with Mikhail Ippolitov-Ivanov. After teaching in Moscow he studied conducting in Berlin (1905–07), first appearing in Russia as a conductor in 1908, the same year his tone poem *The Sirens* was enthusiastically received. Glière taught at the Kiev Conservatory and was appointed director in 1914, but he returned to Moscow in 1920, teaching at the conservatory there. He became involved in studying Russian folk music, traveling widely to collect material. The opera *Shah Senam* (first performed 1934) resulted from his study of Azerbaijan music, and Uzbek elements appear in the music drama *Hulsara* (1936).

After the Revolution Glière achieved a high place in Soviet musical activity largely because of his interest in national styles. He organized workers' concerts and directed committees of the Moscow Union of Composers and Union of Soviet Composers. For this work he was decorated by the government.

Glière's music today is principally performed in Communist countries, although his ballet *The Red Poppy* (1927) won international popularity for a time. Also well regarded were the ballet *The Bronze Knight* (1949) and his Symphony No. 3 (*Ilya Muromets*, 1912). Although he was highly respected by Soviet writers, Glière's often politically motivated works—*e.g.*, the overture *Twenty-five Years of the Red Army* (1943) and *Solemn Overture for the 20th Anniversary of the October Revolution* (1937)—were criticized by others for lack of depth and originality. Nevertheless, his influence on younger Soviet composers was profound; among his pupils were Prokofiev, Nikolay Myaskovsky, and Aram Khachaturian.

RECORDINGS: Ballet suites *The Bronze Knight* and *The Red Poppy;* Concerto for coloratura soprano; Duo for violin and cello; Harp Concerto in E-flat Major; Symphony No. 3.

Glinka, Mikhail (Ivanovich) (June 1 [May 21, old style], 1804–February 15 [February 3, old style], 1857) The first Russian composer to win international recognition and the acknowledged founder of the Russian national school, Mikhail Glinka was born in the village of Novospasskoe (Smolensk government). He was 10 or 11 years old before his interest in music was aroused by his uncle's private orchestra. From 1817 to 1822 he studied at the Chief Pedagogic Institute at St. Petersburg, also taking piano lessons from John Field and Charles Mayer. From 1824 to 1828 he served in the ministry of communications but was too indolent and unambitious for an official

career. As a dilettante he composed songs and a certain amount of chamber music, but three years in Italy brought him under the spell of Bellini and Donizetti and ultimately "homesickness gradually led me to the idea of writing music in Russian."

He studied composition seriously for six months with Siegfried Dehn in Berlin, where he began a *Sinfonia per l'orchestra sopra due motive russe* (1834). Recalled to Russia by his father's death, he married and settled down to the composition of the opera that first won him fame, *A Life for the Tsar* (originally named, and since the Revolution renamed, *Ivan Susanin*), produced at St. Petersburg on December 9, 1836, in the presence of the tsar. A month later he was appointed master of the Imperial Chapel, though he resigned this post in 1839. During this period Glinka composed some of his best songs and in 1840 the music to N. V. Kukolnik's play *Prince Kholmsky*. In 1842, on the sixth anniversary of *A Life for the Tsar*, his second opera, *Ruslan and Lyudmila*, was produced; the fantastic-Oriental subject and often boldly original music of *Ruslan* won neither imperial favor nor popularity, though Liszt was at once struck by the novelty of the music.

Disgruntled and with his marriage broken though not finally dissolved, Glinka left Russia in 1844 and consoled himself with a succession of mistresses. He had the satisfaction of hearing excerpts from both his operas performed in Paris under Berlioz (March 16, 1845—the first performance of Russian music in the West) and others. From Paris he went to Spain, where he stayed for two years (until May 1847) collecting the materials used in his two Spanish overtures, the *Capriccio brillante on the Jota aragonesa* (1845) and *Summer Night in Madrid* (1848). Glinka returned to Russia for a short period but spent most of his time in Warsaw, where he wrote *Kamarinskaya*, an orchestral piece on two Russian folk tunes (1848). Between 1852 and 1854 he was again abroad, mostly in Paris, until the outbreak of the Crimean War drove him home again. He then wrote his highly entertaining memoirs (first published in St. Petersburg, 1887)—musical, social, and amorous—which give an unconscious self-portrait of his indolent, amiable, hypochondriacal character. His last notable composition was *Festival* Polonaise for Alexander II's coronation ball (1855). After the war he decided to study Bach and "the old church modes" with Dehn in Berlin, and in that city he died.

Glinka may be fairly described as a dilettante of genius. Though small in bulk, his work is the foundation of almost all later Russian music of any value. *A Life for the Tsar,* Italianate as some of it is, showed how much could be written "in Russian"; *Ruslan* provided models, not only in its Oriental and "fantastic" conventions (whole-tone scale, etc.) but also in lyrical melody and colorful, transparent harmony and orchestration, on which Balakirev, Borodin, and Rimsky-Korsakov formed their styles. Tchaikovsky, who preferred the earlier of the two operas, wrote that "the present Russian symphonic school is all in *Kamarinskaya* just as the whole oak is in the acorn." Likewise the brilliant scoring of the Spanish overtures provided the basis of Rimsky-Korsakov's orchestral technique.

BIBLIOGRAPHY: Gerald E. H. Abraham, *Studies in Russian Music* (1935; reprint, 1976) and with Michel D. Calvocoressi, *Masters of Russian Music* (1936; reprint, 1971); Donald Brook, *Six Great Russian Composers* (1946); David Brown, *Mikhail Glinka* (1974).

RECORDINGS: *Jota aragonesa; Kamarinskaya; A Life for the Tsar;* overture to *Ruslan and Lyudmila;* Trio *pathétique* for clarinet, bassoon, and piano; Valse-Fantaisie (orchestra); songs.

glissando The rapid execution of adjacent notes. On a keyboard instrument it consists of using the nail of (usually) the thumb or third finger in a sweep of all white or all black keys. It is a much used device in playing the harp. Mozart used a glissando in parallel sixths in his piano Variations on "Lison dormait" and Beethoven octave glissandi in his *Waldstein* Sonata. The action of the piano of that period was considerably lighter than 20th-century instruments, and what is now a next-to-impossible feat was relatively routine. Ravel, however, calls for sadistic glissandi in thirds and fourths in his *Alborada del gracioso.* Berlioz in his *Symphonie fantas-*

tique asks for downward woodwind glissandi that must be suggested rather than executed, and Gershwin begins his *Rhapsody in Blue* with a clarinet glissando that was the trick specialty of Ross Gorman, clarinetist in Paul Whiteman's orchestra. The glissando on stringed instruments, the trombone, and the human voice is confused with portamento and is widely disputed.

glockenspiel A percussion instrument of steel bars of varying lengths and definite pitches. It was originally a set of graduated bells; later steel bars arranged chromatically in two rows on a frame were substituted. The compass is from $2\frac{1}{2}$ to 3 octaves; the music is written two octaves lower than the notes sound. The bars are struck with small hammers of wood or ebonite or occasionally metal. A keyboard mechanism is added when chords are to be played as, for example, in Mozart's *Magic Flute.* The glockenspiel is used with great effect in Handel's *Saul;* in "The Bell Song" from Léo Delibes' *Lakme;* in Tchaikovsky's *Nutcracker* Suite; in *Die Walküre* and *Die Meistersinger* by Wagner; by Elgar in *The Dream of Gerontius.* A lyre-shaped glockenspiel is used in military bands.

glockenspiel   *Boosey & Hawkes, Ltd.*

Gluck, Christoph Willibald (July 2, 1714–November 15, 1787) The German composer and reformer of music drama during the second half of the 18th century, Christoph Willibald Gluck was born at Erasbach near Berching in the Upper Palatinate.

Gluck's father probably intended him to

continue in the family employment of forestry, but at an early age he showed a strong inclination toward music. In order to escape from disagreements with his father, the young Gluck finally left home. Supporting himself by his music, he made his way to Prague, where he played in several churches and presumably completed his musical studies. He went to Vienna in the winter of 1735–36 and was discovered by a Lombard nobleman, Francesco Saverio Melzi, who took the young musician with him to Milan. In addition to fulfilling his duties in the Melzi family chapel, Gluck spent four years studying composition with Giovanni Battista Sammartini, from whom he learned the new Italian style of instrumental music. Probably the Six Trio Sonatas printed in London in 1746 were the fruits of his studies with Sammartini.

Gluck's first dramatic success was with his first opera, *Artaserse* (1741; Teatro Ducal in Milan), to a libretto by Pietro Metastasio. Until 1745 there followed an annual succession of operas for this theater: *Demofoonte* (1742), *Arsace* (in collaboration with Giovanni Battista Lampugnani, 1743), *Sofonisba* (1744), and *Ippolito* (1745). In addition Gluck wrote *Cleonice* or *Demetrio* (1742), and a pasticcio

Christoph Willibald Gluck,
painting by Joseph Siffred Duplessis, 1775
courtesy, Kunsthistorisches Museum, Vienna

La finta schiava (1744) for Venice, *Il Tigrane* (1743) for Crema, and *Poro* (1744) for Turin. In these Gluck largely follows the existing operatic fashion that was dominated by Metastasio as librettist and Johann Adolph Hasse as composer, though occasional passionate outbursts and the beginning of characterization foreshadow the great dramatic composer he later was to become.

In 1745 Gluck, who was now well known as an operatic composer, was invited to London at the instigation of Lord Middlesex, director of Italian opera at the Haymarket Theatre, to appear in opposition to Handel. The plan failed because the Stuart uprising forced all theaters in London to close before Gluck arrived. Later theatrical activities recommenced with the performance of Gluck's opera *La Caduta de' giganti* on January 18, 1746; the libretto was by Francesco Vaneschi glorifying the Duke of Cumberland, who was considered to be the hero of the day. This work, as well as Gluck's second London opera *Artamene* (produced on March 15, 1746), consisted largely of music from his own earlier works from lack of time. Neither opera met with success. Shortly after the production of *Artamene* Handel and Gluck gave a concert in the Haymarket Theatre consisting of works by Gluck and an organ concerto by Handel. Gluck had won Handel's interest, and the latter's much-quoted criticism—that Gluck "knows no more counterpoint than my cook"—must not be taken too seriously. Gluck himself, according to the Irish singer Michael Kelly, tried for the remainder of his life to emulate Handel, whom he described as the "divine master of our art."

After he left England (possibly in 1746) Gluck came into contact with two traveling opera companies; one performed his opera-serenade *La Nozze d'Ercole e d'Ebe* at Pillnitz Castle near Dresden on the occasion of the double wedding between the electoral families of Bavaria and Saxony. By the beginning of 1748 at the latest, Gluck was back in Vienna at work on Metastasio's *Semiramide riconosciuta,* with which the Burgtheater was inaugurated—a brilliant success for the composer. As conductor of the Mingotti Opera Company, Gluck traveled via Hamburg to Copenhagen and composed the opera-serenade *La Contesa dei Numi* in celebration of the birth (January 29, 1749) of the heir to the Danish throne. During the following two winters Gluck was with the Locatelli Opera Company in Prague, where he wrote *Ezio* (1750) and *Issipile* (1752).

On September 15, 1750, Gluck was married to Marianne Pergin in Vienna. Their marriage was harmonious but childless; later Gluck adopted his niece, Marianne. But before the young couple set up a permanent home in Vienna in the winter of 1752–53, Gluck took his wife to Naples for the summer of 1752, where he composed music for Metastasio's drama *La Clemenza di Tito.*

In Vienna Gluck soon found a patron in the imperial field marshal Prince Joseph of Saxe-Hildburghausen, who engaged him first as leader of his orchestra and later as Kapellmeister. Gluck gave successful performances of his symphonies and arias at weekly concerts at the prince's palace and made a particular impression with his opera-serenade *Le Cinesi* (1754) in the presence of the emperor and empress. This success may have contributed to the decision of Count Giacomo Durazzo, director of the court theater, to entrust the provision of the "theatrical and academic music" for the imperial court to Gluck. *La Danza* and *L'Innocenza giustificata,* the libretto for which Count Durazzo had himself assembled from arias by Metastasio and recitatives of his own, were both performed in 1755 at the imperial castle of Laxenburg. The following year (1756) Vienna saw *Il Re᾿ pastore* and *Tetide,* while the first performance of the opera *Antigono* was given during a visit to Rome. In Rome Gluck was created a Knight of the Golden Spur.

After his return to Vienna Gluck began to conquer new fields. Count Durazzo had ordered a number of French vaudeville comedies that he wished Gluck to set to music; *Tircis et Doristée* (1756) may have been a first attempt at this genre. After 1758 Gluck proceeded more independently and composed such works as *La Fausse esclave* and *L'Ile de Merlin* (1758), *La Cythère assiégée, Le Diable à quatre,* and *L'Arbre enchanté* (1759), *L'Ivrogne corrigé* (1760), and *Le Cadi dupé* (1761), which contained, in addition to the overture, a steadily increasing number of airs nouveaux in place of the original vaudevilles. In *La Rencontre imprévue* (Vienna, 1764) no vaudeville remains at all, resulting in a perfect example of opéra comique. Gluck gave the scores of *Le Cadi dupé* and *La Rencontre imprévue* particular charm by using Oriental instrumental effects. In many of the arias tuneful melody and programmatic writing foreshadow later stylistic development; the first examples of complex scene development are noticeable in *L'Ile de Merlin* and *L'Ivrogne corrigé* (four and two years before *Orfeo*).

Reform came to Vienna in 1761 in the person of the Italian poet and librettist Ranieri Calzabigi. Though originally an admirer of Metastasio, he had been influenced in Paris by such literary personages as Diderot, Rousseau, and Voltaire and had come with a libretto for *Orfeo ed Euridice* conceived in the new spirit. This was greeted enthusiastically by Durazzo, who put him in touch with Gluck. Their first work of collaboration, the dramatic ballet *Le Festin de pierre (Don Juan),* was premiered on October 17, 1761, to be followed by the three Italian "reform" operas *Orfeo ed Euridice* (1762), *Alceste* (1767), and *Paride ed Elena* (1770). An additional collaborative effort in ballet was *Semiramide* (1765). Gluck explained the new aims in his foreword to *Alceste:* "to restrict music to its true office of serving poetry by means of expression and by following the situations of the story, without interrupting the action or stifling it with a useless superfluity of ornaments. . . ." The ultimate objective was "simplicity, truth and naturalness." As Gluck himself confessed, the impulse toward opera reform came from Calzabigi, but important new musical features (*e.g.,* the complex scene development) were the contributions of Gluck. Though identified with the reform movement, Gluck was not so committed that he could not turn to Metastasio librettos in three new operas and a revision of the earlier *Ezio* in the years 1763–65.

In the autumn of 1772 Gluck played his newly completed opera *Iphigénie en Aulide* (text by the marquis François Gand-Leblanc du Roullet after Racine) for the English music historian Charles Burney, who was spending some time in Vienna. The Paris Opéra agreed to stage this work, and he went to Paris in the autumn of 1773. The performances of *Iphigénie* in April 1774 and of the French version of *Orfeo* the following summer met with tremendous success, but the new version of *L'Arbre enchanté* in 1775 brought little success, and the completely rewritten *Cythère assiégée* proved a failure. The French version of *Alceste* (1776) also met with disapproval.

Two opposing parties began to form: the Gluckists and the Piccinnists after Niccolò Piccinni, who was prevailed upon to come to Paris in the summer of 1776 to write opera in opposition. At the first performance of *Armide* (1777), the war of the theaters reached a climax, but after the performance of Piccinni's *Roland* (1778) the struggle abated. Gluck retired to Vienna, and his last visit to Paris began at the end of 1778, when he took with him his two latest completed dramatic works, *Iphigénie en Tauride* and *Écho et Narcisse.* The performance of *Iphigénie* in May 1779 brought him his greatest success in Paris, but *Écho* a few months later met with little appreciation. Gluck, who had suffered a stroke during the rehearsals of *Écho,* left Paris for the last time at the beginning of October.

Gluck's French reform operas are more strongly governed by the principle of contrast than his Italian works; the declamatory style of the vocal line is more marked than in the Viennese operas, and the power and orchestral color are more intense. The works are constructed in shorter sections, which frequently follow each other without a break, and the spacious conception of the scenes is partly sacrificed to achieve a greater degree of dramatic and psychological flexibility.

Gluck spent the last eight years of his life in Vienna and in Perchtholdsdorf nearby. His attention turned to Friedrich Gottlieb Klopstock's *Hermannsschlacht,* which had occupied him as early as 1770; he revised *Écho et Narcisse* and, together with the Viennese poet Johann Baptist von Alxinger, produced a German version of *Iphigénie en Tauride* (Vienna, 1781) on the occasion of the visit by Grand Duke Paul Petrovich, later Tsar Paul I. Only a few years before his death he published his *Klopstock Odes* (only seven survive), which must have been written soon after 1770 and are the first examples of his mature style. At his death he was buried in the central cemetery in Vienna amid general mourning. The requiem mass included Gluck's own *De Profundis,* conducted by Antonio Salieri.

BIBLIOGRAPHY: Ernest Newman, *Gluck and the Opera* (1895); Hector Berlioz, *Gluck and His Operas* (1915); Martin Cooper, *Gluck* (1935); Alfred Einstein, *Gluck* (1936); Patricia Howard, *Gluck and the Birth of Modern Opera* (1964).

RECORDINGS: Operas *Alceste, Iphigénie en Aulide,* and *Orfeo ed Euridice;* Chaconne; *Don Juan;* Flute Concerto in G Major.

Godowsky, Leopold (February 13, 1870–November 21, 1938) A pianist of pianists, the Polish-born Leopold Godowsky was largely self-taught. He studied briefly in Berlin and was later a protégé of Saint-Saëns, but the development of one of the greatest techniques of all time is largely a mystery. Although he was a major concert pianist, his most remarkable feats were at private gatherings with the possible exception of his debut in Berlin

Leopold Godowsky   *Brown Brothers*

(1900). He taught in New York City, Philadelphia, Chicago, Berlin, and Vienna and settled permanently in the United States at the outbreak of World War I. He composed many piano pieces and studies with particular emphasis on the left hand. An ingenious set of 53 studies on Chopin's Études are technically complex to the extreme.

Goldberg Variations: *see* BACH, JOHANN SEBASTIAN (Leipzig); BAROQUE ERA (Handel and Bach); CANON; VARIATIONS.

Goldmark, Karl (May 18, 1830–January 2, 1915)   A Hungarian composer of operas and violin music, Karl Goldmark was the son of a poor Jewish cantor. He studied violin in Vienna with Leopold Jansa and Joseph Böhm; in composition he was self-taught. Following the success of a quartet in 1860, he wrote the overture *Sakuntala* (1865) and a successful opera, *Die Königin von Saba* (Vienna, 1875). During this period he was also known as a piano teacher and critic. Among his later operas are *Götz von Berlichingen* (Budapest, 1902) and *Ein Wintermärchen* after Shakespeare's *A Winter's Tale* (Vienna, 1908). His work shows the influence of Hungarian folk music and of Mendelssohn and Wagner; it includes two violin concertos, two symphonies, and choral and chamber works.

His nephew Rubin Goldmark (1872–1936) was a pupil of Dvořák, taught Copland, Gershwin, and other U.S. composers, and in 1924 became head of the composition department of the Juilliard School in New York City.

RECORDINGS: *Rustic Wedding* Symphony; Violin Concerto in a minor.

goliard song   A 10th- to 13th-century Latin song written by wandering scholar-poets. Although vernacular song traditions were emerging in all European languages, it was predictably the Latin songs that traveled, and their manuscript sources are still spread across western Europe. The largest and best known collection of goliard songs is the so-called *Carmina Burana* manuscript at Munich. It was written in Bavaria in the late 13th century, but many of its songs are also to be found, for instance, in the important Cambridge Songbook written in England some 200 years earlier.

The subject matter of the songs varies: political and religious satire; love songs of an unusual directness; and songs of drinking and riotous life. The music is normally notated in diastematic neumes, a kind of musical shorthand that can be read only by comparison with another version fully written out. In musical style the amorous songs are similar to those of the trouvères in the French language (indeed in several cases the same melody appears in both repertoires), but the more goliardic songs have a simpler metrical form, more syllabic melodies, and an unsophisticated repetitive style.

Golschmann, Vladimir (December 16, 1893–March 1, 1972)   Educated in Paris, the French-U.S. conductor Vladimir Golschmann founded and conducted the Concerts Golschmann in Paris (1919–24). He became conductor for Diaghilev's Ballet Russe and was guest conductor of orchestras in Belgium, Spain, and Norway before accepting the post of conductor of the Scottish orchestras of Glasgow and Edinburgh (1928–31). Following guest appearances in the United States, he was conductor of the St. Louis Symphony (1931–57), building it into a major orchestra. He was music director of the Denver Symphony for the 1969–70 season. He recorded much of the music of Samuel Barber as well as the complete *L'estro armonico* of Vivaldi.

Gomberg, Harold (b. November 30, 1916)   A graduate of the Curtis Institute and a faculty member of the Juilliard and Manhattan schools, the U.S. oboist Harold Gomberg played principal oboe in the National Symphony in Washington, D.C., and with the Toronto and St. Louis orchestras before joining the New York Philharmonic. He retired from the latter post in 1978. A specialist in Baroque music, he has recorded oboe concertos of Vivaldi, Telemann, and Handel with the Gomberg Baroque Ensemble. His brother Ralph Gomberg became principal oboist with the Boston Symphony in 1949 and is on the faculty of Boston University.

Gombert, Nicolas (*c.* 1500–*c.* 1556)   One of the foremost Flemish composers of his generation, Nicolas Gombert traveled widely as singer and *magister puerorum* of the domestic chapel of the emperor Charles V, later holding positions with the cathedral chapters of Courtrai and Tournai. A follower and possibly a pupil of Josquin des Prés, he wrote sacred music developing the imitative technique of Josquin but using a freer, less symmetrical design. Some of his chansons recall the naturalistic onomatopoeia of Clément Janequin. Of his works 10 masses, eight Magnificats, about 160 motets, and about 60 chansons survive in printed and manuscript sources.

RECORDINGS: *Missa Je suis déshérité; Missa Da pacem.*

gong A percussion instrument of Oriental origin consisting of a circular metal plate, cast or hammered, with the outer edge turned down. It hangs in a frame and is struck with a heavy-ended beater covered with felt or leather. There are two types of orchestral gongs, each with its individual tone quality: the large, flat, Chinese gong (tam-tam) with a deep, dark tone of indefinite pitch; and the Burmese gong of heavy metal with a raised boss in the center, which produces a bell-like note of definite pitch. Puccini uses a set of tuned gongs in *Turandot.*

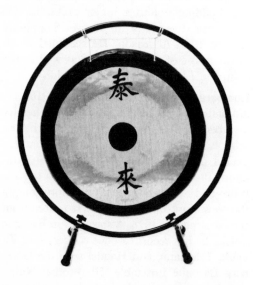

gong   *courtesy, Ludwig Industries*

Goodman, Benny, real name, Benjamin David Goodman (b. May 30, 1909) The U.S. clarinetist and jazz band leader Benny Goodman studied with Reginald Kell at the Lewis Insti-

tute in Chicago. In 1934 he formed his own band with which he popularized the jazz style "swing," becoming known as the "king of swing." The first jazz concert ever held in Carnegie Hall was by Goodman and his band January 16, 1938 (commemorated 40 years later with a similar Goodman concert there). This part of his career is chronicled in his autobiography *The Kingdom of Swing* (1939). Also a classical performer, he has recorded concertos of Mozart and Carl Nielsen. Stravinsky's *Ebony* Concerto, Copland's Clarinet Concerto, and Bartók's *Contrasts* for clarinet, violin, and piano were written for him. He has appeared in 10 motion pictures, including *The Benny Goodman Story* (1956), and on numerous television and radio shows. Honors include the International Jazz Critics Award and membership in the Downbeat Hall of Fame.

Goossens, Eugene (III) (May 26, 1893–June 13, 1962) The son and grandson of reputed conductors, the English conductor and composer Eugene Goossens was educated in Belgium and London, where he studied with Charles Stanford. After an apprenticeship with Thomas Beecham and the Queen's Hall orchestra, he formed his own orchestra (1921) at the same time he was appearing at Covent Garden. His U.S. career included conducting posts with the Rochester Philharmonic (1923–31) and the Cincinnati Symphony (1931–46), after which he went to Australia and conducted in Sydney until 1956. He was knighted in 1955. His compositions include two operas (*Judith,* 1929; *Don Juan de Mañara,* 1937), two symphonies, chamber music, piano music, songs, and Oboe Concerto (1930), written for his brother, the oboist Leon Goossens. He made several notable recordings on 78s (Glazunov's *Scènes de ballet*) and an early LP recording of the Serenade for tenor, horn, and strings by Britten.

RECORDING: Oboe Concerto.

Goossens, Leon (b. June 12, 1897) One of a well-known musical family, the English oboist Leon Goossens studied at London's Royal College of Music. He played principal oboe in the Royal Opera House orchestra, the Royal Philharmonic, and the Queen's Hall orchestra before holding that position with the London Philharmonic from its inception (1932) to 1939. He toured Europe and the United States as a recitalist and taught in London at the Royal College and the Royal Academy. He has recorded oboe concertos of Bach and Handel, Mozart divertimenti, and played with George Melachrino's orchestra.

Götterdämmerung: *see* LEITMOTIV; WAGNER (life).

Gottschalk, Louis Moreau (May 8, 1829–December 18, 1869) Though refused entrance to the Paris Conservatoire because he came from "savage America," Louis Moreau Gottschalk became the first major U.S. pianist and the first national composer.

He studied piano in Paris with Charles Hallé and Camille Stamaty, and from the time of his debut there he was considered one of the great pianists. His compositions incorporated Latin-American and Creole folk themes and rhythms and had an impact on European audiences not understood by later generations; major critics even compared him with Chopin. Late in the 20th century, however, his music underwent a considerable revival. His output included two operas, two symphonic poems, about 90 piano pieces, and a dozen songs. Gottschalk was no less popular in America; but his recital programs were increasingly confined to his own works, and his playing apparently deteriorated with his growing fame. Written in French, his diary was translated and published as *Notes of a Pianist* (1881); it reflects mid-19th-century American life in a charming and witty manner.

RECORDINGS: *Escenas campestres cubanas* for orchestra; *Gran Tarantella* for piano and orchestra; Symphonic poem *La Nuit des Tropiques;* piano pieces.

Götz, Hermann (December 7, 1840–December 3, 1876) The German composer Hermann Götz is known for his comic opera based on Shakespeare's *The Taming of the Shrew.* He went to Berlin in his youth, where he studied with Hans von Bülow and Hugo Ulrich. In 1863 he was appointed organist at Winterthur, Switzerland, and about this time formed a lasting friendship with Brahms. From 1870 he lived at Zürich, where he was music critic

of the *Neue Zürcher Zeitung.* His opera *Der Widerspenstigen Zähmung (The Taming of the Shrew)* was produced at Mannheim in 1874 and achieved immediate success for its spontaneous style and lighthearted characterization. A later opera, *Francesca da Rimini,* completed by Ernst Frank (Mannheim, 1877), was less successful. Götz also wrote chamber and choral works, an overture, a piano concerto, and a symphony. George Bernard Shaw rated him as one of the outstanding masters of 19th-century music.

RECORDINGS: *Frühlingsouverture;* Overtures to *Der Widerspenstigen Zähmung* and *Francesca da Rimini;* Piano Concerto; Piano Quintet; Piano Trio; Quartet for piano and string trio; Symphony in F Major; piano pieces.

Goudimel, Claude (*c.* 1514–August 28?, 1572) A French composer noted for his settings of the metrical psalms, Claude Goudimel was born in Besançon. He worked there and also in Paris, Metz, and Lyons, where he died in the anti-Huguenot riots. Though he also wrote Latin church music and chansons, Goudimel is remembered for his vernacular psalm settings. The incomplete collection of 1551–56 presents an extended motetlike treatment of the text; the 1564 cycle sets only the first verses with the traditional tune usually in the treble. The 1565 book is written in the simplest note-against-note style; the tenor normally has the melody. It proved enormously popular and was widely adopted by the Reformed churches.

BIBLIOGRAPHY: Waldo Selden Pratt, *The Music of the French Psalter of 1562* (1939).

Gould, Glenn (b. September 25, 1932) Educated at the Royal Conservatory in Toronto, the Canadian pianist Glenn Gould is one of the few late 20th-century keyboardists to specialize in playing Bach on the piano. However, he plays music of all schools, including jazz. By the late 1960s he confined his appearances to radio and television and to recording.

BIBLIOGRAPHY: Geoffrey Paysent, *Glenn Gould: Music and Mind* (1978).

Gould, Morton (b. December 10, 1913) A prodigy who began to compose and improvise at age four, the U.S. composer Morton Gould studied composition with Vincent Jones and piano with Abby Whiteside. By 1934 he was producing and conducting weekly radio programs for the Mutual Broadcasting System on which he introduced much of his own music. A fine orchestrator, Gould combines instrumental textures in an original way. His early music is light and programmatic, incorporating popular music, jazz, and folk songs (*Symphonettes,* 1936, 1939, 1940; *A Foster Gallery,* 1940; *Interplay,* ballet, 1943). Later works are abstract, absolute music, more contrapuntal, and often dodecaphonic (*Prisms,* 1962). *Venice* (1966) uses two antiphonally placed orchestras, as does the 17th-century-based *Vivaldi Gallery* (1967) for quartet and divided orchestra. Gould wrote two musicals, three film scores, and the music for a 39-part television documentary, *World War I* (1964).

RECORDINGS: *American Salute; Columbia; Derivations* for clarinet and band; *Latin American Symphonette; Soundings; Spirituals* for orchestra; Suite for tuba and three horns; *Symphonette* No. 2; Symphony No. 4 *(West Point); World War I;* marches.

Gounod, Charles (François) (June 17, 1818– October 18, 1893)   The fame of the French composer Charles Gounod rests chiefly on his opera *Faust,* a model of 19th-century French operatic style. His father, François Gounod, was a painter of some distinction, and his mother, a woman of wide education, was a capable pianist who gave Gounod his early training in music. He was educated at the Lycée St. Louis, where he remained until 1835. After taking his *baccalauréat* in philosophy he began to study music with Anton Reicha. On Reicha's death in 1836 Gounod entered the Paris Conservatoire, where he studied with Fromental Halévy and Jean-François Lesueur, winning the Prix de Rome in 1839 with his cantata *Fernand.* In Italy he devoted much of his attention to the study of Palestrina and was so influenced by him that a mass in imitation of the style of the Italian master was among his earliest important compositions. After completing his course in Rome he proceeded to Vienna, where a mass and a requiem composed in Italy were performed in 1842

and 1843 respectively. On his return to Paris Gounod spent four days in Leipzig with Mendelssohn, who arranged for him to hear a performance of Mendelssohn's *Scottish* Symphony. He was also taken to the Thomaskirche, where Mendelssohn played for him a recital of organ works by Bach.

Gounod became organist and maître de chapelle at the Church of the Missions Étrangères, and for two years he was mainly occupied with the study of theology and the writing of religious music. In 1846 he attended a course at the seminary of St. Sulpice, and it was expected that he would take orders. But in 1847 he decided against entering the priesthood and, abandoning a projected Requiem and Te Deum, turned his attention to composing for the operatic stage.

His first operas, *Sapho* (1851) and *La Nonne sanglante* (1854), together with his incidental music for François Ponsard's tragedy *Ulysse* (1852), were favorably reviewed by Berlioz, although in general their reception was not enthusiastic. In his *Messe solennelle à Ste. Cécile* (1855) he attempted to blend the sacred with a more secular style of composition. An excursion into comic opera followed with *Le Médecin malgré lui* to a libretto based on Molière's comedy. From 1852 Gounod worked on *Faust,* based on Goethe's tragedy (semi-disowned by the Germans, who perform it but call it *Margarethe*); its production in 1859 marked a new phase in the development of French opera. This work has continued to overshadow all his subsequent stage works, including the fairly successful *Mireille* (1864) and *Roméo et Juliette* (1867), as well as his later oratorios.

In 1852 Gounod became conductor of the Orphéon choral society in Paris for which he wrote a number of choral works, including two masses. From 1870 he spent five years in London, where he formed a choir that eventually became the Royal Choral Society. In his later years Gounod devoted himself almost entirely to the writing of oratorios, many of which were first produced in England. He was made a grand officer of the Legion of Honor in 1888.

Among other works were *Gallia,* a lamentation for soprano, chorus, and orchestra inspired by the French military catastrophe of 1870 and first performed at the Albert Hall in London in 1871; the oratorios *La Rédemption* and *Mors et Vita,* first performed at the Birmingham Festival in 1882 and 1885 respectively; 13 operas (one unfinished); music for plays, including *Les Deux Reines,* a drama by Ernest Legouvé, and *Jeanne d'Arc* by Jules Barbier; a large output of church music; orchestral music; piano solos; and songs.

Gounod introduced an original sense of melody though it often deteriorated into sentimentality. He wrote well for the voice and he was a skillful orchestrator. His sacred music lacked fervor. His "Meditation" (Ave Maria) adapted from the first prelude of Bach's *Well-Tempered Clavier* illustrates his sentimental manner. *Faust,* particularly the ballet music, *Mireille,* and *Le Médecin malgré lui* (1857) show his melodic vein at its best.

BIBLIOGRAPHY: James Harding, *Gounod* (1973).

RECORDINGS: Fantasy on the Russian National Hymn for piano and orchestra; *Faust; Messe Solennelle (St. Cecilia): Roméo et Juliette.*

grace note   A note printed smaller than adjacent notes to indicate that its time value must be subtracted from a neighboring note. One type is the short appoggiatura, which is normally performed sharply just ahead of the beat. A 19th-century device, the grace note developed into groups of grace notes such as in Chopin's piano Nocturnes, where they are played freely and expressively (and sometimes total more than a whole measure's time value).

Graffman, Gary (b. October 19, 1928)   Educated at the Curtis Institute and at Columbia University, the U.S. pianist Gary Graffman studied with Horowitz and Rudolf Serkin. He won the Leventritt competition (1949), and his repertoire ranges from Beethoven to Prokofiev.

Grainger, Percy (Aldridge), originally George Percy Grainger (July 8, 1882–February 20, 1961)   Pianist, composer, and collector of folk music, the Australian Percy Grainger was educated in Melbourne and in Germany, where he studied briefly with Busoni. An eccentric personality and a keyboard original,

he was a gifted pianist and champion of the new music of his day (Albéniz, Debussy, Frederick Delius). From 1906 he was a close friend of Grieg, and he became known for his performances of Grieg's Piano Concerto. Through Grieg he became interested in folk music, and Grainger's prolific output was heavily influenced by the genre, including the orchestral works *Molly on the Shore, Shepherd's Hey,* and *Mock Morris.* In his chamber music, notably the two *Hill Songs* for 23 and 24 solo instruments, he experimented with novel rhythmic and structural problems. He also perceived the possibilities of electronic music. From 1914 he lived in the United States, teaching in Chicago and in New York City. In 1935 he established the Percy Grainger Museum at the University of Melbourne for the preservation "of all things bearing upon the musical life of Australia."

BIBLIOGRAPHY: John Bird, *Percy Grainger* (1977).

RECORDINGS: *Faeroe Island* Dance, *Lads of Wampray* March, and *Lincolnshire Posy* for band; piano pieces.

Granados, Enrique (July 27, 1867–March 24, 1916)   The Spanish pianist and composer Enrique Granados was a leader of the late 19th-century nationalist school. He made his debut as a pianist at the age of 16. About 1883 he studied composition with Felipe Pedrell in Barcelona, supporting himself by playing in a café, and in 1887 he went to Paris for two years, perfecting his piano technique with Charles de Bériot, Jr. He returned in 1889 to Barcelona, where he reappeared at concerts and established himself as a player of the front rank; his *Danzas españolas* aroused great interest and popularity. The first of his seven operas, *María del Carmen,* was successfully produced in Madrid in 1898. In 1900 he founded a classical concerts society (that proved short-lived) and his own piano school, in which he produced many distinguished players. He wrote extensively and fluently for the piano in a somewhat diffuse post-Lisztian style; his masterwork was the two sets of *Goyescas,* imaginative and poetic reflections of Goya's paintings and tapestries. (His interest in the 18th century is also exemplified in the attractive *Colección de Tonadillas, escritas en estilo antiguo.*) The *Goyescas* were composed in 1911–13 and then amplified into an opera that was accepted for Paris but because of war conditions received its premiere in New York City in 1916. It was on his way back from this performance that Granados was drowned when the "Sussex" was torpedoed by a German submarine.

BIBLIOGRAPHY: Gilbert Chase, *The Music of Spain,* 2nd ed. (1960).

RECORDINGS: *Colección de Canciones amatorias* (7), *Colección de Tonadillas, escritas en estilo antiguo* (4), and other songs; *Allegro di concierto, Danzas españolas* (12), *Goyescas* (6), and other piano pieces; Symphonic poem *Dante.*

Grandi, Alessandro (died 1630) The Italian composer Alessandro Grandi was the first to use the word cantata in the modern sense. He was known to have been director of music to a religious confraternity in Ferrara in 1597, and he remained in that city in various capacities until 1617, when he became a singer at St. Mark's in Venice. Three years later he became Monteverdi's assistant there. In 1627 he left Venice to direct the music at Sta. Maria Maggiore in Bergamo. He produced several fine books of songs called *Cantade et Arie,* published between 1620 and 1629. In these he shows himself to be a pupil of Monteverdi. His cantatas are the precursors of the ground bass songs of Purcell, the voice varying the melody over a repeated bass. He also wrote religious songs in the same style, and these were known and copied by Heinrich Schütz.

RECORDINGS: Motets.

Grandjany, Marcel (Georges Lucien) (September 3, 1891–February 24, 1975) Recipient of a first prize at the Paris Conservatoire at the age of 13, the French harpist and composer Marcel Grandjany made his U.S. debut in 1924. He taught at the American Conservatory at Fontainebleau before becoming head of the harp department at the Juilliard School in 1938, where he remained until his death. He was also on the faculty of the Manhattan School (1956–66). In 1962 he founded the American Harp Society. His numerous compositions for harp include *Poem* for harp, horn, and orchestra. He has recorded albums of his own works.

RECORDINGS: *Aria in Classic Style* for harp and strings; *Children's Hour; Rhapsodie pour la harpe.*

Graun, Karl Heinrich (*c.* 1704–August 8, 1759) A German composer known for his sacred music, Karl Heinrich Graun was a chorister in his youth at Dresden. At an early age he composed a number of sacred cantatas and other pieces for the church service. He completed his studies under J. C. Schmidt and profited much from the Italian operas performed at Dresden under Antonio Lotti. In 1725 Graun made his debut as a tenor in opera at Brunswick in a work by Georg Kaspar Schürmann, but, not being satisfied with the arias assigned to him, he rewrote them and was commissioned to compose an opera for the next season. This work, with five other operas and two settings of the passion, belong to his Brunswick period. In 1735 the crown prince of Prussia, later Frederick the Great, engaged Graun at Rheinsberg, where he composed a number of cantatas. On Frederick's accession to the throne in 1740, he sent Graun to Italy to engage singers for a new opera company to be established in Berlin. On his return to Berlin he was appointed Kapellmeister and composed about 30 operas to Italian words. Graun's passion cantata, *Der Tod Jesu* (1755), long held a place in Germany similar to that enjoyed by Handel's *Messiah* in England, being regularly performed in Holy Week for a century and a half after its composer's death. The Te Deum written in 1757 to celebrate the Prussian victory at Prague was also a favorite work with German audiences.

Johann Gottlieb Graun (*c.* 1703–71), an elder brother of Karl Heinrich, was a composer, violinist, and conductor known for his chamber music and symphonies. He entered the service of Frederick the Great at about the same time as his brother and was a conductor at Berlin and Potsdam from 1740.

BIBLIOGRAPHY: A. Yorke Long, *Music at Court* (1954).

RECORDINGS: Karl Heinrich Graun— *Montezuma* (opera); Johann Gottlieb Graun —Bassoon Concerto in B-flat Major.

Grechaninov, Aleksandr (Tikhonovich) (October 25, 1864–January 3, 1956) A Russian composer notable for his religious works and music for children, Aleksandr Grechaninov was born in Moscow and studied piano with Vassily Safonov and composition with Sergey Taneyev and Anton Arensky at the Moscow Conservatory; from 1890 to 1893 he worked at composition and orchestration with Rimsky-Korsakov in St. Petersburg. He soon became known for his songs, the First String Quartet (1893), and the first of his five symphonies (1894). His opera *Dobrinya Nikitich* was produced in Moscow in 1903. The later *Soeur Beatrice* was produced in 1912 but had to be withdrawn at once on religious grounds. He composed in all media, producing a great quantity of piano music, songs, and choruses, but his music lacks any strong personal stamp. His church music brought him an imperial pension, though his later religious music (from 1912 onward) introduces instruments and cannot be used in the Eastern Orthodox liturgy. With the 1917 Revolution he lost his pension, and after several visits to the West he settled in Paris in 1925. There he published an autobiography (translated as *My Life,* 1952). In 1940 he fled to New York City and became a U.S. citizen.

Greek music, ancient The literature of Greco-Latin antiquity and the Church Fathers, the plastic and graphic representations, and the findings of archaeology indicate an ancient Greek musical culture extending over more than 2,000 years.

history The first Greek-speaking European peoples reached Greece about 2000 B.C., doubtless bringing their folk music with them. Greece gradually came under the Minoan (Cretan) influence, with its Aegean and Egyptian elements, and about 1550 this influence promoted the first distinctively Greek culture, the Mycenaean. Greece early obtained from the Mediterranean area both instruments and musical and dance forms. Mycenaean remains include fragments of a lyre of Cretan type, while a smaller lyre (Phoenician type) and a bronze trumpet indicate Asiatic influence. Musical life was characterized by a strong ritual element.

The Mycenaean and Minoan cultures declined with the invasion of the Dorians from Asia Minor, and myths indicate extensive new foreign influences. The legend in which the Greek Apollo flays the Phrygian Marsyas recalls the early Greek preference for the lyre, the instrument of the Apollo cult, above the *aulos,* or reed pipe, an instrument associated with the wine-god Dionysus. The precedence of lyre over pipe would seem to foreshadow the supremacy of reason in the artistic life of classical times. The Asiatic influence was nonetheless substantial. Tradition says the Phrygian Olympus (*c.* 900 B.C.) introduced the dactylic meter, the enharmonic genus, the *aulos,* and melody patterns called *nomos* (pl. *nomoi*).

From Homer's time Greek music was closely based on poetry. Poet-musicians, the professional bards of noble families, chanted epics in recitative style, accompanying themselves on the cithara (lyre). The *nomos* on a prescribed melody pattern gave rise to solo (nonrecitative) vocal compositions that were cyclic in form without strophic repetitions, had a prescribed number of movements, and were accompanied by the reed pipe or the lyre. There was also a purely instrumental *nomos* for the reed pipe with descriptive associations. The dithyramb was originally a strophic melody sung by Dionysus worshipers. It developed into a choral genre *c.* 600 B.C., when it was sung and danced to the reed pipe by a circular chorus of 50 men and boys. Hymns and dances were also performed chorally in other cults and at weddings and funerals; they were sometimes accompanied by the bardic lyre. Music also figured in the competitive festivals: the Olympia from 776 B.C. and later the Delphic Pythia, the Spartan Carnea, and the Panathenia. From the 7th century—after the Homeric epics were committed to writing—poets turned to more popular themes sung to a smaller lyre called *lyra,* from which modern lyric poetry derives its name; others wrote for choral performance. Important among lyric poet-musicians were Archilochus of Paros, Tyrtaeus, Alcaeus, Sappho, and Anacreon.

Greek culture now created the classical drama, developed certain basic attitudes to music, and reached its zenith in Athens—the classical period, *c.* 600–400 B.C. The plays were essentially musicodramatic works written by poet-musicians but descended from cult rituals. *Tragoedia* (tragedy) means literally "goat song" after the ritual of the Dionysian dithyramb, while comedy kept the latter's ritual trappings (masks, etc.). The drama was at first mainly choral, though the chorus also gave a semicircular dance *(orchesis)* on that part of the stage called *orchestra.* The single actor was earlier the leader of the dithyrambic dance choir. A second actor was introduced by Aeschylus and a third by Sophocles. The spoken dialogue alternated with solo songs (with lyre) or choruses (unaccompanied, or with lyre or *aulos*).

Music, with the other arts, was regarded as inspired by the nine Muses. The Greek word *mousike* had two meanings: it meant the culture of the intellectual faculties, which, with *gymnastike,* or bodily culture, provided a liberal education; and it signified the poetic text, its melody, and the accompanying dance. The morally uplifting influence of music was taught by the school of Pythagoras (*c.* 585–*c.* 479), which thought it possible by means of sensual harmony to reestablish the primary intellectual harmony of the soul; *i.e.,* the harmony inhabiting the heavens before animating human bodies. Hence the doctrines of the harmony of the spheres, the ethos or characteristic influence of the various musical modes and the efficacy of numbers.

The 4th century B.C. saw the emergence of Greek science and the first formulations of music theory. The most practical approach was that of Aristoxenus, while Euclid expounded Pythagorean theory, and Plato wrote on important musical themes. Theory received further serious attention only from the 1st century A.D., the most important work being that of Ptolemy, the neo-Pythagorean mathematician and astronomer. Before the first theory was written, however, music and poetry had begun to diverge, and the styles of Aristophanes, Miletus, and Philoxenus show a progressively popular trend, after which drama rapidly degenerated into pantomime.

The only surviving examples of Greek music belong to this late period, and it is little indeed compared with survivals from other arts. Of about 20 possible fragments—written variously in a vocal and an instrumental notation—two remain unauthenticated, and three or more are probably Byzantine reconstructions. Of the remainder three are important: the two Delphic hymns to Apollo carved on marble at Delphi (late 2nd century B.C.) and the epitaph of Seikelos for his wife chiseled on a tomb at Tralles (Aidin), Turkey (1st century B.C. or later). The remainder, in papyri, are to be seen in Cairo, Berlin, Oslo, Michigan, and Oxford; the oldest fragment of all, a few choral lines from Euripides' *Orestes,* is in the Rainer papyrus in Vienna (3rd–2nd century B.C.).

forms and principles of composition The fragmentary relics hardly allow structural analysis, though certain fundamental principles of construction are known: poetic meter, verbal contour, and musical time.

The units of poetic meter (feet comprising short and long syllables) fell into three main groups, exemplified by the *dactyl* — ◡◡ ; *iamb* ◡ — (*cf. trochee* — ◡); and *paeon* — ◡◡◡ . The equivalent musical units comprised short and long notes: *duple* ♩ ♫, $\frac{2}{4}$; *triple* ♪ ♩ (or ♩ ♪), $\frac{3}{8}$; and *multiple* ♩. ♩, $\frac{5}{8}$, as found respectively in the hymn to Helios, hymn to the muse, and first Delphic hymn.

Declaimed poetry also had verbal contours—inherent tonal elements represented by the three speech accents: acute (rising), grave (falling), and circumflex (rising followed by falling, or level)—which *melopoeia,* the Greek art of melody making, aimed to enhance. The two principles, poetic meter and tonic accent, are seen in combination in the hymn to Helios with its strictly anapaestic meter and 12 out of 16 acute accents matched by a rising melodic contour.

Greek poetry, conceived without any dynamic stress of its own, could hardly escape the influence of the accompanying instruments and dance, which by their very nature required strong and weak beats, or musical time. Thus the noisy *thesis* (downbeat) of the choral dance leader's foot clapper was inevitably followed by a silent *arsis* (lifting).

Moreover in postclassical times music already imposed its own formal patterns on poetic structure: the four metrically different lines of the epitaph of Seikelos are equally adjusted to a melody in $\frac{12}{8}$ time. According to Dionysius of Halicarnassus the *Orestes* of Euripides went still further toward purely musical form: its melody did not rise and fall with the speech accents; it was identical in two rhythmically paired strophes.

The Greek arts, whether plastic or dramatic, favored linear form; hence rhythm took precedence over elements of color. In music the latter were no doubt represented by occasional decorative two-note chords plucked on the lyre, by a drone on one of the *aulos* pipes accompanying the melody on the other, and by the accompaniment of a vocal melody in heterophonic variation. But the single line of melody remained paramount, and its intervals were classified in Greek music theory.

theory The Greeks referred their music to the intervals of an octave (diapason), fifth, and fourth, and they knew all the intervals of Western music and more. The interval of a fourth was the practical unit of their tonal space; when divided into four notes it was known as a tetrachord. Of these notes the outer two were fixed, the inner two movable; and the position of the latter determined one of three *genera* whose intervals (reading downward) were: tone, tone, *leimma* (Latin *limma,* "remainder" of the interval of a fourth after the subtraction of two tones) in the diatonic, as in the epitaph of Seikilos; minor third, semitone, semitone in the chromatic; and ditone, quarter tone, quarter tone in the enharmonic, as in the *Orestes* fragment. Finer intervals were classified in subgenera called *chroai* ("shades").

Three primary (diatonic) modes correspond to the three possible (descending) orders in which the intervals of the tetrachord run: Dorian (tone, tone, *leimma*), Phrygian (TLT), and Lydian (LTT). Such structures occur respectively in the second Delphic hymn, epitaph of Seikilos, and an instrumental piece from J. F. Bellerman's *Anonymous* (of late date). Two tetrachords joined together formed a *harmonia* (octave scale), and in the diatonic genus the seven such scales in use (with notes reading downward as on the white keys of the piano but allowing for differences in tun-

ing) were as follows: a to A, Hypodorian (Aeolian); g to G, Hypophrygian (Ionian); f to F, Hypolydian; e to E, Dorian; d to D, Phrygian; c to C, Lydian; and b to B, Hyperdorian. These *harmoniai* are called modes today, but they were only the scaffolding for the true modes (*tropos,* pl. *tropoi*) or melodic styles or contours (perhaps comparable with the Indian *raga* and Arabic *maqam*)—each with its particular ethos, or characteristic effect. A five-note scale was also early introduced into Greece from Asia. It is found as late as the second Delphic hymn.

To embrace all the notes of the seven *harmoniai* in each of their three *genera* within the compass of a single octave, the Greeks had a theoretical scale of 21 sounds (greater perfect system); the seven *harmoniai* they related to each other in a continuous two-octave scale *(disdiapason);* for modulation they used an 11-note series (lesser perfect system); and to bring any scale within the limited compass (that of the Dorian *harmonia*) of the lyre, they had a transposing system.

The surviving musical fragments well illustrate certain aspects of classical theory and yet show differences that suggest only a frail link with the music of classical times. To what extent the theory represents musical practice at any one period may be legitimately questioned, for the theorists often disagree among themselves with considerable confusion in terminology.

instruments Ancient Greece appears never to have had a developed instrumental art. The role of its few instruments—all derived from non-Greek sources—was the accompaniment of poetry and the dance.

The all-important national LYRE existed in preclassical forms: *phorminx, citharis, chelys,* and in classical forms: cithara (professional), *lyra* (lyric poets, amateurs), *barbiton.* The harp was played by women: *magadis* (large), *pectis* (smaller), *psalterion* (later). The reed pipe *(aulos),* usually double and next in importance after the lyre, played *nomoi* and accompanied dithyramb and drama. The *syrinx* (shepherd's panpipe) was played to the flocks, and the *salpinx* (straight metal trumpet) had a military function. The *hydraulis* (water organ, Alexandria, 3rd century B.C.) became more popular in Rome. Percussion instruments were introduced with the Dionysus and Cybele cults: *tympanon,* hand-beaten frame drum (Mediterranean); *crotala,* hand clappers; *croupala,* foot clappers; and *cymbala,* cymbals.

heritage Though nothing remains of ancient Greek musical practice and few instruments survive, the influence of classical theory was wide and lasting. The Greek empire carried it to Egypt and the Asiatic coasts and possibly as far as India. In early Christian times the Gnostics used the Greek scale in their incantations, and Byzantium adopted the Greek modes (*see* BYZANTINE CHANT). The Romans acknowledged Greek musical leadership and transmitted Greek theory to Europe through Boethius (*c.* A.D. 480–524), and the early church drew upon its modes. But Islam is the principal heir to Greek theory through the Persians, Arabs, and Turks, whose writings further influenced Europe from the 9th century. Thus Greek music, itself the heir to so much from the world's three most ancient civilizations, helped to create that of at least three more. *See* ANCIENT MUSIC.

BIBLIOGRAPHY: Curt Sachs, *The Rise of Music in the Ancient World* (1943); Oliver Strunk, *Source Readings in Music History* (1950); Egon Wellesz, ed., *Ancient and Oriental Music* (1957), Vol. 1 of *New Oxford History of Music;* Edward A. Lippman, *Musical Thought in Ancient Greece* (1964; reprint, 1975); Solon Michaelides, *The Music of Ancient Greece* (1978).

Green, (William) Martyn (April 22, 1899– February 8, 1975) The English actor and lyric baritone Martyn Green made his reputation in the character and comedian roles of Gilbert and Sullivan operettas (Major General Stanley in *The Pirates of Penzance;* Ko-Ko in *The Mikado;* the Lord Chancellor in *Iolanthe*). A student at the Royal College of Music in London, he joined the D'Oyly Carte Opera Company in 1922, remaining with the group until 1951. A master of the patter song and eccentric dancing, he also had success as a serious actor in Eugene O'Neill's *The Iceman Cometh* and Sean O'Casey's *Red Roses for Me.* In 1953 he went to the United States, where he made numerous television appearances and starred in movies of *The Mikado* and a life of Gilbert and Sullivan. In 1973– 74 he directed the Simsbury (Connecticut) Light Opera Company. His autobiography *Here's a How-de-do* appeared in 1952, and *Martyn Green's Treasury of Gilbert and Sullivan* was published in 1961.

Greenberg, Noah (April 9, 1919–January 9, 1966) A scholar and performer of early music, the U.S. conductor Noah Greenberg is best known for reconstructing and staging the medieval *Play of Daniel* and *Play of Herod.* In 1952 he founded the New York Pro Musica Antiqua (later the New York Pro Musica), which toured Europe and Israel and annually presented the *Play of Daniel* in New York City during Greenberg's lifetime. Greenberg was editor of the *Pro Musica Choral Series* and collaborated with W. H. Auden on *An Elizabethan Song Book.*

Gregorian chant: *see* PLAINCHANT.

Grétry, André (Ernest) Modeste (February 10/11, 1741–September 24, 1813) Known during his lifetime as "the Molière of music," André Modeste Grétry was a leading composer in the evolution of French opéra comique from light popular plays with music into semi-serious musical drama. He studied singing, violin, and harmony in his native Liège and in 1759 was sent to Rome to study composition. In 1766 he went to Geneva as a music teacher. There he met Voltaire, at whose suggestion he went to Paris in 1767. He produced more than 50 works for the stage, including *Le Tableau parlant* (1769; "The Speaking Picture") and *Zémire et Azor* (1771). His masterpiece, *Richard Coeur de Lion* (1784), is considered one of the earliest examples of French Romantic opera.

Grétry's music is noted for its finesse and melodic grace (patches of it are quoted for their Rococo atmosphere in Tchaikovsky's *Queen of Spades* and in the Fifth Violin Concerto of Henri Vieuxtemps), and he excelled in the development of dramatic scenes through melody and the careful setting of words. Widely honored during his life, he received a pension from Napoleon in 1802. In 1789 he published his *Mémoires, ou essais sur la musique.*

RECORDINGS: Ballet music from *Céphale et Procris* and *La Caravane du Caire;* Flute Concerto in C Major.

Grieg, Edvard (Hagerup) (June 15, 1843–September 4, 1907) The great Norwegian Romantic composer Edvard Grieg was the founder of the Norwegian national school. The Grieg (formerly Greig) family was of Scottish origin; his mother, Gesine Hagerup, belonged to a well-established Norwegian family. From the age of six Grieg received piano lessons from her, and in 1858, at the recommendation of violinist Ole Bull, he entered the Leipzig Conservatory, where he studied with Ignaz Moscheles and Karl Reinecke. During this period he suffered a severe attack of pleurisy from which he never really recovered. In 1863 he went to Copenhagen, where he studied with Niels Gade and Emil Hartmann, both illustrating a sentimental rather than a radical aspect of the Scandinavian temperament. Grieg developed through his association in 1864 with the young Norwegian nationalist composer Rikard Nordraak. "Through him," said Grieg, "I first learned to know the northern folk tunes and my own nature." Together they organized the Euterpe Society for the production of works by young Scandinavian composers. In 1867 he married his cousin, the singer Nina Hagerup. He spent the winters of 1865–66 and 1869–70 in Rome, where he first met the Norwegian playwright Henrik Ibsen and also Liszt, who was roused to enthusiasm by his Piano Concerto that had been first heard in Copenhagen with Grieg as soloist (1869). In 1866 he settled in Christiania (Oslo), remaining there until 1874, when he was granted an annual stipend by the Norwegian government that made possible his indulging his desire to live in the western mountains, where he later built his home "Troldhaugen" (1885, near Bergen). In spite of poor health, Grieg made several tours in Scandinavia, on the Continent, and in England, playing his Piano Concerto in London in 1888.

Rooted in the national folk tradition of Norway, Grieg's music displays a refined lyrical sense. Between 1867 and 1901 he wrote ten collections of *Lyric* Pieces for piano. His spirited rhythms often have a folk music association. His harmonies are novel, developed from the late Romantic style, and anticipate the Impressionists. In his relatively few works in the larger forms, the Piano Concerto, the Quartet in g minor, and the three violin and piano sonatas, he makes use of a free sonata form. His original Ballade for piano is a set of variations on a folk theme. Among his most popular works are his incidental music to Ibsen's *Peer Gynt* and the *Holberg* Suite. His arrangements of Norwegian dances and songs (Opp. 17 and 66) and especially his *Norwegian Peasant Dances (Slåtter)* show his characteristic sense of rhythm and harmony. His vocal works include songs on texts of Aasmund Olafsen Vinje and the *Haugtussa* cycle. Intuitively he identified himself with the poet's imagery in these songs and discovered its musical equivalent.

BIBLIOGRAPHY: David Monrad-Johansen, *Edvard Grieg* (1938); Gerald E. H. Abraham, ed., *Grieg; a Symposium* (1948); John Horton, *Grieg* (1974).

RECORDINGS: Piano—Concerto in a minor, *Lyric* Pieces (10 sets), *Norwegian Peasant Dances (Slåtter), Poetic Tone-Pictures* (6), Sonata in e minor; orchestra—*Holberg* Suite, *Peer Gynt* Suites (2), *Sigurd Jorsalfar* Suite, *Symphonic Dances, Two Elegiac Melodies;* chamber music—Cello Sonata, First Quartet in g minor, Violin Sonatas (3); piano pieces; songs.

Griffes, Charles (Tomlinson) (September 17, 1884–April 8, 1920) The first and most important U.S. Impressionist composer, Charles Griffes intended to be a concert pianist but came under the influence of Engelbert Humperdinck in Berlin and turned to composition. He returned to the United States in 1907 and taught at the Hackley School in Tarrytown, New York, from 1908. His compositions reflect two main interests—Orientalism and Impressionism as exemplified in the then new French music of Debussy and Ravel. Griffes' best known work is *The White Peacock,* originally the first of *Four Roman Sketches* (1918) for piano but orchestrated by the composer a few months later for a ballet (and a first concert performance by the Philadelphia Orchestra under Stokowski late in 1919). His tone poem after Coleridge, *The Pleasure Dome of Kubla Khan* (1919), and *Poem* (1919) for flute and orchestra are among the most important of his output cut short by his early death.

BIBLIOGRAPHY: Edward M. Maisel, *Charles T. Griffes; the Life of an American Composer* (1943).

RECORDINGS: Orchestra—*The Pleasure Dome of Kubla Khan, Poem, The White Peacock;* piano—Sonata in F Major, *Three Tone Pictures, The White Peacock; Two Sketches on Indian Themes* (quartet); songs.

Grigny, Nicolas de (1672–November 30, 1703) The French organist and composer Nicolas de Grigny was a member of a Reims family of musicians. He probably studied with Nicolas Lebègue in Paris and became organist of the Abbey of Saint-Denis in 1693. He returned to Reims in 1695 (or perhaps later) as organist of the cathedral, where he remained until his premature death. His organ works were published in 1699 in a collection entitled *Premier Livre d'orgue,* which includes an organ mass, five hymns of three to five settings each, and the concluding *Point d'orgue sur les grands jeux.* It ranks with Couperin's two organ masses as the culmination of the Classical French organ school. J. S. Bach was sufficiently impressed that he copied the book for his own use.

RECORDINGS: *Livre d'orgue.*

Grisi, Giulia (July 28, 1811–November 29, 1869) Admired by Rossini and Bellini (who wrote the roles of Adalgisa in *Norma* and Elvira in *I Puritani* for her), the Italian soprano Giulia Grisi made her debut in 1828 as Emma in Rossini's *Zelmira.* She had great success in Paris from 1832, when she appeared there at the Théâtre Italien as Rossini's Semiramide, until 1849. From 1834 to 1861 she was popular in London as the successor to Giuditta Pasta.

Grosse Fuge: *see* BEETHOVEN (last years); CHAMBER MUSIC; COUNTERPOINT (Classical period); FUGUE (after Bach and Handel).

ground or **ground bass** (Italian, *basso ostinato*) A term used to describe a bass pattern several times repeated on which a musical composition is constructed. The immediate ancestry of the ground bass is found in the 15th-century cantus firmus dances of Italy and France. In the 16th century the practice of composing counterpoint on a repeated bass pattern became popular in Italy and Spain, and such well-known grounds as the *passemezzo antico, Romanesca, folia* (all closely related), *Ruggiero,* and *passemezzo moderno* spread throughout Europe. The early grounds implied an invariable harmonic structure that provided an ideal framework for improvisation. Many 16th- and 17th-century dances were written on preexisting or newly composed grounds. Closely allied to the harmonic ground is the melodic ground that first appeared in the 17th century. In this the harmony may be varied at each repetition, the phrase lengths of the upper parts may overlap those of the ground, and the ground itself may be transposed during the course of the piece.

The use of the ground bass has a more or less continuous history from the 16th to the 20th century; it was particularly popular in the Baroque era in the form of CHACONNE and PASSACAGLIA. Among composers who have employed it with success are Monteverdi, Purcell, Bach, Beethoven, Brahms, Britten, and Berg. *See* VARIATIONS.

Grove, George (August 13, 1820–May 28, 1900) An English writer on music, George Grove began his career as a civil engineer and then became secretary to the Society of Arts in 1850 and to the Crystal Palace in 1852. He collaborated with William Smith in the *Dictionary of the Bible* and was largely responsible for organizing the Palestine Exploration fund in 1865. In addition to having a beneficial influence on the choice of music at the Crystal Palace, for more than 40 seasons Grove wrote analytical notes for the concerts; these notes were marked by enthusiasm, insight, and thoroughness and established a standard that was long admired. In 1867 he visited Vienna with Arthur Sullivan and discovered the part books of the whole of Schubert's music to *Rosamunde,* which had been left unregarded for 44 years. Grove was editor of *Macmillan's Magazine* from 1868 to 1883, and during the years 1879–89 his famous *Dictionary of Music and Musicians* was published. When the Royal College of Music was founded in 1882, Grove was appointed its first director and was knighted. His book *Beethoven and His Nine Symphonies* was published in 1896.

Grumiaux, Arthur (b. March 21, 1921) Awarded the Prix de Virtuosité by his government at the age of 19, the Belgian violinist Arthur Grumiaux joined the faculty of the Brussels Conservatory in 1949. He has toured extensively in Europe and North America. Recordings include a cycle of Beethoven sonatas with Clara Haskil, Mozart's violin concertos with the London Symphony, and works by Berg, William Walton, and Stravinsky.

Guarneri A celebrated family of violin makers, the Guarneris were originally from Cremona. The first was **Andrea** (*c.* 1626–December 7, 1698), who worked with Antonio Stradivari in the workshop of Nicoló Amati (son of Girolamo). Violins of a model original to him are dated from the "sign of St. Theresa" in Cremona. His son **Giuseppe** (November 25, 1666–*c.* 1739) made instruments at first like his father's but later in a style of his own with a narrow waist; his son **Pietro** "of Venice" (April 14, 1695–April 7, 1762) was also a fine maker. Another son of Andrea, **Pietro Giovanni** (February 18, 1655–March 26, 1720), moved from Cremona to Mantua, where he too worked "sub signo Sanctae Teresae." His violins showed considerable variations from those of the other Guarneris. George Hart, in his work on the violin, says, "There is increased breadth between the sound holes; the sound hole is rounder and more perpendicular; the middle bouts are more contracted, and the model is more raised."

The greatest of all the Guarneris was a nephew of Andrea, **Giuseppe,** known as "Giuseppe del Gesù" (August 21, 1698–October 17, 1744), whose title originates in the I.H.S. inscribed on his labels. He was much influenced by the earlier works of the Brescian school, particularly those of Giovanni Paolo Maggini, whom he followed in the boldness of outline and the massive construction that aim at the production of tone rather than visual perfection of form. The great variety of his work in size, model, and related features represents his experiments in the direction of discovering this tone. A stain or sap mark running parallel with the fingerboard on both sides appears on the bellies of many of his instruments. Since the middle of the 18th century, spurious instruments ascribed to the master have been abundant. It was not until Paganini played on a "Joseph" that the taste of amateurs turned from the sweetness of the Amati and the Stradivari violins in favor of the more robust tone of the Giuseppe Guarneri. Paganini's instrument is preserved in the Municipal Palace of Genoa.

BIBLIOGRAPHY: Horace Petherick, *Joseph Guarnerius* (1906; reprint, 1977); Alfred Hill *et al, Violin Makers of the Guarneri Family, 1626–1762* (1963).

Guerrero, Francisco (May 1527–November 8, 1599) An outstanding composer of the Spanish polyphonic school of the 16th century, Francisco Guerrero was born in Seville, where he spent nearly all his working life. Guerrero received his early musical training from his brother Pedro, and in 1545, at the unusually early age of 18, he was appointed maestro de capilla at the Jaén Cathedral. In 1548 he was appointed cantor at the Seville Cathedral under Pedro Fernández de Castilleja, and in 1551 he assumed the effective directorship and became maestro de capilla in 1574.

A most accomplished contrapuntist, Guerrero wrote music that is eminently vocal and strongly Spanish in character. His compositions include 18 masses, two requiems, settings of two passions (St. Matthew and St. John), motets, and a volume of *Canciones y Villanescas espirituales* (1589).

Guido of Arezzo (*c.* 990–1050) An Italian musical theorist who developed the system of modern musical notation, Guido was of Italian descent and a monk at the Benedictine Abbey of Pomposa. Driven from the monastery as a result of jealousies aroused by his musical innovations, he probably settled at Arezzo. After travels that may have taken him to France, he appears to have spent his last years at the Camaldolite Monastery of S. Croce di Fonte Avellana in Umbria. Theories suggesting that Guido was French or that, as an Italian, he had settled at St. Maur near Paris derive from a confusion of names and monasteries. Guido certainly traveled, but knowledge of his journey to France is scanty. It is known only that staff notation, obviously derived from Guido's research in this field, appeared early in the north of France (though not at St. Maur) as it did in central Italy.

Guido established the staff of four lines as well as the names of the degrees of the hexachord. At the same time he developed the alphabetic notation now common to the Germanic countries. It is not possible, however, to ascribe to him the invention, widely used in the Middle Ages, of the "Guidonian hand," in which notes are represented by the joints of the five fingers; though the theory of notation based on this invention bears his name, it is not mentioned in his works.

The staff was the most far-reaching of his achievements. Before Guido's time melodies were learned by rote, since neumes were unable to express intervals precisely. Guido declared that with his system the ten years normally required to become an ecclesiastical singer could be reduced to five months.

The disadvantage of Guido's system was that melodies tended to become desiccated. Many of the ornaments that appear in early manuscripts on neumes are not to be found in those on staves. However, the West was ready to establish the diatonic system, and this movement was followed by Guido, who may not have been entirely appreciative of the earlier significance of neumes. Guido's discovery allowed the diffusion of musical theory, a precise notation of polyphony, and the development of the modern musical language.

Guido is credited with the composition of the Latin hymn to St. John the Baptist, *Ut queant laxis;* the first syllable of each line, *ut, re, mi, fa, sol, la,* is used in Latin countries as the name of the first six ascending notes of the C major scale. Probably he modified the hymn so that the first notes of the lines formed this succession. Before Guido an alphabetical system of musical notation is found in France using the letters of the alphabet from A to P. Guido used forms consisting of a series of capital letters, small letters, and double small letters from A to G.

Guillaume de Machaut: *see* MACHAUT, GUILLAUME DE.

Guillaume Tell: *see* ROMANTIC PERIOD (non-German music of the 19th century); ROSSINI.

Guilmant, (Félix) Alexandre (March 12, 1837–March 29, 1911)   The son of an organist and one of the finest organists of his time, Alexandre Guilmant studied in his native France and in Belgium. From 1871 to 1901 he was organist at the Parisian church of La Trinité, and he taught at the Paris Conservatoire from 1896 until his death. In 1894, with Charles Bordes and d'Indy, he founded the Schola Cantorum for the study of plainchant and liturgical music of the 16th century. He toured widely and inaugurated the organs of St. Sulpice and Notre-Dame de Paris. His compositions include liturgical music and sonatas and two "symphonies" for the organ; he edited two collections, *École classique de l'orgue* and *Archives des maîtres de l'orgue,* which preserved much early French organ music.

guitar   A plucked stringed instrument with a wide, flat shallow body of waisted outline. Although deriving ultimately from the common stock of medieval necked stringed instruments played with plectrum, fingers, or bow, the guitar probably originated in Spain in the early 16th century and was probably a development of the gittern. With seven gut strings arranged in three pairs, or courses, and a single top string, the tuning (two fourths with a third in the middle) of the early guitar was by means of pegs in a viol-like pegbox fitted to a long neck on which gut frets were tied. The neck was mortised into an end block, and the fingerboard was flush with the table (belly). In the table was a circular sound hole that was often elaborately decorated. The bridge was glued to the table, thus sustaining the direct pull of the strings. This instrument was closely related to the *vihuela de mano,* which in Spain took the place of the lute. Books of vihuela music from the middle years of the 16th century often include music for the four-course guitar.

Before the end of the 16th century a fifth course was added, tuned a fourth below the fourth course. This instrument, small bodied and narrow in outline, with a flat, slightly reflexed head in place of the earlier pegbox, remained popular mainly with amateurs during the 17th and 18th centuries, although some music of interest was written by virtuoso professional players.

In the late 18th century a sixth course was added, the stringing subsequently being reduced to six single strings tuned E-A-d-g-b-e', which has since remained standard. At this period the fingerboard remained flush with the table, the frets were of metal or ivory, the 12th or octave fret was at the junction of the neck with the body, and five higher frets were mounted on the table itself.

Thereafter most European makers sought to produce greater sonority. In Spain the tradition of guitar playing remained unbroken, and it was there in the early 19th century that further developments were introduced. The body became broader and shallower with a very thin table, an important internal feature of which was the spreading of radial bars from just below the sound hole in place of the earlier transverse bars. The base of the neck was formed into a shoe that projected a short distance inside the body and was glued to the back; this gave extra stability against the pull of the strings. A raised hardwood fingerboard with metal frets extended down the neck and upper part of the table as far as the sound hole.

Elsewhere in Europe makers on the whole favored a narrow-waisted body and a rather heavier construction. Radial bars were adopted, however, together with the raised fingerboard and the shoe. Most northern instruments were fitted with machine heads instead of pegs for tuning.

The guitar in its modern form was introduced by the Spanish maker Antonio Torres in the mid-19th century; this large instrument with a fuller, deeper tone is suitable for use in the concert hall. The strings of the classical guitar were of gut and metal-covered silk, but plastics later largely replaced gut for the upper strings. Other modern developments include the dance band guitar, metal strung and played with a plectrum; the *cello* guitar, with a violin-type bridge and tailpiece; the Hawaiian guitar, in which the strings are stopped with a metal bar that is used to produce a

Narciso Yepes with 10-stringed guitar
courtesy, Mariedi Anders Artist Management, Inc.

portamento effect; and the electric guitar, where the tone depends not on body resonance but on amplication.

From the 16th to the 18th century guitar music was written either in TABLATURE or in a system of chord symbols known as *abecedario Italiano*. Sometimes the two were combined. Since the 18th century the method normally used is a single staff on which the music is notated an octave higher than it sounds.

The guitar grew in popularity during the 17th century as the lute and vihuela declined. It remained an amateur's instrument from the 17th to early 19th century. A few virtuoso guitarists, however, became known in Europe, among them Gaspar Sanz (flourished 1674), Robert de Visée (*c.* 1650–*c.* 1725), Fernando Sor (1778–1839), and Joseph Kaspar Mertz (1806–56). Modern classical-guitar technique owes much to the Spaniard Francisco Tárrega (1852–1909), whose transcriptions of works by Bach, Mozart, and other composers formed the basis of the repertoire.

In the 20th century Andrés Segovia gave the guitar further prominence as a recital instrument, and composers such as Heitor Villa-Lobos, de Falla, Britten, and Joaquín Rodrigo wrote serious works for it; others (*e.g.,* Pierre Boulez) scored for the guitar in chamber ensembles.

The guitar is widely played in the folk and popular music of many countries. In jazz ensembles it is part of the rhythm section and is occasionally played as a solo instrument.

BIBLIOGRAPHY: A. P. Sharpe, *The Story of the Spanish Guitar,* 4th ed. (1968); Frederic V. Grunfeld, *The Art and Times of the Guitar* (1974); Harvey Turnbull, *The Guitar from the Sixteenth Century to the Present Day* (1974); Frederick Noad, *The Baroque Guitar* (1975) and *The Classical Guitar* (1976); Tom and Mary Anne Evans, *Guitars: From the Renaissance to Rock* (1977).

Gurrelieder: *see* MODERN PERIOD (disintegration of tonality); ROMANTIC PERIOD (20th-century transition); SCHOENBERG.

Gutierrez, Horacio (b. August 28, 1948) Educated at the Juilliard School, the Cuban pianist Horacio Gutierrez made his debut with the Havana Symphony at age 11. He has performed with orchestras in the United States and Europe and has appeared on television programs for the BBC. In 1970 he received a silver medal in the Tchaikovsky competition in Moscow. Recordings include the First Piano Concertos of Tchaikovsky and of Liszt.

gymel A medieval style of two-part polyphony, possibly of popular origin, in which the voices move mainly in consecutive thirds or sixths. Crossing of parts is frequent. Although compositions in gymel form have been preserved in manuscripts dating from the beginning of the 13th century, the name itself (from *cantus gemellus,* "twin song") is first found in a 15th-century detailed description by the theoretician Guilielmus Monachus. Gymel seems to have been favored in England during the 13th century, and the style had a marked influence on the development of English polyphony in the following century. In late 15th- and early 16th-century English choral music the word gymel denotes a duo and the splitting of one part into two parts.

H

Habeneck, François-Antoine (January 22, 1781–February 8, 1849) The first conductor to promote the Beethoven symphonies in France, François-Antoine Habeneck was a product of the Paris Conservatoire, studying violin with Pierre Baillot, and later a professor there. He was a conductor at the Opéra from 1824 and founded (1826; first performance 1828) the Société des Concerts du Conservatoire, described by Mendelssohn as "the best orchestra I have ever heard." According to Wagner, Habeneck "was not a conductor of special genius," but his unlimited rehearsals and more than 150 performances of Beethoven symphonies assured his reputation. His discipline of the orchestra and his dedication to the integrity of the score were both novelties in his day.

Hadley, Henry (Kimball) (December 20, 1871–September 6, 1937) A U.S. conductor and composer of operatic and symphonic music in a neoromantic manner, Henry Hadley studied composition with George Whitefield Chadwick in Boston. He went to Germany in 1904 and in 1909 conducted his one-act opera *Safié* in Mainz. His later operas, *Azora, Daughter of Montezuma* (1917), *Bianca* (1918), and *Cleopatra's Night* (1920), were given in Chicago and New York City.

His orchestral works include five symphonies (1897–1934); the symphonic poems *Salomé, Lucifer,* and *The Ocean;* and the symphonic suites *San Francisco* and *Streets of Pekin.* He also wrote choral works, chamber music, and about 150 songs. His music is cast in a Wagnerian mold with occasional Impressionistic touches.

Hadley conducted the Seattle Symphony (1909–11), the San Francisco Symphony (1911–15), and the Manhattan Symphony (1929–32). From 1920 to 1927 he was associate conductor of the New York Philharmonic. He organized the Berkshire Symphonic Festival (1934) at Tanglewood, Massachusetts, that eventually became the Berkshire Music Center, the summer home of the Boston Symphony.

RECORDING: Piano Quintet.

Haffner Serenade and **Haffner Symphony:** *see* MOZART (early life) and (later life).

Hahn, Reynaldo (August 9, 1875–January 28, 1947) A French composer of light operas and songs in the tradition of Offenbach and André Messager, Reynaldo Hahn was born at Caracas, Venezuela; he went to Paris when a child and studied at the Conservatoire under Massenet. In 1898 his *L'Île du rêve* was given at the Opéra-Comique, and from then until 1939 he produced many light operas, the best of which is *Ciboulette* (1923); ballets, notably *La Fête chez Thérèse* (1910), and *Le Dieu bleu* (1912); and incidental music for plays by Edmond Rostand, Sacha Guitry, and others. His songs include the *Chansons grises* and the *Chansons latines* and the well-known "Si mes vers avaient des ailes." He was also known as a conductor of the operas of Mozart and gave *Don Giovanni* at Salzburg. His piano suite *Portraits de peintres* was inspired by early poems of Marcel Proust, who portrayed Hahn in his novel *Jean Santeuil*. He was music critic of *Le Figaro* from 1934 and was appointed director of the Paris Opéra in 1945. His work is melodious, usually slender, but gracefully written. With Messager he was responsible during his day for the main developments in the French operetta which had been established by Offenbach. His memoirs are valuable sources for the musical and literary life of his time.

Haitink, Bernard (b. March 4, 1929) A student at the Amsterdam Conservatory, the Dutch conductor Bernard Haitink began his career as a violinist and later as conductor of the Netherlands Radio Philharmonic. A short conducting tour with the Amsterdam Concertgebouw in 1958–59 led to his appointment as co-conductor with Eugen Jochum in 1961 and permanent conductor in 1964. In 1958 he made his U.S. debut with the Los Angeles Philharmonic. He became principal conductor of the London Philharmonic in 1967 and its artistic director three years later (until 1979), and in 1977 he was named musi-

cal director of the Glyndebourne Festival, where he conducted from 1972. His recordings are many and include complete cycles of the symphonies of Beethoven, Brahms, Bruckner, and Mahler, and he was the first to record all the tone poems of Liszt.

Halévy, (Jacques François) Fromental (Élie) May 27, 1799–March 17, 1862) The French composer Fromental Halévy was known for his Romantic opera *La Juive*. Born in Paris of a Jewish family originally named Lévy, he studied under Henri Berton and Cherubini. In 1819 he won the Prix de Rome with his cantata *Herminie*. He wrote more than 30 operas, from *L'Artisan* (1827) to *La Magicienne* (1858). Among the earlier operas *La Dilettante d'Avignon* (1829) was a satire on the poverty of contemporary Italian librettos. In 1835 he wrote the five-act grand opera *La Juive* on a libretto by Eugène Scribe, based on episodes from *The Merchant of Venice* and *Ivanhoe*. Remarkable for its choral writing, psychological characterization, and imaginative orchestration, *La Juive* was, with Meyerbeer's *Les Huguenots,* the prototype of early French Romantic opera. Equally successful was *L'Éclair* (1835) in which Halévy revived the 18th-century traditions of opéra comique. *La Tempesta,* based on *The Tempest,* was written in Italian for production in London (1850) and introduced the air by Thomas Arne, "Where the bee sucks." His last opera *Noé* was completed by his pupil Bizet, who married Halévy's daughter Geneviève, later portrayed as the Duchesse de Guermantes in Proust's *À la recherche du temps perdu*. Halévy was influenced by Meyerbeer and was in his day overshadowed by him, though some of Meyerbeer's more delicate orchestral effects were borrowed from *La Juive*. He published *Souvenirs et portraits* (1861) and *Derniers Souvenirs* (1863).

BIBLIOGRAPHY: Mina Curtiss, *Bizet and His World* (1958; reprint, 1977).

RECORDING: Selections from *La Juive*.

Hallé, Charles, originally Karl Halle (April 11, 1819–October 25, 1895) Founder of the Hallé Orchestra in Manchester, England, the German-born pianist and conductor Charles

Hallé was educated in Darmstadt and in Paris (with Friedrich Kalkbrenner), where he became part of the circle of musicians that included Chopin, Liszt, and Berlioz. In 1848 he moved to England, making his home in Manchester. He was probably the first pianist to play all of Beethoven's piano sonatas in a recital series (1861), and he did much to promote Beethoven and Berlioz in England. He was the first head of the Royal College of Music in Manchester (1893) and is also remembered for inventing an automatic page turner. Hallé was knighted in 1888.

Hamlet: see PROGRAM MUSIC (problem of form); SYMPHONIC POEM; TCHAIKOVSKY (later life and works).

Hammerklavier Sonata (No. 29): see BEETHOVEN (last years); CRITICISM (theory).

Hammerschmidt, Andreas (1612–November 8, 1675) An Austro-Bohemian composer known for his sacred music, Andreas Hammerschmidt was born at Brüx, Bohemia. Nothing is known of his youth or education. He was in the service of Count Rudolf von Bünau in 1633, in 1635 he was organist at the Peterskirche, Freiberg, and about 1639 he became organist at the Johanneskirche, Zittau, where he remained until his death. His considerable output is important in the history of Lutheran music, and most of the chorale tunes in the Lutheran service are taken from his work. In form his cantatas foreshadow those of the 18th century, though they have little variety in mood or treatment. Hammerschmidt's sources are mainly the chorales and the German Bible; his style is a simple one. His works include 17 short Lutheran masses (Kyrie and Gloria only), unaccompanied sacred madrigals (*Geistliche Madrigalien*), a set of sacred symphonies (*Geistliche Symphonien*) for one or two voices with strings and continuo, and a book of secular songs (*Weltliche Oden*).

Hammerstein, Oscar, II: see MUSICAL COMEDY.

Handel, George Frideric, German form, Georg Friedrich Händel (February 23, 1685–April 14, 1759) One of the greatest composers of the late Baroque period, George Frideric

George Frideric Handel
oil painting after Thomas Hudson, 1756
courtesy, National Portrait Gallery, London

Handel was born in Germany but spent most of his adult life in England, where he successfully combined the techniques of German, French, Italian, and English musical styles in an outpouring of about 40 operas, 20 oratorios, and numerous other vocal pieces, instrumental works, and church music. His work ultimately became a factor in the popularization of European music throughout the world.

life Handel was born at Halle in Saxony, where his father was a barber-surgeon. At the age of seven he already showed signs of musical talent, and it is said that he practiced the clavichord secretly at night, as his father was opposed to the idea of his son's following music as a profession. But when his father took him to the court of Saxe-Weissenfels, the duke was impressed with the boy's talent and persuaded the senior Handel to allow his son to study music seriously. He was placed with Friedrich Wilhelm Zachau, organist of the Liebfrauenkirche in Halle, but at the same time the boy was required to pursue a general education at the Lutheran Gymnasium. After his father's death in 1697 young Handel entered Halle University as a law student, although he had already begun to earn a living as an organist at the Halle Cathedral. Among the friends that Handel made at this time was Georg Philipp Telemann, soon to be regarded as the leading composer in north Germany.

Handel decided to make music his career, and, having finished his legal studies in accordance with his father's wishes, he left Halle about 1703 and went to Hamburg, then a notable center for German opera. The Hamburg Opera was under the direction of Reinhard Keiser, one of the most gifted opera composers of the day, and Handel found a position as violinist and later harpsichordist in the opera orchestra. He made friends with Johann Mattheson, a young singer and composer who later became well known as a writer on music. The two young men went on an expedition to Lübeck in the hope that one or the other might succeed the celebrated but aged Buxtehude as town organist; but the appointment also entailed marriage with Buxtehude's daughter, and as neither wished to undertake this responsibility they returned to Hamburg. Handel composed a *St. John* Passion that was performed in Holy Week in 1705, and in the same year he produced his first opera, *Almira,* in which he showed a gift for writing memorable tunes. It was a success, and he soon followed it with another, *Nerone.*

He then made a journey to Italy, where he met many of the leading Italian musicians of the day, including Corelli and Alessandro and Domenico Scarlatti. Among the works he composed there were *La resurrezione; Il trionfo del tempo; Aci, Galatea e Polifemo;* the operas *Rodrigo* and *Agrippina;* and a number of chamber cantatas. His fame spread throughout Italy and from there to Germany, and in 1710 he was appointed Kapellmeister to the elector of Hanover, the future King George I of England. Soon after his appointment he applied for leave of absence and went to England, where he found favor with Queen Anne. Attempts had been made to found an Italian opera in London, with scores and singers brought over from Italy, but it was only

with the production of Handel's *Rinaldo* in February 1711 that Italian opera became firmly established in England. *Rinaldo* was a work full of youthful fire and energy, and it created for Handel an immense reputation. Although it became necessary for him to return to Hanover, he soon was back again in England, where he produced further Italian operas: *Il pastor fido* (1712) and *Teseo* (1713), as well as a Te Deum to celebrate the peace of Utrecht and a birthday ode for Queen Anne, who granted Handel an annual pension of £200. A year later the queen died, and his neglected master succeeded her on the English throne as George I. It has been said that Handel composed *Water Music* to win his way back to royal favor, but this has been rejected by modern scholars, although part, at least, of *Water Music* seems to date from the early years of the king's reign, and it is known that Handel directed music for a royal water party on the Thames in 1717. As the new king confirmed Handel's pension, it seems that they must have soon been reconciled.

Meanwhile Handel was composing and directing his operas, a task that was to absorb the greater part of his energies for the next 20 years or so. Eighteenth-century opera seria was to be aptly defined by Dr. Johnson as an "exotic and irrational entertainment," for the texts were in Italian, a language understood by only a very few of the audience; the plots were incredibly involved, full of disguisings and counterdisguisings; and the librettos were as often as not written in great haste by hack writers employed by theatrical managers. The composers were concerned not so much with dramatic effectiveness as with showing off the phenomenal accomplishments of the singers, chief of whom were the castrati. Both male and female singers were notoriously vain, and Handel frequently found himself at variance with them over the presentation of his music.

Handel was more independent than many of his contemporaries, but he was not above accepting a measure of patronage; he lived at Burlington House for a time as the guest of Lord Burlington and there met many famous wits, authors, and fellow artists. From 1718 to 1720 he was composer to the Duke of Chandos at the duke's mansion of Cannons near Edgware in Middlesex. It was for Chandos that Handel composed the series of *Chandos* Anthems, which were sung by the musicians of the duke's private chapel. Other works that Handel wrote for Chandos include the English masques *Esther* and *Acis and Galatea;* the latter was akin to, but by no means the same as, his Italian serenata *Aci, Galatea e Polifemo.* The English *Acis* is one of Handel's most delightful works.

Handel soon became involved again in operatic rivalries; feuds sprang up not only among singers but also among the partisans of several composers, such as Bononcini, Attilio Ariosti, Nicola Antonio Porpora, and Johann Adolph Hasse, who were at one time or another all advanced as Handel's rivals. But Handel, in spite of all difficulties, artistic or financial, continued to compose and direct opera after opera. Among those of the 1720s were *Floridante* (1721), *Ottone* (1723), *Giulio Cesare* (1724), *Rodelinda* (1725), and *Scipione* (1726). His first London operas were written for Aaron Hill, manager of the King's Theatre in the Haymarket.

Handel became a naturalized British subject in 1726 and the next year was commissioned to compose four of the anthems sung at the coronation of the new king, George II. He was already music master to the royal family, and this appointment was confirmed in the new reign with his pension increased to £400 a year. His *Admeto* and *Riccardo I* were produced in 1727, and in 1728 *Siroe* and *Tolomeo* were performed. But the opera establishment was now in serious financial difficulties, partly the result of the immense success of the *Beggar's Opera* by John Gay and John Christopher Pepusch, which was produced at the theater in Lincoln's Inn Fields in January 1728. However, a new Italian opera company was formed, and Handel went to Italy in search of fresh talent. On his return journey he revisited Halle and saw his aged mother and married sister. Back in London he produced *Lotario* (1729), the first of a new series of brilliant Italian operas. Of more importance was a pirated perfomance of *Acis and Galatea* that convinced Handel of the profit to be made from his compositions set to English words.

After producing several new operas *(Ezio, Sosarme, Orlando),* he composed the English oratorio *Deborah* to a poor libretto; but when it was performed in conjunction with revivals of his earlier pieces such as *Esther,* it had sufficient success to warrant his considering other works in the same genre. In 1733 he was invited to make a professional visit to Oxford, where he produced *Esther* and *Deborah* and a new oratorio, *Athalia.* Handel was still busy with Italian operas, and early in 1734 London saw *Arianna* (or *Ariadne*), remembered chiefly for the minuet in its overture—one of the most popular of all 18th-century tunes.

The marriage of the princess royal and the prince of Orange in March 1734 gave Handel the opportunity of putting on the serenata *Parnasso in festa,* which was largely a pasticcio from the music to *Athalia.* He also composed a wedding anthem for the royal pair and performed some of the concerti grossi that were published as his Opus 3. He revived *Sosarme* and *Il pastor fido* in a new version at the King's Theatre in the Haymarket. During the summer of 1734 he was engaged to write operas for John Rich, the prosperous producer of pantomimes and ballad operas who had founded and was running Covent Garden Theatre, and so began Handel's long association with the theater that was to become London's chief opera house. A third version of *Il pastor fido,* preceded by *Terpsicore,* was produced at Covent Garden in the autumn. Handel now found himself composing not only operas but also ballet music for Rich's French protégée, the ballerina Mlle Sallé. Accordingly Handel's new operas, *Ariodante* and *Alcina,* although still primarily Italian in character, have a certain amount of dance music in the French style and of a quality superior to that of much of the music in his opera seria. He set to music John Dryden's ode *Alexander's Feast,* which was produced with much success in 1736; he produced *Atalanta* in Italian during the same year and *Arminio* and *Giustino* in 1737.

The opera was again in serious difficulties. Throughout his London career Handel had suffered competition not only from rival composers but also from rival opera houses in a London that could barely support even one Italian opera in addition to its English theaters. Moreover the opera was supported by the world of fashion; when fashion changed even the finest singers and the best music might lose its audience, and as a result Handel often played to empty houses. In 1719 a Royal Academy of Music had been formed in imitation of the French Académie Royale de Musique (both institutions were founded to perform operas, not to teach music). In 1733 an "opera of the nobility" had been formed to perform at the theater in Lincoln's Inn Fields, but about 1738 both this and Handel's company went bankrupt. Handel became seriously ill. After a course of treatment at the baths at Aachen, he was restored to health and was soon at work again, composing among other things the *Funeral* Anthem for the obsequies of Queen Caroline. Handel became composer to a new operatic venture in which the remnants of the two old companies were united. For this new company he set *Faramondo* and *Serse*, his one attempt at comic opera, and compiled a pasticcio *Alessandro Severo*, all performed early in 1738. He also wrote two of his most celebrated English oratorios, *Saul* and *Israel in Egypt* (performed early in 1739). He was now at the height of his powers, and whatever his personal fortunes his reputation as a composer was immense. In recognition of his popularity Jonathan Tyers, the proprietor of Vauxhall Gardens, had his statue by the French sculptor Louis François Roubillac erected there.

In 1739 he composed his finest set of orchestral concertos, the Twelve *Grand* Concertos, Op. 6, and a setting of Dryden's *Ode for St. Cecilia's Day.* Yet he was still setting and producing Italian operas, with *Imeneo* appearing in 1740 and *Deidamia* in 1741. They were lighter in character than some of their predecessors, but they had little success, and again Handel was overtaken by serious financial difficulties. Even his oratorios were not paying. Yet in spite of his troubles 1741 was the year of his masterpiece, *Messiah,* and its scarcely less inspired successor, *Samson,* composed in a matter of weeks. About this time he received an invitation to go to Dublin, and it was in that city that *Messiah* was first heard on April 13, 1742. It was received with tremendous enthusiasm, but when Handel produced it a little later in London it was somewhat coldly received and only gradually won its way to popularity—and then largely because of its identification with charitable causes, in particular with its annual performance at the Foundling Hospital.

Handel finally abandoned opera, but he still had a liking for classical subjects, and his search for suitable texts for music led him to William Congreve's *Semele,* written years before as an English opera. Handel set it as a masque but produced it in 1744 without dramatic action "after the fashion of an oratorio." It contains some of his most charming music, including the famous aria "Where'er you walk," but it had little success in his lifetime. His next true oratorio was *Joseph* (1744). It suffers from an unusually banal libretto and has rarely been revived. He also composed a fine Te Deum (1743) for the peace of Dettingen. He then returned to classical mythology for subject matter and composed the secular oratorio *Hercules;* this and another fine work, the biblical drama *Belshazzar,* were produced in 1745 with little response from the public. In spite of his prodigious efforts Handel was again in serious financial difficulty, and to add to his troubles his health broke down once more. Early in 1746 Handel produced the successful *Occasional* Oratorio to celebrate the Duke of Cumberland's victories over Prince Charles Stuart. More successful still was the bellicose *Judas Maccabaeus,* produced in 1747. *Judas* was the turning point in Handel's fortunes; he had begun to create a new public among the people of the rising middle classes, who would have turned away in moral indignation from the Italian opera but who were quite ready to be edified by a moral tale from scripture set to suitably dignified and by now rather old-fashioned music.

Gradually his financial position improved. He had found a new librettist in the clergyman Thomas Morell, who, though perhaps not a very good poet, could tell a semidramatic tale in sufficiently smooth verse to please Handel's new audiences. Handel composed *Alexander Balus* and *Joshua* in 1747 and produced them during the Lenten season of 1748; *Solomon* and *Susanna* were produced in 1749. The latter year was made even more memorable by the composition and performance of his instrumental *Fireworks Music,* commissioned by the king for the celebration of the peace of Aix-la-Chapelle. It was performed by a large band of musicians as a musical accompaniment for Signor Servandoni's display of fireworks in the Green Park, and, although the fireworks were not a complete success, Handel's music was enthusiastically received. In July of that year (1749) he finished his oratorio *Theodora,* a work that he valued highly but one that, from its first production in 1750, never won popularity. In gratitude for his work for the Foundling Hospital, he was elected a governor and continued to give a performance of *Messiah* in the chapel every year. In his will he left the hospital a complete set of parts for the performance of *Messiah.*

Handel now began to experience trouble with his eyesight. He managed with much difficulty to finish his last great oratorio *Jephtha* and produced it in 1752, but blindness was fast descending upon him. At first he handed over the direction of his oratorio seasons to others, but later he again took part in the performances with the assistance of his faithful friend and amanuensis, John Christopher Smith the younger. Although in failing health he participated in a performance of *Messiah* during the Lenten season of 1759. A week later he died in his house on Brook Street, London, esteemed and respected in England as the greatest composer of his age. After all the financial straits of earlier years, he died a wealthy man. He was buried in Westminster Abbey, where his monument by Roubillac still stands.

Handel had a dry sense of humor and a way of expressing himself in a mixture of several languages at once, retaining a strong German accent to the end of his life. He was impatient and peremptory, and his temper was quickly lost, but he rarely bore malice and would apologize quickly if he felt he was in the wrong. He was generous and charitable, even when in financial trouble himself, and was one of the founder-members of the Fund for Decayed Musicians (now the Royal Society of Musicians). He was a warmhearted and kindly man although perhaps a rather solitary one. A lifelong bachelor, Handel was by no means averse to female company, but of his emotional life nothing is known. In all business matters he was scrupulously honest, but he seems to have seen nothing wrong in adopting other composers' material and incorporating it into his own compositions. This habit of plagiarizing has been excused as an extension of the easygoing artistic habits of an age of pasticcio makers, but it is more noticeable in Handel than in other composers of the time.

works   The first basis of Handel's style was the north German music of his childhood, but it was soon completely overlaid by the Italian style that he acquired during his travels in Italy. The influences of Corelli and Alessandro Scarlatti, both of whom he greatly admired, can be detected in his work to the end of his long life; the French style of Lully and his followers also influenced him, especially in his overtures and dance music; finally in England he came under the influence of Purcell. There is a robustness in his later music that gives it a very English quality, and 18th-century English critics recognized it as such, welcoming what they called "the manly style of Handel." Above all his music is eminently vocal, and his directness of style makes him one of the great masters of choral music. His choruses have a power and effectiveness that have never been surpassed, and in these his writing is remarkable for the manner in which he interweaves massive but simple harmonic passages with contrapuntal sections of great ingenuity—the whole most effectively illustrating his text. His writing for the solo voice was outstanding in its suitability for the medium and its unerring melodic line. Handel was also able to depict character in music in a single scene—or even an individual aria. The scene in which the giant Polypheme enters in *Acis and Galatea* is perhaps Handel's most obvious example of graphic character drawing in music, but there are many other such examples to be found in his works, both in the Italian operas and in the English oratorios.

Although the bulk of his music was vocal, Handel was nevertheless one of the greatest instrumental composers of the late Baroque era. His long series of overtures, mostly in the French Style; his orchestral concertos (Opus 3 and Opus 6); his large-scale concerted music for strings and wind (such as the *Water Music* and the *Fireworks Music*); the massive double concertos and organ concertos—all show him to have been a complete master of the orchestral means at his command. Indeed the revival of interest in early methods of performance has shown Handel to be one of the surest of orchestral composers.

As can be seen from his biography, Handel had a lifelong attachment to the theater—even his oratorios were usually performed on the stage and not in church or the concert room. Until almost the end of his life, he loved Italian opera, and only after it involved him in ever-increasing financial losses did he abandon it for English oratorio. Like other composers of his time he accepted the conventions of Italian opera with its employment of male sopranos and contraltos and the formalized sequences of stylized recitatives and arias upon which opera seria was constructed; using these conventions he produced many masterpieces. Such works as *Sosarme, Giulio Cesare,* and *Alcina* still make impressive stage spectacles with scenes of great dramatic power bursting through the stiff Baroque grandeur. To dismiss the Italian operas as mere stepping-stones toward the English oratorio is a mistake; many of Handel's Italian operas have been revived in the 20th century, and some can still thrill a modern audience. Handel's Italian vocal works also comprise many cantatas to Italian words—some with simple basso continuo accompaniment, others with orchestra.

There are also a number of "chamber duets," some of which he reworked as choruses for *Messiah;* a well-known example is "No, di voi non vo fidarmi," which is better known as "For unto Us a Child Is Born." Finally there are some serenatas and oratorios, mostly dating from the time of his Italian travels, that he later adapted to English words with varying success.

It was circumstance that turned Handel into a composer of English oratorios, but having finally made his choice he devoted his final years to the form that he himself had virtually created. Paradoxically enough his oratorios now seem much more dramatic than his operas, and they can mostly be performed on the stage with remarkably little alteration. The

great exceptions are *Messiah* and *Israel in Egypt,* neither of which is characteristic of Handelian oratorio in general. Most of the others—from the earliest attempts like *Esther* to the consummate mastery of the later works such as *Saul, Samson, Belshazzar,* and *Jephtha*—can be presented as stage spectacles and rank among the great dramatic masterpieces of the 18th century. With *Israel* and *Messiah* the emphasis is quite different—*Israel,* because of its uninterrupted chain of massive choruses, does not lend itself to stage presentation, and *Messiah* is a meditation on the life of Christ rather than a dramatic narration of his passion. Although *Messiah* is unique in Handel's output, it is commonly regarded as his most typical oratorio just as it is his most popular work. Handel also used the dramatic oratorio form for a number of secular works; chief among these were *Semele* and *Hercules,* both based on stories from Greek mythology and both splendid works that are eminently suitable for modern dramatic production. But his greatest work in this genre is *Acis and Galatea,* composed originally for private performance at Cannons. There is a youthful magic about it that he never quite recaptured, even in *Semele.* One of the most English of all Handel's larger vocal works is *L'Allegro, il penseroso* after the poems by John Milton, which in spite of its Italian title is a haunting evocation of the English countryside. In common with other composers of English and foreign birth then resident in London, Handel set various odes for St. Cecilia's Day, which was long celebrated with special musical events throughout Britain. Chief of these was his setting of Dryden's *Alexander's Feast,* a brilliant work though perhaps lacking in depth and feeling. Special mention must be accorded to a delightful work that has been called a "comic oratorio"; this is *Susanna,* a piece that has been revived with much success. All these, like the Italian operas that preceded them, contain innumerable arias that exhibit Handel's gift of writing easy natural melodies for the solo voice as well as numerous choruses that display his genius in writing for massed voices.

Handel's most notable contribution to church music is his series of large-scale anthems. Foremost among these are the *Chandos* Anthems, 12 pieces written for a small group of singers and instrumentalists but conceived on a grand scale. Closely following these works were the four anthems written for the coronation of King George II; of these the most celebrated is *Zadok the Priest,* a striking example of Handel's achievement of massive grandeur with the simplest means. Other occasional vocal works are the *Utrecht* and *Dettingen* Te Deums, the *Funeral* Anthem for Queen Caroline, and the wedding anthems for the princess royal (1734) and the Prince of Wales (1736). He also set two German passions: one to the text of the Gospel according to St. John (1704), the other to a text by Barthold Hinrich Brockes (*c.* 1716). There are also several Latin works written mostly in his early years and during the Italian tour. Finally there are the *Foundling Hospital* Anthem and three hymns to words by Charles Wesley, the best known of which is "Rejoice, the Lord Is King."

Handel wrote much instrumental music—some in connection with his operas and oratorios and some for concert use. By far the greater part of his orchestral music consists of the overtures, usually in the French style of Lully, that begin with his earliest operas and continue to his latest oratorios; they total about 80 and (published separately from the vocal works from which they originally came) were still a major feature of English concerts long after Handel's death. There were also various sinfonie that originated as act tunes; these, however, mostly fell into disuse with the operas for which they were intended, although one or two were published, together with dances from the operas, in the form of chamber trios as his Opus 5.

Handel was equally at home in the larger orchestral forms of his day, especially the concerto grosso, in which he generally followed the pattern set by Corelli; *i.e.,* with four or more movements. There are a few solo oboe concertos, mostly early works. Then come the six concertos published in 1734 as his Opus 3 and generally called the *Hautboy* Concertos because of the inclusion of oboes and other wind instruments in the score. His next purely

orchestral collection was the set of Twelve *Grand* Concertos, published in 1739. These represent not only Handel's noblest contribution to orchestral music but also the peak of the Baroque concerto grosso for stringed instruments. A further type of Handelian concerto is the large-scale concerto for wind and string bands that seems to have originated in his *Fireworks Music* of 1749. The group of concertos published in the Händelgesellschaft edition (Volume 47) is not large, but the overall concept of the music is on the grandest scale. Finally there are the *Water Music* and *Fireworks Music* suites themselves, closely related to the suites of *Tafelmusik* such as were composed by Handel's friend Telemann.

Handel was a notable organist and a great exponent of the art of keyboard improvisation. He composed something closely approaching an organ concerto movement as early as 1708 for his Italian oratorio *Il trionfo del tempo.* He then seems to have forgotten the form until the 1730s, when he realized the joint possibilities of the organ concerto and his own prowess as an organist. Accordingly he took some of his own earlier trio sonatas and expanded them into organ concertos, which he then played between the acts of his English oratorios. This was so successful that the practice was continued long after Handel's death. Handel published in 1738 a set or organ concertos as his Opus 4. John Walsh issued a second set about 1740, but only two of these were true organ concertos; the others were arrangements of some of his grand concertos. Finally a third set was published posthumously in about 1760 as his Opus 7; these were in many places scarcely more than outline sketches with many gaps left marked ad libitum at the points where Handel himself would have improvised solo passages. One or two other examples of organ concertos (some plagiarized from Telemann's music) are printed in Volume 48 of the Händelgesellschaft edition, and there remains also a fragment of a concerto for two organs and orchestra. It must be remembered that in general Handel's concertos were written for a comparatively small organ and that very few English organs of the time had pedalboards. His instrumental treatment is consequently more akin to harpsichord technique than to that of the organ style of Bach and the other north Germans.

Handel left very little solo organ music apart from six fugues, which were equally suitable for the harpsichord. He published a certain amount of harpsichord music, however, beginning with the first set of *Suites de Pièces pour le Clavecin* in 1720, followed by a second set in 1733. These two sets of suites, 17 in all, represent his finest contribution to the harpsichord repertoire. His third collection of harpsichord music was the set of fugues mentioned above, and finally a fourth collection of miscellaneous pieces from various sources was published by Karl Franz Friedrich Chrysander in Volume 2 of the Händelgesellschaft edition. Much later a selection of harpsichord music found in the collection of Handel manuscripts formerly owned by the Aylesford family, and now in the Royal Music Library in the British Museum, was published under the title of *The Aylesford Music* (1928). Various minuets and dance tunes were published in harpsichord arrangements, with or without his consent, during his own lifetime.

In common with most of his contemporaries, Handel wrote sonatas for one or more solo instruments with basso continuo accompaniment for harpsichord and optional viola da gamba. Some of these were published in his own lifetime; his *opera prima,* for example, was the set of *Twelve Solos for a German Flute, Hautboy or Violin,* published in both London and Amsterdam. Three others were added to these in a later publication, and the resulting 15 were gathered together and printed by Chrysander in Volume 27 of the Händelgesellschaft edition, and a further three appeared in the Händelgesellschaft Volume 48. Several other sonatas for flute, violin, etc., remain in manuscript in the Fitzwilliam Musem, Cambridge, and elsewhere. There is also a sonata for viola da gamba and basso continuo printed in the Händelgesellschaft Volume 48. The favorite chamber music form of the Baroque era, however, was the trio sonata for two solo instruments—violins, oboes, or flutes—with basso continuo. Handel began to write such trio sonatas very early in his career; his first

large set was a group of six sonatas for two oboes and continuo, written when he was still in Germany, that display an astonishing mastery of counterpoint. He continued to write trio sonatas, some of which are known from editions printed during his lifetime; the chief of these is his Opus 2, which consisted originally of six sonatas for two violins, oboes, or flutes, first published in Amsterdam about 1722. Three others are added to these in various editions and are often loosely referred to as belonging to the Opus 2 set, although this is not strictly correct. These trio sonatas are mostly four-movement works, majestic and dignified in character, more akin to the *sonata da chiesa* than to the chamber sonata, the latter being recognizable by the inclusion of dance movements. Handel's last trio sonatas, *Seven Trios for Two Violins, Hautboys or German Flutes,* published by Walsh in 1739 as Handel's Opus 5, definitely belong to the *sonata da camera* class; they are much lighter than his Opus 2 and contain many dance movements taken chiefly from his stage works such as *Alcina* and *Ariodante.* Handel apparently wrote a number of other trio sonatas, as many of the overtures to his *Chandos Anthems*—to say nothing of the well-known overtures to *Saul* and *Esther*—were obviously derived from trio sonatas, sometimes with very little alteration. There are also several rather doubtful works discovered during the 20th century, including the two so-called *Concerti a quattro,* which may or may not have been by Handel. Most of the genuine trio sonatas are published in Volume 27 of the Händelgesellschaft edition.

assessment   Although Handel was highly regarded in his own day, his influence was by no means as paralyzing to British music as some historians believe. During his own lifetime many highly competent English composers (Arne, William Boyce, Charles Avison, John Stanley, and many others) wrote in their own version of the late Baroque style, sometimes closely akin to Handel's, sometimes more closely related to that of the new school of the younger Italian composers—Arne, for example, was a much more "modern" composer than Handel himself. Handel's own style was becoming old-fashioned by the time of his death. About 1760 an immense change took place in the music played and composed in London that coincided with the return of Lord Kellie from Mannheim and the advent of Johann Christian Bach and his friend Karl Friedrich Abel, who set the pattern for the more up-to-date of the younger English musicians with the new manner of the Mannheim and gallant composers. Handel's influence dwindled in all fields but that of the oratorio, church music, and the organ voluntary. Even the organ concerto, Handel's own special contribution to instrumental music, took on a gallant air after about 1765 in keeping with the times and in open imitation of J. C. Bach's style. It was the Handel commemoration of 1784 (erroneously intended to be the centenary of his birth) that turned Handel into the semi-ecclesiastical lay figure of later legend. Even so the only field in which his influence was really marked was that of the oratorio. True there was a brief interest just after the commemoration in what was called "the ancient style," and composers wrote a few works, usually overtures, in a late Baroque idiom—often apologizing for doing so. However, this interest in a bygone style was only superficial and was similar to the interest displayed by Mozart and other continental composers in what they called the "learned style" of J. S. Bach and Handel. In England Handel's influence was largely superseded by that of Haydn in the latter part of the 18th century and by Mozart in the early 19th. The most obvious sign of Handelian influence was the festival movement, which grew out of the Handel commemoration of 1784 and into the mammoth Handel festivals given in the Crystal Palace in the late 19th century. The ADDITIONAL ACCOMPANIMENTS (which began with Mozart's extra wind parts written for Baron von Swieten's concerts in Vienna) was absolutely imperative when orchestras tried to struggle with such vast choral bodies as those that took part in the Crystal Palace festivals, and Handel's scores were subjected to gross indignities in the name of musical progress. With the publication of Handel's original scores as edited by Chrysander for the Händelgesellschaft (for all their faults they represented Handel's

original intentions more closely than those in general use at the time), a movement was begun that eventually led to the reinstatement of Handel's position as a competent orchestrator of his own music. His works are now usually performed with respect for the original text and with Handel's own instrumentation. In some fields Handel's reputation is higher than ever; his concerti grossi have never been more admired than they are today, while his operas are frequently revived.

editions Most of Handel's works were printed, though often in wretchedly incomplete editions, in his own lifetime or soon afterward. In the 1790s Samuel Arnold began the preparation of a complete edition, the first complete edition of any composer's works to be published. It was full of errors and misprints, but it was a remarkable achievement and opened the way for the *opera omnia* editions of the major composers published in the following century. An abortive attempt at another complete edition of Handel's works was made by the London Handel Society, formed in 1843; about a dozen works were printed before publication ceased in 1855. By then Chrysander had begun his monumental work on Handel. The first prospectus of his German Händelgesellschaft was published in 1856, and eventually he saw through the press the greater part of Handel's work in a much more correct and complete edition than those of the earlier editors. Since this edition was defective by modern standards of musicology and had long been out of print, a new complete edition was proposed after World War II. This publication by Bärenreiter (1955–   ) incorporates much new material from sources unknown to, or unused by, Chrysander.

BIBLIOGRAPHY: Percy Marshall Young, *Handel* (1949; rev. ed., 1963); Gerald E. H. Abraham, ed., *Handel: A Symposium* (1954); Otto Erich Deutsch, *Handel, a Documentary Biography* (1955); Winton Dean, *Handel's Dramatic Oratorios and Masques* (1959) and *Handel and the Opera Seria* (1969); Paul Henry Lang, *George Frideric Handel* (1966).

RECORDINGS: Numerous recordings of most works.

Handl, Jakob, also known as Jacobus Gallus (July 31, 1550–July 18, 1591)   An Austrian composer celebrated for his sacred music, Jakob Handl was born in Slovenia (now part of Yugoslavia). He traveled in Bohemia, Moravia, and Silesia; was a member of the Viennese court chapel in 1574; was Kapellmeister to the Bishop of Olmütz (Olomouc) from 1579; and was cantor at St. John's Church in Prague from 1585 until his death.

Nearly all of his masses are parody masses (four books published 1580), but more important are his motets in from four to 24 parts in the four volumes of *Opus musicum* (1586–91), a collection of 374 texts covering the entire liturgical year. His eclectic style blends archaism and modernity and has been described as a "fusion of the Netherlands and the Venetian styles." Some of his harmonic progressions seem old-fashioned; yet his daring chromatic transitions (*Mirabile mysterium,* for instance) foreshadowed the breakup of modality. He enjoyed word painting in the style of the madrigal, but he could write the simple *Ecce quomodo moritur justus* that was later employed by Handel in his funeral anthem, "The Ways of Zion Do Mourn."

Handy, W. C.: *see* JAZZ (W. C. Handy).

Hanslick, Edward: *see* CRITICISM (development).

Hanson, Howard (b. October 28, 1896) Sometimes called "the American Sibelius," the composer, conductor, and educator Howard Hanson represents the Romantic tradition in U.S. music. Of Swedish ancestry, he studied with Percy Goetschius in New York City and spent three years (1921–24) in Italy as the winner of the Prix de Rome. On his return to the United States, he was appointed director of the Eastman School of Music in Rochester, New York, a post he retained for 40 years. He established annual festivals of American music and conducted hundreds of new works by young composers, among them many of his own pupils. In 1958 he organized the Eastman Philharmonia, a student orchestra, and in 1961–62 toured with it through Europe, the Soviet Union, and the Middle East.

Primarily a symphonist, Hanson has written six symphonies. symphonic poems, and other orchestral works; an opera, *Merry*

Mount, commissioned by the Metropolitan Opera (produced 1934); concertos; choral works; chamber music; and songs. His sense of harmony and form is derived from Romantic models, his rhythms are strong and varied, and his orchestration is effective. He published a textbook for advanced students, *Harmonic Materials of Modern Music* (1960).

BIBLIOGRAPHY: Henry Cowell, ed., *American Composers on American Music* (1933; reprint, 1962).

RECORDINGS: Suite from *Merry Mount;* Piano Concerto; Quartet; Symphonies (Nos. 2 and 6); orchestral and choral works.

Harbison, John H. (b. December 20, 1938) A student of Earl Kim and Roger Huntington Sessions at Princeton University, the U.S. composer and conductor John H. Harbison has been most influenced by his activity as a performer of jazz and chamber music. He was composer in residence at Reed College in Oregon (1968–69) and then began teaching at the Massachusetts Institute of Technology. In addition to chamber music he has written Sinfonia (1963) for violin and double orchestra; Violin Concerto (1967); the opera *Winter's Tale* (1973); and *Elegiac* Songs (1975) on texts by Emily Dickinson.

RECORDINGS: *Bermuda Triangle* for jazz ensemble; *Confinement* for 12 players; *Five Songs of Experience* for soloists, chorus, quartet, and percussion; *Parody-Fantasia* for piano.

harmonica A term applied both to the mouth organ and, earlier, to a musical instrument of glass resonators sounded by friction (*see* GLASS HARMONICA). The mouth organ was first produced by Friedrich Buschmann of Berlin in 1821 as the *Mundäoline*. It consists of a number of free metal reeds fixed in slots in a small wooden box enclosed in metal plates and supplied with wind through two parallel rows of wind channels. The notes of the diatonic scale are obtained by the player alternately blowing and sucking as he moves the instrument across his lips and uses his tongue to cover those channels not required. Chromatic models have two sets of reed chambers pitched a semitone apart, a finger-operated mechanism enabling the player to use either set at will. Compass varies between two and four octaves, and bass models are used in harmonica bands. The virtuosity of some modern players has inspired several eminent composers to write for the instrument; an example is Milhaud's Suite (1947) for harmonica and orchestra, written for Larry Adler.

harmonic series: *see* OVERTONE.

harmonium or **reed organ** A free-reed keyboard instrument with wind supplied by foot bellows through a pressure-equalizing air reservoir. The reeds comprise metal tongues, or vibrators, screwed over slots in metal frames. Different tone colors in imitation of the organ are provided mainly through separate sets of reeds, each set varying in the size and shape of the tone chamber surrounding each reed. Constricted chambers, for instance, induce powerful vibration and incisive tone. Volume is controlled by an air valve operated by a knee lever or directly from the bellows pedals by an expression stop that allows the wind supply to bypass the reservoir. The U.S. equivalent of the harmonium, the American organ, or melodeon, differs in the detail of reeds and chambers and in the direction of air flow, the bellows exhausting the reservoir instead of filling it.

harmonium by Jacob Alexandre (1804–76), Paris
Behr Photography

The earliest instrument of the harmonium group was the physharmonica, invented in 1818 by Anton Haeckl in Vienna. His invention was inspired by the Chinese mouth organ, or *sheng,* which, brought to Russia *c.* 1770, had introduced the free reed to Europe and aroused the interest of certain physicists and musicians. Other types now extinct (such as John Green's seraphine) appeared before Alexandre Debain produced his harmonium in Paris in 1840. The main improvements after 1850 were made by builders Victor Mustel in Paris and Jacob Estey in the United States.

The harmonium was a popular church and household instrument until the electronic organ drove it from the market after the 1930s. Compositions for the instrument include solo works by Franck, Louis Vierne, Max Reger, and Sigfrid Karg-Elert and *Bagatelles* for two violins, cello, and harmonium by Dvořák. Schoenberg used it in *Herzgewächse* (1911) and in several of his arrangements.

BIBLIOGRAPHY: Robert F. Gellerman, *The American Reed Organ* (1973); S. G. Earl, *Repairing the Reed Organ and Harmonium* (1976); Horton Presley, *Restoring and Collecting Antique Reed Organs* (1977).

harmony In its earliest English sense the term harmony is applied to any pleasing arrangement of musical sounds, but technically it is confined to the science of the simultaneous combination of sounds of different pitch without regard to their quality of tone or timbre, a matter that belongs to the province of instrumentation. The sense of the word harmony is further restricted to the study of combinations rather as blocks of sound than as textures. The fundamental aesthetic texture of harmony is COUNTERPOINT.

But while the abstraction of harmony from instrumentation is as legitimate and necessary as the abstraction of draftsmanship from color, the abstraction of harmony from counterpoint cuts music adrift from its foundations and leads to no better results than the abstraction of sound from sense. Harmony is to classical music what perspective is to pictorial art. But visual perspective is a science, whereas musical perspective is wholly an art. The present article attempts to show that its laws are true to the nature of art and are no mere rules of a game. But we must not impute the meaning of its laws to any music earlier than the 14th century, and in the spacious days of Elizabeth and Palestrina there were many things in harmony that had meanings distinctive to the period.

origin of concord and discord The diatonic major scale (or something very like it) may be found by playing eight successive white notes from C to c on the piano. It would be better to accept this as a scientific definition than to begin the study of harmony with questions such as whether the first hen preceded or followed the first egg. The interesting fact is that the ancient Greeks showed a latent harmonic sense by developing the diatonic scale, which has proved itself capable of bearing our classical system of harmony.

The one ostensible effort the Greeks made at organizing simultaneous notes of different pitch was the practice of *magadizing.* The *magadis* was a stringed instrument with a bridge that divided the strings at two-thirds of their length. The shorter portion of the string then sounded an octave higher than the longer. To *magadize,* therefore, was to get the voices of children or women to sing in octaves above the voices of men.

We may begin our survey of harmonic combinations with two propositions. First, any two notes an octave apart are harmonically identical. From this may be drawn two useful inferences—that doubling in octaves never was and never will be a process of harmonization, and that a combination does not change its meaning by the addition or subtraction of an octave. The second fundamental proposition is that harmonies are built upward from the bass. This will be denied by some theorists, but the present line of thought is not an a priori theory but the observation of facts. By low notes we mean sounds produced by slow vibrations and by high notes sounds produced by rapid vibrations.

The harmonic identity of notes an octave apart was a matter of physical sensation before the dawn of history. In 1862 Helmholtz explained it and a great many other facts in musical aesthetics. He solemnly warned musical theorists against hastily applying his scientific results to the art of music and warned them in vain. But we may safely draw some inferences from his discovery that the timbre of a note depends on the selection and proportion of a series of overtones in the vibration ratios of aliquot parts of the fundamental note. Thus a note adds nothing to a lower note if it is at the distance of an overtone; except that if the distance is not exactly one or more octaves, the combination will assume the harmonic sense of its difference from an octave; *i.e.,* a 12th is equivalent to a fifth.

Distances of pitch are called intervals. They are reckoned (numerically and inclusive of both notes) up a diatonic scale. From the fundamental (or tonic) note of a major scale, all intervals within that scale are major, and the fourth, fifth, and octave are called perfect. Intervals a semitone less than major are called minor except in the case of perfect intervals, which become imperfect, or diminished, when reduced by a semitone. Otherwise a diminished interval is a semitone less than minor. An augmented interval is a semitone greater than major. The terms augmented and diminished should be applied only to chromatic intervals; that is, to intervals of which one note is foreign to the scale of reference. There is in every scale one fourth that is greater than perfect (F to B in the scale of C) and one imperfect fifth (B to F). This diatonic enlarged fourth is called the tritone. Intervals are inverted by raising the lower note to a higher octave; thus the imperfect fifth is the inversion of the tritone fourth.

Helmholtz's discovery of the nature of timbre proves that certain aspects of harmony are latent in nature. Conversely the art of harmony constantly produces effects of timbre apart from those of the particular instruments in use. But musical elements interact in ways that quickly carry musical aesthetics into regions far removed from any simple relation between harmony and timbre. What acoustics can tell us of concord and discord is not only inadequate for our musical experience but contrary to it. Acoustics tell us that the rapid beats that distress the ear in harsh combinations are the result of periodic reinforcements and weaknesses that occur as the waves get in and out of phase with one another. When these beats are so rapid as to produce a note of their own, this resultant tone may or may not be pleasant; the painful stage of beats is that in which they are noticeable as a flickering light is noticeable. Combinations that are out of beating distance may set up beats between the upper note and the octave harmonic of the other. On this criterion thirds and sixths, especially the minor sixth, are rougher than many combinations that rank as discords or than some never digested in classical harmony such as the seventh overtone.

The art of music had not attained the simplest scheme for dealing with discords before it traversed the acoustic criterion in every direction. It became a language in which sense dictated what should be accepted in sound. The minor sixth, as the inversion of the major third, occurs in many positions of what has come to be the most fixed chord in music—the major triad. But a discord beyond beating distance will have no beats if it is produced in a timbre that has no octave overtones; if its sense has come to be that of a discord, its timbre will not make it a concord.

Theorists of the 16th century shrewdly regarded the major triad as really a chord of six notes in the ratios of 1, 2, 3, 4, 5, 6, which they called the sestina:

Example

Long before this natural phenomenon had been recognized, music had organized many other elements into its language, and harmony had become (what it has ever since remained apart from experiments) counterpoint. This arose slowly and painfully out of devices diametrically opposed to it. The organum of the 10th century amounted to a *magadizing* in all the perfect concords; *i.e.,* in fourths or fifths doubled by octaves:

Example 2

etc.

Its intention was that of a glorified unison, and it survives—unheard except as artificial timbre—in the guise of an aura of brilliance above the notes of the organ when that instrument is using its mixture stops.

The problem of counterpoint was attacked in two ways. First there was a slow evolution through experiments in ornamenting one or more voices of an organum. This gradually took shape as the art of discant and was slow to move far from the foundation of parallel perfect concords. But a violent frontal attack was made by the motets of the 13th and 14th centuries, which had no connection with the sublime motet form of 16th-century church music but consisted in the simultaneous singing of several melodies that were independent and perhaps preexisting; the combination was rough-hewn into perfect concords at the strong accents with the remainder of the harmony taking care of itself. We are likely to misread our documents by forgetting that the note that is now double the length of the longest note in normal use originally deserved its name of breve. A Hungarian band produces a general harmonic effect more like that of Brahms's *Hungarian* Dances than like any less classical music; but if the details of the Hungarian ornamentation and part writing were written in breves, whole notes, and half notes, we should find them remarkably like medieval counterpoint.

pure polyphony   The first matter of principle that emerged from the chaos was that if the parallel movement of perfect concords was correct, everything else was wrong. A few compositions show an evenly-balanced conflict of opposing principles. The English rota "Sumer is icumen in" sounds to us like a tuneful six-part double canon spoiled or rendered quaint by numerous consecutive fifths. Its contemporaries were more likely to have regarded it as a beautiful scheme of perfect concords spoiled or illuminated by dangerous licenses. There was no room for prolonged doubt as to where the path of progress and freedom lay. And if the basis of harmony was to be independent melody, then one of the main cares of the composer was to prevent independent melodies from lapsing into duplications. Fifths and octaves will still form (as they do at the present day) cardinal points in every chord that is dwelt upon; but no two voices can double each other for two consecutive octaves or fifths without dissolving their integrity in a false resonance.

As to discords the criterion ceased to be acoustical. After centuries of trial and error musicians accepted thirds and sixths as concords, and all discords became equal to one another in mildness when they occurred as unaccented passing tones proceeding by diatonic conjunct notes between one concord and the next. Polyphony made musical accents far stronger than those of speech, and so the behavior of accented discords was more restricted. The accented discord must be prepared by first appearing as a concord; it then becomes a discord by being held, or suspended, while the other voices move against it; and finally it must resolve by a step downward. Upward resolutions are harsh and of complex import, intelligible only in a later system, and so are discords that skip.

Passing tones (marked *) are shown moving up and down between concords:

Example 3

The tied C is a suspension, prepared by having begun as an octave, becoming a discord by colliding as a fourth against a fifth, and resolving by stepping down to a third:

Example 4

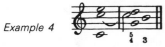

Four three-note chords attained the rank of concords. (Two of them were only inversions of the other two.) First, of course, was the major triad, the upper three notes (4, 5, 6) of the sestina (Example 1). All doublings and differences of octave are negligible in the distribution of a chord so long as they do not bring its middle or upper notes into the bass. All the following examples are concords identical with the sestina and with one another, though the positions that leave two parts low at a distance from the upper parts or that

double the third are acoustically as rough as many a discord. Positions *(d)* and *(e)* could be justified only in circumstances of great polyphonic or instrumental interest.

Example 5

The essential intervals are those of position *(a)* and comprise a perfect fifth (G–D), a major third from the bass (G–B), and a minor third above (B–D).

In listening to polyphony the mind can appreciate the parts two at a time, and 16th-century theorists avoid reasoning as if the mind could do more. They were probably right as well as cautious; nor is it necessary that the mind should attempt more. For any fault in the aggregate of the richest polyphony must be a fault between two parts. If it concerns more it is more than a single fault, and if there are no faults the ear enjoys the faultless aggregate whether it can distinguish the parts or not. Accordingly the question arises: will the ear resent an aggregate that corresponds to nothing in nature but that contains no intervals that have not already been accepted in the sestina? In other words, can we treat as a concord a triad that puts the minor third below the major?

Example 6

The history of harmony not only answers this in the affirmative but shows that the contrast between this artificial concord and the major triad is essential to the formation of a flexible musical language. Some theorists, fascinated by the ways in which minor harmonies behave like major harmonies reversed, invented schemes with roots of minor chords as their top notes. The way in which minor chords happen in music does not support any theory that makes Example 6 anything other than an artificial alteration of Example 5 with the same fundamental behavior of the same bass note in every relevant musical context. The artificiality of the chord is not arbitrary or conventional; it is of the very nature of art and is far more self-explanatory than most of the phenomena of spoken language.

Both major and minor triads are found in inverted positions. An inversion is not a reversal but a position in which one of the upper notes of the normal chord has become the bass note. When the third of a triad is in the bass, we have the chord of the sixth:

Example 7

And now arises a phenomenon wholly unintelligible to acoustics and unpredictable by theory. The once perfect concord of the fourth becomes a discord when taken from the bass. Between any higher parts it is a concord, but from the bass it will not do except as a passing tone or a properly prepared and duly resolved suspension. The reason for this is purely contingent. It happens that almost every context in which an accented fourth occurs from the bass implies a fifth above it, as in Example 4. If instead of the fifth a sixth is substituted, a chord will be obtained that is theoretically a second inversion of a triad.

Example 8

But no amount of logic will persuade the ear that this sixth is more than another appoggiatura demanding as urgently to resolve on the fifth as the fourth demands to resolve on the third. The fact is an accident of far-reaching importance but as unamenable to grammatical logic as the reason why a modern English poet should not apply the epithet "blooming" to his lady's cheek. Find a context for a fourth from the bass that does not imply the $\frac{5}{4}$ 3 of Example 4, and that fourth will cease to be a discord. But it will be some strange and pregnant language not to be taken in vain like the cry at the beginning and end of the Allegretto of Beethoven's Seventh Symphony. And even there the ear expects the true bass and remembers it at the end.

The harmonic materials of 16th-century polyphony are thus the major and minor triads, their inversions as chords of $\frac{6}{3}$, and the discords of the second and seventh and (from the bass) the fourth treated either as suspensions or as passing tones. The scale in which the flux of polyphony moved through transient discord from concord to concord was the diatonic scale preserved from ancient Greece and handed down directly from the Greco–Roman or Ptolemaic system to the church music of the Middle Ages, doubtless with conflation from Jewish sources.

modal tonality Tonality is the element that groups a succession of musical sounds intelligibly around a center. With the development of polyphony tonality becomes as important as the concord–discord system itself, and indeed that system could not have existed without tonal guidance at every point. Discord is transition; concord is finality. The task of tonality is to organize various degrees of finality among concords. The first decision made by pure polyphony (but revoked in a later age) was that the minor triad, though it might be a concord, could never be final. A bare fifth or even a bare octave would be more acceptable as a potential major triad. The final chord, whether complete or not, requires an approach by chords in a well-defined relationship to it. Two types of full close, or cadence, thus came into existence—the authentic in which the final chord is preceded by a major chord whose bass is a fourth below or a fifth above the final bass; and the plagal in which the penultimate chord is based a fourth above or a fifth below the final and is major or minor according to the mode:

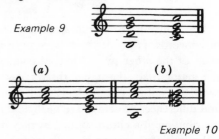

Example 9

Example 10

The modes were named after those of ancient Greece but wrongly identified, and theory clung to terms derived from non-harmonic notions long after the practice of composers had become inveterately harmonic. An aesthetically correct account of Palestrina's tonality is much more easily achieved by a description in terms of Beethoven's key system than by any attempt to refer it to orthodox modal theory.

According to the finally prevalent statement of that theory, there were ideally 14 modes—two based on each degree of the diatonic scale (*see* MODE [medieval modes]). Practically the modes based on B were impossible, as the diatonic fifth from B is imperfect. The numbers of these imaginary modes, XI and XII, were piously retained for them together with the name of Locrian. The authentic modes ran from the final, or fundamental note, to its octave. Each authentic mode was allied to a plagal mode having the same final but lying a fourth lower. This is an important distinction in purely melodic music and can be clearly recognized in folk songs. Thus "The Bluebell of Scotland" is authentic, while "Auld Lang Syne" is, except for an isolated top note, typically plagal. In polyphonic music the difference between an authentic mode and its plagal companion is a vague matter settled by the position of the tenor voice.

The word modulation was used in the theory of modal music to denote the formation of full closes on notes other than the final. The 16th-century composer developed a perfect sense of key around cadences and knew very well how to avoid stimulating that sense elsewhere. Subordinate cadences were selected on no more cogent principle than the avoidance of monotony. The composer was like a painter whose draftsmanship is faultless in faces and figures but who sees no objection to implying a different horizon for each detail. And harmony has no such relation to external nature as can justify critics in calling modal tonality archaic. Palestrina's tonality is one of the most mature and subtle things in music, and later developments cannot lessen its truth to the nature of art.

Here are the 12 modes that theoretically underlie the tonality of the 16th century. Every composition was writ-

ten in one of these modes, and its incidental modulations were not regarded as visits to another mode, though that is aesthetically what they really were. The diagram gives the name of the authentic position above each scale and the plagal name and position below. The white note is the final. The imaginary Locrian modes (with B as final) are omitted. (See Example 11.)

In practice these modes are not always easy to ascertain. The B-natural in Lydian tonality is so difficult to handle that the great masters almost always flattened it permanently and put the flat as a key signature, thus producing an Ionian mode transposed, or plain modern F major. (All modes could be thus written a fourth higher, and apart from this the actual pitch of performance was determined by convenience and was bound by no fixed standard.) The Phrygian mode cannot form an authentic cadence, and its plagal cadence (Example 10*b*) sounds to our ears like a half-close on the dominant of a minor. This is quite final enough for modal harmony, but a very slight impulse may make Palestrina reverse the cadence and so end with a chord of A. This does not make the mode Aeolian, and though the Aeolian mode looks as if it was the origin of our minor scale true Aeolian polyphony is of all harmonic styles the most remote from modern music. The Dorian and Phrygian modes are much nearer to our conception of a well-grounded minor key. The Ionian mode is iden-

Example 11

359

tical with our major key, and Mixolydian tonality is like a major key with either an excessive emphasis on the subdominant or a top-heavy and finally prevalent dominant.

Extraneous sharps constantly come into modal music because authentic cadences require major penultimate chords as well as final major thirds for minor modes. Flats were no less often necessary to correct the tritone fourth between F and B (hence the shape of the flat and Morley's naming of it as the B clef). The rules governing these accidentals were so well known that singers resented signs where the need of such musica ficta was self-evident. But many of the most mystical harmonies, such as the opening of Palestrina's *Stabat Mater,* were the gifts of creative imagination equally remote from modal theory and modern tonality. Brahms understood modal harmony much better than the critics who blame him for violating the modes of folk songs. If old tunes are to be set without using leading tones and changes of key, they should not be harmonized at all.

essential discords and rigid tonality The strict theory of suspensions and passing tones was diversified by many idioms that grew up charmingly and illogically. Logic admitted harshnesses that the pure taste of Victoria and Palestrina rejected without the judgment of theorists. For instance, the Tudor masters shared with many other composers outside the Hispano–Roman orbit a keen intellectual pleasure in violent collisions between a major and a minor third over the same bass, some third being essential to the harmony and each of the conflicting voices having unanswerable reasons for its own version. But these false relations, as they are now called, are both archaic and provincial for all their logic. The overlapping of harmonic ideas produced many results both more pleasant and more fruitful.

Here is an extreme case in which the ordinary rules of musica ficta give results that strain the 19th-century theorist and compel the discovery of double roots:

The bass singer knowing the rules of musica ficta would be insulted at such a "donkey's mark" as a flat to the B for the purpose of correcting the inadmissible tritone between F and B. The treble singer would automatically sharpen G under the impression that the close was on A; and so the augmented sixth, one of the most complex discords known to Bach and Mozart, did frequently occur in 16th-century performances and was not always regarded as a blunder. In Example 12 the treble singer would happen to be mistaken in sharpening the G, for it is not really part of a close on to A. The close is on to D, and the middle singer would recognize its leading tone without the aid of "donkey's marks." For our insensitive age we require a flat to the B in the bass and sharps for the penultimate Cs in the middle part. If the 16th-century composer intended to produce an augmented sixth, the soprano would be provided with a sharp to the G in order to reassure the singer.

But the beginning of the 17th century saw a musical revolution far beyond the scope of any accumulation of licenses on the polyphonic basis. The feeble efforts of the first monodists—Jacopo Peri, Emilio del Cavaliere, and other pioneers of opera and solo vocal declamation with lute or keyboard accompaniment—had already drawn attention to the value of any and every chord as a thing in itself, apart from its position in a polyphonic flux, when the masterful spirit of Monteverdi gave to the new movement all the power of his intellect and rhetorical instinct. Only a polyphonist can appreciate the real aesthetic values of monody, and Monteverdi was a vigorous though decadent polyphonist both before and after he took up monody. But not even his mastery could organize the chaos that overwhelmed the art of music when the limitations of the golden age had been broken down. For one thing pure polyphony dealt with what was primarily vocal music. When instruments were treated as additional elements in serious music, the polyphonic hypothesis became inadequate, and several new sets of laws had to be found by experiment. A century was no long time for such a task.

Monteverdi's chief innovation is popularly said to be the invention of the dominant sev-

Example 12

enth and of other so-called essential discords. An essential discord is merely a discord that through custom has ceased to require preparation, and to attribute its invention to any particular author is like naming the first writer who used a metaphor instead of a full-blown simile. Most—if not all—discords that have become essential are based on that part of the key that we call the dominant for the reason that all harmonic phenomena gravitate toward the full close as inevitably as all verbal statements consist of a subject and predicate. The dominant of a key is the bass of the penultimate chord of an authentic cadence. Opposed to the dominant there is another center, the subdominant, which supports the penultimate chord of a plagal cadence. A key, therefore, has three cardinal points: the key note, or tonic; the dominant, the chief means of orientation in modulations; and the subdominant, whose function we should understand more readily if we called it the anti-dominant.

The chief and not wholly unconscious aim of the successors of Monteverdi (that is, the composers of the mid-17th century) was to establish the tonic–dominant–subdominant orientation of major and minor keys in a system that could digest essential discords. A modal composition visited other modes than its own whenever it made a cadence other than on its own final, but it did not establish itself in the visited modes, and still less did it go into regions that produced its own mode at a different pitch.

Throughout the 17th century the various streams of music were trickling gently toward a mighty lake from which all later music takes its origin. Alessandro Scarlatti is now less known than his wayward son Domenico, whose harpsichord music is in a genre by itself. But Alessandro, more than any other composer in history, deserves to be considered the founder of a great classical tradition. He is called the founder of the Neapolitan school, and classical tonality is primarily Neapolitan. It recognizes only two modes—the major and the minor. The loss of modal subtleties is more than compensated by the dramatic and architectonic values of clearly-established keys with a capacity for modulation to similar keys in relations of clear harmonic significance.

The eight measures in Example 13 below from the end of the first recitative in Handel's *Messiah* epitomize several normal features of the system:

Before discussing this example we must further explain the system of major and minor keys. Example 14 shows the first six degrees of the scale of C major (which, without sharps and flats, is taken as the standard key) with a triad, or common chord, on each. The notes of these triads are all within the key. The functional names of each degree are given below and the number above in Roman figures. Capital figures indicate major chords and small figures minor.

The seventh degree, or leading tone, bears no common chord within the key, for its triad has an imperfect fifth. The submediant is so called because the subdominant is not conceived as the note below the dominant but as an anti-dominant, a fifth below the tonic, so that there is a submediant as a third between it and the tonic just as there is a mediant as a third between the tonic and dominant.

Another most important gain of the new tonality as against the modal system is that the minor mode can now so firmly support its tonic by its other chords that a minor tonic chord becomes convincing as a final. The contrast between major and minor keys acquires a high emotional value. We must clearly un-

"The voice of one that crieth in the wilderness"

Example 13

Example 14

I   ii   iii   IV   V   vi

Tonic   Super-tonic   Mediant   Sub-dominant   Dominant   Sub-mediant

derstand that the minor mode, like the minor triad, is identified with the major mode on the same tonic. The so-called relative major is one of five equally direct relations to a minor tonic, and the relative minor is one of five to a major tonic. The minor mode of C is not (as the tonic sol-fa system will have it) a minor, but c minor.

In the minor mode a strict confinement to cardinal harmonies produces a melodically awkward augmented second between the flat sixth and the necessarily sharp leading tone. Accordingly the external form of the scale varies, and the variations have harmonic results. Example 15 below shows the so-called harmonic and melodic minor scales. The melodic form avoids the augmented second by sharpening the sixth in ascent and flattening both sixth and seventh in descent.

classical key relationships A fundamental proposition in the aesthetics of tonality is that key relationship subsists between two tonics only and has nothing to do with the intervention of a third tonic. Observe the word tonic; the proposition commits us to no specified mode on either side of the relation.

Direct relationship exists between two keys when the tonic chord of one is among the common chords of the other. If the first key is major its related keys are simply identified with its common chords other than its tonic; thus Example 14 shows that C major is directly related to five keys: d minor the supertonic, e minor the mediant, F major the subdominant, G major the dominant, and a minor the submediant.

The relatives of a minor tonic must be discovered by a converse process, for the minor scale is so unstable that the evidence of its common chords is conflicting and misleading. For instance, the dominant chord of a minor key is major. But you will receive a shock if you try answering the subject of Bach's g minor Fugue, Book I, No. 16, of *The Well-Tempered Clavier,* in D major instead of d minor!

Evidently the only directly related dominant key to a minor tonic is also minor. This being so the subdominant must be minor also, for it is the converse of the dominant, the key to which the tonic is dominant. To reach it the tonic chord must become major, a pathetic effect constantly found near the end of classical slow movements in minor keys.

The other relations of a minor tonic are converse to the relations of a major tonic. Thus if d minor is the supertonic of C major, the relation of C major to d minor requires a name. We run up the scale of d minor and find that C is its flat seventh. Similarly if e minor is the mediant of C major, then C major is the flat sixth or submediant of e minor; and if a minor is the submediant or relative minor of C major, then C major is the mediant or relative major of a minor. And so the relations of a minor tonic may be obtained by reading Example 14 backward with a minor as the key of reference. Transposing Example 14 so that vi becomes c minor, the following five relations are obtained: B-flat major the flat seventh, A-flat major the submediant, g minor the dominant, f minor the subdominant, E-flat the mediant (or relative major).

It is now easy to describe the drift of the Handelian chords of Example 13. The key signature is that of E major, a key that differs only in pitch and in minute instrumental technicalities from all other major keys. (Ideas as to the characters of keys in themselves are entirely subjective, and no agreement is to be expected about them.) The first chord is a common chord of B major, the dominant of E. In its present context it represents not only the dominant chord but the dominant key, for it happens to be the close of a passage in B major. The next chord is still a dominant chord but effects a return to E, being the last inversion of the dominant seventh thereof. The seventh is in the bass and duly resolves on G-sharp in the next chord, a first inversion of E (measure three). Handel would have had less compunction than many later writers in letting the bass skip down to E, so long as the G-sharp was somewhere in the chord, but here he is making his bass regularly descend the scale. The next

Example 15

step, F-sharp, supports another dominant chord, that of c-sharp minor (vi from our tonic) in its last inversion like that in measure two. It also resolves in measure five. The sixth measure passes to the subdominant (A major), and the seventh establishes that key in a manner that removes all doubt by striking its subdominant chord, which is wholly outside the range of E major. The natural result is the full close in A major in measure eight. Such is the normal way of using key relations in the essentially Neapolitan art of Handel, and all the intensity of Bach's thought adds nothing to its essential elements. When Bach modulates more widely, his purpose is not to explain but to astound.

Another great change had to enlarge the art of music before key relationships could attain their full meaning, but this time the change was accomplished without a period of chaos. Its first effect on harmony was shown in a drastic simplification of style; for music had now become dramatic, and there was no musical resource of more cardinal dramatic importance than changes of key. Consequently the baldest facts of key relation became dramatically significant out of all proportion to their direct intellectual import. A musical historian can make no graver blunder than to mistake Mozart's and Haydn's harmonic simplicity for an intellectual simplicity. To prolong a preparatory harping on the dominant of a new key is equivalent to working up the entry of an important person in a drama.

The problem that Alessandro Scarlatti solved in his youth 100 years earlier might be described as that of finding the dominant. The simple-seeming Mozart is as often as not mocking us with the riddle "When is a dominant not a dominant?" Musical perspective has gained another new depth in its command of planes. A modulation may establish a new key firmly enough for an incident in the course of a melody but not nearly firmly enough for a new stage in the whole scheme. Conversely a passage that at first sounded like vehement emphasis on the local dominant may long afterward, when the dominant key has been firmly established, be given note for note at the same pitch with a triumphantly tonic effect. And the dimensions over which Mozart's

tonality maintains its coherence are enormous—sometimes almost on Beethoven's largest scale.

Music, which in Palestrina's age was "a linked sweetness long drawn out" with the links extending only from one accent to the next, had by the beginning of the 18th century trained the mind to measure harmonic relations over melodic periods of eight or more measures, and the mighty polyphony of Bach and Handel broke down the melodic regularity but did not greatly enlarge the range over which the listener must depend on memory. These masters can visit the same key several times in a composition without inciting the listener to notice the fact either as a purpose or as a tautology. But Mozart, Haydn, and Beethoven built confidently on a knowledge of the exact effect that a modulation in one passage would have on a passage five or even 10 minutes later. Beethoven's enormous architectural and dramatic power enabled him to discover and command the whole range of key relationship theoretically possible within any definite meaning of the term. There is no limit to the possible range of modulation, as Bach took pains to show; but "the unity of the chromatic scale" is a feeble dogma on which to base the opinion that Beethoven should have treated all keys as equally related instead of drawing the line where he did. Great artists discover facts and resources—not licenses and vagaries.

Haydn, Mozart, Beethoven, Schubert, Brahms, and Wagner all agreed in one simple and cogent method of extending the direct or natural series of key relations. They merely changed the modes of either or both numbers of a directly related pair. Certain reservations were necessary; the supertonic of a major key that is quite happy as a minor neighbor completely fails to sound like a major key in its own right and behaves merely like dominant preparation for the ordinary dominant. An analyst who imputes the key of A major to measures 19–24 of the first movement of Beethoven's G Major Sonata, Op. 14, No. 2, when heard in their context should not attempt to discuss key relationship until the difference between a passage on the dominant and a passage in the dominant can be ascertained.

What is true of one key relationship will be true of its converse: the key of the flat seventh refuses to assert itself as a real key in relation to a major tonic. A dozen accessory chords in D major would not make the seventh measure of Example 13 amount to more than the subdominant chord in A major until they included a chord of G. The testimony of such openings as those of Beethoven's Sonatas, Op. 31, No. 1, and Op. 53, is emphatic.

In the rare cases where such keys do not thus explain themselves away, their effect is startling. (Ineptitudes may be neglected.) The passage that follows the return of the main theme in the first movement of Beethoven's *Eroica* Symphony is one of the supreme dramatic strokes in music. The hard-won tonic of E-flat gives way first to F major and then to the opposite extreme a third lower, D-flat. Another third down brings us safely to the dominant chord.

One other type of key relation is derived from a special form of the minor scale in which the lower tetrachord is made to correspond with the upper:

Example 16

The first inversion of its flat supertonic chord is known as the Neapolitan sixth; and the Neapolitan key relations are the flat supertonic major, equally related (as the E-natural in Example 16 shows) to a major and a minor tonic, and the converse relation of the sharp seventh. A minor tonic has no direct converse relation, for the Neapolitan chord is major. But, as Schubert shows at the end of the first movement of his d minor Quartet and in the slow movement of his String Quintet in C, an indirect relation may be established by making the Neapolitan chord minor.

We must beware of imputing relationship to keys separated by discursive modulation unless we have strong collateral evidence from the key functions of a musical design. Tonality and form are inseparable, and great composers do not even expect the tonic to be recognized after long wanderings without some such con-

clusive evidence as the return of the opening theme.

Tables A and B indicate by Roman figures the whole scheme of key relationships—first from a major tonic, secondly from a minor tonic. Flats indicate degrees flattened in comparison with those of the major scale of reference, and in Table 2 sharps are used to distinguish cases where the key is a semitone above the corresponding degree of a minor scale. Thus if C is the tonic, E major will be represented by III in Table A and by III♯ in Table B. In either table the figure iii♭ would, reckoned from C, be e-flat minor.

The characters of key relationships are solid facts, and they probably have some bearing on the various subjective ideas that many music lovers entertain of the character of keys in themselves; for no one can name a key without being aware of its distance from C major. But it is an undisputed fact that modulations in a dominant direction have an effect of action, whereas modulations toward the subdominant have an effect of retirement. With a major tonic the three remaining directly related keys are minor, a contrast that outweighs their other distinctive characters. To move from a major tonic to the relations of its tonic minor, such as III♭ and VI♭, is to pass into deep and warm shadow. Such modulations form characteristic purple patches in the course of Mozart's second subjects.

Changes from a major tonic to the major mode of its mediant or submediant are extremely bright. Haydn, who explored all the range of tonality in contrasts between whole movements or between a minuet and its trio, is fond of using them in this way in his later works. Beethoven incorporates them in the most highly organized functions of his sonata movements. The Neapolitan relations appearing once as a paradox in Haydn's last piano sonata are completely rationalized by Beethoven, Schubert, and Brahms. The flat supertonic casts a deep warm shadow over the tonal scheme and becomes sheer blackness in the rare cases where it is changed to minor. Conversely the move a semitone downward from the tonic (to VII♯ or vii♯) is a move into mysterious brightness. Other extreme depths are sounded in the double changes from a major tonic to iiib or vib, which (with convenient change of notation) may be found in Beethoven's Sonata, Op. 106, and Schubert's last piano sonata. The converse relations III♯ and VI♯ from a minor tonic are very bright, the only really bright contrasts that the minor key relations possess. Beethoven's c minor Concerto shows III♯, and his f minor Quartet shows VI♯.

TABLE OF KEY-RELATIONSHIPS
A. From Major Tonic.

	I Direct Relationships	ii	iii IV V	vi
Indirect through both i and the second key			iv v	
Indirect through i IIIb VIb / Indirect through the second key			III	VI
Doubly indirect through the former indirect keys iiib vib				
Neapolitan direct		IIb	VII and vii	
Neapolitan, indirect		iib		
Unconnected	IV♯ and iv♯ = Vb and vb and all enharmonic synonyms of other keys			
Ambiguous			II VIIb and viib.	

TABLE OF KEY-RELATIONSHIPS
B. From Minor Tonic

	i Direct Relationships	IIIb iv v	VIb VIIb
Indirect through both I and the second key		IV V	
Indirect through i iii♯ vi♯ / Indirect through the second key		iib	vib
Doubly indirect through the former indirect keys III♯–VI♯			
Neapolitan, direct		IIb	
Neapolitan, indirect		iib	VII♯ and vii♯
Unconnected	IV♯ and iv♯ = Vb and vb and all enharmonic synonyms of other keys		
Ambiguous	ii II vib		

thoroughbass The great classical tradition cares little for the study of chords as things in themselves, and the art of harmony perishes under a discipline that separates its details from counterpoint and its larger issues from form. An excellent means of mastering a good harmonic vocabulary is to practice the filling out of classical figured basses at the keyboard; in other words, to exercise the function of the continuo player who, from the time of Monteverdi to that of Beethoven's organ teachers, supplied accompaniments from a bass with figures indicating the gist of the chords required. Fluency in such a practice does not of itself confer the ability to produce original harmony, but it means that music can be read with understanding. It is an empiric craft. But it had the misfortune to become a science, when early in the 18th century Rameau discovered the theory of the fundamental bass. This is an imaginary bass (best when most imaginary) that gives roots to all the essential chords of the music above it. The conception is true only of the most obvious harmonic facts; beyond them it is as vain as the attempt to ascertain your neighbor's dinner from a spectrograph of the smoke from his chimney. The augmented sixth that arose so innocently in Example 12 requires a double root. The first chord of Beethoven's Sonata in E-flat, Op. 31, No. 3, is an 11th with its root on the dominant in flat defiance of the fact that the dominant is the most inconceivable bass note in the whole passage until it arrives as a climax in the sixth measure. But musical fundamentalists refuse to look six measures ahead.

Carl Philipp Emanuel Bach, in conversation with Charles Burney (*The Present State of Music in Germany . . .* , 1773, 1775), said that Rameau's theory was "childish, for it reduces all music to full closes." This is perfectly true, and the theory did no harm to 18th-century French music, which eschewed long sentences and seldom strayed far from the regions of the full close. But in England Rameau's doctrine raged unchecked by taste or common sense and culminated in Alfred Day's famous application of homeopathy to the art of music. This would have mattered less if Dr. Day had not gained the ear of the leading English academic musicians of mid-Victorian times. As Charles Villiers Stanford aptly says *(Musical Composition)*, Dr. Day's theory "irrigated a wide area of low-lying ground, and we are still suffering from the effects of its miasma." The remedy lies in cultivating vivid impressions of the actual relations between counterpoint and harmony in detail, between tonality and form in general, and between key relations and chromatic chords. To this end thoroughbass should be cultivated not on paper but at the keyboard with passages (graded according to difficulty) from the continuos of Bach's cantatas and Mozart's church music.

temperament and just intonation Even in pure 16th-century polyphony the ideal diatonic scale implies distinctions of intonation beyond the capacity of any mechanical instrument with a limited number of notes. In the Ionian mode or major scale of C, the interval C–D is not the same kind of whole tone as the interval D–E but differs as 8:9 from 9:10.

The normal position for the supertonic is a major tone (8:9) above the tonic; but even so common a discord as the dominant seventh will set up a conflict, the dominant requiring its fifth to be as 9:8 above the tonic, while the seventh will want to make a true minor third from a supertonic in the position of 10:9. Such conflicts are about very minute distinctions, but every discord produces them if it is dwelt upon. Nevertheless the 12 notes that human hands can negotiate within a span-stretched octave suffice to express the most chromatic harmony with less average inaccuracy than is cheerfully permitted in human singing and violin playing. Singers and violinists can and do constantly achieve a purer intonation than that of keyed instruments; but the only aesthetic issue between free voices and tempered instruments is the difference between a human intonation liable to human error and an instrumental intonation with an inherent systematic error. The human error is often not only accidentally but deliberately in excess of the systematic error, for the slightest vibrato is larger than the quantities involved.

The subject of just intonation is fatally fascinating to people whose mathematical insight has not accepted approximation. In art, as in mathematics, accuracy lies in estimating the relevant degree of approximation rather than in unrolling interminable decimals. Music is no more to be heard through Helmholtz resonators than pictures are to be enjoyed through microscopes. The true musical ear will recognize the real meaning of harmonies though the practical intonation confounds them with homonyms. Bach introduced no new musical thought when he arranged *The Well-Tempered Clavier* to stimulate the adoption of equal temperament by providing music in every major and minor key for which the keyboard had notes. Systems of unequal temperament tuned the commoner keys as well as possible in the hope that remoter keys would never be visited. Bach decided that it was better to have all keys equally out of tune than to have some keys intolerable. The miraculous modulations of his *Chromatic* Fantasia deliberately emphasize all the chords that were wolves in unequal temperament, and thus Bach devoted his highest efforts of imagination to a humble practical purpose. But Luca Marenzio had modulated as far in madrigals written in the purest golden-age polyphony. No true harmonic ideas are based on equal temperament any more than a true geometry is based on exclusively rational quantities. *See* TUNING AND TEMPERAMENT.

methods of modulation The commonest way of establishing a change of key is to emphasize the dominant chord of the new key until only the new tonic can be expected. This we will call dominant modulation, leaving out of consideration how the new dominant is reached (it was probably surrounded by its own dominant-of-dominant, which could be reached from various other directions).

A more interesting type of modulation begins with Beethoven, arising out of hints given by Haydn and Mozart. It may be called functional modulation and consists in placing indirectly related keys into positions that make their exact relation appear vividly. If the first chord of the second key is a dominant, the relation will still appear in high relief, but any further decoration of that dominant will reduce the result to an ordinary modulation. (Compare measures 22 and 23 of the first movement of Beethoven's *Waldstein* Sonata with the drastic process of measures 37 and 38 in the first movement of Opus 106.) Functional modulation might well be called natural if that term had not been commonly assigned to modulation within the five directly related keys, irrespective of method.

Mere juxtaposition of tonics will suffice for the purposes of a functional modulation. If Beethoven had wished to explain the presence of f-sharp minor (vib) in the scheme of Opus 106, the natural (or functional) process would consist of the following four chords:

Example 17

Closely akin to this method is Beethoven's dramatic way of reducing a chord to a single note and then building up therefrom a quite remote chord, as in Opus 90 and Opus 81a.

All such devices show the listener what is really happening. The object of enharmonic modulation is frankly to mystify. It is popularly supposed to belong especially to tempered scales, but it really presupposes just intonation. All discords set up a conflict in their intonation, and an enharmonic modulation is merely a conflict so coarse-grained that it appears in the notation by some such mark as a change from G-sharp to A-flat. An ill-motived enharmonic modulation is like a bad pun; a great enharmonic modulation is a sublime mystery. Here is the commonest pivot of enharmonic changes—the diminished seventh—with its four vastly different resolutions:

Example 18

I	II	III	IV

Of course these are really four different chords. If the true theory of just intonation demanded that the minor scale should be rigid, a chord of the diminished seventh would be much harsher than the tempered scale makes it. But what really happens in just intonation is that two notes of the minor scale become

so unstable in the stress of discord that it becomes a small matter to shift the strains to whichever notes are wanted. Even with a limited keyboard the ear imagines a change of intonation when the unexpected resolution appears. This is why chromatic intervals are difficult to sing; the singer loses confidence when the aim is toward a note that will not stand still.

Not every change of notation represents a genuine enharmonic modulation. Modulate diatonically from A to F and transpose the modulation down a semitone. It will start in A-flat, but if the composer has much to say in the second key the preference will be to write it as E instead of F-flat. Sad nonsense has been written by many commentators on the most ordinary harmonies disguised by convenience in notation.

Nevertheless a merely notational change may eventually have an enharmonic result, for it may be part of an enharmonic circle. If the harmonic world is round why should just intonation be plane? Adjustments infinitely smaller than those of temperament will suffice to make the ends of an enharmonic circle meet in the course of a long composition. The first movement of Brahms's F Major Symphony, played with its repeat, goes four times around an enharmonic circle of major thirds (F, D-flat, B double-flat = A, F). Every time the key written as F returns, it identifies itself by the opening theme. If the pitch rose to G double-flat, it would scarcely be noticed after the intervening passages, and when the pitch had risen noticeably we should complain. Temperament keeps the pitch, but just intonation could do so by an even distribution of infinitely smaller adjustments.

It now becomes clear why keys a tritone fourth apart cannot become related. That interval (which modal musicians identified with the devil) constitutes the kink in musical space. It sets up an enharmonic short circuit; a modulation from C to F-sharp is exactly the same as one from G-flat back to C; and whichever key is first, the other will sound like the dominant of a Neapolitan key instead of asserting its own rights. No sensible person forbids the modulation; its effect may be excellent, but it is not the effect of a key relation.

Wagnerian harmony Wagner's sense of key is exactly the same as Beethoven's; but it has hours in which to exercise itself, whereas Beethoven's designs seldom stretch without break over 15 minutes and always show their purport within five. But take, for example, the conflict between two major keys a tone apart. The jealous Fricka did hope (in F major) that the domestic comforts of Walhalla would induce Wotan to settle down. Wotan, gently taking up her theme in E-flat, dashes her hopes by this modulation more effectively than by any use of his artillery of tubas and trombones.

But the most distinctive feature of Wagner's harmony is his use of long auxiliary notes in such a way as to suggest immensely remote keys, which vanish with the resolution. Chopin anticipates Wagner in what Sir Henry Hadow finely describes as "chromatic iridescence."

Example 19

Example 19 shows the evolution of the opening of *Tristan und Isolde*.

post-Wagnerian harmony The line of evolution traced thus far has evidently no a priori limits, though it has principles. Any new system is destined either to starve for lack of nourishment from the main sources of music or become absorbed in them. Systems derived from equal temperament are crude fallacies. The whole-tone scale that readily arises on the piano, *e.g.,* C, D, E, F♯ (= G♭, A♭, B♭, C), amused Debussy in a few dozen songs and short pieces and played a much less predominant part in his *Pelléas et Mélisande* than is generally supposed. It is really no more a whole-tone scale than the diminished seventh is a major sixth bounding a series of minor thirds. Walford Davies pointed out that this scale is a six-note chord projected into a single octave and capable, like the diminished seventh, of an enharmonic turn to each of its

Three concords (tonic, first inversion of subdominant, and dominant of a minor—a possible 16th-century cadence in the Phrygian mode)

The same with chromatic passing notes * and appoggiaturas †

The same chords varied by a suspension *

The last two chords of the above attacked unexpectedly, the first appoggiatura * prolonged until it seems to make a strange foreign chord before it resolves on the short note at ‡, while the second appoggiatura † is chromatic

The same with the further addition of a double suspension * and two passing notes ††

The same enharmonically transformed to become a variation of the dominant ninth of c minor; the G♯ at * is really A♭, and ‡ is no longer a note of resolution but a chromatic passing note

The same with a chromatic alteration of the second chord * and an "essential" discord (dominant seventh) at †

notes. Here is one of several possible ways of showing the six resolutions of this scale:

Example 20

Enthusiasts for new systems are naturally infuriated when the systems fade into the light of common or Wagnerian day. Nevertheless the pleasure given by every effort at revolutionary harmony results from the fact that the new chords enter our consciousness with the meaning they would bear in a classical scheme. Not only Wagner but Bach and Palestrina lurk behind every new harmonic sensation and cannot long be prevented from making sense of it. After sense has been made the fundamental theorists will prove that many quite commonplace chromatic progressions contain the triskaidekahyperhendekaenneaheptachord of Example 20 with the omission of not more than four of its notes.

Other new theories are not less quickly worn out, even when invented by gifted composers. Aleksandr Scriabin, each of whose last five sonatas is built around its own new chord, complained shortly before his untimely death that he had not succeeded in getting away from a sophisticated dominant seventh. This complaint recalls Carl Philipp Emanuel Bach's criticism of Rameau's theory, and its cause lies deep in the very nature of articulate thought. If you wish to compose freely do not fix your mind on new harmonic propositions. Language is not extended by declining to use what is known of it.

Schoenberg's harmonic theory is often masterly in its analysis of classical music, but it is extremely disappointing in its constructive aspect. Schoenberg refutes the absurd old theory of added thirds, but he invents a new theory of added fourths that has even less foundation. The theory of added thirds was no more scientific than a classification of birds by the color of their feathers. But birds do have feathers of various colors, and classical music does build up chords by sequences of thirds. Schoenberg's theory rests on no observation at all, for the piling up of fourths has no origin in classical harmony and only a quickly exhausted melodic value. However, it can be carried around the tempered scale in 12 steps and ad infinitum in just intonation. To find the composer of the *Gurrelieder* fathering such theories is as disconcerting as to discover Einstein telling fortunes.

theoretic possibilities Harmony has not yet found a place for so simple a natural phenomenon as the seventh note of the harmonic series. Example 21 shows the first 16 notes from bass C as the fundamental. Many a clang contains them all in appreciable strength; yet no fewer than three (in addition to the octave of No. 7) are outside our system, Nos. 7 and 13 being much flatter than the notes here written, and No. 11 much sharper.

Though resultant tones are audible enough to save organ builders the expense of 32-ft. pipes by means of devices that reinforce the resultant tone and obliterate its generators, they have played no acknowledged part in musical aesthetics. A theory that builds upon them must abandon the hypothesis that all harmony grows upward from the bass. Abandon it by all means if your musical intuitions inspire you with ideas based on resultant tones. But you must mean something different from harmony whose ideal bass lies in its resultant tones, for that will be merely another conception of fundamental bass, differing from Rameau's but again forcing you to regard harmony as rising from the bass. And after all the hypothesis is not a theory but an experi-

Example 21

ence. The language of music has in fact taken shape without guidance from resultant tones just as the art of painting has until recently made no conscious use of complementary colors except by instinctively avoiding ugly or unintelligible effects.

Schoenberg rightly says that *der Einfall,* the inspiration that comes without theorizing, is the sole criterion of musical truth; and perhaps some composers may have *Einfälle* so convincing in their use of Nos. 7, 11, and 13 as to compel the building of new instruments for them. And so with the use of a resultant tone or inverted harmonic system. The quartets of Alois Hába have not made quarter tones sound convincingly unlike faulty intonation. We must not blame our ears, which often appreciate much smaller measurements. The just intonation of a Wagner opera would comprise some 1,000 notes to the octave. The question is not how many notes are used in the long run but how small a direct measurement is of interest.

Many other modern harmonic tendencies are essentially matters of instrumentation. If, abandoning the polyphonic hypothesis, we use chords—simple or complex—as mere unanalyzed tone colors, we can start a new polyphony with moving cords instead of moving single parts. (See Example 22.)
Our problem then will be to keep the planes of tone distinct. Organ mixtures, if not dominated by fundamental tones, would shock the boldest multiplanar harmonist by the mess they would make of classical harmony.

Extremes meet, and we are recovering a sense of the values of unharmonized melody—not melody that wants to be harmonized nor melody that achieves harmonic sense by draftsmanship but the austere achievement, far more difficult than any atonality, of a melody that neither needs nor implies harmony.

BIBLIOGRAPHY: Jean-Philippe Rameau, *Treatise on Harmony* (1722; Eng. trans., 1971); Ebenezer Prout, *Harmony, Its Theory and Practice,* rev. ed. (1903; reprint, 1971); Matthew Shirlaw, *The Theory of Harmony* (1917; reprint, 1969); Paul Hindemith, *The Craft of Musical Composition,* 2 vols. (1941–42), and *A Concentrated Course in Traditional Harmony,* 2 vols. (1943–53); Roger Sessions, *Harmonic Practice* (1951); Heinrich Schenker, *Harmony* (1954; reprint, 1974); Vincent Persichetti, *Twentieth-Century Harmony* (1961); Walter Piston, *Harmony,* 3rd ed. (1962); Leonard Ratner, *Harmony: Structure and Style* (1962); Richard F. Goldman, *Harmony in Western Music* (1965); Elie Siegmeister, *Harmony and Melody,* 2 vols. (1965–66); Arnold Schoenberg, *Structural Functions of Harmony,* rev. ed. (1969), and *Theory of Harmony* (1978).

Harnoncourt, Nikolaus (b. December 6, 1929) Educated at the Academy of Music in Vienna, the German gambist, conductor, and musicologist Nikolaus Harnoncourt founded the Concentus Musicus of Vienna (1954) to revive performance of pre-Classical works on the original instruments. With this group he has recorded the *St. Matthew* Passion and some 30 cantatas of Bach as well as other music—mostly Baroque. He has published editions of Bach's choral works and edited scores for Monteverdi's *L'Incoronazione di Poppea* and *Il Ritorno d'Ulisse in patria.*

Example 22
Vaughan Williams, *Pastoral* Symphony
triplanar harmony and doubling of melodies in whole chords

Harold en Italie: *see* BERLIOZ; CYCLIC FORM; LEITMOTIV.

harp　A plucked stringed instrument of great antiquity. Typically the harp is either triangular or bow-shaped with one string for each note and with a resonator to which the plane of the strings is perpendicular or nearly so. The gradation of string length from short to long corresponds to the gradation from high to low pitch. The word harp is often used inaccurately to describe instruments that are properly zithers or lyres.

The modern harp is a combination of the basic structure and method of sound production of ancient harps with a complex mechanism to obtain a full chromatic range. The

double-action pedal harp
courtesy, Lyon & Healy

modern double-action pedal harp covers six and one-half octaves (three below and three and one-half above middle C) and consists of a hollow sound box, rectangular or semicircular in section to which the belly, or sounding board, is attached; the harmonic curve, or neck, carrying the tuning pins, a set of wrest pins and two sets of rotating brass disks; the forepillar, which joins the end of the neck to the base; the strings (of gut or nylon and, in the bass, bound wire), which at the upper end are fixed through the tuning pins and at the lower end are pegged to holes in the belly; and the mechanism, concealed inside the forepillar and the deep metal plates that run along both sides of the neck. This mechanism is worked from seven pedals (one for each string in the harp's seven-note octave) set in the base of the harp; each of these pedals acts on all the strings of a certain pitch name throughout the harp's compass. Depression of the pedal to the first notch (single action) shortens the appropriate strings by a semitone; to the second notch (double action) by a whole tone; the shortening is effected by means of the rotating disks on the neck that grip the string at the appropriate point. This harp is normally tuned diatonically in C-flat; thus depression of all pedals to the first notch puts it into C and to the second notch into C-sharp. Its technique demands skilled coordination between the hands, which pluck the strings with the fleshy part of the finger tips, and the feet, which select the pedals for the necessary pitch changes on the strings.

True harps of great size are depicted in the tomb of Ramses III (*c.* 1200 B.C.), and harps of various forms and sizes were much used in ancient Mediterranean civilizations. Exceptions were Greece and Rome, where the lyre and cithara were more important. There are few extant specimens of these ancient harps, but their use ultimately spread to Africa and the Far East, and the form of the small Egyptian bow harp survives in the tribal harps of east Africa and the old Burmese harp. Ancient harps had no forepillar and presumably were strung at rather low tension.

The frame harp, with a forepillar joining the forward ends of neck and sound box, appears to have developed in northern Europe in the 10th and 11th centuries A.D. From the 12th century two main forms are recognizable—one Irish and one European. The characteristic features of the Irish harp, or *clarsach,* were a huge sound box carved from a solid block of wood, a heavy neck, and a deeply curved forepillar. It was designed to bear great tension from thick brass strings, which were plucked by long fingernails to produce a ringing, bell-like sound. It belonged to the world of strongly colored medieval instruments, but because of the static nature of the aristocratic Irish society of which it was a part, it survived almost unchanged to the end of the 17th century. Its long resonance was out of keeping with the harmonic nature of 18th-century music, and by the end of that century it had disappeared.

The modern harp is derived from the more delicate European harp, which differed from the Irish in having a thin, shallow sound box, slender neck and forepillar, and at least from the 16th century gut strings plucked with the finger tips. The simple 16th-century form is preserved in the rustic harps of Latin America, taken there by the Spaniards and adopted by the Indians, who still play vivacious dance music on them together with drums, guitars, and maracas.

From the 17th century the harp was progressively mechanized to give it the chromatic notes demanded by changing musical styles. The first attempt was made by Tirolean harp makers, who placed a number of hooks on the neck close to the strings to be turned by hand when required. Although this mechanism made it possible to sharpen the pitch by a semitone, it also pulled the hooked strings out of plane, and its operation left only one hand free to play. In 1720 the Bavarian Celestin Hochbrucker attached hooks to a series of levers in the forepillar (which henceforth became hollow) that were controlled by seven pedals. In 1750 Cousineau of Paris replaced the hooks by metal plates that gripped the strings while leaving them in plane. In 1792 Sébastien Érard substituted the rotating disk for the metal plate and in 1810 added a second disk for each string and produced the double action for the pedals; Érard's changes virtually established the modern form of the harp.

The Welsh triple harp with three parallel ranks of strings and the chromatic harp invented and improved by members of the Pleyel firm in Paris in the late 19th century were attempts to chromaticize the harp without using mechanism. The so-called Irish harp of the 19th and 20th centuries is derived from the gut strung pedal harp and has little connection in construction or technique with the historic Irish harp.

In the absence of exact instrumentation medieval harp music can only be inferred. Much 17th- and 18th-century solo music is alternatively for harp or keyboard instruments and is, with the exception of Mozart's Concerto for flute and harp, unremarkable. The tonal and technical possibilities of the modern harp, particularly its sweeping glissandi and mysterious harmonics, make it most effective in Impressionist music, and it has been used especially well by Debussy and Ravel.

Parts specifically written for the harp are rare in early concerted music; Monteverdi's *Orfeo* (1607), Handel's *Esther* (1730), and Gluck's *Orfeo ed Euridice* are notable exceptions. The double-action pedal harp, however, became a standard part of the orchestra from 1830.

BIBLIOGRAPHY: William H. Grattan Flood, *The Story of the Harp* (1905; reprint, 1977), Otto Andersson, *The Bowed-Harp* (1930; reprint, 1977); Roslyn Rensch, *The Harp: Its History, Technique and Repertoire* (1969); Gildas Jaffrennou, *Folk Harps* (1973).

Harper, Heather (b. May 8, 1930)   At home in both opera and lieder, the English soprano Heather Harper studied at Trinity College of Music in London. She sang with several small English and Welsh opera companies before receiving acclaim at Glyndebourne, Covent Garden, and Sadler's Wells. Since 1957 she has sung regularly at the London Promenade Concerts. Among her best-known roles are Violetta (Verdi's *La Traviata*), Mimi (Puccini's *La Bohème*), and Belinda (Purcell's *Dido and Aeneas*). She created the soprano role in Britten's *War* Requiem in 1962; her nonoperatic recordings include Bach, Handel, and Mahler.

harpsichord   A keyboard instrument with strings that are plucked. It has one or two (rarely three) manual keyboards and has sometimes been equipped with a pedal keyboard (for the feet) as well.

mechanism Each note normally has three, sometimes two, strings made of steel except for those of the lowest octave, which are of brass. The strings are plucked by jacks, vertical strips of pearwood or beech that rest on the far ends of the keys and pass through a lower fixed jack guide and an upper jack slide level with the soundboard. Above this point is a pivoted tongue that is pierced in its upper half to take a small plectrum of crow's quill. The tongue is kept upright by a weak spring of hog's bristle or wire. When the key is depressed the jack rises, and the quill plucks the string. When the key is released the quill again meets the string, but the tongue swings back and allows the quill to drop back past the string without replucking it. At this moment a small square of cloth, let into the top of the jack, rests on the string and damps the vibrations. A padded wooden jack rail that passes about one-half inch above the jacks keeps them from jumping out of their slots. This rail has been removed in the illustration to show the jacks and jack slides.

Two sets of strings at unison (8-ft.) pitch are hitched to pins in a strip of wood fixed just inside the curved side. They pass over the curved 8-ft. bridge on the soundboard, between the rows of jacks, over the near bridge, or nut, and around the tuning, or wrest, pins fixed in an oak plank over the keys. As the jacks for each note must be in line with their key, the two 8-ft. strings pass on either side of the jacks. Consequently the jacks face in opposite directions, and the principal 8-ft. strings are slightly longer than the corresponding second unison strings. The strings that make up the third set sound an octave higher at 4-ft. pitch, are half the length of the 8-ft. strings, have a separate bridge in the middle of the soundboard, and have their own third row of jacks. The different sets may be used separately or together by small sideways movements of the jack slides. The sustained tone of a harpsichord depends on the proportions, lightness, and resonance of the soundboard and case and the scaling of the strings.

Registers signify particular combinations of strings and jacks that give various tone qualities, therefore resembling organ stops. These differences of tone quality depend on the relative plucking point. This point varies from about 10 percent of the length of the string in the bass to 20 to 30 percent for the principal 8-ft. register and to about 40 percent for the second unison in the top octave. Thus the principal 8-ft. is brilliant, and the second unison is rounder in tone, especially in the treble.

history Little information on the early history of the harpsichord is available before the manuscript treatise of Henri Arnault of Zwolle (d. 1466), which includes a drawing of a *clavicimbalum* ("keyed dulcimer," the origin of the Italian name for the instrument *clavicembalo* or *cembalo* and the French *clavecin*) with nearly three octaves, B to a″, adequate for all the music in the *Buxheim Organ Book* (*c.* 1470). The alternative hammer mechanism described by Arnault suggests that the harpsichord may have developed from an earlier pianoforte of inefficient mechanism.

From the early 16th century Italy produced a series of fine though simple instruments. They were lightly constructed, usually of cypress and with boxwood topped keys, and could be lifted out of their protective outer cases. Their design and construction differed little in 250 years. They have a rich and brilliant sound and served as well for Domenico Scarlatti's sonatas as for the music of Frescobaldi written *c.* 1600.

Antwerp also produced fine harpsichords, especially from 1570 to 1680, a large proportion made by members of the Ruckers family and circle. This school was apparently the first to build harpsichords with a regular 4-ft. stop and with a second keyboard. The additional manual was initially for transposition, but after the middle of the 17th century the keyboards were changed to the same pitch. At the same time the registers were rearranged to give one 8-ft. stop on the upper manual with the other 8-ft. and the 4-ft. on the lower manual. The upper 8-ft. stop could be added to the lower keyboard by means of a coupler. These four-octave Flemish harpsichords largely supplied the demand throughout most of northern Europe. The rapidly developing keyboard schools of the second half of the

17th and early 18th centuries demanded an increased compass, especially in the bass.

By this time the old Flemish harpsichords were so highly prized for their tone that they were conserved by adding a few extra notes in place of the key blocks and eventually enlarged to accommodate a five-octave compass, especially in France where the process was known as *ravalement*. This enlargement usually meant replacement of everything except the soundboard and sometimes part of the casework. This enlarged instrument, without the modern 16-ft. register, was the one for which Bach, Handel, the Couperins, and all the other great Baroque masters wrote and on which their music sounds best.

Many Italian instruments were imported into England in the 16th century. Comparatively few English harpsichords were built before 1720, but after that date England rapidly became a leading center for harpsichord building largely because of the work of Burkat Shudi (or Tschudi) and Jacob Kirkman. These differed from the harpsichord of *c.* 1700 by

having the two 8-ft. rows of jacks placed together, with the 4-ft. farthest from the player, and allowing the principal 8-ft. jacks to play from both manuals. Thus a key depressed on the upper manual lifts only the near 8-ft. jack, while one on the lower manual lifts all three jacks. The instrument illustrated shows the changing styles in harpsichord design by having a Hans Ruckers soundboard of 1612 extended in the treble, an early 18th-century case and compass, and the English disposition of jacks. Most English harpsichords also included the lute stop, an extra row of jacks that plucked the principal 8-ft. strings at the four percent position, providing an attractive dry, almost brittle, sound.

Few harpsichords were produced in Germany, but in the middle of the 18th century the Hass family built some fine specimens with the English disposition, one or two exceptional and elaborate instruments with 16-ft. registers, and one with three manuals and a 2-ft. stop. These are indicative of a change in musical taste after Bach's time. In Germany builders

harpsichord with soundboard by Hans Ruckers, Amsterdam, 1612
from the National Trust Property, Fenton House, Hampstead
by gracious permission of Her Majesty Queen Elizabeth, the Queen Mother

tended to design the harpsichord like an organ; in France it was made to sound like a piano through the use of plectra of soft buff leather.

By 1790 it was accepted that the piano was more suitable for the new Romantic music, and throughout most of the 19th century the harpsichord was considered quaint and old-fashioned. But the growing interest in older music after the middle of the century resulted in a revival of the commercial manufacture of harpsichords in the late 1880s with the piano manufacturing firms of Érard and Pleyel in Paris and in 1895 with Arnold Dolmetsch in England.

Twentieth-century harpsichords vary considerably because of the different demands of two repertoires: the great masters of the past, requiring only two 8-ft. and one 4-ft. stops but great resonance; and the growing modern repertoire, demanding 16-ft. pitch, greater contrasts and variety in tone color, rapid stop control, and a frame that will resist strenuous conditions. The great Polish harpsichordist Wanda Landowska led the revival from her first public appearance in 1903, inspiring composers such as de Falla and Poulenc to write concertos for the instrument and promoting interest in early keyboard works.

See also FORTEPIANO; SPINET; VIRGINAL.

BIBLIOGRAPHY: Raymond Russell, *The Harpsichord and Clavichord; An Introductory Study* (1959); Hanns Neupert, *Harpsichord Manual* (1960); Frank Hubbard, *Three Centuries of Harpsichord Making* (1965); Donald H. Boalch, *Makers of the Harpsichord and Clavichord, 1440–1840,* 2nd ed. (1974).

Harrell, Lynn (Morris) (b. April 30, 1944) Educated at the Juilliard School and the Curtis Institute, the U.S. cellist Lynn Harrell made his debut at Carnegie Hall in 1963 and the same year joined the Cleveland Orchestra, later becoming the youngest principal player in its history. He shared the first Avery Fisher Prize (1975; with pianist Murray Perahia) and has taught at Juilliard since 1977. His recordings include the Dvořák Concerto and 20th-century works.

Harris, Roy (Ellsworth) (b. February 12, 1898) A composer who helped establish the distinctive features of the modern U.S. school, Roy Harris was born in Lincoln County, Oklahoma. His musical development came relatively late. After studying in California with Arthur Farwell, Arthur Bliss, and others, he went to Paris in 1926 to study with Boulanger. His first significant work was a concerto for clarinet, piano, and string quartet (1927). After returning to the United States in 1929, he accepted various teaching positions, spending the longest period at the University of California at Los Angeles (1961–73).

Harris' works are marked by broad tonal melodies and asymmetrical rhythms. Some of his works reflect scenes of U.S. life. Of his 14 symphonies the best known is the Third (1939), written in a single movement with contrasting sections of lyrical and dramatic nature. In chamber music Harris follows Classical models. He also has written numerous works for chorus and solo voice and piano and organ pieces.

BIBLIOGRAPHY: Henry Cowell, ed., *American Composers on American Music* (1933; reprint, 1962); Aaron Copland, *The New Music: 1900–1960,* rev. ed. (1968; originally *Our New Music,* 1941).

RECORDINGS: *American Ballads* for piano; *Epilogue to Profiles in Courage: J.F.K.* for orchestra; Piano Quintet; Piano Sonata; Symphonies (Nos. 3, 4, and 5); Violin Sonata.

Harrison, Lou (b. May 14, 1917) An early collaborator with John Cage (1934–35), the U.S.-born Lou Harrison is best known as a composer of music for dance and as a designer and builder of musical instruments. He studied with Henry Cowell and taught at Mills College in California (1937–40). He later studied with Schoenberg and began using serial and aleatory techniques. In 1961 he visited the Far East, where he became interested in Asian instruments and rhythms in combination with those of Western music (*Pacifika Rondo,* 1963) and alone (*Moo gung kwa, Se tang ak* for classical Korean court orchestra, 1961). He also employs medieval polyphonic techniques, and much of his vocal music, for which he prefers the open vowels of Esperanto, is intoned rather than sung. His music is basically melodic, often backed by the unconventional sounds of brake drums, coffee cans, and tack piano (featured in *Solstice,* 1950; and Symphony on G, completed 1961). He has written a mass (1939–49), an opera (*Rapunzel,* 1954), a flute concerto, a puppet opera (*Young Caesar,* 1970), songs, and much music for percussion (*Canticles 1, 3;* 1940, 1941). Harrison edited several works of Ives, including the Third Symphony, which he conducted in its first performance (1947). Also prominent as a critic, from 1943 to 1947 he wrote for the *New York Herald Tribune* and for *Modern Music.* He has taught at San José (California) State College since 1967.

RECORDINGS: *Canticle* No. 1 for percussion; Concerto for organ and percussion; Concerto for violin and percussion; Concerto *in Slendro;* Fugue for percussion; *Song of Quetzalcoatl;* Suite for percussion; Symphony on G.

Harty, (Herbert) Hamilton (December 4, 1879–February 19, 1941) After an early career as an organist in Belfast and Dublin, the Irish conductor Hamilton Harty went to London in 1900 and made a reputation as a composer and accompanist. In 1920 he was successful as a conductor with the Hallé Orchestra in Manchester, where he remained until 1933. His compositions, which are romantic and conventional, include a violin concerto (1909) and a symphonic poem (*With the Wild Geese,* 1910), as well as arrangements of Irish folksongs and of Handel's *Water Music* and *Music for the Royal Fireworks,* suites that have become more popular than the originals. An admirer of Berlioz, he revived the Requiem and recorded many of the overtures. He was a pioneer in early electrical recording.

Háry János: *see* KODÁLY.

Haskil, Clara (January 7, 1895–December 7, 1960) A student of Alfred Cortot and Fauré in Paris and of Busoni in Berlin, the Romanian-Swiss pianist Clara Haskil made her debut in Vienna at seven. Noted as an interpreter of Classical and early Romantic music, she specialized in Mozart and Beethoven; she gave recitals of the latter's chamber music with Georges Enesco, Eugène Ysaÿe, and Casals and recorded with Arthur Grumiaux the full cycle of Beethoven violin sonatas.

Hasse, Johann Adolph (March 25, 1699–December 16, 1783) A German composer known for his operas, Johann Adolph Hasse began his career as a singer and made his debut as a composer at Brunswick in 1721 with the opera *Antioco.* He went to Italy to complete his studies with Nicola Antonio Porpora; but his relationship with Porpora proved unfortunate, and Hasse became a student of Alessandro Scarlatti. His first Italian commission, a serenade for two voices, was first performed by two of the greatest singers in Italy, Vittoria Tesi and the castrato Farinelli, and contributed greatly to Hasse's popularity. In 1726 his opera seria, *Sesostrate,* written for the royal opera at Naples, made him famous throughout Italy as "Il Sassone" ("the Saxon"). He spent several years in Venice, where he married the singer Faustina Bordoni, with whom he was invited to Dresden by the Elector of Saxony. Hasse later lived in Dresden from 1739 until 1763, when he and his wife retired from court service. They then went to Vienna, where Hasse wrote several more operas. His last stage work was *Ruggiero* (1771), written for the wedding of Archduke Ferdinand at Milan. Hasse returned to Venice in 1773.

Hasse's compositions include 56 operas, as well as oratorios, masses, and instrumental works. The popularity of his music during his lifetime was enormous. The two airs that Farinelli sang every evening for 10 years to the melancholy King Philip V of Spain were both by Hasse. The chief characteristics of Hasse's music were melodic beauty and formal balance. His operatic overtures had a considerable influence upon the development of the symphony, especially in north Germany.

RECORDINGS: Overture to *Euristeo;* Mandolin Concerto in G Major.

Hassler, Hans Leo (October 26, 1564–August 19, 1612) The most famous German composer of his day, Hans Leo Hassler was born in Nürnberg and presumably studied music with his father, the organist Isaak Hassler. After mastering the imitative techniques of Orlando di Lasso and the fashionable polychoral style of the Venetians, he traveled to Venice in 1584 to study with Andrea Gabrieli, in whose nephew and pupil Giovanni Gabrieli he found a close friend. The light, elegant secular music of Orazio Vecchi, Baldassare Donati, and Giovanni Giacomo Gastoldi and the keyboard works of the Venetian school soon attracted him. In 1585 he returned to Germany as organist to the Augsburg banking family of Fugger. By 1591 he enjoyed the favor of Emperor Rudolph II, who later ennobled him. In 1600 he was appointed director of music for the city of Augsburg, moving to a similar post in Nürnberg in 1601. In 1608 he became organist to the elector of Saxony.

Hassler's style is a remarkable fusion of German counterpoint and Italian form. His *Madrigali* (1596), though avoiding the harmonic experiments of Luca Marenzio, are among the finest of their time. His instrumental compositions and his church music—Protestant and Roman Catholic—were widely imitated. His German songs owe much to the homophonic dance rhythms of Gastoldi; the best-known collection was the *Lustgarten* (1601), which contains the charming "Mein Gemüth ist mir verwirret." This tune reappears in Bach's *St. Matthew* Passion under the title "O Haupt voll Blut und Wunden."

Hawkins, John (March 30, 1719–May 21, 1789) Author of the first history of music in English, John Hawkins was a musical and literary amateur but a diligent scholar. Born in London, he was articled as a clerk to John Scott of Bishopsgate and became a solicitor. A legacy from his brother-in-law enabled him to sell his practice in 1759; he was a Middlesex magistrate from 1761 and was elected chairman of the Quarter Sessions in 1765. Personal application to the earl of Rochford in 1772 brought him a coveted knighthood.

Hawkins entertained literary ambitions early: he wrote an "Essay on Honesty" for the *Gentleman's Magazine* (1739) and cantata texts (1742–43) for the organist John Stanley. These were followed by, among other works, an annotated edition of Walton's *Compleat Angler* (1760), articles on legal matters, and a biography of Samuel Johnson, a close friend, that was superseded only by Boswell's. The biography was published with his edition of Johnson's works in 1787.

Hawkins is remembered chiefly as a writer on music. *A General History of the Science and Practice of Music* was published in five volumes in 1776, having occupied him for 16 years. No earlier work provided a model; Hawkins consulted primary musical and theoretical sources and gathered extensive biographical material from original documents, musical acquaintances, and gravestones. It is principally as a mine of detailed information, some of it unavailable elsewhere, that the *History* continues to be invaluable.

Hawkins did not sympathize with the music of his own generation, but he had a great admiration for early music. The *History* covered music from the time of the ancients to the mid-18th century, and his antiquarianism was satirized. His *History* was eclipsed by Charles Burney's. Other musical writings included biographical articles and a history of the Academy of Ancient Music.

Haydn, (Franz) Joseph (March 31, or April 1, 1732–May 31, 1809) Often called the father of the symphony and of the string quartet, Joseph Haydn in effect founded the Viennese Classical school. Living from the end of the Baroque to the beginning of the Romantic period, he presided over the musical transition between them, creating his distinct style by combining elements of the pompous and complex idiom of the Baroque, the lighthearted gallant style from Italy and France, and the emotional expressive *empfindsamer Stil* ("sensitive style") of the north Germans. Though 24 years older, he became the friend and collaborator of Mozart and was a major influence on his pupil Beethoven.

early years Born at Rohrau, Lower Austria, Haydn was the second child and eldest son of Mathias Haydn and Anna Marie Koller. Most of Haydn's ancestors came from the border state of Burgenland. Though Hungarian, Croatian, German, Austrian, and Gypsy elements were spread throughout this state, modern research has left little doubt that Haydn's forefathers were German and Austrian peasants and that he was not, as was once believed, of Croatian origin.

Concerning his early years Haydn wrote in 1776: "My father was a wheelwright by profession, and served Count Harrach [whose coun-

Joseph Haydn, portrait by Thomas Hardy, 1791
courtesy, Royal College of Music, London

try castle was at Rohrau], a great lover of music. [My father] played the harp without knowing a note of music and, as a boy of five, I sang all his simple little pieces correctly: this induced my father to entrust me to the care of my relative, the school rector in Hainburg, in order that I might learn the rudiments of music and other juvenile requirements . . . When I was seven, the late Kapellmeister von Reutter [the elder Georg Karl von Reutter, 1708–72] passed through Hainburg and quite by accident heard my weak but pleasant voice. He forthwith took me to the choir house [of St. Stephen's Cathedral in Vienna] where, apart from my studies, I learned the art of singing, the harpsichord, and the violin—and from very good masters. Until my 18th year I sang soprano with great success, not only at St. Stephen's but also at court. Finally I lost my voice, and then had to eke out a wretched existence for eight whole years . . . I never would have learned what little I did, had I not, in my zeal for composition, composed well into the night. I wrote diligently, but not quite correctly, until at last I had the

good fortune to learn the true fundamentals of composition from the celebrated Herr Porpora [Nicola Antonio Porpora], who was then in Vienna . . ."

Not many of these diligent early compositions have survived, but two masses, the *Missa brevis* in F and the *Missa brevis alla cappella* "Rorate coeli desuper" (rediscovered in 1957 at Göttweig Abbey) certainly date from the period *c.* 1750; the latter mass also contains sufficient "not quite correct" passages to suggest that it may be Haydn's earliest surviving work. Probably some of the early piano sonatas were written during these formative years.

About the year 1757 Haydn was invited by an Austrian nobleman, Count Carl Joseph von Fürnberg, to spend the summer in Weinzierl Castle near Melk. On this occasion Haydn wrote his first quartets, probably those contained in what is known as Opus 1 and four of the six contained in Opus 2. Before this date he had written a comic opera, *Der krumme Teufel,* for the Viennese comedian and impresario Joseph Felix Kurz-Bernadon. Although the piece was a great success and was played all over Germany, as well as in Prague and Pressburg, the music remains lost.

In 1759 Haydn was engaged as music director to Count Ferdinand Maximilian Morzin, whose summer castle was at Lucaveč in Bohemia. There he wrote his first symphony and numerous divertimenti for wind band or for wind instruments and strings. Haydn stayed only a short time with the Morzins, for the count fell into financial difficulties, and the musicians were dismissed; but while the band was still intact Prince Pál Antal Esterházy seems to have heard Haydn and subsequently invited him to become assistant Kapellmeister of the Esterházy court orchestra. He accepted, and the contract dates from May 1, 1761. In 1760 he had married Maria Anna Keller, daughter of the wigmaker Johann Peter Keller who had befriended him 10 years before. His childless marriage was unhappy, and Haydn's animosity to his wife increased as the years went by.

Esterházy service   The engagement as assistant Kapellmeister to the Esterházy court at Eisenstadt and, in the winters, at Vienna proved decisive for Haydn's career. He remained in the family's service until his death. He was in command of a small but brilliant orchestra, a church choir, and, at the beginning, a few operatic singers. The instrumentalists and vocalists were supplemented by local musicians from Eisenstadt.

In 1762 Prince Pál Antal died and was succeeded by his brother Miklós József "the Magnificent," under whose reign the Esterházys became known throughout Europe as patrons of the arts. The prince was a passionate lover of music and played the baryton for which Haydn was required to write an enormous number of divertimenti. Miklós enlarged the band and the operatic forces, and a regular opera season was soon inaugurated. The singers were mostly Italian and the prince preferred opera buffa to all other kinds of opera. At the beginning Haydn's relationship to his patron was one of master and servant, but, in the course of years, he turned Miklós from a despotic and often ruthless ruler into a kindly and tolerant protector. Haydn's letters to Miklós, discovered in 1955, show the composer to have been a born diplomat.

In 1766 Miklós opened an enormous new castle at the south end of the Neusiedler See called Esterháza. It was intended to be a Hungarian Versailles, and it was one of the most luxurious and fantastic aristocratic residences of the 18th century. There was an opera house that seated 500, and strolling players were housed in the castle for several months of the season. When the prince was in residence there was theatrical performance, a concert, an opera, or a marionette performance every night.

During the 1760s Haydn's fame began to spread throughout Europe. The Austrian and Czech monasteries did much to disseminate his church music and also his symphonies, divertimenti, sonatas, and concertos. Many of Haydn's secular works are preserved only in one or more of the great monastery collections. Aristocratic patrons in south Germany, Italy, and the Austro-Hungarian empire assiduously collected his music, and their libraries are among the most important sources for his work. It spread rapidly to France, where G. B. Venier in Paris published a Haydn symphony as early as 1764, and R. de la Chevardi-

ère followed with the first quartets in the same year. J. J. Hummel of Amsterdam and Berlin and Robert Bremner of London also printed these quartets. Within five or six years a large number of Haydn's instrumental works had been printed, most of them in Paris. It was not until 1774, however, that Haydn himself actually arranged to have any of his works published and not until 1780 that he found a firm, Artaria of Vienna, that was willing to issue all his new music. It is probable that Haydn never knew of the existence of half the music printed under his name in Paris.

Apart from moving from one Esterházy castle to the other, Haydn traveled little. He and the other musicians were obliged to remain available to Prince Esterházy almost without interruption. The story of the *Farewell* Symphony (No. 45 in f-sharp minor) is associated with the long stays that the prince made in Esterháza. In 1772 the musicians asked Haydn to write a piece of music that would suggest to Miklós that they thought it time to return to Vienna and their families. When Luigi Tomasini and Haydn, left alone at the end of the symphony, were blowing out their candles, the prince is reported to have said, "Well, if they go, we might as well leave, too." Whereupon the court departed the next day. The anecdote shows Haydn's tact in handling his princely patron, but it does not entirely explain the passionate Romanticism of the symphony and indeed of all Haydn's music during this period. The "Romantic crisis," which begins about 1768 and continues until about 1774, inaugurates Haydn's maturity; the music written then, from the great *Stabat Mater* (1767) to the large-scale *Missa Sanctae Caeciliae* (c. 1773), would be sufficient to place Haydn among the ranks of the great.

The succeeding decade (1774–84) shows a tendency to popularization. After the great quartets of Opus 20, the Piano Sonata in c minor, No. 20, and the symphonies in minor keys (especially the so-called *Trauersymphonie* in e minor, No. 44), the ensuing compositions seem in part pallid. This is not true, however, of the Quartets, Op. 33, which Mozart acknowledged as models, nor of the operas produced in this decade. Here Haydn's swift imagination fills page after page of beautiful music. He wrote about 10 operas and sing-spiele in this decade, but until his operas become generally known his importance as a composer in the genre must be left undecided. *Il mondo della luna* (1777) on a text by Carlo Goldoni was revived in 1959 with great success; *Orfeo (L'anima del filosofo)* was revived in 1951; *L'infedelta delusa* (1773) in 1961; *La vera costanza* (1779) in 1973–74; and *La canterina* (1767) in 1974.

Toward the end of the 1780s the composer's letters begin to show restlessness and dissatisfaction. He longed for his Viennese friends, among them Mozart, who in 1785 had dedicated to him six of his finest quartets. In fact, Haydn longed for artistic freedom. In 1790, just as this situation threatened to become intolerable, Prince Miklós died. His successor Antal cared nothing for music, dismissed the whole band, and retained only Haydn as nominal Kapellmeister and a few musicians for the hunt. The composer was free to go. Meanwhile, one of London's leading impresarios, Johann Peter Salomon, hearing of the death of the prince, hastened to the Austrian capital. He offered Haydn a double contract—one for 12 new pieces of music to be performed at public concerts in the Hanover Square rooms in London, and one from Sir John Gallini for a new Italian opera to be produced at the King's Theatre. Haydn needed no persuasion, and the two men set off on December 15, 1790, journeying through Munich, Wallerstein, Bonn, and Brussels to London.

London In his artistic development Haydn's visits to England were the most important events in his life. Esterháza, beneficial though it was, had outlived its usefulness. It is doubtful that he would have become the great master he did were it not for the enormous stimulation provided by the English public. He was feted, lionized, and treated as a genius. The public received his new "overtures" (actually the *Salomon,* or *London,* Symphonies) with "shouts of applause." Although his new opera *L'anima del filosofo* was completed, court intrigues prevented its being given, and it was not performed until 1951 in Florence.

At the end of the first concert season in June 1791, Salomon persuaded Haydn to stay another year. Salomon's undertaking had of course excited the jealousy of rival organizations, and the "Professional Concerts" engaged Ignaz Pleyel, Haydn's former pupil, to come to London for the 1792 season and to organize a rival concert series. But the excitement soon died down because neither Haydn nor Pleyel would stoop to disfavor the other; both series played to sold-out houses. The strain of producing so many new pieces, of a constant social life, and many fashionable pupils rather tired the aging composer, however, and it was with considerable relief that he returned to the Continent. En route to Vienna in the summer of 1792, he stopped again at Bonn, where Beethoven was introduced to him. Haydn accepted the tempestuous young man as his pupil. In a letter of 1793 to Beethoven's patron, the elector of Cologne, Haydn stated that "Beethoven [then aged 23] will one day be considered one of Europe's greatest composers, and I shall be proud to be called his teacher."

Haydn's return to Vienna was scarcely noticed in the Viennese newspapers. "I had to go to England to become famous in my own country," he often bitterly remarked. The curiously cool reception on his return in 1792 may have strengthened his decision to make a second journey to England in January 1794.

The principal compositions of the second London journey were the second set of *Salomon* Symphonies (Nos. 99–104) and the six *Apponyi* Quartets (erroneously known by two different opus numbers, each containing three works, 71 and 74). On his second London visit, Haydn reached even greater heights of inspiration, particularly in the last three symphonies (Nos. 102–104), of which No. 102, in B-flat major, is one of the greatest of all symphonies. The public no longer regarded him as a sensation but as an old and well-loved friend. George III earnestly invited him to stay in England, but Haydn—for reasons that have never been made clear—preferred to return to his native Austria to serve a new Prince Esterházy, Miklós II.

late oratorios Again his arrival in Vienna in the early autumn of 1795 was greeted with stony silence, and Haydn's success with the Viennese public was first established with the late oratorios, *The Creation* and *The Seasons.* Haydn seems to have received the text of *The Creation* from Baron Gottfried van Swieten while still in England. He began work on it in 1796, and the first performance on April 29 and 30, 1798, at the Schwarzenberg Palace in Vienna was an instantaneous success.

Haydn's duties with Prince Miklós II, an unpleasant and despotic patron with whom Haydn preserved only a conventional politeness, consisted primarily in writing a yearly mass for the name day of Princess Maria. His last six masses (1796–1802) are his greatest church works and the worthy successors to the London symphonies. They were performed in the Bergkirche at Eisenstadt, where the prince resided when he was not in Vienna.

During this period Haydn composed the six *Erdödy* Quartets known as Opus 76, most of which were completed by 1797. He also rewrote the earlier oratorio, *The Seven Words of the Saviour on the Cross* (1785), adding vocal parts, the text of which was also by van Swieten (first performed at Eisenstadt, 1797). Honors were awarded to him in succession from Holland and Sweden and from Paris and St. Petersburg. Finally Vienna conferred on him the coveted "Salvator" medal and the honorary citizenship of the city.

In 1799 Haydn began *The Seasons,* the text of which van Swieten adapted from James Thomson's poem. "Spring" was finished rapidly and was performed at the Schwarzenberg Palace on March 17, 1799; the remaining three parts were not completed until 1801. On April 24 of that year the first semiprivate performance of the complete work took place.

"*The Seasons* broke my back," Haydn is reported to have said; and indeed, apart from the last two masses of 1801 and 1802, he undertook no more large-scale works. During the last years of his life, shadowed by illness and the Napoleonic Wars, Haydn's thoughts were constantly of death; he felt himself incapable of further work, and on his 74th birthday he made the pathetic statement to his biographer, G. A. Griesinger: "Music is boundless, and that which could be done is far greater than that which has hitherto been accomplished; I often have ideas which would increase the boundaries of the art far beyond its present scope, but my physical powers are not equal to the task."

In 1809 Napoleon besieged Vienna and in May entered the city. Haydn refused to leave his house and take refuge in the inner city. Napoleon placed a guard of honor outside Haydn's house, and the enfeebled composer was much touched by the visit of a French hussars' officer who sang an aria from *The Creation.* On May 31 Haydn died peacefully and was buried two days later. "Not one single Viennese Kapellmeister was there to accompany his last journey," a contemporary report acidly notes.

achievement Haydn's creative activity spans half a century—50 years that witnessed one of the most profound stylistic revolutions in the history of music. Not only is he the first of the three great names of the Viennese Classical style—Haydn, Mozart, and Beethoven—but he also was a deciding factor in forming this style. At Haydn's death his achievement was obvious to musicians throughout Europe. But during the 19th century, as fewer and fewer of his early and middle period works were played, his importance became obscured. It was not until the middle of the 20th century that his position again became clear.

His achievement, however, is still considerably confused by the fact that an enormous number of works were wrongly attributed to him. In the 18th century publishers and professional music copyists did not hesitate to publish and circulate in manuscript under Haydn's name works by Johann Baptist Vanhal, Carlos d'Ordoñez, Leopold Hofmann, Karl Ditters von Dittersdorf, and a score of others. It was not until about 1955 that research was completed by which most of this staggering amount of spurious Haydn could be attributed to correct authors. Just how staggering the numbers are may be seen in one instance: for 107 authentic symphonies there are nearly 200 spurious. The difficulty in determining the genuine works is, moreover, complicated by the large stylistic gap that Haydn's music bridges, ranging from the outgoing Baroque to the advent of Romanticism.

Haydn's early style is rooted in the Austrian and south German Baroque, to which the Italian opera buffa added a stylistic admixture typical of Austrian music about 1750. On the one hand there is in Haydn the strongly Baroque *Missa brevis* in F and on the other fresh gaiety, as in the Viennese street serenade or the Divertimento in G for string quintet of *c.* 1754. During the 1760s Haydn began to solidify and deepen his style. The new technique of working with small motifs to tighten the fabric of the sonata form turns the first movement of sonata, quartet, and symphony into a little drama. Haydn worked simultaneously at a number of genres—church music, the symphony, the piano sonata, the divertimento (in the narrower sense; *i.e.,* music for strings, or wind instruments, or both), the string quartet, the opera, the cantata, the concerto. It is only in the last form that he never displayed much more than a passing interest.

During the Romantic crisis between 1768 and 1774 Haydn's music took on a deeper hue; the intellectualization that had steadily increased throughout the 1760s found its natural outlet. An important change in his outlook occurred in 1785. The profound music to *The Seven Words* did much to restore the emotional strength that so much of his work had lost after the outburst of the early 1770s. The *Paris* Symphonies (1785–86) are miracles of beauty and formal perfection combined with great profundity, noticeable especially in the slow movement of No. 86 in D.

The London visits injected a new force in Haydn's music, but side by side with a greatly increased nervous tension his works began to take on an emotional depth often characteristic of the music of an aging composer. Haydn began to explore new harmonic fields; *e.g.,* third-related keys, his interest in new harmonic structures being particularly apparent in the late piano trios. On his return to Vienna Haydn concentrated almost exclusively on vocal music and the string quartet. The last six masses are pillars of symphonic strength and grandeur, ranging from the brightness of the *Missa in tempore belli* to the terse drama of the *Missa in Angustiis* (*Nelson* Mass) in d minor. Here the symphonic principles brought to perfection in the *London* Symphonies are brilliantly combined with older contrapuntal forms. Solo voices are blended with vocal

quartet and choir, and there is a constant juxtaposition of the available forces. The same musical principles are employed, but in the purely orchestral passages ("Chaos" at the beginning of *The Creation*) Haydn showed his ability to discover new tonal continents.

Haydn's last instrumental works were the Quartets, Op. 76 (*Erdödy*), Op. 77 (1799), and the unfinished Opus 103. In these works the art of the quartet was brought to a new pinnacle. "I never received more pleasure from instrumental music," Charles Burney wrote to the composer about Opus 76 in August 1799. "They are full of invention, fire, good taste, and new effects, and seem the production, not of a sublime genius who has written so much and so well already, but of one of highly-cultivated talents, who had expended none of his fire before."

The full scope of Haydn's achievement only began to emerge as the result of advances in musicology in the first half of the 20th century. Gradually he was seen to be a musical giant whose one hand touches the fading Baroque—the world of Bach and Handel—and whose other hand calls to life the evergreen freshness of the young Romantic movement at the beginning of the 19th century.

BIBLIOGRAPHY: Karl Geiringer, *Haydn: A Creative Life in Music* (1946; rev. ed., with Irene Geiringer, 1963); Rosemary Hughes, *Haydn* (1950); H. C. Robbins Landon, *The Symphonies of Joseph Haydn* (1955), *The Collected Correspondence and London Notebooks of Joseph Haydn* (1959), *Haydn* (1972; with Henry Raynor), and the series *Haydn: Chronicle and Works,* Vol. 3, *Haydn in England, 1791–1795* (1976), Vol. 4, *Haydn: The Years of "The Creation," 1796–1800* (1977), and Vol. 5, *Haydn: The Late Years, 1801–1809* (1977); G. A. Griesinger, *Joseph Haydn: Eighteenth-Century Gentleman and Genius* (1963); Charles Rosen, *The Classical Style* (1971).

RECORDINGS: Numerous recordings of many works.

Hayes, Roland (June 3, 1887–December 31, 1976) Educated at Fisk University (Tennessee) and in Europe, the U.S. tenor Roland Hayes toured as a recitalist and in 1925 sang for King George of England and Queen Mother María Cristina of Spain. He sang with the principal orchestras of Europe and the United States but was known primarily as an interpreter of lieder and folk songs in many languages. Hayes was awarded the Spingarn medal (1925), and he edited *My Songs: Aframerican Religious Folksongs* (1948).

Hebrides Overture: *see* MENDELSSOHN; OVERTURE; PROGRAM MUSIC (imagery) and (program symphony).

heckelphone A woodwind instrument resembling the hautbois baryton, or baritone OBOE. It was perfected by Johann Adam Heckel in 1904 as a result of a request from Wagner about 20 years earlier for an instrument of low register combining the qualities of the oboe and the alphorn. It is an instrument of conical bore with a bent metal crook and a wooden bell. The commonest form is built in C an octave below the oboe with an extended lower register. Other forms are the smaller terzheckelphone in E-flat and the piccolo heckelphone in F. It was most effectively used by Richard Strauss in his opera *Salome.*

Heifetz, Jascha (b. February 2, 1901) Perhaps the greatest violinist of the mid-20th century, the Russian-born violinist Jascha Heifetz began his career as a child prodigy. He performed the Mendelssohn Concerto at age six and made his first European tour six years later. A student of Leopold Auer at the St. Petersburg Conservatory, he

heckelphone
L. G. Aubin—EB Inc.

fled Russia during the revolution in 1917 and the same year made his U.S. debut, becoming a U.S. citizen in 1925. He has transcribed works for violin ranging from Vivaldi to Poulenc and has commissioned much new music. Two examples are the concertos of Mario Castelnuovo-Tedesco (1933) and William Walton (1939). He teaches at the University of Southern California, where he and cellist Gregor Piatigorsky formed the nucleus of a chamber music group that performed until the latter's death in 1976.

Jascha Heifetz   *courtesy, RCA Victor*

Heiller, Anton (b. September 15, 1923) A Baroque scholar and professor at the Vienna Academy of Music since 1945, the Austrian organist, harpsichordist, and composer Anton Heiller received first prize at the International Organ Contest in Haarlem, The Netherlands, in 1952. He has composed for organ, orchestra, chorus, and piano and has recorded much of the music of Bach, as well as albums demonstrating Renaissance and Baroque ornamentation. He also conducts Baroque chamber music.

Heldenleben, Ein: *see* COUNTERPOINT (Romantic period); ROMANTIC PERIOD (20th-century transition); STRAUSS, RICHARD.

heldentenor: *see* TENOR.

Hellmesberger, (Johann) Georg (April 24, 1800–August 16, 1873)   The Austrian violinist and pedagogue Georg Hellmesberger was a fellow chorister with Schubert in the Imperial Chapel. In 1820 he entered the Vienna Conservatory, where he was appointed a professor 13 years later. Among his best known students were Leopold Auer and Joachim. He became conductor of the Imperial Opera in 1829.

hemiola   A rhythmic relationship of three to two. It occurs in Renaissance and Baroque music as a sudden change from $\frac{6}{4}$ to $\frac{3}{2}$, or vice versa, and is a characteristic of the courante in the Baroque instrumental suite. In the 19th century such composers as Chopin, Schumann, and Brahms used the device frequently.

Hendl, Walter (b. January 12, 1917)   A student of Fritz Reiner at the Curtis Institute, the U.S. conductor Walter Hendl worked with Serge Koussevitzky and in 1945 became assistant conductor of the New York Philharmonic. From 1949 to 1958 he conducted the Dallas Symphony, and from there was appointed assistant conductor of the Chicago Symphony and music director of the Ravinia (Illinois) Festival. He replaced Howard Hanson as director (1964–72) of the Eastman School of Music in Rochester, New York. He has recorded much U.S. music for the American Recording Society in Vienna.

Hendricks, Barbara (b. November 20, 1948)   The U.S. soprano Barbara Hendricks majored in chemistry and mathematics at the University of Nebraska (B.S., 1969) and then studied voice at the Juilliard School with Jennie Tourel. She was acclaimed in the first performance (1976) of David Del Tredici's *Final Alice* with the Chicago Symphony and that same season sang her Town Hall debut recital in New York City. Hendricks appeared at Salzburg (Mahler's Second Symphony) and at both Spoleto festivals (Haydn's *The Seasons*) in 1977, and she has sung with many of the major orchestras in Europe and the

United States. Operatic performances have included the title role in Janáček's *The Cunning Little Vixen* with the Santa Fe Opera (1975).

Henschel, (Isidor) George (February 18, 1850–September 10, 1934)   An English singer, conductor, and composer, George Henschel was born at Breslau. He made his first public appearance as a pianist in Berlin in 1862. Subsequently he took up singing, having developed a fine baritone voice. He studied in Leipzig and Berlin and later became friendly with Brahms. He went to England in 1877, and in 1881 he married the U.S. soprano Lillian Bailey, with whom he gave many recitals in Britain and the United States. From 1881 to 1884 he was the first conductor of the Boston Symphony. Returning to England he organized and conducted choral and orchestral concerts in London, and from 1893 to 1895 he conducted the Scottish Orchestra in Glasgow. In 1907 he married Amy Louis, also a singer. He was knighted in 1914 and continued singing and teaching until he was over 80. Among his compositions are two operas; choral works, including a *Stabat Mater* and a Requiem Mass; and songs.

Henselt, Adolf von (May 9, 1814–October 10, 1889)   One of the great 19th-century pianist who performed rarely in public (and then usually for small groups), the German-born Adolf von Henselt studied piano at Weimar with Johann Nepomuk Hummel (though with mutual dislike) and theory in Vienna with Simon Sechter. Mendelssohn stated that his specialty was "playing widespread chords, and that he went on all day stretching his fingers over arpeggios played *prestissimo*"; as a result, he had particularly strong fingers and was known for a special legato. He composed numerous studies and other piano works that required his unusual technique, but they do not fit most pianists' hands. Henselt spent most of his professional life in St. Petersburg as official court pianist.

BIBLIOGRAPHY: Wilhelm von Lenz, *The Great Piano Virtuosos of Our Time* (1971).
RECORDING: Piano Trio in a minor.

Henze, Hans Werner (b. July 1, 1926)   A leading German opera composer of his generation, Hans Werner Henze has composed operas, ballets, symphonies, and other works that are marked by an individual and advanced style.

Henze was a pupil of Wolfgang Fortner, and he later studied with René Leibowitz. His Violin Concerto (1947) demonstrates his mastery of 12-tone technique, but he never became exclusively attached to that method. His early works, up to his Second Symphony (1949), Henze considers simple, even primitive; they depend greatly upon the effectiveness of his melodies. His later works show greater independence of melody, texture, and rhythm (the ballet *Der Idiot,* 1952; the Quartet, 1955).

The opera *König Hirsch* (1956; *King Stag*) shows Henze at maturity, though he was well established in 1951, when he won the Schumann Prize for his Piano Concerto and finished his first opera, *Boulevard Solitude.* In 1950–52 Henze was ballet adviser at the Staatstheater Wiesbaden; there he received the impetus for much of his later ballet music, including *Undine* (1958), a classical work incorporating jazz elements. Henze's operas have been widely performed: *Das Wundertheater* (1949), *Der Prinz von Homburg* (1960), *Elegy for Young Lovers* (1961), *Der junge Lord* (1965), *Die Bassariden* (1966), *Das Floss der Medusa* (1972), and *Rachel, La Cubana* (1975, produced for television). In his symphonies as well as his stage works, Henze reveals himself as eclectic in his choice of styles—several may combine in a single work—and romantic in temperament. His Sixth Symphony (1970) for two chamber orchestras draws on both serialism and elements of traditional tonality and utilizes microtonal intervals, amplified instruments, and a large percussion section.

Henze's conversion to Marxism in the late 1960s had considerable influence on his later works, exemplified by two semi-stage pieces, *El Cimmarón* (1970), a "recital for four musicians" based on *The Autobiography of a Runaway Slave* as dictated to the Cuban writer Miguel Barnet; and *Natascha Ungeheuer* (1970) for one singer and 17 others (including percussion, jazz band, and tape), described by more than one critic as an exercise in radical chic. Two contrasting instrumental works were *Heliogabalus Imperator* (1972), a flamboyant piece commissioned to celebrate the 80th anniversary of the Chicago Symphony, and *Compases para Preguntas Ensimismadas* (1973), "music for viola and 22 players," a sensuous and delicate piece of chamber music. Henze's *Essays* (1964) reveal him as a highly articulate spokesman for modern music.

RECORDINGS: *Kammermusik* for tenor, guitar, and eight instruments; *Ode to the Westwind* for cello and orchestra; Piano Sonata; Variations für Klavier; Violin Concertos (2); *Die weisse Rose* for chamber orchestra.

Herbert, Victor: *see* OPERETTA; POPULAR MUSIC (the 20th century).

Herod, Play of: *see* GREENBERG.

Hérold, Louis Joseph Ferdinand (January 28, 1791–January 19, 1833)   A French composer of early Romantic operas, Louis Joseph Ferdinand Hérold was a pupil of Charles Simon Catel and Joseph Méhul, winning the Prix de Rome in 1812. His first opera *La Gioventù di Enrico V* (its overture became known under its French title, *La Jeunesse de Henri V*) was produced in 1815 at Naples, where Hérold was court pianist. On his return to Paris he collaborated with François Adrien Boieldieu in the opera *Charles de France* (1816); he produced 12 light operas at the Opéra-Comique between 1817 and 1830. In 1823 he collaborated with Daniel François Esprit Auber in *Vendôme en Espange;* it was produced at the Paris Opéra, where four of his ballets were given between 1827 and 1829, including the four-act *La Belle au bois dormant.*

Zampa (1831) and *Le Pré aux clercs* (1832) were produced at the Opéra-Comique. Though they were later to be known only by their overtures, they revealed a novel use of instrumental color derived from Weber and a subtle sense of characterization. His last opera *Ludovic* was completed by Fromental Halévy. Like Auber and Boieldieu, Hérold brought the opéra-comique to the borders of Romantic opera and anticipated in his later works the style of Berlioz. Hérold was also a prolific composer of piano and chamber music, including four piano concertos and works for unusual combinations of wind instruments.

RECORDINGS: Ballet *Fille mal gardée;* Overture to *Zampa.*

Herz, Henri (January 6, 1803–January 5, 1888) A student and later professor (1842–74) at the Paris Conservatoire, the Austrian pianist, teacher, and composer Henri Herz modeled his interpretations after the pianism of Ignaz Moscheles, with whom he played chamber music. Herz played with a brilliancy and bravura popular at the time but soon out of favor. He toured widely in Europe and the Americas and wrote *Mes Voyages en Amérique* (1866). Also a maker of pianos, he built instruments that took first prize at the Paris Exposition Universelle in 1855. He wrote more than 200 compositions for piano, including eight concertos and numerous pieces in variation form, almost none of which remains in the standard repertoire.

RECORDING: Études; Variations.

Hess, Myra (February 25, 1890–November 25, 1965) Educated at the Royal Academy of Music in London, the English pianist Myra Hess studied there with Tobias Matthay. Known especially for her playing of Bach and Mozart, she cultivated an intimate chamber music style, and it was in that manner that she also played Schumann, especially his Piano Concerto. She was created a Dame Commander of the British Empire in 1941.

Myra Hess, c. 1935   *J. R. Freeman & Co., Ltd.*

Heure espagnole, L': *see* OPERA (the 20th century); RAVEL.

hexachord A series of six diatonic notes as organized in the theory and teaching practice of the later Middle Ages and the Renaissance. In SOLMIZATION the names of the degrees of the hexachord are ut, re, mi, fa, sol, la. The essence of the hexachordal system is that each hexachord includes only one semitone that is always in the same position—between mi and fa. In the hard hexachord starting on G, mi is B and fa is C. In the natural hexachord starting on C, mi is E and fa is F. In the soft hexachord starting on F, mi is A, but fa cannot be B since that would be a tone and not a semitone above A; fa is therefore B-flat.

The pupil learned the scale by singing the hexachordal names and positions so that the location of the semitone interval mi to fa was always known. Ascending the hard hexachord to its fourth note, C fa, the first note, C ut, of the natural hexachord is found. The full name of this note is therefore C fa ut. The hexachords overlap in a system called mutation, but the best note on which to mutate depends on the context. The system had the advantage of helping the learner to keep tonal bearings; modifications of it to an octave system are still in use.

Heyward, DuBose: *see* GERSHWIN.

Hiller, Johann Adam (December 25, 1728–June 16, 1804) A German composer who played a prominent part in the development of the singspiel and the lied, Johann Adam Hiller was born at Wendisch-Ossig near Görlitz. He went to Leipzig in 1751, earning his living by playing the harpsichord and the flute, singing, and composing. He promoted public concerts in Leipzig that led to the establishment of the Gewandhaus concerts in 1781. From 1776 he was associated with the Leipzig theater. For production there he wrote a number of light German operas in the style of the future singspiel, derived from the Italian opera buffa and the French opéra comique. *Die Liebe auf dem Lande* (1768) and *Die Jagd* (1770) were among his successes in this form. Among the first to popularize Handel in Germany, Hiller conducted several of his oratorios, including *Messiah,* which he gave in Berlin in 1786. He published *Wöchentliche Nachrichten* (4 vols., 1766–70), the first German musical review concerned with current musical affairs. Other writings include books on singing and the violin, and Hiller edited numerous collections of works by his contemporaries. In 1789 he became cantor of the Thomasschule in Leipzig.

Hiller, Lejaren: *see* CAGE; COMPUTER MUSIC.

Hillis, Margaret (b. October 1, 1921)   A student of Robert Shaw, the U.S. conductor Margaret Hillis became music director of the American Concert Choir in 1950 and four years later founded the American Choral Foundation. From 1952 she was choral conductor of the American Opera Society in New York City. In 1957 she became director of the Chicago Symphony Orchestra chorus, where she prepared the chorus for the recordings of Prokofiev's *Alexander Nevsky* and of Beethoven's Ninth Symphony, and in 1969 she was appointed to the same position for the Cleveland Orchestra chorus. She was a conductor and choral director of the Santa Fe Opera in 1958–59 and has been resident conductor of the Chicago Civic Orchestra since 1967. She has taught at Union Theological Seminary in New York City (1950–60), the Juilliard School (1951–53), and Northwestern (Illinois) University (1969–77).

Hindemith, Paul (November 16, 1895–December 28, 1963)   One of the principal composers of the first half of the 20th century and a leading musical theorist, Paul Hindemith sought to revitalize tonality, the system underlying Western music for three centuries, which had begun to disintegrate. As a teacher of composition he exerted an influence on most of the composers of the generation that followed him.

Born in Germany near Frankfurt, Hindemith at first earned his living playing the violin in cafés, dance bands, and theaters. His undertaking of almost any kind of musical job may have contributed to the facility and matter-of-factness with which he later composed. Studying music in Frankfurt, at 20 he became leader of the Frankfurt Opera Orchestra.

Paul Hindemith   *Karlheinz Bauer, Bamberg*

Meanwhile his own compositions were being heard at international festivals of contemporary music. Early works included chamber music composed for the Amar-Hindemith Quartet, in which he played the viola; the song cycles *Die junge Magd* (1922) and *Das Marienleben* (1923; rev. 1948); and the opera *Cardillac* (1926). By the late 1920s Hindemith was regarded as the foremost German composer of his generation.

He wrote music for children's games, youth groups, brass bands, radio plays, and other practical purposes that was labeled Gebrauchsmusik ("utility music"), an epithet that stuck—to his irritation. He also collaborated with Kurt Weill on the music for a radio cantata by Bertolt Brecht, *Lindberghflug* (1929; "The Lindbergh Flight").

His greatest work, *Mathis der Maler,* an opera about the painter Mathias Grünewald and his struggles with society, caused a public imbroglio in Nazi Germany when Wilhelm Furtwängler conducted the symphony derived from it with the Berlin Philharmonic in 1934 and vigorously supported the opera in the press. The Nazi cultural authorities banned the opera. Furtwängler was barred briefly from conducting for his advocacy of a man denounced by Goebbels as a "cultural Bolshevist" and "spiritual non-Aryan."

Hindemith, who had been professor of composition at the Berlin Hochschule für Musik since 1927, left Germany for Turkey, where he set up a music-education system on Western lines. He taught at the Ankara Conservatory (1935–37); at Yale University (1940–53); and at the University of Zürich (1951–58).

His early music was considered anti-Romantic and iconoclastic, but it also showed humor, exuberance, and inventiveness. His *Kammermusik* series—for small, unconventional, astringent groups of instruments—is outstanding. About 1936 he began a series of sonatas for each orchestral instrument and three sonatas each for piano and for organ. He also produced concertos for violin, cello, piano, and organ; *Symphonic Metamorphoses on Themes of Carl Maria von Weber* (1944); the operas *Die Harmonie der Welt* (1957; symphonic version, 1952) and *The Long Christmas Dinner* (1960); a number of choral works; and considerable chamber music.

A vigorous opponent of the 12-tone school of Schoenberg, he formulated the principles of a harmonic system based on an enlargement of traditional tonality. He also rewrote certain of his works from the 1920s, notably *Das Marienleben,* to adjust their harmony to his later views. His *Unterweisung im Tonsatz* (1937–39; *The Craft of Musical Composition,* 1941, rev. 1945) is a theoretical statement of his principles. He also wrote *A Concentrated Course in Traditional Harmony* (2 vols., 1943, 1953) and *Elementary Training for Musicians* (1946).

BIBLIOGRAPHY: Ian Kemp, *Hindemith* (1970); Geoffrey Skelton, *Paul Hindemith: The Man Behind the Music* (1975).

RECORDINGS: Numerous recordings of many works.

hocket (Latin, *hoketus, oketus, ochetus;* Italian, *ochetto;* French, *hocquet, hoquet*)   In medieval polyphony, the device of alternating between parts single notes or groups of notes.

The result is a more or less continuous flow with one voice resting while the other voice sounds. Some scholars feel that the term is derived from the Arabic *īqā'āt* ("rhythm" or "music"). Others suggest that the word was coined in imitations of a hiccup.

The hocket was a popular device in the motet and cantilena forms of the 13th and 14th centuries. It appears rarely in the early 15th century. Although hocket technique generally is found in short passages (often at the endings of sections or phrases) within a larger composition, it is used pervasively in Guillaume de Machaut's *Hoquetus David,* in which the two upper voices are in hocket above the slower moving tenor. The form is for instruments, probably winds, and is one of the earliest instrumental forms known.

Hoffmann, E(rnst) T(heodor) A(madeus) January 24, 1776–June 25, 1822)   The German writer, composer, music critic, and caricaturist E. T. A. Hoffmann wrote tales of the supernatural and fantastic, first collected as *Die Serapionsbrüder* (4 vols., 1819–21) and *Die Lebensansichten des Katers Murr* (2 vols., 1820–22), that have been translated many times and were the inspiration of Offenbach's opera *The Tales of Hoffmann* (1881), Léo Delibes' ballet *Coppélia* (1870), and later musical works by Busoni and Hindemith (the opera *Cardillac,* 1926). Hoffmann himself wrote two operas, *Aurora* (c. 1811) and *Undine* (first performed 1816). He was a perceptive and original critic whose essays on Beethoven constitute the first valuable commentary on that master's music. He changed his name Wilhelm to Amadeus in honor of Mozart.

Hofmann, Josef (Casimir) (January 20, 1876–February 16, 1957)   One of the first of the great modern pianists (*i.e.,* with textual integrity), the Polish-born Josef Hofmann was, like most pianists destined to be great, a child prodigy. At age 11, however, he was so musically mature that he could be judged as an adult. His New York City debut was a sensation, and he was exploited (52 appearances in about 10 weeks), raising the public concern of the New York Society for the Prevention of Cruelty to Children. A patron emerged, and he was returned to Europe for study with

Josef Hofmann, with his son, Anton
courtesy, Steinway & Sons

Moritz Moszkowski and Anton Rubinstein. Resuming his public career in 1894, he lived mainly in the United States after 1898. His style was described by the critic Harold C. Schonberg as "the quintessence of aristocracy." Hofmann was director of the Curtis Institute in Philadelphia (1926–38), and he composed a symphony, five piano concertos, and a quantity of solo piano music, some of it published under the pseudonym of Michel Dvorsky. He was also the author of three books on piano playing.

Hofmannsthal, Hugo von: *see* LIBRETTO (19th-century influences); STRAUSS, RICHARD.

Holborne, Anthony (?–1602) and **William** (*c.* 1575–?) Two English brothers and composers, Anthony and William Holborne were both probably lutenists and cittern players. In 1597 Peter Short published *The Cittharn Schoole* by "Antony Holborne, Gentleman," which contained 33 peices for solo cittern (a small flat-backed, fretted instrument with plucked metal strings), 23 for cittern and bass (viol), and two for either cittern or three melody instruments. This publication also included "Sixe short Aers" by William Holborne. It is the description of these as "the first fruits of composition done by him" that has suggested the probable date of William's birth. Anthony Holborne states that he was induced to publish the airs because of the circulation of pirated versions. In 1599 appeared *Pavans, Galliards, Almains and other short Aeirs .. in five parts for Viols, Violins, or other Musicall Winde Instruments*—Anthony Holborne's most important work—consisting of 65 pieces. His music also appears in other contemporary collections: Füllsack and Hildebrand's 1607 publication (Hamburg) and Robert Dowland's *Musical Banquet* (1610) and *Varietie of Lute Lessons* (1610). The latter describes him as gentleman usher to Queen Elizabeth. He wrote commendatory verses to Thomas Morley's *Plain and Easie Introduction* (1595) and to Giles Farnaby's *Canzonets* (1598).

BIBLIOGRAPHY: Ernest Meyer, *English Chamber Music* (1946; reprint, 1970).

RECORDINGS: *Pavans, Galliards, Almains and other short Aeirs.*

Holliger, Heinz (b. May 21, 1939) Educated in his native Switzerland and at the Paris Conservatoire, oboist and composer Heinz Holliger played first oboe in the Basel Orchestra from 1959 to 1964. In 1966 he became professor of oboe at the Musikhochschule in Freiburg im Breisgau, Germany. A composition student of Pierre Boulez, he has written music for voice and instruments, *Erde und Himmel* (1961) and *Glühende Rätsel* (1964): *Der magische Tänzer* (1965) for singers, dancers, actors, choir, orchestra, and tape; *Pneuma* (1970) for 34 winds, organ, percussion, and radio; and *Cardiophonie* (1971) for one wind player. Better known as an oboist through his many recordings of music from Bach to Berio, he specializes in contemporary music and little-known 19th-century oboe concertos. Berio, Ernst Krenek, Hans Werner Henze, André Jolivet, Krzysztof Penderecki, and Stockhausen have composed for him.

Holst, Gustav (Theodore) (September 21, 1874–May 25, 1934) Combining an international flavor with a continuation of English Romanticism, the composer and teacher Gustav Holst was the son of a Swedish father and English mother. From 1893 to 1898 he studied at the Royal College of Music, where he joined Sir Charles Villiers Stanford's composition class. His solo instrument was the trombone, and for some years he made his living as a trombone player in the Carl Rosa Opera Company and in various orchestras. He became music master at St. Paul's School for girls in 1905 and director of music at Morley College in 1907, retaining both posts until the end of his life.

Holst's pioneering methods, which entailed a rediscovery of the English vocal and choral tradition (folk song, madrigals, and church music), were still influential in music education in many English schools in the mid-20th century. Many of Holst's smaller choral works, folk song arrangements, and instrumental pieces, *e.g.*, the *St. Paul's* Suite for strings (1913), reflect the musical interests he sought to promote as a teacher. In this part of his creative output he shares common ground with Vaughan Williams, his friend and contemporary. Holst's stubbornly independent, exploring mind had need, however, of a musical language less limited and more flexible than that offered by the English folk song school. He found fresh creative stimuli in the "new" European music, *e.g.*, the innovations of Stravinsky, whose impact Holst registered in his orchestral suite *The Planets* (1918), and also in Hindu literature, which gave rise to his so-called "Sanskrit" period when the opera *Savitri* and four sets of Choral Hymns from the Rig-Veda were composed in the years 1908–12. It is the cosmopolitanism of Holst's style, rare in English music of the period, that lends him a special historical significance. In works like *Egdon Heath* for orchestra (1928), the *Choral Fantasia* (1930), and the *Fugal* Concerto for flute, oboe, and strings (1923), he anticipated many of the trends associated with a later generation of English composers who were to turn away from the self-consciously national style bred by the folk song revival.

Holst's works include the operas *Sita* (composed 1899–1906), *The Perfect Fool* (1923), *At the Boar's Head* (1925), and *Tale of the Wandering Scholar* (1934); *Hymn of Jesus* (1920) and *Ode to Death* (1922) for chorus and orchestra; *Choral* Symphony (1925); Concerto for two violins (1930); and Prelude and Scherzo for orchestra (1931).

BIBLIOGRAPHY: Edmund Rubbra, *Gustav Holst* (1947); Ralph Vaughan Williams and Gustav Holst, *Heirs and Rebels* (1959); Imogen Holst, *The Music of Gustav Holst,* 2nd ed. (1968), and *Gustav Holst,* 2nd ed. (1969); Gustav Holst, *Gustav Holst: Letters to W. G. Whittaker* (1974); Michael Short, *Gustav Holst, 1874–1934: A Centenary Documentation* (1974).

RECORDINGS: *Choral Hymns* from the Rig-Veda; *Choral* Symphony; *Egdon Heath; Hammersmith,* Prelude and Scherzo; *Medieval Lyrics* (Seven Partsongs for female voices and strings); ballet music from *The Perfect Fool; The Planets; St. Paul's* Suite; *Savitri;* Suites for band (2); *Tale of the Wandering Scholar; Terzetto* for flute, oboe, and viola; songs.

Homer, Louise, before her marriage, Louise Dilworth Beatty (April 30, 1871–May 6, 1947) Educated in Boston and Paris, the U.S. soprano Louise Homer made her debut in Vichy, France, in 1898 in Donizetti's *La Favorita.* The following year she made her Covent Garden debut as Amneris in Verdi's *Aida,* the same role in which she first sang at the Metropolitan Opera (1900). Remaining there until 1918, she created the role of the witch in the first *Hänsel und Gretel* by Engelbert Humperdinck performed there and the witch in the premiere of that composer's *Die Königskinder* (1910). Other important roles were Suzuki in Puccini's *Madama Butterfly* and Dalila (Saint-Saëns) to Caruso's Samson. On leaving the Metropolitan she sang for three seasons with the Chicago Civic Opera with occasional guest appearances there until 1926. She was noted as a Wagnerian soprano in her later years and was popular as a concert artist in recitals and with orchestra. She made several early acoustic recordings, notably duets with Geraldine Farrar.

homophony A chordal style is part music, where all parts move together rather than as independent melodies as in POLYPHONY. It can also refer to music in which one part, usually the highest, predominates while the accompaniment is more or less chordal. Note-against-note writing originated in the earliest part music known as organum (9th–12th centuries) but was then displaced by contrapuntal styles. The secular frottola in Italy at the end of the 15th century led to the recultivation of homophony in 16th-century secular music, but it was not until the 17th century that homophony dominated musical style.

Honegger, Arthur (March 10, 1892–November 27, 1955) The French-born Swiss composer Arthur Honegger was closely associated with the modern movement in French music during the first half of the 20th century. Born at Le Havre, he studied at the Paris Conservatoire with André Gédalge, Charles-Marie Widor, and d'Indy. He came into prominence after World War I as a member of the group of young composers known as LES SIX, but he was bound to them more by ties of friendship than by any real aesthetic affiliation. He asserted his own strong personality in the work that was to bring him international fame, the "dramatic psalm" *Le Roi David,* first performed at Mézières, Switzerland, in 1921. This was followed by two of his best-known orchestral works, *Pacific 231* (1924), an inspired impression of a locomotive in action, and *Rugby* (1928)—both of which reflect the composer's love of speed and virile sports. He was a prolific composer and made notable contributions to opera *(Judith, Antigone, Amphion),* ballet *(Skating Rink, Sémiramis, L'Appel de la montagne),* choral and symphonic music *(Cantiques des Cantiques, La Danse des morts,* and five symphonies), chamber music (three string quartets and sonatas for violin, viola, and cello), and music for films *(La Roue, Pygmalion, Cavalcade d'amour,* to cite only a few). He also wrote a number of songs, mostly settings of works by contemporary French poets such as Jean Cocteau, Guillaume Apollinaire, and Paul Claudel. Other works are *Jeanne d'Arc au bûcher,* a stage oratorio on a text by Claudel (Basel, 1938); the early *Pastorale d'été* for chamber orchestra; and the striking Fifth Symphony *Di tre re* (composed 1951), which was almost his last work. In all his music a strong personality expresses itself in a bold and uninhibited musical idiom that, while indebted for certain harmonic audacities to the French avant-garde, was nevertheless more Germanic than Gallic in its essence.

RECORDINGS: *Christmas* Cantata; *Danse de la chèvre* for flute; *Pacific 231; Pastorale d'été;* Prelude *d'Aglavaine et Sélysette* for orchestra; *Quatre Poèmes* (songs); *Le Roi David; Rugby;* Piano Concertino; Sonatinas (for clarinet and piano; for violin and cello; for two violins); Symphonies (Nos. 2, 3, and 4).

Hook, James (probably June 3, 1746–1827) An English organist and composer, James Hook studied music in his native Norwich and performed keyboard concertos in public concerts when still a child. His father died when Hook was 11, and he then began earning his living by music. About 1763–64 he went to London, where he became organist at White Conduit House, one of the numerous tea-houses in the London area. When Samuel Arnold took over the management of Marylebone Gardens, he appointed Hook organist and composer; from there the young man went to a similar appointment at Vauxhall Gardens. It was for Vauxhall that he wrote most of his 2,000 songs as well as a number of organ concertos. He composed numerous operas—some produced at the gardens—including *The Double Disguise* (1784), for which his wife wrote the libretto. Later operas had librettos by their sons, James and Theodore. Hook was a fashionable piano teacher, and his popular textbook, the *Guida di Musica* (1785), went into many editions and was a standard work for many years. As a composer he is notable for his melodic gifts, which are best exemplified in songs such as "The Lass of Richmond Hill."

horn A class of wind instruments sounded by vibration of the player's tensed lips applied to a mouthpiece; these instruments are primarily derived from animal horns blown at the truncated narrow end, or, as among many tropical peoples, at a hole in the side. Metal construction, at first imitating natural shapes, dates as far back as the Danish Bronze Age luren, cast in the shape of mammoth tusks. From the oxhorns of medieval huntsmen and watchmen, sounding but one or two notes of

XVII   *Corno Raddoppiato*

man blowing horn
from Filippo Bonanni's Gabinetto armonico,
18th century *courtesy, Dover Publications, Inc.*

the natural harmonic series, later and modern metal horns have been developed by refining the bore profile (which remains mainly conical except at points where this is impracticable, as through valve mechanism) and bell form and such prolongation of the bore as may be desired to lower the fundamental pitch and so bring higher notes of the tube's natural series within the upper frequency limit of a player's lip vibration, thereby extending the instrument's melodic possibilities. Horns conserving the curved shape but with lengthened tube include the 18th-century BUGLE horn. An English straight-built group, derived from early 19th-century hunting horns, includes the brass post horn (sounding harmonics Nos. 2 to 5, written C G C E but sounding in the key of A-flat) and copper coach horn—both lengthened versions—and the 20th-century English hunting horn, a reduced version with one note only.

Accommodation of increased length by making one or more coils in the tube was

well known in the 16th century; small once-coiled horns have led to various continental European small hunting horns and post horns (the ancestor of the CORNET) and closed-coiled helical horns with five or more feet of tubing. The large circular French hunting horn, *trompe* (or *cor*) *de chasse,* from which the orchestral horn (*see* FRENCH HORN) is derived, appeared about 1650. It has varied in diameter and number of coils. As played in modern France and Belgium by huntsmen, horn-playing clubs, and brass bands, it is usually 15 inches (38 centimeters) across, thrice-coiled with 15 feet (4.6 meters) of tubing. It is held on the arm with one hand alone; the harmonics most used are from No. 4 to No. 12 (written as shown in the example below, but sounding in D, a seventh lower), though Nos. 2 and 3 are used for brass notes when the horns are played in harmony.

BIBLIOGRAPHY: Horace Fitzpatrick, *Horn and Horn-Playing and the Austro-Bohemian Tradition from 1680 to 1830* (1970).

Horne, Marilyn (b. January 16, 1934) After a debut in a small part in Smetana's *The Bartered Bride* in San Francisco, the U.S. contralto Marilyn Horne appeared primarily in concert performances until 1954, when she sang for Dorothy Dandridge in the film *Carmen Jones.* Two years later she went to Europe, where she sang at the Municipal Opera at Gelsenkirchen, West Germany, until 1959. In 1960 she returned to the United States for successes in Berg's *Wozzeck.* She has become known for her coloratura contralto roles in Rossini and Bellini's operas,

Natural harmonics of the French horn (also *trompe de chasse*) at their written pitch. Those marked with X are not in tune with the tempered scale and are used only exceptionally on the valved horn; Nos. 7 and 14 (both too flat) are regularly used only on the hand horn; Nos. 11 (very sharp) and 13 (too flat) are used also on the *trompe.* No. 2 is often notated in bass clef as the C below the staff. Very high harmonics in the range 17 to 24 were used by horn virtuosos of the 18th and early 19th centuries but not extensively.

which she has recorded with Joan Sutherland as the soprano. Also acclaimed is her recording of *Carmen.*

Horner, Anton (1877/78–December 4, 1971) The Austrian-born horn player Anton Horner emigrated to the United States in 1885, returning to Europe to attend the Leipzig Conservatory (1891–94). He played in the Pittsburgh Symphony (1899–1902) under Victor Herbert, toured Europe with John Philip Sousa's band in 1900, and joined the Philadelphia Orchestra as principal horn (1902–30) in its second season, remaining in the section until his retirement in 1946. Horner taught at the Curtis Institute (1924–42), training a whole generation of symphony horn players.

hornpipe A Renaissance dance believed to have been performed to the rustic instrument of that name. At times it meant a jig, a reel, or a country dance. As an Irish, Scottish, or English solo dance, the hornpipe is in $\frac{4}{4}$ time and is related to the jig and the solo reel. It has intricate steps and often imitates a sailor's dance. Hornpipes are often danced with clogs, especially in northern England.

In the suite the hornpipe is a stylized version of a country dance in $\frac{3}{2}$ time. A well-known example occurs in Handel's *Water Music Suite.*

The instrument is a single-reed pipe with a cowhorn bell (sometimes two parallel pipes with a common bell) and is often converted into a bagpipe. Known since antiquity, it is today played in Spain and North Africa, east to Arabia and parts of Russia.

Horowitz, Vladimir (b. October 1, 1904) Celebrated for his flawless technique and the almost orchestral quality of his tone, the pianist Vladimir Horowitz was educated in his native Kiev, studying piano with Felix Blumenfeld. He preferred composition, but family misfortune caused by the Russian Revolution forced him to the piano. His reputation was assured when at age 20 he played about 25 recitals in Leningrad, performing more than 200 works and never duplicating a piece. He married Arturo Toscanini's daughter Wanda in 1933 and settled in the United States in 1940. Although he continued to record, Ho-

Vladimir Horowitz
courtesy, Shaw Concerts, Inc.
photograph, Christian Steiner

rowitz withdrew from the recital stage in 1953; his return in 1965 was a major musical event. A gala performance of Rachmaninoff's Third Piano Concerto with the New York Philharmonic in Carnegie Hall in January 1978 marked the 50th anniversary of his U.S. debut—Horowitz' first public performance with an orchestra in 25 years. He is known for his powerful performances of Liszt, Rachmaninoff, and Prokofiev, but his interpretations of keyboard miniatures, such as those by Domenico Scarlatti and Schumann, are noted for their delicacy and simplicity.

Hotter, Hans (b. January 19, 1909) Educated in Munich, the German baritone Hans Hotter made his debut in 1930 and sang at the German Theater in Prague (1932–34) and at the Hamburg State Opera (1934–37). In the latter year he joined the Munich State Opera, where he appeared in the premieres of Richard Strauss's *Friedenstag* (1938) and *Capriccio* (1942). His greatest successes came at the Metropolitan Opera (debut in Wagner's *Der fliegende Hollander,* 1950) and at Bayreuth (1952). He is at home in opera and

393

lieder; best-known recordings include Schubert's *Winterreise* and the Wagnerian roles of Wotan *(Der Ring des Nibelungen)* and the Dutchman.

Hotteterre, Jacques (-Martin) (*c.* 1684–*c.* 1761)   A member of an illustrious family of wind players and instrument makers, the French flutist Jacques Hotteterre (called "le Romain" after an extended stay in Italy) was also known as a composer and teacher. His playing of the then-new German transverse flute was so impressive that it contributed to the decline of the recorder *(flûte-à-bec)* in France. He played bass oboe and violoncello in the Grande Écurie ensemble in Paris and composed for flute and musette. He published extensive teaching methods, although his authorship of the long-influential *Traité de flûte* (1707) is now disputed.

RECORDINGS: *Pièces pour la flute traversière;* Sonata in D Major; Suite for flute and continuo.

Hovhaness, Alan (b. March 8, 1911)   A prolific U.S. composer of Armenian and Scottish descent, Alan Hovhaness is notable for his eclectic choice of material from non-European traditions. Hovhaness studied piano and composition at the New England Conservatory and later with the noted Czech composer Bohuslav Martinů at Tanglewood, Massachusetts. He taught at the Boston Conservatory (1948–51) and traveled and composed extensively. At age 30 he became interested in Armenian music, an interest that later broadened to include music of the Near and Far East. He toured Europe and Asia in the early 1960s as conductor and pianist, and in India he studied with native musicians. Hovhaness' music draws on many exotic rhythmic, melodic, and instrumental resources, as is indicated by the descriptive titles he favors.

RECORDINGS: *Fantasy on Japanese Woodprints* for xylophone and orchestra; *Floating World* and *Fra Angelico* for orchestra; *Khaldis* for piano, 4 trumpets, and percussion; *Koke no niwa* for English horn, harp, and percussion; *Lady of Light;* Magnificat; *Mysterious Mountain; Requiem and Resurrection* for brass and percussion; Symphonies (4, 6, 9, 11, 19,

21, 23, 24, 25); songs; choral works; chamber music.

Hubay, Jenö (September 15, 1858–March 12, 1937)   The Hungarian violinist Jenö Hubay studied first with Joachim and then with Henri Vieuxtemps, whom he was to succeed in 1882 as professor at the Brussels Conservatory. In 1886 he succeeded his father as professor at the Budapest Conservatory, later becoming its director. His best-known student was Joseph Szigeti. In addition to music for the violin, he wrote six operas and four symphonies.

RECORDINGS: *Hejre Kati* for violin and orchestra; Violin Concerto in g minor.

Hucbald (*c.* 840–*c.* 930)   Mention of the scholar and humanist Hucbald is found at Nevers, St. Amand (near Valenciennes), St. Omer, Reims, and again at St. Amand, where he died. A pupil of his uncle, the scholar Milo of St. Amand, he became magister scholarum and later an abbot and appears to have spent his life teaching. He is the author of the treatise *De harmonica institutione,* which describes the gamut and the eight modes. He was also the author of a number of poems, metrical prayers for the offices, and hymns.

His homonym, known as Pseudo Hucbald, lived somewhat later. J. Smits van Waesberghe identifies him with Count Otger of Laon, a lay abbot of St. Amand. Almost no information is available concerning his activities, but his theoretical works are of great importance. These include *Musica enchiriadis* (more correctly *Enchirias de musica*), *Scholia enchiriadis,* and *De alia musica,* a treatise dealing with a notational system known as daseian notation. Pseudo Hucbald was the first theorist to describe the theory of parallel organum, put forward not as a new theory, however, but as based on ancient writings that unfortunately have not survived.

Hugh the Drover: *see* BALLAD OPERA; OPERA (the 19th century); VAUGHAN WILLIAMS.

Huguenots, Les: *see* MEYERBEER.

Humfrey, Pelham (1647–July 14, 1674)   The English composer and lutenist Pelham Humfrey became one of the first choristers of the restored Chapel Royal under Captain Henry Cooke in 1660 and when still a boy showed his skill in composition. At the age of 17 he was sent by Charles II to Italy and France to continue his studies and, while abroad, was appointed royal lutenist and gentleman of the chapel. On his return to England in 1667, he received further court appointments and succeeded Cooke as master of the children, one of his pupils being the young Purcell. He also became Composer in Ordinary for the Violins to His Majesty and had many sacred and secular works performed at court. He died at Windsor and was buried in Westminster Abbey. Humfrey produced many fine works, principally anthems. He wrote odes for the king's birthday and some theater music, including songs for plays by William Wycherley and John Dryden and incidental music for *The Tempest.* Many of his songs appear in the numerous collections published by John Playford.

Hummel, Johann Nepomuk (November 14, 1778–October 17, 1837)   A pupil of Mozart, Clementi, Johann Georg Albrechtsberger, Antonio Salieri, and Haydn, the Hungarian pianist, composer, and conductor Johann Nepomuk Hummel was also the teacher of Czerny, Adolf von Henselt, Sigismond Thalberg, and Ferdinand Hiller. He was perhaps the greatest improviser of his day, his only rival being his fellow student Beethoven. His influence as a composer is evident in the early works of Chopin and Schumann; his piano method was the major influence in the field during the first half of the 19th century.

One of the last of the Classical pianists, Hummel played and conducted throughout Europe. His official appointments consisted of positions as Kapellmeister for the Esterházy family (1804–11, succeeding Haydn) and at Stuttgart (1816–19) and Weimar (1819–37). His works totaled 124 opus numbers, including nine operas, three masses, ballets, concertos, numerous piano pieces, and chamber music; they were popular during his lifetime but fell into oblivion at his death. Hummel's concertos, piano pieces, and chamber music have been much revived in the 20th century.

RECORDINGS: Concertos (bassoon, mandolin, four for piano, piano and violin, trumpet); Études (24) for piano; Fantasy in g minor for viola, two clarinets, and strings; Piano Trios (2); Quintet; Septets (2); Sonatas (for flute, mandolin, and piano); Trios.

humoresque (German spelling, *Humoreske*) A 19th-century character piece, usually for the piano, expressing a good-humored mood or vague nonmusical idea. Among the best known are Dvořák's Opus 101, No. 7, and Schumann's Opus 20, which atypically is a long sectional piece with contrasting moods. Schumann's Opus 88, No. 2, is a humoresque for violin, cello, and piano.

Humperdinck, Engelbert (September 1, 1854–September 27, 1921)   A German composer known for his children's opera *Hänsel und Gretel,* Engelbert Humperdinck studied with Ferdinand Hiller at Cologne and Franz Lachner and Joseph Rheinberger at Munich. In 1879 a Mendelssohn scholarship enabled him to go to Italy; there he met Wagner, who invited him to assist in the production of *Parsifal* at Bayreuth. He taught at the Barcelona Conservatory (1885–87) and at Frankfurt (1890–96), where he was also music critic of the *Frankfurter Zeitung.* Early works were the choral ballads *Die Wallfahrt nach Kevelaar* (1878), *Das Glück von Edenhall* (1879), and the *Humoreske* (1880) for orchestra. *Hänsel und Gretel,* conducted by Richard Strauss, was produced at Weimar in 1893. The libretto, by the composer's sister Adelheid Wette, was based on the folk tale made familiar by the brothers Grimm. Between 1895 and 1919 Humperdinck produced six further operas, including *Dornröschen* (Frankfurt, 1902) and *Königskinder* (New York City, 1910), but none of them, nor the pantomime *The Miracle* (London, 1911), achieved much success. He also wrote incidental music for plays by Aristophanes, Shakespeare, and Maeterlinck, a *Moorish Rhapsody* for orchestra (1898), a quartet, piano works, and songs.

RECORDINGS: *Hänsel und Gretel.*

Hungarian Rhapsodies: *see* LISZT.

hurdy-gurdy A medieval stringed instrument, a kind of squat fiddle with the strings sounded by the rosined rim of a wooden wheel turned by a handle. The tunes are made on one string, or on a pair of strings, stopped

woman playing hurdy-gurdy
from Filippo Bonanni's Gabinetto armonico,
18th century *courtesy, Dover Publications, Inc.*

by means of short wooden jacks pressed sideways against the string or strings *(i.e.,* from below as the hurdy-gurdy hangs from its carrying sling) by the fingers of the left hand. Further strings, up to four in number, are not stopped and sound a drone. Described as *organistrum,* the instrument is first mentioned in the 10th century by Bishop Odo of Cluny. It was then a church instrument for two—one turning, the other fingering.

During the 13th century single-player forms called symphonia appeared and were used in secular music. These remained in use sporadically until the middle of the 20th century, played either by folk musicians or by beggars, notably in central France, where the *vièlle à roue* (wheel fiddle) was perpetuated by the pastoral fashions cultivated during the reign of Louis XIV. The Swedish *nyckel-harpa* has similar stopping mechanism but is played with a bow. Because of the hurdy-gurdy's handle-operated wheel and its association with street musicians, the term is sometimes mistakenly applied to mechanical instruments such as the barrel organ.

hymn A song of praise to God from the Greek *hymnos,* which signified a song composed in honor of gods, heroes, or famous men. All civilizations have examples of songs (associated in some with dances) composed for religious or panegyric purposes. The word hymn can still be used in this sense, but usually its use presupposes a Christian association.

In Christian use the form, though not the name, has Hebrew origins, which are to be found chiefly in the Old Testament Psalms. In the worship of the synagogue the exalted public style of many of the Psalms suggested at once to primitive Christians a style in which new songs of praise might be composed. Where St. Paul exhorts Christians to edify one another with "psalms and hymns and spiritual songs," it is at least possible that he had in mind not only the psalms but new hymns, especially when the prophetic and even ecstatic content of the word spiritual in the Old and New Testaments is remembered. The earliest Christian hymn text that has survived in full is the *Phos hilaron* ("O gladsome light"), a hymn used at a lamplighting ceremony, which dates from *c.* A.D. 200 or earlier. But it was the post-Constantinian church that began the systematic development of hymnody. For Greek hymnody *see* BYZANTINE CHANT.

Latin hymnody In the West the earliest hymn writer was probably Hilary of Poitiers, who composed *c.* 360 a book of lyrics. Not much later Bishop Ambrose of Milan instituted the singing of "hymns and psalms after the manner of the Eastern churches, to keep the people from being altogether worn out with anxiety and want of sleep." St. Ambrose has been credited with a number of hymns, but only three can be ascribed to him with certainty: *Deus creator omnium, Aeterne rerum conditor,* and *Iam surgit hora tertia.* Hymn singing seems from the foregoing quotation to have been taken over from the Eastern churches; the form of these hymns (iambic octosyllables in four-line stanzas—in English usage known as Long Meter) was influenced by Christian Latin poetry of the period; their content is ascetic, trinitarian, and associated with the night.

In imitation of Ambrose's technique a considerable corpus of Latin hymnody developed. Much of it was inspired by the liturgical reforms of Pope Gregory I. The hymns in this group (dated roughly 500–1000) are either in Long Meter or Sapphic Meter (11. 11. 11. 5), but Christian Latin poets such as Prudentius and Venantius Fortunatus experimented with other lyric meters, especially the six-line trochaic verse, 87. 87. 87.

medieval hymns The next important development in hymnody was the invention of the sequence. Notker Balbulus (d. 912), a monk of St. Gall, composed a prose that was designed to fill the pause between the alleluia and the Gospel in the mass, making use of the extended musical phrase that had become customary to sing to the alleluia's final syllable. This composition is preserved in translation as "The strain upraise." Inspired by this example later authors wrote sequences for the Christian seasons, of which the best known is *Victimae Paschali,* written before 1100. A natural development was the writing of sequences in meter, and this led to the composition of some of the most exquisite of all Christian lyrics, notably *Veni Sancte Spiritus,* probably by Stephen Langton (d. 1228), and *Dies irae* by Thomas of Celano (d. *c.* 1260). St. Thomas Aquinas composed a few hymns especially for the office of Corpus Christi, of which the best known are *Pange lingua gloriosi corporis mysterium* in imitation of Fortunatus' *Pange lingua gloriosi lauream certaminis* and *Verbum supernum prodiens,* imitating an Ambrosian hymn beginning with the same words.

Medieval devotional Latin hymnody has produced through translation a number of well-known English hymns. *Dulcis Jesu memoria,* an anonymous poem probably by a Cistercian monk *c.* 1200, has given us "Jesu, the very thought of thee"; and the monumental poem *Hora novissima* by Bernard of Cluny, in 2,966 lines of invariable dactylic hexameter, has provided among other selections "Jerusalem the golden." The solemn and epigrammatic *Veni Creator Spiritus* (uncertainly ascribed to Rabanus Maurus; d. 856) is an early example of extraliturgical Latin hymnody.

Somewhere between the liturgical and the devotional groups come *Gloria, laus et honor* by Theodulf of Orléans (750–821), a carollike hymn in elegiacs translated by John Mason Neale as "All Glory, Laud and Honour," and Peter Abelard's *O quanta qualia,* written for use at the abbey of which Héloise was prioress.

The Te Deum, the most universally used of all Latin hymns, is beyond doubt a hymn but in both provenance and form mysterious. The story that it was antiphonally improvised by St. Ambrose and St. Augustine at Augustine's baptism is without doubt legend. It has been plausibly ascribed to Niceta, Bishop of Remesiana (d. *c.* 414). But it reads like a mosaic of traditional credal utterances, and its curious form suggests a historic origin (in its present form) some time between 318 and *c.* 350. The music with which these various forms of hymnody were associated is discussed in the article PLAINCHANT.

German Reformation Medieval hymnody was not congregational; congregational singing associated with the central acts of worship was established only with the Reformation. Before then popular praise took the form of the CAROL rather than the hymn.

Martin Luther's conception of hymnody was considerably influenced by the form of contemporary popular and secular song. In the chorale "Ein feste Burg," for instance, a repeated initial phrase is followed by development material and a final short phrase recapitulating the first, a pattern often found in the music of late medieval court musicians.

German hymnody has had a continuous history from the publication of the *Encheiridion* (1524), edited by Luther and Johann Walther, but its classical period runs from 1524 to the death (1676) of Paul Gerhardt. The chief authors (who were sometimes composers as well) apart from Luther himself are Michael Weisse of the Bohemian Brethren, Justus Jonas, Paul Eber, and Philipp Nicolai in the 16th century; and in the 17th Matthäus Apelles von Löwenstern, Martin Rinkart (author of the original of "Now thank we all our God"), and Gerhardt himself.

The three last mentioned are authors characteristic of the period of the Thirty Years' War, which produced much noble hymnody.

Gerhardt was the greatest of them all both in output and in quality. His best-known hymn is "Befiehl du deine Wege" (translated by John Wesley as "Commit thou all thy griefs"). Gerhardt's period of activity corresponded with that of Johann Crüger (*see* CHORALE), and together they brought German hymnody to the highest point reached since its inception— a height to which it has not risen again.

later German hymnody Pietism brought a new lyrical and subjective note into German hymnody. The hymns of Johann Scheffler (Angelus Silesius) and the tunes of G. Joseph (flourished 1657) are good early examples. Johann Georg Ebeling (1637–76) and C. Peter (1626–69) wrote music of a high standard, and some strong hymns came from Joachim Neander (1651–81), notably the hymn translated as "Praise to the Lord, the Almighty."

After the turn of the 18th century, the best work in German hymnody was in the devotional rather than the congregational context. The Enlightenment brought much doctrinal skepticism but also some fresh hymn writing in the work of Matthias Claudius and Carl Johann Philipp Spitta. In music a devotional style that was perhaps first seen in the psalm tunes of Heinrich Schütz was developed among pietist composers, and the finest examples of this are to be found in the works of Johann Freylinghausen and Bach.

In the 19th century the writing of new hymns came almost to a halt, and in music more work was done by editors than by composers. The previous output and high quality of hymnody discouraged the later writing of hymns in Germany and set a higher standard than later authors and composers found themselves able to reach.

Genevan psalmody It was during his brief ministry in Strasbourg (1538–41) that John Calvin caused his first metrical and musical psalter to be collected. This was a small volume, published in 1539, containing 19 psalms and two other pieces; the music, austerely set for unison singing, was edited by M. Greiter. On moving to Geneva (1541) Calvin engaged the services of Loys Bourgeois as musical editor, and in successive editions between 1542 and 1551 Bourgeois composed or adapted settings for 83 of the 150 psalms, the words of

which were partly based on the psalms of Clément Marot and partly written by other poets. Unison singing without accompaniment remained the Genevan rule, but Bourgeois published an edition in five-part harmony at Lyons in 1549. After the resignation of Bourgeois the work was completed by several successors, the most eminent of whom was Claude Goudimel (d. 1572). The final psalter—with 150 psalms, 125 tunes, and 110 different meters—was published in 1562.

Meanwhile certain English and Scottish exiles who had taken refuge at Geneva during the reign of Queen Mary (1553–58) were impressed by the Genevan style and sought to adapt Genevan tunes or compose new tunes in the same style for English metrical psalms. Thus were published three Anglo-Genevan psalters in 1556, 1558, and 1561, which brought the Genevan tunes (often severely modified to suit English ballad meter) to England and Scotland. *See also* PSALMODY.

English psalmody The English psalters proved a dynamic source of new music, and during the period 1558–1677 many editions of the English psalter were published, of which musically the most significant were those of Thomas Este (1592) and Thomas Ravenscroft (1621), and in Scotland those of Andro Hart (1615) and Edward Miller (1635). It soon became clear that the complexity of most of the Genevan tunes, written for French meters, exacted too much of British congregations, and so the custom of singing each psalm to its proper tune was soon dropped: in most places a few tunes were used for the whole psalter. The English psalter used only a few meters, and it was easy for a group of common tunes to gain favor at the expense of the Genevan tunes. Moreover, although the English adaptation of Genevan tunes normally formed itself in four 14-syllable lines, the common tune was content with two such lines, and thus Common Meter (8. 6. 8. 6), still the archetypal English meter for hymns, came into currency. The use of common tunes also made it necessary to identify hymn tunes not by the number of their psalm (as "Old 100th" or "Old 124th") but by names. This practice was first systematically used by Thomas Ravenscroft.

Alongside the official psalter many private

versions were published. A few of these are of special musical importance, such as that of Matthew Parker for which Tallis composed eight tunes, and that of William Sandys for which several tunes were composed by Henry Lawes. Hymns as such were not yet composed (apart from metrical versions of the commandments, the Gospel canticles, and the Lord's Prayer, which were authorized with the psalter), but George Wither composed two books of lyrics and hymns, *Hymns and Songs of the Church* (1623) and *The Hallelujah* (1641), the first of which involved him in legal proceedings. It was distinguished by its accompanying tunes, which were the work of Gibbons.

new English hymnody It was Isaac Watts who in 1707 began the fashion of modern hymnody by publishing the first edition of his *Hymns and Spiritual Songs*. In four books (1705–19) Watts published about 750 hymns and psalm versions. Although he was capable of startling bathos, he established himself as the "father of English hymnody." Examples are "When I survey the wondrous Cross," "There is a land of pure delight," "Our God, our help in ages past," and "Jesus shall reign." Watts was an Independent (or Congregationalist), and he was followed in the same communion by Philip Doddridge, a lesser but still important author most famous for the original of "O God of Bethel." The evangelical revival under John and Charles Wesley finally established hymnody on the English scene. Charles Wesley's 9,000 lyrics use many experimental meters, and John Wesley's translations fertilized the field by introducing many of the finest German hymns to Englishmen. This sudden expansion of hymnody brought with it new musical styles. The Wesleys imported many German tunes, and their later editions contain much music in a post-Handelian style. Later editions of Watts produced music in a post-Purcellian style, which under Jeremiah Clarke and William Croft had distinguished the early music editions of the "New Version" (1696) of the metrical psalter.

The development of hymnody throughout the 18th century was thus a phenomenon of the dissenting and evangelical churches in England. Scotland stood aloof, remaining loyal to the psalter of 1650. The only Scottish concession was in the *Paraphrases* (1745, 1781); among these were versions of a number of New Testament passages that were largely drawn from the work of Watts and Doddridge.

Anglican hymnody The Church of England (of which the Wesleys regarded themselves as nondissenting priests to the end of their lives) regarded hymnody as technically illegal, for the rubrics did not provide for the introduction of hymns into the services appointed in the Book of Common Prayer. In 1820 a controversy at Sheffield, where the vicar of St. Paul's Church had been using hymns and had published a hymnbook for use in his church, led to a reexamination of the church's law, and consequently hymnody was declared legitimate. One of the central figures in this controversy was James Montgomery, a layman of Scottish descent who ranks as the greatest nonclerical hymnwriter before Robert Bridges. Among his famous hymns are "Hail to the Lord's Anointed," "Songs of praise the angels sang," and "For ever with the Lord." His only 18th-century competitor for that title is William Cowper, who with John Newton wrote the *Olney Hymns* (1779). This was a parish hymnbook typical of those produced by Anglican evangelicals but famous as the source of many well-known hymns, such as "God moves in a mysterious way" and "How sweet the name of Jesus sounds."

The legalization of hymnody in the Church of England came close to the beginning (1833) of the Oxford Movement. Between the two dates, however, stand two important collections: *Hymns, Adapted to the Weekly Church Service of the Year* (1827), edited by Bishop Reginald Heber, and *The Christian Year* (1827) by John Keble. Heber's book can be called the first hymnary of the Church of England. Most of it was of his own composition, and it is the source of "Holy, Holy, Holy," among many other well-known hymns. It also printed for the first time one of the greatest of 19th-century hymns, Dean Milman's "Ride on, ride on in majesty." Keble's book was not a hymnbook but a book of poems, many of which have been made into hymns, such as "New every morning."

The Oxford Movement introduced a new

interest in hymns in relation to the liturgy, a host of hymn writers who wrote hymns suitable for use with the Book of Common Prayer, many hymns for liturgical seasons and holy days, and research into and revival of medieval hymns in translation. The most eminent hymn writers of the Oxford Movement were Bishops Christopher Wordsworth, author of "Gracious Spirit, Holy Ghost," and W. W. How (1823–97), who wrote "For all the Saints." Of translators the most prolific was John Mason Neale. John Henry Newman's "Praise to the Holiest" was not written as a hymn, but after its appearance (1868) in the hymnbook became one of the most famous of the Oxford Movement's hymns.

Hymns Ancient and Modern   The publication in 1861 of *Hymns Ancient and Modern* marked the beginning of the modern era of hymnody. It was distinguished by its austerity of style, its close conformity to the Prayer Book, and its setting of each of its 273 hymns to its own tune. It so combined authority and practicality that it became and has remained the most widely used hymnary in English. Its first presiding musician was William Henry Monk, and among the composers whom it brought to prominence were John Dykes and John Stainer. Since 1558 English hymnody had been strangely insular, but at about that time, with the widening of musical culture, many German chorales were introduced although often in an anglicized form. Catherine Winkworth (1827–78) was the leader of a school of translators who sought to translate German hymns in their original meters; "Now thank we all our God" is the most famous of the many translations she made.

new standards   It was Robert Bridges, however, who in his *Yattendon Hymnal* (1899) showed to what literary heights the translator and hymnographer might aspire. In the 19th century the great demand for new hymns and easier music publishing had sadly inflated the repertoire with hymns of little value, both in words and music. Bridges was a truculent and outspoken enemy of this tendency, and the minor cultural revolution he began was communicated through the work of Percy Dearmer and Vaughan Williams in their joint editorship of the *English Hymnal* (1906).

Where *Hymns Ancient and Modern* had resisted the overdemonstrative tendencies of evangelical hymnody, the *English Hymnal* in its turn resisted the use of an overyielding musical idiom. The *English Hymnal* introduced several folk tunes to hymnody, such as "King's Lynn," and some strong new tunes, one that has become especially popular, "Sine Nomine." A number of hymn tunes based on Welsh folk music were also included, such as "Aberystwyth" and "Bryn Calfaria." The advance in musical and literary taste to which the *English Hymnal* committed English congregations was taken to succeeding stages by *Songs of Praise* (1926, 1931) and *The BBC Hymn Book* (1951). The former was greatly influenced by the work of the composer Martin Shaw.

United States   Colonists coming to America brought their hymn traditions with them, the Moravians and the Mennonites in Pennsylvania singing in German and the English settlers singing their English hymns. The first significant U.S. contribution was the shapenote hymnal incorporating many folk hymns and utilizing a special musical notation. The hymns were normally in three- or four-part harmonizations. Traditional rules of European harmony were consistently disregarded, giving rise to a spare, vigorous style. Important hymnals were John Wyeth's *Repository of Sacred Music, Part Second* (1813), Ananias Davisson's *Kentucky Harmony* (1816), William Walker's *Southern Harmony* (1835), and Benjamin Franklin White's and E. J. King's *Sacred Harp* (1844), with the popular "Wondrous Love" and "Amazing Grace."

A special contribution from the United States has been the gospel hymn, especially associated with the names of the evangelist Dwight L. Moody and the composer Ira D. Sankey. In the hands of Sankey the gospel hymn was a simple, repetitive hymn of evangelical emphasis set to a naive carollike tune (the best example is "There were ninety-and-nine in the wilderness"). The form became fatally easy to imitate and debase; it can be seen at its best and worst in *Sacred Songs and Solos*. Its use in England can be dated from 1872, the year of Sankey's and Moody's first English evangelical crusade.

mid-20th century With folk and popular music coming into churches in the 1950s, an entirely new aspect of hymnody was introduced. Though texts often remained the same, hymn tunes came from many idioms, and accompanying instruments also changed radically. The guitar, both alone and in rhythm bands, became the most popular.

After Vatican II the Roman Catholic Church found itself in need of a new hymnody, its vast storehouse of Latin hymns almost unknown to its people. Lacking the long tradition of congregational hymn singing, it adopted the new folk/popular style more rapidly even than Protestantism; the "folk mass" became a standard parish occurrence. It also, however, made use of many standard hymns from other traditions. *See also* CHURCH MUSIC.

BIBLIOGRAPHY: John Julian, *A Dictionary of Hymnology* (1892; rev. ed., 1977); Ira D. Sankey, *My Life and the Story of the Gospel Hymns and of Sacred Songs and Solos* (1907; reprint, 1974); Waldo S. Pratt, *The Music of the French Psalter* (1939); Henry W. Foote, *Three Centuries of American Hymnody* (1940; reprint, 1968); Maurice Frost, *English and Scottish Psalm and Hymn Tunes c. 1543–1677* (1953) and *Historical Companion to Hymns Ancient and Modern,* rev. ed. (1962); Erik Routley, *The Music of Christian Hymnody* (1957); Arthur Pollard, *English Hymns* (1962).

Hypoaeolian mode The second of the four additions by the 16th-century Swiss theorist Henricus Glareanus to the eight medieval church modes. Its general range comprises the eight natural notes from the E below middle C to the E above. Melodies in Hypoaeolian, or Mode X, have A as the *finalis,* or final note, and C as the *tenor,* or reciting note.

Hypodorian mode The second of the eight medieval church modes. Its general range comprises the eight natural notes from the second to the first A below middle C. Melodies in Hypodorian, or Mode II, usually have D as the *finalis,* or final note, and F as the *tenor,* or reciting note.

In ancient Greek music Hypodorian was one of several names for the scale pattern, or octave species, conventionally represented in modern writings as A-A.

Hypolydian mode The sixth of the eight medieval church modes. Its general range comprises the eight natural notes from the C below middle C to middle C. Melodies in Hypolydian, or Mode VI, usually have F as the *finalis,* or final note, and A as the *tenor,* or reciting note.

In ancient Greek music Hypolydian referred to the scale pattern, or octave species, conventionally represented in modern writings as F-F.

Hypomixolydian mode The last of the eight medieval church modes. Its general range comprises the eight natural notes from the D below middle C to the D above. Melodies in Hypomixolydian, or Mode VIII, usually have G as the *finalis,* or final note, and C as the *tenor,* or reciting note.

Hypophrygian mode The fourth of the eight medieval church modes. Its general range comprises the eight natural notes from the second to the first B below middle C. Melodies in Hypophrygian, or Mode IV, usually have E as the *finalis,* or final note, and A as the *tenor,* or reciting note.

In ancient Greek music Hypophrygian was one of several names for the scale pattern, or octave species, conventionally represented in modern writing as G-G.

I

Iberia: *see* ALBÉNIZ.

Ibert, Jacques (François Antoine) (August 15, 1890–February 5, 1962) The French composer Jacques Ibert was known for his wit and humor and on his more serious side a neo-Impressionism and colorful orchestration. He was a pupil of Fauré and Paul Vidal at the Paris Conservatoire and won the Prix de Rome in 1919. Ibert was director of the French Academy in Rome (1937–55) and of the combined management of the Paris Opéra and Opéra-Comique (1955–57). Among his best-known orchestral works are *La Ballade de la geôle de Reading* (1922), based on Oscar

Wilde's poem, *Escales* (1924), and Divertissement (1930), the latter based on his score for René Clair's film, *The Italian Straw Hat* (1927). He wrote seven operas (two with Honegger), five ballets, radio and film music, chamber music (including a number of pieces featuring flute and harp), solo voice and choral works, and concertos for cello, saxophone (Concertino *da Camera*), flute, and oboe (*Symphonie concertante*).

RECORDINGS: *Bacchanale; La Ballade de la geôle de Reading;* Concertino *da Camera; Deux Interludes* for flute, violin, and harp; Divertissement; *Escales;* Flute Concerto; *Jeux* for flute and piano; *Pièce* for unaccompanied flute; *Ouverture de fête; Trois pièces brèves* for woodwinds.

Ice Break, The: *see* OPERA (the 20th century); TIPPETT.

idiophone A class of instruments in which a resonant solid material, such as wood, metal, or stone, vibrates to produce the initial sound. In many cases, as in the gong, the vibrating material itself forms the instrument's body. Other examples include xylophones and rattles. Idiophone and membranophone (membrane instruments; *e.g.,* drums) replace the looser term percussion instruments when a precise, acoustically based classification is required. *Compare* AEROPHONE; CHORDOPHONE; ELECTROPHONE; MEMBRANOPHONE.

Idomeneo: *see* CLASSICAL PERIOD (vocal music, 1750–1800); MOZART (early life); OPERA (the 19th century).

Illica, Luigi: *see* PUCCINI.

Images: *see* DEBUSSY.

Imbrie, Andrew W(elsh) (b. April 6, 1921) A composer of symphonies and chamber music, U.S.-born Andrew W. Imbrie studied with Boulanger and with Roger Sessions. From the latter he developed his principle of contextualism, whereby the problems of composition are solved by their contexts rather than by predetermined or abstract properties. In Imbrie's music harmony arises from the counterpoint in a linear idiom. He has written four quartets, three symphonies, operas, including *Christmas in Peebles Town* (1960) and *Angle of Repose*

(1976), *Legend* for orchestra (1959), sonatas for piano (1947) and for cello (1966), and Flute Concerto (1977). He won the New York Music Critics' Award in 1944 and the Prix de Rome three years later. He has taught at the University of California at Berkeley since 1947.

RECORDINGS: Cello Sonata; Impromptu for violin and piano; Quartets Nos. 2 and 3; Serenade for flute, viola, and piano; Symphony No. 3; Violin Concerto.

Impressionism Borrowed from painting, the word impressionism was principally applied as a musical term to the music of Debussy and later adopted to describe music of French associations of the post-Wagnerian period. An early use occurred in a letter of Renoir in 1882 in which, referring to a conversation with Wagner, he wrote "We spoke of the Impressionists of music." In 1887 the *Journal Officiel* criticized the "vague impressionism" of Debussy's *Printemps.* The term was used in a laudatory sense by Belgian critics in 1894 in reference to Debussy's String Quartet, which was played in the hall of an exhibition of paintings by Renoir, Pissarro, Sisley, Gauguin, and others. On the same occasion Maurice Kufferath spoke of Debussy's "musical pointillism" and stated that his music suggested "the neo-Japanese canvases painted in Montmartre."

The term was later used by Jean d'Udine to describe the subtle orchestration of Debussy's *Nocturnes* and by Romain Roland in writing of *Pelléas et Mélisande.* Though Debussy himself compared the original form of his *Nocturnes* to "a study in grey in painting" and frequently sought the musical equivalent of a visual image, there was no conscious imitation of Impressionist methods in his music nor in that of Chabrier, who possessed an important collection of Impressionist paintings. Comparisons in technique, such as that between the broken chords in Debussy's *Reflets dans l'eau* and the reflection of clouds in water in Monet's "La Grenouillère" or between a bold use of solo instruments in the orchestration of Chabrier and the use of primary colors by the Impressionist painters, were therefore conjectural.

In the first quarter of the 20th century, the

term was applied in a general sense to the works of many other composers (not all of them French), including Ravel, Frederick Delius, Aleksandr Scriabin, and Stravinsky. Since an affinity with the aesthetic of the Impressionist painters in the work of such composers was remote, Impressionism acquired a period sense that was comparable to the use of the terms Classical and Romantic and was used loosely to describe a variety of trends in post-Wagnerian music.

BIBLIOGRAPHY: Christopher Palmer, *Impressionism in Music* (1974).

impromptu A name used in the 19th century as the descriptive title of pieces for the piano from the French *impromptu,* "extemporary" or "improvised." The style of the music is similar to that of other compositions of this period with such titles as *fantaisie,* caprice, and bagatelle. The name impromptu first appeared in 1822 as the title of piano pieces by Jan Hugo Voříšek and Heinrich August Marschner. In 1824 Liszt wrote an Impromptu on Themes of Rossini and Spontini. These and the impromptus by Chopin, Schumann, and others may have been intended to convey the impression of improvised pieces, but as they first appeared in their published form they were not actually extempore works. This also applies to the first set of impromptus by Schubert so called by his publisher. An improvised impromptu of this period is the 13-measure "Allegretto quasi andante" dedicated by Beethoven to a granddaughter of Charles Burney. No definite form is prescribed for the impromptu, which may resemble a prelude, a set of variations, or be freely conceived in the form of a fantasia. Among the impromptus of a later period are those of Fauré and Aleksandr Scriabin.

improvisation or **extemporization** Composing and performing simultaneously, or creating music spontaneously. Music originated as improvisation and is still extensively improvised in Eastern traditions and in the modern Western tradition of jazz, but this is an offshoot of African music with a higher proportion of genuinely primitive inspiration than is usually realized.

In antiquity and in many Eastern schools with ancient traditions, elaborate modes developed for codifying melodic and rhythmic patterns. Different subjects, different emotions, and even different localities are associated with different modes, between which any possibility of confusion is rigorously resisted. Knowing their modes well and preserving them jealously, musicians can improvise long compositions within the boundaries thus set. Important examples of this method of improvisation are encountered in the early history of European church music, including the Byzantine school of the so-called dark ages and the astonishing Notre Dame school of music in medieval Paris. There the foundation was written down as plainchant and maintained according to strict and conservative rules; yet it was the originally improvised additions to it that led to a written art of flexible melody subtly combined into "horizontal" harmony by counterpoint; *e.g.,* the Renaissance polyphony of Josquin des Prés, Byrd, or Palestrina.

Outside this central tradition in Western music, full "vertical" harmony was already being improvised within conservatively established modes (orally transmitted) by Welsh and other harpers of the Celtic fringe. The nearest surviving equivalent (though it is melodic rather than harmonic) is the highly developed and sophisticated Hindu tradition. Another and vast field in which improvisation has always played a vital part is folk music.

The delight taken by Renaissance organists, harpsichordists, lutenists, viol players, and other instrumentalists in adapting plain vocal compositions to the idiosyncracies of their instruments by insinuating the most elaborate variations impromptu did more than anything else to develop the specifically instrumental idioms that have been the glory of Western music since the 16th and 17th centuries.

Certain types of composition came into being through the same spontaneous outpouring of invention. The prelude and the toccata were at first informal improvisations to loosen the fingers, check the tuning (*e.g.,* of a lute), establish the tonality, and put both performer and audience at their ease. The chorale prelude started as improvisations on a hymn tune by church organists in the service. The theme and variations grew out of that most sophisticated of early parlor games: improvising contrapuntal descants on a given plainchant, or free variations on a ground bass, or the like.

A favorite 18th-century development of this, continued frequently in the 19th century and occasionally (*e.g.,* by French virtuoso organists) in the 20th, was improvising not merely variations but a formal fugue on a theme handed up by a member of the audience—not necessarily an accomplice of the performer. The art was quite genuine; and there were listeners who put it on record that the improvisations of John Bull and Frescobaldi, of Bach and Handel, of Mozart and Beethoven, of Liszt and Busoni were as highly organized as the written-out compositions of these composers and in some ways even more moving.

The impression may have been in part the excitement of hearing great music spontaneously shaped and no sooner shaped than lost. Some allowance must also be made for the composer's bringing memory to the aid of invention; no one can genuinely improvise except in an existing tradition that is intimately familiar. But this is a condition that applies almost as strictly to composition in its ordinary written form. An existing tradition can be modified only by a composer who has the indispensable advantage of having grown up within it.

BIBLIOGRAPHY: Gertrude P. Wollner, *Improvisation in Music* (1963).

incidental music A type of music so called because it is incidental or subservient to the action of a play, film, or radio or television program and is intended to reflect or enhance a dramatic situation rather than to form an integral part of it. The best of such music, originally written to form part of a dramatic performance, has acquired a life of its own and can be played and heard without reference to the work for which it was intended, although it is in a sense PROGRAM MUSIC, *i.e.,* music written to express a literary idea rather than a purely musical one.

The place of music in drama is closely bound with the origins of both drama and opera. It is not really possible to describe the music in Greek drama or in Oriental drama, with its ritual associations, as incidental, al-

though the songs in Menander's comedies seem to have been forerunners as do the flute accompaniments to speeches in Roman plays. Knowledge of this music can only be inferred from stage directions, and it is difficult to determine how far it was regarded as essential, or whether it always took the same form. The gradual emergence of drama from the liturgy of the church in the late Middle Ages was marked by a development of a more truly incidental music. But it was not until the 16th century that the use of music in the theater began to approximate modern practice.

In Italy attention was concentrated on opera and oratorio and in England on the spoken drama; thus it was in England that incidental music developed. It took the form of songs within the plays themselves, interludes between acts, and instrumental music accompanying the interpolated dumb shows, or masques, or even offstage (indicated by the frequent stage direction "music within") as a means of heightening dramatic effect. Early examples of such music are the comic songs in Nicholas Udall's *Ralph Roister Doister* (*c.* 1553), the dumb-show music in *Gorboduc* (1562), and the music between the acts in *Gammer Gurton's Needle* (*c.* 1559).

Incidental music was used in a variety of ways by Shakespeare. The use of songs serves many dramatic purposes, and instrumental music not only forms an accompaniment to the masque scenes (as in *Timon of Athens, Much Ado About Nothing,* and *The Tempest*) and to the dances that sometimes ended the plays but also heightens the dramatic tension (as in the casket scene in *The Merchant of Venice*) and introduces supernatural characters (as in *Cymbeline, Pericles,* and *As You Like It*). Knowledge of this music is derived both from Shakespeare's own stage directions (*e.g.,* "music! ho") and from the inventories of Elizabethan theaters, which show the types and number of instruments used and make possible a reconstruction of the manner of performance. Settings of Shakespeare's songs were made by such contemporary composers as Robert Johnson, Thomas Morley, and John Wilson.

In the Restoration theater elaborate scores of incidental music were written by Purcell for adaptations of *A Midsummer Night's*

Dream and *The Tempest,* for John Dryden's *King Arthur,* and for *The Indian Queen* by Dryden and Sir Robert Howard. Purcell also wrote incidental music for about 40 other plays by Thomas D'Urfey, Beaumont and Fletcher, John Dryden, Thomas Shadwell, William Congreve, and others.

In France Lully, in association with Molière, wrote a series of *comédies-ballets,* forming interludes in the plays for *la troupe du Roi* (Louis XIV). The king and princes of the blood themselves took part in the performances of these ballets, which fell into two categories: majestic ballets such as in *Les Amants magnifiques* and comic ballets such as in *Monsieur de Pourceaugnac* and *Le Bourgeois gentilhomme.* Since vocal items were introduced into these ballet interludes, the former was held to have anticipated the French opera and the latter the opéra comique.

In the 18th century there was relatively little incidental music, though Handel wrote music for Ben Jonson's *The Alchemist* (1732) and Mozart for T. P. von Gebler's *Thamos, König in Aegypten* (1779). Where opera and drama were performed in the same subsidized theater, as at the 19th-century German and Austrian courts, the orchestra was also available for dramatic productions, resulting in incidental music by Beethoven for Goethe's *Egmont* (1810), by Mendelssohn for *A Midsummer Night's Dream* (1826), and by Schumann for Byron's *Manfred* (1849). These scores, like those by Bizet for Daudet's *L'Arlésienne,* Grieg for Ibsen's *Peer Gynt,* and Fauré for Maeterlinck's *Pelléas et Mélisande,* were later performed independently, sometimes outliving the plays for which they were written. Among later associations of playwrights and composers of incidental music are those of Paul Claudel and Milhaud, Virgil Thomson and Ernest Hemingway, and Britten and W. H. Auden.

Toward the middle of the 20th century, developments in motion picture productions and in radio and television programs created an enormous demand for incidental music. Much of it was ephemeral, but some of the scores by composers who experimented with new forms of film and broadcast music, among them Vaughan Williams and Prokofiev, survived in their own right. These new opportunities in film and radio for incidental music increasingly supplied the main sources of income for many composers. Motion pictures and radio also made use of experiments with electronic music in Germany, Italy, and France. In contrast two particularly fine films used music from the past: Jean Cocteau's *Les Enfants terribles* (1950) with music by Vivaldi and *Elvira Madigan* (1967) with music by Mozart.

Incoronazione di Poppea, L': *see* BAROQUE ERA (beginnings); MONTEVERDI (Venice); OPERA (beginnings).

Indian music   History and tradition require that the music of the Indian subcontinent be viewed as a whole. Over a period of about 6,000 years numerous peoples have flowed into this region. Some tribal melodies and rhythms preserve elements of ancient origin, and a wealth of more developed folk music has always been connected with the agricultural year. Such elements can have changed little in their essential character over long periods. Certain higher cultures also appeared in prehistoric times such as that of the artistic people (related to the Sumerians) who brought an early harp to the Indus Valley (2500–1500 B.C.).

Vedic and early classical tradition   The Aryans reached India from western Asia with sacred teachings and rituals that they later wrote down in four Vedas (*veda,* "knowledge"); each of these books (Rig, Sama, Yajur, and Atharva) had its own style of recitation. The Rigveda ("Knowledge of Hymns"), for instance, where the words are all-important, is austerely chanted on three pitch accents, its basic forms still being used in Hindu temples. The Samaveda ("Knowledge of Chants"), using words as little more than a vehicle for the voice, employs more or less elaborate melody. The Vedic tradition, crossed with the traditional songs of the south where the dark Dravidian peoples already enjoyed something of a higher culture, helped the development of a secular art of music about 2,000 years ago, and these beginnings underlie the familiar classical raga music of later times.

India's first known musical theorist, Bharata, in his work on the arts of the theater, *Natya Shastra* (*c.* 6th century B.C.), devotes six chapters to the subject of music. Called *Samgita* in Sanskrit, the classical art consisted of *gita*, or vocal music, always of primary importance in India; *vadya*, or instrumental music, for long very subordinate; and dependent upon these, *nrtya*, dance. The *Bharata Natyam*, the classical temple dance of south India, goes back to Vedic origins; *Kathakali*, the dance-drama of Kerala, though later in its form, is no less inspired by the ancient Hindu epics, *Ramayana* (c. 5th century B.C.) and *Mahabharata* (400 B.C.–A.D. 400).

classical system of ragas After a period of Hellenic and Buddhist predominance (c. 250 B.C.–A.D. 600), during which the classical tradition was somewhat overshadowed, a period of religious revival followed, and India once again became Hindu. Many forms of the drum had long been popular, though the basis of music remained vocal. Temple sculptures show many new instruments, including those of the lute and fiddle classes. Despite their variety these instruments were played not as orchestras but as solo instruments or in small ensembles. Musical theorists and writers began to appear, and important works on classical theory include Matamga's *Brihad deshi* (8th century or earlier), Narada's *Naradiya Shiksha* (10th century or earlier), and Sarngadeva's *Samgita Ratnakara* (early 13th century).

Indian theory recognizes the octave (*saptaka*, "set of seven") as a complete cycle of sounds comprising, as in the Western scale, seven main steps, or notes (*svaras*), called for short: *sa, ri, ga, ma, pa, dha, ni.*

The octave is further divided into 22 more or less equal *srutis*, microtonal steps used in various groupings of two, three, and four to form the intervals of the various scales and modes. In classical theory there are two fundamental seven-note (*sampurna*, "complete") scales (*grama*), which also have six-note and five-note forms. These, conceived as a sequence of ascending intervals measured in *srutis*, are the *Sa Grama* (4 3 2 4 4 3 2) and the *Ma Grama* (4 3 4 2 4 3 2). The first figure (4) in these scales represents the number of *srutis* not between *sa* (tonic) and *ri* but between the note below *sa* and *sa*. A scale has seven modal forms according to which one of its seven notes is considered the tonic. From the two scales of *sa* and *ma*, therefore, 14 theoretical *murcchanas* ("extensions") were formulated, seven of which were deemed suitable for practical use. From these were formed seven principal (and 11 mixed) *jatis*, or species of melodic germ cell, each having its own special hierarchy of notes.

The *jatis* form the basis for more complex structures called ragas, of which there are normally considered to be 132. The raga ("color," "feeling") is a characteristic Oriental melody type, and each raga is defined by its scale, melodic tessitura, characteristic melodic contours, and the emphasis given to a particular note (*vadi*) that forms a contrast with the tonic, as well as by the choice of subtle ornaments (*gamakas*) that give the melody its flexibility. Each raga is conceived to excite and (when performed at length) sustain a particular mood in the listener. The name is first found in the 8th century—though the idea is much earlier, for the moods had already been classified by the Aryans in antiquity. In time the ragas came to express moods appropriate to different hours of the day and night, and later they acquired an extensive mythology illustrating their right and wrong use as well as allusions to the planets and the elements. The reality of such associations in the Indian mind is indicated by the traditional paintings conveying the essence of the ragas in pictorial form.

In performance any given raga needs a time measure. This is called *tala*, and in south Indian tradition there are seven main *talas*, each having five forms. A given *tala* has a fixed number of beats arranged in distinctive groupings determined by stress and quantity (longs and shorts). Some are simple, like Western common time, others asymmetrical. The *tala* is thus a point of departure for the music's rhythm and as such is normally played on the drums. Within a given complete period of a *tala*, two performers (singer or instrumentalist and drummer) may go their own way with rhythmical variants, but they must coincide on the first beat (*sam*) of each new period.

In the formal basis of a musical performance, the first element heard is the *alapa*, a prelude in free but slow time without drumming in which the performer eases into the mood of the raga material and establishes its main features. Then follows the main body of the work, called *ghat,* when the drum comes in with the *tala;* this section is usually in a moderate tempo. Here the recurrent period of the *tala* underlies the formal structure. The proportion of *alapa* to *ghat* is no more definite than the length of a single raga performance, which varies from a few minutes to two hours or longer.

The two elements raga and *tala,* together representing music's rhythmitonal structure, are completed by a drone that acts as a tonic measuring note (or notes) throughout the piece; since there is no modulation in Indian music, the drone is regarded as immovable. It is often played by a long-necked unfretted lute called *tambura,* whose four strings are normally tuned to fundamental, fifth (occasionally fourth), and two octaves. When played in cyclic sequence the strings, having a considerable reverberation time, give the impression of a continuous sound. This sound, rich in harmonic partials, provides a harmonic reference frame for the art of raga and *tala.* The addition of further harmony would completely destroy the fine melodic-harmonic balance of the system.

Having selected a raga appropriate to the hour, the performer subordinates individual creative tendencies to its laws but exercises maximum ingenuity and skill in extemporizing within the prescribed framework—indeed a far more creative role than the modern Western performer.

Muslim influence The raga principle belongs to the whole of India, but the style of performance, as well as the choice of actual ragas, differs much in north and south. The differentiation began in early times, as racial movements always tended to push the earlier inhabitants southward. Moreover the north was successively influenced by the Indus Valley and Greco-Buddhist cultures, the Persian Empire (5th and 4th centuries B.C.), the Parsees, and the Arab occupation of Gujarat (8th century A.D.).Thus Persian and Arabic influence was not new at the time of the Muslim conquest. The new rulers were, moreover, devoted to music, and this art reached a high

point at the late Mogul courts, especially under the emperor Akbar (1542–1605).

Muslim influence was never comparable in the south; the music of the south, Carnatic music that was Aryan in form and largely Dravidian in content, remained architectural, sublime, and restrained, whereas the Hindustani music of the north, already a blend of Aryan and Hindu, absorbed new melodies and styles from Persia and the Middle East and reached a new elegance and vitality—as well as becoming more secular in atmosphere. It also favored certain instruments.

instruments Many Indian instruments have ancient origins and some are indigenous, but most of those in 20th-century use are either of Middle Eastern origin or are the result of a fusion of older Hindu instruments with new Persian and Arabic forms.

Stringed instruments include the plucked stringed instruments vina (especially in the south), sitar, and sarod (especially in the north); and the bowed reedy-toned fiddles, sarangi and *esraj,* and the more recently adopted European violin (in the south). Wind instruments include the cross flute and vertical flute; shawms, *shahnai* (north) and *nagasuaram* (south); the ceremonial conch shell; and the snake charmer's reed pipe. Drums are very numerous, including the classical *tabla* (north), consisting of two drums (*daina* and *bayan*); the *mridamga* (south); the hourglass drum *damaru;* the stick-struck drums *dhol* and *dholak;* and the kettledrums *naqira.* Idiophones are represented by various cymbals, bells, and clappers.

modern developments While the Mogul Empire declined British influence in India grew, and the British raj (1757–1947) saw great changes in India's musical life. A decline in feudalism and hence in musical patronage led to a fall in the musician's status and ultimately in artistry. The process was accelerated in the 19th century because of misguided attempts to foist Western harmony onto a fully developed modal system and by the introduction of instruments tuned in equal temperament such as the harmonium (whose principle is found in the *sruti*-box, which now often replaces the traditional *tambura* as a drone).

With the adjustments of modern life Indian

musicians work somewhere between the extremes of preserving their own tradition and of following Western ideals. On the popular level the influence of Western dance and film music seriously threatens the integrity of traditional music. The fate of the classical raga music, however, is still in the balance. Some of its leading exponents are influenced by what they heard on visits to the West. Some Indian musicians were trained in Western methods of composition, and they write music of various hybrid types; others are engaged in finding forms suitable for radio and concert hall.

heritage Indian music periodically influenced that of other regions. During the early centuries of the Christian era, it traveled with Buddhism into Tibet, China, Korea, and Japan, where surviving forms still attest its influence. Hindus in southeast Asia and Indonesia, especially from the 8th century, stimulated the development of music in those regions. Its influence survives in Burma and Thailand in the boat-shaped harp and in Bali in certain musical forms. The gypsies carried Indian ragas to Arabia and Europe. In the middle of the 20th century Indian classical musicians began to visit Europe and the United States, and a growing number of recordings provided a means of study. Indian classical music forms an important part of the great surviving Eastern traditions and is beginning to invite study by Western musicians.

BIBLIOGRAPHY: E. Clements, *Introduction to the Study of Indian Music* (1913; reprint, 1977); Arthur Henry Fox-Strangways, *Music of Hindostan* (1914; reprint, 1975); H. A. Popley, *The Music of India* (1921; 3rd ed., 1970); Swami Prajnanananda, *Historical Development of Indian Music* (1960; rev. ed., 1973); S. Krishnaswami, *Musical Instruments of India* (1967); Walter Kaufmann, *Ragas of North India* (1968), *Ragas of South India* (1976), and *Music of India* (1976).

Indy, (Paul Marie Theodore) Vincent d' (March 27, 1851–December 1, 1931) The French composer and teacher Vincent d'Indy was remarkable for his attempted and partially successful reform of French symphonic and dramatic music along the lines indicated by Franck.

Born in Paris of an aristocratic family, he studied with Albert Lavignac, Antoine Marmontel, and Franck. In 1874 he was admitted to the organ class of the Paris Conservatoire, and in the same year his second *Wallenstein* Overture was performed at one of the Pasdeloup concerts. In 1876 d'Indy visited Bayreuth—an experience that confirmed and completed his musical creed: he considered French 19th-century music and the tradition of the Paris Opéra (Meyerbeer, Gounod, Massenet), of the Paris Conservatoire, and of French "decorative" symphony (Saint-Saëns) to be superficial, frivolous, and unworthy to compete with the teutonic Bach-Beethoven-Wagner tradition.

D'Indy's most important stage works were *Le Chant de le Cloche* (1883), *Fervaal* (1895), *Le Légende de Saint Christophe* (1915), and *Le Rêve de Cinyras* (1923). Among his symphonic works Symphony on a French Mountain Air (1886) with solo piano, based on one of the folk songs he had collected in the Ardeche district, and *Istar* (variations, 1896) represent his highest achievement. His 105 scores also include keyboard works, secular and religious choral writings, and chamber music. Among the latter are some of his best compositions: Quintet (1924); Suite for flute, string trio, and harp (1927); and the Third Quartet (1928–29). He also arranged hundreds of folk songs that he collected in the Vivarais.

In 1894 d'Indy was one of the founders of the Schola Cantorum in Paris, and it was through courses at this academy that he spread his theories and initiated the revival of interest in plainchant and in the music of the 16th and 17th centuries. D'Indy published studies of Franck (1906), Beethoven (1911), and Wagner (1930). In France Paul Dukas, Albert Roussel, and Déodat de Sévérac were among his disciples. Outside France his influence was great and lasting: in Greece, Bulgaria, Portugal, and Brazil he was counselor of those who endeavored to shape folk music into symphony.

BIBLIOGRAPHY: Martin Cooper, *French Music, from the death of Berlioz to the Death of Fauré* (1951); Norman Demuth, *Vincent d'Indy, 1851–1931; Champion of Classicism* (1951).

RECORDINGS: Piano Sonata in E Major; Symphony on a French Mountain Air; Trio in B-flat Major; Violin Sonata in C Major.

in nomine An English instrumental form of the 16th and 17th centuries that used the plainchant antiphon *Gloria tibi trinitas* (Vespers of Trinity Sunday) as a cantus firmus. The *in nomine* owes its name to an instrumental arrangement of the section "in nomine Domini" of the Benedictus in the Mass *Gloria tibi trinitas* by John Taverner (*c.* 1495–1548?), which in the mid-16th century began to serve as a model for numerous new compositions. Although the instrumental styles changed, the title and cantus firmus remained the same through the Elizabethan and Jacobean periods and continued in use until the time of Purcell.

intermezzo In the 16th century, an entertainment performed between acts of a play, consisting of solo songs, madrigals, dance, and occasionally spoken dialogue. Intermezzo, or *intermedio,* is Italian for interlude; the French word is *intermède.* An early example of the form was in the comedy *Calandria* by Bernardo Cardinal Bibbiena given at Urbino in 1513. By 1600 it was frequently an elaborate spectacle that attracted more attention than the play. Comic intermezzi were performed between acts of the 17th- and 18th-century opera seria. Usually for soprano and bass and sung throughout, they gave rise to OPERA BUFFA, the characteristic Italian form of comic opera. Pergolesi's famous and influential comic opera *La serva padrona* (1733) was originally a series of such intermezzi performed between the acts of his serious opera *Il prigionier superbo.* Operatic intermezzi of this kind were so successful that they were later performed as comic operas complete in themselves.

In the 19th century intermezzo was the title for a character piece, usually for piano, similar in style to a fantasia, impromptu, or capriccio; there are examples by Schumann and by Brahms. Mascagni's one-act opera *Cavalleria rusticana* (1890) has an orchestral intermezzo as an interlude between its two sections.

interval The distance in pitch between one tone and another, sounded simultaneously as in a chord (harmonic interval), or successively as in (melodic interval). Simple intervals encompass one octave or less. Compound intervals include more than one octave and are heard as varieties of their simple counterparts: a 10th (octave plus a third) is recognized by the ear as a third (an interval encompassing three notes: for example, C-D-E).

There are four perfect (P) intervals: the unison (P1), octave (P8), fourth (P4), and fifth (P5). The other intervals (seconds, thirds, sixths, sevenths) have major (M) and minor (m) forms that differ in size by a half step (semitone).

Intervals may be modified to a point that the ear may not recognize them outside a musical context. Perfect and major intervals may be augmented (A) or enlarged by a semitone: for example, C-E (M3) and C-E♯ (A3); or C-G (P5) and C-G♯ (A5). Perfect and minor intervals may be diminished (d), or narrowed, by a semitone: for example, E-G (m3) and E-G♭ (d3), or F-C (P5) and F♯-C (d5). ENHARMONIC intervals are those that in the system of equally tempered tuning (*see* TUNING AND TEMPERAMENT) sound identical and on a keyboard use the same keys: for example, C-E♯ and C-F. They are differentiated by their musical context.

invention A seldom-used term that is known primarily through Bach's set of 15 two-part Inventions for clavier.

Its exact meaning is rather vague and ill defined, but it has been affixed to compositions of a novel, progressive character; *i.e.,* compositions that do not fall within any traditional form or genre. The earliest known use of the term in a musical context is the *Inventiones musicales* (1555) of Clément Janequin, a publication containing examples of original and unorthodox programmatic chansons that contain extramusical images, such as battle sounds for which that composer became well known. Later inventions of a similarly capricious or novel aspect include John Dowland's *Invention for Two to Play upon One Lute* (1597): Lodovico da Viadana's *Cento concerti ecclesiastici . . . Nova inventione* (1602), and Vivaldi's *Il cimento dell'armonia e dell'invenzione* (1720).

The best known collection of inventions is

the set by Bach and his three-part Sinfonias (often called Three-Part Inventions). Each of these pieces is characterized by the thorough elaboration of a single melodic idea through the use of counterpoint. A possible model for these pieces may have been Francesco Bonporti's *Invenzioni* for violin and bass (1712), several of which were copied by Bach and were for a time thought to have been composed by him.

A number of 20th-century composers have used the title, including Berg, Boris Blacher, Wolfgang Fortner, and Alexander Tcherepnin. Their pieces are more directly inspired by Bach's Inventions than by the earlier, more unorthodox compositions.

inversion The rearrangement of top-to-bottom elements in an interval, a chord, a melody, or a group of contrapuntal lines.

The inversion of chords and intervals is utilized for various purposes; *e.g.,* to create a melodic bass line or (with certain chords) to modulate to a new key. To invert a chord or an interval is to rearrange its notes so that the original bottom note becomes an upper note; for example,

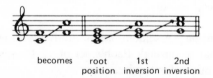

becomes   root   1st   2nd
           position inversion inversion

An interval (c'-f') and its inversion (f'-c") are complementary: together they form an octave. A three-note triad can be inverted twice from its original, or root, position.

Inversions of melody and counterpoint enable a composer to elaborate on basic musical material; they are common in fugues. To invert a melody means to change its ascending intervals to descending ones and vice versa; for example:

becomes

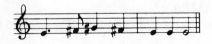

In inverted counterpoint the original order of the contrapuntal lines is rearranged; in this way a line sounds above the line that it originally sounded beneath; for example,

becomes

Invitation to the Dance: *see* WEBER.

Iolantha: *see* TCHAIKOVSKY (later life and works).

Ionian mode The third of the four additions by the 16th-century Swiss theorist Henricus Glareanus to the eight medieval church modes. Its general range comprises the notes middle C to the C above, a pattern identical to the major scale. Melodies in Ionian, or Mode XI, usually have C as the *finalis,* or final note, and G as the *tenor,* or reciting note.

In ancient Greek music Ionian was one of several names for the scale pattern, or octave species, conventionally represented in modern writings as G-G.

Iphigénie en Tauride: *see* CLASSICAL PERIOD (vocal music, 1750–1800); GLUCK.

Ippolitov-Ivanov, Mikhail (Mikhailovich) (November 19, 1859–January 28, 1935) A Russian composer of instrumental music, operas, and songs, Mikhail Ippolitov-Ivanov entered the St. Petersburg Conservatory in 1875; there he studied with Rimsky-Korsakov. In 1882 he went to Tbilisi (Tiflis), where he founded and conducted regular symphony concerts and directed a music school. In 1893 he joined the staff on the Moscow Conservatory (director 1906–22) and until 1906 was conductor of Mamontov's opera company. He visited Tbilisi in 1924–25 to reorganize the Georgian State Conservatory, which had developed from his former music school, but returned to Moscow in 1925 as director of the Bolshoi Theater. Ippolitov-Ivanov's 11 years in the Caucasus led to a lifelong interest in Georgian folk music and inspired some of his most successful orchestral compositions: *Armenian* Rhapsody, the symphonic poem *Mtsyri,* and five suites, of which *Caucasian Sketches* (1895) won widespread popularity. None of his seven operas has held the stage, nor has his completion of Mussorgsky's *Marriage.*

RECORDINGS: *Caucasian Sketches.*

Ireland, John (Nicholson (August 13, 1879– June 12, 1962) The English composer John Ireland entered the Royal College of Music in 1893, studying with Charles Villiers Stanford. Later he taught composition there; his pupils included Ernest John Moeran and Britten. His first important work was the song cycle *Songs of a Wayfarer* (1912). The bulk of Ireland's large output consisted of songs, piano pieces, and church music; orchestral works included Symphonic Rhapsody *Mai-Dun* (1923) and *A London* Overture (1937). His motet *Greater Love Hath No Man* (1912) and a piece for organ, *The Holy Boy* (1919; arranged for strings, 1941), have enjoyed popularity.

RECORDING: *A London* Overture.

Isaac, Heinrich, also spelled Hendryk Isaak and other ways (*c.* 1450–1517) The leading Flemish composer of his generation, Heinrich Isaac was probably born in Brabant. He may have been in Italy *c.* 1474–82, initially as a pupil of the Florentine organist Antonio Squarcialupi. He was certainly at the imperial court in Innsbruck in 1484. He then moved to Florence, where he taught in the household of Lorenzo de' Medici and set to music some of Lorenzo's own carnival songs. He apparently left Florence during the Medicean exile, returning to imperial service in 1494–95; he was officially appointed court composer in 1497, but he spent most of his life elsewhere. Between 1497 and 1514 he traveled extensively, finally settling in Florence.

Isaac's most important publications were a collection of masses (*Misse henrici Izac;* Venice, 1506) and the posthumous *Choralis Constantinus* (Nürnberg, 1550–55). The latter is the first complete polyphonic setting of the proper of the mass for all Sundays (and other feasts); it also contains five settings of the ordinary. At least part of the work was commissioned for the Diocese of Constance in 1508 and employs plainchants unique to the Constance liturgy. Isaac left his great monument unfinished; the task of completing it fell to his pupil, Ludwig Senfl.

In his sacred music Isaac treats cantus firmus with infinite resourcefulness, placing the chant in any voice or sharing it between two parts, either in long notes or embroidered with shorter values; he also uses it as the thematic basis of contrapuntal imitations—a technique that came to dominate 16th-century music. Though cosmopolitan and eclectic, Isaac remains Flemish in his rather hollow harmonies and his love of mensural intricacies. His famous "Innsbruck, ich muss dich lassen" recalls the style of the frottola. This song was later reworked as a chorale, "O Welt, ich muss dich lassen," familiar today as a hymn and through arrangements most notably by Bach and Brahms.

RECORDINGS: *Missa carminum; Missa O praeclara;* motets and chansons.

Isle of the Dead, The: *see* PROGRAM MUSIC (problem of form); RACHMANINOFF; SYMPHONIC POEM.

isorhythm A 14th-century variation technique by rhythmic means used frequently in the motet, especially in the tenor. The melodic pattern of the cantus firmus is called the *color,* the rhythmic pattern the *talea.* The two patterns are typically of different lengths with, say, four repetitions of the *talea* to two of the *color* or in uneven ratios that make possible overlappings. Though the system is artificial and often elaborate, it creates interesting variations of texture. The isorhythmic principle was basic for the tenor, but its use was extended to the upper parts, usually in a freer form.

Isorhythm was an outgrowth of the 13th-century rhythmic modes, which were fixed, short rhythmic patterns repeated throughout a piece of music. The isorhythmic motet was a development of the ars nova (the new musical style of the 14th century), and examples may be found in the works of Guillaume de Machaut (*c.* 1300–77), the Burgundian Guillaume Dufay (*c.* 1400–74), and other composers.

The isorhythmic principle (*i.e.,* the repetition of rhythmic formulas) is sometimes a unifying feature of primitive musical styles of North America, as in peyote cult songs of American Indians.

Israel in Egypt: *see* FUGUE (Handel) and (after Bach and Handel); HANDEL (life) and (works); ORATORIO (Handel).

Istomin, Eugene (b. November 26, 1925) Winner of the Leventritt award (1943), the U.S. pianist Eugene Istomin studied at the Curtis Institute with Rudolf Serkin. He appeared regularly from 1950 at the Casals Festival, first in Prades, France, and from 1957 in Puerto Rico. He married Pablo Casals' widow Marta in 1975.

Italian Concerto: *see* BACH, JOHANN SEBASTIAN (Leipzig); BAROQUE ERA (Handel and Bach); CONCERTO (concerto grosso).

Italian Symphony (Fourth): *see* MENDELSSOHN; PROGRAM MUSIC (program symphony).

Iturbi, José (b. November 28, 1895) The Spanish pianist, conductor, and composer José Iturbi was educated in Valencia and at the Paris Conservatoire (1913). He served as conductor of the Rochester (New York) Philharmonic (1935–44) and appeared in a number of U.S. motion pictures in the 1940s. He and his sister Amparo Iturbi have played as duo pianists.

Ivan the Terrible: *see* MAID OF PSKOV, THE.

Ives, Charles (Edward) (October 20, 1874– May 19, 1954) A significant U.S. composer whose innovations anticipated most of the later musical developments of the 20th century, Charles Ives received his earliest musical instruction from his father, George Ives, a bandleader, music teacher, and acoustician who experimented with quarter tones. To sharpen his son's musical perception, George Ives had him sing "Swanee River" in one key while he accompanied him in another key. At 12 Charles played organ in a local church, and two years later his first composition was played by the town band. In 1893 or 1894 he composed *Song for the Harvest Season,* a fugue in four parts—for voice, trumpet, violin,

Charles Ives   *Clara E. Sipprell*

and organ—each in different keys. That year he began to prepare for a career in business at Yale University and studied music with Horatio Parker, then a foremost academic composer. His unconventionality disconcerted Parker, for whom Ives turned out a series of "correct" compositions.

After graduation in 1898 Ives became an insurance clerk and part-time organist in New York City. In 1907 he founded a highly successful insurance partnership, in which he was involved until his retirement in 1930. Until the beginning of World War I, he divided his energies between his business and composition. After a heart attack in 1918 his health gradually deteriorated, and he became more and more reclusive.

Although most of his composing had ended by 1916, his music remained mostly unperformed, unpublished, unknown. Ives himself published his *Concord* Sonata for piano in 1920 and his *114 Songs* in 1922 (along with the accompanying *Essays before a Sonata*), but these were distributed privately to friends; it was not until the late 1920s that the composer Henry Cowell printed some of Ives's pieces in his *New Music* and for the first time attracted the attention of the avant-garde. Additional landmarks in the discovery of Ives were first performances of *Three Pieces in New England* (also known as *Orchestral Set No. 1*) by Nicolas Slonimsky conducting his Chamber Orchestra of Boston (New York City, 1931); *Concord* Sonata by the pianist John Kirkpatrick (New York, 1939); Third Symphony by Lou Harrison conducting the Little Symphony of New York (1946; it then received the 1947 Pulitzer Prize); Second Symphony by Bernstein conducting the New York Philharmonic (1951); the publishing of *A Temporary Mimeographed Catalogue of the Music Manuscripts and Related Materials of C.E.I.* by Kirkpatrick (1960); and the first complete performance of the Fourth Symphony by Stokowski conducting the American Symphony (1965). Finally in the 1970s—20 years after Ives's death—his true stature was generally recognized; that before Stravinsky he had employed polyrhythm and polytonality, before Schoenberg atonality, before Cowell tone clusters, before Alois Hába microtones, and before John Cage indeterminacy, or chance music.

Like the works of most composers, they can be grouped into three basic periods: formative until about 1896, developing until about 1905, and mature. Significant examples of the early period are the Variations on *America* (1891–94) for organ, the earliest known piece using polytonality; the earlier mentioned *Song for the Harvest Season;* and his First Quartet "A Revival Service" (1896). The first three symphonies, violin sonatas, and First Piano Sonata all date from the middle period, but Ives's greatest inventiveness occurs in his various Psalm settings (mostly 1896–1900) and the three *Harvest Home* Chorales (1898?–1902) with their complex polyrhythms. *The Unanswered Question* (before 1908) for quartet or string orchestra is one of the earliest examples of chance music. The culmination of his genius is evident in the large-scale works of his mature period: the two *Orchestral Sets* (the first has two bands approaching and passing each other, each playing its own music in its own key, tempo, and rhythm); the *New England Holidays* Symphony ("Washington's Birthday," "Decoration Day," "Fourth of July," and "Thanksgiving and Forefathers' Day"); the monumental *Concord* Sonata (in four sections echoing the spirit of the New England Transcendentalists Emerson, Haw-

thorne, the Alcotts, and Thoreau); and the mammoth Fourth Symphony.

BIBLIOGRAPHY: Henry and Sidney Cowell, *Charles Ives and His Music,* 2nd ed. (1969); Vivian Perlis, *Charles Ives Remembered: An Oral History* (1974); Rosalie S. Perry, *Charles Ives and the American Mind* (1974); Frank R. Rossiter, *Charles Ives and His America* (1975).

RECORDINGS: Numerous recordings of many works.

J

Jackson, William (May 29, 1730–July 5, 1803) The English composer and author William Jackson was a chorister at Exeter Cathedral and was appointed organist there in 1777. He published many vocal works, including Twelve Songs (1755) and Twelve Canzonets for Two Voices (*c.* 1770), two operas, of which the first, *The Lord of the Manor* (London, 1780), held the stage for many years, and 14 harpsichord sonatas. He is associated with a service of doubtful authenticity known as "Jackson in F," written in a deliberately simple style for provincial singers. His literary works include a pamphlet *Observations on the Present State of Music in London* (1791) and essays on music and painting in *Thirty Letters on Various Subjects* (1782) and *Four Ages* (1798). As an amateur painter he enjoyed the friendship and correspondence of Thomas Gainsborough.

Jacobs, Paul (b. 1930) A graduate of the Juilliard School and a student of Ernest Hutcheson, the U.S. pianist and harpsichordist Paul Jacobs has played with numerous ensembles devoted to 20th-century music. He lived in Europe from 1951 to 1960, where he performed, recorded, and lectured on American music. Since 1961 he has been the pianist for the New York Philharmonic and its harpsichordist since 1974. He has taught at Brooklyn College since 1968.

Janáček, Leoš (July 3, 1854–August 12, 1928) The leading Czech composer of the early 20th century, Leoš Janáček was born at Hukvaldy, then in northern Moravia, and studied at Brno, Prague, and later at Leipzig, St. Petersburg (1878), and Vienna (1879–80), where he was a pupil of Franz Krenn. From 1881 to 1919 he was director of the college of organists at Brno. He devoted himself to criticism and research on folk music, which he undertook with František Bartoš, and between 1884 and 1888 published the journal *Hudební Listy*. His first opera, *Šárka* (1887–88; produced in Brno, 1925), was a Romantic work in the spirit of Wagner and Smetana. In 1896 he again visited Russia; influences are evident in his opera *Kát'a Kabanová* (Brno, 1921) and his orchestral rhapsody *Taras Bulba* (Prague, 1924).

Earlier he created a distinctive Czech style in his opera *Její pastorkyňa,* later called *Jenůfa* (Brno, 1904). The production of *Jenůfa* in Prague in 1916 finally established the reputation of this retiring and idealistic composer, then past 60. His later operas, produced in Brno and Prague in 1926, include *The Makropulos Affair* (1926), *From the House of the Dead* (1930), the satire *Mr. Brouček's Excursion* (1920), and the comic opera *The Cunning Little Vixen* (1924), which achieved success in Germany and England.

His instrumental works include Sinfonietta, Concertino for piano and chamber orchestra, Capriccio for piano (left hand) and chamber ensemble, Sextet *Mládí* ("Youth") for wind instruments, three quartets, and piano pieces. His vocal works, both sacred and secular, show his manner of modeling the writing for voices on the inflection of his native language. They include *Glagolitic* (also called *Slavonic*) Mass (1926), *Diary of One Who Vanished* (1917–19), and *Říkadla* (*Nursery Rhymes,* 1925–27).

BIBLIOGRAPHY: Jaroslav Vogel, *Leoš Janáček; His Life and Works* (1962).

RECORDINGS: Capriccio; Concertino; *Diary of One Who Vanished; Glagolitic* Mass; *Idyll* for strings; *In the Mist* for piano; *Jenůfa; Kát'a Kabanová; Lachian* Dances; Sextet *Mládí;* Sinfonietta; Suite for strings; *Taras Bulba;* Violin Sonata.

Janequin, Clément (*c.* 1485–1558) The French master of the 16th-century descriptive chanson, Clément Janequin was probably born in Châtellerault. He worked in Bordeaux and Anjou before settling in Paris in 1549. From 1555 he was in the service of Henry II, but he died a pauper. Though he was a priest and set religious texts, Janequin's fame lies in his 286 chansons. His well-known onomatopoeic pieces such as the early *Chant des Oiseaux* are not entirely typical of his style, which is distinguished by elegant restraint, subtle prosody, and perfect formal balance as in *Guerre de Renty.*

Janigro, Antonio (b. January 21, 1918) The cellist and conductor Antonio Janigro studied in his native Milan and then toured Europe, South America, Africa, and Asia. In 1939 he joined the faculty of the Zagreb (Yugoslavia) Conservatory, remaining until 1953. He founded the chamber group I Soloisti di Zagreb in 1954 and conducted it until 1967, making numerous recordings that included much Bach, Mozart, Telemann, and Vivaldi. He has taught at the Robert Schumann Conservatory in Düsseldorf since 1965 and has been permanent conductor of the Chamber Orchestra of the Saar since 1968.

Janis, Byron, real name, Byron Yanks (b. March 24, 1928) Making his debut with the Pittsburgh Symphony when he was but 15, the U.S. pianist Byron Janis studied with Horowitz. Like his teacher, he is known for his performances of Liszt and Rachmaninoff.

Janissary music The music of the Turkish military establishment—particularly of the Janissaries (*Yeniçeri,* "new soldier"), an elite corps of royal Ottoman bodyguards (disbanded 1826)—that inspired a particular repertoire of European music. Characteristic was its use of a variety of drums and bells and the combination of bass drum, triangle, and cymbals. Janissary music probably appeared in Europe for the first time in 1720, when it was adopted by the army of the Polish ruler Augustus II. The novel clangor of its colorful instruments led to their wide use throughout Europe, where they became an integral part of the military spectacle. They were occasionally used in opera scores—*e.g.,* Gluck, *Le Recontre imprévue* (1764), and Mozart, *The Abduction from the Seraglio* (1782)—because of their exotic color.

In the late 18th and early 19th centuries, compositions in naive imitation of the Turkish military style enjoyed a short-lived vogue. Well-known examples of the "alla turca" genre are the final movement of Haydn's *Military* Symphony (1794); the final movement of Mozart's Piano Sonata in A Major, K.331; the "Turkish" March from Beethoven's incidental music to *The Ruins of Athens;* and the tenor solo from the finale of Beethoven's Ninth Symphony. So great was the popularity of the Turkish style that many pianos and harpsichords of the time were provided with a Janissary stop, which produced a percussive accompaniment of indefinite pitch.

See TURKISH MUSIC for a discussion of the music of Turkey.

Japanese music   By the 8th century the documentary history of Japanese music had begun. Although this claim predates an equal state of Western music history by some 100 years, certain parallels between the two traditions can be made. Both seem more clearly established in the same general 200-year period, a short time when compared to Chinese music studies. Both developed a musical nomenclature heavily influenced by the music of religious organizations: the Roman Catholic Church in the West, Buddhism in Japan. Both traditions were equally influenced by theories of a foreign culture from over the nearest sea: Greece in Italy and China in Japan. Herein many differences arise, one of the most significant being that in Japan the foreign tradition of China at the time of its first major influence was alive and strong and could apply practical musical information and instrumentations as well as theories, whereas the Greek tradition was long dead when European monks turned to it for guidance. Nevertheless, one can see that the general length and beginning of each history is comparable. An attempt should be made to envision general characteristics, realizing that in doing so the tendency is to apply aphorisms to music that stretches over a series of styles as old and varied as the music of Europe from plainchant through Debussy. With that caveat general guidelines for the appreciation of Japanese traditional music can be put forth.

These guidelines fall under three general concepts: the sound ideal, the structural ideal, and the artistic ideal; but these three things are not clearly separate in any musical event.

In general the most common sound ideal of Japanese music is to produce the maximum effect with a minimum amount of material. For example, the *taiko* drum of the Nō drama consists of a barrel-shaped body over which are lashed two cowhide heads some 20 inches in diameter stretched over iron rings. Wooden sticks are used to hit one head. Obviously the sound potentials of the drum are many, but they are deliberately suppressed. The sticks are made of very soft wood, and the strokes are applied only to a small circle of soft deerskin in the center of the head. The *taiko,* like Japanese ink paintings, accomplishes a great deal by concentrating on carefully chosen limitations of the medium.

Another feature of much Japanese traditional music could be called the chamber music sound ideal. No matter how large an ensemble may be, one finds that the various instruments are set in such a way that the timbre of each can be heard. This can be understood in Western chamber music and contrasts with the Western orchestral sound ideal in which the primary intention is to merge all the instrumental sounds into one glorious color. The color separation of Japanese music is evident in the large court ensemble *(gagaku)* as well as in drama music and actual chamber ensembles such as the *sankyoku* for koto zither, samisen plucked lute, and the end-blown *shakuhachi* flute.

The structural intents of Japanese music are as varied as those of the West, but one of special interest is the frequent application of a three-part division of a melody, a section of a piece, or an entire composition. This is in contrast with the more typical two-part division of Western music. The fundamental terminology of the Japanese tripartite form is *jo-ha-kyū,* the introduction, the scatterings, and the rushing toward the end. A Western musician might compare this with sonata allegro form and its three parts (exposition, development, recapitulation). But the Western example relates to a complete event and involves the development of certain motives or

415

melodic units (such as first and second theme), whereas the Japanese concept may be applied to various segments or complete pieces that are generally through-composed. Japanese music reveals its logic and its forward motion not by themes but by a movement from one section to another different one until the final section is reached. Forward motion in motivic Western music was often derived during the classical periods from the tension created by chord progressions. In Japanese music such sonic events generally are not used. Nevertheless, the need for aurally recognizable patterns falling into a progression that the informed listener can anticipate is necessary in all music. In Japan such stereotyped patterns are melodic or rhythmic, not harmonic. The recognition, whether intellectual or aural, of the existence of such recurring patterns is essential to the appreciation of any music.

One of the artistic ideals of Japanese music is equally clear in all of East Asia. It is the tendency for much of the music to be word oriented either through actual sung text or through pictorial titles to instrumental pieces. With the exception of variation pieces *(danmono)* for the Japanese koto zither, one can seldom find a purely instrumental piece in the spirit of, for example, the Western sonata or symphony. Japanese ensemble pieces, like those in China and Korea, are either dance pieces, instrumental versions of songs, or descriptive. This ideal in all of East Asia was not weakened until recent times, when such music was forced to compete with Western idioms.

The ideal of the composer as genius, so dear to 19th- and 20th-century Western hearts, had little place in earlier East Asian music. In Japan, as in China and Korea, the names of many composers are known, but the actual setting of their music was and still is often done by a group of fairly anonymous people. One may know who was helping out at a given time and in a given place, but in any written form of the music their names, or the name of "the" composer, may often be missing. In the Orient, particularly in Japan, the performer is often the person remembered and noted. Such an ideal is understood in the West by fans of popular music. Although this ideal

has given way to the Western composer star system in modern Japan, it does depict an important social setting for any appreciation of the older Japanese classical traditions.

In keeping with this artistic ideal one should add that often there is not one correct version of a given piece. Most traditional music is organized under guild systems, and each guild may have its secret version of a well-known piece. A given guild will play its version precisely the same way in each performance, for improvisation has practically no role in any of the major genres of East Asian music. Differences are maintained between guild versions, however, in order to identify a given group's musical repertoire as separate from all the others. A fascinating example of the tenacity of this ideal is found in the present-day imperial court orchestra. It was formed in the late 19th century by the combination of previously separate ensembles from the courts and temples. The musicians played the same-named pieces but could not always agree on many musical details, so they continued to play their disparate versions at the same time, creating a kind of polyphony that is now accepted as the correct ancient tradition in Japan, although, as with such composers as Ives, it sometimes represents two things going on at once. The separation of guild styles can be carried further to one more artistic ideal, which holds that it is not just what one plays on an instrument, it is how one plays it. For example, in the case of the *taiko* drum mentioned above, the manner in which a player sits, picks up the sticks, strikes the drum, and puts the sticks away will reveal the name of the guild in which membership is held and also can be used to judge skill in performance. No Japanese instrument is merely played. One could almost say that its performance practice is choreographed. Such distinctions exist in the music of other East Asian cultures as well, although the clues to their understanding have not yet been revealed to outside listeners and viewers.

Nara period Documents from the Nara period (710–784) demonstrate how very active music was in the newly established capital in Nara. The general term for court orchestra music, *gagaku,* is merely a Japanese pronunciation for the same characters used in China for *ya yüeh* and in Korea for *a-ak*. As Japan absorbed more and more of the outside world, the music of the court, like that of T'ang dynasty China of the same general centuries, received an increasing variety of styles. In 702 these styles were organized under a music bureau *(gagaku-ryō)*, and by the early 9th century an additional *Ōuta dokoro* (the "Big Song Hall") was created for handling Japanese-composed additions to the repertoire. Among foreign genres the musical styles of the nearby three kingdoms of Korea were some of the first imports, Silla music being called in Japanese *shiragi-gaku*, Paekche music, *kudara-gaku,* and Koryŏ music, *kōkurigaku*. Music from these three kingdoms was sometimes called collectively *sankangaku*. Under all these terms were found still other Chinese and north Asian traditions in addition to music purported to have come from India as early as 736. The date of 736 is also assumed for the entrance of music from Indochina, which survived for several centuries in a form of music called *rinyūgaku*. Although this tradition is now lost, there are extant detailed pictures of the ensemble along with other ancient instruments and a variety of dances in sources such as the 14th-century copy of the 12th-century *Shinzeigakuzu* scroll.

The dominant musical style of early *gagaku* was naturally from China and was called T'ang music *(tōgaku)*. In Japan, as in Korea, the establishment and maintenance of such a music has made it possible for modern listeners to hear foreign versions of famous pieces long forgotten in the country of their origin. For example, there are names of pieces played and dances performed in Japan that are also found in T'ang Chinese lists. Unlike China, however, many of these works are still played in Japan, and a few of the original costumes and masks used at that time are preserved.

Heian period Further images of Japanese musical life can be captured from the Heian period (794–1185). In the first chapter of the 10th-century *Ochikubo monogatari,* Japan's earliest novel, the sad fate of the heroine is noted by the fact that she was never able to learn how to play the Chinese seven-stringed *ch'in* zither, although she did have some train-ing in Japanese koto zither music. The famous 11th-century works, such as Murasaki Shikibu's *The Tale of Genji,* are filled with romantic koto, *biwa,* and flutes as well as *gagaku* and *bugaku* performances and the singing of many songs. Diaries also show that the courtiers, now moved to Kyōto, found music to be a useful and frequent adjunct to their insular courtly life.

It was in this period that the many forms of official court music were organized into two basic categories. The so-called music of the left was called *tōgaku* and contained the Chinese- and Indian-derived pieces. The music of the right was called *komagaku* and contained all Korean and Manchurian examples. In both categories there were pieces that by this time may have been Japanese arrangements or original compositions. The terms left and right were derived from the Confucian-based administration system of the new capital, which divided the entire government into such categories. In *bugaku* they controlled the costumes of the dancers, left dances emphasizing red, right dances green. In *gagaku* these two major divisions standardized the instrumentation of the ensembles. When playing dance accompaniments stringed instruments were deleted, but the two orchestras for purely instrumental performances were complete. Each used plucked 12-stringed zithers with movable bridges called *gaku-sō* or by the generic term koto. The string section was completed by a four-stringed plucked lute, the *gaku biwa*. A small hanging gong *(shōko)* and a large hanging drum *(tsuri daiko)* were found in both. The leader of a *tōgaku* piece would use a barrel drum *(kakko)* with two lashed heads struck with sticks, while a *komagaku* piece would be led by an hourglass *san no tsuzumi* drum. The standard melodic instrument for both was the double-reed *hichiriki,* a *komabue* flute being added in *komagaku* and a *ryuteki* flute in *tōgaku*. The Japanese *shō* mouth organ appears in both.

Nō music The Kamakura period (1192–1333) marks the end of Heian court splendor and the start of a new military government located in Kamakura far away from Kyōto. In such a context it is not surprising to find the development of long narratives of military history and the flourishing of plebeian theatricals. The story of the defeat of the Heike clan (the *Heike monogatari*) was known in mansions, war camps, and temple grounds primarily as sung by *biwa*-playing bards. As in the traditions of ancient Greece and Europe, these minstrels were often blind or built their style in that of the blind priest lute tradition *(moso biwa)* in which mendicant monks recited sutra (scriptures) from house to house or at temples. More lucrative forms of entertainment grew under the circus acts that developed out of the *san-gaku* (folk theatricals), its companion comic acts *saru-gaku* (literally, "monkey music"), and theatricals derived from folk rice-planting dances, *den-gaku*. Street parades *(fūryū)* and Buddhist entertainments *(en-nen)* also were part of the colorful scene. By the subsequent Muromachi period (1338–1573) the terms *saru-gaku-no-Nō* and *den-gaku-no-Nō* had become the dominant terms for temple and shrine pantomime and dialogue dramas, while the comic interludes of such plays were called *kyōgen*. Through the support of the military rulers and the efforts of individual artists, the first major form of Japanese theater developed. It became known eventually as Nō.

The music of Nō as it is performed today consists of vocal music *(yōkyoku)* with an instrumental ensemble known collectively as the *hayashi*. The singing is done by the actors or by a unison chorus *(jiutai)*. The four instruments of the *hayashi* are a flute *(Nō-kan)*, the *taiko* stick drum, a small hourglass drum *(ko tsuzumi)* held on the right shoulder, and a larger one *(o tsuzumi)* placed at the left hip.

Kabuki theater The *nagauta* ("long song") form of lyric music, like most of the other narrative forms, began with a close relation to the Kabuki popular theater of the Edo period (1603–1867). The first Kabuki performances used instruments *(hayashi)* from the Nō drama. Because Kabuki was related to the flourishing demimonde of the major cities, however, the music of the party houses and brothels was soon added to the theater. By the mid-17th century the names of *nagauta* singers and samisen players were listed on posters along with the cast.

Kabuki musical events can be divided into onstage activities *(debayashi)* and offstage groups *(geza)*. The most common dance scene today is one in which the onstage group consists of *nagauta* musicians and the Nō *hayashi*. The samisen and singers are placed on a riser at the back of the stage, and the *hayashi* sit before them on floor level. There are as many different types of dances that require different kinds of music as there are in Chinese or Western opera. In a classical repertoire of hundreds of set pieces, there are many different combinations, but to many listeners these situations seem rather puzzling at first hearing, with apparently two kinds of music going on at the same time. If the situation is from a play derived from a former Nō drama and uses the full *hayashi*, one notes first that the flute is not in the same tonality as the samisen, nor is it playing the same tune. The drums in turn do not seem to relate rhythmically to the melody. If a given situation is analyzed in detail, it is found that the drums and flute are playing named stereotyped patterns normally of eight-beat length as in the Nō. The essential difference between them and the samisen melody is that they do not seem aurally to have the same first beat. Many times a given samisen melody will make room through silence for an important vocal call in the drum patterns, but the deliberate lack of coordination of beat "one" creates a vital rhythmic tension that makes the music drive forward until resolve is accomplished at a common cadence. This important compositional device can be called a slide-rule effect: each part is internally rigid and progressive, but its conflict with the other parts forces the music (and the listener) to move the musical event through a time continuum toward a mutual completion. In Kabuki dance music, as in Western music, there are three kinds of musical needs. In the West they are melody, rhythm, and harmony. In this music they are melody, rhythm, and a third unit of one drum and a flute that functions like harmony although its sound is totally different. If this third Japanese feature is called the dynamism unit, then it can be said that *nagauta* dynamism and Western traditional harmony both serve to color the line, to create tension that drives the music onward and help to standardize the formal design of the piece by clarifying cadences or by creating the need for them.

The music offstage is rather different. This *geza,* or *kagebayashi* (shadow *hayashi*), music is normally placed in a small room on stage right with a view of the drama through a bamboo curtain. This music consists of special samisen and vocal pieces and a great variety of percussion signals. For example, a huge *o daiko* barrel drum with two tacked heads signals the beginning of a program, in keeping with the sounds given by the same drum from a tower over the entrance of very early Kabuki theaters. Other drums, bells, gongs, and clappers are used to reinforce stage action, and special offstage songs may set the mood or location of a scene, particularly in those scenes in which onstage musicians do not appear. As in Western musical theater and films, many of the sounds are naturalistic, whereas others are traditional means of evoking desired responses from an audience.

The specific musical devices used in a given Kabuki play are under the control of a headman, *hayashi gashira,* who works with the first samisenist, the actors, and the director to produce the desired results. Thus the musical contents of a given play may change with different productions. In Kabuki the combination of offstage and onstage music creates a total atmosphere that has few parallels in other world theaters. Perhaps it comes as close as anything to Wagner's ideal of the all-embracing art form *(Gesamtkunstwerk).*

notation   There exist three different notation systems in traditional Japanese music: tablature, pitch designations, and neumes. Tablature is used for lute *(biwa)* and zithers (koto, *wagon*); flute, *hichiriki,* and mouth organ *(shō)* notations indicate the exact pitch but use a different nomenclature and different symbols for each of the instruments. All vocal music is written in florid neumes derived from the *shōmyō* neumes imported from China by the Buddhist monk Ennin (posthumously named Jikaku Daishi, 794–864) and modified or simplified for courtly songs and Nō recitation.

scale system and theory   Scales differ with each type of music. Court music uses the two pentatonic modes *ryo* (d e f♯ a b d) and *ritsu*

(d e g a b d) and a number of auxiliary notes. Buddhist chant is built on a small number of melodic nuclei of restricted range, hardly ever exceeding the range of a perfect fourth or a diminished fifth and provided with elaborate embellishments and microtone shadings. Nō melody moves around three tonal centers—high, middle, and low *(jo, chu, ge)*— at intervals of the fourth:

Koto music of the Tokugawa period makes use of the two secular *(zokugaku)* scales, *hirajoshi* and *kumoi-joshi:*

Found in all kinds of Japanese music is an open or veiled pentatonic basis, the drone element, prominence being given to the tritone, to onomatopoeic effects, to embellishments and microtone deviations, and to a prolonged trailing sound at the end of phrases. Coloristic elements replace harmony, which is unknown in the Western sense to Japanese music.

Westernization   The modern period dates from the opening of the country and the reinstatement of the emperor in 1868, known as the Meiji restoration. French military music (bugles) had already been introduced by some independent feudal lords *(daimyō)* who maintained armies of their own. In the 1870s the imperial court pressed for the immediate introduction of Western music. Under the baton of the Englishman William Fenton, the imperial musicians were the first to perform an all-Western orchestral concert (1877).

Public-school music was organized by a member of a Meiji educational search team, Izawa Shūji, and a Boston music teacher, Luther Whiting Mason, who was brought to Japan in 1880 to help form a music curriculum for public schools and start a teacher-training program. Though there was much talk of combining the best of East and West, the results of the sincere efforts of an American late-Victorian and a Japanese bureaucrat were less than glorious. The teacher-training school became the Tokyo Music School by 1890 and included instruction in koto and, because of the lack of proper violins, the bowed *kokyu*. The music department of the modern University of Fine Arts is still located at the spot of the original school in Ueno Park, Tokyo, with a bust of Beethoven beside the entrance. Koto, samisen, Nō music, and Japanese music history are now found there along with extensive offerings in Western music. But until very recent times music education was totally Western in orientation.

It has often been felt that no true combination of Japanese and Western music would be possible until there was some composer who was equally knowledgeable in both Western and Japanese traditional styles. Takemitsu Toru seems a likely candidate to fill the void. His music is totally contemporary and never directly "orientale"; yet some of his senses of timing, texture, and structure are characteristically Japanese.

In modern Japan all styles of music are available, from the traditional to the most avant-garde. Fully professional performances of Kabuki music are matched by complete Beethoven symphonic series. Huge choruses singing polemics of every type and mass bands of children bowing violins in the widely imitated method of instruction developed by Suzuki compete for audiences with intimate recitals of Heike *biwa* music and hundreds of other events. Research in Japanese traditional music has flourished among native sholars as well as among an increasing number of foreign devotees. National, private, and academic organizations have been founded for the collection, study, and publication of material dealing with all aspects of Japanese musical life; and the commercial record companies periodically enter into prestige contests that result in stunning, well-documented albums concerning nearly every type of Japanese music from Buddhist chant and folk songs to electronic music and prewar popular tunes. *See also* CHINESE MUSIC.

BIBLIOGRAPHY: Francis T. Piggott, *The*

Music and Musical Instruments of Japan (1909; reprint, 1971); William P. Malm, *Japanese Music and Musical Instruments* (1959) and with J.I. Crump, *Chinese and Japanese Music-Dramas* (1975); Eta Harich-Schneider, *A History of Japanese Music* (1973); Robert Garfias, *Music of One Thousand Autumns: The Togaku Style of Japanese Courtly Music* (1976).

Jaques-Dalcroze, Émile (July 6, 1865–July 1, 1950) The Swiss composer and educator Émile Jaques-Dalcroze was a pioneer in the teaching of eurhythmics, a term designating the representation of musical rhythms by bodily movements. Born in Vienna of French parents, he was reared and educated in Geneva, later studying with Bruckner and Robert Fuchs in Vienna and Léo Delibes in Paris. He became an instructor of harmony at the Geneva Conservatory in 1892. He founded his first institute at Hellerau near Dresden in 1910, transferring it to Geneva in 1914, where it became known as the Institut Jaques-Dalcroze. Additional schools were established in London, Paris, Berlin, Vienna, Stockholm, and New York City. He composed three quartets, two violin concertos, and numerous piano pieces and arranged many songs for the teaching of eurhythmics. His *Eurhythmics, Art and Education* was published in an English translation in 1930.

jazz The word has been applied to many kinds of American music and to some European derivative light and concert pieces as well. It is more usefully and more commonly applied to a kind of improvisational U.S. music with an empirically identifiable history, evolution, and body of work from the past that is preserved on recordings. Jazz has characteristics that have persisted, but it is difficult to be definitive about them as jazz is a living and still-evolving form of music. Various attempts at definition have included the ideas that jazz is played with a fixed and constant rhythmic pulse, that it uses only a limited number of time signatures, that the use of so-called "blue notes" will make any piece jazz— even that it is a kind of cacophonous noise and not really music at all. None of these ideas will serve as part of a valid definition.

Throughout its history jazz has borrowed melody and harmony—and even larger forms—from European music, but only certain European characteristics have taken root. For example, although the modern jazz musician seems to be turning to atonal improvising, it is in a manner perhaps more characteristic of the jazz heritage than of the Schoenberg school. Also the jazz musician finds incompatible certain harmonic inversions that have been common in Western concert music for centuries.

origin and early development Jazz was first of all the secular music of the Negro people of the United States. The evolution of jazz has been looked at geographically, by styles, and as the gradual adoption and transmutation of various vocal, instrumental, formal, and orchestral techniques. Perhaps the most meaningful way to see it historically is as a swing toward composition and form alternating with an opposite tendency toward major innovations in basic musical language brought about by great individual improvisers. The trend toward composition and orchestration has shown itself in the very early minstrel and cakewalk popularizations, in the ragtime style in the orchestral work of Ferdinand "Jelly Roll" Morton in the 1920s, in the compositional orchestral works of Edward "Duke" Ellington in the 1930s and '40s, and in the work of Thelonious Monk in the '50s. The great innovators were trumpeter (and singer) Louis Armstrong in the late 1920s and '30s and alto saxophonist Charlie Parker in the '40s. Jazz is probably unique in native U.S. art in that it has retained its identity and life while expanding its range as it adopts new techniques. Another fact that emerges from such a view of jazz is that each of its important innovative steps has a unique rhythmic basis along with the constant and integrated harmonic and linear changes.

African music has a rhythmic complexity that the Western ear often cannot grasp, and such music must have been somehow transplanted by Negro slaves into the United States. But a rhythmically complex, highly percussive music does not necessarily remain complex after its practitioners gradually adopt European ideas of melody, harmony, and rhythm.

Afro-Cuban music has retained a percussive complexity; in Afro-American music some earlier forms are less rhythmically complex than later ones, and the tendency seems to have been to try to get the rhythmic complexity into the melodic lines. And when these lines were transferred from voice to instrument, they retained vocal characteristics. Furthermore, at the same time in the mid-19th century that Negro singers or players were making simple cakewalks out of broad assimilations of European folk melodies or marches for the popular minstrel stage, a complex voodoo drum ceremony might be taking place in New Orleans. And elsewhere a kind of *ur*blues or spiritual might be shaping up from the influence of Baptist hymns on more or less specifically African ideas of melody and rhythm and on the African idea of harmony; that is, nonunison singing by several voices. All of those levels of musical culture might exist and interplay simultaneously; in a sense several of them still do.

The difficult and subtle task of adapting simplified, popularized but apparently African ideas of rhythm to certain European folk standards produced in the cakewalk a rhythmic pulse based (as nearly as can be determined) on a heavily accented half note. In the compositional, pianistic style of the turn-of-the-century ragtime, the rhythm was based on a half note with syncopation. Between 1910 and 1930 this was broken up (sometimes with tangolike syncopations) in the first improvisational, orchestral jazz style that had evolved in New Orleans by 1900. By the late 1920s Louis Armstrong had made rhythm based on evenly accented quarter notes irrevocable, and in the middle '40s the jazzman had again variously subdivided that rhythm. By the late '50s a new rhythmic change (both a sixteenth-note melodic phrasing and a uniquely free use of meter) was definitely taking shape. Throughout most of its history—and certainly since the '20s—the complex jazz rhythm (the rhythm in its melodies as well as in its percussion) has been characterized by a particular flowing movement or momentum for which the term swing has been appropriated; this movement has never been defined, but it persists empirically.

blues The history of jazz cannot be discussed without commenting on the fundamental, flexible, musical–poetic form called the blues. For all the discussions of spirituals, works songs, and chants called field hollers, the blues form is undeniably a crucial fact in jazz. The blues is the only original musical form to have evolved in the United States. By the mid-20th century it was known and used by musicians and singers throughout the world. It is not known where the blues form came from or how or when it evolved. It can only be said—on the basis of what happened to become described or notated—that an interplay of apparently African and European musical traditions gradually produced a definite musical and verse form—the blues. It probably was at first a free, poetic–musical expression whose stanzas consisted of a sentence or phrase chanted several times and another sentence or phrase completing or complementing the first repeated thought and with its last word rhyming with the last word of the repeated first line. As the blues became more formal, the first line was changed or sung only twice, both lines became approximately pentameter in verse form, and the musical form of each stanza usually was 12 measures. To take an example from an even more formal and later day:

> Don't the moon look lonesome,
>   shining through the trees?
> Don't the moon look lonesome,
>   shining through the trees?
> Don't a man seem lonesome when
>   his woman packs to leave?

Gradually a blues stanza came to have a standard 12-measure musical form. Also there are less common blues forms of eight and 16 measures. The blues form has often been described according to the manner in which it was later written down and formally harmonized in piano scores. Thus the so-called blues tonalities were given in terms of flatting the third and seventh (and sometimes fifth) notes in a scale. But these devices are actually attempts to approximate vocal sounds—the bent blue notes, or bent quarter tones, of the voice; later of stringed instruments; and still later of wind instruments. It has also been said that the vo-

cal–instrumental blues scale is a diatonic scale with mobile third and seventh steps that are these blue notes. That is true enough as an approximation, but the blue notes may appear at any interval. And in more formal instrumental versions of authentic blues, the "blue" effects also may appear in various forms. A comparable use of such approximate quarter tones is found in performance in almost all the world's music except in Western concert music.

Like most folk musical–poetic forms the blues was played with a certain amount of improvisation. As instrumental jazz developed and became more sophisticated, the idea of improvisation not only was retained but also became more sophisticated and more important. In addition the musical principles that evolved from the improvised blues came to be applied to materials from other sources.

Archetypical, elementary blues then is a poetic–musical 12-measure form consisting of three rhyming, iambic pentameter (approximate) lines, the first two of which are identical. If the singer is self-accompanied blue notes will be played in the general pitch area of the voice, most probably on a stringed instrument. In the late 1920s and after it became more formal and harmonized, the blues form could sustain the songs of a Bessie Smith and also, in its uniquely percussive piano form later called boogie woogie, such a fine piece of descriptive impressionism as *Honky Tonk Train* (1929) by Meade Lux Lewis.

ragtime At an almost opposite pole from such free and expressive development was ragtime. It was a formal, almost neoclassical, compositional piano music with very limited rhythmic resources. It gave jazz a crucial sense of melody, of form, and probably of harmony. Ragtime was "in the air" in various places by 1880, but its creative centers were first Sedalia, Missouri, and then St. Louis, and its first major composer was Scott Joplin, whose best-known work was *Maple Leaf Rag* (1889). Rags are built like marches, or like their analogues—polkas or mazurkas—on several themes. Improvisation (or at least embellishment) was apparently used in performance, but composition was more important. There were several important rag composers, but after Joplin the most important was probably James Scott. The music became enormously popular by 1895 and was quickly exploited and commercialized, but Joplin continued to experiment within it, and Joseph Lamb was still writing authentic rags in the 1950s.

W. C. Handy Between ragtime and the later emergence of orchestral jazz came the important work of W. C. Handy. Fundamentally a kind of creative folklorist–orchestrator, Handy often took his themes from the blues performers he heard around him, wrote them down, and harmonized them with tonic, dominant, and subdominant "church" chords, using the flattened third and seventh intervals to approximate the blue notes. He also showed excellent taste in selecting and building his multithematic blues *(Memphis Blues, St. Louis Blues, Beale Street Blues)* on the multithematic model of rags; his formal contribution to jazz was large. Some blues were published before Handy's, but as a result of his dissemination of formally harmonized blues jazz players by the late 1920s were freely improvising and spontaneously inventing melodies (in the European sense of invention) on blues chord sequences. By the 1930s the typical form of such improvisational blues would comprise—for a chorus in B-flat—B-flat (four measures), E-flat (two measures), B-flat (two measures), F (two measures), and B-flat (two measures); but both simpler and more complex blues chord sequences appear in all jazz styles.

orchestral style The first orchestral jazz style that developed was the so-called New Orleans style, first popularized by the Original Dixieland Jazz Band in 1917 and probably best preserved on records by the 1923 groups of Joseph "King" Oliver and by "Jelly Roll" Morton's Red Hot Peppers in 1926–30.

King Oliver's band was a group of improvisers who played blues pieces and pieces modeled on rags and marches. Their music might be called an orchestral ragtime improvised on by good blues players, using primary triads (I, IV, V) and some secondary ones, and with a rhythm both more free and more complex than in ragtime. There are closely harmonized passages, but the general characteristic is a kind of polyphony with the two trumpets playing lead melodies, clarinet improvising embellishments and fills (arpeggio or countermelody), trombone in a kind of ground bass, and rhythm instruments (banjo or guitar, string bass or tuba, piano, drums) in an integrated accompaniment. There was also an occasional solo chorus (single horn with rhythmic accompaniment) that pointed to future developments.

Morton's music was more formal. He had a larger perspective that led him to integrate heterophony, polyphony, harmony, solo, written music, sketched parts, and improvisation into a total form and development. By the time he was recording such orchestral jazz, however, a revolution was in effect. It was being staged by Louis Armstrong, who earlier had been a member of Oliver's group.

By the late 1920s Armstrong had developed into a virtuoso trumpet soloist with innovative ideas about rhythm, melody, harmony, and by implication the future of the improvisational aspect of jazz as a soloist's art. He is to many commentators the greatest single figure in jazz. Armstrong's instrument, the trumpet (and its brass cousins), is the one instrument most affected by the innovative techniques of jazz players: in range, sound, use of a variety of mutes, and melodic function. Among other avant-garde players of the period were pianist Earl "Fatha" Hines and soprano saxophonist Sidney Bechet. There was also cornetist Leon "Bix" Beiderbecke, who was originally inspired by the Original Dixieland Band's cornetist Dominick "Nick" La Rocca (among others). His Impressionistic ideas of melody and harmony also made a contribution to the future development of jazz.

At the same time jazz soloists were emerging, efforts were being made to orchestrate for larger groups and to set off the solo improviser. The arranger Don Redman and the orchestra of Fletcher Henderson sought to convert a conventional U.S. dance band with its brass, reed, and rhythm sections into a jazz band. Henderson had fully succeeded by the early 1930s, and it was chiefly his style scores that sustained Benny Goodman's orchestra when swing style found public popularity a few years later.

Duke Ellington began with a dance band; but because he had to provide rather theatrical backgrounds for a night club floor show and because of his own outstanding compositional and orchestral talents, he led his group and his fine improvising soloists (*e.g.,* trumpeter James "Bubber" Miley) into what is sometimes regarded as the highest formal achievements in jazz up to that time, reaching a peak between 1938 and 1941. His orchestra's interpretations of Ellington's own compositions—such as *Subtle Lament, Azure, Ko Ko, Harlem Airshaft,* and *Concerto for Cootie*—are often mentioned as being among his best works, but there are high achievements from all periods of his career. Indeed it has become increasingly common to hear Ellington acclaimed as the great American composer–orchestrator, and—particularly since his death—his longer works such as *Black, Brown, and Beige* and others have received renewed critical attention.

By the 1930s jazz improvising was taking on the form of the invention of new melodic lines on preset chord sequences of the blues and of popular songs. (The latter device might be called playing in a blues style of the chords of "I Got Rhythm," "You're Driving Me Crazy," "Sweet Sue," etc., instead of inventing on blues chords.) In the avant-garde of such invention were chiefly trumpeter Roy Eldridge; pianist Teddy Wilson, vibraphonist Lionel Hampton; Ellington's alto saxophonist Johnny Hodges; alto saxophonist Benny Carter; tenor saxophonists Coleman Hawkins, Ben Webster, and Lester Young, perhaps the most original soloist after Armstrong; trombonist William "Dickie" Wells; drummer Sidney Catlett; singers Billie Holiday and Ella Fitzgerald; and guitarist Charlie Christian. Counter to the movement to invention was the work of pianist Art Tatum, who developed a style of keyboard virtuosity, melodic embellishment, and astonishing harmonic imagination. At this time also appeared the rhythmic perfection of the Count Basie orchestra, a product of Kansas City and the Southwest. Basie was the first pianist to drop timekeeping with his left hand on all the beats.

the 1940s The mid-1940s saw the crisis of rhythmic perfection overcome by a change

that also involved an attempt to make jazz—by then again played mostly by small ensembles—far less a dance (or atmosphere) music and more a listener's music. The most brilliant member of the new movement (at first called be bop after a rhythmic device) was alto saxophonist Charlie Parker, who—like Armstrong before him—had new ideas of jazz rhythm, melody, and phrase length and had a great harmonic imagination in improvisation. Following the lead of Basie, of his drummer Jo Jones, of bassist Walter Page, and of Ellington's bassist Jimmy Blanton, the new rhythm sections dispensed with the rhythm (timekeeping) guitar and lightened or sometimes even discontinued timekeeping by the drummer's foot on the bass drum pedal so that the new rhythm the soloists were making could be more freely accented. Other leaders of the movement were trumpeter John "Dizzy" Gillespie, drummers Kenny Clarke and Max Roach, pianist Earl "Bud" Powell, and trombonist J. J. Johnson. Pianist Thelonious Monk often is mentioned with this group, but his intentions became more formal.

Sarah Vaughan, the most accomplished singer associated with 1940s jazz, has gone on to develop one of the most flexible and resourceful voices in contemporary music, transforming U.S. popular songs into a kind of sublime contemporary bel canto.

Efforts were made in the late 1940s and '50s to formalize the new jazz language. One of the first efforts to attract attention was the so-called cool style. Its main achievement was a series of orchestral recordings for a medium-sized group led by trumpeter Miles Davis. One of the participants was pianist and composer–arranger John Lewis, who later sought musical form for the Modern Jazz Quartet (with vibraphonist Milt Jackson) partly by adopting and assimilating aspects of classical counterpoint for collective jazz improvisation. Another formal development was the unique work of Thelonious Monk, whose compositions for small groups—*Four in One* and *Criss Cross* are good examples—and thematically developed improvisations found musical form within the jazz tradition; his rhythmic and metric virtuosity suggested further innovation. Under such inspiration tenor saxophonist Theodore "Sonny" Rollins became the first horn player in jazz to play an extremely long improvisation with thematic development and cohesion. A further effort was that of virtuoso bassist Charlie Mingus, who combined composition and group improvisation in a manner suggesting the earliest jazz styles. Another advanced instrumentalist was tenor saxophonist John Coltrane, whose later works proved strikingly parallel to that of Ornette Coleman.

In the late 1950s Gunther Schuller wrote a so-called "third stream" work called *Conversations* that succeeded in integrating jazz and concert music. He did not sprinkle a classical form with blue notes and syncopation or write a blues movement in a sonata; instead he pitted writing for and improvising by jazzmen against writing for a string quartet and produced an integrated work.

recent developments Although it had immediate precursors as well as grounding in the jazz tradition as a whole, the music of Ornette Coleman—even in its formative stage—possessed striking originality. As with Armstrong and Parker, Coleman's most important innovations were rhythmic, not only in the rhythm section in his groups (drummer and bass player even provided different time signatures simultaneously) but also in the phrasing of his improvised melodic lines. Intonation was also frequently free, as if Coleman had elevated the blue notes and vocalized inflections so that they encompassed whole melodic phrases and lines. For the first time in jazz, improvisation was based not on a chord structure implied by a theme melody but on invention within the general area of pitch that the theme outlined. Coleman's improvising was predominantly modal, although certain atonal notes were also brought in. Coleman's solos were organized around the development and fragmentation of key phrases so that they became sequential melodies—often ingenious permutations and alterations of a brief opening phrase. Musicians began to refer in the late 1950s to such modal jazz music—and to some more academically oriented experiments with atonality—as "the new thing."

Parallel to Coleman's efforts (and independent of them) were the late 1950s, modally-oriented pieces by Miles Davis such as *Milestones, So What, Flamenco Sketches,* and others that were inspirational to Davis' saxophonist John Coltrane, whose modal and scalar improvisation became prominently a part of the new thing. In view of Coleman's (and Coltrane's) free use of microtones, it is striking that their followers in the 1970s should have been two pianists—Keith Jarrett, who frequently used Coleman's musical associates in his ensembles, and McCoy Tyner, who had worked with Coltrane.

Martin Williams

BIBLIOGRAPHY: Hugues Panassié, *Hot Jazz: The Guide to Swing Music* (1936; reprint, 1970) and *The Real Jazz* (1960; reprint, 1973); Wilder Hobson, *American Jazz Music* (1939; reprint, 1976); Frederic Ramsey, Jr., and Charles E. Smith, eds., *Jazzmen* (1939; reprint, 1977); Nat Shapiro and Nat Hentoff, eds., *Hear Me Talkin' to Ya* (1955; reprint, 1966); André Hodeir, *Jazz: Its Evolution and Essence* (1956; reprint, 1975); Marshall W. Stearns, *The Story of Jazz* (1956); Nat Hentoff and Albert J. McCarthy, eds., *Jazz: New Perspectives on the History of Jazz* (1959; reprint, 1974); Francis Newton, *The Jazz Scene* (1959; reprint, 1975); Leonard Feather, *The Encyclopedia of Jazz,* rev. ed. (1960), *The Encyclopedia of Jazz in the Sixties* (1967), and *The Encyclopedia of Jazz in the Seventies* (1976); Benny Green, *The Reluctant Art: The Growth of Jazz* (1962; reprint, 1975); Rudi Blesh and Harriet Janis, *They All Played Ragtime,* rev. ed. (1966); Martin Williams, *Jazz Masters of New Orleans* (1967), *The Jazz Tradition* (1970), and *Jazz Masters in Transition, 1957–1969* (1970); Donald Kennington, *The Literature of Jazz: A Critical Guide* (1970); George T. Simon, *The Big Bands,* rev. ed. (1975); Stanley Green, *Kings of Jazz,* rev. ed. (1978).

RECORDINGS: The *Smithsonian Collection of Classic Jazz* is an introductory, historically oriented six-LP set. Among other significant jazz recordings are those by Louis Armstrong, Count Basie, Bix Beiderbecke, Ornette Coleman, Miles Davis, Duke Ellington, Dizzy Gillespie, Fletcher Henderson, Billie Holiday, Keith Jarrett, Charlie Mingus, the Modern Jazz Quartet, Thelonious Monk, Jelly Roll Morton, King Oliver, Charlie Parker, Sonny Rollins, Bessie Smith, Art Tatum, Sarah Vaughan, and Teddy Wilson.

Jephtha: *see* CARISSIMI; HANDEL (life) and (works); ORATORIO (Handel).

Jerusalem: *see* PARRY.

Jeux: *see* BALLET (Diaghilev Ballet); DEBUSSY; MODERN PERIOD (new paths).

Jewels of the Madonna, The: *see* GIOIELLI DELLA MADONNA, I.

jig: *see* GIGUE.

Joachim, Joseph (June 28, 1831–August 15, 1907) The great Hungarian violinist and teacher Joseph Joachim was noted for a technical proficiency that never overshadowed musical exigency and for his interpretations of Bach, Beethoven, and Mendelssohn. He first studied at Pest, then at Vienna with Georg Hellmesberger and thus was in contact with both the French and German schools of playing. In 1844 he was successfully sponsored in London by Mendelssohn. After positions as concertmaster at Weimar (1849) and Han-

Joseph Joachim
F. Bruckmann Verlag Bildarchiv

over (1853), Joachim became director in 1868 of the Berlin Hochschule für ausübende Tonkunst, where students from all over Europe sought him out. The next year he formed the celebrated Joachim Quartet, which specialized in the late quartets of Beethoven. In 1881–83 he was the first conductor of the Berlin Philharmonic but found that he preferred the violin to the baton. He aligned with Brahms and Clara Schumann in a long polemic against Liszt and the "new music." The Violin Concerto of Brahms, Schumann's *Fantasy,* and the Concerto No. 2 in d minor of Max Bruch were dedicated to him, as was Dvořák's Concerto in a minor, which Joachim did not premiere. Joachim helped to popularize public concerts that programmed music of the past and was responsible for the public acceptance of much of Bach and Mozart. He composed many virtuoso pieces for the violin, the best known of which is his *Hungarian* Concerto (1860).

RECORDINGS: *Hungarian* Concerto.

Jochum, Eugen (b. November 1, 1902) A conductor at the German opera houses of Lübeck, Mannheim, Munich, and Berlin, the Bavarian conductor Eugen Jochum studied at the Augsburg Conservatory and at the Munich Academy of Music. He founded the Bavarian Radio Symphony in 1934, the same year that he succeeded Karl Muck as music director of the Hamburg State Opera. After 10 years as conductor of the Radio Orchestra of Munich, he became co-conductor (with Bernard Haitink) of the Amsterdam Concertgebouw (1961–64) and then permanent conductor of the Bamberg Symphony. Guest appearances at festivals include Bayreuth, Salzburg, Lucerne, and Edinburgh. His best recordings include a Bruckner cycle and Carl Orff's *Carmina Burana.*

Jolas, Betsy (b. August 5, 1926) A student of Milhaud and Messiaen at the Paris Conservatoire, the French composer and writer Betsy Jolas has since 1955 edited *Écouter aujourd'hui,* the journal of the French radio and television network. Her music is primarily for vocal combinations: two radio cantatas, *L'Oeil égare* (1961) and *Dans la chaleur vacante* (1963), *Quatuor II* (1964) for coloratura soprano and strings, *Points d'aube* (1968) for alto and 13 winds, Sonata *à* 12 (1970), and *Onze Lieder* (1978). For orchestra she composed *Tales of a Summer Sea* (1977). Her music, delicate in texture, is marked by concentration and power in gesture and form.

RECORDING: *Quatuor III* (9 études).

Jolivet, André (August 8, 1905–December 19/20, 1974)   The French composer André Jolivet is noted for his sophisticated experiments with rhythm and new sonorities. Interested in drama, painting, and literature as a young man, he became the only composition pupil of Edgard Varèse. His early Quartet and Andante for string orchestra (both 1934) demonstrate his familiarity with the techniques of Bartók, Schoenberg, and Berg. In 1935 Jolivet was a founder of La Spirale, later called La Jeune France (the name originated with Berlioz), dedicated to fostering modern nationalist music. He joined the Comédie-Française as a conductor in 1943, becoming music director (1945–59) and professor of composition at the Paris Conservatoire (1965–70).

Jolivet was interested in primitive religions and mysticism, reflected in *Mana* (1935) for piano and *Cosmogonie* (1938) and *Psyché* (1946) for orchestra. An expressive melodic style is exemplified in the virtuoso Concertino for trumpet, strings, and piano (1948) and Flute Concerto (1949). He experimented with the ondes Martenot and produced *3 Poèmes* (1935) and a Concerto (1948) for the electronic instrument. His Piano Concerto (1951) has a complex and enormous orchestration that features extensive percussion.

In addition to 12 concertos and much chamber music, Jolivet's compositions include ballets (*Guignol et Pandore,* 1943, and *L'Inconnue,* 1950), a comic opera (*Dolorès, ou Le Miracle de la femme laide,* 1942), vocal and choral pieces, works for radio, and five symphonies.

RECORDINGS: Concerto No. 2 for trumpet, brass, piano, and percussion; Concertino for trumpet, strings, and piano; Flute Concerto; *Suite en Concert* for flute and percussion.

Jommelli, Niccolò (September 10, 1714–August 25, 1774)   Sometimes called the "Italian Gluck," the Neapolitan composer Niccolò Jommelli produced his first opera in Naples, *L'Errore amoroso,* in 1737 and *Odoardo* the following year. He went to Rome in 1740, producing two new operas there, and then to Bologna, where he was influenced by Giovanni Battista Martini. In 1749 he went to Vienna, where he formed a close friendship with Pietro Metastasio. He was appointed in 1753 as Kapellmeister to Duke Karl Eugen of Württemberg at Stuttgart, where he stayed until 1769 and wrote his best operas, including *L'Olimpiade* and *Fetonte.* On Jommelli's return to Italy he was criticized for the French character his music had acquired. His last composition was a *Miserere* for two voices and orchestra that was long his best-known work. Jommelli introduced in his 70 operas a free use of accompanied recitative but broke with the tradition of the da capo aria, thus anticipating Gluck. The style of his overtures influenced the early symphonies of Johann Stamitz.

Jones, Robert (fl. 1600–1611)   Robert Jones was one of the school of English lutenist songwriters that flourished *c.* 1580–1620. Details of his life are scanty. He received his B. Mus. degree at Oxford in 1597. In 1610, together with Philip Rosseter and two other partners, he was granted a patent to train a group of children in London, to be called "The Children of the Revels to the Queene," but when the building in which they were to play was nearly finished the privy council issued an order against its completion and it was demolished. Jones's works include a set of madrigals (1607), now incomplete, and five books of songs for voice and lute published between 1600 and 1611. These songs are mostly light in character, full of melodic inventiveness and rhythmic ingenuity.

Jongen, Joseph (December 14, 1873–July 13, 1953)   The Belgian composer Joseph Jongen was born at Liège and studied at the conservatory there. After winning the Belgian Grand Prix de Rome in 1897 with his cantata *Comala,* he studied in Italy, Germany, and France. In 1903 he became professor of harmony at Liège. As a refugee in England during World War I, he formed a piano quartet with Désiré Defauw, Lionel Tertis, and Émile Doehaerd. He became professor of composition at the Brussels Conservatorie in 1920 and director, 1925–39. Of his numerous works the most widely known are Harp Concerto (1944), *Concert à cinq* (1923), three quartets, and two piano trios. His *Symphonie Concertante* (1926) for organ and orchestra has been associated with the organist Virgil Fox.

RECORDING: *Symphonie Concertante.*

Joplin, Scott (November 24, 1868–April 11, 1917)   Called the king of ragtime composers, the U.S. pianist and songwriter Scott Joplin played jazz piano in the 1890s in St. Louis and Chicago, where he wrote some of his best known rags (*Maple Leaf Rag,* 1899; *The Entertainer,* 1902, popularized as the sound track for the movie *The Sting,* 1973) and a folk ballet (*Rag Time Dance,* 1902). After moving to New York City Joplin wrote numerous rags and an unsuccessful opera, *Treemonisha* (1911), which was successfully revived in New York in the 1970s. In 1970 his piano rags were edited and recorded by pianist Joshua Rifkin, beginning a U.S. revival of ragtime and especially of Joplin's music.

BIBLIOGRAPHY: James Haskins and Kathleen Benson, *Scott Joplin* (1978).

RECORDINGS: *Treemonisha;* complete piano works.

Joseffy, Rafael (July 3, 1852–June 25, 1915) Called "the Patti of the piano," the Hungarian pianist and pedagogue Rafael Joseffy was a pupil of Ignaz Moscheles, Carl Tausig, and Liszt. He was known both as a miniaturist and as a brilliant virtuoso, playing both Chopin and Liszt. After his New York City debut in 1879, he lived in the United States, where he taught extensively and promoted the then relatively unknown works of Brahms. He published an edition of Chopin's works and an important piano method.

Josquin des Prés (*c.* 1440–August 27, 1521)   A Flemish composer whose works mark the transition from the late Middle Ages to the Renaissance, Josquin des Prés was the most renowned musical figure of his time. Born at Condé-sur-L'Escaut or elsewhere in the province of Hainaut, he was probably a chorister at the collegiate church of St. Quentin. He was a singer in the Milan Cathedral

(1459–72), in the service of Duke Galeazzo Maria Sforza in Milan (1473–*c.* 1479), and the papal chapel (1486–*c.* 1494). Between his service in the papal chapel and 1503, when he became choirmaster of the chapel of Ercole I, Duke of Ferrara, he seems to have had connections with the chapel of Louis XII of France and probably also with the cathedral of Cambrai. In Ferrara he wrote in honor of his employer the Mass *Hercules Dux Ferrariae* (based on the theme *re ut re ut re fa mi re,* the Guidonian syllables corresponding to the vowels of the title), and his motet *Miserere* was composed at the duke's request. At the death of the duke (1505), Josquin seems to have left Ferrara. On the conclusion of an alliance between the Netherlands and England, he composed the chanson *Plus nulz regretz.* He spent the remainder of his life as provost of the collegiate church of Notre Dame in Condé.

Josquin des Prés
drawing by Joris van der Straeten, 16th century
courtesy, The Bettmann Archive, Inc.

Of the 20 masses that survive in their entirety and are certainly written by him, 17 were printed in his lifetime in three sets (1502, 1505, and 1514) by Ottaviano del Petrucci. His motets and chansons were included in other Petrucci publications from the *Odhecaton* of 1501 onward. Three musical laments on his death by Nicolas Gombert, Benedictus Appenzeller, and Hieronymus Vinders are extant. Luther expressed great admiration for Josquin's music, calling him "master of the notes, which must do as he wishes; other composers must do as the notes wish." Adrian Petit Coclico, self-styled pupil of Josquin, described and praised his methods of teaching. Until late in the 16th century his works were widely copied, examples of his technique were cited by theorists, and his pieces were used as models by many composers.

In his masses Josquin developed notably the methods inherited from Guillaume Dufay, Jean d'Ockeghem, and Jakob Obrecht, progressing from the cantus-firmus type to the paraphrase and parody mass. His motets and antiphons show a parallel growth in integration by the use of imitative and antiphonal techniques; many of his secular chansons employ canonic and closely imitative writing.

BIBLIOGRAPHY: Edward E. Lowinsky, ed., *Josquin: A Comprehensive Report on the Present State of Josquin Studies, Biographical and Musical* (1976) and with Ferdinand Schevill, ed., *Josquin des Prez* (1977).

jota   A traditional dance of northern Spain, especially popular in Aragon. It is danced in couples in bouncing ¾ rhythm, usually accompanied by castanets and singing. Its lively jumps make it effective in theatrical adaptations for solo, duo, or group performance. A popular jota tune was used by Liszt in his *Rhapsodie espagnole* No. 16 and by Glinka in his *Jota aragonesa*. Other examples are to be found in the works of Saint-Saëns, Albéniz, and de Falla.

Judas Maccabaeus: *see* HANDEL (life).

Juilliard, Augustus D. (April 19, 1836–April 25, 1919)   A U.S. banker and industrialist, Augustus D. Juilliard bequeathed the bulk of his large fortune for the advancement of musical education and opera production. The Juilliard Foundation established (1924) the Juilliard Graduate School in New York City. In 1926 the foundation formed a second board of directors to operate, under the title Juilliard School of Music, both the Juilliard Graduate School and the Institute of Musical Art (founded by Frank Damrosch and James Loeb in 1905). The two institutions were combined into a single school in 1946. A dance department was added in 1951 and a drama division in 1968; in that year, in preparation for moving into a new building at the Lincoln Center

for the Performing Arts (1969), the name was shortened to the Juilliard School.

Juive, La: *see* HALÉVY.

Jullien, Louis Antoine (April 23, 1812–March 14, 1860)   The most flamboyant conductor-showman of the 19th century, Louis Antoine Jullien left his native France for London in 1840 and produced promenade concerts on a monumental scale. Although the circus-like atmosphere turned off serious musicians, Jullien introduced occasional pieces by Beethoven and other major composers and probably contributed considerably to the uplifting of public taste. He was engaged by P. T. Barnum for a series of extravaganzas in the United States (1853–54). In the last year of his life he became insane.

junge Lord, Der: *see* HENZE; OPERA (the 20th century).

Jupiter Symphony (No. 41): *see* COUNTERPOINT (Classical period); MOZART (later life).

just intonation: *see* TUNING AND TEMPERAMENT.

K

Kabalevsky, Dmitry (Borisovich) (b. December 30, 1904)   The Soviet composer Dmitry Kabalevsky studied at the Scriabin Music School and the Moscow Conservatory. He began to compose at the age of 18, primarily for piano. As a pianist he made several European tours after World War II, playing his own music. In 1932 he was appointed to the Moscow Conservatory faculty.

Kabalevsky's early music shows the influence of his teachers Aleksandr Scriabin and Nikolay Myaskovskiy. A personal style characterized by clear tonality and energetic rhythm developed later, though his music showed influences of Mussorgsky, Borodin, and Tchaikovsky. Early works include Four Preludes for piano and the First Piano Sonata (all 1928). Most of Kabalevsky's work has reflected the social and political aims of the Soviet Union. His opera *Colas Breugnon* (1938;

revised 1971) is about a 16th-century Burgundian craftsman with overtones of 20th-century proletarian concepts. In his First Symphony (1932) Tsarist Russia is portrayed by a dark combination of cello, double bass, and bassoon; the Third Symphony (1934) is a memorial on the 10th anniversary of Lenin's death. Folk music elements are evident in *Colas* (French), First Symphony (Russian), *The Golden Spikes* ballet (1940; Byelorussian), and *The Folk Avengers* (1942; Ukrainian) for chorus and orchestra.

Additional operas include *Under Fire* (1943), unsuccessful because of a poor libretto; *The Family of Taras* (1947; revised 1950), which incorporates much of the music from *Under Fire; Nikita Vershinin* (1955); *The Sisters* (1969); and an operetta *Spring Sings* (1957). He has also written much music for children, concertos, chamber music, seven symphonies, and miscellaneous instrumental works.

BIBLIOGRAPHY: Gerald E. H. Abraham, *Eight Soviet Composers* (1943); Stanley D. Krebs, *Soviet Composers and the Development of Soviet Music* (1970).

RECORDINGS: *Colas Breugnon; The Comedians* for orchestra; Piano Concerto No. 3; Piano Sonata No. 3; Violin Concerto.

Kalkbrenner, Friedrich (Wilhelm Michael) (November 7, 1785–June 10, 1849) Educated at the Paris Conservatoire and winning first prizes in piano and harmony, the German pianist and composer Friedrich Kalkbrenner had a facile technique, a vain ego, and a shallow, "brilliant" style of composition. His career was successful, but his pretensions were derided by his colleagues.

RECORDINGS: *Grand sonate brillante* in A-flat; Piano Concerto in d minor; Quintet in a minor for piano, clarinet, horn, cello, and double bass.

Kapell, William (September 20, 1922–October 29, 1953) One of the most promising U.S. pianists after World War II, William Kapell was killed in an airplane crash returning from an Australian concert tour. He was a pupil of Olga Samaroff and won a Naumburg award (1941). His playing was forceful and rhythmically vital and was known especially in 20th-century works.

Karajan, Herbert von (b. April 5, 1908) One of the first conductors of the Austro-German school to devote himself to a cosmopolitan repertoire, Herbert von Karajan has been an internationalist physically as well. At one point in his career he simultaneously headed the Berlin Philharmonic (from 1955), the Vienna State Opera (1956–64), and the Salzburg Festival (1956–62) and was a leading conductor at La Scala and of the Philharmonia in London.

A child prodigy on the piano, Karajan studied at the Mozarteum in Salzburg and at the Vienna Academy. His early conducting was at Ulm and Aachen, and from 1938 to 1944 he led the Berlin State Opera. He succeeded Wilhelm Furtwängler at the Berlin Philharmonic. A Nazi party member, Karajan was exonerated by an Allied tribunal after World War II, but his U.S. debut in 1955 precipitated public protests. For many years his interpretations were noted for their precision and objectivity, but a more personal style developed in his mature years.

BIBLIOGRAPHY: Paul Robinson, *Karajan* (1975).

Herbert von Karajan
courtesy, Deutsche Grammophon/Lauterwasser

Karelia: *see* SIBELIUS.

Karg-Elert, Sigfrid, originally Sigfrid Karg (November 21, 1877–April 9, 1933) The German organist and composer Sigfrid Karg-Elert studied at the Leipzig Conservatory with Karl Reinecke and Salomon Jadassohn and in 1919 became a teacher of piano and composition there. Influenced by Debussy, Schoenberg, and Scriabin, he developed a style of organ music based on the Baroque with Impressionistic overtones. Many of his works, including the 33 *Stilstudien,* were written for a type of harmonium built by Victor Mustel. Among his best-known organ works are his 66 *Chorale Improvisations* (1908–10), *Pastels from Lake Constance* (1919), and *Cathedral Windows* (1923).

Karr, Gary (Michael) (b. November 20, 1941) A graduate of the Juilliard School, the U.S. double bassist Gary Karr has given numerous recitals and workshops throughout the United States and Canada, especially since forming the Karr-Lewis Duo in 1971 with keyboard player David Harmon Lewis. He has premiered solo works by Hans Werner Henze and Paul Ramsier and has recorded music of Serge Koussevitzky.

Kay, Ulysses (Simpson) (b. January 7, 1917) A nephew of the New Orleans jazz trumpeter Joe ("King") Oliver, the U.S. neoclassical composer Ulysses Kay played jazz saxophone as a boy; later he turned to piano, violin, and composition. After earning his B.A. at the University of Arizona (1938), he studied at the Eastman School with Howard Hanson, the Berkshire Music Center, and Yale (with Hindemith) and Columbia (Otto Luening) Universities.

After naval service in World War II as a performer, composer, and arranger for dance bands, Kay composed Suite for strings (1947), Concerto for orchestra (1948), and the film *The Quiet One* (1949). He worked in Rome (1949–52) as recipient of the Prix de Rome and a Fulbright grant. Since 1968 he has taught at the City University of New York.

Kay's music is characterized by melodic lyricism and tonal orientation supplemented by chromaticism. In his later works he also uses quartal harmony, or chords built of tones a fourth apart. His works include many film and television scores, among them *An Essay on Death* (1964), a tribute to John F. Kennedy. In addition to a variety of large orchestral works, including a symphony (1968), Kay has written chamber music, choral works such as the cantata *Song of Jeremiah* (1947), organ and piano music, short band pieces, and two one-act operas, *The Boor* (1955) and *The Juggler of Our Lady* (1956).

RECORDINGS: *Fantasy* Variations; *Markings;* Short Overture; Six Dances for strings.

Keiser, Reinhard (baptized January 12, 1674–September 12, 1739) A German composer of operas and church music, Reinhard Keiser received his early education from his organist father and later attended the Thomasschule in Leipzig. About 1697 he settled in Hamburg and became the most celebrated opera composer of his day. His many operas include *Octavia* (1705), written to compete with Handel's lost opera *Nero; Der angenehme Betrug,* with arias by Christoph Graupner (1707); *Croesus* (*c.* 1710); and the comic opera *Der laecherliche Printz Jodelet* (1726). In 1700 he started a series of winter concerts in Hamburg in the form of a combination concert and banquet. In 1712 he married a well-known singer, Barbara Oldenburg, and in 1728 became cantor and canon of the Hamburg Cathedral.

Keiser's outstanding gifts for melody foreshadow the gallant style. With his colleagues Johann Mattheson and Telemann, he attempted to establish at Hamburg a distinctively German form of Baroque opera. Though he long remained a favorite with the public, his aims remained unfulfilled. In his later years he turned to church music, including oratorios, motets, cantatas, and psalms in a more severe style.

Kempe, Rudolf (June 14, 1910–May 11, 1976) Educated in Dresden, the German conductor and oboist Rudolf Kempe directed the state opera there (1949–52) and in Munich (1952–54). A noted interpreter of Wagner, he conducted at the major music festivals, including Bayreuth, Salzburg, and Edinburgh, and at opera houses in Europe, Australia, and South Africa. He made his conducting debut

431

at the Metropolitan Opera in Wagner's *Tannhäuser* in 1955. He was also associated with the Royal Philharmonic (London) from 1961, becoming principal conductor in 1970. He was appointed artistic director of the Tonhalle Orchestra of Zurich in 1965, music director of the Munich Philharmonic in 1967, and principal conductor of the BBC Symphony in 1975. Recordings include operas of Wagner (two *Meistersingers, Lohengrin*) and operas (notably *Ariadne auf Naxos*) and orchestral music of Richard Strauss.

Kempff, Wilhelm (Walter Friedrich) (b. November 25, 1895)   The German pianist Wilhelm Kempff studied in Berlin and taught in Stuttgart (1924–30). He is known especially as an interpreter of Beethoven, Schubert, and Schumann and has recorded their works extensively. Kempff has also composed operas, ballets, symphonies, and concertos for piano and for violin.

Kern, Jerome: *see* MUSICAL COMEDY; POPULAR MUSIC (the 20th century).

Kertész, István (August 28, 1929–April 17, 1973)   Educated at the Franz Liszt Academy (Budapest) and the Accademia di Santa Cecilia (Rome), the Hungarian conductor István Kertész taught briefly at the Budapest Academy before devoting his time principally to conducting. After positions in Budapest and in Augsburg and appearances at the Salzburg Festival, he toured North America with the Hamburg Radio Orchestra (1963). Guest appearances throughout the world were scheduled around positions as music director of the Cologne Opera (from 1964) and as principal conductor of the London Symphony (1965–68). He has recorded all the symphonies of Dvořák, a Brahms cycle, and notable performances of Kodály's *Háry János* and Bartók's *Bluebeard's Castle*.

kettledrum: *see* TIMPANI.

key   The concept of interrelated chords based ultimately on the notes of the diatonic major and minor scales. Each of the pitches, or tones, used in Western music can serve as a tonic note, or keynote, for a major or minor key. Thus the key of G major refers to a system of fixed relations between chords based on the

tones of the major scale beginning on the note G, its tonic note. In musical notation key is indicated by the key signature, a group of sharps or flats at the beginning of each line of music: *e.g.,* in the key of G one sharp; in the key of C no sharps or flats; in the key of D-flat five flats.

The concept of key is an essential part of the system of TONALITY. Different keys are closely or distantly related to one another according to the number of tones their diatonic scales share: the keys of C major and G major have six of their seven tones in common and are closely related. The distantly related keys of C major and C-sharp major have no tones in common. The ability of a listener to sense key relationships is exploited in musical forms such as the sonata. The broader term tonality is sometimes used as a synonym for key.

The word key is also used to refer to the visible end of a lever in the action of a keyboard instrument and to the comparable lever on the side of a woodwind instrument.

keyboard instruments   Instruments played from a keyboard. The PIANO, HARPSICHORD (including its several variants), and CLAVICHORD all make use of strings and are often grouped together. Other examples are the ORGAN, HARMONIUM, CELESTA, ONDES MARTENOT, SYNTHESIZER, and carillon (*see* BELL).

key signature   The sharps or flats (or lack thereof) at the beginning of a staff immediately following the clef that indicate the major or relative minor key. For instance, two sharps indicate either the key of D major or b minor (*see* example). A new key signature may also be inserted at a change of key within a piece.

Khachaturian, Aram (Ilich) (June 6, 1903– May 1, 1978)   A student at the Gnesiny State Musical and Pedagogical Institute in Moscow and of Nikolay Myaskovskiy at the Moscow Conservatory, and professor at both from 1951, the Soviet composer Aram Khachaturian was influenced as a youth by contemporary Western music, particularly that of Ravel. In his First Symphony (1934) and later works this influence was superseded by interest in his national heritage of Armenian folk music as well as in other folk sources of Georgia, Russia, Turkey, and Azerbaijan. His Second Symphony (1943) was written for the 25th anniversary of the Bolshevik Revolution. Other works include the ballets *Happiness* (1939), the popular *Gayane* (1942), and *Spartak* (1956); concertos for piano (1936), viola (1940), violin and cello (*c.* 1944), and cello (1946); a symphonic suite *Masquerade* (1944); Third Symphony (1947); and a series entitled Concerto-Rhapsody for a solo instrument with orchestra: piano (1961), violin (1961), and cello (1963). Khachaturian was twice the recipient of the Stalin Prize, and he composed the music for the Armenian national anthem.

With Shostakovich and Prokofiev, Khachaturian was accused in 1948 by the Central Committee of the Communist Party of bourgeois tendencies in his music, but after Stalin's death he publicly condemned the accusation. The Khachaturian family was prominent in Soviet cultural affairs, and Aram's nephew Karen is also a composer.

BIBLIOGRAPHY: Gerald E. H. Abraham, *Eight Soviet Composers* (1943); Stanley D. Krebs, *Soviet Composers and the Development of Soviet Music* (1970).

RECORDINGS: *Armenian* Dances; Cello Concerto; *Gayane; Masquerade;* Piano Concerto; Piano Sonata; *Spartak;* Symphony No. 3; Trio for clarinet, violin, and piano; Violin Concerto.

Khan, Ali Akbar (b. 1922)   The Indian master of the sarod Ali Akbar Khan was a pupil of his father, Allauddin Khan, and learned vocal music, drums, and other Indian instruments before concentrating on the sarod. He played his first public performance when he was 14 and became court musician for the Maharajah of Jodhpur while in his early 20s. Khan first visited the United States in 1955 at the request of Yehudi Menuhin, playing at the Museum of Modern Art in New York City, making his first Western recording, and appearing on U.S. television. He has since

toured regularly and with his brother-in-law, the sitarist Ravi Shankar, has promoted Indian music in the Western world. He founded Ali Akbar College of Music in Calcutta in 1956 and a branch in Marin County, California, in 1967. Khan has composed music for 18 films, including the award-winning *Hungry Stones.* Honors include the Sangeet Natak Academy award and the rarely-given Padma Bhushan award by the government of India. *See* photograph at SAROD.

Khovanshchina: *see* MUSSORGSKY; ROMANTIC PERIOD (non-German music of the 19th century).

Kincaid, William (Morris) (April 26, 1895–March 27, 1967)   Educated at the Institute of Musical Art (now the Juilliard School), the Hawaiian-born flutist William Kincaid joined his teacher Georges Barrère as flutist in the New York Symphony. From 1921 to 1960 he was first flutist with the Philadelphia Orchestra, with whom he made 135 appearances as a soloist. He was on the faculty of the Curtis Institute and the Manhattan (New York City) School. He attributed his phenomenal breath control to rigorous training in swimming, when he was the protégé of the Olympic champion Duke Kahanamoku.

Kinderscenen: *see* SCHUMANN, ROBERT (early career).

Kindertotenlieder: *see* MAHLER (middle period).

King Priam: *see* LIBRETTO (modern status); OPERA (the 20th century); TIPPETT.

King Stag: *see* HENZE.

Kipnis, Alexander (February 1, 1891–May 14, 1978)   The Russian bass Alexander Kipnis studied at the conservatories of Warsaw and Berlin after relinquishing plans to become a merchant. Interned during World War I, he made his debut in 1916 at the Hamburg Opera. After three years at Wiesbaden he joined the German Opera at Berlin-Charlottenburg, where he remained until 1930, coupling this activity with regular performances (1924–32) at the Chicago Civic Opera. He became principal bass at the Berlin State Opera (1932–35) and was celebrated at the Bayreuth and

Salzburg festivals. A member of the Metropolitan Opera (1940–46), he remained in the United States to teach. Reputed for his lieder and for the Russian operatic repertoire, he also achieved success in the roles of Sarastro (Mozart's *Die Zauberflöte*) and Gürnemanz (Wagner's *Parsifal*). His son Igor Kipnis became a well-known harpsichordist.

Kipnis, Igor (b. September 27, 1930) The German-born U.S. harpsichordist Igor Kipnis, son of the singer Alexander Kipnis, was educated at Harvard University (1952) and taught at the Berkshire Music Center, Tanglewood (1964–67), and since 1971 at Fairfield University, Connecticut. In addition to extensive recitals and recording, he has been active in record reviewing and in radio. He edited *A First Harpsichord Book* (1970).

Kirchner, Leon (b. January 24, 1919) Educated at the University of California at Berkeley (1940), the U.S. composer and conductor Leon Kirchner also studied with Schoenberg, Stravinsky, Bloch, and Roger Sessions. He taught at the University of Southern California (1950–54), Mills College (1954–60), and at Harvard University since 1961. Kirchner's music has an emotional excitement but is carefully controlled and not composed according to any standardized system or technique. His principal works include three quartets (1948, 1958, 1966); two piano concertos (1953, 1963); Toccata (1956) for strings, winds, and percussion; Concerto (1960) for violin, cello, 10 winds, and percussion; and an opera, *Henderson* (1977), after Saul Bellow's novel, *Henderson the Rain King*.

RECORDINGS: Quartet No. 3; Sonata Concertante for violin and piano; Toccata for strings, winds, and percussion.

Kirkpatrick, Ralph (b. June 10, 1911) Active in the revival of early keyboard instruments in the United States, Ralph Kirkpatrick became a noted performer on the harpsichord and the clavichord, specializing in the works of Bach and of Domenico Scarlatti. A graduate of Harvard University (1931), he studied with Landowska, Boulanger, Arnold Dolmetsch, and Günther Ramin. His research on Scarlatti resulted in a performing edition of *Sixty Sonatas* (1953; also recorded by Kirk-

patrick), a biography *Domenico Scarlatti* (1953), and an edition of Scarlatti's *Complete Keyboard Works in Facsimile from the Manuscript and Printed Sources* in 18 volumes (1971). He also published a valuable edition of Bach's *Goldberg* Variations and served on the faculty at Yale University from 1956.

kit A small 16th- to 18th-century fiddle with a muted tone carried in dancing masters' pockets. A last descendant of the medieval REBEC, the kit evolved as a narrow, boat-shaped instrument usually with three or four strings. Later narrow violin-shaped kits were also built. Dancing masters used it in teaching to play the dance melody and rhythm. Instruments were frequently carved or inlaid with ivory, tortoiseshell, or gems. A frequent tuning was middle C-G-D.

rebec- and violin-shaped kits
Leslie Lindsey Mason Collection of Musical Instruments (formerly the Galpin Collection) Museum of Fine Arts, Boston

Klangfarbenmelodie A term meaning "tone-color melody" employed by Schoenberg in his *Harmonielehre* in arguing that tone color (timbre) is a structural element of composition comparable in importance to duration, pitch, etc. The idea was further explored by his pupil Webern and by his followers in serial and electronic composition.

Klavierstücke XI: *see* ALEATORY MUSIC; MODERN PERIOD (rediscovery of serialism); STOCKHAUSEN.

Kleiber, Carlos (b. July 3, 1930)   The son of conductor Erich Kleiber, Carlos Kleiber was born in Berlin, grew up in Buenos Aires, and followed in his father's footsteps after beginning an education in chemistry at Zurich. After brief engagements in Munich and Potsdam, Kleiber conducted eight seasons at the Deutsche Oper am Rhein in Düsseldorf (from 1956) and the Zurich Opera (from 1964). In 1966 he began conducting in Stuttgart and two years later at Munich, but he refuses to take a permanent appointment. He made his debut at Bayreuth in 1974 with Wagner's *Tristan und Isolde*. His first operatic recording was Weber's *Der Freischütz* (1973), followed two years later by Beethoven's Fifth Symphony and still later the Seventh (both with the Vienna Philharmonic).

Kleiber, Erich (August 5, 1890–January 27, 1956)   Educated in Vienna and Prague, the Austrian conductor Erich Kleiber appeared in Darmstadt, Düsseldorf, and Mannheim before becoming general music director of the Berlin State Opera (1923). He made his U.S. debut with the New York Philharmonic-Symphony in 1930 and conducted the NBC Symphony (1945–46). In 1935 he left Germany for political reasons and conducted for a year at La Scala. He then worked in South America, conducting German opera in Buenos Aires (1936–49) and directing the Havana (Cuba) Philharmonic (1944–47); in these two cities he gave the first Latin American performances of standard repertoire from Beethoven's *Missa solemnis* to Richard Strauss's *Die Frau ohne Schatten*. In 1950 he had great success at Covent Garden with Mozart's *Magic Flute,* Richard Strauss's *Rosenkavalier,* and Tchaikovsky's *Queen of Spades.* Interested in contemporary music, he conducted the premieres of Berg's *Wozzeck* (1925) and Luigi Dallapiccola's *Due pezzi* (1947). He has made notable recordings of operas of Mozart and Richard Strauss.

Klemperer, Otto (May 14, 1885–July 10, 1973)   Despite numerous accidents that left him physically impaired, Otto Klemperer was the last surviving member of the 19th-century Austro-German school of conducting, though he was one of the few to promote 20th-century

Otto Klemperer
courtesy, Angel Records

music of the new school. Klemperer studied in Frankfurt and Berlin and on the recommendation of Mahler was made conductor of the German Opera at Prague in 1907. Between 1910 and 1927 he conducted opera at Hamburg, Strasbourg, Cologne, and Wiesbaden and then became director of the Kroll Opera in Berlin, where he introduced works by Janáček, Schoenberg, Hindemith, Stravinsky, and Ernst Krenek. With the rise of the Nazis he was compelled to leave Germany, settling in the United States for a time with the Los Angeles Philharmonic (1933–39) and making many guest appearances. He returned to Europe as director of the Budapest Opera (1947–50) and from 1951 conducted the Philharmonia and (after 1964) New Philharmonia orchestras in London. Klemperer's *Minor Recollections* was published in an English translation in 1964, further amplified by Peter Heyworth's *Conversations with Klemperer* (1973).

Knot Garden, The: *see* LIBRETTO (modern status); OPERA (the 20th century); TIPPETT.

Köchel catalog: *see* MOZART (Köchel catalog).

Kodály, Zoltán (December 16, 1882–March 6, 1967)   A Hungarian composer and authority on Hungarian folk music, Zoltán Kodály was a chorister in his youth at Nagyszombat (renamed Trnava), where he wrote his first compositions, and in 1902 he studied composition with Hans Koessler in Budapest. In 1905 he undertook his first folk song expedition. In the following year he met Bartók and also graduated from Budapest University with a thesis on the structure of Hungarian folk song. After studying for a short time with Charles-Marie Widor in Paris, he was appointed teacher of theory and later composition at the Budapest Academy (1907–41). Further researches on folk music were made until the outbreak of World War I; in 1923 he wrote his *Psalmus Hungaricus* to celebrate the 50th anniversary of the union of Buda and Pest. In 1926 he produced his comic opera *Háry János,* and his reputation was further established with two sets of Hungarian dances for orchestra, *Marosszéki táncok* (1930) and *Galántai táncok* (1933). Other works include Te Deum (1936), Concerto for orchestra (1941), *Missa brevis* (1945), and the opera *Czinka Panna* (1948). His Symphony was first performed in 1961. Kodály created an individual style derived from Hungarian folk music, contemporary French music, and the religious music of the Italian Renaissance. With Bartók he published editions of folk songs (1906; 1921), and his folk song collection formed the basis of *Corpus Musicae Popularis Hungariae* (1951). He revolutionized Hungarian music education, bringing it to the people through singing—particularly solmization and Hungarian folk song.

BIBLIOGRAPHY: Zoltán Kodály, *Folk Music of Hungary* (1960) and *Selected Writings of Zoltán Kodály* (1974); László Eösze, *Zoltán Kodály: His Life and Work* (1962); Percy M. Young, *Zoltán Kodály, a Hungarian Musician* (1964; reprint, 1976); Erzsébet Szönyi, *Kodaly's Principles in Practice* (1973); Lorna Zemka, *Kodaly Concept: Its History, Philosophy, Development,* 2nd ed. (1977).

RECORDINGS: Numerous recordings of many works.

Koechlin, Charles (November 27, 1867–December 31, 1950) A French composer and teacher of many of the younger composers of his time, Charles Koechlin did not take up music seriously until he was 22 after having studied at the École Polytechnique. Among his teachers at the Paris Conservatoire were Massenet and Fauré. He later studied privately with Fauré and was to some extent influenced by him. As a teacher he influenced composers of his own and younger generations, including "Les Six." As a composer he experimented with new techniques, polytonality, atonality, and serialism. His works, many of which are still unpublished, range from songs, piano music, and chamber combinations to symphonic and choral works, lyric dramas, ballets, music for films, and educational exercises in polyphonic composition. Among the sources of his inspiration was Kipling's *Jungle Book,* from which he set three poems for chorus and orchestra (1899–1910) and four symphonic poems (1925–39); *e.g., La Course de printemps* and *Les Bandar-Log.* His theoretical writings include treatises on modal polyphony, harmony, and orchestration and an essay on polytonal and atonal music. He also wrote biographies of Debussy and Fauré and orchestrated Debussy's ballet *Khamma,* Chabrier's *Bourrée fantasque,* and Fauré's incidental music for *Pelléas et Mélisande.*

RECORDINGS: *Les Bandar-Log; Cinq Chorals dans les modes du moyen-âge;* Partita for chamber orchestra; Trio for flute, clarinet, and bassoon.

Kogan, Leonid (Borisovich) (b. November 14, 1924) A student (with Abram Yampolsky) and later teacher at the Moscow Conservatory, the Soviet violinist Leonid Kogan toured and recorded with a trio including Emil Gilels and Mstislav Rostropovich. He won first prize at the Brussels Competition in 1951 and made his North American debut in 1958. A People's Artist of the U.S.S.R., he won the Lenin Prize in 1956. He has recorded concertos of Brahms, Prokofiev, Tchaikovsky, and Aram Khachaturian.

Kondrashin, Kiril (b. February 21, 1914) Educated at the Moscow Conservatory, the Russian conductor Kiril Kondrashin began conducting at the Leningrad Academic Maly Theater and five years later at the Bolshoi

Theater. He headed the Moscow Philharmonic (1960–76), recording most of the Shostakovich symphonies and much of the standard Russian Romantic and 20th-century repertoire. He has appeared as a guest conductor throughout the Soviet Union, Europe, and the Americas. Kondrashin was named a "People's Artist of the Soviet Union" in 1972, but in 1978 he defected to the West.

König Hirsch: *see* HENZE.

Korngold, Erich (Wolfgang) (May 29, 1897–November 29, 1957)   Best known as a composer of film music, the Moravian-born composer Erich Korngold began composing while a boy; his pantomime, *Der Schneemann,* written at age 11, was presented at the Vienna Court Opera in 1910. His father, Julius Korngold, was Vienna's most influential music critic. His output includes operas (*Die tote Stadt,* 1920), quartets, choral works (*Psalm,* 1941), a violin concerto (1945), and a symphony (1950), and in the 1970s there was renewed interest in this part of his work. In 1934 he went to Hollywood to adapt Mendelssohn's incidental music for Max Reinhardt's production of *A Midsummer Night's Dream* and later established a career there. His scores for the films *Anthony Adverse* (1936) and *The Adventures of Robin Hood* (1938) won academy awards and, with *Of Human Bondage* (1945), have become classics of their genre.

RECORDINGS: *Much Ado About Nothing;* Piano Trio; Piano Quintet; Piano Sonatas; *Der Schneemann;* Symphony in F-sharp; *Die tote Stadt;* Violin Concerto; Violin Sonata; film music; songs.

Kosleck, Julius (December 1, 1825–November 5, 1904)   A composer and arranger of works for brass instruments, the German cornetist and trumpeter Julius Kosleck taught at the Berlin Hochschule für Musik. He organized the Kaiser Cornet Quartet, which was enlarged to become the official brass band of the state. Kosleck was one of the first (1871) to experiment with "Bach" trumpets—then thought to be impossible to play in the high range called for by Bach and usually replaced by clarinets and the like. He used a straight trumpet in A with two valves for a performance (1884) of the b minor Mass at Eisenach.

Kossuth: *see* BARTÓK.

koto   A Japanese 13-stringed board zither with movable bridges. Though derived from

woman playing koto at Ikuta School   *Tadashi Kimura*

continental Asian models, it has developed structural and musical characteristics that make it specifically Japanese. It is played by plucking the strings with the thumb and first two fingers of the right hand, either bare or with ivory attachments (*tsume,* "plectrum"). In traditions after the 16th century the left hand may alter the pitch or ornament the sound of each string by pressing or manipulating the strings on the other side of each bridge. Many tunings are used. The koto has enjoyed popularity from the earliest periods of Japanese music to the present in ensemble, chamber, and solo music repertoires.

Koussevitzky, Serge (July 26, 1874–June 4, 1951)   The first important Russian conductor, Serge Koussevitzky began as a virtuoso on the double bass, for which he composed a concerto and some small pieces. Trained at the Moscow Conservatory, he became interested in conducting from observing Arthur Nikisch in Berlin. He married (1905) the daughter of a wealthy tea merchant and in 1908 hired the Berlin Philharmonic for his conducting debut. Though he had certain weaknesses in conducting technique and in score reading that he never completely over-

Serge Koussevitzky   *EB Inc.*

came, he was naturally musical and possessed a dynamic personality that affected players and audiences alike. He returned to Russia in 1909 and founded his own orchestra in Moscow and also a publishing house, whose catalog listed such composers as Rachmaninoff, Prokofiev, Stravinsky, and Aleksandr Scriabin (whose music Koussevitzky especially championed). After the Revolution of 1917 he was appointed to the State Symphony (until 1920), conducted in Paris (from 1921), and finally began his long association (1924–49) with the Boston Symphony. In Boston (he seldom conducted elsewhere and rarely engaged guest conductors) he promoted new music in great quantity, giving first performances of works by young Americans (Samuel Barber, his protégé Bernstein, Copland, Gershwin, Roy Harris, Howard Hanson, Walter Piston, William Schuman, and many others) and Europeans (Bartók, Hindemith, Honegger, Prokofiev, Stravinsky, etc.). He took over the fledgling Berkshire Festival at Tanglewood, Massachusetts, in 1936 and established it as America's major summer festival, adding a school in 1940. He organized the Koussevitzky Foundation (1942) to commission and perform new works.

   BIBLIOGRAPHY: Arthur Lourié, *Sergei Koussevitzky and His Epoch* (1931; reprint, 1971); Hugo Leichtentritt, *Serge Koussevitzky, the Boston Symphony Orchestra and the New American Music* (1946; reprint, 1976).

   RECORDINGS: Double Bass Concerto; *Valse miniature* for double bass.

Krainis, Bernard (b. December 28, 1924) Co-founder (with Noah Greenberg) of the New York Pro Musica Antiqua (1953), the U.S. recorder player Bernard Krainis majored in economics and anthropology at the University of Denver, later turning to musicology at New York University. He served as associate director and recorder soloist with the Pro Musica (1953–59) and later formed the Krainis Recorder Consort and the Krainis Baroque Ensemble. He taught at Kirkland College, Clinton, New York, beginning in 1970, Columbia University from 1973, and Smith College, Northampton, Massachusetts, from 1976. He teaches summer sessions at Aston

Magna in Great Barrington, Massachusetts, and performs with the group. His recordings include Telemann and Vivaldi.

Kraus, Lili (b. April 3, 1905)   Educated at the Budapest Academy, where she studied with Bartók and Kodály, the Hungarian pianist Lili Kraus also studied in Vienna and with Artur Schnabel. She taught in Vienna, became a British subject in 1948, and has lived in the United States since 1967. Although her repertoire ranges from Bach to Bartók, she is known primarily for her Mozart: she played all of his piano concertos in a single season in New York City (1966–67 and has recorded them), and all of the piano sonatas the next.

Krebs, Johann Ludwig (October 10, 1713– buried January 4, 1780)   The German organist and composer Johann Ludwig Krebs studied music first with his father and in 1726 entered the Thomasschule at Leipzig, where he became a pupil of Bach. He held posts as organist at Zwickau, Zeitz, and at Altenburg. Krebs's organ music is composed in the forms used by Bach and leans heavily on his master's style. It is technically accomplished and includes some fine trio sonatas. He also wrote sonatas for flute and harpsichord and some sacred vocal music.

RECORDING: Guitar (harpsichord) Concerto in G.

Kreisler, Fritz (February 2, 1875–January 29, 1962)   One of the greatest violinists of the first half of the 20th century, the Viennese musician Fritz Kreisler studied in Vienna and then at the Paris Conservatoire, where he won the Grand Prix de Rome at the age of 12. After a successful concert tour of the United States in 1888–89, he studied medicine in Vienna and art in Paris and Rome before continuing his musical career. His playing was characterized by an intense vibrato (continuing the tradition of his teacher Lambert-Joseph Massart), resonant tone, and economy in bowing. Elgar dedicated his Concerto in b minor (1910) to him. Kreisler wrote many short, descriptive pieces, which he passed off as obscure works by Vivaldi, Couperin, and Stamitz; in 1935 he admitted that these "classical manuscripts" arrangements were actually his own compositions.

Kremer, Gidon (b. February 27, 1947)   Born to a family of violinists, the Soviet violinist Gidon Kremer entered the Moscow Conservatory in 1965 and studied with David Oistrakh for eight years. He won the Paganini Competition in Genoa in 1969 and the Tchaikovsky in Moscow in 1970. His debut with the London Symphony in 1975 brought critical acclaim and a recording of the Brahms Violin Concerto with Herbert von Karajan and the Berlin Philharmonic. Two years later he played his first recital in New York City's Avery Fisher Hall with equal success.

Krenek, Ernst (b. August 23, 1900)   A prominent exponent of serial technique, the Austrian-born composer Ernst Krenek studied in Vienna and Berlin and was assistant conductor at the opera houses of Kassel (1925–27) and Wiesbaden (1927–28). In 1938 he emigrated to the United States, taught compo-

Fritz Kreisler   *EB Inc.*

sition at Vassar (1939–42) and Hamline (1942–47), became a U.S. citizen in 1945, and in 1947 settled in California.

Krenek's earliest compositions were influenced by Mahler (his father-in-law from 1923 to 1925). In his first operas, however, he turned to a dissonant, expressionist style, as in *Zwingburg* (1924; *Dungeon Castle*). He gained international success with the opera *Jonny Spielt Auf!* (1927; *Johnny Strikes up the Band!*), written in an idiom that mixed dissonance with jazz. After a period in which he espoused the Romanticism of Schubert, he began in the 1930s to use the 12-tone technique of Schoenberg. His first significant 12-tone work was the opera *Karl V* (1933; produced 1938). Other important 12-tone works were the Second Piano Concerto (1938) and the Fourth Symphony (1947).

Krenek experimented widely with styles and techniques. In *Sestina* (1957) he used total serialization; in his Third Piano Concerto he temporarily abandoned the 12-tone method for traditional tonality; his Fifth Symphony is atonal but avoids serial technique; in his oratorio *Spiritus Intelligentiae* (1958) he utilized electronically produced sound; in *Pentagram* for wind quintet (1952; revised 1958) and in *Fibonaci Mobile* (1965) mathematical ideas influence the musical content. Krenek's other compositions include sonatas for harp and for organ; Twelve Short Piano Pieces, an introduction to 12-tone technique; *Eleven Transparencies* for orchestra; and operas, among them *Pallas Athene Weint* (1955; *Pallas Athena Weeps*).

Krenek's books include *Music Here and Now* (1939); *Studies in Counterpoint* (1940); *Self-Analysis* (1953), an autobiography; and *Johannes Ockeghem* (1953).

RECORDINGS: *Aulokithara* for oboe, harp, and tape; *Echoes from Austria* for piano; Harp Sonata; *Kleine Blasmusik; O Tape and Double; Pentagram* for winds; *Santa Fe Timetable* for chorus; Toccata for accordion; Trio for clarinet, violin, and piano; Violin sonata; *Wechselrahmen* (song cycle).

Kreutzer, Rodolphe (November 16, 1766–January 6, 1831) The founder of the French school of violin playing, Rodolphe Kreutzer studied with Anton Stamitz and in 1795 was appointed a professor at the Paris Conservatoire. He played solo violin at the Théâtre Italien and the Paris Opéra and was chamber musician to Napoleon and to Louis XVIII. Beethoven dedicated his Sonata in A Major (Op. 47; published 1805) to him; although this is now known as the *Kreutzer* Sonata, Kreutzer himself never performed it. He was an expert improviser and had a brilliant technique. His 40 Études, or Caprices, summarize the entire range of violin technique and, with the *Méthode de violon* (written with Pierre Baillot and Pierre Rode), are still standard exercises.

Kreutzer Sonata (No. 9): *see* BEETHOVEN (approaching deafness).

Krieger, Johann Philipp (February 25, 1649–February 7, 1725) The German composer Johann Philipp Krieger studied at Nürnberg and Copenhagen and was appointed organist at Bayreuth in 1670. He made a study tour of Italy, working under Johann Rosenmüller in Venice and Bernardo Pasquini in Rome. After a brief return to Bayreuth he was appointed Kapellmeister to the court of Halle and Weissenfels in 1680. Krieger was a prolific composer of sacred music, but of the 2,000 or so cantatas he is known to have written only about 80 are extant. He also composed suites of outdoor music for wind instruments and about 200 secular strophic *Arien*. Of Krieger's operas only a few arias remain.

Krips, Josef (April 8, 1902–October 13, 1974) A student of Felix Weingartner, the Austrian-born Josef Krips made his early reputation as an opera conductor with the Vienna Volksoper and in Dortmund and Karlsruhe before becoming conductor of the Vienna State Opera (1933). He conducted opera in Belgrade (1938–39) and in 1945 returned to Vienna to help rebuild its post-war musical life. He was principal conductor of the London Symphony (1950–54), the Buffalo (New York) Philharmonic (1954–63), and the San Francisco Symphony (1963–70). He was a fine Bruckner conductor, although he left no recordings of the symphonies. His recordings include Mozart and Johann Strauss the Younger, and he was the first conductor to record with Artur Rubinstein a cycle of the Beethoven piano concertos.

Krumpholz, Johann Baptist (May 8, 1745– February 19, 1790)   A composition student of Haydn while attached to the Esterházy chapel (1773–76), the Bohemian harpist Johann Baptist Krumpholz was an innovator in developing improvements for his instrument. The greater part of his career was spent in Paris performing and teaching. His compositions for harp include six concertos, 32 sonatas with violin, and symphonies for harp and chamber orchestra.

Kubelík, Jan (July 5, 1880–December 5, 1940)   The violinist Jan Kubelík, Czech-born but later a Hungarian citizen, was taught initially by his father, who was a gardener. He then studied with Otokar Ševčik at the Prague Conservatory and made his professional debut in Vienna in 1898. His playing was considered a parallel to Paderewski's in virtuosity and dramatic power, but his career was curtailed in World War I and did not regain momentum. His son is the conductor Rafael Kubelík.

Kubelík, (Jeronym) Rafael (b. June 29, 1914)   Son of violinist Jan Kubelík, the Czech conductor and composer Rafael Kubelík studied at the Prague Conservatory and made his debut at 19 conducting the Czech Philharmonic, of which he became conductor two years later. He held that position until 1948 except for two years (1939–41) as music director of the Brno (Czechoslovakia) Opera. He was music director of the Chicago Symphony (1950–53) and of the Royal Opera at Covent Garden (1955–58). From 1961 he conducted the Bavarian Radio Symphony, and in 1973–74 he was the first music director of the Metropolitan Opera. Important in his programming and recording are Czech music and contemporary music. His own compositions include four operas, two symphonies, four string quartets, and chamber music, concertos, and songs.

L

Lablache, Luigi (December 6, 1794–January 23, 1858)   Admired as both a musician and actor, the Neapolitan-French bass Luigi Lablache made his debut in Naples at age 18 in Valentino Fioravanti's *La molinara*. He subsequently achieved success in buffo roles, especially as Geronimo in Cimarosa's *Il matrimonio segreto*. He was singing teacher to England's Queen Victoria (1836–37) and sang the bass aria of Mozart's Requiem at Beethoven's funeral (1827). He was one of a quartet for which Donizetti wrote *Don Pasquale,* and Schubert wrote songs for him.

lai   A medieval form cultivated especially among the trouvères in the 12th and 13th centuries and among their slightly earlier Provençal-language counterparts, the troubadours; it was called *Leich* by the German minnesingers.

The lai was a long poem with nonuniform stanzas of about six to 16 or more lines of four to eight syllables. One or two rhymes were maintained throughout each stanza. The text might address the Virgin or a lady or in some cases might be didactic.

In musical form the lai was influenced by the sequence, a long liturgical hymn having the general musical pattern *x aa bb cc . . . y;* the repeated pairs are termed double versicles. In lais, however, the triple and quadruple repetitions and unrepeated lines might occur, and the first and last lines of music were not always unrepeated. Each stanza had its own music.

This basic form could be varied. A set of several double versicles could be repeated, giving musical unity in the setting of a long poem; the last few notes of a melody might be altered on the repetition, the first ending called *ouvert* (open), the second *clos* (closed); and the melody might be varied on the repetition. Shorter variants and offshoots of the lai included patterns such as *aabb* set to short poems, and strophic songs using short double versicle patterns such as *abbc*.

The lai was monophonic music, but in the 14th century Guillaume de Machaut set two of his 18 lais polyphonically, using a form called the *chace,* a three-part canon at the unison. Machaut typically wrote lais of 12 stanzas, the last of which shared the melody and poetic form of the first; within each stanza he used double or quadruple versicles.

Lakmé: *see* DELIBES.

Lalande, Michel Richard de (December 15, 1657–June 18, 1726)   The finest French composer of sacred music in the first part of the 18th century, Michel Richard de Lalande was born in Paris, the 15th child of a tailor, and was a chorister at the church of St. Germain l'Auxerrois. He learned to play various instruments, but he excelled as an organist and in this capacity was appointed to four Paris churches simultaneously. Because of his youth he was refused the post of royal organist to Louis XIV but was asked to superintend the musical education of the princesses. In 1683 he was one of four appointed as *surintendants* of the Chapel Royal; by 1704 he was in control of all the sacred music at court as well as the royal chamber music. He died at Versailles, having been in court service for 45 years.

Lalande's fame rests on his 42 motets for chorus and orchestra written for the chapel at Versailles and published posthumously in 1729. His counterpoint is firm, his handling of the texts masterly, and his admixture of French and Italian styles well contrived. What Lully did for opera in France Lalande did for sacred music. Of his instrumental music the *Symphonies pour les soupers du roy* was so appreciated by Louis XIV that he ordered André Danican Philidor to copy the complete set in 1703. He also wrote secular cantatas and pastorals and music for the sacred tragedies produced by the Jesuit college in Paris.

RECORDINGS: *Symphonies pour les soupers du roy.*

Lalo, (Victor Antoine) Édouard (January 27, 1832–April 22, 1892)   The French composer Édouard Lalo was born into a military family of Spanish descent. In 1839 he entered the Paris Conservatoire, studying violin with François Habeneck. His first songs were published in 1848, and in 1855 he became violist in the Armingaud-Jacquard Quartet. Though he composed chamber music and the opera *Fiesque* (1866), his works were not successful until his Violin Concerto in F (1874) and *Symphonie espagnole* (1875) for violin and orchestra, both performed by Pablo de Sarasate. His gift for orchestration was further shown

in Cello Concerto (1877) and the ballet *Namouna* (1882), one of the first ballets that claimed attention more for its musical score than for its choreography (as such, it was not popular until movements were made into a suite and transferred to the concert hall). His Symphony in g minor was performed in 1887, and the following year he completed the opera *Le Roi d'Ys*. Another opera, *La Jacquerie*, left unfinished at his death, was completed by Arthur Coquard and produced in 1895.

RECORDINGS: Cello Concerto; *Namouna* (excerpts); *Rapsodie norvégienne* for orchestra; Overture to *Le Roi d'Ys; Symphonie espagnole;* Symphony in g minor; Violin Concerto in F; Violin Concerto *russe;* Violin Sonata.

Lambert, Constant (August 23, 1905–August 21, 1951)   An English composer, conductor, and critic who played a leading part in establishing the ballet in England, Constant Lambert studied at the Royal College of Music with Vaughan Williams. While still a student he was commissioned by Sergey Diaghilev to write the ballet *Romeo and Juliet* (1926). *Pomona,* his second ballet, was given the following year. He was associated with the Sitwell family, and his choral work, *The Rio Grande,* on a poem of Sacheverell Sitwell, was given in 1929. In the same year he became conductor of the Camargo Society, formed to continue the work of Diaghilev; the society led to the creation of the Sadler's Wells Ballet, which Lambert directed until 1947. He produced two further ballets, *Horoscope* (1938) and *Tiresias* (1951), and made numerous arrangements for the ballet of works by William Boyce, Purcell, Handel, Liszt, and others. His compositions also include a piano concerto, a piano sonata, and a song cycle, *Eight Chinese Songs.* As a conductor he was known for bringing little-known works before the public and for 20th-century music. Lambert was also a perspicacious critic. His assessment of the contemporary scene, *Music Ho! A Study of Music in Decline* (1934), in which he foresaw developments of the succeeding generation, was long held to be one of the most illuminating studies of 20th-century music.

RECORDING: *The Rio Grande.*

Lamoureux, Charles (September 28, 1834–December 21, 1899)   A major French conductor of the 19th century, Charles Lamoureux received a first prize in violin at the Paris Conservatoire (1854) and played in Paris orchestras for many years. With Édouard Colonne and others he founded (1860) a chamber music society and was the first in France to play the sextets of Brahms. He established (1873) a society for the performance of large-scale works for chorus and orchestra (*Messiah, St. Matthew* Passion, *Judas Maccabaeus,* and Massenet's *Eve*) and was subsequently appointed to the Opéra-Comique (1876–77) and the Opéra 1877–79. Lamoureux founded the Nouveaux Concerts (later called the Concerts Lamoureux) in 1881, producing many works by contemporary French composers and leading the Wagnerian movement in his native country. Technically he was the best conductor of his generation, and he polished his orchestra to a degree unequalled at that time in France.

Landini, Francesco, also spelled Landino (*c.* 1335–September 2, 1397)   The best known and most prolific Italian composer of the 14th century, Francesco Landini was also a noted organist. Born at Fiesole near Florence, the son of "Jacopo the painter," Landini was blinded in early childhood from smallpox. Despite his handicap he acquired a reputation for learning in philosophy, astrology, and above all in music. He was crowned with a laurel wreath as the winner of a poetry contest at Venice in 1364. At his death he was buried in Florence's Church of San Lorenzo, where he had long served as organist. Landini's surviving works include 140 ballate (91 for two voices, 49 for three), 12 madrigals, and a lively caccia depicting a fishing scene.

The Landini cadence, though much used by Landini, was a conventional cadential formula of the period consisting of the insertion of the sixth degree of the scale (Landini sixth) between the leading tone and the tonic.

ländler   A traditional pair dance in triple measure properly belonging to alpine Austria and Bavaria (from *Landl,* "little land," the provincial name for Upper Austria). Characteristic of the dance are complicated turns with the partners holding hands. Belonging to the ländler family are many variants, including the *Steyrischer* in Styria, in which the men improvise satirical verse followed by syncopated hand clapping, and the well-known *Schuhplattler* in Bavaria, which calls for acrobatic displays by the men. Musicians on the Danube barges early in the 19th century carried ländler airs to Vienna, where they became exceedingly popular. The tradition is that the city folk discarded all but the last figure of the dance, which became the famous Viennese ballroom waltz, but this origin of the waltz has been much disputed. Concert forms of ländler airs were composed by Mozart, Schumann, Beethoven, Mahler, and others.

Landowska, Wanda (Louise) (July 5, 1879–August 16, 1959)   Initiating the revival of the harpsichord in the 20th century, Wanda Landowska was one of the greatest exponents of the instrument and of early music. Born in Warsaw and trained as a pianist, she studied composition in Berlin and established herself in Paris, playing the harpsichord in public for the first time in 1903. After years of teaching, lecturing, writing, and playing, World War II forced her to leave France, and in 1941

Wanda Landowska, 1953   *UPI Compix*

443

she made her permanent home in the United States. The first modern works to be composed for the harpsichord were written expressly for her: Concerto (1926) by de Falla and *Concert champêtre* (1929) by Poulenc.

Langlais, Jean (b. February 15, 1907)   A pupil of André Marchal, Marcel Dupré, and Paul Dukas, the French organist Jean Langlais has taught at the French National Institute for the Blind since 1931 and at the Schola Cantorum in Paris since 1961. He became organist at the Basilica of Ste. Clothilde in 1945. He has toured and appeared on radio and television in Europe and North America. His compositions include choral music and pieces for the organ.

RECORDINGS: *Messe solennelle;* organ pieces.

Lanier, Nicholas (baptized September 10, 1588–February 1666)   An English composer, singer, and painter of French descent, Nicholas Lanier painted the scenery, composed the music, and sang in Ben Jonson's masque *Lovers Made Men* (1617); he also wrote music for masques by Thomas Campion. He was appointed master of the king's music for Charles I after 1626 and after the Restoration (1660) for Charles II.

Lanier's use of the recitative style is a landmark in the influence of Italian music on English composers. His experimentation with speech rhythms, in imitation of the Italian style, sowed the seeds of a tradition later to be reaped by John Blow and Purcell.

Larrocha, Alicia de (b. May 23, 1923) Educated in Barcelona, the Spanish pianist Alicia de Larrocha is known for her playing of Spanish works, though her repertoire is eclectic.

La Rue, Pierre de, also known as Pierchon and Petri de La Rue and other forms (*c.* 1460– November 20, 1518)   The celebrated Franco-Flemish composer Pierre de La Rue was possibly a pupil of Jean d'Ockeghem. From 1492 he worked in Brussels, where he served Philip the Handsome and (from about 1508) Margaret of Austria, regent of the Netherlands; with them he visited France and Spain. He spent the final two years of his life as canon at Cour-

trai. More than 35 masses survive, five of them published by Ottaviano Petrucci in the composer's lifetime (Venice, 1503), proof of his reputation. About 45 motets and 32 secular pieces also survive; his style tended toward austerity and grave seriousness.

Lasso, Orlando di, Latin form, Orlandus Lassus (*c.* 1532–June 14, 1594)   The composer who stands at the apex of the Flemish school, Orlando di Lasso was a choirboy at St. Nicholas in Mons. Because of his beautiful voice he was kidnapped three times and was finally taken into the service of Ferdinand of Gonzaga, general to Emperor Charles V. He traveled with the imperial army during its French campaign in 1544 and accompanied Gonzaga in 1545 to Italy, where he remained for 10 years. After some years in Milan and Naples, he was appointed maestro di capella of the papal church of St. John Lateran at Rome (1553–54), an honored position in which he was later succeeded by Palestrina. This post was followed by a sojourn in Antwerp (1555– 56). In 1556 Duke Albrecht V appointed him to the court chapel in Munich, where he remained for the remainder of his life except for some incidental journeys. In 1558 Lasso married a daughter of one of the clerks at the Bavarian court; the four sons of this marriage were all musicians.

Of Lasso's more than 2,000 compositions many appeared in print between 1555, when his first book of Italian madrigals was published in Venice, and 1604, when a posthumous collection of 516 Latin motets, *Magnum opus musicum,* was published in Munich by his sons. From this wealth of music certain volumes may be singled out as significant landmarks in Lasso's career: the first collection of motets (Antwerp, 1556) established his mastery in a field to which he contributed all of his life; a comprehensive anthology of his French chansons appeared in Paris in 1570 and helped to consolidate his position as the leading composer in this genre. At the invitation of his publisher, Adrian Le Roy, Lasso visited Paris, where he received flattering offers from the King of France. These he declined, retaining his post at the court of Munich (which attracted many distinguished composers from Lasso to Wagner). The German emperor raised him to the nobility in 1570; and when Lasso dedicated a collection of his masses (Munich, 1574) to the pope, he received the knighthood of the Golden Spur. Lasso's best-known work is probably his collection *Psalmi Davidis poenitentiales* (Munich, 1584).

Lasso was a master in the field of sacred music and was equally at home in secular composition. In the latter field his internationalism is striking, as he wrote French chansons as well as Italian madrigals and German part songs. Lasso was an unchallenged master of vocal composition. His style was less conservative and at times more chromatic than that of Palestrina, but he always exhibited an unmatched ability to express the meaning of the words.

BIBLIOGRAPHY: Geoffrey B. Sharp, *Lassus and Palestrina* (1972).

RECORDINGS: Madrigals; masses; motets; psalms.

Last Rose of Summer, The: *see* FLOTOW.

Latin-American music The greater part of Latin-American folk music resides in two great culture areas: the Antillean-Brazilian zone, whose influence reaches from the Caribbean to just south of Rio de Janeiro, Brazil, and the Andean zone, set mainly within the territory of the old Inca empire from southern Colombia to central Chile and across to western Bolivia and northwestern Argentina. In the Antillean-Brazilian complex the most characteristic music is part European, part African. In the Andean complex the music is made up of varying mixtures of European and Indian—mainly Quechua—elements. The two complexes interacted on each other to some extent, especially in their later developments. In both zones the mass of folk music is not only ethnically hybrid but is also derived from two different social sources, the one of relatively recent urban influence, the other of earlier, more rural influence. Between these sources there is constant interaction, and the student of Latin-American music often finds it difficult to determine a specific Negro (or

Indian) music as opposed to entirely white—utterly urban in contrast to exclusively rural.

In pre-Columbian times the musics of Central and South America were already varied and stratified. The high culture of the Aztec, Maya, and Inca civilizations was very different from the primitive culture of the interior. The Aztecs maintained music schools with an *ometochtli* or priestly director of performances, a *tlapizcatzin* (maker and teacher of instruments), and a *cuicapicque* (composer and teacher of songs). But apparently the music of the old Central American civilizations was in too weak a condition to resist the music of the Spanish conquerors, and it crumbled until only a few vestiges remained, notably among the Indians of the Mexican northwest. With Indian music weak and African music scanty (in the absence of large numbers of Negro slaves), folk song in the territory of the former Aztec empire has for some centuries been predominantly European. In the territory of the former Inca empire, on the other hand, a fund of vigorous well-formed native melody combined with Spanish song to make an attractive hybrid of remarkable durability.

Andean Probably the Andean songs that most clearly kept their Indian character are the *bahualas* with tritonic melodies based on an octave scale of three notes, usually *do fa la (do)*. Originally they were sung as free recitative, but the adoption of the Spanish octosyllabic verse line imposed a regular shape. The texts are among the gravest and most profound of any in South America, and the *bahualas* have been called "the blues of the Andes." Like the U.S. country blues, they are the property of the lowest social classes though also esteemed by city intellectuals with an interest in folk song. These three-note songs are limited mainly to the eastern slopes of the central Andes, roughly from Oruro, Bolivia, to Catamarca, Argentina.

A greater area of diffusion is enjoyed by the pentatonic melodies that abound in a wide band stretching from Ecuador, through Peru and western Bolivia, to northwestern Argentina. These melodies, almost exclusively binary in rhythm, are much used for a variety of attractive types of dance and song with

Spanish hybrid, or Indian names such as *carnavalito, huachi-torito, huaino,* etc. The greater part of the tunes used by the large Indian and mixed populations of the central Andes are of this type.

Another powerful kind of music, of later origin and of more European and less Indian influence, exists in the western part of South America. Much of this music evolved in colonial times with bimodal scales of heptatonic character. The commonest rhythms are $\frac{6}{8}$ and $\frac{3}{8}$, and the harmony of two voices in parallel thirds is typical. Unlike the tritonic and pentatonic melodies, the tunes of this category (called "colonial ternary" by the Argentine folklorist Carlos Vega) were by no means exclusive to the lower classes. On the contrary, many of them originated in the ballrooms of the Pacific cities and spread only gradually to the countryside, where they underwent characteristic alteration. To this category belong such types as the *zamacueca* (called the *cueca* in Chile and the *zamba* in Argentina), the *chacarera,* the *gato,* and the *vidala.* In rural districts the melody in this kind of music was chiefly entrusted to the human voice, especially in duets in parallel thirds. Among instruments the harp, the *quena* (Indian flute), and more rarely the fiddle were used for melody, supported by a monotonous rhythm from guitars, *charangos* (small guitars made partly of the carapace of the armadillo), and the European bass drum or the small flat *caja* drum.

During the 19th century, following the wars of independence and the consequent broadening of cultural horizons in many South American states, the flow of popular and folk music from the central Andes met another musical current, of more modern European influence, sweeping up from Buenos Aires and Santiago, that had the effect of liberating the rather limited tonal, rhythmic, and harmonic system of "colonial ternary" music. *Quena* and harp (except in Paraguay) retreated to the remoter villages before the advance of the guitar, which now became the dominant instrument for melody as well as for rhythm. The use of the drum likewise declined, and accordion and *bandoneon* became increasingly common, especially in villages within reach of town influence. Most of the Argentine, Chilean, and Par-

aguayan music heard from popular stage performers in Europe and the United States belongs to this later stage of development.

Antillean-Brazilian In Europe and the United States, Latin-American music of the Atlantic seaboard is more familiar than that of the Pacific coast and the Andes, chiefly because of the international success of such dances as the ballroom versions of the Cuban rumba and the Brazilian samba. In this area the give-and-take between town and country musics has been so widely effected that what scholars call authentic folk music is difficult to find. The music is mainly compounded of west European and west African elements. Negro slaves on the plantations of Cuba, Trinidad, Venezuela, Brazil, etc., were in close contact with the whites, and their vigorous music mingled with that of their Hispanic masters from early times; this is testified by such songs as the celebrated "Son de Má Teodora," notated in Havana, Cuba, in 1598. Nevertheless this mulatto music, now regarded as typical of eastern Latin America, waited long for proper recognition. In colonial countries African musical ways were despised by white intellectuals, and the first publicized music was that derived from European models—the ballads, lyrical songs, and courtly dances; later came such popular productions as the waltz, polka, mazurka, and quadrille, which were given a certain Latin-American spice but showed little of Africa in form, rhythm, or accompaniment.

During colonial times African musical usages were mainly confined to the slave barracks and the urban slums. By the beginning of the 19th century, however, Negro musicians were establishing themselves in the small orchestras of the towns, playing a dance music repertoire that varied from Iberian or creole folk tunes and old courtly pieces to more recent bourgeois romantic compositions. Gradually, during the 19th century, African instruments—rhythm sticks, gourd rattles, and various drums—were added to the flutes, clarinets, fiddles, and cellos of these orchestras. But it was only after the proclamation of Brazilian independence in 1882 and the liberation of Cuba in 1898 that the black musician came fully into his own in this vast zone where the folk music is much colored by the popular productions of Havana and Rio de Janeiro.

Lower-class blacks throughout the area had preserved certain African traditions almost intact, particularly in the music attached to the African-style religions that are known under various local names such as Voodoo, Vodun, *shango, candomble,* and *macumba* in Haiti, Cuba, Brazil, and elsewhere. This more-or-less purely African music was declining in the mid-20th century, and the working population was left with a folk music that was becoming either black diluted with European or vice versa. Influences from old Europe still flourished, notably in certain *corridos* and *romances* (topical and lyrical ballads), in lyrical songs such as the *polos* of eastern Venezuela, and in song dramas such as the celebrated *Nau Catarineta* of Brazil, but the most characteristic music is an interracial, even international, hybrid.

Humble professional minstrelsy is still a feature of rural life, especially in northeastern Brazil where the ballad singer, often a blind man, may be heard intoning in public his accounts of chivalry or banditry or, rather curiously, the exploits of remarkable animals such as the brave ox that fights for its freedom and is killed as a rebel. An urban example of the minstrel is provided by the calypso singers of Trinidad who specialize in the composition and performance of narrative songs relating to passing events, local or otherwise. Generally the music of the Antillean-Brazilian area has been dominated by dance melody, and even the purely diversionary lyrical songs tend to move in one or other characteristic dance rhythm, frequently syncopated and often of admirable variety and subtlety.

Throughout the area the guitar is paramount, either in its conventional form or smaller and with fewer strings, such as the *tres* of Cuba, the *cuatro* of Venezuela, and the *cavaquinho* of Brazil. The Indian flute *(quena)* is not heard in the folk and popular music of the Atlantic coast, but the array of percussion instruments is far vaster than on the Pacific side. All kinds of drums, entirely wooden or with membrane, played by hand or sticks, are encountered, along with stamping tubes, rhythm sticks *(claves),* scrapers *(reco-recos),* gourd rattles with seeds or pellets inside (maracas) or outside *(cabaças),* and tube rattles consisting of cylinders containing pellets *(chocalhos, ganzas).* With the vogue for Antillean-Brazilian popular music, many of these ancient primitive percussion instruments became familiar in the ballrooms of Europe and the United States during the first half of the 20th century.

art music A decree of 1574 granted the Jesuits, who had settled in Brazil, control of the Indians, and the early Jesuits taught the musical natives to sing, make and play musical instruments, and to compose. Also in the 16th century the Spanish composer Fernando Franco was active in Guatemala and was later maestro de capilla in Mexico City. He wrote Magnificats and other religious works, some of which, on texts in the Nahuatl language, were written for use by missionaries.

During the 17th and 18th centuries the church was still the center of music, but after the Jesuits were expelled (1759 and 1767) the trend was toward secular music. One of the earliest composers of secular music was a Brazilian mulatto, José Maurício Nunes García, an organist who produced choral and instrumental works and a grand opera, *Le due Gemelle* (1821). The opera *O Guaraní* (La Scala, 1870) brought fame to Carlos Gomes, but it was the symphony and the piano that were to prevail in Brazil. The first real symphonist was Alberto Nepomuceno (1864–1920); his contemporary Ernesto Nazaré (1863–1934) was much influenced by Chopin, but his carioca music prepared the way for the great Brazilian nationalist composer Heitor Villa-Lobos, who was also a major force in promoting music education throughout the country. His fellow nationalists included Milan-trained Francisco Mignone (b. 1897), Paris-trained Mozart Camargo Guarnieri (b. 1907), and the more adventurous Radamés Gnattali (b. 1906). Serialism was introduced to Brazil by the arrival of the German-born Hans-Joachim Koellreutter in 1937. His contemporaries César Guerra-Peixe and the Paris-trained Cláudio Santoro wrote 12-tone music for many years; a later generation is represented by Edino Krieger (b. 1928), who turned toward neoclassicism with a nationalist flavor after 1953. There is but one opera house in Brazil—

at Manaus in the heart of the Amazon jungle—but there are three symphony orchestras in Rio de Janeiro and one each in São Paulo and Porto Alegre.

By 1850 opera and ballet were established in Argentina, where the first Teatro Colón was inaugurated (1857) in Buenos Aires. The major musician of his generation was Alberto Williams (1862–1952), a pupil of Franck who founded his influential Conservatorio Williams in 1893. Williams was primarily a symphonist, but his contemporary Arturo Berutti (1862–1938) wrote operas *(Pampa, Los Heroes);* both composers showed nationalist tendencies. Juan José Castro (1895–1968) led the next generation; his opera *Proserpina e Straniero* (1952) won the Verdi Prize given by La Scala. The first Argentine composer to win international acclaim was Alberto Ginastera (b. 1916), who has progressed from an early nationalist period through neoclassicism, serialism, and atonality to aleatory techniques. In addition to the Teatro Colón, Buenos Aires boasts three large conservatories, seven symphony orchestras, and two chamber orchestras.

Though the Teatro Municipal in Santiago, Chile, was opened in 1857, the first real impetus given to serious music in Chile was by the Spanish-trained Domingo Santa Cruz (b. 1899), who after the first world war established a Bach society, a faculty of fine arts at the University of Chile, a symphony orchestra, and a system of music examinations and revolutionized the conservatory. As a composer Santa Cruz writes in a neoclassical idiom as does his later colleague Juan Orrego-Salas (b. 1919). Humberto Allende (1885–1959) was the leading nationalist composer. Carlos Isamitt (b. 1887) and Gustavo Becerra (b. 1925) have led the way in using serial techniques and Becerra in experimental music. Chile's best-known export to the international musical world is the noted pianist Claudio Arrau.

In Mexico José Mariano Elízaga (1786–1842) founded a philharmonic society in 1825, and two years later Manuel García introduced opera. A Mexican opera, *Ildegonda,* by Melesio Morales was produced in Florence in 1868. Present-day art music in Mexico begins with Manuel Ponce (1882–1948). Trained in Bolo-

gna and in Berlin, Ponce incorporated folk music idioms into a neoromantic style, developed further by his pupil Carlos Chávez (1899–1978). Chávez was also a noted conductor and founded the Orquesta Sinfónica de Mexico in 1928, directing it for more than 18 years. His contemporary Silvestre Revueltas became known primarily for his film scores and symphonic poem *Sensemayá* (1938).

Cuba's Conservatorio Municipal of Havana was founded in 1837 as a branch of the conservatory in Madrid, but it ceased to function and was re-established in 1877 and once again in 1884 by Cuba's first symphonist, Paris-trained Ignacio Cervantes. Present-day Cuban music dates from Madrid-trained Amadeo Roldán (1900–1939) and Paris-trained Alejandro García Caturla (1906–1940), who established a nationalist style from Afro-Cuban elements. José Ardévol founded (1943) the Grupo Renovación Musical, which rejected nationalism for the avant-garde. A prominent export is the pianist Jorge Bolet.

Venezuela produced the great 19th-century pianist Teresa Carreño, who lionized Europe, and the composer Reynaldo Hahn, though he left his native country as a child. Vicente Emilio Sojo (b. 1887) founded the Orquesta Sinfónica Venezolana and the Orfeón Lamas (both 1930) and in 1936 became director of the Escuela Nacional de Música. The leading nationalist composer was the U.S.-trained Juan Vicente Lecuna (1894–1954).

Colombia's musical life was reformed in 1910 by Guillermo Uribe-Holguín. The country's most promising composer is Luis Antonio Escobar (b. 1925). Puerto Rico produced the pianist Jesús María Sanromá (b. 1902) and was the home of the famous Casals Festival from 1956.

BIBLIOGRAPHY: Juan Orrego-Salas, *The Young Generation of Latin American Composers* (1963) and *Music in Latin America* (1977); Gilbert Chase, ed., *A Guide to the Music of Latin America,* rev. ed. (1972); Nicolas Slonimsky, *Music of Latin America,* rev. ed. (1972); Raoul Gordon, ed., *Puerto Rican Music* (1976).

Lawes, Henry (baptized January 5, 1596– October 21, 1662) The English composer

Henry Lawes and his brother William were pupils of John Coperario. Henry Lawes was a gentleman of the Chapel Royal from 1626 and "musician in ordinary for the lutes and voices" from 1631. He provided music for Thomas Carew's masque, *Coelum Britannicum* (1634), and Milton's *Comus* (1634) and collaborated with his brother in Sir William Davenant's *Triumphs of the Prince d'Amour* (1636). The Civil War led to his relinquishing his court appointments, but he regained them at the Restoration. He provided some of the music to Davenant's *Siege of Rhodes* (1656) and wrote an anthem for Charles II's coronation. He was buried in Westminster Abbey.

BIBLIOGRAPHY: W.McC. Evans, *Henry Lawes: Musician and Friend of Poets* (1941).

Lawes, William (baptized May 1, 1602–September 1645)   The English composer William Lawes, brother of Henry Lawes, entered the household of the Earl of Hertford *c.* 1612 to study with John Coperario and became a "musician in ordinary" to Charles I in 1635. He joined the royalists at the outbreak of the Civil War and was killed at the siege of Chester. Although he was greatly esteemed by contemporaries, none of his music was printed until after his death, when it appeared in several publications. His instrumental music includes *Harpe Consorts* for violin, bass viol, theorbo, and harp; fantasias; and a collection of dance suites called *The Royall Consort*. His daring harmonies employ dissonances unusual in English music of the time. Of his masque music, only that to James Shirley's *Triumph of Peace* (1634) and Sir William Davenant's *Triumphs of the Prince d'Amour* (1636; in collaboration with his brother) was known until the mid-20th century, when the music to Davenant's *Britannia Triumphans* (1638) and Shirley's *Triumph of Beautie* (*c.* 1644) was discovered. These works show William Lawes to have been a masque composer of great importance; of the music to court masques extant, his contribution is the longest.

BIBLIOGRAPHY: Murray Lefkowitz, *William Lawes* (1960).

RECORDING: *Great Consort.*

leading tone   The seventh degree of the diatonic scale, a semitone below the tonic. It is so-called because of its strong tendency to lead into the tonic, a frequent occurrence in most music since the 17th century.

Leclair, Jean-Marie (May 10, 1697–October 22, 1764)   The French violinist and composer Jean-Marie Leclair began his career as ballet master at Turin. In 1728 he began playing violin at the Concert Spirituel in Paris and appeared on its programs until 1736. After that date he devoted himself principally to composition. His excellence as a violinist can only be inferred from the intricacy of his violin music. In addition to music for strings he wrote operas and ballets. He was murdered at his home.

RECORDINGS: *Concerti* (6) for strings, Op. 7; Sonatas for two violins; Trio Sonatas; Violin Sonatas (48).

Lecocq, (Alexandre) Charles (June 3, 1832–October 24, 1918)   One of the principal French composers of operettas after Offenbach, Charles Lecocq was born a cripple in Paris. He studied harmony at the Conservatoire with François Bazin, composition with Fromental Halévy, and organ with François Benoit. Though he became proficient at the organ, he was prevented from continuing his studies by his diseased hip. His first operetta was *Le Docteur Miracle* (1857), written for a competition organized by Offenbach, that shared the prize with a setting of the same libretto by Bizet. Between 1859 and 1867 he produced six one-act operettas, but it was not until the production of his three-act *Fleur de thé* (1868) that he achieved success. Nine of Lecocq's operettas were produced during the next four years; following the success in Brussels of *Les Cent Vierges* (1872), *La Fille de Madame Angot* was given there in December the same year. Acclaimed as his masterpiece, it was performed three months later in Paris, where it ran for 411 nights. Within a year it was performed in 103 provincial towns in France and thereafter was frequently revived in most European countries and in the United States. In 1947 some of the music was arranged by Gordon Jacob as a ballet and given as *Mam'zelle Angot.* From 1874 to 1911 Lecocq continued to write operettas, produced mainly in Paris, of which the most successful was *Le Petit Duc* (1878). His single attempt at opéra comique, *Plutus* (1886), was a failure. He also wrote polkas, mazurkas, schottisches and other dances, and five volumes of songs. Lecocq kept alive the spirit of Offenbach in the French operetta, adapting it to the more sober view of light opera that came into fashion after the Franco-German War.

RECORDINGS: *La Fille de Madame Angot.*

Lehár, Franz (April 30, 1870–October 24, 1948)   A Hungarian composer of operettas, Franz Lehár achieved worldwide success with *Die lustige Witwe (The Merry Widow)*. He entered the Prague Conservatory in 1882 and later studied with Zdenko Fibich. Encouraged by Dvořák to follow a musical career, he assisted his father in conducting a military band and from 1890 traveled in Austria as a bandmaster. In 1896 he achieved his first success with his operetta *Kukuschka,* produced at Leipzig. In *The Merry Widow* (Vienna, 1905), on a libretto by Viktor Léon and Leo Stein, he created a new style of Viennese operetta, introducing waltz tunes and imitations of the Parisian cancan dances as well as a satirical element. Its success was such that two years later it was being played at Buenos Aires at five theaters simultaneously. Many other operettas followed, first in Vienna but also in England and the United States under their English titles, *The Man with Three Wives* (1908), *The Count of Luxembourg* (1909), *Gypsy Love* (1910), and *The Land of Smiles* (1923). Several of his works were filmed, including *The Merry Widow* and *The Land of Smiles*. He wrote a single grand opera, *Giuditta* (Vienna, 1934), which was less successful.

RECORDINGS: *The Merry Widow.*

Lehmann, Lilli (November 24, 1848–May 17, 1929)   The German Wagnerian soprano and lieder singer Lilli Lehmann made her debut in Prague (1865) in a minor role in Mozart's *Die Zauberflöte.* By 1870 she was singing the coloratura role of the Queen of the Night in that opera. Wagner coached her for the first Bayreuth performance (1876) of *Der Ring des Nibelungen,* where she sang a Rhinemaiden (*Das Rheingold* and *Götterdämmerung*) and the Forest Bird *(Siegfried).* She later sang dramatic soprano roles and was unequalled as Wagner's Isolde *(Tristan und Isolde)* and as Beethoven's Leonore *(Fidelio).* She made her Metropolitan Opera debut in 1885 as Bizet's Carmen. A noted Mozart singer, she had a repertoire of 170 operatic roles and 600 lieder. She wrote *How to Sing* (1902) and an autobiography, *My Path Through Life* (1914; in German in 1913). She was not related to the German Wagnerian soprano Lotte Lehmann.

Lehmann, Lotte (February 27, 1888–August 26, 1976)   After her first major appearance (1910) as Freia (Wagner's *Das Rheingold*) in Hamburg, the German lyric-dramatic soprano Lotte Lehmann sang at the Vienna State Opera. There she met Richard Strauss, who wrote the title role in his *Arabella* for her (1933) and chose her for other roles in his operas; her greatest triumph was as the Marschallin in *Der Rosenkavalier.* She was popular in England after 1913 and in the United States after 1930, with a Metropolitan Opera debut in 1934 as Sieglinde in Wagner's *Die Walküre.* She sang primarily Wagnerian roles for the remainder of her years at the Metropolitan but was also much admired as a lieder singer, especially in the music of Schumann. She retired in 1961 but continued to teach. She is the author of three books of memoirs.

Leider, Frida (April 18, 1888–June 4, 1975)   The German Wagnerian soprano Frida Leider studied in Berlin and Milan before receiving an engagement at the Berlin State Opera. In 1928 she sang at Bayreuth and the same year made her U.S. debut as Brünnhilde in Wagner's *Die Walküre* at the Chicago Civic Opera. Her Metropolitan Opera debut was as Wagner's Isolde in 1933. Her repertoire included all the dramatic soprano Wagnerian roles, and Leonore in Beethoven's *Fidelio.* She retired from singing in the 1940s for political reasons. After World War II she directed opera in East Berlin and taught at the West Berlin Conservatory (1948–58). Her autobiography *Das war mein Teil, Erinnerungen einer Opernsängerin* ("That Was My Part, Remembrances of an Opera Singer") appeared in 1959.

Leinsdorf, Erich (b. February 4, 1912)   Educated in his native Vienna, the conductor and cellist Erich Leinsdorf was assistant to Bruno Walter and Toscanini at the Salzburg Festival. He conducted opera at Bologna, San Remo, and Trieste before making his Metropolitan Opera debut in 1937 as assistant conductor, becoming full conductor the following year. After a year as conductor of the Cleveland Orchestra, he joined the U.S. Army (1944) and remained in Europe until 1947, when he became conductor of the Rochester (New York) Philharmonic (until 1956), with which he did some notable recordings of standard repertoire. He returned to the Metropolitan in 1958 after a season with the New York City Opera. He was conductor of the Boston Symphony (1962–69) and was named chief conductor of the Radio Symphony of West Berlin in 1978.

leitmotiv or **leitmotif**   Used first in connection with the later works of Wagner, leitmotiv (leading motif) is a term for a type of recurring theme invented not by him but by the writers who first analyzed his music dramas. The meaning of the word is inexact as applied to the representative themes that are the outstanding characteristic of Wagner's later dramatic and quasi-symphonic style, and the sense in which these themes are said to be leading never has been defined properly. The designation has, however, become useful for a particular technical procedure in composition; its intended significance is universally understood, and it therefore may be accepted for current use in musical terminology.

Although Wagner did not originate the use of the leitmotiv any more than he invented the term, he brought it to its logical conclusion, not because of any superiority to great composers who worked before his time, but because he found in the course of his development as a creative artist that it was the natural expression of his particular genius. Such close thematic workmanship as is found in his work from the *Ring* onward (with *Tristan* and *Die Meistersinger* interrupting the tetralogy) does not necessarily suggest the greatest power of invention. In a sense it obviates invention to a great extent, substituting thematic development for the constant devising of new ideas. But if Wagner's recurring motifs call for com-

paratively little further effort of invention, they do demand gifts of the highest order in the way of logical and skillful contrivance as well as the keenest intelligence in making the themes work, not only in a symphonic way that is musically satisfying, but at the same time so as to enrich the dramatic happenings with constant references called for by the words and action.

It is Wagner's awareness of such suggestions and his subtlety in weaving them into his musical fabric to awaken in the listener's mind all kinds of extramusical ideas relevant to the dramatic events that make him the greatest exponent of the leitmotiv system. Nothing was done by any later composer to expand or improve upon his procedure. Richard Strauss, for instance, makes elaborate use of it but on the whole with less close reference to the dramatic action and more often as material for purely musical development. It is in his symphonic poems rather than his operas that his use of leitmotiv is most dramatic for the simple reason that there is no stage action to carry on the plot.

The leitmotiv has two distinct dramatic functions, which may operate separately or together: one is allusion, the other transformation. Both go back a good way beyond Wagner. Mozart's

Co - si fan tut - te

for example, is allusive but appears in a rudimentary form as a motto rather than a leitmotiv, somewhat like Alfred de Musset's play titles (*Il ne faut jurer de rien,* etc.). Another good early example of such allusive use occurs in Weber's opera *Der Freischütz* at the moment when Max hesitates to descend into the wolves' glen and the orchestra urges him on derisively with an echo of the mocking chorus that had teased him in the first act. But Weber also used the leitmotiv symphonically to some extent in *Euryanthe,* where Sir Donald Tovey finds no fewer than 13 motifs that are transformed or developed. Transformation is also found early in Berlioz' *Symphonie fantastique*

451

and *Harold en Italie;* in the former work the *idée fixe,* as he calls it, appears in different forms—first like the poet's thought of his beloved as an ideal and lastly in a nightmarish distortion, where he fancies her taking part in the witches' Sabbath. But in a sense this is still a motto, like the fate motif in each movement of Tchaikovsky's Fifth Symphony, and indeed it has not yet become an entirely organic part of the musical structure, as proved by the fact that the "March to the Scaffold" was taken from an earlier work and the *idée fixe* simply inserted into it like a patch of foreign material.

In Wagner allusion and transformation are both used in rich abundance, either separately or in combination. Purely allusive, for instance, is the death theme in *Tristan und Isolde:*

which tells us that a character is thinking of death, or that a situation suggests it, but does not undergo development, though it can be used simultaneously with other material like a symphonic theme. The most familiar example of Wagnerian transformation is the horn call in the second act of *Siegfried,* which later—in *Götterdämmerung* turned from $\frac{6}{8}$ into $\frac{4}{4}$ time—becomes the theme for the matured and heroic Siegfried and—further modified in rhythm and enriched in texture—forms the basis for the great orchestral threnody after his death. To quote a less obvious example, here is the Rhine maidens' joyful song about the as yet unravished treasure in *Rheingold:*

and here the new form of the theme representing the evil power the gold has acquired in the hands of Alberich:

Wagner contrives endless ingenuities both of allusion and of transformation not to speak of symphonic development; on the other hand it is possible for commentators to see connections where none may have been intended, as between the theme of Wotan's spear throughout the *Ring:*

and that of Brünnhilde's self-justification in the third act of *Die Walküre:*

Strauss's transformations are more often than not musical developments rather than dramatic references. Allusions he often uses with quite as much subtlety as Wagner, as for example where the princess in *Der Rosenkavalier* tells Ochs that she has a headache, while the theme of her love for Octavian in the orchestra apprises us that it is really a heartache from which she suffers. Other followers of Wagner, however, have done less than nothing to improve on his methods, partly because he left them little to do and partly because they happened to be composers of much smaller stature. On the whole the leitmotiv never again showed the same flexibility and power.

Wagner's great original contribution to the use of leitmotiv is that of allusion; transformation was not his invention, for it was already well advanced not only in the works by Berlioz but also in Liszt's symphonic poems, where musically it was applied too mechanically but where it does a great deal to clarify the outline of the program. Post-Wagnerian composers too could be unduly mechanical in its application; *e.g.,* Rimsky-Korsakov and, on a lower level, Gustave Charpentier.

Debussy, on the other hand, used the principle in the most purely musical manner of which it is capable and never, as he said maliciously but not altogether unjustifiably of Wagner's method, to make the characters on the stage present their visiting cards. This does happen in Wagner's work, but there is very much more in it than that. In some other later composers there is much less; but like Bizet or Puccini, for instance, they can be very effective when they do use representative themes. However, Puccini and others often do little more than indulge in sentimental reminiscence, which can be very moving if it is used with the mastery of Verdi, who was fond of recalling past happiness during a final tragic situation by means of a melody associated with it earlier.

With lesser masters, or those who are not masters at all, the device degenerates into the naivete of the theme song, which is not a modern invention except for its name; a good example is a song as early as "Home, Sweet Home" in Henry Rowley Bishop's *Clari* (1823), where moreover we already find rhythmic transformation.

BIBLIOGRAPHY: Robert Donington, *Wagner's Ring and Its Symbols; the Music and the Myth* (1963).

Le Jeune, Claude (*c.* 1530–September 1600) A leading French composer of vocal music, Claude Le Jeune was born in Valenciennes, Flanders, and was in Paris by 1564. He was choirmaster to François d'Anjou, brother of Henry III, from about 1579 to 1584. Le Jeune's most original compositions are his *musique mesurée,* in which he set French verse written according to the rules of classical prosody, working in collaboration with the poet Jean Antoine de Baïf. He also composed chansons, madrigals, motets, and particularly psalms. A Huguenot, he set the *French,* or *Genevan,* Psalter in four and five voices (pub-

lished 1613) that were widely used in the Reformed churches of France and the Netherlands and were even translated into German and English. *Douze Psaumes de David,* in motet style for two to seven voices, were included in *Dodecacorde* (1598).

RECORDING: Chansons.

Lekeu, Guillaume (January 20, 1870–January 21, 1894) A Belgian composer who was a follower of Franck, Guillaume Lekeu first learned music from the organist of his native village. At school at Poitiers he made an intensive study of the quartets of Beethoven. In 1888 he took his degree in philosophy at the University of Paris and then studied music there with Gaston Vallin. He visited Bayreuth in 1889 and on his return was a pupil of Franck. Deeply affected by Franck's death in 1890, he was guided in his studies by Franck's pupil, d'Indy. In 1891 he wrote a piano sonata and a piano trio and placed second in the Belgian Prix de Rome with his cantata, *Andromède,* a scene of which he conducted in Brussels in 1892. As a result of this performance the Belgian violinist Eugène Ysaÿe commissioned him to write a violin sonata, performed by Ysaÿe in 1893; Ysaÿe also conducted his *Fantaisie symphonique* on two folk songs of Anjou. At Lekeu's untimely death many works remained unpublished, including two early quartets, a suite for cello and orchestra, a symphonic study on the subject of *Hamlet,* and *Epithalame* for strings, trombones, and organ. His cello sonata and piano quartet were completed by d'Indy.

RECORDING: Violin Sonata in G.

Lemmens, Nicolas (Jacques) (January 3, 1823–January 30, 1881) A student of François-Joseph Fétis at the Brussels Conservatory and of Adolf Hesse at Breslau, the Belgian organist and composer Nicolas Lemmens became a professor at the former in 1849. He lived for many years in England but returned to Belgium to open a school in Mechelen for training in Catholic liturgical music (1879). He is important historically as the link between the German tradition of organ playing from Bach (through Johann Christian Kittel and Johann Christian Heinrich Rinck to Hesse) to the French school, established by

453

Lemmens through his pupils Alexandre Guilmant and Charles-Marie Widor. Lemmens also wrote an important organ method (adopted at the Paris Conservatoire as well as Brussels, Madrid, etc.), masses, motets, and a method (1886) for accompanying plainchant.

Leo, Leonardo (Ortensio Salvatore de) (August 5, 1694–October 31, 1744)   An Italian composer noted for his comic operas, Leonardo Leo entered the Conservatorio della Pietà dei Turchini at Naples in 1709, where his earliest known work, a sacred drama, *L'infedeltà abbattuta,* was performed by his fellow students in 1712. In 1714 he produced an opera, *Pisistrato,* for the court theater. He later held various posts at the royal chapel and taught at the conservatory. His operas include *La 'mpeca scoperta* (1723), a comic opera in Neapolitan dialect; *Demofoonte* (1735) and *L'Olimpiade* (1737), both serious operas; and the comic opera *Amor vuol sofferenze* (1739). His sacred works include six or seven oratorios, of which *S. Elena al Calvario* (1732) was particularly esteemed; five or six masses; and a *Miserere* for double choir. He also wrote instrumental works, among them six concerti for cello and strings and harpsichord toccatas.

RECORDING: Cello Concerto in A.

Leoncavallo, Ruggero (April 23, 1857–August 9, 1919)   An Italian *verismo* opera composer whose fame rests on his *Pagliacci,* Ruggero Leoncavallo was born at Naples and studied at the conservatory there. After graduating he supported himself by playing at cafés and teaching singing and piano. During this time he worked on an opera based on Alfred de Vigny's *Chatterton* and on *I Medici,* the first part of a projected trilogy inspired by the Italian Renaissance. These works failed to attract attention, and he accordingly composed *Pagliacci* under the influence of the *verismo* style of Mascagni. It was produced at the Teatro dal Verme in Milan and achieved an immediate success. As a result *I Medici* was given there the following year. An opera based on Murger's *La Vie de Bohème* (Venice, 1897) suffered from comparison with Puccini's work on the same subject produced the previous

year. *Zazà* (Milan, 1900) was more successful, but the ambitious *Der Roland,* commissioned by the German Emperor Wilhelm II to glorify the Hohenzollerns and produced in Berlin in 1904, revealed Leoncavallo's deficiency in musical inspiration. A number of slighter works followed that achieved passing success. For most of his operas he was his own librettist, and he showed a literary ability and a flair for theatrical effect.

RECORDINGS: *Pagliacci.*

Leonhardt, Gustav (M.) (b. May 30, 1928)   Though known primarily as a harpsichordist, the Dutch Gustav Leonhardt is also organist, conductor, and musicologist. He was educated in The Netherlands and studied with Eduard Müller in Switzerland. He has toured widely in Europe and the United States, and his Leonhardt Consort has recorded extensively, especially the works of Bach. His thesis, *The Art of Fugue, Bach's Last Harpsichord Work; an Argument* (1952), became a center of controversy.

Leppard, Raymond (John) (b. August 11, 1927)   Associated with the English Chamber Orchestra since its inception, the English conductor Raymond Leppard has been principal conductor of the BBC Northern Symphony Orchestra since 1973. He has conducted opera in the United States, England, and Norway and has performed his own score realizations of operas by Monteverdi and Francesco Cavalli. He has conducted film scores and more than 100 recordings of Classical and pre-Classical music.

Leschetizky, Theodor (June 22, 1830–November 14, 1915)   One of the great piano teachers of all time, the Polish pianist Theodor Leschetizky produced a whole generation of great pianists, including Paderewski, Gabrilowitsch, Fanny Bloomfield Zeisler, Alexander Brailowsky, Annette Essipoff (his second wife), Frank La Forge, Ignaz Friedman, Benno Moiseiwitsch, and Artur Schnabel. Although in the Romantic tradition (Schnabel became a notable exception), his teaching resulted in such a variety of style in his pupils that no method can be detected. Indeed, he denied that he had a method. A pupil of Czerny at the Vienna Conservatory, he taught at the St. Petersburg

Theodor Leschetizky
The Bettmann Archive, Inc.

Conservatory (1862–78) and then in Vienna. Although his playing was eclipsed by his teaching, there is evidence that as a performer he "was more than masterly even past 70." Leschetizky was also a composer, including an opera and chamber music, but only his piano pieces remain of interest.

Lesueur, Jean-François (February 15, 1760–October 6, 1837)   A French composer of religious and dramatic works, Jean-François Lesueur helped to transform musical taste during the Revolution. He acquired his musical training as a chorister at Amiens. In 1781 he was appointed chapelmaster at the cathedral of Dijon and in 1786 at Notre-Dame in Paris. There he aroused controversies by introducing a large orchestra to accompany his masses, which, he maintained, should make a dramatic appeal. Though Lesueur's masses, admired by operagoers, caused Notre-Dame to be described as *L'Opéra des gueux* ("the beggars' opera"), he succeeded in blending the sacred and secular styles, anticipating the religious works of Berlioz and Gounod. He left Notre-Dame in 1788 and retired to the country. After 1789 he wrote several odes and chants for performance at the open-air celebrations of the Revolution by vast numbers of choristers and instrumentalists; between 1793 and 1796 he wrote three operas, and in 1795 he became

inspector of the Paris Conservatoire. In 1804 he was made director of music to Napoleon I, to whom he dedicated his opera *Ossian ou les Bardes,* and later was appointed director of music to Louis XVIII. In 1818 Lesueur became professor of composition at the Conservatoire, where his pupils included Berlioz, Gounod, and Ernest Guiraud.

Levi, Hermann (November 7, 1839–May 13, 1900)   A prominent Wagnerian conductor who directed the premiere of *Parsifal* at Bayreuth, the German-born Hermann Levi studied with Vincenz Lachner at Mannheim and then at the Leipzig Conservatory. He directed German opera at Rotterdam before being appointed a conductor of the Court Theater in Munich (1872–96). On a visit to London in 1895, he conducted one performance at the Queen's Hall. He conducted the music at Wagner's funeral (1883). The composer of songs and piano music, he revised the librettos of Mozart's *Così fan tutte, Don Giovanni,* and *Le nozze di Figaro.*

Levine, James (b. June 23, 1943)   A child prodigy as a pianist making his debut at age 10 with the Cincinnati Symphony, the U.S. conductor James Levine studied piano with Rosina Lhévinne and Rudolf Serkin and conducting with Jean Morel, Max Rudolf, Alfred Wallenstein, and George Szell. While a student of the latter he became apprentice conductor of the Cleveland Orchestra (1964) and then its youngest associate conductor. After guest appearances with many major U.S. orchestras and with the San Francisco Opera, he made his Metropolitan Opera conducting debut in Puccini's *Tosca* in 1971. Two years later he became the first in the history of Metropolitan to hold the position of principal conductor. He has been director of the Ravinia (Illinois) Festival since 1973. His recordings include several Italian operas, Brahms and Mahler cycles, and music for cello and piano (with Lynn Harrell, cello).

Lhévinne, Josef (December 13, 1874–December 2, 1944)   A pupil of Vassily Safonov at the Moscow Conservatory, the Russian pianist Josef Lhévinne won the Rubinstein Prize in 1895. A modern Romantic who did not distort the music, he taught at Tiflis, Moscow, and

Berlin until 1919, when he moved to the United States. He and his wife, Rosina Lhévinne, taught at the Juilliard School from 1924.

Lhévinne, Rosina (March 28, 1880–November 9, 1976)   One of the leading mid-20th-century pedagogues in the United States, the Russian pianist Rosina Lhévinne was a pupil of Vassily Safonov at the Moscow Conservatory. In 1899 she married her fellow student and occasional teacher Josef Lhévinne and subordinated her playing career to his, though the two often appeared as duo pianists. From 1924 she taught at the Juilliard School and taught such successful pianists as Van Cliburn, John Browning, Ralph Votapek, Misha Dichter, and Jeffrey Siegel and the pianist-conductor James Levine.

Liadov, Anatol (Konstantinovich) (May 11, 1855–August 28, 1914)   A student of Rimsky-Korsakov, the Russian composer Anatol Liadov researched his native folk music and compiled more than 130 Russian national songs. In 1878 he joined the faculty of the St. Petersburg Conservatory, where he remained until his death. Among his composition students was Prokofiev. He is remembered principally for his symphonic poems, *Baba Yaga* (1904) and *The Enchanted Lake* and *Kikimora* (both 1909), and a large quantity of piano music in the style and forms of Chopin.

BIBLIOGRAPHY: Michel D. Calvocoressi and Gerald E. H. Abraham, *Masters of Russian Music* (1936; reprint, 1971).

RECORDINGS: *Baba Yaga;* Eight Russian Folksongs for orchestra; *Kikimora.*

libretto   The text that is set to music by the composer of an opera or operetta; the term is less commonly used of works not intended for the stage. The word is a diminutive of the Italian *libro* ("book") and derives from the practice of printing the texts of Venetian operas (from 1637) in a miniature format (about three-quarters the size of a modern miniature score). It originally applied simply to a published text of this kind but by a natural transference acquired the broader meaning. In the 19th century it became an international term, except that the French preferred their own diminutive *livret*. In Germany a printed libretto is normally called a *Textbuch*. A libretto may be in verse or in prose; it may be designed for a particular composer, or it may provide raw material for several; it may be wholly original or an adaptation of an existing play or novel; it may even in certain cases be the actual text of a play, either in the original language or in translation or adaptation.

origins   The earliest operas, beginning in Italy with Ottavio Rinuccini's *Dafne* (1597), set by Jacopo Peri, were court entertainments, and the printing of the words was intended more as a commemoration of the festivity than as a convenience for the aristocratic audience. Once opera became a public spectacle (Venice, 1637), the printed libretto served a very practical purpose and was often used by the audience to follow the performance—a practice that was made easier by the fact that the auditorium was not plunged into darkness when the curtain rose. There was a further difference in style. The earliest librettists regarded their works as poetic dramas, which might offer occasional opportunities for lyricism and for choral episodes but which for the most part the composer was expected to set with a faithful regard for the accents—as well as the mood—of the text. The same attitude was observed in France when opera was established on a permanent footing by Lully and his librettist Philippe Quinault in 1673. Lully's operas, which included a prologue in honor of Louis XIV, were described as *tragédies mises en musique*. In Venetian opera great stress was laid on the dramatic spectacle, but a tendency toward lyrical treatment of the text affected the relationship between librettist and composer. The composer was no longer merely providing music for a poetic drama; he was using the libretto as the material for creating something new. But the librettist had the satisfaction of seeing his name in print, often without any reference to the composer, and he could count on a steady remuneration from the sale of copies, whereas the complete score of an opera was rarely published. Since operas were often modified for revivals, fresh librettos had to be printed, and this provided the author with an additional source of income. For the modern historian printed librettos are a valuable source of information, as they generally give full details about the occasion for which they were published, the performers who took part, and the various scenes in the course of the work—details that are rarely found in composers' scores.

emergence of historical subjects Early 17th-century librettists developed material out of the pastoral drama of the 16th century, which dealt with mythological subjects. It was no accident that Orpheus, representing the power of song, was the subject of Ottario Rinuccini's *Euridice* (1600), set by Jacopo Peri (also by Giulio Caccini), and of Alessandro Striggio's *Orfeo* (1607), set by Monteverdi. The Venetian opera public, however, did not share this enthusiasm for classical mythology. Hence the appearance of Giovanni Francesco Busenello's *L'Incoronazione di Poppea* (1642), set by Monteverdi, which deals with incidents in the life of Nero. From this time historical subjects became increasingly popular in Italy, and no one worried about the superimposition of details for which there was no authority. Such subjects could be treated in a way that would appeal both to the man in the street and to princely patrons. The aristocratic appeal was important in a good many opera centers that, unlike Venice or Hamburg, were largely dependent on royal favor. The public could enjoy the love intrigues that became an indispensable feature of the text, while authority was flattered by the representation of rulers remarkable for their magnanimity: the best-known example is Pietro Metastasio's *La clemenza di Tito,* which was set to music by some 20 composers beginning with Antonio Caldara in 1734 and ending with Bernardo Ottani in 1798 (Mozart's setting of an adaptation of the text dates from 1791).

This flattery was practiced particularly in Vienna, where Apostolo Zeno was poet to the imperial court from 1718 to 1729, followed by Metastasio from 1730 until his death in 1782. Zeno aimed at raising the standard of the contemporary libretto by excluding comic characters from serious opera and by creating a poetic drama nearer the style of French tragedy. It was he who established the curious convention of late Baroque opera in which a character who has sung an aria immediately leaves the stage. Metastasio had similar ideals and cultivated an elevated style that made his librettos equally suitable for performance as spoken drama. He also had the advantage of being a practiced musician and in his arias adopted a relatively simple style that appealed to a large number of composers. There was, however, a strong feeling among many 18th-century critics that opera of this kind was unnatural and in the case of the conventional da capo aria absurd. The pursuit of a more dramatic style can be observed in the operas of Niccolò Jommelli and Tommaso Traetta but is most noticeable in the works of Gluck. When Johann Adolph Hasse was about to write *Attilio Regolo* (1750), Metastasio sent him a good deal of detailed advice; but he had not written the libretto expressly for him. Ranieri Calzabigi also advised Gluck on the setting of *Orfeo ed Euridice* (1762); but in this case he had the composer in mind when he wrote the libretto, and the two men worked together in close collaboration. It is noticeable that in this work Calzabigi reverted to Greek mythology, which had for long been the staple fare of French opera. Several of Gluck's later operas are on subjects drawn from this source, but there was a growing tendency in the late 18th century to turn aside from material so remote from the contemporary world. Comic opera had always dealt with scenes from everyday life, even if they were treated with a certain artificiality. These now became the background for works that were largely serious in intention, even though in France they still retained the name of OPÉRA COMIQUE because of the use of dialogue. The heroism of ordinary men and women and resistance to tyranny were subjects that acquired an even stronger significance after the outbreak of the French Revolution and inspired Beethoven to write *Fidelio* (1805).

19th-century influences Romanticism encouraged the setting of texts dealing with medieval history or legends of the supernatural, *e.g.,* Helmina von Chézy's *Euryanthe* (1823) and Friedrich Kind's *Der Freischütz* (1821), both set by Weber; and even in Italy, which was virtually untouched by Romanticism, librettos were concocted from the works of Schiller and Sir Walter Scott. Meanwhile in

France historical subjects were popular in grand opera; for example, in the librettos written for Meyerbeer by Eugène Scribe. Composers were often as critical of their librettists as Mozart had been and just as often accepted texts that were devoid of any literary quality. It was partly dissatisfaction with the ordinary librettos of his time and partly egotism that decided Wagner to write his own texts, as Berlioz did in the case of *Les Troyens* (1859) and *Béatrice et Bénédict* (1862). Comparatively few later composers followed their example and not always with the happiest results. The ideal solution is for librettist and composer to work together as Calzabigi and Gluck did. Examples of such close collaboration are Arrigo Boito and Verdi (*Otello,* 1887, and *Falstaff,* 1893); Hugo von Hofmannsthal and Richard Strauss (*Elektra,* 1909; *Der Rosenkavalier,* 1911; *Ariadne auf Naxos,* first version 1912, second version 1916; *Die Frau ohne Schatten,* 1919; *Die ägyptische Helena,* 1928; *Arabella,* produced 1933, though Strauss collaborated with Hofmannsthal before his death in 1929); Montagu Slater and Britten (*Peter Grimes,* 1945); and W. H. Auden, Chester Kallmann, and Stravinsky (*The Rake's Progress,* 1951). In such cases temperamental differences between librettist and composer are less important than a common desire to create a work of art. The setting of existing plays demands particular care from the composer in abridgment and, if necessary, adaptation. Successful examples of such treatment are rare: Debussy's setting of Maeterlinck's *Pelléas et Mélisande* (1902) and Strauss's of a German translation of Oscar Wilde's *Salomé* (1905) are exceptions to the general rule that music does not readily accommodate itself to a text designed to be spoken.

modern status Since the latter part of the 19th century, there has been an increasing demand for librettos of a high literary quality. This has affected the way in which operas are described on the title page. Berlioz described his own libretto for *Les Troyens* as a "poème lyrique"; *Der Rosenkavalier* is entitled "Komödie für Musik von Hugo von Hofmannsthal: Musik von Richard Strauss." This does not mean that the wheel has come full circle from the early 17th century, but it does indicate a more serious view of the librettist's function than was accepted by many 19th-century composers. At the same time the growth of realism in spoken drama has had a corresponding influence on opera, which from the time of Bizet's *Carmen* (1875), based on Prosper Mérimée's novel, has frequently represented neurotic situations and scenes of savage violence. Puccini's *Tosca* (1900) and Berg's *Wozzeck* (1925) on a libretto that was an abridged form of the play by Georg Büchner belong to this category. Much of the success of Menotti's operas, notably *The Medium* (1946) and *The Consul* (1950), was the fact that the librettos were the work of the composer. Other examples of the composer-librettist are Hindemith in his operas *Mathis der Maler* (1938) and *Die Harmonie der Welt* (1957) and Sir Michael Tippett in his *The Midsummer Marriage* (1955), *King Priam* (1962), and *The Knot Garden* (1970).

The librettist not only must see that the text, whether verse or prose, is worth setting but must ensure that it is heard as clearly as the composer will allow. Elaborate literary artifices, particularly inversions, have no place in a libretto because they present the audience with unnecessary problems. The English and German languages have a wealth of monosyllables, which are much easier to catch in the theater than more elaborate alternatives. Repetitions are a further aid to understanding as are phrases that have associations for the listener. These principles apply equally to translations, which can often be made more effective than the original text. A librettist obviously must have a sense of the stage but must also realize that music moves at a slower pace than the spoken word and that the orchestra can suggest emotions that would need to be made explicit in a play. A plain, simple language is the most appropriate for music; colloquialisms, except in comic opera, are nearly always out of place and tend to destroy the illusion that opera attempts to create. The composition of an opera is a major undertaking, but the librettist's task can be almost equally severe.

lied, plural **lieder** The German word for song used in English to denote the particular form of the 19th-century German song written by Schubert, Schumann, Brahms, and others; *i.e.,* the lied form. It is also used for the 16th-century German form of polyphonic SONG.

Lied von der Erde, Das: *see* MAHLER (last period).

Lieutenant Kije: *see* PROKOFIEV.

Life for the Tsar, A: *see* GLINKA; OPERA (the 19th century).

Ligeti, György (b. May 28, 1923)   A pioneer in the use of shifting blocks of sound and tone colors, the composer György Ligeti studied and taught music in his native Hungary until 1956. Later he was associated with centers of new music in Cologne, Darmstadt, Stockholm, and Vienna. Since 1973 he has been on the faculty of the Hamburg Music Academy.

Ligeti has composed electronic music (*Artikulation,* 1958) as well as music for performers. In the early 1960s he caused a sensation with his *Future of Music—A Collective Composition* (1961) and *Poème symphonique* (1962). The former consists of the composer regarding the audience from on stage and their reaction to this; the latter is written for 100 metronomes, operated by 10 performers.

In Ligeti's music specific musical intervals, rhythms, and harmonies are often not distinguishable but act together in a multiplicity of sound events to create music sometimes of smooth stillness, sometimes of dynamic anguished motion. Examples occur in *Atmosphères* (1961) for orchestra and Requiem (1963–65) for soprano, mezzo-soprano, two choruses, and orchestra. In the mime-dramas *Aventures* (1962) and *Nouvelles Aventures* (1962–65) Ligeti attempts new ways of disintegrating the differences between vocal and instrumental sounds. In the Cello Concerto (1966) the concerto contrast between soloist and orchestra is minimized in very long lines and slowly changing, nontraditional textures. His first opera, *Le Grand Macabre,* was produced in Stockholm in 1978 with librettist Michael Meschke after a play (1934) by the Belgian author Michel de Ghelderode. It was described as "totally absurd."

RECORDINGS: *Atmosphères; Aventures; Étude No. 1; Harmonies; Lux aeterna* for chorus; *Nouvelles Aventures;* Ten Pieces for wind quintet; *Volumina* for organ.

light opera: *see* COMIC OPERA.

Lind, Jenny, originally Johanna Maria Lind (October 6, 1820–November 2, 1887)   Called the "Swedish Nightingale," soprano Jenny Lind made her debut (1838) in Stockholm as Agathe in Weber's *Der Freischütz* and then went to Paris to study with Manuel García. Meyerbeer and Verdi wrote for her (the roles of Vielka in *Ein Feldlager in Schlesien* [later *L'Étoile du Nord*] and Amelia in *Il masnadieri*). Among her most popular roles was that of Alice in Meyerbeer's *Robert le diable,* and she also had tremendous success on the concert stage, especially with simple songs and ballads. Her voice had great agility over a wide range. She taught at the Royal College of Music in London from 1883 to 1886.

Jenny Lind
miniature on ivory
courtesy, New-York Historical Society,
New York City

Linde, Hans-Martin (b. May 24, 1930) Renowned as a chamber music performer and music historian when most flutists earn their reputation as solo or orchestral players, the German flutist Hans-Martin Linde studied flute with Gustav Scheck and composition with Konrad Lechner at the State Music Academy at Freiburg im Breisgau. He has played chamber music with the West German Radio musicians in Cologne and with the Cappella Coloniensis. A proficient performer on the recorder and Baroque transverse flute, Linde has written a *Handbook on Playing the Recorder* and several books on ornamentation. In 1957 he joined the staff for teaching historical instruments at the Schola Cantorum of the Music Academy at Basel. He has been head of the Conservatory at Basel since October 1976.

Linley, Thomas (January 17, 1733–November 19, 1795)   An English musician and father of a large family of musicians, Thomas Linley studied music at Bath and settled there as a singing master and conductor. From 1774 he was engaged in the management of the oratorios at Drury Lane Theatre in London. He composed or compiled the music for many dramatic pieces, including *The Duenna* by his son-in-law Richard Brinsley Sheridan. In 1777 he was elected a member of the Royal Society of Musicians.

Linz Symphony (No. 36): *see* MOZART (later life).

Lipatti, Dinu (March 17, 1917–December 2, 1950)   Educated in his native Bucharest, the pianist Dinu Lipatti studied in Paris with Alfred Cortot, Charles Munch, Paul Dukas, and Boulanger. His repertoire was all-inclusive, and he was well established before his premature death. He taught at the Geneva Conservatory from 1943 and composed a variety of works, mostly involving piano.

lira   A pear-shaped bowed instrument with three to five strings. Closely related to the medieval rebec and, like the rebec, a precursor of the medieval fiddle, the *lira* survives essentially unchanged in several Balkan folk instruments, among them the Bulgarian *gadulka,* the Aegean *lira,* and the Yugoslavian *gusla.* Its tuning and range vary.

The name *lira,* a misapplication of *lyra,* the ancient Greek lyre played with a plectrum, had appeared by the 9th century for the Byzantine form of the Arab *rabāb,* the ancestor of all European bowed instruments. The Byzantine *lira* spread westward through Eu-

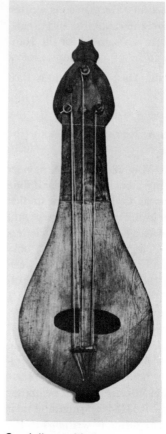
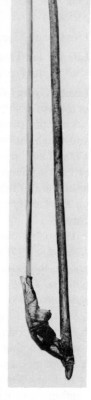

Greek lira and bow
courtesy, Pitt Rivers Museum, Oxford

rope, where its precise evolution is unclear; writers in the 11th and 12th centuries often used the words fiddle and *lira* interchangeably. Unlike the *rabāb* and rebec but like the medieval fiddle, the *lira* has rear tuning pegs set in a flat peg disk.

The lira da braccio, a predecessor of the violin, was a 15th-century fiddle with three to five melody strings plus two off-the-fingerboard drone strings. Its bass version was the *lira da gamba,* or *lirone.*

lira organizzata: *see* HURDY-GURDY.

Liszt, Franz, Hungarian form, Ferencz Liszt (October 22, 1811–July 31, 1886)   The greatest piano virtuoso of his time, the Hungarian Franz Liszt was also a composer of enormous originality and a principal figure in the Romantic movement.

Born at Raiding, Hungary, he was the son of Ádám Liszt, an official in the service of

Prince Miklós Esterházy. Ádám Liszt was a talented amateur musician, and at the age of six Liszt began to listen attentively to his father's piano playing and showed an interest in church and gypsy music; he also developed a strong religious sense that remained with him throughout his life. He began to play the piano at the age of seven and to compose a year later; when only nine he made his first appearance in public as a pianist at Sopron and Poszony, and as a result a number of Hungarian magnates subscribed to the expenses of his musical education. In 1821 he moved with his family to Vienna, where he studied piano with Beethoven's pupil Czerny and composition with Antonio Salieri. He was extremely successful in Vienna and had many public and private engagements. He was among 50 Austrian composers invited to contribute a variation each on a waltz by Diabelli, to which Beethoven sent 33. In 1823, still only 12 years of age, Liszt moved with his family to Paris, giving concerts in Germany on the way. Having been refused admission to the Paris Conservatoire by Cherubini on the grounds that foreigners were not allowed, he studied privately with Ferdinando Paër. As

Franz Liszt
lithograph by Joseph Kriehuber, 1846
courtesy, Museo Teatrale alla Scala, Milan

a pianist he soon was a success in Parisian society and toured England in 1824, 1825, and 1827, as well as the French provinces and Switzerland. In 1825 his one-act opera *Don Sanche, ou Le Château de l'amour* was performed at the Paris Opéra, and Liszt also composed a number of piano works in these years, including the first version of the *Transcendental* Études.

In 1827 Liszt had a nervous collapse after a concert in London and expressed the wish to become a priest (never to be fulfilled); he was taken to Boulogne by his father, who died there. Liszt then returned to Paris, where he earned his living as a piano teacher. In the following year he fell in love with one of his pupils, Caroline, daughter of the Comte de Saint-Cricq; but the comte insisted that the attachment be broken off. After this Liszt became ill for some time. After a period of doubt and pessimism he decided to give up his career as a virtuoso. He met a number of poets, including Lamartine, Victor Hugo, and Heine, and began to read widely. Between 1830 and 1832 he met the three men who were to influence him the most: Berlioz, from whom he learned the command of the Romantic orchestra and also that species of diabolism that remained with him for the rest of his life; Paganini, who disclosed to him new possibilities of virtuoso composition and performance; and Chopin, whose poetic style inspired many of Liszt's works.

In 1834 Liszt, who had written little for some years—though he had achieved the seemingly impossible feat of transcribing Berlioz' *Symphonie fantastique* for piano—composed his first mature works, the single piece *Harmonies poétiques et religieuses* and the three *Apparitions*. In the same year he met George Sand and Comtesse Marie d'Agoult. He began an affair with the comtesse, and in 1835 she left her husband and family to join Liszt in Switzerland. For the next four years they lived together, mainly in Switzerland and Italy, though returning to Paris for occasional visits (during one of which occurred the celebrated "duel" in which Liszt defeated Sigismond Thalberg in virtuoso performance). Their three children were born in this period. Liszt wrote the first versions of the Swiss and Italian books of the *Années de pèlerinage* and the second version of the *Transcendental* Études, as well as numerous transcriptions (including six of Paganini's Études) and operatic fantasies.

In 1839 relations with the comtesse became strained, and she returned to Paris with the children, while Liszt embarked on a series of tours that took him all over Europe for the next eight years. This was the period of his greatest brilliance and success as a performer: he was adulated everywhere; gifts and decorations were showered on him; and he had numerous mistresses, including Lola Montez and the original "Dame aux camellias." He still continued to compose, writing songs for the first time as well as piano works. He revisited Hungary and again became interested in the music of the gypsies, which he transcribed for piano in his *Hungarian* Rhapsodies. He also visited England three times in 1840–41. In 1844 he finally separated from Comtesse d'Agoult, and in 1847 he met Princess Carolyne von Sayn-Wittgenstein at Kiev. She persuaded him to give up his career as a pianist, and he spent the winter with her at Woronince in Poland.

Liszt had been appointed director of music extraordinary to the Weimar court in 1843 but spent little time there until in 1847 he decided to settle there and devote himself entirely to composition and conducting. Many of his greatest works were written during the ensuing period. Princess Sayn-Wittgenstein came to join him in Weimar, and after unsuccessfully trying to obtain a divorce from her husband she lived with Liszt in the Altenburg. There he wrote the first 12 symphonic poems, the *Faust* and *Dante* Symphonies, the piano sonata, the two piano concertos, the *Totentanz* for piano and orchestra, revised versions of the first two books of the *Années de pèlerinage* and of the *Transcendental* and *Paganini* Études, and numerous other works. He also conducted performances of his own works and of many by other composers, including Wagner's *Tannhäuser* and *Lohengrin* (the latter for the first time on any stage), Berlioz' *Benvenuto Cellini,* Schumann's *Genoveva* and *Manfred,* and operas by Verdi and Donizetti. But this fruitful period began to end in the late 1850s;

the grand duke's interest in music flagged, and the intrigues of the Intendant Dingelstedt undermined Liszt's position. In 1858, after a hostile demonstration at the first performance of his pupil Peter Cornelius' opera *Der Barbier von Bagdad,* Liszt tendered his resignation to the grand duke. In 1859 his son Daniel died, and in the following year the princess left Weimar for Rome, where she hoped to obtain her divorce. Liszt joined her there in October 1861, and they planned to marry on his 50th birthday; but at the last moment the pope revoked his sanction of her divorce. Both remained in Rome in separate establishments.

During the next eight years Liszt lived mostly in Rome, and his thoughts turned more and more toward religious music: he wrote the big oratorios *St. Elisabeth* and *Christus,* the *Hungarian Coronation* Mass, and many other smaller works. In 1865 he received the four minor orders of the Roman Catholic Church, though he never became a priest. In 1869 he returned to Weimar as a teacher, and from then until the end of his life he made regular journeys between Rome, Weimar, and Budapest, where he also taught at the Academy of Music. His music began to lose some of its brilliant quality and became starker, more introverted, and more experimental in style, looking forward to the music of the 20th century. Meanwhile his daughter Blandine had died, and his second daughter Cosima had left her husband, Hans von Bülow, and had married Wagner, straining the relations between the two composers. Nevertheless Liszt regularly attended the Bayreuth Festivals, though he only appeared in public as a pianist at charity concerts. The younger generation of composers of many countries, including Borodin, Grieg, Albéniz, and Debussy, visited him and learned from his methods. In 1886, at the age of 74, he undertook his last tour, visiting Florence, Venice, Budapest, Liège, Paris, and London, where he had not been for 45 years and where several concerts were given in his honor, including a performance of *St. Elisabeth.* After further performances at Antwerp and Paris, he caught a cold that turned finally to pneumonia; he died at Bayreuth.

As a composer Liszt radically extended the

technique of piano writing, giving the instrument not only brilliance but a full and rich, almost orchestral sound. Most of his pieces bear titles and are representations of some natural scene or of some poetic idea or work of art; a rare major abstract work is the Sonata in b minor. Apart from introducing a new poetic note into music, Liszt extended the harmonic language of his time, even in his earlier works, and his later development of chromatic harmony led eventually to the breakdown of tonality and ultimately to the atonal music of Schoenberg and his followers. Liszt's "transformation of themes" was fully developed by Wagner in his system of leitmotiv, and the invention of the one-movement symphonic poem was also ascribable to Liszt. In his last works Liszt anticipated the style of 20th-century composers such as Debussy and Bartók, and one of his last pieces is actually called "Bagatelle sans tonalité." As a pianist he was the first to give complete solo recitals, and he also popularized the works of Beethoven, Schubert, Berlioz, Wagner, and others by transcribing them for piano and playing them in his concerts at a time when they were insufficiently appreciated. He campaigned to raise the status of the artist from that of a superior domestic servant, and he was always willing to help musicians of the younger generation. He came in contact with almost every important artist of his time, and his influence has been enormous on the music of his century and, indirectly, on that of the 20th.

BIBLIOGRAPHY: Liszt's letters—*Letters of Franz Liszt* (1894 and 1968), *Letters of Liszt and von Bülow* (1898), *Correspondence of Wagner and Liszt,* 2 vols. (1897; new ed., 1969), *Liszt, As Sketched in the Letters of Borodin* (1895), *The Letters of Franz Liszt to Marie zu Sayn-Wittgenstein* (1953); Sacheverell Sitwell, *Liszt,* rev. ed. (1955; reprint, 1966); Bence Szabolcsi, *The Twilight of Ferenc Liszt* (1959; reprint, 1973); Alexandr Buchner, *Franz Liszt in Bohemia* (1962); Humphrey Searle, *The Music of Liszt,* rev. ed. (1966); Ernest Newman, *The Man Liszt: A Study of the Tragi-comedy of a Soul Divided against Itself* (1969); Ludwig Nohl, *Life of Liszt* (1970); Victor Ilytch Seroff, *Franz Liszt* (1970); Alan Walker, *Franz Liszt: The Man and His Music* (1970) and *Liszt* (1971); Herbert Westerby, *Liszt, Composer, and His Piano Works* (1970); James Gibbons Huneker, *Franz Liszt* (1971); Wilhelm von Lenz, *The Great Piano Virtuosos of Our Time* (1971); Claude Rostand, *Liszt* (1972).

RECORDINGS: Numerous recordings of many works.

Litaize, Gaston (b. August 11, 1909) The blind French organist and composer Gaston Litaize studied at the Paris Conservatoire (organ with Marcel Dupré), winning first prizes in organ, improvisation, fugue, and composition and the second Grand Prix de Rome (1938), unprecedented for a blind person. Litaize became organist at the church of Saint-François Xavier in Paris and has taught at the French National Institute for the Blind. His compositions are mostly for organ and for chorus.

liturgical drama A medieval play acted within or near a church that depicted a religious story. Although it had its roots in the Christian liturgy, it was not a part of the service. The language was Latin, and the dialogue was frequently chanted to simple monophonic melodies. Music was also used in the form of incidental dance and processional tunes.

The earliest traces of the liturgical drama are found in manuscripts dating from the 10th century. Its genesis may perhaps be found in the chant "Quem quaeritis" ("Whom seek ye"), a TROPE to the introit of the Easter mass. In *Regularis concordia* (mid-10th century) St. Aethelwold of Winchester described the manner in which the "Quem quaeritis" trope was performed as a small scene at matins. The dialogue represents the well-known story of the three Marys approaching the tomb of Christ: "Whom do you seek?" "Jesus of Nazareth." "He is not here. He has arisen as was prophesied. Go. Announce that he has arisen from the dead."

The liturgical drama, gradually increasing in both size and sophistication, flourished particularly during the 12th and 13th centuries. The most popular themes were derived from biblical tales (the three Marys, Daniel in the lion's den, the foolish virgins, the story of the passion and death of Jesus, etc.) as well as from the stories of the saints (the special class known as the miracle plays). Eventually the connection between the liturgical drama and the church was severed as the plays came under secular sponsorship and adopted the vernacular. This later development (continuing through the 16th century) is most correctly referred to as the mystery play.

Locatelli, Pietro (September 3, 1695–March 30, 1764)   A student of Corelli in Rome, the Italian violinist and composer Pietro Locatelli settled in Amsterdam, where he regularly gave public concerts. He was the first of the great violinists who practiced virtuosity for virtuosity's sake, thereby extending the vocabulary of the instrument. Some of the bravura effects in his studies and caprices, which anticipate those of Paganini, overstep the legitimate bounds of music. But these are ostensibly exercises, and in his sonatas and concertos, of which he composed several sets, Locatelli proves himself to be a serious musician capable of elegant and expressive melody.

RECORDINGS: *L'arte del violino; Concerti a quattro* (6); Concerti grossi (12); Sonata in F for flute and guitar; Violin Sonata, Op. 6, No. 7.

Locke, Matthew (*c.* 1630–August 1677)   A leading English composer for the stage before Purcell, Matthew Locke was a chorister at the Exeter Cathedral under Edward Gibbons. At the age of 18 he visited the Low Countries. With Christopher Gibbons, nephew of his former teacher, he wrote the music for James Shirley's *Masque of Cupid and Death* (1653). He also wrote part of the music for Sir William Davenant's *The Siege of Rhodes* (1656), usually considered to be the first operatic entertainment produced in England, and sang in it as well. In the same year appeared his *Little Consort of Three Parts* for viols. By 1660 he had been appointed Composer in Ordinary to the King. Locke wrote the music for the "king's sagbutts and cornetts," used when Charles II "progressed" from the Tower of London to Whitehall the day before his coronation; he also wrote several anthems for the Chapel Royal. After his conversion to Catholicism he was appointed organist to the queen.

Much of his later music of importance is concerned with the stage: for Thomas Shadwell's *Psyche* (1673), Davenant's *Macbeth* (1663), and Shadwell's *The Tempest* (1674). Locke's instrumental music lacks the harmonic daring so typical of his vocal style, but the consort music mentioned above and other works for viols remain some of the most masterly instrumental music of the century. In the *Tempest* music Locke uses for the first time in English music such markings in the vernacular as "soft," "louder by degrees," and uses tremolos for string instruments. His treatise, *Melothesia* (1673), contains his "Certain General Rules for playing upon a Continued Bass."

Loeffler, Charles Martin (Tornow) (January 30, 1861–May 19, 1935)   The composer Charles Martin Loeffler was born at Mulhouse, Alsace, France, the son of a German writer and agriculturist who was employed intermittently in Russia, Hungary, and Switzerland when Loeffler was a child. At the age of 14 he was sent to Berlin, where he studied violin with Joachim, and later to Paris, where his teachers were Joseph Massart in violin and Ernest Guiraud in composition. He emigrated to the United States in 1881 and in 1882 was engaged as a violinist in the Boston Symphony, resigning in 1903 to devote himself entirely to composition.

Loeffler's childhood in eastern Europe is reflected in his symphonic poem, *Memories of My Childhood,* subtitled *Life in a Russian Village* (1924), but his musical home was France with leanings toward Impressionism. He wrote numerous works for various instruments and voices with orchestra, most of which were first performed by the Boston Symphony. Of these the most enduring and musically significant is *A Pagan Poem.* His *Canticum Fratris Solis* for voice and chamber orchestra on a text of Francis of Assisi was first performed at the opening concert of the Coolidge series at the Library of Congress, Washington, D.C. (1925), and *Evocation* for women's voices and orchestra was commissioned for the inauguration of Severance Hall, Cleveland (1931). In smaller forms Loeffler wrote Two Rhapsodies for oboe, viola, and piano (1905); Music for Four Stringed Instruments (1917); other chamber music, songs, and piano pieces.

RECORDINGS: Music for four stringed instruments; *Pagan Poems;* Two Rhapsodies for oboe, viola, and piano.

Lohengrin: *see* ROMANTIC PERIOD (Wagnerian development); WAGNER (life) and (development).

London, George, real name, George Burnstein (b. May 30, 1919?)   A Canadian of Russian heritage, the bass-baritone George London made his debut as Dr. Grenvil in Verdi's *La Traviata* in 1942 at the Hollywood Bowl. He subsequently appeared in operettas and musical comedy and made world tours with a trio that included Frances Yeend and Mario Lanza. London first appeared at the Vienna State Opera (as Amonasro in Verdi's *Aida*) in 1949 without rehearsal. Two years later he first sang at Bayreuth and at the Metropolitan Opera; his debut at the latter was again as Amonasro. A capable actor, he was best known in roles of Mozart, Wagner, and Mussorgsky.

London Symphonies (Nos. 93–104): *see* CLASSICAL PERIOD (instrumental music, 1750–1800); HAYDN (London).

Louise: *see* CHARPENTIER, GUSTAVE; OPERA (the 19th century).

Love for Three Oranges, The: *see* PROKOFIEV.

Love of Three Kings, The: *see* AMORE DEI TRE RE, L'.

Lucia di Lammermoor: *see* DONIZETTI; OPERA (the 19th century).

Ludford, Nicholas (*c.* 1485–*c.* 1557)   One of the most important English composers of the early Tudor period, Nicholas Ludford is mentioned in Morley's list of English authors consulted in the preparation of his famous *Plaine and Easie Introduction to Practicall Musicke* (1597); Ludford otherwise went unnoticed until the 20th century. Very little is known of his life. He was admitted in 1521 to the Fraternity of St. Nicholas, the guild of parish clerks of the city of London, and was identified as a verger in the dissolution certificate of the collegiate church of St. Stephen's, Westminster, in 1547; he was still receiving a pension in 1555–56. Eleven of his masses have survived complete. These comprise a set of seven daily Lady masses complete with propers that are unique in English music and four large-scale festal masses; there is also a Magnificat that is musically related to his Mass *Benedicta.*

Luening, Otto (b. June 15, 1900)   The U.S. composer, conductor, and flutist Otto Luening is notable for his innovative experiments in composition employing tape. While in his teens he studied with Busoni in Zürich, where he first came in contact with electronic music. He performed in the United States and Europe (flute, piano) and later taught at the Eastman School, the University of Arizona, Bennington College, and (from 1944) Barnard College.

An early development was his formulation of acoustic harmony in which overtones are manipulated and reinforced. In 1954 Luening collaborated with Vladimir Ussachevsky in *Rhapsodic* Variations for tape recorder and orchestra, the first time tape had been combined with live performers. Luening's and Ussachevsky's other works include *Poem in Cycles and Bells* (1954) and incidental music for Shakespeare's *King Lear.* Luening's more than 275 compositions include several for flute on tape (*Fantasy in Space,* 1952; *Low Speed,* 1952; *Moonflight,* 1967).

Co-director of the Columbia–Princeton Electronic Music Center from 1959, Luening has also composed a considerable body of music for traditional instruments, including two Symphonic Fantasias (1924 and 1939–49), *Kentucky* Concerto for orchestra (1951), chamber music for winds and strings, and three solo Violin Sonatas (No. 3 premiered 1971). His opera *Evangeline,* written in 1932, was not produced until 1948.

RECORDINGS: Fugue and Chorale Fantasy with electronic doubles for organ and tape; Piano Sonata; Quartet No. 2; Short Suite for woodwind trio; *Synthesis* for orchestra and electronic sound; Trio for flute, cello, and piano; Violin Sonata No. 3.

Luisa Miller: *see* VERDI.

Lully, Jean-Baptiste, Italian form, Giovanni Battista Lulli (November 28, 1632–March 22, 1687)   The most important French court and operatic musician of the 17th century, Jean-Baptiste Lully was born in Florence of Italian parents; he changed his name to its French form when he became a naturalized Frenchman. His early history is obscure but it is probable that he was taken to France by the Duke of Guise. He entered the service of Mme de Montpensier and became a member of her string band but was dismissed for having composed some scurrilous verses and music. He joined the court band of Louis XIV in 1652 as a violinist and soon became composer of dance music to the king and leader of the newly formed *Petit Violons*. In 1658 he began to compose music for the court ballets, and from 1662 to 1671 he collaborated with Molière in such works as *Les Fâcheux, Le Mariage forcé, La Princesse d'Élide,* and *Le Bourgeois Gentilhomme.* From 1672 until his death he worked with the librettist Philippe Quinault. The subjects of the works produced by this partnership vary from the classical *Alceste* (1674) to the heroic *Roland* (1685) and the pastoral *Le Temple de la paix* (1685). Lully died in Paris from blood poisoning resulting from a wound in his foot caused by his long conducting stick.

His rise from violinist in Louis XIV's court

Jean-Baptiste Lully
detail of a portrait by an unknown artist.
17th century. Giraudon

band was meteoric and was accomplished by brazen and merciless intrigue. By 1662 he had gained complete control of the court music by the royal appointments of *Brevet de la charge de Composition de la Musique de la chambre du Roi* in 1661 and *La charge de Maître de Musique de la Famille royale* in 1662. He then acquired from Abbé Perrin and Robert Cambert their patents of operatic production, and by 1674 no opera could be performed anywhere in France without Lully's permission. In 1681 he received his *lettres de nationalisation* and his *lettres de noblesse.* He also became one of the *secrétaires du roi,* a privilege usually held only by the French aristocracy.

At the outset of his career Lully's operatic style was similar to that of the Italian masters Francesco Cavalli and Luigi Rossi. He quickly assimilated the contemporary French idiom, however, and created a new and original style of writing that was widely imitated in Europe. In his ballets he introduced new dances such as the minuet and made use of a higher proportion of quicker ones such as the bourrée, gavotte, and gigue; he also introduced woman dancers to the stage. The texts in both ballets and operas were French.

He established the form of the French overture and abandoned the recitativo secco style. This last he replaced by an accompanied recitative of great rhythmic freedom with careful word setting and declamation. This led to a lessening of the demarcation between the recitative and the aria so that French opera acquired much more continuity. The arias themselves, however, retain many Italian characteristics. Each is written in a particular style and mood: *chanson à couplets, air-complainte* (arioso), and *air déclamé.* His operas frequently end with a chaconne movement, and in this he was followed by both Rameau and Gluck.

Among Lully's other works are several sacred compositions, including the famous *Miserere* and 17 motets; dances for various instruments; suites for trumpets and strings, a form that became very popular in England during the Restoration; and the *Suites de Symphonies et Trios.*

BIBLIOGRAPHY: R. H. F. Scott, *Jean-*

Baptiste Lully (1973; U.S. ed., *Jean-Baptiste Lully: The Founder of French Opera,* 1977).

RECORDINGS: *Alceste; Le Triomphe de l'amour* (ballet suite); *Xerxés* (ballet); fanfares, marches, and motets.

Lulu: *see* BERG; COUNTERPOINT (modern period); OPERA (the 20th century).

lute A plucked stringed instrument originally brought to Europe from the Near East. Much used in European music from the Middle Ages to the 18th century, it was still in use in many Arab countries in the 20th century. In Western music it enjoyed a revival in the late 20th century.

The distinguishing feature of the lute is the shape and complex structure of its body, which resembles half an almond or filbert, having a vaulted or barrel-shaped back, convex in each direction and wider toward the bottom end. This back is composed of several ribs, or staves, bent over a prepared mold, the edges brought together, glued, and lined with strips of paper or parchment. Much at-

man playing lute
from Filippo Bonanni's Gabinetto armonico,
18th century courtesy, Dover Publications, Inc.

tention is paid to the shaping and proportions of the mold.

The earliest European lutes followed the contemporary Arab pattern in having four strings; they were played with a quill plectrum. By the middle of the 14th century, the strings had become pairs, or courses. Existing representations of the lute in the 15th century show it then to have had a body usually composed of nine staves and five courses of strings (*i.e.,* nine strings, the lower courses in pairs, the highest single) laid on a short, flat neck carrying seven gut frets.

The soundboard contains a circular sound hole, set nearly central, with a perforated ornament—the rose—cut in the soundboard wood. The bridge is of the tension type, glued directly to the lower part of the soundboard. The head or pegbox is sharply reflexed and turns back from the nut at the top of the fingerboard at nearly a right angle. The purpose of this reflection seems to be twofold: to reduce overall length on this rather large instrument so that there is easier access to the pegs in tuning, and to ensure firm bearings at the nut for the very thin, slack double gut strings.

In the 15th century the use of the plectrum was generally abandoned in favor of the fingers of the right hand, and by the 16th century the classic form and stringing of the lute were established. The great Bolognese and Venetian schools of makers had arisen; these makers—Laux and Sigismond Maler, Hans Frei, Nikolaus Schonfeld and the Tieffenbruckers—by their fine workmanship and the tonal proportions of their instruments contributed much to the popularity of the lute in the late Renaissance and prepared the way for its extensive and noble literature of solo music (fantasias, dance movements, chanson arrangements), song accompaniments, and consort music. The neck was lengthened to take nine, later 10, semitone frets, and the standard stringing was six courses tuned to G c f a, d' g'. Its technique was systematized and its music expressed in TABLATURE, a form of notation representing not the musical sounds played but the strings and fret positions used in order to produce those sounds. These positions were indicated by a stave of horizontal lines representing the courses of the lute, letters or figures

467

being placed on these lines to denote the fret to be stopped by the left hand and the strings to be played by the right hand.

Toward the end of the 16th century, further bass strings were added, the neck and head being enlarged to take them. These diapasons, which reached four in number, were usually tuned to a diatonic scale downward from the sixth course. From about 1600 modifications in the tuning were introduced by French lutenists and by about 1630 had generally replaced the old tuning. Further diapasons were added, resulting in an instrument known as the French lute, primarily a solo instrument. Its repertoire required a highly mannered and ornamented style of performance and a new technique of broken chords and slurred notes that had a marked influence on the 17th-century French harpsichord composers. With the introduction of the additional diapasons, problems of tonal balance arose, and the lower strings were often lengthened beyond the normal nut and carried by means of an extension of the neck to a separate nut and pegbox.

man playing chitarrone, or archlute
from Filippo Bonanni's Gabinetto armonico,
18th century courtesy, Dover Publications, Inc.

The theorbo, or theorboed lute, was often a large instrument that continued to use the old tuning and had the diapasons carried on a second head. Because of its greater string length, which made only the simplest chordal playing practicable, it was mainly used for continuo purposes. A larger form of theorbo, the chitarrone, or archlute, was developed in Rome about 1600. Usually about six feet (not quite two meters) long, it had a normal lute body, six to eight strings running over the fingerboard to a pegbox positioned midway in an extended neck, and six to eight additional bass strings (diapasons) lying off the fingerboard and running to a second pegbox at the end of the neck. Having a sonority approaching that of the contemporary harpsichord, it was used as a continuo instrument in 17th-century chamber ensembles.

BIBLIOGRAPHY: Thomas Robinson, *The School of Musicke, Wherein Is Taught the Perfect Method of True Fingering of the Lute, Pandora, Orpharion and Viol da Gamba* (1603; reprint, 1973); Curt Sachs, *The History of Musical Instruments* (1940); Sibyl Marcuse, *A Survey of Musical Instruments* (1975).

Lutoslawski, Witold (b. January 25, 1913) The Polish composer Witold Lutoslawski studied theory and composition at the Warsaw Conservatory and mathematics at the University of Warsaw. His early works, most of which were destroyed in World War II, were within the system of traditional Western tonality, sometimes using material from Polish folk tunes. The Symphonic Variations (1938) and Variations on a Theme of Paganini for two pianos (1941) are traditional. His *Little* Suite (1951) for orchestra was performed at the first Warsaw Festival of Contemporary Music in 1956. *Funeral Music* (1958) for string orchestra was a turning point in his style; dedicated to the memory of Bartók, it is a 12-tone work that received recognition from UNESCO's Tribune Internationale des Compositeurs. It was followed by Lutoslawski's first use of aleatory operations in *Venetian Games,* written for the Venice Festival of 1961. In this work Lutoslawski uses non-staff, optically suggestive notation to guide the performer in the various improvisatory operations.

Lutoslawski has written piano pieces, children's songs, choral works, a Quartet (1964), two symphonies, and a Cello Concerto (1970). He was honored with a government prize in 1955 soon after having composed his Concerto for orchestra based on folk themes. In demand as a lecturer, he has taught intermittently in the United States and Sweden since 1962.

RECORDINGS: Cello Concerto; Concerto for orchestra; *Funeral Music;* Quartet; Variations on a Theme of Paganini; *Venetian Games.*

Lutyens, (Agnes) Elisabeth (b. July 9, 1906) The composer of more than 100 radio and film scores, British-born Elisabeth Lutyens is the daughter of the architect Sir Edwin Lutyens. She studied at the Royal College of Music in London and at the École Normale de Musique in Paris. She was a co-founder (1931) of the Macnaghten-Lemare Concerts in London, and in 1954 she founded the Composers Concourse there for the performance of new music. She has written chamber music; an opera, *The Numbered* (1967); and vocal music with far-ranging texts, including *The Valley of Hatsu-se* (1965; early Japanese poetry), *Akapotik Rose* (1966; text by Eduardo Paolozzi), *Essence of Our Happinesses* (1968; texts from 9th-century Arabic sources, John Donne, and Arthur Rimbaud), and *The Tyme Doth Flete* (1968; texts from Ovid and Petrarch); and a lyric drama with libretto by the composer, *Isis and Osiris* (1969). Her music has been dodecaphonic since 1939 (Concerto for nine instruments), and she has produced a great deal of incidental music for the stage. Her autobiography, *A Goldfish Bowl,* was published in 1972. Lutyens was made a commander in the Order of the British Empire in 1969.

Lydian mode The fifth of the eight medieval church modes. Its general range comprises the eight natural notes from the F below middle C to the F above. Melodies in Lydian, or Mode V, usually have F as the *finalis,* or final note, and C as the *tenor,* or reciting note.

In ancient Greek music Lydian referred to the scale pattern, or octave species, conventionally represented in modern writings as C-C.

lyre A type of stringed instrument that was widespread in the ancient Mediterranean world and Near East and is still used in Arabia and parts of Africa. It is characterized by a sound box from which project two arms joined by a yoke; the shape of the sound box varies. The strings run from the sound box over a bridge to the yoke, where they are tuned by means of twisted thongs or pegs; they are plucked with the fingers or with a plectrum.

The lyre is known in Mesopotamia from the Sumerian period onward; it was introduced into Egypt not later than the 19th century B.C. Size, construction, and number of strings vary greatly. Splendid specimens have survived from Ur (25th century B.C.). These are about three and one-half feet (slightly more than one meter) high. Giant lyres that stand on the ground and are played by a seated player are seen on Mesopotamian reliefs from

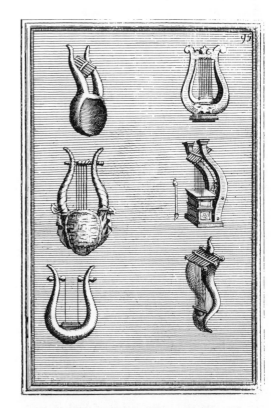

classical Greek lyres and a cithara
the lyre is shown correctly in the left row center opposite the cithara; the conventional symbolic form of the lyre is shown upper right; the three remaining items are imaginary; from Filippo Bonanni's Gabinetto armonico, *18th century courtesy, Dover Publications, Inc.*

the 3rd millennium and later in Egypt (Amarna period). Smaller, portable instruments (Babylonia, Egypt, Syria, Assyria) were held horizontally or lying in the arms; their construction was often asymmetrical. The Hebrew *kinnor* was probably a lyre.

In Greek lands there is evidence of lyre-type instruments with seven or more strings—probably related to Asiatic types—during the Minoan-Mycenaean civilizations. Vase paintings of the 8th century B.C. show a simple variety with from three to five strings that can be identified with the phorminx of Homer. From the 7th century B.C., probably under renewed Asiatic influence, the main classical varieties became established, at first with seven strings.

The *lyra* had a sound box made of tortoise shell (later wood) and slender curved arms. This was the instrument of the schoolboy and the amateur; players are generally shown seated with the lyre resting on the left hip. The *barbiton,* a subtype of the *lyra,* had longer strings and lower pitch.

The instrument of the professional was the cithara, which was larger and more solidly built, the hollow arms forming a substantial prolongation of the sound box. The *citharoedus* (singer to the cithara) stood on a small platform, his decorative instrument resting against his body and supported in position by a band attached to his left wrist. There were two main varieties of cithara: an elaborately constructed instrument with a flat base; and a much simpler instrument with a rounded base, favored by less pretentious players.

With both the *lyra* and the cithara, the left hand was spread over the strings while the right hand held a plectrum. The precise function of the two hands is still uncertain. Though strings numbering up to 12 were added to the cithara by virtuosos of the late 5th century B.C., the number seven was canonical in the classical period. It is debated whether each string provided one note only or whether it was possible to obtain notes of higher pitch by stopping.

During the Roman period new varieties of cithara emerged. The lyre of medieval Europe (rote) tended to depart from the type by the addition of a fingerboard and the use of a bow; *e.g.,* the Welsh CRWTH, which was still played in the early 19th century. A similar instrument, the kantele, is still played in Finland and Estonia.

In Africa, *e.g.,* Sudan, Ethiopia, Uganda, the lyre survives in a form not unlike that of the ancient world and is used, as in Homer's day, to provide an accompaniment for the professional singer.

BIBLIOGRAPHY: Francis W. Galpin, *The Music of the Sumerians* (1937; reprint, 1970); Curt Sachs, *The History of Musical Instruments* (1940); Sibyl Marcuse, *A Survey of Musical Instruments* (1975).

Lytton, Henry A(lfred), real name, Henry Alfred Jones (January 3, 1865–August 15, 1936)   One of the most famous of the Savoyards, the baritone Henry A. Lytton joined the chorus of the D'Oyly Carte Opera Company briefly in 1884, making his solo debut in 1887 in the role of Robin Oakapple (*Ruddigore*). He became a regular soloist in 1897, singing intermittently until he became a mainstay of the company from 1908 until his retirement in 1934. In that time he sang 30 Gilbert and Sullivan roles, his favorite being Jack Point in *The Yeomen of the Guard.* Though he was not the original in any of his famous portrayals, and he did not read music, he is generally considered the leading singing actor in the history of the company. He was knighted in 1930.

M

Maazel, Lorin (b. March 5, 1930)   A musical prodigy who at age nine conducted at the World's Fair and at the Hollywood Bowl, the French-born U.S. conductor Lorin Maazel had conducted many major U.S. orchestras by the time he reached his teens. After study in Italy he toured Europe and South America. He was appointed director of the Berlin Radio Symphony in 1964 and was music director of the Deutsches Oper in Berlin (1965–71). In the latter year Maazel became associate principal conductor of the New Philharmonia of London and since 1972 has been music director of the Cleveland Orchestra. He was named principal guest conductor of the National Orchestra of France in 1977. He has conducted opera at Bayreuth and the Metropolitan Opera (both 1962), at Vienna (1966), and at La Scala (1966–67). His many recordings span music from Bach to Stravinsky.

McCormack, John (June 14, 1884–September 16, 1945) Trained in Milan after winning a gold medal at the National Irish Festival (1902), the Irish tenor John McCormack made his operatic debut at Covent Garden in 1907 as Turiddu in Mascagni's *Cavalleria rusticana.* His New York City debut at the Manhattan Opera was in Verdi's *La Traviata* in 1909. He was a member of opera companies in Boston (1910–11) and Chicago (1912–14) and made many guest appearances at the Metropolitan Opera. He also sang oratorio, lieder,

John McCormack   *courtesy, RCA Records*

and sentimental ballads, and he was unsurpassed in Irish songs. His operatic roles included the tenor leads in Verdi's *Rigoletto,* Donizetti's *Lucia di Lammermoor,* Puccini's *Tosca,* Mozart's *Don Giovanni,* and Victor Herbert's *Natoma.*

McCracken, James (b. December 16, 1926) The U.S. tenor James McCracken began his career in musical comedy and operetta. He studied at the Metropolitan Opera studio, where he sang bit roles (1952–56). The following year he studied in Milan and achieved his first success in Zürich in 1959. Since 1960 he has appeared regularly as a guest at the Vienna State Opera, and he became a full member of the Metropolitan in 1965. He developed his voice to that of a heldentenor and has been admired as Otello (Verdi) and Manrico (Verdi's *Il Trovatore*). In 1977 he sang his first major Wagnerian role on the stage (Tannhäuser) at the Metropolitan.

Macbeth: *see* VERDI.

MacDowell, Edward (Alexander) (December 18, 1860–January 23, 1908) A U.S. composer known for his piano pieces, Edward MacDowell helped establish an independent American school. He first studied in New York City with Teresa Carreño and then went to Paris, where he was a pupil of Antoine Marmontel (1876–78) at the Conservatoire. In 1878 he went to Germany to study composition with Joachim Raff at the Frankfurt Conservatory, and he later taught piano at Darmstadt. In 1882 Raff introduced MacDowell to Liszt, who arranged for him to play his First *Modern* Suite at the Allgemeiner Musikverein at Zürich. He returned to the United States in 1888 and the following year played in New York City the first performance of his Second Piano Concerto in d minor, his most successful large-scale work.

In 1896 he was invited to establish a department of music at Columbia University. He undertook the task with enthusiasm but was frustrated in carrying out his plans. As a result of disagreement with university authorities, he resigned in 1904, becoming the subject of much unpleasant publicity. His mental balance was gravely undermined, leading to a collapse and eventually to a recession to infantilism from which he never recovered. After his death his widow organized the MacDowell Colony at their residence in Peterborough, New Hampshire, as a summer residence for U.S. composers and writers.

MacDowell's music derives from the contemporary Romantic movement. His lyrical style suggests Grieg and his harmony Schumann and sometimes Liszt. Almost all his works have literary or pictorial associations. His early symphonic poems include *Hamlet and Ophelia* (1885), *Lancelot and Elaine* (1888), *Lamia* (1889), and *The Saracens* (1891). More distinctive is his orchestral *Indian* Suite (1897), depicting American Indian life and rituals and based on authentic Indian tunes. His songs, though derivative, are genuinely lyrical, but he is at his best in his piano music, particularly in small pieces where he shows the gifts of a sensitive miniaturist. The best of his piano works are *Sea Pieces* (1898), *Woodland Sketches* (1896), *Fireside Tales* (1902), and *New England Idylls* (1902). His four piano sonatas, *Tragica* (1893), *Eroica* (1895), *Norse* (1900), and *Keltic* (1901), are ambitious attempts at programmatic music in classical forms.

BIBLIOGRAPHY: Marian MacDowell, *Random Notes on Edward MacDowell and His Music* (1950).

RECORDINGS: *Indian* Suite; *Modern* Suite No. 2; Piano Concertos (2); Piano Sonatas (3); *Sea Pieces;* Suite No. 1 for orchestra; *Woodland Sketches.*

Machaut, Guillaume de (*c.* 1300–1377) The poet and musician Guillaume de Machaut was greatly admired by contemporaries as a master of French versification and regarded as the leading French composer of the ars nova. Although he wrote both lyrics and longer forms such as the *dit* (extended debates in dialogue with allegorical content), it is on his shorter poems and his musical compositions that his reputation rests. He was the last great poet in France to think of the lyric and its musical setting as a single entity.

He took holy orders and in 1323 entered the service of John of Luxembourg, King of Bohemia, whom he accompanied on his wars as chaplain and secretary. He was rewarded with an appointment in 1337 as canon of Reims Cathedral. After the king's death he found another protector in the king's daughter, Bonne of Luxembourg, wife of the future King John II of France, and in 1349 in Charles II, King of Navarre. Honors and patronage continued to be lavished by kings and princes on Machaut at Reims until his death.

Machaut's music has been preserved in 32 manuscripts, representing a large part of the surviving music from the period. The ars nova style in which he composed was named after the title of a treatise on the new 14th-century music, which was more refined and expressive than what had preceded it. He was the first composer to write a unified polyphonic setting of the ordinary of the mass, a work sometimes called *Messe Notre-Dame.* In most of this four-part setting he employs the characteristic ars nova technique of isorhythm.

Machaut's secular compositions make up the larger part of his musical output. His three- and four-part motets number 23. Of these 17 are in French, two are Latin mixed with French, and four are in Latin. Love is often the subject, and all but three employ isorhythm. Machaut's 19 lais are based on a complex type of lyric poem and are usually for a single part, though two are for three parts, and one is for two parts. His 33 virelais are also based on a lyric genre. Of these 25 consist solely of a melody, and they, along with the bulk of his lais, represent the last of such songs composed in the tradition of the trouvères. The remainder of his virelais have one or two additional parts for instrumental accompaniment, and these are typical of the accompanied solo song that became popular in the 14th century. He also wrote rondeaux and ballades. The wide distribution of his music in contemporary manuscripts reveals that he was esteemed not only in France but also in Italy, Spain, and much of Europe.

RECORDINGS: *Messe Notre-Dame;* ballades; motets; rondeaux; virelais.

Mackenzie, Alexander Campbell (August 22, 1847–April 28, 1935) The Scottish composer Alexander Campbell Mackenzie was born in Edinburgh and at the age of 10 was sent to study music in Germany at Sondershausen, where he also played violin in the ducal orchestra. Returning to Britain, he continued his studies at the Royal Academy of Music. Then followed some years in Edinburgh as composer, conductor, and violinist until, encouraged by Hans von Bülow, he settled in Florence to devote himself to composition.

Cantatas *The Bride* (1881) and *Jason* (1882) belong to this time, as do his first two operas, *Colomba* (1883) and *The Troubadour* (1886). From 1888 to 1924 he was principal of the Royal Academy, and he was also active as a conductor and lecturer. He was knighted in 1895. Among other works were an oratorio *The Rose of Sharon, Scottish* Piano Concerto, three *Scottish* Rhapsodies, and Overture *Britannia.* His autobiography, *A Musician's Narrative,* was published in 1927.

Mackerras, (Alan) Charles (b. November 17, 1925)   Educated in New South Wales (Australia) and in Prague, where he studied with Václav Talich, the U.S.-born Australian conductor Charles Mackerras began his career as an oboist with the Sydney Symphony (1945–47). He became a conductor at the Sadler's Wells Opera in London, of which he was made musical director in 1970. He was conductor of the BBC Concert Orchestra (1954–56) and principal conductor of the Hamburg State Opera (1966–69). Though his repertoire includes a wide variety, Mackerras is somewhat of a Janáček specialist (having introduced three of his operas to London). He conducted the first performance of Britten's *Noye's Fludde* (1958) and the opening concert at Sydney's new opera house (1973).

MacMillan, Ernest (Campbell) (August 18, 1893–May 6, 1973)   A student at the universities of Toronto (B.A., 1915) and Oxford (Mus. D., 1918), the Canadian organist, conductor, and composer Ernest MacMillan had made numerous concert appearances and been made an associate of the Royal College of Organists by the time he was in his teens. Interned during World War I, he conducted a prison orchestra in Germany and composed a setting for Charles Swinburne's ode *England.* He was principal of the Toronto Conservatory (1926–42), dean of the music faculty at the University of Toronto (1926–52), and conductor of the Toronto Symphony (1931–56) and the Mendelssohn Choir (1942–57). He was chairman of the Canadian Music Council (1949–66) and in 1935 became the first Canadian musician to be knighted. His compositions include works for chorus and orchestra as well as chamber music. He edited

and arranged two books of Canadian folk songs (*A Canadian Song Book* and *Vingt-et-une chansons canadiennes,* both 1928).

Madama Butterfly: *see* OPERA (the 19th century); PUCCINI.

Maderna, Bruno (April 21, 1920–November 13, 1973)   An Italian conductor and composer, of avant-garde and electronic music, Bruno Maderna studied with Malipiero and Hermann Scherchen. In 1941 he received his degree in composition at Rome from the Conservatorio di Musica Santa Cecilia. After World War II he became associated with the Internationale Ferienkurse für Neue Musik at Darmstadt, West Germany. With Berio, Maderna founded the Studio di Fonologia Musicale at Milan Radio in Italy in 1954; the studio became a major laboratory for electronic music in Europe. They also founded a review devoted to electronic and avant-garde music, *Incontri Musicali.* Maderna later taught composition in Milan, at the Dartington Summer School of Music, Devon, and elsewhere.

Maderna's music is expressive and lyrical as well as experimental. His *Serenata* (1954) is a colorful orchestral work with subtle sonorities and polyrhythms. The *Notturno* for tape (1956) and *Sintaxis* for four different, unspecified electronic timbres display his interest in new sonorities. His Oboe Concerto (1962) uses small-scale aleatory operations. He has written a Concerto for two pianos (1948), a Flute Concerto (1954), and a theater piece, *Hyperion.*

Maderna conducted widely and recorded extensively, including many works of his contemporaries.

RECORDINGS: *Dedication; Giardino Religioso; Honeyrêves* for flute and piano; *Pièce pour Ivry; Serenata; Viola.*

madrigal   A form of concerted vocal music, Italian in origin. The earliest school of madrigal writing flourished in northern Italy in the 14th century and is quite distinct from the later one that began about 1530.

The early madrigal, like the ballade or the ballata, is a poetical form as well as a musical one. Two or three strophes of three lines each are followed by a final ritornello of two lines;

in each strophe two lines rhyme with one another. For this type of madrigal the suggested derivation from *mandria* ("sheepfold") may well be correct, as early writers associate it with the *pastourelle* of the troubadours, and its subject matter is generally idyllic and contemplative if not exactly pastoral. The principal composers in this form were Jacopo da Bologna and Giovanni da Cascia (or da Firenze); their settings are for two or three voices, of which the topmost is usually very ornate.

The madrigal was already becoming obsolete by the time of Francesco Landini (d. 1397), and it fell into complete oblivion in the 15th century. When it was revived by the humanistic circle that gathered about Cardinal Pietro Bembo in the early years of the 16th century, it is probable that, whatever its original derivation had been, *madrigale* was thought of simply as equivalent to *matricale,* meaning "in the mother tongue"; *i.e.,* Italian and not Latin, for it is applied to poems without any fixed form. The madrigals of this period were intended as a literary return to the more elevated style of antiquity, in contrast to such current forms as the frottola and the *strambotto.* The music to which they were set was likewise intentionally dignified, and it drew on the style of the contemporary sacred motet and upon Josquin des Prés's sonorous chansons; nevertheless the break was not a sudden one, and the first of these madrigals (published in 1533) are still similar to frottole.

The earliest group of 16th-century madrigal composers includes Philippe Verdelot, Jacob Arcadelt, Adriaan Willaert, and Costanzo Festa. It will be noted that northern (French and Flemish) composers predominate, and it was not until the middle of the century that native Italian composers began to play a large part in the composition of madrigals. Whereas the earlier madrigalists had aimed at a placid, almost abstract, musical accompaniment to the words, Cyprien de Rore, Andrea Gabrieli, Philippe de Monte, and Orlando di Lasso cultivated a new and detailed expressiveness with words such as *acerbo* ("bitter"), *ira* ("anger"), *pianti* ("weepings") underlined by dissonances and *gioia* ("joy") or *riso* ("laugh") set to swiftly running figures. Although the applica-

tion of these expressive symbols at times appears naïve, the result was the rapid development of a new musical language, one that had repercussions on the setting of words to music throughout Europe.

The final stage of the Italian madrigal, although it produced much superb music, can be seen as a decline from this intimate fusion of music and poetry. In the hands of such composers as Luca Marenzio, Carlo Gesualdo, and Monteverdi, the musical language of the madrigal became ever richer and more varied, but with this went a tendency to set stilted and epigrammatic poems of negligible literary value. The increasing independence of the separate voice parts eventually resulted in the complete breakup of the old polyphonic texture. In the later madrigals of Monteverdi, for example, passages for one or more solo voices are punctuated with sonorous passages for the full group, and unity is achieved not by continuity of texture but by the use of an accompanying basso continuo. From this type of accompanied madrigal it was a comparatively short step to the cantata, which in the 17th century was to take its place as the most elevated form of secular vocal music.

In France, Germany (notably Hassler), and Spain the Italian madrigal made its influence felt on the native forms of secular part song, but nowhere was it so enthusiastically imitated or so completely naturalized as in England. Madrigals had been known at court since the later years of Henry VIII, but it was not until the 1580s that they achieved real popularity. In 1588 Nicholas Yonge published a large collection of Italian madrigals in English translation under the title *Musica Transalpina,* and similar collections followed it. Byrd was already a mature artist and was little influenced in his secular music by the Italian style, but his pupil Morley embraced it wholeheartedly and had two sets published in an Italian version as well as in the original English. Morley excelled in the lighter and more cheerful types of madrigal, such as canzonets ("little short songs," as he calls them) and balletts; the latter he modeled on the *balletti* of Giovanni Giacomo Gastoldi but achieved a more elaborate musical development and a stronger sense of harmonic direction. John Wilbye and Thomas

Weelkes brought to the English madrigal a new depth of feeling and on occasion a profound melancholy that is not characteristic of the Italian school; Wilbye is the purer stylist, but Weelkes the bolder and more individual.

Of the later English madrigal publications, those of Gibbons and Thomas Tomkins, published in 1612 and 1622 respectively, are the best. Although the fashion for madrigals lasted only about 40 years in England, it had in that comparatively short time produced a remarkable quantity of fine music.

The tradition of madrigal singing was revived in England in the early 18th century. The Madrigal Society (founded by John Immyns in 1741) and John Christopher Pepusch's Academy of Ancient Music kept the practice alive in London, and it also flourished among the lay clerks of cathedral and collegiate churches throughout the country. At the meetings of these groups both English and foreign madrigals were sung, together with later compositions in imitation of their style.

BIBLIOGRAPHY: Thomas Ravenscroft, *A Briefe Discourse of the True Use of Charact'ring the Degrees in Measurable Musicke* (1614; reprint, 1971); Edward F. Rimbault, *Bibliotheca Madrigaliana* (1847); William A. Barrett, *English Glee and Madrigal Writers* (1877; reprint, 1977); Charles K. Scott, *Madrigal Singing* (1931); Edmund H. Fellowes, *The English Madrigal Composers,* 2nd ed. (1948), and *English Madrigal Verse,* 3rd ed. (1967); Alfred Einstein, *The Italian Madrigal,* 3 vols. (1949; reprint, 1971).

Maeterlinck, Maurice: *see* DEBUSSY; DUKAS; FAURÉ.

Magic Flute, The: *see* CLASSICAL PERIOD (vocal music, 1750–1800); GLOCKENSPIEL; MOZART (later life); OPERA (the 19th century).

Mahillon, Victor Charles (March 10, 1841–June 17, 1924) A Belgian musical scholar and authority on wind instruments, Victor Charles Mahillon was the son of Charles Mahillon, founder of a firm of wind-instrument makers, and entered the firm in 1865. As curator of the museum of the Brussels Conservatoire, he formed a collection of more than 1,500 instruments; he published an analytical catalogue (1880–1922) with theories of construction and a methodical classification. He had copies made of rare instruments and adapted some of them, notably the Bach trumpet, for modern use. Mahillon published *Les Éléments d'acoustique musicale et instrumentale* (1874) and numerous monographs on instruments, and he organized concerts of historical works played on old instruments.

Mahler, Gustav (July 7, 1860–May 18, 1911) The last notable exponent of the Austro-German symphony, Gustav Mahler was one of the most important forerunners of 20th-century musical developments. But his music was long rejected, and it is only since about 1960 that his true stature has been recognized, thanks in part to the lifelong efforts of his friend and disciple Bruno Walter and to such later conductors as Bernstein.

childhood Mahler was the son of an Austrian Jewish tavern keeper living in the Bohemian village of Kaliště (German Kalischt) in the southwestern corner of modern Czechoslovakia, but the family moved to the nearby town of Jihlava (German Iglau), where Mahler spent his childhood and youth. As part of a German-speaking Austrian minority, he

Gustav Mahler
The Mansell Collection, London

475

was an outsider among the indigenous Czech population and as a Jew an outsider among that Austrian minority; later in Germany he was an outsider as both an Austrian from Bohemia and a Jew. Mahler's life was also complicated by the tension between his parents. His father, a self-educated man of fierce vitality, had married a delicate woman from a cultured family; coming to resent her social superiority, he resorted to maltreating her physically. In consequence Mahler was alienated from his father and had a strong mother fixation, which even manifested itself physically: a slight limp was unconsciously copied in imitation of his mother's lameness. Furthermore he inherited his mother's weak heart, which was to cause his death at age 50. Finally there was a constant childhood background of illness and death among his 11 brothers and sisters.

The unsettling early background may explain the nervous tension, the irony and skepticism, the obsession with death, and the unremitting quest to discover some meaning in life that was to pervade Mahler's life and music. But it does not explain the prodigious energy, intellectual power, and inflexibility of purpose that carried him to the heights as both master conductor and composer. Despite his inherited heart trouble, he was an extremely active man—a ruthless musical director, a tireless swimmer, and an indefatigable mountain walker.

His musical talent revealed itself early and significantly. About the age of four, fascinated by the military music at a nearby barracks and the folk music sung by the Czech working people, he reproduced both on the accordion and the piano and began composing. The military and popular styles, together with the sounds of nature, became main sources of his mature inspiration. At 10 he made his debut as a pianist in Jihlava and at 15 was so proficient musically that he was accepted as a pupil at the Vienna Conservatory. After winning piano and composition prizes and earning a diploma, he supported himself by sporadic teaching while trying to win recognition as a composer. When he failed to win the conservatory's Beethoven Prize for composition with his first significant work, the cantata *Das*

klagende Lied (1880; *The Song of Complaint*), he turned to conducting for a more secure livelihood, reserving composition for lengthy summer vacations.

The next 17 years saw his ascent to the very top of his chosen profession. From conducting musical farces in Austria, he rose through various provincial opera houses, including important engagements at Budapest and Hamburg, to become artistic director of the Vienna Court Opera in 1897. As a conductor he won general acclaim, but as a composer he encountered the public's lack of comprehension that was to confront him for most of his career.

Since Mahler's conducting life centered in the opera house, it is at first surprising that his whole mature output was entirely symphonic (his 40 songs are not true lieder but embryonic symphonic movements, some of which provided a partial basis for the symphonies). But Mahler's unique aim, partially influenced by the school of Wagner and Liszt, was essentially autobiographical—the musical expression of a personal view of the world. And for this purpose song and symphony were more appropriate than the dramatic medium of opera—song because of its inherent personal lyricism and symphony (from the Wagner and Liszt point of view) because of its subjective expressive power.

first period Each of Mahler's three creative periods produced a symphonic trilogy. The three symphonies of his first period were conceived on a programmatic basis, the programs (later discarded) concerned with establishing some ultimate ground or existence in a world dominated by pain, death, doubt, and despair. To this end he followed the example of Beethoven's *Pastoral* Symphony and Berlioz' *Symphonie fantastique* in building with more than the then traditional four movements; of Wagner's music dramas in expanding the time span, enlarging the orchestral resources, and indulging in uninhibited emotional expression; of Beethoven's Ninth Symphony in introducing texts sung by soloists and chorus; and of some of Schubert's chamber works in introducing music from his own songs (settings of poems from the German folk anthology *Des Knaben Wunderhorn* [*The*

Youth's Magic Horn] or of his own poetry in a folk style).

These procedures, together with Mahler's own tense and rhetorical style, vivid orchestration, and ironic use of popular music, resulted in three symphonies of wide contrasts but unified by his creative personality and command of symphonic structure. The program of the purely orchestral First Symphony (one of the five movements was later discarded) is autobiographical of his youth. The five-movement Second, or *Resurrection,* Symphony begins with the death obsession and culminates in an avowal of the Christian belief in immortality (a huge finale with a setting of Friedrich Klopstock's resurrection ode with soloists and chorus). The even vaster Third Symphony also includes soloist and chorus.

The religious element in these works is highly significant. Mahler resolved his disturbing early background by identifying with Christianity. That this was a genuine impulse there can be no doubt, even if there was an element of expediency in his becoming baptized early in 1897 because it made it easier for him to be appointed to the Vienna Opera post. The ten years there represent his more balanced middle period. His newfound faith and his new high office brought a full and confident maturity, which was further stabilized by his marriage in 1902 to Alma Maria Schindler, who bore him two daughters.

middle period As director of the Vienna Opera (and for a time of the Vienna Philharmonic Concerts), Mahler achieved an unprecedented standard of interpretation and performance, which proved an almost unapprochable model for those who followed him. A fanatical idealist, he drove himself and his artists with a ruthless energy that proved a continual inspiration and with a complete disregard for personal considerations that won him many enemies. He made a number of tours and became famous over much of Europe as a conductor. He continued devoting his summer vacations in the Austrian Alps to composing; and as this involved a ceaseless expenditure of energy, he placed an intolerable strain on his frail constitution.

Most of the works of this middle period reflect the fierce dynamism of Mahler's full maturity. An exception is the Fourth Symphony, which is more of a pendant to the first period; conceived in six movements (two of which were eventually discarded), it has a *Wunderhorn* song finale for soprano, which was originally intended as a movement for the Third Symphony. In dispensing with an explicit program and a chorus and coming near to the normal symphony, it foreshadows the middle-period trilogy, the Fifth, Sixth, and Seventh Symphonies. These are all purely orchestral, with a new, hard-edged, contrapuntal clarity of instrumentation and devoid of programs altogether; yet each clearly embodies a spiritual conflict that reaches a conclusive resolution. The Fifth and Seventh (both in five movements) move from darkness to light. Between them stands the work Mahler regarded as his *Tragic* Symphony—the four-movement Sixth in a minor, which moves out of darkness only with difficulty and then back into total night. From these three symphonies onward, he ceased to adapt his songs as whole sections or movements, but in each he introduced subtle allusions to his *Wunderhorn* songs or to his settings of poems by Friedrich Rückert, including the cycle *Kindertotenlieder (Songs on the Deaths of Children).*

At the end of this period he composed his monumental Eighth Symphony for eight soloists, double choir, and orchestra—a work known as the Symphony *of a Thousand* from the large forces it requires, though Mahler gave it no such title. This stands apart as a later reversion to the expansive metaphysical tendencies of the first period and represents a consummation of them—the first continuously choral and orchestral symphony ever composed. The first of its two parts, equivalent to a symphonic first movement, is a setting of the medieval Pentecost hymn *Veni Creator Spiritus;* part two, amalgamating the three-movement types of the traditional symphony, has for its text the mystical closing scene of Goethe's *Faust* drama (the scene of Faust's redemption). The work marked the climax of Mahler's confident maturity and at its first performance in 1910 was received enthusiastically—the first unqualified success he had experienced.

last period In 1907 his resignation was demanded at the Vienna Opera. Thus began Mahler's last period in which at the age of 47 he became a wanderer again. He was obliged to make a new reputation for himself and went to the United States, directing performances at the Metropolitan Opera and becoming conductor of the Philharmonic Society of New York; yet he went back each summer to the Austrian countryside to compose his last works, finally returning to Vienna.

The three works comprising his last-period trilogy, none of which he ever heard, are *Das Lied von der Erde (The Song of the Earth)*, the Ninth Symphony, and the Tenth in f-sharp minor, left unfinished in a comprehensive full-length sketch. All are dark works, written under the shadow of his impending death. The first of the three began as a song cycle (to Chinese poems in German translations), growing into "A Symphony for Tenor, Baritone (or Contralto) and Orchestra" in six movements. The first of the four movements in the purely orchestral Ninth has been called "the first work of new music." The third movement, entitled "Rondo-Burleske," is Mahler's most modern and prophetic, evoking horror and bitterness; and the finale ends with an extraordinary, long-drawn disintegration of the musical texture, dying away on pianissimo strings. Mahler wanted the sketches of the Tenth destroyed, but his widow preserved them. Two movements were completed by Ernst Krenek and heard for the first time in 1924, and a realization of the complete work by the British musicologist Deryck Cooke was first performed in 1960.

assessment Modern critical opinion recognizes Mahler's powerful influence during a period of musical transition. In his works may be found pervasive elements foreshadowing the radical methods employed in the 20th century: these elements include progressive tonality; dissolution of tonality; a breakaway from harmony in the total ensemble in favor of a contrapuntal texture for groups of solo instruments; continually varying themes rather than merely restating them; ironic quotation of popular styles and of sounds from everyday life (bird calls, bugle signals, etc.); and a new way of formally unifying the symphony through the adoption of techniques subtly derived from Liszt's cyclic method. In terms of the personal content of his art, it can be said of Mahler more than of any other composer that the man is the music.

BIBLIOGRAPHY: Bruno Walter, *Gustav Mahler* (1941; reprint, 1973); D. C. Mitchell, *Gustav Mahler: The Early Years* (1958); Hans Ferdinand Redlich, *Bruckner and Mahler,* rev. ed. (1963); Alma Maria Mahler, *Gustav Mahler: Memories and Letters* (1968); Gabriel Engel, *Gustav Mahler, Song-symphonist* (1970); Kurt Blaukopf, *Gustav Mahler* (1973); Henry Louis de La Grange, *Mahler,* Vol. 1 (1973); Michael Kennedy, *Mahler* (1974); Egon Gartenberg, *Mahler: The Man and His Music* (1978).

RECORDINGS: Numerous recordings of most works.

Maid of Pskov, The: *see* OPERA (the 19th century); RIMSKY-KORSAKOV.

Malcolm, George (John) (b. February 28, 1917) The English harpsichordist George Malcolm is also a pianist, organist, and conductor and is known especially as a continuo player. Educated at the Royal College of Music and at Oxford University (Balliol College), Malcolm was master of music at London's Westminster Cathedral (1947–59) and artistic director of the Philomusica of London (1962–66).

Malibran, Maria, before her marriage, María Felicità García (March 24, 1808–September 23, 1836) The daughter and student of tenor Manuel García, the French-born Spanish mezzo-soprano Maria Malibran first sang on stage at age five and made her operatic debut in 1825 as Rosina in Rossini's *Il barbiero di Siviglia*. The same year she sang with her father's company in New York City. Malibran appeared at the Théâtre des Italiens in Paris from 1828 and the following year was acclaimed at the Gloucester (England) Festival. She toured successfully in Italy, France, and England until her death. After an unsuccessful marriage to a French merchant, she married and toured with the violinist Charles de Bériot. A fall from a horse precipitated her early death. Her sister was the equally well-known mezzo-soprano, Pauline Vardot.

Malipiero, Gian Francesco (March 18, 1882–August 1, 1973) An Italian composer and musicologist, Gian Francesco Malipiero was born in Venice but studied harmony at the Vienna Conservatory in 1898 and later composition at Venice and Bologna with Enrico Bossi. In 1921, after a journey to Paris where he was influenced by contemporary French music, he was appointed professor of composition at the Parma Conservatory. Subsequently he became director of the Istituto Musicale Pollini at Padua and in 1939 director of the Liceo Marcello in Venice. With Alfredo Casella he played a leading part in Italian music in the 1920s. Rebelling against the principles of *verismo,* the realistic aesthetic that inspired Puccini, he rediscovered the qualities of Italian pre-Romantic music. His work reflects the spirit of 17th- and 18th-century Venetian music, and his operas, inspired by Monteverdi, represent a fusion of modern and archaic styles. His instrumental music avoids both development of themes and contrapuntal elaboration.

His more than 30 operas include two trilogies, *L'Orfeide* (1925) and *Il mistero di Venezia* (1932), two after Shakespeare, *Giulio Cesare* (1936) and *Antonio e Cleopatra* (1938), and *Il figliuolo prodigo* (1953). Orchestra music includes 11 symphonies, three sets of pieces entitled *Impressioni dal vero* (1910–22), and *Pause del silenzio* (1917–26). He wrote numerous concertos—two for violin (1932, 1963), six for piano (1934–64), and flute (1968); chamber music (including seven quartets); choral works; and songs. Between 1926 and 1942 he published the complete works of Monteverdi in 16 volumes and later collaborated in the collected edition of the works of Vivaldi.

mandolin A small stringed instrument remotely derived from the lute. The earlier Milanese mandolin was in effect a miniature, rather deep-bodied lute with either five or six courses of strings, played with a plectrum. It had the usual lute characteristics of a tension bridge glued to the flat table, the fingerboard flush with the front plane of the instrument, and a violin-type pegbox and tuning pegs. The frets were fixed, however, and were either of ivory or metal.

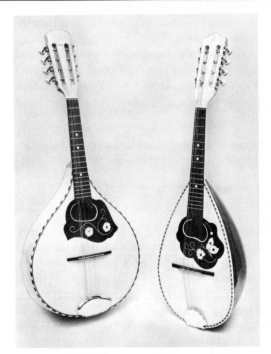

Neapolitan mandolins
courtesy, Boosey & Hawkes, Ltd.

The instrument as known and played in the 20th century owes its form and proportions to the maker Pasquale Vinaccia of Naples (1806–82). This Neapolitan mandolin has four pairs of steel strings tuned at violin pitch in fifths. The body is deeply vaulted and pear shaped. The fingerboard is slightly raised and is continued down from the neck to the border of the oval sound hole in the upper part of the belly; it carries 17 fixed metal frets. The table of the mandolin is reflexed downward at its widest part, forming an angle on which the bridge is set. The strings pass over the bridge and are attached to a metal plate at the bottom of the instrument. Thus the cutaway table has the effect of increasing the pressure of the strings on the bridge over which they pass at a marked angle, giving the instrument a brilliant soprano tone of great carrying power. Tuning is effected by a machine head.

A characteristic feature of the plectrum technique of the mandolin is the tremolo, obtained by the rapid oscillation of the plectrum across a unison pair of strings for the duration of the written note. In expert hands this has almost the effect of a sustained sound. The table usually has a tortoiseshell plate below the striking position to protect it from damage by the plectrum.

Vivaldi wrote a concerto for mandolin and two concertos for two mandolins; Mozart used it in *Don Giovanni;* and Beethoven composed two sonatinas and an adagio for mandolin and piano.

Manfred Overture: *see* SCHUMANN, ROBERT (larger works) and (assessment).

Manfred Symphony: *see* TCHAIKOVSKY (later life and works).

Mannheim school   A group of 18th-century composers in Mannheim under the patronage of Duke Karl Theodor (reigned 1743–99), the elector Palatine. They distinguished themselves particularly in their instrumental music, which proved to be of great significance in the development of the mature Classical style. Many contemporary visitors to the Mannheim court, such as the historian Charles Burney, wrote glowing accounts of the musical establishment there. Especially impressive to these travelers was the outstanding orchestra, which was famous throughout Europe for its highly disciplined virtuosity and its ability to produce certain novel and arousing effects. These effects, such as lengthy crescendos, abrupt dynamic changes, and swiftly ascending melodic figures (the famous "Mannheim rocket"), were cultivated in the symphonic works of the Mannheim composers. More important historically than these rather naïve and superficial devices was the tendency of these composers (especially Johann Stamitz) to articulate the various components of the symphonic form to a greater degree than had previously been the case. Their role in the evolution of the Classical symphony is therefore of some importance, although most scholars now agree that these changes occurred nearly simultaneously at various other centers, such as Berlin and Vienna.

The Mannheim school consists chiefly of two generations of composers. The first includes Johann Stamitz, Ignaz Holzbauer, and Franz Xaver Richter. These men established the supremacy of the Mannheim school and, in their orchestral works, initiated many of the effects that were to popularize it. The com-

posers of the second generation are Anton Filtz, Johann Christian Cannabich, Carl Stamitz, and Franz Beck.

Manon: *see* MASSENET.

Manon Lescaut: *see* PUCCINI.

Manzoni Requiem: *see* FUGUE (after Bach and Handel); MASS (requiem); VERDI.

Mara, before her marriage, Gertrud Elisabeth Schmeling (February 23, 1749–January 20, 1833)   Exploited as a child prodigy on the violin, the Prussian soprano Mara (the surname of her husband, which she used professionally) studied voice after being advised that the violin was an unfeminine instrument. She studied in Leipzig and made a successful debut in Dresden in 1771, after which she was engaged at the Berlin and Potsdam courts of Frederick II. After several unsuccessful appearances in Vienna and Munich and a slightly better reception in Paris, Mara went to London (1784), where she had her greatest success. She was acclaimed in a Handel commemoration performance that led to the role of Cleopatra in Handel's *Giulio Cesare* as well as appearances in concerts and oratorio. In 1902 she went to Moscow and after the burning of the city (1812) settled in Reval (Livonia) to teach.

maraca   A Latin-American gourd rattle, usually used in pairs. Invented by Indians in South America, the dry gourd filled with seeds had magical connotations. Maracas used in the modern orchestra and dance band are based on the Cuban variety.

maracas   *courtesy, Ludwig Industries*

Marais, Marin (March 31, 1656–August 15, 1728)   The Parisian gambist Marin Marais was apprenticed as a choirboy at Sainte-Chapelle and studied viola da gamba with Hottemann and his pupil Sainte-Colombe and composition with Lully, to whom he dedicated his first book of viol duets. Some of his innovations with the gamba were to improve its sonority and the development of a new fingering method that had an effect on performance practice. He shared the post of conductor at the Académie Royale de Musique and entered the royal orchestra as a soloist in 1685. Marais wrote several operas; in *Alcione* (1706) there is a tempest scene that represents an early attempt at stage realism.

Marbeck or **Merbecke, John** (*c.* 1505–*c.* 1585) An English composer, organist, and author, John Marbeck is known for his setting of the Anglican liturgy. Marbeck was apparently in Windsor in 1531 and as far as is known remained there throughout his life. His name appears in the records of St. George's Chapel, Windsor, as organist (1541–42). In 1544 he was sentenced to the stake for heresy but was pardoned through the intervention of Bishop Gardiner of Winchester. At that time his "greate worke," his English *Concordance* to the Bible, was taken from him and destroyed. On his release he began it again, and under Edward VI it was published in 1550 in an abbreviated form; in the same year his most famous musical accomplishment, *The booke of Common praier noted* (*i.e.,* set to musical notes), was printed. This setting of the liturgy was superseded by the revisions of 1552, but interest in it was revived by the Oxford Movement in the 19th century. By that time, however, the traditional context of Marbeck's work had been lost. Nevertheless, it has remained in use in many churches of the Anglican Communion. During the last 10 years of his life Marbeck published six books on religious subjects that show an uncompromising dedication to the principles of the Calvinist Reformation. Of his music only three Latin compositions survive complete: *Missa Per arma justitiae,* an antiphon, and a carol.

Marcello, Benedetto (August 1, 1686–July 24, 1739) The Italian composer Benedetto Marcello was born in Venice of a patrician family and was intended by his father for the law, but he became a pupil of Antonio Lotti and Francesco Gasparini. In 1711 he was a member of the Council of Forty and in 1730 went to Pola (Istria) as governor. After eight years he retired to Brescia as chancellor.

Marcello is remembered primarily for two works: the operatic satire *Il teatro alla moda* (1720), an important document in the early history of opera; and *Estro poetico-armonico* (1724–26), a setting for voices and instruments of the first 50 psalms in an Italian paraphrase by Girolamo Giustiniani. An edition with English words was published in London in 1757. Marcello's other compositions include operas, oratorios, cantatas, concertos, and sonatas. He was also a poet and translated John Dryden's *Timotheus* as a text for one of his own cantatas and wrote a libretto for Giovanni Maria Ruggeri's opera *Arato in Sparta* (1709). The celebrated Concerto in d minor (sometimes transposed into c minor) for oboe and strings, long attributed to Benedetto, is now known to have been composed by his brother Alessandro (1684–*c.* 1750).

BIBLIOGRAPHY: Oliver Strunk, *Source Readings in Music History* (1950).

RECORDINGS: Benedetto—*Concerti a cinque* (12); Flute Sonatas (12); Cello Sonata No. 2 in e minor. Alessandro—Oboe Concerto.

march Music originally written to facilitate marching. It is in simple, regular rhythms, such as $\frac{6}{8}$, $\frac{2}{4}$, $\frac{4}{4}$. As a musical form the march consists of an initial march (M) alternating with one or more contrasting sections, or trios (T): MTM or MTMTM. One of the earliest examples, by Thoinot Arbeau, appeared in 1589. In 17th-century France the military band of Louis XIV played marches of Lully. Handel and Wagner in widely different eras used marches in their operas; Beethoven included slow, solemn funeral marches in several of his symphonies. Mozart and Schubert used the march as an art-music form. In the 1880s and '90s in the United States, John Philip Sousa excelled as a composer of military marches.

Marchal, André (b. February 6, 1894) Blind from birth, the great Parisian organist André Marchal is noted especially for his improvisations and for his interest in the revival of classical traditions in French organ building and performance practices. A pupil of Eugène Gigout at the Paris Conservatoire, he won first prizes in organ and in improvisation (1913) and in counterpoint (1917). He was organist of Saint-Germain-des-Prés (1915–45) and of Saint-Eustache (1945–63). Among his many pupils was Jean Langlais. He has recorded the complete organ works of Bach and of Franck.

Marchesi (de Castrone), Mathilde, before her marriage, Mathilde Graumann (March 24, 1821–November 17, 1913) The teacher of the most prima donnas in vocal history, Mathilde Marchesi was a German mezzo-soprano who went to Paris (1845) to study with Manuel García and made her debut in 1849. She married the Italian baritone and nobleman Salvatore Marchesi in 1852, and together they made numerous concert tours. Having already proven her teaching ability when she took over García's class temporarily while still his student, she accepted an appointment as professor of singing at the Vienna Conservatory (1854–61) and began her notable career (continued in Paris) as a foremost teacher of singing. Among her pupils were Emma Calvé, Emma Eames, and Nellie Melba; almost alone she extended the traditions of the bel canto into the 20th century. Marchesi published works on the technique of singing and a volume of reminiscences, *Marchesi and Music* (1897). Her daughter Blanche Marchesi (1863–1940) was a Wagnerian soprano and also a teacher.

Marenzio, Luca (1553/54–August 22, 1599) The greatest Italian madrigalist of his generation, Luca Marenzio was born in Coccaglio. He may have served as a choirboy in the nearby town of Brescia. By 1578 he was in service with Cardinal Luigi d'Este in Rome, where he remained until 1586. In 1588 he went to Florence, where he worked with the circle of musicians and poets associated with Count Giovanni Bardi, and later returned to Rome to serve Cardinal Cinzio Aldobrandini. In 1594 he visited Sigismund III of Poland, was in Rome in the summer of 1595, and returned to Poland in 1596. In 1598 he was in Venice and was later appointed musician at the papal court. He died in Rome.

Marenzio published a large number of madrigals and villanelle and five books of motets. His sacred works are colorful and impressive, but he is best known for his madrigals. Marenzio's early works are influenced by Marco Antonio Ingegneri, but he soon developed an individual technique rarely surpassed in elegance and expressiveness. His extended forms depend upon subtle contrasts of emotional tension. He liked writing for high voices but varied his brilliance with sentiment and gravity. His chromaticism occasionally leads to advanced enharmonic modulations, and he sometimes leaves dissonances unresolved for dramatic effect. He exerted a strong influence on Monteverdi, Carlo Gesualdo, and Hassler and was much admired in England, where his works were first printed in Nicholas Yonge's *Musica Transalpina* (1588).

BIBLIOGRAPHY: Denis Arnold, *Marenzio* (1965).

Maria Stuarda: *see* DONIZETTI.

marimba   A XYLOPHONE with resonators below the keys that originated in Java. It was taken to Africa, where it spread across the center of the continent and was taken by the slave trade to Central America. In the United States the name has been applied to an orchestral xylophone, with large keys and soft beaters, used mainly for light music. In the Javanese instrument the keys are of bronze and the resonators of bamboo. Elsewhere the keys are of wood, and the resonators are gourds or wooden boxes (except in the orchestral instrument, which has brass tubes). In South African mining compounds marimbas are made from floorboards and tin cans. In Africa and Central America the resonators usually have a hole near the bottom covered by a membrane that adds a buzz to the tone. The instrument is invariably played with soft beaters. The tuning always follows the two original Javanese scales, the pentatonic *sléndro* and the heptatonic *pélog* (*see* GAMELAN). Concertos for marimba have been written by Paul Creston (1940) and Milhaud (1949).

marine trumpet or **tromba marina** (German, *Trumscheit,* "drum log")   A stringed instrument of medieval and Renaissance Europe that was highly popular in the 15th century,

marimba   *courtesy, Ludwig Industries*

surviving into the 18th. It had a long narrow body and one or two strings, which the left thumb touched lightly to produce the notes of the harmonic series as on a natural trumpet.

103

LXII   *Tromba Marina*

man playing marine trumpet
from Filippo Bonanni's Gabinetto armonico,
18th century courtesy, Dover Publications, Inc.

The strings, originally plucked, were by the 15th century sounded by a bow played between the fingering and the tuning pegs. The tone was brassy and substantial. One foot of the bridge was free and rattled loosely on the belly when the strings vibrated. The stationary bridge foot served as a sound post, extending through the belly to the instrument's back and transmitting the string vibrations to it. In the 17th century seven or eight sympathetic strings were set inside the body.

Mario, (Giovanni Matteo), Cavaliere di Candia (October 17, 1810–December 11, 1883) Known only by his Christian name professionally to avoid compromising his aristocratic family's pride, the Italian tenor Mario achieved his greatest popularity as a singer of operatic romances. After sporadic and brief study he made his debut in the title role of Meyerbeer's *Robert le diable* (1838) at the Paris Opéra. His popularity in London and Paris was aided by his flawless sense of stage manner and costume and his skill as an actor. He retired in 1867.

Markevitch, Igor (b. July 27, 1912)   A student of Hermann Scherchen and Boulanger, the Russian conductor and composer Igor Markevitch became musical director of the Montreal Symphony in 1955, the same year that he made his U.S. debut with the Boston Symphony. He was permanent conductor of

483

the Lamoureux Orchestra (Paris) from 1957 to 1961. In 1965 he conducted the Spanish National Radio and Television Orchestra and in 1968 became artistic director of the Monte Carlo Opera (to 1972). Since 1973 he has conducted the orchestra of the Accademia di Santa Cecilia in Rome. His noted recordings are of 19th-century French and Russian music. His compositions include orchestral and chamber music, ballet scores, and two cantatas (1930; 1935–36). A prolific writer for musical journals, he wrote *Introduction to Music* (1940) and with Claude Rostand, *Point d'orgue* (1959).

Marpurg, Friedrich Wilhelm (November 21, 1718–May 22, 1795) A German composer and writer on music, Friedrich Wilhelm Marpurg was born at Marpurgsdorf, near Seehausen, Brandenburg. Nothing is known of his musical training, but in 1746 he is heard of as secretary to a Prussian general in Paris, where he met Voltaire, Jean le Rond d'Alembert, and Rameau. Later he lived in Berlin and Hamburg, and from 1763 to 1795 he was director of the Prussian state lottery. Although he composed for the harpsichord, it is as a theoretical and critical writer that he is remembered. Such works as the *Historisch-kritische Beyträge* (Berlin, 1754–78) and his introductions *(Anleitungen)* to different branches of the art, of which perhaps *Abhandlung von der Fuge* (Berlin, 1753–54) is the most important, are of great value. Marpurg's published compositions include *6 Sonaten für das Cembalo* (1756) and *Fughe e caprice* (1777).

Marriage of Figaro, The: *see* NOZZE DI FIGARO, LE.

Marriner, Neville (b. April 14, 1924) A student of Pierre Monteux, the English conductor Neville Marriner also studied at the Royal College of Music and at the Paris Conservatoire. Formerly a violinist in the London Symphony, he founded in 1959 a chamber orchestra called the Academy of St. Martin-in-the-Fields at a London church of that name. He has edited most of the group's repertoire and with it has made more than 120 recordings of music from Corelli to Shostakovich; he has won the Edison Award five times. Similarly in 1969 he founded the Los Angeles Chamber Orchestra. He was appointed music director of the Minnesota Orchestra beginning in 1979.

Marschner, Heinrich August (August 16, 1795–December 14, 1861) A German composer who helped to establish the style of German Romantic opera, Heinrich August Marschner was born at Zittau, Saxony. He studied at Leipzig and about 1815 met Beethoven in Vienna. Weber produced his *Heinrich IV und d'Aubigné* (1820) at Dresden, where Marschner was later appointed director of the opera. In 1827 he was appointed director at Leipzig, where in 1828 he successfully produced *Der Vampyr* and the following year *Der Templer und die Jüdin* with a libretto based on Sir Walter Scott's *Ivanhoe.* In 1831 he became director at Hanover, and in 1833 he produced his more successful opera, *Hans Heiling,* at Berlin. Between 1836 and 1863 five further operas were produced (the last posthumously), among them *Kaiser Adolf von Nassau* (1845), which was conducted by Wagner. None of these, however, achieved the success of his earlier works.

Martha: *see* FLOTOW.

Martin, Frank (September 15, 1890–November 21, 1974) Influenced by Joseph Lauber and Ernest Ansermet, the Swiss composer Frank Martin was mostly self-taught. He directed the Technicum Moderne de Musique in Geneva (1933–39) and taught composition at the Hochschule für Musik at Cologne (1950–57). His chamber music is best exemplified by the Ballades for various instruments, and he has written two operas (*Der Sturm,* 1956; and *Monsieur de Pourceaugnac,* 1962; after Shakespeare and Molière respectively), a ballet (*The Fairy-Tale of Cinderella,* 1941), and five oratorios that show a devotion to Bach. Martin studied the technique, but rejected the aesthetics, of Schoenberg; he never abandoned beauty as a musical objective, and in his 12-tone music the row always has a harmonic as well as a linear function. He uses asymmetrical, chromatic melodies and jazz rhythms. His reputation rests primarily on his *Huit Préludes* for piano (1948), the Ballades, the secular oratorio *Le Vin herbé* (1941), and the sacred oratorio *Golgotha* (1948). Concertos include those for piano (1934, 1969), seven winds (1949), violin (1951), harpsichord (1952), and cello (1966).

RECORDINGS: Ballade for flute and piano; Ballade for piano and orchestra; Ballade for trombone and orchestra; Cello Concerto; Concerto for seven winds, strings, and percussion; Études for strings; Harpsichord Concerto; *Huit Préludes; Monologe* (6) *aus Jedermann;* Passacaglia for organ; *Petite Symphonie concertante;* Piano Concerto No. 2; *Pièces brèves; Sonata da chiesa* for viola d'amore and strings; Violin Concerto.

Martini, Giovanni Battista, called Padre Martini (April 24, 1706–October 4, 1784) The Italian composer, theorist, and teacher Giovanni Battista Martini was born at Bologna. He learned the rudiments of music from his violinist father and later studied singing, harpsichord, and organ with Luc' Antonio Predieri and counterpoint with Antonio Ricieri. He was ordained in 1722 and in 1725 was appointed maestro di cappella of the church of S. Francesco at Bologna. He opened a school of music, and the fame of his teaching made Bologna a place of pilgrimage for musicians from all countries. Among his pupils were Giuseppe Sarti and Johann Christian Bach. Martini was a zealous collector of musical literature; his library, which Charles Burney estimated at 17,000 volumes, passed at his death to the Imperial Library at Vienna and to the city of Bologna. He was a prolific composer of sacred and secular music; his works include the *Litaniae* (1734), 12 *Sonate d'intavolatura* (1741), 6 *Sonate per l'organo ed il cembalo* (1747), and the *Duetti da camera* (1763). His most important literary works are the *Storia della musica* (1757–81), unfortunately never completed, and the *Esemplare o sia Saggio fondamentale pratico di contrappunto* (1774–75).

Martinon, Jean (Franisque-Étienne) (January 10, 1910–March 1, 1976) A pupil in composition with Albert Roussel and in conducting with Charles Munch at the Paris Conservatoire, the French conductor Jean Martinon began his career as a concert violinist. He be-

came assistant to Munch at the Société des Concerts de Conservatoire (1944–46) and conducted the orchestra in Bordeaux before being appointed artistic director of the Lamoureaux Concerts in Paris (1950–57). He held the same position with the Israel Philharmonic from 1958 to 1960. He made his U.S. debut in 1957 with the Boston Symphony and returned to the United States from 1963 to 1968 as conductor of the Chicago Symphony. In 1968–73 he was music director of the French National Radio Orchestra. He conducted the orchestra of The Hague from 1974. His compositions include four symphonies, an opera (*Hecuba,* 1949), chamber music, and early politically-inspired works (*Absolve Domine,* 1940, in honor of the French war dead; *Psalm 136–Chant des captifs,* 1940–43).

Martinů, Bohuslav (December 8, 1890–August 28, 1959) A Czech composer whose music is a mixture of French and Czech influences in classic forms, Bohuslav Martinů studied violin from the age of six, attended and was expelled from the Prague Conservatory, and in 1913 joined the Prague Philharmonic. After the success of his ballet *Istar* and symphonic poem *Mizející půlnoc (Vanishing Midnight),* both 1922, he studied under Josef Suk, a leader of the nationalist movement in Czech music. In 1923 he went to Paris to study with Albert Roussel, whose music combined Impressionist, Oriental, and neoclassical influences. In 1940 Martinů fled the German invasion of France and settled in the United States, where he taught at Princeton University and at the Berkshire Music Center at Tanglewood. He returned to Prague in 1946 and taught at the conservatory there. In 1957 he was in Rome as composer in residence at the American Academy.

His orchestral works *Polička (Half-Time,* 1925) and *La Bagarre* (1928) were inspired by contemporary events: a Czech-French football (soccer) game and the crowds that met Lindbergh's plane as it ended its transatlantic flight. Of Martinů's later works, the Concerto grosso (1941) for chamber orchestra shows his skill in polyphonic writing; the Double Concerto (1940) for two string orchestras is a powerful work expressing Czech suffering after the partition of Czechoslovakia; and his *Memorial to Lidice* (1943) is a short symphonic poem commemorating Czechs killed by the Nazis at Lidice. Other works include six symphonies; violin, piano, cello, and flute concertos; six quartets; and compositions for piano, harpsichord, voice, and unaccompanied cello and violin.

Martinů was a prolific composer whose works varied greatly in quality; at his best his music shows vitality, charm, and originality. He assimilated rhythmic and melodic traits of Czech folk music into a modern, neoclassical idiom that shows a clarity and precision characteristic of French music.

RECORDINGS: Duo for violin and cello; Études and Polkas for piano; Flute Sonata No. 1; Symphony No. 5; Trio for flute, cello, and piano; *Trois Danses tchèques* for piano.

Marx, Joseph (May 11, 1882–September 2, 1964)   Primarily known as the composer of more than 120 songs, the Austrian composer, critic, and teacher Joseph Marx taught (1914–52) at the Imperial Musical Academy (director, 1922–27) in Vienna and at the University of Graz (1947–57). Calling himself a Romantic realist, his style is at the same time Romantic, Impressionist, and traditionally Viennese, with influences of Debussy, Liszt, and Brahms. Marx has written choral and orchestral works and chamber music, of which the most representative is the quartet "in modo antico" (1940).

Mary, Queen of Scots: *see* MUSGRAVE; OPERA (the 20th century).

Mascagni, Pietro (December 7, 1863–August 2, 1945)   One of the principal exponents of the *verismo* operatic style, the Italian composer Pietro Mascagni studied at the conservatory at Milan. Unable to submit to the discipline of his master, Amilcare Ponchielli, he left in 1884 to join a traveling opera company. In 1889 he won first prize in a competition with his one-act opera, *Cavalleria rusticana,* a setting of a Sicilian melodrama by Giovanni Verga. Produced at the Teatro Costanzi in Rome (1890), it was an instant success and subsequently maintained its popularity, usually being given with Leoncavallo's *Pagliacci*

as a companion piece. *Le maschere* (1901), reviving the commedia dell'arte, is musically superior, though it had little success. Among Mascagni's other operas are *L'amico Fritz* (1891), *Iris* (1898), and *Nerone* (1935), the latter glorifying Benito Mussolini. He succeeded Toscanini as musical director of La Scala in 1929.

RECORDINGS: *L'amico Fritz; Cavalleria rusticana.*

Masked Ball, The: *see* BALLO IN MASCHERA, UN.

Mason, Daniel Gregory (November 20, 1873–December 4, 1953)   A grandson of Lowell Mason and son of Henry Mason of the piano manufacturers Mason and Hamlin, the U.S. composer Daniel Gregory Mason studied with John Knowles Paine at Harvard University and later with d'Indy in Paris. In 1910 he joined the faculty of Columbia University and taught there until his retirement in 1942. His music was in the German Romantic style with elements of French Impressionism and Russian modernism. He wrote three symphonies, a festival overture *Chanticleer,* chamber music, and several books of essays and teaching guides.

RECORDINGS: Prelude and Fugue for piano and orchestra; Quartet on Negro Themes.

Mason, Lowell (January 8, 1792–August 11, 1872)   A pioneer of musical education in the United States and a composer of hymn tunes, Lowell Mason founded the Boston Academy of Music in 1832 and later trained music teachers. He promoted festivals of choral music and published many song collections and hymns; among the latter, "Nearer My God to Thee" became famous. His son William became known as a concert pianist, piano teacher, and composer of light piano pieces. His son Henry was a co-founder of the firm of Mason and Hamlin, well known piano manufacturers.

mass   The setting of the eucharistic liturgy of the Roman Catholic Church.

ordinary   Settings of the Kyrie, Gloria, Credo, Sanctus and Benedictus, and Agnus dei have been created in the forms of chant, polyphony, and concerted music over a period of nearly 1,400 years. The *Ordinarium missae* contains not only those items mentioned above, which make up the standard polyphonic or concerted mass familiar to musicians, but also a final section, either *Ite, missa est* or *Benedicamus domino,* not always included in the usual musical settings (as well as the normally unchangeable prayers and parts sung or read by the celebrant and other sacred ministers of the mass). In the Middle Ages the texts of the ordinary were not as standardized as they have been since the 16th century, and the texts sometimes varied from day to day; the tropes (additions of music and text) to the Kyrie, Gloria, Sanctus, and Agnus changed according to the feast or season. Although the trope texts are no longer in use, the numerous settings of the Kyrie in PLAIN-CHANT are still distinguished by their old titles.

The modern *Roman Kyriale* is a collection of chants for the ordinary, the main part being a group of 18 composite masses. Various chants are in different styles and modes, and they stem from different epochs in the development of plainchant. Tradition and usage account for their manner or grouping, though no hard-and-fast rule need be observed. Chants from one mass may be interchanged with chants from another, and to give added variety there follow a number of plainchant settings of every section of the ordinary, including the Credo.

Florid settings for one, two, or three voices of tropes to the Kyrie, Gloria, Sanctus, Agnus, and *Benedicamus* were written down as early as the 14th century and formed part of the repertoire of the Notre Dame school of Paris that spread rapidly throughout the Western world. There is even a troped *Sursum corda,* which belongs to the preface sung by the celebrant. At first these different settings were combined with considerable freedom so as to constitute mass cycles for daily use, and this custom persisted into the 14th and 15th centuries, when manuscript choirbooks often contained hundreds of individual settings grouped together under Kyrie, Gloria, and so on. The 14th century saw the beginnings of a tendency to paired movements, usually Gloria–Credo

or Sanctus–Agnus, and about this same time the masses of Toulouse, Tournai, and Besançon give evidence of further progress in the combination of four or more items to make a unified ordinary. In some cases these experiments were not entirely successful; but when Guillaume de Machaut wrote his mass, it became clear that homogeneous style and liturgical fitness were not incompatible.

Parts of Machaut's mass were built on a plainchant cantus firmus, and this method of construction was followed by John Dunstable, Guillaume Dufay, Jean d'Ockeghem, Jakob Obrecht, Josquin des Prés, Robert Fayrfax, and many Renaissance composers to the time of Palestrina and Victoria. There was, however, a gradual change from masses containing at least one clearly instrumental part to those whose polyphonic texture was entirely vocal, even though instruments may have been used to double the voices. Early in the 17th century concerted music greatly influenced ecclesiastical music, and many of the masses by Tarquinio Merula, Michel Angelo Grancino, Orazio Tarditi, and Francesco Cavalli prepared the way for the Baroque extravagances of the masses of Orazio Benevoli. In Germany the chief composers of masses were Heinrich von Biber, Johann Heinrich Schmelzer, and Johann Caspar Kerll, while in France the outstanding composer was Marc-Antoine Charpentier.

Operatic music inevitably made a profound impression on concerted masses, with the result that elaborate solos began to be incorporated into the choral and orchestral background. Bach's b minor Mass was probably never used liturgically, although the masses of Johann Adolph Hasse, Francesco Durante, Johann Joseph Fux, Haydn, and Mozart successfully adorned the services of their time and place. Beethoven's C Major Mass was conceived as a liturgical work, but his *Missa solemnis* is basically a work for concert performance. Large-scale masses continued to be written in the 19th century by Cherubini, Schubert, Weber, Liszt, Franck, Gounod, and Bruckner, and in the 20th century some of them were occasionally heard in the concert hall if not in church. Toward the middle of the 20th century a sharp distinction arose between masses written in imitation of the Renaissance style, such as those by Lorenzo Perosi, and the more original and forward-looking examples by Vaughan Williams, Poulenc, Kodály, Edmund Rubbra, Stravinsky, Britten, Hindemith, and William Walton.

The ordinary of the mass was not always assigned to voices, or voices and instruments. Sometimes the organist was allowed to alternate with the plainchant of choir or congregation, and composed settings for organ are generally termed organ masses. Early 15th-century Italian and German organ masses set the pattern for most subsequent developments, which gave rise to complete settings of the ordinary by Johann Buchner, Pierre Attaignant, Philip ap Rhys, Girolamo Cavazzoni, Claudio Merulo, Frescobaldi, Nicolas Lebègue, François Couperin, and Nicolas de Grigny, to name only the most important.

proper As the items comprising the *Proprium missae* vary according to the feast and season, they are clearly more bound to the liturgy and its immediate needs than the ordinary is. A mass proper has not made its presence felt in the concert hall, though it is of prime importance in the service. Its principal sections are: introit, gradual, alleluia (or tract), sequence, offertory, and communion. Once again the earliest noteworthy polyphonic settings are those of the Notre Dame school of Paris, beginning in the last decade of the 12th century. Léonin and after him Pérotin set most of the great responsorial chants for two, three, or four voices, and their lead was followed by English and Spanish composers. Isolated compositions are found in the 14th century, but no large-scale settings of the proper preceded those of Dufay, presumably written from 1430 onward.

The seven choirbooks at Trent preserve many settings of the proper, though these are not invariably grouped as a cycle; it was customary to keep texts of one kind together, as in collections of the *Ordinarium missae*. Choirbooks similar in type to those of Trent, and again containing a large selection of items from the proper, are to be found in Jena and Weimar, but the earliest and most ambitious venture of the 16th century was Heinrich Isaac's *Choralis Constantinus,* printed at Nürnberg after the composer's death. Isaac's polyphonic monument provided music for all the principal feasts of the church year as well as for the Common of Saints and Martyrs, and although there were other printed collections of the time (the Lyon *Contrapunctus* of 1528 and Georg Rhau's editions of 1539 and 1545) the *Choralis Constantinus* is unrivaled in its scope and excellence.

Both Orlando di Lasso and Palestrina wrote complete cycles of the offertory, and many of their unclassified motets could be assigned to the proper. But it was not until Byrd's two books of *Gradualia* appeared in 1605 and 1607 that a truly great scheme made itself felt in the world of church music. Even then Byrd's work did not receive the recognition it deserved, as England was no longer a Catholic country and the number of copies exported must have been small. The Baroque era saw only isolated settings of texts for the proper. The earliest made considerable use of divided choirs *(cori spezzati)* and reached a minor peak of excellence in the work of Mikałaj Zieleński, Steffano Bernardi, Giovanni Felice Sances, and Francesco Foggia.

The concertante style was exploited by J. Hofer, Simone Mayr, V. Rathgeber, Vincenzo Ruffo, Niccolò Jommelli, Giovanni Battista Martini, and Michael Haydn, to mention only a few of a vast and active group of church composers. Subsequent contributions to the mass proper were, on the whole, desultory rather than broadly conceived, though contributions were made by a few composers of good standing. Settings of the proper for organ, alternating with plainchant, are comparatively rare, but there is a notable and reasonably complete setting of the proper for Easter Day by the Tudor composer Thomas Preston and a set for 51 Sundays and feasts by the 20th-century French composer Charles Tournemire entitled *L'Orgue mystique.*

requiem The plainchant of the *Missa pro defunctis* combines parts of the ordinary and the proper: introit, Kyrie, gradual, tract, sequence, offertory, Sanctus, Agnus, and communion. Not all of these are set in polyphonic and concerted requiem masses; on the other hand, additions are sometimes made, as in Verdi's Requiem, which ends with the responsory "Libera me" taken from the burial service that follows the mass, and the "Pie Jesu" and "In paradisum" in Fauré's. One of the earliest polyphonic settings is that of Ockeghem; others followed in the 16th century by Pierre de la Rue, Johannes Prioris, Antoine de Fevin, Morales, Francisco Guerrero, Lasso, Palestrina, and Victoria. Later settings by Kerll and Biber emphasized the dramatic element, especially in the "Dies irae," and this is largely true of the requiems by Jommelli and Mozart. Outstanding among the 19th-century settings are those of Berlioz, Cherubini, Dvořák, Verdi, Bruckner, and Fauré. (Brahms's *Ein deutsches Requiem* [1868] is not based on the mass text but on texts from the Bible.) Notable in the 20th century are Maurice Duruflé's (1947) and Britten's *War* Requiem (1962), based on a text consisting of both the Latin prayers and the war poems of Wilfred Owen. *See also* CHURCH MUSIC.

Massenet, Jules (Émile Frédéric) (May 12, 1842–August 13, 1912)   A French composer and teacher who helped establish the late 19th-century style of French opera, Jules Massenet entered the Paris Conservatoire in 1853, studying piano with Adolphe Laurent and composition with Ambroise Thomas. His knowledge of instrumentation was partly acquired from his practical experience as a timpanist in the orchestra of the Théâtre Lyrique. He won the Prix de Rome in 1863. He was professor of composition at the Paris Conservatoire (1878–96); his pupils included Alfred Bruneau, Gabriel Pierné, Florent Schmitt, Charles Koechlin, and Gustave Charpentier.

With the production of *La Grand' Tante* (1867) Massenet embarked on a career as a composer of operas and incidental music. The latter includes the score for Leconte de Lisle's *Les Erinnyes* (1873), containing the song "Élégie." In the same year his sacred drama *Marie Magdeleine,* later produced as an opera, established his characteristic style, which made both religious and erotic appeals; *Eve* and *La Vierge* were other choral works of this kind. His opera *Hérodiade* (1881) was followed by his masterpiece *Manon* (Opéra-Comique, 1884), which displayed his gifts for sensuous melody and characterization. Thereafter he remained the principal composer of French op-

era of his time, admired for his lyrical though often sentimental qualities. His reputation spread beyond France to the extent that he was sometimes described without malice by his detractors as "Mlle Wagner." Among his later operas, produced between 1889 and 1910, are *Esclarmonde, Werther, Thaïs, Le Jongleur de Notre-Dame,* and *Don Quichotte.* He also composed seven suites for orchestra (1865–81), *Fantaisie* for cello and orchestra (1897), a piano concerto (1903), about 200 songs, and piano pieces.

RECORDINGS: Operas—*Le Cid, Esclarmonde, Manon, La Navarraise, Thaïs, Thérèse, Werther;* Cello *Fantaisie,* Orchestral Suites Nos. 2, 3, 4, 7; Piano Concerto; *La Vierge.*

Mathews, Max V.: *see* COMPUTER MUSIC; ELECTRONIC MUSIC (computers as musical instruments).

Mathis der Maler: *see* FUGUE (after Bach and Handel); HINDEMITH; LIBRETTO (modern status); MODERN PERIOD (new paths).

Matthay, Tobias (Augustus) (February 19, 1858–December 15, 1945)   A student and later teacher at the Royal Academy of Music (1876–1925), the English pianist and pedagogue Tobias Matthay founded his own piano school in 1900. Among many successful pupils was Myra Hess. He taught a revolutionary piano method based on analysis of touch controlled by weight and relaxation (he published *The Act of Touch* in 1903) and wrote articles on the association of psychology with piano technique. Some of his more important texts are *Commentaries on the Teaching of Pianoforte Technique* (1911), *The Rotation Principle* (1912), and *Musical Interpretation* (1913). His numerous compositions for the piano have been essentially forgotten.

Mattheson, Johann (September 28, 1681–April 17, 1764)   A German composer and writer on musical theory and practice, Johann Mattheson was a singer at the Hamburg Opera (1690–1705), and from 1699 he also worked there as composer and conductor. In 1704 he was appointed tutor to Cyrill, son of Sir John Wich, the English resident in Hamburg, and in 1706 he became secretary to Sir John and his successors until 1755. He also was organist at the Hamburg Cathedral from 1715 to 1728.

His musical activities were hampered by ear trouble that started in 1705 and led to total deafness.

Mattheson's compositions—operas, church music, serenades, and chamber music—are of average quality, but as a writer on music his influence was great. He advocated the merging of Italian, French, and German styles; revitalizing church music; the use of equal temperament; the inclusion of women in church choirs; good musical education for musicians and adequate payment for their services. He fought against the use of solmization and against corruption and simony in musical life. His books are an inexhaustible source of information on German music of the 18th century and include *Grosse General-Bass-Schule* (1731) and *Kleine General-Bass-Schule* (1735) on the figured bass; *Der vollkommene Capellmeister* (1739), an encyclopedia of his musical ideas; and *Grundlage einer Ehrenpforte* (1740), with biographies of 148 composers and details of his own life. He translated English pamphlets, periodicals, and books into German; *e.g.,* Daniel Defoe's *Moll Flanders* (1723) and John Mainwaring's *Memoirs of the Life of . . .Handel* (1761) with additional notes.

Maurel, Victor (June 17, 1848–October 22, 1923)   After studying at the conservatories in Marseilles and Paris, the French baritone Victor Maurel made his debut with the Paris Opéra in 1868. In 1873 he made his U.S. debut as Amonasro in the U.S. premiere of Verdi's *Aida.* By this time he was considered the best baritone of his generation in the Italian repertoire. He sang in all parts of the world during the subsequent 30 years and was a member of the Metropolitan Opera (1894–99). He had some acting experience and from 1883 to 1885 was a member of the directorate of the Théâtre des Italiens in Paris. A celebrated interpreter of Verdi, he was chosen by the composer to create the role of Posa in *Don Carlo* in 1871. Other Verdi premieres included Iago (*Otello,* 1887) and Falstaff (1893). Retiring in 1904, he continued teaching until his death. His autobiography *Dix ans de carrière* was published in Paris in 1897.

Maxwell Davies, Peter (b. September 8, 1934)   A student at the Royal Manchester College of Music and then of Goffredo Petrassi in Rome and Roger Sessions at Princeton, the English composer Peter Maxwell Davies was composer in residence at the University of Adelaide (1966). In 1967 he and Harrison Birtwistle formed the Pierrot Players (later called the Fires of London), a chamber music group that premiered much of Maxwell Davies' music. His earliest compositions (1950s) set rhythmic complexity against lyrical vocal lines (Five Motets, 1959), and later works use a huge percussion section and such instruments as stereo tape, gramophone horn, and player piano (*Revelation and Fall,* 1965; *L'homme armé,* 1968). Many pieces contain quotations from medieval and Renaissance music and were inspired by the literature of that period. Representative works are *Eight Songs for a Mad King* (1969) for instrumental ensemble and actor-singer, based on writings of King George III, and *Vesalii icones* (1970) for dancer-pianist and instrumental ensemble, based on the 1543 textbook of Andreas Vesalius and the Stations of the Cross. Maxwell Davies' interests then centered on new forms of musical theater (the opera *Taverner,* 1972) and electronic media but took a new turn in a monumental symphony (1978) that shows the considerable influence of Sibelius.

RECORDINGS: *Antechrist* for piccolo, bass clarinet, violin, cello, and three percussion; *Dark Angels* for soprano and guitar; *Eight Songs for a Mad King;* Fantasia on "O magnum mysterium" for organ; *Saint Michael* Sonata for 17 winds; Second Fantasia on Taverner's "In nomine"; Sonata for trumpet and piano; *Taverner* ("Points and Dances"); *Vesalii icones.*

Mayr, Richard (November 18, 1877–December 1, 1935)   Advised by Mahler to become a singer, the Austrian bass Richard Mayr left the study of medicine to sing at the Vienna Imperial Opera, where Mahler was conductor. His debut was in 1902 at Bayreuth as Hagen (Wagner's *Götterdämmerung*), and he also was known there for his Gurnemanz (*Parsifal,* 1908–14). His debut in Vienna was as Don Gomez (Verdi's *Ernani*), and he remained a member of the company until his death. In 1924 he first sang at Covent Garden as Baron

Ochs (Richard Strauss's *Der Rosenkavalier*), which was one of his finest roles, along with Rocco (Beethoven's *Fidelio*) and Sarastro (Mozart's *Die Zauberflöte*). He sang for three seasons at the Metropolitan Opera (1927–30), making his debut there as Pogner (Wagner's *Die Meistersinger*) and specializing in roles of Wagner and Richard Strauss.

mazurka   A Polish national dance in $\frac{3}{4}$ or $\frac{3}{8}$ time, the accent falling on the second beat of the measure. Danced in couples in multiples of four, it has more than 50 different steps, of which the most typical combines a skip and a slide. Characterized by stamping feet, clicking heels, and a proud carriage of the body, the mazurka was popular in western Europe as well as in Poland and Russia in the late 19th century. It has been effectively introduced in *Coppélia, Swan Lake,* and other ballets and is especially well known in Chopin's set for piano.

meantone temperament: *see* TUNING AND TEMPERAMENT.

measure (French, *mesure;* Italian, *misura;* German, *Takt;* Spanish, *compás;* British, bar)   The metrical unit enclosed by two bar lines, containing a group of beats, the first of which is normally accented.

mechanical instruments   Devices designed to reproduce music mechanically without the aid of a performer. Until the end of the 19th century, all such instruments were operated by a barrel-and-pin mechanism that was activated by hand or a mechanical clockwork. Carillons were so operated as early as the 14th century, and by the 16th century harpsichords and organs had such devices.

The most extensive use of the hand-operated mechanism was in the English BARREL ORGAN, and one of the most popular applications of clockwork was the *Flötenuhr* ("flute clock"). Some of the finest organ builders supplied the organ components for this instrument, and skilled clockmakers built the clockworks. Frederick the Great was fond of the *Flötenuhr,* and composers of his court composed for the instrument, including Quantz and Carl Philipp Emanuel Bach. Thirty-two pieces by Haydn exist for musical clocks dated 1772, 1792, and 1793 with from 17 to 29 stopped 4-ft. pipes each. The masterpiece for such a device is undoubtedly Mozart's Fantasy in f minor, K.608, one of three pieces Mozart wrote for the *Flötenuhr.*

The musical clock gave way late in the 18th century to the MUSIC BOX with a revolving brass cylinder and a comb of tuned metal teeth replacing the pipes. Larger versions had a brass disk in place of the cylinder.

The 19th-century successor to the barrel organ was the orchestrion in imitation of the orchestra. The most memorable example was the Panharmonicon (1804), built by Johann Nepomuk Maelzel (whose name is erroneously attached to the metronome), for which Beethoven wrote *Die Schlacht bei Vittoria* (*Wellington's Victory,* 1813, later scored for orchestra). A monstrous version was the Apollonicon, exhibited in 1817 by Flight and Robson of London, that was 24 feet (seven meters) in height, 20 feet (six meters) wide and deep, and contained more than 1,900 pipes in 46 registers; it could be played by five performers as well as three huge barrels. Another monstrous variant was the calliope (1856), a steam-driven organ that could be played either from a cylinder or a keyboard.

An advance over the barrel-and-pin mechanism was a paper roll in connection with a pneumatic action, patented by Michael Welte in 1887. A further application was in the Pianola, patented in 1897 by a U.S. engineer, Edwin S. Votey. Music was notated in perforations on a paper roll that passed over a tracker bar. Pedals and levers controlled pneumatic devices that released air, moving hammers that struck the piano keys. In the early 20th century player-piano rolls were made that reproduced with considerable accuracy performances by distinguished figures, such as Alfred Cortot and Debussy. The player piano also attracted composers, who could write pieces without concern for the limitations of the human hand. Such works include Stravinsky's Étude for Pianola (1917) and Hindemith's Toccata for mechanical piano (1926).

Welte-Mignon applied the player device to the organ, and famous organists of the early 20th century also made rolls, such as Eugène Gigout, Joseph Bonnet, and Lynnwood Farnam.

BIBLIOGRAPHY: John E. T. Clark, *Musical Boxes; a History and an Appreciation,* 3rd rev. ed. (1961); Romke De Waard, *From Music Boxes to Street Organs* (1967); Harvey N. Roehl, *Player Pianos and Music Boxes: Keys to a Musical Past* (1968); Q. David Bowers, *Encyclopedia of Automatic Musical Instruments* (1972); Heinrich Weiss-Stauffacher and Rudolf Bruhin, *The Marvelous World of Music Machines* (1976).

Medea: *see* BENDA; CLASSICAL PERIOD (vocal music, 1750–1800); MELODRAMA.

Médée: *see* CHARPENTIER, MARC-ANTOINE; CHERUBINI; MILHAUD.

mediant   The third tone of the diatonic scale halfway between the tonic and the dominant.

Medium, The: *see* LIBRETTO (modern status); MENOTTI; OPERA (the 20th century).

Medtner, Nikolai (Karlovich) (January 5, 1880 [old style, December 24, 1879]–November 13, 1951)   A Russian composer of piano music and songs, Nikolai Medtner studied piano with his uncle, Aleksandr Goedicke, and later at the Moscow Conservatory (1892–1900). In 1900 he won a first honorable mention in the Rubinstein competition at Vienna and then embarked on a career as pianist and composer, teaching at the Moscow Conservatory for a short time in 1909 and again from 1914 to 1921. He settled in 1921 in Germany, in 1925 in France, and in 1936 in England, making extensive concert tours of the United States in 1924–25 and 1930.

Medtner's work consisting almost entirely of piano music and solo songs, stands apart from the main tradition of Russian music but in close relationship to that of late 19th-century Germany. He was a master of rich and complicated pianistic textures, which, however, sometimes overload his song accompaniments. Thoughtful and introspective, his music makes no concessions to either popular or fashionable taste.

RECORDINGS: Piano—Concerto No. 3, *Fairy Tales,* Sonata in g minor, Sonata-Ballade, Sonata *Tragica;* songs.

Mefistofele: *see* BOITO.

Mehta, Zubin (b. April 29, 1936)   The Indian conductor Zubin Mehta studied in Bombay, where his father founded a symphony orchestra, and in Vienna. After guest appearances with European orchestras he visited the United States in 1961 and made his debut with the Los Angeles Philharmonic, of which he became musical director in 1962. He held that position with the Montreal Symphony from 1961 to 1967 and in 1968 became musical adviser to the Israel Philharmonic. He made his Metropolitan Opera debut in 1965 conducting Verdi's *Aida.* In 1969 he was director of the Maggio Musicale in Florence, Italy. In 1978 he became conductor of the New York Philharmonic. His numerous recordings include a cycle of Richard Strauss's tone poems.

BIBLIOGRAPHY: Martin Bookspan and Ross Yockey, *Zubin: The Zubin Mehta Story* (1978).

Méhul, Étienne (Nicolas) (June 22, 1763–October 18, 1817)   One of the principal composers at the time of the French Revolution, Étienne Méhul studied in Paris from 1778 with Jean Frédéric Edelmann and in 1782 produced a cantata at the Concert Spirituel on a text by Rousseau. Under the influence of Gluck he turned to dramatic music and from 1787 wrote more than 40 operas, produced at the Opéra-Comique, of which the most successful were *Le Jeune Henri* (1797), *Les Deux Aveugles de Tolède* (1806), *Uthal* (1806), and his masterpiece *Joseph* (1807). He also wrote patriotic works demanding great choral and orchestral resources to mark festive occasions of the Revolution, such as the *Hymne à la Raison* (1793) and *Chant de Départ* (1794). In this sphere, with Cherubini and Jean François Lesueur, he anticipated Berlioz. Though he had a bold sense of harmony and original gifts as a dramatist and orchestrator, he was poorly served by his librettists, and only some of the overtures survived. In addition to dramatic works he wrote piano sonatas, chamber music, and orchestral works.

Meistersinger   A German poet–musician (German for "master singer") in the 14th–16th centuries. A middle-class continuation of the aristocratic MINNESINGER tradition, Meistersingers claimed to be heirs of 12 old masters, accomplished poets skilled in the medieval *artes* and in musical theory (Heinrich von Meissen, called Frauenlob, was said to be their founder). Later—since music and poetry were crafts to be taught and learned—these fraternities became *Singschulen* ("song schools"), organized like craft guilds, and their principal activity became the holding—still in church—of singing competitions. Composition was restricted to fitting new words to tunes ascribed to the old masters; subject matter, meter, language, and performance were governed by an increasingly strict code of rules *(Tabulatur)*. These deadening restrictions led Hans Folz (d. *c.* 1515), a barber-surgeon from Worms, to persuade the Nürnberg *Singschule* to permit a wider range of subjects and the composition of new tunes. These reforms, adopted elsewhere, restored some life to the *Singschulen;* henceforth a member, having passed through the grades of *Schüler, Schulfreund, Singer,* and *Dichter,* became a *Meister* by having a *Ton* of his own approved by the *Merker* ("adjudicators"). In this freer atmosphere Hans Sachs flourished—though some regard the 16th century as a period of decline rather than of flourishing.

Nevertheless, music, form, and subject matter remained remarkably constant through the centuries. The music, derived from plainchant, determined the meter (*Ton* meant both "meter" and "melody"). Each strophe *(Gesätz)* consisted of two identical *Stollen,* forming the *Aufgesang,* and an *Abgesang* with its separate metrical scheme—a form derived from *Minnesang.* Verses were based on syllable counting regardless of stress or quantity; rhyme schemes were often elaborate. Three strophes, or a multiple of three, constituted a song *(Bar);* for large subjects several *Töne* were used. Songs were unaccompanied solos. For the *Singschulen* in church a wide range of religious subjects (*e.g.,* the nature of the Trinity, episodes from the Bible and from Jewish history, praise of the Virgin Mary) were versified, learnedly but without much original thought; after the Reformation the text of Luther's Bible was rigidly adhered to. From the 15th century serious secular subjects are also found. At the *Zechsingen,* held afterward in a tavern (perhaps not an official part of the *Singschule*), subjects were humorous, sometimes obscene.

From the earliest centers—Mainz, Worms, and Strasbourg—the movement spread all over south Germany and to Silesia and Bohemia; north Germany had individual Meistersingers but no *Singschulen.* The best documented center is Nürnberg. The Meistersingers were not popular figures, as Wagner's opera *Die Meistersinger* suggests; they were largely ignored by professional men, humanists, and the general populace; their craft was esoteric and their songs were not published; and they produced few outstanding artists or songs. Their importance lies rather in their devotion to their art in a troubled age and in their constant efforts to inculcate religious and moral principles. After 1600 attempts—mostly unsuccessful—at modernization were made; but the *Singschulen* slowly declined and disappeared, though the last one at Memmingen was not disbanded until 1875.

BIBLIOGRAPHY: Archer Taylor, *Literary History of Meistergesang* (1937); Mary Juliana Schroeder, *Mary-verse in Meistergesang* (1942; reprint, 1970); Clarence W. Friedman, *Prefiguration in Meistergesang* (1943; reprint, 1970); Robert W. Linker, *Music of the Minnesinger and Early Meistersinger* (1962); Romain Goldron, *Minstrels and Masters: The Triumph of Polyphony* (1968).

Meistersinger, Die: *see* GLOCKENSPIEL; LEITMOTIV; ROMANTIC PERIOD (20th-century transition); WAGNER.

Melba, Nellie, originally Helen Porter Mitchell (May 19, 1859–February 23, 1931)   After early training in piano and theory and later in voice with Mathilde Marchesi in Paris, the Australian soprano Nellie Melba (an adaptation of the name of her native Melbourne) made her debut in Brussels in 1887 as Gilda in Verdi's *Rigoletto.* The following year she made a London debut as Donizetti's Lucia di Lammermoor and in 1889 her first Paris performance as Ophélie in Ambroise Thomas's *Hamlet.* Her debuts at La Scala and at the Metropolitan Opera (both 1893) were as Lucia. For the 1897–98 season she toured the United States with her own opera company, then returning to London. She joined the Manhattan Opera Company in 1907. Melba was last heard in the United States in 1920 and gave a formal farewell in London

Nellie Melba
engraving by an unknown artist, 1894
courtesy, trustees of the British Museum
photograph, J. R. Freeman & Co., Ltd.

six years later. She was considered to be the finest lyric coloratura at the turn of the century; her favorite roles were Mimi (Puccini's *La Bohème*), Marguérite (Gounod's *Faust*), Léo Delibes' Lakmé, and Desdemona (Verdi's *Otello*). She was created a Dame of the British Empire in 1918. Her memoirs, *Melodies and Memories,* were published in 1925, and the following year she became president of the Melbourne Conservatorium.

Melchior, Lauritz (Lebrecht Hommel) (March 20, 1890–March 18, 1973) The Danish-American heldentenor Lauritz Melchior made his debut (1913) as a baritone in the role of Silvio in Leoncavallo's *Pagliacci* at the Royal Opera in Copenhagen. He began singing tenor roles there five years later. After leaving Denmark in 1921 to study in London, Berlin, and Munich, Melchior was such a success at Covent Garden (1924) that he became an annual guest performer there. Considered the greatest Wagnerian tenor of his time, he sang at Bayreuth (1924–31) and performed in opera houses throughout Europe and the United States. After his Metropolitan Opera debut in 1926 in Wagner's *Tannhäuser,* he was a leading member of the company until

1950 (he sang more than 200 performances of Wagner's *Tristan und Isolde* and more than 100 of *Siegfried*). He also appeared in films, operettas, and musical revues.

melodrama A stage work with spoken dialogue alternating with music, the music sometimes serving as a background to pantomime. The first full melodrama was Jean Jacques Rousseau's *Pygmalion* (1762, first performed 1770), followed by *Ariadne auf Naxos* and *Medea* (both 1775) by Georg Benda. Mozart provided two melodramatic monologues in *Zaïde* (1780), Beethoven the gravedigging scene in *Fidelio* (1805), and Weber the incantation scene in *Der Freischütz* (1821). In Schubert, Schumann, and Liszt the music no longer alternates but becomes a continuous background for the dialogue. Later examples are Richard Strauss's setting of Tennyson's *Enoch Arden* (1898); Schoenberg's *Erwartung* (1909), *Kol Nidrei* (1939), *Ode to Napoleon* (1943), and *A Survivor from Warsaw* (1947); a section of Milhaud's *Christophe Colomb* (1930); Stravinsky's *Perséphone* (1934); and the part of Joan in Honegger's *Jeanne d'Arc au bûcher* (1938).

The term *melodramma* in Italian signifies serious opera, replacing the earlier term *dramma per musica,* and has no connection with the English word melodrama—the Italian for the latter being *melologo.*

melody The organization of successive musical sounds in respect to pitch (Greek, *melodia,* "a choral song," from *melos,* "tune," and *ode,* "song"). In its most primitive state it is inseparable from rhythm; but it can develop freely without the aid of harmony, which removes it into another category. Thus a melodic scale is a scale based on a modal rather than on a harmonic system.

Attempts to define the term are found in the writings of several ancient Greek philosophers and music theorists. Aristotle accepts a common philosophical classification of melody into three groups: ethical melodies, melodies of action, and passionate melodies. A distinction of another kind is made by Aristoxenus (late 4th century B.C.), who states that the order (or lack of order) in melodious and unmelodious compositions resembles that in the arrangement of letters in language, as only certain arrangements of given letters will produce a syllable. Pseudo-Euclid (2nd century A.D.), known as Cleonides, indicates four methods of forming a melody: *agoge,* conjunct motion; *ploke,* disjunct motion, *petteia,* the repetition of a single note; and *tone,* the prolongation of a single note.

In the Middle Ages the word melody was often used synonymously with song or plainchant. Odo of Cluny (d. 942) showed that the monochord could be made to produce melody, which in this context means plainchant, or more specifically an antiphon. In France during the 12th and 13th centuries the creation of melodies was brought to a high standard by the trouvères and troubadours, who were imitated in Germany by the minnesingers and less successfully by the Meistersingers. Re/naissance composers, for all their occupation with polyphony, always based their music on melodic ideas and strands that were woven together in a texture of great beauty and complexity. In both sacred and secular music one voice part was occasionally allowed to stand forth as a cantus firmus; *i.e.,* as a solid melody that could nevertheless be decorated. The growing importance of solo song was responsible for the new refinement of melody, which coincided happily with the emergence of opera and cantata.

The conception of melody as tunefulness belongs to the 19th century and depends on symmetries of harmony and rhythm that seldom occur in music written before the 16th century and are accidental, if frequent, potentialities in older folk music. By the beginning of the 20th century a melody was considered to be the surface line in a series of harmonies. Harmonic rationality and symmetrical rhythm thus combined to produce a tuneful melody that helped to generate the sonata form.

A large number of resources are used to produce the melodic surface of music. They include:

1. A theme is a melody not necessarily complete in itself, except when designed for a set of variations, but recognizable as a pregnant phrase or clause. Thus a fugue subject is a theme, and the expositions and episodes in sonata form are more or less complex groups of themes.

2. A figure is the smallest fragment of a theme that can be recognized when transformed or detached from its surroundings. The grouping of figures into new melodies is the main resource of the development, or working out, in sonata form and the means by which fugues are carried on when the subjects and countersubjects are not present in their entirety. In 16th-century polyphony melody often consists of figures broken off from a cantus firmus.

3. A sequence is the repetition of a figure or group of chords at different levels of pitch. A real sequence repeats the initial group exactly and therefore changes its key (for example, in the first movement of Beethoven's *Waldstein* Sonata, measures 5–8 are a step in real sequence below measures 1–4). A tonal sequence repeats the figure within the key and modifies details accordingly, tolerating things that would be inadmissible in the initial group (*e.g.,* in the first movement of the *Waldstein* Sonata, the theme, with a brilliant counterpoint above, is treated in tonal sequence 40 measures from the end). Repetition at the same pitch is not sequence.

4. Polyphony is harmony made of melodic threads. Some classical melodies are polyphonically composite, requiring an inner melody that appears through transparent places in the outer melody to complete the sense. This well suits the piano with its evanescent tone, but it is even more frequent in music for earlier keyboard instruments, as in the keyboard works of Bach. Beethoven often divides a melody between voices (*e.g.,* measures 35–42 of the first movement of the *Waldstein* Sonata).

5. Conjunct motion is movement along adjacent degrees of the scale. Disjunct motion is movement proceeding by intervals of more than one step, often producing arpeggio-type melodies.

Conjunct and disjunct melodies are strongly contrasted in the music of ancient civilizations. Japanese music is predominantly conjunct, its melodies proceeding by small adjacent or scalic intervals, while Chinese music employs wider intervals. The use of wider intervals in melody is believed to be a sign of musical evolution toward a relaxed or static emotional state as opposed to the tension generated by melodies built on a succession of small intervals. This is illustrated by a comparison of the arpeggio-like melodies in works of Mozart and Beethoven with the severity of plainchant.

Melody types is a term used by mid-20th-century writers to describe the melodic formulas, figurations, progressions, and rhythmic patterns used in the creation of melodies in certain forms of non-European and early European music. These melody types are often characteristic of one mode or another, and they provide a means of forming melodies radically different from that based on the 19th-century conception of melody as being original or inspired. They include the Greek *nomoi* (literally "laws") and in a broader sense the melody types of folk music.

membranophone A class of instruments in which a stretched membrane vibrates to produce sound. In addition to drums the class includes the mirliton, or kazoo, and the friction drum (sounded by friction produced by drawing a stick back and forth through a hole in the membrane). Membranophone and idiophone (instruments whose solid, resonant body vibrates to produce sound) replace the looser term percussion instruments when an acoustically based classification is required. *Compare* AEROPHONE; CHORDOPHONE; ELECTROPHONE; IDIOPHONE.

Mendelssohn (-Bartholdy), (Jakob Ludwig) Felix (February 3, 1809–November 4, 1847) One of the pivotal figures of 19th-century Romanticism, the composer, pianist, and conductor Felix Mendelssohn was also a major force in the revival of Bach's music. Born at Hamburg of Jewish parents, he was the grandson of the philosopher Moses Mendelssohn and the son of Abraham Mendelssohn. His mother was Lea Salomon, from whom he and his sister Fanny took their first piano lessons. Though the Mendelssohns were proud of their ancestry, they considered it desirable, in accordance

Felix Mendelssohn
drawing by Aubrey Beardsley (1872–98)
The Mansell Collection, London

with 19th-century liberal ideas, to mark their emancipation from the ghetto by adopting the Christian faith. Accordingly Felix, together with his brother and two sisters, was baptized in his youth as a Lutheran. The name Bartholdy, a family property on the Spree, was held by a wealthy maternal uncle who had embraced Protestantism. When the fortune of this relative passed to the Mendelssohns, his name was adopted by them.

During the French occupation of Hamburg in 1811, the family moved to Berlin, where Mendelssohn studied piano with Ludwig Berger, a pupil of Clementi, and composition with Carl Friedrich Zelter. Other teachers in the Mendelssohn household gave lessons in literature and landscape painting, with the result that at an early age Mendelssohn's mind was widely cultivated. He was one of the first composers of the Romantic era to be nourished by a broad knowledge of the arts and stimulated by learning and scholarship, becoming the most accomplished and original letter writer among 19th-century composers. He traveled with his sister to Paris, where he took further piano lessons and where he seems to have become acquainted with the music of Mozart. He wrote numerous compositions during this boyhood period, among them five operas, 11 symphonies for strings, concertos, sonatas, and fugues, most of which were long preserved in manuscript in the Preussische Staatsbibliothek at Berlin but are believed to have been lost in World War II.

Mendelssohn made his first public appearance as a pianist in 1818, and in 1821 he was taken to Weimar to meet Goethe, for whom he played works of Bach and Mozart and to whom he dedicated his Quartet in b minor. A remarkable friendship developed between the aging poet and the 12-year-old musician. In Paris in 1825 Cherubini discerned his outstanding gifts, which now developed rapidly. The next year he reached his full stature as a composer with the overture to *A Midsummer Night's Dream*. The atmospheric effects and the fresh lyrical melodies in this work reveal the mind of an original composer, while the airy texture of the orchestration looks forward to the orchestral manner of Rimsky-Korsakov. Mendelssohn also became active as a conductor. On March 11, 1829, at the Singakademie in Berlin, he gave the first performance since Bach's death of the *St. Matthew* Passion, thus inaugurating the Bach revival of the 19th and 20th centuries. In the meantime he had visited Switzerland and had met Weber, whose opera *Der Freischütz* (Berlin, 1821) encouraged Mendelssohn to develop a national character. The greatest work of this period was the Octet (1825), displaying not only technical mastery and an almost unprecedented lightness of touch but great melodic and rhythmic originality. Mendelssohn developed in this work the genre of the swift-moving scherzo, also shown in the incidental music to *A Midsummer Night's Dream*.

In the spring of 1829 Mendelssohn made his first journey to England, conducting his Symphony in c minor at the London Philharmonic Society. In the summer he went to Scotland, of which he gave many poetic accounts in his evocative letters. He went there "with a rake for folk-songs, an ear for the lovely, fragrant countryside and a heart for the bare legs of the natives." At Abbotsford he met Sir Walter Scott. The literary, pictorial, and musical elements of Mendelssohn's imagination are often merged. Describing in a letter written from the Hebrides the manner in which the waves break on the Scottish coast, he noted down in the form of a musical symbol the opening bars of the *Hebrides* Overture. Between 1830 and 1832 he traveled in Germany, Austria, Italy, and Switzerland and in 1832 returned to London, where he conducted the *Hebrides* Overture and published the first book of his *Lieder ohne Worte (Songs without Words)*, completed in Venice in 1830.

In 1833 he was in London again to conduct his *Italian* Symphony, and in the same year he became music director at Düsseldorf, where he introduced into church services the masses of Beethoven and Cherubini and the cantatas of Bach. At Düsseldorf he began his first oratorio, *St. Paul*. In 1835 he became conductor of the celebrated Gewandhaus Orchestra at Leipzig, where he not only raised the standard of orchestral playing but made Leipzig the musical capital of Germany. Chopin and Schumann were among his friends there.

In 1835 Mendelssohn was overcome by the death of his father, whose dearest wish had been that his son should complete *St. Paul.* He accordingly plunged into this work with renewed determination and the following year conducted it at Düsseldorf. The same year at Frankfurt he met Cécile Jeanrenaud, the daughter of a French Protestant clergyman, and though she was ten years younger than he, they were married on March 28, 1837.

Works written over the following years include the Variations *sérieuses* for piano, *Hymn of Praise, Psalm CXIV,* the Second Piano Concerto, and chamber works. In 1838 Mendelssohn began the Violin Concerto. Though he normally worked rapidly, throwing off works with the same facility as one writes a letter, this final expression of his lyrical genius compelled his arduous attention over the next six years. In the 20th century the Violin Concerto is still admired for its warmth of melody and its vivacity and is the Mendelssohn work that for nostalgic listeners enshrines the elegant musical language of the 19th century. Many of Mendelssohn's works are cameos, delightful portraits or descriptive pieces, held to lack characteristic Romantic depth. But occasionally, as in the Violin Concerto and certain of the chamber works, these predominantly lyrical qualities convey a sense of the deeper Romantic wonder.

In 1843 Mendelssohn founded the Leipzig Conservatory, where he and Schumann taught composition. Visits to London and Birmingham followed, entailing an increasing number of engagements. These would hardly have affected his normal health; he had always lived on this feverish level. But after the death of his sister Fanny in May 1847, his energies deserted him, and following the rupture of a blood vessel he died at Leipzig a few months later.

Mendelssohn's main reputation was made in England, which in the course of his short life he visited no less than ten times. At the time of these visits the character of his music was held to be predominantly Victorian, and indeed he eventually became the favorite composer of Queen Victoria herself. Mendelssohn's subtly ironic account of his meeting with the queen and the prince consort at Buckingham Palace in 1843, to both of whom he was affectionately drawn, shows him also to have been alive to the pomp and sham of the royal establishment. His *Scottish* Symphony was dedicated to Queen Victoria. The fashion for playing the "Wedding March" from *A Midsummer Night's Dream* at bridal processions originates from a performance of this piece at the wedding of the Princess Royal in 1858. In the meantime he had given the first performances in London of Beethoven's *Emperor* and G Major Concertos. He was among the first to play a concerto from memory in public—Mendelssohn's memory was prodigious—and he also became known for his organ works. Later the popularity of his oratorio *Elijah* (Birmingham, 1846) established Mendelssohn as a composer whose influence on English music equaled that of Handel. After his death this influence was sometimes held to have had a stifling effect. Later generations of English composers, enamored

of Wagner, Debussy, or Stravinsky, revolted against the domination of Mendelssohn and condemned the sentimentality of his lesser works. Nevertheless he succeeded in arousing the native musical genius—at first by his performances and later in the creative sphere—from a dormant state.

BIBLIOGRAPHY: Ferdinand Hiller, *Mendelssohn: Letters and Recollections* (1874; reprint, 1972); Sebastian Hensel, *Mendelssohn Family, 1729–1847, from Letters and Journals,* 2 vols. (1882; reprint, 1969); Schima Kaufman, *Mendelssohn: A Second Elijah* (1934; reprint, 1971); Philip Radcliffe, *Mendelssohn* (1954); Heinrich Eduard Jacob, *Felix Mendelssohn and His Times* (1963; reprint, 1973); Michael Hurd, *Mendelssohn* (1970); Karl Mendelssohn-Bartholdy, *Goethe and Mendelssohn, 1821–1831,* 2nd ed. (1970); John Horton, *Mendelssohn Chamber Music* (1972); Herbert Kupferberg, *The Mendelssohns; Three Generations of Genius* (1972); George Richard Marek, *Gentle Genius* (1972); Felix Mendelssohn, *Felix Mendelssohn: Letters* (1973); Wilfrid Blunt, *On Wings of Song* (1974); Mozelle Moshansky, *Mendelssohn* (1978).

RECORDINGS: Numerous recordings of many works.

Mengelberg, (Josef) Willem (March 28, 1871– March 21, 1951)   One of the last of the great romantic conductors, Willem Mengelberg was long associated with the Amsterdam Concertgebouw (1895–1941), which he transformed into one of the world's great ensembles. Educated in his native Utrecht and at the Cologne Conservatory, Mengelberg began his conducting career in Lucerne. Though he excelled in a style that was fast becoming unfashionable— the antithesis of his contemporary Toscanini, with whom he shared conducting duties at the New York Philharmonic (1928–30)—he was noted for his interpretations of large-scale, dramatic music, especially that of Mahler and of Richard Strauss. Because of his collaboration with the Nazis in World War II, he was exiled from The Netherlands in 1941 and lived in Switzerland until his death.

Mennin, Peter, original name, Peter Mennini (b. May 17, 1923)   The U.S. composer Peter Mennin is primarily a symphonist. A student of Normand Lockwood at the Oberlin Conservatory and of Bernard Rogers and Howard Hanson at the Eastman School, Mennin taught composition at the Juilliard School (1947–58), was director of the Peabody Conservatory (1958–62), and then president of Juilliard. His music is characterized by long, diatonic melodic lines and conventional registration of instruments. He has written seven symphonies (1941–63; the fourth, *The Cycle,* 1949, is for chorus and orchestra), Concertato *Moby Dick* (1952), and concertos for cello (1956) and for piano (1958). His extensive vocal and choral music includes the cantata *The Christmas Story* (1949) and *Cantata de virtute* (1969). His style combines neoromanticism and Impressionism.

RECORDINGS: *Canto* for piano; Cello Concerto; Quartet No. 2; Symphonies (Nos. 4 and 5); Toccata for piano.

Menotti, Gian Carlo (b. July 7, 1911) A composer and librettist of realistic operas, the Italian-born Gian Carlo Menotti wrote his first opera, *The Death of Pierrot,* at age 11. He studied at the Verdi Conservatory in Milan and in 1927 emigrated to the United States, where he continued his studies at the Curtis Institute (1927–33).

Somewhat influenced by Puccini, Verdi, and Mussorgsky, Menotti uses largely traditional harmonies in which dissonance and polytonality heighten dramatic effect. His highly successful opera, *Amelia Goes to the Ball* (1937), is a witty satire on society manners and morals. It was followed by a radio opera, *The Old Maid and the Thief* (1939), and *The Island God* (Metropolitan Opera, 1942). These works were less successful, and Menotti turned to writing chamber operas on melodramatic subjects. His first opera of this type, *The Medium* (1946; motion picture, 1951), was a tragedy about a medium who becomes a victim of her own fraudulent voices. It was followed by a one-act comic opera, *The Telephone* (1946). In 1947 the two operas were paired in an unprecedented Broadway run.

In 1950 his political opera, *The Consul,* which won a Pulitzer Prize, was produced on Broadway. *Amahl and the Night Visitors* (1951), the first opera composed specifically for television, was in the late 1970s performed more often in the United States than any other

opera. With *The Saint of Bleecker Street* (1954) Menotti won a second Pulitzer Prize. His "madrigal fable," *The Unicorn, the Gorgon, and the Manticore* for chorus, instruments, and dancers, was produced in 1956. He wrote the librettos for Samuel Barber's operas *Vanessa* (1958) and revised *Antony and Cleopatra* (1974–75). His grand opera *Maria Golovin* (1958) was less successful than his earlier tragic operas. In 1963 he produced a cantata, *Death of the Bishop of Brindisi;* a television opera, *Labyrinth,* which utilizes special camera effects; and a comic opera, *The Last Savage,* for which he wrote the libretto in Italian and had it translated. His instrumental works include the symphonic poem *Apocalypse* (1951), concertos for piano (1945) and for violin (1952), and a ballet, *Sebastian* (1944). In 1958 Menotti established the Festival of Two Worlds for opera, music, and drama, in Spoleto, Italy, and its New World branch in Charleston, South Carolina, in 1977. His two-act, anti-war opera *Tamu-Tamu* (1973) is sung in English and Indonesian; it was commissioned by the International Congress of Anthropological and Ethnological Sciences.

BIBLIOGRAPHY: John Gruen, *Menotti: A Biography* (1978).

RECORDINGS: *Amahl and the Night Visitors; The Medium;* Piano Concerto in F; *Sebastian.*

mensural notation: *see* NOTATION (mensural notation).

mensuration canon: *see* CANON.

Menuhin, Yehudi (b. April 22, 1916) The U.S.-born violinist and conductor Yehudi Menuhin studied with Louis Persinger, Adolf Busch, and Georges Enesco. He made his debut in the Mendelssohn Concerto at the age of seven and in New York City played the Beethoven Concerto at the age of 11. His first world tour at 15 included 73 cities in 13 countries. In 1963 he opened the Yehudi Menuhin School in Stoke d'Abernon, England, for musically gifted children. He has sponsored new music, both in performances and in commissions, that includes Bartók's Sonata for solo violin. He regularly presides over music festivals in England and Switzerland and conducts the Bath Festival Orchestra. He appears in

Yehudi Menuhin
courtesy, Columbia Artists Management, Inc.

recitals with his sister, the pianist Hephzibah Menuhin. His autobiography, *Unfinished Journey*, appeared in 1977.

BIBLIOGRAPHY: Robert Magidoff, *Yehudi Menuhin; the Story of the Man and the Musician* (1955); Lionel Menuhin Rolfe, *The Menuhins; A Family Odyssey* (1978).

Mer, La: *see* DEBUSSY.

Merry Widow, The: *see* LEHÁR.

Merry Wives of Windsor, The: *see* NICOLAI; OPERA (the 19th century).

Messager, André (Charles Prosper) (December 30, 1853–February 24, 1929) A French conductor and composer of operettas, André Messager was a pupil of Saint-Saëns. After composing a symphony (1876) and a cantata, he completed Firmin Bernicat's comic opera *François les Bas-bleus* (1883). His reputation became established with his operetta *La Béarnaise* (Paris, 1885). Between 1890 and 1926 he produced 14 operettas, including *Madame Chrysanthème,* based on the novel by Pierre Loti (Paris, 1893), *Mirette* (London, 1894), *Véronique* (Paris, 1898), *Fortunio,* based on Alfred de Musset's *Le Chandelier* (Paris, 1907), and *Monsieur Beaucaire,* based on the novel by Booth Tarkington (Birmingham, England, 1919). Messager wrote in a light style, but he brought to the operetta a melodic

elegance that made it acceptable to the more serious-minded musical public. He wrote three ballets of which the best known was *Les Deux Pigeons* (1886). In 1898 he was appointed director of the Opéra-Comique, where in 1902 he conducted the first performance of Debussy's *Pelléas et Mélisande*. He was artistic director of Covent Garden (1901–06) and later associate director of the Paris Opéra, where he conducted Wagner's *Der Ring des Nibelungen*.

Messiaen, Olivier (Eugène Prosper Charles) (b. December 10, 1908) One of the most original composers of the 20th century, organist, and influential teacher, Olivier Messiaen was the son of Pierre Messiaen, a scholar of English literature, and of the poet Cécile Sauvage, who wrote "L'Âme en bourgeon" at the birth of her son. Messiaen grew up in Grenoble and Nantes, began composing at the age of seven, and taught himself to play the piano. At 11 he entered the Paris Conservatoire, where his teachers included Marcel Dupré and Paul Dukas. During his later years at the Conservatoire, he began an extensive private study of both Western and Eastern rhythm, birdsong, and microtonal music. In 1931 he was appointed organist at the church of the Trinité, Paris, the only major 20th-century composer who is a church organist (as were many composers of earlier periods).

Messiaen became known with the perfor-

Olivier Messiaen

mance of *Les Offrandes oubliées* in 1931 and *La Nativité du Seigneur* (1935) for organ. In 1936, with André Jolivet, Daniel Lesur, and Yves Baudrier, he founded La Jeune France to promote new French music. He taught at the Schola Cantorum and the École Normale de Musique from 1936 until the outbreak of World War II in 1939. As a soldier he was taken prisoner and interned at Görlitz, where he wrote *Quatuor pour la fin du temps* (Quartet *for the End of Time*), performed at the prison camp in 1941. Repatriated in 1942, he resumed his post at the Trinité and became professor of harmony and later of composition at the Conservatoire. His students include two of the major figures of 20th-century music, Stockhausen and Pierre Boulez. Much of Messiaen's music is inspired by Roman Catholic theology, interpreted in a quasi-mystical manner, notably in *Trois Petites Liturgies de la présence divine* (1944) for women's chorus and orchestra; *Vingt Regards sur l'Enfant Jésus* (1944) for piano; *Visions de l'amen* (1943) for two pianos; and *Messe de la Pentecôte* (1950) and *Livre d'orgue* (1951) for organ. His most important orchestral works are *L'Ascension* (1935; also transcribed for solo piano and solo organ); *Turangalîla-Symphonie* (1948) in 10 movements with a prominent solo piano part, percussion instruments in the manner of the gamelan, and ondes Martenot; and *Chronochromie* (1960) for 18 solo strings, winds, and percussion. *Le Réveil des oiseaux (The Awakening of the Birds,* 1953); *Oiseaux exotiques* (*Exotic Birds,* 1956), and *Catalogue d'oiseaux* (*Catalog of Birds,* 1959) incorporate meticulous notations of birdsong. Important later works include *Couleurs de la cité céleste* (1964) for piano, three clarinets, three xylophones, brass, and percussion; *Et exspecto resurrectionem mortuorum* (1964) for woodwinds, brass, and percussion; and *La Transfiguration de Notre Seigneur Jésus-Christ* (1965–69) for piano, flute, clarinet, cello, xylorimba, vibraphone, marimba, chorus, and orchestra.

The key to Messiaen's method of composition is expounded in his treatise *Technique de mon langage musical* (1944; *The Technique of My Musical Language,* 1957), which contains his theories on rhythm, modes, harmony,

and musical structure. His other writings include *Traité de rythme,* begun in 1948. His "Mode de valeurs et d'intensités" (1949; one of the *4 Études de rythme* for piano) was influential in propounding the theory of rhythmic modes to serialists of the 1950s.

BIBLIOGRAPHY: Robert Sherlaw Johnson, *Messiaen* (1975); Roger Nichols, *Messiaen* (1975).

RECORDINGS: *Apparition de l'Église éternelle* for organ; *L'Ascension; Le Banquet céleste* for organ; *Catalogue d'oiseaux; Chronochromie; Les Corps glorieux* for organ; *Couleurs de la cité céleste; Et exspecto resurrectionem mortuorum; 4 Études de rythme; 7 Haïkaï* for piano, xylophone, marimba, and orchestra; *Merle noir* for flute and piano; *Messe de la Pentecôte; La Nativité du Seigneur; Oiseaux exotiques; O sacrum convivium* (motet); *Poèmes pour mi* for soprano and piano; *Preludes for piano; Quatuor pour la fin du temps; Le Réveil des oiseaux; Turangalîla-Symphonie; Vingt regards sur l'Enfant Jésus; Visions de l'amen.*

Messiah: *see* ADDITIONAL ACCOMPANIMENT; FUGUE (Handel); HANDEL (life) and (works); ORATORIO (Handel).

Mester, Jorge (b. April 10, 1935) The Mexican-born U.S. conductor Jorge Mester studied with Jean Morel at the Juilliard School, joining the faculty there when he was but 22. He also played viola with the Beaux Arts Quartet. He became musical director of the Louisville Orchestra in 1968 and the Aspen Festival in 1969, and served as principal guest conductor of the St. Paul Chamber Orchestra for the 1978–79 season. Equally at home in opera and ballet, he has conducted at Spoleto and recorded Menotti's *The Medium* with the Washington Opera Society. His recordings with the Louisville Orchestra include a wide range of 20th-century music, but his repertoire is eclectic.

metallophone Any percussion instrument consisting of a series of struck metal bars (*compare* XYLOPHONE with struck wooden bars). Examples include the *saron* and *gender* of the Indonesian GAMELAN orchestra and the Western CELESTA, GLOCKENSPIEL, and VIBRAPHONE.

Metastasio, Pietro: *see* CLASSICAL PERIOD; GLUCK; JOMMELLI; LIBRETTO (emergence of historical subjects); MOZART (early life) and (later life); OPERA (developments in the 18th century); OPERA SERIA; PASSION (Bach); PORPORA.

meter The arrangement of rhythmic groups, each containing an equal number of temporal units called beats. Each group is a measure (or bar) and is set off from those adjoining it by bar lines. A time, or meter signature, found at the beginning of a piece of music, indicates the number of beats in a measure and the value of the basic beat. For example, $\frac{3}{4}$ meter has three quarter-note beats per measure. The time signature implies that an accent regularly occurs on the first beat of each measure. Simple meters are duple ($\frac{2}{2}$, $\frac{2}{4}$), triple ($\frac{3}{4}$, $\frac{3}{8}$), or quadruple ($\frac{4}{4}$, $\frac{4}{8}$). Compound meters are also duple ($\frac{6}{8}$, $\frac{6}{16}$), triple ($\frac{9}{8}$), or quadruple ($\frac{12}{8}$) but have time signatures that indicate the number of beats to be a multiple of three. Thus in $\frac{6}{8}$, for example, both beats of the basic duple division are divisible into three sub-units, yielding a total of six. Some meters that occur less frequently are neither duple nor triple ($\frac{5}{4}$, $\frac{7}{4}$) but may be considered a combination of duple and triple—such as $\frac{2}{4} + \frac{3}{4}$ or $\frac{3}{4} + \frac{2}{4} + \frac{2}{4}$.

The concept of regular rhythmic groups first appeared in music as early as *c.* 1200, when short rhythmic formulas called RHYTHMIC MODES came into use, implying repetition of simple triple patterns. From 1300 to 1600 both duple and triple meters were recognized in music theory, but in practice rhythm was often complex and involved combinations of meters. From the 17th to the 20th century regular meters as used today became the standard. Such 20th-century composers as Stravinsky often used frequent changes of time signature and complicated combinations of meters.

metrical modulation A term coined by William Glock for the polyrhythmic technique, introduced by Elliott Carter, for altering the pulse (not necessarily the meter) between sections by introducing a cross rhythm to the established pulse, thereby establishing a new pulse for the succeeding material.

metronome An instrument for denoting the tempo of a composition. Its invention is generally, although erroneously, ascribed to Johann Nepomuk Maelzel, but it was actually invented by a Dutch musician named Dietrich Nikolaus Winkel (*c.* 1812). The metronome consists essentially of a pendulum swung on a pivot; below the pivot is a fixed weight and above it is a sliding weight. The rate at which the pendulum swings is adjusted by moving the sliding weight up or down. In its simplest form the metronome is put in motion by hand and allowed to continue swinging until it is stopped or comes to rest. A scale of numbers, usually from 40 to 208, is marked on the pendulum above the pivot; the upper edge of the sliding weight is placed under the number that indicates the speed at which the music is to be played; *e.g.,* M. M. (Maelzel's metronome) ♩ = 60. ♩ = 72 or ♪ = 108. The number 60 shows that 60 oscillations are to occur each minute and that a half note will receive one beat. Lower numbers denote slower, and higher numbers quicker, beats. The conventional metronome, housed in a pyramidal case, is actuated by a hand-wound clockwork whose escapement makes a ticking sound at each beat; the device continues beating and ticking until the works run down. Many versions of the metronome have been made. One can be made to strike a bell at the first of any number of beats; other models are operated by electricity or can be carried in a pocket.

Meyerbeer, Giacomo, real name, Jakob Liebmann Meyer Beer (September 5, 1791–May 2, 1864) A German opera composer who established in Paris a vogue for spectacular Romantic opera, Giacomo Meyerbeer was born at Tasdorf near Berlin of a wealthy Jewish family. He studied composition with Carl Friedrich Zelter and Bernard Weber in Berlin and from 1810 with Georg Joseph Vogler at Darmstadt, where he formed a friendship with Carl Maria von Weber. His early German operas, produced at Munich, Stuttgart, and Vienna, were failures, and after a journey to Paris and London he settled in 1816 in Italy, where he produced five operas in the style of Rossini. The best of these was *Il Crociato* (Venice, 1824), given the following year in London and Paris.

Giacomo Meyerbeer
lithograph by Delpech
after Maurin's drawing from life
courtesy, Musikinstrumenten-Museum des
Staatlichen Instituts für Musikforschung
Preussischer Kulturbesitz, Berlin

His first French opera, written in association with Eugène Scribe, was *Robert le Diable* (Paris, 1831), produced on a lavish scale and calculated to appeal to the current Romantic taste for medievalism, the supernatural, and the macabre. Its success was immediate, establishing this work as the model of French grand opera. *Les Huguenots* was similarly successful in 1836. In 1842 Meyerbeer temporarily returned to Berlin, where he became music director to the King of Prussia and where he promoted the production of Wagner's *The Flying Dutchman*. From this period date his German opera *Ein Feldlager in Schlesien* (1844), in which Jenny Lind took the principal part, and the incidental music for the play *Struensee* by his brother Michael Beer. His third Romantic opera on a libretto of Scribe, *Le Prophète*, was given in Paris in 1849. He then turned to a lighter style and produced two works in the tradition of the opéra comique, *L'Etoile du Nord* (1854) and *Le Pardon de Ploërmel* (1859). His last opera, *L'Africaine,* was in rehearsal at the time of his death in Paris in 1864 and was not given until the following year.

Meyerbeer enjoyed an enormous vogue in his day, but later generations judged his music to be superficial; his reputation, based on his four Paris operas, did not survive long. Yet he had a considerable influence on the development of opera. This influence derived from his conception of big character scenes, his dramatic style of vocal writing, and his original sense of the orchestra, particularly the novel use of the bass clarinet, the saxophone, and the bassoon. Berlioz came under his influence, and operas such as Verdi's *Don Carlos* and Puccini's *Turandot* owe to Meyerbeer not only their spectacular elements but also their effective manipulation of ensembles and arias. Meyerbeer also wrote a number of choral works and songs.

BIBLIOGRAPHY: Arthur   Hervey, *Meyerbeer* (1913).

RECORDINGS: *Les Huguenots; Le Prophète;* lieder.

mezzo-soprano   A voice with a range (A below middle C to the second G above) between the alto and the soprano voices (*mezzo* is Italian for "half"). The tone quality is usually in the direction of the latter as opposed to mezzo-contralto, though the distinction is not universally made. The term is frequently shortened to mezzo.

Michelangeli, Arturo Benedetti (b. January 5, 1920)   The major Italian pianist of the 20th century, Arturo Benedetti Michelangeli is a virtuoso with great technical prowess. He was educated in his native Brescia and at the Milan Conservatory. Basically a romantic pianist, his playing is noted for being exceptionally clear.

Middle Ages   Music in the Middle Ages, the period before the RENAISSANCE, is usually reckoned as spanning the years roughly 500 to 1450. For music earlier than this, *see* ANCIENT MUSIC; GREEK MUSIC, ANCIENT.

chant   During the first seven centuries of its existence, the Western church had gradually acquired a large body of music for celebrations of its rite. Far from being uniform, it existed in a number of different repertoires and melodic dialects corresponding to localized liturgical practices. Beginning about 750 and continuing for about a century, Frankish rulers made continual efforts to establish a single liturgy throughout their domain. The rite they imported from Rome along with its music. Just how successful they were in achieving their goal can be seen from the remarkable uniformity of the earliest notated manuscript sources for chant (*c.* 900); but it is also clear that the melodies had undergone certain changes of style and form and were no longer what they had been two centuries earlier. It is this northern version that we know as Gregorian chant. *See* PLAINCHANT.

In the succeeding centuries—indeed almost to the present day—composers enlarged the repertoire by composing other chants in similar style. But they also began writing in a new manner and in new forms—chants for the ordinary of the mass (Kyrie, Gloria, Sanctus, and Agnus Dei) and the sequence, trope, and hymn. Placed alongside the old melodies, these new ones seem remarkably modern even to our own ears, for they have more clearly defined contours and strongly defined tonal centers as well as bolder shapes and more lucid types of organization.

During the 11th century another type of melody arose—one that matched the shapes of rhyming—accentual poetry. Poetic couplets were set as melodic couplets with a single line of music, varied—if at all—only at the cadence. The form was sometimes strophic, sometimes through-composed; when strophic it often used refrains. Independent pieces in this style are called *versus,* or conductus, but their features were incorporated into older forms as well, particularly the sequence. Liturgical drama like the *Play of Daniel* relies heavily on this style.

secular monophony The oldest preserved secular repertoires began taking form in the 12th century and show many of the characteristics found in the *versus,* or conductus. The goliards, wandering students, wrote Latin songs in this manner but on ribald themes. *Carmina Burana* is a large collection of them.

Song in the vernacular flourished too. In the 12th and 13th centuries hundreds of TROUBADOUR and TROUVÈRE songs were written. The forms varied widely. Most were strophic, but some were open-ended and designed for narration. Couplets were common, and most songs began with one. Refrains were

used in a number of ways. Toward 1300 forms using them crystallized as the ballade and rondeau. Like the *versus,* the melodies of the troubador and trouvère tended to be syllabic (one note per syllable) or nearly so and reserved melismatic flourishes (many notes per syllable) for cadences or special effects.

These melodies spread throughout Europe and gave rise to several national repertoires. The troubadour was also at home in Spain and wrote what was called the *cantiga.* In Germany the MINNESINGER adapted German words to French melodies or wrote entirely new songs imitating them. In Italy too there were troubadours, and large numbers of popular sacred song called the *lauda* were written. Monophonic secular composition retained its importance longer in Italy than in the north—well into the 14th century, when the madrigal and ballata were written for one voice as well as for two or three.

early polyphony From the same period that the earliest sources for Gregorian and medieval chant originate came the first testimonies that church musicians were interested in grappling with the problems of writing music in two or more parts. A Frankish treatise from about 900 A.D., *Musica Enchiriadis,* gives the earliest examples of notated polyphony; this little manual explains how to sing in parallel with a given melody at a distance of an octave (as men and boys might sing) or a fifth or fourth (as lower and higher men's voices might sing). As only one melody is involved such singing in parallel is hardly polyphonic; but several examples found here and in its companion commentary *Scholia Enchiriadis* show oblique and contrary motion, for the purposes of avoiding dissonant tritones, and beginning or ending on a unison. Singing in more than one part was nothing new at this time, of course. The ancient world seems to have done it, and it seems unlikely that the practice would have been absent from the intervening centuries. What these treatises seem to mark is the beginning of efforts to control composition—as opposed to improvisation—in this note-against-note contrapuntal style.

For the next two centuries most information regarding the development of compositional control continues to come from theory treatises. But from the end of the 10th century we have a series of practical sources giving many examples of ORGANUM, as these early two-part pieces are called. The only large collection of organa before 1100 is also the earliest monument of polyphonic music. Dating from perhaps as early as 975, the manuscript comes from Winchester Cathedral in the south of England. It is known as the Winchester Troper, for it—like all these early practical sources—is primarily a chant book. The notation of the pieces does not clearly represent pitch or melodic contour, nor does that of many organa found in other manuscripts. From those that can be read, however, we get a fairly clear picture of what two-part music was like during this period, and it conforms to principles espoused by theorists. The pieces are note-against-note settings of chant melodies, most often alleluias or responsories, sequences, or mass ordinary chants. They move primarily from one perfect consonance (an octave, fifth, fourth, or unison) to another, with contrary motion becoming more important in later pieces.

That a tremendous advance in part writing took place during the 11th century is shown by the independence of the voices in organa from the first major collections of pieces that can be accurately read—and thus the first that can be performed with confidence that what we hear bears some close likeness to what was intended. The earliest of these collections is from St. Martial; dating from about 1100, it contains only a dozen or so two-part pieces, but they seem to represent what is found in the others: three more sources from the south of France and one (the so-called *Codex Calixtinus*) from Santiago de Compostela, the final goal of a long pilgrimage route stretching from the north of France through Limoges and on to the northwestern coast of Spain. What is new in these repertoires is a manner of writing in which the upper voice is more elaborate than the lower voice. While the older note-against-note style is not neglected—the simplest pieces making regular use of it, the more florid ones reserving it for contrast—the typical piece moves faster in its upper voice than in its lower voice. The added counterpoint is free—both melodically and rhythmically—

from the constraint of sounding perfect consonances determined largely by the movement of the lower voice and the rule of contrary motion. Within a piece the relation between the two voices often varies from syllabic or melismatic note-against-note writing to neumatic or melismatic organal style, in which the upper voice has somewhere between two and 20 notes against each note of the lower voice; the simplest and most florid extremes are used carefully to highlight the form with melismas falling usually at cadences. As the notation does not indicate note duration, modern performances sometimes use freely flowing, undifferentiated rhythm and at other times something closer to the modal patterns found in music of the following century.

Notre Dame polyphony   The 12th century saw the rise of Paris to preeminence as a center for culture and learning, and its reputation attracted men of particular talent from all of Europe. Sometime after mid-century, coincidental with the construction of the new cathedral of Notre Dame, there grew up an entire school of composers responsible for the most important musical developments of this period. Two of these men we know by name, or rather by reputation, from the report of some unknown Englishman studying in Paris a century later who said that Léonin had written a great book of organum and that Pérotin had been the best composer of discant.

This *Magnus liber organi,* said to be by Léonin, is preserved in several large anthologies alongside works by Pérotin and other of their contemporaries. It is a cycle of organa in two parts for all the major feasts of the year, pieces for the office (responsories for vespers or matins) as well as the mass (graduals and alleluias). No longer compositions designed to fit unobtrusively into the liturgy, these magnificent organa set polyphonically the most elaborate Gregorian chants and stretched them out to unheard of lengths as they embellished them with seemingly endless melismatic flourishes. The chants themselves were responsorial, and the alternation between soloist and choir was preserved; only the soloistic sections were set polyphonically, the remainder being sung in unison by the choir. The chant was placed in the lower voice (called the tenor), slowed down to accommodate on every note melismas of 10, 20, 40, or even 70 notes in the upper voice (called the *duplum*). At times, usually when the tenor is moving through a melisma itself, the two voices come together in a passage that approaches note-against-note style called a discant section, or CLAUSULA. In such passages the upper voice moves along in a fairly regular pattern of alternation between long and short notes (called longs and breves) in what is called modal rhythm. This particular pattern, the first mode, is the only one used by Léonin in his discant; but it is one of six patterns that became standardized during the next few decades (*see* RHYTHMIC MODES). The lower voice moves almost as fast in notes of equal value, corresponding to the entire long-short pattern. The surrounding passages of organum may well have used the same kind of rhythmic pattern, but the notation is unclear about this. Suffice it to say that most modern performances use modal rhythm even for the organal passages.

Pérotin and other composers also wrote organa in three and four parts as well as two. Our anonymous author specifies that Pérotin wrote two organa *a* 3 and two *a* 4. Aside from the compositions he names there are in the same manuscripts 28 others in three parts and one in four; the latest version of the *Magnus liber organi,* moreover, shows enlargement from about 50 to nearly 100 pieces. The organa in three and four parts no longer show the sharp contrast between organum and discant that characterizes Léonin's work; although in organal passages the tenor still moves as slowly as ever, and even more slowly, the upper parts move in modal rhythm throughout so that they form a layer of voices moving note-against-note. While Léonin's upper voice showed a tendency toward repetition of melodic as well as rhythmic patterns, the upper voices in the larger organa to a much greater extent reveal motivic repetitions, sequential patterns, and imitation.

These men wrote CONDUCTUS as well—works in one, two, or three (occasionally four) parts—with all voices singing the same text, moving along syllabically in note-against-note style, and with melismas occurring sometimes at beginnings and ends of phrases but in all

voices at the same time. The conductus were not based on chant; they began with new poetic text and new tenor melodies. They moved—or at least the melismas did—in the same rhythms found in discant and in organum *a* 3 or *a* 4. More than any other type of Notre Dame composition, conductus placed emphasis on homogeneity of texture rather than differentiation of voices. While melodic repetition and sequence were common, the technique of voice interchange developed here. These features, along with regular, syllabic declamation of text and a propensity for composition *a* 3 with rich sonorities, often make the conductus immediately appealing to the modern listener.

But the most innovative work of Pérotin and his contemporaries involved Léonin's great cycle of organa. At first it was directed toward modernizing the organa, recomposing sections in organal or discant style. The most striking result was the replacement of large sections in organal style with much shorter sections of discant. In the end the organa were shorter, but the more important change was one of musical style, for these new discant settings began to show rhythmic control and structural features unknown in Léonin's originals. An entire group of 153 such abbreviations is collected in one source, where they seem to be intended for ad libitum substitution. The same source contains another 300 clausulae, most of which correspond to Léonin's discant passages; more advanced in style than the abbreviations, these clausulae seem to have been the working ground for any number of developments that came to characterize 13th-century music. One—perhaps the most important—was the establishment of regular rhythmic patterns in the tenor; whereas before the tenor moved through discant in phrases of irregular lengths, now it began to move in groups of three notes followed by a rest, which made two-bar phrases or, in longer groups, four-bar phrases. Against these regular patterns in the tenor, the *duplum* could now be phrased in any number of ways—so as to coincide with the tenor, to overarch two or three of its phrases, or even to contradict it by beginning and ending in the middle of the tenor's patterns without any synchronization. Another development was enlargement of the clausula by repeating the segment of chant that made up the tenor. On repetition the tenor was usually unchanged but sometimes was given a new rhythmic pattern.

Another innovation, one that would be exploited later, was the systematic use of rhythms other than the first mode pattern alternating long and short notes ♩♪. The reverse pattern, breve-long ♪♩, began to appear, as did one that was entirely made up of short notes ♪♪♪ and another that combined the ternary long used by the tenor with either the first mode or the reverse pattern breve-long ♩. ♩♪ or ♩. ♪♩.

As the *duplum* took up these new modal rhythms, the tenor for the most part continued to move along at a slightly slower pace, providing a regular beat that coincided with the basic ternary units of the upper voice. Increasingly often, however, the tenor would move as fast as the upper voice. The new rhythmic patterns, which generally began and ended with the same note values, were soon classified according to the modal system.

motet From the discant clausula the MOTET was born, and it drew its characteristics from the structural and rhythmic innovations outlined above. The process of converting clausula to motet by placing Latin text underneath the upper voice was begun sometime early in the 1200s; and while organum, conductus, and clausula were gradually abandoned by composers, the motet continued to preoccupy them throughout the 13th century and into the next. To place a new text underneath the *duplum* of a clausula was to give it a new identity, one that removed it from the context of the organum and rationalized it by articulating its design—its rhythm with changes of syllable, its phrasing with lines of rhyming poetry. Even if the music had been written first, the newly refashioned motet must have seemed designed to fit its particular text. The texture before had been one of two nearly equal voices, but now it was differentiated, and all the musical and textual interest seemed to reside in the upper voice.

While the earliest motets did not involve any new composition, they did establish a new genre, and composers soon began adding new upper voices above the familiar chant melismas. If a few clausulae *a* 3 had been turned into motets, now motets *a* 2 were given new *tripla* with phrases matching those of the *dupla;* this type of motet, with the same text in two—or even three—upper voices, resembled the conductus enough to earn the name conductus-motet. Soon they were given new texts too, as French *contrafacta* were substituted for the Latin originals. A new generation of French motets *a* 2 were made from clausulae, sometimes from those most recently composed, and using the second mode, or having tenor patterns with short as well as long notes. If a *duplum,* now called a *motetus,* used one of the refrain forms of secular poetry, it required a melody shaped to fit and a tenor adjusted to the design of the *motetus.* Until this time the motet continued to be dependent on the clausula. It developed along with the clausula the techniques of overlapping and noncoincidental phrasing, which when articulated by a text only served to further dissociate the voices. It seems that clausulae were composed almost as long as motets *a* 2; one of their functions, quite likely, was to provide notational models for the motet, as during this time only melismatic notation could express rhythm unambiguously.

The earliest motet sources contain almost exclusively pieces *a* 2 with the exception of the conductus-motet. Sometime perhaps in the second quarter of the century, composers returned their attention to motets *a* 3 but this time using the stylistic traits of the most modern motets *a* 2. They began writing double motets, sometimes adding a new *triplum* to a motet *a* 2 but often composing entirely new pieces in three parts. The *motetus* and *triplum* each had their own text. The texture was now that of three independent voices, each one moving at its own pace, in its own rhythms, with its own phrasing. Coincidental phrasing in all three voices came to be reserved for especially important cadences, sometimes only the final one. One device, borrowed from the clausula, that underlined this rhythmic independence was the hocket, in which the upper voices alternate with each other, one voice singing while the other one rests, each voice being fractured into segments of one or two isolated notes. New types of tenors, even secular melodies, were sometimes used, and the traditional chant melismas were treated more freely. The *triplum* often moved faster than the other voices, even dividing the short notes of the sixth mode syllabically, which retarded the tempo. Motets in this style precipitated revisions in the notational system, which are associated with a theorist named Franco of Cologne; both the new manner of notation and motets written in this style, with lively declamation in the upper voice (often in the pattern ♪♪ ♪ ♪ or ♪♪♪ ♪ are referred to as Franconian.

Some of these newer features, which first appeared as isolated experiments, became more common toward the end of the 13th century. When pushed to an extreme they strained against the traditional confines of the form. Indeed it could be argued that they moved beyond those bounds to become new forms; at the very least it can be said that composers were less often content to write motets in one of the customary manners and looked more often to unique and novel formal solutions. While some motets use longer and more complicated rhythmic patterns in their tenors, a greater number dispense with the modal patterns altogether, leaving the tenor phrasing irregular and without any structural import. A few pieces, at least two of which are by Petrus de Cruce (Pierre de la Croix), concentrate melodic interest in the *triplum* by making it move in yet smaller note values— five, six, even nine semibreves to the breve— thereby slowing the pace of the tenor and *motetus*. Others speed up the tenor. When its melody is short and not segmented into regular rhythmic patterns, it functions as an ostinato. While in the Petronian motet we have one fast moving voice above two slower ones, in this type all three voices move at the same pace. Other unusual features include binary rhythm in place of ternary modal rhythm, and voice exchange in which two upper voices exchange parts phrase-by-phrase over a specially constructed tenor called a *pes*, each phrase of which is repeated to allow for the exchange. As if to counter the trend, the Latin double motet returned to more conservative techniques, including identical rhythms in the upper voices and coincidental phrasing with the tenor.

Music from the Parisian repertoire was disseminated all over Europe and continued to be sung long after it was composed. But away from Paris—in French provincial centers, in England, Spain, and Germany (there are no sources for polyphonic music from Italy during this period)—composition itself led a course more or less independent of the specialized techniques of the Notre Dame organa and clausulae and the motets derived from them. Composers in these areas continued to write polyphonic settings of entire chants, not just graduals, alleluias, and responsories, as at Notre Dame, but a wide variety of types. The settings are in note-against-note style and typically in two parts except in England, where three- and four-part writing was also common. Enough has survived from the English repertoire to give evidence of musical sophistication equal to that of the Parisian repertoire, but with its own national style emphasizing the rich sonorities of the third and the sixth, a strong sense of tonal center (the result sometimes of restriction to only a few harmonies), and a homogeneous texture with all voices moving and often even cadencing together. Voice exchange is a common feature. Tenors are often freely composed, and when chants are used they are treated more freely than on the Continent. Together these traits can give English 13th-century music a richer and even smoother sound than its Parisian counterpart. None of these features was exclusively English, and from time to time French composers showed some interest in them, yet for the most part the French motet shows a different conception, one emphasizing differentiation of texture. Nevertheless the presence of English motets in continental collections testifies that their sound had the same broad appeal to medieval ears as to our own.

ars nova At the end of the 13th century the motet seemed to be heading in several different directions at once, and composition showed an interest in highly individualized formal solutions. But soon after the turn of the century, whatever had held the secular and sacred together within the confines of a single form lost its force. While for some time

French secular pieces still retained ties to the old motet—most notably the use of a slow-moving instrumental tenor—during the course of the 14th century composers began to set French poetry as accompanied song rather than double motet. Now the controlling structural feature came to be the text with its *forme fixe,* the BALLADE, RONDEAU, or VIRELAI; the musical flow became freer as the upper voice (called the *cantus*) was designed to fit its text, and the tenor was no longer restrained by modal patterns or rigid schemes. While a number of polyphonic chansons survive from the 13th century (anonymous except for 16 by Adam de la Halle and one by Jehannot de l'Escurel), the new genre soon flourished. One new type of special interest was the *chace,* a canon in two or three parts often imitating birdcalls, instruments, or sounds of the hunt. This realistic manner is also characteristic of the virelai.

The motet was redefined and given a stronger, if more narrowly circumscribed, identity during the 1310s, one that would retain its vitality more than a century. Latin was its language, but its subject was as often political as religious. The most important element in the new identity was the reassertion of large-scale organization according to repeated rhythmic patterns in the tenor voice, but its corollary was the reimposition of order on the rhythmic flow of the smallest note values. That much of this was the accomplishment of Philippe de Vitry we can see from his motets, a dozen or so, which are the first to show these characteristics. In 1316 some were inserted by Chaillou de Pesstain into the *Roman de Fauvel,* a long poem by Gervais de Bus that satirized political and clerical corruption. The new style depended partly on its hierarchical rhythmic control and was linked with a new manner of notation described in Philippe's treatise *Ars nova,* whose title is often used in referring to music of this era. No longer confined to ternary modal values, rhythm could now be duple or triple at every level; with the help of a new note shape (the minim), the varied and multiple divisions of the breve were given values proportional to those on other levels.

Philippe's motets are larger than those of his predecessors, and his texture is more stratified than theirs. The upper voices, always two, move in semibreves and minims, smaller values than ever before, so that the long and breve are slowed once again. Underneath them the tenor (and sometimes another low voice called a *contratenor*) keeps a slow pace; sometimes its patterns are extended by using longer values than in the old modal tenors, but the more interesting ones use a longer and more varied series of values that can even effect a change of meter. The tenor pattern, now called a *talea,* is repeated any number of times; the tenor melody, called the *color,* is stated two or three times, the last time often in reduced values. The large-scale rhythms of phrase and *talea* are articulated as much by rests as anything else; they become a conspicuous characteristic of the style—long rests in the tenor pattern, long rests as one upper voice or the other drops out after completing a phrase, shorter rests alternating between the upper voices and placed so as to coincide with changes of meter or some other feature of the tenor pattern. In some of Philippe's motets rests in the upper voice recur over the same part of every *talea* so that the recurrent rhythms of the tenor correspond to recurring rhythms in the upper voices. At times the rests form hockets, which can appear over each statement of the *talea;* but they show up more often toward the end of a motet, where over a final repetition of the *color,* with diminished values for the *talea,* the upper parts can even give themselves over entirely to hocketing. Periodic recurrence of rhythmic values in all voices is called ISORHYTHM. At first it encompassed only short passages, often just a few measures long; but once its utility was established the device spread out further over each *talea* until in the second half of the century many motets were completely isorhythmic.

Alongside the new type of motet and the new polyphonic song forms arose a body of polyphony for the ordinary of the MASS, the Kyrie, Gloria, Credo, Sanctus, Agnus Dei, and Ite missa est. As most settings of these texts are preserved in two manuscripts from Avignon, it seems that much of the repertoire may have been written for the papal court, which made its home there during the century.

The pieces vary widely in style. The simplest ones are note-against-note with the same text in all voices. Others have two voices above an instrumental tenor and something of the manner of the motet. Another type has only one vocal part above two instrumental ones. Few display the complexity of the motet or the lyricism of polyphonic song; the mass movements generally present a plainer face. Chant settings of the same texts, which continued to be composed throughout the Middle Ages, had been grouped together since the 12th century, both as Kyrie–Gloria and Sanctus–Agnus Dei pairs and as cycles including all four texts. During the 14th century composers began to group polyphonic settings in the same manner. Five such cycles have been preserved.

The most famous of these early polyphonic mass cycles is by Guillaume de Machaut, perhaps the greatest composer of the Middle Ages and the first to leave a large body of works both secular and sacred—one mass, 23 motets, and more than 100 secular songs in one, two, three, or four parts. For all these forms he doubtless had his models, and if we were to judge by the motets it would seem that he changed scarcely anything. Yet he may well have taken the lead in reshaping the ballade, virelai, and rondeau—in giving them their own manner of sophistication. It is in his works that we first see secular song rivaling the motet. What sets Guillaume apart from his contemporaries and successors, other than his fame and the number of preserved works, is his excellent craftsmanship and highly personalized style, characterized by colorful melodic and harmonic inflections and constantly shifting rhythms and syncopations—all bound within gracefully balanced phrases and forms. His music was known throughout Europe, and for more than half a century it set a standard for other composers to emulate.

Italian music of the trecento Polyphonic composition did not take root in Italy nearly so early as in France, and it was not until the 14th century that it began to flourish there. When it did it was in connection with secular poetry rather than liturgical texts. What it may have been like beforehand is hard to say, but it must have been largely improvised. At first its resemblance to anything French was minimal; if its contrapuntal technique was not so very different, its melodic and rhythmic expression were. Over the course of the century, however, it gradually adopted a northern manner until composers were setting French texts. Then for one reason or another the native art died out, and soon after the beginning of the 15th century northerners came to outnumber Italian musicians in their own country.

Perhaps the most distinctive feature of early trecento music was its entirely vocal nature. Until after mid-century the MADRIGAL was the predominant form; it was typically written for two voices, both singing the same text, changing syllables together, moving in similar rhythms and in phrases of the same length. The upper voice was florid. While the tenor was largely unornamented and thus moved more slowly, at times it shared even the fastest rhythms of the upper voice. Both parts moved through the text syllabically but regularly had melismas at beginnings and ends of phrases. In later examples the voices became more nearly equal and even took up imitation.

In form the madrigal had two sections. The first was repeated to accommodate two or three strophes of text; the second (the ritornello) provided a contrast—often in meter, sometimes in texture. Pieces written in three parts were exceptional; their upper two voices were often canonic. When canonic they resembled the CACCIA, which had two upper voices in canon usually over a free instrumental tenor. In spirit and style the caccia resembled the French chace and had little of the florid decoration so characteristic of the madrigal.

While Jacopo da Bologna and Giovanni da Cascia were among the best composers of the first half of the century, and thus masters of the madrigal, the one most respected after mid-century was Francesco Landini. By his time the popularity of the madrigal had declined, and composers were turning more and more to the BALLATA, a refrain form like the French virelai. Almost from the start the ballata tended to avoid the peculiarities of the madrigal. The voices were more nearly equal, sometimes even homorhythmic, and melismas were either avoided or carefully integrated into the melodic flow. But it underwent considerable change and gradually came to resemble French accompanied song *a* 3. Thus in texture the ballata varies more than other secular forms of the period. Yet the change went further than that, for along with the French influence on texture came modifications in melodic and contrapuntal style, affecting the very substance of trecento music and undercutting its native characteristics. Italian composers at the end of the 14th century and at the beginning of the 15th more and more gave way to influence from the north and came to write in French forms, to French texts, and in a French manner.

The same French influence can be seen in the *Faenza codex* (*c*. 1420), the earliest sizable source of keyboard music. It contains transcriptions and arrangements of both French and Italian pieces from the second half of the 14th century.

French music at the end of the Middle Ages During the second half of the 14th century and even the first quarter of the 15th, French composers continued to write in the established forms—motet, mass movement, and polyphonic song. The ballade became particularly important: it grew to larger proportions and took on a ceremonial function. Especially in these pieces composers tended to move toward stylistic extremes—extremes of harmonic expression or rhythmic complexity on the one hand, or contrapuntal simplicity and formal clarity on the other. In this they may have been following the lead of Guillaume, for it is possible to see him—along with the entire group of composers who delighted in intricacy and artifice—as being somewhat off the main path of musical development. Indeed it should be possible to trace this path from Petrus de Cruce and Philippe de Vitry to Guillaume Dufay without being deflected by untoward dissonance, ungainly syncopation, difficult notation, or unusual twists of phrase. The path, however, leads mostly through anonymous works until the end of the century, after which even a composer like Matheus da Perusio—best known for his extraordinarily complex rhythms—wrote uncomplicated rondeaus. There was a school of composition, centered perhaps in Avignon but extending into

Spain and northern Italy, that gave itself over to intricacy of detail, using either a variety of meters and a system of proportional values to give each voice maximal rhythmic independence, or unexpected melodic and harmonic events to give the piece an unusual cast. It is known through the works of a number of men—Jacopin de Senleches, Solage and Trebor, Matheus, and Antonellus da Caserta, as well as others—none of whom has left any great number of compositions. The movement had importance in its time, and many of its products well reward a listening; but its peculiarities evidently left little impression on the following generation of composers.

English music at the end of the Middle Ages What survives of the English medieval repertoire is almost entirely sacred—polyphonic elaborations of canti firmi or freely composed settings of liturgical or devotional texts. The mass ordinary and its tropes continued to attract composers, but during the 14th century they set the Gloria and Credo in increasing numbers. While the Gloria and Credo were generally free, the Sanctus and Agnus Dei were usually based on plainchant. Motets were written too but continued to show traditional English features such as freely composed tenors or free treatment of canti firmi.

English chant settings from this period are marked by several characteristics. They move in note-against-note style, the cantus firmus typically being placed in the middle voice and often transposed up a fifth. In certain pieces the chant would be elaborated or extended; in others it would move from one voice to another. Free compositions were generally written in similarly simple style but sometimes with an emphasis on parallel motion in thirds and sixths. Both types of pieces had an English sound, emphasizing the rich sonority of full triads in a homophonic texture and avoiding dissonances except in passing. While the top voice was most ornamental, all parts were vocal.

The only large source from this period is the Old Hall manuscript, an anthology of nearly 150 pieces from the second half of the 14th century and the first two decades of the 15th. It is almost entirely devoted to mass movements but also includes motets and antiphon settings. Many of the pieces for the ordinary are set in the simple styles described above. Another large group shows the influence of secular continental style with melodic interest being centered in the top voice. Others are isorhythmic or use canonic imitation in the upper parts. Whatever the style, these pieces had a character that was peculiarly English. During the early part of the 15th century, French musicians had ample opportunity to hear the music of English composers such as John Dunstable and Leonel Power. The sound impressed them. For the next few decades English music was circulated and collected on the Continent in large numbers and left its mark on continental style.

BIBLIOGRAPHY: Gustave Reese, *Music in the Middle Ages* (1940); Oliver Strunk, *Source Readings in Music History* (1950); Richard L. Crocker, *A History of Musical Style* (1966); Frederick W. Sternfeld, ed., *Music from the Middle Ages to the Renaissance* (1973); Albert Seay, *Music in the Medieval World,* 2nd ed. (1975); John Caldwell, *Medieval Music* (1978); Richard H. Hoppin, *Medieval Music* (1978).

David Bjork

Midsummer Marriage, The: *see* LIBRETTO (modern status); OPERA (the 20th century); TIPPETT.

Midsummer Night's Dream, A: *see* BRITTEN; INCIDENTAL MUSIC; MENDELSSOHN; OPERA (the 20th century).

Mignon: *see* THOMAS, AMBROISE.

Milán, Luis (*c.* 1500–?) A Spanish vihuela player, composer, and courtier, Luis Milán was born in Valencia and seems to have lived there at the brilliant and cultivated court of Germaine de Foix, which he described in a manual of behavior (1561); he also published a book of parlor games. His fame rests on *El Maestro* (1536), a collection of pieces for the vihuela and songs with vihuela accompaniment. This was the first of a series of such publications of vihuela music by various composers that continued to appear until 1576; the series is one of Spain's most distinctive contributions to 16th-century culture. The music in Milán's book is arranged in order of increasing difficulty, its apparently didactic purpose being suggested by the title. The

songs—Spanish and Portuguese *villancicos, romances,* and Italian sonnets—are often of great beauty, and the instrumental writing is infinitely varied and resourceful.

Milanov, Zinka (b. May 17, 1906) The Yugoslavian soprano Zinka Milanov studied in Zagreb, Milan, and Berlin. After appearing for 10 years with opera companies in Ljubljana, Zagreb, and Prague, she was chosen by Toscanini as soloist in the Verdi Requiem for the Salzburg Festival in 1937. The same year she made her Metropolitan Opera debut as Leonora in Verdi's *Il Trovatore;* she was to sing more than 400 performances with that company in the next 28 years. She also had a successful concert career during those years. She recorded widely in the Italian repertoire, especially in Verdi and Puccini, and was most noted for the roles of Aida (Verdi) and Desdemona (Verdi's *Otello*).

Milhaud, Darius (September 4, 1892–June 22, 1974) A major French composer of the 20th century known for his development of polytonality, Darius Milhaud was born of a Provençal Jewish family and studied with Paul Dukas and d'Indy at the Paris Conservatoire. As a student he met the writer Paul Claudel, who engaged Milhaud as his secretary (1917–18) while ambassador to Brazil in Rio de Janeiro. In 1920 the critic Henri Collet included Milhaud in the group of young composers he called LES SIX. For the next 20 years Milhaud taught in Paris and traveled extensively until his appointment in 1940 at Mills College in Oakland, California. After 1947 he taught at the Paris Conservatoire. In his later years he suffered from crippling arthritis, but he continued to compose and conduct.

Milhaud's bold, individual, dissonant style is exemplified in the ballets *L'Homme et son désir* (1918; scenario, Paul Claudel), *Le Boeuf sur le toit* (1919; scenario, Jean Cocteau), and *La Création du monde* (1923; scenario, Blaise Cendrars). He composed the incidental music for Claudel's *Protée* (1920) and for Claudel's translations of the Aeschylean tragedies *Agamemnon* (1913), *Choéphores* (1915), and *Les Euménides* (1917–22). Whips and hammers are introduced in the orchestration of this trilogy, a work of great dramatic force, in which the chorus is required to groan, whistle, and shriek. His other operas include *Christophe Colomb* (1930; text by Claudel), *Le Pauvre Matelot* (1926; *The Poor Sailor;* text by Cocteau), *Médée* (1939), *Bolivar* (completed 1943; Paris Opéra, 1950), *David* (1954), and *Saint Louis* (completed 1971).

The style of his music was largely inspired by his admiration for Berlioz, Bizet, and Chabrier. He was the first to analyze (though not the first to use) polytonality and to develop that technique consistently. Although his style became simplified in later years, its harmonic basis remained predominantly polytonal. Although dissonant, his music retains a lyrical quality.

A prolific composer, Milhaud wrote more than 400 works, including radio and motion picture scores, a setting of the Jewish Sabbath Morning Service, symphonies (12 for large orchestra, six for small orchestra), choral works, and the two-piano suite *Scaramouche* (1936; later arranged for saxophone or clarinet and orchestra). His chamber music includes the Suite for violin, clarinet, and piano, and 18 quartets. Among his songs are settings of poems by Claudel, Christina Rossetti, and Mallarmé. His autobiography was published in an English translation, *Notes without Music,* in 1952.

RECORDINGS: Numerous recordings of many works.

Military Symphony (Haydn, No. 100): *see* BAND; BASS DRUM; CYMBALS; JANISSARY MUSIC.

Milnes, Sherrill (Eustace) (b. January 10, 1935) Most noted as a Verdi singer, the U.S. dramatic baritone Sherrill Milnes studied with Rosa Ponselle and Boris Goldovsky. He made his debut at the Metropolitan Opera as Valentin in Gounod's *Faust* in 1965, after winning the American Opera auditions the preceding year. He has sung throughout Germany and the United States, at the Vienna State Opera, and at the Paris Opéra. Some of his best known roles are Macbeth, Rigoletto, Iago *(Otello),* and Don Carlo *(La Forza del destino),* all of Verdi; Don Giovanni (Mozart); and Figaro (Rossini's *Il barbiere di Siviglia*).

Milstein, Nathan (b. December 31, 1904) The Russian violinist Nathan Milstein studied with Leopold Auer in St. Petersburg and then with Eugène Ysaÿe in Brussels. He established U.S. citizenship and toured the United States in sonata recitals with Horowitz, as well as making annual European tours through all but the war years. He is known both for unaccompanied Bach and for works from the Romantic repertoire, and he has made many transcriptions for the violin.

BIBLIOGRAPHY: Bernard Gavoty, *Nathan Milstein* (1956).

minnesinger The German poet-musician of the 12th and 13th centuries. In the usage of the poets themselves, the term *Minnesang* denoted only songs dealing with courtly love *(Minne),* but it has come to be applied to the entire poetic-musical body *Sprüche* (political, moral, and religious song) as well as *Minnesang.*

The minnesinger, like his Romance counterparts the TROUBADOUR and TROUVÈRE, usually composed both words and music and performed songs in open court so that his art stood in an immediate relationship to his public. Some were of humble birth; at the other end of the social scale were men such as Emperor Henry VI, son of Frederick I Barbarossa. Most, however, were *ministeriales,* or members of the lower nobility, who depended on court patronage for their livelihood; from the vicissitudes of such an existence come many of the motifs in their poetry.

In form the music follows in the main the tripartite structure taken over from the Provençal canso: two identical sections, called individually *Stollen* and collectively *Aufgesang,* and a third section, or *Abgesang* (the terms derive from the later MEISTERSINGER); the formal ratio between *Aufgesang* and *Abgesang* is variable. The basic *aab* pattern was subject to much variation.

On a larger scale was the *Leich,* analogous to the French lai. It was an aggregation of short stanzas (versicles), typically couplets, each line of which was sung to the same music and each versicle having its own music. The *Leiche* were often several hundred lines long, and many incorporated religious motifs (such as the veneration of the Virgin Mary) that are also found in the shorter lyrics. Musical unity in both the *Leich* and the shorter forms was often achieved by the recurrence and variation of brief motifs, or even entire phrases.

Some of the early songs were probably sung to troubadour melodies, as their texts closely resemble Provençal models. Yet the German songs in the main differ in general musical character from the Romance songs. For example, the melodies are more often basically pentatonic (based on a five-tone scale). Popular song and plainchant are other musical roots of the style.

The poems of the earliest minnesinger known by name, Kürenberger (flourished 1160), and a few anonymous early poems suggest that before the force of the new troubadour-stimulated art was felt, native poetic traditions were sustained by quite different attitudes and conventions. Kürenberger's realistic verses show a proud, imperious knight with a woman pining for his love. But by the end of the century, the courtly love themes of the troubadours and trouvères had taken control.

The climax of the Romance-inspired *Minnesang* is reached at the turn of the 12th century in the work of the Thuringian Heinrich von Morungen, whose poetry is marked by an intensity of feeling and moral involvement unusual for the period, and the Alsatian Reinmar der Alte, who brings to their consummation the formal and conceptual values of the courtly love lyric as an expression of defined social ideals, and who was taken by his contemporaries as the most representative poet of pure *Minnesang*.

Walther von der Vogelweide, the greatest lyric poet of the Middle Ages, absorbed much of his teacher Reinmar's craftsmanship, but he went far beyond the artificial conventions with which the *Minnesang* had been governed and introduced an element of practical realism, both in his love poetry and in his *Sprüche*. By the time of Neidhart von Reuenthal, a Bavarian squire (d. *c.* 1250), the knight had turned his attention from the ladies of the castle to the wenches of the villages; Neidhart's melodies likewise have a certain affinity with folk song.

Whereas poets like Ulrich von Lichtenstein strove to keep the conceits of chivalry alive, others—among them Reinmar von Zweter, the Marner, and Konrad von Würzburg (mid-13th century)—cultivated didactic poetry, which Walther von der Vogelweide, building on the work of earlier poets, had already raised to a high level. At the end of the 13th century stands Frauenlob (Heinrich von Meissen), who by his versatility, his power of rhetoric, and his technical refinement points to the stylized art of the later Meistersingers.

BIBLIOGRAPHY: Adolph Ernst Kroeger, *The Minnesinger of Germany* (1873); Robert W. Linker, *Music of the Minnesinger and Early Meistersinger* (1962); Ronald J. Taylor, *Art of the Minnesinger* (1968).

minstrel A professional secular musician from the 12th to the 17th century, superseding the earlier term jongleur (Old French). Minstrelsy denoted any entertainment in which music played a part: hence minstrel was used loosely for many entertainers not primarily musicians such as dancers, jugglers, etc. More precisely minstrel referred to an instrumentalist; this supports the suggested derivation of the Old French *ménestrel* from the Latin *ministerium* ("a craft"), for the playing of an instrument required professional training.

The minstrel profession antedates the term. The *gléoman* of the Angles and the Teutonic *scôp,* first found in the 4th and 6th centuries respectively, were harper-singers, usually itinerant. Although many of these adapted themselves to the Christian culture, the profession had degenerated by the 8th century, and the church did not approve of it. The best gleemen nevertheless kept their relatively high social position and by the 11th century were often paid retainers in noble households. The most respectable instruments for a jongleur to play were the strings, both plucked and bowed, but the bagpipe, the one-man pipe and tabor, and the chimebells were also used. Some Arab instruments, such as trumpets, shawms, and nakers (small kettledrums), probably came to Western Europe at the time of the Crusades.

By the 15th century civic minstrels were established in Germany, France, and England. Originally they formed shawm-and-trumpet bands, but in the 16th century they were more versatile, singing and playing soft instruments such as the viol and recorder. Civic minstrels survived in some places until the 18th century, although minstrelsy otherwise died out in the 17th century.

Minstrelsy was an itinerant profession, for even household minstrels were not required at their posts throughout the year. The division between skilled liveried minstrels and independent entertainers, already apparent in the 8th century, later forced the better minstrels to protect their standards and privileges. In 1313 a minstrel school was held at Ypres, at which minstrels met to improve their technique and repertoire. Several more such schools were held at Bruges, Mechelen, Brussels, Mons, and Audenarde before the last-known school, again at Ypres, in 1432.

Membership in a guild also offered protection, and many minstrels joined merchant or trade guilds. Fraternities of minstrels were set up in the late 13th and early 14th centuries at Vienna, Lucca, Paris, and London, and later elsewhere. These discouraged unskilled minstrels by demanding a toll of any nonmember before he was allowed to perform.

The minstrel guilds did not flourish, however, and were unable to control the activities of nonmembers. In the 16th century the church's continual criticism led to the complete discrediting of independent minstrels. But even the liveried minstrels were now an anachronism. They could not normally read measured notation: their repertoire was based on memory and improvisation on well-known tunes, and medieval iconography clearly distinguishes between singers reading from a book and minstrels playing from memory. Only with the simpler notation of the 16th century and the increasing dissemination of printed part music did it become both possible and necessary for a minstrel to read music. Some adapted themselves and survived; but most did not, and the 16th century saw the end of minstrelsy as the Middle Ages knew it.

Of the great variety of medieval instruments, those with drones (bagpipe, fiddle, hurdy-gurdy) or drum (pipe and tabor) were most suitable for solo minstrelsy and were used for dances. In the 14th and 15th centuries a band of a trumpet and two or three shawms was also standard for dances and ceremonial music. Trumpets, fiddles, and viols were often played in pairs, while one bowed and one plucked instrument also formed a standard combination. The voice was usually accompanied by a plucked or bowed stringed instrument. In church the organ was joined (in plainchant but apparently not in polyphony) by shawms, trumpets, and chime-bells on special occasions.

The amount of minstrel music to be found in pre-16th-century manuscripts is very small indeed and consists almost entirely of dance music for unspecified instruments. The sources are few and the number of pieces meager. The reasons for this lack of notated evidence are partly the improvisatory nature and traditions of the music and partly the lack of regard in which minstrelsy was held in musically literate circles. Like many 20th-century performers of popular music, most minstrels were unable to write down their music and may also have been unwilling to have their repertoires and techniques known outside the profession. Their noble patrons were content to dance to and be entertained by minstrel music, but when a scribe was commissioned to copy music for the patron's library he would be expected to confine himself to composed music.

Early in the 16th century the invention of music printing and the emergence of a large amateur public resulted in the spread of printed and manuscript collections of dance music for instrumental ensemble and particularly for solo lute. By the late 1500s the dance forms were being used by composers as a framework for composition rather than for improvisation or variation; this converging of the hitherto distinct styles of minstrelsy and art music coincided with the decline of the minstrel profession in Western Europe. *See also* POPULAR MUSIC.

BIBLIOGRAPHY: Romain Goldron, *Minstrels and Masters: The Triumph of Polyphony* (1968).

minstrel show: *see* POPULAR MUSIC (the 19th century).

minuet An elegant couple dance that dominated aristocratic European ballrooms, especially in France and England, from *c.* 1650 to *c.* 1750. Reputedly derived from the French folk dance branle de Poitou, the court minuet (from French *menu,* "small," for the dance's small steps) became slower and increasingly etiquette-laden and spectacular. Dancers, in the order of their social position, often performed versions with especially choreographed figures, or floor patterns, and prefaced the dance with stylized bows and curtsies to partners and spectators. The basic floor pattern outlined by the dancers was at first a figure 8 and later the letter Z.

Musically the minuet is in triple time (as $\frac{3}{4}$ or $\frac{3}{8}$) with two sections: minuet and trio (actually a second minuet, originally for three instruments, derived from the ballroom practice of alternating two minuets). Each consists of two repeated phrases (AA-BB), but the repetition may be varied (AA'-BB'). The overall form is minuet-trio-minuet. The minuet frequently appears in 18th-century suites; in Mozart's opera *Don Giovanni* onstage musicians play a minuet in the fourth act. Typically the third movement of a Classical sonata or symphony is a minuet. In his symphonies Beethoven often replaced the minuet with a scherzo, similar or identical in form, but much faster and more exuberant.

Miraculous Mandarin, The: *see* BARTÓK.

Missa in tempore belli: *see* CLASSICAL PERIOD (vocal music, 1750–1800); HAYDN (achievement).

Missa pro defunctis: *see* MASS (requiem).

Missa Sanctae Caecilia: *see* HAYDN (Esterházy service).

Missa solemnis: *see* BEETHOVEN (last years); MASS (ordinary).

Mitropoulos, Dimitri (March 1, 1896–November 2, 1960) One of the earliest major conductors to promote 12-tone music, Dimitri Mitropoulos was educated in his native Athens, later studying piano with Busoni and conducting with Erich Kleiber. A fine pianist, he turned to conducting about 1930 and headed the Minneapolis Symphony (1937–49) and the New York Philharmonic (1950–58), later conducting at the Metropolitan Opera and La Scala. An excellent musician with a faultless memory, Mitropoulos conducted without a baton and was noted for his choreographic beat. A champion of 20th-century music, he introduced works by Samuel Barber, Bloch, Carlos Chávez, Copland, Morton Gould, Hindemith, Ernst Krenek, and Milhaud. He sometimes conducted piano concertos from the keyboard.

Mixolydian mode The seventh of the eight medieval church modes. Its general range comprises the eight natural notes from the G below middle C to the G above. Melodies in Mixolydian, or Mode VII, usually have G as the *finalis,* or final note, and D as the *tenor,* or reciting note.

In ancient Greek music Mixolydian was one of the names for the scale pattern, or octave species, conventionally represented in modern writings as B-B.

mode The word mode (from Latin *modus,* "manner," "measure," "mood") has two meanings in music: (1) the ways of ordering the notes of a scale according to the intervals they form with the tonic note, thus providing a theoretical framework for melodic music; in this sense the term is generally used in reference to the modes defined by the Roman Catholic Church for the classification of plainchant, but it also includes the modern major and minor scales as well as modes found in ancient and Oriental music and in folk music the world over. (2) RHYTHMIC MODES are a way of ordering long and short notes to form metrical (rhythmical) patterns, used chiefly in the 13th century.

medieval modes The modes in Europe owe something of their structure and terminology to the octave species *(harmoniai)* of ancient Greece, which early influenced the Christian church. But because of medieval Europe's own musical instincts and certain differences among musicians in the interpretation of Greek music theory, European modal theory went its own way *(see* GREEK MUSIC, ANCIENT).

St. Ambrose (*c.* 340–397), Bishop of Milan, was the first to organize the melodies of the church in four modes *(protus, deuterus, tritus, tetrardus,* corrupt forms of the Greek words for first, second, third, and fourth; that is I,

Name	Greek name (wrongly applied)	Authentic	Plagal	Notes	Finalis	Tenor
Protus authenticus	Dorian	I		D E F G A B C D	D	A
Protus plagalis	Hypodorian		II	A B C D E F G A	D	F
Deuterus authenticus	Phrygian	III		E F G A B C D E	E	C
Deuterus plagalis	Hypophrygian		IV	B C D E F G A B	E	A
Tritus authenticus	Lydian	V		F G A B C D E F	F	C
Tritus plagalis	Hypolydian		VI	C D E F G A B C	F	A
Tetrardus authenticus	Mixolydian	VII		G A B C D E F G	G	D
Tetrardus plagalis	Hypomixolydian		VIII	D E F G A B C D	G	C
The Additions of Glareanus						
	Aeolian	IX		A B C D E F G A	A	E
	Hypoaeolian		X	E F G A B C D E	A	C
	Ionian	XI		C D E F G A B C	C	G
	Hypoionian		XII	G A B C D E F G	C	E

Church modes

III, V, and VII of the Table). Each of these consists of an octave scale comprised of tones and semitones in different orders; a keynote to which all the intervals of this scale are referable called *finalis,* as a melody written in such a mode ends on this note; a *tenor,* so-called as it was the holding note, or reciting note, on or around which most of the recitation occurred. The *tenor* is normally, though not always, an interval of a fifth above the *finalis,* a feature that divides the mode into two conjunct segments: a lower pentachord (series of five notes forming the interval of a fifth); and an upper tetrachord (series of four notes forming the interval of a fourth). These four modes came to be called authentic (original). The Greek names applied to them, as to all other medieval modes (*see* Table), are through a medieval error quite different from those referring to Greek modes of comparable structure.

Subsequently Pope Gregory (*c.* 540–604) provided more variety by introducing four new modes, or rather a new form of each of the four original modes of Ambrose. These new forms (II, IV, VI, and VIII in the Table) each kept the same *finalis* as their parent modes but occupied a lower range of the voice. Thus the original lower segment (pentachord) was retained, the original upper segment (tetrachord) being transposed an octave lower; *i.e.,* it was placed below the pentachord instead of, as formerly, above it. The *finalis* now occupied the middle of the scale, and the scale ran from the authentic *tenor* to its octave. But in order to avoid the reciting note's being at the extreme ends of the scale, the *tenors* were given new places as shown. These new modes were called plagal (from Greek *plagios,* "oblique"), and their adopted Greek names were given the prefix *hypo-* ("below") in refer-

517

ence to their compass being lower than that of the authentic modes. A mode of more extended compass—*i.e.,* including both authentic and plagal notes—is called a mixed mode.

By the end of the 8th century, a considerable time after Pope Gregory's redaction of the original corpus of melodies, this system of eight modes—known as the *oktoechos*—became the basis for classifying the melodies of PLAINCHANT. Many of the chants are indeed thus adequately classified, though others do not conform to the modes under whose appellation they appear, while others again have been deliberately modified to conform more closely. But the system has always remained the official basis of church music, and its modes are usually called church modes, or ecclesiastical modes, though they were also the principal basis for the works of composers in general until about 1500 and are found in folk music.

The next enrichment of modal theory came from the Swiss monk Henricus Glareanus. Recognizing that each of the seven notes of the scale could form the *finalis* of a mode, Glareanus described in his *Dodecachordon* (1547) three further pairs of modes on the notes A, B, and C. The authentic mode on B (Locrian) and its plagal derivative (Hypolocrian) he rejected as they had no true pentachord or tetrachord but possessed only the imperfect fourth F-B, called *diabolus in musica.* But the mode on *finalis* A (Aeolian with its plagal derivative Hypoaeolian) and the mode on *finalis* C (Ionian with its derivative Hypoionian) he admitted (IX, X, XI, and XII in the Table), thereby completing the set of 12 modes underlying melodic music.

The Aeolian and Ionian modes, virtually the modern minor and major scales (the *finalis* now called the tonic, and the *tenor* becoming the dominant), had been rejected by the medieval church, the Ionian called *modus lascivus* because of its popularity in secular music in which it is found from the 11th century at the latest. But of all the modes it lent itself most to the harmonic feeling that was awakening in Europe, though it was not officially recognized by the church until the 16th century. Meanwhile the efforts of musicians to avoid the tritone interval explains not only why the

tenors of modes III and VIII settled on C rather than (by analogy with other modes) on B but also why altered notes gradually crept in, first B-flat, later F-sharp, then E-flat, C-sharp, and G-sharp to create a system called musica ficta in which these accidentals, although often not written, were executed by performers according to certain rules. This practice, used especially at cadences, also modified the modes in the direction of the modern major and minor scales. *See also* HARMONY (modal tonality).

modes since 1600   From 1600 to 1900 the major and minor scales (*i.e.,* virtually the Ionian and the Aeolian modes in their authentic forms) came to be used exclusively. For the major and minor scales are no less modes than the medieval structures. They are to be distinguished from keys, which are a device for transposing a given mode. A given mode can indeed be taken in any key. All major keys are modally identical (*i.e.,* their notes always have the same relation to the tonic), the difference between one major key and another being in the pitch of the tonic. Similarly all the different modes can be transposed so as to start from the same key note; thus, following the notes of the piano from C to c: the Lydian has F-sharp; the Ionian is all on the white keys; the Mixolydian has B-flat; the Dorian B-flat and E-flat; the Aeolian B-flat, E-flat, and A-flat; and the Phrygian B-flat, E-flat, A-flat, and D-flat.

In modern times the minor mode has three forms (*see* SCALE). Two of these are for melodic purposes: descending (mode IX, Aeolian); and ascending, where the upper tetrachord is major, *viz.,* A̲ B̲ C̲ D̲ E̲ F♯ G♯ A̲. In the third form, the harmonic minor, the upper tetrachord is in the Greek sense a chromatic genus, *viz.,* A̲ B̲ C̲ D̲ E̲ F G♯ A̲; that is, its tetrachord has two intervals of a semitone and one interval of a minor third as opposed to the diatonic genus, which in its patterns of tones and semitones characterizes all the other Western modes.

During the period of the greatest popularity of the major and minor modes—*i.e.,* that of "classical music"—the church modes, still kept for plainchant, tended to disappear in other music. Though the traditional material used by Bach is sometimes modal, his treatment of it is rarely so. After his time modal thinking is exceptional, though rare instances occur in Beethoven's Quartet in a minor in which the slow movement has a Lydian theme, and in Bruckner's Sixth Symphony in which the finale has a Phrygian theme. But a freer use of the modes was again found around the beginning of the 20th century as a result of the awakening interest in folk music and in plainchant and of the tendency to use archaisms. The interest in folk music also reintroduced the modes of the anhemitonic (*i.e.,* without semitones) pentatonic scale.

ancient and Oriental modal systems Toward the middle of the 20th century, the Western world became aware of living modal systems in the music of the Orient and of some of the systems used in antiquity. These systems are different from those of the West in many ways. The differences concern the range of notes (octave in Byzantine and Roman chant and in Indian classical music; tetrachord in Persia as in ancient Greece); the direction of the modal scale (descending in ancient Greece; ascending in the West; both directions in India); the size of the intervals (diatonic only in Europe; often finer shades of interval in the East); and the number of focal notes that may be added to the dominant. Yet despite these differences all these systems are related through their fundamental principle, namely, the relationship of each note to a permanent and immovable tonic and hence to each other. This tonic may be sounded only occasionally and only in the melody as the Western *finalis* or tonic; or it may be permanently (or intermittently) sounded as a reference note throughout a performance as in the Indian *chhandovati sruti,* Byzantine *ison,* and the bagpipe drone. Even European sacred music made considerable use of drones until at least the 12th century. The constantly sounding tonic lends the melody notes a far more certain expression than they have when left without a continuous point of reference.

The modal systems of music (ancient Egyptian and Mesopotamian, Greek, Jewish, Indian, Persian, and Arab; Byzantine and Roman Christian; European until *c.* 1600) are different in principle from systems employing transposition (with a measure of modulation). The latter systems, based not on the division of a string (and its octave unit) but on the cycle of fifths (as in the music of Pythagorean Greece, China, and Europe since *c.* 1600), favor the development of harmony, though this is, strictly speaking, incompatible with a full modal system. The two systems, the divisive (modal) and the cyclic (transposing), were first confused by the later Greeks; the confusion continued in Europe, though European harmony first developed within the Western modal system.

modal ethos The essence of mode lies in its mood. Indeed the eight medieval Western modes have been described as being respectively: I, grave; II, sad; III, mystical; IV, harmonious; V, joyful; VI, devout; VII, angelic; VIII, perfect. Here is an echo of the Greek concept of ethos, or moral effect of modes. Some ancient peoples still traditionally regard music as, in its own language, reflecting the pattern of the universe or of divine nature. They regard *phenomena* (things apparent to the senses) as ideally reflecting *noumena* (principles lying behind all appearances)—Plato's *mimesis*—and in this view a mode of music is part of a larger mode running through all existence. *Modus* also means measure; that is, the precise measure of a modal note in relation to its tonic, which indeed goes hand-in-hand with mode's particular expression (mood) and manner. This measure can be expressed as a ratio of string lengths or (in modern times) of vibration frequencies. Hence the number correspondence and number symbolism inevitably connected with ethos. Tribute is paid to the ancient beliefs about modal ethos in the myths that have come down—myths telling of marvelous music that can create and destroy, kill and cure, music that can influence and indeed control man's every mood. *See also* ANCIENT MUSIC.

BIBLIOGRAPHY: Gustave Reese, *Music in the Middle Ages* (1940); Egon Wellesz, *Eastern Elements in Western Chant* (1947; reprint, 1967), and ed., *Ancient and Oriental Music* (1957), Vol. 1 of *The New Oxford History of Music;* Dom Anselm Hughes, ed., *Early Medieval Music up to 1300* (1954), Vol. 2 of *The New Oxford History of Music.*

modern dance The advent of U.S. modern dance is conventionally dated from the first years of the 20th century, when it was correctly perceived that European BALLET was spiritually sere and technically ossified. Revolt was apt against exhausted traditions; yet the sweeping revolution that occurred, with Americans in the vanguard, must be viewed and evaluated as a movement in itself and not as the genesis of modern dance as we have come to know it either technically or in terms of emotional content.

Three performers might be mentioned as having played a crucial part in establishing a nonballetic art form with a profile of its own. Isadora Duncan, born in 1878 in San Francisco, began her career as a show dancer in Chicago but soon moved to New York City, where she devoted herself to perfecting her danced interpretations of concert scores. Her career was conceived as a celebration of the energy inherent in the ruined civilization of ancient Greece, and this led to her adoption of the classical flowing tunic as her basic and most beloved costume. As well as dancing throughout Europe, she founded academies in France, Germany, and Russia that she vainly hoped would become international forces of ethical education.

So far as can be judged her choreography depicted large and noble issues in equally broad strokes. Among the works she interpreted were Gluck's *Iphigénie en Aulide,* Tchaikovsky's *Marche slav* and his Sixth Symphony, Wagner's "Dance of the Apprentices" from *Die Meistersinger,* and Beethoven's Fifth Symphony. Having neither devised a notational system that might have preserved the shape of her dances nor long-term disciples to perform them, Isadora's legacy is a legend of iconoclastic independence.

The life of Ruth St. Denis (born Ruth Dennis in 1877) was decisively changed by a poster that showed the goddess Isis advertising Egyptian Deities cigarettes. From an undistinguished theatrical dancer she became a tireless explorer of movements based on Eastern dance.

What ancient Greece was to Isadora, the Orient was to Miss Ruth, as St. Denis was ubiquitously known. From the iconography that is extant, both printed and on film, we get a picture of an artist whose aim was the creation of cosmetic illusion. Essentially St. Denis made static vignettes with neither kinetic drive nor dramatic development. Unlike Isadora's dances St. Denis's were short; whereas Isadora tried to paint the epic canvas, St. Denis remained content throughout her career with the finely etched miniature. In the scope of their accomplishments the more than 150 dances St. Denis made in the 50 years after 1906 cannot be said to have deepened in ambitions or attainments. Her earliest works such as *Radha* (1906; music from Léo Delibes's *Lakmé*) and *Nautch* (1908), because of their freshness, remained her best.

Edwin Meyers Shawn—Ted Shawn—was 14 years younger than St. Denis but became her partner, her husband, and her colleague in their school—called Denishawn, an amalgam of their names. Founded in Los Angeles in 1915, Denishawn was decidedly successful, counting among its students Martha Graham, Doris Humphrey, and Charles Weidman, all of whom would dance with the Denishawn company before its dissolution in 1932.

More important perhaps to the future of U.S. modern dance than his performances with St. Denis was Shawn's creation in 1933 of an all-male company. With vigor and style in works such as *Cutting the Sugar Cane* (1933) and as Pierrot in the *Dead City* (1934), Shawn staked out the terrain for the male modern dancer.

If these three artists prepared the soil in which U.S. modern dance would grow, it was Martha Graham who first reaped a harvest of both public acclaim and critical respect for dances that were theatrically gripping and impeccably crafted. Unlike her precursors, who relied for much of their effect on exotic postures and attitudes, she built her works on a technique that was kinetically forceful and emotionally direct. After studying at Denishawn in 1916 and dancing with the company from 1919 until 1923, Graham struck off on her own, first dancing with the Greenwich Village Follies and in 1925 assuming a teaching position at the Eastman School of Dance and Dramatic Action in Rochester, New York.

Although she first formed her own company and began showing her works in New York City in 1926, it was five years later that she choreographed what was considered her first masterpiece, *Primitive Mysteries* (1931). A dance for an ensemble of 19 women, the work had the formal scope, the mystical overtones, and the direct emotional resonance that would set Graham apart for decades to come.

Stylistically Graham moved through several phases. For a decade from the mid-1930s, her works were tinged by a strongly patriotic feeling that manifested itself in pieces such as *American Provincials* (1934), *American Document* (1938), *Salem Shore* (1943; music by Paul Nordoff), culminating in Copland's *Appalachian Spring* (1944). There followed a series of works inspired by ancient Greek and Hebraic myths, including *Errand into the Maze* (1947; Menotti), *Clytemnestra* (1958; Halim el-Dabh), and *Circe* (1963; Alan Hovhaness). Complementing these trends were individual works of great beauty, the elegiac *Lamentation* (1930; Kodály), the serenely abstract *Diversion of Angels* (1948; Norman Dello Joio), and works to literary themes such as *Letter to the World* (1940; Hunter Johnson), inspired by Emily Dickinson, and *Seraphic Dialogue* (1955; Dello Joio), after the story of Joan of Arc. Although her company still existed under her watchful eye in the late 1970s, it could not be said to perform with the riveting excitement that was its hallmark when Graham herself was in her prime.

Hanya Holm, although German born, was the second of a trio of women who lent their characters to the first generation of U.S. modern dance and who spawned the successive generation. A disciple of Mary Wigman in Dresden, Holm emigrated to America in 1931 and served as her mentor's emissary until 1936, when she formed her own dance company and gave her own name to her school.

At its most successful Holm's work reflected her perceptions of contemporary society, as in a satire called *Trend* (1937; Wallingford Riegger and Edgard Varèse) or a spoof called *Metropolitan Diary* (1938; Gregory Tucker). Starting in the late 1940s she refocused her energies toward more frankly theatrical productions and created dances for many musicals, including *Kiss Me Kate* (1948), *My Fair Lady* (1956), and *Camelot* (1960). As much as for her choreography Holm is remembered as a transcontinental link with the Wigman tradition and for her tutelage of prominent members of the second generation of U.S. modern dance.

Doris Humphrey, another alumna of Denishawn, which she joined in 1918 and toured with until the late 1920s, was a choreographer of exemplary intelligence and a teacher of rare effectiveness. Her major compositions include *Water Study* (1928), danced in silence by 15 women; *The Shakers* (1930), a moving tribute to the Quaker sect; and the Passacaglia in c minor (1938), a visualization of Bach's composition. As an educator she played a central role in establishing a dance department at the Juilliard School in New York City, and she enriched the literature with her sensible treatise, *The Art of Making Dances* (1959). From 1927 until 1945 she was intimately associated with Charles Weidman as both performer and teacher with the company and school that they jointly ran. Although Weidman was also active as a choreographer—his best works include *Fables for Our Times* (after James Thurber, 1947) and *Brahms Waltzes,* Op. 39 (1967)—his gifts were slighter than Humphrey's.

A second generation of U.S. modern dance was dominated by artists associated with Graham. Two predominate. Merce Cunningham danced with Graham from 1939 until the mid-1940s, when he began to choreograph and perform on his own. Of all modern dancer-choreographers Cunningham was the most indebted to ballet. He created a work for the Ballet Society in 1947 and taught a modern dance class at the School of American Ballet, the bastion of George Balanchine. His own works are notable for their clarity of line and for their breathtaking range of tempi—from an attenuated slow motion to a fleet and clean allegro.

Cunningham prided himself on his collaborations and on the aesthetic freedom he endowed upon each of his colleagues. Composers with whom he worked included John Cage and David Tudor, and set designers included Robert Rauschenberg, Jasper Johns, and

Andy Warhol. With each partner pursuing his own discrete way, formidable works were created, including *Winterbranch* (1964) and *Rainforest* (1968).

Paul Taylor, who danced with Graham from the mid-1950s until the early 1960s when he formed his own troupe, was far more frankly theatrical than Cunningham. His work was made accessible in ways that Cunningham's was not: through the use of traditional music, clearly plotted dramatic scenarios, and steps drawn from a variety of vernacular movements.

Taylor's versatility embraced a host of differing styles. *Aureole* (1962), a sweet-tempered plotless piece that seems balletic in sentiment, was in the repertoire of the Royal Danish Ballet in the 1970s. *Big Bertha* (1971), belying its carnival setting, was an allegorical gloss on the potential destructiveness of the machines that run our lives. *American Genesis* (1974) was an evening-length triptych that fused American history with biblical stories, the one strain enhancing the other. And *Esplanade* (1975) was a tour de force whose choreographic vocabulary consisted entirely of walks, runs, skips, turns, and other movements drawn from everyday life. Although he ended his dancing career in 1975, Taylor has continued to choreograph works of remarkable sensitivity and perception and to serve as an inspiration for a younger generation of artists.

What Taylor and Cunningham were to Graham, Alwin Nikolais was to Hanya Holm. From his base at the Henry Street Settlement Playhouse in New York City, Nikolais refined the core of expressionism he learned from Holm. A sophisticated array of light projections and sound effects gave his works a look that was unique on the U.S. stage, although the roots of his visual imagery can be traced beyond Holm to Wigman and to such Bauhaus masters as Oskar Schlemmer. If many of his pieces shared a similar look, several are considered outstanding, including *Totem* (1960), *Sanctum* (1964), and *Tent* (1968).

José Limón was another towering figure of the second generation of U.S. modern dance. A student of Humphrey and Weidman and a member of their company throughout the 1930s, he formed his own troupe in 1940. His foremost works, which took keen advantage of his commanding stage presence, include *The Moor's Pavane* (1949; music by Purcell; in the repertoire of the American Ballet Theatre and the Joffrey Ballet in the late 1970s); and *Emperor Jones* (1956; Heitor Villa-Lobos). As well as being a performer and choreographer, Limón was a teacher of great importance and until his death in 1972 enjoyed long associations with both the Juilliard School and the American Dance Festival at Connecticut College in New London. Two members of his company who also won acclaim for their own choreography were Pauline Koner and Lucas Hoving.

By the mid-1960s a third generation of prominent U.S. modern dancers had appeared. Twyla Tharp, perhaps the most celebrated choreographer of the 1970s, danced with Taylor in the early 1960s before forming her own ensemble in 1966. In the subsequent decade she created a repertoire that was brilliantly diverse and entertaining. As well as works for her own company—*The Bix Pieces* (1972; Haydn and 1920s songs) and *The Raggedy Dances* (1972) were ingenious examples of modern dance influenced by both ballet steps and social dancing—she made works for the Joffrey Ballet—*Deuce Coupe* (1973; Beach Boys) and *As Time Goes By* (1973; Haydn)—and for the American Ballet Theatre, where she choreographed expressly for the gifted Mikhail Baryshnikov in *Push Comes to Shove* (1976; Haydn). By working repeatedly with ballet companies she helped blur the demarcation line that traditionally separated the techniques of classical and modern dance.

Other former members of Taylor's troupe who carved independent careers include Senta Driver, who in 1974 founded a group named Harry that offered whimsical choreographic commentaries on both balletic and modern dance conventions; Dan Wagoner, who in 1969 formed his own group to express his antic theatricality; and Cliff Keuter and Elizabeth Keen, choreographers who showcased their works at the Judson Memorial Church on Washington Square in New York City, making it a mecca for the avant-garde in the mid-1960s.

Viola Farber, another artist to exhibit her works at the Judson Memorial Church, stayed choreographically pure in the manner of her mentor, Merce Cunningham. A member of his company from 1953 to 1965, Farber produced dances that were hard-edged, precise, and yet infused with a palpable personality. In pieces such as *Route 6* (1972), performed with her husband Jeff Slayton, Farber's elegant sparseness was informed by a sense of human fallibility that made her message touching and direct.

Murray Louis studied with Nikolais at the Henry Street Settlement Playhouse and performed with his troupe before pursuing a choreographic career of his own. Among the most brilliant of modern dancers, he brought to his choreography the wit and precision that characterized his performances. His most admired works include *Junk Dances* (1964), a manic parody of modern life, and *Charade* (1966), a work that is closer in style to those of Nikolais, who composed the score for this solo. Phyllis Lamhut, Beverly Schmidt, and Jeff Duncan are other former Nikolais dancers who formed their own ensembles.

One of the most magnetic performers associated with José Limón was Louis Falco, who in 1967 established a company to dance his own works. Noteworthy among his creations has been *Huescape* (1968), which he performed with Jennifer Muller, another principal dancer with the Limón ensemble and herself a respected choreographer.

Expanding the boundaries of modern dance in the late 1960s and 1970s was Meredith Monk, whose iconoclastic pieces incorporated dance elements in pursuit of a larger dramatic end. Her most moving tableaux included the autobiographical *Education of the Girl Child* (1973) and *Chacon* (1974), created with her collaborator Ping Chong. Intensely personal amalgams of traditional theatrical elements, Monk's works reflected a concern for keeping modern dance infused with fresh ideas.

BIBLIOGRAPHY: John (Joseph) Martin, *The Modern Dance* (1933); Louis Horst and Carroll Russell, *Modern Dance Forms in Relation to the Other Modern Arts* (1961); Selma J. Cohen, ed., *The Modern Dance: Seven Statements of Belief* (1966); Irma Duncan, *Duncan Dancer* (1966); UNESCO, *Ten Years of Films on Ballet and Classical Dance, 1955–1965* (1968); Margaret Lloyd, *Borzoi Book of Modern Dance* (1970); Martha Graham, *The Notebooks of Martha Graham* (1973); James Klosty, *Merce Cunningham* (1975); Joseph H. Mazo, *Prime Movers: The Makers of Modern Dance in America* (1976).

George Gelles

modern period   The development of music in the 20th century has shown a radical rebellion against the long-held concepts and assumptions about the nature, structure, and function of music. As sophisticated music grew to reach a larger public through the radio and phonograph, the scope for revolutionary techniques increased. The result was a far wider range of production and the gradual acceptance of all manifestations of sound as potentially musical material.

disintegration of tonality   Mahler and Richard Strauss followed the general style and aesthetics of Wagnerian Romanticism. Grand in scale and lavish in orchestration, their works satisfied the audience's craving for emotional indulgence. This craving led to the expressionist movement in Germany; its effect on music had already been felt in Wagner's *Tristan,* in which emotional tension was conveyed by unresolved harmony and shifting chromaticism. The traditional basis of musical construction—dramatic sonata form linked with diatonic tonality—was collapsing.

Schoenberg composed his *Gurrelieder* (1901–13) in a similar style, and he explored the psychological depths of EXPRESSIONISM in *Erwartung* (1909). The complexity of his musical ideas led him to abandon traditional forms of tonality, although he spoke merely of "emancipating dissonance." Around 1913 the public began to hear his works performed, particularly the chamber cantata *Pierrot Lunaire* (1912), which vividly realized the claustrophobic atmosphere of the poems in an atonal but closely organized idiom. World War I forced him to pause and consider his ideas. By 1921 Schoenberg had evolved a method of composition in which the 12 chromatic notes acquired equal importance, arranged in serial order in both linear and vertical planes (*see* SERIALISM). Many of his masterworks, including the opera *Moses und Aron* (1932–54) and the Fourth Quartet (1936), are composed according to serial methods. Late in life he returned to a more conventional tonal organization.

Schoenberg's pupil Berg had even more affinity with expressionism. In his opera *Wozzeck* (1921) the acts are built on suite, sonata, and variation forms that grow from leitmotiv technique; intense dramatic tension is still conveyed by varying harmonic complexity, often with comparatively tonal implications. Like his teacher, Berg adopted fully serial methods but frequently retained tonal references.

It was his fellow pupil Webern who fully realized the serial revolution. In his Symphony, Op. 21 (1928), the tone-row contains internal mirror-cells, so that the number of transpositions possible is limited. The form of the work reflects this inward unity; each note has a special significance as well as harmonic and melodic meaning.

The development of serial techniques more or less halted in Europe with World War II; many musicians considered that the method was sterile—too abstract and cerebral in the case of Webern, too complex and unmemorable in that of Schoenberg.

new paths The restrained delicacy of Webern's aural imagination is also found in the work of Debussy. Although he reluctantly acknowledged the current fascination for Wagner and for large orchestras, Debussy rejected Germanic ostentation in his opera *Pelléas et Mélisande* (1902). He used a quasi-chromatic idiom, partly diatonic and modal, evoking an ambivalent, suggestive world where man is helpless against fate. Debussy discovered the music of the Javanese gamelan at the Paris Exposition of 1889 and recalled its clear sonorities and hypnotic rhythmic patterns in his later works. The ballet *Jeux* (1913), written for Diaghilev, was built from mosaic-like motives and contained the scale based on whole-tone steps, used to suggest ambiguity of mood and tonality.

Again for Diaghilev, Stravinsky used the primitive nature of Russian folk music to defy Romanticism in his ballet *Le Sacre du prin-*

temps (1913). Shocked audiences heard the symmetry of classical rhythm and romantic rubato shattered by unpredictable shifts of meter and accent. His use of melodic repetition was static and ritualistic, and this became a recurrent feature of his music, which underwent many stylistic changes as the century progressed. In the 1920s he abruptly abandoned much of his former style and became interested in reinterpreting classical forms, as in the Violin Concerto (1931).

The French had their own answer to the humorlessness of Schoenberg's school. Satie cultivated a form of musical Dadaism in which elegance and absurdity replaced content and form. Following him, the group of composers known as Les Six supported Stravinsky's neoclassical eclecticism. Stravinsky's later work might be characterized as serious and austere, as in the Symphony in Three Movements (1945) and the Mass (1948).

Bartók moved from the influence of Liszt toward the barbarism of the early Stravinsky, seeking new vitality through folk rhythms of Hungary. This vitality continued throughout his work, which grew less barbarous and more chromatic. He evolved strong formal structures, combining motivic growth with architectural arch forms (A B C B A). His six quartets (1908–39) were admired not only for the extension of string sonority and technique but for their individual idiom and formal perfection. Later works, such as the Concerto for orchestra (1943) and the Third Piano Concerto (1945), show the full range of his music but witness his return to a slightly less revolutionary style.

Hindemith by contrast attempted the evolution of new tonal principles. He used the thick textures and stable rhythms of German music, but he opposed serialism as being an arbitrary system. His sense of social responsibility led him to advocate GEBRAUCHSMUSIK ("music for use"), which would provide all instrumentalists with interesting music suited to their instruments and capabilities. He constructed a theory of harmony based on the laws of acoustics that he hoped would provide a natural extension of the tonal system. His opera *Mathis der Maler* (1938) is preoccupied with the social responsibility of the artist.

It is this social responsibility that burdened Soviet composers after the Revolution. Prokofiev and Shostakovich used neodiatonic styles, partly flavored by Russian folk song, but their experiments were often modified by government declarations that music should be immediately comprehensible and relevant to the people.

In England composers inherited a strong vocal tradition that was fundamentally opposed to the acrobatic techniques of Schoenbergian atonal melody and *Sprechstimme*. Britten and Michael Tippett concluded that true melodic beauty needed a setting with a diatonic foundation. Britten's operas, particularly *Peter Grimes* (1945), established a renaissance of the form.

rediscovery of serialism At the end of World War II, European music was dominated by Stravinsky, Bartók, and Hindemith; serialism had not made much impression on the public; and the nationalistic and folk song movements—so important at the beginning of the century in England, Scandinavia, and Hungary—had lost impetus.

After the war a new school of post-Schoenberg serialists was noticed, and again Stravinsky reflected the change. He came to accept serialism through motivic development and a consciousness of related medieval techniques that he used in the *Canticum sacrum* (1956). His serial works, such as *Threni* (1958) and *Movements* for piano and orchestra (1959), were usually based on a free approach to the row order; his musical textures became sparser. Hans Werner Henze, Roberto Gerhard, and Luigi Dallapiccola also composed significant works with serial methods.

Also significant was the rediscovery of Webern, which occurred in France. Messiaen began with a post-Impressionist style and an interest in Eastern culture even stronger than Debussy's. His *Turangalîla-Symphonie* (1948), the largest of his earlier works, is based on Oriental modes and rhythmic patterns, while the sensual harmony and scoring show much influence of Oriental immobility. Messiaen adopted Debussy's technique of mosaic form in which motives are repeated without development. His rhythmic innovations were the most influential since *Le Sacre du prin-*

temps; he created patterns like sprung rhythms in poetry by using added values on the basic beat.

After World War II Messiaen began to study Webern's approach to serialism. Searching for total musical unity, Messiaen extended serial organization beyond pitch to include rhythm, duration, and intensity; this may be seen in his *Quatre Études sur rhythme* (1949) for piano. But he was concerned with transcendent experience rather than with mathematics, and he soon combined highly serialized structure with one of his former religious metaphors—birdsong—to produce a series of works incorporating the colors and rhythms of natural birdsong (*Catalogue d'oiseaux,* 1958, for piano).

Messiaen's numerous pupils believed that total serialization would remove the arbitrariness of Schoenberg's system by uniting all musical dimensions. Pierre Boulez attempted this in his two-piano *Structures* (1955). When all compositional elements are evenly distributed by mathematics, the result is total uniformity; Boulez concluded that total serialization was an unwieldy monster and that interesting music required the decisions of the composer. In his Third Piano Sonata he introduced elements of chance (*see* ALEATORY MUSIC), and in *Le Marteau sans maître* (1955) he allowed sound-logic to determine how he serialized rhythmic and motivic cells, which evolve like crystals. In spite of its technical complexity, *Le Marteau* has a gamelan-like beauty of sound.

Like Boulez, Stockhausen discovered the paradox that perfect order is actually perceived as total disorder—because a united whole has no structural architecture, no form. Stockhausen therefore introduced other elements. In *Klavierstücke XI* (1956) he allowed the pianist to choose the sequence of musical events; indeterminacy humanizes inevitability. In *Zeitmässe* (1956) for five woodwinds the performers must often choose individual tempos. In *Gruppen* (1957) the audience is surrounded by three orchestras, which call to one another from superimposed layers of sound— again he attempted to differentiate musical space. In *Momente* (1964) Stockhausen used evocative fragments of human noises to form

525

sound patterns—abstract but with emotional associations—which introduce another element into serialized music.

music in the United States U.S. composers have been less hampered by tradition than their European contemporaries. Most experimental techniques were explored in the United States long before they appeared in Europe. Ives believed that all natural sounds are potentially music, and he expressed this through atonal, heterophonic, polytonal, even indeterminate material, as in the Fourth Symphony (1916). In his *Concord* Sonata (1909–15) he acknowledged New England philosophy, thereby bringing the metaphysical element into music many years before Messiaen. His friend Henry Cowell not only wrote music to be played inside the piano (*e.g., The Banshee,* 1925) but explained tone clusters and the proportionate relationship between pulsations of rhythm and vibrations of pitch, which were to become an element in Stockhausen's theories.

Copland was influenced by U.S. folk music and the primitive vitality of jazz; in such works as *Music for a Great City* (1964) he expressed the effect of environment in a dissonant and crushing idiom. Elliott Carter, like Copland and many other leading U.S. composers, studied under Boulanger in Paris, but he remained closer to serial techniques. He developed musical structures based on crystal formation in nature; in his Cello Sonata (1948) he evolved a practical way of controling tempo changes through METRICAL MODULATION.

The exile of many great European composers before World War II brought new influences to the United States. Schoenberg arrived in 1933 and established the serial tradition among his pupils; but because their activities were centered on the patronage of universities, the composers were often divorced from contact with the concertgoing public. Milton Babbitt, working with the private RCA electronic sound synthesizer at Princeton, said that the composer's duty is the advancement of art and that the average man cannot understand advanced art.

Edgard Varèse, like Ives, explored the relationship between musical sound and disordered noise; *Octandre* (1924) and *Arcana*

(1927) are among his best-known works. It was logical for Varèse to include electronic sounds in his *Déserts* (1954), which concerns the impact of mechanization on man. In *Poème électronique,* written for the Brussels Exhibition (1958), he extended the multidimensional nature of electronic music to include stereophonic involvement of the audience.

John Cage, like Ives, saw that a metaphysical approach to music led to indeterminacy. He rejected modern Western aesthetics and sought to make composers and performers the vessels of infinite possibilities of sound. In such works as *Music of Changes* (1951), Cage chose the notes by chance operations. His book *Silence* (1961) was in many ways more influential than his music and provided stimulating thought for others who cultivate Oriental immobility and nonevent in art—particularly such composers as Earle Brown, Morton Feldman, and Christian Wolff. Because Cage denies the artist's will, submits to chance, and takes silence as his goal, his music is closely akin to theatrical and religious ritual, as in *4'33"* (1952) in which nothing happens but the audience's expectancy.

electronic music Luigi Russolo produced his catalog *L'Arte dei rumori (The Art of Noises)* in 1916, but the search for new sounds and sound producers depended on the development of electronics. The first electronic instruments were used largely as novel additions to orchestral works. Ernst Toch and Hindemith experimented with sounds on magnetic tape, but it was not until the establishment under Pierre Schaeffer in Paris of a studio equipped to produce MUSIQUE CONCRÈTE that the electronic medium was taken seriously. *Concrète* was a method of transforming natural sound into montage. After 1950 the machines producing true synthetic sound were evolved, and Schaeffer, together with Boulez, Jean Barraqué, and Michel Phillipot, began to create ELECTRONIC MUSIC. Interest spread slowly and chiefly in the United States, where Otto Luening and Vladimir Ussachevsky were composing electronic music a year before the foundation in 1951 of the Cologne Radio Studio in Germany under the direction of Herbert Eimert and of Stockhausen. Stockhausen's *Gesang der Jünglinge* (1956) remains one of the classics of early electronic music.

There have been signs of composers trying to overcome the gap between contemporary music and alienated audiences, and between the performer and electronically produced sound, by placing the audience in the middle of the sound (Stockhausen, in *Carré,* 1960); by giving new responsibility to the performer to choose or improvise material (with the example of such performers as Cathy Berberian and David Tudor); and by encouraging musical education. The problems are many. Since Varèse and Cage any kind of sound can be used as music, and form has been declared as a meaningless concept. Consequently there are very few manifestations of sound or even of silence that cannot be regarded as music. The greatest problems here are perhaps for the critic and the historian.

BIBLIOGRAPHY: Rene Leibowitz, *Schoenberg and His School* (1949; reprint, 1975); Aaron Copland, *Music and Imagination* (1952) and *The New Music: 1900–1960,* rev. ed. (1968); Paul Henry Lang, *Problems of Modern Music* (1962), *Stravinsky: A New Appraisal of His Work* (1963), and with Nathan Broder, eds., *Contemporary Music in Europe* (1968); William Austin, *Music in the Twentieth Century* (1966); Eric Salzman, *Twentieth-Century Music* (1967); Pierre Boulez, *Boulez on Music Today* (1971); Virgil Thomson, *American Music since 1910* (1971); Leon Dallin, *Techniques of Twentieth-Century Composition,* 3rd ed. (1974); Reginald S. Brindle, *The New Music* (1975); Robert Craft, *Current Convictions: Views and Reviews* (1977); Paul Griffiths, *A Concise History of Modern Music from Debussy to Boulez* (1978); George Perle, *Serial Composition and Atonality,* 4th ed. (1978).

modes, rhythmic: *see* RHYTHMIC MODES.

modulation   A term signifying the transition in diatonic harmony from one key to another achieved by the use of chords common to both keys. In the harmonic technique of the 18th-century sonata form, modulation determines the breadth and range of expression of a movement, allowing developments of themes on different tonal planes. At the end of the 19th century it became identified with chromaticism. There are three main methods of modulation in classical harmony: diatonic, in which a pivot chord is common to two tonalities; chromatic, in which a note or notes in the pivot chord require alteration by a semitone; and enharmonic, in which the notes of the pivot chord assume different names (*e.g.,* the chord C-sharp E-sharp G-sharp changed enharmonically to D-flat F A-flat). Modulation may be transitory, as a means of giving depth to thematic development, or it may be structural. The latter type is a principal consideration in the design of a musical form. *See* CHROMATICISM; ENHARMONIC; HARMONY (methods of modulation).

Moeran, Ernest John (December 31, 1894–December 1, 1950)   An English composer whose pastoral idiom resembles that of Frederick Delius and his teacher John Ireland, Ernest John Moeran was influenced by folk song and made arrangements of tunes that he collected, chiefly from Norfolk and Suffolk. His individuality is best seen in his many solo and choral songs, which include settings of Shakespeare, Robert Herrick, A. E. Housman, James Joyce, and Seumas O'Sullivan. Among larger works are a symphony (1937), concertos for violin and cello, and several chamber works.

RECORDINGS: Rhapsody in F-sharp Major for piano and orchestra; Sinfonietta; Symphony in g minor.

Moiseiwitsch, Benno (February 22, 1890–April 9, 1963)   One of the last of the great romantic pianists, Benno Moiseiwitsch studied in his native Odessa, Ukraine, and with Leschetizky in Vienna. He made his home in England from World War I. In the early years of his career his repertoire was large (20 concertos in one season), and his playing was always distinguished by impeccable taste.

Molinara, La: *see* PAISIELLO.

Moments musicaux: *see* SCHUBERT (final years).

Monk, Thelonius: *see* JAZZ (origins and early development) and (the 1940s).

monochord   An instrument of musical science employed by ancient Greek and later theorists for measuring musical intervals. It consisted of a single string stretched over a calibrated sound box with a movable bridge. In the Middle Ages it was also developed as a musical instrument called the manichord (later clavichord) by the addition of further strings and, eventually, a keyboard mechanism for striking them.

man playing monochord
from Filippo Bonanni's Gabinetto armonico,
18th century courtesy, Dover Publications, Inc.

monody   A style of accompanied solo song in which a melody is accompanied by simple, often expressive, harmonies. It developed about 1600, particularly in Italy, as a reaction to the contrapuntal style of 16th-century vocal music forms such as the madrigal and motet. In part it was an attempt to emulate ancient Greek music. The words were considered of prime importance, and recitative-like vocal lines were accompanied by figured bass. The monodies of Giulio Caccini in *Le nuove musiche* (1602) exemplified the new ideas, which are also represented in early Italian operas and oratorios.

The term is also used, especially in Britain,

interchangeably with MONOPHONY, music consisting of only one voice, as plain-chant.

monophony   Music made up of a single melody with no accompanying parts in contrast to POLYPHONY, music in several simultaneously sounding parts, or voices. Monophony is the earliest type of music known. Gregorian and Byzantine chants and Hebrew cantillation (intoned recitation) are ancient forms of monophonic religious music. The secular music sung by medieval trouvères, troubadours, Meistersingers, and minnesingers was monophonic. Primitive music of non-Western cultures and European and American folk music are often monophonic.

The term MONODY is sometimes used synonymously with monophony, especially in Britain, but it more properly refers to a style of accompanied solo song that flourished in the early 17th century.

Monte, Philippe de (1521–July 4, 1603)   An outstanding composer of the Flemish school, Philippe de Monte was born in Mechelen. After an early period spent in Naples, he visited England in 1554–55 with the choir of Philip II of Spain, befriending the 13-year-old Byrd. He then returned to Italy. In 1568 he became court musical director to the Habsburg emperors and held this position until his death in Prague. Prolific but never perfunctory, fluent but not experimental, he excelled in subtle contrasts of register and voice grouping. His 38 masses and 319 motets stand comparison with Palestrina. He was also one of the last Flemish masters of the Italian madrigal, publishing more than 1,200 in 42 books.

Montemezzi, Italo (August 4, 1875–May 15, 1952)   The Italian composer Italo Montemezzi studied at the Milan Conservatory and established himself as an operatic composer with *Giovanni Gallurese* (Turin, 1905). His greatest success was *L'Amore dei tre re* (La Scala, 1913). Based on the play by Sem Benelli, it obtained its atmosphere of brooding tragedy from a fusion of Italian melody with French Impressionism. *La Nave* (1918), on a libretto after Gabriele d'Annunzio, was less successful. Orchestral works include *Paolo e Virginia* (1930) and *Italia mia, nulla fermerà il tuo canto* (1944), inspired by Italy's defeat in

World War II. In 1939 Montemezzi emigrated to California, returning to Italy after World War II.

RECORDING: *L'Amore dei tre re.*

Monteux, Pierre (April 4, 1875–July 1, 1964) One of the few 20th-century French conductors of international stature, Pierre Monteux was international in his repertoire as well. A master of baton technique, he achieved the normal French transparent clarity, adding grace and charm to a monumental strength.

A product of the Paris Conservatoire (first prize in violin in 1896), Monteux played viola in orchestras until his founding of the Concerts Berlioz (1910). While conductor of Sergey Diaghilev's Ballets Russes (1911–14), he led the premieres of Stravinsky's *Petrushka* and *Le Sacre du printemps,* Ravel's *Daphnis et Chloe,* and Debussy's *Jeux.* He also conducted at the Opéra, founded the Société des Concerts Populaires (1914), was at the Metropolitan Opera (1917–19), headed the Boston Symphony (1919–24), was associated with the Concertgebouw in Amsterdam (1924–34), founded and conducted the Orchestre Symphonique de Paris (1929–38), was head of the San Francisco Symphony (1936–52), and was appointed musical director of the London

Pierre Monteux
courtesy, Boston Symphony Orchestra

Symphony (1961). His son Claude Monteux had an early career as a flutist and then turned to conducting.

Monteverdi, Claudio (baptized May 15, 1567– November 29, 1643) One of the most important composers in the transition from the Renaissance to the Baroque era, Claudio Monteverdi was both a pioneer and a preservationist. He based his work on the belief that music must "move the whole man"; that is, it must express man's deepest feelings, even in the lightest songs, and that to do so it must be joined with words. Even in his earlier madrigals he demonstrated his skill in combining contrasting emotions into a satisfying unit. But he did not totally abandon the polyphony of the past, infusing it with new life and establishing the two "practices" that coexisted through the revolutionary changes of the new operatic age.

early career Monteverdi was baptized in the north Italian town of Cremona, the son of a barber-surgeon and chemist. He studied with the director of music at the Cremona Cathedral, Marcantonio Ingegneri, a well-known musician who wrote church music and madrigals of some distinction. Monteverdi was obviously a precocious pupil; he published several books of religious and secular music in his teens, all of them containing competent pieces in a manner not far from that of his master. The culmination of this early period occurred in two madrigal books published in 1587 and 1590. They are full of excellent, attractive works, somewhat more modern in approach than Ingegneri's. As yet, however, Monteverdi's aim appears to be to charm rather than to express passion, exemplified at its best in such a madrigal as the setting of "Ecco mormorar l'onde" ("Behold the Murmuring Sea") by Torquato Tasso, the greatest Italian poet of the late Renaissance.

It is not known exactly when Monteverdi left his hometown, but he entered the service of the Duke of Mantua around 1590 as a string player. He immediately came into contact with some of the finest musicians of the time. Most influential seems to have been the Flemish composer Giaches de Wert, a modernist who was still in the middle of an avant-garde movement of the 1590s. The crux of his style

529

Claudio Monteverdi
oil painting by Bernardo Strozzi (1581–1644)
courtesy, Museum Ferdinandeum, Innsbruck

1605, both of which contain masterpieces. The avant-garde manner was now better assimilated into his idiom. His aim was still to follow the meaning of the verse in great detail, but he solved the purely musical problems of thematic development and proportion.

It was the advanced musical means, especially the use of intense and prolonged dissonance, that provoked attacks by the conservatives on Monteverdi, who became a figurehead of the avant-garde group. The attacks by the Bolognese theorist Giovanni Maria Artusi in a series of pamphlets made Monteverdi the most famous composer of the age and provoked him to reply with an important aesthetic statement of his view on the nature of his art. He disclaimed the role of revolutionary, saying that he was only the follower of a tradition that had been developing for the last 50 years or more. This tradition sought to create a union of the arts, especially of words and music, so that he should not be judged simply as a composer using conventional musical devices. Moreover the artwork must be powerful enough to "move the whole man," and this again might mean the abandonment of certain conventions. On the other hand, he declared his faith in another and older tradition represented by the pure polyphony of such composers as Josquin des Prés and Palestrina. Thus there were two "practices," as he called them; and this view, which became immensely influential, was to prove the basis of the preservation of an old style in certain types of church music as opposed to a modern style in opera and cantatas, a dichotomy that can be found well into the 19th century.

If the madrigals of this time gave him a reputation well outside northern Italy, it was his first opera *Orfeo* (performed in 1607) that finally established him as a composer of large-scale music rather than of exquisite miniatures. Monteverdi may have attended some of the performances of the earliest operas, those composed by the Florentine composers Jacopo Peri and Giulio Caccini, and he certainly had written some stage music in previous years. In *Orfeo* he showed that he had a much broader conception of the new genre than did his predecessors. He combined the

was that music must exactly match the mood of the verse and that the natural declamation of the words must be carefully followed. It had an immediate effect on Monteverdi, whose next book of madrigals, published in his first year at Mantua, shows the influence, though his understanding was imperfect. It represented a complete change of direction; the melody is angular, the harmony increasingly dissonant, the mood tense to the point of neurosis.

The new style and ambience seems to have upset his productivity. Although he went on composing, he published very little for the next 11 years. In 1595 he accompanied his employer on an expedition to Hungary and four years later to Flanders. About 1599 he married a singer, Claudia Cattaneo, by whom he had three children, one of whom died in infancy. When the post of maestro di cappella to the duke became vacant on the death of Wert in 1596, Monteverdi was embittered at being passed over, but in 1602 he achieved the position at the age of 35. He published two more books of madrigals in 1603 and

opulence of dramatic entertainments of the late Renaissance with the straightforwardness of a simple pastoral tale told in recitative, which was the ideal of the Florentines. His recitative is more flexible and expressive than theirs, based on the declamatory melody of his madrigals rather than on their theories about heightened speech. Above all he had a greater gift for dramatic unity, shaping whole acts into musical units rather than assembling them from small sections. He also showed a sense of matching the climaxes in the drama by musical climaxes, using dissonance, the singer's virtuosity, and instrumental sonorities to create the sense of heightened emotion.

A few months after the production of *Orfeo*, Monteverdi suffered the loss of his wife, seemingly after a long illness. He retired in a state of depression to his father's home at Cremona, but he was summoned back to Mantua almost immediately to compose a new opera as part of the celebrations of the marriage of the heir to the duchy, Francesco Gonzaga, to Margaret of Savoy. Monteverdi returned unwillingly and was promptly submerged in a massive amount of work. He composed not only an opera but also a ballet and music for an intermezzo to a play. Further disaster occurred when the opera *L'Arianna* was in rehearsal, for the prima donna, a young girl who had been living in Monteverdi's home, possibly as a pupil of his wife, died of smallpox. Nevertheless the part was recast, and the opera was finally produced in May 1608. It was an enormous success. The score has been lost except for the famous "Lamento," which survives in various versions and is the first great operatic *scena*.

After this enormous effort Monteverdi returned again to Cremona in a condition of collapse, which seems to have lasted for a long time. He was ordered back to Mantua in November 1608 and refused to go. He eventually returned, but thereafter he hated the Gonzaga court, which he maintained had undervalued and underpaid him, though he gained a raise in pay and a small pension for his success with *L'Arianna*. He does not, however, appear to have been uncreative, though the music he wrote in the next year or so reflects his depres-

sion. He arranged the "Lamento" as a five-voiced madrigal and wrote a madrigalian threnody on the death of his prima donna, published later in the sixth book of madrigals, which represents the peak of dissonant, agonized music in this style. In a more vigorous vein he wrote some church music, which he published in 1610 in a volume containing a mass in the old style and music for vespers. The mass was a remarkable achievement, a deliberate attempt to show that the polyphonic idiom was still possible when everywhere it was dying. Still more remarkable is the vespers music, a virtual compendium of all the kinds of modern church music possible at the time—grand psalm settings in the Venetian manner, virtuoso music for solo singers, instrumental music for interludes in the service, even an attempt to use up-to-date operatic music to set the expressive, emotional words of the Magnificat. Yet, though this music is as advanced as possible, Monteverdi makes it an extension of the old tradition by using plainchant as the thematic material.

The volume containing this music was dedicated to Pope Paul V, and Monteverdi visited Rome apparently to present it in person. He may also have been seeking a new post in order to leave Mantua, but nothing came of this. Nothing is known of his life for the next two years. Then Francesco Gonzaga succeeded to the duchy on the death of his father and suddenly dismissed Monteverdi from his service in July 1612 for reasons that are unknown. Without a job Monteverdi again went back to his father's house with his two sons and remained there for about a year.

Venice   When the maestro di cappella of St. Mark's in Venice died, Monteverdi was invited to take his place after an audition of some of his music in the basilica. He finally took up his appointment in the autumn of 1613. Although Monteverdi had not been primarily a church musician, he took his duties extremely seriously and within a few years completely revitalized the music in the basilica. He hired new assistants (including two future composers of note, Francesco Cavalli and Alessandro Grandi), wrote much church music, and insisted on daily choral services. He also took an active part in music making elsewhere in the city, directing the music on several occasions for the fraternity of S. Rocco, an influential philanthropic brotherhood, on the annual festival of its patron saint.

His letters in those early years in Venice reveal a complete change in his state of mind from what it was in Mantua. He felt fulfilled and honored, well and regularly paid, and he seems to have been reasonably prolific. He kept up his links with Mantua, largely because there was little chance of producing opera in Venice, while opportunities came quite regularly from the Gonzaga court. In his correspondence a philosophy of dramatic music emerges that was not only to mold Monteverdi's later work but also to influence the history of opera in general. The older type of opera had developed, on the one hand, from the Renaissance intermezzo, a short, static musical treatment—often allegorical and with scenery—of a subject from the play with which it was given, emphasizing the wishes of the gods; and, on the other hand, from the pastoral, with its highly artificial characterizations of shepherds and shepherdesses. Monteverdi, however, was concerned with the expression of human emotions and the creation of recognizable human beings with their changes of mind and mood. Thus he wished to develop a greater variety of musical means, and in his seventh book of madrigals (1619) he experimented with many new devices. Most were borrowed from the current practices of his younger contemporaries, but all were endowed with greater power. There are the conversational "musical letters," deliberately written in a severe recitative melody in an attempt to match the words. The ballet *Tirsi e Clori*, written for Mantua in 1616, shows on the contrary a complete acceptance of the simple tunefulness of the modern aria. All this work shows an astonishing renewal for a man of about 50 years of age.

The War of the Mantuan Succession broke his link with the Gonzagas, who were ruined by the war. Monteverdi may have written an opera for performance in Venice in 1630, but the plague that broke out in that year effectively stopped all musical activities in Venice and the provinces for about 18 months. Monteverdi and his family seemed to have emerged

unscathed, and Monteverdi himself took holy orders during this period. He wrote a grand mass for the thanksgiving service in Saint Mark's when the epidemic was officially declared over in November 1631. The Gloria from it still survives and shows him applying some of the theories concerning the diversity of mood suggested by the words. Both this and some other church music probably written about this time, however, show a calm and majestic approach rather than the passion of his earlier years. A book of lighthearted songs and duets published in the following year is much the same. There is also a detached quality about much of the music in the final collection of his madrigals assembled by Monteverdi himself in 1638. A vast retrospective anthology of music dating from 1608 onward, it sets out to display Monteverdi's theories, as its title, *Madrigali guerrieri et amorosi (Madrigals of War and Love)*, denotes.

Though this collection, put together when Monteverdi was over 70, might seem the end of his career, chance played a part in inspiring him to an Indian summer of astonishing productivity: the first public opera houses opened in Venice in 1637. As the one indigenous composer with any real experience in the genre he naturally was involved with them almost from the beginning. *L'Arianna* was revived, and no fewer than four new operas were composed within about three years. Only two of them have survived in score—*Il ritorno d'Ulisse in patria (The Return of Ulysses to his Country)* and *L'incoronazione di Poppea (The Coronation of Poppea)*—both masterpieces. Although they still retain some elements of the Renaissance intermezzo and pastoral, they can be fairly described as the first modern operas. Their interest lies in revealing the development of human beings in realistic situations. There are main plots and subplots, especially in *Poppea,* allowing for a great range of characters, and the music expresses their emotions with astonishing accuracy. Monteverdi shows how the philosophy of music evolved during his early years in Venice could be put to use, using all the means available to a composer of the time—the fashionable arietta, duet, and ensemble—and how they could be combined with the expressive and less fashionable recitative of the early part of the century. The emphasis is always on the drama: the musical units are rarely self-contained but are usually woven into a continual pattern so that the music remains a means rather than an end. There is also a sense of looking toward the grand climax of the drama, and there are enough memorable melodies for the opera to seem musically attractive.

With these works Monteverdi proved himself to be one of the greatest musical dramatists of all time. That he was held in the highest esteem by his Venetian employers is shown by their gifts of money in these last years and by their granting him leave to travel to his native city in the last few months of his life. The Venetian public showed its esteem at his funeral; he was buried in the Church of the Frari, where a monument to him still remains.

BIBLIOGRAPHY: Henry Prunieres, *Monteverdi: His Life and Work* (1926; reprint, 1973); Hans F. Redlich, *Claudio Monteverdi; Life and Works* (1952); Denis Arnold, *Monteverdi* (1963), *Monteverdi Madrigals* (1969), and with Nigel Fortune, eds., *The Monteverdi Companion* (1968; reprint, 1972); Denis Stevens, *Monteverdi: Sacred, Secular, and Occasional Music* (1977).

RECORDINGS: Numerous recordings of many works.

Montoya, Carlos (b. December 13, 1903)   Influenced by his mother's playing but primarily self-taught, the Spanish gypsy flamenco guitarist Carlos Montoya was the first to legitimize that style as serious music. After performing in cafés and touring as an accompanist for singers and dancers (notably La Argentina and La Teresina), he began to play flamenco guitar recitals (from 1948). He has toured the United States, Europe, and the Orient, made many recordings, and composed music for flamenco guitar, including a Suite *flamenca* for guitar and orchestra.

Moonlight Sonata (No. 14): *see* BEETHOVEN (achievement).

Morton, Ferdinand "Jelly Roll": *see* JAZZ (origin and early development) and (orchestral style).

Moore, Douglas (Stuart) (August 10, 1893– July 25, 1969)   A student of Horatio Parker, d'Indy, and Bloch, the U.S. composer Douglas Moore wrote in a tonal, melodic idiom with clearly defined counterpoint. He composed nine operas, three of which (*The Devil and Daniel Webster,* 1938; *The Ballad of Baby Doe,* 1956; and *Carry Nation,* 1966) use American stories and indigenous music. In form, the set pieces and recitatives are reminiscent of French and Italian 19th-century opera. His songs use texts by U.S. poets, many of whom were his friends (Archibald MacLeish, Vachel Lindsay, Stephen Vincent Benét). Moore's vocal writing follows the natural line of English prosody with rhythms deriving from folk songs, ragtime, dances, hymns, and marches. These song and dance patterns are also the bases for much of the instrumental music (*The Pageant of P. T. Barnum,* 1924; *Farm Journal,* 1947). Other works of note are the symphonic poem *In Memoriam* (1943), Suite *Down East* (1944; violin with piano or orchestra), a clarinet quintet (1946), and his most extensive opera, the three-act *Giants in the Earth* (1950). Moore's writings about music include *Listening to Music* (1932; revised 1937) and *From Madrigal to Modern Music* (1942).

In 1926 Moore joined the faculty at Columbia University, where he was music department chairman from 1940 to 1962.

RECORDINGS: *The Ballad of Baby Doe; Carry Nation; The Devil and Daniel Webster; The Pageant of P. T. Barnum.*

Morales, Cristóbal de (1500?–1553)   One of the most important Spanish composers of the 16th century, Cristóbal de Morales was born in Seville and prided himself on being a native of a city with such a rich musical heritage. His first post was as maestro de capilla at the cathedral at Ávila (1526–29). After a short stay at Plasencia he joined the papal choir in Rome (1535), where he remained for 10 years, during which time he published several collections. His work and travels with the papal choir greatly advanced his fame, as it gave him the opportunity of performing his works before European rulers and other influential people. His health seems to have suffered during this period, and he returned to Spain in 1545, where he was appointed maestro de capilla at the Toledo Cathedral the same year.

He left after two years, and after a period at Marchena in the service of the Duke of Arcos he was appointed maestro de capilla at Málaga in 1551.

Morales' music is solemn and powerful, displaying both technical and expressive genius. He enjoyed remarkable fame during his lifetime, and his reputation continued to grow after his death. Apart from his numerous publications in Rome, his works were published in Antwerp, Louvain, Nürnberg, and Wittenberg during his lifetime and quickly found their way to cathedrals as far away as Cuzco in Peru. The earliest printed polyphony prepared for use in the New World was Morales' 1544 book of masses, now part of the cathedral treasure of Pueblo, Mexico. Of his 21 masses, 16 were published in Rome in 1544 under Morales' personal supervision.

He was the first Spanish composer to write Magnificats in all eight ecclesiastical modes. They were unquestionably the most popular of his works in the 16th century and were widely reprinted. Palestrina paid Morales the compliment of adding an additional *si placet* part to more than one of them. Of his many motets, two have been repeatedly singled out for mention, *Lamentabatur Jacob* and *Emendemus in melius,* both *a* 5. No less a figure than Palestrina parodied a Morales motet for his Mass *O sacrum convivium.* Among Morales' other compositions are three sets of Lamentations *a* 4, *a* 5, and *a* 6, published in 1564. There are a few hymns, settings of the Marian antiphons—*Regina coeli* and *Salve Regina*—and a setting of the Office for the Dead *a* 4. His compositions to texts other than Latin include three short Spanish pieces and an Italian madrigal *a* 4.

RECORDINGS: *Lamentations;* Magnificats; motets.

Morini, Erica (b. January 5, 1908?) A student of Otakar Ševčik, the Viennese violin prodigy Erica Morini completed the Vienna Conservatory course at the age of eight. She played with the Gewandhaus Orchestra under Arthur Nikisch in 1918. At age 16 she was the only soloist to appear with the Vienna Philharmonic during its musical festival week. Subsequent to a successful U.S. debut in 1921, she toured Europe, Australia, and the Orient. A resident of New York City, she has been soloist with nearly every major U.S. orchestra.

Morley, Thomas (1557/58–1603?) The first of the great English madrigalists, Thomas Morley held a number of church musical appointments, first as master of the children at Norwich Cathedral (1583–87), then by 1589 as organist at St. Giles, Cripplegate, in London, and by 1591 at St. Paul's Cathedral. In 1592 Morley was sworn in as a gentleman of the Chapel Royal. By 1597 he was in ill health, and his place at the Chapel Royal was filled in 1603. Since the appointment as gentleman was normally made for life, it seems likely that he died earlier that year.

It is probable that Morley became a Roman Catholic early in life, perhaps under the influence of his master Byrd, who remained a Catholic until his death. By 1591 Morley had defected, for in that year he engaged in espionage work among the English Catholics in the Netherlands. The mission nearly cost him his life, but he obtained useful information against the Catholic Party in England. Evidently Morley realized the possibilities offered by the new popularity of Italian madrigals fitted with English texts and began publishing sets of madrigals of his own composition (in 1593, 1594, 1597, and two sets in 1595). These include a considerable proportion of Italian madrigals, which Morley reworked and published with no acknowledgment of the original composers, a practice not uncommon at the time. In 1598 Morley published a volume of English versions of selected Italian madrigals; in that year he received the license to print music in England for 21 years (this monopoly, originally granted to Byrd and Tallis in 1575, had expired in 1596). In 1597 he published his textbook, *A Plaine and Easie Introduction to Practicall Musicke,* one of the most important contributions to modern knowledge of the theoretical basis of composition of Morley's own time and of earlier generations whose work was based on strict modal structure.

Morley's compositions are written in two distinct styles that many be chronologically separate. As a pupil of Byrd he was brought up in the pre-madrigalian English style of broad and strong polyphony. In 1576 he wrote two of a number of Latin motets that survive in manuscript sources; all these motets may well belong to his earlier period of presumed Catholicism. But his madrigal volumes of the 1590s employ the style of the Italian madrigal and are characterized by a direct effectiveness, gentle harmonic warmth, springy rhythms, and clarity of texture. His *First Booke of Consort Lessons* (1599), containing compositions by Morley himself and various contemporaries arranged for an instrumental sextet composed of treble and bass viols, flute, cittern, lute, and bandora, is one of the few remaining examples of music for a group of instruments commonly in use at the time. In 1601 Morley edited *The Triumphs of Oriana,* a collection of 25 madrigals by various composers in praise of Oriana, who may or may not be identified with Queen Elizabeth I. His last volume of original compositions, *The First Booke of Ayres* (1600), contains "It was a lover and his lass." Morley is not always at his best when composing for voice and lute, and the volume suggests a definite falling off in creative power. His masterpieces are the six-voice motets *Laboravi in gemitu meo* and *De profundis clamavi.*

BIBLIOGRAPHY: Thomas Morley, *A Plaine and Easie Introduction to Practicall Musicke* (1597; reprint, 1969); Edmund H. Fellowes, *The English Madrigal Composers,* 2nd ed. (1948).

RECORDINGS: *First Booke of Ayres; First Booke of Consort Lessons;* madrigals.

Moscheles, Ignaz (May 30, 1794–March 10, 1870) Perhaps the most significant pianist to bridge the transition between the Classical (Clementi school) and Romantic traditions as exemplified by Chopin, Liszt, and Sigismond Thalberg was the Bohemian Ignaz Moscheles. Educated in Prague, he was sent to Vienna to work with Johann Georg Albrechtsberger and Antonio Salieri, and in his early years he was clearly a member of the Classical school. One of the first to play Beethoven sonatas in public, he was the teacher and close friend of Mendelssohn, and he tried to adapt to the new ways. The music of Chopin, however, remained a mystery to him, although

he admitted its success when played by its composer. Moscheles did accept the music of Schumann. In 1826 he moved to London, and he conducted the first performance in England of Beethoven's *Missa solemnis* (1832). Mendelssohn invited him to become the first professor of piano at the Leipzig Conservatory in 1846, and he remained there as a most successful teacher. Moscheles was also a prolific composer.

RECORDINGS: Concertante in F for flute, oboe, and orchestra; *Grande Sonate symphonique* for two pianos; Piano Concerto in g minor; Piano *Sonate caractéristique;* piano pieces.

Moses und Aron: *see* COUNTERPOINT (modern period); MODERN PERIOD (disintegration of tonality); OPERA (the 20th century); SCHOENBERG.

Moszkowski, Moritz (August 23, 1854–March 4, 1925) A German pianist and composer of Polish descent, Moritz Moszkowski studied piano at Dresden and Berlin, where he gave his first concert in 1873. His two books of *Spanish* Dances (1876) for piano duet and later in many different arrangements were long popular as an example of national music in a light style. Other attempts with national idioms were less successful. His opera *Boabdil* (1892) was known chiefly for its ballet. He also wrote concertos and chamber music. He lived in Paris from 1897.

RECORDINGS: Piano Concerto in E Major; *Spanish* Dances; Suite No. 3 for orchestra; Violin Concerto in C Major; *Virtuoso* Études.

motet A form of vocal composition that has undergone numerous transformations through several centuries; typically it is a Latin religious unaccompanied choral composition, but it can be secular or a work for soloist(s) and instrumental accompaniment, in any language, with or without a choir.

The motet (from French *mot,* "word") originated in the early 13th century, a period later called ARS ANTIQUA, as an application by composers of the NOTRE DAME SCHOOL of a new text to older music, specifically to the wordless upper voice parts of a discant CLAUSULA. Clausulae were short sections of organum, consisting of a plainchant melody in the tenor, above which were added one, two, or three simultaneous melodies; in discant clausulae, as opposed to other organa, all the voice parts were set in short, repeated rhythmic patterns called rhythmic modes.

In forming motets from discant clausulae, two or even three parts were each given a text. Although the earliest motets were usually in Latin and intended for church use, there later arose bilingual motets (French–Latin, English–Latin) on secular and sacred texts or combinations of both. Particularly during the late 13th century the motet was secular in its added texts, which were often all in French. Tenors were sometimes chosen from French popular songs rather than from plainchant. Rhythmic patterns became freer and more varied, and the rhythmic modes fell into disuse. Instruments apparently played the lower voice parts as accompaniment to a singer's performance of the upper part, so that the motet became an accompanied solo song.

In the 14th century secular motets were largely serious in content (*e.g.,* on historical topics) and were used for ceremonial occasions. Both sacred and secular motets often used the technique of ISORHYTHM: the repetition of an often complex rhythmic pattern throughout the composition. This pattern often overlapped but did not always coincide with the repetition of a melody.

By the second half of the 15th century, motets were normally sung in all voice parts. Nearly always all parts now shared the same text; the musical texture was largely contrapuntal. Syllables and words were not always sung simultaneously in the different voice parts except in contrasting sections based on chords. The tenor melodies were largely chosen from plainchant, and sacred texts predominated.

Motets were frequently written for a particular holy day and were sung at mass between the Credo and Sanctus or at vespers in the Divine Office. Such motets were often based on plainchants associated with their texts. The music of the mass might also be founded on the same musical themes, giving the entire service a musical unity not approached in any later church music. Even when a motet was not founded on a plainchant fragment, it was

possible for a composer to design a motet and a mass setting on the same themes. Titles of 16th-century masses often indicate either the motet or the plainchant on which they are founded. Thus, the *Missa Nos autem gloriari* by the Roman composer Francesco Soriano was based on the motet *Nos autem gloriari* by Palestrina. When a motet was in two movements, or self-contained sections, the second movement usually ended with the last musical phrases and text of the first.

After about 1600 the term motet came to indicate any composition setting a serious non-liturgical but often sacred text. In the late 16th century Venetian composers such as Giovanni Gabrieli wrote motets for multiple choirs and contrasting instruments. In the 17th and 18th centuries the musical style varied from instrumentally accompanied motets for solo voice to the large choral motets of Bach, which may have been sung with instrumental accompaniment. In Lutheran Germany motets were based on the texts, and often the melodies, of chorales. In England a motet with English text for use in Anglican services was called an ANTHEM. Anthems were either for chorus (full anthems) or for soloist(s) and chorus (verse anthems). Instrumental accompaniment was common in both types. After the end of the Baroque era in the mid-18th century, the motet became a less prominent form, but motets continued to be written; *e.g.,* by Mozart in the 18th century, Brahms in the 19th century, and in the 20th century by Ernst Pepping, Hugo Distler, and Poulenc.

Mother Goose: *see* RAVEL.

Mother of Us All, The: *see* OPERA (the 20th century); THOMSON.

Mottl, Felix (August 24, 1856–July 2, 1911) A student of Bruckner at the Vienna Conservatory, the Austrian conductor and composer Felix Mottl was a noted Wagnerian whose career began at the Academical Richard Wagner Society in Vienna. In 1876 he was stage conductor for performances of *Der Ring des Nibelungen* at Bayreuth and served as chief conductor there in 1886. At the recommendation of his teacher, Felix Otto Dessoff, Mottl was conductor of the opera house at Karlsruhe (1880–1903), where he produced all the operas of Wagner and Berlioz. He was also conductor of the Philharmonic Society there until 1892. His English career included many concert performances of Wagner and a *Ring* cycle at Covent Garden in 1898. He conducted at the Metropolitan Opera (remaining for only one season, 1903–04), where he produced Mozart's *Die Zauberflöte* for the first time in German. He became general music director in Munich in 1903 and director of the Munich Opera in 1907. Mottl wrote three operas and many songs; he edited music of Bach and Berlioz and orchestrated music of Wagner and Liszt.

mouth organ: *see* CHINESE MUSIC (musical practice); HARMONICA; JAPANESE MUSIC (Heian period) and (notation).

Mouton, Jean (*c.* 1470–October 30, 1522) A French composer known for his sacred music, Jean Mouton was a chorister in Nesle from 1477 to 1483 and worked in Amiens and Grenoble from 1500 to 1502 before joining the French Chapel Royal. He died in St. Quentin. Mouton apparently studied with Josquin des Prés and taught Adriaan Willaert. A book of five masses *a* 4 (printed by Petrucci in 1508) was an early example of a single book devoted to one composer. Mouton's known printed works include nine masses, about 75 motets and psalms, and a few chansons. A master of counterpoint, he excelled especially in canon.

RECORDINGS: *Missa Alleluia.*

movement One of a number of separate, comparatively independent divisions (usually in the same or related keys) that comprise a larger work such as a symphony, sonata, or suite.

Movements: *see* MODERN PERIOD (rediscovery of serialism); STRAVINSKY.

Mozarabic chant The music and text of the Mozarabic, Hispanic, or Visigothic liturgy that formed the eucharistic rite of Spanish Christians before the 11th century. The term Mozarabic is derived from *musta'rib,* the Arabic name for Christians who lived in Aragon, Castile, León, and other parts of Spain under Moorish rule (711–1085). The music of the Mozarabic church dates, however, from before the Moorish invasion. A Mozarabic *Pater noster,* the oldest liturgical Latin hymn with a refrain, is believed to date from the 4th century, and the form of the Mozarabic liturgy had been defined between the 5th and 7th centuries by the bishops of Seville, Toledo, and Saragossa. Though most of the music of the Mozarabic church is preserved, the notation—even when the manuscripts were copied by a later hand—is in neumes of a type with Eastern and Byzantine elements that remain indecipherable. The Mozarabic *Pater noster* is known from a copy in a Visigothic hymnal of the 9th or 10th century in diastematic notation; *i.e.,* the neumes are arranged around an imaginary horizontal line. In Aragon, Castile, and León the Mozarabic chant survived until the second half of the 11th century, when the *Lex romana* was introduced in an attempt to unify the chant and liturgy of European churches. The Mozarabic chant was, however, retained in some monasteries and in the six old parishes of Toledo. Unfortunately, though the diastematic notation was at this time spreading rapidly, the musicians of Toledo did not transcribe their chant into the new notation, and the bulk of the music became indecipherable. In the 16th century an attempt was made by Francisco Cardinal Jiménez de Cisneros to revive the Mozarabic liturgy at Toledo, but even then the key to the ancient melodies had been lost. Only the recitative sections of the sung mass, preserved by oral tradition, survived.

BIBLIOGRAPHY: Dom Anselm Hughes, ed., *Early Medieval Music up to 1300* (1954), Vol. 2 of *The New Oxford History of Music.*

Mozart, Wolfgang Amadeus (January 27, 1756–December 5, 1791) Regarded by many as the greatest musical genius of all time, Wolfgang Amadeus Mozart was one of the world's three or four leading operatic composers and one of the central figures of the Viennese Classical school.

early life Mozart was born in Salzburg. His parents were Leopold Mozart, composer and vice Kapellmeister to the Archbishop of Salzburg, and his wife, Anna Maria, *née* Pertl, daughter of an official from St. Gilgen. Of their seven children only two survived: a daughter, Maria Anna (known as Nannerl),

Wolfgang Amadeus Mozart
unfinished oil portrait by Joseph Lange, 1789
courtesy, Internationale Stiftung Mozarteum,
Salzburg, Austria

born in 1751, and Wolfgang, who was christened Joannes Chrysostomus Wolfgangus Theophilus (in German, Gottlieb, in Latin, Amadeus; later Mozart generally signed his letters and compositions "W. A. Mozart" or "Wolfgang Amadé Mozart"). Both children showed profound musical talent and were taught music by Leopold, who was not only a well-known violinist and composer but the author of a celebrated theoretical treatise, *Versuch einer gründlichen Violinschule,* published at Augsburg the year of Wolfgang's birth and in numerous editions in various languages until long after its author's death.

At the age of five Wolfgang was beginning to compose minuets and other pieces—a sufficient number of them have been preserved to show his immediate grasp of musical forms—and he soon became proficient both on the harpsichord and on the violin. By the end of the 1770s he was gradually to abandon any public performances on the violin and

concentrate on the piano, one of its foremost virtuosos.

Leopold considered that his children's talents might be better displayed and put to more profitable use than in provincial Salzburg, and he therefore began a series of journeys throughout Europe in which Nannerl and Wolfgang played separately and together. The first tours in 1762 included Munich (for the elector), Vienna (where Wolfgang had an unprecedented success at the imperial court), Pressburg, Vienna, and back to Salzburg.

The first grand European tour lasted from June 1763 to November 1766 and included the principal towns of southern Germany, the Rhineland, Brussels, and Paris (for the first winter, 1763–64, where Wolfgang published his first compositions, four violin sonatas K.6–9 in Köchel's catalog of 626 items), followed by a year and a half in London. There Johann Christian Bach became a friend of the family, and in London Mozart wrote his first symphonies (K.16, 19) under the influence of J. C. Bach and his colleague Karl Friedrich Abel; the J. C. Bach influence was a vital one, lasting for many years. The Mozarts spent the winter of 1765–66 in Holland and then returned to Austria via Brussels, Paris, Geneva, Berne, and Munich.

The family left Salzburg for a second trip to Vienna in September 1767 and returned in January 1769. In Vienna Wolfgang composed his first German operetta, *Bastien und Bastienne,* K.50, and his first Italian opera, *La finta semplice,* K.51 on a libretto by Marco Coltellini, who also provided books for Gluck and Haydn. Although the Italian opera was ordered by the emperor, intrigues prevented its being produced. This is the beginning of a sorry tale of such resistance not only to Mozart but also to Haydn, whose opera *La vera constanza* (composed 1776, produced 1779), commissioned by the court opera, was withdrawn by the composer in the face of strong opposition from the Italian party, led (more or less openly) by the composer Antonio Salieri. For the consecration of the Waisenhäus (Orphanage) Church in 1768 Wolfgang composed a new mass (recently identified as K.139 in c minor) and other works, which he conducted before the emperor and the court. On his return to Salzburg the benevolent Archbishop Sigismund von Schrattenbach, always a friend and patron of the Mozart family, had the rejected *La finta semplice* performed in the archiepiscopal palace and made Wolfgang his *Konzertmeister* (without salary, since Wolfgang was hardly ever in Salzburg).

The first Italian tour, which lasted from December 1769 to March 1771, included Rovereto, Verona, Milan, Parma, Bologna, Florence, Rome, and Naples. On their return Leopold and Wolfgang spent three months in Bologna, where Wolfgang studied counterpoint with Giovanni Battista Martini, and more than an equal period at Milan, where he executed a commission for a new opera, *Mitridate, rè di Ponto,* K.87, which was first produced at the Teatro Reggio Ducal in December 1770 with a large orchestra (14 first and 14 second violins; in all about 60 players) and repeated 20 times with enormous success. In March 1771 they were at Padua, where Wolfgang was asked to write a new oratorio, *La Betulia liberata,* K.118, "which he can do at his leisure."

On the second Italian journey, which lasted from August to December 1771, Wolfgang went to Milan to compose and produce a dramatic serenata, *Ascanio in Alba,* K.111, commissioned by the empress Maria Theresa for the marriage of her son Archduke Ferdinand to Princess Maria Beatrice d'Este of Modena. He composed the whole score in four weeks, and it was performed with such success in October 1771 that Leopold wrote that "Wolfgang's serenata has killed Hasse's opera," which had been performed the day before.

On his third Italian journey, from October 1772 to March 1773, Mozart returned to Milan to execute the new commission for the Teatro Reggio Ducal, *Lucio Silla,* K.135, an opera seria first performed in December 1772. Two weeks later Leopold could write, "Thank God, the opera is an extraordinary success, and every day the theater is surprisingly full"; the opera ran for about 20 performances. *Lucio Silla* is a significant milestone in Mozart's stylistic development; it is full of felicitous details, and the orchestration is particularly full and rich. Meanwhile Archbishop Schrattenbach had died, to be succeeded by Hierony-

mus, Count Colloredo, Bishop of Gurk, with whom the Mozarts never had the same friendly relations that they had enjoyed with his predecessor. For the new archbishop's installation in April 1772, Mozart composed the festival opera *Il sogno di Scipione,* K.126. While at Milan he wrote the motet *Exsultate, jubilate,* K.165, for the celebrated castrato Rauzzini, one of the singers in *Lucio Silla.*

The Mozarts visited Vienna again from July to September 1773. Father and son hoped to secure an appointment for the latter at the imperial court—but to no avail. In Vienna, however, Mozart came under the profound influence of Haydn's music, whose style—in common with that of many Austrian composers of the early 1770s (*e.g.,* Florian Leopold Gassmann, Carlos Ordoñez, J. B. Vanhal)—had undergone a radical change. From light-hearted rococo music the new Haydn style now swerved abruptly to the *Sturm und Drang.* The Austrian musical revolution preceded that in German literature by some years, and the *Sturm und Drang* style began with Haydn as early as *c.* 1767–68.

Mozart composed six string quartets (K.168–173) under the shadow of Haydn's Opus 20 quartets of 1772; and Mozart's stormy Symphony in g minor, K.183, is a typical and excellently composed product of the restless Viennese symphonic style of this period—even the use of four, rather than two, horns is characteristic (see Vanhal's Sinfonia in g minor and Haydn's Symphony No. 39 in g minor for two obvious precursors in the field). For the remainder of 1773 and almost all of 1774, the family remained at Salzburg, Wolfgang diligently composing. Perhaps his best known compositions of this interlude are the Bassoon Concerto in B-flat Major, K.191, and four symphonies (K.199–202), of which the A Major, K.201, is the most popular.

Leopold and Wolfgang went to Munich from December 1774 to March 1775, where Wolfgang carried out a commission for an opera buffa, *La finta giardiniera,* K.196. The day after its performance in January 1775 at the Residenz-Theater, Wolfgang writes: "Thank God! My opera was performed yesterday, the 13th, for the first time, and was such a success that it is impossible for me to describe the applause . . . the whole theater was . . . packed." If Mozart hoped to enter the elector's service, nothing came of the plan, and he returned to Salzburg, where he remained until 1777. A very large quantity of music was composed, including the opera *Il rè pastore,* K.208, an attractive and sophisticated piece on a rather over-used libretto by Pietro Metastasio; several masses, in which Wolfgang attempted to create a popular, folklike mass— of these the brilliant Mass in C Major *(Credo Mass),* K.257, is particularly successful; the five famous violin concertos (K.207, 211, 216, 218, 219); various serenades and divertimenti, foremost among them the enchanting *Serenata notturna,* K.239, for strings and kettledrums, and the grand and lengthy Serenade in D Major *(Haffner* Serenade, out of which Mozart later created a symphony, adding kettledrums and making some other alterations), which has curiously escaped attention and has not even a Köchel number. Mozart also wrote several works for the piano, an instrument that was gradually assuming great importance in his artistic world (six sonatas for Baron Dürnitz, K.279–284; the Triple Concerto, K.242; two concertos, K.238, 246; etc.).

Mozart's relations with Archbishop Colloredo became increasingly strained, and sometime in August 1777 (the document is undated) the composer applied for discharge from his duties. On August 28 the archbishop dictated his reply, that "father and son have permission to seek their fortune elsewhere, according to the Gospel"; however, the final break between Mozart and the archbishop did not occur until 1781.

In September 1777 Mozart and his mother left Leopold behind and started on a long journey through Germany to Paris, where Wolfgang hoped to find some permanent appointment. They went to Munich, then to Mannheim, where Mozart fell in love with Aloysia, second daughter of the prompter and copyist Fridolin Weber. Aloysia had an exceptionally well trained coloratura soprano voice, and Mozart entertained the idea of going with her to Italy, but his father sternly forbade it. In Paris Mozart did not really gain any foothold, and in July 1778 his mother died. He slowly returned home, arriving at Salzburg

in the middle of January 1779. When on his return journey he stayed with the Webers, who had meanwhile moved to Munich, Aloysia scarcely seemed to recognize him ("Today," writes Mozart, "I can only weep . . ."). Of the various compositions written on this trip, the best known are the six violin sonatas (K.301–306), to which should be added a seventh (K.296), some piano sonatas (including the famous a minor, K.310), the music to *Les Petits riens* (a ballet by Jean-Georges Noverre, written in Paris), and three symphonic works for Joseph Legros of the Concert Spirituel, of which only one—the Symphony No. 31 in D Major *(Paris* Symphony), K.297—has survived in its authentic and original state. Meanwhile various court musicians had died at Salzburg, and Mozart applied in January 1779 for the position of court organist. His request was granted. The whole of 1779 and most of 1780 were spent in Salzburg, where Mozart's music enters its first period of consistent greatness. This new maturity, with dark-hued undertones that were to assume an ever-increasing importance in his style, is found in everything Mozart composed—the series of church music (particularly the two great C Major masses, the *Coronation* Mass, K.317, and the solemn and grandiose *Missa solemnis* in C Major, K.337); the dramatic and extremely modern music to *Thamos, König in Ägypten,* K.345; two symphonies, of which the Symphony No. 34 in C Major, K.338, is outstanding among Austrian symphonies of that time; the celebrated Sinfonia concertante in E-flat Major for violin, viola and orchestra, K.364; and his greatest and most profound Serenade in D Major *(Post Horn* Serenade, K.320, which Mozart later shortened and adapted into a symphony like that fashioned from the *Haffner* Serenade.

While in Salzburg Mozart, through friends at Munich, received a commission to compose a new opera seria, *Idomeneo,* K.366 (and the ballet music K.367). He went to Munich early in November 1780, and in January the new opera was most enthusiastically received; the archbishop being in Vienna at that time, Leopold and Nannerl came to Munich to witness Wolfgang's new triumph. For *Idomeneo* was the first stage work that revealed Mozart at the summit of his powers; although it is cast in the antiquated form of an opera seria, the music is so profound, so brilliantly composed, and so astonishingly orchestrated, that it retains its dramatic impact despite the stereotyped libretto by the Salzburg court chaplain Abbate Varesco. Of other compositions written in Munich, the Kyrie in d minor, K.341, and the exquisite Serenade in B-flat Major, K.361, for 13 wind instruments are outstanding—the latter showing an entirely new and original treatment of the wind band as a whole and the clarinet family (including basset horn) in particular. Mozart always preserved a special affection and aptitude for the clarinet, whose beauty had been scarcely realized by his precursors (Haydn, for example, had hardly used it since a few wind-band works of *c.* 1760).

Early in March 1781 the archbishop summoned Mozart to Vienna. Mozart enjoyed the patronage of many members of the Viennese aristocracy, including Countess Thun and Count Cobenzl, and the archbishop enjoyed the reflected glory of his young composer; but Colloredo did not allow him to play in houses other than his own and forced him to eat with the servants. The already strained relations between the two soon came to a head; in a shameful scene the Prince-Archbishop of Salzburg addressed Mozart in the language of the street (using the third person singular reserved for low-grade servants), and Mozart resigned. Shortly afterward, not having received his official dismissal, Mozart brought it in person, only to be subjected to more street language from the archbishop's high steward, who actually kicked Mozart out "on his behind" (Mozart's own words).

later life   Mozart was now entirely on his own, the first composer after Handel who risked an existence without some official patronage. After years of waiting Emperor Joseph II finally engaged him in December 1787 as chamber composer at 800 gulden annually (Gluck, his predecessor, had received 2,000 gulden). At the beginning of 1781, however, Mozart's prospects—despite Leopold's dismayed reactions from Salzburg—seemed favorable. Apart from his success at various concerts, at which the emperor also applauded,

Mozart soon received a commission to write a German opera for the National Singspiel, founded by the emperor in 1778. This work, *Die Entführung aus dem Serail (The Abduction from the Seraglio),* on a libretto by Gottlieb Stephanie, the younger, after Christoph Friedrich Bretzner, was produced with great success in July 1782, though a strong cabal had already aligned itself against Mozart. Meanwhile he had moved in with the Webers, who had come to Vienna from Munich, and he fell in love with the third daughter, Constanze. Despite Leopold's strenuous protests Mozart married Constanze at St. Stephen's Cathedral on August 4, 1782. There has been a great deal of criticism about Constanze— that she was fickle, a bad manager of finances, and so on—but they were very fond of each other, and Mozart wrote her affectionate letters all his life. The considered opinion of the 19th-century Austrian scholar C. F. Pohl was that "she was a good and loving wife, accommodated herself in everything to her husband's disposition, and restrained him from many heedless actions."

Mozart soon came to hold his own subscription concerts, either at the Burgtheater or the Mehlgrube, which consisted of a full orchestra with one or more vocal soloists and Mozart himself playing his own concertos for piano and improvising on that instrument; his improvisations were much admired. It was for these concerts that Mozart wrote most of his great piano concertos from K.413 to K.595. Some of his improvisations may possibly be gathered from such a work as the Fantasy in c minor, K.475. Mozart was not only a great pianist but was profoundly interested in the mechanical aspects and construction of the piano, to the development and perfection of which he contributed a great deal.

Despite an intense activity as a pianist, Mozart's finances were never very secure. He perhaps reached the apex of his worldly gains shortly before he composed *Figaro* and was living in comfortable quarters at the Domgasse behind St. Stephen's. Gradually from 1785 to 1791 his financial situation became more and more catastrophic, and he was forced to borrow ever-increasing sums from his friends and particularly his Masonic brothers—Mozart was an ardent Freemason and a member of the Lodge "Zur gekrönten Hoffnung." It was from his fellow Mason, the banker Michael Puchberg, that Mozart borrowed most freely. The ever-present threat of these debts hung over Mozart's until his death.

Wolfgang and Constanze visited Leopold and Nannerl in Salzburg in August to October of 1783; the visit was not a success, and Constanze was not much liked by the Salzburg Mozarts. Mozart performed the Kyrie and Gloria of his great (unfinished) Mass in c minor, K.427, in St. Peter's in August 1783; although a torso, the mass is a noble work, showing Mozart's renewed study of Bach and Handel at the Sunday concerts of Baron Gottfried van Swieten, director of the National Library in Vienna, who was later to be closely connected with Haydn and to become a patron of the young Beethoven.

Mozart had little time in the last 10 years of his life to compose symphonies, but those he did manage to write are all masterpieces: the *Haffner,* K.385, reduced from another serenade for that Salzburg family; the *Linz,* K.425, composed on the way back from Salzburg to Vienna in October and November 1783; the *Prague,* K.504, written for the Bohemian capital; and the last three (E-flat Major, g minor, and *Jupiter* in C Major of 1788, K.543, 550, 551). The last four in particular carry the art of the 18th-century symphony far beyond anything hitherto achieved except in a few of Haydn's works.

Leopold returned the visit to his son and daughter-in-law from February to April 1785 and was witness to his son's material and artistic successes. Mozart was in the process of completing the six quartets dedicated to Haydn (K.387, 421, 428, 458, 464, 465), and when the last three were played to Haydn in Mozart's flat, Haydn said to Leopold: "Before God and as an honest man I tell you that your son is the greatest composer known to me either in person or by name." The quartets also show Mozart to have mastered the form in a way far superior to anyone except Haydn; the ensuing works, particularly K.499 in D Major, but even the more superficial *Prussian* quartets for Berlin, show his complete grasp of this central form of chamber music. His quartets indeed are perhaps only surpassed in quality by the string quintets (of which the C Major and g minor, K.515 and 516, are the most popular, though a lesser known one in D Major, K.593, is equally fine).

The great operas that were composed after *Die Entführung* in these last 10 years are as follows: *Le nozze di Figaro,* K.492, the first of three masterpieces written on librettos by Lorenzo da Ponte, first performed with enormous success in May 1786 at the Burgtheater in Vienna and later repeated with even more approbation at Prague; *Don Giovanni,* K.527, again on a libretto by da Ponte, first played at the National Theater, Prague, in October 1787 with sensational success (but when repeated at Vienna the next year, it was a failure, although a few—among them Haydn—violently defended it); *Così fan tutte,* K.588, the last da Ponte opera, produced at the Vienna Burgtheater in January 1790, was not entirely successful partly because of the death of Emperor Joseph II, throwing Vienna into some confusion; but *Così* was perhaps too richly scored, too cynical, too erotic, and too overpoweringly intense for the easygoing Viennese, who were amused by *Figaro* but less enchanted by its political undertones; *La clemenza di Tito,* K.621, an opera seria on a libretto by Metastasio, was commissioned by the Estates of Bohemia for the coronation of Emperor Leopold II at Prague in 1791; it was given there on September 6 but was badly sabotaged by the court in general and the empress in particular, who referred to it as a *porcheria tedesca* ("German muck"). *Die Zauberflöte* (*The Magic Flute;* libretto by Emanuel Schikaneder), K.620, was written for the little Theater auf der Wieden and made Schikaneder wealthy and famous. The first performance took place on September 30, 1791, and, while the initial reception was rather cool, audiences soon took to its fairy-tale machine comedy world, with its strong Masonic elements, the whole made immortal by Mozart's fantastic music. (Beethoven was to admire it particularly because, he said, in it Mozart wrote in every kind of form; it is certainly true that in *Die Zauberflöte* we find everything from north German *Choral-Vorspiel* to fugue, and from coloratura aria to *Volkslied.*)

In another attempt to save his failing finances, Mozart undertook an extensive concert tour, leaving Vienna in April 1789 with his pupil and noble patron, Prince Karl Lichnowsky, who was later to be a firm supporter of Beethoven. Mozart went to Dresden, Leipzig (where he studied Bach's manuscripts), Berlin, and Prague, returning to Vienna in June 1789; the financial results of the tour were negligible, as were those from his last concert tour to Frankfurt am Main, where Emperor Leopold II was crowned in October 1790. His financial position was now catastrophic, for he was deeply in debt.

In the summer of 1791 a stranger commissioned the Requiem Mass, K.626, from Mozart under rather mysterious circumstances; in fact the man behind it was Count Franz von Walsegg, an amateur musician who ordered works from professional composers and performed them under his own name. Mozart was not able to complete the Requiem, but from oral instructions and sketches (some have come to light as late as 1960), his pupil Franz Xavier Süssmayr was able to finish the work and present it to Walsegg.

Mozart became seriously ill in the late autumn of 1791, and his rapid decline and death soon led people to whisper that he had been poisoned. But in the mid-20th century the medical research of Carl Bär showed that Mozart's heart had been strained by his youthful attacks of rheumatic fever and that his final attack of that same fever in December 1791, plus excessive bloodletting, contributed to the failure of his heart. He died in Vienna and was buried, unattended by anyone except the gravedigger, at St. Mark's Cemetery. Constanze was left brokenhearted and in a state of nervous collapse with hugh debts. She later married the Danish diplomat Georg Nicolaus von Nissen and died in Salzburg in 1842.

assessment Because most of Mozart's major works were not printed until after his death—and some not until the middle and end of the 19th century—Mozart did not create a school. Although his operas were widely circulated all over Germany by 1795, it was many years before his work *in toto* was known to the average European musician; London in 1795, for instance, knew hardly anything of Mozart's music. During the Romantic age Mozart became the object of a veneration such as has hardly ever been accorded to any other musician except—later—Bach and Beethoven; and even today the sheer beauty, perfection, and profundity of his music continue to astonish and delight us. If Mozart wrote with staggering ability in every single form—including even dance music—perhaps his greatest single achievement is in the characterization of his operatic figures. They are not only subtle and very human but are also capable of changing as the course of the drama unfolds. After Mozart perhaps only Verdi ever succeeded in creating such vital operatic personalities. Altogether it is possible that in Mozart the music of Western civilization reached an apex of perfection to which future ages will look back just as for centuries men regarded with nostalgia the products of ancient Greece at the summit of its achievements.

Köchel catalog The Köchel catalog forms the basic list of the works of Mozart. The compositions of Mozart are almost always identified by the letter K. followed by an Arabic numeral, which indicates the chronological order in which the work was composed.

Ludwig Ritter von Köchel is best remembered for the monumental *Chronologisch-thematisches Verzeichnis,* a thematic catalog that lists in chronological order of composition all the works of Mozart. Mozart did not always date his compositions; as a result, there was confusion as to the order and period of his works. It was to the task of bringing order out of chaos that Köchel set himself.

The Köchel catalog was published by Breitkopf and Härtel in 1862 and appeared in six editions. The third and definitive revision of the catalog is Alfred Einstein's (1937); he assigned new numbers of more accurate chronology. This revision in turn was supplemented by its author, and in 1947 these supplements appeared as an appendix to the 1937 revision.

BIBLIOGRAPHY: Alfred Einstein, *Mozart: His Character, His Work,* 2nd ed. (1956); Edward Joseph Dent, *Mozart's Operas: A Critical Study,* 2nd ed. (1960); Paul Henry Lang, ed., *The Creative World of Mozart* (1963); Otto Erich Deutsch, *Mozart, a Docu-*

mentary *Biography* (1965); H. C. Robbins Landon and Donald Mitchell, eds., *The Mozart Companion,* 2nd ed. (1965); Emily Anderson, ed., *Letters of Mozart and His Family,* 2nd ed. (1966).

RECORDINGS: Numerous recordings of many works.

Muck, Karl (October 22, 1859–March 3, 1940) Though born in the middle of the Romantic movement, the German conductor Karl Muck was one of the founders of the modern school (together with Felix Weingartner, Richard Strauss, and Toscanini). Educated at Heidelberg (Ph.D. in philology, 1880), he studied at the Leipzig Conservatory and made his debut as a pianist. He began conducting (1884) in minor opera houses and worked his way up to the Berlin Opera (1892–1912; conducting 1,071 performances of 103 operas), Bayreuth (1901–31; with Wagner's *Parsifal* his specialty), the Boston Symphony (1906–08 and 1912–18), and the Hamburg Philharmonic (1922–33). As a result of anti-German hysteria in the United States during World War I, he was interned for six months in 1918 and then deported. Known as an efficient disciplinarian who was intensely dedicated to the musical text, Muck especially liked Bruckner and Mahler, but he performed all schools, including avant-garde works with which he had little sympathy.

Muffat, Georg (*c.* 1645–February 23, 1704) Of Scottish extraction, the German organist and composer Georg Muffat studied for six years in Paris. He was appointed organist at Strasbourg and at Salzburg and later visited Vienna and Rome. In 1682 he published *Armonico tributo,* a set of five-part sonatas, and *Apparatus musico-organisticus* was published in Augsburg in 1690, in which year he went to Passau as organist, becoming Kapellmeister to the bishop in 1695. His most famous work, 12 orchestral suites, *Florilegia,* appeared in two sets (Augsburg, 1695, and Passau, 1698). These works and their prefaces contain valuable information concerning the late 17th-century French style of performance. In 1701 Muffat published a set of concerti grossi under the title of *Auserlesene mit Ernst und Lust gemengter Instrumental-Musik,* in which

he paid an early tribute to the new Italian style.

His son Gottlieb (1690–1770) was a pupil of Johann Joseph Fux in Vienna, becoming organist to the emperor in 1717. His two most important works were *Versetten oder Fugen* for organ (Vienna, 1726) and *Componiment musicali* (*c.* 1739), from which Handel borrowed heavily.

BIBLIOGRAPHY: Oliver Strunk, *Source Readings in Music History* (1950).

RECORDINGS: *Apparatus musico-organisticus;* Concerti Grossi (12).

Mühlfeld, Richard (February 28, 1856–June 1, 1907) Trained as a violinist and self-taught on the clarinet, the German clarinetist Richard Mühlfeld was for most of his life associated with the Grand Ducal Orchestra of Meiningen (Germany) as violinist, first clarinetist, and associate conductor. He performed at Bayreuth (1884–96) and played chamber music in England after 1892. Brahms wrote his Clarinet Quintet, Op. 115, and his two Clarinet Sonatas, Op. 120, for Mühlfeld.

Munch, Charles (September 26, 1891–November 6, 1968) The eminent French conductor Charles Munch was trained as a violinist in his native Strasbourg (and later in Paris and Berlin) and served as concertmaster of the Strasbourg Orchestra (1919–26) and of the Gewandhaus Orchestra in Leipzig (1926–32). He made his conducting debut in 1932 in Paris and founded the Paris Philharmonic in 1935, heading it until his appointment to the Paris Conservatoire Orchestra (1938–47). In 1949 he succeeded Serge Koussevitzky at the Boston Symphony, where he led 39 world premieres and 17 first U.S. performances. From 1951 he also directed the Berkshire Festival at Tanglewood, leaving both positions in 1962 to found the Orchestre de Paris. Always a specialist in French works, he devoted his last years almost exclusively to them. His autobiography was translated into English as *I Am a Conductor* (1955).

Münchinger, Karl (b. May 29, 1915) Founder and director of the Stuttgart Chamber Orchestra, the German conductor Karl Münchinger toured with this group in Europe, South Africa, and the Far East. After study in Stuttgart and Leipzig, he made his U.S. debut with the San Francisco Symphony in 1953. In 1966 he founded the Klassische Philharmonie in Stuttgart. He has recorded much of Bach, including oratorios, orchestral suites, and the *Brandenburg* Concertos, and music of Corelli and Pergolesi.

Munrow, David (John) (August 12, 1942–May 15, 1976)   Founder (1967) and director of the Early Music Consort of London, the English musicologist, composer, and recorder player David Munrow played bassoon in the Royal Shakespeare Theatre wind band. While teaching with a volunteer corps in Peru, he became interested in primitive instruments, which led to the investigation of instruments of the Middle Ages. In 1967 he lectured at Leicester University. He wrote and arranged music for the BBC, including more than 500 television programs *(Henry VIII and His Six Wives; Elizabeth R.)*. Credits include period music for Ken Russell's *The Devils* (1971) and Vincent Malle's *La Course en tête* (1974). He recorded much music of the Middle Ages and the Renaissance.

Muris, Jean de (*c.* 1290–*c.* 1351)   The French philosopher and mathematician Jean de Muris was born in Normandy. His musical treatise *Ars novae musicae* (1319) demonstrates his enthusiasm for the great changes in musical style and notation generally associated with Philippe de Vitry and the ars nova. An attack on these changes known as *Speculum musicae* was mistakenly attributed to Jean de Muris, but its true author is now known to be Jacques de Liège. Muris knew many of the great composers of his day, especially Vitry, with whom he exchanged letters. His treatise is much concerned with medieval ideas of numerical perfection based on multiples of three, and his defense of notational improvements relies to a considerable extent on mathematical reasoning.

BIBLIOGRAPHY: Oliver Strunk, *Source Readings in Music History* (1950).

musette   A small bagpipe that was fashionable in French court circles in the 17th and 18th centuries; also a musical composition.

The bagpipe was bellows-blown with a small, cylindrical double-reed chanter beside which the instrument maker Jean Hotteterre (*c.* 1650) placed a short stopped chanter with six keys giving notes above the main chanter compass. It employed a shuttle drone: a short cylinder with about 12 narrow channels variously connected in series to supply four drones, each sounded with a double reed and tuned or silenced by slider keys moving in the slots through which the bores vented to the exterior. The bag was typically covered with silk or velvet; the pipes were of ivory.

As a composition the musette is a slow, pastoral dance with delicate figurations played over a pedal bass, or drone. It was originally played on the musette accompanied by the *vielle à roue* (hurdy-gurdy) and later on other instruments. Well-known examples are found in Bach's *English* Suites (Nos. 3 and 6) and in Mozart's *Bastien et Bastienne.*

Musgrave, Thea (b. May 27, 1928)   A student of Mary Grierson at Edinburgh University and of Boulanger in Paris, the Scottish composer Thea Musgrave lectured (1959–65) at the University of London and since 1970 has taught at the University of California at Santa Barbara. Increasingly a dramatic composer, her operas include *The Abbot of Drimock* (1962), *The Decision* (1967), *The Voice of Ariadne* (Aldeburgh, 1974), and *Mary, Queen of Scots* (Edinburgh, 1977). Her instrumental music, too, has a dramatic element. In the Clarinet Concerto (1968) the soloist moves around the stage, joining groups of players in opposition to the conductor; in her Horn Concerto (1971) the horn section moves, answering the soloist. Her output includes much chamber music, and the horn holds special interest: in addition to the concerto there is *Music for Horn and Piano* (1967), *Night Music* for two horns and orchestra (1969), and in *Mary, Queen of Scots* Musgrave specified a new horn fingering that made possible a quarter-tone passage at the end of the first act. Other works include a ballet, choral works, and *Soliloquy* (1969) for guitar and tape.

RECORDINGS: Chamber Concerto No. 2; Clarinet Concerto; Concerto for orchestra; Horn Concerto; *Night Music.*

musica ficta or **musica false**   The theory of nondiatonic tones in medieval and Renaissance music; that is, the addition by performers of unwritten sharps and flats. This practice was responsible for the introduction of accidentals into musical notation. It also influenced the evolution of the major and minor keys on which most Western music came to be based, for it modified the medieval church modes to resemble the major and minor scales.

Musica ficta occurs both in the purely melodic music of plainchant and in polyphony. While the rules of its usage are known, medieval and Renaissance music theorists disagreed about details; their views lagged behind changes in performance practice; and modern scholars differ in their opinions as to how extensively the practice was carried out. Musical manuscripts offer some clues, but accidentals were frequently omitted, for they were often considered an insult to the performer. Consequently two modern editions of the same Renaissance piece may show slight differences in their notation of the musica ficta for the modern performer.

Certain rules of musica ficta are believed to have been commonly applied. Generally the tritone, for example, F–B, was avoided both in melodies and between the voices of polyphonic music, with, in this case F-sharp or B-flat substituted as appropriate. The leading tone was often used: the seventh tone of the mode was raised a half step (for example, F might become F-sharp) when it led, or ascended, to the final note of the mode (in this case, G). For purely aesthetic reasons an upper neighbor note might be altered (for example, A–B–A might become A to B-flat to A). Other rules were applied in other instances. For example, the final chord of a piece was often altered to major, which was considered a more appropriate conclusion.

musical comedy or **musical**   A form of dramatic and musical entertainment, usually utilizing a plot and dance, that is often sentimental and amusing. A specific application of the term to a genre of stage piece in which popular songs, dances, and production ensembles are festooned upon a farcical plot was first made in the early 1890s by George Edwardes, manager of the Gaiety Theatre in London, who called his production of *A Gaiety Girl* musical comedy to distinguish it from his previous burlesques. These musical comedies were brought from the Gaiety to the United States, where they formed the basis for the entertainment that has since persisted and developed to the point of being called "America's foremost indigenous theatrical form."

Musical comedy, as it has been known in 20th-century U.S. and English theaters, differs from comic opera and the OPERETTA in that it adheres to a more vernacular style in its music, dances, lyrics, and dialogues. It differs from variety or vaudeville—to which it is indebted for many of its elements of song, dance, and humor—in its possession of a plot, however minimal, and also as a rule in the elaborateness of its physical production. It differs from the revue largely in its use of a story line; the mainstays of that medium—satire, parody, and topical thrusts—are also used in musical comedy. U.S. musical comedy, as it came into being just before the beginning of the 20th century, developed through a fusion of the elements of six earlier types of musical entertainment—extravaganza, pantomime, variety, burlesque, farce-comedy (in the special sense the term acquired in the 1870s), and European comic opera.

The extravaganza (in France, the *féerie*) was originally an imaginative spectacle leaning upon the devices of ballet; *The Black Crook* by Charles M. Barres (1866) was a celebrated example in the United States. After French Romantic ballet dropped out of favor, almost any spectacular piece using elaborate machinery for the production of illusions was called extravaganza.

Pantomime, still popular in England, was a short-lived importation in the United States, disappearing in the 1870s.

Variety served as a proving ground for performers who later graduated into musical comedy; many songs and dance routines (including those from blackface minstrel shows) became the stock in trade of musical comedy.

Burlesque, still true to its name, was taken to the United States in 1868 by Lydia Thompson of London and was given a homely U.S. showing by Edward E. Rice in *Evangeline* (1874). Among the distinguishing marks of burlesque in the 19th century were its girls in tights, playing so-called male roles, its comedians with baggy pants and red noses, and its coarse humor.

Farce-comedy derived from the work of the Roman comic dramatist Plautus, with its metric recitations accompanied by the flute *(tibia)*, and became in the mid-1870s a vernacular form of entertainment popular in England. The Vokes family of England and an American troupe called Salsbury's Troubadours introduced hanging variety specialties on a slender plot.

These shows stood in contrast to English and Viennese comic opera and Offenbach's French opéra bouffe, which at best constituted a more aristocratic form produced by better craftsmen.

Borrowing from all these sources and adding a native drive and ingenuity, U.S. musical comedy began to develop. In the second decade of the 20th century, ballroom dancing and the ragtime of Irving Berlin moved musical comedy out of the world of imaginary Balkan principalities into the present. As the impact of the new continental inventions in staging—led by Max Reinhardt and Josef Urban—invaded the theater, the artistic level of musical comedy rose considerably.

In the depression years of the 1930s, political satire per se appeared; *Of Thee I Sing* by George S. Kaufman, Morrie Ryskind, and Ira and George Gershwin became the first piece of this kind to win the Pulitzer Prize (1931). In the late 1930s and early 1940s such choreographers as George Balanchine (*On Your Toes,* 1936) and Agnes de Mille (*Oklahoma!,* 1943) won for the dance a serious participation in the musical comedy form. Music and the lyric theater took on more importance; score, scenery, ballet, costumes, and play were taken seriously.

In choreography Jerome Robbins began a new era of influence, evolving from the choreographer in *On the Town* (1944) to director-choreographer in *West Side Story* (1957; music by Bernstein) and his last Broadway production before devoting himself exclusively to ballet, *Fiddler on the Roof* (1964; Jerry Bock). The importance of the choreographer was now established and continued with Michael Kidd (*Guys and Dolls,* 1950), Onna White (*The Mu-*

sic Man, 1957), Hanya Holm (*Kiss Me Kate,* 1948); *Camelot,* 1960), Bob Fosse (*Sweet Charity,* 1966; *Dancin',* 1978), Gower Champion (*Bye-Bye, Birdie,* 1960), and Michael Bennett (*A Chorus Line,* 1975).

From a series of intimate musical comedies initiated by Jerome Kern, Guy Bolton, and P. G. Wodehouse with *Very Good, Eddie,* the musical theater gradually took on believable plot construction and characterization, which grew into such dramatically superior works as *Lady in the Dark* (1941) by Moss Hart and Kurt Weill and *Oklahoma!* (1943), *Carousel* (1945), and *South Pacific* (1949), all by Richard Rodgers and Oscar Hammerstein II. The use of plays by such dramatic authors as Eugene O'Neill, Sidney Howard, and George Bernard Shaw became great popular successes in musical comedy form as *New Girl in Town* (1954) by George Abbott and Bob Merrill, *Most Happy Fella* (1955) by Frank Loesser, and *My Fair Lady* (1956) by Alan Jay Lerner and Frederick Loewe. Later successes, such as *Hello, Dolly!* (1964) by Jerry Herman and *The Man of La Mancha* (1965) by Mitch Leigh and Joe Darion were again based on dramatic plays. *The Sound of Music* (1959) by Rodgers and Hammerstein and *Applause* (1970) by Charles Straus and Lee Adams were based on a popular book and a successful movie.

Although the musical as it flourished in the decades of 1920–60 seemed to be on the wane, a notable vehicle for social comment opened in 1967: *Hair* by Galt MacDermot, Gerome Ragni, and James Rado blended amplified rock music, strobe lighting, a degree of audience participation, youthful irreverence, and nudity. Rock combined with religion four years later in *Godspell* by Stephen Swartz and *Jesus Christ Superstar* by Andrew Lloyd Webber and Tim Rice. Erotic themes were explored in The Open Window's *Oh! Calcutta!* (1969) and four years later in *Let My People Come* by Earl Wilson, Jr. *A Chorus Line* by Marvin Hamlisch and Edward Kleban almost dispensed with the usual theatrical sets, costumes, plot, and dialogue. These innovations—along with the unconventional music, adult themes, and imaginative flights of staging and dance utilized in Stephen Sondheim's

Company (1970), *Follies* (1971), *A Little Night Music* (1973), and *Pacific Overtures* (1976), with three of them based on original scripts—may portend a growing maturity of the musical comedy form.

BIBLIOGRAPHY: Julian Mates, *The American Musical Stage Before 1800* (1962); David Ewen, *Complete Book of the American Musical Theater*, rev. ed. (1970); Tom Vallance, *The American Musical* (1970); Stanley Green, *The World of Musical Comedy*, rev. ed. (1974), and *Encyclopaedia of the Musical Theatre* (1976); Lehman Engel, *The American Musical Theater*, rev. ed. (1975); Ethan Mordden, *Better Foot Forward: The History of American Musical Theater* (1976); Arthur Jackson, *The Best Musicals from Show Boat to A Chorus Line* (1977); Gerald Bordman, *The American Musical Theatre: A Chronicle* (1978).

Musical Offering: *see* BACH, JOHANN SEBASTIAN (last years); BAROQUE ERA (Handel and Bach); COUNTERPOINT (Baroque era).

music box A mechanical instrument that sounds when a revolving brass cylinder with properly spaced pins plucks graduated steel tongues cut in a comb or flat plate. Harmonics are generated in the solid steel back of the comb. A spring and clockwork move the cylinder, and a fly regulator governs the rate.

Probably invented *c.* 1770 in Switzerland, the music box was a popular domestic instru-

German music box, c. 1900,
with disk in playing position
*courtesy, Musical Wonder House, Wiscasset, Maine
photograph, L. Douglas Henderson*

ment in the 19th century until displaced by the phonograph and player piano. Large models had teeth plucked by projections on the lower side of a brass disk about 30 inches (75 centimeters) in diameter. The disks could be changed to allow different selections, as could the cylinders on some instruments of the other type. *See* MECHANICAL INSTRUMENTS for bibliography.

music hall: *see* POPULAR MUSIC (the 19th century).

Music of Changes: *see* ALEATORY MUSIC; CAGE; MODERN PERIOD (music in the United States); NOTATION (20th-century notation).

musicology The scientific study of music in all its aspects. The term, first used in English in the first quarter of the 20th century, is derived from *musicologie,* introduced into French shortly before 1914. The French term was taken from the German *Musikwissenschaft,* used for the first time by Friedrich Chrysander in 1863. A much earlier use of a similar term is found in the Latin title of a work by Athanasius Kircher, *Musurgia universalis* (1650).

Musicology inevitably covers a wide and heterogeneous area of research and is concerned with the study not only of European and Oriental art music but also of all folk music. The scope of musicology may be summarized as covering the study of the modern, the historical, and the developmental aspects of: (1) performance (including the voice, musical instruments, tone quality and its analysis, the effect of acoustical surroundings and performing styles); (2) the style of the music itself; (3) theory (of intervals, temperament, and composition); (4) notation and pitch; (5) the lives of composers, performers, and instrument makers; and (6) the place of music in the life of the community.

The beginnings of European musicology are found in the works of the theorists of Greek antiquity. These writers were concerned principally with speculative philosophy and with moral and aesthetic concepts of music. The numerical theories of the Greeks were preserved by later Arab and Christian theorists, though in a corrupted form, and their classification of the modes survived in medieval Europe.

The innovations of Guido of Arezzo (*c.* 990–1050), which included the use of the hexachord and the development of musical notation, brought about a radical change in the methods of music teaching, and subsequent theorists became increasingly concerned with the dissemination of the principles of notation and the more practical elements of music theory.

The Renaissance gave rise to the publication of a considerable number of works dealing with the aesthetics, theory, and practice of music. Detailed drawings and descriptions of the construction of musical instruments begin with the manuscript treatise of Arnault de Zwolle (*c.* 1440); in his *De inventione et usu musicae,* Johannes Tinctoris gives an account of instruments and their function. The first printed book of music, Sebastian Virdung's *Musica getutscht* (1511), contains indications of instrumental practice and technique as well as woodcuts of instruments.

In the 17th century musicians began to apply scientific principles to recording the details of contemporary vocal and instrumental practice as well as the exact measurement of instruments. Toward the end of the century a new interest in the music of the past resulted in a certain musical antiquarianism, a gathering of facts as curiosities as well as for their historical interest.

Histories of European music first appeared in the 18th century. They include Giovanni Battista Martini's *Storia della musica* (1757–81), left uncompleted, and Antonio Eximeno's *Dell'origine e delle regole della musica* (1774), which opposes the theory that music should be composed according to rules. By maintaining that sensibility is the basis of musical theory, Eximeno established himself as a practical musicologist, laying foundations for the later Romantic developments in music. Important English histories of music of the 18th century are Charles Burney's *General History of Music* (1776–89) and Sir John Hawkins' *General History of the Science and Practice of Music* (1776).

Modern musicology, with its practical as well as its historical approach to the music of the past, may be said to have started about the middle of the 19th century when such pioneers as Samuel Wesley and Mendelssohn inaugurated a wide-scale interest in the performance of the music of earlier composers. The 19th century also saw the publication of the *Gesellschaft* editions of Handel and Bach, backed by the new musicological scholarship. After the turn of the century the research of such scholars as Johannes Wolf resulted in the study of medieval systems of notation and in the transcription and publication of the works of many medieval and Renaissance masters.

The new sciences of psychology and ethnology exerted an influence on musicology. The German scholars August Wilhelm Ambros, Guido Adler, Chrysander, Philipp Spitta, and Hugo Riemann added greatly to the historical and theoretical knowledge of music, and Adler, in his *Methode der Musikgeschichte* (1919), presented a practical system of historical procedure dealing with musical paleography, instruments, aesthetics, pedagogics, and comparative studies connected with folklore and ethnography. The main contributions in French were François Joseph Fétis's *Histoire générale de la musique* (1869–76) and Albert Lavignac's *Encyclopédie de la musique* (begun 1913).

In the 19th century the study of the relationship between the life and the work of a composer began to assume a new importance; the subsequent steady stream of biographies provided in many cases an increased insight into the music itself.

The investigation of the music of ancient or non-European civilizations, known as ETHNOMUSICOLOGY, developed greatly as a science in the 20th century, but it originated in the 18th century with Jean Amiot's *Mémoire sur la musique des Chinois* (1779), followed by works on ancient Egyptian and other Oriental music by Guillaume André Villoteau. Ethnomusicology is divided into two categories: that connected with the invention and growth of instruments (organology); and that concerned with the investigation of musical civilizations maintained by oral traditions. Curt Sachs was the pioneer in research on instruments, notably in his *Geist und Wer-*

den der Musikinstrumente (1929), while in the realm of aesthetics John Ellis' *On the Musical Scales of Various Nations* (1885) was followed by Carl Stumpf's *Die Anfänge der Musik* (1911).

Toward the middle of the 20th century musicology became part of the curriculum of many U.S. and European universities, and the subject then covered such wide and varied fields of research that not only musicologists but also their many societies and journals showed an ever-increasing specialization.

The results of musicological scholarship have an importance for the layman as well as for the performer and composer. Transcription of early notations and research into performing practices widens musical experience. Analyses of the physical nature of sound and the means of its production may be directly connected with the manufacture of instruments and also with the acoustical properties of concert halls and opera houses. The sense of hearing and its relation to the phenomenon of music has a bearing on musical education. Other physiological matters, such as the use of muscles or methods of breathing, may help to clarify problems in the performance of music, both instrumental and vocal. Studies in aesthetics and the philosophy of music, primarily belonging to music criticism, also bring a fresh view to the works of philosophers who have dealt with music, from Pythagoras to Herbert Spencer. Investigations into musical theory may reveal new territories to composers.

BIBLIOGRAPHY: Manfred F. Bukofzer, ed., *The Place of Musicology in American Institutions of Higher Learning* (1957; reprint, 1977); Frank L. Harrison, ed., *Musicology* (1963; reprint, 1974); James W. Pruett, *Studies in Musicology* (1969; reprint, 1976); Barry S. Brook, ed., *Perspectives in Musicology* (1975); John W. Grubbs, ed., *Current Thought in Musicology* (1976).

musique concrète A technique of composition developed around 1948 by the French composer Pierre Schaeffer and his associates at the Studio d'Essai of the French radio system. The fundamental principle of *musique concrète* lies in the assemblage of various natural sounds recorded on tape (or originally on disks) to produce a montage of sound. During the preparation of such a composition, the sounds selected and recorded may be modified in any way desired: played backward, cut short or extended, subjected to echo-chamber effects, varied in pitch, intensity, and other characteristics. The finished composition thus represents the combination of varied auditory experiences into an artistic unity.

A precursor to the use of electronically generated sound, *musique concrète* was among the earliest uses of electronic means to extend the composer's sound resources. The experimental use of machinery in *musique concrète*, the random use of ingredients, and the absence of the traditional composer-performer roles characterize the technique as a pioneering effort that led to further developments in ELECTRONIC MUSIC and computer music.

Compositions in *musique concrète* include *Symphonie pour un homme seul* (1949–50; Symphony for One Man Only) by Schaeffer and Pierre Henry; and *Déserts* (1954) for tape and instruments and *Poème électronique* (performed using 400 loudspeakers at the 1958 Brussels Exhibition), both by Edgard Varèse.

Mussorgsky, Modest (Petrovich) (March 21, 1839–March 28, 1881) The most important of the Russian nationalist composers, Modest Mussorgsky was born at Karevo in the district of Pskov, the son of a landowner. At 13 he was sent to the army cadet school in St. Petersburg, and it was his meetings there in 1857 with Mily Balakirev, Aleksandr Dargomyzhsky, and César Cui that led to his serious application to music. In 1858 he left his regiment, having earlier in the year begun to study with Balakirev. Financial difficulties caused by the liberation of the serfs obliged him to take a post in the civil service in 1863. But in addition to composing several piano and orchestral works, he had made his first attempts in the two genres in which he was to excel—opera and song. In 1865 the death of his mother caused the first serious symptoms of dipsomania, which was to affect him increasingly.

He achieved artistic maturity in 1866 with a series of remarkable songs such as "Darling

Modest Mussorgsky
portrait by Ilya Repin, 1881
The Bettmann Archive, Inc.

Savishna," "Hopak," and "The Seminarist." In 1868 he reached the height of his conception of musical realism with the first song of the cycle *The Nursery* (published 1870) and a setting of the first act of Gogol's *The Marriage*. He also began his masterpiece *Boris Godunov* (based on Pushkin's drama), finished at the end of the following year. Its lack of love interest caused its rejection, and Mussorgsky subjected it to a thorough revision; it was eventually performed with success at St. Petersburg in February 1874. In the same year *Pictures at an Exhibition* for piano, in memory of the painter Victor Hartmann, and the relatively introspective song cycle *Sunless* were written, and in 1875 he resumed work on a new historical opera, *Khovanshchina*. But in 1876 he turned to Gogol's *Sorochinsky Fair,* and henceforth he worked on both operas simultaneously without completing either. The last of his major works was the cycle *Songs and Dances of Death,* finished in 1877.

Mussorgsky's importance and influence on later composers is quite out of proportion to his relatively small output. Few composers were less derivative or evolved so original and bold a style. His 65 songs, many to his own texts, describe scenes of Russian life with great vividness and insight and realistically reproduce the inflections of the spoken Russian language. His power of musical portrayal, his strong sense of characterization, and the importance of the role of the chorus—all expressions of his anti-Romantic convictions—established *Boris Godunov* as a historical masterpiece. Shortly after his death Mussorgsky's original harmonic and instrumental style was unjustifiably criticized, and it was with the well-meaning intention of purging Mussorgsky's works of what he considered to be harmonic eccentricities and instrumental weakness that Rimsky-Korsakov edited and "corrected" almost his entire output, of which his widely performed edition of *Boris Godunov* is best known. From about 1908, however, there was a growing demand for Mussorgsky's original versions, which began to be made available in 1928.

BIBLIOGRAPHY: Gerald E. H. Abraham, *Studies in Russian Music* (1935; reprint, 1976), *On Russian Music* (1939; reprint, 1976), and with Michel D. Calvocoressi, *Masters of Russian Music* (1936; reprint, 1971); Donald Brook, *Six Great Russian Composers* (1946); Michel D. Calvocoressi, *Mussorgsky* (1946); Jay Leyda and Sergei Bertensson, *The Mussorgsky Reader: A Life of Modest Petrovich Mussorgsky in Letters and Documents* (1947; reprint, 1970).

RECORDINGS: *Boris Godunov; Khovanshchina; Night on Bald Mountain; Pictures at an Exhibition; Songs and Dances of Death; Sorochinsky Fair.*

Muti, Riccardo (b. July 28, 1941) Educated at the conservatory at Naples, the Italian conductor Riccardo Muti made his conducting debut with the orchestra of the Maggio Musicale in Florence in 1968; he later served as principal conductor there until 1973. In that year he became conductor of the New Philharmonia of London. He has conducted opera at the Salzburg Festival and at the Vienna State Opera. He was awarded first prize in the Guido Cantelli competition in 1967. He first conducted the Philadelphia Orchestra in 1972, was named principal guest conductor in 1977, and appointed music director beginning in 1980.

N

Nabucco: *see* VERDI.

nachtanz: *see* AFTERDANCE.

Nadermann, François-Joseph (*c.* 1773–April 2, 1835)   One of a family of harp-makers, the French harp virtuoso François-Joseph Nadermann studied with Johann Baptist Krumpholz. He played at the Paris Opéra and taught at the Conservatoire from 1825. He composed concertos, solos, and chamber music for the harp. The Nadermann harps were superseded during François-Joseph's lifetime by the double action harps made by Sébastien Érard.

Nápravník, Eduard (Franzevich) (August 24, 1839–November 23, 1916)   Important in the development of Russian opera, the Czech composer and conductor Eduard Nápravník became associated in 1863 with the Russian Imperial Opera and was appointed principal conductor in 1869. He also conducted symphonic concerts of the Russian Musical Society from 1870 to 1882. He wrote four operas (including *Francesca da Rimini,* 1903), four symphonies, songs, and chamber music in which may be seen the influence of Tchaikovsky. During his career he conducted 4,000 opera performances, of which 80 were first productions and approximately 40 were Russian.

Nardini, Pietro (April 12, 1722–May 7, 1793)   Reputed for the beauty and emotional power of his playing, the Italian violinist Pietro Nardini was a student of Giuseppe Tartini. From 1753 to 1767 he was soloist in the court orchestra at Stuttgart, and in 1770 he became music director to the Duke of Tuscany. He was a prolific composer, and his violin compositions are still valued as technical studies.

natural   A note that is neither sharp nor flat; the sign ♮ that cancels a sharp or flat in the key signature or earlier in the same measure;

a term for a horn or trumpet without valves such as the bugle.

Neapolitan   The 18th-century school of composers of OPERA SERIA centered in Naples is sometimes referred to as the Neapolitan school. A favorite chord used by these composers, especially in cadences, is the first inversion of the flatted supertonic (F, A-flat, D-flat in the key of C), a sixth chord that has come to be known as the Neapolitan sixth.

Nelson Mass: *see* CLASSICAL PERIOD (vocal music, 1750–1800); HAYDN (achievement).

neoclassicism   A 20th-century stylistic movement that began as a reaction against the excesses of Romanticism and post-Romanticism. One of the earliest examples was Prokofiev's *Classical* Symphony (1918). Neoclassical compositions most often have their aesthetic or technical roots in music of the 18th century. The term neobaroque might be an equally valid designation, for the style owes allegiance both to the last half of the 18th century, which falls in the Classical period, and to the first half, which falls in the Baroque era. Regardless of terms, it is often difficult to point to individual compositions from the 18th century that are the prototypes of modern neoclassical works. But some composers have transformed specific music from earlier eras: Stravinsky wrote *Pulcinella* (1920) on themes from Pergolesi; Hindemith wrote *Symphonic Metamorphoses* (1943) on themes of Weber. Parody and satire are also involved in some neoclassicism, as can be seen from the titles of some of the works of Satie; *e.g., Embryons desséchés* (*Desiccated Embryos,* 1913) and *Trois Morceaux en forme de poire* (*Three Pieces in the Shape of a Pear,* 1903). Hindemith's opera *Neues vom Tage* (*News of the Day,* 1929) parodies many conventions of 18th-century opera, and Milhaud has written three full operas, each of which lasts about eight minutes.

In general neoclassical works tend to be objective and intellectual, subtle in emotional appeal, and aloof from sentiment in an inherently abstract formal logic. It is perhaps this desired emphasis on order and design, clarity, and lack of frills that led neoclassical composers to hold up the 18th century, rightly or wrongly, as a model. A renewed interest in the music of Bach led composers to experiment with new types of counterpoint and the use of Baroque forms (Bloch's Concerto Grosso, 1925; Alfredo Casella's Partita for piano and orchestra, 1925; Walter Piston's Toccata for orchestra, 1948).

neume   A sign that shows one or more successive musical pitches, an early form of musical NOTATION. Neumes are used to notate Jewish and Christian liturgical chants. In the Middle Ages they were also used to notate polyphony and some secular music consisting of a single melodic line. Early neumes, thin squiggles written without a musical staff, developed from Greek textual accents that were gradually modified into various shapes showing pitch direction and vocal ornament. These staffless, or chironomic, neumes enabled a singer to recall a memorized melody and were capable of indicating subtle nuances. By the 11th century in European music, neumes were heighted, or arranged to suggest melody line. A musical staff of four lines evolved in Europe in the 10th and 11th centuries. Neumes placed on the staff showed exact pitch, allowing a singer to read an unfamiliar melody. By about 1200 neumes had assumed a characteristic square shape. Whether and how neumes indicated rhythm is unknown and a subject of controversy. Musical notes with time values evolved from neumes in the last half of the 13th century.

Climacus   Torculus   Porrectus

A distinct system of neumes is used for the notation of Japanese Buddhist chant.

Newman, Anthony (J.) (b. May 12, 1941) Known both as harpsichordist and organist, Anthony Newman was educated at the Mannes School in New York City and at Harvard and Boston Universities. He has toured and recorded extensively in both capacities.

New World Symphony: *see* DVOŘÁK; PROGRAM MUSIC (program symphony).

Nicolai, (Carl) Otto (Ehrenfried) (June 9, 1810–May 11, 1849)   A German composer known for his comic opera *The Merry Wives of Windsor* on the comedy by Shakespeare, Otto Nicolai was exploited by his father in his youth as a prodigy. In 1827 he studied in Berlin and later under Giuseppe Baini in Rome, producing from 1838 several successful operas in Italy and Vienna. In 1841 he became court conductor in Vienna and founded the Philharmonic Society there the following year. In 1848 he was appointed conductor of the opera at Berlin, and in March 1849 he produced there *The Merry Wives of Windsor,* which remained one of the most popular comic operas throughout the 19th century.

RECORDINGS: *The Merry Wives of Windsor.*

Nicolet, Aurèle (b. January 22, 1926) Educated at the Paris Conservatoire, the Swiss flutist Aurèle Nicolet has been heard in orchestral and solo repertoire from Bach to Poulenc at many of the world's music festivals. From 1950 to 1959 he was first flutist in the Berlin Philharmonic. He won the Association of German Critics Award in 1963.

Nielsen, Carl (August) (June 9, 1865–October 3, 1931)   The outstanding Danish composer of his time, Carl Nielsen entered the Copenhagen Conservatory in 1884, where he studied with Niels Gade. He was violinist in the court orchestra at Copenhagen intermittently from 1886 to 1905, conductor at the court theater (1908–14), and director of the *Musikforeningen* (Music Society) from 1915 to 1927. In 1915 he was appointed professor at the Copenhagen Conservatory. Nielsen's early music was influenced by Romanticism, but his later works were more enterprising and made use of polytonality. He became known for his six symphonies, particularly the Second, *The Four Temperaments* (1902), the Third, *Sinfonia espansiva* (1911), and the Fourth, *The Inextinguishable* (1916); all are richly scored. He also wrote three concertos—for violin, for flute, and for clarinet; operas *Saul og David* (1902) and *Maskarade* (1906); four quartets, two quintets, and organ and piano music. His early *Hymnus amori* reveals an influence of Palestrina. Two of his books have been translated into English: *My Childhood* and *Living Music* (both 1953).

RECORDINGS: *At a Young Artist's Bier* for strings; Clarinet Concerto; *Commotio* for organ; Flute Concerto; *Helios* Overture; *Pan and Syrinx* for orchestra; Symphonies (6); Violin Concerto; Woodwind Quintet.

Nights in the Gardens of Spain: *see* FALLA; PROGRAM MUSIC (problem of form).

Nikisch, Arthur (October 12, 1855–January 23, 1922)   The most celebrated conductor of his day, the Hungarian-born Arthur Nikisch was educated at the Vienna Conservatory (1874) and began his way in the musical world as a violinist. Although he held distinguished appointments elsewhere, his conducting career began (1878) and ended in Leipzig, whose musical life he came to dominate (the Opera, Conservatory, Stadttheater, and the Gewandhaus Orchestra from 1895). He was conductor of the Boston Symphony (1889–93), the Royal Opera and the Philharmonic concerts in Budapest (1893–95), and the Berlin Philharmonic (from 1897), as well as a regular guest with the Hamburg Philharmonic, the London Philharmonic, and the London Symphony. A quiet conductor with an economy of movement, Nikisch was responsible for a new baton technique (primarily from the wrist and fingers instead of the arm and fist) and was described as mesmerizing both players and listeners.

Nilsson, Birgit (b. May 17, 1918)   Educated at the Royal Academy in her native Stockholm, soprano Birgit Nilsson made her debut there as Agathe in Weber's *Der Freischütz* with the Royal Opera in 1946. Her greatest early triumph was as Electra (Mozart's *Idomeneo*) at Glyndebourne in 1951. Her voice gradually changed from lyric to dramatic, and in 1954 she was acclaimed as Elsa (Wagner's *Lohengrin*) at Bayreuth, where she has since appeared annually. She sang in the United States in 1956 at the San Francisco Opera (as Brünnhilde in Wagner's *Die Walküre*) and made her Metropolitan Opera debut three years later as Wagner's Isolde. She is celebrated throughout the world as the greatest living interpreter of Isolde and of Brünnhilde (in *Walküre* and *Götterdämmerung*) as

Arthur Nikisch
courtesy, Boston Symphony Orchestra

Birgit Nilsson
courtesy, Eric Semon Associates

well as for Beethoven's Leonore *(Fidelio)* and Puccini's Turandot.

Noces, Les: *see* BALLET (United States after 1932); STRAVINSKY.

Noches en los jardines de España: *see* NIGHTS IN THE GARDENS OF SPAIN.

nocturne A form found principally in the 19th century. It originated from the Italian *notturno,* an 18th-century form associated with (or to be played during) the night as opposed to *serenata,* an evening piece. *Notturnos* for various combinations of instruments and in several movements were written by Haydn, Adalbert Gyrowetz, and Mozart, whose *Eine kleine Nachtmusik* also comes under this heading. The French form *nocturne* was first used in 1814 by John Field as the title of piano pieces in different styles and later by Chopin, who established the Romantic or introspective character of the nocturne. A similar conception is seen in the nocturnes for piano by Fauré. The term was also used by Mendelssohn for an interlude in his *Midsummer Night's Dream* music and by Debussy as the title of three pieces for orchestra. The German form of the word, *Nachtstück,* was used for pieces by Schumann and Hindemith.

Noé: *see* HALÉVY.

Noehren, Robert (b. December 16, 1910) The U.S. organist and organ builder Robert Noehren was educated at the Institute of Musical Art (now the Juilliard School) and the Curtis Institute and later at the University of Michigan. He taught at Davidson (North Carolina) College (1946–49) and was university organist and a professor at the University of Michigan (1949–75). One of the early leaders of the Baroque revival, he turned in 1954 to a more eclectic style when he began building instruments, which include those in St. John's Roman Catholic Cathedral in Milwaukee, the First Unitarian Church in San Francisco, and the First Presbyterian Church in Buffalo. A recipient of the Grande Prix du Disque, Noehren has recorded all schools from the Baroque to Messiaen.

Nono, Luigi (b. January 29, 1924) A leading Italian composer of electronic, aleatory, and serial music, Luigi Nono studied with Bruno Maderna and Hermann Scherchen. Nono came to public attention in 1950 with his orchestral variations on a 12-tone theme of Schoenberg. Since then he has continued to explore avant-garde techniques and has lectured widely in Europe and the United States. He is married to Schoenberg's daughter Nuria.

Nono's music is distinguished by its clarity of form. Polyphony, monophony, and rhythm are explored in a straightforward manner in his *Polifonica–Monodia–Ritmica* (1951) for seven instruments. *Il canto sospeso (The Suspended Song,* 1955–56), a serial setting for solo voices, chorus, and orchestra of letters written by victims of Nazism, passes its melody among the instruments and voices with each performer rarely playing more than a single note at a time. Nono also adopted this technique of fragmentation in several works involving voices and percussion. *Per Bastiana Tai-yang Cheng (For Bastiana the Sun Rises,* 1967), based on a Chinese folk song and celebrating the birth of Nono's daughter, is somewhat aleatory and calls for three instrumental groups playing in quarter tones and for magnetic tape.

Among Nono's works incorporating texts of social concern and protest are *Intolleranza* (1961), an opera attacking prejudice and reaction, and the dramatic cantata *Sul ponte di Hiroshima (On the Bridge of Hiroshima,* 1962), on a text dealing with the implications of nuclear warfare. His *Epitaffo per Federico García Lorca* (1952) is a set of three pieces in memory of the Spanish poet.

RECORDINGS: *Espressione; Polifonica–Monodia–Ritmica.*

Nordica, Lillian, originally Lillian Norton (May 12, 1857–May 10, 1914) A student at the New England Conservatory, the U.S. soprano Lillian Nordica gave her first concert at age 17. Three years later she toured the United States and Europe with Gilmore's American Band and then studied in Milan. Her early triumphs were as Donna Elvira (Mozart's *Don Giovanni*) and Violetta (Verdi's *La Traviata*). She was at the Metropolitan Opera from 1891 (debut as Valentine in Meyerbeer's *Les Huguenots*) to 1909. In 1894 she sang Elsa (Wagner's *Lohengrin*) at Bayreuth. Her repertoire covered the entire soprano literature from coloratura to Wagnerian roles.

Norma: *see* BELLINI.

Norman, Jessye (b. September 15, 1945) The U.S. soprano Jessye Norman was educated at Howard University, the Peabody Conservatory, and the University of Michigan, studying at the latter with Pierre Bernac. She made her operatic debut (1969) at the Deutsche Oper (Berlin) in the role of Elisabeth in Wagner's *Tannhäuser*. Three years later she made first appearances at La Scala and the Hollywood Bowl (Verdi's *Aida*), Aldeburgh, Tanglewood, Edinburgh, and Covent Garden (singing Cassandra in Berlioz' *Les Troyens*). Norman's first operatic recording was in 1971 (Mozart's *The Marriage of Figaro*), followed by a wide variety of Haydn, Verdi, Weber, and Wagner to Berg, Poulenc, and Michael Tippett.

notation A system of written symbols used to record musical sound. A notational system should convey the relationship in duration and pitch of musical sounds that are successive and of those that are simultaneous. The system should also convey the tempo, dynamic force, and quality of the sounds. In practice even the most sophisticated notations only approach exactitude in conveying the pitch and relative duration of the intended sounds.

definitions A NOTE is a written symbol indicating the pitch and usually the duration of a musical sound. The STAFF (or stave) consists of horizontal, parallel lines that represent the tones (steps) and semitones (half steps) of the musical scale. The CLEF is a sign placed at the beginning of a staff to define the pitch and, in conjunction with the key signature, the order of the tones and semitones that are represented by the lines and spaces of the staff. A grouping of signs for sharp (♯) or flat (♭) notes placed at the beginning of the staff after the clef is called the KEY SIGNATURE. It defines the order of tones and semitones on the staff and thus indicates the key of the music. After the key signature the staff carries a TIME SIGNATURE that indicates meter by means of a fraction. An ACCIDENTAL signifies that the

note to which it is attached must be raised, lowered, or restored to its original pitch.

The illustration consists of a staff with a treble, or G, clef; a key signature of two sharps that indicates D major or b minor; a time signature indicating four beats to the measure with each quarter note receiving one beat; and one measure of four quarter notes, two on the pitch G and two on D, followed by a bar line that marks the end of the measure.

development in Western music The ancient Greeks used systems of notation founded on letters of the Phoenician and Ionic alphabets. It is from Jewish liturgical recitation signs and Greek grammatical accents, however, that the whole notational system of European music first sprang. These accents gradually came into use for the melodies of Christian liturgical chants, serving as mnemonic aids to a tradition that was handed down orally in the manner of folk music. From early times the church required that the authentic melodies and manner of performance be taught and preserved, and although embellishment and improvisation were introduced their use was discouraged. The need thus arose for more accurate notation.

The NEUME developed from the ancient signs / *acutus* (high voice) and \ *gravis* (low voice), indications for rise and fall. They changed their shapes in the early Christian centuries to / • /⌣/. The last two of these indicate pairs of notes. These neumes were placed above the words and gave no precise indication of duration or pitch. They were expressive aids to the memories of singers well trained in the singing of traditional liturgical chants.

These simple neumes were gradually altered in shape, increased in number, arranged in height to convey approximate pitch relationship, and then arranged on staff lines with clefs to indicate real pitch relationships. These developments took place between the 8th and 12th century. The square forms of the neumes had become fixed by 1200, and various compound neumes (ligatures) of two or more notes had developed:

In the two centuries from about 1190 to 1390, notation changed and developed more rapidly than in any other period before or since. Square-shaped neumes, joined in numerous ligatures of two, four, and even five notes, were organized in a system of rhythmic modes in which the temporal values were controlled by set patterns of long and short notes. The system of rhythmic modes gave way as two distinct temporal values were adopted; the old *virga* ◆ and *punctum* ■ became the longa and brevis respectively, and the old diamond-shaped *punctum* ▟ became the semi-

brevis (*see* the chart below). The ligatures took on precise values (they had been variable under the modal system), and the rigid rhythmic patterns of modal notation disintegrated with a musical style that was freer and yet more accurately notated. Petrus de Cruce (flourished *c.* 1280) introduced larger groups of semibreves (*e.g.,* five and seven); these are typical of late 13th-century motets.

mensural notation   In the first quarter of the 14th century, Philippe de Vitry in his treatise *Ars nova* (*c.* 1320) described a notational system that is basically that of the modern system. In brief duple time was recognized as equal in status to triple time, and shorter note values appeared; with the introduction of shorter notes the longer note values began to fall into disuse.

A time signature system developed to define and govern the number of shorter notes that were to be performed in the time of a longer

Names and shapes of commonly used note values from the 13th century onward

old terminology	longa	brevis	semibrevis	minima	semiminima	fusa	semifusa
c. 1225 to c. 1300	▟	■	◆	—	—	—	—
c. 1300 to c. 1430	▟	■	◆	♦	♪	♪	(♪) rare
c. 1430 to c. 1600	⊟	⊟	◇	◇	♦	♪	♪
c. 1600 to the 20th century	—	⊟ ◪ gradually disused	𝅝	𝅗𝅥	♩	♪	♪
modern terminology	not used	breve (rarely used)	semibreve or whole note	minim or half note	crotchet or quarter note	quaver or eighth note	semiquaver or sixteenth note
RESTS late Middle Ages and Renaissance	▬ or ▬	▮	▾	▪	⌐	⌐	☰
modern	not used	▮	▬	▬	⌐ or 𝄽	𝄾	𝄿

value. This system, called mensural notation, prevailed until 1600. It assumed one basic tempo—about the rate of the human pulse—and became complex but very precise as befitted music that was highly sophisticated and sometimes, as in the 14th century, mannered in its rhythms to an extraordinary degree. Time signatures and special notational devices multiplied.

Soon after 1400 the appearance of notation underwent an important alteration when it changed from what is called black full notation to white void notation (*see* Table). The old black full notation remained in scattered use well into the 15th century, and it is found in some English manuscripts as late as 1500.

In the 15th century musical style lost many of the mannered complexities of the preceding century, and in the time of Josquin des Prés a radical simplification of musical style took place. Notation reflects the style of the music it represents, and progressively from about 1450 notation became simpler; many of the complications of the mensural system disappeared. About 1500 many of the time signatures became obsolescent as the ternary division of breve and semibreve fell into disuse.

rests   At the bottom of the Table are given the signs defining lengths of rests; *i.e.,* silent pauses within a continuing piece of music. In the case of the rest for the value of a long, it should be noted that when the stroke covers two spaces the rest equals two breves; when it covers three spaces it equals three breves. In the early mensural notation the other rests were treated usually in the same way as actual note values; *e.g.,* the rest sign for the value of a breve could also have the value of two or three semibreves according to the context.

modern system   From 1600 to modern times note shapes and the principles governing their use did not change to any appreciable degree. Some important developments, however, must be noted: The use of bar lines became standard practice, and score arrangement of music for more than one instrument or voice replaced the old use of unbarred separate parts. Time signatures ceased to indicate the various ways in which the breve and semibreve could be divided into two, three, or more notes of a lower value. They now became frac-

tions indicating the number of a particular value contained in one measure. A large number of abbreviations, signs, and written terms were introduced to indicate expression, manner of performance, degrees of intensity, etc. Many signs came into use, especially in the 17th and 18th centuries, to indicate ORNAMENTATION. Whereas the old mensural notation presupposed a basic tempo (called *integor valor*) that could be varied only by changes of time signature, modern notation and time signatures have been used so freely that tempo is made clear only by written directions and METRONOME marks.

Timbre and volume are specified through a variety of additional signs: symbols such as $>$ (stress) and ——————— (increase in volume), verbal instructions (frequently in Italian) such as forte (loud) and col legno (with the wood of the bow) placed above or below the staff wherever space permits. Additional symbols may also provide information about pitch and duration: the dot for staccato, the hold sign, or fermata ($\frown$), the phrase mark, indications of amount of vibrato, and so forth. Other verbal instructions indicate the general manner of performance (*pesante,* "heavy"; cantabile, "songlike"; etc.) or expression (con dolore "with suffering"; giocoso, "playfully"; etc.). There are also technical signs for each type of instrument, as for bowing, breathing, tonguing, or use of mutes.

twentieth-century notation   Two developments in musical style in the 20th century have placed great strain on staff notation: integral SERIALISM—in which the music is controlled by a mathematical system—and indeterminacy, or ALEATORY MUSIC. In the former every note in a texture may have its individual dynamic marking and type of attack (for example, in Messiaen's *Mode de valeurs et d'intensités* and in parts of *Structures I* and *II* of Pierre Boulez). There may also be extensive use of unconventional playing techniques. Since staff notation indicates volume, attack, and technical effects in a comparatively clumsy manner, the written page becomes cluttered and unclear. In indeterminate and aleatory music the notation must offer choices to the performer or be deliberately imprecise. Staff notation is for these purposes often too specific. In addition ELECTRONIC MUSIC, composed with such devices as graphs, mathematical symbols, and diagrams, is not easily translated into a readable score for publication.

Notation has moved in two directions: toward adaptation of staff notation and toward the devising of new notational systems. Music using microtonal intervals (less than a semitone) has tended to adapt by modifying the standard accidental signs:

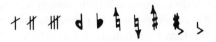

—meaning one-third sharp, two-thirds sharp, and so on (*e.g.*, in Krzysztof Penderecki's *Anaklasis*). So-called space time notation is a further adaptation that reasserts the graphic nature of staff notation. It abandons symbolic indication of note values and replaces it by the spacing out of note heads horizontally on the staff, accompanied by an instruction such as "1 inch = 1 second." The principle may then be amplified by using different note heads

(○. □. ◇,) to signify short, medium, and long sustaining of a note, thus obviating the use of rests, and by beaming together notes to be performed in one breath or bow (*e.g.*, Witold Lutoslawski's *Trois poèmes d'Henri Michaux* and John Cage's *Music of Changes*).

Indeterminate music requires constant experimentation with notation. A composer may offer directions for one element of the music— as rhythm or pitch contour—and leave the performer to improvise the remaining elements. Or the general character of a passage may be described by resorting to a specially designed symbol, a verbal description, or even an impressionistic drawing (as in Earle Brown's *Hodograph*). At the extreme John Cage supplies materials (lines, dots, shapes) and leaves the performer to attach musical significance to them. For electronic music published scores have so far adopted either strict graph form (Stockhausen's *Electronic Study II*) or pictorial form, using patterned drawings to represent different timbres (as in Henri Pousseur's *Electre* and Stockhausen's *Kontakte*).

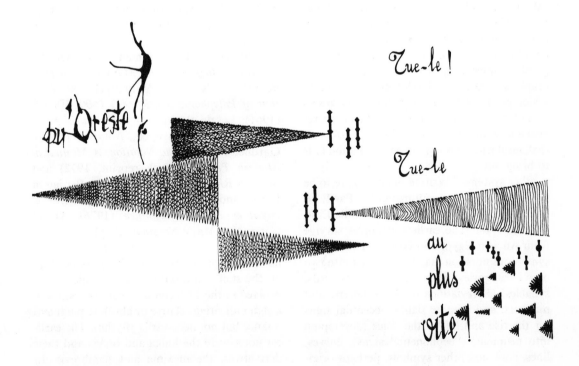

page from score of *Electre* by Henri Pousseur

courtesy, Universal Edition, Vienna

adaptation to non-Western music Notations evolve with the musical styles they serve, and they reflect the underlying aesthetics of their own cultures. Thus staff notation is ill-equipped to cope with non-Western scales and tunings, with music to which the idea of the note (a stable, sustained pitch) is foreign, or with music whose subtlety lies as much in delicate gradations of volume or timbre as in pitch and rhythm. Ethnomusicologists have developed a range of supplementary symbols—*e.g.,* for notes of uncertain pitch, glissandi (slides), slight lengthening of a value, half-voiced notes, and other sounds. They have also experimented with staffs of fewer or more lines. The Western system of proportional note values (for example, quarter note equals half of a half note) does not easily cope with fine fluctuations of value; instead constant changes of metronome tempo mark may be necessary. Among the most complex uses of staff notation in ethnomusicology are the transcriptions of Serbo-Croatian and Romanian folk song by Bartók. Other transcribers have used graph paper to draw a curve of pitch against time. Many significant mechanical methods of transcription have been devised. The two most notable are the melograph, invented by the ethnomusicologist Charles Seeger, which traces a pitch/time graph immediately above a volume/time graph, and a device developed by Dahlbeck, which produces two similar graphs by means of a cathode-ray tube. These methods can reveal a level of interpretation by the performer that aural transcription into staff notation fails to bring out.

other systems Written notations are to be found in the musical cultures of the Far East, Southeast Asia, South Asia, the Middle East, and the West. The earliest examples survive from Ancient Egypt and Greece. The written symbols of notation may be classified into two broad categories: phonetic symbols—words, syllables, abbreviations of these, letters, and numbers; and graphic signs—accentual signs for the rise and fall of the voice (developing into neumelike "ecphonetic" signs), curves, lines, dots, and other symbols, perhaps originally depicting hand signs, and neumes. Symbols in both categories may denote simple sounds or stand for groups of successive sounds. In the West they are read in lines from left to right, whereas in the Orient many are read from right to left or read vertically in columns.

A second fundamental distinction is that between representational notations that depict the sound of the music and tablatures that instruct a player as to the technical means of producing a sound. Phonetic symbols play an important role in both types of notation, while graphic signs contribute mainly to representational notations. A prime example of non-Western representational notation is the *kraton* notation used in music for the Javanese gamelan orchestra, its grid using the graph principle found in Western staff notation but oriented at a 90° angle relative to the latter.

In conclusion it must be said that if oral tradition—and in music this also means aural—were to be completely broken, no notation could convey the authentic manner of performance. Debased or almost completely lost traditions make it difficult to revive old music with any certainty of authenticity. This is not, however, to deny the value of research or the aesthetic value of modern performances of old music. *See also* PLAINCHANT; RHYTHM; TABLATURE.

BIBLIOGRAPHY: Emanuel Winternitz, *Musical Autographs from Monteverdi to Hindemith,* 2 vols. (1955); Willi Apel, *The Notation of Polyphonic Music, 900–1600,* 5th ed. (1961); Laszlo Boehm, *Modern Music Notation* (1961); John Cage, ed., *Notations* (1969); Gardner Read, *Music Notation: A Manual of Modern Practice* (1969; reprint, 1972) and *Modern Rhythmic Notation* (1978); Benjamin Boretz and Edward T. Cone, *Perspectives on Notation and Performance* (1976); David Cope, *New Music Notation* (1976).

note A sign indicating pitch by its position on the staff and duration by its shape. Notes evolved in the 13th century from the NEUME, a sign indicating relative or absolute pitch and nuance but not necessarily rhythm. The earliest notes were the longa and brevis and their derivatives, the maxima and semibrevis. In modern notation the brevis and semibrevis correspond to the double whole note and the whole note. Other modern notes, in diminishing time value, are the half note, quarter note, eighth note, sixteenth note, thirty-second note, and sixty-fourth note (*see* Table in NOTATION).

Note may also refer to a tone, the sound produced by a singer or musical instrument or represented by a pitch name (as G, or sol), a neume, or a written note.

Notre Dame school An important group of composers and singers in the late 12th century and early 13th who worked under the patronage of the Cathedral of Notre-Dame in Paris. The Notre Dame school is important because it produced the earliest repertoire of polyphonic music to gain international prestige and circulation. Its four major forms are ORGANUM, a setting for two to four voices of a plainchant melody in which the chant is sung in sustained notes beneath the florid counterpoint of the upper voice(s); CLAUSULA, actually a section within an organum corresponding to a melismatic section of the chant and characterized by a decisive acceleration of pace in the voice having the chant; CONDUCTUS, a processional composition in chordal style not derived from any preexistent chant; and MOTET, similar to the clausula, from which it evidently evolved, but with the addition of new texts, often secular, in the upper parts.

The composers of the Notre Dame school are all anonymous except for two, Léonin, or Leoninus (late 12th century), and Pérotin, or Perotinus (flourished *c.* 1200), both of whom are mentioned in a 13th-century treatise by an anonymous Englishman studying in Paris. According to the treatise Léonin excelled in the composition of organa and composed the *Magnus liber organi* that contains a series of two-part organa for the entire liturgical year. Pérotin, the apparent successor to Léonin, is cited for his three- and four-voice organa as well as his "substitute clausulae," newly composed clausulae intended for insertion within the older organa.

Nourrit, Adolphe (March 3, 1802–March 8, 1839) The son of Louis Nourrit, a leading tenor at the Paris Opéra, the French tenor Adolphe Nourrit was encouraged by Manuel

García to become a singer. His debut was in 1821 as Pylades in Gluck's *Iphigénie en Tauride* at the Opéra. He succeeded his father there five years later and created roles in much of the standard repertoire of the time: Arnold in Rossini's *Guillaume Tell;* Daniel Auber's *La Muette de Portici;* and Meyerbeer's Robert le Diable, Eleazar in *La Juive,* and Raoul in *Les Huguenots.* He assisted in the librettos of some of these operas and wrote ballet scenarios. In 1837 he left the Opéra and toured Italy and the French provinces with success. He taught at the Conservatoire from 1828 to 1837 and introduced the songs of Schubert to Paris. He committed suicide in Italy.

Novaës, Guiomar (February 28, 1895–March 7, 1979) Isidore Philipp's greatest pupil was the Brazilian pianist Guiomar Novaës. When she applied for entrance to the Paris Conservatoire in 1909, she won admittance over nearly 400 applicants. Called the "Paderewska of the pampas" (despite inaccurate geography), she was a major 20th-century performer of the large-scale romantic type, though Harold C. Schonberg described her playing as "intensely poetic and intensely feminine" and "strikingly reminiscent of Josef Hofmann's."

Novák, Vítězslav (December 5, 1870–July 18, 1949) The Bohemian composer and teacher Vítězslav Novák studied at the Prague Conservatory with Dvořák and in 1909 joined the teaching staff there. His early music was influenced by the Romantic school, but after he made a visit to Moravia his music showed a nationalist character. He was also influenced by Debussy and Richard Strauss.

His works include four operas, two ballets, and the orchestral *V Tatrach* ("In the Tatra"), *Slovakian* Suite, and others inspired by Hans Christian Andersen and František Ladislav Čelakovský. *De Profundis* for orchestra and the *May* Symphony were among those written during World War II. He also wrote chamber music, songs, and many choral works, including the *Autumn* Symphony.

Novello, Vincent (September 6, 1781–August 9, 1861) The English composer and publisher Vincent Novello was organist at the Portuguese embassy chapel (1797–1822), where he directed the first English performances of masses by Haydn and Mozart; from 1840 to 1843 he was organist at the Roman Catholic chapel at Moorfields. An original member of the Philharmonic Society, he had a distinguished circle of friends, including the Lambs, Leigh Hunt, Percy Bysshe Shelley, and John Keats. Novello was a prolific composer, but his work as editor and publisher forms his chief claim to fame. His *Collection of Sacred Music* in two folio volumes appeared in 1811 and marks the founding of the publishing house of Novello. In 1849 he went to live at Nice.

His eldest son Joseph Alfred (1810–1896) began a career as a bass singer, but in 1829 he became active in music publishing, and it was he who developed the house of Novello and who introduced inexpensive editions of large-scale choral works. The fourth daughter of Vincent Novello, Clara Anastasia (1818–1908), was one of the most famous sopranos of her time, receiving high praise from Mendelssohn, Schumann, and Rossini.

Noye's Fludde: *see* BAND; BRITTEN; ORATORIO (late 19th century).

nozze di Figaro, Le: *see* MOZART (later life); OPERA (the 19th century).

Nutcracker: *see* BALLET (Russia before 1900); CELESTA; GLOCKENSPIEL; TCHAIKOVSKY (later life and works).

O

obbligato An essential but subordinate instrumental part. The word is Italian for "obligatory." In an 18th-century aria with trumpet obbligato, the trumpet part, although serving as accompaniment to the voice, may be as brilliant in its writing as that of the voice itself. The term obbligato accompaniment has a more specialized meaning in some 18th-century music (*see* ACCOMPANIMENT).

Oberon: *see* OPERA (the 19th century); WEBER, CARL MARIA VON.

oboe A treble woodwind instrument with a conical bore and double reed. It is used chiefly as a component of the orchestra but also has a considerable repertoire of solo work.

Hautbois (French, "high wood"), or oboe, was one of the names applied to the SHAWM, the violently powerful instrument of outdoor ceremonial. But the oboe proper (*i.e.,* the orchestral instrument) was the mid-17th-century invention of two French court musicians, Jean Hotteterre and Michel Philidor, and was designed to play indoors with the large bands of strings that were becoming common. This instrument, almost certainly softer and less brilliant in quality than the modern oboe, was probably first used in public in Lully's *Ballet de l'amour malade* (1657). Before the end of the 17th century, it had become the principal wind instrument of the orchestra and military band and, next to the violin, the most important solo instrument of the time.

The early instrument, which had only two keys, could produce a fairly even chromatic scale by the use of cross fingering somewhat similar to that used by recorder players. The compass, at first two octaves from middle C, was soon extended, and solo works of the period of Mozart include the F above the treble staff. The instrument remained essentially the same into the middle period of Beethoven.

In the early years of the 19th century, however, the increasing complexity of music coincided with a number of improvements in the manufacture of keywork, particularly the introduction of metal pillars in place of the wooden ridges on which the keys had been mounted. This reduced the threat to the airtightness of the instrument formerly associated with the introduction of additional

"Gillet model" oboe and oboe d'amore
courtesy, T. W. Howarth & Co., London

keys, and in France by 1839 the number of keys had been gradually increased to ten.

Before 1800 French players had adopted the narrow modern type of reed. Guillaume Triébert (d. 1848) had begun his experiments, which were continued by his son Frédéric (d. 1878) and resulted by the 1860s in an instrument almost identical with the modern oboe, both in bore and complexity of mechanism. This was essentially the expressive, flexible, and specifically French instrument of the 20th century. The instrument in which the finger-holes are covered by perforated metal plates, now widely used in the United States and in France, was produced by François Lorée and Georges Gillet in 1906.

The centralized institutions of France probably helped to preserve the musical standards that made this evolution economically possible. The working lives of the Triéberts roughly correspond to the greatest period of French grand opera; the new sensitive, lyrical oboe writing of Berlioz coincides with the early development of the new instrument; the gaiety, variety, and agility in the scores of Léo Delibes mark its completion.

In other countries the decay of patronage and the public enthusiasm for military band music resulted in radically different traditions in oboe playing and manufacture. In Germany and Austria the rise of the many-keyed instrument occurred earlier than in France and was accompanied by a development of the bore and reed that produced an increased loudness clearly of military inspiration. After Beethoven this resulted in a long period of neglect for the oboe. It is strange to consider that the dramatic solo in *Fidelio,* the high point of 19th-century German writing for the oboe, was almost certainly played on the Baroque type of instrument with two keys. With the exception of the obbligato in Weber's *Der Freischütz* (1821), there is little in later German scores that calls either for much sensitiveness or much technique until the end of the 19th century, when Richard Strauss campaigned successfully against the prevailing standards of playing. After a period of experiment with an extremely small reed, which was ill suited to the large German bore, the French oboe was generally adopted by about 1925.

A chief factor in playing the oboe is the making of the reed and its control by the lips and breath. Most serious players make their own reeds, though in modern times ready-made reeds are available. The raw material of the oboe reed is the plant *Arundo donax,* which resembles bamboo in appearance. It grows in warm temperate or subtropical regions, but only the crops of *départements* of Var and Vaucluse in the south of France are satisfactory for reedmaking.

The revival of the oboe as a solo instrument that began to some extent in the 1930s accelerated rapidly after the end of World War II. Though a number of modern concertos (Richard Strauss, Lukas Foss) and solo works (sonatas by Hindemith, Poulenc) were written for the instrument, the rich repertoire of the early 18th century still remains the stock in trade of the oboe soloist.

There are several larger varieties of oboe. The ENGLISH HORN, or cor anglais, is pitched in F a fifth below the oboe and is a normal component of the modern orchestra, to which it was restored largely by the example of Berlioz and Wagner. It had been used intermittently, however, as a special effect since its earlier vogue in Bach's time, when the straight alto or tenor oboe of the 17th century made way for a curved instrument covered with leather and fitted with a globular bell. The origin of the name is unknown, but it was to this form that the term English horn was specifically applied, and Bach's *oboe de caccia* was almost certainly the same instrument. The curved form survived late in Germany and was used in Italy until about 1900. The *oboe d'amore* in A, a minor third below the oboe, is made with a globular bell like that of the English horn. Introduced in Germany about 1720, it was much employed by Bach. It was revived by Victor Charles Mahillon in 1878 for Bach performances and is also used in 20th-century works.

Instruments pitched an octave below the oboe are more rare. The hautbois baryton, or baritone oboe, resembles a larger and therefore lower-voiced English horn both in its tonal quality and in its proportions. Despite several early examples, notably those by Henri Brod and the Triéberts, its effective history dates from François Lorée's model of 1889. The HECKELPHONE, with a much larger bore and reed than the hautbois baryton, has a more distinctive tone but is rather heavy in the low register. It was first used by Richard Strauss in *Elektra* and *Salome*.

BIBLIOGRAPHY: Anthony Baines, *Woodwind Instruments and Their History,* rev. ed. (1963); Philip Bate, *The Oboe: An Outline of Its History, Development, and Construction,* 3rd ed. (1975); Sibyl Marcuse, *A Survey of Musical Instruments* (1975).

Obraztsova, Elena (Vasilievna) (b. July 7, 1939)   First heard in the United States in the Bolshoi Opera's production of Mussorgsky's *Boris Godunov* at the Metropolitan Opera in 1975, the Soviet soprano Elena Obraztsova was acclaimed the same year as Azucena in Verdi's *Il Trovatore* at the San Francisco Opera. Her own Metropolitan debut was in 1976 as Amneris (Verdi's *Aida*). Educated at the Leningrad Conservatory, she made her Bolshoi debut in 1965 as Marina *(Boris Godunov)* and sings roles by Verdi, Bizet, and Wagner (Kundry in *Parsifal* and Ortrud in *Lohengrin*) as well as the Russian operas of Mussorgsky, Rimsky-Korsakov, Borodin, and Tchaikovsky. She has been awarded gold medals at the first Glinka All-Union Competition (1963) and the 1970 Tchaikovsky Competition.

Obrecht, Jakob (November 22, 1452–1505)   A Flemish composer known chiefly for his sacred music, Jakob Obrecht was the son of Willem Obrecht, a trumpeter in the service of the Duke of Cleves. Willem Obrecht had journeyed to Sicily and Mantua, and his musical contacts in Italy were ultimately to prove useful for his son. It has been suggested that the young Obrecht was trained at Ferrara, a city he later visited at the height of his fame. But his first certain appointment dates from 1484, when he served as instructor of the choirboys at the Cambrai Cathedral. In the following year he became succentor of the Cathedral of St. Donatien at Bruges, but he soon applied for leave of absence to visit Italy. Obrecht served the Duke of Ferrara briefly but was back in Bergen op Zoom (his birthplace) by June 1488. He resumed his duties in Bruges and was nominated chaplain of the

altar of St. Jodocus at the Antwerp Cathedral in 1498. He journeyed to Ferrara again in 1504 and in 1505 died of the plague that ravaged the city.

Although Obrecht is best known for his liturgical music, he also wrote secular songs, which include settings of Dutch, Italian, and French texts. Twenty-five of these survive along with a number of motets, most of which have Marian texts. Twenty-seven settings of the mass are extant, most of them for four voices.

BIBLIOGRAPHY: Gustave Reese, *Music in the Renaissance,* rev. ed. (1959).

RECORDINGS: *Missa Fortuna desperata; Missa Sub tuum praesidium.*

O'Carolan, Turlogh, or Terence Carolan (1670–March 25, 1738)   One of the last of the Irish harper-composers and the only one whose songs survive in both words and music in any significant number, Turlogh O'Carolan became blind from smallpox at age 18 and was apprenticed to a harper for three years. As an itinerant harper he traveled widely in Ireland and enjoyed a considerable reputation as a song writer and composer of extemporary verse, though as a performer he was never regarded as a master. One of his 220 known melodies was used by Thomas Moore for his song "Oh! the sight entrancing."

Ockeghem, Jean d' or **Johannes,** also spelled Okeghem (*c.* 1420–*c.* 1495)   A Flemish composer and singer known for his church music and chansons, Jean d'Ockeghem was a singer at the Antwerp Cathedral (1443–44) and served similarly in the chapel of Duke Charles of Bourbon (1446–48) and later in the royal chapel. He acted as chaplain and composer to three successive French kings (Charles VII, Louis XI, and Charles VIII) and was given the title of *maître de la chapelle du roy* (1465). As treasurer of the wealthy abbey of St. Martin at Tours, he received a handsome salary. Like many of his Flemish contemporaries, Ockeghem traveled widely and used his visits to distant cities to improve his musical knowledge.

Ockeghem knew Gilles Binchois and mourned his death in a lament of touching beauty. He was a follower of Guillaume Dufay and John Dunstable. If his mature work sounds richer than theirs, it is because instrumentally supported vocal lines were being gradually modified to make way for sonorous choral harmony and not because he invented (as is claimed) a polyphonic texture knit together by constant melodic imitation. There is little imitation in his magnificently austere *Missa pro defunctis* and only the slightest trace of canon, a device of which he was a master. His ten motets include Marian texts such as *Ave Maria, Salve regina, Alma redemptoris mater,* and a complete setting of the responsory *Gaude Maria.* Fourteen masses have survived, but two consist of Kyrie, Gloria, and Credo only. He often uses preexistent material, as in the masses based on chansons. The *Missa Prolationum* and the *Missa Cuiusvis toni* are examples of his highly developed contrapuntal and canonic technique. There are about 20 chansons.

BIBLIOGRAPHY: Ernst Krenek, *Johannes Ockeghem* (1953); Gustave Reese, *Music in the Renaissance,* rev. ed. (1959).

RECORDINGS: Chansons; *Missa Au travail suis; Missa Caput; Missa Ecce ancilla; Missa Ma maistresse; Missa pro defunctis;* motets.

octave The eighth tone of the diatonic scale. As an interval of the eighth, it is the most perfect consonance, with the higher note having a frequency twice that of the fundamental. Because of the close acoustical relation between the two notes, the second is perceived by the listener almost as a repetition of the first. It is the only interval to appear as a constant in the musical scales of nearly all cultures. The term octave is also used to encompass all eight tones of the diatonic scale.

Oedipus Rex: *see* STRAVINSKY.

Offenbach, Jacques, originally Jakob Eberst (June 20, 1819–October 5, 1880) The French, originally German, composer Jacques Offenbach created a type of light burlesque French comic opera known as the *opérette,* which became one of the most characteristic artistic products of the Second Empire. Born at Cologne, he was the son of a Jewish cantor from Offenbach am Main known as "Der Offenbacher" (*i.e.,* the man from Offenbach), and

the composer was known only by his assumed name, Offenbach. Attracted by a more tolerant attitude to Jews in Paris, Offenbach's father took him there in his youth, and in 1833 he was enrolled as a cello student at the Paris Conservatoire. In 1844, having been converted to Roman Catholicism, he married Herminie d'Alcain, the daughter of a Spanish Carlist. In 1849, after playing the cello in the orchestra of the Opéra-Comique, he became conductor at the Théâtre Français. He opened a theater of his own in 1855, the Bouffes-Parisiens, which he directed until 1866 and where he gave many of his celebrated operettas, among them *Orpheus in the Underworld* (1858). He then produced operettas at Ems in Germany and an opera-ballet in Vienna (*Die Rheinnixen,* 1864), returning in 1864 to Paris, where at the Variétés he produced his successful operetta *La Belle Hélène* (1865). Other successes followed, including *La Vie Parisienne* (1866), *La Grande-Duchesse de Gérolstein* (1867), and *La Périchole* (1868). He directed the Théâtre de la Gaîté (1872–76), producing a revised version of *Orpheus,* described then as an "opéra-féerique." This venture was a financial failure, and in 1876 he made a tour of the United States. The remaining years of his life were devoted to composition. His only grand opera, *The Tales of Hoffmann,* remained unfinished at his death. It was orchestrated and provided with recitatives by Ernest Guiraud and, described as an "opéra-fantastique," produced at the Opéra-Comique in February 1881.

Writing in a fluent, elegant style and with a highly developed sense of characterization and satire (particularly evident in his irreverent treatment of mythological subjects), Offenbach was appropriately named by Rossini "our little Mozart of the Champs Élysées." Indeed he was almost as prolific as Mozart, writing more than 100 stage works, many of which remained in the repertoire into the 20th century.

BIBLIOGRAPHY: Siegfried Kracauer, *Orpheus in Paris; Offenbach and the Paris of His Time* (1938; reprint, 1972).

RECORDINGS: *La Grande-Duchesse de Gérolstein;* Overture to *Orpheus; Le Papillon* (ballet); *La Périchole; Tales of Hoffmann; La Vie Parisienne.*

Ohlsson, Garrick (b. April 3, 1948) A student of Rosina Lhévinne and Sascha Gorodnitski, the U.S. pianist Garrick Ohlsson appeared as soloist with the Boston Symphony in 1969 and with the Philadelphia Orchestra in 1970. He has toured as a recitalist in Europe and the United States. He won first prize in the Busoni piano competition in Italy (1966) and in 1970 was the first American to win the Warsaw International Chopin Competition. He has recorded music of Chopin and Liszt.

Oistrakh, David (Fyodorovich) (September 30, 1908–October 24, 1974) An exponent of the Russian school of violin playing, David Oistrakh was educated at the Musical and Dramatic Institute at Odessa. In 1934 he joined the faculty of the Moscow Conservatory, becoming a full professor there in 1939. In 1935 he won the Wieniawski Competition (Poland) and in 1937 the Ysaÿe Competition (Belgium); he was awarded the Stalin Prize in 1942. Oistrakh appeared in London and Paris in 1953 and two years later made his U.S. debut. He recorded 20th-century Russian works as well as the standard repertoire. His son Igor Oistrakh also became a well-known violinist.

Oistrakh, Igor (Davidovich) (b. April 27, 1931) Son and student of David Oistrakh, the Soviet violinist Igor Oistrakh received first prize in the Wieniawski Competition in Poland in 1952, four years after his debut and 17 years after his father had won the same award. He has toured Europe and the United States as a soloist and in joint recitals with his father; together they recorded duos of Bach, Haydn, Louis Spohr, and Mozart. He has recorded concertos of Tchaikovsky and Prokofiev.

Oliver, Joseph "King": *see* JAZZ (orchestral style).

Oliveros, Pauline (b. May 30, 1932) A proponent of group improvisation and mixed media, the U.S. composer Pauline Oliveros began writing for electronic equipment in 1963 after several works for chorus (*Sound Patterns,* 1961) and for small groups (Trio for flute, piano, and page turner, 1961; and Outline for flute, percussion, and string bass, 1963). Since 1966 she has written for multichannel tape and accompanying theatrical material, much of which is composed directly on tape rather than through precomposition processes (*I of IV,* 1966). Other works include *Night Jar* (1968) for viola d'amore, tape, film, and mime; *To Valerie Solanas and Marilyn Monroe in Recognition of Their Desperation* (1970) for orchestra, chorus, electronics, and lights; and *Postcard Theater* (1972). Much of her music is written for specific players. Oliveros cofounded and then directed the San Francisco Tape Music Center. In 1967 she joined the faculty of the University of California at San Diego. She won the 1977 Beethoven Prize for her "city-music" piece *Bonn Feier.*

RECORDINGS: *Outline; Sound Patterns.*

ondes Martenot An electronic instrument demonstrated in 1928 in France by the inventor Maurice Martenot, it is also called *ondes musicales,* French for "musical waves." Oscillating tubes produce electric pulses at two supersonic frequencies. They in turn produce a lower frequency within audible range equal to the difference in their rates of vibration that is amplified and converted into sound through a loudspeaker. Many timbres can be created by filtering out upper harmonics of the audible tones.

In the earliest version the player's hand approaching or moving away from a wire varied one of the high frequencies, thus changing the lower frequency and altering the pitch. Later a wire was stretched across a keyboard; the player touched the wire to vary the frequency. A version also exists in which the frequency changes are controlled from a functioning keyboard. Works for the ondes Martenot include those by Honegger, Milhaud, Messiaen, and Samuel Barber.

opera A dramatic work in which the words are wholly or partly sung to an instrumental accompaniment almost always assigned to an orchestra. The music of an opera may be divided into separate, formal pieces for single or combined voices (arias, concerted numbers), and sometimes for instruments only (overtures, interludes, dances), connected either by spoken dialogue or by sung recitative; or it may be composed continuously in a more

ondes Martenot   *Photo Lauros*

or less symphonic manner, with structural sections still discernible or entirely submerged in an organization spread over whole acts. Whatever the composer's procedure, which depends partly on his individual disposition and partly on his place in operatic history, there must be musical structure of some kind. Most operas before the early 19th century began with an overture, but after that time this practice gradually died out.

Public taste is to a great extent responsible for the different emphases placed at different times on the elements of opera as a whole. Audiences in the 17th century often paid more attention to elaborate spectacle than to words, music, or performance; a strong element in the 18th century preferred natural, simple opera to formal, artificial opera, the audience for which seemed to pay too much attention to the brilliant performances of rival singers; probability and improbability have each been exalted in turn, as have topicality (evident or

veiled), remoteness from everyday life, naturalistic staging, and the use of a picture-frame stage.

beginnings The opening date of the history of opera can be placed in the year 1600, when Jacopo Peri's *Euridice* was produced at Florence, though he had collaborated in 1594–98 with Jacopo Corsi in a setting, now almost entirely lost, of Ottavio Rinuccini's *Dafne*. But opera has a long prehistory, which with justification can be traced back to Greek tragedy of the Periclean age, portions of which were undoubtedly sung. The share music may have had in the Roman theater and in quasi-dramatic performance up to the Middle Ages is so uncertain as to be unprofitable to speculate upon, but from the 10th century onward the medieval church had an elaborate form of sacred music drama that was performed on particular feast days by clergy in costume, with the chancel for a stage, and intoned in plainchant. Allowing for the conditions of the time,

567

these performances had every feature of opera, including probably instrumental accompaniment. An outstanding example is *The Play of Daniel* (Beauvais, *c.* 1140). *See* LITURGICAL DRAMA.

Outside the church and nearer the time of opera proper, performances of mystery and miracle plays made enough of music, then certainly instrumental as well as vocal, to show distinctly operatic ingredients; out of them grew in Italy a special type of acted oratorio or allegorical drama with music, the 16th-century *rappresentazione.* The most famous, and one of the last before opera came into its own, was Emilio del Cavaliere's *La rappresentazione di Anima e di Corpo,* performed in Rome in February 1600. The soul and the body of the title are impersonated by human characters, and so are various abstractions such as virtues and vices.

Cavaliere also wrote incidental music for at least three pastoral dramas. Here was another genre, going back at least to the *Orfeo* of Poliziano (Angelo Ambrogini), performed at Mantua between 1472 and 1483, that can be seen as a forerunner of opera. More important than pastorals or even *rappresentazioni* were the *intermedii* performed at the leading ducal courts—notably at the Medici court at Florence in the intervals of plays. Their texts were usually a static, allegorical treatment of subjects from the plays with which they were given. The words might be set as solos or choruses, many instruments might be used, and the scenery might be elaborate. The last two conditions were invariably fulfilled in *intermedii* performed at wedding celebrations, and in the most sumptuous of these, which marked the wedding in Florence in 1589 of Grand Duke Ferdinando I de' Medici and Christine of Lorraine, the vocal music too was extremely elaborate. These *intermedii* were planned by Giovanni Bardi of Vernio, who, as one of the moving spirits behind the first CAMERATA, revealed himself as an ardent enemy of complex polyphony and in favor of simply accompanied song as the ideal medium for communicating emotions to an audience. The composers included such diverse figures as the traditional madrigalist Luca Marenzio and the dramatically inclined Cavaliere.

The madrigal comedy, of which Orazio Vecchi's *L'Amfiparnaso* of 1594 is the best-known example, was anticipated by Alessandro Striggio and others and imitated by Adriano Banchieri and others; but it cannot really be regarded as a direct forerunner of true opera except insofar as it was a kind of dramatic form. Vecchi, however, did not intend his works of this kind to be staged, though there is evidence that Banchieri did.

Thus it can be seen that various kinds of dramatic music were current in the 1580s and '90s at about the time that the first of the three cameratas was deliberating about monodic music and the last two about its application to drama. The Peri–Corsi *Dafne,* as presumably the first through-composed dramatic work and hence the first true opera, was thus the first work to show this application in practice. It cannot have been very different from Peri's *Euridice,* or from Giulio Caccini's setting of the same libretto (also by Rinuccini), also of 1600. Here the entire story moves forward in recitative, exiguously accompanied from the basso continuo and interrupted only occasionally by ensembles or instrumental pieces. The declamation, notably in Peri's score, is sometimes eloquent, but it pales beside that of Monteverdi's *Orfeo* (Mantua, 1607), the first incontestably great opera. Monteverdi, apart from being a much greater composer, did not make the mistake of throwing overboard the musical forms of the previous century; madrigals and instrumental pieces therefore appear along with recitative and songs in a unified whole, while the large ad hoc orchestra is of exactly the kind that appeared in *intermedii* in the 16th century. An even greater surviving work by Monteverdi is his last, *L'incoronazione di Poppea* (Venice, 1642), interesting also for its treatment of a subject from history instead of mythology. Thus two chief sources evolved from which serious opera during the 17th century was to draw its librettos exclusively.

At Venice Monteverdi, who moved from Mantua in 1613, took part in the establishment of opera as public entertainment as distinct from a court function. In his last years four public theaters in the city were devoted to music. An important feature in Venice and one that remained true of opera on the whole for some 150 years was that the orchestra was small; it was based on strings and continuo. The chief Venetian composers succeeding Monteverdi before 1660 were Francesco Cavalli, Pietro Antonio Cesti, Francesco Sacrati, and Pietro Andrea Ziani. Their works were elaborately spectacular, and there is little doubt that the staging was regarded as more exciting than either the plot or the music, both of which were likely to stiffen into conventions that escaped being tedious only in the best composers' best moments. Nowhere else did opera yet flourish outside the courts. For example, in Rome, where Stefano Landi, Luigi Rossi, and Domenico Mazzocchi were the main composers, operas were usually presented in the cardinals' palaces.

Meanwhile there had been an abortive beginning in Germany. A German adaptation of Rinuccini's *Dafne* libretto by Martin Opitz was set as an opera (now lost) by Heinrich Schütz and produced at Torgau in 1627. But Schütz was diverted into other activities and never again wrote an opera. Nor did any other German composer for half a century; even then there was only one public opera house in all Germany (at the free Hansa city of Hamburg, which had no court). The courts themselves cultivated Italian opera, and a little later some of them fostered French opera. Had it not been for the German princes, who vied with each other in keeping up luxurious establishments, opera might have suffered the same neglect in Germany as it did in England, for it was from the courts that the larger towns gradually inherited the tradition in the 19th century that opera must be subsidized.

The neglect in England seems to have been rooted in a typically English compromise and in that insularity that has so often kept England lagging as much as 50 years behind the Continent in musical matters. Italianate recitative simply did not take root in England—at least not in stage works—and a love of compromise was displayed by the continuing English adherence to the hybrid form of the masque, which was not through-composed and where indeed music did not have first claim on the audience's attention. What is usually referred to as the first English opera is

lost: *The Siege of Rhodes* (1656) with text by Sir William Davenant and music by Matthew Locke, Henry Lawes, and three lesser composers. Even late in the 17th century the play with music (including masques) remained the favorite English stage entertainment involving the use of music. Most of Purcell's greatest stage music takes this form; *e.g.,* the five masques he wrote for *The Fairy Queen* (1692) are really independent of the play in which they appear. He wrote four other "semi-operas" of this kind; only *King Arthur* (1691) with text by John Dryden was specifically conceived as such; the others were adaptations of existing plays. John Blow's *Venus and Adonis* (c. 1682) and Purcell's *Dido and Aeneas* (1689/90) are the only two real operas surviving from 17th-century England. Both are untypical of opera elsewhere in being very short (about an hour in performance); both show more French than Italian influence. *Dido* is a masterpiece of the first order—intensely inventive and dramatic—and shows what Purcell might have achieved within a vital operatic tradition. But this was his only chance; his isolated, insular position conspired with his early death, the absence of any sufficiently strong successor, and any system of patronage in damming up what might have grown into an operatic mainstream in Britain.

In France tournaments and masquerades led to the immediate predecessor of opera, the court ballet; the most famous specimen, *Le Ballet comique de la reine* (1581), shows operatic elements. But its composer Baldassarino de Belgiojoso (Balthazar de Beaujoyeulx) was Italian-born. The first real French opera is sometimes claimed to have been *Andromède* (1650); but in this play by Corneille the words immeasurably overpowered what was little more than incidental music by Charles Coypeau d'Assoucy. A better claim to priority is made for Michel de La Guerre's *Le Triomphe de l'amour* (1655) and Robert Cambert's *Pastorale d'Issy* (1659). The latter is rather more important musically, but both pieces are pastorals—lyrical and spectacular—and both give as much scope to dancing as to drama. The earliest French operas had some influence in London, particularly those of Cambert, who went there to live.

In Paris the next great figure, indeed the first truly great one in French opera, was Lully, again originally an Italian but belonging to French music as much as Handel later did to English. Nevertheless it is significant that before him Italian opera was cultivated in Paris to some extent. Lully's musical technique is limited, and he tended to avoid counterpoint except in the fugal allegro section of his overtures, where he created a type of instrumental piece that remained in force—by no means only in France—until well into the 18th century, being used frequently, for example, by Bach and Handel. Lully had a great fund of graceful and sometimes pathetic melody, and he laid much stress, especially in his recitatives, on correct declamation of the French language, a difficult problem where so little syllabic stress occurs and yet one to which the French attached great importance.

French recitative, more dignified and more melodic than the Italian, was accompanied by the orchestral strings, whereas in Italian opera recitative was accompanied by the harpsichord that played the continuo throughout the opera and was supported in the recitatives by bass strings alone.

late 17th-century Italy During the last third of the 17th century, while France and Italy continued to develop opera in their several ways—with Marc-Antoine Charpentier, Pascal Colasse, André Campra, Henri Desmarets, and André Cardinal Destouches as new figures in France and Antonio Draghi, Bernardo Pasquini, Alessandro Stradella, and Agostino Steffani in Italy—there were some isolated events in Spain and Germany. They were the work of Juan Hidalgo in Madrid, Johann Theile at Hamburg, and Nicolaus Adam Strungk there and at Leipzig. Heinrich von Biber at Salzburg brought out the first work by an Austrian (strictly speaking, a Bohemian) in 1687. But this had an Italian libretto, and the court in Vienna had already patronized Italian opera on a lavish scale, with Pietro Antonio Cesti's *Il pomo d'oro* (1666) as the most extravagantly spectacular work.

Alessandro Scarlatti was the finest Italian opera composer of the time. He did nothing, however, to alter the Italian operatic conventions, which by his time had become too rigid to be easily upset; he simply did first-rate work within their limitations. Among these conventions was an exclusively Italian phenomenon—which, however, found its way until well into the middle of the 18th century into opera elsewhere—that of the male soprano and contralto. The practice of castrating boys before their voices broke began in the church, where woman singers were not allowed (*see* CASTRATO). It became the fashion to admire artificial treble voices in opera, especially since these singers were capable of performing incredibly difficult florid passages—not only those written for them by the composers but also those passages the singers themselves improvised in long cadenzas as elaborate as those inserted later into instrumental concertos. The apparent incongruity of seeing male sopranos and contraltos taking the roles of heroes and sometimes even of women was accepted as one of the ordinances of opera. There were, of course, many brilliant female opera singers too; parts for tenors and basses, however, were usually of lesser importance.

Scarlatti's numerous and splendid operas are among the chief exemplars of this phase of excessive artifice, which causes them to survive all too precariously as historical curiosities. It has also robbed other composers of this period of any but the slenderest chance of survival, however fine the music of such men as Antonio Caldara, Leonardo Vinci, Leonardo Leo, Johann Adolph Hasse, Nicola Antonio Porpora, and Bononcini may have been. Reinhard Keiser is also an offshoot of this school—he brought the Hamburg Opera to its culmination with works of the Scarlatti type in a mixture of German and Italian words set to wholly Italianate music. Johann Mattheson was associated with him; so was the youthful Handel, who thus knew the Italian style of the day before his visit to Italy and his settling in England. Handel's first opera was like Keiser's and appeared at Hamburg in 1704. Those produced by him in London (36 works between 1711 and 1741) are all Italian and contain much fine music. It is true that this work is confined mainly to arias, there being far fewer ensembles, choruses, and instrumental pieces; though in these too he reaches a higher level than his contemporaries, as he also does in some of his more dramatic, impassioned recitatives. Handel, who was one of the greatest melodists who ever lived, wrote more arias than Schubert did songs; these are frequently of the utmost beauty, and time and again they reveal his acute psychological insight. They are mostly examples of the da capo ARIA, but sometimes he turns this conventional form to dramatic ends. A number of important mid-20th-century revivals, notably in England and Germany, show that Handel's operas when well sung and imaginatively produced are not the shapeless, undramatic works they were too long assumed to be and are not necessarily less stageworthy than his admittedly dramatic oratorios.

developments in the 18th century The greatest 18th-century librettist was Pietro Metastasio. It was chiefly he who influenced composers to persist in an artificial kind of opera, which he handled with consummate skill. Between 1724 and 1771 most of the important and many of the unimportant opera composers in Italy and abroad set Metastasio's texts, many of which were used repeatedly. He worked exclusively in the field of OPERA SERIA. Another species—the OPERA BUFFA— then began to emerge in Italy and to revitalize the musical stage with characters more directly in touch with the audiences than the gods and heroes of antiquity, though even they at first appeared in the conventional guise of the harlequinade figures of the commedia dell'arte. The first Italian comic operas were not independent works but instead were interludes inserted, scene by scene, between the acts of the serious operas to enliven the evening. These intermezzi (*see* INTERMEZZO) were very slight, and only one is still much performed: *La serva padrona* by Pergolesi (1733).

It was this work that in 1746 brought the opera buffa to Paris, where on reappearing six years later it was used as a model for French comic opera; it also then unleashed the quarrel known as *la guerre des bouffons.* This dispute lasted until 1754 and was nothing more than an argument, for argument's sake, between the partisans for Italian and for French opera, between men of letters rather than musicians. It is significant that the first

French comic opera—*Le Devin du village* (1752)—was written by Rousseau, a man of letters who was also a musician.

The next great figure in French serious opera after Lully was Rameau, another fine composer whose operas—by far his greatest achievement—were neglected after his death. He worked within the Lully tradition, but his orchestral writing and his dramatic choruses, with their consummate counterpoint, are superior to Lully's. He also anticipated some of Gluck's reforms. His works are as nobly classical in their way as the tragedies of Corneille and Racine, and they are bigger and much more distinguished than the French type of comic opera that developed in the hands of small-scale but delightful composers like Antoine Dauvergne, François-André Philidor, Pierre Alexandre Monsigny, and a little later André Modeste Grétry and Nicolas-Marie d'Alayrac. Their pieces were often tearfully sentimental though freshly and charmingly human. Out of them developed the quite peculiar OPÉRA COMIQUE, which is not necessarily comic but always contains spoken dialogue. As late a work as Bizet's *Carmen,* with its original dialogue, is still an opéra comique for all its tragic ending, and so were the "rescue" operas of the Revolution period, one of which—Pierre Gaveaux's *Léonore*—led by way of a close translation of its libretto straight to Beethoven's *Fidelio,* which is thus also in a sense an opéra comique. In Italy the opera buffa continued, and one of its major composers, Baldassare Galuppi, had the advantage of finding a playwright of genius, Carlo Goldoni, for his librettist.

In Germany opera in the vernacular at last began to emerge in mid-18th century. It did so as modestly as the English so-called opera, which had started with the most famous BALLAD OPERA, *The Beggar's Opera* (1728), and was to continue for a long time with slight pieces by Arne, Samuel Arnold, Charles Dibdin, William Shield, and others. Indeed the first impulse came to Germany from England; a translation of Charles Coffey's ballad opera *The Devil to Pay,* with music by J. C. Standfuss, given at Leipzig in 1743, began the vogue of the SINGSPIEL, a simple, sentimental and naively humorous play with music restricted mainly to songs and choruses of an easy, popular kind. The first full-scale German opera, Mozart's *Die Entführung aus dem Serail, (The Abduction from the Seraglio),* was still 40 years off, and even this retained some elements of the singspiel.

With Gluck began the period that still supplies the regular modern repertoire, although in the mid-20th century a few isolated works of earlier date were added. But Gluck himself was slow to produce anything capable of surviving a first production; indeed until nearly the end of the 18th century operas were not intended to do so. His numerous Italian operas, not all of them written before his *Orfeo ed Euridice,* are in fact technically weaker than those by the best of his contemporaries such as Domingo Terradellas, Niccolò Jommelli, and Tommaso Traetta. There is more vitality in his French comic operas, written for the Viennese court, but they are little more than plays with songs. For German opera he did nothing; indeed, like Handel, he set very few German words to music.

Orfeo ed Euridice, Gluck's first reform opera, appeared in Vienna in 1762, and *Alceste* followed in 1767. French versions of both (1774 and 1776), together with his four splendid French serious operas (1774–79), spread his influence to Paris (though he was himself influenced by Rameau to some extent), and they provoked another literary dispute there among his partisans and those of Niccolò Piccinni, an Italian who wrote as nobly as Jommelli but remained conservative. He and Gluck respected each other and took no part in the quarrel. Gluck's reforms—which did away with vocal virtuosity for its own sake, suited the character of the music to the situation, and turned stock figures into human beings—were really as much the librettist Ranieri Calzabigi's as Gluck's, but that the composer knew very well what he was doing is evident from his preface to *Alceste.* Gluck still had to concede conventionally happy endings, however, and in the works written for Paris he was obliged to retain the traditional ballet, which remained a feature of French grand opera.

the 19th century When what may be called the modern repertoire is reached, it is possible to survey the remainder of operatic history much more briefly because its major works are still familiar or at least accessible.

The entry of Mozart into German opera with *The Abduction from the Seraglio* has already been mentioned; in his last year he was to reach the heights of the singspiel with *Die Zauberflöte* (1791; *The Magic Flute*), which still belongs to the category, exalted and for the most part solemn and uplifting though it be. But he had already written several Italian works and produced *Idomeneo,* his first masterpiece in that class, in 1781. The three greatest, which place him with Wagner and Verdi in the triumvirate of opera composers who have so far remained unmatched, are *Le nozze di Figaro* (1786), *Don Giovanni* (1787), and *Così fan tutte* (1790).

In some ways Mozart stands alone in supreme mastery. Never has opera achieved such ideal balance among the conflicting elements that go into the making of it. In him alone music of the purest shape and quality and of the most flawless workmanship is reconciled with all the dramatic claims made by a libretto: perfect delineation of characters, faultless timing of every situation, simultaneous handling of conflicting emotions in unified concerted pieces.

Some minor Germans continued to set Italian words; others tried their own language. But the first great opera in German was Beethoven's *Fidelio* (1805, revised 1806, 1814), though its model was French and the musical influences behind it were Franco-Italian (Cherubini, Ferdinando Paër, Étienne Nicolas Méhul). As an opera it is not perfect, and the spoken dialogue lowers its temperature; but its high moral tone is divested of smugness or ingenuousness by the incomparable elevation of the composer's musical thinking and feeling. *Fidelio* had no influence on later German works: its form was unsatisfactory and its music unapproachable.

The progress of German opera was threatened at the outset by the enormous success of Rossini, whose first opera was produced in 1810. His new type of opera buffa, with its enticing, peppery music, was made as welcome in Vienna and Germany as anywhere and interfered with the operatic careers of

Germanic composers—making Schubert's impossible and Weber's difficult and driving Meyerbeer first to Italy and then to Paris. But in 1821 Weber managed to bring out *Der Freischütz* in Berlin, and here for the first time was a musically important opera that was thoroughly German in every respect—so much so that it never took a firm footing anywhere else. It was also the first Romantic opera of any consequence.

Romanticism, by this time established in literature, poured into opera after Weber's lurid story of the magic bullet. He also dealt with a French subject in *Euryanthe* (1823) and set an English libretto in *Oberon* (London, 1826). In Germany, though, a strongly Romantic vein had already been apparent by 1816 in E. T. A. Hoffmann's *Undine,* a musically rather feeble work by a man whose major gift was literary, and to a lesser extent in Louis Spohr's *Faust.* Soon, however, Romanticism in German opera verged on hysterical extravagance, as in Heinrich August Marschner's *Der Vampyr* (1828) and *Hans Heiling* (1833). Marschner also wrote *Der Templer und die Jüdin* (1829), an opera based on Sir Walter Scott's *Ivanhoe.* Another *Undine* (1845) by Albert Lortzing enjoyed some favor in Germany in the mid-19th century, but Lortzing's talent was particularly suited to comic opera, which flowered charmingly in Paris during the first half of the century and whose composers include Daniel François Esprit Auber, François Adrien Boieldieu, Adolphe-Charles Adam, and Louis Joseph Ferdinand Hérold. Two other comic operas, Otto Nicolai's somewhat Italianate *Merry Wives of Windsor* (1849) and Peter Cornelius' more Wagner-influenced *Der Barbier von Bagdad* (1858), should also be mentioned; both are among the lesser masterpieces of the time.

In France Romanticism took a rather different, semihistorical form in Auber's *La Muette de Portici* (1828), a revolutionary opera, and in Meyerbeer's works, especially *Robert le Diable* (1831). These belong to a type usually known as grand opera with a strong accent on rather sensational spectacle.

Even in Italy, which was far less open to conventional Romanticism, a streak of it is perceptible in works based on Sir Walter Scott:

Rossini's *La Donna del lago* (1819) and Donizetti's *Lucia di Lammermoor* (1835). But both Rossini and Donizetti were at their best in opera buffa, which, with the exception of the suavely lyrical works by the short-lived Bellini, remained the most vital operatic phenomenon in Italy until the advent of Verdi. Verdi furnished only two examples of opera buffa, a failure in 1840 and *Falstaff* (1893); the latter, written when the composer was 79, is one of his most perfect works and, unlike the operas of his earlier years, is incomparably refined. It improves immeasurably on conventional opera buffa by removing its heartlessness and by adding poetry.

Verdi up to *Otello* (1887), and even there once or twice, could be crude. His *Aida,* for example, is a traditional grand opera. But from the first he never failed to be strikingly effective, and at his best he had not only an unfailing sense of the stage and a wonderful melodic gift but also great technical mastery and a discriminating and resourceful musicianship far exceeding that of any of his Italian, and most of his other, contemporaries. He also possessed much more mastery in technical matters than is generally acknowledged. He was matched in skill only by Wagner, his exact contemporary, who, however, matured later.

Wagner's *Rienzi* (1842), another grand opera, still shows the influence of Spontini, Marschner, and Meyerbeer, whose works he knew well as a conductor. Wagner also knew what to his mind was feeble, artificial, and illogical in conventional opera and by much theorizing arrived gradually at a thoroughgoing reform. Though this reform did not prove as vital in the hands of his imitators as he doubtless hoped (and it found even less general acceptance among later composers), it was more than suited to his own needs. What ultimately saved his work for future generations was not his feat of turning opera into music drama; rather it was his eminence as a composer. His resources are endless and serve his special requirements perfectly; his use of the LEITMOTIV is wonderfully eloquent and flexible not only because it allows the orchestra to express what the characters on the stage are doing and even thinking but also because his handling of these themes developed into the very highest art of symphonic composition.

In Russia, which came on the operatic scene with Glinka, opera took a rather different turn, its subjects being as a rule either historical or fairy-tale material of national interest. Glinka's two operas represent both tendencies: *A Life for the Tsar* (1836) and *Ruslan and Lyudmila* (1842) followed the historical and the fairy-tale patterns respectively. They also show features commonly found in later Russian operas: episodic treatment of plot, negligible love interest, the use of exotic melodies and bare and uncompromising harmonies, and a lack of musical development that can be heard only as a fault by ears overaccustomed to German procedures. Subsequent historical works were Mussorgsky's *Boris Godunov* (1874), easily the greatest Slav opera; Borodin's *Prince Igor* (posthumous, 1890); and Rimsky-Korsakov's *The Maid of Pskov* (1873). Most of Rimsky-Korsakov's librettos were based on fairy tales. All these were nationalist composers, but Tchaikovsky was more cosmopolitan. Except for *Eugene Onegin* (1879), however, he was never quite happy in his choice of subjects; his inspiration was unequal and his dramatic sense weak, but his technical competence and lyrical charm are considerable.

The nationalist operas of Smetana are the most distinguished outside Russia; those of the other great Bohemian composer of the day, Dvořák, are less important. There were similar though lesser figures in other musically awakening countries; *e.g.,* Stanislaw Moniuszko in Poland and Francisco Asenjo Barbieri in Spain. Not until the 20th century was there comparable nationalist opera in England (*e.g.,* Vaughan Williams' *Hugh the Drover*), another instance of the time-lag mentioned above; 19th-century English operas palely reflect German or Italian opera, though Arthur Sullivan's light pieces proved successful counterparts to the much more sophisticated operettas of composers like Offenbach and Johann Strauss the Younger.

The greatest French operas of the 19th century are without doubt those of Bizet and Berlioz, which are in marked contrast to the stuffiness or sentimentality of operas by composers such as Gounod or Massenet. Bizet's work culminated in the inventive, realistic, and splendidly scored *Carmen* (1875), Berlioz' in *Les Troyens* (composed 1856–58 but not performed in its entirety until 1967). *Les Troyens,* one of the greatest of all operas, is really a grand opera treated with classical restraint in Berlioz' original style deriving ultimately from Gluck. The realistic operas of Alfred Bruneau at the end of the century stem from *Carmen,* though Gustave Charpentier's *Louise* (1900) is probably the most successful later French work of this kind.

In Italy the corresponding school of VE-RISMO began at that time. Amilcare Ponchielli, Leoncavallo, Mascagni, and Umberto Giordano turned out crudely effective works. Puccini followed the same lines but with better musicianship and a rather more refined artistic conscience. Especially his earlier operas—*La Bohème* (1896), *Tosca* (1900), and *Madama Butterfly* (1904)—but also his later works— the three one-act operas *Il Tabarro, Suor Angelica,* and *Gianni Schicchi* (1918) and *Turandot,* completed by Franco Alfano—remained popular well beyond the middle of the 20th century.

the 20th century   Two of the most important younger composers of the day then turned to the writing of opera. Richard Strauss's *Feuersnot* (1901) was still Wagnerian in its music, but Strauss attempted to scandalize the public by a modern and "immoral" libretto. Debussy's *Pelléas et Mélisande* (1902) made a new departure from operatic convention by using a spoken play by Maeterlinck instead of a specially written libretto, and it shocked its hearers as much as Strauss's work had done—though in quite a different way—by disappointing every expectation of accustomed procedures. It was uneventful, unemphatic, undervitalized, and almost devoid of action. But those who looked for musical quality of the finest kind and were not to be put off by understatement and harmonic innovations learned to cherish this ultrarefined work, which remained unique, for Debussy never wrote another opera. Strauss did write more operas after *Feuersnot,* continuing into old age and retaining his mastery to the last but falling back too often on what had served him well before. Even at his best he is uncertain in style and taste but astonishingly inventive and vibrant. *Der Rosenkavalier* (1911), a sort of "grand operetta," is his most glamorous success, *Elektra* (1909) his most expressionistic and uncompromising score, and *Ariadne auf Naxos* (1912) his most enchanting although just beginning to show the first cracks of decay.

Eugène d'Albert (*Tiefland*, 1903), Riccardo Zandonai, Italo Montemezzi, and Ermanno Wolf-Ferrari (in *I gioielli della Madonna*) continued along the line of *verismo*. Wolf-Ferrari also revived the Goldonian comedy of the 18th century with a charm that seemed faded and a humor more Germanic than Italian. High comedy of the most sophisticated kind is represented by Ravel's brilliant *L'Heure espagnole* (1911). Busoni's operas, revealing both German and Italian elements, are extremely eclectic.

One of the most interesting figures of the 20th century is the Moravian Janáček, as thorough a nationalist as Mussorgsky and one of the most original minds in all opera; he was untouched by any fashion and was free from preconceived theories except those connected with the natural declamation of words, which unfortunately make his work almost untranslatable. He was the leading 20th-century nationalist, far more important operatically than his counterparts like Manuel de Falla in Spain or Vaughan Williams in England. The extremely concentrated, atonal, expressionist operas of Schoenberg, such as *Erwartung* (1909) and *Moses und Aron,* his later 12-tone opera (unfinished), belong to the central European tradition at its most fruitful time. Berg in his remarkable *Wozzeck* (1925) and his unfinished *Lulu* (posthumous, 1937) used the 12-tone system only as far as it would bend to his intentions. What is more remarkable about his works is that they are cast in various traditional musical forms scene by scene without allowing the least constraint to appear in the dramatic events, though these forms are not necessarily perceptible to the listener. The operas of the outstanding mid-20th-century Italian composer Luigi Dallapiccola, *e.g., Il Prigioniero* (broadcast 1949; stage premiere 1950), owe something to Berg.

Two other great figures of cardinal importance in 20th-century music have, like Schoen-berg and Berg, composed only one or two operas, though these are highly distinctive. Bartók's *Duke Bluebeard's Castle* (1918) is a one-act work of great power owing something to Debussy. Stravinsky wrote two Russian operas in his earlier years, but his major achievement in this sphere is *The Rake's Progress* (1951), an 18th-century pastiche that sounds nevertheless typically Stravinskyan—brilliant, refined, and witty, and first-rate entertainment. Hindemith and Prokofiev are two figures of the age who showed more persistent interest in opera and put some of their best music into their diverse works in this medium: most notably Hindemith in *Mathis der Maler* (1933–34; first staged 1938) and Prokofiev in *The Love for Three Oranges* (1921) and *War and Peace* (1946).

Carl Orff and Kurt Weill, two German composers, won great reputations by writing operas whose importance is enchanced by music that is not consciously great but is effective, whether in the naive works of Orff or in the savage social commentaries of Weill. Hans Werner Henze is the most recent major operatic composer to come out of Germany. The works of his most likely to be encountered in the opera house are *Elegy for Young Lovers* (1961), his first collaboration with the poets W. H. Auden and Chester Kallman, and *Der junge Lord* (1965; *The Young Lord*), which satirizes German provincial life. More recent operas are *Das Floss der Medusa* (1972) and *La Cubana* (1975).

U.S. operas have also earned some success by their composers' skillful handling of popular elements of various kinds, whether jazz in the left-wing, socially critical works of Marc Blitzstein and, with other Negro elements, Gershwin's *Porgy and Bess* (1935) or the Puccinian realism in the work of Menotti. Using his own librettos he has produced in a variety of structural styles a series of melodramas and sentimental tragedies of considerable popular appeal, among them *The Medium* (1946), *The Consul* (1950), *Amahl and the Night Visitors* (composed for television performance, 1951), and *The Saint of Bleecker Street* (1954). He also wrote the libretto for the first, mildly successful, opera of Samuel Barber, *Vanessa* (1958; awarded 1958 Pulitzer Prize). Barber's second large opera, *Antony and Cleopatra*

(1966; libretto derived from Shakespeare by Franco Zeffirelli), commissioned to inaugurate the Metropolitan Opera House in New York City's Lincoln Center, was a failure and vanished quickly from performance, though it was rewritten to a new libretto by Menotti and produced at the Juilliard School in the 1974–75 season.

A unique niche is occupied by the two operas that Virgil Thomson composed to texts by Gertrude Stein arranged by Maurice Grosser: the Spanish-tinted *Four Saints in Three Acts* (1934) and *The Mother of Us All* (1947), a delicious flow of invention around the figure of Susan B. Anthony. Their fragile but real durability has resulted from Thomson's singable, apt folk-based setting of texts that alternate among the apparently nonsensical, the satiric, and the emotionally moving. Within the United States—not to count the workshop operas and simplified semi-folk near-operas that many U.S. composers recently have favored—two of the most frequently performed recent American operas are the folklike "Western" *Ballad of Baby Doe* (1956) by Douglas Moore and the melodramatic "Southern" *Susannah* (1955) by Carlisle Floyd.

The most arresting feature of the international scene after World War II was the emergence of an Englishman, working within no established tradition, as the outstanding new operatic composer. Britten is the first English composer to write more than one great opera and is the first to earn an international reputation (mainly through opera). English operas produced before the war contained charming things but were often undramatic and scarcely held the stage. Britten's *Peter Grimes* (1945), his first surviving opera, continued to show every sign of doing so by observance of traditional (in this case somewhat Verdian) operatic methods: the music, of high quality, is psychologically penetrating and constantly used for characterization. Some of his more mature operas are even more distinguished through greater terseness and musicodramatic organization and through solution of the problem of what to do to keep going between climaxes in the absence of recitative or symphonic organization. This is shown in *Billy Budd* (1951), possibly his masterpiece; *The Turn of the Screw* (1954), one of a series for chamber forces; and *A Midsummer Night's Dream* (1960) and *Owen Wingrave* (1971), originally for television. He turned to more austere church parables, inspired by Japanese Nō plays and medieval plainchant: *Curlew River* (1964), *The Burning Fiery Furnance* (1966), and *The Prodigal Son* (1968)—all with librettos by William Plomer.

Britten's example prompted several other English composers to write operas, though none has shown anything like his flair for the stage allied to fine music. Arthur Benjamin offered the former quality and Michael Tippett the latter in *The Midsummer Marriage* (1955), *King Priam* (1962), *The Knot Garden* (1970), and *The Ice Break* (1977). Acclaimed "a potential classic," the Scottish composer Thea Musgrave's *The Voice of Ariadne* (1974) after Henry James gave evidence of a major talent, shown further in her *Mary, Queen of Scots* (1977).

BIBLIOGRAPHY: Sutherland Edwards, *History of the Opera: From Monteverdi to Donizetti* (1862; reprint, 1977); Alfred Loewenberg, ed., *Annals of Opera: 1597–1940,* 2nd ed. (1955; reprint, 1970); Edward J. Dent, *Mozart's Operas: A Critical Study,* 2nd ed. (1960); Donald J. Grout, *A Short History of Opera,* 2nd ed. (1965); Patrick Smith, *The Tenth Muse: A Historical Study of the Opera Libretto* (1970); David Ewen, *Opera: Its Story Told through the Lives and Works of Its Foremost Composers* (1972); Gustav Kobbe, *The New Kobbe's Complete Opera Book,* rev. ed. by the Earl of Harewood (1976); Irving Kolodin, *The Opera Omnibus: Four Centuries of Critical Give and Take* (1976); Leslie Orrey and Gilbert Chase, eds., *The Encyclopedia of Opera* (1976); May S. Teasdale, *Handbook of 20th-Century Opera* (1976); Peter Conrad, *Romantic Opera and Literary Form* (1977).

opera buffa (French form, opéra bouffe) A genre of comic opera originating in Naples in the mid-18th century. It developed from the INTERMEZZO that was performed between the acts of serious opera. Opera buffa plots center on two groups of characters: a comic group of (usually) five male and female personages, and a pair (or more) of lovers. The dialogue is sung. The operatic finale, a long formally organized conclusion to an opera act, including all principal personages, developed in opera buffa. The earliest opera buffa still regularly performed is Pergolesi's *La serva padrona* (1733; *The Maid as Mistress*).

opéra comique The French form of opera in which spoken dialogue alternates with self-contained musical numbers. The earliest examples were satirical comedies with interpolated songs and compared with BALLAD OPERA in England and SINGSPIEL in Germany. The form later developed into serious musical drama distinguished from other opera only by its spoken dialogue.

The term was first used in 1715. Opéra comique developed from the entertainments of comedians who had long performed at fairs, but the traditional characters stemming from the commedia dell' arte were gradually supplanted by those from everyday life, especially (under the influence of Rousseau and the French Encyclopédistes) by the *ingénu,* male and female. The genre also received a musical impetus from the Italian opera buffa. Originally purely comic entertainment, it grew into satire and became with some a form of social criticism. Rousseau himself composed an early example, *Le Devin du village* (1752), which Mozart parodied in *Bastien und Bastienne* (1768). Lesser 18th-century French composers, such as Nicolas-Marie d'Alayrac, Egidio Duni, Pierre Alexandre Monsigny, and François-André Philidor, specialized in opéra comique, but Gluck, writing for audiences in Vienna, was the only great composer to devote himself extensively to it. The tradition continued through the work of André Modeste Grétry, François Adrien Boieldieu, and Daniel François Esprit Auber, who treated more serious and romantic subjects and made a more evocative use of the orchestra. The form merged toward 1830 with grand opera and gradually lost both its comic and later socially significant character. Bizet's *Carmen* (1875) is a late, isolated example of opéra comique; it has spoken dialogue but deals with a tragic theme.

BIBLIOGRAPHY: Martin Cooper, *Opéra Comique* (1949).

opera seria A style of Italian opera dominant in 18th-century Europe except France. It emerged in the late 17th century, notably in the work of Alessandro Scarlatti and other composers working in Naples, and is thus frequently called Neapolitan opera.

The primary musical emphasis of opera seria was on the solo voice and on BEL CANTO, the florid vocal style of the period. Chorus and orchestra played a circumscribed role. High voices were cultivated, both in women and in the castrati. Music and text were divided into recitative, which advanced the dramatic action, and the ARIA, a solo that reflected a character's feelings and also served as a vehicle for vocal virtuosity. Arias characteristically took the da capo form (ABA), the first section (A) being repeated after the B section, but with improvised embellishments.

Apostolo Zeno and Pietro Metastasio were the leading masters of the required libretto style, which presented characters from classical mythology or history and avoided diversionary comic episodes. Among examples of opera seria are *Rinaldo* by Handel, *Demofoonte* by Niccolò Jommelli, *Didone abbandonata* by Nicola Antonio Porpora, and *Artaserse* by Johann Adolph Hasse.

BIBLIOGRAPHY: Winton Dean, *Handel and the Opera Seria* (1969); Michael F. Robinson, *Naples and Neapolitan Opera* (1972).

operetta Originally a short comic opera but by the 19th century a long play with music in which the action was farcical, usually including elements of social or political satire and musical burlesque. This form of entertainment became especially popular in Paris during the second empire, its most successful practitioner being Offenbach, whose *Orpheus in the Underworld* (1858) and *La Belle Hélène* (1864) satirized contemporary Parisian life under the guise of classical Greek mythology. Offenbach's influence spread to London, where from the end of the 1870s Gilbert and Sullivan created a characteristic English form of operetta, satirizing the follies of contemporary society and parodying current operatic conventions. The English operetta, however, lacked the cynical and other daring elements of the French models.

In Vienna from about 1870 another distinct form of operetta appeared; it was more sentimental in style and relied on a warm melodiousness rather than on the garish brilliance characteristic of Offenbach. The chief composers of this school were Johann Strauss the Younger, whose *Die Fledermaus* (1874) remains the best example of the Viennese type; Franz von Suppé, who produced *Boccaccio* (1879); and Karl Millöcker, composer of *Der Bettelstudent* (1882).

Toward the end of the 19th century, perhaps influenced by the gentler quality of Viennese operetta, the French style became itself more sentimental and less satirical, stressing elegance over parodic bite. Viennese successors to Strauss, such as Franz Lehár (Hungarian by birth), Oscar Straus, and Leo Fall, and French composers such as André Messager contributed to the evolution of operetta into what is now called MUSICAL COMEDY.

The operetta traditions of Austria, France, Italy (Puccini made one contribution, *La rondine,* 1917), and England began to wane but found new life in the United States. Victor Herbert, Reginald De Koven, Rudolf Friml, and Sigmund Romberg were all significant transitional figures, adding to U.S. musical life such operettas as, respectively, *Babes in Toyland* (1903), *Robin Hood* (1890), *Rose Marie* (1924), and *The Student Prince* (1924).

BIBLIOGRAPHY: M. Sterling Mackinlay, *Origin and Development of Light Opera* (1927); Eric Walter White, *The Rise of English Opera* (1951); David Ewen, *The Book of European Light Opera* (1962; reprint, 1977); Gervase Hughes, *Composers of Operetta* (1962); Leslie Ayre, *The Gilbert and Sullivan Companion* (1972).

ophicleide   A brass wind instrument with a cup-shaped mouthpiece and padded keys; it is the bass version of the old key BUGLE from which it was derived by the inventor Jean Hilaire Asté, known as Halary, in 1817. The name (from the Greek *Ophis*, "serpent," and *cleides*, "keys") alludes to its improvement over the military band upright serpent through the provision of 11 brass keys to replace open fingerholes. The ophicleide was normally built in C or B-flat, with the same compass as a euphonium and with a similar tone. It was extensively used in French and British bands and orchestras until replaced by the tuba near the end of the 19th century.

oratorio   A large-scale composition for solo voices, chorus, and orchestra on a sacred or semi-sacred subject but not intended for liturgical use. No completely accurate definition is possible. The meaning of the term varies, and indeed in Handel's England it bore two almost contradictory meanings at once. It has been applied to anything from a secular cantata to a biblical opera. A certain latitude is therefore necessary in tracing its development.

There are three principal schools of oratorio: the Italian, in essentials a form of religious opera; the German, developed from the liturgical treatment of the passion story; and the English, created by Handel from a synthesis of several forms. All three reached their climax in the work of Bach and Handel, the German and the English forms drawing sustenance from Italy. A more or less dramatic method is used in all successful oratorios, together with a contemplative or an epic quality.

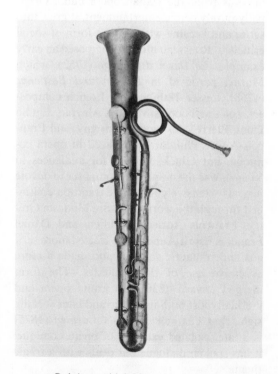

Belgian ophicleide
courtesy, Musée Instrumental, Brussels
photograph, © A.C.L. Brussels

Oratorios may or may not be produced with theatrical action. Practice varied at different periods, and some works are obviously less suited to theatrical action than others. The association of the oratorio exclusively with concert performance tends to sever the link with the dramatic principle. From the middle of the 18th century to the middle of the 20th century only three or four oratorios attained the rank of masterpieces, a decay possibly the result of the inability of composers to find a new formal framework.

beginnings Oratorio, like opera, was an Italian invention. Its name derives from the oratory of the Church of Sta. Maria in Valli-cella in Rome, where St. Philip Neri (1515–95) instituted musical entertainments designed to reform the youth of the city. These entertainments were divided in two by a sermon; hence the two-act form common in early Italian oratorio. The models were the traditional mystery plays, or *sacre rappresentazioni,* which included dramatic action, dances, and religious songs in the vernacular *(laudi spiri-tuali),* often based on secular tunes provided with new words. These in turn can be traced back to the LIGURGICAL DRAMAS of the Middle Ages. The aim of all these productions was to reinforce a popular allegory or the moral of a tale from the Bible or from the lives of the saints by means of drama and spectacle. The passion story itself was scarcely ever treated in this way.

The earliest surviving work sometimes classed as an oratorio—though the term was not so used until a generation later—is *La rappresentazione di anima e di corpo* by Emilio del Cavaliere, produced in St. Philip's Church in Rome in 1600 with elaborate dramatic action, including ballet. This is a morality play with allegorical characters written for choruses in the manner of the *laudi spirituali* and introducing the new monodic style of contemporary opera. It was followed by many similar works, some of them highly spectacular. Toward the middle of the 17th century Carissimi introduced a more sober type with a Latin text based on the Old Testament. Carissimi's oratorios are short, simple in texture, and free from extravagance. The story is told by a narrator, and the composer aims at generalized expression rather than characterization. Nevertheless the style is predominantly operatic, and the most memorable episodes are those in which the narrative is interrupted and the characters express their emotions.

A distinction is sometimes drawn between oratorio (with a narrator) and religious opera *(dramma sacro),* but it was seldom observed in practice. Arcangelo Spagna in 1706 published his sacred librettos under the title *Oratorii ovvero melodrammi sacri.* The Latin and Italian types continued in use, but the latter (known as *oratorio volgare*), sung by virtuoso singers including castrati, was the more popular and flourished to the end of the 18th century. It became a Lenten substitute for opera and musically indistinguishable from it. Alessandro Scarlatti's oratorios reduce the chorus to a minimum and employ all manner of operatic devices. It is not clear when or to what extent stage action was abandoned; it certainly continued into the 18th century, and the oratorio librettos of Apostolo Zeno were designed for use with or without it as circumstances required. The medieval habit of inserting comic interludes still persisted: oratorios as late as Nicola Antonio Porpora's *Sta. Eugenia* (1721) and Pergolesi's *La Con-versione di S. Guglielmo d'Aquitania* (1731) have parts for comic characters who sing in Neapolitan dialect. New Testament subjects, such as those used in Alessandro Stradella's *S. Giovanni Battista* (1676) and Handel's *La resurrezione* (1708), received an equally operatic treatment.

Schütz The history of German oratorio begins with Heinrich Schütz, who wrote an Easter oratorio in 1623, a setting of the Seven Last Words about 1645, and a Christmas oratorio in 1664. His style, like Bach's after him, is a judicious blend of German and Italian elements. Having spent two periods of study in Italy, he was able to graft the monodic arioso of Monteverdi and the instrumental splendor of Giovanni Gabrieli onto the solid contrapuntal trunk of German church music. His oratorios are confined to subjects taken from the Gospels. His handling of the text shows great powers of emotional expression, and his vigorous treatment of the *turba* choruses anticipates Bach; but the dramatic content is always at the service of the devotional. In the *Easter* Oratorio he retains the old convention of setting the words of each character polyphonically for two or more voices. Schütz's oratorios achieve a balance between the austerity of the unaccompanied passions (*St. Luke,* 1664; *St. John,* 1665; *St. Matthew,* 1666) and the exuberance of the psalms, which profoundly affected the history of the oratorio form in Germany.

By the end of the 17th century, this balance had been disturbed. The early German PASSION settings had been strictly liturgical, but the introduction of congregational chorales, meditative arias, instrumental tone painting, and other features led gradually to the establishment of an independent passion oratorio; and increasing Italian influence gave it a strong tilt in the direction of the theater. A species of biblical opera had flourished for a few years at Hamburg, where the first opera house in Germany was opened in 1678 with Johann Theile's *Adam und Eva,* which included a ballet. Clerical opposition seems to have broken this link (an all too familiar event in Protestant countries) with the result that German opera soon died and German oratorio became more and more secular. Reinhard Keiser omitted both the chorales and the evangelist's narrative from his 1704 passion, *Der blutige und sterbende Jesus.* His eloquent and eclectic style, in which Italian and French elements are as conspicuous as German, influenced both Bach and Handel. The passion oratorio texts of this period, when they are not openly operatic, often abandon the words of the Bible for a mixture of rhymed paraphrase and lyrical commentary of a more or less sentimental nature.

Bach   Bach's two great passion oratorios (*St. John,* 1723; *St. Matthew,* 1729) deliberately reversed the German trend then current and restored the balance attained by Schütz, though they are written on a far greater scale and are enriched by the introduction of the later Italian aria style. Bach, in addition to increasing the significance of the chorale, brought back the evangelist's narrative as a framework binding the dramatic element (the words of the characters and the *turba* choruses) to the contemplative or epic sections

(arias, chorales, opening and final choruses). There is nothing novel about Bach's settings except their genius, which holds the long and complex structure in perfect balance. The other works of Bach that bear the name oratorio are more properly church cantatas. The *Christmas* Oratorio was conceived not as a single work but as a series of six cantatas for performance on successive days in Christmas week. Bach's passions, considered old-fashioned in their own day, were soon forgotten and remained so until the Bach revival in the 19th century.

The biblical narrative again succumbed to the attractions of pietist verse. The most popular German passion oratorio of the 18th century, Karl Heinrich Graun's *Der Tod Jesu* (1755), though it preserves the form of the north German model (including chorales), lacks the spiritual stature of Bach's works; it belongs to an age of reason rather than faith. By this time German oratorios on subjects other than the passion were common. Johann Christian Schieferdecker, who was active in Hamburg and Lübeck, sought to combine the allegorical abstractions of the passion commentary with Old Testament stories. The numerous Hamburg oratorios of Johann Mattheson were conceived wholly as dramas and sung by opera singers in church; in 1739 Mattheson defined oratorio as "merely a sacred opera." Some works of this kind, such as Johann Hugo von Wilderer's *Esther* at Mannheim (1724), were played on the stage. Telemann, the most prolific composer of the age, wrote many oratorios as well as 44 passions.

Handel   Bach's passions, partly dramatic in structure, are religious in spirit. The oratorios of Handel are essentially theatrical; they reflect his experience as an opera composer, his cosmopolitan background in Hamburg, Italy, and London, and the broad humanity of his temperament. Before settling in London he had attempted the Italian *oratorio volgare* and the north German passion oratorio with little success. His English oratorio, a largely fortuitous creation, was fed by many tributaries: Italian opera, English stage masque, German cantata, and the choral tradition of all three countries. There was also a French strain: the original version (1720) of his first oratorio *Esther* was a stage masque based on Racine's drama after the model of Greek tragedy with sung choruses. This link was repeatedly confirmed later. Greek tragedy with its compound of drama, ritual, and myth and its double role of the chorus as actor and commentator is the artistic ancestor of Handel's oratorios. They were performed by opera singers in the theater, though ecclesiastical prejudice forbade stage action, and have no connection with the church to which their often pagan spirit, not to mention their musical style, is quite unsuited.

Handel's achievement has been distorted by the almost exclusive concentration of posterity, largely for nonmusical reasons, on the two oratorios with biblical words, *Israel in Egypt* (1739) and especially *Messiah* (1742). Neither is typical; *Messiah,* well described by the compiler of the text as "a fine entertainment," reveals only one side of Handel's genius. Most of the oratorios, while varying widely in subject and design, are concerned with the sufferings of men and women as individuals or as nations in their conflict with life and death. Handel's mastery of characterization and every type of choral utterance is crowned by a deep and sympathetic pondering of the issues involved, and if the librettist's proffered moral contradicts his experience, he does not hesitate to ignore or subvert it. In his last two oratorios, *Theodora* (1750) and *Jephtha* (1752), in which he explores the problems of man's enforced subjection to destiny, the music transcends the facile piety of the text. There is no difference in kind between the oratorios on Old Testament and Apocryphal stories and the classical masques *(Acis and Galatea, Semele, Hercules),* sometimes loosely known as secular oratorios. This was not Handel's title; the confusion results from the double meaning of the word oratorio: a drama on a sacred subject, whether staged or not; and any performance—even a mixed concert—given in the theater without action.

late 18th century Handel's oratorios had few rivals in England during his lifetime. His successors made the double error of imitating his style and misinterpreting his aim, which they took to be ethical rather than aesthetic, and they were content to turn almost any part of the Bible into three hours of music for as large a body of players and singers as they could muster. A tradition founded on such premises was bound to collapse; although works of some merit, such as Arne's *Judith* (1761) and William Crotch's *Palestine* (1812), appeared from time to time, the vast brood of English oratorios remained undistinguished for nearly a century and a half.

Oratorio on the Continent was less subject to extraneous considerations, but it can scarcely be said to have prospered; never after the death of Bach and Handel did it represent a vital, creative tradition. Nearly every Italian composer of opera, serious or comic, from Leonardo Leo and Nicola Antonio Porpora to Giovanni Paisiello, Cimarosa, Antonio Salieri, and Ferdinando Paër, wrote an occasional oratorio, but they seldom achieved more than a parody of the operatic style. Niccolò Jommelli's *La Passione* (1749), a setting not of the Scriptures but of a poem by Pietro Metastasio, treats the subject with a lyrical charm apt for sentimental comedy. Carl Philipp Emanuel Bach's oratorios, notably *Die Israeliten in der Wüste* (published 1775), combine something of his father's intensity of expression with the sensibility of Graun and a vigor suggesting Haydn, but this scarcely adds up to a satisfying whole. The first oratorio of Haydn himself, *Il Ritorna di Tobia* (1775), belongs to the Italian type and suffers from a feeble libretto and a surfeit of long da capo arias; but it contains some fine choruses. *The Creation* (1798) shows very clearly the impact made on Haydn by Handel's oratorios in London. One striking detail, the blaze of C major at the words "Let there be light," is borrowed straight from *Samson;* the massive simplicity of the whole conception, the free polyphony of the choruses, and the picturesque treatment of the text bear witness to the same inspiration. The influence of Mozart's operas may also be traced in the solo music. It is the fusion of these epic and dramatic elements with Haydn's mature mastery of the symphonic style that gives the work the cohesion of a masterpiece. Haydn called *The Seasons* (1801) an oratorio, though its content is secular and its form a loosely articulated series of genre pieces; its vivid pictures of nature have a pantheistic quality that links it once more to Handel, as well as to the world of Beethoven and Schubert. Beethoven's single oratorio, *Christus am Ölberge* (1803), is a failure not because it uses the language of the opera house but because it does so without discriminating between the spiritual levels of the characters.

late 19th century The multiplication of large halls, choral societies, and festivals in the 19th century increased the flow of oratorios, especially in Germany and England. Most German oratorios of the Romantic period were produced by minor composers and have long been forgotten. Schubert's only work of this class, the religious drama *Lazarus,* remained unfinished. Louis Spohr's three oratorios enjoyed much success in their time. Mendelssohn's *Elijah* (1846) is one of the few 19th-century oratorios still heard in modern times.

Mendelssohn's promotion of the Bach revival and his experience with Handel's music, both in Germany and England, led him to attempt in his own works a fusion of the two styles, perhaps without fully understanding the source of their strength. *Elijah* is remarkable for the vitality of the choruses. *St. Paul* (1836) suffers from Mendelssohn's inability to express religious emotion except in terms of a respectable complacency.

Elijah remained the most popular of many oratorios written by foreign composers for English choral festivals. Others include Sigismund Neukomm's *David* (1834), Spohr's *Fall of Babylon* (1842), Michael Costa's *Eli* (1855) and *Naaman* (1864), Gounod's *The Redemption* (1882) and *Mors et Vita* (1885), Dvořák's *St. Ludmilla* (1886), and Saint-Saëns' *The Promised Land* (1913). All were more or less adapted to the English taste, which was not improved when the style of Spohr, Mendelssohn, and later Gounod replaced that of Handel. A masterpiece of 20th-century English oratorio is Elgar's *Dream of Gerontius* (1900). Cardinal Newman's poem has unity and a sufficiently dramatic framework within which the fervent, wayward, and individual character of the music could expand without becoming disorderly. In Elgar's later oratorios, *The Apostles* (1903) and *The Kingdom* (1906), the first two parts of an unfinished trilogy, the absence

of a firm design forced him into a systematic and almost didactic use of the leitmotiv that only emphasized their episodic nature.

Italian oratorio remained in abeyance after the 18th century. Germany produced little of consequence after Mendelssohn, unless Brahms's *Deutsches* Requiem, a setting of passages from Luther's Bible, is classed as an oratorio. Liszt's two works in this form, *St. Elisabeth* (1865) and *Christus* (1873), reflect a characteristic intention to combine the devotional and the theatrical on the grandest scale. *St. Elisabeth,* with its choruses of German and Hungarian bishops, leans toward the theater where it has been staged; *Christus* is more restrained in keeping with a Latin text based partly on the liturgy. Apart from Dvořák's *St. Ludmilla,* which belongs to the same class as *St. Elisabeth,* Slavonic composers have produced few oratorios. Anton Rubinstein wrote sacred operas on subjects varying from *The Tower of Babel* (1870) to *Christus* (1888), but they belong rather to the German school and left little mark.

Nor has France nourished a tradition of oratorio. Marc-Antoine Charpentier in the 17th century introduced *histoires sacrées* after the manner of his master Carissimi, and François Joseph Gossec wrote several for the Concert Spirituel in the following century. There were occasional biblical operas, from Michel Pignolet de Montéclair's *Jephté* (1732) and Rameau's *Samson* (composed 1733, never performed) to Étienne Nicolas Méhul's *Joseph* (1807) and Jean François Lesueur's *La Mort d'Adam* (1809). But the first (perhaps the only) French oratorio of major importance is Berlioz' sacred trilogy *L'Enfance du Christ* (1854), a series of loosely linked tableaux with a strong theatrical flavor. Berlioz' detachment from orthodox Christianity led him to view the story almost as a classical myth; his music is reverent but wholly free from religiosity. Later French composers of oratorios include Gounod, Franck, Massenet, Saint-Saëns, and d'Indy. The many oratorios of Honegger and Milhaud were inspired by both religious and historical subjects.

The 20th century largely abandoned the large-scale festival oratorio. Frederick Delius in *A Mass of Life* (1905, text from Nietzsche) and Hindemith in *Das Unaufhörliche* (1931, poem by Gottfried Benn) attempted a philosophical oratorio without finding a substitute for the dramatic framework. Kodály's *Psalmus Hungaricus* (1923) is a strongly nationalist work in which the composer drew heavily on old Hungarian folk elements. Stravinsky's opera-oratorio *Oedipus Rex* (1927), with a Latin text translated from a French adaptation of Sophocles, was most successful in the opera house. Michael Tippett in *A Child of Our Time* (1941) grafted traditional oratorio elements onto an ethical theme, employing Negro spirituals in the manner of chorales.

In England the long-delayed reaction against the past led to a preference for shorter choral works on sacred texts; but Gustav Holst's *Hymn of Jesus* (1917), Vaughan Williams' *Sancta Civitas* (1926), and William Walton's *Belshazzar's Feast* (1931) should perhaps be classed as reflective or dramatic cantatas rather than oratorios. There were also modern settings of the medieval mysteries, one of the roots of oratorio. Rutland Boughton set the Coventry play *Bethlehem* in 1915, and Britten's *Noye's Fludde* (1958) was designed for dramatic performance in church. Vaughan Williams' opera *The Pilgrim's Progress* (1951), based on the text of John Bunyan, which the composer described as a morality, belongs partly to the oratorio tradition.

A most active composer in this field in the mid-20th century was the Swiss Frank Martin. His works include *Le Vin Herbé* (1942), a secular oratorio on the Tristan story; the passion oratorio *Golgotha* (1949); and *Le Mystère de la Nativité* (1959), a setting of a 15th-century French mystery play intended for stage or concert performance. The last two make a deliberate return to the early forms of the oratorio. A major choral work with the dimensions of an oratorio was *Prayers of Kierkegaard* (1954) by Samuel Barber, and an important passion oratorio was Krzysztof Penderecki's *St. Luke Passion* (1965).

BIBLIOGRAPHY: Howard E. Smither, *The Oratorio in the Baroque Era,* 3 vols. (1977).

orchestra An instrumental group of varying size and composition. Although applied to various ensembles found in Western and non-Western music, the term usually refers to the typical Western music ensemble of bowed stringed instruments complemented by winds and percussion that has—at least in the strings—more than one player per part. The word stems from the Greek *orchēstra,* the part of the ancient Greek theater in front of the proscenium where the dancers and instrumentalists performed in a semicircle.

In the Middle Ages and the early Renaissance, music that can be identified as instrumental was of chamber size, though large ensembles were used for festive occasions. The first known works to indicate specific instruments for each part were the *Sacrae symphoniae* (1597) by Giovanni Gabrieli, namely cornets, trombones, and violins.

A notable example of the antecedent of the modern symphony orchestra is that required for Monteverdi's *Orfeo* (1607): two violins, 10 viols, three bass viols, two double-bass viols, one regal, two cornetts, one small recorder, one high trumpet, three soft trumpets, four trombones, two harpsichords, two organs of wooden pipes, one harp, two bass lutes, and kettledrums (unspecified). In the late 17th century Lully directed for the royal court an orchestra dominated by stringed instruments but including woodwinds, such as oboes and bassoons, and sometimes also flutes and horns. In the 18th century in Germany Johann Stamitz and other composers of the Mannheim school established the basic composition of the modern symphony: four sections, consisting of woodwinds (flutes, oboes, and bassoons), brass (horns and trumpets), percussion (two timpani), and strings (first and second violins, violas, cellos, and double basses). Clarinets were added in this period, while earlier mainstays, such as the harpsichord, lute, and theorbo, were gradually dropped.

The 19th century was a fertile period. Woodwinds were increased from two to typically three or four of each instrument, and the brass section was augmented by a third trumpet, third and fourth horns, and the inclusion of trombones. Composers such as Berlioz, Wagner, Rimsky-Korsakov, and—into the 20th century—Richard Strauss, Mahler, and Stravinsky added their imagination and skills to producing orchestras of unprecedented size and tonal resources. The large orchestra typical of the late 19th through late 20th century incorporates an average of 100 performers and may include a wide variety of instruments and devices required in specific works. *See also* CHAMBER ORCHESTRA.

BIBLIOGRAPHY: Esther Singleton, *Orchestra and Its Instruments* (1917; reprint, 1976); Adam Carse, *The Orchestra from Beethoven to Berlioz* (1948); John H. Mueller, *The American Symphony Orchestra* (1951; reprint, 1976); Reginald Nettel, *The Orchestra in England: A Social History* (1956; reprint, 1972); Charles Sanford Terry, *Bach's Orchestra* (1961; reprint, 1972); Paul Bekker, *Orchestra* (1963; originally *The Story of the Orchestra,* 1936); Henry Raynor, *The Orchestra: A History* (1978).

Orfeo: *see* ARIA; BAROQUE ERA (beginnings); CHAMBER ORCHESTRA; HARP; HAYDN (Esterházy service); MONTEVERDI; OPERA (beginnings) and (France); ORNAMENTATION (Baroque); OVERTURE.

Orfeo ed Euridice: *see* CLASSICAL PERIOD (vocal music, 1750–1800); GLUCK; HARP; OPERA (developments in the 18th century).

Orff, Carl (b. July 10, 1895) The German composer Carl Orff studied at the Munich Academy of Music. Later he conducted at Munich, Mannheim, and Darmstadt and wrote incidental music for the theater. In 1921 he studied with Heinrich Kaminski and became interested in musical education. With Dorothea Günther he established an institute for gymnastics, dance, and music (1924–43) and experimented with music education techniques, publishing *Schulwerk* (1930–35; revised 1950–54), which has been influential in many countries. He also edited early musical dramatic works, notably Monteverdi's *Orfeo,* and staged passions by Heinrich Schütz and Bach. In 1937 he produced *Carmina Burana,* a scenic oratorio on medieval secular poems preserved in a manuscript at the monastery of Benediktbeuern, Bavaria; it achieved much success. Later dramatic works were inspired by the Greek theater and by medieval mystery plays. His *Catulli carmina* (1943) were musical plays on the poetry of Catullus, and the

trilogy begun with *Carmina Burana* was completed by *Trionfo di Afrodite* (1953). Other dramatic works on Greek subjects were *Antigonai* (1949) and *Oedipus der Tyrann* (1959). In his operas *Der Mond* (1939) and *Die Kluge* (1943), followed by *Die Bernauerin* (1945) and *Astutuli* (1946), he was inspired by Bavarian secular poetry. Some of his later works were inspired by religious subjects, including an Easter play *Comoedia de Christi resurrectione* (1957) and the Christmas story *Ludus de nato infanti mirificus* (1960).

BIBLIOGRAPHY: Andreas Liess, *Carl Orff* (1966).

RECORDINGS: *Carmina Burana; De temporum fine comoedia; Entrata; Der Mond; Trionfo di Afrodite.*

organ A keyboard instrument in which the sound is produced by pipes to which wind is supplied through a mechanism. The word organ is derived from Greek *organon* and Latin *organum,* "instrument." By common usage organ has come to embrace any keyboard instrument capable of producing indefinitely sustained sounds, but these should be particularized as HARMONIUM or ELECTRONIC ORGAN. Organ alone implies an organ with pipes, and the term pipe organ is redundant.

basic parts An organ is divided into three main parts. At one end of the instrument are the keyboards, or manuals, and other controls that collectively are called the console. At the other end are the pipes that produce the tone. Between these two is the mechanism, or action, that accounts for a large park of the bulk and cost of any organ. The simplest type of organ has one keyboard and one pipe to each note. The pipes stand in a row on an airtight box, or chest, that is supplied with wind through a trunk from bellows. Under each pipe is a valve, or pallet, connected by a system of cranks and levers to its respective key on the keyboard. A reservoir interposed between the bellows and the windchest is appropriately weighted to keep the supply of wind at a constant pressure. This reservoir has a blowoff valve that comes into operation when the reservoir is full. Although the bellows may resemble basically the familiar domestic type that is operated by hands or feet, wind is normally supplied from an electrically driven rotary blower.

The pitch of each note is determined by the length of the pipe; the longest pipe makes the lowest note, the shortest pipe the highest. If two comparable pipes sound an octave apart, the effective length of the higher-pitched pipe is exactly half that of the lower-pitched.

Since the tone of a pipe sounding on a constant pressure of wind is immutable, both as to quality and quantity, the uses of an organ with only one pipe to each note are strictly limited. Even the smallest organs, therefore, have at least three pipes to each note, and large organs have as many as 100 or more to each note. These sets, or ranks, of pipes are arranged in parallel rows on the windchest. The pallet controlled from each note admits wind to all the pipes belonging to that note; but in order that the organist may be able to use at will all, none, or any of the sets of pipes, an intermediate mechanism is provided by which any set or sets of pipes may be stopped off. From this function the control at the console for this purpose has come to be known in English as a stop, a term also used loosely for each rank of pipes.

mechanism   The operative part of the stop mechanism lies between the pallet and the footholes of the pipes. It normally consists of a strip of wood or plastic running the full length of the set of pipes, or stop. In it is drilled a series of holes. One hole registers exactly with each pipe. The strip of wood is placed in a close-fitting guide in which it may be moved; when it is moved longitudinally a short distance, so that its holes no longer register with the pipes, wind will no longer reach that set of pipes, even when the organist opens the pallets. These strips are therefore called sliders, and windchests in which the stops are operated in this way are called slider chests. There are other ways of working the stops, both ancient and modern, but the slider chest was in almost universal use before the 20th century, and many modern organ builders consider it the best. The slider is connected to the console by a system of levers and cranks, and it terminates in a knob that the organist pulls to bring the stop into play or pushes to silence it.

Organs of more than seven or eight stops usually have two or more manuals, each controlling its separate windchest and stops. Each manual division is self-contained, so that the organ is really a composite instrument. The organist, therefore, may vary the sounds in one or both of two ways: by changing the stops on the manuals or by changing from one manual to another.

Since the 18th century there has been yet a third way of controlling the volume of sound. The pipes of one or more manuals are placed in a box, one side of which consists of hinged and movable shutters (similar to Venetian blinds) that are connected to a pedal at the console. By opening and closing the shutters the sound from the division concerned is made louder or softer. Such boxes are called swell boxes.

Since the 14th century one division of the organ has commonly been played from a keyboard, or more properly a pedalboard, controlled by the organist's feet. The pedal division is basically like the manual divisions but controls the longer pipes.

The organist sometimes wishes to combine the stops of two different manuals or to couple one or more of the manuals to the pedals. This is effected by a simple mechanism called a coupler that is controlled by a stop knob at the console (stops that control a set of pipes are called speaking stops).

Certain combinations of stops on each manual are more commonly needed than others; in order that these combinations may be readily available, the console is provided with a number of short pedals disposed above the pedalboard. Each of these pedals is connected to a commonly needed combination of stops. When a pedal is depressed, the stops connected to it are drawn on, and any others that are already drawn are pushed off. These pedals are called combination (composition) pedals.

In the simplest mechanical action the connection from key to pallet is by a series of cranks and levers. The overall distance may be considerable, and the main distance is bridged by trackers, slender strips of wood, metal, or plastic that always work in tension.

The mechanism of the organ as described

so far is entirely mechanical, and such organs are said to have tracker action. Tracker action is used in many modern organs, especially in Germany, The Netherlands, Scandinavia, and increasingly in the United States and Canada; many organists prefer it to all other forms because it is so direct and sensitive in response. Organs may, however, have pneumatic, direct electric, or electropneumatic action, although these actions result in a loss of touch and responsiveness. In very large organs with tracker action, considerable strength may be necessary to depress the keys. Where the layout of the building is inconvenient and the divisions of the organ must be widely separated, tracker action is not practicable. To overcome these difficulties, especially with the objective of lightening the touch, other forms of action were devised.

The first effective system was developed (after a device invented by David Hamilton of Edinburgh in 1833) by Charles Spackman Barker, an Englishman. It consisted of a series of small, high-pressure pneumatic bellows, or motors, one attached to each note of the main manual at the console. When a note was depressed compressed air was admitted to the motor, which in turn operated the tracker action. Lacking encouragement at home, Barker went to France, where the great French builder Aristide Cavaillé-Coll employed the Barker lever almost exclusively from 1840 on.

Later trackers were supplanted by lead tubes, and the connection from key to pallet was solely by compressed air traveling through these tubes. This system was called tubular pneumatic action. At its best it was remarkably effective—reliable, long-lived, reasonably silent in action, and perfectly prompt in operation—at anything but its best it was none of these things, and its worst fault usually lay in sluggish operation. Tubular pneumatic action is almost never used in modern times.

As early as 1860 electric action was used experimentally, and in 1888 it was employed by the English builder Henry Willis at Canterbury Cathedral. His action remained in satisfactory use there for 50 years before it needed to be replaced. The modern type of electric action was pioneered by Robert Hope-Jones in Britain at the end of the 19th century. Direct electric action may be used, but a combination of electric and pneumatic mechanism is more general. In this system the depression of a key completes an electrical circuit, which energizes an electromagnet, allowing wind to enter a pneumatic motor attached to the windchest, and this motor opens the pallet. The stops may be operated in exactly the same way, but where they are operated electrically the sliders are often replaced by a series of valves, one to each pipe. The organ is then said to have a sliderless chest, and the most usual type is the pitman chest, so called because it contains a type of floating valve called a pitman. This action is commonly known as electropneumatic.

The combination pedals can also be operated electropneumatically or electrically. They are usually supplemented by a series of buttons, or pistons, placed in the keyslips on each manual, where they are conveniently operated by the organist's thumbs. The pistons may easily be made adjustable so that the organist can quickly alter the combination of stops controlled by each one.

No electric action has yet lasted more than 50 years without needing a comprehensive rebuilding, and many have lasted for much shorter periods. But with improvements in design and standardization of parts, it may be anticipated that rebuilding will become less frequent and expensive. On the other hand, there are small tracker-action organs working satisfactorily after 300 years, and even large ones have continued to operate for more than a century despite almost total neglect.

A compromise has been used successfully with tracker action for each division with the coupler action operated electrically. This arrangement has considerable merit, as the coupling together of three or four manuals with tracker action results in a heavy touch. Electric stop action may also be combined with tracker key action, enabling the use of electric (including solid-state) combinations—an invaluable aid, especially in larger instruments.

tone production The pipes are the most important part of an organ. There are two main categories: flues and reeds.

Flue pipes (made either of wood or metal; their construction is basically similar in princi-

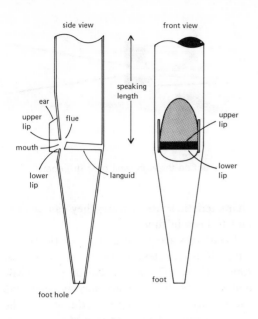

Figure 1
typical flue pipe (principal)

ple) account for about four-fifths of the stops of an average organ. Figure 1 shows a front view and a vertical section of the most typical sort of metal flue pipe. The pipe consists of three main parts: the foot, the mouth, and the speaking length.

The pipe stands vertically on the windchest, and wind enters at the foothole. The foot is divided from the speaking length by the languid, a flat plate; the only airway connection between the foot and the speaking length is a narrow slit called the flue. The wind emerges through the flue and strikes the upper lip, producing an audible frequency, the pitch of which is determined by and amplified in resonance by the speaking length of the pipe. A pipe of this kind is in fact identical in principle with a recorder or a tin whistle; but, whereas they have holes along the speaking length, which the player covers and uncovers with his fingers to secure the notes of the musical scale, in an organ there is a separate pipe for each note.

The tone of a pipe is determined by many factors, including the pressure of the wind supply, size of foothole, width of flue, height and width of mouth, and the scale, or diameter, of the pipe relative to its speaking length. The material of which the pipe is made also exerts an influence; it may be metal (*i.e.*, an alloy of lead and tin), wood, or more rarely pure tin or copper, and for the bass pipes zinc. The pipes may also vary in shape, a common variant being an upward taper in which the pipe is smaller in diameter at the top than at the mouth. Or the top of the pipe may be completely closed by a stopper. Such a pipe is said to be stopped; a stopped pipe sounds an octave lower in pitch than an open pipe of the same speaking length.

Open pipes of large diameter are said to be of large scale, and open pipes of small diameter are said to be of small scale. Large-scale pipes produce a dull or foundational quality of tone that is free from the higher harmonics. Small-scale pipes produce a bright quality of tone that is rich in harmonics. Stopped pipes can be particularly foundational in tone, and they favor the odd-numbered at the expense of the even-numbered partials. Tapered pipes are somewhere between stopped and open pipes in tone quality.

Flue pipes are tuned by increasing or decreasing the speaking length. In the past several methods of tuning were employed, but in modern times this is often done by fitting a cylindrical slide over the free end of the speaking length and sliding it up and down, lengthening or shortening the pipe as required. In stopped pipes the stopper is pushed farther down to sharpen the pitch or is pulled upward to lower it.

The pipe maker thus broadly fixes the type of tone that a pipe will produce; but this is further controlled within fairly wide limits by the wind pressure and finally by the voicer, who adjusts the tone of each pipe by manipulating the foothole, flue, and upper and lower lips. The attack of the note may also be greatly influenced by cutting a series of small nicks in the edge of the languid. Heavy nicking, so commonly practiced in the early 20th century, produces a smooth and sluggish attack. Light nicking or no nicking, as used up to the 18th century and in more advanced modern organs, produces a vigorous attack, or chiff, somewhat like tonguing in a woodwind instrument. This enhances the vitality and clarity of an organ. The voicer is the craftsman upon whom the ultimate success of any organ depends, although the tonal designer, or architect, is hardly less important, specifying the stops, their disposition, and the scales to be followed by the pipe maker. A completely successful organ depends upon the effective cooperation of designer and voicer.

Reed stops have beating reeds of a kind that finds several counterparts in the orchestra, and no doubt organ reeds were originally copied from instrumental prototypes.

The shallot, seen in cross section in Figure 2, is roughly cylindrical in shape, with its lower end closed and the upper end open. A section of the wall of the cylinder is cut away and finished off to a flat surface, as shown in the inset to Figure 2. The slit, or shallot opening, thus formed is covered by a thin brass tongue that is fixed to the upper end of the shallot. The tongue is curved and normally only partially covers the shallot opening. But when wind enters the boot the pressure of the wind momentarily forces the tongue against the shallot, completely closing the opening. Immediately the elasticity of the brass asserts itself, and the tongue reverts to its curved shape, thus uncovering the opening. This process is repeated rapidly. The frequency of the pulsations of air that enter the shallot is determined by the effective length of the reed and in turn determines the pitch of the note. Thence the pulsations pass out into the tube, or resonator, which further stabilizes the pitch and decides the quality of the note. Most reed resonators have a flared shape, as shown in Figure 2. As in flue pipes a wide scale favors a fundamental tone and a narrow scale a bright tone. Cylindrical resonators produce an effect similar to that of stopped flue pipes, the note being an octave lower than the equivalent flared pipe and the tone favoring the odd partials. Some reed pipes, such as the Vox humana, have very short resonators of quarter or eighth length. Pipes whose resonators have no mathematical relationship to the pitch are known as regals; the REGAL stops were very popular in the 17th century, particularly with the North German school, and their use has been revived in modern times. Their short resonators have varying and peculiar shapes, which produce a highly

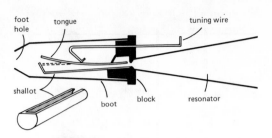

Figure 2
section through reed pipe (trumpet)

characteristic snarling tone; they can be difficult to keep in tune.

Reed pipes are tuned by moving the tuning wire, thus shortening or lengthening the tongue (Figure 2). As in flue pipes the scale and shape of the resonator largely determine the quality of tone to be produced; but the wind pressure, shape and size of the shallot, and thickness and curvature of the tongue also have important influence. The tongues may also be weighted with brass or felt; this weighting produces a smoother quality of tone, especially in the bass notes.

It has already been explained that the pitch of a pipe is proportional to its length. Most modern organs have a manual compass of five octaves, from the second C below middle C to the third C above; an open pipe sounding the low C is about eight feet (2.5 meters) in speaking length (64 vibrations per second). The shortest pipe in the same rank is thus about three inches (eight centimeters) long (2,048 vibrations per second). The most characteristic tone of the organ is produced by its diapason, or principal, stops. These are of medium scale (usually about 6-in. scale at the 8-ft. open pipe) and moderate harmonic development—i.e., neither particularly dull nor bright. Such a tone quality becomes boring if heard for a long time. Also when greater power is required, there is a distinct limit to what can be done by adding more stops of unison pitch. From the earliest times stops, especially the principals, were arranged in choruses, and the principal chorus is the backbone of the organ.

A chorus consists of stops of similar quality and power but at a great variety of pitches.

A unison principal is known as Principal 8 ft. because of its longest (8-ft.) pipe, and the figure 8 appears on the stop knob or tablet (rocking tablets are often used in place of knobs with electric action) at the console to give an indication of its pitch. The first step toward a chorus is to add a stop sounding an octave above 8-ft. ranks (*i.e.,* at octave pitch), the largest pipe of which is therefore four feet long. Next comes a 2-ft. stop, while in the other direction the suboctave pitch may be represented by a 16-ft. stop. The top pipe of a 2-ft. stop has a speaking length of only three-quarters of an inch, and this is about the practical upper limit. Nevertheless, an organ with nothing higher in pitch than a 2-ft. stop would be lacking in brilliance, especially in the lower parts of the compass.

From the earliest times, therefore, organs have been supplied with what are known generically as mixtures, with several high-pitched pipes to each note. But since, for example, a 1-ft. rank cannot be carried to the top note, it breaks back an octave at some convenient point in the compass. Ranks pitched even higher will break back more than once. Thus in the bass a mixture adds definition to the slow-speaking, low-pitched pipes; in the treble, where the small pipes tend to be lacking in power, it duplicates the unison and octave ranks. A mixture, therefore, helps to maintain a balance of power between bass and treble while adding harmonious power of a kind that is completely peculiar to the organ and can be produced in no other way.

Mixtures also contain ranks sounding at pitches other than octaves. In chorus mixtures these sound at a fifth above the unison (*e.g.,* G above C), although ranks sounding at a third above and even at a flat seventh (*e.g.,* E and B-flat above C) and their respective octaves are also found; but these are best restricted to mixtures intended for somewhat special effects. The theoretical justification for these quint- (fifth) and third-sounding ranks is that they reinforce the natural upper partials of the harmonic series, but they were included in organs long before this was understood. The fact is that they were found to sound well, and any attempts to build organs without

mixtures and off-unison ranks have been completely unsuccessful. The colorfulness and vitality of any organ depend largely on copious, artistically voiced mixtures.

Off-unison ranks are also available as separate stops, mostly sounding at an interval of a 12th (an octave and a fifth; $2 \frac{2}{3}$ ft.), 17th (two octaves and a third; $1 \frac{3}{5}$ ft.), or 19th (two octaves and a fifth; $1 \frac{1}{3}$ ft.) above the unison. These are used melodically to color the unison and octave stops, and they may be wide or narrow in scale. Such stops are known as mutation stops, as opposed to the mixtures, or chorus stops. Their use is essential for the historically (and therefore artistically) correct performance of organ music written before 1800 and of much modern music as well. After a period of disuse throughout the 19th century, they are again included in all modern organs that have any pretensions to being artistically competent.

early history The earliest history of the organ is so buried in antiquity as to be mere speculation. The earliest surviving record is of the Greek engineer Ctesibius, who lived in Alexandria in the 3rd century B.C. He is credited with the invention of an organ very much on the lines of the single-manual, slider-chest organ already described, except for its wind supply, which made use of a principle that was most ingenious, though applicable only to a very small instrument. A piston pump supplied air through an ordinary clack valve to a reservoir; at its upper end this reservoir communicated directly with the wind-chest. The reservoir, cylindrical in shape and with no bottom, was placed in a large drum-shaped container that was partly filled with water. As the reservoir became filled with air, the air would escape around its lower edge. In this way a more or less equal pressure of air was maintained inside the reservoir. Because of this arrangement the instrument was known as a hydraulis. A clay model of a hydraulis was discovered in 1885 in the ruins of Carthage (near modern Tunis, Tunisia), and the remains of an actual instrument were found in 1931 at Aquincum near Budapest.

The development of the organ in the early Middle Ages is obscure, but by the 8th or

9th century it was used in Christian churches. In the 10th century the famous instrument in the cathedral at Winchester, England, was constructed, of which the monk Wulfstan left a much quoted but manifestly garbled description ending: "the music of the pipes is heard throughout the town and the flying fame thereof is gone out over the whole country."

The artistic history of the organ begins with the development of the chromatic keyboard in the late 12th and early 13th centuries. By 1361 the cathedral organ at Halberstadt, Germany, had three chromatic keyboards and pedals; the keys, however, were much wider than those of the modern keyboard. The modern size of keys was fairly generally established by the end of the 15th century. Although the Halberstadt organ had three manuals, it had no stop mechanism. The main keyboard controlled a huge mixture stop, and the other keyboards controlled reduced groups of stops.

Ctesibius' slider arrangement was probably rediscovered some time in the early 15th century, and it became common soon after 1450. Reed stops began to appear at the same time,

performing on a positive
engraving by Israel van Meckenem (c. 1450–1503) courtesy, Bibliothèque Nationale, Paris

and by 1500 the organ had reached a stage in northern Germany in which all the important features of the modern organ were present. Each division had separate choruses; stopped, tapered, and open flue pipes; mutation stops; and reeds. The north German organ builders continued to be preeminent until about 1700, when the southern German builders took the lead.

During the Middle Ages and the Renaissance, three diminutive forms of the organ were widely used. The positive (in which category are included most chamber organs of the period) was a small organ capable of being moved usually by two men either on carrying poles or on a cart. The second type, the portative, was smaller still, with only one set of pipes and a manual of very short compass. It was carried by the player and was supported by a strap around his neck. The bellows were worked with one hand and the keys played with the other. Such instruments were used in processions and possibly in concerted instrumental ensembles. A third type, the regal, usually had a single regal stop as previously described.

Of the basic medieval organ, prior to the development of national styles, little if any material survives except in the old cathedral at Sion in Switzerland, where a large proportion of the seven-stop organ appears to date from about 1400. Although voiced on very low wind pressure, the tone of the chorus is brilliant, colorful, and amazingly powerful. Not much is known about the precise uses of church organs in the Middle Ages. The organ hardly began to possess a literature of its own before the last portion of the 15th century.

Italy Italy is mentioned first because its organs developed to their maturity soon after 1500 and remained relatively unaltered until about 1800. The Italian organ had one manual and usually only an octave of pedal keys, which had no pipes of its own (except an occasional independent 16-ft. *contrabasso*) but was coupled permanently to the manual. The manual chorus *(ripieno)* had the peculiarity that there was no collective mixture; all the ranks were drawn by separate stops. Each rank broke back an octave as it reached the

figure playing portative
from M. Severinus Boetius,
De Arythmetica, de musica, 14th century
courtesy, Biblioteca Nazionale, Naples
photograph, Antonio Beuf

$1\frac{1}{2}$-in. pipe. In addition there were flute stops of 4-ft., $2\frac{2}{3}$-ft., and 2-ft. pitch and a register called the *fiffaro* or *voce umana* (not to be confused with the French *voix humaine* or German Vox humana, which are regals), a principal rank found only in the treble and tuned sharp so that when it is played together with the *principale* one hears an audible beat. It was the forerunner of the similarly constructed *voix céleste* stop popular in the 19th-century Romantic organ. The scale of the classic Italian *principale* was not much different from its counterpart in the north, but its mouth was narrower, its voicing more delicate, and there was a notable lack of chiff. Reeds were not found until late in the 16th century and were never considered essential. There are well-preserved 16th-century instruments surviving, especially in Brescia and Bologna.

These simple resources were adequate for the performance of the keyboard works of the Gabrielis and Frescobaldi. Organ music of these men and their contemporaries was not clearly differentiated from that for harpsichord, as indicated by the collections *"per organo o cembalo."* The organ enjoyed some popularity: in Rome, according to Baini, no less than 30,000 people flocked to the square of St. Peter's hoping to find entrance to the cathedral to hear Frescobaldi's magic organ playing.

Spain and Portugal   The Iberian organ followed the Italian tradition, but later many reeds were added, most notably the *trompetas reales* ("royal trumpets") and other horizontal *(en chamada)* reeds arrayed in fanlike projections from highly ornamental cases. These reeds were on extremely low wind pressure and achieved amazingly full sounds that filled the huge edifices.

Like their Italian counterparts Spanish and Portuguese organs had only a few rudimentary pedals. The manuals, however, were divided, with notes up to middle C controlled by a drawknob to the left and notes up from C-sharp by a drawknob to the right. This enabled the playing of a solo voice against an accompaniment on the same manual.

The leading composers of this era wrote for the instruments at hand. Their music is exciting on these instruments but is seldom effective elsewhere. Likewise, northern European literature is not satisfactory on the Iberian instrument. Cabezón (1510–66) is the most illustrious of the historic Spanish composers. Others include Sebastián Aguilera de Heredia (1570–?) and Cabanilles (1644–1712). Carlos Seixas (1704–42) is known as the Portuguese Bach.

Germany   From 1500 to 1800 Germany led the world in organ building and the composition of organ music. The organ builders reached the peak of their achievement about 1700 in the work of Arp Schnitger. His was the organ of the high Baroque; but his countrymen Andreas and Gottfried Silbermann were equally masters of the slightly later, more sophisticated style of the mid-18th century.

Schnitger made organs with four manuals, pedals, and as many as 60 speaking stops, but he made some instruments with fewer than 30 speaking stops that are capable of dealing with the whole pre-Romantic repertoire. The finest surviving examples in this size are at Steinkirchen, near Hamburg, and at Cappel,

591

near Cuxhaven. Two great larger examples are at Zwolle and Alkmaar, The Netherlands, both restored to excellent condition in the mid-20th century.

Seventeenth- and 18th-century German organs were usually constructed on *Werk*-principle lines: each division of the instrument, or *Werk*, was separately cased, the Hauptwerk

organ by Christian Müller, 1738, in the Grote Kerk, Haarlem, The Netherlands
courtesy, International Orgel Improvisatie Concours Zomer Academie voor Organisten

(main manual) in front of and above the player, with the Pedals at each side and the Positiv (auxiliary manual) behind on the gallery railing. Each division, including the Pedal, had its own principal chorus complete up to at least one mixture. All divisions were roughly equal in power but varied in pitch, having divisions respectively a 16-ft., 8-ft., and 4-ft. preponderance (and 32-ft. and 2-ft. as well in larger instruments). Each manual division also had a set of flutes and mutations and at least one reed.

The earliest organ music consisted of simple arrangements of vocal and instrumental music. A significant development in ornamented versions of such compositions for other mediums is the *Fundamentum organisandi* (Nürnberg, 1452) by Konrad Paumann, organist at the court of Bavaria. By the end of the 15th century, the polyphonic style was establishing itself in an independent form for the organ as a separate and distinct instrument. Pedal notes were ideally suited for a long-note cantus firmus against manual counterpoint. The great Amsterdam organist Jan Pieterszoon Sweelinck (1562–1621), having studied in Venice (a tradition already established from northern Europe), developed a notable school of organ playing and composition that dominated a significant part of the musical world for almost two centuries, culminating in the genius of Bach. Among its composers were one of Sweelinck's greatest pupils, Samuel Scheidt of Halle, Johann Adam Reinken of Hamburg, and Dietrich Buxtehude of Lübeck. In Austria and south Germany a pupil of Frescobaldi, Johann Jakob Froberger of Vienna, was noted for his improvisational style. Johann Pachelbel of Nürnberg was the agent by which Italian and south German influences were again transported to northern Germany. By the time of Bach the written CHORALE PRELUDE (as opposed to the improvised prelude to the chorale within the Lutheran service), prelude and fugue, toccata, passacaglia, chaconne, and trio were firmly established forms for the organ— probably never again to be surpassed.

France   As far as the manual divisions are concerned, French organs differed little from the German type, but the principal choruses were generally larger in scale. The separate,

large-scaled Tierce ($1\frac{3}{5}$ ft.) was also universal, and there were many cornet stops. These mixture stops consisted of five pipes to each note: a stopped unison (8 ft.) and large-scale open 4 ft., $2\frac{2}{3}$ ft., 2 ft., and $1\frac{3}{5}$ ft. They extended only from middle C upward and were largely melodic in use. They were never drawn with the principal chorus (Plein Jeu) but generally were used with the reed chorus (Grand Jeu). Apart from this the Plein Jeu, Grand Jeu, and Jeux de Mutation were seldom or never intermixed in French music.

The pedal division of the French organ prior to 1700 was regarded largely as a sort of solo cantus firmus section that consisted usually of only 8- and 4-ft. flutes and 8- and 4-ft. trumpets. Only in the largest 18th-century organs were 16-ft. stops included, although there were often as many as three on the Grand Orgue (the manual analogous to the German Hauptwerk and the English Great Organ). When French organs had more than two manuals (Grand Orgue and Positif), the others (Récit and Écho) were usually of short compass; but if there was a fifth manual, it was a Clavier de Bombardes, consisting of 16-, 8-, and 4-ft. trumpets and a cornet. Unlike its German counterpart the main case housed all divisions except the Positif, which was in its usual location on the gallery railing.

French organs were notable for their reeds, and the highly stylized French music of the 17th and 18th centuries calls for their frequent use. Surviving specimens in good order are rare; but unaltered, late 18th-century, four-manual organs survive at Poitiers Cathedral (by the noted builder François-Henri Clicquot) and at Saint-Maximin, Provence (by Jean-Esprit Isnard).

Jean Titelouze (1563–1633) of Rouen may be considered the father of French organ music. A great tradition of playing and composing developed with a single dynasty presiding at a single church, Saint-Gervais in Paris, for more than 150 years: the Couperin family, including Louis, François, Charles, and culminating in François le Grand (1668–1733), whose two famous masses are repertoire staples even today. Contemporaries included the Paris organist Nicolas Lebègue and his pupil Nicolas de Grigny of Reims; Louis Nicholas

Clérambault, known for two modal suites; and Louis Claude Daquin, a great favorite in Paris who played his popular *Noëls* at the royal chapel.

Great Britain British organs before the Commonwealth (1649–60) seem to have been very immature. Only a few had two manuals, and none had pedals. Mixtures and reeds seem to have been unknown, and mutations were restricted to a single twelfth.

After 1660 a new school rapidly grew up, and although the two principal builders had both been abroad during the Commonwealth (Bernard Smith in Germany or Holland and Renatus Harris in France), their British work owed little to foreign influence. Only the Great Organ had a complete diapason chorus, and the Choir, or Chayre, organ usually extended upward only to a single 2 ft. Almost every organ had a Cornet, and the reeds in common use were Trumpet, Vox humana, and Cremona, or Krummhorn, with half-length, cylindrical resonators. There were no pedals, but the manual compass almost invariably extended to the third G below middle C. If there was a third manual it consisted of a short-compass Echo division in which all the pipes were shut up in a box to produce the echo effect. In 1712 the builder Abraham Jordan first fitted the echo box with shutters that were controlled by a pedal at the console; this arrangement produced what Jordan described as the swelling organ, but it was not to reach its full development until 150 years later; no 18th-century organ music demands a swell box. There are hardly any surviving examples of British instruments of this period in original condition, and the only one of any size is the 14-stop, two-manual organ at Adlington Hall, near Macclesfield, dating from the last quarter of the 17th century. It is possibly the work of Bernard Smith, is entirely original, and was restored to perfect order in 1959.

Such instruments were adequate for the music of John Lugge, John Blow, Purcell, Handel, John Stanley, and even early 19th-century composers such as Samuel Wesley.

the Romantic organ Because of the increasing interest in orchestral and operatic music, the organ fell out of favor in the 18th century, and by 1800 it survived only as an ecclesiastical drudge. From the middle of the 19th century, however, a revival took place under the leadership of two great builders, Aristide Cavaillé-Coll of France and Henry ("Father") Willis of England. The German Edmund Schulze, who brought to England an organ built by his father's firm in central Germany, was also influential, especially in his flue choruses. In Britain during the first half of the 19th century, the introduction of pedals under the influence of Henry John Gauntlett made it possible for the first time to play the organ music of Bach and his German contemporaries and predecessors. While retaining respectable vestiges of the classical chorus, Cavaillé-Coll and Willis developed the solo stops, especially reeds, and Willis, in particular, provided new aids to registration.

The work of Cavaillé-Coll was directly responsible for a new school of organ composition—most notably the works of Franck but also Saint-Saëns, Alexandre Guilmant, Charles-Marie Widor, Louis Vierne, Charles Tournemire, Marcel Dupré, Messiaen, Poulenc (a lone concerto), Jean Langlais, and Maurice Duruflé.

Parallel to the French movement German-born Mendelssohn, though working primarily in England, revived an interest in the works of Bach and composed sonatas and preludes and fugues for the organ. Liszt and the German Julius Reubke added to the repertoire several flamboyant, pianistic pieces, and Brahms wrote chorale preludes and several preludes and fugues. A composer of monumental chromatic fantasies and fugues, as well as simple chorale preludes, was Max Reger.

Organists found that they could play effective arrangements of orchestral music on the new Romantic-style organ. Since orchestral music was popular and respectable orchestras very rare and other forms of public entertainment even more so, the organ suddenly regained an immense popularity hardly rivaled by that of the 17th and 18th centuries, when it was the acknowledged "king of instruments." Organ builders naturally responded by making their instruments increasingly orchestral in character, culminating at the end of the 19th century in the work of the English builder Robert Hope-Jones, who entirely abandoned the chorus and mutation stops and relied instead upon diapasons of vast scale on heavy-pressure wind, with reeds to match, backed up by huge-scaled flutes, tiny-scaled string stops (with keen-sounding flues), and powerful stops of his own invention called diaphones. Hope-Jones emigrated to the United States, and, although a semblance of classical design returned to England soon after 1900, his influence continued to be felt throughout the first half of the 20th century. This discredited the organ as a musical instrument in the eyes of serious musicians and composers.

The first organs in America had been imported from England beginning about 1700. This was the period after the Commonwealth, and the Puritan view of the unsuitability of an organ in church was inherited by the colonies. Only parishes of the Church of England (later known as Protestant Episcopal Church) and Lutheran and Moravian churches in Pennsylvania would admit instruments. Another century elapsed before the New England Puritans did likewise. The only builder of note was the German-American David Tannenberg. A U.S. school of builders began to emerge in the early 1800s with such names as Henry Erben, Elias and George Hook, George Jardine, William A. Johnson, J. H. and C. S. Odell, and Hilborne and Frank Roosevelt. Perhaps the inevitable end of the U.S. "romantic" era was reached in Ernest M. Skinner, who lived until the middle of the 20th century. In Canada, Joseph Casavant built his first organ in Quebec province in 1837. Two of his sons visited France in 1878–79 and brought back to North America the Cavaillé-Coll tradition.

organ revival Albert Schweitzer wrote *Deutsche und französische Orgelbaukunst und Orgelkunst* ("The Art of German and French Organ Builders and Players") in 1906 outlining the inadequacies of the 19th-century organ for the performance of Bach and his contemporaries. It was not until 1926, however, with the influential Karl Straube, that the revival began. He renounced his earlier approach to the organ and called for a return to the instrument of Schnitger and the high Baroque. Since then the movement has spread among such builders as Karl Kemper, Rudolph von Beck-

erath, and Johannes Klais in Germany; Victor Gonzalez in France; Sybrand J. Zachariassen and Th. Frobenius in Denmark; Dirk A. Flentrop in The Netherlands; Th. Kuhn in Switzerland; and Walter Holtkamp, G. Donald Harrison, and Herman Schlicker in the United States. These were the pioneers of the neoclassical movement; the firms they founded and their imitators have reestablished the traditions of the past and combined them with new materials and mechanical improvements so that the organ can once again be taken seriously as a musical instrument.

BIBLIOGRAPHY: Edward F. Rimbault, *The Early English Organ Builders and Their Works* (1865; reprint, 1976); Wallace Goodrich, *The Organ in France* (1917; reprint, 1977); Cecil Clutton and Austin Niland, *The British Organ* (1963; reprint, 1977); Michael Wilson, *The English Chamber Organ: History and Development, 1650–1850* (1968); Poul-Gerhard Andersen, *Organ Building and Design* (1969); Fenner Douglass, *The Language of the Classical French Organ* (1969); E. N. Matthews, *Colonial Organs and Organ Builders* (1969); Jean Perrot, *The Organ from Its Invention in the Hellenistic Period to the End of the Thirteenth Century* (1971); Orpha Ochse, *The History of the Organ in the United States* (1975); William Leslie Sumner, *The Organ*, 4th ed. (1978).

organum A medieval Latin term denoting any musical instrument, later specifically an organ; or a polyphonic setting in certain specific styles of plainchant (9th–13th century). In its earliest written form, found in the treatise *Musica enchiriadis* (c. 900), two melodic lines moved simultaneously, note against note. Sometimes the second, or organal, voice ran parallel to the chant melody, or principal voice, a fourth or a fifth lower (as G or F below C, etc.). In others the two voices started in unison but moved to wider intervals during each phrase. Both melodies might in turn be doubled at the octave, making three- or four-voice polyphony. Such polyphony during the 9th to 11th century was probably spontaneously produced by specially trained singers (*e.g.*, at the cathedrals of Chartres and Fleury in France and Winchester in England).

In more elaborate forms of organum a freely composed melody was sung above the plainchant, as in manuscripts from the abbeys of Santiago de Compostela, Spain (*c.* 1137), and Saint-Martial at Limoges, France (*c.* 1150). The plainchant was sung or played in long notes, called the tenor, and an upper melody, called the *duplum,* consisted of unmeasured melismas much like those in a gradual or responsory verse. The new style continued being called organum, and the term discant was now applied to the earlier note-against-note form. Gradually the upper voice took on a more measured form, culminating in the late 12th century in the composers of the NOTRE DAME SCHOOL, who brought the style to its greatest floridity. One of them, Léonin, is credited with organal settings of graduals, alleluias, and responsories for all the major feasts that are collected in *Magnus liber* (*c.* 1170). Here is found a contrasting section called the CLAUSULA, which was more measured and quicker moving. Around 1200 the composer Pérotin modified this collection and wrote florid organa for three and four voices.

Ormandy, Eugene, real name, Eugene Blau (b. November 18, 1899)   Long identified with the luscious "Philadelphia sound," the Hungarian conductor of the Philadelphia Orchestra Eugene Ormandy began as a violinist, the youngest student ever to be admitted to the Budapest Conservatory (at the age of five). He played in various orchestras in Europe, coming in 1921 to the United States, where he was soon concertmaster of the Capitol Theatre orchestra in New York City. Ormandy began conducting in 1924; he was appointed to the Minneapolis Symphony in 1931, as Stokowski's associate in Philadelphia in 1936, and as music director in 1938, retiring in 1980. He is a romanticist who specializes primarily in the post-Romantics and early moderns.

ornamentation   The embellishment of a melodic line either by elaboration or by rhythmic modification. In Western music ornamentation is ideally something added in order to make it more pleasing (early writers called it "spice," "salt," etc.). In all arts badly conceived or badly executed ornaments may have

the effect of causing confusion and a disintegration of the basic structure.

From at least the Middle Ages until the end of the 18th century, the practice of improvised ornamentation was part of a singer's or an instrumentalist's traditional technique. The composer provided the composition and the performer vocal agility or instrumental technique to heighten the expressive power of the music by florid embellishment and sensitive articulation. That ornamentation was sometimes debased by a tasteless display of technical virtuosity is attested by writers of many periods.

In instrumental music some styles of ornamentation are the direct result of the technical limitations of an instrument; *e.g.,* repeated notes of the same pitch are impossible to play on most bagpipes and must be simulated by means of ornamentation:

Ornamentation was also the result of a natural desire to add variety to the repetition of a section of a work or of a short piece, such as a dance, that was repeated many times. This practice led logically to the variation form.

The apparatus of ornamentation varies greatly from age to age and from country to country. It is a traditional vocabulary that reflects and often influences the development of musical style. In its most creative sense ornamentation is closely linked with improvisation and therefore with composition itself.

When a musical work is transferred from one medium to another, as in a keyboard transcription of a vocal composition, the instrumental style and ornamentation appropriate to the new medium may alter entirely the character of the music.

A decorated arrangement is often a creative reworking of the original material and may reflect not only the instrumental style of the new medium but also the personal style of the arranger. This is found in the harpsichord transcriptions by Bach of violin works by Vivaldi and later in the elaborate arrangements and fantasias for piano made by Liszt of operatic excerpts and orchestral works.

The European concept of ornamentation as an addition to an already musically complete composition is something foreign to the music of ancient civilizations and to the classical music of many modern Oriental countries. In this primarily melodic music the boundaries between ornamentation, improvisation, and composition are impossible to define. Composition is improvisation, and improvisation is the organization, within the limits of a specific mode, of a traditional vocabulary of melody fragments and ornamentation formulas proper to the mode.

Middle Ages   In the Middle Ages the practice of vocal ornamentation in sacred music was strongly opposed by the church and was prohibited by papal bull and denounced by bishops as being detrimental to the purity of the plainchant. Precise details of early medieval ornamentation were not recorded. All that is known is that some notational signs signified an ornament and that in vocal music the trill was known from at least the 3rd century. Guido of Arezzo wrote that Italian singers were best fitted to perform the ornaments notated in the plainchant and that foreigners who were unable to perform these ornaments adequately should rather sing the music undecorated.

Both the monophonic and the polyphonic music of the 13th century contain what appears to be written vocal ornamentation. The first notated dance tunes date from this time, and these show certain features of a purely instrumental style of ornamentation:

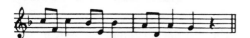

Although no particular instrument is specified, this is typical writing for bowed stringed instruments tuned in fifths and in fact was later to become a commonplace of violin figuration.

Italian secular music of the 14th century contains much notated vocal and instrumental ornamentation. In this mu-

sic one of the fundamental techniques of ornamentation was established: that of diminution (the 16th-century English word was division); *i.e.,* the dividing of the basic notes of the melodic line into groups of notes of a shorter duration. The first measure shows the melody undecorated, followed by three possible methods of ornamentation:

In the 14th century this technique became codified, and the performer could choose one of several diminution patterns to ornament a given melodic phrase. These diminutions were generally performed at certain foreseen developments in the composition such as at cadences.

The most elaborate diminution was often reserved for the end of a section, as in this florid example from "De'l non fugir" by Landini (d. 1397):

This practice of cadential embellishment became a feature of vocal and later instrumental ornamentation. The following is the unornamented form of the last two bars of "Pandolpho" by Robert Parsons (d. 1570) and a contemporary decorated version in which the first bar is significantly extended to three bars in order to give the singer full scope for virtuosity:

Some pi - ty Pan - dol - pho.

Some pi-ty Pan   dol-pho

It thus came about that the 18th-century CA-DENZA, from which the cadenzas of the great 19th-century instrumental virtuosos developed, had its origin, as its name implies, in the earlier cadential ornamentation.

Renaissance Despite the codification of diminution in the 14th century, it was not until the following century that the first theoretical works on the subject appeared. One of these, the *Buxheim Organ Book* (*c.* 1460–70), contains many ornamented keyboard settings of French, German, and English vocal music and examples showing 15th-century methods of improvisation in which appears the sometimes inflexible and stereotyped style of diminution typical of German lute and keyboard ornamentation.

In the Renaissance vocal ornamentation was one of several subjects coordinated in a musician's training. Jean Petit Coclico records that Josquin des Prés taught his pupils singing, vocal ornamentation, improvised counterpoint, and composition.

In the 16th century many printed books appeared containing instructions on diminution. These books, mostly by Italian authors, were directed to the amateur musician, though they were not necessarily of a popular nature. Among these, *Fontegara* (1535) by Sylvestro Ganassi is one of the most comprehensive ever published on the subject. In common with all writers on ornamentation from the 16th to the 18th century, Ganassi deals with the ornamentation of intervals—a systematic survey of the intervals of the second, third, fourth, and fifth in various ornamented forms—and with the ornamentation of conventional cadences. All the treatises on ornamentation from Ganassi to Quantz in the 18th century follow this principle. A copy of *Fontegara* contained in Ganassi's own hand 300 different ways to ornament a single cadence.

Sixteenth-century vocal ornamentation was conceived as an abstract musical expression rather than as an expression of literary ideas. It was primarily concerned not with underlining the words but with reflecting the mood of the text. Therefore the singer's approach to diminution was basically the same as that of the instrumentalist. In fact the title page of Ganassi's work describes it as "teaching . . . diminution suitable to wind and stringed instruments as well as to those who delight in singing."

Baroque A decisive change in vocal and instrumental styles occurred in Italy and France in the early years of the 17th century and also two distinct national styles of ornamentation. With the revival of interest in the literature of classical Greece and with the founding of the literary academies, poets and musicians began to collaborate in an attempt to recreate the musico-poetic art of the classical world. Music was to be the servant of poetry, and vocal ornamentation was used to heighten the emotional content of the words. To achieve this a new emotionally expressive style of melodic writing was developed together with a rhythmically mannered vocabulary of vocal ornamentation.

In Italy diminution was still practiced in vocal as well as in instrumental music, but the new style of ornamentation was reserved for solo vocal music. The following example from the opera *Orfeo* (1607) by Monteverdi shows the intense dramatic passion conveyed by the early 17th-century Italian vocal ornamentation, with its jerky rhythms and groups of rapidly repeated notes (called *trilli;* trills were known as *gruppi*):

The principles of diminution were preserved in the 17th-century French style of vocal ornamentation associated with the performance of the *airs de cour*. They also survived in a relatively simple form in the doubles, or varied repeats, found in the harpsichord works of François Couperin. In early 17th-century French lute music, a tradition was current using a large number of small ornaments for the purpose of articulation and accentuation as well as rhythmic modifications of the written notes. These ornaments became an important stylistic feature of French harpsichord music, while the rhythmic modifications used by the lutenists were incorporated in the later French instrumental style—notably in that of the French overture with its characteristic double-dotted rhythms.

Small ornaments such as mordents and turns, derived from the lute compositions of the École de Paris in which Denys Gaultier was a prominent figure, were transformed and codified for use in the harpsichord music of Couperin and are set out in his *L'Art de toucher le clavecin* (1717). The following examples are typical of this style of ornamentation:

written   played   written played   written played

Following the ornamented vocal styles of Monteverdi and his contemporaries, the Italian instrumental style remained elaborately florid. The performance of solo works in the mid-18th century required great creative skill in improvisation on the part of the performer, as it was customary for the composer to write only the main structural notes of the melody. This led eventually to the debasement of the Italian style in the vocal and instrumental gymnastics practiced by virtuosos of the late 18th and early 19th centuries.

The following shows the first measure of an adagio from a violin sonata by Giuseppe Tartini (d. 1770), first in its simple form and then in a typically elaborate version published about 1788:

The French and Italian styles of ornamentation remained distinct throughout the greater part of the 18th century. A composer such as Bach, not born to either one, could use both dispassionately.

In the works of Haydn and Mozart, variations of themes incorporated written ornaments in a manner that announces the absorption of ornaments in the accepted musical language. In the 19th century many of the features of ornamentation, such as turns and accented grace notes (which take the form of appoggiaturas or anticipations), became an integral part of the musical language but without being left to the discretion of the performer. Improvisation ceased to form part of the performer's equipment except in vocal ornamentation (deplored by contemporary critics) in Italian opera; but its spirit persisted in a crystallized form of established harmonic and contrapuntal procedures. Many examples of florid turns, anticipations, and suspensions in the works of Chopin and Wagner can be traced back to earlier forms of ornamentation.

In essence the art of ornamentation is dependent on a certain distribution of responsibility between composer and performer. This concept was foreign to early 20th-century music, though the ancient tradition reappears in spontaneously conceived examples of ornamentation in jazz. Here, however, as in the series of stereotyped ornamented cadenzas provided by the composer Quantz in the 18th century, the uninitiated jazz trumpeter is provided with a series of "hot breaks" in the form of cadenzas. These cadenzas have their origin in practices reaching back to the beginnings of music.

BIBLIOGRAPHY: Sylvestro Ganassi, *Fontegara* (1535; Eng. trans., 1959); Arnold Dolmetsch, *The Interpretation of the Music of the XVII and XVIII Centuries* (1915; reprint, 1969); Carl Philipp Emanuel Bach, *Essay on the True Art of Playing Keyboard Instruments* (1949); Walter Emery, *Bach's Ornaments* (1953); Johann Joachim Quantz, *On Playing the Flute* (1966); Thurston Dart, *The Interpretation of Music,* 4th ed. (1967); Robert Donington, *A Performer's Guide to Baroque Music* (1973) and *The Interpretation of Early Music,* rev. ed. (1974); Howard Mayer Brown, *Embellishing Sixteenth-Century Music* (1976).

Ornstein, Leo (b. December 11, 1895) A student at the Imperial Conservatory in St. Petersburg and the Institute of Musical Art in New York City, the Russian pianist and composer Leo Ornstein concertized throughout North America and Europe from 1911 to 1913. Two years later he gave a series of lecture-recitals in New York City, where he introduced his own music as well as that of Debussy, Ravel, and Aleksandr Scriabin. After 1935 he devoted himself to teaching and composition and established the Ornstein School of Music in Philadelphia. In 1974 he gave all his music manuscripts to the Yale University library. A pioneer in dissonance, his music alternates tonal melodies with atonal complexities and contrapuntal rhythms. His principal compositions are for piano (*Three Moods,* 1913; four sonatas; two concertos), orchestra (*Nocturne and Dance of the Fates,* 1937), chamber music (a quartet, a piano quintet, and a sonata and six preludes for cello and piano), and songs.

RECORDINGS: Cello Sonata; *Nocturne and Dance of the Fates;* Piano Quintet; Piano Sonata No. 4; Preludes (3) for cello and piano; *Three Moods;* piano music.

Orpheus in the Underworld: *see* OFFENBACH; OPERETTA.

ostinato A short phrase repeated persistently in a composition or section thereof, usually in close succession. It is normally repeated at the same pitch in the same voice with little or no variation; hence, the Italian word for "obstinate." The ostinato appears as early as the 13th century and frequently after 1450 in ostinato motets, a well-known example being Morales' *Emendemus in melius* in the 16th century. It was particularly common in 16th-century dance pieces, notably in the bass, where it is called a basso ostinato, or ground bass (see GROUND). The ostinato has been revived by such 20th-century composers as Bartók and Hindemith.

Otello: *see* BOITO; LIBRETTO (19th-century influences); OPERA (the 19th century); ROMANTIC PERIOD (non-German music of the 19th century).

overtone A faint tone sounding above the fundamental when a string or air column vibrates simultaneously as a whole, producing the fundamental (or first partial, or first harmonic); if it vibrates in sections it produces overtones (upper partials, or harmonics). The listener normally hears the fundamental pitch clearly; with concentration the faint overtones can be heard.

Harmonics are a series of overtones resulting when the partial vibrations are of equal sections (*e.g.,* halves, thirds, fourths). As the vibrating sections become smaller, the harmonics are higher in pitch and successively closer together. The frequencies of the upper harmonics form simple ratios with the frequency of the first harmonic, or fundamental (*e.g.,* $2:1$, $3:1$, $4:1$).

Some instruments whose sounds result from the vibration of metal, wood, or stone bars; from cylinders; from plates (*e.g.,* cymbals, bells, marimbas); or from membranes (drums) produce nonharmonic overtones—that is, tones whose frequencies (and therefore pitches) lie outside the harmonic series. *See* COMBINATION TONE.

overture A piece originally serving as an introduction to an opera, later developed into an instrumental work associated with both the suite and the symphony, and ultimately into an independent piece for large orchestra.

The earliest operas usually opened with a trumpet fanfare (of which a surviving example is the short toccata repeated three times in Monteverdi's *Orfeo*) or with a prologue sung in recitative. The first attempt to establish the form of an organized work as an appropriate introduction to operatic entertainment is found in the overtures to the French operas of Lully. These, *e.g.,* the overture to *Thésée* (1675), open with a slow section in a pompous double-dotted rhythm followed by a quick section in a fugal style. The third section of the Lullyan, or French, overture was either a repetition of the opening slow section or a slow dance movement, sometimes a minuet or a gavotte. Another type of overture, the Italian opera overture (or *sinfonia avanti l'opera*), was established after 1680 by Alessandro Scarlatti; it is also in three sections, the two outer sections in quick time and the central one in slow (allegro–adagio–allegro).

The form of the French overture was widely copied and not only by opera composers. It appears also as an introduction to oratorios. Purcell's *Dido and Aeneas* and Handel's *Messiah* are among the many 17th- and 18th-century works provided with an overture on the Lullyan model. It was also adopted in purely instrumental music. Many German composers used the form for the opening movement of harpsichord suites, the remaining movements consisting of dances. It was natural that the gavotte or the minuet that formed the final section of the Lullyan overture should be followed by other dances, and so this type developed into the orchestral suite. Handel's seventh harpsichord suite, opening with a movement entitled Overture, and Bach's four orchestral *ouvertures,* in which there is an extended first movement followed by a series of dances, are works of this kind. This form of suite, based on the French overture, persisted until the middle of the 18th century. But the form of the Italian opera overture served as a model for the three-movement 18th-century symphony illustrated in works by Johann Gottlieb Graun, Carl Philipp Emanuel Bach, and Georg Benda. This form was cultivated until Johann Stamitz added the minuet. The term overture, however, was used for the symphony in England until the end of the 18th century. It appears as a description of Haydn's symphonies performed in London in 1791.

A more modern form of the opera overture was established by Gluck. In his dedication of *Alceste* (1769) he declared that an overture should "prepare the audience for the plot of the play." Instead of the overture's ending before the rise of the curtain, it was designed to merge into the mood of the opening act. Gluck's overture to *Iphigénie en Tauride* contains an example of this device, foreshadowing similar use by Wagner in *Tristan und Isolde*. Gluck's recommendation was followed by Mozart, notably in the overtures to *Don Giovanni* and *Die Zauberflöte* with allusions to themes from the opera. Similar allusions were used with great dramatic effect in Beethoven's *Leonore* Overtures No. 2 and No. 3 and with great evocative effect in Weber's *Der Freischütz* and Wagner's *Tannhäuser*. The most

highly developed is Wagner's overture to *Die Meistersinger,* in which the principal themes from the opera are combined contrapuntally.

Toward the end of the 19th century the opera overture was frequently replaced by a shorter introductory prelude, particularly in Wagner's *Lohengrin* and *Parsifal*. This was an entirely new conception. By establishing the mood of the opening act quickly, such preludes were thought to merge more effectively into the dramatic action. Following the Wagnerian model introductions to later operas, as in Debussy's *Pelléas et Mélisande* and Britten's *Peter Grimes,* consist of only a few measures. A successful experiment was an aria as the prologue to Leoncavallo's *Pagliacci.*

Based on the style of the overtures to Romantic operas, the concert overture was established in the 19th century as an independent work of a descriptive or programmatic nature. Mendelssohn's *Hebrides* Overture, Dvořák's *Carnival,* and William Walton's *Portsmouth Point* are examples. Unity is achieved by the development and contrast of themes in the manner of the symphony, but the descriptive nature dictated a rhapsodic rather than a classical form. The concert overture thus took on the character of a symphonic poem. Another category belongs to incidental music or music for the spoken drama. Overtures to plays, such as Mendelssohn's *Midsummer Night's Dream* and Beethoven's *Coriolan,* were intended for occasions when a large orchestra was available at the performance of a stage play but are in modern times heard exclusively in the concert hall.

Owen Wingrave: *see* BRITTEN; OPERA (the 20th century).

Ozawa, Seiji (b. September 1, 1935) Educated in Tokyo and then in Europe with Herbert von Karajan, the Japanese conductor Seiji Ozawa was awarded the Koussevitzky Memorial Scholarship at the Berkshire Music Center in 1960, where he worked with Leonard Bernstein. He served as Bernstein's assistant at the New York Philharmonic (1961–62; 1964–65). After a brief tenure with the Japan Philharmonic, Ozawa returned to the United States and was director and conductor of the Ravinia (Illinois) Festival (1964–68), overlapping the same position with the Toronto Symphony. In 1970 he succeeded Josef Krips as director of the San Francisco Symphony and was appointed joint artistic director (with Gunther Schuller) of the Berkshire Center. In addition to the San Francisco post, he became music director of the Boston Symphony in 1973, leaving San Francisco in 1977. Notable among his numerous recordings are large choral works, such as Berlioz and Messiaen.

P

Pachelbel, Johann (baptized September 1, 1653–March 3, 1706)   One of the great German organ masters of the generation before Bach, Johann Pachelbel studied in Altdorf and Regensburg and held posts as organist in Vienna, Stuttgart, and other cities. In 1695 he was appointed organist at the Sebalduskirche in Nürnberg, where he remained until his death. All Pachelbel's work is in a clear and contrapuntally simple style. His organ compositions show a knowledge of the Italian forms such as the toccata, derived through Johann Jakob Froberger from Frescobaldi. Of special importance are his chorale preludes, which did much to establish the chorale melodies of Protestant north Germany in the more lyrical musical atmosphere of the Catholic south. Pachelbel also wrote harpsichord music without much feeling for that instrument's individuality and other instrumental music, including six suites for two violins (1691) and *Hexachordum Apollinis* (1699), six sets of variations on airs. His popular Canon in D Major was written for three violins and continuo and published with a Gigue in the same key. His son Wilhelm Hieronymus Pachelbel (1686–1764) was also an organist and composer.

RECORDINGS: *Hexachordum Apollinis;* Canon; organ music; suites.

Pachmann, Vladimir de (July 27, 1848–January 6, 1933)   The pianist Vladimir de Pachmann studied in his native Odessa, Ukraine, and in Vienna with Joseph Dachs. Though his early recitals were successful, he was severely self-critical, and he withdrew for long periods. He was known as a Chopin interpreter, but his eccentricities increased with age, and he was called "the Chopinzee" and "a pianissimist" by his detractors.

Paderewski, Ignacy (Jan) (November 18, 1860–June 29, 1941)   The most famous pupil of Leschetizky, the Polish pianist Ignacy Paderewski was a legend in his own time. No one since Liszt had such a hold on the public. Adulation stopped short of his professional colleagues, however. He had problems of technique that plagued him from childhood, and it was not until his exposure to Leschetizky at age 24 that he had any success. His magic with the public, nevertheless, knew no bounds. He produced a unique sound, and he could shape a lovely phrase, making his Chopin something special. Paderewski had teaching posts at the conservatories in Warsaw and Strasbourg, and he taught privately at his home in Switzerland. His compositions were performed widely during his lifetime, but only his Minuet in G has survived. He was also a staunch Polish patriot, and he worked diligently for the independence of Poland after World War I and served as its first prime minister in 1919. During World War II he was chairman of the Polish National Council in Paris.

Ignacy Paderewski ·   *EB Inc.*

Paër, Ferdinando (June 1, 1771–May 3, 1839)   An Italian opera composer, Ferdinando Paër was much influenced by the French opera of the period. His first opera, *Orphée et Euridice* (Parma, 1791), was a setting of a French version of the Orpheus legend. In the same year he went to Venice as maestro di cappella, and from there he moved to Vienna where he produced his most successful opera, *Camilla* (1799). In 1803 he was appointed Kapellmeister at Dresden and there produced *Leonora* (1804), a setting in Italian of Jean Nicolas Bouilly's libretto that was the basis of Beethoven's *Fidelio*. In 1806 he accompanied Napoleon to Poland and in 1807 was appointed his maître de chapelle in Paris. In 1812 he succeeded Gasparo Spontini as director of Italian opera at the Odéon, where he remained until 1827.

Paganini, Niccolò (October 27, 1782–May 27, 1840) Called by Schumann the "turning point in the history of virtuosity," the Italian violinist Niccolò Paganini inspired the romantic mystique of the musical virtuoso. He first performed at age nine and toured at 13, playing many of his own compositions. In 1805, after several years' absence from the stage because of dissolute living, he became music director at the court of the Princess of Lucca. He stayed there until 1813, when he toured Europe with great success. It was on his request for a viola solo that Berlioz composed his *Harold in Italy* (1833). He revolutionized violin technique with his use of harmonics, pizzicati, and new methods of fingering and tuning. To guard these technical secrets he published few of his own works (the 24 Caprices and some chamber music for strings with guitar, which he also played). Posthumously published were five concertos and sets of variations, and many works remain in manuscript. He had great influence on subsequent performers, especially Eugène Ysaÿe, Pablo de Sarasate, and Liszt.

RECORDINGS: Caprices (24); Quartet No. 7 for violin, viola, cello, and guitar; *Romanze* in a minor for guitar; Sonatas for violin and guitar, Opp. 2 and 3; *Le streghe* for violin and orchestra; Trio in D; Variations on "Di tanti palpiti"; Variations on "God Save the Queen"; Variations on "Nel cor più non sento"; Viola Sonata, Op. 35; Violin Concertos (6); Violin Sonata *appassionata*.

Niccolò Paganini
etching by Luigi Calamatta after a drawing by Ingres, 1818 The Granger Collection

Paganini Études: *see* LISZT.

Paganini Rhapsody: *see* RACHMANINOFF.

Paganini Variations (Brahms): *see* VARIATIONS.

Pagliacci: *see* LEONCAVALLO; VERISMO.

Paine, John Knowles (January 9, 1839–April 25, 1906) Educated principally in Germany, the U.S. organist and composer John Knowles Paine became the first musician to hold a chair of music at a U.S. university when he was appointed professor of music at Harvard (1875). Paine was one of the first U.S. composers to write significantly for orchestra and chorus. He wrote a mass, an oratorio, an opera, four cantatas, two symphonies, and symphonic poems—all in a conservative idiom. Perhaps his best known work is the *Centennial Hymn,* written for the opening of the U.S. centennial (1876) in Philadelphia. His students included Frederick S. Converse and Arthur Foote.

RECORDINGS: Organ pieces—Concert Variations on "The Star-Spangled Banner," Fantasy on "Ein' fest Burg," Variations on "Austria"; Mass in D.

Paisiello, Giovanni (May 9, 1740–June 5, 1816)   An Italian composer of opera, Giovanni Paisiello studied at the Conservatorio di S. Onofrio at Naples, where he later taught (1759–63). While a student he wrote intermezzi for the conservatory theater, one of which attracted so much notice that he was invited to write two operas, *La Pupilla* for Bologna and *Il Marchese di Tulipano* for Rome. His reputation established, he settled for some years at Naples, where he produced a series of successful operas, among them *Le finte contesse* (1766), *L'Idolo cinese* (1767), and *La Frascatana* (1774). In 1776 Paisiello was invited by Empress Catherine II to St. Petersburg, where he remained for eight years, producing *Il barbiere di Siviglia* (1782).

In 1784 Paisiello left Russia and after a brief sojourn in Vienna, where he composed for Joseph II, he entered the service of Ferdinand IV of Naples. During his 15 years as music director there he composed several of his best operas, including *La Molinara* (1788) and *Nina* (1789). He was invited to Paris in 1802 by Napoleon, whose favor he had won five years previously by composing a march for the funeral of Gen. Lazare Hoche. Napoleon treated him munificently while neglecting the resident musicians Cherubini and Étienne Nicolas Méhul. Paisiello conducted the music of the court in the Tuileries; the Parisian public, however, received his opera *Proserpine* (1803) without enthusiasm. Disappointed at the failure of his only opera with a French libretto, he asked to return to Italy, pleading his wife's delicate health. On his arrival at Naples Paisiello was reinstated in his former appointment by Joseph Bonaparte and Joachim Murat, but he was unable to meet the demands for new works. Paisiello's fortunes fell with those of the Bonaparte family.

Paisiello is known to have composed about 100 operas. His church music comprises about 40 masses and many smaller works; his instrumental music includes symphonies, a harp concerto, quartets, and sonatas for harp and for violin and cello.

RECORDING: Piano Concerto in F.

Palestrina, Giovanni Pierluigi da (*c.* 1525–February 2, 1594)   One of the greatest composers of church music in the late Renaissance, Palestrina was long held as the pinnacle of perfection in Catholic church music. His technical proficiency is of such a level as to make his legendary status almost true.

Born probably in the town of Palestrina near Rome, he is known to have been one of the choirboys at Sta. Maria Maggiore in 1537 when he was about 12 years old, but in all probability he had gone to Rome a few years previously. Giacomo Coppola and Robin Mallapert were choirmasters at Sta. Maria Maggiore between 1537 and 1539, and Palestrina probably studied with them. Fermin le Bel became choirmaster in 1540 and may have helped him in organ playing, for in 1544 Palestrina was engaged as organist and singer in the cathedral of his native town. His prowess there attracted the attention of the bishop who later became Pope Julius III.

In 1547 Palestrina married Lucrezia Gori, and three sons were born to them. In 1551 the family was in Rome, where Palestrina took up the first of his papal appointments, maestro di cappella of the Julian Chapel. Before he was 30 he published his first book of masses

Giovanni Pierluigi da Palestrina,
*portrait bust by an unknown artist
courtesy, Vatican Museums*

(1554), dedicated to Julius III, and the following year he was singer in the pontifical choir. About this time he became composer to the papal chapel. Yet he did not neglect the secular side of his art, for his first book of madrigals appeared in 1555, unfortunately at a time when the lenient regime of Julius III had given way to the sterner discipline of Paul IV. A *motu proprio* of the new pope forbade married men to serve in the papal choir, and Palestrina together with two of his colleagues received a small pension by way of compensation for their dismissal.

For the next five years Palestrina directed the choir of St. John Lateran, but his efforts were continually thwarted by singers whose quality was almost as limited as their number. Eventually he broke away from this uncongenial milieu and returned to Sta. Maria Maggiore, the scene of his first musical training. About 1566 he taught at the Roman seminary. He was in the service of Cardinal Ippolito d'Este II in Tivoli from 1567 to 1571. In 1583 he was invited to Mantua, but his terms (as when he had been invited to Vienna in 1568) were too high. From 1571 until his death Palestrina served continuously as maestro di cappella of the Julian Chapel in Rome.

Pope Gregory XIII commissioned Palestrina and Annibale Zoilo to restore the plainchant to something like its pristine condition, but the task proved to be too great and Palestrina's editorial work gave way to a new flow of creative music. In the last 12 years of his life, he published four books of masses, three of motets, three of madrigals, as well as offertories, litanies, hymns, and Magnificats.

Palestrina's 105 masses embrace many different styles. The time-honored technique of using a plainchant cantus firmus is found in such masses as *Ecce sacerdos magnus, L'homme armé, Ut re mi fa sol la, Ave Maria, Tu es Petrus,* and *Veni Creator Spiritis;* his mastery of contrapuntal ingenuity may be appreciated to the fullest extent in his canonic masses, including *Repleatur os meum, Sacerdotes Domini,* and *Ad coenam agni providi;* his ability to ornament and decorate a solemn plainchant is evident in masses based on hymn melodies such as *Jesu nostra redemptio, Aeterna munera Christi, Jam Christus astra*

ascenderat, and *Sanctorum meritis;* and on antiphons as in *Sacerdos et pontifex, Ave Regina coelorum, Regina coeli laetare,* and *Beatus Laurentius.* By far the greatest number employ the parody technique as on his motets *Lauda Sion, O magnum mysterium, Sicut lilium inter spinas, Tu es Pastor ovium,* and *Veni sponsa Christi.* Yet another type is demonstrated by the nine works written for Mantua; in these the Glorias and Credos are so arranged that plainchant and polyphony alternate throughout. Finally there is a small but important group in free style, the musical material being entirely original. Perhaps the best-known are the *Missa brevis* for four voices and the *Missa Papae Marcelli* for six.

Palestrina's motets, of which more than 250 are extant, display almost as much variety of form and type as do his masses. Most are in some clearly defined form, occasionally reflecting the shape of the liturgical text; comparatively few are based on plainchant, though many paraphrase the chant. The six-part *Assumpta est Maria,* three settings of *Alma Redemptoris Mater,* and three settings of *Lauda Sion* all follow the plainsong fairly closely though sometimes only at the beginning. On the same level as the canonic masses are such motets as *Cum ortus fuerit* and *Accepit Jesus calicem,* the latter apparently a favorite of the composer as he is depicted holding a copy of it in a portrait now in the Vatican.

His 29 motets based on texts from the *Song of Solomon* afford numerous examples of "madrigalisms": the use of suggestive musical phrases evoking picturesque features. In the offertories he completely abandons the old cantus firmus technique and writes music in free style, whereas in the hymns he paraphrases the melody usually in the highest voice. In the *Lamentations of Jeremiah* he contrasts the Hebrew and Latin texts—the former melismatic and the latter simple and solemn. His Magnificats are mainly in four sets on each of the eight tones with *alternatim* structure as in the Mantua masses.

Although Palestrina's madrigals are generally considered of less interest than his sacred music, they show as keen a sense for pictorial and pastoral elements as in any of his contemporaries. He is to be remembered for his early exploitation of the narrative sonnet in madrigal form, notably in *Vestiva i colli,* which was frequently reprinted and imitated. His settings of Petrarch are also excellent.

Palestrina, unlike Bach, did not have to be rediscovered in the 19th century, but the view that Palestrina represented the loftiest peak of Italian polyphony was in some ways detrimental to his reputation. Even more unfortunate was the insistence on counterpoint in the style of Palestrina as a *sine qua non* in the examination requirements of academies and universities. Generations of fledgling composers were taught to revere the music of Palestrina as a symbol of all that was pure in ecclesiastical counterpoint. Indeed the greater part of his musical output, and in particular his masses (where his unerring sense of tonal architecture may be heard at its best), still remains worthy of admiration.

BIBLIOGRAPHY: Zoe K. Pyne, *Giovanni Pierluigi da Palestrina, His Life and Times* (1922); Henry Coates, *Palestrina* (1938); Knud Jeppesen, *The Style of Palestrina and the Dissonance,* 2nd ed. (1946; reprint, 1970); Gustave Reese, *Music in the Renaissance,* rev. ed. (1959); Jerome Roche, *Palestrina* (1971); Malcolm Boyd, *Palestrina's Style: A Practical Introduction* (1973).

RECORDINGS: Masses—*Aeterna munera Christi, Ascendo ad patrem, Assumpta est Maria, Missa de Beata Virgine, Missa brevis, Già fu chi m'ebbe cara, Papae Marcelli, Veni sponsa Christi;* Magnificat; motets; ricercari.

paraphrase In Renaissance music, the use of an elaborated plainchant melody from one composition in another, usually a mass or motet but also in keyboard works. The melody is frequently broken up with notes added, but occasionally the melody is condensed (Palestrina). The paraphrased melody may appear in one voice part, as in the motet *Alma Redemptoris Mater* by Guillaume Dufay, or in all voice parts through the technique of melodic imitation, as in the *Missa Pange lingua* by Josquin des Prés.

Paris Symphonies: (Nos. 82–87): *see* CLASSICAL PERIOD (instrumental music, 1750–1800); HAYDN (achievement).

Paris Symphony (No. 31): *see* MOZART (early life).

Parkening, Christopher (b. December 14, 1948) A pupil of Pepe Romero and Andrés Segovia, the U.S. classical guitarist Christopher Parkening was chosen by composer Mario Castelnuovo-Tedesco to premiere his Second Concerto in C for guitar (1966). His first tour of the United States and Canada was in 1968, and he made his New York City debut recital at Alice Tully Hall in 1972. Recordings include music of Bach and albums "In the Classic Style" and "In the Spanish Style." Parkening has taught guitar at the University of Southern California and Montana State University at Bozeman and is the author of a guitar method.

Parker, Charlie: *see* JAZZ (origins and early development) and (the 1940s).

Parker, Horatio (William) (September 15, 1863–December 18, 1919) A U.S. composer, conductor, and teacher who helped establish the character of U.S. music at the beginning of the 20th century, Horatio Parker was educated in Boston and Munich (1882–85), studying with Joseph Rheinberger. On his return to America he served as organist and choirmaster at churches in the New York City area and in Boston. His reputation was established with his oratorio *Hora Novissima* (1893), and in 1894 he was appointed professor of music at Yale University, where he remained until his death. He founded the New Haven Symphony. His works include two operas, *Mona* (1912) and *Fairyland* (1915); the ode *Hymnos Andron,* written for the bicentenary of Yale, and the morality *The Dream of Mary;* and many organ works and songs. His book *Music and Public Entertainment* (1911) deals with social aspects of music.

parody A Renaissance technique in which several voices of a preexistent composition are creatively reworked to form a new composition as in the parody mass *(missa parodia).* This technique is not to be confused with CANTUS FIRMUS, where a single line only of the original is employed, or *contrafactum,* where the original music is merely provided with a substitute text.

The earliest known parody masses are from the late 14th century, but the procedure became common in the 15th and 16th centuries. The composer of a parody mass used as his model a vocal work such as a chanson, madrigal, or motet, freely reorganizing and expanding the original material and often inserting new sections between borrowed, modified passages. A parody mass is known by the name of its model, as *Missa Malheur me bat,* by Josquin des Prés, a reworking of Jean d'Ockeghem's chanson *Malheur me bat.* Nearly three-quarters of the masses of Palestrina and Orlando di Lasso are parody masses.

The process of parody was also utilized in arrangements of vocal works for lute or keyboard, as in Peter Philips' arrangement for virginal of the chanson *Bon Jour, mon coeur* by di Lasso.

Parody in the more familiar sense of the word, *i.e.,* as a form of humor, has in music a restricted field of expression. Unless the composer is concerned with a broad form of humor, it is difficult to differentiate between the style of the parody and the object parodied. Parody is thus often indistinguishable from pastiche, as the oversubtle parody of 18th-century opera in Stravinsky's *Mavra.* More successful examples of musical parody are *Ein musikalischer Spass* of Mozart, concluding with glaringly wrong notes; and the absurd repetitions in quick tempo of the word Amen by the chorus in Berlioz' *L'Enfance du Christ.*

parody mass: *see* PARODY.

Parry, (Charles) Hubert (Hastings) (February 27, 1848–October 7, 1918) An English composer, writer, and teacher who helped revive the creative spirit in English music at the end of the 19th century, Hubert Parry studied at Eton, Oxford, and Stuttgart and later with William Sterndale Bennett. Parry was appointed choragus of Oxford University in 1883 (professor, 1900) and in the same year joined the staff of the Royal College of Music, becoming director in 1894. His writings on music, which had much influence in their day, include *Studies of Great Composers* (1886), *The Evolution of the Art of Music* (1896), *Johann Sebastian Bach* (1909), and *Style in Musical Art*

(1911). He was knighted in 1898 and created a baronet in 1903.

Parry's gifts as a composer developed especially in chamber music and later in choral music, where he showed a gift for spacious writing and massive effects with a strong lyrical element. In 1880 his *Scenes from Prometheus Unbound* was produced at the Gloucester Festival, followed by the ode *Blest Pair of Sirens* (1887), and the oratorios *Judith* (1888), *Job* (1892), and *King Saul* (1894). Other successful works were *Songs of Farewell* (1916–18) and his song *Jerusalem* (1916), a setting of words from William Blake's *Milton,* which became almost a second national anthem during and after World War I. He also wrote five symphonies, *Symphonic* Variations (1897), chorale preludes for organ, and many songs. His anthem *I Was Glad,* composed for the coronation of Edward VII (1902), has been performed at succeeding coronations and has become a standard for church choirs.

RECORDINGS: *Blest Pair of Sirens; I Was Glad; Jerusalem.*

Parsifal: *see* WAGNER (life) and (achievement).

Parsons, Robert (d. 1570) One of the most distinguished English composers of church music of the mid-16th century, Robert Parsons was appointed gentleman of the Chapel Royal in 1563. He died by drowning in the River Trent at Newark. Parsons' contrapuntal writing has considerable strength and shows a virile and sometimes original treatment of dissonance. His best-known composition, "Pandolpho," a song with viol accompaniment, is remarkable not only for its expressive power but also for its intense motivic organization.

Partch, Harry (June 24, 1901–September 3, 1974) A U.S. visionary and eclectic composer and instrument builder, Harry Partch was largely self-taught. His compositions are remarkable for the complexity of their scores (each instrument has its own characteristic notation, often involving 43 tones to each octave) and their employment of unique instruments of his invention. Partch's early works are mainly vocal, based on texts collected during his travels as a hobo during the Depression (*Barstow—8 Hitchhiker Inscriptions from a California Highway Railing,* 1941; *The Letter, a Depression Message from a Hobo Friend,* 1943).

Later his interest in mythology and the occult led to the magical sounds of common materials such as light bulbs and bowls. The result was instruments such as the boo (bamboo marimba, 1955–56), marimba eroica (1951–55, the largest plank eight feet [2.4 meters] long), cloud chamber bowls, mazda marimba, and many others; some were exhibited at the San Francisco Museum of Art (1966) and at the Whitney Museum in New York City.

Typical of his works of the 1950s are *Oedipus* (1951; Partch's first large dramatic work), the theater piece *Plectra and Percussion Dances* (1952), the dance satire *The Bewitched* (1955), and the filmtrack of *Windsong* (1958). The enormous suite *And on the Seventh Day Petals Fell in Petaluma* (1963–64, revised 1966) comprises 23 one-minute duets and trios among 20 instruments, followed (by means of electronic dubbing) by 10 quartets and quintets and a final septet. The traditional process of development is ignored; musical ideas are simply stated, then abandoned.

Later Partch was involved with tactile theater pieces that have the nature of rituals. He summarized his esoteric theories in a book, *The Genesis of a Music* (1949), and in 1953 he began issuing his own recordings. He won an award (1966) from the National Institute of Arts and Letters.

RECORDINGS: *And on the Seventh Day Petals Fell in Petaluma; Barstow; Castor and Pollux; Daphne of the Dunes; Delusion of the Fury; Plectra and Percussion Dances.*

partial: *see* OVERTONE.

Pasdeloup, Jules (-Étienne) (September 15, 1819–August 13, 1887)   The first Wagnerian conductor in France, Jules Pasdeloup was educated at the Paris Conservatoire (piano and composition), and he began a career in government with leisure to devote to composition. His lack of performances forced him to found the Société des Jeunes Artistes du Conservatoire (1851), which developed into the Con-

certs Populaires (1861–84). Here he introduced many new compositions to France, including contemporary French works, but his interest was the music of the Austro-German school. Though important historically, Pasdeloup did not have the respect of his musical colleagues.

passacaglia   A form in slow $\frac{3}{4}$ time, the passacaglia (Italian variant of Spanish *pasacalle*—"street song") appeared in the French theater of the 17th and 18th centuries as a dance of imposing majesty. Its musical structure is identical with that of the CHACONNE, but futile attempts have been made to discover differences between them. Baroque composers used both terms indiscriminately, writing fine examples of the rondo, theme and VARIATIONS, and passacaglia forms under both designations. The true passacaglia form consists of a series of divisions (like variations) over a GROUND BASS. Bach's great Passacaglia is an outstanding example.

passepied   A gay, charming dance of Breton origin in rather lively $\frac{3}{4}$ or $\frac{3}{8}$ time. It was a fashionable court dance (*c.* 1660 to 1760) in which lords and ladies emulated the pastoral characteristics of shepherds and shepherdesses. Its name probably derives from the basic step in which the feet crossed and recrossed while gliding forward, one foot often striking the other. The music, beginning with an upbeat in fairly rapid time, is usually syncopated in cadence measures when three two-count facets occur against two three-count measures. It appears occasionally in the suite, notably in Bach's Fifth Partita and Fifth *English* Suite.

passion   Musical settings of the passion of Christ—that is, his suffering in his last days on earth and especially his crucifixion—based either on biblical texts or poetic elaborations of them, date from the 4th century onward. They range from unaccompanied plainchant to compositions for soloists, chorus, and orchestra. Various terms, many of them confusing or inaccurate, were invented to describe different kinds of settings in different epochs and countries. The best guides, however, are the liturgical performances of passion music.

Much confusion was created by a mistranslation from the German. The usual German

term for plainchant is *Gregorianischer Choral,*
often shortened to *Choral,* with the result that
a plainchant passion according to SS. Matthew, Mark, Luke, or John is called a
Choralpassion. This was unfortunately translated into English as "choral passion," a mis-
nomer because from the 4th to the 15th century the passion was sung by a single deacon.
The chorus, even if one were available, had
nothing to do with the performance.

Middle Ages   In the medieval passion the
deacon sang the entire text, changing his manner of declamation according to certain signs
in the manuscripts from which he sang. A
range of only 11 notes was required, but this
was divided clearly into three parts: the lowest
four notes (c–f) were used for the part of
Christ, the middle register (f–c') for the
Evangelist (*i.e.,* Matthew, Mark, Luke, or
John), and the top register (c'–f') for the
turba ("crowd"), which comprised all the
other characters, such as Peter, Pilate, soldiers, and high priests. Each of the three vocal
ranges was further distinguished by a characteristic method of performance: the part of
Christ was sung in a slow and solemn manner,
marked *t* (for *tarde*), the Evangelist more rapidly (*c* for *celeriter*), and the crowd in high
and excited tones (*s* for *sursum*). These signs
were given new interpretations in the Middle
Ages, when the *t* was taken for a cross, *c* for
Chronista and *s* for *Synagoga,* meaning Evangelist and crowd respectively.

From the 15th century the three parts often
were chanted by three deacons, especially in
larger churches and cathedrals, and in consequence the dramatic nature of the text was
heightened, and the congregation could follow
the narrative more easily. The passion according to St. Matthew was assigned to Palm Sunday, St. Mark to Tuesday of Holy Week, St.
Luke to Wednesday, and St. John to Good
Friday (this tradition held until late in the
20th century, when the first three were prescribed for annual rotation on Palm Sunday).

In the 13th century the passions were
adapted as music drama on the same principle
as the earlier plays of the resurrection. Two
versions, mainly in Latin but with some
German text, and accompanied by neumes of
indeterminate pitch (*see* NOTATION [develop-

ment in Western music]), are found in the
German Benediktbeuren manuscript *Carmina Burana.* Later passion plays abound in
France, Germany, and England, and the tendency was for them to become longer and
more complex as time went on.

polyphonic development   In the early 15th
century royal and other wealthy establishments had small choirs capable of singing polyphony, and something had to be found for
them to sing during Holy Week. The most
obvious choice was the *turba* music, and one
of the first composers to set this music polyphonically was Gilles Binchois, who was
handsomely rewarded for his labors in 1438.
It is usually assumed that this music is lost
without trace, but there is a possibility that
the two anonymous passions (*Matthew* and
Luke) in a British Museum manuscript of
about 1450 may be his or early imitations;
the music in three-part harmony resembles
some of the liturgical music of Binchois, who
is known to have served the Duke of Suffolk
for some time. This type of passion, in which
plainchant alternated with polyphony, was set
by Richard Davy and Byrd in England, by
the Italians Giovanni Matteo Asola (three settings) and Francesco Soriano (four), by the
Spaniards Victoria and Francisco Guerrero,
by the Frenchmen Claude de Sermisy and
Loyset Compère (not strictly liturgical), and
by the Netherlander Orlando di Lasso, who
composed music for all four versions.

Latin and German texts of the passion were
used in Germany in the early years of the
Reformation. Luther's friend and musical adviser Johann Walther composed a *St. Matthew*
passion first performed about 1550; it was still
popular in Nürnberg in 1806. Other German
passions adopted a different style, commonly
known as the motet passion because the entire
text—not only the *turba*—is set polyphonically. The prototype of the through-composed
passion is a work by the 16th-century French
composer Antoine de Longaval (but long ascribed wrongly to Jakob Obrecht). Longaval's
setting, based on a conflation of all four accounts of the passion, makes extensive use of
the chant formulas but is more concerned with
declamation than with elaborate polyphony.
It was thus a good model for the Germans,

among whom Johannes Galliculus, Joachim a Burgk, Johann Heroldt, Leonhard Lechner, Jakob Handl, and Bartholomäus Gesius produced worthy and dignified settings that did not, however, remain in the liturgical repertoire as long as Walther's passion.

The Longaval setting inspired motet passions by the 16th-century Franco-Flemish composer Maistre Jhan, also known as Johannes Gallus (Jean Lecocq), who worked at the court of Ferrara; and Cyprien de Rore, another Netherlander who spent much time in Italy. Antonio Scandello (1517–80), an Italian composer working at Dresden, produced an effective yet hybrid passion according to St. John in German. He chose to amalgamate the two types by setting the *turba* music for five voices, contrasting this not simply with the single line of the Evangelist but also with three-part settings of the words of Peter, Pilate, and other minor characters, while the words of Jesus are in four-part harmony. Motet passions of a more regular type were written by Johann Steurlein, Johann Machold, and Christoph Demantius.

The influence of Italian recitative, and indeed of polychoralism, made itself felt first of all in north Germany, especially in Hamburg where Thomas Selle (1599–1663) produced at least three settings (two of St. John, one of St. Matthew) for voices and instruments. Selle's *St. Matthew* Passion makes extensive use of double chorus, while his larger setting of St. John brings in a group of six instruments and calls for a "distant choir" after the manner of Giovanni Gabrieli and his Venetian contemporaries. The maximum contrast between the various interlocutors is achieved by assigning a particular instrument or group of instruments to the character concerned. Thus the Evangelist is accompanied by two bass viols (or bassoons) and two bandores, and Christ by two violins and two lutes. In addition to the normal text Selle interpolates three extra musical items, each with the title of "Intermedium." This tendency was carried further by Johann Sebastiani in his *St. Matthew* Passion, which brings in several chorales simply scored for unison voices and strings "for the awakening of greater devotion" among the congregation. Germany wel-

comed this innovation, and chorales were similarly introduced into passions by Johann Theile, Johann Valentin Meder, and Johann Kuhnau, who preceded Bach as cantor of the Thomaskirche, Leipzig.

Schütz   Although Heinrich Schütz studied with Gabrieli and was considerably influenced by that master in his earlier works, the three passions (*St. Matthew, St. Luke,* and *St. John*) indicate a return to the more austere type of passion of Walther's day. Schütz does not even allow the modest instrumental resources used in his earlier *Seven Last Words,* where the words of Christ are accompanied by an instrumental trio. The three passions leave the Evangelist's words without any form of accompaniment, and the only harmony apart from the *turba* choruses appears in the duet for the false witnesses. Notwithstanding this apparent austerity, Schütz's music is moving and dramatic, both in the flexible and expressive solo line and in the vivid choruses, which are far more truly polyphonic than many of the earlier German passions. Schütz does not avoid simple musical devices for heightening the meaning of the text, for his wish was to combine sincerity and devotion with a message that might easily be grasped. He allows an imitation of the cock's crowing and hints at the rolling of the stone from the sepulchre and the descent of an angel from heaven by rolling and falling musical figures respectively. His only additions to the biblical narrative are the "Exordium" at the beginning of each passion and the "Gratiarum actio" at the end, though the *St. John* Passion is exceptional in its use of a stanza from *Christus der uns selig macht* at the very end.

Settings of the passion were rare in 17th-century Italy and France, as music of an elaborate nature was unwelcome during Holy Week, instruments especially being frowned upon by the church. The passion according to St. John of Alessandro Scarlatti is, however, a strictly liturgical work in that it follows the text with scrupulous accuracy and refrains from undue elaboration in the brief *turba* choruses. A four-part string orchestra accompanies these choruses and the words of Christ, but the other characters are supported only by the continuo. The Evangelist, usually a tenor voice, is here an alto or male counter-tenor and is only occasionally placed against an orchestral background. When Scarlatti set the story of the passion once more in later life, he chose to adopt the oratorio style and made use of a specially composed text *La Vergine addolorata* (Naples, 1722). In France Marc-Antoine Charpentier also was attracted to the oratorio style and displays in his *Le Reniement de St. Pierre* an intensity of emotion and a contrast of color that is typical of the age of Louis XIV, although there is a noticeable restraint in the matter of musical realization of the key words in the text.

Hamburg, which had seen the first German imitation of Venetian musical splendor, witnessed early attempts at sacred opera and operatic settings of the passion based on new libretti that paraphrased rather than borrowed phrases from the Bible. Two of the most popular of the passion libretti were those by Christian Friedrich Hunold-Menantes and Barthold Hinrich Brockes, the latter being set by such composers as Reinhard Keiser, Telemann, Handel, and Johann Mattheson. These rhymed and sentimental accounts of the passion greatly appealed to German audiences of the time, but they were not entirely approved by the clergy, who objected to the abandonment of Bible narrative. The dramatic element maintained its hold for some time, and strong traces are found in passion oratorio texts by Johann Ulrich von König (1688–1744), Joachim Beccau, and Benjamin Neukirch, who even goes so far as to add stage directions.

Bach The inevitable reaction to this trend came with Christian Heinrich Postel's version of the *St. John,* set by Handel in 1704, and with the *St. John* and *St. Matthew* by Bach, who used his own adaptation of the text of Brockes for the first work, and of a text by Picander (pseudonym of Christian Friedrich Henrici) for the second. Bach's passions, which are really cantata cycles, placed the texts once more in a position of importance and dignity and wedded to them music of remarkable fervor and beauty, heightening the drama by skillful interplay of choral and instrumental forces that alternate with arias and recitatives accompanied by the organ. Bach not only avoided many of the artistic pitfalls that his predecessors had fallen into, he also succeeded in reuniting seemingly disparate elements of musical style that in his expert hands are both musically convincing in their sincerity and devotional in their general approach. It was the custom in Leipzig to perform Bach's passions at vespers on Good Friday, alternately at the Thomaskirche and at the Nicolaikirche.

Carl Philipp Emanuel Bach wrote two passions, both of them for use in Hamburg, and Johann Ernst Bach contributed a *Passionsoratorium* that did not detract from the high reputation of J. S. Bach's settings. These were seriously challenged only by Karl Heinrich Graun's *Der Tod Jesu,* first performed in 1755 and famous even outside Germany. The specially composed libretto found favor in Italy, where theatrical performances of the passion story outside church at last freed composers of restrictions regarding the use of instruments. *La Passione di Gesù Cristo* of Pietro Metastasio was set by numerous composers, the most successful among them Antonio Caldara, Niccolò Jommelli, Francesco Morlacchi, and Antonio Salieri.

later passion music Throughout the Classical and Romantic periods it was the oratorio style of the passion that was most usually set, and by this time the use of a large orchestra and chorus was common. Haydn's *Seven Last Words* was originally written as an instrumental work for the cathedral at Cadiz, but its subsequent adaptation by the composer proved to be an artistic success. Beethoven's *Christus am Ölberge* (1803), although not free from faults in planning and balance of narrative and dramatic elements, set a fashion in the writing of passion oratorios that was followed by Louis Spohr in his *Des Heilands letzte Stunden* (1835) and by lesser composers. Sir John Stainer's *The Crucifixion* (1887) achieved great popularity in English-speaking countries. Works by English composers of the 20th century include *The Passion of Christ* by Arthur Somervell and a *St. Mark* passion by Charles Wood. In Italy Lorenzo Perosi wrote a *St. Mark* passion; in Germany Kurt Thomas (*St. Mark,* 1927) and Hugo Distler (*Choralpassion,* 1933) showed a return to the ideals and techniques of Bach, while the St. Matthew settings by Hans Friedrich Micheelsen (1948) and Ernst Pepping (1950) are motet passions. Oratorio passions were produced by the Swiss Frank Martin (*Golgotha,* 1948) and the Polish Krzysztof Penderecki on the St. Luke text (1965). *See also* ORATORIO.

BIBLIOGRAPHY: Basil Smallman, *The Background of Passion Music: J. S. Bach and His Predecessors,* rev. ed. (1970); Anthony Lewis and Nigel Fortune, eds., *Opera and Church Music 1630–1750* (1975), Vol. 5 of *The New Oxford History of Music.*

Pasta, Giuditta, before her marriage, Giuditta Negri (April 9, 1798–April 1, 1865) After unsuccessful appearances in Italy, France, and England, the Italian dramatic soprano Giuditta Pasta conquered Paris in 1822 and London in 1824. Bellini wrote the title roles of *La Sonnambula* (1831) and *Norma* (1832) for her as did Donizetti his *Anna Bolena.* Some of her best roles were the leads in Verdi's *Otello* and Rossini's *Tancredi* and *Semiramide.*

Pastoral Symphony (Sixth): *see* BEETHOVEN (wider recognition); PROGRAM MUSIC.

Pathétique Symphony (Sixth): *see* PROGRAM MUSIC (program symphony); TCHAIKOVSKY (later life and works).

Patti, Adelina (Adela Juana Maria) (February 19, 1843–September 27, 1919) One of the most famous bel canto singers of all time, the Spanish soprano Adelina Patti first sang in concert at age 7 in New York City and continued to sing for five years, "retiring" to study until she reached 16. Then she made her formal debut in New York (1859) as Donizetti's Lucia di Lammermoor, and two years later she sang the role of Amina (Bellini's *La Sonnambula*), one of her most popular roles that served for both London (1861) and Paris (1862) debuts. She sang at Covent Garden for 23 years and had a command of 42 roles; her specialties were those of Rosina (Rossini's *Il barbiere di Siviglia*), Zerlina (Mozart's *Don Giovanni*), and Violetta (Verdi's *La Traviata*). After several farewell tours in the United States, she officially retired in 1906 but continued to sing benefit performances until 1914.

Patzak, Julius (b. April 9, 1898) Educated as a conductor in his native Vienna, tenor Julius Patzak sang in Reichenburg in 1926 and the following season at the Brno State Opera (both in Czechoslovakia). This was followed by engagements at the Munich State Opera until 1945. From 1946 he sang at the Vienna State Opera and at the Salzburg Festival. A notable Mozart singer, he taught at the Salzburg Mozarteum. Known also for recitals and oratorio, he was the first Austrian to sing for the BBC after World War II. An interest in contemporary music is evident from his performances of songs of Ernst Krenek and the premiere of Gottfried von Einem's *Dantons Tod* (1947). He is heard in recordings of Beethoven (Ninth Symphony), Mahler *(Das Lied von der Erde),* and Haydn *(The Creation),* and operas of Richard Strauss *(Salome)* and Wagner *(Das Rheingold* and *Siegfried).*

pavane A majestic processional dance of the 16th- and 17th-century European aristocracy. The term is probably derived from Pava, a dialect form of Padua. Adapted from the *basse danse,* the pavane presumably traveled from Italy to France and England by way of Spain. Its basic movement in $\frac{2}{2}$ or $\frac{4}{4}$ time consisted of forward and backward steps; the dancers rose onto the balls of their feet and swayed from side to side. The pavane was customarily followed by its afterdance, the vigorous galliard.

Examples date from Giovanni Ambrogio Dalza's *Intabolatura de lauto* (1508). The form reached its zenith with the English virginalists such as Byrd, Gibbons, Morley, and John Dowland. It also appears briefly in Germany—e.g., the *padouanen* in the suites (1617) of Johann Hermann Schein—and later in Saint-Saëns' opera *Étienne Marcel* (1879), Fauré's Pavane for orchestra (1887), Ravel's Pavane *for a Dead Princess* (1899), and in Vaughan Williams' ballet *Job* (1930).

Pavarotti, Luciano (b. October 12, 1935) Educated in Mantua, the Italian lyric tenor Luciano Pavarotti made his debut at the opera in Reggio Emilia as Rodolfo (Puccini's *La Bohème*) in 1961, the same year he won the Concorso Internationale there. After touring Europe he sang in Australia (1965) with Joan

Sutherland, with whom he has recorded extensively (Donizetti's *Lucia di Lammermoor* and *La Fille du régiment;* Puccini's *Turandot*). His U.S. debut was in San Francisco in 1967, and he sang Rodolfo at the Metropolitan Opera the following year. One of the outstanding lyric tenors of the 1970s, he is best known as Edgardo *(Lucia),* Tonio *(La Fille du régiment),* and Alfredo (Verdi's *La Traviata*).

Pearl Fishers, The: *see* BIZET.

Pears, Peter (b. June 22, 1910) Educated at London's Royal College of Music, the English tenor Peter Pears toured the United States with the New English Singers (1936–37). His London debut was in Offenbach's *Tales of Hoffmann* (1942). After singing for two years with the opera company at Sadler's Wells, he joined the British Opera Group in 1946. He was closely associated with Britten, premiering his songs and 12 operas, including *Peter Grimes* and *Owen Wingrave,* and collaborating with Britten on editions of the music of Purcell. In 1948 he was one of the founders of the Aldeburgh Festival; he was knighted in 1978. In addition to the music of Britten, Pears has recorded oratorios of Bach and Heinrich Schütz, songs of Schubert, Schumann, and Gustav Holst, and 17th- and 20th-century music with lutenist-guitarist Julian Bream.

pedal: *see* HARP; HARPSICHORD; ORGAN (mechanism); PIANO (actions).

pedal point A sustained note, ordinarily in the bass, over which changing harmonies are played. The term may derive from the low tones sustained by organ pedals, although a pedal point can occur in the middle voices or soprano. Pedal points are usually important notes in a key (normally the tonic or dominant), and they create tension as other harmonies are heard against them. The second fugue in Bach's *Well-Tempered Clavier* ends with a pedal point on the tonic. In the sonata-allegro form pedal points on the dominant often appear in the retransition (the passage preceding the recapitulation of the principal themes in the tonic key). This persistent dominant tone leads the listener to anticipate the eventual return to the tonic. An example occurs in the first movement of Mozart's *Jupiter*

Symphony. Pedal points are special instances of the use of DRONE and are occasionally called bourdons.

Pedrell, Felipe (February 19, 1841–August 19, 1922) A Spanish composer and scholar, Felipe Pedrell was devoted to the development of Spanish nationalism from its folk songs and musical heritage. As a choirboy his imagination was fired by contact with early Spanish church music. Largely self-taught, he composed several operas, *El último Abencerraje* (Barcelona, 1874) on a text by Chateaubriand, a trilogy, *Los Pirineos* (1902), to a Catalan libretto, *La Celestina,* and *Raimundo Lulio*—the latter two never performed. In 1891 he published his manifesto *Por nuestra musica,* which attracted much attention though it was misunderstood as advocating Wagnerian reforms. Following his theories he published an invaluable four-volume collection of folk songs and a vast quantity of early Spanish church, stage, and organ music, including the keyboard works of Cabezón and the complete works of Victoria. As a composer Pedrell was hampered by technical shortcomings, but his influence on later Spanish composers, especially through his pupil de Falla, was incalculable; his editions of early Spanish music laid the foundations of Spanish musicology.

Peerce, Jan, originally Jacob Pincus Perelmuth (b. June 3, 1904) The U.S. tenor Jan Peerce received his early musical experience playing violin in dance bands and singing in synagogues. In 1933 he appeared at Radio City Music Hall in New York City. His operatic debut occurred in 1938 as the Duke (Verdi's *Rigoletto*) in Philadelphia, and the following year he made his New York recital debut. In 1941 he first sang at the Metropolitan Opera (as Alfredo in Verdi's *La Traviata*) and continued to sing there through the subsequent 25 years, specializing in Italian roles. He gave 14 performances with Toscanini, including a Beethoven Ninth Symphony and a broadcast of Puccini's *La Bohème.* In the 1960s he sang with the Bach Aria Group. He has recorded operas of Beethoven, Verdi, and Puccini, arias of Handel, and Jewish sacred and folk music.

Peer Gynt: *see* GRIEG; INCIDENTAL MUSIC.

Pelléas et Mélisande: *see* DEBUSSY; FAURÉ; IMPRESSIONISM; INCIDENTAL MUSIC; LIBRETTO (19th-century influences); MODERN PERIOD (new paths); OPERA (the 20th century).

Penderecki, Krzysztof (b. November 23, 1933) The Polish composer Krzysztof Penderecki, whose novel and masterful treatment of orchestration has won worldwide acclaim, studied composition at the Superior School of Music in Kraków (graduated 1958), subsequently becoming a professor there. He first drew attention in 1959 at the third Warsaw Festival of Contemporary Music, where his *Strophes* for soprano, speaker, and ten instruments was performed. *Anaklasis,* premiered at the Donaueschingen Festival, and the now-classic *Threnody for the Victims of Hiroshima* for 52 strings, both in 1960, followed. Inspired by the bombing of Hiroshima, *Threnody* makes use of quarter-tone clusters, microtone glissandi, whistling harmonics produced by partial string vibrations, and other effects. These techniques were extended to Penderecki's vocal work *Dimensions of Time and Space* in 1961. His uses of elements of musical collage owe much to Witold Lutoslawski and Iannis Xenakis. The *Psalms of David* (1958) and *Stabat Mater* (1962) are simpler and more linear. The *Stabat Mater* combines traditional and experimental elements and led to his other well-known masterpiece, the *St. Luke* Passion (1966), in which Penderecki makes use of traditional forms such as the passacaglia, chant-like freedom of meter, and a twelve-tone row based on B-A-C-H. The *Threnody* too shows Penderecki's debt to traditional forms; one section is in strict melodic imitation. The 1962 Canon for 52 strings and two tapes makes use also of Renaissance polyphonic techniques. On the other hand, he uses aleatory freedoms, percussive vocal articulation, non-traditional notation, and other devices of the European avant-garde. Later works include the operas *The Devils of Loudun* (1968) and *Paradise Lost* (1978), *Utrenja* (1971), Cello Concerto (1972), Magnificat (1974), and *Utrenja,* Part II: *The Resurrection of Christ* (1977).

RECORDINGS: *Anaklasis* for strings and percussion; Canon; Capriccio No. 2 for violin and orchestra; Cello Concerto; *De natura sonoris* for orchestra (2); *The Devils of Loudun; Dies irae* (oratorio); *Emanationen* for two string orchestras; *Fluorescences; Fonogrammi* for flute and chamber orchestra; *Kosmogonia;* Magnificat; Partita for harpsichord and orchestra; *Polymorphia* for 48 strings; *Utrenja.*

pentatonic: *see* SCALE.

Pepusch, John Christopher, originally Johann Christoph Pepusch (1667–July 20, 1752) The Anglo-German musician, composer, theorist, and teacher John Christopher Pepusch was born in Berlin and settled in England about 1700. In 1712 he became music director to the Duke of Chandos and not long after was appointed music director at Lincoln's Inn Fields Theatre. Among much other music for the theater, he arranged tunes and composed the overture for John Gay's *Beggar's Opera* (1728) and its sequel *Polly* (unperformed until 1777). In 1737 he became organist of the Charterhouse and was in some demand as a teacher; William Boyce was among his pupils. He collected a magnificent library of music books and scores and was deeply interested in music of the Renaissance and that of ancient Greece and Rome. He had a strong influence on the early development of musical antiquarianism in England, which led to the publication of such collections as Boyce's *Cathedral Music* and to the performance of old music by societies of enthusiasts.

performance practice An increased sensitivity to earlier styles of performance and a heightened respect for historical authenticity has been a concomitant of scholarly research. Although the proper realization of music from earlier eras is an issue that has been raised intermittently since the mid-19th century, the scope and sophistication of the inquiry have deepened appreciably in the latter half of the 20th century.

It is no longer sufficient to interpret earlier music with the characteristic impasto of our age. Through scholarship wedded with informed intuition, we have learned that periods prior to our own conformed to different and differing standards in music's crucial parameters: timbre, tuning, and articulation were variables subject to the dictates of fashion as well as to technical refinements. Baroque music has benefited most from these insights. It is no longer a novelty, although not yet the norm, to hear a performance that is properly phrased by an aptly-sized ensemble using instruments from the period tuned to the proper intonation. The fountainhead for such performances has flourished since World War II in Amsterdam, home of harpsichordist Gustav Leonhardt, flute and recorder virtuoso Frans Brüggen, and violinist Jaap Schröeder. Through their teaching, touring, and recorded performances, they have redefined the sound and the sense of Baroque music and redeemed it from the mindless grip of modern-day conventions.

Medieval and Renaissance music has also been restored a good measure of its stylistic integrity. Among the chief questions concerning the interpretation of this repertoire is the relationship between voices and instruments, since precise scoring is the exception rather than the rule. Recent studies have resulted in performances that are thought to approximate more closely than before the circumstances of performance in which the scores were first heard. Another matter that has been clarified to the music's advantage is the application of discretionary accidentals, since much chromatic coloring was implicitly called for.

Although modern scholarship has won a greater understanding of earlier theory and practice, it has yet to touch meaningfully those eras that are closest in time to our own. Music of the Classical and Romantic periods has been scrutinized for inherent stylistic attributes, and many of these traits have been learned. We know, for instance, about the changing disposition of the orchestra through the 18th and 19th centuries, about nuances of articulation, and about a variety of techniques for ornamental embellishment. In practice, however, this knowledge is infrequently applied. Contemporary orchestras and ensembles, and soloists as well, rarely attempt to approximate stylistic authenticity. Modern-day ideals of technique and temperament are loosely based on late 19th-century models. While this insures a level of competence that in many respects is high indeed, this competence is paid for by the sacrifice of authentic-

ity, a loss that leads ultimately to a dilution of substance and a distortion of style.

George Gelles

BIBLIOGRAPHY: Frederick Dorian, *The History of Music in Performance* (1942; reprint, 1966); Arnold Dolmetsch, *The Interpretation of the Music of the XVII and XVIII Centuries,* rev. ed. (1946; reprint, 1969); Thurston Dart, *The Interpretation of Music* (1954); Richard L. Crocker, *A History of Musical Style* (1966); Mary Vinquist and Neal Zaslaw, eds., *Performance Practice: A Bibliography* (1971); Robert Donington, *The Interpretation of Early Music,* rev. ed. (1974), *A Performer's Guide to Baroque Music* (1974), and *String Playing in Baroque Music* (1977).

Pergolesi, Giovanni Battista (January 4, 1710–March 16, 1736)   An Italian composer whose intermezzo *La serva padrona* was one of the most celebrated stage works of the 18th century, Giovanni Battista Pergolesi was born at Jesi near Ancona, the son of a surveyor. His family name was Draghi, but having moved to Jesi from Pergola, the family was called Pergolesi or Pergolese, meaning "of Pergola."

From 1726 Pergolesi attended the Conservatorio dei Poveri at Naples, where his masters included Leonardo Leo and Francesco Durante and where he earned a high reputation as a violinist. In 1731 his oratorios *La conversione di S. Guglielmo d'Aquitania* and *La morte di S. Giuseppe* and his opera *Salustia* were performed at Naples but with little success. In 1732, when he had become acquainted with the work of Alessandro Scarlatti, he was appointed maestro di cappella to the Prince of Stigliano at Naples and produced a Neapolitan opera buffa, *Lo frate 'nnammorato.* In December of the same year a mass commissioned as a thanksgiving for delivery from an earthquake at Naples was also performed with success. In August 1733 his most important stage work was first produced: the gay little intermezzo *La serva padrona* on a libretto by Gennaro Antonio Federico inserted between the acts of his opera seria, *Il prigionier superbo,* which received the cool reception usually reserved for his serious operas. In February 1734 Pergolesi was appointed deputy maestro di cappella of Naples and in May went to Rome to direct the performance of his Mass in F. He produced *Adriano in Siria* with the intermezzo *Liviette e Tracollo* at Naples in October and on his return to Rome his best opera seria, *L'Olimpiade.* His comic opera *Flaminio* was well received in Naples in 1735; but his health was now failing, and in February 1736 he left Naples for the Capuchin monastery at Pozzuoli near Naples. There he finished his last work, the celebrated *Stabat Mater.* He died in extreme poverty at the age of 26 and was buried at the cathedral at Pozzuoli.

When Pergolesi died his fame had scarcely penetrated beyond Rome and Naples, but later in the century his reputation grew enormously. After the posthumous success of *La serva padrona* and particularly after its performance in 1752 in Paris, where it led to *la guerre des bouffons,* forgers produced spurious Pergolesiana, and a number of works are either known to be by other composers or are of doubtful authenticity. These include some ascribed to Pergolesi by Stravinsky in arrangements he made for his ballet *Pulcinella* in 1920. Pergolesi's serious style is best illustrated in his *Stabat Mater,* his ability to wield large choral and instrumental forces in his masses, and his gift of comic characterization in *La serva padrona.*

RECORDINGS: Magnificat; *La serva padrona; Stabat Mater.*

Peri, Jacopo (August 20, 1561–August 12, 1633) A Florentine singer and the first composer of opera, Jacopo Peri was born in Rome of noble stock and studied in Florence, entering the service of the Medici about 1590. He became a member of Count Bardi's camerata, the learned coterie that attempted to reconstruct the authentic presentation of ancient Greek drama. The group held that plays were sung throughout, and their desire to find a form of music completely subservient to the words and dramatic action led them to abandon traditional polyphony and to experiment with recitative. Ottavio Rinuccini's *Dafne* was set to music in this style by Peri (with some contributions from Count Corsi) and performed with great success in 1597. The music of *Dafne,* the first opera, is almost entirely

lost, but Peri's next work (a setting of Rinuccini's *Euridice*) was printed and survives; it was commissioned for the wedding of Maria de' Medici and Henry IV of France in 1600. *Tetide* (1608) and *Adone* (1620), written for Mantua, apparently remained unperformed and are now lost. Marco da Gagliano's *Flora* (Florence, 1628), for which Peri wrote and sang the part of Clori, survives. From 1609 to 1625 Peri composed or collaborated on ten ballets, *feste,* masquerades, and interludes for the Florentine court; none of these found a printer, and most have disappeared. Further short pieces in manuscript and printed collections, together with *Euridice* and the fine continuo madrigals of *Le varie musiche* (1609), show Peri as a sensitive composer, remarkable as much for his control as for his daring.

RECORDING: *Euridice.*

period A unit of melodic organization made up of several related consecutive phrases. Often the period has two phrases, the antecedent and the consequent. The implication of finality is usually avoided at the end of the first phrase, but the period ends with a cadence; thus a period is the expression of a complete musical thought.

In the 20th century the term has been extended to include rhythmic and harmonic elements and even tonal vibrations.

Perle, George (b. May 6, 1915) A student of Ernst Krenek, the U.S. composer George Perle writes in the 12-tone idiom, on which he has also written numerous essays (*e.g.,* "Evolution of the Tone-Row: The Twelve-Tone Modal System," 1945). He has taught at the University of Louisville, University of California at Davis, Juilliard School, and at Queens College (New York) since 1961. He has composed two symphonies, a cello concerto (1966), six quartets, three wind quintets (1959, 1960, 1967), and music for piano. His book *Serial Composition and Atonality, An Introduction to the Music of Schoenberg, Berg, and Webern* is in its fourth edition (1977).

RECORDINGS: Inventions for solo bassoon (3); Quartet No. 5; Six Preludes for piano; Three Movements for orchestra; Toccata for piano.

Perlman, Itzhak (b. August 31, 1945)   Of the young violinists who became prominent in the 1960s, perhaps the most admired was Israel's Itzhak Perlman. Stricken with crippling poliomyelitis at the age of four, his arms remained unimpaired; he played his first solo recital at the age of 10 and three years later was brought to the United States by Ed Sullivan to perform on the latter's weekly television program. He entered the Juilliard Preparatory School and continued his college education at Juilliard, where he studied with Dorothy DeLay and Ivan Galamian. In 1966–67 he made a world tour that included 50 appearances. In 1964 he won the Leventritt Competition, although the theft of the Stradivarius violin, lent to him for the competition from the Juilliard library of musical instruments, attracted more attention than the actual prize (the violin was later recovered). Perlman's repertoire ranges from Bach to Berg; he has played the Stravinsky Concerto with the composer conducting and has performed music written for him by Robert Mann, founder of the Juilliard Quartet.

Persichetti, Vincent (b. June 6, 1915)   Noted for his succinct polyphonic style, forceful rhythms, and generally diatonic melodies, the U.S. composer Vincent Persichetti began piano lessons at age 5, studied theory at 8, and produced his first two works at 14. Among his later teachers were Roy Harris and Fritz Reiner. In 1942 Persichetti began teaching at the Philadelphia Conservatory, and from 1947 he taught at the Juilliard School. He has been music editor for the Elkan-Vogel Company since 1952. Among his many published works are several for band (*Parable* IX, 1972) and various chamber combinations and the highly regarded Piano Quintet (1955). He has written nine symphonies and many piano concertos as well as more than 70 songs, solo sonatas (including one for harpsichord; 1951), ballet music, and 13 serenades. He is the author of *Twentieth-Century Harmony: Creative Aspects and Practice* (1961), *Essays on Twentieth-Century Choral Music* (1963), and *Essays on Twentieth-Century Orchestral Music* (1970).

RECORDINGS: *Bagatelles;* Cello Sonata; *Hollow Men* for trumpet and strings; *Pageant;* *Parable* IV for solo bassoon; *Psalm;* Serenades (5); Sonato for two pianos; *So Pure the Star;* Symphonies Nos. 6 and 8.

Peter and the Wolf: *see* PROKOFIEV.

Peter Grimes: *see* BRITTEN; LIBRETTO (19th-century influences); MODERN PERIOD (new paths); OPERA (the 20th century); PROGRAM MUSIC (imagery).

Petrassi, Goffredo (b. July 16, 1904)   A student and later teacher (since 1934) at the Accadèmia di Santa Cecilia in Rome, the Italian composer Goffredo Petrassi has worked in styles from neoclassical to serial. His early works (1930s) show the influence of Stravinsky and Hindemith; 20 years later his music demonstrates acquaintance with that of Schoenberg. Important works are the seven Concertos for orchestra (1933–64) through which can be traced several periods of development; two operas, *Il Cordovano* (1944–48) and *Morte dell'aria* (1949–50); a cantata (*Noche oscura,* 1950–51), Flute Concerto (1960), and *Estri* (1966–67) for 15 instruments. Petrassi has promoted contemporary Italian music through governmental and private organizations. He was president of the International Society for Contemporary Music from 1954 to 1956.

RECORDINGS: Concertos for orchestra; *Noche oscura; Nonsense* (a cappella chorus).

Petri, Egon (March 23, 1881–May 27, 1962)   Busoni's best pupil was the German pianist Egon Petri. Petri was the son of the Dutch violinist Henri Petri, and he learned that instrument first, playing second violin in his father's quartet. He was educated in Dresden, and he also studied piano with Teresa Carreño. Petri was known for his playing of large-scale works, especially those of Liszt, Beethoven, Chopin, and Brahms. He also enjoyed a fine reputation as a pedagogue, teaching in Manchester, Basel, Berlin, and finally in the United States at Cornell University and Mills College (Oakland, California).

Petrucci, Ottaviano (June 18, 1466–May 7, 1539)   An Italian printer of music whose collection of chansons *Harmonice Musices Odhecaton A* (1501) was the first book of part music to be printed from movable type, Ottaviano

Petrucci was born at Fossombrone near Ancona, moving to Venice about 1490. He held music printing monopolies first at Venice, where he worked from 1498 to 1511, and later at Fossombrone. At the request of the Venetian Senate, he returned to Venice in 1536. His 61 music publications contain masses, motets, chansons, and frottole by many of the foremost composers of the 15th and early 16th centuries, among them Josquin des Prés, Jean d'Ockeghem, and Loyset Compère. He also published the first book of printed lute music, Francesco Spinaccino's *Intabolatura de lauto* (1507).

Petrushka: *see* ARRANGEMENT; BALLET (Diaghilev Ballet); POLYTONALITY; STRAVINSKY.

Pettersson, Gustaf Allan (b. September 19, 1911)   The Swedish composer Gustaf Allan Pettersson was a student of Honegger and of Karl-Birger Blomdahl. A violinist and violist, he has written a concerto for violin and quartet (1949), seven sonatas for two violins (1951), three concertos for strings (1950, 1956, 1957), and 12 symphonies (1953–73).

BIBLIOGRAPHY: Paul Rapoport, *Opus Est: Six Composers from Northern Europe* (1979).

RECORDINGS: *Barefoot Songs;* Symphony No. 7.

Pfitzner, Hans (Erich) (May 5, 1869–May 22, 1949)   A German composer who upheld traditional ideals during the post-Wagnerian era, Hans Pfitzner was born in Moscow and was a pupil at Frankfurt of Iwan Knorr. Between 1892 and 1934 he held posts as teacher and conductor in several German cities, including Strasbourg, where he was director of the conservatory and of the opera and conductor of the orchestra. His five operas include *Der arme Heinrich* (Mainz, 1895), *Die Rose vom Liebesgarten* (Eberfeld, 1901), and *Palestrina* (Munich, 1917), the last his best-known work. His output includes 12 orchestral and concerted works, chamber music, and over 100 songs; they were widely performed in Germany but made little impression elsewhere.

RECORDING: *Palestrina.*

Philipp, Isidore (September 2, 1863–February 20, 1958)   The Hungarian-born pianist Isidore Philipp grew up in France and was educated at the Paris Conservatoire (pupil of Georges Mathias), winning the first prize in piano (1883) and 20 years later becoming professor of piano there (until 1934). From World War II he made his home in the United States. Philipp is remembered primarily as a pedagogue; his greatest pupil was the Brazilian pianist Guiomar Novaës.

Philippe de Vitry: *see* VITRY, PHILIPPE DE.

Philips, Peter (1560/61?–1628?)   An important English composer of madrigals, motets, and keyboard music, Peter Philips was a Roman Catholic; in 1582 he left England for Italy, where he became organist of the English College in Rome. In 1585 he entered the service of Thomas, Lord Paget, with whom he traveled extensively. After Lord Paget's death in 1590 Philips went to Antwerp, and in 1597 he moved to Brussels, where he was appointed organist of the royal chapel of Archduke Albert of Austria. In 1593 he was accused by the Dutch authorities of planning the murder of Queen Elizabeth I, but after imprisonment and trial he was released. He probably took holy orders, for in 1610 he was appointed to a canonry.

Philips published volumes of madrigals to Italian texts in 1596, 1598, and 1603. Eight volumes of his church music were published between 1612 and 1633. A posthumously published volume of masses is lost. Philips evidently enjoyed a considerable reputation during his lifetime, for many of his compositions appeared in contemporary collections, including Morley's *First Booke of Consort Lessons* (1599) and the *Fitzwilliam Virginal Book,* which contains 19 keyboard pieces by him. Philips' style reveals Italian and Dutch as well as English traits; Jan Pieterszoon Sweelinck was a powerful influence, and his firm polyphonic passages are at times reminiscent of Byrd.

Phrygian mode   The third of the eight medieval church modes. Its general range comprises the eight natural notes from the E below middle C to the E above. Melodies in Phrygian, or Mode III, usually have E as the *finalis,* or final note, and C as the *tenor,* or reciting note.

In ancient Greek music Phrygian referred to the scale pattern, or octave species, conventionally represented in modern writings as D-D.

piano A keyboard instrument in which the sound is produced by the action of hammers striking strings stretched across a resonating soundboard. Though early makers adopted the form of the harpsichord and clavichord, the principle of piano tone production really derives from the dulcimer, in which the strings are struck with hammers held in the hand.

The invention of the piano may be attributed to the desire to make the harpsichord "expressive"; to make the clavichord louder; and to bring the dulcimer under the control of a keyboard.

The name of the piano, a shortening of the more proper pianoforte (meaning literally "soft-loud"), is derived from its ability to produce gradations of volume by touch. In mid-18th-century England it somewhat confusingly began life as a FORTEPIANO, but the name was changed to pianoforte toward the end of the century.

early development Credit for priority of invention has been much disputed, but there is little doubt that it belongs to Bartolommeo Cristofori, who devised his *gravicembalo col piano e forte* in Florence probably in the 1690s. This was not the first instrument using keyboard striking action: the *dulce melos* described by Henri Arnault of Zwolle in about 1440 and an instrument said to be dated 1610 in the Belle Skinner Collection, Holyoke, Massachusetts, are early examples of the piano principle. Not long after Cristofori's first piano independent inventions were demonstrated by Jean Marius in France and Christoph Gottlieb Schröter in Germany, the latter inspired by the accomplished dulcimer playing of Pantaleon Hebenstreit. But these were inferior to Cristofori's invention. By 1726 Cristofori had arrived at all the essentials of the modern piano action: escapement, check, dampers, and una corda mechanism. It is from Cristofori that the modern piano stems. But not until

piano by Bartolommeo Cristofori, 1720
courtesy, Metropolitan Museum of Art
The Crosby Brown Collection of Musical Instruments, 1889

the 19th-century development of metal bracing, leading to the full metal frame, were the potentialities of Cristofori's remarkable action fully realized. Three of Cristofori's grand pianos have survived: the oldest, dated 1720, is in the Metropolitan Museum of Art in New York City.

Cristofori's work received little recognition in his lifetime. In 1732, the year after his death, appeared 12 sonatas for *cimbalo di piano e forte* by Lodovico Giustini—the first music published specifically for the new instrument. Despite the fact that Italy was the birthplace of the new expressive music in the 16th century, the piano attracted no Italian composers of great distinction. It would certainly be wrong to suppose that the developed Cristofori piano was incapable of satisfying a sensitive performer. On the evidence of the New York example, his instruments had a surprisingly wide dynamic range, a light, shallow, and sensitive touch, and a balance between treble and bass that was better than many 18th-century English pianos. Domenico Scarlatti had access to several Italian pianos, however, and the style of some of his sonatas suggests that he may have been the first eminent composer to take account of the new instrument.

As Italy abandoned the piano it was quickly taken up in Germany. A description of Cristofori's early mechanism by Scipione Maffei was published in Hamburg in 1725. This and probably the immigration of Italian workmen led to the adoption in 1726 of the Cristofori grand action by the German organ builder Gottfried Silbermann. Silbermann's pianos were criticized by Bach for their weak trebles and deep, heavy touch, but by 1745 they had improved sufficiently to gain Bach's approval. In fact he wrote for the instrument and acted as Silbermann's agent. But during the period *c.* 1740–*c.* 1770 German development was largely in the rectangular or square form of the instrument. This derived from the clavichord, the domestic instrument invariably preferred to the wing-shaped harpsichord by German music lovers, for whom the new grand piano was too large, expensive, and heavy of touch. Endeavors to make an action smaller, lighter, and cheaper than the Cristofori grand type resulted in a square piano action of comparatively crude craftsmanship and limited musical effect. The invention of the square has been attributed to Gottfried Silbermann's pupil Christian Ernst Friederici, but the earliest known example, dated 1742, is by Johann Söcher.

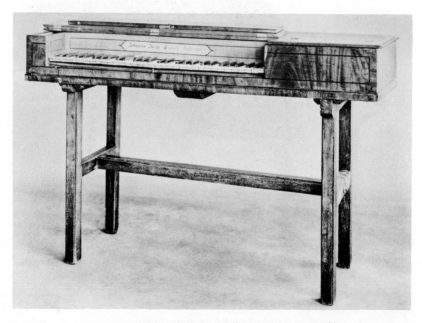

square piano by Johann Christoph Zumpe, 1767
courtesy, Victoria and Albert Museum, London

About 1760 a dozen German piano makers, jobless because of the Seven Years' War, settled in London, bringing with them the Cristofori tradition. Among them probably was Johann Christoph Zumpe, a pupil of Silbermann's, who entered the London factory of the Swiss harpsichord maker Burkat Shudi (or Tschudi), the founder of John Broadwood and Sons, Limited, which became the leading firm of piano makers. Thereafter England became the center of piano development. Zumpe became exclusively concerned with the manufacture of square pianos, which were immensely popular. As the harpsichord was the prevalent English domestic instrument, the horizontal grand piano also found favor, and this was fitted with action on the Cristofori principle, achieving such fame that it became known as the English action.

Of the early composers for the piano, Carl Philipp Emanuel Bach continued to prefer the more delicately expressive clavichord; in his *Versuch über die wahre Art das Klavier Zu spielen* (1753, 1762) he mentions his endeavor "to play the pianoforte, despite its deficiency in sustaining tone, as much as possible in a singing manner—this is by no means an easy task, if we desire not to leave the ear empty, or to disturb the noble simplicity of the *cantabile* by too much noise." Johann Christian Bach, however, played the piano by choice and was largely responsible for popularizing it in England, where he gave the first public piano recital on a Zumpe square in 1768. But both of Bach's sons lived in a period of transition. It was left to Mozart and Clementi to develop an exclusively pianistic style of playing and composing; by 1780 the piano had become fully established as the foremost of the keyboard instruments.

The piano first reached maturity, not with the English action but with a fundamentally different mechanism—the German, or Viennese, action. Invented, probably by Johann Andreas Stein, about 1770, the important feature of this action was the application of an escapement to the *Prellmechanik*, a primitive form of square piano action that had in turn evolved from the clavichord. In Stein's grand pianos the frame and stringing were for the first time well matched to the action. The light

hammers gave a blow that the strings could sustain, resulting in a singing tone of considerable charm. In the English grands the comparatively powerful and sonorous bass tends to overpower the trebles, which incline toward hardness in an attempt to keep up the power. The English touch was heavier and deeper than the Viennese, and repetition was not so good—or at least was harder to achieve. But with Stein's instruments the trebles were well matched to the bass, and the touch was light and shallow, approaching the clavichord in sensitivity. It is difficult to escape the conclusion that Stein was seeking to achieve a louder clavichord, whereas members of the Cristofori-English school were thinking in terms of an expressive harpsichord. Herein lies the fundamental difference between the two schools.

Mozart first played a Stein piano in 1777, and he wrote to his father extolling the excellence of damping, equality of tone, and the importance of the escapement in avoiding "blocking": "not one in an hundred makers bothers with escapement, and yet, without it, it is absolutely impossible for a note not to jingle or continue vibrating after being struck." The Viennese pianos were perfectly suited to Mozart's style of playing—singing tone, a quiet steady hand, and smoothness of execution in which passage-work "flowed like oil."

Clementi became known as the "father of the pianoforte." His influence in popularizing the instrument and systematizing its technique was considerable, particularly in England, where he eventually settled and became engaged in piano manufacture. His Sonatas, Op. 2 (1773), are considered to be the first music entirely suitable for the piano, and his *Gradus ad Parnassum* (1817) was the first piano instruction book. Clementi preferred the English pianos with their greater power and sonority.

Thus by 1780 there were two fully established schools of piano making, each with its own virtues. Each developed an individual style and technique determined by the nature of the instrument: the Viennese suited best to lightness, rapidity, and elegance; the English to larger musical forms and brilliance of execution.

The Viennese school culminated with Johann Nepomuk Hummel, Mozart's favorite pupil and probably the greatest virtuoso of the day. Even when virtuoso technique had outstripped the Viennese action, some players continued to prefer it, and it was made by the Bösendorfer firm for its cheaper instruments as late as 1914. But while the then-imperfect English piano was to improve by further development, the already perfected Viennese instrument deteriorated by it. The mature Viennese piano of the 1770s remains the ideal instrument for authentic Mozart performance. On any modern piano his music must be scaled down in volume if it is not to sound intolerable. But on a Stein it can be rendered life-size with the full resources of the instrument and with a lightness and transparency of tone that the modern piano can never achieve. In modern times the artistic merits of the Viennese piano are so greatly appreciated that many excellent reproductions have been made for concert use (*see* FORTE-PIANO).

actions The four basic types of action of the 18th-century piano are here explained in further detail.

The single action, a very simplified form of the Cristofori action, was introduced into England by Zumpe. It is shown diagrammatically in Figure 1. The key is pivoted at the pivot point. This strikes the hammer by means of the projecting jack, or mop stick, throwing the hammer upward to hit the string, from which it immediately falls back. Simultaneously the tail of the key raises the damper by means of the damper stick, the damper being otherwise held against the string by a whalebone spring. The sole merit of this action is simplicity. There is very little control over the tone, which at its loudest is quite feeble. If the key is struck too hard the hammer may bounce back and block the tone.

The expressive qualities of a Zumpe are in every way inferior to a large clavichord. Its popularity in England can only be explained by fashion and the fact that the English never appreciated the clavichord.

Zumpe provided two hand-operated stops to the left of the keyboard for raising the bass and treble dampers respectively. The sympathetic resonance of all the strings could thus be brought into effect for the duration of entire movements. This characteristic of the dulcimer (called the Pantaleon effect after its famous exponent) was so admired that some early pianos were entirely undamped. Even when the damper-raising forte pedal or knee lever was introduced, it was still the Pantaleon effect that was admired. Clementi's pupil John Field was probably the first to develop the modern selective technique of the sustaining pedal.

The double action illustrated in Figure 2 is Cristofori's action of 1726. The key is pivoted at the pivot point. Fixed to the key is the escapement, which conveys the thrust to the hammer by means of the intermediate lever. After hitting the string the hammer falls back but is held against the check until the key is fully released. The damper is not shown. This action avoids most of the shortcomings of the single action, the most important improvement being the escapement. The jack,

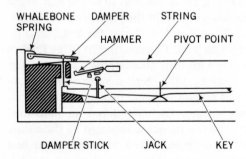

Figure 1
Zumpe single action, 1760
*from R. E. M. Harding, The Piano-Forte (1933)
published by Cambridge University Press*

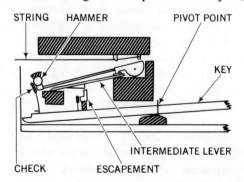

Figure 2
Cristofori double action, 1726
*from R. E. M. Harding, The Piano-Forte (1933)
published by Cambridge University Press*

instead of being rigidly fixed to the key, is hinged in such a way that as soon as it has given its impulse it is deflected, so that even if the note is held the hammer can return to its position of rest. This, together with the check, is an almost complete safeguard against blocking. A weakness of the single action is the slow hammer velocity, resulting in a limited dynamic range. In the double action the intermediate lever conveys the thrust to the hammer butt, giving increased velocity to the hammer and consequently greater control. The "English double action," as it came to be called, eventually superseded the single action in the better classes of square piano such as were made by Broadwood.

For grand pianos a modification of the Cristofori double action was developed in the 1770s by the Dutch Americus Backers, his apprentice Robert Stodart, and John Broadwood. This action is shown diagrammatically in Figure 3. The working principle is similar to that of the double action except that the intermediate lever has been eliminated, the thrust conveyed directly to a notch in the butt of the hammer by means of the escapement, or hopper, the play of which is regulated by an adjustable screw. This action, in various stages of improvement, continued to be made in English grands until late in the 19th century. The hammers of the early English grands are lightly constructed and covered with leather. Experiments were made with various materials such as cloth over leather and leather over felt, and all-felt hammers were introduced by Jean Henri Pape in 1826. Stringing is trichord throughout (brass in the

bass and steel in the treble), and no strings are overspun, or covered. The result is an entirely characteristic tone quality, full but brilliant, on which the full left-hand chords of Beethoven do not sound thick and cloudy as they do on most modern pianos. Many early English pianos have been ruined by being fitted with heavy felt hammers. Dampers are light and consequently by no means instantaneous in effect; but contemporary performers do not seem to have found this objectionable, as good damping would not have been difficult to achieve.

In the Viennese, or German, action, as shown in Figure 4, the key is pivoted at the pivot point. The hammer is mounted in a fork, or Kapsel, which is rigidly fixed to the key. Also shown are the string, the escapement, and the escapement return spring. The damper is not shown. The essential difference between the Viennese and the other actions is that the hammer is mounted on the key and not on the frame. When the key is depressed the tail of the hammer engages in the escapement notch, causing the hammer to rise and hit the string. Further pressure pushes the escapement aside, allowing the hammer to fall to rest.

The differences between the Viennese and English instruments are considerable. The Viennese damping is more effective. The hammers, like the English, are leather covered, but they are lighter, sometimes hollow, and probably achieve a higher velocity. Viennese stringing is generally bichord and significantly thinner than the English, and the relationship between frame, soundboard, and case of each

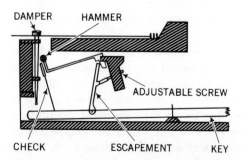

Figure 3
English grand action, 1795
from R. E. M. Harding, The Piano-Forte (1933)
published by Cambridge University Press

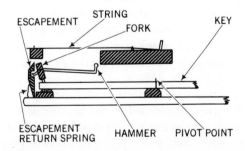

Figure 4
Viennese action, 1773
from R. E. M. Harding, The Piano-Forte (1933)
published by Cambridge University Press

school is quite differently contrived. These are factors that contribute to the tonal difference between the two types of instruments.

Grand pianos were rare until about 1780, but thereafter they were made in increasing numbers. Meanwhile the square piano remained popular as a domestic instrument with increased size. Toward the end of the 18th century, the widespread interest in the orchestra, stimulated by the music of Haydn and Mozart, led to a demand for two- and four-hand transcriptions of orchestral works. The piano compass was consequently extended to keep pace with that of the orchestra, and it had increased from Cristofori's four and one-half octaves to a universal five and one-half to six octaves in grands by 1800. For many years square pianos were restricted to five octaves (F′ to f′′′′) since any extension either curtailed the soundboard or made the instrument too long. In 1794 William Southwell of Dublin overcame this difficulty by placing a subsidiary frame for the extra treble notes under the soundboard, the hammers rising through a small slit to reach the strings.

In the 18th century pianos were provided with various timbre-creating stops in an effort to please those who found it difficult to escape the habits of the harpsichord. Three of these survive in modern instruments: the previously mentioned forte pedal that raises the dampers; and two soft effects, una corda (shifting the keyboard so that the hammers strike only one or two strings in each set, the free strings vibrating sympathetically) and *celeste* (interposing a strip of soft material between hammers and strings). These stops were first worked by hand stops or knee levers. Later pedals were applied, Broadwood taking out a patent in 1783. By about 1790 the two loud and soft pedals found in the modern instrument had become almost universal. In the period from about 1800 to 1840 a vogue for percussion and other special effects (under the influence of Turkish music) led to the construction of pianos with as many as eight pedals. But such trivialities earned the condemnation of serious teachers and performers. One device from this period, however, survives in many modern upright pianos: this is the piano pedal, which shortens the radius of the hammer, thereby

significantly reducing the strength of its blow on the strings.

Early upright pianos followed the design of upright harpsichords with the strings rising from keyboard level. They were consequently very tall, and many were made in elegant shapes such as the lyre, giraffe, and pyramid. But by taking the strings down to floor level, the upright was made shorter and more suitable for small rooms. This was first done by a progressive maker, John Isaac Hawkins, in 1800. The essentials of the modern upright action were contained in the tape-check action of Robert Wornum that was patented in 1842 but probably was invented several years earlier.

development of the modern piano After 1800 the piano, as a result of the increasing demands of composers and performers, began a rapid growth to its modern form, which for practical purposes it reached by 1859. The main stimulus was the gigantic pianism of Beethoven (according to Czerny, "marked by enormous strength, incredible bravura, and fluency"), followed by the efforts of others to emulate his style and to excel in his works.

Earlier virtuosos brought to the piano a style of playing essentially legato, something between harpsichord and clavichord technique. Beethoven's playing opened new vistas of dramatic quality and expression beyond the capacity of existing instruments. He made no secret of his preference for the English piano with its greater sonority and brilliance. During this period the famous heads of piano houses gathered around them a brilliant circle of pianists and composers, and the incentive to develop instruments capable of matching the rapidly increasing musical demands was intense.

After Beethoven the composer-pianists who most influenced piano development were John Field, Chopin, and Liszt. Field's influence on Chopin was considerable, and he was probably the first to use the forte pedal artistically for the sustaining of widespread chords. Chopin, whose technique derived from C. P. E. Bach, was much opposed to a forceful touch, preferring a square or small upright piano to a more sonorous grand. Field and Chopin developed the intimate character of the piano. Like Schumann's their music demands a degree of softness, evanescence, and sustained treble tone that none of the earlier instruments possessed.

The teaching of Beethoven's pupil Czerny paved the way for Liszt, the consummate piano virtuoso of the age. Liszt's playing (influenced by Chopin on one hand and Paganini on the other) combined musicianship and showmanship to an unprecedented degree, and his technique transcended that of all his contemporaries. He adopted a high-seat position in a quest for greater power, but his playing combined great strength with softness and delicacy, and he never sacrificed good tone to noise. Many of his successors were less artistic, so that in the 1870s piano makers felt compelled to fortify their instruments by increasing the touch weight to as much as four ounces, more than twice the weight of a Viennese action. This did not last long, however, and by the end of the 19th century a lighter touch once again became normal.

In the period 1800 to 1859 the efforts of piano makers were directed toward evolving methods of improving the volume, sustaining power, and sonority of the instrument. In practice this involved heavier stringing, frames capable of carrying the increased tension, and a scientific approach to the covering of the hammer and its striking place on the strings.

An inherent structural weakness of the early pianos was the gap across the full width of the soundboard through which the hammers came up. The early makers strengthened this with light wooden braces, but the first maker to tackle the problem seriously was Americus Backers, who placed metal arches from wrest plank to soundboard of his grands as early as 1772. A few 19th-century makers sought a solution in the down-striking action, which made the gap unnecessary.

The weakness of the all-wooden frames became seriously apparent with the extension of the treble compass, where the tension is

modern Steinway grand piano with overstrung frame
courtesy, Steinway & Sons

highest. Makers found the solution in an increased use of metal. Systems of metal resistance were evolved independently by Joseph Smith and by Hawkins in about 1780, but Broadwood first applied iron tension bars to the treble of grands in 1808. William Allen and James Thom, employees of the Stodart firm, invented a metal grand frame in 1820, but this was primarily intended to compensate the differing coefficient of expansion of brass and steel strings under heat. In 1827 Broadwood combined iron tension bars with a fixed iron string plate, and its first complete iron-frame grand was produced for the Crystal Palace Exhibition of 1851. Much of the metal frame development took place in the United States, however, where the first complete iron frame was made by Alpheus Babcock of Boston for a square as early as 1825. The idea was adopted by other U.S. firms, and in 1859 came the Steinway overstrung frame, which has been the model for all successful modern grand frames.

Overstringing, or cross-stringing, is a method in which the strings are slightly fanned out, and the bass strings cross over the tenor ones. This has the advantage of allowing greater string length within a relatively shorter case (Pape introduced it into uprights in 1828), but its primary object is to spread the strings so that they affect the soundboard area of maximum resonance and are better disposed for sympathetic resonance when the sustaining pedal is used.

The striking place of the hammer on the string is an important factor in determining the tone quality. Makers of the harpsichord and early piano were aware of this acoustical fact, but they made no attempt to achieve uniformity throughout the scale. The first piano maker to strive for uniformity was Broadwood, who in 1788 obtained scientific advice and modified his design to provide a uniform striking distance of one-ninth vibrating length throughout most of the compass.

In the 1830s improvements in the tempering of steel wire and the introduction of overspun bass strings made possible the increased sustaining power obtainable from heavier stringing and greater tension. It was also found that the felt-covered hammers introduced by Pape had the effect of damping the more dissonant harmonics; as the tendency was toward fullness and mellowness of tone rather than brilliance, the use of felt became widespread—though not universal until after 1855.

After a slow start in the 18th century, another school of piano manufacture had grown up in France under the leadership of Sébastien Érard, a progressive maker who experimented with metal bracing more or less simultaneously with Broadwood. By 1821 he perfected his double escapement repetition action on which the modern grand action is directly based. Early 19th-century piano music is full of repeated notes in imitation of the violin *tremolando*. Érard's action made possible the repetition of a note without materially raising the key. Its working principle is so much like the modern grand action that a separate description here is unnecessary.

In the early 19th century the compass of the piano continued to spread, reaching the standard seven octaves (A_2 to a'''') by 1836. In the 1890s a further three notes to c''''' were added in the treble.

Thus by 1859 the piano had reached its modern form in all essential details. The subsequent period has been largely one of detail development and standardization. Among post-1859 developments must be mentioned a third pedal (invented by Claude Montal in 1862) for sustaining only the notes of a given chord, the remainder staying damped. This is invariably provided by Steinway and is essential for the performance of the works of certain modern composers. Another Steinway feature is the duplex scale (a revival of an idea patented by W. F. Collard in 1821), in which the surplus length of the treble strings is used for sympathetic reinforcement of the tone. Blüthner of Leipzig went further with its aliquot scaling, which provided independent octave-tuned treble strings for sympathetic vibration.

Among numerous 20th-century developments the most significant is probably the double keyboard of Emmanuel Moór, with the upper keyboard an octave higher than the lower. This permits widespread chords and other effects impossible for two hands on a normal keyboard. Although admired by

Ravel, this clever invention seems destined to share the oblivion of any instrumental innovation that does not attract the imagination of leading composers and performers.

String tension, determined at 16 tons in 1862, increased to as much as 30 tons in modern instruments. The result is a dynamic range, sostenuto, and tonal spectrum unknown to Chopin, Beethoven, and even Liszt.

modern actions The modern grand action (Figure 5) is a refinement and simplification of Érard's action of 1821. It must be remembered that details vary between one maker and another. The key, pivoted at the pivot point, raises the carriage. This carries the hopper, or bell crank lever, the tip of which imparts the thrust to the hammer by means of a small roller attached to the underside of the hammer shank. Escapement is caused by the engagement of the prolongation of the L-shaped hopper with the adjustable set-off button. Before the key is fully released the repetition lever (through which the tip of the hopper passes) rises against the pressure of the spring until it is checked by a screw. The repetition lever then supports the roller and enables the hopper to regain its position under the roller in order to be ready for a second blow before the key is materially raised. Shown also are the check and the damper, the working of which is self-explanatory.

The modern upright action (Figure 6) is derived from the tape-check action of Wornum. The key pivoted at the pivot point conveys the thrust to the carriage lever on which are mounted the hopper and check. Thrust is conveyed by the hopper to a notch in the hammer butt, and escapement is caused by the engagement of the hopper prolongation with the set-off button. The spring ensures the return of the hopper. A special feature is the tape, which is tightened by the rise of the hammer and pulls it back to assist repetition. The damper, held against the string by a spring, is raised by the action of the pin as the key is depressed.

BIBLIOGRAPHY: Edgar Brinsmead, *History of the Pianoforte* (1879; reprint, 1969); Daniel Spillane, *History of the American Pianoforte* (1890; 2nd ed., 1968); Oscar Bie, *History of the Pianoforte and Pianoforte Players* (1899; 2nd ed., 1966); Alfred Dolge, *Pianos and Their Makers: A Comprehensive History of the Development of the Piano from the Monochord to the Concert Grand Player Piano* (1911); Alfred J. Hipkins, *A Description and History of the Pianoforte* (1929; reprint, 1975); Rosamond E. Harding, *The Piano-Forte: Its*

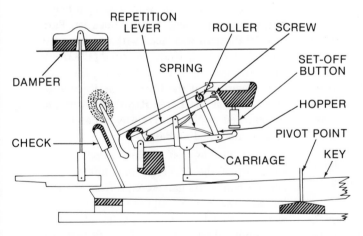

Figure 5
modern grand action
from E. Q. Norton, Tuning and Care of the Pianoforte

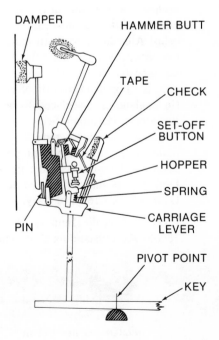

Figure 6
modern upright action
from E. Q. Norton, Tuning and Care of the Pianoforte

History Traced to the Great Exhibition of 1851 (1933); Ernest Closson, *History of the Piano,* rev. ed. (1974); Helen R. Hollis, *The Piano: A Pictorial History of Its Ancestry and Development* (1975); Cyril Ehrlich, *The Piano: A History* (1976); William Leslie Sumner, *The Pianoforte,* rev. ed. (1978).

Piatigorsky, Gregor (April 17, 1903–August 6,1976)   Noted for his interpretations of the Romantic repertoire, the Russian-born cellist Gregor Piatigorsky was an example of his own definition of a virtuoso: one who shows how good the music really is. While in his teens he began his career with the Imperial Opera Orchestra, but in 1921 he fled the Soviet Union, swimming across a river to Poland holding his cello above his head. He became first cellist (1924–28) in the Berlin Philharmonic under Wilhelm Furtwängler and made his U.S. debut the following year, playing the Dvořák Concerto in b minor, which he subsequently recorded three times. He taught at the Curtis Institute (1942–44), and in 1949 he joined the faculty at the University of Southern California, where he and Heifetz formed the nucleus of a chamber ensemble. His autobiography *Cellist* appeared in 1965.

Piatti, Alfredo Carlo (January 8, 1822–July 18, 1901)   Elected a member of the theater orchestra at Bergamo at the age of eight after playing there as a substitute, the Italian-born cellist Alfredo Carlo Piatti entered the Milan Conservatory at age 10. After touring Europe he appeared for nearly 40 years (1859–98) with the Popular Concerts of chamber music (in England) and replaced Robert Lindley in the Sacred Harmonic Society concerts there. His technical control, pure tone, perfect intonation, and cantabile phrasing had a great influence on later cellists and cello playing. King Umberto designated him *commendatore* in the Order of the Crown of Italy.

Piccinni, Niccolò (January 16, 1728–May 7, 1800)   An outstanding representative of the Neapolitan school, Niccolò Piccinni wrote in both the comic and serious styles but was chiefly remembered as a rival of Gluck. Born at Bari, he received his early musical education in Naples. In 1754 his first opera buffa was produced there. He was a prolific composer, writing about 140 operas. His first opera seria *Zenobia* was given in Naples in 1756. Two years later he achieved a triumph with *Alessandro nell' Indie,* but the masterpiece of his early years was *La buona figliuola,* also known as *La cecchina* (Rome, 1760).

In 1773 intrigues created in Rome by Pasquale Anfossi forced Piccinni to leave for Naples and later for Paris, where he was invited in 1776 by the supporters of Italian opera. Piccinni was thus condemned to play a role in a continuation of *la guerre des bouffons.* His French operas *Roland* (1778) and *Atys* (1780), both on librettos of Philippe Quinault, were compared to the operas of Gluck. Piccinni maintained the traditional sequence of arias and recitatives, whereas Gluck was laying the foundations of an operatic reform. In order to incite controversy both composers were commissioned to write operas on *Iphigénie en Tauride.* Gluck's was given in 1779, but Piccinni's not until two years later. Piccinni continued to admire the art of Gluck and did nothing to encourage his own partisans in the journalistic war waged on behalf of the two composers. When Gluck left Paris in 1779 Piccinni was faced with another rival, Antonio Sacchini, whose *Renaud* (1783) was to be dwarfed by Piccinni's *Didon* the same year. Deprived at the time of the Revolution of his post at the École Royale de Musique, he returned to Naples. He was in Paris again in 1798 and died at Passy.

piccolo   The highest pitched woodwind instrument of the orchestra and military and concert bands. Its name comes from the Italian *flauto piccolo,* "small flute," as it is a small wood or metal transverse FLUTE of conical or cylindrical bore fitted with the Boehm key-

modern wooden piccolo   *courtesy, Conn Corporation*

work system and sounds an octave higher than the ordinary concert flute and an octave above the written notes. Its compass extends three octaves from the second D above middle C. Its orchestral use dates from the late 18th century, when it replaced the flageolet (also called *flauto piccolo*). A six-keyed piccolo in D-flat was formerly used regularly in military bands to facilitate playing in flat keys.

Pictures at an Exhibition: *see* EUPHONIUM; MUSSORGSKY.

Pierrot Lunaire: *see* ATONALITY; MODERN PERIOD (disintegration of tonality); SCHOENBERG; SPRECHSTIMME.

Pilkington, Francis (?–1638?) An English composer of madrigals and lute songs of great charm, Francis Pilkington earned a bachelor of music degree from Lincoln College, Oxford, in 1595. In 1602 he was appointed "chaunter"—a term Pilkington used in describing himself—in Chester Cathedral and about 1612 became a minor canon. He held various benefices in and near Chester until his death, which probably occurred in 1638. His *First Booke of Ayres* (1605) contains 21 songs, which can be performed either with four voices or with solo voice and lute, and a "Pavin for the Lute and Bass Viol." This book was followed by two sets of madrigals published in 1613 and 1624. Although Pilkington's madrigals are not of the first rank, almost all are well constructed. The madrigal considered by some to be his best, "O Softly Singing Lute" for six voices, is among the second set of madrigals (1624), his last known published work. A small number of lute solos by Pilkington have survived in manuscript.

Pines of Rome: *see* RESPIGHI.

Pinkham, Daniel (b. June 5, 1923) On the faculty of the New England Conservatory since 1959, the U.S. organist, harpsichordist, and composer Daniel Pinkham studied with Walter Piston, Copland, Honegger, and Samuel Barber, as well as with Landowska and E. Power Biggs. In 1948 he co-founded the Cambridge Festival Orchestra, and 10 years later he became music director at King's Chapel in Boston. He also tours as a recitalist and lecturer. His early compositions are neo-

classical (Concerto for celesta and harpsichord, 1954); his later works are dodecaphonic with experimental sonorities, but all his music exhibits clarity of form and contrapuntal skill. Much of his music is religious in orientation: *Christmas* Cantata (1957); *St. Mark* Passion (1966); *Lamentations of Jeremiah* (1967); *Martyrdom of St. Stephen* (1967) for chorus and guitar; *Liturgies* (1974).

RECORDINGS: *Christmas* Cantata; *For Evening Draws On; Liturgies; Signs of the Zodiac* for narrator and orchestra; Toccatas *for the Vault of Heaven.*

Pinza, Ezio (May 18, 1892–May 9, 1957) With a wide range of repertoire the Italian bass Ezio Pinza sang in Vienna and Paris and made a La Scala debut before appearing in the United States. His Metropolitan Opera debut was as Pontifex Maximus in Spontini's *La Vestale* (1926), and he was a member of the company for more than 20 years. In addition to roles at the Metropolitan that ranged from Don Giovanni (Mozart) to Mussorgsky's Boris Godunov and Golaud in Debussy's *Pelléas et Mélisande,* he sang many U.S. premieres, including the roles of Podesta in Ildebrando Pizzetti's *Fra Gherardo* (1929) and Tcherevik in Mussorgsky's *Sorochinsky Fair* (1930). Following his departure from the operatic stage (1948), he was successful in musical comedy on stage and film; notable was the role of Émile de Becque in Rodgers and Hammerstein's *South Pacific* (1949).

Pique Dame: *see* QUEEN OF SPADES, THE.

Piston, Walter (Hamor) (b. January 20, 1894) Influential in the development of the 20th-century neoclassical style in the United States, composer Walter Piston studied at Harvard University and in Paris with Boulanger and Paul Dukas (1924–26). On his return to the United States, he taught at Harvard until 1960. His style is neoclassical with romantic overtones and is noted for its structural strength and rhythmic vivacity. He wrote little program music except for the orchestral suite *Three New England Sketches* (1959); his only composition for the theater is the ballet *The Incredible Flutist* (1938). He composed eight symphonies, the third (1947) and seventh (1960) of which were awarded Pulitzer prizes.

He also wrote concertos (orchestra, 1933; violin, 1939 and 1960; viola, 1957; two pianos, 1959; clarinet, 1967), Capriccio for harp and strings, and *Lincoln Center Festival* Overture (1962). Chamber music includes a Divertimento for nine instruments, five quartets, piano quintet, and wind quintet. His musical idiom has not changed to reflect contemporary techniques. He published three textbooks, *Harmony* (1941), *Counterpoint* (1947), and *Orchestration* (1955).

RECORDINGS: Chromatic Study on B-A-C-H for organ; Concertino for piano and orchestra; Concerto for orchestra; Flute Sonata; *The Incredible Flutist;* Passacaglia for piano; Piano Trio No. 1; Quartet No. 5; Suite for oboe and piano; Symphonies (Nos. 2, 5, 7, and 8); Three Pieces for flute, clarinet, and bassoon; Wind quintet.

pitch A measure of the position of a single sound in the complete range of sound. The term is more particularly applied in relation to a performance or an instrument. A precise designation of pitch is needed if singers and instrumentalists are to perform together; this is effected by reference to the pitch of one note—almost always A above middle C.

Pitch is expressed with greatest convenience as the frequency of oscillation of the sounding instrument (or of the air through which the sound waves are propagated) in cycles per second (c.p.s.). Thus A = 440 means that standard-pitch A is the sound of a tuning fork vibrating at 440 c.p.s.

history Before 1500 the main evidence concerning pitch is found in the written compass of vocal music, especially plainchant, which was sung by average voices with no special vocal training. From such evidence it would appear that pitch throughout the Middle Ages was not very different from that of today.

From the period 1500 to about 1670, large numbers of woodwind instruments survive; the pitch of most of these is remarkably constant at about A = 466, or one semitone above A = 440, because most were made in Venice in the workshop of one excellent manufacturer and his pupils and successors, all of whom used identical measurements. The pitch of church music in this period was governed by the pitch of the organ. It was usual to specify that the lowest pipe (which might be F or C) should be either five, six, eight, or ten feet long. In England and much of Europe five or ten feet was the standard. However, organists of the time were required to transpose at sight in order to bring the more extreme plainchant tones into the middle of the vocal range, and they sometimes regarded this lowest note as F and sometimes as C. In the former the pitch was about a third higher and in the latter about a third lower than A = 440. This is why the church music of Byrd, Gibbons, and Thomas Tomkins is written either a third lower or a third higher than the pitch at which it should sound.

About the middle of the 17th century, the Hotteterres, instrument makers in Paris, were remodeling the entire woodwind family. They used the Paris organ pitch of about A = 415, or a semitone below A = 440. Within 20 to 30 years they and their pupils and followers effectively set European pitch for the next 100 years. This new, or Baroque, pitch (known in Germany as *Kammerton*) was thus one tone below the old Renaissance pitch *(Chorton)*. An old trumpet in C was now in effect in D at the new pitch; this is why nearly all Baroque music with trumpets is in D.

After about 1760 the pitch rose, reaching A = 440 around 1820. It then rose more rapidly and by the latter half of the 19th century reached the Old Philharmonic Pitch of A = 452. However, the inconvenience of the high pitch, which strained singers' voices and made wind instruments quickly out of date, was eventually realized. An international commission, meeting in Paris in 1858–59, fixed a compromise pitch called diapason normal (known in the United States as French Pitch, or International Pitch) at A = 435. England in 1896 adopted the New Philharmonic Pitch at A = 439 and in 1939 adopted the U.S. Standard Pitch of A = 440, which is practically identical. After the middle of the 20th century pitch again tended to creep up; some continental makers started making woodwind instruments at A = 444 unless otherwise specified, thus repeating the tendencies of the 19th century.

When frequency numbers are not used for

a particular pitch, a system of lowercase and capital letters indicates the octave in which it occurs. The notes in the octave below middle C are indicated by lowercase letters from c to b; the notes of the second octave below middle C are shown as C to B; the notes of the next lower octave as C_1 to B_1. Middle C is shown as c′, and the notes in the octave above as d′, e′, . . . b′. The C above is shown as c′′, and the next octave as c′′′.

absolute pitch The ability to identify any note—at some standard pitch—by ear or to sing a specified note at will without recourse to an instrument is popularly called absolute pitch. Fully developed absolute pitch is uncommon. It appears in early childhood and is evidently an acute form of memory or recollection of sounds of a particular instrument such as the home piano. Some musicians slowly acquire some degree of absolute pitch if only for the familiar concert A.

plainchant or **plainsong** A general term for a style of monophonic music comprising chiefly the church music called Gregorian, which belongs to Rome, and that called Ambrosian, which comes from Milan. Other collections of Western church music much less well known than these and a good many groups of Eastern church music could also quite properly be put under this heading (see AMBROSIAN CHANT; ARMENIAN CHANT; BYZANTINE CHANT; GALLICAN CHANT; MOZARABIC CHANT). The term is a translation of *cantus planus,* meaning unmeasured music, not regular in rhythm, as contrasted with *cantus mensurabilis,* measured music.

Gregorian chant is named after St. Gregory I the Great, pope from 590 to 604. It was collected and codified during his reign. Charlemagne, King of the Franks (768–814), imposed Gregorian chant on his kingdom, where another liturgical tradition—Gallican chant—was in common use. During the 8th and 9th centuries a process of assimilation took place between Gallican and Gregorian chants, and it is the chant in this evolved form that has come down to the present.

ordinary The ordinary of the mass includes those texts that remain the same for each mass. Sung by the choir and/or congregation are the Kyrie, Gloria, Credo, Sanctus (sometimes divided into Sanctus and Benedictus), Agnus Dei, and Ite Missa Est or Benedicamus Domino. The chant of the Kyrie ranges from neumatic (patterns of one to four notes per syllable) to melismatic (unlimited notes per syllable) styles. The Gloria appeared in the 7th century. The psalmodic recitation (*i.e.,* using psalm tones, simple formulas for the intoned reciting of psalms) of early Glorias attests to their ancient origin. Later Gloria chants are neumatic. The Credo, or profession of faith, was accepted into the mass about the 11th century. Its melodies resemble psalm tones. The Sanctus and Benedictus are probably from apostolic times. The usual Sanctus chants are neumatic. The Agnus Dei was brought into the Latin mass from the Eastern Church in the 7th century and is basically in neumatic style. The Ite Missa Est or its substitute Benedicamus Domino is the final chant of the service; both usually have the melody of the opening Kyrie.

proper The proper of the mass is made up of texts that vary for each mass to bring out the significance of each feast or season. The introit is a processional chant. Its original form was that of a psalm with a refrain, or ANTIPHON, sung between each verse. By the 9th century it had received its present form: refrain in a neumatic style—a psalm verse in psalm-tone style—refrain repeated. The gradual, introduced in the 4th century, also developed from a refrain between psalm verses. Later it became: opening melody (chorus)—psalm verse(s) (soloist), a virtuosically embellished psalmodic structure—opening melody (chorus), repeated in whole or in part. The alleluia is of 4th-century Eastern origin. Its structure is somewhat like that of the gradual. The tract replaces the alleluia in penitential times. This chant is a descendant of synagogue music.

The SEQUENCE originated about the 9th century. In its modern form the texts are sacred poems with double-line stanzas having the same accentuation and number of syllables for every pair of lines. The melody of the first line was repeated for the second line of the stanza, a new melody given to the next stanza; the music is syllabic. The offertory originally consisted of a psalm and refrain, but by the

12th century only the refrain remained. The music is quite melismatic. Peculiar to the offertory alone is repetition of text. The communion is, like the offertory, a processional chant; the music is neumatic in style. *See also* MASS.

canonical hours The canonical hours comprise the official prayer worship of the church, consisting of eight prayer services: matins, lauds, prime, terce, sext, none, vespers, and compline. Each of the eight hours includes antiphons, or refrains, short texts that precede or follow each psalm and are set mostly in syllabic chant; psalms, each psalm set to a PSALM TONE; hymns, usually strophic and metrical set in a neumatic style; responsories, which follow the lessons of matins and the chapter (brief lesson) of the other hours and have the form response—psalm verse—partially or entirely repeated response. The RESPONSORY is related to the form and style of the gradual.

theory Plainchant is based on a series of eight scales called church (or ecclesiastical) modes (*see* MODE). It uses the old diatonic scale of the Greek theorists (equivalent to the white notes of the piano with the addition of B-flat), but the modes themselves are different from the old Greek modes, and the use of the old Greek names only leads to confusion. The eight-mode system is probably the same as that underlying Eastern church music, but the origins are obscure in East and West alike. The scheme seems to go back at least to St. John of Damascus (d. *c.* 752), but it is known in the West only in theoretical treatises derived through the Byzantine teachers at the court of Charlemagne at the end of the 8th century. This modal theory does not fully account for all the procedures of classical plainchant, but these eight modes form the foundation of the music, whether responsorial or antiphonal.

In the Middle Ages the *cantilena Romana* was handed on by tradition; in the 9th century it was recorded in staffless neumes. The later notation on a staff, while it fixed accurately the pitch of each note, failed to indicate the rhythmical delicacies of performance. Hence the renaissance of classical plainchant was based on a return to the neumes as interpreted by subsequent tradition. *See* NOTATION (development in Western music).

modern revival The rise of the art of harmony diverted attention from the monody of plainchant, and part singing had the effect of measuring music so that it fell into regular time and was no longer free or plain. Under these influences the old plainchant was progressively debased, and with the development of the harmonic concept plainchant declined. Not until the 19th century did this decline cease. The efforts then made in various quarters to recover alike the true rhythm and tonality of the old music culminated in the work of the Benedictines of Solesmes Abbey in France and their followers and in the revival that produced the new Vatican gradual and antiphonal. With the recovery of the music came a new insistence upon its use and study as the official music of the Roman Church until Vatican II (1962–65), after which its use became sporadic.

BIBLIOGRAPHY: Alec Robertson, *The Interpretation of Plainchant* (1937; reprint, 1970); Joseph Smits van Waesberghe, *Gregorian Chant and Its Place in the Catholic Liturgy* (1947); Dom Anselm Hughes, ed., *Early Medieval Music up to 1300* (1954), Vol. 2 in *The New Oxford History of Music;* Willi Apel, *Gregorian Chant* (1958); Eric Werner, *The Sacred Bridge; the Interdependence of Liturgy and Music in Synagogue and Church during the First Millennium* (1959).

Planché, James Robinson: *see* WEBER.

Plançon Pol (-Henri) (June 12, 1851–August 12, 1914)   A student of Jean-Baptiste Sbriglia, the French bass Pol Plançon made his debut at Lyons in Meyerbeer's *Les Huguenots* (1877) in the role of St. Bris. He first sang at the Paris Opéra in 1883 (as Méphistophélès in Gounod's *Faust*), the role in which he made his London debut at Covent Garden in 1891. Two years later he first sang in the United States as Jupiter in the Metropolitan Opera's production of Gounod's *Philémon et Baucis.* He retired in 1908 after appearances as Sarastro (Mozart's *Die Zauberflöte*), Comte des Grieux (Massenet's *Manon*), and both Abimelech and the Old Hebrew (Saint-Saëns' *Samson et Dalila*). Although best known in

French opera, especially as Mephistopheles, he sang in Italian and German, the latter including Wagnerian roles of Pogner *(Die Meistersinger)* and the Landgrave *(Tannhäuser).* An unusual quality of his voice was the florid melismas in a bass range.

Planté, Francis (March 2, 1839–December 19, 1934)   The most acclaimed French pianist of his day (until Raoul Pugno), Francis Planté was a product of the Paris Conservatoire and Antoine-François Marmontel. As a teenager he joined the distinguished violinist Delphin Alard and cellist Auguste Franchomme as their pianist in a trio, a spot formerly filled by Sir Charles Hallé.

player piano: *see* MECHANICAL INSTRUMENTS

Playford, John (1623–*c.* November 1686) An English bookseller and music publisher, John Playford had established his business by 1648 in London, where he became a clerk of the Temple Church and moved to the Inner Temple. His numerous publications, which include songs, catches, and instrumental music for cittern, lyra viol, and harpsichord, reflect the taste of English amateur musicians of the latter half of the 17th century. The friend as well as publisher of most of the English composers of his time, Playford was himself a competent musician, as may be seen from his songs and psalm settings in his collections. His best-known work, *The English Dancing-Master,* is a collection of tunes for country dances set for the fiddle; it went into numerous editions between 1650 and 1728. *A Brief Introduction to the Skill of Musick,* a handbook on music theory and practice, went into many editions between 1654 and 1730. In 1694 it was revised by Purcell, who rewrote the section on composition originally by Thomas Campion with additions by Christopher Simpson. Other Playford publications include: John Hilton's *Catch that Catch can* (1652); *Select Ayres and Dialogues* (1652–69); *Court Ayres* (1655); and *Musick's Handmaid* (1663). Of the several elegies on Playford's death, "Gentle Shepherds, You That Know" by Nahum Tate was set to music by Purcell.

Playford's son Henry Playford (1657–*c.* 1709) continued the family business, which

from 1696 he conducted in his own name. As well as bringing out new editions of his father's publications, he issued a small number of new works, notably John Blow's "Ode on the Death of Mr. Henry Purcell" (1696) and two posthumous collections of music by Purcell, *Orpheus Britannicus* (1698–1702) and *A Choice Collection of Lessons for the Harpsichord or Spinnet* (1696).

Pleyel, Ignaz (Joseph) (June 1, 1757–November 14, 1831)   An Austrian composer and founder of one of the principal French firms of piano makers, Ignaz Pleyel was the 24th child of a poor village schoolmaster. He studied piano with Jan Křtitel Vanhal and composition with Haydn, whose close friend he became. In 1776 he produced at Esterháza the puppet opera *Die Fee Urgele* on a libretto derived from Voltaire and Chaucer, and in 1780 his opera *Ifigenia in Aulide* was produced in Naples. In 1783 Pleyel was appointed deputy and in 1789 principal maître de chapelle at the cathedral in Strasbourg, where in 1791 he became involved in the troubles of the French Revolution and barely escaped the guillotine. In 1795 he moved to Paris, where he opened a music shop, published the first complete set of Haydn's quartets, and in 1807 founded the piano factory that still bears his name. Pleyel was a prolific composer with a facile and spirited invention. A few of his numerous symphonies, concertos, serenades, and quartets were revived toward the middle of the 20th century.

His son Camille Pleyel (1788–1855) was also a pianist and composer who married Marie Moke. Under the name Marie Pleyel, she became one of the major pianists of her day.

RECORDING: Sinfonia Concertante in B-flat for violin and viola.

Pleyel, Marie (Félicité Denise), before her marriage, Marie Félicité Denise Moke (September 4, 1811–March 30, 1875)   Greatly admired by Mendelssohn, Liszt, and Schumann, the French pianist Marie Pleyel studied with Henri Herz, Ignaz Moscheles, and Friedrich Kalkbrenner. Berlioz was in love with her, but she married Camille Pleyel, son of the founder of the piano manufacturing firm bearing the family name. Mme Pleyel headed the piano department of the Brussels Conservatoire from 1848 to 1872.

Plomer, William: *see* OPERA (the 20th century).

polka A lively courtship dance in ⅔ time of Bohemian origin. It is characterized by three quick steps and a hop. Introduced in Paris about 1843, it became an extraordinary craze in the ballroom and on the stage, sweeping rapidly across Europe and the Americas. It has retained considerable popularity as a social dance and has been used by composers of art music as in Smetana's *The Bartered Bride* (1866), William Walton's *Façade* (1922–23), and Jaromir Weinberger's *Schwanda the Bagpiper* (1927).

polonaise A dignified ceremonial dance in ⅔ time. From the 17th to 19th century it frequently served to open court balls and other royal functions. Originally a folk dance or warriors' triumphal march, it was adopted by the Polish nobility as a formal march as early as 1573. In its aristocratic form the dancers, in couples, walked around the ballroom in stately procession with slightly accented steps. As a musical form the polonaise was occasionally employed by Beethoven, Mozart, and Handel and was highly developed by Chopin. The polonaise has been introduced in opera (Mussorgsky's *Boris Godunov,* 1874) and ballet (Tchaikovsky's *The Sleeping Beauty,* 1890).

Polovtsian Dances (Borodin): *see* BALLET (Diaghilev Ballet).

polyphony A term derived from the Greek *polys,* "many," and *phonos,* "sound," used of music in which the parts are independent of each other though forming an acceptable harmony. It is thus a synonym of COUNTERPOINT, though the term counterpoint is generally associated with the technique of polyphonic music. The term polyphony is used of vocal works of the 16th century, *e.g.,* a polyphonic chanson, madrigal, or motet, as opposed to HOMOPHONY, used of music in which the conception is predominantly harmonic. It is also the converse of MONOPHONY, music consisting of one part alone, and monody, a solo song with continuo.

polyrhythm Varied rhythmic patterns in different parts of a composition used simultaneously. The term polyrhythm usually means conflicts of rhythm, or cross rhythms. One such conflict may occur within the same meter; for example, two eighth notes against triplet eighths. There may also be conflicts of meter or accent.

polytonality The simultaneous use of different tonalities. Usually two different tonalities—known as bitonality—were used as in the passage for trumpets in C major and f-sharp minor in the second tableau of Stravinsky's *Petrushka* (1911), expressive of the puppet's pathos. Alfredo Casella's *Pezzi infantili* (1920) are among children's pieces in which this device was used. Prokofiev's *Sarcasms* (1912) for piano boldly juxtaposes the keys of f-sharp minor in the right hand and b-flat minor in the left, while Milhaud's *Saudades do Brazil* (1920–21) has a melody in C with an accompaniment in A-flat major. Such combinations may also be analyzed as highly inflected forms of chromatic harmony whose dissonances are evantually resolved. The passage from *Petrushka* may be said to be based on the harmony of c-sharp minor, to which it resolves, and the passage from Milhaud's work on the key of the accompaniment in A-flat. The simultaneous combination of three or more keys leads to harmonic or contrapuntal combinations that are even more difficult to define and that belong to the technique of ATONALITY. The technique of polytonality was first analyzed by Milhaud, who maintained that it could be traced back to the simultaneous use by Bach of two keys in a canon at the fourth.

Pomp and Circumstance: *see* ELGAR.

Ponchielli, Amilcare (August 31, 1834–January 16, 1886) An Italian composer best known for his opera *La Gioconda,* Amilcare Ponchielli studied at Milan and produced his first opera, *I promessi sposi* (1856; on the novel of Alessandro Manzoni), at Cremona. In a revised version it was frequently given in Italy and abroad. Between 1873 and 1875 he wrote two ballets and four operas and became the most important of Verdi's Italian contemporaries. *La Gioconda* (La Scala, 1876) on a libretto by Arrigo Boito, based on Victor Hugo's *Angelo,* achieved wide success at the end of the 19th century. Later it was chiefly known for its ballet "Dance of the Hours" but returned to the repertoire of Italian opera houses in the 1950s. From 1881 to 1886 Ponchielli was musical director at the Bergamo Cathedral, where he wrote several sacred works.

RECORDINGS: *La Gioconda;* Wind Quartet in B-flat with piano accompaniment.

Pons, Lily, real name, Alice Josephine Pons (April 12, 1898–February 13, 1976) After early experience as an actress the French coloratura soprano Lily Pons made her operatic debut in Alsace in 1928 in Léo Delibes's *Lakmé,* one of her best-known roles. In 1931 she made her Metropolitan Opera debut as Donizetti's Lucia di Lammermoor, singing there for more than 25 years. Her appearances included the first commercial broadcast from the Metropolitan, Ambroise Thomas's *Mignon.* Pons made several Hollywood films from 1935 and gave many benefit performances, especially for the blind and for U.S. veterans. A popular and glamorous artist, she appeared in concert occasionally until 1972.

Ponselle, Rosa, originally Rosa Melba Ponzillo (b. January 22, 1897) A vaudeville and café singer in her youth, the U.S. soprano Rosa Ponselle made her operatic debut at the Metropolitan Opera in 1918 as Leonora in Verdi's *La Forza del destino* with Caruso. During her 20 years there she sang the French and Italian repertoire, becoming best known for Rachel in Meyerbeer's *La Juive,* Mathilde in Rossini's *Guillaume Tell,* and the title role in Bellini's *Norma.* She also sang Bizet's Carmen and Mozart's Donna Anna *(Don Giovanni).* Her London debut (1930) was in the role of Norma. Ponselle retired from the Metropolitan in 1937 and became artistic director of the Baltimore Civic Opera (from 1954).

Ponte, Lorenzo da: *see* MOZART (later life).

Popper, David (December 9, 1843–August 7, 1913) A student of Georg Goltermann at the Prague Conservatory, the German-Bohemian cellist David Popper taught at the Royal Conservatory of Budapest from 1896 to 1913, during which time he was made a *Hofrat* of the Austro-Hungarian Empire. He had a large, expressive tone and a classical style of interpretation. A prolific composer for the cello, he wrote concertos, methods, and pieces as well as a *Requiem* for three cellos.

popular music Inhabiting the broad domain that lies between folk music and fine art music, popular music is a domain with no clearly defined frontiers, merging at both extremes. But for the most part the distinction between folk, popular, and fine art music is clear enough.

In general popular music—unlike folk music proper—is produced by professionals and mainly in urban centers. But it is in many cases—unlike fine art music—diffused by oral means. In important examples such as Spanish flamenco, central European gypsy music, and a great deal of jazz, it flourished without the aid of print. These three considerations—professionalism, urbanism, and the relative degree of its oral transmission—have for centuries affected the nature of popular music in many parts of eastern and western Europe, North and South America, and much of Asia. After the mid-20th century, with the global expansion and dominance of Western music, a worldwide uniformity of popular music began to be apparent, derived in large part from U.S. models.

antiquity and the Middle Ages In antiquity another layer of music was interposed between the music of the peasantry and that of the upper classes. Cities such as Rome and Alexandria attracted Greek minstrels, Syrian dancers, Negro musicians, singers from the Italian countryside, and former slaves or smallholders who made a living by providing music for the urban crowds at circuses or in theaters, in processions or dances. The phenomenon of the popular "hit" song, spreading from the theater into the streets, was already familiar in Roman times. The Roman writer Suetonius reports that when Galba was made emperor in A.D. 68, the audience in a theater roared out a song then in vogue that satirized Galba's avarice.

When in 6th-century Europe the by then degenerate theater of antiquity disappeared during the barbarian invasions, dispossessed musicians were driven afoot to mingle with the bards of various peoples—Teutonic, Celtic, Slav—in that miscellaneous body of entertainers who haunted the towns and thoroughfares of the Middle Ages. Before long a general European popular music idiom began to show itself in which national differences were to some extent masked by a stylization that resulted from the cosmopolitanism of the professional musicians' calling—but to some extent only. It is true that the popular performances of medieval Europe were far more international in character than those of folk music, which often varied enormously in style from country to country and even from province to province. Yet there were characteristic differences between the analogous melody forms and utterances of such varieties of poet-musician as the northern French trouvères, Provençal troubadours, German minnesingers, Spanish *juglares,* and English minstrels. A 14th-century proverb of French origin indicates the manner of popular singing among various nations: "The French sing, the English carol, the Spaniards wail, the Germans howl, the Italians bleat." In the high and late Middle Ages, popular music covered a wide social and artistic range. Minstrels might be of the court or the tavern, they might be large landowners or beggars, wandering scholars or illiterates, virtuosos or strummers. The repertoire ranged from aristocratic hero ballads through lyrical songs, courtly or crude, to rustic dance tunes. Musicians' earnings varied as widely as their grades, and the wealthy troubadours were as scornful of the ragged jongleurs as minnesingers and Meistersingers were of the itinerant *Spielleute* of the German countryside and back streets. The fortunes of popular musicians in the Middle Ages were subject to the same ups and downs as those experienced by the star performers today. Thus the talented jongleur Bernard de Ventadour (flourished late 12th century), a baker's son, attained the courtly rank of troubadour and entered the aristocracy; but his contemporary, the equally gifted Raimbaut de Vaqueyras, a dispossessed nobleman, sank down into the ranks of the *juglares,* playing and singing on fairgrounds and in market squares.

International traffic in popular music, exemplified in modern times in the worldwide spread of jazz and rock 'n' roll, was already foreshadowed in the Middle Ages by itinerant professional musicians who might wander anywhere within a territory bounded by Edinburgh, Santiago de Compostela, Cyprus, and Tallinn on the Baltic. Paris-based minstrels would operate in France between Roncesvalles and Metz; German musicians based in Nürnberg might be in Cracow for the summer and in Verona for the winter. French, Italian, Spanish, and Portuguese minstrels were frequent guests in England. In the towns on the Adriatic coast, Serbian, Greek, and Croatian musicians played alongside instrumentalists from the German principalities and from Transylvania (Romania). French popular musicians, settled in the Hungarian wine-growing districts, accompanied the annual Tokay caravans through Slovakia and across the Carpathians into central Poland. All these musicians exchanged melodies, musical ideas, and instrumental techniques.

Nor was the influence of the Near East unimportant. Urban popular music of Arabic-Persian origin was early spread over parts of southwest Europe by the Moors in Spain, southern France, and southern Italy. From this culture came the short-necked lute with bent-back pegbox, the instrument now popularly associated with medieval minstrels. Later, with the Turkish invasions and occupations, music of similar provenance was spread among occupational musicians in the towns of southeast Europe, notably Bulgaria, Romania, Serbia, Bosnia, and Albania. It was carried mainly by gypsy professional entertainers into Central Europe, where it mingled with the local musical stock to create the peculiar, hybrid, semi-Oriental kind of popular music that Mozart used in his *alla turca* compositions.

Renaissance As feudalism merged into early capitalism (15th and 16th centuries in western Europe, later elsewhere), popular musicians became more settled, and generally only those in the lowest reaches of the profession remained itinerant. An active traffic between urban and rural culture became the normal condition of popular song. Some of the agents of this process were amateur composers among the rural middle class, making formalized arrangements of folk tunes; domestic servants bringing village music into towns and taking town music back into the villages with them; fairground and marketplace singers; street showmen; booth-theater actors; peddlers of cheap songbooks and broadsides (from the 16th century onward).

Various institutions helped in the formation of popular music idioms. In England from Tudor times the municipalities employed town waits, instrumentalists who combined the functions of perambulating night watchmen and town bandsmen. They played for official visits, for the mayor on market days, and for summer evening concerts from the guildhall roof or a roadside scaffolding. In Coventry, for instance, they also played softly at various corners of the city five nights a week from midnight to four for the reassurance of citizens. Their repertoire consisted mainly of adapted folk melodies, humble amateur compositions, popular dance tunes, theater music, and marches. In France, from the time of François Villon and Rabelais onward, popular city cabarets put into circulation a large number of songs—sentimental, satirical, or comic—most of which enjoyed only a brief vogue, though some proved lasting.

An even more powerful source of popular music was the secular theater that established itself firmly in France, Spain, and Italy in the 15th and 16th centuries. The theaters performed short plays—often four pieces in an evening—acted usually on open platforms of a movable kind by companies consisting partly of professionals and partly of amateurs, including women and at times children. Many of these plays began and ended with a song in the manner of an overture-finale frame, and most of them were punctuated with chansons, *villancicos,* and villanelle during the course of the action. Some of the actors played instruments and at times would perform pieces from the regular minstrel repertoire in the absence of music especially written for the theater.

In Germany—where after the Reformation printed music, the popular choral movement, and the activities of educated amateur musicians, parsons, and schoolmasters worked with especially powerful effect on lower class music making—a vast amount of folk song was transformed into popular song by the imposition of the conventions and usages of art music. This was accomplished by simplifying rhythms, converting old modes into modern scales, tidying the structure of melodies, and encouraging a standard kind of voice production. A characteristic institution of the early capitalist period in Germany was that of the MEISTERSINGER—most were small merchants, artisans, and tradesmen—who assembled, usually in the guildhall on Sunday afternoons, to practice their new, often homemade songs that belonged firmly to the realm of popular music, being neither folk song nor fine art compositions.

Baroque In 17th-century England the powerful expansion of bourgeois ways of life and manners of thought was accompanied by a flourishing of urban popular music that became equally as important as folk music and art music. Significant landmarks were the extremely successful publication of John Playford's *The English Dancing-Master,* a collection of contredanse tunes—many based on popular song and ballad airs—that ran into 17 editions between 1650 and 1728, and Henry Playford's *Wit and Mirth. An Antidote against Melancholy* (1682) gained great fame when it was re-edited in 1699 with the subtitle of *Pills to Purge Melancholy.* Rather unjustly Thomas D'Urfey gets the most credit for this collection of popular songs—serious or saucy—of aristocratic, bourgeois, or lower class origin. New volumes were added over the years and reprintings constantly ordered. By 1720 the work had grown to six volumes and contained more than 1,000 songs, giving a wide view of the popular music of the time in parlor and kitchen, tavern and pleasure garden.

The pleasure gardens that sprang up, notably in the 18th century, in the cities and spas, or watering places, gave an important stimulus to popular music through their evening entertainments. Thousands of songs were written specifically for performance in these places and, at least from the middle of the century, were profusely printed on leaflets or in books. In London between 1769 and the early years of the 19th century, at least one book of Vauxhall Gardens songs was published annually, as were songs from Marylebone Gardens. One composer, James Hook, wrote more than 2,000 songs mainly for the "gardens crowd," and another, Charles Dibdin, wrote nearly 1,000; several other composers were scarcely less diligent. A comparable flood of lyrical popular music flowed at a slightly later time from the beer garden entertainments of German and Austrian towns.

Meanwhile in most larger towns of 18th-century continental Europe, popular comedies with music could be seen in the puppet and marionette tents and on the fairground or back-street stages, often with stereotyped figures derived from the Italian commedia dell'arte such as Pantaloon, Harlequin, and Pulcinella. A report from 1711 tells that at the fairs of Saint-Germain and Saint-Laurent in Paris theater audiences habitually joined the actors in singing favorite songs of the day; the actors had only to sing the opening bars, and the audience knew the rest.

Later in the century, when the French royal opera forbade actors to sing in the popular theaters on grounds of its exclusive privilege for such performance, actors would cause a scroll to unfurl each time they came to a song, the instrumentalists would introduce the melody, and the entire audience would roar out the song, reading the words from the scroll. Usually in this kind of performance the text was more important than the music, which more often than not was derived or adapted from well-known tunes similar to the BALLAD OPERA. Probably the most important of the ballad operas and one that had great effect internationally was *The Beggar's Opera* by John Gay, an aggressively satirical piece and a favorite with the populace. It was first staged in 1728 and was an immediate success; within a few years it had been played on countless stages in England, Ireland, and Scotland. In 1733 it was performed in Jamaica and in 1750 in Paris and New York. Its triumph encouraged others. By the end of 1729 London had seen 15 ballad operas and by 1733, 70. Some 700 popular tunes were used in these works with librettos sometimes written by hack writers, sometimes by such eminent literary men as Jonathan Swift, Henry Fielding, and Richard Sheridan. In later years this form of light

Baroque lyrical theater was to have considerable influence on continental popular music, notably in Germany.

the French Revolution The years of the French Revolution comprise a singular period in the history of popular music. Admired singers would set up their little platforms in the squares or near the bridges of Paris to amuse the public by singing topical songs. In many parts of the city the audiences were so large that coach-and-wagon traffic was seriously hindered, and the municipal authorities were at length obliged to provide special vantage points where singers might perform. At the height of revolutionary enthusiasm there was hardly a gathering of any kind where patriotic, satirical, or general popular song was not heard. In his compendious work *Les Hymns et chansons de la Révolution* (1904), the musicographer of the French Revolution, Constant Pierre, reports: "For a certain period the theaters were literally invaded and treated as an annexe of the public highway; the audiences displayed their opinions by themselves singing songs of political tendency or by demanding performances, there and then, of their preferred ditties."

Singing invaded the National Convention itself with one deputation after another announcing its revolutionary fervor and then singing its favorite song to the accompaniment of drums and other instruments brought along for the purpose. Deputies habitually stood in the convention and intoned lengthy ballads written on some topical point or other until in March 1794 Georges Danton, a prominent revolutionary leader, proposed a resolution "That henceforth this platform hears nothing but reason in prose." The motion was carried, and from then on singers were rarely heard in the convention hall except by invitation. The course of the torrent of revolutionary popular songs is not without interest. In 1789 a mere 100 songs on political or social themes were published. In the enthusiasms of 1793 the number rose to 590, and the next year 701 such songs were issued. With the reaction to the execution of the revolutionary leader Robespierre, the numbers declined steeply. Only 137 new songs on topical themes were issued in 1795, and by the end of the century the flow of directly political songs had all but ceased. This example serves to remind that popular music is far more sensitive to the important moments of history than either fine art music or folk music, at least in the Western tradition. Thus the American Revolution and the Civil War both produced a flood of popular songs but only a few occasional pieces for the concert hall, while—contrary to general belief—the reflection of these events in folk song proper was minimal.

the 19th century   The period of industrial capitalism saw the greatest spread of specifically popular music. The growth of large towns meant bigger audiences, which in turn gave rise to an entertainment industry of vast scope: at first in Europe, later in the Americas, and then in Africa and Asia. Conditions favoring an oral culture weakened, and the masses of working people evolved away from self-made folk song toward the products of music hall, dance hall, and popular theater.

Particularly in the early part of the 19th century in western and central Europe and the Americas, popular social song developed enormously in all its forms—sentimental, patriotic, comic, satirical. The remarkable evidence of the democratization on musical life—after the French Revolution and the growth of the industrial proletariat—was the appearance of the British music hall, which was to have an even more decisive influence on the trends of popular music than the cabarets of Paris or the operetta theaters of Vienna. The music halls first sprang up in the big industrial cities as workingmen's beer halls with entertainment. Gradually, during the second half of the 19th century, the entertainment became more important than the drinking, and the beer halls evolved into theaters-with-a-bar, providing shows that largely consisted of humorous, satirical, or sentimentally emotional songs mainly of lower class life. In the earlier years of the 19th century, visiting entertainers from the British music halls were instrumental in stimulating the U.S. entertainment industry that in a later time, in the domain of popular music as in other fields, was to become the dominant influence throughout the world.

During the whole of the 19th century the process by which music "from below" in the social scale is taken over and formalized by educated composers for the benefit of a middle and even upper class audience was vigorously under way. Out of the topical songs and festive dances (the carmagnole, for example) of the French Revolution emerged the tradition of Parisian cabaret song and such boisterous gallops as the can can. Describing these songs and dances as he experienced them in lower class city dives, the German poet Heinrich Heine wrote: "They make fun not only of sexual relations but of bourgeois relations too, and of everything else that seems good and fair . . . patriotism, faith, belief, family relations, heroism and godliness in every shape and form." This originally proletarian satirical tradition was transformed to provide the basis for the lively bourgeois operettas of Offenbach, Hervé, Charles Lecocq, and others. *See* OPERETTA.

Also powerful in its effect on the popular musical theater was the less mordant, more sentimental Viennese tradition represented by the younger Johann Strauss and by Franz von Suppé. This tradition had derived much from the *Liedertafel* ("table song") movement of popular harmony-singing clubs and from waltz music that had grown out of the Ländler dances of the Austrian and Bavarian peasantry put into evening dress and performed amid the glitter of high bourgeois candelabra. This style even invaded the realm of fine art music and reached its peak in Richard Strauss's opera *Der Rosenkavalier*.

Even in the less developed parts of Europe and in Central and South America, popular music was expanding and undergoing transformation. In Spain flamenco music was growing away from its folk origins, becoming progressively more showy and exotic in the cabarets and small theaters that sprang up around the middle of the century, notably in the Andalusian seaports. In Lisbon the fado developed in much the same way. About the same time in the Balkans, the emancipation of serfs and the weakening of the Turks' grip meant that many private orchestras belonging to nobles and officials—playing an Orientally tinged music—were broken up. This released a flood of popular instrumentalists seeking employment in restaurants and night spots of towns and cities. The result was the stylized, idiom loosely called gypsy music, in which—as with flamenco—the exotic aspects were often exaggerated to satisfy the customers.

In Latin America the great developments in popular music were in the domain of the dance. Fashionable travelers from Europe brought to Havana, Rio de Janeiro, Buenos Aires, and Lima the minuets, gavottes, schottisches, polkas, and waltzes of Paris and Vienna. In upper class ballrooms these dances were performed as received, but as they seeped down to the lower classes—which, from the Caribbean to Brazil, were mainly comprised of Negroes and mulattoes—the dances and the music accompanying them became altered with the choreography, melody, and rhythm current among the working people. These developed into rumbas, sambas, and congas that were later to invade the ballrooms and dance halls of North America and Europe and have influence on urban popular music over some parts of Africa.

In the United States an important development toward the middle of the 19th century was the emergence of the blackface minstrel shows, with white performers disguised as blacks presenting mainly a burlesque of Negro song and humor. Touring groups such as Daniel Emmett's Virginia Minstrels, who made their debut in 1843, and the Christy Minstrels, who followed shortly after, gave widespread currency to a vast number of popular songs, some of which are still sung. Companies such as these, as well as the growing number of vaudeville theaters in U.S. towns, promoted on a vast scale the compositions of such songwriters as Stephen Foster, the composer of "Oh! Susanna" and "Old Folks at Home"; Henry Clay Work, who wrote "Marching Through Georgia" and "The Year of Jubilo"; and George F. Root, whose best known songs are "The Battle Cry of Freedom" and "Tramp, Tramp, Tramp." A more peripheral but ultimately influential development was the emergence of a stratum of rural musicians who became entertainers with medicine shows and on the country–town vaudeville circuits, playing a stylized music of folklore origin. It was these minstrels who laid the foundations for the powerful hillbilly industry and its subse-

quent analogues—country and western and bluegrass in the mid-20th century.

the 20th century In the early years of the 20th century, the upper, more genteel reaches of popular music were still dominated by European operetta and opéra bouffe. This tradition, characterized by Offenbach and even more by Johann Strauss the Younger, was prolonged in the 20th century by such composers as Victor Herbert, who wrote some 40 operettas, including *Babes in Toyland* (1903) and *Naughty Marietta* (1910). Prominent among Herbert's rivals were Rudolf Friml, born in Prague, and the Hungarian-born Sigmund Romberg, both of whom had emigrated to the United States in the early years of the century. Among Friml's greatest successes were *Rose Marie* (1924) and *The Vagabond King* (1925). Romberg is best remembered for *The Student Prince* (1924) and *The Desert Song* (1926).

At the same time that these talented composers were producing their European-style works—sweetly lyrical, making heavy use of waltz time, and in the main presenting unrealistic and exotic subjects—a new kind of musical play known as MUSICAL COMEDY, or just musical, was emerging in the United States. It is a genre that is somewhat brash in character with breezy rhythms, usually offering scenes of American life in relatively realistic terms. Representatives of this vigorous trend were Jerome Kern, whose *Show Boat* (1927) became a classic; and Gershwin, who had a brilliant run of successes from *Lady Be Good* (1924) to the quasi-opera *Porgy and Bess* (1935). The boisterous folkways of the American frontier provided two outstanding successes in Richard Rodgers' and Oscar Hammerstein's *Oklahoma!* (1943) and Irving Berlin's *Annie Get Your Gun* (1946). More sophisticated and silken were the works of the composer-lyricist Cole Porter, whose urbane musical comedies skillfully combined the traditions of New York, Paris, and Vienna, notably in such works as *The Gay Divorcee* (1932) and *Can-Can* (1953). Bernstein's *West Side Story* (1957) was a continuation of the tradition of realistic American urban musical comedy, begun in the opening years of the century by the vaudeville performer George M. Cohan with such works as *Little Johnny Jones.*

Throughout the first half of the 20th century and to an ever increasing degree, the popular music of the cities and towns in a great part of the Western world (and ultimately beyond) was nourished mainly from the United States, with songs from the musical shows and other lyrical pieces composed by such well-known musicians as those named above. Although most of these compositions, following the common fate of much commercial popular music, proved brittle and ephemeral, certain of them have lingered on over the years to become standard songs in the popular repertoire; for instance, Berlin's "Alexander's Ragtime Band" (1911), "What'll I Do?" (1924), "How Deep Is the Ocean?" (1932), and "I'm Dreaming of a White Christmas" (1942) or Gershwin's "Swanee" (1918), "The Man I Love" (1924), and "Summertime" (1935).

Most of the creations of the musical comedy composers leaned heavily on the conventions of serious music for their idiom and manner of performance. But as the half-century progressed they were more and more influenced by the world of jazz. Indeed the most powerful development in the field of popular music in the 20th century has been the emergence of jazz as a commercially viable entertainment for a public of the broadest social range. Jazz developed first of all as a synthesis of European ballroom dance music (via ragtime), brass band music, and the songs of black laborers (especially folk blues) and—to a lesser extent—white workers. It became such a powerful trend in mass music because conditions in post-slavery America favored a synthesis of black African and white European music, attractive through its exotic coloring and informal atmosphere. Moreover the growing drift of country workers into urban areas meant that a new current began to flow into the culture of the cities, always avid for novelty. At the same time the most propitious economic and technical conditions developed in America for the marketing of this new music, for adapting it to suit the tastes of various layers of society, and for stimulating its mass production, dissemination, and global export.

Formally JAZZ is in essence a synthesis of European shapeliness and African rhythmic ingenuity. The synthesis began at the point where folk music merges into commercial popular music, and it first began to show itself in such places as the railway construction camps in the course of musical exchanges between black and white laborers, each possessing a fairly rich rural repertoire. These exchanges were reinforced and formalized by the constant flow of humble occupational musicians who drifted from one construction camp to another as entertainers. When in the early years of the 20th century these pre-proletarians began to drift into the cities in large numbers, they brought their musical adaptations with them and developed them further in their new urban surroundings. So out of the almost formless paramusical hollers of field workers grew the shapely urbanized complaint songs called the blues. Out of a synthesis of plantation song and white folk music came a repertoire of rhythmically attractive lyrical airs. Likewise the dynamic rhythms of the gang work songs were adapted to European-style march tunes by brass-band musicians who accompanied carnival and funeral processions through the streets of cities (following the Civil War and the Spanish-American War of 1898, ex-Army wind instruments had become available at cheap prices in several U.S. towns, a decisive factor in the composition of early jazz bands).

Since the various kinds of jazz were cradled among the lower strata of society, it followed that at the outset those bearers of the tradition who sought to become occupational musicians were restricted for employment to the rougher places of entertainment. Hence the early reputation of jazz as a music of the gin mills and honky-tonks, a music inherently immoral, appealing to the basest instincts and threatening to disintegrate the very fabric of society. This reputation at first inhibited, but failed to prevent, the flowing of the jazz idiom into the mainstream of popular commercial music.

Significantly the first kind of jazz to make an impact on the broad popular music market was precisely the genre lying closest to conventional fine art music, namely ragtime. The ragtime composers were mostly Negro pianists trained in European music, often men of considerable artistic pretensions. The structures of ragtime derived largely from French or

American light music models, rather mechanically infused with syncopations from Negro tradition. Prominent among ragtime composers were Scott Joplin (1868–1917) and the slightly younger James P. Johnson. Incidentally, both composers tried their hand at more ambitious forms, Joplin with a ragtime opera, Johnson with symphonies and concertos, none successful. With its basically conventional idiom ragtime was easily absorbed into the mainstream of commercial popular music, and by 1900 Tin Pan Alley had taken it over. Already in 1899 a writer in the *Musical Record* had forecast: "Ragtime will find its way gradually into the works of some great genius and will thereafter be canonised," as if he foresaw Debussy's "Gollywog's Cakewalk" (1906–08) and *Ragtime* (1918) of Stravinsky.

Only a few years later a deeper, more original jazz style, the blues, entered the popular music market by way of professional woman performers on the music hall stage. The pioneer blues singer Ma Rainey (Gertrude Pridgett) obtained her first vaudeville engagements in 1902, and subsequently in company with such as Bessie Smith and Bertha Hill she established a bold, expressive, essentially professional if sometimes brassy style that some call classic blues, a style that like other authentic kinds of jazz was out of the range of the great entertainment corporations. Eventually, however, in diluted and polished forms, with its realistic passions replaced by the poetry of bourgeois dreams, the blues was adapted for general show business exploitation, whether in the most expensive night clubs or the cheapest suburban dance halls.

For all that, it was the lyrical dance music of small jazz bands, rather than the piano rags or vocal blues, that attracted the most energetic attention of large-scale commercial promoters. From 1910 onward, as jazz music and jazz musicians moved northward from such centers as New Orleans to the large industrial cities such as Chicago and New York, elements of jazz flowed easily and to an increasing extent into the sweet pop music that was the dominant product of the entertainment industry. It infused at least a semblance of life into what has been described as "the unchanging nullity of the Palm Court orches-

tra," adding spice to the general run of musical comedy songs and positively liberating certain light music composers such as Gershwin, who extended the realm of popular music into the great concert halls with a jazz-influenced *Konzertstück* entitled *Rhapsody in Blue* (though some of the success of this piece must be attributed to its skillful orchestration by Ferde Grofé).

Prominent among Negro composers who profited from the discoveries and inventions of a great army of nameless jazzmen, black or white, was Duke Ellington, whose compositions over the last half century moved progressively closer to the realm of "service" music—graceful, subdued, rather Delius-like, a high-quality popular music belonging firmly within the economic setting of the modern general entertainment industry rather than within the specialized jazz business. It must be realized that jazz is not a single category but a kind of music presenting a vast range of transformations, in fact a microcosm of the whole sphere of popular music, simultaneously being performed at the level of urban folklore (exemplified, say, by McKinley "Muddy Waters" Morganfield), light salon music (Glenn Miller), "big band" dance music (Count Basie), popular symphonic music (certain works of Gershwin and Ellington), concert chamber music (Modern Jazz Quartet), even reaching to a far-out form of intellectualized musical Dadaism (Charlie Mingus)—a range that synchronically corresponds to something like the development of musical history from Adam de la Halle to John Cage. As far as the mainstream of popular music is concerned, the vitalizing effect of jazz was most felt on the standard popular lyrical song, with its 32-bar AABA chorus, the great mainstay of the 20th-century light music industry.

Jazz was not the only music coming from below to mingle with and ultimately to affect the direction taken by popular music in the 20th century. Just as in the lowland South the rapid industrialization of postbellum America had resulted in the emergence of the predominantly Negro hybrid music called jazz, so in the upland South similar factors produced the predominantly white hybrid music called hillbilly.

Until the mid-19th century the secular music tradition of the southern uplands—particularly the Appalachians and Ozarks—had been almost exclusively domestic, amateur, folkloric. Following the Civil War, however, rapid economic and social changes ensued, itinerant workers came into contact with workers from different cultural regions, and whole families moved from the remote countryside into mill towns. Construction camps, mines, and manufacturing plants altered not only the economy but also the lower class music of the mountaineers. Many folk music performers became part of itinerant show business—attached to traveling medicine shows, playing at fairs, appearing in the vaudeville theaters—performing (mainly to a white audience) a music based on mountain folk tradition but adapted by simplification of form, virtuosity of performance, and the projection of easily-absorbed emotion to make an instant impression on a public of mixed regional culture. Thus arose the art form loosely called hillbilly music, which in its later developments—as country and western, etc.—neatly expressed the polarization of country and city, frontier and metropolis.

For much of the 20th century this music played but small part on the general scene of popular music. Shortly after World War I a number of the newly-established country radio stations began to draw on the growing tradition of hillbilly musicians, interspersing local advertising with brief musical interludes provided—often free—by performers appearing in the neighborhood. By 1924 it was realized that there was even a northern market for this music; the first successful barn dance program was established on WLS, Chicago, mainly using country musicians from Kentucky. Around the same time the recording industry began to interest itself in the music, intending to issue disks mainly for sale in rural crossroads stores. To their surprise they soon found there was some national demand—at first modest—for the product.

Unlike jazz, which was mainly based on wind instruments, hillbilly music relied on strings. Instruments such as violin, guitar, and banjo had become widely available in rural areas through urban contact and mail order houses and were found relatively cheap, easy to combine in ensemble, and well-suited for a repertoire that had to a large extent grown out of folk fiddle music.

By the 1930s the place of country music in the mainstream of popular music was consolidated, and through the commercial success of such performers as the Carter family from upland Virginia and the former railroad worker Jimmie Rodgers it had gained status not only with a section of the urban audience but with the entertainment corporations too. The repertoire of country music performers represents a jumble of musics deriving from folk dance tunes, white adaptations of Negro blues, sacred songs contrasted with lyrics of drink and violence, broadside-like accounts of railroad disasters and hard times in the cotton mills, and above all a range of songs of commercialized pathos treating of dying mothers, orphaned children, bereft lovers, and lonely men far from home.

During the 1930s the music inevitably became less folkloric, tending more and more toward the general conventions of professional popular music. Gradually the more folkloric southeastern, or mountain, tradition exemplified by the Carter family, the Monroe brothers, and the highly successful Roy Acuff and his Smoky Mountain Boys was overtaken on the commercial market by the southwestern tradition of such performers as Jimmie Rodgers, Gene Autry, and the like—a tradition affected both by the blues and by cowboy music and centered particularly on Oklahoma and Texas, areas of broader acculturation than the Appalachian regions.

During World War II country music expanded enormously through intense promotion by the popular entertainment industry, probably because the strong nostalgic bias of the music was particularly appealing during a time of widespread shifts of population into urban industrial plants and the armed forces. By the end of the war and notably during the decade following, country music had come into the orbit of the star–hit system, involving rapid sales, large profits, and a voracious demand for new material.

During the 1950s the growth of a profitable market among adolescents, combined with the invention of electronic instruments allowing the easy production of a powerful and impetuous sound, stimulated the enormous diffusion of rock 'n' roll music, which relies largely on amplification for its exciting effects and which proved irresistible to many young people throughout the world. Subsequent modifications of pop music have retained the metronomic quality present in the music of Elvis Presley and later rock 'n' roll performers but have also reinforced its blues ingredient. Rather paradoxically what was originally an intensely American kind of popular music was to find some of its most characteristic modifications and its greatest commercial successes in England with such performers as the Rolling Stones and most notably and influentially with the four young men who comprised the group known worldwide as the Beatles.

Toward the end of the 1960s a new force began to enter the world of professional popular music, coming mainly from the white middle class, particularly the more libertarian fringes of the intelligentsia. This music was derived in large measure from a parody of the blues, with the old Negro slum preoccupation transposed into bourgeois terms, complaining of spiritual rather than material deprivation and commenting, at times frenetically, on the general dilemmas of the world rather than on personal domestic tragedies. In its various nuances such as folk, acid, and hard rock, this form of music, sometimes called progressive pop, existed successfully alongside the more conventional popular music, at times approaching the aleatory fragmentation characteristic of some present-day serious music.

Concurrently the folk-rooted blues tradition persisted in the cities, reflecting the culture of the black ghetto-dweller, yet appealing also to audiences beyond the ghetto. The older city blues evolved into the urban blues style—marked by freer vocal phrasing and often larger, more electronically amplified ensembles—and through urban blues into soul music, which fuses blues with jazz and gospel music influences.

summary Initially formed mainly in the south and west of Europe, Western popular music has gradually spread throughout the entire world, at first to the ends of Europe, then to the colonized Americas, then to the cities of the Orient, and now into the maize and paddy fields and even the jungles of peoples who had hitherto remained primitive. The rise of the United States to a position of economic and political power accelerated the process by which Western popular music replaces the proper musical arts of Asians, Africans, and other peoples, a process already begun with the weakening of tribal and feudal traditions and the introduction of formal education through Western colonialism. Missions, schools, trade, radio, television, films, and development aid projects have all played a part in encouraging a taste for Western popular music. Simultaneously in the Communist world sovietization carried the more formal idioms of popular European music across a vast area of the globe, acclimatizing it by means of political rather than commercial propaganda.

Throughout the Communist world popular music has become mainly identified—at least officially—with stylized folk music performed in a diluted manner, while in the Western world and throughout the sphere of Western influence jazz music has seemed progressively to shrink into an intellectually rarefied atmosphere, replaced in the affections of the younger mass audiences by the emotional and musical simplifications of rock 'n' roll and its successors. After a gradual decline musical comedy—both in the theater and in motion pictures—showed new signs of life in the late 1960s and '70s, but salon music was fading. For the global intrusion of Western popular music, the Orient extracted a mild revenge with the introduction in the 1970s of one or two Eastern instruments (such as the sitar) and a few tentative Oriental intonations into popular instrumental ensembles of both the United States and Europe.

BIBLIOGRAPHY: Sigmund G. Spaeth, *A History of Popular Music in America* (1948); Reginald Nettel, *Seven Centuries of Popular Song* (1956); Marshall W. Stearns, *The Story of Jazz* (1956; reprint, 1970); Claude M. Simpson, *The British Broadside Ballad and Its Music* (1966); Bill C. Malone, *Country Music U.S.A.; a Fifty-Year History* (1968); Harry

Oster, *Living Country Blues* (1969); Charlie Gillett, *The Sound of the City: The Rise of Rock and Roll* (1970); Carl Belz, *The Story of Rock,* 2nd ed. (1972); Charles Boeckman, *And the Beat Goes On: A History of Pop Music in America* (1972); David Ewen, ed., *Great Men of American Popular Song,* rev. ed. (1972), and *All the Years of American Popular Music* (1977); Ronald Pearsall, *Victorian Popular Music* (1973) and *Popular Music of the Twenties* (1976); Arnold Shaw, *The Rockin' Fifties: The Decade that Transformed the Pop Music Scene* (1975); Irwin Stambler, *Encyclopedia of Pop, Rock and Soul* (1977); Giles Oakley, *The Devil's Music: A History of the Blues* (1978).

Porgy and Bess: *see* GERSHWIN; OPERA (the 20th century); POPULAR MUSIC (the 20th century).

Porpora, Nicola Antonio (August 17, 1686–March 3, 1768)   An Italian opera composer and singing teacher, Nicola Antonio Porpora was born at Naples, and his first three operas were produced there. Others followed in Rome, Vienna, and Venice. He taught in Naples and Venice: among his pupils were the celebrated castrati Antonio Uberti (known as Porporino), Farinelli, and Caffarelli and the poet and librettist Pietro Metastasio. After visiting Vienna in 1725 Porpora settled for a while in Venice, where he taught at the Ospedale degli Incurabili, a music school for girls. In 1733 he went to London as a rival to Handel and as chief composer of the "Opera of the Nobility" at the theater in Lincoln's Inn Fields and at the King's Theatre in the Haymarket. While in London he wrote five operas, among them *Polifemo, Davide e Bersabea,* and *Ifigenia in Aulide,* with parts for his remarkable pupil Farinelli. In 1737 he was teaching at Venice and two years later at Naples, where he also produced two comic operas. In 1747 he taught singing at Dresden and the following year was appointed Kapellmeister there. Later he was at Vienna, where he gave composition lessons to the young Haydn. He died in poverty at Naples.

RECORDING: Cello Concerto in G Major.

portative: *see* ORGAN (early history).

Porter, Cole: *see* POPULAR MUSIC (the 20th century).

positive: *see* ORGAN (early history).

post horn: *see* CORNET; HORN.

post-Romanticism   A term applied to music of the last decades of the 19th century and first decades of the 20th century that displays exaggerated characteristics of 19th-century Romanticism such as extreme largeness of scope and design, a mixture of musical forms (*e.g.,* opera and symphony), and heightened contrapuntal complexity. Often post-Romanticism embraces vivid religious or mystical fervor, a sense of longing, and a sense of the grim and the grotesque. The term overlaps neoromanticism, although the former is more often applied to compositions showing links in style and approach between Romanticism and early 20th-century modernism. Composers often considered part of the school include Mahler, Bruckner, Busoni, Max Reger, and Schoenberg.

Pothier, Joseph (December 7, 1835–December 8, 1923)   A French monk and scholar, Joseph Pothier was part of the plainchant reform movement centered at Solesmes. He took vows as a Benedictine monk at Solesmes in 1860, was prior of Ligugé in 1893, and appointed abbot of Saint-Wandrille in 1898. Soon after he entered Solesmes he collaborated with Paul Jausions on a new edition of the choir books based on plainchant manuscripts. Dom Jausions died in 1870, but his contribution was acknowledged in the preface to Dom Pothier's publication *Les Mélodies grégoriennes d'après la tradition* (1880), which became the standard work on the subject. In 1883 he published the *Liber gradualis,* which also included research earlier undertaken by Dom Jausions. The two works marked the beginning of a reform in liturgical chant. In 1889 he was associated with his disciple André Mocquereau (1849–1930) in the foundation of the publication *Paléographie musicale* for the dissemination of medieval liturgical manuscripts. In 1904 Pope Pius X appointed him chairman of a commission for the reconstitution of the music of the Roman Catholic Church. Many of the controversial theories regarding the intervention of plainchant were published in the *Revue du chant grégorien* (1892–1914), edited by Dom Pothier.

Poulenc, Francis (January 7, 1899–January 30, 1963) One of the French composers known as LES SIX, Francis Poulenc studied piano with Ricardo Viñes and in 1917 produced *Rapsodie nègre,* followed in 1918 by *Mouvements perpétuels* and Sonata for piano duet, and in 1919 by songs on poems by Guillaume Apollinaire and Jean Cocteau. From 1921 to 1924 Poulenc studied composition with Charles Koechlin. His ballet *Les Biches* was produced by Sergey Diaghilev in 1924. Settings of poems by Pierre de Ronsard and *Chansons gaillardes* (1926) began a series of song cycles, chiefly on poems by Apollinaire and Paul Éluard. Becoming one of the greatest exponents of the art song in the 20th century, Poulenc produced more than 50 songs and song cycles, many of which became known in the extensive recital tours by the French baritone Pierre Bernac accompanied by Poulenc. Éluard poems provided the text for his cantata *Figure humaine* (1945) and Apollinaire for the comic opera *Les Mamelles de Tirésias* (Opéra-Comique, 1947). Poulenc's other operas were *Dialogues des Carmélites* (La Scala, 1957) on a libretto by Georges Bernanos and *Voix humaine* (Opéra-Comique, 1959) on the monodrama by Cocteau. He was working on a fourth opera at his death.

Litanies à la Vierge Noire de Rocomadour (1936) marked the beginning of numerous religious works that made Poulenc one of the most important composers of liturgical music. His Mass (1937) and motets (1938–52) for unaccompanied chorus and *Stabat Mater* (1951), Gloria (1960), and *Sept Répons des Ténèbres* (1961) for soloists, chorus, and orchestra are all important, as are his several sets of chansons for unaccompanied chorus.

At the suggestion of Landowska he wrote *Concert champêtre* (1928) for harpsichord and orchestra, to be followed by a series of concertos for piano, two pianos, and organ. Poulenc also produced solo piano works, much chamber music (never writing for the same combination twice), ballets, incidental music, and film scores. Predominantly lyrical and traditional in harmony, Poulenc's music revived the ironic spirit of Emmanuel Chabrier and also the elegance of French 18th-century composers.

BIBLIOGRAPHY: Pierre Bernac, *Francis Poulenc: The Man and His Songs* (1978).

RECORDINGS: Numerous recordings of many works.

Pousseur, Henri (b. July 23, 1929) Educated at the conservatories in Liège and Brussels, the Belgian composer Henri Pousseur has written music for many different combinations of performers (*e.g., Les Ephémérides d'Icare* II, 1970, for soloist, concertino of three players, and ripieno of 16 players) as well as for electronic instruments only (*Scambi,* 1957). Influenced by such composers as Webern, Stockhausen, and Berio, Pousseur has written serial as well as aleatory music. In *Répons pour sept musiciens* (1960) the course of the composition is partly determined by lottery and by the players' free choice based on moves on a checkerboard. In Pousseur's opera-like *Votre Faust* (1968), the Faust story is given new twists; which one of four possible denouements a particular performance presents is determined by audience vote. Much of his music defines its form in the use of opposites, or extremes, of pitch, tempo, timbre, and dynamics (*Exercises pour piano,* 1956).

Pousseur has taught music in Europe and the United States. He also helped establish electronic music studios in Cologne (1954), Milan (1956), and Brussels (1958). In his theoretical writings he has argued that certain older methods of discussing and appraising music are no longer valid for recent music that makes use of new musical aims, resources, and techniques.

RECORDINGS: *Madrigal* III; *Trois visages de Liège.*

Power, Leonel (d. June 5, 1445) An English composer and theorist, Leonel Power began an association with Christ Church Priory, Canterbury, in 1423. In the last four years of his life he received a yearly allowance of livery, presumably for musical assistance either as composer or as composer and organist. In previous years he could have served in a less exalted capacity than the *armigeri* (esquires) among whom his name appears, and he may well have acted as instructor in music. As a composer he was closely in touch with developments in France and made use of the chanson style in such works as the *Missa Alma redemptoris mater* and the motet *Mater ora filium*. The *Missa Rex seculorum* may also be his, though it is ascribed to John Dunstable in some sources. Slightly more than 30 of Power's compositions have survived.

Praetorius, Michael (February 15, 1571–February 15, 1621)   The German music theorist and composer Michael Praetorius was highly regarded by his contemporaries. He adopted the latinized form of the German name Schultheiss. After studying at Frankfurt an der Oder, he was organist and Kapellmeister to the Bishop of Halberstadt and from 1612 was Kapellmeister at the court of Wolfenbüttel.

An admirer of Italian music, Praetorius had a predilection for rich and varied settings for voices and all kinds of instruments. His output was considerable and various. The most important collections are the settings of evangelical church songs called *Musae Sioniae* (nine parts, 1605–10), partly for eight to 12 voices in the Venetian double choir style and partly in simple four-part style; and the *Puericinium* (1621), where the hymn strophes receive varied treatment, foreshadowing the cantata. Praetorius published much music other than his own, and in his collection *Terpsichore* (1612) he introduced several hundred foreign dance pieces to Germany. The three completed parts of Praetorius' great work *Syntagma Musicum* (1614–18) comprise a Latin treatise on music theory, a lavishly illustrated account of instruments, and an exposition of musical forms and methods of performance; the fourth part on counterpoint was not completed.

RECORDINGS: Selections from *Polyhymnia* and *Terpsichore*.

Prague Symphony (No. 38): *see* MOZART (later life).

prelude   A composition generally of brief and introductory function or character; originally a piece performed before something else such as a religious service. Church organists still frequently perform a prelude before worship and a postlude afterward; the piece can be of any type, depending on the occasion. Prelude similarly may designate a piece preceding an act of an opera that is not long enough to constitute an overture.

The prelude as a musical form began as an introductory fantasia to a longer or more rigorously worked out piece, especially a fugue. Bach used the term praeludium in this sense and gave each prelude its own distinct character, often not at all improvisatory; some are similar to arias, others to dance forms, toccatas, or inventions.

The freedom with which the name prelude has since been used can be seen in the preludes of Chopin and Debussy. These are brief, self-contained pieces varying widely in character and not introducing anything at all. Chopin, for example, wrote études that are in no structural way distinct from some of his preludes, and Debussy's two books of preludes bear descriptive titles reflecting their evocative, sometimes rhapsodic moods.

Preludes and fugues have been written in the 20th century, notably a set of 24 by Shostakovich. But the prelude no longer constitutes a distinct genre. Perhaps the only thing that Debussy's *Prélude à l'après-midi d'un faune* and the set of preludes for orchestra by Romanian-born Marius Constant have in common with the works of Bach is a general tendency toward conciseness.

Prélude à l'après-midi d'un faune: *see* BALLET (Diaghilev Ballet); DEBUSSY; PRELUDE; SYMPHONIC POEM.

Préludes, Les (Liszt): *see* ROMANTIC PERIOD (Wagnerian development); SYMPHONIC POEM.

Preston, Simon (b. April 4, 1938)   Educated at the Royal Academy of Music in London and at King's College, Cambridge, the English organist, harpsichordist, and conductor Simon Preston served as sub-organist at Westminster Abbey for five years before his appointment as a tutor in music at Oxford and organist and choirmaster at Christ Church Cathedral there. As a recitalist he appears regularly both in Europe and in North America. His organ recordings range from Handel to Messiaen; harpsichord, English Renaissance and Bach; and as a conductor, Orlando di Lasso to Poulenc.

Previn, André (George) (b. April 6, 1929) Born in Germany and a naturalized U.S. citizen, the conductor, pianist, and composer André Previn was educated in Berlin, Paris, and California. His early professional career was as a jazz pianist. He then worked in films, conducting and arranging, and won Academy Awards for his work in the music for *Gigi* (1958), *Porgy and Bess* (1959), and *My Fair Lady* (1964). After touring the United States and Europe as a concert pianist, he devoted his time to conducting, which he had studied with Pierre Monteux. He was conductor of the Houston Symphony (1967–69) and music director and conductor of the London Symphony (1968–79). He taught at the Guildhall (London) School of Music and was director of the South Bank Festival there. Previn became conductor of the Pittsburgh Symphony in 1976. His recordings include 19th- and 20th-century Russian symphonic music and 20th-century English music; in progress are symphonic cycles of Rachmaninoff, Prokofiev, and Vaughan Williams as well as a project to record all the orchestral music of William Walton. He has composed concertos for cello (1968), violin (1969), and guitar (1970), chamber music, piano music, and songs.

RECORDING: Guitar Concerto.

Prey, Hermann (b. July 11, 1929) Acclaimed in opera, lieder, and oratorio, the German baritone Hermann Prey joined the company of the Hamburg State Opera in 1953 after a year of singing at Wiesbaden, where he made his debut in Eugène d'Albert's *Tiefland*. Since 1956 he has sung regularly at the Berlin and Vienna state operas and is a frequent guest at the Salzburg and Edinburgh festivals. He first toured the United States as a recitalist in 1952 and four years later made his Metropolitan Opera debut as Wolfram in Wagner's *Tannhäuser*. He has recorded operas of Mozart, Richard Strauss, and Weber, an operetta of Albert Lortzing, songs of Mahler and Schubert, and oratorios of Bach. He won first prize in the Meistersinger competition in Nürnberg in 1952.

Price, (Mary) Leontyne (b. February 10, 1927) After study at the Juilliard School, the U.S. lyric *spinto* soprano Leontyne Price was invited in 1952 by Virgil Thomson to appear in his *Four Saints in Three Acts* in New York and Paris. She made a reputation in contemporary music, singing premieres of music by Stravinsky, Samuel Barber, and Lou Harrison before appearing regularly in opera: she sang Tosca (Puccini) with the NBC Opera in 1955, Leonora (Verdi's *Il Trovatore*) at the Metropolitan Opera in 1961, and Aida (Verdi) in Vienna in 1968. Her debuts at the Rome (1967) and Paris (1968) operas were as Aida, and her first appearance at the Teatro Colón, Buenos Aires, in 1969, was as Leonora. Her recordings include operas of Verdi, Puccini, and Mozart, songs by Schumann, Berlioz, and Samuel Barber, Negro spirituals, and selections from Gershwin's *Porgy and Bess*.

Price, Margaret (Berenice) (b. April 11, 1941) Best known as a Mozart singer, the Welsh soprano Margaret Price studied at London's Trinity College of Music and made her debut with the Welsh National Opera as Cherubino in Mozart's *Le nozze di Figaro*. Her U.S. debut with the San Francisco Opera in 1969 was as Pamina (Mozart's *Die Zauberflöte*). A 1971 appearance as Donna Anna in *Don Giovanni* at the Cologne Opera led to an invitation to sing all the Mozart repertoire there and elsewhere in Germany. In 1974 she first sang at the Paris Opéra (as the Countess in *Le nozze*) and at the Salzburg Festival. Her non-Mozart roles include Mimi (Puccini's *La Bohème*), Desdemona (Verdi's *Otello*), and Agathe (Weber's *Der Freischütz*). She has appeared in recitals in the United Kingdom and Europe and has twice toured the United States.

Prigioniero, Il: *see* DALLAPICCOLA; OPERA (the 20th century).

primitive music The concept of primitive music is understood in this survey to refer to vocal and instrumental sounds produced in primitive societies. Its meaning cannot be precise because usage of the words primitive and music has undergone changes. This reflects the evolution of new interests and attitudes among Western observers and in illiterate societies in relation to these sounds. Anthropologists have come to suspect the term primitive of being too ambiguous and to avoid it because of its pejorative associations. Western musicians doubt whether their concept of music, which refers to the music of artists, can legitimately be applied to the sound making of so-called primitives. The impasse has been overcome to some extent by the art historians. They think of primitive music as a process and speak of premusical sounds organized for rhythmization of work and ritual, for stimulation, and perhaps for magical purposes and of a long premusical period in which "the elementary *materials* of music became established."

origins Interest in primitive music began in Europe with the discovery of new routes to other continents. Explorers occasionally mentioned music of indigenous peoples. In 1615 Michael Praetorius could assume sufficient interest among his readers to include 30 illustrations of African, American, and Asian musical instruments in his famous *Syntagma musicum* with remarkably clear detail, though not all his examples were primitive. Yet the study of primitive music received little support until Walter Fewkes recorded songs of North American Indians on phonograph cylinders in 1889. Two years later B. I. Gilman was able to demonstrate the existence of a new field of musical studies in his "Zuni melodies," which were based on these recordings.

Collections grew with improved communications and more efficient apparatus, and recordings are now available from almost every country. Yet sooner or later primitive music will be extinct as a living tradition, largely because modern conditions break down the isolation that had been its main protection, and the recordings will be the only way by which it can be heard.

Primitive music was found to be more diverse and complex than the lexicographic meanings of the word primitive suggest. Sound enters most activities of humans and other animals. Gibbon monkeys use sterotyped vocalizations that produce characteristic reactions in their fellows, and expression is given to "aggressive or defensive behavior." Wolfgang Köhler noted that chimpanzees formed a circle, decked themselves out with twigs and leaves, and made rhythmic noises by stamping on the ground. But man's acoustic utterance is invested with yet another quality: the supernatural. According to students of primitive religion the supernatural took different forms at different stages of prehistory, but whatever the form it is acted out and danced out. The elementary materials of music were thus nurtured and became established.

To speculate on the place of primitive music within the supernatural is not the same as speculating on the origin of music itself. The following have at one time or another been held responsible for the genesis of music: competition in courting; imitation of bird calls; rhythms demanded by working procedures; the lulling of an infant; the release of passion; patterns of speech or more specifically a primeval tonal communication that gave rise to both language and music; and calling from a distance, which requires an essentially musical treatment in order that the voice may carry. The comparative merits of these theories are discussed by Jaap Kunst in *Ethnomusicology* (1959).

supernatural It is unreasonable to expect that the birth of music could be witnessed as the division of cells can be seen under a microscope. But with regard to the supernatural in music making among primitive societies, field work has produced ample evidence of its effects. A revealing example is the music of the Dogon tribe of West Africa. The Dogon see their environment in the light of a dualistic order of the universe that is transmitted and sanctioned in myths of creation. This is acted out in Dogon music in several ways; a song will either have a binary or ternary rhythm according to the significance of the song in a female or a male context. The onion harvest is accompanied by female rhythms because the crop grows in the womb of the earth, but the ritually important millet requires work songs in a male ternary beat. The two notes of a pair of drums are interpreted as being female for the higher note and male for the lower note. The four strings of the harp-lute are divided into pairs, one male and one female. Because the craft of weaving is important in the myth of creation, the harp-lute is likened to a loom, and the strings are strung like the threads on a loom. Dogon believe that a wrong note on this instrument confuses the spirits and play such a note to prevent evil. The tempo of their songs is sometimes accelerated toward the end, even in a work song where change of tempo might run counter to the even rhythm demanded by the work; acceleration adds spiritual vitality, as does the raising of the pitch in tuning the harp-lute. Extensive song cycles are performed at funerals and marriages that require sequences of different chants to match the stages of the ritual.

artistic form The Dogon examples illustrate what the anthropologist and student of Dogon culture Marcel Griaule meant when he said "certain types of art are directed toward a spiritual rather than a human audience." That this approach does not occur everywhere at the same level of intensity is clearly demonstrated by comparison between two practices of superficial resemblance: both the xylophone of the Soga of East Africa and the lithophone of the Maa of southern Vietnam are sprinkled with the blood of a sacrificial animal. With the Soga this has become a perfunctory gesture that has no connection with the entertainment that follows, and it is almost forgotten that the offering is for the spirit of the tree from which the keys are carved. With the Maa the sole purpose of the playing of the instrument is said to be its "feasting on the meat." These examples illustrate an evolutionary trend in primitive music away from the vital spiritual level toward empty convention, a trend that eventually leads to the awarenes of artistic form and the end of the premusical period.

rise of instruments It is no accident that vocal elements dominate theories on the origin of music; vocal sounds are universal. Instrumental sounds in music are said to be absent among the inhabitants of the interior of Ceylon and are notably limited among many nomadic tribes; for instance, those of the Horn of Africa. At the crudest level, among the inhabitants of Tierra del Fuego in South America no instruments are known that are especially designed for sound. "Instead they blow into the windpipe of a newly killed duck or at their death dances they pound the earth with pairs of thick, long poles or drum on a rigid rolled piece of hide. Men bellow into the hollow of their hands placed against the earth, knock sticks and branches against the frame of the festival hut for rhythm or simply beat the floor of the hut with bare fists" (E. M. Hornbostel).

An interesting attempt has been made to distinguish different levels of achievement by arranging musical instruments in accordance with their diffusion throughout the world. This was based on the assumption that diffusion progressed from a few important centers like ripples spreading in water. The earliest types of instrument traveled farthest and survived here and there on their way toward the periphery, while they may have become extinct near the center. Instruments of similar range of diffusion were taken to be nearer in age and more closely related in origin even though they did not necessarily belong to the same culture. This scheme, put forward by Curt Sachs in 1929, retained its usefulness as a working hypothesis even though the ethnological theory from which it derived was severely criticized.

The acoustic devices in these early instruments are manifold. The lowest (Paleolithic) levels show man stamping, shaking, rubbing, scraping, and blowing, armed with common objects turned to musical purpose ad hoc, and later employing rattles, bull-roarers, and flutes without finger holes. The subsequent prehistoric levels add to these the slit drum, stamping tubes, flutes with finger holes, trumpets, and the earliest stringed instruments, including the musical bow.

With the invention of the bow, man succeeded in concentrating and controlling energy. To a 20th-century person it may be plausible that this must have been for shooting an arrow; to Neolithic man it may have been equally plausible to use the energy of the bow for communicating with the supernatural by making sounds. A prehistoric cave painting at Les Trois Frères in France shows the bow thus used in ritual.

melody and pitch With flutes and strings on which to experiment, man had the opportunity of observing the harmonic series and of making overtones the focal points for casual musical conventions. The Kalahari Bushmen have adopted a pentatonic mode based on the partials they discovered in the strings of their shooting bows. They also mastered another musical trick: by stopping and unstopping the end of an open flute, access is obtained at will to the harmonic series of either open or stopped pipes in the same instrument, and by selecting from the pitch material thus offered to the player a pentatonic scale can be constructed.

Yet it would be rash to conclude that such five-note patterns developed in this way decisively influenced primitive music. In primitive melody a stressed note, vocal or instrumental, stands out in contrast to an unstressed note. They make pairs of light and heavy (or light and dark) sounds that are indistinguishable from bitonal melody. The addition of a middle register makes tritonal tunes possible, and the repetition of either pattern (in sequences on different levels of pitch) accounts for even wider forms. Their intervals may be narrow steps or wide jumps or where more than one interval is involved a combination of both. None of these forms depends on the experience that the Bushmen applied to strings and flutes, an experience that may be no more than the rationalization of earlier practices stimulated by contact with civilizations that were not primitive. Primitive melody need not have recourse to the pentatonic mode of the acoustician or even develop a concept of scale.

Western theory has been greatly influenced by speculation about the intrinsic excellence of the simple frequency ratios in the octave, fifth, and fourth. In primitive music such intervals are far from universal; where they do occur they are difficult to identify. It would be unwarranted to treat them as if they were, by virtue of these frequency ratios, better fitted for survival.

polyphonic forms Neither the harmonic series nor the simple frequency ratios were needed to account for the rise of primitive polyphony. The same song may be sung by different persons at the same time, but through vocal incompetence or sheer exuberance their renderings will differ widely. Their concerted action might be governed by the pattern of their social purpose or by the participation of groups of different status. From Australia has been reported the simultaneous perfor-

mance of two songs intended to be different when people gathered in two groups divided according to moiety. The oldest forms of polyphony are the simultaneous execution of variants of the same tune, singing in parallel lines (which may or may not give the impression of unison), the canon, and the drone.

Yet polyphony is not universal. Three main regions have been distinguished: Polynesia, Melanesia, Indonesia, India, and the Philippines; the region stretching from the southern Caucasus to Europe; and Africa south of a line between Mombasa and Freetown.

rhythm As to rhythm scholars generally agree that its wealth is unlimited, but that only later cultures tend to use definite metrical schemes. Others find primitive rhythm mostly asymmetrical. It is difficult to isolate rhythm from other elementary materials of music. Thus the difficulty is understandable in identifying any survivals of rhythm from the lowest levels of the premusical period. Western civilization has a striking example of such survival in its children's rhymes. They are built to an underlying scheme of eight values, arranged in four pairs of two eighth notes, each pair read in $\frac{2}{8}$ time. Widely differing structures in many languages have been found to adapt their individual features to this scheme. The children's rhymes of Europe correspond to examples of adult singing among the Kabyle, Tuareg, the Negroes of Senegal, Dahomey, and the Sudan, and the indigenous peoples of Formosa.

The polyrhythmic forms observed in African drumming contrast strongly with the simplicity and wide distribution of the eight values of the children's rhythms (*see* AFRICAN MUSIC). They are constructed on the principle of simultaneous performance of different rhythms with their own method of cohesion. They may well be of more recent origin than other less complex patterns, but so little is known of the growth of rhythm that even speculation must cease.

ethnomusicology Primitive music forms part of a new branch of study called ETHNOMUSICOLOGY. In Anglo-Saxon countries it is the task of the anthropological and ethnological sciences rather than a matter for music historians and musicians. The development of

651

electronic devices and of new techniques for analysis is likely to give greater insight into primitive music than the musician, conditioned to hear in his own tradition, could ever hope to achieve.

BIBLIOGRAPHY: Curt Sachs, *The Rise of Music in the Ancient World* (1943); Bruno Nettl, *Music in Primitive Culture* (1956); Egon Wellesz, ed., *Ancient and Oriental Music* (1957), Vol. 1 of *The New Oxford History of Music;* Frank Llewellyn Harrison, *Time, Place and Music: An Anthology of Ethnomusicological Observation, c. 1550–c. 1800* (1973).

Primrose, William (b. August 23, 1904) The Scottish violist William Primrose studied violin at the Guildhall School in London and in Belgium with Eugène Ysaÿe, who recommended that he become a violist. He joined the London String Quartet and traveled with it through Europe and the Americas between 1930 and 1935. In 1937 Toscanini chose Primrose as first violist in the NBC Symphony. Two years later he founded the William Primrose Quartet. He commissioned a viola concerto from Bartók, which was unfinished at the time of the composer's death. In 1956 Primrose became violist with the Festival String Quartet. His autobiography *The North Side of the Street* was published in 1978.

Prince Igor: *see* BALLET (Diaghilev Ballet); BORODIN; OPERA (the 19th century).

Prinz von Homburg, Der: *see* HENZE.

Prodigal Son, The: *see* BALLET (Diaghilev Ballet); BRITTEN; OPERA (the 20th century); *see also* ENFANT PRODIGUE, L'.

program music Instrumental music that carries with it some extramusical meaning; *i.e.,* a literary idea, scenic description, personal drama, or national legend. It is contrasted with absolute or abstract music in which the artistic interest is confined to tonal relationships, purely musical arguments, and abstract constructions in sound. Descriptive music is by contrast often regarded as less pure and by implication less good. Yet most of the great composers have been unable to resist the pleasure of depicting the sort of experiences that graphic artists put into genre painting, portraits, and conversation pieces. Byrd wrote

The Battell, a work in 15 sections for virginal; Bach the Capriccio *on the Departure of a Beloved Brother;* Beethoven *Wellingtons Sieg* and the *Pastoral* Symphony. These (except the symphony) are admittedly not among their composers' best works, but they show that external ideas, natural scenery, solid objects, even a railway engine (Honegger's *Pacific 231*) can go into music and that there is nothing reprehensible in a composer's including them.

Composers of instrumental music explored the possibilities at an early period. The *Fitzwilliam Virginal Book* (early 17th century) contains pieces about the weather, hunting, and battle. A little less than a century later Johann Kuhnau wrote six *Biblical* Sonatas in which he indulges in many curious realistic effects in the representation of Saul and David, the healing of Hezekiah, and David and Goliath. In the last named the flight of the slingstone is a quick upward scale. This sort of realism can be naive and even ridiculous: some of the formulas and clichés used to accompany silent films in the early days of the cinema were of the same order as Victorian descriptions of battles, camels in the desert, and similar absurdities for drawing-room pianists. But with the development of the orchestra, the range of experience expressible in music was enormously expanded, although certain specific references could not be immediately identified without verbal clues. Controversy about the validity of program music developed into an issue of musical aesthetics in the second half of the 19th century when the "new" music of Liszt and Wagner was put into the scales against the Classicism of Brahms, who never went so far down the Romantic road as to give descriptive names or fancy titles, as Schumann did, to his piano pieces. In the late 20th century the issue was still alive; Stravinsky went so far as to deny that music needed any expressive powers at all; it was just music. Though there was a truce of live-and-let-live during the 20th century, some new arguments were made available—namely, symbolism from Freudian psychology and semantics from philosophy.

imagery As in most other subjects program music can be discussed historically for the facts and critically for the values. Either approach must deal with one vital fact of the musical imagination: composers have always set words to music; *i.e.,* they have gained some sort of conceptual content in music whose thought is nonconceptual—they have illustrated the meaning of the words by flux and motion. They have even gone in for word painting, as in Thomas Weelkes's madrigal "As Vesta was from Latmos' hill descending," where the personages go up and down hill in rising and falling scale passages, two by two in two-part harmony and three by three in three-part harmony, leaving their goddess all alone in a brief soprano solo. Half the business of the accompaniment to a song is to evoke the mood of the poem by suggestion; the other half is to provide the harmonic context and support. Such suggestion operates through images: images of pitch to suggest height, depth, and position and acuity, stress, or slackness of tension; images of tone-color to suggest qualities of touch such as warmth or hollowness; images of rhythm to suggest any kind of temporal phenomenon, spatial movement, gesture, duration, reiteration, repose, agitation, speed, etc. These images constitute a language of music that was analyzed with a wealth of illustration in Deryck Cooke's *The Language of Music* (1959). Being images they are the material with which the musical imagination works. Musical imagery of all sorts, amassed by the composer from hearing music already in existence, is employed indifferently in vocal, symphonic, and program music.

In addition to these true images, which are capable of taking on further symbolic meanings, there are sounds in nature that can be imitated in music. Bird song is an obvious example. Messiaen is the only composer who has made a sustained effort to integrate bird calls into serious composition. The cuckoo of course had a long run: Louis Claude Daquin's harpsichord piece *Le Coucou,* Beethoven's *Pastoral* Symphony, and Frederick Delius' tone poem *On Hearing the First Cuckoo in Spring* immediately come to mind. Songs about the nightingale usually stylize the bird's performance. More like onomatopoeia are storms, of which opera can provide instances from Rossini's *Il barbiere di Siviglia* to Wil-

liam Walton's *Troilus and Cressida.* Fire in Wagner's hands is presented not only with the crackle of flames but with their visible edges perceptible by means of this mysterious process of the imagination. Water is ubiquitous in music: fresh in Schubert, salt in Debussy—but the sea has many moods: boisterous in the overture to Wagner's *The Flying Dutchman;* calm and lapping the shore with a phrase in the shape of a wave in Mendelssohn's *Hebrides* Overture; or keen in scent, sound, and sight (seagulls, ozone, and shingle) in the first of the interludes in Britten's *Peter Grimes,* where the sea is an arpeggio of superimposed triads and the dry land a chord of A major. But this is far beyond onomatopoeia, which includes man-made sounds of ships' sirens, steel anvils, church bells, striking clocks, and the rumble of railway trains—all of which can be accommodated in small quantities for dramatic or descriptive purposes, though they invariably stick out.

problem of form The powers of music to evoke situations in life, as well as to express human feelings, have been recognized by composers from the beginning; after all imitation is instinctive. Thus vocal music has always used the descriptive devices of musical technique for every kind of expression. Though vocal music is excluded from the definition of program music, its relevance to the aesthetic issue cannot be ignored in quite the airy way that led the combatants in the 19th-century controversy to declare that music presented two separate sets of phenomena and aroused two sorts of emotion. Music is surely one—not two. But without cleaving the art in two, it is possible to recognize the difference between a symphony and a symphonic poem. This difference is fundamentally one of logic and form—or perhaps the logic of form.

The ground plan of a symphony is four movements. In Beethoven's *Eroica,* for example, the first movement is in sonata form with its exposition of two groups of themes in different but related keys, its middle section a development of these thematic ideas, and a recapitulation rounded off by a coda. The slow (second) movement is, somewhat exceptionally, a funeral march; the third a scherzo (with trio); and the fourth a set of variations. This is a satisfactory scheme for presenting some sort of experience—in this case heroism—in its several aspects, but it is singularly inept for depicting the life history of Napoleon (to whom the symphony was originally dedicated), for the hero is buried in the second movement and is fuller of life than ever in the third. Symphonic order is thus not to be reconciled with chronological order. Furthermore, if in the first movement any indication of the events in Napoleon's career had been the composer's intention, he would have found that recapitulation would have made redundant nonsense of what had already been narrated in full. Sonata form is thus not to be reconciled with traditional narrative or drama, which moves on and does not go back. Hence the incongruity of using symphonic movements for ballets with a program, however sketchy, of biographical, historical, or dramatic events. When Richard Strauss wants to portray Don Juan's erotic adventures, Don Quixote's chivalric adventures, or (in the *Domestic* Symphony) a day in his family life, he does not employ sonata form but modifies freely more episodic forms such as the rondo and variation form or writes in the form of a loose rhapsody held together only by key coherence and the recurrence of themes symbolizing, like Wagner's leitmotiv, the persons and events of the story. He writes in fact a symphonic poem. Both the SYMPHONIC POEM, in which the form is subservient to the subject matter, and the term itself were invented by Liszt, who was thus the cause of all the controversy.

Tchaikovsky's *Hamlet* is a true symphonic poem; however, the story is told in a kind of sonata form, and this is done by dissolving the chronological element of Shakespeare's play. When Robert Helpmann choreographed a ballet to it, he began with Hamlet's body on a bier and the motto "Our little lives are rounded with a sleep," which fits Tchaikovsky's scheme wonderfully well. For if at the moment of death his past life flitted past Hamlet's eyes, it made no difference in what order the gravedigger and Ophelia and the ghost occurred. They were episodes that could be presented in symphonic order with their relationships expounded by themes, rhythms,

keys, and orchestration (the oboe for Ophelia, for instance). Once the problem of logical sequence is solved, the composer can proceed to make music out of anything except specific statements such as that angles at the base of an isosceles triangle are equal, or propositions about monetary theory or the gold standard. Strauss did it, saying in a moment of bravado and in answer to a challenge, that he could set a knife and fork to music. If he did not do that exactly, he bathed his baby, he disturbed a flock of sheep, he hanged a rogue, he produced the smell of ethyl chloride at a death bed, he confounded his critics, and he made love—but then love does not count as program music as it is all-pervasive.

The Romantic and nationalist movements greatly enlarged the range of subjects that composers desired to express. Literature was well to the fore with *Faust* (Liszt and Wagner), *Romeo and Juliet* (Berlioz and Tchaikovsky), *Falstaff* (Elgar). Then came legend with *The Water Sprite* (Dvořák), *Tamara* (Balakirev), *The Sorcerer's Apprentice* (Paul Dukas), *Sheherazade* (Rimsky-Korsakov), and *The Swan of Tuonela* (Sibelius). Geography added a whole gallery of picture postcards: *The Steppes of Central Asia* (Borodin), *Bohemia's Woods and Forests* (Smetana), *The Fountains of Rome* (Respighi), *Paris* (Frederick Delius), *Cockaigne* Overture (Elgar), *Nights in the Gardens of Spain* (de Falla), Sinfonia *Antarctica* (Vaughan Williams), and *El Salón México* (Copland). Even philosophy was tried by Strauss in *Also sprach Zarathustra* (after Nietzsche), and pictures by Rachmaninoff in *The Isle of the Dead* (after Arnold Böcklin) and Liszt in *Hunnenschlacht* ("The Battle of the Huns" after Wilhelm von Kaulbach). The concert overture form provided a rather shorter medium for program pieces such as William Walton's overtures *Portsmouth Point* (after Thomas Rowlandson's picture) and *Scapino* (after the commedia dell'arte).

aesthetic considerations The earlier examples of program music began an aesthetic battle that led the Viennese critic Eduard Hanslick to formulate a case against the genre in his book *Vom Musikalisch-Schönen* (1854; Eng. trans., "The Beautiful in Music," 1891). Hanslick argued that the aim of music was not expression but beauty and that the conveyance of feeling was incidental and subsidiary to its main purpose. Later avant-garde musicians of the 20th century claimed that in music only sound and how to manipulate it mattered—a doctrine readily understood in an age dominated by technology.

program symphony Between the symphony and the symphonic poem there is an intermediate stage, the program symphony, illustrated by the *Pastoral* Symphony. Before Beethoven, Haydn had in his humorous way infused an element of external reality in small doses into the *Farewell,* the *Surprise,* and the *Clock* Symphonies. But Beethoven in the *Pastoral* Symphony went the whole way and indicated in words what he was depicting: cheerful impressions on arriving in the country, the brook, the peasants, the storm, the shepherds' hymn—though he appeared to have some qualms about it, for he added, quite untruly, that it was more an expression of feeling than painting. From the *Pastoral* stemmed a line of program symphonies in which the form was musically self-sufficient but the content contained extramusical matter in varying degrees of density: very thick in Berlioz' *Symphonie fantastique,* which purports to depict episodes in the life of an artist, and minimal in Mendelssohn's *Scottish* and *Italian* Symphonies. Mendelssohn's *Hebrides* (or *Fingal's Cave*) Overture is probably the most beautifully balanced of such combinations as there is Mendelssohn's own testimony that the programmatic and the thematic idea of it were conceived simultaneously on the spot—at the cave. In Tchaikovsky's Fourth and Fifth Symphonies the notion of fate embodied in the motto theme is elaborated to the extent vouched for in Tchaikovsky's own explanation; in his Sixth Symphony the title *Pathétique* is used in a general sense as far as a program permeates the music—at least until the extraordinary slow finale that is a clear premonition of death. Similarly in Dvořák's *New World* Symphony there is no detailed program but an allusion to the Negro in the slow movement. Vaughan Williams' *London* Symphony has rather more specific programmatic content in that it incorporates actual sounds from the London scene and employs the unusual combination of nocturne and scherzo, which somehow conveys the animation of London at night. The Soviet composers load their symphonies with significance or have them loaded for them by commentators: Shostakovich's Seventh *(Leningrad)* Symphony was composed with the events of the defense of that city in mind. But in general the program symphony has grown less programmatic as the symphonic form has grown more ambitious.

summary Program music increased in extent and status within the art through the program symphonies and symphonic poems of the 19th century. At the outbreak of World War I, the aesthetic debate as to the propriety of program music had been going on for more than half a century. The swing of the pendulum after each of the world wars was toward neoclassicism, absolute music, sound manipulation, and aural austerity in reaction to the enormous enrichment of the repertoire, the extension of orchestral resources, and the subtlety of music's expressive power in the previous heyday of the symphonic poem.

BIBLIOGRAPHY: Frederick Niecks, *Programme Music in the Last Four Centuries* (1907; reprint, 1969); Ernest Newman, *Musical Studies* (1910; reprint, 1969); Lawrence Gilman, *Nature in Music and Other Studies in the True-Poetry of Today* (1914; reprint, 1966).

program notes The practice of providing those attending a concert with historical and analytical information about the works to be heard seems to have been started in Berlin by Johann Friedrich Reichardt, who in 1783 organized the *Concert Spirituel* on the model of the Paris series.

In England program notes first appeared in the 1830s and by mid-century were standard. U.S. orchestras provided explanatory information from their inception. Among the most notable annotators were Henry Krehbiel (1854–1923), for many years associated with the New York Philharmonic, and the Boston Symphony's Philip Hale (1854–1934).

Sir Donald Francis Tovey (1875–1940), however, set a standard that has not been equalled with his notes for the Reid Orchestral

Concerts at Edinburgh University, where he was Reid Professor of Music. These "Essays in Musical Analysis" display an infallible feeling for the broad sweep of history, a keen sensitivity to compositional detail, and a literary wit and brio that is altogether rare.

BIBLIOGRAPHY: Donald Francis Tovey, *Essays in Musical Analysis,* 6 vols. (1935–39).

George Gelles

Prokofiev, Sergey (Sergeyevich) (April 23 [April 11, old style], 1891–March 5, 1953). One of 20th-century Russia's most gifted composers, Sergey Prokofiev wrote instrumental music, operas, and ballets. He began to compose at the age of six and wrote an opera at nine. After private lessons from Reinhold Glière he entered the St. Petersburg Conservatory, where he studied composition with Anatol Liadov, orchestration with Rimsky-Korsakov, and piano (1904–14), with Annette Essipoff, winning the Rubinstein Prize in 1914 with a performance of his own First Piano Concerto. The concerto had already been performed publicly in 1912 and the Second in 1913; while still at the conservatory Prokofiev

Sergey Prokofiev   *Sovfoto*

was already the young hero of the Russian modernists. In the three years before the Revolution he did much to justify their hopes, producing the First Violin Concerto, the *Classical Symphony,* an opera *The Gambler,* the *Scythian* Suite for orchestra, the Third and Fourth Piano Sonatas, and a number of songs and short piano pieces. In the summer of 1918 he left Russia and traveled by way of Japan and Honolulu to the United States. There he wrote an opera, *The Love for Three Oranges,* for the Chicago Civic Opera Company (1921), and began *The Flaming Angel* (the score was left in Paris and never performed during the composer's lifetime). In the meantime Sergey Diaghilev had invited him to Europe for the Paris and London productions of his ballet *The Buffoon* (1921). He made his home first at Ettal in Bavaria, then (autumn 1923) in Paris, working on the *Angel,* Fifth Piano Sonata, Third Piano Concerto, and Second Symphony. In Paris he wrote two more ballets for Diaghilev, *Le Pas d'acier* (1927) and *L'Enfant prodigue* (1929), and *Sur le Borysthène* (1932) for the Paris Opéra. The Third and Fourth Symphonies were based respectively on material from *The Flaming Angel* and *L'Enfant prodigue.*

In 1927 Prokofiev visited the Soviet Union; a number of his works were performed at that time in various cities. He paid another visit in 1929, and at the end of 1932 he returned permanently to his native land. In the music written after his return, Prokofiev emphasized the naive and lyrical aspects of his art and modified the asperities of his harmony, but there is evidence that in doing so he was following the curve of his natural development— not merely bowing to the official demand for socialist realism. In the period before World War II, he was prolific: the witty orchestral suite *Lieutenant Kije* (1934); the Second Violin Concerto (1935); the ballet *Romeo and Juliet* (1938); the opera *Simeon Kotko* (1940); and a quantity of lesser works such as *Peter and the Wolf* (1936). The chief works of the World War II years were the Tolstoyan opera *War and Peace* (first version finished in 1942), the Fifth Symphony (1944), three piano sonatas, and a quantity of chamber music. In the artistically reactionary period after World War II,

Prokofiev suffered official rebuffs: his Sixth Symphony (1947) was only half approved, the Third Violin Sonata (1947) remained unperformed, and the opera *Story of a Real Man* (1948) was suppressed on the eve of production. Bowing to criticism, he produced in his last years "democratically acceptable" works such as the ballet *Tale of the Stone Flower* (1954), the oratorio *On Guard for Peace* (1950), the Seventh Symphony (1952), and a revised version of *War and Peace* (1952).

Prokofiev's early reputation as an enfant terrible was unjust. He was from first to last a creator of vigorous, clean-cut pure music. Being of his age he was not a romantic; his marked lyrical gift was never placed at the service of subjective expression. But he commanded a genuine epic power that showed itself first in the *Scythian* Suite and very markedly in the film score *Alexander Nevsky* and other works of his Soviet period. *War and Peace* shows both his lyrical and his epic invention at their best. At the other end of the scale he had wit and simple charm. He showed marked skill in accepting the requirements of socialist realism without, except in a very few instances, compromising his artistic integrity.

BIBLIOGRAPHY: Gerald E. H. Abraham, *Eight Soviet Composers* (1943); Israel Nestyev, *Prokofiev* (1960); Claude Samuel, *Prokofiev* (1971); Sergei Prokofiev, *Prokofiev on Prokofiev: A Composer's Memoir* (1979).

RECORDINGS: Numerous recordings of most works.

Prometheus: *see* BALLET (dramatic ballet); BEETHOVEN (Beethoven and the theater) and (achievement); SCHUBERT (maturity); SCRIABIN; VARIATIONS.

Prophète, Le: *see* MEYERBEER.

psalmody The singing of psalms in worship or a collection of psalms. In biblical times professional singers chanted psalms at Jewish religious services. Occasionally the congregation interpolated a short refrain between the chanted verses. The alternation of soloist and chorus was called responsorial psalmody (*see* RESPONSORY). Another method, antiphonal psalmody, was the alternation by two half choirs in the singing of psalm lines or half

lines (*see* ANTIPHON). Psalms were also sung without either refrain or alternating singers (direct psalmody). These methods of psalmody were adopted by the early Christian Church in the East and West. Psalmody in the early church was the germ from which evolved both the classical plainchant and also the Byzantine, Ambrosian, and other Christian chants (*see also* PSALM TONE).

In 16th-century Reformed churches congregational singing was reintroduced. Until about 1700 all except Lutherans excluded hymns having nonbiblical texts. Metrical, strophic translations of the psalms were set to composed or borrowed melodies for congregational singing (metrical psalmody). The most noted collection of metrical psalms is the *French,* or *Genevan,* Psalter of 1539–62 with melodies by Loys Bourgeois and translations by the poet Clément Marot and the theologian Théodore de Bèze. Soon composers were setting the metrical psalms in parts, including Bourgeois (1547, 1560), Claude Goudimel (1564, 1565), Claude Le Jeune (1564, 1606), and Jan Pieterszoon Sweelinck (1604–21).

Later psalters in English of significance were the *Anglo-Genevan* Psalter (1561), *English,* or *Old Version* (by Thomas Sternhold and John Hopkins, published by John Day, 1562), *Scottish* (1564), *Ainsworth* (Amsterdam, 1612), *Ravenscroft* (1621), *Bay Psalm Book* (America, 1640), *Playford* (1671, 1673), and *New Version* (by Nahum Tate and Nicholas Brady, 1696).

In the 18th century the hymn began to replace psalm singing in English-speaking Protestantism, though the Church of Scotland did not authorize the singing of hymns until 1861.

BIBLIOGRAPHY: Henry A. Glass, *The Story of the Psalters* (1888; reprint, 1972); Waldo S. Pratt, *Music of the French Psalter of 1562* (1939); Henry W. Foote, *Three Centuries of American Hymnody* (1940; reprint, 1968); Hamilton C. Macdougall, *Early New England Psalmody: An Historical Appreciation, 1620–1820* (1940; reprint, 1969); Erik Routley, *Exploring the Psalms* (1975).

psalm tone A recitation formula used in the singing of psalms and canticles in the canonical hours, or divine office. In the plainchant repertoire there are eight psalm tones corresponding to the eight church modes (plus the *tonus peregrinus*). Because each psalm verse is divided into two halves, the psalm tone has a binary form. The first part consists of the *initium,* or intonation; *tenor,* or recitation notes; (*flexa,* or downward inflection, used only if the first half of the verse is long); and *mediatio,* or middle cadence. The second part comprises the *tenor* and *terminatio,* or final cadence.

Each psalm is preceded and followed by an ANTIPHON composed in one of the eight modes. The psalm tone chosen corresponds to the number of the mode of the antiphon. *Differentiae* (various endings) are used to make a smooth transition between the end of a psalm tone and the beginning of an antiphon.

psaltery An instrument related to the dulcimer and ZITHER with gut or metal strings stretched over a flat soundbox. Its outline is characteristically trapezoid, often in the Middle Ages with incurving sides. The psaltery was then plucked with the fingers or with a pair of quill plectra. The strings are all open, none stopped to give different notes as on a true zither. Probably of Near Eastern origin in late classical times (and inheriting the Greek harp name *psalterion*), the psaltery reached its greatest popularity in the West in the 13th to the 15th century. No medieval specimen survives. The Russian *gusli* and Finnish *kantele* are rudimentary psalteries played across the knees. The large Egyptian

man playing psaltery
from M. Severinus Boetius,
De Arythmetica, de musica, 14th century
courtesy, Biblioteca Nazionale, Naples
photograph, Antonio Beuf

psaltery, *qanun,* is played with two bone plectra worn in rings on the forefingers.

Puccini, Giacomo (Antonio Domenico Michele Secondo Maria) (December 22, 1858–November 29, 1924). The greatest Italian opera composer of his period, Giacomo Puccini represented the fifth (and last) generation of a musical dynasty that dated from the first half of the 18th century. Four of his ancestors held the post of maestro di cappella at the Cathedral of S. Martino at Lucca. It was intended that he should follow the family tradition, and he accordingly studied at the Istituto musicale Pacini (now Istituto musicale Luigi Boccherini); but a performance of *Aida* at Pisa in 1876 revealed his true vocation for opera. In the autumn of 1880 he entered the Milan Conservatory, where he remained for three years. His principal teachers there were Antonio Bazzini and Amilcare Ponchielli, the composer of *La Gioconda.* In the summer of 1883 he graduated with an instrumental work, Capriccio *sinfonico,* whose success attracted attention.

In the same year he entered *Le villi* in a competition for one-act operas. Though it failed to win a prize it was produced with great success in Milan in 1884. The publisher Giulio Ricordi acquired the work and commissioned him to write another: thus began Puccini's lifelong association with the house of Ricordi, whose head was to become a staunch paternal friend and counselor. While at work on the commissioned opera *Edgar,* based on a verse-drama by Alfred de Musset, Puccini lived with Elvira Gemignani, the wife of a Lucchese grocer. In 1886 she bore him a son, Antonio; in 1904, after the death of her husband, her union with Puccini was legalized.

Edgar (Milan, 1889) was a failure, but with *Manon Lescaut* (Turin, 1893), based like Massenet's *Manon* on the celebrated 18th-century novel by Antoine François Prévost, he achieved his first international success. In 1891 during the composition of *Manon Lescaut* he settled at the simple fishing village of Torre del Lago on the Lake of Massaciuccoli, remaining there until he moved to Viareggio just three years before his death. *Manon*

Giacomo Puccini
Mansell-Alinari, London

Lescaut was followed by Puccini's three most popular operas, which established him as the most remarkable Italian opera composer since Verdi. *Lá Bohème* (Turin, 1896), based on the autobiographical novel *Scènes de la vie de Bohème* by Henri Murger; *Tosca* (Rome, 1900) after Victorien Sardou's five-act drama; and *Madama Butterfly* (first version, Milan, February 1904; second version, Brescia, May 1904) after David Belasco's one-act play. In all three operas the librettists were Luigi Illica and Giuseppe Giacosa, who complemented each other and were the composer's best collaborators. With *La Fanciulla del West* (*The Girl of the Golden West;* New York City, 1910), also after a Belasco play, Puccini temporarily abandoned his lyrical style for technical experiments in harmony and orchestration under the influence of Debussy and Richard Strauss. His single attempt at operetta, *La Rondine* (Monte Carlo, 1917), was unsuccessful. Then came *Il Trittico* (New York City, 1918), consisting of three strongly contrasted one-act episodes: the somber, horrific *Il tabarro* after Didier Gold's *La Houppelande (The Cloak);* the sentimental tragedy *Suor Angelica* on a libretto by Giovacchino Forzano; and the comedy *Gianni Schicchi,* also on a libretto by Forzano derived from Dante's

Inferno. Puccini's last opera—some consider it his greatest—was *Turandot* (Milan, 1926), based on the play *Turandotte* by Carlo Gozzi. He died before its completion. The last two scenes of the opera were completed from Puccini's sketches by Franco Alfano.

Puccini's approach to dramatic composition is expressed in his own words: "The basis of an opera is its subject and its treatment." The fashioning of a story into a moving drama claimed his attention, and he devoted as much labor to it as to the music. The action of his operas is uncomplicated and self-evident, so that the spectator readily comprehends what takes place on stage.

Puccini's conception of diatonic melody is rooted in the tradition of 19th-century Italian opera, but his harmonic and orchestral style show that he was aware of contemporary developments, notably the work of the Impressionists and of Stravinsky. Though he allowed the orchestra a more active role, he upheld the traditional vocal style of Italian opera in which the singers carry the burden of the music. In many ways a typical *fin-de-siècle* artist, Puccini nevertheless can be ranked as the greatest exponent of operatic realism.

BIBLIOGRAPHY: Giacomo Puccini, *Letters of Giacomo Puccini; Mainly Connected with the Composition and Production of His Operas* (1973); Stanley Jackson, *Monsieur Butterfly; the Story of Giacomo Puccini* (1974); Mosco Carner, *Puccini: A Critical Biography,* 2nd ed. (1977); William Weaver and Paul Hume, *Puccini: The Man and His Music* (1977).

RECORDINGS: All of the operas.

Pugnani, Gaetano (November 27, 1731–June 15, 1798) A student of Giuseppe Tartini, the Italian violinist and pedagogue Gaetano Pugnani toured between 1754 and 1770, primarily in Paris and England; in the latter he was concertmaster of the London Italian Opera. In 1770 he returned to Turin, where he had been concertmaster of the court orchestra, to regain his former position and later to direct the orchestra and teach at a violin school there. Among his pupils was Giovanni Battista Viotti. He wrote operas, cantatas, and chamber music, including 14 violin sonatas.

659

Pugno, (Stéphane) Raoul (June 23, 1852–January 3, 1914) Though remembered primarily as a pianist, the French Raoul Pugno spent the early years of his career as pedagogue, organist, and chorus master. A student of Georges Mathias at the Paris Conservatoire, Pugno won first prizes in piano, solfège, harmony, fugue, and organ. He was professor of harmony there (1892–96) and of piano (1896–1901). In 1896 he joined the Belgian violinist Eugène Ysaÿe in a duo, and from 1903 he made a number of early recordings.

Pulcinella: *see* BALLET (Diaghilev Ballet); NEOCLASSICISM; PERGOLESI; STRAVINSKY.

Punto, Giovanni, originally Jan Václav Stich (1748–February 16, 1803). Although born a serf, the Bohemian horn player Giovanni Punto (the name was taken professionally) was educated by his master in Prague, Munich, and Dresden. He returned for three years of service and then ran away. In 1781 he played in the court band of the Prince Archbishop of Würzburg and the following year in that of the Comte d'Artois in France. Punto met Mozart (1778) and Beethoven (1800), both of whom composed for him (Symphonie Concertante, K.297b, and the Horn Sonata, Op. 17). He toured Europe with the pianist Jan Ladislav Dussek and composed for the horn, including a book of daily exercises (1795) and a method (1798).

Purcell, Henry (*c.* 1659–November 21, 1695) The most important English composer of his time, Henry Purcell was the son of a gentleman of the Chapel Royal, where he himself received his earliest education as a chorister under Henry Cooke and then under Cooke's son-in-law Pelham Humfrey. When his voice broke in 1673 he was appointed assistant to John Hingston, keeper of the king's instruments, whom he succeeded in 1683. From 1674 to 1678 he tuned the organ at Westminster Abbey and was employed there in 1675–76 to copy organ parts of anthems. In 1677 he succeeded Matthew Locke as composer for Charles II's string orchestra (the "24 violins") and in 1679 was appointed organist of the abbey, succeeding John Blow. A further appointment as one of the three organists of the Chapel Royal followed in 1682. He re-

tained all his official posts through the reigns of James II and of William III and Mary. He married in 1680 or 1681 and had at least six children, three of whom died in infancy. His son Edward (1689–1740) was also a musician, as was Edward's son Edward Henry (b. 1716). Purcell seems to have spent all his life in Westminster. His final illness prevented him from finishing the music for *The Indian Queen,* which was completed by his brother Daniel (d. 1717).

Purcell's music covers a wide field: the church, the stage, the court, and private entertainment. In all these branches he showed an obvious admiration for the past combined with a willingness to learn from the present, particularly from his contemporaries in Italy. With an alert mind went an individual invention, marking him as the most original English composer of his time and one of the most original in Europe. This originality is found not only in his outstanding gifts as a melodist but also in his capacity for producing unexpected harmonic progressions by means of contrapuntal ingenuity.

The first evidence of his mastery is an in-

Henry Purcell
*portrait by John Closterman (1658–1713)
courtesy, National Portrait Gallery, London*

strumental work—a series of fantasias (or "fancies") for viols in three, four, five, six, and seven parts. The nine four-part fantasias all bear dates in the summer of 1680, and the others can hardly be later. Purcell was reviving a form that was out of date and doing it with the skill of a veteran. It was probably about the same time that he started to work on a more fashionable series of sonatas for two violins, bass viol, and organ (or harpsichord). Twelve of these were published in 1683 with a dedication to Charles II, and a further nine (together with a chaconne for the same combination) were issued by his widow in 1697. The foreword to the 1683 set claimed that the composer had "faithfully endeavour'd a just imitation of the most fam'd Italian Masters"; but along with an Italianate manner there was much derived from the English tradition of chamber music.

It is the instrumental movements that are the most striking part of the earliest of Purcell's "Welcome Songs" for Charles II—a series of ceremonial odes beginning in 1680. Possibly he lacked experience in writing for voices, at least on the scale required for works of this kind, or perhaps he had not yet achieved the art of cloaking insipid words in significant music. By 1683 he had acquired a surer touch, and from that time until 1694, when he wrote the last of the birthday odes for Queen Mary, he produced a series of compositions for the court in which the vitality of the music makes it easy to ignore the poverty of the words. The same qualities are apparent in the last of his odes for St. Cecilia's Day (1692).

Purcell's genius as a composer for the stage was hampered by the fact that there was no public opera in London in his lifetime. Most of his theater music consists simply of instrumental music and songs interpolated into spoken drama, though occasionally there were opportunities for more extended musical scenes. His contribution to the stage was in fact very modest until 1689, when he wrote *Dido and Aeneas* for performance at a girls' school in Chelsea; this miniature opera achieves a high degree of dramatic intensity within a narrow framework. From that time until his death he was constantly employed in writing music for public theaters. These productions included some that gave scope for more than merely incidental music—notably *Dioclesian* (1690), adapted by Thomas Betterton from the tragedy *The Prophetess* by John Fletcher and Philip Massinger; *King Arthur* (1691) by John Dryden, designed from the first as an entertainment with music; and *The Fairy Queen* (1692), an anonymous adaptation of Shakespeare's *A Midsummer Night's Dream* in which the texts set to music are all interpolations. In these works Purcell showed not only a lively sense of comedy but also a gift of passionate expression that is often more exalted than the words. The tendency to identify himself still more closely with the Italian style is noticeable in the later dramatic works, which often demand considerable agility from the soloists.

Purcell's four-part fantasias, his first court ode, and his first music for the theater, *Theodosius,* all date from 1680. Some of his church music may be earlier than that, but it is not possible to assign definite dates. Most of his anthems, whether full anthems or verse anthems, were written between 1680 and 1685, the year of Charles II's death. The decline of the Chapel Royal in the reigns of James II and William and Mary may have been responsible for the comparatively few works he produced in that period; or he was so busy with stage music and odes that he had little time or inclination for church music. The style of his full anthems, like that of the fantasias, shows a great respect for older traditions. His verse anthems were obviously influenced by Humfrey, who had acquired a knowledge of continental styles during his travels abroad. The most notable feature of these later works is the use of expressive vocal declamation that is pathetic without being mawkish. The same characteristics appear in the sacred songs he wrote for private performance. Since composers for the Chapel Royal in Charles II's reign had the string orchestra at their disposal, Purcell took the opportunity to include dignified and lively overtures and ritornellos. The most elaborate of his church compositions are the anthem *My heart is inditing,* performed in Westminster Abbey at the coronation of James II, and the festal canticles Te Deum and *Jubi-*

late, written for St. Cecilia's Day in 1694. Of these the anthem is the more impressive; the canticles suffer on the whole from a forced brilliance that seems to have faded with the passage of time.

Though the main period of Purcell's creative activity lasted for little more than 15 years, he managed to crowd into it a large number of compositions, including more than 100 secular songs and about 40 duets as well as those he contributed to plays. Many of the songs are quite substantial pieces, incorporating recitative and arias on the lines of the Italian solo cantata. A favorite device in Purcell's secular music, though rarely in his anthems, was the ground bass. This can have an invigorating effect in lively pieces; and in laments such as Dido's farewell it can intensify the expression of grief. The chaconne in the second set of sonatas uses the same technique with impressive results. Works of this kind represent the composer at the height of his capacity. The numerous catches, though accomplished enough, are little more than an experienced musician's contribution to social merrymaking. Purcell seems to have abandoned instrumental chamber music after his early years. His keyboard music forms an even smaller part of his output, consisting of suites and shorter pieces (many adapted from other works) for harpsichord and a handful of pieces for organ.

Apart from many songs that appeared in vocal collections, very little of Purcell's music was published in his lifetime. The principal works were the *Sonnatas of III parts* (1683); *Welcome to all the pleasures,* an ode for St. Cecilia's Day (1684); and *Dioclesian* (1691). After his death his widow published a collection of his harpsichord pieces (1696), instrumental music for the theater (1697), and the Te Deum and *Jubilate* (1697); the publisher Henry Playford issued a two-volume collection of songs entitled *Orpheus Britannicus* (1698 and 1702) that went through three editions. A few dramatic works, odes, and anthems were printed in the late 18th and early 19th centuries; but it was not until 1876, when the Purcell Society was founded, that a serious attempt was made to issue all of Purcell's works.

BIBLIOGRAPHY: William H. Cummings, *Purcell* (1881; reprint, 1969); Dennis D. Arundell, *Henry Purcell* (1927; reprint, 1971); Edward J. Dent, *Foundations of English Opera* (1928; reprint, 1965); Arthur K. Holland, *Henry Purcell: The English Musical Tradition* (1932); Imogen Holst, *Henry Purcell* (1961); Robert E. Moore, *Henry Purcell and the Restoration Theatre* (1961; reprint, 1974); Franklin B. Zimmerman, *Henry Purcell, 1659–1695: His Life and Times* (1967); Jack A. Westrup, *Purcell,* 7th ed. (1973).

RECORDINGS: Numerous recordings of many works.

Puritani, I: *see* BELLINI.

Pythagorean temperament: *see* TUNING AND TEMPERAMENT.

Q

quadrille   A lively dance executed by four couples arranged in a square. A form of contredanse known by 1710, the quadrille crystallized about 1815 in the general form popular since then consisting of five figures: *le pantalon, l'été, la poule, la pastourelle,* or *la trénise,* and the finale. The music was often based on operatic melodies; dance patterns were subject to great variation. Although steps and figures have undergone considerable modification, quadrilles such as the lancers are still among the most popular square dances. In theatrical terminology quadrille has denoted: small groups of dancers in 18th-century ballet; Paris nightclub dancers of the 1890s, immortalized by Henri de Toulouse-Lautrec; and divisions of ensemble dancers at the Paris Opéra in the 20th century.

Quantz, Johann Joachim (January 30, 1697– July 12, 1773)   The German flutist, theorist, and composer Johann Joachim Quantz played double bass, harpsichord, violin, and oboe before beginning to learn the flute. In 1728 he became flute teacher to Crown Prince Frederick of Prussia, visiting the court biannually to give lessons to the prince. Upon Frederick's accession as Frederick II (the Great), Quantz was invited to the court as chamber musician and court composer; there he wrote 300 flute concertos and approximately 200 pieces for solo and multiple flutes. Quantz improved the fingering and intonation of the instrument. His treatise *Versuch einer Anweisung die Flöte traversiere zu spielen* (1752; *On Playing the Flute,* 1966) has long been authoritative on such general musical matters as ornamentation, performance practice, music criticism, and aesthetics.

RECORDINGS: Flute Sonatas, Op. 1 (6); Trio Sonatas in a minor and D Major.

quartet A composition for four instruments or voices; also the group of four performers. Although any music in four parts can be performed by four individuals, the term has come to be used primarily in referring to the string quartet (two violins, viola, and cello)—the predominant genre of chamber music since *c.* 1750; its derivatives piano quartet, flute quartet, oboe quartet, etc.—usually a string trio combined with a non-stringed instrument; quartets of mixed instruments such as woodwind or brass quartet; and the vocal quartet (soprano, alto, tenor, and bass)—especially in opera, oratorio, church music, and such notable examples as Brahms's two sets of *Liebeslieder* Waltzes, *Zigeunerlieder,* and Quartets, Opp. 31, 64, 92, and 112.

The development of the string quartet occurs in the works of Haydn, who established it as the principal chamber music genre. His early quartets show soloistic writing for the first violin and the dependence of the viola on the cello, whose melodic line it frequently duplicates. Later works show progressive integration of the first violin and increased participation by the lower pitched instruments. In his Opus 33 he brought the form to its mature Classical style, achieving a texture characterized by equal participation of all four instruments and establishing the genre's standard formal outlines.

Specifically the string quartet follows the sonata's division into several movements and its principles of form and development. Haydn's early quartets follow the divertimento in having five movements; but in his Opus 17 he established four as the standard number. The genre became infused with the sonata principle of contrast between keys.

Typically its first movement utilizes sonata form.

Mozart's quartets—notably the six dedicated to Haydn and the three dedicated to Frederick William II of Prussia—are cast in the mature form established by Haydn and in turn influenced Haydn. Beethoven's early quartets fall into the established framework, but in his *Razumovsky* Quartets he expanded the length and scope of the genre. His late quartets puzzled contemporaries by their conciseness, profundity, and complexity.

The Classical tradition was inherited by Schubert, Brahms, Borodin, and other Romantic composers. In the 19th century there was a tendency (*e.g.,* in the quartets of Dvořák) to move away from the intimate workmanship of the Classical quartet to a more orchestrally conceived texture. The genre was largely untouched by the Romantic tendency to program music; a rare example is Smetana's quartet *Z mého života (From My Life).*

In the 20th century changing styles have proved highly suitable to the quartet. The Impressionism of Debussy and Ravel is revealed in the coloristic harmonies and textures of their quartets. The genre is equally adaptable to the rhythmic drive of Bartók, the quarter-tone experiments of Bloch, and the polytonality of Milhaud. It is also an effective medium for the atonality and 12-tone method of Schoenberg and his followers.

BIBLIOGRAPHY: Robert Sondheimer, *Haydn: A Historical and Psychological Study Based on His Quartets* (1951); Charles Rosen, *The Classical Style* (1971); Reginald Barrett-Ayres, *Joseph Haydn and the String Quartet* (1974).

Queen of Spades, The: *see* GRÉTRY; TCHAIKOVSKY (later life and works).

Quinault, Philippe: *see* LIBRETTO (origins); LULLY; PICCINNI.

quintet A composition for five instruments or voices; also the group performing such music. The string quintet normally includes two violins, two violas, and cello. Mozart's six works for this medium are usually considered his greatest achievement in chamber music. Boccherini favored two cellos in place of two violas (he was a virtuoso cellist) and composed

113 quintets for this combination (plus a dozen for the more conventional instrumentation). Only Schubert followed his example, in the well-known Quintet in C. The piano quintet—usually piano and string quartet—has been a popular medium with composers (another dozen by Boccherini), though Schubert's famous *Trout* Quintet is for piano, violin, viola, cello, and double bass. Flute, oboe, clarinet, etc. are also combined with four strings. Boccherini composed 18 quintets for flute or oboe and the normal complement of strings. Vocal quintets are usually for two sopranos, alto, tenor, and bass; much literature for five parts exists—16th-century madrigals, for example—but the term quintet is rarely used for it.

quodlibet A humorous composition in which the melodies of existing songs are combined either simultaneously or, less frequently, sequentially. Quodlibet can also refer to an amalgamation of different song texts.

The simultaneous combination of two or more melodies is found at least as early as the 13th century (motets using, for example, a chant melody and a secular tune) and became popular in the 15th and 16th centuries. In Germany numerous quodlibets of folk songs are found in manuscript collections of polyphonic songs. A similar English example is the *Cries of London* by Gibbons. Perhaps the most famous example of a quodlibet is the last of Bach's *Goldberg* Variations for harpsichord (1742). Quodlibets of hymn and plainchant melodies were also occasionally written.

R

Raaff, Anton (May 6, 1714–May 27, 1797) A close friend of Mozart, who wrote the title role in *Idomeneo* for him (1781), the German tenor Anton Raaff studied in Munich and Bologna before singing in Italy, Austria, and Portugal from 1738 to 1755. In the latter year he sang with Farinelli in Madrid, remaining until 1759. From 1770 he was in the service of the elector Karl Theodor in Mannheim, and after 1779 in Munich.

Rachel, La Cubana: *see* HENZE; OPERA (the 20th century).

Rachmaninoff, Sergei (Vasilyevich) (April 1 [March 20, old style], 1873–March 28, 1943) The last of the great Russian Romantic composers, Sergei Rachmaninoff was also the leading piano virtuoso of his day and a gifted conductor. After a period of unsuccessful study at the St. Petersburg Conservatory (1882–85), he was sent to Moscow, where he studied piano with Nikolay Zverev and his cousin Aleksandr Siloti and composition with Sergey Taneyev and Anton Stepanovich Arensky. He completed his piano course in 1891 and his composition course the following year, winning a gold medal with his one-act opera *Aleko.* His First Piano Concerto dates from the same period. During the next two or three years he produced piano pieces (including the famous Prelude in c-sharp minor that he came to despise) and songs, *Elegiac* Trio in memory of Tchaikovsky, an orchestral fantasia *The Rock,* and his First Symphony in d minor. The disastrous first and only performance of this First Symphony in St. Petersburg in March 1897 caused him to suffer a nervous collapse; he composed nothing more until 1900. From 1896 to 1898 his only musical occupations were as second conductor of the Mamontov Opera in Moscow and as a piano teacher in a girls' school. The popular Second Piano Concerto in c minor, originally performed in 1900 without the first movement (written in 1901), marked the resumption of Rachmaninoff's creative career. It is dedicated to the psychiatrist who is credited with leading Rachmaninoff out of his depression. The concerto was soon followed by a cello sonata, the cantata *The Spring,* and more songs and piano pieces. A brief appointment as conductor of the Bolshoi Theater in Moscow (1904–06) led to the composition of two short operas, *The Miserly Knight* and *Francesca da Rimini.* He also conducted orchestral concerts, putting new life into Tchaikovsky and even Mozart—both "traditionally" performed slowly and lifelessly.

From the autumn of 1906 to the summer of 1908 Rachmaninoff lived in Dresden, where he wrote four major works: Second Symphony

Sergei Rachmaninoff
Bassano and Vandyk, Elliott and Fry

in e minor (1907), Piano Sonata in d minor
(1907), the symphonic poem *The Isle of the
Dead* (1909; suggested by Arnold Böcklin's
painting), and the Third Piano Concerto in
d minor, composed for a concert tour of the
United States in the autumn of 1909 in which
he appeared as composer, pianist, and conductor. (London had heard him in all three roles
as early as 1899.) From 1910 to the Revolution
Rachmaninoff again made his home in Moscow, appearing as conductor (*e.g.,* of the Philharmonic concerts from 1911 to 1913) more
often than as pianist. His compositions of that
period include the *Liturgy of St. John Chrysos-
tom* (1910), a choral symphony based on Poe's
"The Bells" (1913), the Second Piano Sonata
(1913), and the *Vesper* Mass (1915). At the
end of 1917 Rachmaninoff left Russia for
Scandinavia; in 1918 he went to the United
States, where he made his principal home for
the remainder of his life. After 1917 he devoted himself mainly to the establishment of
a career as a major piano virtuoso, an amazing
feat for a man in his middle 40s. He refused
conductorships of both Boston and Cincinnati
Symphonies. But the Fourth Piano Concerto
in g minor was written in 1927, and in the

1930s he composed Variations on a Theme
by Corelli for piano (1932), Rhapsody on a
Theme by Paganini for piano and orchestra
(1934), the Third Symphony (1936), and three
Symphonic Dances (first performed 1941).

Rachmaninoff was a superb pianist, and all
his most characteristic works—the concertos
and the *Paganini* Rhapsody, the solo preludes
and *Études-Tableaux* (1916–17), and the
songs—are marked by rich, euphonious, and
highly effective piano writing. He had a modest but real gift for somewhat elegiac melody
but no great creative range, and he never made
any serious attempt to go beyond the harmonic idiom of his youth.

BIBLIOGRAPHY: Sergei Rachmaninoff,
*Rachmaninoff's Recollections Told to Oskar
von Riesemann* (1934); Watson Lyle, *Rach-
maninoff: A Biography* (1939; reprint, 1976);
Victor I. Seroff, *Rachmaninoff* (1950; reprint,
1970); Sergei Bertensson and Jay Leyda, *Ser-
gei Rachmaninoff: A Lifetime in Music* (1956);
Robert Threlfall, *Sergei Rachmaninoff; His
Life and Music* (1973); Patrick Piggott,
Rachmaninov Orchestral Music (1974) and
Rachmaninov (1977).

RECORDINGS: Numerous recordings of
most works.

Raff, (Joseph) Joachim (May 27, 1822–June
24/25, 1882)   A Swiss composer who wrote
in the style of Mendelssohn and Liszt, Joachim
Raff composed more than 300 works, including 11 symphonies, chamber music, choral
works, and many piano pieces. He was long
known for his "Cavatina" for the violin. Raff
became a schoolteacher and taught himself
piano, violin, and composition. In 1844 he
went to Zürich, where he devoted himself to
composition and teaching. In 1848 Hans von
Bülow played Raff's *Concertstück* at Stuttgart,
and in 1850 his opera *König Alfred* was given
at Weimar. Between 1856 and 1877 he was
a piano teacher at Wiesbaden, producing seven
symphonies and his comic opera *Dame Ko-
bold*. In 1877 he was appointed director of
the Konservatorium at Frankfurt am Main.

RECORDINGS: *Ode to Spring* for piano
and orchestra; Piano Concerto in c minor;
Suite in d minor for piano; Symphonies Nos.
3 and 5.

Raïsa, Rosa, originally Rosa Burstein (May 30, 1893–September 28, 1963)   Long identified with the Chicago Opera, soprano Rosa Raïsa performed as a child in her native Poland and then studied at the Naples Conservatory. In 1913 she made her debut at Parma, Italy, and the same year sang in the United States as Verdi's Aida in Chicago. She created the role of Puccini's Turandot as the composer's choice at La Scala in 1926; two years earlier she had created the leading role of Asteria in Arrigo Boito's *Nerone.* She appeared at Covent Garden, at the Teatro Colón in Buenos Aires, and was a familiar singer in European opera houses. Her best known roles included Malliela (Ermanno Wolf-Ferrari's *I gioielli della Madonna*), Puccini's Suor Angelica, Bellini's Norma, Mozart's Donna Anna *(Don Giovanni),* and Richard Strauss's Marschallin *(Der Rosenkavalier).* She also premiered contemporary operas, including Riccardo Zandonai's *Francesca da Rimini* (Chicago premiere, 1917), Italo Montemezzi's *La Nave* (U.S. premiere, 1919), and Lodovico Rocca's *The Dybbuk* (U.S. premiere, 1938). She was heard in early acoustic and electric recordings.

Rake's Progress, The: *see* ARIA; LIBRETTO (19th-century influences); OPERA (the 20th century); STRAVINSKY.

Rameau, Jean Philippe (baptized September 25, 1683–September 12, 1764)   The greatest French composer of the 18th century, Jean Philippe Rameau is known also for his theoretical works on harmony. The son of an organist, at 18 he decided to become a musician and went to Italy, but he only reached Milan and returned a few months later. He became organist successively at Avignon, Clermont-Ferrand, Paris, Dijon, Lyons, and again at Clermont-Ferrand, leaving in 1722 for Paris, where he settled for the remainder of his life. Until 1753 he was in the service of the financier Le Riche de La Pouplinière, conducting his private orchestra and ministering to his musical needs.

Before the age of 50 Rameau had published harpsichord pieces, a few motets, and some solo cantatas and had written a little light music for the stage; but it was only later, from his position in La Pouplinière's circle, that

Jean-Philippe Rameau
portrait by Jacques-André-Joseph Aved (1702–66)
Snark International

he was able to turn fully to opera in which he produced his masterpieces. In 1733 his *Hippolyte et Aricie* was produced at the Paris Opéra. From then until 1760 he wrote tragic operas, various forms of ballet-opera, pastorals, and comic operas. His tragic operas and pastorals are in the form created by Lully and Philippe Quinault; his ballet-operas follow the form used by André Campra and Antoine Houdar de La Motte; and in *Platée* (1745) he adapted for the first time the form of the *tragédie lyrique* to a comic plot.

None of his librettists, not even Voltaire, was a great dramatist, and Rameau himself was too unheeding of dramatic structure to criticize their plots, though he would dwell on details. Yet when the plot allowed it, he identified himself with his characters—*e.g.,* Thésée in *Hippolyte et Aricie* and Iphise in *Dardanus*—entering into their feelings with great imagination. He was also able to portray a tragic situation vividly; *e.g.,* Hippolyte's death and the tragic suspense in the second entry of *Les Fêtes d'Hébé.* His recitative, unlike that of Italian opera composers, is expressive and shades away smoothly into the airs.

His harmony is rich and dense and his bass line interesting, its coherence and power often making his harmonies more telling than the vocal line itself. His many choruses are outstanding. The orchestral accompaniment is often of great beauty and interest in itself. Though consisting only of strings, woodwinds, horns, and occasionally trumpets, Rameau's orchestra is used with an almost impressionistic resourcefulness. The orchestra is used alone in the *symphonies,* in the dances during the interludes, *ballets figurés,* and sections of dumb show. His masterpieces are the comedy *Platée,* his first two ballet-operas *Les Indes galantes* (1735) and *Les Fêtes d'Hébé* (1739), and his first three tragedies: *Hippolyte, Castor et Pollux* (1737), and *Dardanus* (two versions, 1739 and 1744).

Rameau's three books of solo harpsichord pieces and his five trios *(Pièces de clavecin en concert)* are more advanced than François Couperin's in keyboard technique and show the same harmonic vigor and concentrated expression as his operas. The trios are early examples of chamber music with an independent keyboard part instead of merely a figured bass. His four motets and his solo secular cantatas, all early, are among the less distinctive examples of his work. Among his theoretical works the *Traité de l'harmonie* (1722), based on the acoustic discoveries of the mathematician Joseph Sauveur, offers an explanation of the harmonic practice of the time.

BIBLIOGRAPHY: Cuthbert Girdlestone, *Jean-Philippe Rameau: His Life and Work,* rev. ed. (1969).

RECORDINGS: *Acanthe et Céphise* (excerpts); *Castor et Pollux; La Guirlande; Harpsichord Suites in a minor and E Major; Les Indes galantes; Les Paladins* (excerpts); *Pièces de clavecin; Pièces de clavecin en concert; Platée; Thétis* (solo cantata); *Zoroastre* (excerpts).

Rampal, Jean-Pierre (Louis) (b. January 7, 1922)   Perhaps the best known flute virtuoso of the latter part of the 20th century, the French flutist Jean-Pierre Rampal has been heard in solo and chamber music performances in Europe, Asia, Africa, and the Americas. He performs regularly at music festivals and has recorded extensively, for which he has won the Grand Prix du Disque seven times. He began his studies with his father at the Marseille Conservatory and, after several years in medicine, returned to the conservatory to work with Gaston Crunelle. He made his U.S. debut in 1958 and has been an editor for the International Music Company in New York City since that year. Now a professor at the Paris Conservatoire, he is a chevalier of the Légion d'Honneur.

Rape of Lucretia, The: *see* BRITTEN; CHAMBER MUSIC.

Rapsodie espagnole: *see* RAVEL.

Ravel, (Joseph) Maurice (March 7, 1875–December 28, 1937)   One of the most original French composers of his time, Maurice Ravel was of mixed Swiss-Basque descent. While still a student at the Paris Conservatoire, which he entered at the age of 14, he published a *Menuet antique* for piano (1895), some songs, and the *Pavane pour une infante défunte* for piano (1899), which established his reputation almost overnight, although he judged it severely in later life. His failure, after three attempts, to win the coveted Prix de Rome for composition—the works he submitted were judged too advanced—caused a scandal. Indignant protests were published, and liberal-minded musicians and writers, including Romain Rolland, supported Ravel, denouncing the narrow-mindedness of his judges. The director of the Conservatoire, Théodore Dubois, was forced to resign in 1905, and his place was taken by Fauré, with whom Ravel had been studying composition since 1898.

By the time Ravel was 30 he had published his Quartet (1903), the song-cycle *Shéhérazade,* the Sonatina and *Miroirs* for piano, and the *Introduction et Allegro* for harp, string quartet, flute, and clarinet. One of his earliest piano pieces, *Jeux d'eau* (1901), inaugurated a new era in the use of the piano's technical resources, and in 1931 he wrote two piano concertos; the one for the left hand alone is among his most original works. Several of his piano works were later orchestrated by him, notably *Ma Mère l'Oye* ("Mother Goose") and *Valses nobles et sentimentales.*

His chamber works include a remarkable

Maurice Ravel
courtesy, French Embassy,
Press and Information Division, New York City

trio for violin, cello, and piano, a violin and piano sonata, and a sonata for violin and cello; but it was in his symphonic works, the *Rapsodie espagnole,* the ballet *Daphnis et Chloé* (1909–12), and *Boléro* (1928) that he reached his height. As a songwriter Ravel achieved distinction with his imaginative *Histoires naturelles* (1906), *Trois Poèmes de Mallarmé* (1913), and *Chansons Madécasses* (1925–26). In opera he produced two little masterpieces of wit and fantasy, *L'Heure espagnole* (1907) and with Colette as librettist *L'Enfant et les sortilèges* (1925).

In everything he wrote Ravel was an exquisite craftsman, striving always for perfection of form and style, which he judged more valuable than an expression of personal feelings. Though he worked in the classical form and was never a revolutionary, he created an individual harmonic language as unmistakably his own as any page of Bach or Chopin. Although it is incorrect to bracket him with Debussy, the two composers nevertheless had certain features in common, notably their attraction to Baudelaire and Mallarmé, and a delight in rare and precious sensations. In tempera-

ment, however, and in methods and technique they were vastly different. A highly distinctive composer in everything he wrote, Ravel, as Roland-Manuel wrote, "is one of the rare French composers who have left so strong an imprint on their art that music after them can never be the same as it was before they appeared on the scene."

BIBLIOGRAPHY: Roland-Manuel, *Maurice Ravel* (1947; reprint, 1972); Vladimir Jankelevitch, *Ravel* (1959; reprint, 1976); Rollo H. Myers, *Ravel: Life and Works* (1960; reprint, 1973); Laurence Davies, *Ravel Orchestral Music* (1970); Arbie Orenstein, *Ravel: Man and Musician* (1975).

RECORDINGS: Numerous recordings of many works.

Ravenscroft, Thomas (*c.* 1583–*c.* 1633) An English composer remembered chiefly for his social songs and his collection of psalm settings, Thomas Ravenscroft was a chorister of St. Paul's Cathedral, London. In 1607 he received his B. Mus. at Cambridge, and from 1618 to 1622 he was music master at Christ's Hospital. Ravenscroft's *Whole Booke of Psalmes* (1621), comprising more than 100 metrical psalm tunes, proved extremely popular. Ravenscroft himself harmonized about half the melodies, commissioning or compiling the remainder from other composers. Several of his versions are still in use. His secular collections are full of interest for the sociologist or historian of popular music. *Pammelia* (1609), containing 100 catches and rounds, was the first anthology of its kind; *Deuteromelia* (1609) has 31 items, including "Three blind mice"; *Melismata* (1611) has 23 songs for the "court, city, and country humours"; and his theoretical work *Briefe Discourse* (1614) appends further characteristic pieces. Ravenscroft aimed cunningly to please a middle-class lay public very different from the educated elite who enjoyed the madrigal or the ayre.

Rawsthorne, Alan (May 2, 1905–July 24, 1971) A student at the Royal Manchester College of Music and a private piano pupil of Egon Petri, the English pianist and composer Alan Rawsthorne worked solely as a free-lance composer after 1935, following three years as music director of the school of dance-mime at Dartington Hall. He wrote three symphonies (1950, 1959, 1964), two pianos concertos (the second, 1951, is important in his musical development), a ballet (*Madame Chrysanthème*, 1955), and chamber music for strings, winds, and piano (piano quintet, 1968; three quartets; quintet for piano, oboe, horn, violin, cello, 1971).

RECORDINGS: *Elegy* for guitar; Symphonic Studies; Symphony No. 1.

Razumovsky Quartets (op. 59): *see* BEETHOVEN (Beethoven and the theater); CHAMBER MUSIC; COUNTERPOINT (Classical period); QUARTET.

rebec A bowed stringed instrument of Middle Eastern origin that was in general use in Europe in the Middle Ages and early Renaissance; it is still commonly used in the folk music of the Balkans. The medieval rebec (the name is derived from the Arabic *rabab*) had a violin-type bridge and tailpiece and a vaulted back like the lute, either carved from a solid block of wood or constructed from separate ribs glued together over a mold. The European instrument differed from the *rabab* in that the table or soundboard was of wood rather than of skin. It had no soundpost, and the two or three gut strings were generally tuned in fifths. Although in western Europe a fingerboard was added at an early date, the Oriental method of stopping the strings with the sides of the fingernails of the left hand persisted in some countries until modern times. The medieval rebec was often held against the chest or under the chin; but when the player was sitting the instrument was sometimes held in the Oriental manner, the bottom of the instrument resting on the player's left thigh.

The medieval rebec appears to have been a treble instrument, but by the late 15th century rebecs were being made in several sizes from treble to bass. The family of rebecs was superseded by the viols by about the middle of the 16th century; the treble rebec, however, survived in western Europe to the 18th century as an instrument for rustic music making and in a miniature form as the dancing master's fiddle (*see* KIT). In modern times the rebec in various forms and tunings is found in the folk music of Greece, Bulgaria, and Yugoslavia as well as in its original form in the art music of the Middle East. It also appears increasingly in authentic performances of old music.

recapitulation In sonata form, the third major section in which the musical material stated in the exposition and altered, expanded, restructured, and subjected to harmonic change in the development is restated more or less in its original form. In contrast to the exposition in which the material is stated in contrasting keys, in the recapitulation the restated material is typically in the tonic key.

recitative A declarative vocal style in opera, oratorio, and cantata that emphasizes the rhythms and accents of the spoken language. The earliest significant form of monody, recitative developed in the late 1500s in opposition to the polyphonic style of 16th-century choral music.

The earliest operas, such as Jacopo Peri's *Euridice* (1600), consisted almost entirely of recitativo arioso, a lyric form of recitative intended to communicate the emotion of the text. In operas of the late 17th century the expression of emotion was left to the lyric outpouring of the aria, and the recitative carried

modern rebec by Arnold Dolmetsch, Ltd., 1962
courtesy, Howard Mayer Brown
photograph, EB Inc.

the dialogue and advanced the action of the plot. In oratorios and cantatas it often serves the similar function of advancing the narrative.

Two principal varieties developed. Recitativo secco ("dry recitative") is sung with a free rhythm dictated by the accents of the words. Accompaniment, usually by continuo (such as harpsichord and cello), is simple and chordal. The melody approximates speech by using only a few pitches. Recitativo *stromentato,* or accompanied recitative, has stricter rhythm and more involved, often orchestral accompaniment. Used at dramatically important moments, it is more emotional in character. Its melody is more lyric, and it frequently leads into a formal aria.

recorder An instrument of the flageolet class, also described as fipple flute from the shape of the part that the player holds to the lips. Most modern recorders, made since the instrument's revival by Arnold Dolmetsch in 1919, follow the early 18th-century or Baroque design: the cylindrical head joint is partially plugged to direct the wind against the sharp edge below; the body tapers, and its lowest part is usually made as a separate foot joint; there are seven finger holes and one thumbhole. Often the lowest two holes are each arranged as a pair of holes, one of which is left open to produce the semitone above the note made by covering both. The upper register at the octave is obtained by pinching the thumbhole; *i.e.,* flexing the thumb to make a narrow opening above the thumbnail. The larger instruments may have one or more keys, allowing holes to be pierced at points otherwise out of reach of the fingers. Recorders are made in the following sizes: sopranino in f‴; descant (soprano) in c″; treble (alto) in f′; tenor in c′; bass in f; and (rarely) great bass in c. (These notes refer in each case to the instrument's lowest note.) The treble and tenor recorders sound at written pitch; the sopranino and descant sound an octave higher than written; the bass, whose music is written in the bass staff, also sounds an octave higher.

The recorder is a 14th-century improvement upon kindred instruments played earlier in the Middle Ages. The English name may

derive from Old Italian *ricordo,* a keepsake. The first instructions are found in books by Sebastian Virdung (1511) and Sylvestro Ganassi (1535), written at a time when recorder consorts were approaching the height of their popularity. The Baroque repertoire, which includes many works by Handel and Bach, is almost exclusively for treble recorder (then described as flute or common flute), after which time the instrument lay obsolete until its flourishing modern revival.

recording It is probable—with further historical perspective—that the invention of recording will be seen as an event comparable in its social impact to the introduction of print-

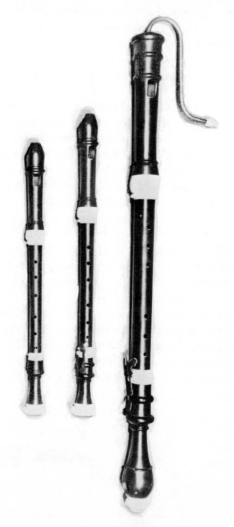

recorders by P. J. Bressan, 18th century
courtesy, Grosvenor Museum, Chester, England

ing from movable type. Since the close of the second world war the technology developed for the electronic recording of sound has been applied to preserving a vast range of information both visually—in the form of television pictures—and in computer memories. We view a future in which electronic data processing will eliminate the majority of tasks that traditionally were done with paper and pen.

The history of the phonograph falls into two periods of nearly equal length: 1877–1925, when sound recording was accomplished by mechanical means; and from 1925 to the present, when mechanical steps in the recording and playback process have successively been replaced by electronic devices. The last significant mechanical step—cutting a disk and recovering information from its grooves through a pickup stylus—remains a central part of the industry, but it can be replaced by the direct electronic transmission of information from magnetized tape.

Recording technology does not show a pattern of slow, steady development but rather one in which major developments burst upon the scene, introducing a period of rapid growth; conditions then return to stability for a number of years. It is only since the 1950s that the phonograph could be accepted by musicians as a device for the accurate reproduction of their performances, and although earlier recordings have obvious value and interest, their limitations must be accepted.

early history   Although many of the basic components of the earliest phonographs were known to Greek science and its acoustical amplification system is found in the sketchbooks of Leonardo da Vinci, the development of a working apparatus for the reproduction of sound was a by-product of investigations into electromagnetic devices. The idea of preserving sound and reproducing it at will attracted a number of investigators in Europe and the United States; Thomas A. Edison is the most important because he was the first to design a machine that worked successfully as both a recorder and a reproducer. The French honor Charles Cros, who had worked out the theory of sound recording using disks to store the information; but in 1877 when Cros's phonograph was still to be realized in a work-

ing model, Edison's device was already in operation.

Paradoxically Edison did not set out to record music or speech but was interested in perfecting a "talking telegraph" to store and repeat messages; and although he was involved with electromagnetic problems, he designed a mechanical rather than an electronic device. Its immediate ancestor was a mechanism to emboss telegraph messages on a strip of paper tape. Edison concluded that if he could record dots and dashes, he could also preserve telephone messages, and, apparently without realizing the full implications of this line of thought, he sent the sketch for his first phonograph to his machine shop in August 1877.

The first Edison phonograph consisted of a metal cylinder with a spiral groove cut in its surface. The cylinder was covered by tinfoil, and a stylus, attached to a mouthpiece by a diaphragm, was set at the end of the groove. Turning a crank moved the cylinder on a lead screw from right to left past the stylus, which embossed the vibrations of the diaphragm into the bottom of the groove. Edison invented vertical, or hill-and-dale, recording, a technique that was later replaced by Cros's lateral recording in which the information was contained in the movement of the groove from side to side. The modern stereo record, which contains both vertically and horizontally recorded information, unites the approach of these two pioneers.

Edison's tinfoil recordings were of very poor quality and could not be duplicated. The first machine to create this possibility (although it went unrealized for some years) was the Graphophone, a modification of the Edison machine by Alexander Graham Bell, his cousin Chichester A. Bell, and Charles Sumner Tainter in 1881. The grooves in the cylinder were filled with wax in which the recording stylus incised a deep groove that produced sound of much higher quality. This quickly led to the development of a wax-coated cardboard cylinder to replace tinfoil as the recording medium.

The musical potential of the phonograph was quickly grasped. "Imagine an opera or oratorio, sung by the greatest living vocalists, thus recorded and capable of being repeated as we desired," the editor of *Scientific American* wrote in November 1877, anticipating events that would not take place on the scale he prophesied for another half century. Although the commercial recording of cylinders in the 1890s provided a repertoire for the coin-slot phonograph industry, the mass marketing of records awaited the development in 1894 of a technique for the duplication of cylinders in celluloid. Further advances of cylinder recording in the Edison Blue Amberol cylinders of 1912 produced recordings that often are superior to disks of the same period, but the research necessary to make the cylinder acceptable unfortunately came after the public at large had come to regard it as obsolete.

It was the laterally-cut disk record, made commercially feasible through the work of Emile Berliner, that made the phonograph the prime source of entertainment and the symbol of culture in the U.S. living room of the early 20th century. The disk phonograph, with its clockwork motor and inexpensive, mass-produced records, was within the means of all but the very poor. And the possibility—exploited by the advertising copywriters of the Victor Talking Machine Company—of having Caruso singing in your home on Christmas morning was a powerful stimulus to sales.

Berliner's first machine, called a Gramophone, was a hand-cranked device patented in 1887. It was midway in the '90s, however, before these machines had any impact on the market. The British Gramophone Company dates from 1898, and the Victor Company was founded by Berliner's colleague Eldridge Johnson in 1901. Johnson's efforts to make a record with less surface noise and wider dynamics than the earliest disks were influential in the rapid acceptance of the Victrola and its rivals the world over. By 1912 Edison was producing disk phonographs, although his records continued to be cut vertically. He apparently remained convinced that the cylinder (which always turns at the same speed) was inherently superior to a disk in which the actual playing speed changes as the stylus moves from the long outer grooves of the disk to the shorter ones near the center. Edison continued to offer cylinders until he left the record business entirely in 1929.

technical revolutions The transition from cylinders to disks in the years before the first world war might be called the first great technical revolution in the recording industry. The second came in the mid-1920s with the introduction of electrical recording and reproduction. Although the Victor Orthophonic machines of this period were markedly better than those of the early part of the century, the inherent limitations of acoustic recording horns and reproducers were too great to permit the industry to survive on this basis. The immediate competition of radio facilitated the introduction of a technology based on electronic devices: microphones, vacuum tube amplifiers, and loudspeakers. But the new radio in the living room with its seemingly limitless supply of free music was the severest competition the phonograph had faced. This, plus the beginning of the great depression in 1929, produced years of grave crisis. Just as Edison in 1926 offered unsuccessfully a record that played for 20 minutes, so Victor (now owned by RCA) tried to improve sales in 1931 by offering an electrically recorded long-playing disk. The quality was not outstanding, and the public response was weak. What eventually brought new life to the phonograph was an improvement in the national economy and the fact that radio could not offer free music in varieties to satisfy every taste. The Victor advertising slogan of the '30s, "The music you want when you want it," stated the theme.

The repertoire of the parlor Victrola had consisted almost entirely of music that could be put on a single playing surface: operatic arias, songs, and instrumental works of four minutes duration or less. Only rarely were larger compositions attempted. With the advent of electrical recording complete symphonies, operas, and other longer works could be offered in multiple disk sets, and the widespread use of the record changer in the 1930s permitted this music to be heard with reasonable continuity. But it was clear at the close of the second world war that continued growth in recording, now faced by the prospect of competition from FM broadcasting and television, required major improvements in the quality of records.

The third revolution in the industry came

from the introduction of magnetic recording on oxide-coated tape rather than on the wax or acetate disks that had been used from the early part of the century. Tape not only permitted higher quality work, but, unlike a disk, it could be edited, thus permitting a note-perfect performance to be assembled from several takes. The principle of magnetic recording was the product of the research of a Danish investigator, Valdemar Poulsen, who established the basic technique for recording on a wire in 1898. But the potential of his device, the Telegraphone, could not be realized until the development of the vacuum tube amplifier. Magnetic recording as we know it today is the result of work in the United States and Germany in the 1940s, and the technique was first put to widespread use by the German radio networks during the second world war. After the war tape recording quickly became the new international standard for making master recordings, which, when edited, were then transferred to disks for duplication. This led immediately to the fourth revolution in the industry, which came from the U.S. Columbia Records in 1948 with the introduction of a microgroove long-playing record that turned at less than half the speed of the old shellac disks ($33\frac{1}{3}$ versus 78 RPM) and exploited the fact that a vinyl record would accept the accurate impression of a groove only a third the width of the older disks. The long-playing record, moreover, offered "high fidelity," a term the industry had been using for years but that first started to have musical validity after the war when British Decca offered its FFRR (full frequency range recording) product on shellac disks. The shellac record provided an almost ideal playing time for popular songs, and after a brief war of speeds it was replaced by the 45-RPM disk, first introduced by RCA.

Recording binaurally to reproduce the space perceptions of normal hearing was a matter of research for many years. Multiple channel recording, in which a complex sound source was divided into several elements to be reproduced in synchronization with the others, was first widely known through the Walt Disney film *Fantasia* (1940) with a nine-channel soundtrack developed by RCA to ful-

fill the requirements of conductor Stokowski. Stereophonic (or two-channel) tapes were offered in 1955, but it was not until 1958 that a stereophonic record, in which the right and left sides of the groove conveys different information, was placed in the mass market. This quickly proved to be the fifth revolution in the industry.

Efforts to produce a sixth major change by extending the number of channels from two to four were attempted in the early 1970s but did not win the acceptance of either the record producers or the general public necessary to achieve success. Emphasis returned to the issue of greater realism by minimizing noise and distortion and increasing the dynamic range of records. One way to do this was to eliminate tape mastering and return to the older technique of recording directly on disks. Another was to use a new type of tape recorder that encoded sound in binary numbers at the rate of 640,000 digits per second and used a computer to reconstruct the original wave form.

social impact Through most of Western music history emphasis in performance has been on current work. Scholars might be familiar with earlier compositions, but the general public was primarily aware of contemporary musical thought. This process began to change in the early 19th century; the public recognized the existence of a music literature and began to see the musician as one who draws on this repertoire. Today, as we take for granted that literature, drama, painting, and sculpture of every period and style are available for our study and enjoyment, we look to recordings to provide examples of every type of music since antiquity, and we look to musical scholarship to ensure that these performances will be as faithful to the originals as possible. We can, if we wish, become musically sophisticated beyond the possibility of any other generation in history, although the fullest implications of this situation are yet to be seen. Edison was searching for a telegraph that talked, but he invented something far more important in its far-reaching implications—a music manuscript that played and sang in any home without the repeated intervention of a skilled performer. Caruso could sing in millions of living rooms on Christmas morning. Thanks to recording, the influence of music and the exceptional musician has never been more widely felt in history.

Robert C. Marsh

BIBLIOGRAPHY: Frederic William Wile, *Emile Berliner: Maker of the Microphone* (1926; reprint, 1974); Frederick W. Gaisberg, *The Music Goes Round* (1942; reprint, 1977); Matthew Josephson, *Edison* (1959); Robert E. Runstein, *Modern Recording Techniques* (1974); Jerrold Northrop Moore, *A Matter of Records* (1976); Oliver Reed and Walter Welch, *From Tin Foil to Stereo,* 2nd ed. (1976); Roland Gelatt, *The Fabulous Phonograph: 1877–1977,* rev. ed. (1977).

reed instruments Wind instruments (aerophones) that sound when the player's breath or air from a wind chamber causes a reed (a thin blade of cane or metal) to vibrate, thereby setting up a sound wave in an enclosed air column (in reed pipes) or in the open air (usually free reeds).

Reed pipes have single or double reeds. Double reeds (as in the oboe) are believed to be older. They were originally tubes of cane pinched flat to form a slit whose edges vibrated in and out under the player's breath. Later two blades were tied together, or (in Europe) one was doubled back and slit. Single reeds may hit against a frame (beating reeds) as in a clarinet mouthpiece or may vibrate freely through a closely fitting frame (free reeds) as in an accordion; the term single reed usually refers to a beating reed.

Reed pipes, such as clarinets and oboes, follow the acoustical principles of pipes, the pipe length determining pitch and the shape of its bore strongly affecting timbre. An exception is a regal pipe of an organ, which is built so that the pipe acts solely as a timbre-influencing resonator; the beating reed itself determines the pitch as with free reeds.

A free reed may be cut from the material of its frame, leaving one end attached (as in Southeast Asia), or may be a separate blade attached to the frame (as in Europe). Its thickness and length determine its pitch. The simplest example is a ribbon reed—a blade of grass or bark held taut in front of the player's mouth and vibrated by breath. Its use in so-

phisticated instruments originated in ancient Southeast Asia and reached Europe in the 18th century. Because free-reed instruments cause sound vibrations in unenclosed air, they are classified as free aerophones (as opposed to pipes). But in Southeast Asia free-reed pipes are also made.

The ancient beating reed continues to be used in peasant reed pipes and hornpipes in Europe and Asia and in the bagpipe. Its use in European art music, apart from the medieval regal, dates from the late 17th century in experiments leading to the clarinet. The ancient double reed appeared in the Greek aulos and its precursors and later in the shawm and its relatives played from Mediterranean lands eastward to China. *See* BAGPIPE; BASSET HORN; BASSOON; CLARINET; CONCERTINA; ENGLISH HORN; HARMONICA; HARMONIUM; HECKELPHONE; HORNPIPE; MUSETTE; OBOE; ORGAN (tone production); REGAL; SAXOPHONE; SHAWM.

regal A small bellows-blown keyboard instrument popular in the 16th and 17th centuries. Its sound is produced by beating reeds that have either no resonators or very short ones. The reeds are placed immediately behind the keys, and the two hand-blown bellows are placed horizontally behind the reeds. In addition to reeds some regals had a Cymbal stop, presumably a very small mixture. One form of the instrument, the bible regal, can be folded when not in use and when closed resembles a large book. The regal's highly colored buzzing tone made it especially suitable for accompanying brass instruments, and in this context it is specified by Monteverdi as one of several continuo instruments in his opera *Orfeo* (1607).

A set of regal pipes is sometimes included as a stop in the organ.

Reger, (Johann Baptist Joseph) Max(imilian) (March 19, 1873–May 11, 1916) A German composer and teacher who developed the neoclassical tradition inherited from Brahms, Max Reger studied at Weiden and in 1888 visited Bayreuth, where he heard *Die Meistersinger* and *Parsifal*—but the Wagnerian influence was short-lived. From 1890 to 1893 he studied with Hugo Riemann at Sondershausen and at Wiesbaden, where he also taught piano, organ, and theory. From this period dates his friendship with Busoni and with the Leipzig organist Karl Straube, who introduced Reger's organ music. He returned to Weiden in 1898. In 1901, in spite of much opposition to his traditional methods, he established himself as a composer, pianist, and teacher in Munich. After writing many organ, piano, and chamber works, he produced in 1906 his first orchestral work, the Sinfonietta, Op. 90. The following year he was appointed professor of composition at the Leipzig Conservatory and musical director at the University of Leipzig. There he wrote many choral and orchestral works, chamber music, and songs. In 1911 he was appointed conductor of the court orchestra at Meiningen, where he wrote his *Böcklin* Suite and one of his finest works for orchestra, the Variations and Fugue on a Theme by Mozart.

In an age of bold harmonic experiments, Reger used the conventional musical language, but he developed it in a personal way. One of the last composers to infuse life into the 19th-century style, he influenced forward-looking composers of the following generation, among them Honegger and Hindemith. His organ pieces, notably his Fantasy and Fugue on B-A-C-H, and his songs, some of them dedicated to the memory of Schubert and Hugo Wolf, are best known. A Reger Society was established in Germany in 1920.

RECORDINGS: Allegro in A for two violins; Canon and Fugue; Cello Suites (3); Clarinet Quintet; Clarinet Sonata No. 3; *Comedy Overture*; *Der Einsiedler* and Requiem for chorus and orchestra; Quartets (5); Serenades (2); String Trios; Variations and Fugue on a Theme by Mozart; organ pieces; piano pieces.

Reich, Steve (b. October 3, 1936) A pupil of Berio and Milhaud and with a degree in philosophy, the U.S. composer Steve Reich expounded his theories of music in the essay "Music as a Gradual Process," which de-

Swiss regal, 17th century
courtesy, Musée Instrumental, Brussels photograph, © A.C.L., Brussels

675

scribes his music as the slow unfolding of a musical process in time. His thinking was influenced by books on music of Africa and Indonesia, although his compositions do not reflect exoticism. In 1964–65 he was a composer-performer at the San Francisco Tape Center, from which he established his own electronic music studio in New York City. Principal compositions include *Pitch Charts* (1963) for any number of any instruments; *Violin Phase* (1967) for violin, tape, or four violins; *Four Organs* (1969) for four electronic organs and maracas; *Piano Store* (1969) for a store full of pianos; and *Drumming* (1971) for tuned bongo drums, marimbas, glockenspiels, and voices.

RECORDINGS: *Drumming; Four Organs;* Music for mallet instruments, voices, and organ; *Six Pianos.*

Reiche, Gottfried (February 5, 1667–October 1734) Considered to have been one of the first instrumentalists in Bach's orchestra at Leipzig, trumpeter Gottfried Reiche probably played a high *tromba da caccia* and a *Jagdtrompete* with four coils (as shown in his portrait by E. G. Haussmann), somewhat similar to a valveless horn. In 1696 he published a volume of 24 quartets for cornet and three trumpets.

Reinecke, Carl (Heinrich Carsten) (June 23, 1824–March 10, 1910) Violinist, pianist, composer, and conductor, the German musician Carl Reinecke studied with his father and in 1843 toured Scandinavia as a pianist, becoming attached to the court in Copenhagen (1846–48). In 1851 he was appointed to the faculty of the Cologne Conservatory, followed by positions at Barmen, Breslau, and Leipzig, where he conducted the Gewandhaus Orchestra (1860–95) and taught at the conservatory (1860–1902). During this time he continued his recital tours. His compositions include five operas, an oratorio, cantatas, choral works, and chamber music. He wrote more than 40 cadenzas to standard piano concertos and numerous analyses of orchestral works and operas.

RECORDINGS: Ballade for flute and piano; Flute Concerto; Flute Sonata *(Undine);* Piano Concerto No. 1.

Fritz Reiner
courtesy, Chicago Symphony Orchestra

Reiner, Fritz (December 19, 1888–November 15, 1963) Known as a conductor's conductor, the Hungarian Fritz Reiner was a master of baton technique and was a noted teacher of that technique. Educated in his native Budapest, Reiner spent his early years in the opera houses of Budapest, Ljubljana (now in Yugoslavia), and Dresden. He was conductor of the Cincinnati Symphony (1922–31), headed the opera and orchestra departments at the Curtis Institute (1931–41), and was musical director of the Pittsburgh Symphony (1938–48), and the Chicago Symphony (from 1953), conducting at the Metropolitan Opera in the intervening years. Though born in the 19th century Reiner was a modernist from the beginning, and his repertoire was broadly based. He was noted for his small beat, his frightening personality, and his ability to achieve extreme clarity from the most complicated of scores.

Renaissance The Renaissance in music is generally understood to have spanned the period from about 1425 to 1600. As with all style periods such chronological limits are necessarily arbitrary. For techniques of the MIDDLE AGES continued to run side by side with new practices of the Renaissance until the late

15th century, while stylistic changes that fore-shadow the oncoming BAROQUE ERA began to appear as early as the 1580s—long before the creative forces inspired by Renaissance ideals were fully spent. The classical style of the Renaissance was established by the turn of the 16th century. In this style, particularly as it was applied to sacred music, several voices of equal importance arranged within a homogeneous contrapuntal or chordal texture are made to unfold their free-flowing melodies so as to produce richly sonorous harmonies. Dissonance is carefully regulated, and much attention is given to the correct accentuation and representation of the text. The classical style, however, was not shared simultaneously by all countries, for it appeared earlier in some and much later in others.

Modern writers have found it convenient to subdivide the era into a number of shorter periods. These in turn are often associated with major figures. The early Renaissance is usually dated c. 1425–90 and has been defined as the "age of Dufay" in its initial stages and as the "age of Ockeghem" in its last phase. Likewise the period 1490–1520, when the classical style was established, is generally referred to as the "age of Josquin" or the high Renaissance. The decades following Josquin's death until the end of the 16th century are frequently called the late Renaissance with the music of Palestrina, an Italian whose musical style sums up the achievements of his northern predecessors, invoked as its culmination. The period before 1550 has also been characterized as the "age of the Netherlanders" in reference to the leading role played by composers from the present-day regions of Belgium, The Netherlands, and northern France. In recent times the terms Franco-Flemish and Franco-Netherlandish have gained wide acceptance because they more accurately describe the cultural–geographical milieu that produced most of the major composers born in the 15th and early 16th centuries. *See* FLEMISH SCHOOL.

None of these designations, however, can be used to describe precisely the amalgamation of Franco-Netherlandish and Italian techniques that characterizes the classical style found in the music of the greatest figure of the high Renaissance, Josquin des Prés, whose influence was felt throughout the remainder of the era. During the late 15th century many of the leading Franco-Netherlanders made their way to Italy, where they obtained positions at courts and cathedrals in major cities throughout the peninsula. It was there that many of them, like Josquin, spent long and fruitful years. Much of their music, written for Italian patrons and preserved exclusively in manuscripts and prints of Italian origin, was naturally influenced by Italian concepts—both musical and philosophical. Clearly the cultural influence of the peninsula must be mentioned in any account of the classical style of the Renaissance, even though there were few if any Italian composers of stature who took the lead in shaping it.

The use of the terms Franco-Flemish and Franco-Netherlandish are also somewhat restrictive in describing other currents in the 16th century such as the development of independent instrumental forms and the stylistic innovations introduced by the avant-garde madrigalists. Finally it should be stressed that in the last half of the 16th century the main stream of European polyphony was represented by almost as many composers of different nationalities—the Italian Palestrina, the English Byrd, the Spanish Victoria, the Franco-Netherlandish Orlando di Lasso in Germany and Philippe de Monte in Austria, to name only the most outstanding—as there were local dialects of the pan-European musical language that had been established almost a century earlier in the Low Countries, France, and Italy by the men of the North.

printing The printing of polyphonic music, introduced at the beginning of the 16th century by Ottaviano Petrucci in Venice, was an event of far-reaching importance. It made possible the dissemination of far greater quantities of music at far less cost than ever before. Manuscripts in the form of elegantly decorated songbooks or in the large choir-book format needed by church musicians continued to be written, but it was in printed copies that most music was now circulated. Petrucci's *Odhecaton* of 1501, a collection of chansons for three and four voices, was the first of some 60 volumes of sacred and secular works, all printed in multiple impression, that he issued during the next two decades. His example was followed elsewhere in Italy and in other countries by a number of enterprising publishers. Probably the most important of them was the Parisian Pierre Attaignant, who successfully introduced the more commercially viable method of printing polyphony by single impression in the late 1520s. It was also in the early 16th century that the nucleus of the first great music library was put together in Seville by Fernando Colón, son of the discoverer of America. Later collections of importance were those of the popes in Rome, the Fuggers in Augsburg, and the Bavarian dukes in Munich.

social conditions   Hand in hand with the invention of music printing went new attitudes toward music making and performance. Changing social and economic conditions now fostered widespread practice of the art so that it was no longer the province of prince and prelate but also of a larger well-to-do class that had the leisure and the means to cultivate it. Excellent music making on an amateur level became the rule, for educated people were expected to be able to sing from part books or to play instruments. Moreover the virtuoso performer emerged as a prominent figure in society. Early in the 16th century, for example, the lutenist Francesco da Milano, hailed by his contemporaries as "il divino," was an honored guest at the Vatican and at the royal court of France. Toward the end of the 16th century, Alessandro Striggio, a nobleman in the service of the Florentine duke, did not consider it below his dignity to be recognized as a virtuoso performer on the viol, and the fame of the "three noble ladies of Ferrara," singers without peer, echoed throughout Italy's courts.

Musical patronage also became a fact to be reckoned with. Most of the princely courts maintained their own chapels of singers who performed at religious, social, and political functions, as well as their own bands of instrumentalists who played at private and public ceremonies indoors and out. Indeed there was often intense competition among the various courts as they vied with one another to procure the services of the best musicians. Cathedrals in most major cities employed chapels of professional singers who performed polyphony and plainchant at religious services and at church festivals. Schools of singing were often associated with these churches, and some of them, such as the one at Cambrai, became internationally famous as training grounds for young talented musicians.

The numbers of singers employed in the chapels at various times reflect the performance practices of the period. As might be expected, these changed from decade to decade and from place to place. Through the 1470s, for example, it was customary for Italian cathedrals to have no more than six or seven adult singers. These were often assisted by a number of choirboys. By the 1520s, however, the number of adults had increased to 12 in some chapels and to as many as 18 in others. The papal chapel, with its usual complement of 20 or more singers, stood somewhat apart from these, as did that at St. Mark's in Venice, which had two concurrent groups of singers from the 1520s onward. Throughout most of the Renaissance polyphony was performed a cappella by these chapels, although it is possible that at times the organ accompanied the singers or alternated with them in certain kinds of music. On occasion other instruments were also used. By the late 16th century, however, the unaccompanied homogeneous sounds of vocal polyphony were being replaced in many churches by those of voices and instruments, a result of the ever-increasing predilection for variety and color.

Most secular vocal music was normally performed with one person to a part, although this was not an immutable rule. As the occasion demanded an instrument or two might double the voices or even play the lower parts of a composition while the singer performed the highest part. Solo singing with instrumental accompaniment was more widespread than is often thought, as can be seen by the continuous stream of published lute songs from the time of Petrucci to that of John Dowland more than a century later.

The principal forms of Renaissance sacred vocal polyphony were masses, motets (generally biblical texts), psalm settings, Magnificats, and hymns. It is within these musical settings that the major stylistic trends leading to the development of the classical style are best observed.

compositional techniques Composers had at their disposal several compositional techniques that enabled them to create unity in larger or smaller formal structures. The cantus-firmus technique, one of the principal legacies of the medieval period, utilized a preexistent melody, either sacred or secular, as the basis for a new piece. The borrowed melody was often, though not always, presented in one part in longer notes, around which the other parts wove lively contrapuntal lines, sometimes based on the borrowed melody itself. That composers had recourse to the technique throughout the Renaissance is illustrated by the masses written over the course of a century by such figures as Dufay, Josquin, and Palestrina on the popular *L'homme armé* tune. *See* CANTUS FIRMUS.

The two compositional techniques that in the late 15th century began to supersede cantus firmus in popularity were those known as PARAPHRASE and PARODY. In the former the phrases of a preexistent melody became part and parcel of the entire musical fabric, often supplying material for various imitations or appearing in decorated form in various voices. Josquin's mass on the *Pange lingua* hymn tune is one of the most inspired examples of the use of the technique. Parody differs notably from cantus-firmus and paraphrase techniques in that all parts of a previously composed polyphonic work are employed in the formation of a new one. Thus a single voice or the complete musical complex may be drawn upon and quoted in whole or in part and interspersed with sections in which the composer develops some of the preexistent materials or writes passages of entirely new music. Excellent examples of the technique in its various forms a group of masses composed by Adriaan Willaert, Morales, Palestrina, and de Monte, all of which are based on Josquin's motet *Benedicta es, coelorum regina,* itself a paraphrase piece based on a plainchant melody of the same name.

Dufay and Ockeghem The classical style of the Renaissance was preceded in the 15th century by a number of different styles and techniques that a glance at the music of Guillaume Dufay and Jean d'Ockeghem will suffice to illustrate. Dufay's works in particular reveal the dichotomy between medieval practices and the new musical concepts of the Renaissance, many of which he himself formulated. Much of his music is constructed according to the discant–tenor technique, an outgrowth of the medieval method of composing each voice of a polyphonic composition successively. In this technique the discant (top) and tenor parts are written first. To the framework they create are added one or more voices that enrich the harmonies and vary the rhythms. The result is a texture of contrasting parts dominated by the treble voice, which itself sometimes was an elaboration of a preexistent melody. In some of his later works Dufay makes sporadic use of imitation. It is clear that by now he was adopting the technique of simultaneous composition; that is, writing all of the parts at the same time. This technique, first described by the early 16th-century theorist Pietro Aron, helps create the more homogeneous and smoother texture that was preferred and brought to perfection by later composers.

In many of his large-scale works written before the mid-15th century, Dufay uses the old isorhythmic technique of organizing his cantus firmus. In his later works, however, he puts the cantus firmus to new use by systematically exploiting it—in longer or shorter note values, in its entirety or in segments—as a means of giving unity, balance, and coherence to a large cyclic structure such as the ordinary of the mass. In his mature style Dufay also moves the cantus firmus to the tenor voice in a four-part texture and composes below it a freely moving bass line that is now made to give direction to the harmony.

Harmonically Dufay's music looks forward as well. He integrated what has been called the "contenance angloise" into his own style. This sound-ideal, inherited from Dunstable and other English composers of the early 15th century, makes use of the interval of a third and sometimes triads and chords of the sixth, thus producing a fuller, richer sound than was previously known in continental music. After this time the triad—in root position and in first inversion—continued to be used more and more as the basis for Renaissance harmony, although changing concepts about how and where these chords should progress, as well as the introduction of chromaticism on a wide scale after 1540, considerably altered the sounds so effectively introduced by Dufay almost a century earlier.

The art of writing counterpoint and treating dissonance was also refined throughout the Renaissance. It is a long road indeed from the free dissonance treatment found in the music of Dufay, and even in that of Josquin, to the highly codified system for preparing and resolving dissonances at the time of Palestrina. Nevertheless the roots of Renaissance counterpoint are firmly embedded in Dufay's mature works, particularly those in which the new technique of voices imitating other voices makes its appearance.

Much of Ockeghem's sacred music was written during Dufay's mature years. In many ways, however, it seems to be a throwback to earlier times. For although Ockeghem makes occasional use of new techniques such as parody and imitation, his works are constructed in a seemingly endless flow of polyphony whose individual melodic lines spin out in a manner reminiscent of plainchant. His harmonies too are firmly rooted in the modes of the chant and lack the more modern tonal bias noticeable in the works of Dufay's mature style. Ockeghem is renowned for his complete mastery of the intricacies of Franco-Netherlandish polyphony. His skill is perhaps best revealed in his *Missa prolationum* in which a series of double canons is presented in the several movements at different melodic intervals and in various combinations of time signatures.

Paralleling these developments in the North was the appearance in Italy of the secular FROTTOLA style. This style, which is perhaps an outgrowth of the unwritten musical practices of Italian poet-improvisers of the later 15th century, emphasizes the homophonic, or chordal, concept of music rather than the linear one favored by the Franco-Netherlanders. Used primarily for settings of poetry known collectively as frottole, the Italian style features a clearly phrased, tuneful upper voice supported by a chordal or slightly animated chordal texture of similar rhythms. The Italian predilection for harmonic clarity and tonal direction is reflected in the simple chord progressions that generally stress the primary tones of the mode. This is the style encountered by the Franco-Netherlanders who began arriving in Italy toward the end of the 15th century. Its impact upon them opened a new chapter in the history of European music.

Josquin The classical style of the Renaissance, which appeared in definitive form near the end of the 15th century, was the creation of one of the most gifted generations of composers known to European music. These included, to name only the most outstanding, Jakob Obrecht, Heinrich Isaac, Johannes Martini, Alexander Agricola, Loyset Compère, Pierre de La Rue, and the incomparable Josquin des Prés. All of them, but particularly Josquin, took the foundations laid by Dufay and Ockeghem and built upon them a massive stylistic edifice that was to dominate music, especially sacred music, until the early 17th century.

Josquin's style was the product of two cultures—of the North where he was born and trained and to which he later returned, and of the South where he reached artistic maturity and spent many of the most productive years of his life. It is small wonder that the techniques and styles of the two regions exist side by side in his music and that he had recourse to them throughout his long career. In many of his works the contrapuntal artifices of the Franco-Netherlanders and the chordal, harmonically controlled style of the Italians are fused into a rich and expressive language that has as its primary goal the perfect union of words and music.

At the heart of Josquin's style is the technique of imitation or the "point" of imitation, as the English theorist Morley called it in his *Plaine and Easie Introduction to Practicall Musicke* of 1597. In this technique each of the parts has an equal share in stating and exploiting the principal melodic material. One voice presents a melody at the beginning of a line, a phrase, or sometimes even a single word of the text. As each of the voices enters successively, it repeats the melody (or a portion of its opening) at a pitch and interval of time determined by the composer, thus creating the point of imitation. The texture may be dense or airy, depending upon the frequency with which the various parts enter and upon whether or not all parts sing continuously throughout a musical phrase.

During the course of a piece the points, each with a new melody, follow one another, sometimes overlapping and sometimes not. The process thus creates an evolving musical form based on the length, placement, and arrangement of the points. In any work further variety is obtained by the various ways in which the composer applies the imitative technique, by dropping voices from the overall texture and allowing vocal duets or trios to alternate with one another, and by interspersing the imitative sections with others in chordal style or in free counterpoint. This was the legacy bequeathed by Josquin and his contemporaries to succeeding generations. Its almost universal adoption throughout the remainder of the 16th century in both vocal and instrumental music—sacred and secular—gives a unity to the music of the period that transcends formal considerations and national boundaries.

Palestrina The twilight of the Renaissance is best reflected in the music of Giovanni Pierluigi, who is known by the name of his birthplace—Palestrina—which he added to his surname. Of the post-Josquin composers— a group that includes Nicolas Gombert, Jacob Arcadelt, Clemens non Papa, Adriaan Willaert, Luca Marenzio, and Tomás Luis de Victoria—Palestrina has left a repertoire of sacred works that most clearly exemplifies the stylistic ideals sought by Pope Marcellus in 1555 and seconded by the Council of Trent in 1563. According to notes of the papal secretary, Marcellus was concerned that "the Passion and Death of the Saviour . . . be sung in a suitable manner, with properly modulated voices . . . so that everything could be both heard and understood properly."

Compared to the music of Josquin, Palestrina's scores represent a retrenchment. In their use of dissonance, in the scope of their tonality, and in their melodic fancies, they are distinctly more conservative. Furthermore the balance between line and harmony is less perfectly realized than in Josquin's finest works, where structure and sonority are inseparable concepts. Yet Palestrina's distillation of contemporary techniques was unequaled in its purity, and his application of polyphony to music for the church was unrivaled by the music of his colleagues. Palestrina's scores were composed in inspired conformity to rules that regulated dissonance and insured a smooth sense of line through a regular flow of accent and stress. He was uninterested in a self-conscious chromaticism that would disrupt the clear comprehension of his texts, and he had use for neither the excessively polyphonic style of Gombert nor the quasi-dramatic manner of Willaert and other "moderns." Though admittedly he broke no new ground, Palestrina achieved a clarity and a sense of repose that have become an aural emblem for an era.

Reformation With the Reformation new forms of music reflecting the ideals of Luther, Calvin, and their followers came into being. Particularly important from the point of view of congregational. participation were the growth and development of the German CHORALE and the French metrical psalm. Luther himself wrote texts for some of the earliest chorale tunes, many of which were adaptations—known as *contrafacta*—of Catholic chants, German religious songs, and popular secular melodies. Almost from the beginning these chorales, sung in unison by the congregation, were regarded by Protestant composers as a repository of melodies to be treated as canti firmi or paraphrased—much in the same way that Catholic composers used the traditional plainchant in masses and motets. The first and one of the most celebrated collections of polyphony issued for use in the new church was Johann Walther's *Geystliche Gesangk Buchleyn* of 1524, which contains elaborate contrapuntal as well as simple homophonic settings of some of the earliest chorales.

In Geneva under Calvin's guidance the singing of rhymed metrical psalms in French translation was established as a form of popular piety. These were eventually collected into the *Genevan* Psalter of 1562, which contained melodies that were both derived from secular sources and composed expressly by Loys Bourgeois, who also furnished some of them with simple chordal settings. In France later in the 16th century, composers such as Claude Goudimel and Claude Le Jeune made effective use of many of these melodies in motet-like works and in simple homophonic arrange-ments. The *Genevan* Psalter also served as a model for similar collections in other languages, especially the English and Scottish psalters of 1562–64. Its influence furthermore is traceable as late as Henry Ainsworth's Amsterdam psalter of 1612, a collection that accompanied the Pilgrims to New England and remained in use long after the publication of the first American psalter, the *Bay Psalm Book* of 1640. *See also* PSALMODY.

The Reformation in England brought about the creation of a large body of sacred music in the English language, although some composers, notably Byrd, also composed to Latin texts. The principal forms evolved by the new Anglican church were the service and the anthem. The service is designated as either great or short depending upon whether it is composed in elaborate contrapuntal or in simple chordal style. There are two types of anthems. The full anthem is an unaccompanied imitative work for chorus alone, while the verse anthem is an extended work for soloists and instruments as well as chorus. Both reflect parallel developments in the Catholic motet of the later 16th century.

chanson   Secular vocal polyphony was dominated by the chanson and the madrigal, the former inherited from the Middle Ages, the latter a creation of the 16th century. Other forms such as the lied in Germany, the *villancico* in Spain, and the part song in England were important because of their contributions to the rise of national styles in those countries. But it was in the chanson and madrigal that the principal stylistic traits of Renaissance secular music were most fully displayed. The CHANSON passed through several phases during the period. Those of Dufay and Gilles Binchois are cast in fixed forms in which the music exactly mirrors the complicated repetition schemes of poems such as the rondeau, the virelai, and the ballade. Typically for three voices, these works are in a treble-dominated style that features long, flowing melodic lines arranged in clearly articulated phrases. In some of Dufay's later chansons imitation is used with telling effect, a trend that is noticeable also in the works of his immediate successors.

By Josquin's time the chanson was undergo-ing significant changes, for the older fixed forms were being replaced by shorter poems that lent themselves to a variety of formal and musical treatments. Some of the formally concise pieces are arrangements of popular songs, some are intricate structures based on canon and other contrapuntal devices, and some are simple homophonic settings. After Josquin the chanson developed along two distinct paths. The Netherlands chanson, highly imitative and somewhat dense in texture, was cultivated principally by Thomas Crequillon, Jacobus Clemens non Papa, and Nicolas Gombert, all of whom were celebrated for their masses and motets to which their chansons, save for differences of detail, often bear a close resemblance. In contrast the Parisian chanson is characterized by markedly rhythmic melodies, generally homophonic textures, and simple repetition schemes. Examples of these charming miniature pieces, which are typically represented in the works of Claudin de Sermisy and Clément Janequin, began appearing in the late 1520s. Within a few decades the form attained a European vogue that was matched by few other kinds of music. The final synthesis of the Renaissance chanson occurred later in the 16th century in the works of Orlando di Lasso. In his more than 150 chansons the styles and techniques of his predecessors are absorbed and refined within musical settings that are as formally varied as are the many different kinds of poems he favored.

madrigal   The MADRIGAL was a relative latecomer to Renaissance music, for examples of the genre began appearing only in the 1520s; it was not until 1530 that a volume using the word madrigal in its title was printed. A measure of the popularity of the form, however, is evident in the more than 3,000 volumes of madrigals published within a century of its first appearance. Musically the madrigal is descended from the harmonically conceived frottola to which has been added the contrapuntal flexibility of Franco-Netherlandish polyphony. Poetically the typical madrigal consists of an indeterminate number of seven- and eleven-syllable lines arranged in a rhyme scheme of the poet's choice. This freedom is reflected in the musical setting, which emphasizes the mood and meaning of individual words and phrases of the text rather than its formal structure. Accordingly homophonic and imitative textures, free flowing rhythms and strongly metrical patterns, syllabic declamation and melismatic melodies are all utilized by the composer in his efforts to realize musically the thoughts and images of the text.

The earliest madrigal composers include the Italians Bernardo Pisano and Costanzo Festa and the Franco-Netherlanders Philippe Verdelot, Adriaan Willaert, and the renowned Jacob Arcadelt, whose first book of madrigals alone was reprinted more than 50 times after its initial appearance in 1537. Another Franco-Netherlander, Cipriano de Rore, was the first to use chromatic harmony as a means of further enhancing the text. By the late 16th century the madrigal had become established as the dominant form of secular music in Italy and indeed in all of Europe, for it was within this genre that the avant-garde composers Giaches de Wert, Luzzasco Luzzaschi, Luca Marenzio, Carlo Gesualdo, and Monteverdi made their boldest harmonic experiments and developed new modes of dissonance treatment.

Italian madrigals had circulated in England for some time before the publication in 1588 of *Musica Transalpina,* a collection containing works in English translation by celebrated composers such as Marenzio. Within a few years native musicians, principally Morley and then Thomas Weelkes and John Wilbye, succeeded in creating a form that was thoroughly English in content, though based on Italian models, and that quickly became assimilated into Elizabethan and Jacobean musical culture. The ballett (*see* BALLETTO), with its familiar "fa-las," is another imported Italian form that gained widespread popularity in England at this time.

instrumental style It was during the Renaissance that instrumental music freed itself of its dependence upon vocal models and emerged as a genre in its own right. Hand in hand with this phenomenon went the growth of idiomatic instrumental styles and the creation of new instrumental forms. Many works continued to be composed that were "apt for voices or viols," as the Elizabethans put it, but the tendency was overwhelmingly toward the development of music that re-

flected the capabilities of the performer and the technical possibilities of the instrument.

As in the case with vocal music, there was no sharp break with the medieval past. Rather there was an expansion of traditional practices as well as the introduction of new ones, for instrumental music now began to assume a larger role in secular society and in the church. Although instrumental music was composed and performed throughout Europe, it was in Italy (to judge from the number of extant sources and the contributions of a large group of outstanding composers) that it was most widely cultivated and made its most significant advances. Among the best known of these composers are the organists Marcantonio and Girolamo Cavazzoni, Andrea and Giovanni Gabrieli, and Claudio Merulo and the lutenists Francesco da Milano, Vincenzo Galilei, and Antonio Terzi. Composers of international reputation from other lands included the German and Spanish organists Paul von Hofhaimer and Cabezón, the Hungarian and English lutenists Valentin Bakfark and John Dowland, and the famous triumvirate of English keyboard masters Byrd, John Bull, and Gibbons.

Interest in instrumental music is reflected in the many instruction books that began to appear with increasing regularity in the 16th century. Silvestro Ganassi's instruction manuals for flute (1535) and viol (1542) were among the most influential as was Adrian Le Roy's lute method, originally published in French in 1557. This was translated into English and printed in London less than a decade later. Books that taught improvisation and ornamentation and that described instruments were also published in various languages. By far the most comprehensive of the latter is Praetorius' *Syntagma Musicum* (1618), which contains detailed illustrations of the many instruments in use throughout the period. In addition to the lute (the Renaissance instrument par excellence), the harp, and various kinds of keyboard instruments, these include wind, brass, and stringed instruments such as the recorder, shawm, sackbut, crumhorn, cornett, and viola da gamba—many of which were constructed in sets or families of different ranges called consorts or chests.

The principal types of Renaissance instrumental music include pieces based on preexistent materials, independent forms, and various kinds of dances. Transcriptions of polyphonic vocal works were by far the most popular of the pieces based on preexistent materials. Prevalent among these are the arrangements, or intabulations as they were called, of chansons for lute and keyboard. Their continued cultivation eventually led to the creation in the later 16th century of an independent form, the canzona, which retains several features of its original vocal prototype. Cantus-firmus and paraphrase settings of plainchant melodies form the basis of a good deal of liturgical organ music, while much of the literature for lute and keyboard comprises sets of variations on well-known secular tunes or bass patterns such as the *romanesca* and the *passamezzo antico*.

Among the independent forms are preludes, preambles, intonations, toccatas, ricercares, and canzonas. They are usually abstract in content, freely structured, and characterized by differences in texture, length, and mood. Preludes, preambles, intonations, and toccatas are all improvisatory-like pieces. The first three, however, are relatively simple in structure and content and shorter than the toccata, which contrasts sections of brilliant passage work with contemplative or restrained ones in imitation and chordal style. The imitative RICERCARE, which is often likened to the vocal motet, generally has a continuous structure. It is more serious in mood than the metrically varied, sectionalized CANZONA, although both forms sometimes exchange their most obvious features.

Dances such as the *basse danse*, pavane, galliard, branle, *allemande*, and courante appear individually, in related pairs, and in small suites. Most share simple binary or ternary structures and are distinguished from one another by their use of characteristic rhythms and meters. Many dances are independently conceived, while others are based on well-known melodies and bass patterns that are in effect comparable to sets of variations. As the Renaissance ran its course a few dances, notably the pavane and the galliard, became stylized and began to pass from the realm of practical music into that of the abstract instrumental piece. By that time, however, the ideals of a cappella music, of homogeneous sounds, and of free flowing polyphony were also being superseded by the newer practices and styles that heralded the oncoming Baroque.

Frank A. D'Accone

BIBLIOGRAPHY: Manfred F. Bukofzer, *Studies in Medieval and Renaissance Music* (1950; reprint, 1964); Gustave Reese, *Music in the Renaissance*, rev. ed. (1959); Robert Stevenson, *Spanish Music in the Age of Columbus* (1960) and *Spanish Cathedral Music in the Golden Age* (1961; reprint, 1976); Anselm Hughes and Gerald Abraham, eds., *Ars Nova and the Renaissance 1300–1540* (1960), Vol. 3 of *The New Oxford History of Music;* Friedrich Blume, *Renaissance and Baroque Music* (1967); Peter Le Huray, *Music and the Reformation in England, 1549–1660* (1967); Howard Mayer Brown, *Embellishing Sixteenth-Century Music* (1976) and *Music in the Renaissance* (1976); Edward E. Lowinsky and Bonnie J. Blackburn, eds., *Josquin Des Prez* (1977).

repeat   The literal repetition of any segment of a composition. Rather than writing out the segment note for note, composers bracket the portion of the piece to be repeated with the signs ⸬ ‖ In addition, for first movements written in sonata form, they frequently provide first and second endings, the former to be played when returning to the beginning of the exposition, the latter when proceeding to the development.

Although repetition of some sort can be found in virtually all compositions, systematic repeats in Western music assumed a special significance in the Classical era; *i.e.,* the age in which sonata form prevailed. In the opening movements of symphonies or in sonatas per se, it became customary for the initial exposition section to be repeated. While this practice would grow to be merely conventional, it was of prime structural importance for many composers, including Mozart, Haydn, and Beethoven.

Exposition repeats served both to anchor a work's tonality and to provide a foil against which the harmonic motion and thematic transformations of the development could be displayed. In Beethoven's Piano Sonata, Op. 31, No. 3, for example, the two measures before the repeat sign provide either a smooth transition from the tonality of B-flat back to the start of the piece or an equally smooth entrance, by way of an enharmonic reinterpretation of the uppermost voice, to the harmonic activities of the development.

In many first movements of Haydn's symphonies, the exposition repeat seems necessary to provide the proportional weight and stability to balance the harmonic excursions of the development section. In Symphony No. 68, for example, the cadence on F at the repeat sign leads naturally back to the B-flat opening of the piece when the exposition is repeated, and it also provides a well-defined point of departure for the development, which begins in contrast by abruptly dropping down a third to a dominant harmony built on D.

One of the few examples in Classical symphonic literature of a first movement without repeats is provided by Mozart in his *Haffner* Symphony. Although repeat signs were at one point written in the manuscript, and are still clear in the facsimile, the composer eventually crossed them out. It is likely that he did this because the monothematic nature of the first movement—no new thematic material is introduced or exploited in the development—neither justifies nor requires an exposition to be fortified with a repeat. Repeats in the sonata and symphonic repertoire of the Classical period are also found with great frequency in variation movements and in both parts of minuet–trio movements. They are found less regularly at the ends of finales, and in practice this repetition is but rarely observed.

Requiem: *see* MASS (requiem).

Respighi, Ottorino (July 9, 1879–April 18, 1936)   The Italian composer Ottorino Respighi was born at Bologna and studied at the Liceo of Bologna and later with Rimsky-Korsakov in St. Petersburg and Max Bruch in Berlin. From his foreign masters Respighi acquired a command of orchestral color and an interest in orchestral composition. In 1913 he was appointed professor of composition at the Sta. Cecilia Academy in Rome (director, 1924–26).

Respighi had a talent for colorful descriptive music of a lyrical character illustrated in the series of suites *Fountains of Rome*

(1917), *Pines of Rome* (1924), *Vetrate di chiesa* (1927), and *Trittico botticelliano* (1927), the last for chamber orchestra. He was also drawn to old Italian music, which he arranged with skill and taste in three sets of Ancient Airs and Dances. One of his most popular scores was his arrangement of pieces by Rossini, *La Boutique fantasque,* produced by Diaghilev's Russian Ballet in London (1919). In opera Respighi had less success outside his own country. His best works for the theater were a comic opera *Belfagor* (Milan, 1923) and *La fiamma* (Rome, 1934), which transfers the gloomy Norwegian tragedy of H. Wiers Jenssen (known to English-speaking audiences in John Masefield's version as *The Witch*) to Byzantine Ravenna with brilliant effect. In a different, more subdued vein are the "mystery" *Maria Egiziaca* (1932) and *Lucrezia* (completed by his wife, 1937), the latter showing Respighi's interest in the dramatic recitative of Monteverdi, whose *Orfeo* he freely transcribed for La Scala in 1935. His wife and pupil, Elsa Olivieri-Sangiacomo Respighi, was a singer and composer of operas, choral and symphonic works, and songs.

RECORDINGS: Ancient Airs and Dances (3 sets); Overture to *Belfagor; La Boutique fantasque; Brazilian Impressions; Feste romane; Fountains of Rome; Pines of Rome; Rossiniana; Trittico botticelliano; Gli uccelli; Vetrate di chiesa;* Violin Sonata in b minor.

responsorial singing   The alternation of one or more soloists with a chorus. Responsorial singing of the psalms was practiced in ancient Hebrew and early Christian liturgies and became part of plainchant tradition in the Western church (*see* RESPONSORY). It is also found in many folk music cultures; *e.g.,* American Indian, African, and Afro-American. One example from the rural United States is the lining out of hymns: a leader sings a hymn line that is repeated by the congregation. *Compare* ANTIPHONAL SINGING.

responsory   A plainchant melody and text originally sung responsorially; *i.e.,* by alternating choir and soloist or soloists. Responsorial singing of the psalms was adopted into early Christian worship from Jewish liturgical practice. Most frequently the congregation sang a short refrain, such as amen or alleluia, between psalm verses sung by a cantor. As medieval plainchant developed more elaborate refrains (R) were sung by a choir alternating with soloists singing psalm verses (V), producing a musical form R V$_1$ R V$_2$. . .R. The responsory, or refrain, was frequently abbreviated on its repetition. Its text usually related to the meaning of the feast day or the content of the psalm. Only a few such chants survive in this long form, now normally curtailed.

The main places in which responsorial chants occur are in the canonical hours, or divine office, and in the alleluia and gradual of the mass. In most cases the basic pattern is R V R, with the V section being one or a few psalm verses. In the gradual the final refrain, or responsory, is usually omitted, making the form R V. In the earliest polyphony the solo sections of responsorial chants were generally set polyphonically and alternated with the original chant of the choral sections. By the 16th century the great responsories *(responsoria prolixa)* were often composed as responsory motets, with the pattern R in the *prima pars* and V followed by an abbreviated R in the *secunda pars.*

resultant tone: *see* COMBINATION TONE.

Resurrection Symphony: *see* MAHLER (first period).

Reubke, Julius (March 23, 1834–June 3, 1858)   A favorite pupil of Liszt, the German pianist and composer Julius Reubke wrote a sonata and other pieces for piano, some songs, and a monumental Sonata on the 94th Psalm for organ, on which his reputation rests. Much influenced by Liszt, the piece is remarkable from one so young. It is important in the history of the organ as an early example of a work built on a program—a single movement on nine verses of the psalm text.

RECORDINGS: Sonata on the 94th Psalm.

Revueltas, Silvestre (December 31, 1899–October 5, 1940)   Primarily self-taught as a composer, the Mexican musician Silvestre Revueltas studied violin and conducting in Mexico and in the United States. In 1928 Carlos Chávez, with whom he had played chamber music, appointed him assistant conductor of the Orquesta Sinfónica de México that Chávez

had founded. Revueltas remained in that position until 1935, conducting and writing program notes for the orchestra and teaching at the National Conservatory in Mexico City. His early composition is Impressionist, with reliance on folk elements and especially on traditional Indian musical rhythms (*Sensemayá*, 1938, on an Indian snake-killing song). In 1930 *(Esquinas)* he began exploring atonality and tone clusters. He wrote three quartets (1930–32), music for voice and piano, seven film scores (a symphonic suite was arranged from *Redes*, 1935), and an incomplete ballet, *La coronela* (1939; finished by Blas Galindo).

RECORDINGS: Allegro for piano; *Redes; Sensemayá;* Two Little Serious Pieces for winds; *Ventanas* for orchestra.

Rhapsody in Blue: *see* GERSHWIN; GLISSANDO; POPULAR MUSIC (the 20th century).

Rheinberger, Joseph (Gabriel von) (March 17, 1839–November 25, 1901)   A German composer and teacher whose organ sonatas are among the finest 19th-century works for that instrument, Joseph Rheinberger was born at Vaduz, Liechtenstein, and studied organ in his native town, becoming organist at the parish church when only seven years old. He later studied at Feldkirch and Munich and in 1867 became professor of organ and composition at the Munich Conservatory. Among his pupils in composition were Engelbert Humperdinck, Ermanno Wolf-Ferrari, Wilhelm Furtwängler, and the U.S. composers George Whitefield Chadwick and Horatio Parker. In addition to 20 organ sonatas, Rheinberger wrote concertos (two for organ and one for piano), four operas, and much church and chamber music. He received a title of nobility in 1894.

RECORDINGS: Organ Concertos (2); Piano Concerto; *Romantic* Sonata for piano; organ pieces.

Rheingold, Das: *see* LEITMOTIV; ROMANTIC PERIOD (Wagnerian development); WAGNER (life) and (development).

Rhenish Symphony (Third): *see* SCHUMANN, ROBERT (last years).

rhythm   In a general sense, an ordered alternation of contrasting elements. The problem of rhythm is by no means specific to music and language; there are the rhythms of nature and of work, and the term is used in a rather metaphorical sense of painting, sculpture, and architecture. The word is derived from the Greek *rhythmos,* "measured motion."

Attempts to define rhythm in music and poetry have produced much disagreement, partly because rhythm has often been identified with one or more of its constituent but not wholly separate elements such as accent, meter, and tempo. As in the closely related subjects of verse and meter, opinions differ widely on the nature and movement of rhythm. Theories requiring periodicity as the *sine qua non* of rhythm are opposed by theories that include nonrecurrent configurations of movement as in prose or plainchant.

Unlike a painting or a piece of sculpture, which are compositions in space, a musical work is a composition dependent on time. Rhythm is music's pattern in time. Whatever other elements a piece of music may or may not have (*e.g.,* patterns in pitch or timbre), rhythm is the one indispensable element of all music. For instance, rhythm can exist without melody, as in the drumbeats of primitive music, but melody cannot exist without rhythm. In music that has both harmony and melody, the rhythmic structure cannot be wholly separated from the harmonic and melodic structures, and each molds the other to an appreciable extent. Plato's observation that rhythm is "an order of movement" *(kinesis taxis)* provides a convenient starting point for an analysis of rhythm. The first task is to discover the various elements of this order.

beat   The unit division of musical time is called a beat. Just as we are aware of the body's steady pulse, or heartbeat, so in composing, performing, or listening to music we are instinctively aware of a periodic succession of beats. Whether each beat is sounded separately or not, its constant underlying presence is felt.

tempo   The pace of the fundamental beat is called tempo (Italian, "time"). The expressions slow tempo and quick tempo suggest the existence of a normal tempo; *i.e.,* a tempo built on a pulse of 60 to 80 beats per minute—a range comparable with that of the heartbeat

(72 per minute) or a natural walking pace (76 to 80 paces per minute). The tempo as a given number of beats to the minute can be determined by a device called the METRONOME. A piece of music in which the beat runs at 64 to the minute may carry an indication at the opening of the score, ♩ = 64, together with a less precise but more suggestive verbal indication such as andante moderato. In practice the slow and fast extremes of tempo are built on pulses of 32 and 128 beats to the minute; *i.e.,* half of and double the normal 64. Modern metronomes extend to 208 beats per minute, but such beats are felt to be sub-beats of longer units in a slower tempo. The tempo of a piece of music indicated by a composer is, however, neither absolute nor final. In performance it is likely to vary according to the performer's interpretative ideas or to such considerations as the size and reverberation of the hall, the size of the ensemble, and to a lesser extent the sonority of the instruments. A change of tempo within such limits does not affect the rhythmic structure of a work.

The tempo of a work is never inflexibly mathematical. It is impossible to adhere in a musical manner to the metronomic beat for any length of time. In a loosely knit passage a tautening of tempo may be required; in a crowded passage a slackening may be needed. Such modifications of tempo, known as tempo rubato ("robbed time,") are part of the music's character. Rubato needs the framework of an inflexible beat from which it can depart and to which it must return. True rubato never passes the point where the exact basis can no longer be perceived through the inexact. Moreover it cannot alter the rhythmic organization of the work; it is an essential part of it. Rubato, being essentially a matter of instinct, is rarely written as a direction in musical scores. Chopin, however, uses the term in his Mazurka, Op. 24, No. 2.

time-measure   Music is not built on steady, unemphasized beats. The mind seeks some organizing principle; if a grouping of sounds is not objectively present, it imposes one of its own. Experiments show that regular and identical sounds are instinctively grouped by the mind into twos and threes with a stress on every second or third beat. From a monotonous series the mind thus creates a regular succession of strong and weak beats.

In music such grouping is achieved by actual stress, or periodically making one note stronger than the others (dynamic accent); or by duration, or periodically marking one note longer (agogic accent). When the accent occurs at regular intervals, the beats fall into natural time-measures. Though in European music the concept of time-measures reaches back to a remote age, only since the 15th century have they been indicated by means of bar lines.

The length of each beat in a measure may be a unit of short or long duration. The time-measure is indicated at the opening of a piece by a TIME SIGNATURE; *e.g.*, $\frac{2}{4}$, $\frac{4}{8}$, $\frac{3}{4}$, $\frac{6}{8}$. The lower numeral (always a multiple of two) indicates the time unit of the beat; the upper numeral, the number of beats in a measure.

Measures, or bars, of music are part of a larger design known as a PERIOD. The period most commonly found in classical music is of four measures. Periods of three or six measures, though found in the songs of the troubadours and trouvères, are less frequent in later European music. Five-measure periods are still rarer, though Brahms uses a five-measure theme, and certain of Purcell's grounds, *e.g.*, the Chaconne in g minor, are based on a five-measure period. Some 20th-century composers use a recurrent cycle of measures with different time signatures.

The instinct for dynamic accent in music is closely associated with the exertions of the body; for example, the rhythms of music have been much influenced through folk music by occupational movements such as hauling on a rope or rocking a cradle, which are reflected as strong dynamic accents. In art music the influence of the dance has been paramount, and for this reason the types of musical instrument traditionally associated with the dance— *i.e.*, the drum and other percussion instruments—have had an important place in music in most parts of the world. In Europe the cultivation of musical dance forms in the Renaissance has left an important heritage from the keyboard music of the 16th century to the suites of Bach. Perhaps the most popular and influential dance of all has been the minuet, which originated as a French rustic dance; numerous examples are to be found in classical music.

meter   The combinations of long (—) and short (◡) syllables are known in prosody as feet. The system of notating the musical equivalents of feet is derived from the application of prosody to music. For European music the foundations were laid in ancient Greece, where classical music and poetry were regarded as parts of a single art (*see* GREEK MUSIC, ANCIENT). These principles were taken over by the Romans and were transmitted by way of Latin poetry to medieval Europe.

Until the 12th century church music was virtually limited to unadorned PLAINCHANT. The early polyphonic composers found that polyphony required a rhythmical organization to keep the parts together, and for this purpose RHYTHMIC MODES were adopted.

Compared with a hypothetical flow of beats equal in stress, meter adds significance to what was merely a forward flow in time—though the continuation of a metrical pattern may itself become monotonous. Thus meter, though rhythmic by comparison with pulse, is not the whole of rhythm.

Theoretically meter appears to be without dynamic accent, and certainly much polyphonic music of a later period, such as the masses of Palestrina, has an almost stressless flow. Yet despite the absence of strong and weak accents, the rhythmical organization of these works is subtle. At a later period meter and time-measure cannot be wholly separated. In their purest forms they may be extremes, but in music predominantly of one type the other element is rarely wholly absent.

phrase   Tempo, time-measure, and meter may be regarded as the essential means of assessing music's flow in time. These form the straight line of time. But rhythm needs also the curves of time. Curves are achieved not only by the use of rubato, cross-accent, and other means but also by the use of the phrase. Phrases may coincide with periods but more often go across them because of the need to convey the shape and sense of the words or for the observance of breath, whether this breath is actually taken or not. In vocal music this often means shortening the last word—

and therefore the last note—of a phrase and taking an actual breath as at a comma or semicolon in speech. But asymmetrical phrases are not confined to vocal music; instrumental music often displays much ingenuity in their use. Phrasing, however, may be entirely symmetrical; and sometimes, especially in very simple music, it may correspond exactly to the framework of the period.

In broad terms the mathematical framework of music—*i.e.* its time—is comprised of tempo, time-measure and period, and meter; and its rhythmical life hangs on rubato, musical motif (which may already include cross-accent), and metrical variation, as well as on asymmetry and balance of phrase. Whereas the former are more or less mechanical factors, measured and rational, the latter are organically inspired and, numerically speaking, irrational—the very life of the music itself.

word accent   Rhythm, therefore, is not any one of these rational or formal features, nor is it comprised solely of a combination of these factors. Yet rhythm requires the background of a rational framework in order that it may be fully perceived. But this framework need not embrace all the rational factors here described. Plainchant, as it is known in modern times, makes no use at all of measure or of regular meter; yet it is at the same time supremely rhythmical in conception. Whereas so much music has for its framework a regular repetition of underlying accent, whether dynamic or agogic, the framework of plainchant is irregular (non-metrical). While omitting meter, it has developed other factors in greater degree. Its rhythm belongs to the Latin tongue and springs from the accentuation of each word and the dynamic quality already inherent in the grouping of the words.

tonal accent   Although music's structure in time has been examined separately from its structure in tone, no such separation is really possible. Melody and rhythm are intimately connected in the rhythmitonal structure of music. A periodic leap, for instance, in an otherwise conjunct movement in a melody becomes a rhythmical factor, an accent by tone, or tonal accent—the equivalent of the tonic accent in poetry. Moreover various styles of music tend to standardize their melodic cadences and with them their time divisions. Thus a typical cadence of plainchant prolongs the value of the penultimate note.

harmonic rhythm   In music employing harmony the rhythmic structure is inseparable from harmonic considerations. The time pattern controlling the change of harmonies is called harmonic rhythm. In 17th- and 18th-century music harmony tends to limit rhythmic subtleties and flexibility of the melodic elements (as well as determining the basic type of melody), at least in regard to dynamic accents. It is no accident that the polyphonic music of Indonesia and southeast Asia, like much European music, exhibits certain four-square melodic tendencies. By contrast the music of India and the Persian-Arab world employs a melody instrument or voice performing in a given meter offset by a drum playing cross-rhythms or (in the Arab world) a quite different meter; with no harmony (a drone excepted) to impede its flow, the rhythm can reach great subtlety and complexity.

structure and style   In European music the great variety of styles derives from different concepts of rhythm in its relation to melody. They include the strict rhythmic modes of the 13th century, the free oratorical speech rhythms of the Renaissance, the almost stressless flow of Renaissance polyphony, the strong body rhythms of the Baroque era, the rhapsodic freedom of the late Romantics, and the primitivistic rhythms of 20th-century composers with their composite and ever-changing time signatures.

Thus the study of musical history shows a varying attitude to rhythm—sometimes closer to strict rule, sometimes to freedom—as the temper of the times and the relative influence of poetry, dance, and folk music decree. Plato's definition as "an order of movement" might, therefore, be expanded. As a determining factor in the vitality of music, rhythm may be described as "an inspired, organic order of movement," communicating intelligibly to the senses. From the analytical viewpoint it operates in the rational framework described, which it varies in terms of rubato, motif, and phrase. Ultimately rhythm is the organic process of music in time; it is music's direction in time. The quality of rhythm is the quality of life; and however vitally the composer may conceive his music, he is ultimately dependent on the performer to recreate it rhythmically. *See* EXPRESSION.

BIBLIOGRAPHY: Charles F. Abdy Williams, *The Aristoxenian Theory of Musical Rhythm* (1911; reprint, 1977) and *The Rhythm of Song* (1925; reprint, 1977); Émile Jaques-Dalcroze, *Rhythm, Music and Education* (1921; reprint, 1972) and *Eurhythmics, Art and Education* (1930; reprint, 1972); Curt Sachs, *Rhythm and Tempo* (1953) and *The Wellsprings of Music* (1977); Grosvenor W. Cooper and Leonard B. Meyer, *The Rhythmic Structure of Music* (1960); Joseph Schillinger, *Encyclopedia of Rhythms* (1976); Maury Yeston, *The Stratification of Musical Rhythm* (1976).

rhythmic modes The short, constantly repeated patterns in triple rhythm used in the polyphonic music of the late 12th and 13th centuries were the first systematic use of meter known in Western music. The rhythmic modes were originally used in organum, a type of composition in which a plainchant was elaborated by the addition of a countermelody above it. Modal rhythm is especially associated with the organa of the composers of the Paris-centered Notre Dame school *c.* 1200 (*e.g.*, Léonin, Pérotin) and with 13th-century musical forms that grew out of their work. With the emergence of music in three and four parts (with Pérotin and a few three-voiced precedents), such a system was possibly necessary to coordinate the voice parts.

There were six rhythmic modes, analogous to poetic meters:

I	— U	(trochee)	♩ ♫ ♪
II	U —	(iamb)	♫ ♫
III	— U U	(dactyl)	♩. ♫
IV	U U —	(anapest)	♫ ♩.
V	— —	(spondee)	♩. ♩.
VI	U U U	(tribrach)	♫♫ ♫♫

They were notated by placing square neumes on the staff in consistent formulas; *e.g.*, neumes ligatured in groups of three-two-two meant Mode I.

The longer rhythmic patterns used in some non-Western music are occasionally referred to as rhythmic modes. Examples include the Islamic *īqā' āt* and Indian *tāla*.

Ricci, Ruggiero (b. July 24, 1918) The U.S. violinist Ruggiero Ricci studied in San Francisco with Louis Persinger, who had earlier launched the career of Yehudi Menuhin. Ricci's highly successful debut was in the Mendelssohn Concerto at age 10, and he made his first European tour in 1932. A mature musician who plays the standard repertoire from Bach to Hindemith, Ricci is known for his interpretations of music for unaccompanied violin, particularly the Paganini Caprices, and of contemporary music.

ricercare or **ricercar** An instrumental piece with one or more themes developed through melodic imitation that was prominent in the 16th and 17th centuries. The term is Italian for "to search." The earliest ricercari, for the lute, appeared in 1507. Well-suited to the lute, they mixed passages in chordal style, running scale passages, and alternation of high and low phrases suggesting the many-voiced structure of polyphonic music. By 1523 Marcantonio Cavazzoni (and later others) composed ricercari for the organ. By the 1560s such pieces were written for ensembles of viols. In this period the ricercare moved away from the free style of the lute ricercare to a style based on melodic imitation reminiscent of the motet. Like the motet organ ricercari frequently subjected a number of themes to melodic imitation sequentially with slight overlaps to produce a continuous texture. Andrea Gabrieli and other Venetian composers often wrote ricercari based on only one theme treated extensively in the manner of the later fugue—*e.g.*, by stretto (playing the theme against itself with repeated, closely spaced entrances) and augmentation and diminution (in longer or shorter note values). The canzona and fantasia closely resembled the ricercare, particularly in the use of melodic imitation, and the names were often interchanged. Spanish pieces in ricercare style were known as *tientos* ("trials").

Richter, Hans (April 4, 1843–December 5, 1916)   A prominent early modern conductor known for his performances of Wagner, Brahms, and Elgar, the Hungarian-born Hans Richter studied at the Vienna Conservatory. For a short time in 1869 he succeeded Hans von Bülow at the Munich Opera on Wagner's recommendation, and in 1876 he conducted the first performances of Wagner's *Der Ring des Nibelungen* at Bayreuth; he later became principal conductor there. The following year he and Wagner conducted a Wagner festival in London, where Richter's career was to include the first London performances of *Tristan und Isolde* and *Die Meistersinger* (1882). He also directed annual concerts, the Richter Concerts, in London until 1897. He became conductor of the Manchester Hallé Orchestra in 1899 and built it into a highly reputed organization. From 1904 he conducted opera at Covent Garden, including a *Ring* cycle (in English) in 1909. Until 1911 he was principal conductor of the London Symphony.

Richter, Karl (b. October 15, 1926)   A specialist in the music of Bach, the German organist, harpsichordist, and conductor Karl Richter became organist at the Thomaskirche in Leipzig in 1949. Since 1951 he has been on the faculty of the Academy of Music in Munich and conductor of the Bach Choir there. He founded the Munich Bach Orchestra in 1953. He has made concert tours in Germany and abroad and has been awarded the International Bach Prize. His recordings include much Bach and some Handel, Telemann, and Beethoven.

Richter, Sviatoslav (Teofilovich) (b. March 20, 1915)   Trained at the Moscow Conservatory (1947), the Soviet pianist Sviatoslav Richter won the Stalin Prize (1950) and the Lenin Prize (1961). Although he plays very much in the romantic tradition, his repertoire ranges from Bach to Britten. His recordings are voluminous.

Ricordi: *see* PUCCINI; VERDI.

Riegger, Wallingford (April 29, 1885–April 2, 1961)   A prolific and venturesome U.S. composer of orchestral works, modern dance and film scores, and teaching pieces and choral arrangements, Wallingford Riegger began playing cello in a family ensemble in 1900 and studied theory with the noted teacher Percy Goetschius at the Institute of Musical Art (later the Juilliard School; graduated 1907) and later in Germany with Max Bruch.

He conducted opera in Germany (1915–17), returning to the United States to teach at Drake University (Iowa, 1918–22). His earliest works (from this period), conservative, lush scores, won him the Paderewski Prize (1921). From 1924 he taught in New York City; in that year he won the E. S. Coolidge Award for *La Belle dame sans merci* (to the poem by Keats) for four solo voices and chamber orchestra. His 1927 *Study in Sonority* for ten violins or any multiple of ten marked a transition toward a dissonant, contrapuntal style. He then became an early U.S. adaptator of 12-tone technique in *Dichotomy* (1932), based on his study of Schoenberg's music.

Riegger's free use of the 12-tone technique remained expressive while technically advanced. His Third Symphony (1948), which combines 12-tone and conventional writing, brought him wide attention. His later works continued to use strict forms such as canon and fugue and incorporated traditional with experimental material (*Quintuple Jazz*, Variations for violin and orchestra, both 1959).

Riegger's orchestral works are considered more advanced than his choral pieces, and he used pseudonyms for his many choral arrangements and teaching pieces. His modern dance scores were choreographed by Martha Graham and others. Riegger was music director of the Dance Division of the Federal Theater Project in New York City in the 1930s.

RECORDINGS: Brass Nonet; *Dichotomy;* Fantasy and Fugue for orchestra and organ; Movement for two trumpets, trombone, and piano; Music for brass choir; Piano Trio; Quartet No. 2; *Study in Sonority;* Symphony No. 4; Variations for two pianos.

Rienzi: *see* OPERA (the 19th century); WAGNER (life) and (development).

rigaudon   A lively dance of frivolous nature in $\frac{2}{2}$ or $\frac{4}{4}$ time. It should properly begin (although exceptions occur) with two eighth-note upbeats on the count of 4. Most authorities believe it to be French, specifically a Provençal sailors' dance, deriving its name from a Marseilles ballet master named Rigaud who brought it to Paris around 1630. It became popular in England as the rigadoon (Purcell). The dance itself included running, hopping, and turning; also *balancés* done with quick little jumps. The melodic structure of the music closely resembles that of most English hornpipes and is occasionally found in the suite (Johann Pachelbel, Bach, Grieg, Ravel). Lully, André Campra, and Rameau used it in their operatic ballets.

Rigoletto: *see* BAND; ROMANTIC PERIOD (non-German music of the 19th century); VERDI.

Rilling, Helmuth (b. May 29, 1933) Known primarily as a choral conductor, the German conductor and organist Helmuth Rilling received part of his musical training as a seminarian and later at the Staatliche Hochschule für Musik in Stuttgart, where he studied composition with Johann Nepomuk David and conducting with Hans Grischkat. He went to Rome in 1955 to study organ with Fernando Germani at the Conservatorio Santa Cecilia, returning in 1957 to Stuttgart, where he was appointed to the Memorial Church. Soon after he helped to reestablish the Spandauer Kantorei in Berlin. He was appointed to the Hochschule für Musik in Frankfurt am Main in 1966, but he is best known for his touring and recording group, the Bach Collegium and Kantorei Stuttgart.

Rimsky-Korsakov, Nikolay (Andreyevich) (March 18 [March 6, old style], 1844–June 21 [June 8, old style], 1908) One of the principal nationalist figures in Russian music, Nikolay Rimsky-Korsakov was born at Tikhvin in the Novgorod *guberniya*. In 1861, when he was a student at the St. Petersburg naval school, he made the acquaintance of Balakirev and his circle and was inspired to study music and to compose. His First Symphony was partly written on a three-year cruise (1862–65) and was successfully performed in St. Petersburg on his return. In 1871 he was appointed professor at the St. Petersburg Conser-

vatory, though he did not leave the navy until 1873. In that year his first opera, *The Maid of Pskov,* was produced in St. Petersburg. Two further operas, *May Night* (1880) and *Snow Maiden* (1882), were produced in St. Petersburg, and in 1887 and 1888 he wrote three brilliant orchestral works, the Capriccio *espagnol, Sheherazade,* and the *Russian Easter Festival* Overture. About this time he occupied a number of official positions: inspector of naval bands (1873–84), director of the Free School of Music concerts (1874–81), assistant music director of the Imperial Chapel (1883–94), and conductor of the Russian Symphony Concerts (1886–1900). His pupils at the conservatory at this period included some of the outstanding composers of the following generation, notably Anatol Liadov and Glazunov. He also found time to complete, orchestrate or reorchestrate, and edit drastically the unfinished works of his friends Borodin and Mussorgsky. Without his editorial work neither the *Prince Igor* of the one nor the *Khovanshchina* of the other could ever have been staged; but his total rewriting of the completed *Boris Godunov,* however well-intentioned and brilliant in result, was misguided.

Between 1891 and 1893 Rimsky-Korsakov passed through a physical and intellectual crisis marked by an inability to compose and even a distaste for music itself. Recovering, he composed the opera *Christmas Eve* (St. Petersburg, 1895) and followed it with a series of operas produced in Moscow, including *Sadko* (1898), *The Tsar's Bride* (1899), *The Story of Tsar Salton* (1900), and *Kashchei the Immortal* (1902). *Kitezh* was produced in St. Petersburg in 1907, and *Le Coq d'or* was produced posthumously in Moscow in 1909. This series of operas contains much of his finest music.

In the course of the revolutionary disturbances of 1905, Rimsky-Korsakov defended the rights of the conservatory students against the reactionary director; he was dismissed and became a hero of the liberals. Demonstrations after a performance of *Kashchei* led to the imposition of a two-month ban on the performance of all his works, with the result that they became unprecedentedly popular when it was lifted. Rimsky-Korsakov was later reinstated at the conservatory but took advantage of the period of retirement to complete his memoirs, *Letopis moei muzykalnoi zhizni* (1909; English translation, *My Musical Life,* 1942), a book of great interest and importance. In May 1907 he visited Paris to take part in Diaghilev's festival of Russian orchestral music. He had not quite completed another important book, *Principles of Orchestration* (English translation, 1923), when he died.

Rimsky-Korsakov was one of the greatest masters of orchestration in the history of music. His handling of the orchestra influenced not only his pupils Stravinsky and Respighi but Debussy, Ravel, and other French musicians, Gustav Holst, and many others. He was a melodist, but he lacked the dramatic power and architectural sense necessary for a symphonist. His unique contribution was the half-real, half-fantastic world portrayed in the best of his 16 operas.

BIBLIOGRAPHY: Gerald E. H. Abraham, *Studies in Russian Music* (1935; reprint, 1976), *On Russian Music* (1939; reprint, 1976), and *Rimsky-Korsakov: A Short Biography* (1945; reprint, 1976) and with Michel D. Calvocoressi, *Masters of Russian Music* (1939; reprint, 1971); Nikolay Rimsky-Korsakov, *My Musical Life* (1942; reprint, 1972); Donald Brook, *Six Great Russian Composers* (1946); Victor I. Seroff, *The Mighty Five* (1948; reprint, 1970).

RECORDINGS: Operas—*May Night, Snow Maiden, and The Tsar's Bride* (selections); suites—*Christmas Eve, Le Coq d'or, Sheherazade, Tsar Saltan;* Capriccio *espagnol;* Concerto for trombone and band; *Concertstück* for clarinet and band; *Dubinushka* (orchestra); Fantasy on Russian Themes for violin and orchestra; Piano Concerto; Quintet for piano and winds; *Russian Easter Festival* Overture; *Sadko: Song of Oleg the Wise* for soloists, chorus, and orchestra; Symphonies (2); Variations on a Romance by Glinka for oboe and band.

Rinaldo: *see* BAROQUE ERA (Handel and Bach); CANTATA; HANDEL (life); OPERA SERIA.

Ring des Nibelungen, Der: *see* LEITMOTIV; WAGNER.

Nikolay Rimsky-Korsakov
portrait by V. A. Serov (1865–1911)
H. Roger-Viollet

Rinuccini, Ottavio: *see* CAMERATA; LIBRETTO (emergence of historical subjects); OPERA (beginnings); PERI.

Rite of Spring, The: *see* SACRE DU PRINTEMPS, LE.

ritornello   The last two lines of the 14th-century madrigal and caccia that summarizes the content of the verse; hence the Italian "little return."

In 17th-century vocal music the ritornello is a short instrumental introduction or conclusion.

In the Baroque CONCERTO GROSSO the ritornello is the repeating section played by the tutti in alternation with the solo group, or concertino.

Robert le Diable: *see* MEYERBEER; OPERA (the 19th century); ROMANTIC PERIOD (Wagnerian development).

Robeson, Paul (Bustill) (April 9, 1898–January 23, 1976)   Son of a former slave, and holding a law degree from Columbia University, the U.S. bass-baritone singer and actor Paul Robeson attracted attention in 1924 with his appearance on the New York stage as Eugene O'Neill's Emperor Jones. The following year he sang a recital of spirituals in Greenwich Village and the role of Joe in the musical play *Show Boat.* Also a Shakespearean actor, his Otello (from 1943) was the longest running Shakespearean performance on Broadway. Robeson appeared in several films, including *Emperor Jones* (1933) and *Show Boat* (1936). He became affiliated with pro-Soviet politics and lived in Europe from 1958 to 1963. He recorded albums of spirituals and songs, and his autobiography, *Here I Stand,* appeared in 1958.

Rochberg, George (b. July 5, 1918) A student of Menotti at the Curtis Institute, the U.S. composer George Rochberg joined the faculty at Curtis the year following his graduation in 1947. In 1950, while in Rome as a Fulbright fellow, he was influenced by Luigi Dallapiccola and dodecaphony, a principle that he first used in his *12 Bagatelles* (1952). His music has progressively shown influences of Hindemith, Stravinsky, Bartók, Schoenberg, and Mahler, with whom Rochberg most closely identifies (Second Symphony, 1956). In later works he has experimented with durations (*Time-Span,* 1960–62) and densities (*Apocalyptica,* 1964). He has written six quartets (the second with voice) and three symphonies (the third with solo voices, chamber chorus, and double chorus), songs (*Songs in Praise of Krishna,* 1970), chamber music, and a cantata (*David the Psalmist,* 1954). *Contra mortem et tempus* (1965) includes fragments from Berio, Pierre Boulez, Edgard Varèse, and Ives. A neoromantic violin concerto was premiered in 1977. Rochberg has written articles on theory ("Indeterminacy in New Music"; "Duration in Music") and on composers Hugo Weisgall and Schoenberg and *The Hexachord and Its Relation to the Twelve-tone Row* (1955). In 1960 he joined the faculty of the University of Pennsylvania, where he has served as department chairman.

RECORDINGS: *Blake Songs;* Chamber Symphony for nine instruments; *Contra mortem et tempus;* Duo Concertante for violin and cello; Music for the Magic Theater; Quartets (3); *Serenata d'estate; Songs in Praise of Krishna;* Symphonies (2); *Tableaux* for soprano and 11 players.

Rode, (Jacques-) Pierre (-Joseph) (February 16, 1774–November 25, 1830) A student of Giovanni Battista Viotti, the French violinist Pierre Rode toured the Continent (1794) and England and on his return to France was appointed a professor at the newly-opened Paris Conservatoire. On a tour through Spain (1799) he met Boccherini, who is reputed to have orchestrated Rode's early violin concertos. In 1800 he became solo violinist to Napoleon I and then went to Russia to be first violinist in the court orchestra of Tsar Alexander I. Beethoven's Sonata in G Major, Op. 96, was written for him. Rode wrote caprices, études, a method, and 13 concertos for violin.

Rodelinda: *see* HANDEL (life).

Rodeo: *see* BALLET (United States after 1932); COPLAND.

Rodgers, Richard: *see* MUSICAL COMEDY; POPULAR MUSIC (the 20th century).

Rodrigo, Joaquín (b. November 22, 1902) A student of Paul Dukas at the École Normale de Musique in Paris, the blind Spanish composer Joaquín Rodrigo has made world tours as a lecturer and pianist. He has taught music history at the University of Madrid since 1946, acted as musical adviser to the Spanish radio since 1944, and been vice president of the International Society for Contemporary Music since 1954. His composition was influenced by de Falla. He has written concertos for piano (1942), violin (1943), cello (1949), harp (1952), and for one, two, and four guitars (1934, 1967, 1968). He has also written for solo voice (*Cantico de la esposa,* 1934; *4 Villancicos,* 1952) and for chorus (*4 Villancicos* "Canciones de navidad," 1952). His music uses indigenous Spanish musical elements of rhythm and melody.

RECORDINGS: Concert-Serenade for harp and orchestra; *Concierto Andaluz* (four guitars); *Concierto de Aranjuez* (guitar); *Concierto Madrigal* (two guitars); Fantasia *para un gentilhombre* for guitar; *Sones en la Giralda* for harp and orchestra; *Triptic de Mosen Cinto* for voice and orchestra.

Rodzinski, Artur (January 1, 1892–November 27, 1958) Originally a lawyer, the Polish conductor Artur Rodzinski was educated in Vienna and made his debut in Lwów in 1921. He conducted in Warsaw until his appointment as Stokowski's assistant with the Philadelphia Orchestra (1926–29; simultaneously he headed the opera and orchestra departments at the Curtis Institute) and then served as conductor of the Los Angeles Philharmonic (1929–33), the Cleveland Orchestra (1933–43), the New York Philharmonic (1943–47), and the Chicago Symphony (1947–48). Though respected technically and musically, Rodzinski was involved in controversy wherever he worked. He specialized in 20th-century works, conducting premieres of scores by Hindemith, Milhaud, Walter Piston, Schoenberg, William Schuman, and William Walton.

Roger-Ducasse, Jean Jules Aimable (August 18, 1873–July 20, 1954)   A French composer and teacher, Jean Jules Aimable Roger-Ducasse was a pupil of Fauré at the Paris Conservatoire and won the second Prix de Rome in 1902. He was inspector of music in the municipal schools of Paris and from 1935 to 1940 professor of composition at the Conservatoire. His works include two operas, *Orphée* (1926) and *Cantegril* (1931), two quartets, orchestral works *Suite française* (1909) and *Le Joli Jeu de furet* (1920), motets, works for chorus and orchestra, and technical studies for the piano. In 1940 he resigned from the Conservatoire and in 1945 retired to his estate in the Gironde.

RECORDING: Barcarolle for harp.

Rogg, Lionel (b. April 21, 1936)   Educated at the Geneva Conservatory and a professor there since 1961, the Swiss organist and harpsichordist Lionel Rogg has recorded the complete organ works of Bach, the *Art of the Fugue* (Grand Prix du Disque), and the Handel Organ Concertos. He plays throughout Europe and since 1965 has toured North America frequently. Rogg has composed chorale preludes for the organ and has written an organ method and a book on counterpoint (*Éléments de contrepoint*).

Romani, Felice: *see* BELLINI; DONIZETTI.

Romantic period   The beginning of the 19th century marked a change of both musical style and aesthetic attitude that has become identified as Romantic. The term originated in German literature of the late 18th century, illustrating the overlapping of Classical and Romantic attitudes and ideals. The Franco-Swiss writer Mme de Staël articulated the new ideals of the movement in 1813 as original, modern, national, popular, derived from the soil, religion, and prevailing social institutions. Obviously some of these proclaimed Romantic ideals and purposes were the same as those of the 18th-century Classicists. *See* CLASSICAL PERIOD.

The Janus-like figure who marked the transition was Beethoven, the first composer whose personality and character made a purposeful impact on the types and style of music he composed. Inspired by the revolutionary forces prevailing at the time, he declared himself a free artistic agent with neither allegiance nor responsibility to any patron. His early works reflected the 18th-century acceptance of providing music on demand, and he applied his craftsmanship to supplying compositions in hope of financial reward. But in his later works from about 1820 on, he declared his personal independence and wrote only what his imagination and inspiration dictated, thus establishing individuality, subjectivity, and emotional expression as the standard for Romantic composers. Yet the body of music he produced reflects the tastes of the 18th rather than the 19th century in that he was attracted more by the absolute forms of instrumental music than by the dramatic and lyrical forms cultivated by the Romanticists. Symphonies, chamber music (particularly quartets), and piano pieces (including 32 sonatas) far outweigh his one opera, one oratorio, one major mass, and assorted songs and part songs. His lack of interest in dramatic vocal music reflects the Classical side of his nature, though the expressive changes apparent in his instrumental works are evidence of his being the springboard to the Romantic epoch.

With the period comes the development of lyric music in the forms of songs and short piano pieces. Schubert, Weber, Louis Spohr, Mendelssohn, and Schumann would be the Romantic composers in this sense, and many contemporaries would have added Cherubini to the list, for they thought of him not as the martinet who directed the Paris Conservatoire but as the composer of the opera *Les*

Deux Journées (1800). Romanticism was thrilling, and Classicism was cold.

But this list traverses another sense of the term that opposes the Romantic to the Classical. The Classical is in this connection identified with both formalism and mastery. Mendelssohn and Spohr chose romantic subjects to no purpose; their mastery was unromantically slick (there is no other word for it), and Spohr's forms were more thoroughly ascertained than anyone else's except those of Mozart's brilliant pupil, Johann Nepomuk Hummel. Mendelssohn's forms were free; but he never got into difficulties, so how could anybody recognize his freedom? Carl Philipp Emanuel Bach's vein of sentimental rhetoric was not only typically romantic but enabled him to write some genuinely lyrical songs. Johann Schobert is another romantic writer who influenced Mozart at an impressionable time of his youth. Every thrilling modulation in Beethoven's music was romantic, as were the double-bass passages at the beginning of Cherubini's overture to *Les Deux Journées.*

But the facts are more interesting than this generalization. Mastery is not the line of cleavage that ranges Spohr and Mendelssohn on the one side and Schubert, Schumann, and Chopin on the other. Beethoven's later tonality and polyphony made music ready for lyric forms that he himself anticipated in a few of his Bagatelles for piano and in some sporadic good things among his songs. Mendelssohn and Spohr took up songwriting and produced in that line masterpieces for the drawing room. We should not despise the drawing room. Schubert became the supreme master of song, and Schumann achieved greatness there as in his piano lyrics; but you might as well think of Keats and Shelley as writers for the drawing room.

Another line of cleavage separates Schubert from Schumann and Chopin as fundamentally as it separates him from Mendelssohn and Spohr. When Schumann and Chopin handle the large Classical forms they show obvious weaknesses. Schumann makes an effective new artificial sonata form out of his stiff, antithetic, epigrammatic style, as one might construct a landscape in mosaic. Chopin merely shows that he has taken the sonata forms uncritically

from Hummel, though the first two movements of the b-flat minor Sonata are almost as happy in their Classical form as the Ballades are in Chopin's unique way. But Schubert's large forms have only the weaknesses of youth, and their positive qualities and tendencies set him above all schools. The mastery that Schubert lacks is not anything that Spohr could have supplied. Younger composers with new worlds to conquer could with some truth accuse Spohr of playing with Classical forms as one might play chess, but they could never have so accused the Schubert that died young or the Schubert that might have reached old age.

We do not know what Mendelssohn might have achieved if he had lived longer. His influence on the musicians he knew personally was wholly stimulating and good. But he too seemed able to play chess with symphonies, oratorios, and songs with and without words, while other composers were grappling in their music with real life, perhaps confined to one narrow art medium like Chopin; or, like Schumann, deserting lyrics for larger forms or some artificial hypothesis; or, like young Berlioz, kicking right and left against all teaching and all criticism while dreaming new wonders of orchestral sound and correctly dreaming the practical means to them as well.

Meanwhile a greater than Berlioz was arising, a dreamer of new sense as well as sound. Mendelssohn and Schumann saw only the beginning of Wagner's development and could not feel very sure that this voluble and stormy reformer of music drama was really likely to achieve anything better than the tinsel of the astute Meyerbeer who dominated the world of cosmopolitan opera. The early style of Wagner is indeed an alloy of many metals, but even in the 1840s his work marks the eclipse of the first Romantic period and the dawn of another and greater epoch.

The art forms peculiar to the Romantic period have no definite names, though composers began to use many literary titles such as ballade, romance (already used by Mozart for slow movements in sonata form), nocturne, and the like. Dance rhythms, especially those of Poland, were brought into prominence in the piano music of Chopin. Mendelssohn's song without words was very successful but too facile to lead far or even to justify its existence. Fantastic titles, used in the 18th century by the French *clavecinistes,* assumed great prominence in the piano works of Schumann, who created a new type of long connected cycles of epigrammatic little pieces. The crowd of piano composers whose brilliance on that instrument obstructed all wider musical prospects include the respectable Hummel, the less respectable Daniel Steibelt, the flimsy Josef Wölffl, and the Irish writer of beautiful pre-Chopin nocturnes, John Field.

Wagnerian development Wagner formulated his principles of music drama long before he matured his musical style. It is impossible to understand the musical history of the second half of the 19th century until we frankly admit that the composers of instrumental music saw in Wagner not only the subversive operatic theorist and erotic dramatist but the composer who was popular because of the Salvation Army religiosity of the end of the *Tannhäuser* Overture and the downright vulgarity of the entr'acte before the third act of *Lohengrin.* His theories and methods might be controversial, but these lapses never were.

Strange to say Wagner received something like recognition from the doyen of Classical champions Spohr, whose attitude to Beethoven had been merely condescending but who saw in *The Flying Dutchman* and *Tannhäuser* interesting, if faulty, works that well deserved painstaking production at his theater at Kassel. Schumann too, after joining in the general hostility toward *Tannhäuser,* frankly recanted and praised its many noble features. Personally he and Wagner did not get on well; he found Wagner too talkative, and Wagner found that Schumann had nothing to say. Later, when Wagner was in exile, *Lohengrin* found a powerful champion in Liszt at Weimar.

Liszt presented another problem to sober musicians. Wagner himself at first saw nothing in Liszt but the virtuoso who, when asked for music, would give you a fantasia on Meyerbeer's *Robert le Diable.* But persons who became bitterly hostile to all the musical tendencies that Liszt fostered went out of their way to declare that no such wonderful interpreta-

tions and technique as Liszt's piano playing had ever before been heard on any instrument or orchestra. All Liszt's gestures were superb—from his monumental immobility at the piano to his princely and often really self-sacrificing generosity to other musicians. And at the age of 37 he made the most superb of all his gestures in giving up playing in public. And so the one incontrovertible power of his art became a legend, and his actual activity became the championship of unorthodox artists. He took to composing on a more ambitious scale than that of the marvelous piano virtuoso and became himself the leader of a new development of Romantic music. Although he took little pleasure in counterpoint, he had none of Berlioz' clumsiness in harmonic texture; and his orchestration, in which his first efforts had the secret assistance of Joachim Raff, was always brilliant and novel, though it never caught the Berliozian fire or plumbed the Wagnerian depths. Liszt realized no more than did Berlioz the true musical purport of the new ideas that his symphonic poems and Berlioz' symphonic–dramatic phantasmagorias were putting forward under all kinds of literary and pictorial names. While the new Romantic composers purported to be devoting instrumental music to the illustration of literature (*see* PROGRAM MUSIC), they were really struggling with a new musical time scale.

Musical history may be traced in terms of the time limit over which the listener's memory is brought into play. In the 16th century that limit is from accent to accent; by the end of the 17th century it ran from phrase to phrase. The great architectural forms of Bach could stretch it easily to six minutes and in extreme cases to 10. The rise of the dramatic sonata style did not greatly enlarge the time scale; there are few well-constructed sonata movements that exceed a quarter of an hour, though on no smaller scale could Beethoven have prepared the famous harmonic collision that gave such offense in the first movement of the *Eroica* Symphony. Now this 10-minute time scale obviously compelled musicians to handle the action of an OPERA by means of conventions. It is less obvious that it also produced a similarly conventional artifice in the

697

relation of sonata forms to their emotional content. A design may complete itself in 10 minutes while raising emotional issues that cannot be dealt with in less than 40. And so the sonata forms are grouped in from two to four (rarely more) movements as artificially as the musical sections of Classical operas. Wagner's enormous achievement in music drama consisted essentially in giving music the same time scale as that of the drama. As with all first solutions of an art problem, he achieved an extreme case, for his drama became cosmically slow. But from *Das Rheingold* (1869) onward every Wagnerian opening instantly—and without any introductory gestures—established the lines of its vast time scale to the utter bewilderment of his contemporaries, who continued to expect *Das Rheingold* to show its pattern on Beethoven's time scale, just as Beethoven's contemporaries had heard seven pianissimo measures on the chord of E-flat not as that vaulted vacancy appears in the middle of the Andante of the c minor Symphony but as it would have sounded if it were intruded into an andante by Mozart.

No one else before Richard Strauss achieved Wagner's mastery of his new time scale; and few if any of his contemporaries, whether hostile or friendly to him, realized its existence. Liszt was trying in his symphonic poems to make a music that filled its half hour or 40 minutes continuously; but his first effort of the kind, *Ce qu'on entend sur la montagne* (1850), spends the first 20 of its 40 minutes in a series of introductions and the remaining 20 in retracing the series backward. His more successful efforts, such as *Orpheus* (1854) and *Les Préludes* (revised form, 1854), are either essentially lyric or not on the new time scale at all. He never achieved so effective a symphonic poem as Schubert had already long before unwittingly produced in the *Wanderer* Fantasia (1822). Musicians who might not have been repelled by new doctrines of musical form found Liszt's style even more semi-mundane than that Wagner's early works; nor did Liszt show any tendency to purify it. Moreover he rivaled Meyerbeer in the efficiency of his press bureau by which he made propaganda—often in his own fluent French—more generously for others than for himself.

Meanwhile another musical development was arising, conscious of its continuity with the past and, like Judaism as defined by Matthew Arnold, tinged with emotion in the morality of its aesthetic principles. Joachim, as great an interpreter on the violin as Liszt on the piano, at first found in Liszt a congenial friend until he saw his compositions. These horrified him, and the horror completed an estrangement already begun by his dislike of the atmosphere of Liszt's press bureau. He and his younger friend Brahms were united not only in general musical taste but in personal devotion to the heroic widow of Schumann, who, after her husband's tragic and lingering death, was bringing up a large family on the proceeds of her concerts. These three artists soon came to regard the musical atmosphere of Weimar, where the *Lisztianer* gathered around their master, as unhealthy. In the correspondence and mutual criticism of Brahms and Joachim, the word *Lisztisch* became synonymous with devilish; and indeed it is true that any characteristic Lisztian and many Wagnerian idioms would have a disgusting effect if intruded into Brahms's music. Today we can be wise after the event and find matter for regret in the drastic outspokenness of Joachim and Brahms, which elevated matters of taste into questions of artistic honor. If Liszt could have been contented with neutral criticism on definable issues of technique without requiring attestations of sympathy and enjoyment, and if Joachim could have resolved matters of taste into questions of artistic proportion, the neoclassical and neoromantic musicians would have joined forces instead of condemning each other. Similar economies might be effected in nature if lions could be converted to vegetarianism.

The controversy was unequal in two compensating ways. Wagner had a tremendous, if acrid, fluency in prose and did not care where his vitriol might alight. Moreover Wagnerian and Lisztian music was much easier to write about, whether in attack or defense, than music that had no literary aspect. Brahms, like Wagner, needed and found friends who adored his music, but he hated the idea of a press bureau and snubbed anyone whose compliments aroused the least suspicion of flattery. These drawbacks had their own compensation. It might be difficult to write as interestingly about Brahms as about Wagner; but Wagner, whether in exile or enthroned at Bayreuth, had Wagnerian music drama as his whole province, while Brahms reigned over the whole of the remainder of music—instrumental, choral, and lyric. If criticism came to persecution, on the whole the neoclassicists had the worst of it; for Brahms had no equals after Joachim gave up composition, and the position of a champion of Classical forms was easily confused with that of a persecutor of the prophets of progress. Brahms was no anti-Wagnerian and was annoyed when his friends bracketed Wagner with Liszt.

But apart from the clash of flying inkpots, the recognition of Brahms was assured by two facts: the propaganda of his work not by words but by consummate and authoritative performance, and the very fact that his music required an experienced love of music for its understanding. One might become an enthusiastic Wagnerian or even a well-equipped conductor of Wagner's music and be as the brutes that perish about symphonic orchestration, choral music, chamber music, songs, and all piano music except Chopin. But it was long before any musician could venture to tackle Brahms's music on any basis except that of the most comprehensive musical culture and technique. Brahms lived long enough to become worshipped unintelligently, and after his death in 1897 the reaction was more evident than the fashionable worship had been.

The Wagnerians felt deeply that their propaganda was incomplete for lack of a master of purely symphonic music. This they found in Bruckner. Brahms was appalled by the clumsiness of Bruckner's forms, and the most official Wagnerians admitted the frequent lapses of their symphonic master. But Bruckner's *Nibelungen*-tetralogy openings to his symphonies obviously dwarfed the terse themes of Brahms. By the time Brahms and Bruckner had come into their own, the public had long lost all sense of form in its appetite for bleeding gobbets of musical butcher's meat hacked from the living body of Wagnerian music drama. After this it was pedantry to

quarrel with any symphonic composer's form so long as his openings were vast enough. Brahms was no pedant; obvious weakness of form and style did not deter him from being the first to recognize Dvořák, and he was drastic in his rebuff of anyone who thought to flatter him by talking against Wagner.

The song writer Hugo Wolf became recognized too late to be made use of as a lyric pawn in the Wagner–Bruckner party politics of music. As far as his theory of song can be summarized, it consists in the application of Wagnerian declamation to lyric poetry. If his practice were not better than this essentially prose theory of verse rhythm and the perky censorship of Classical musical declamation that goes with it, Wolf's art would not have survived his short and ailing life. But it is deeper than the theories on which it is supposed to rest, and its apparent revolt from lyric melody only partly conceals a powerfully organized lyric form and does not at all conceal a great gift of characterization.

non-German music of the 19th century
While these great issues were being debated in Germany, the music of other countries was awakening from long sleep or outgrowing infancy and provinciality. Since Rameau, France had been remarkably content to have its music dominated by foreigners. Before Rameau French opera was established by the Italian Lully. After Rameau it was reformed by the Austrian Gluck. Early 19th-century French Classicism was dominated by the Italian Cherubini. Another Italian, Rossini, was absorbed by Paris in the prime of his life, and the result was *Guillaume Tell* (1829) with its rich orchestration and grandiose forms. But the crown of French opera was imposed on it by the German Jew Meyerbeer. The pretensions of the native French composers were more modest except for the volcanic eruptions of that typical meridional Berlioz. The popularity of Gounod rested on the same misunderstanding of the meaning of art as the vogue of Gustave Doré in the capacity of an illustrator of the Bible. *Faust* (1859) was a success. Another development, more improvisatorial, uncertain of its style, but fundamentally sincere, was initiated by the Belgian Franck. From him, and not from the more prolific

and facile Saint-Saëns, originates the mainstream of modern French music. His style has too much affinity with Liszt to please the musicians who continued to regard Liszt as the author of all musical evil; but he achieved mastery in a wide range of forms all his own, and he never wrote for effect.

After Rossini music in Italy was long content to imitate the things in which Rossini was imitable. These were the mechanical cultivation of bel canto and the use of a full orchestra to support the voice in a thick unison of the melodic instruments, with a brassy dance rhythm and the big drum and cymbals to mark the rhythm. The genuine melodic inventiveness of Bellini and Donizetti did little to improve the other categories of the art, but in Verdi a new genius was arising together with the Risorgimento. In *Rigoletto, Il Trovatore,* and *La Traviata,* Verdi's dramatic sincerity triumphs over the defects of a musical texture that still clings to traditional squalor, though strokes of genius occur unpredictably in the orchestration of many passages. In *Aida* the style silences all cavil; and in *Otello* (1887; written at the age of 74) and *Falstaff* (1893) Verdi creates a new kind of opera—Wagnerian in its perfect continuity and dramatic movement but utterly independent of Wagner's style and method.

Bold prophets in Beethoven's time had been heard to say that a great musical future was in store for Russia. The fulfillment of this prophecy was long delayed, for when Anton Rubinstein averred that Glinka was the equal or the superior of Haydn and Mozart, he expressed an opinion that could have occurred only to a Russian and then only as a patriotic paradox. Rubinstein himself achieved only a weak cosmopolitanism in his voluminous compositions, though his piano playing remained—for all its waywardness—until almost the end of the century as the most monumental power of interpretation on that instrument after Liszt. The first composer to make a genuinely Russian music recognized over the whole civilized world was Tchaikovsky, whose symphonies were held by some critics to have eclipsed those of Brahms. This was the eclipse of drama by melodrama. The true merits of Tchaikovsky are now eclipsed

by the reputation of his less immediately successful contemporaries. Mussorgsky had the posthumous fortune to have his two great operas *Boris Godunov* and *Khovanshchina* revised by Rimsky-Korsakov, the most brilliant contemporary master of pure orchestral color and texture. This was unquestionably good fortune in so far as it speeded these unconventional works on their way into the wide world; but something like indignation accompanied the later study of Mussorgsky's original scores with the discovery that in addition to altering clumsinesses Rimsky-Korsakov constantly meddled with features in his friend's style that were far beyond his comprehension.

The 19th century was over before any musician on the Continent could be persuaded that there were composers in England. Schumann had repeated St. Gregory's pun about Angles and angels when he hailed William Sterndale Bennett as "ein englischer Componist"; but the trials of English musical life dried Bennett up. All who knew and loved him denied hotly that his music reflected Mendelssohn's; and perhaps a leisurely study of it might vindicate his independence. The renascence of English music began in the work of Hubert Parry and Charles Villiers Stanford. They put an end to the provincial absurdities of the British oratorio tradition and consistently set great literature in a way that revealed to contemporary poets that the antithesis between musical and general culture was false. They also had wide and deep influence as teachers of composition.

But recognition of English music on the Continent was rare and capricious. Englishmen wrote church music for the stage, stage music for the church, organ music for the orchestra, and—as far as there were any orchestral ideas at all—orchestral music for the organ. The one English composer who could be understood on the Continent as saying intelligible things in fit terms was Arthur Sullivan with his Savoy operas. And his serious colleagues and critics urged him with owlish solemnity to produce no more light masterpieces but to go on with his serious and luscious "Golden Legends" and "Martyrs of Antioch" and generally to consummate the final merging of English music into "The Lost

Chord." We may thankfully hope that that chord is now lost forever, but the Savoy operas live and might have risen to the position of great music if Sullivan had had enough stead-fast love of music to finish those parts of his work to which the public did not listen; for example, if he had provided his operas with better orchestral introductions than the per-functory potpourris of favorite tunes he calls overtures that are quite as long as artistically decent overtures would have been.

It is customary to explain the failure of all but the most recent British music by saying that the native art was crushed by the ponder-ous genius of Handel. It is a pity that the united ponderosity of Handel and the middle-weight Mendelssohn could not avail to dam the output of oratorios by composers who might have become good song writers or even acquired some knowledge of orchestration be-yond that of choral accompaniment. The com-plaint of foreign domination is nonsense. No country had its music so long and so com-pletely dominated by foreigners as France, and French music always remained exclusively French and made thoroughly French artists of the foreigners who dominated it. The traces of foreign influence on English music were always echoes of individual phrases or man-nerisms. While Britain echoed—as fashions changed—Mendelssohn, Brahms, and De-bussy, no technical lessons were learned from them.

20th-century transition   The 20th century inherited the last development of the 19th in the symphonic poems and operas of Richard Strauss. Much acrid controversy at first raged around the details of his style, which dashed through all the traffic regulations of Classical part writing. And nothing was easier than to identify all carping critics with *Die Meister-singer's* Beckmesser and to accept humbly Strauss's own self-portrait as the hero of *Ein Heldenleben* (1899). The elements that were sensational in Strauss's symphonic poems have become so familiar that we are in some danger of underestimating the importance of these works as real achievements of the prob-lem in which Liszt failed—not the trivial prob-lem of program music but the vital problem of writing purely instrumental music on the Wagnerian time scale. The power of compo-sition in these works is unquestionable and remains eminent in their facile aftermath, the *Alpine* Symphony, which, designed before the first world war, appeared in 1915. But Strauss had eclipsed the fame of his symphonic works by his operas, which began to be important with *Salome* (1905), a setting of Oscar Wilde's play. Then came the long and fruitful partner-ship with Hugo von Hofmannsthal that ena-bled poet and musician to prove the possibility of many different kinds of modern opera—Wagnerian and non-Wagnerian. The purity of the Straussian metal has been strongly al-loyed with worldly wisdom in every phase of Strauss's career: in the period of the good boy of the conservatory; in the Romantic sym-phonic poet of *Death and Transfiguration* (1890); in the timely musical adaptation of Wilde while he was still a new discovery on the German stage; in the seizing of the oppor-tunity presented by Hofmannsthal's *Elektra* (opera, 1909) after its triumph as a play; and not least in the later phase of naive melodious-ness. But *Die Frau ohne Schatten* (1919) is a grand and Strauss's most grandly realized op-portunity for beauty.

In the early part of the 20th century the large forces employed by late 19th-century composers were still regarded as a natural me-dium for expression. The composition of such works was encouraged by the apparent ab-sence of any serious economic obstacle. As a result there were grandiose works for chorus and orchestra like the Eighth Symphony (1910) by Mahler and the *Gurrelieder* (1913) by Schoenberg. Purely orchestral works were on a similar scale, and opera followed suit. The idioms of Romantic music were also kept alive by a passionate style of writing that clothed a diatonic framework with a generous use of chromaticism. In a sense it was an inter-national style, but it had many local variants. The characteristically Slav melancholy of Rachmaninoff conquered the world as deci-sively as the Italian operas of Puccini. The music of Mahler, Strauss, and Elgar was firmly grounded in diatonic tonality, but other com-posers were not so ready to keep one foot on traditional territory. One development was IMPRESSIONISM, associated particularly with

701

Debussy, who as a young man was strongly influenced by Wagner. The other direction was expressionism, beginning with Schoenberg and his disciples Berg and Webern. Thus the MODERN PERIOD was on its way.

BIBLIOGRAPHY: Daniel Gregory Mason, *Contemporary Composers* (1918; reprint, 1973); Arthur Ware Locke, *Music and the Romantic Movement in France* (1920; reprint, 1972); Cecil Gray, *A Survey of Contemporary Music,* 2nd ed. (1927; reprint, 1972); Irving Kolodin, ed., *The Critical Composer, the Musical Writings of Berlioz, Wagner, Schumann, Tchaikovsky, and Others* (1940; reprint, 1969); Alfred Einstein, *Music in the Romantic Era* (1947); Gerald E. H. Abraham, *Slavonic and Romantic Music* (1968); Friedrich Blume, *Classic and Romantic Music* (1970); Edward Dannreuther, *The Romantic Period,* 2nd ed. (1973); Rey M. Longyear, *Nineteenth-Century Romanticism in Music,* 2nd ed. (1973); Henry Raynor, *Music and Society since 1815* (1976).

Romberg, Bernhard (November 12, 1767–August 13, 1841)   The son of a well-known bassoonist and a member of an illustrious 18th-century musical family, the German cellist Bernhard Romberg performed with the most distinguished musicians of his day. He played a concert with Beethoven in Vienna in 1797, though he disliked the latter's music and is said to have trampled on the score of the First *Razumovsky* Quartet, Op. 59. He performed the music of Louis Spohr and Anton Reicha and played duos with Ferdinand VII of Spain on the violin. After being a member of the court orchestra at Bonn, he became court Kapellmeister in Berlin (1815–19). He composed operas, chamber music, a cello method, and concertos and pieces for cello that greatly extended the acknowledged capabilities of the instrument.

RECORDINGS: Flute Concerto, Op. 17; Sonata in B-flat for harp and cello.

Romberg, Sigmund: *see* OPERETTA; POPULAR MUSIC (the 20th century).

Romeo and Juliet: *see* BERLIOZ; GOUNOD; PROGRAM MUSIC (problem of form); PROKOFIEV; TCHAIKOVSKY.

Romero family   Celedonio Romero (b. March 2, 1918) and his three sons—Celin

Romero (b. November 23, 1940), Pepe Romero (b. March 8, 1944), and Angel Romero (b. August 17, 1946)—are all Spanish guitarists who have been prominent in the 20th-century revival of the classical guitar. They appear individually as soloists, together as a quartet, and in all possible combinations.

Born in Málaga, Celedonio Romero studied at the conservatories in Málaga and Madrid, making his debut in 1940. He moved with his family to the United States in 1958, and from the early 1960s they have toured regularly throughout the world. They commissioned Joaquín Rodrigo to write a concerto for four guitars (*Concierto Andaluz,* 1967, which they recorded), and Rodrigo wrote his *Concierto Madrigal* (1968) for two guitars (recorded by Pepe and Angel Romero) for them as well. Their extensive recordings also include Rodrigo's *Concierto de Aranjuez* (Angel Romero twice) and works from Vivaldi to Celedonio Romero.

rondeau   One of the *formes fixes* in French lyric poetry and song of the 14th and 15th centuries (*compare* BALLADE; VIRELAI). The full form consists of four stanzas. The first and last are identical; the second half of the second stanza is a short refrain, which has as its text the first half of the first stanza.

The earliest rondeaux had stanzas of two or three lines; later, especially in the 15th century, stanzas of four, five, or even six lines were common. Because of the unwieldy length of the refrains in such cases, the literary rondeau (which in the 15th century began to separate itself clearly from the sung rondeau) often curtailed the refrains in the second and fourth stanzas, leaving only a *rentrement* (reentry) of the opening words. This often produced unexpected changes of meaning as a result of the new context.

Such curtailment probably did not take place in the sung rondeau because the musical form required that refrains be complete. The music for the first stanza was always bipartite and was repeated for the third and fourth stanzas; the second stanza returned to the beginning from its midpoint so that the half-stanza refrain could be sung to its correct music. In the following diagram the repeats of music with new text appear in lowercase, while exact repeats (of text and music) are in uppercase:

I	II	III	IV
A B	a A	a b	A B

To adapt this form to include the curtailed *rentrement* would require adjustment tantamount to overthrowing the form. The musical form of the full rondeau had a peculiar strength because the triple repetition of the "a" section in stanzas II and III made the eventual return of the "b" section in the third stanza a moment of immense significance, its weight requiring the balance provided by the final full refrain.

The earliest known rondeaux with polyphonic music are by the 13th-century poet-composer Adam de la Halle. These brief pieces already follow the bipartite musical form strictly. The 14th-century poet and composer Guillaume de Machaut wrote fewer than 30 musical rondeaux, but they constitute the most varied and inventive body of music in his whole output. Partly because of the wide range that Machaut found and demonstrated in the rondeau, it had by the middle of the 15th century virtually supplanted the other song forms. For Machaut and his successors the rondeau was a highly intimate form compared with the other *formes fixes;* and the texts often display the mood of slightly sentimental longing that was to characterize the courtly love tradition in its later stages.

In the 15th century the Burgundian composers Guillaume Dufay and Gilles Binchois wrote many rondeaux. Perhaps the most memorable song of the century is the rondeau "De plus en plus" ("More and More") of Binchois; while the most widely appreciated at the time was the infinitely more delicate "Par le regart de vos beaux yeulx" ("For a Glance From Your Lovely Eyes") of Dufay. Such songs would represent the peak of the rondeau's history were it not for the long, fine songs of their contemporary Hayne van Ghizeghem, written in the last years of the supremacy of the Burgundian dukes. The end of the 15th century saw the abandonment of the medieval *formes fixes.* The rondeau was the only one to have survived 200 years without any significant change in its form or content; it was perhaps ideally designed and balanced to express the spirit of its time.

The collective title rondeaux was also often given to anthologies containing some pieces in other forms. The poet Charles d'Orléans gave the title chanson to those of his rondeaux intended for singing. Theorists writing in Latin used the words *rondellus* or *rotundellus* with two meanings: elements of canonic writing and voice exchange found especially in 13th- and 14th-century English polyphonic music; and a 13th-century form in Latin sacred song containing several stanzas, each having the form aA bB or aA ab AB. The rondeau possibly developed from the second, but the forms are essentially different.

rondo An instrumental form characterized by the initial statement and periodic restatement of a melody (or section), whose various appearances are separated by contrasting material. It developed in the 18th century as a solo piece or as a finale of the sonata and symphonic forms.

In the 13th-century songs of the trouvères and in the polyphonic music of the 14th and 15th centuries, the structure of the RONDEAU consisted of two sections A and B, which constituted the music for both the refrain and the *additamenta,* usually taking the form A B a A a b A B. In the harpsichord rondeaux of Couperin, Rameau, and others, the refrain alternated with episodes according to the scheme A B A C A D, etc. The refrain and the episodes were each 8 or 16 measures in length, and each episode gravitated around a different key such as the dominant or the relative minor. The symphonic rondo of the 18th century was not essentially different from these earlier forms. The number of episodes was reduced, and their alternation with the refrain was conceived in such a way that the form had a ternary character. A common form was A B A C A B A. A highly developed form of the rondo is the finale of Mozart's Piano Concerto in A Major (K.488). This is a movement in nine sections in which the episodes are boldly worked out and contrasted. Sometimes in the 19th-century rondo the refrain was inclined to be repeated mechanically, as in Beethoven's Sonata in e minor, Op. 90, where it is heard no less than eight times in its original form. Weber, Chopin, Mendelssohn, and Saint-Saëns are among the composers who developed the rondo in the 19th century. In the 20th century several works of Messiaen, notably the *Turângalila* Symphony, are built on the principle of the rondo.

Rorem, Ned (b. October 23, 1923)   A prolific composer and widely read author, Ned Rorem studied with his U.S. compatriots Copland and Virgil Thomson and with Bernard Wagenaar. From 1949 to 1958 he lived in Paris and Morocco, where his music assimilated French wit and clarity of form and rhythms, coupled with American jazz idioms, while remaining essentially lyrical. Rorem has taught at the University of Buffalo (1959–61) and the University of Utah (1965–67). He has written several hundred songs to texts by contemporary U.S. poets, sacred and secular music for chorus, and eight operas (including *Miss Julie,* after Strindberg, 1964). His many orchestral works include three symphonies and the companion pieces *Water Music* (1966) and *Air Music:* Ten Variations for Orchestra (1975), which won the Pulitzer Prize in 1976. He has written about his life and ideas in his *Paris Diary* (1966) and *New York Diary* (1967), *Music From Inside Out* (1967), *Music and People* (1968), and *Critical Affairs, A Composer's Journal* (1970).

RECORDINGS: *Ariel* for soprano, clarinet, and piano; *Book of Hours* for flute and harp; *Day Music* for violin and piano; Eleven Studies for eleven players; *Gloria; Ideas* for orchestra; *King Midas* (song cycle); *Lions; Lovers* for harpsichord, oboe, cello, and percussion; Madrigals; Night Music for violin and piano; Piano Concerto in six movements; *Poems of Love and the Rain; Some Trees;* Symphony No. 3; Trio for flute, cello, and piano; *War Scenes; Water Music;* songs.

Rosamunde Overture: *see* SCHUBERT (maturity).

Rosbaud, Hans (July 22, 1895–December 31, 1962)   Noted for his understanding of contemporary music, the Austrian conductor Hans Rosbaud studied in Frankfurt and directed the municipal music school and orches-

tra at Mainz before becoming chief conductor (1928) of the Frankfurt Radio and orchestral society there. He left in 1937 to become director of the opera and orchestra at Münster and then at Strasbourg (1941–44). Rosbaud conducted the Munich Philharmonic for three seasons and was appointed (1948) chief conductor of the Southwest German Radio Symphony (Baden-Baden). He conducted in Zürich (1950–58) as well as at the festival at Aix-en-Provence and in the United States.

Rose, Leonard (b. July 26, 1918)   Educated at the Curtis Institute under Felix Salmond, the U.S. cellist Leonard Rose played in the NBC Symphony with Toscanini, the Cleveland Orchestra, and the New York Philharmonic (1944–51). He joined the faculty of the Juilliard School in 1947 and that of Curtis in 1951. Since 1951 he has limited his appearances to solo performances and chamber music and has toured North America and Europe with regularity. His recording of the Brahms Double Concerto with Isaac Stern won the Grand Prix du Disque in 1957. He has performed extensively with Stern and Eugene Istomin; for the Beethoven bicentennial (1970) the trio gave 50 Beethoven concerts in the Americas, Europe, and Israel. His trademark is a consistency of tone; his repertoire is eclectic.

Rosen, Charles (Welles) (b. May 5, 1927)   Educated at the Juilliard School and at Princeton University, the U.S. pianist and musicologist Charles Rosen was a pupil of Moriz Rosenthal. He made his Town Hall (New York City) debut in 1951 and the same year his first recording—Debussy's Études. He taught modern languages at the Massachusetts Institute of Technology (1953–55) and has been a professor of music at the State University of New York at Stony Brook since 1971. His recordings include Bach's *The Art of the Fugue* and *Goldberg* Variations, the last six sonatas of Beethoven, and Elliott Carter's Double Concerto for piano, harpsichord, and two chamber orchestras. His *The Classical Style* (1971) won the National Book Award in 1972, and he published *Schoenberg* in 1975.

Rosenkavalier, Der: *see* LEITMOTIV; LIBRETTO (19th-century influences) and (mod-

ern status); OPERA (the 20th century); POPU-
LAR MUSIC (the 19th century); STRAUSS,
RICHARD.

Rosenthal, Moriz (December 19, 1862–September 3, 1946)   One of the greatest of Liszt's
pupils (he also studied with Rafael Joseffy),
the Polish pianist Moriz Rosenthal was known
in his early years as a thunderous technician,
but he matured into an artist of great sensitivity as well. Among his colleagues Rosenthal
was also noted for a sharp wit and an even
sharper tongue.

Rossini, Gioacchino (Antonio) (February 29,
1792–November 13, 1868)   The principal
19th-century Italian opera composer before
Verdi, Gioacchino Rossini was born at Pesaro.
His father was a town trumpeter and horn-
player in theaters; his mother was a singer.
As a child Rossini studied singing and piano
at Bologna while his parents performed in theaters in the district. He was engaged to sing
as a treble in churches and theaters, and he
also played the horn. In 1807 he entered the
conservatory at Bologna, but over the following years his knowledge of instrumentation
was gained from independent study of the
quartets and symphonies of Haydn and Mozart. He became known as *il tedeschino* ("the
little German") because of his devotion to Mozart. At age 16 he won a prize for his cantata
Il pianto d'armonia per la morte d'Orfeo. His
first opera, *La cambiale di matrimonio,* was
performed at Venice when he was 18. Between
1810 and 1813 he produced several operas
with varying success at Bologna, Rome, Venice, and Milan. *Tancredi* (Venice, 1813), based
on Tasso's *Gerusalemme liberata* and Voltaire's *Tancrède,* was his first world success.
This was preceded by *Il Signor Bruschina* and
followed by *L'italiana in Algeri* and in 1814
by *Il turco in Italia.* Rossini continued to write
operas for Venice and Milan during the next
few years but without repeating the success
of *Tancredi.*

From 1815 to 1823 he was engaged to write
two operas a year for Domenico Barbaja, the
impresario who managed the theaters at Naples and Milan and the Italian opera at Vienna. Audiences liked *Elisabetta, regina
d'Inghilterra* (Naples, 1815) with Barbaja's
mistress, the Spanish soprano Isabella Col-

Gioacchino Rossini
photograph by Étienne Carjat, c. 1868
George Eastman House Collection

bran, whom Rossini married in 1822. In
Almaviva, ossia La precauzione inutile (Rome,
1816), the libretto by Cesare Sterbini was a
version of Beaumarchais's *Barbier de Séville*—
also the source for the libretto of Giovanni
Paisiello's *Barbiere,* an opera that had enjoyed
European popularity for more than a quarter
of a century. Rossini conducted the work himself, but on the first night the opera was hissed.
A more favorable reception greeted the second
performance, and it was soon realized that
Rossini had created a masterpiece; the result
was that the title of *Il barbiere di Siviglia*
passed inevitably to his opera. It is eminent
among Rossini's best works, which are remarkable for their light, captivating rhythms,
their pictorial effects, particularly the long crescendo passages in his overtures, and their
spontaneous melodies.

Rossini produced numerous operas during
the years of his association with Barbaja.
Otello (1816) is notable for its contrast with
the treatment of the same subject by Verdi
at a similar point in his development. The
comic opera *La Cenerentola,* based on the Cin-

705

derella story, was produced at Rome in 1817, *Mosè in Egitto* at Naples in 1818, and *Zelmira* at Naples in 1822. Rossini conducted his own works in Vienna in 1822 and in London the following year. In 1824 he was appointed musical director of the Théâtre Italien in Paris and was later composer to the king and held the title of *inspecteur-général du chant en France*. At the Opéra he produced French versions of several of his earlier Italian works. *Le Comte Ory* was produced there in 1828, and the production of *Guillaume Tell* in 1829 brought his career as a composer of operas to a close. The music of this final operatic work is largely free from the conventions in his earlier works, and it therefore marks an important transitional stage in operatic development.

Apart from brief stays in Bologna and Madrid, Rossini remained in Paris until 1836. From 1836 to 1848 he lived in Bologna, where he was president of the Liceo Musicale and taught singing. In 1837 he separated from his wife and in 1845 married Olympe Pélissier. In 1848 he moved to Florence, returning to Paris in 1855. His comparative silence from 1832 makes his biography appear almost like the narrative of two lives—the life of swift triumph and the long life of seclusion. Between 1832 and 1839 he wrote a *Stabat Mater;* its success compared favorably with the success of his operas. Among other compositions of his later years were the *Petite Messe solennelle* (1864) and a collection of piano pieces, songs, and instrumental works issued under the title *Péchés de vieillesse* ("Sins of Old Age").

BIBLIOGRAPHY: Francis Toye, *Rossini: A Study in Tragi-Comedy* (1954); Herbert Weinstock, *Rossini: A Biography* (1968); Stendhal, *Life of Rossini*, rev. ed. (1970); James Harding, *Rossini* (1971).

RECORDINGS: Numerous recordings of many works.

Rostropovich, Mstislav (Leopoldovich) (b. March 27, 1927) The son of a musical family, the Soviet-born cellist, pianist, and conductor Mstislav Rostropovich entered the Moscow Conservatory in 1937 and 20 years later became a full professor there. In 1955 he married the Bolshoi Opera soprano Galina

Mstislav Rostropovich
courtesy, Columbia Artists Management, Inc.

Vishnevskaya, whom he regularly has accompanied in recitals in addition to his own full recital schedule on the cello. Noted for his wide repertoire and prodigious memory, he played 41 solo works in 11 consecutive concerts in Moscow and 31 works in nine concerts in London. Although he received the Lenin Prize in 1964, he was later blacklisted in the Soviet Union for his public defense of the dissident Soviet author Aleksandr I. Solzhenitsyn and was placed under a three-year travel restriction. In 1974 he was granted a two-year pass to the United States, but he declared that he would not return to the U.S.S.R. until he was given unequivocal artistic freedom; he was stripped of his Soviet citizenship in 1978. Rostropovich became principal conductor of the National Symphony Orchestra in Washington, D.C., in 1977.

Roussel, Albert (Charles Paul Marie) (April 5, 1869–August 23, 1937) A French composer whose music is notable for its lyrical fervor, its austerely intellectual approach, and its harmonic audacities, Albert Roussel studied at the Collège Stanislas in Paris and at the age of 18 joined the French navy. As a sailor he made several journeys to the Far East, whose exotic impressions he recalled in his later orchestral and dramatic works. At 25 he resigned his commission in the navy and devoted himself to music, becoming a pupil of d'Indy at the Schola Cantorum. After studying there for six years he joined the teaching staff in 1902.

Among his early compositions inspired by the Far East are the three *Évocations* for solo voices, chorus, and orchestra and the opera-ballet *Padmâvatî* (Paris, 1923). The earlier ballet *Le Festin de l'araignée* (1913) long remained in the repertoire of the Opéra-Comique. Other notable stage works are the one-act opera *La Naissance de la lyre* (1925) and the ballet *Bacchus et Ariane* (1931). Of his purely orchestral works the best known are the symphonic poem *Pour une fête de printemps*, four symphonies, the Suite in F, and the Sinfonietta for strings, all of which show his bold, personal style. In spite of his early training at the Schola Cantorum, Roussel soon broke away from the influences of Franck and also the Impressionists. His distinguished chamber music includes two violin and piano sonatas, a quartet, and piano and string trios. His songs show a completely unsentimental approach. Among his large-scale choral works is his setting of Psalm 80 for chorus and orchestra (1928). Piano works include a suite, sonatina, and a concerto.

RECORDINGS: Andante and Scherzo for flute and piano; Suite from *Bacchus et Ariane;* Divertissement for flute, oboe, clarinet, bassoon, horn, and piano; Impromptu for harp; *Joueurs de flûte;* Piano Concerto; Piano Sonatina; Psalm 80; *Segovia* for guitar; Serenade for lute, string trio, and harp; Sinfonietta; Suite in F; Symphonies Nos. 3 and 4; piano pieces; songs.

Rozhdestvensky, Gennady (Nikolayevich) (b. May 4, 1931) Educated at the Moscow Conservatory, the Soviet conductor and pianist Gennady Rozhdestvensky was associated with the Bolshoi Theater from 1951 to 1960. In that year he became chief conductor of the Moscow Radio Symphony until 1965, when he served for five years as principal conductor of the Bolshoi. He conducted the Leningrad Philharmonic on its 1973 tour of the United States. Recordings include much 19th- and 20th-century Russian music, including symphonic cycles of Tchaikovsky and Prokofiev.

rubato A subtle rhythmic freedom and nuance in performance from the Italian *rubare,* "to steal." For greater expression the performer stretches some beats, measures, or phrases and compacts others. The term seldom appears in the musical score, but freedom is taken according to the performer's judgment. Rubato may affect only the melody (as in jazz) or the entire musical texture. In the application of rubato the written note values must not be disregarded, and the performer must return to the original underlying rhythm.

Rubbra, Edmund (b. May 23, 1901) A student of Gustav Holst at the Royal College of Music in London, the English pianist and composer Edmund Rubbra lectured at Oxford University (1947–68) and since 1961 has been on the faculty of the Guildhall School of Music in London. He has written eight symphonies (1937–68), three quartets (1934–68), sonatas for cello (1947), viola (1953), oboe (1959), and violin (No. 3, 1968), as well as works for chorus (*Missa cantuariensis,* 1946; *Missa in honorem Sancti Dominici,* 1949; *Veni, Creator Spiritus,* 1966). Much of his music shows the influence of the 16th-century English choral tradition. He has written a monograph on Holst and a textbook, *Counterpoint: A Survey* (1960).

Rubini, Giovanni Battista (April 7, 1795–March 2, 1854) Most successful in the operas of Rossini, Bellini, and Donizetti, the Italian bel canto tenor Giovanni Battista Rubini had his first notable success in Paris in 1825 after he had sung bit parts with companies throughout Italy. From 1831 to 1843 he spent his time in Paris and London, where he was popular at music festivals. In 1843 he toured Europe with Liszt and then sang in Russia, where he was well received and was made director of singing in the Russian dominions. Equally at home with florid or affectingly simple music, he inspired the tenor role in Donizetti's *Anna Bolena,* which was written for him.

Rubinstein, Anton (Grigoryevich) (November 28 [November 16, old style], 1829–November 20 [November 8, old style], 1894) One of

Anton Rubinstein
Royal College of Music, London

the greatest pianists of the 19th century, the Russian composer Anton Rubinstein was born at Vykhvatintsy, Podolia province. In 1835 his father opened a small factory in Moscow, and the same year his brother Nicholas (d. Paris, 1881) was born. Both were taught the piano, first by their mother and then by Aleksandr Villoing. Anton gave his first public recital in Moscow in 1839, and the following year Villoing took him abroad for a three-year concert tour. He appeared in Paris, London, Holland, Germany, and Sweden, attracting the attention of Chopin and Liszt. From 1844 to 1846 he and his brother studied theory in Berlin with Siegfried Dehn. Anton spent two more years abroad alone, mainly in Vienna, studying piano and composition. On his return to Russia in 1849, he settled in St. Petersburg, where in 1852 his first opera *Dimitri Donskoi* was produced; *Fomka the Fool* appeared the following year, and *The Siberian Huntsmen* in 1854 at Weimar. The original form of his once popular Second Symphony, *The Ocean,* came later. The years 1854–58 were spent abroad. Under the patronage of the Grand

Duchess Elena Pavlovna, Rubinstein founded (1859) the Russian Music Society and later became conductor of its orchestral concerts; in 1862 he founded and became the director of the Petersburg Conservatory, and in 1866 his brother founded the Moscow Conservatory. Rubinstein resigned the conservatory directorship in 1867 but resumed it in 1887 and held the post until 1891. From 1871 to 1872 he directed the Vienna Philharmonic concerts, and the next year he toured the United States with Henryk Wieniawski.

His operas include *The Demon* (St. Petersburg, 1875), *The Maccabees* (Berlin, 1875), and *The Merchant Kalashnikov* (St. Petersburg, 1880). He wrote six symphonies, the oratorio *The Tower of Babel* (Königsberg, 1870), five piano concertos, songs, piano pieces, and numerous chamber works.

BIBLIOGRAPHY: Anton Rubinstein, *Autobiography of Anton Rubinstein* (1890; reprint, 1970).

RECORDINGS: Ballet music from *The Demon;* Cello Sonata No. 2; *Konzertstück* for piano and orchestra; Piano Concertos Nos. 3, 4, and 5; Quintet for piano and winds; Symphonies Nos. 2 and 6.

Rubinstein, Artur (b. January 28, 1887) Probably the leading romantic pianist of the

Artur Rubinstein
courtesy, Eva Rubinstein, photographer

mid-20th century, the Polish-born Artur Rubinstein was trained in Warsaw and in Berlin. A natural pianist, he had a mildly successful early career in Europe, but he was not accepted in England or in the United States. After he married (1932) Aniela Mlynarski, the daughter of a Polish conductor, he reformed his playing, adding intense discipline to what had been mostly an ebullient musical personality. Thereafter his success knew no bounds. He became recognized as the greatest living interpreter of Chopin, though his repertoire is all inclusive. In a series of 10 recitals in less than six weeks (1961, New York City), he played more than 200 pieces. He was still in excellent form as late as his 90th birthday, but he retired from public performances soon after because of failing eyesight. His autobiography, *My Young Years,* was published in 1973.

Rubinstein, Nicholas (June 14, 1835–March 23, 1881)   The brother of the Russian pianist and composer Anton Rubinstein, Nicholas Rubinstein studied with Theodor Kullak in Berlin (1844–46). In 1860 he founded a branch in Moscow of the Imperial Russian Music Society, which developed into the Moscow Conservatory six years later. He remained its director for the remainder of his life and conducted the Music Society concerts there. In 1861 he performed in London. Well reputed as a pianist, he was considered to be a better conductor and teacher than his brother; among his students were Emil von Sauer and Alexander Siloti.

Rudel, Julius (b. March 6, 1921)   Educated in his native Vienna, the conductor and opera impresario Julius Rudel also studied at the Mannes College while he was assistant conductor with various opera companies in the New York City area. In 1944 he became a conductor of the newly-formed New York City Opera (general director, 1957–79) and made his debut there in Johann Strauss the Younger's *The Gypsy Baron.* His interest in U.S. musical theater and opera is reflected in his performances of Cole Porter's *Kiss Me, Kate* at the Vienna Volksoper and Rodgers and Hammerstein's *Carousel* and Carlisle Floyd's *Susannah* in Brussels in 1958. Among his numerous administrative posts was the first

music directorship of the Kennedy Center for the Performing Arts in Washington, D.C. (1971).

Rudolf, Max (b. June 15, 1902)   Educated in Frankfurt, the German-U.S. conductor Max Rudolf began his career as an opera coach in Freiburg (1922–23) and in Darmstadt (1923–25). He was principal conductor at the latter from 1927 to 1929 and then conducted in Czechoslovakia and Sweden until 1940. Affiliated with the Metropolitan Opera from 1945, Rudolf made his conducting debut there in 1947 (in Richard Strauss's *Der Rosenkavalier*) and became artistic administrator in 1950. He was conductor of the Cincinnati Symphony (1958–70) and has since been head of the opera department at the Curtis Institute. His *The Grammar of Conducting* was published in 1949.

Ruffo, Titta (June 10, 1877–July 6, 1953)   Educated in Rome and Milan, the Italian baritone Titta Ruffo made his debut in Rome (1898) as the herald in Wagner's *Lohengrin.* After singing in London, Vienna, and Paris, he made his U.S. debut in Philadelphia as Verdi's *Rigoletto* (1912), the same role and year as his Chicago debut. He sang intermittently in Chicago until 1921, and he made his first Metropolitan Opera appearance as Figaro (Rossini's *Il barbiere di Siviglia*) in 1922, remaining until 1929. He sang leading roles in Leoncavallo's *Pagliacci,* Ambroise Thomas's *Hamlet,* and Verdi's *Un Ballo in Maschera* and *Il Trovatore.*

Ruggles, Carl (March 11, 1876–October 24, 1971)   A controversial and important New England composer, Carl Ruggles played the violin for Pres. Grover Cleveland at the age of nine. Though a close friend of such innovative and influential composers as Ives and Edgard Varèse, he was largely self-taught except for some music study at Harvard. For five years following 1912 he conducted an orchestra that he founded at Winona, Minnesota. He was active in composers' organizations in New York (1923–33) and taught composition in Florida (1937). A patron made it possible for Ruggles to devote most of his energy to composition and painting. Because Ruggles destroyed his early compositions, he is known only through a few remaining works. He was elected to the National Institute of Arts and Letters in 1954, and a Ruggles Festival was held at Bowdoin College in Maine (1966).

Among the works released by Ruggles *The Sun-Treader* (1927–32) for orchestra is the longest and most important. It is highly dissonant and complex, rhapsodic and imaginative, characteristics typical of Ruggles' other works. Fond of mystical poetry, Ruggles, like the English poet William Blake, sought sublime, impressionistic effects; this practice led some critics to attack his compositions as being vague and unclear. Ruggles worked over his compositions so that some exist in several different versions. His works include *Toys* (1919) for voice and piano, *Men and Angels* (1920, 1939) for brass, *Men and Mountains* (1924, 1936) for orchestra, works for orchestra and piano, and the hymn *Exaltation* (1958). In all these he uses highly dissonant, nonmetric melodies, wide dynamic range, and rich coloring.

RECORDINGS: *Evocations* for piano; *Men and Mountains; The Sun-Treader.*

Ruins of Athens, The: *see* BAND; BEETHOVEN (last years); JANISSARY MUSIC.

Ruslan and Lyudmila: *see* GLINKA; OPERA (the 19th century).

S

sackbut The Renaissance name for the TROMBONE from *c.* 1470 until about 1700. The name is derived from the old Spanish *sacabuche,* "draw tube," or old French *sacqueboute,* "pull-push." It has thicker walls than the modern trombone, imparting a softer tone, and its bell is narrower.

Sacre du Printemps, Le: *see* BALLET (Diaghilev Ballet); MODERN PERIOD (new paths) and (rediscovery of serialism); STRAVINSKY.

St. John Passion: *see* BACH, JOHANN SEBASTIAN (Leipzig) and (last years); HANDEL (life); ORATORIO (Schütz) and (Bach); PASSION; SCHÜTZ.

St. Matthew Passion: *see* BACH, JOHANN SEBASTIAN (Leipzig) and (last years); COUN-

TERPOINT (Romantic period); MENDELSSOHN; ORATORIO (Schütz) and (Bach); PASSION; SCHÜTZ.

Saint of Bleecker Street, The: *see* MENOTTI; OPERA (the 20th century).

Saint-Saëns, (Charles) Camille (October 9, 1835–December 16, 1921) A French composer, pianist, and organist known for his symphonic poems and his opera *Samson et Dalila,* Camille Saint-Saëns was born in Paris, studied piano with Camille-Marie Stamaty, and gave his first recital as a child prodigy in 1846. At the Paris Conservatoire he studied organ with François Benoist and composition with Fromental Halévy. His First Symphony was performed in 1853. Saint-Saëns was appointed organist at the Church of Saint-Merry in Paris the same year and at the Madeleine in 1857; Liszt described him as "the finest organist in the world." From 1861 to 1865 he was professor of piano at the École Niedermeyer, where his pupils included Fauré and André Messager, and in 1865 he played his First Piano Concerto at Leipzig. In 1871 after the Franco-German War, he founded (with the singer Romain Bussine) the Société Nationale de Musique, which promoted performances of the main French orchestral works of the following generation. He also began writing symphonic poems: *Le Rouet d'Omphale* (1871), *Phaëton* (1873), *Danse Macabre* (1874), and *La Jeunesse d'Hercule* (1877).

Following the production of his first operas, *La Princesse jaune* (1872) and *Le Timbre d'argent* (1877), his biblical opera *Samson et Dalila,* rejected in Paris because of its subject, was given in German at Weimar in 1877 at the recommendation of Liszt. Despite its success the prejudice in France and elsewhere against the portrayal of biblical characters on the stage persisted, and early performances in London, New York City, and Brussels were given in concert form. It was first given in Paris on the stage in 1890 at the Théâtre Eden and subsequently became Saint-Saëns' most popular dramatic work.

In 1878 Saint-Saëns lost his elder son, who fell to his death from a window, and six weeks later his younger son died in infancy. He separated from his wife three years later and un-

Camille Saint-Saëns
courtesy, Musée de Dieppe, France
photograph, Bernard Delacroix

dertook over the following years extensive tours throughout Europe, the Americas, and the Near and Far East. On these tours he played his five piano concertos and conducted his symphonic works. As a pianist he was admired by Wagner for his brilliant technique and was the subject of a study by Marcel Proust.

From about 1880 until the end of his life his large output covered all fields of dramatic and instrumental music. He wrote ten operas, including *Henry VIII, Les Barbares,* and *Déjanire,* and after 1915 a series of works for wind instruments and piano. His popular Third Symphony (1886) with organ and two pianos, dedicated to the memory of Liszt, shows a romantic tendency. *Le Carnaval des animaux* for small orchestra, written in 1886 but not publicly performed in his lifetime, is a humorous work conceived as "a zoological fantasy"; *Africa* (1891) for piano and orchestra and Caprice *Arabe* (1894) for two pianos show Oriental influences; among the best of his later

works are the Fifth Piano Concerto (1896) and the Second Cello Concerto (1902).

Under the influence of Liszt, Saint-Saëns developed the symphonic poem and wrote for the piano in an elegant, virtuoso style. The clarity of his orchestration long remained a model. Though he lived through the period of Wagnerian influence, he remained unaffected by it, adhered to Classical models, and upheld a conservative ideal in French music that was admired for its polished craftsmanship and sense of form. In his essays and memoirs he described the contemporary musical scene in a shrewd and often ironic manner.

BIBLIOGRAPHY: Camille Saint-Saëns, *Musical Memories* (1919; reprint, 1969); Arthur Hervey, *Saint-Saëns* (1922; reprint, 1970); Watson Lyle, *Saint-Saëns: His Life and Art* (1923; reprint, 1970).

RECORDINGS: Numerous recordings of many works.

Salieri, Antonio (August 18, 1750–May 7, 1825) An Italian composer of operas and sacred music, Antonio Salieri was taken to Vienna in 1766 by his teacher Florian Leopold Gassmann, the imperial court composer and music director, who introduced him to Emperor Joseph II. His first opera, *Le donne letterate,* was produced at the Burgtheater in 1770. A succession of operas followed, among them *Armida* (1771), which was enthusiastically received. On Gassmann's death in 1774 Salieri became Kapellmeister, and on Giuseppe Bonno's death in 1788 he was appointed Hofkapellmeister. He held court office for 50 years, during which time he made frequent visits to Italy and France and composed music for many European theaters; one such work was *Les Danaïdes* (Paris, 1784), commissioned by the Académie de Musique at Gluck's recommendation. His most important work was the opera *Tarare* (1787), later called *Axur, re d'Ormus,* which the Viennese public preferred to Mozart's *Don Giovanni.* Salieri's last opera was *Die Negersclaven.* After its production in 1804 he devoted himself to the composition of sacred music. In 1824 he retired from court office on full salary.

Throughout his life he remained on friendly terms with Haydn and with Beethoven, to whom he had given lessons in counterpoint and who dedicated the Opus 12 violin sonatas to him. Salieri was distrusted by Mozart; there is, however, no foundation for Mozart's belief that Salieri tried to poison him—a legend that formed the basis of Rimsky-Korsakov's opera *Mozart and Salieri* and of Cedric Glover's novel, *The Mysterious Barricades* (1964).

RECORDINGS: Concerto in C for flute, oboe, and orchestra; Sinfonia in D.

Salome: *see* HECKELPHONE; LIBRETTO (19th-century influences); STRAUSS, RICHARD.

Salomon Symphonies (Nos. 93–104): *see* HAYDN (London).

saltarello A medieval and Renaissance court dance and a folk dance of present-day Rome. In the 14th century the saltarello followed the estampie as an afterdance; a few examples survive in manuscript. In the 15th century it followed the *basse danse* and was sometimes called *paso de brabante*. It was light and gay and, like the 14th-century dance, was in triple meter. In the 16th century the saltarello was absorbed into and replaced by the galliard. The folk dance is danced by couples to music in $\frac{3}{4}$ or $\frac{6}{8}$ time.

Salzedo, Carlos (April 6, 1885–August 17, 1961) Educated at the Paris Conservatoire, the French harpist Carlos Salzedo toured Europe and the Americas as a recitalist and with orchestras. He went to New York City, where he (with Edgard Varèse and others) founded the International Composers' Guild (1921) to give first U.S. performances of contemporary music for chamber orchestra. He founded (1921) the magazine *Eolus,* devoted to contemporary music (last issue 1933). On the faculty of the Institute of Musical Art (later the Juilliard School), he organized the harp department at the Curtis Institute, where he taught until his death. In 1931 he founded a summer harp colony at Camden, Maine. He toured the United States with the Salzedo Harp Ensemble and played chamber music with flutist Georges Barrère and cellist Paul Kéfer. In addition to solo harp music he wrote Four Choruses (1914) with harp, piano, and organ interludes; *The Enchanted Isle* (1918) for harp and orchestra; Sonata (1922) for harp and piano; *Préambule et jeux* (1929) for harp

and chamber orchestra; and pieces for multiple harps.

Samaroff, Olga, originally Olga Hickenlooper (August 8, 1822–May 17, 1948) The first U.S. woman to be admitted to the Paris Conservatoire, the pianist and educator Olga Samaroff also studied with Ernest Hutcheson in Baltimore and with Ernst Jedliczka in Berlin. Married to the conductor Stokowski (1911–23), she was music critic for the New York *Evening Post* (1927–29) and taught at the Juilliard School and at the Philadelphia Conservatory. Two of her best-known pupils were William Kapell and Rosalyn Tureck. She published a number of books on music appreciation, including *The Layman's Music Book* (1935; rev. ed., *The Listener's Music Book,* 1947).

Sammartini, Giovanni Battista (*c.* 1698–January 15, 1775) An Italian oboist, organist, and composer of sacred music, Giovanni Battista Sammartini spent most of his life in Milan. As early as 1734 he had composed a four-movement symphony. As his orchestral and chamber music began to be known outside Italy, pupils were attracted to Milan, among them Gluck, who studied with him from 1737 to 1741. Sammartini was a prolific composer—of 2,000 works by some estimates—and was one of the formative influences on the development of the pre-Classical symphony and thus on the Classical style itself. It is impossible, however, to determine whether certain works are his, by his brother Giuseppe Sammartini, by Giovanni Battista Martini, or by one of the numerous forgers who profited from the popularity of his genuine works.

RECORDINGS: Symphonies (24); Viola Pomposa Concerto in C.

Sammartini, Giuseppe (*c.* 1693–June 24, 1751) Often called "St. Martini of London" to differentiate him from his more famous brother Giovanni Battista Sammartini, Giuseppe Sammartini first appeared as oboist of the Milan Opera in the early 1720s. His oratorio *La calunnia delusa* was performed there in 1724. In 1729 he went to London, where he stayed for the remainder of his life, much esteemed by the English public as an oboist at the opera and later as a composer and concert performer. After leaving the opera he entered the service of Frederick Louis, Prince of Wales, for whom he wrote a setting of William Congreve's *The Judgment of Paris.* His works, written in the late Baroque style, include some fine trio sonatas and concerti grossi. He published many of his own works, not always profitably. After his death they were a source of profit to certain music sellers, who reissued them using the composer's plates.

RECORDINGS: Recorder Concertos.

Samson: *see* HANDEL (life) and (works); ORATORIO (late 18th century).

Samson et Dalila: *see* SAINT-SAËNS.

Sándor, György (b. September 21, 1912) A pupil of Bartók and Kodály in Budapest, the Hungarian pianist György Sándor has specialized in performing works by those composers, recording their complete output for piano and playing the world premiere of Bartók's Third Piano Concerto (1946). He has also recorded the solo piano pieces of Prokofiev. Sándor has lived in the United States since 1938 and teaches at the University of Michigan.

saraband or **sarabande** A bawdy dance of medieval Spain, probably of Mexican origin. Suppressed during the reign of Philip II, it was later revived in purer form, playing a prominent part in religious dramas. Transplanted to the French court early in the 17th century, it became a slow, serious, processional dance in triple time. The music, of simple structure, was adapted as an important part of the SUITE in which it generally follows the courante.

Sarasate (y Navascués), Pablo (Martín Melitón) de (March 10, 1844–September 20, 1908) A colorful and idolized musician, the Spanish violinist Pablo de Sarasate was best known in his early career for playing elaborate fantasias on opera themes, most of which he composed himself. He mastered the standard repertoire later but played it with great beauty of tone, flawless intonation, and grace of manner. At age 10 he played for Queen Isabella; there is a legend that she gave him a Stradivarius violin, although later research suggests

that he bought it himself. He was given many gifts by his admiring public during successful world tours, and he willed these gifts to a museum to be established in his native town of Pamplona. He was a student of Delphin Alard at the Paris Conservatoire, where he won first prize for violin in 1857. Among the compositions written for him are Édouard Lalo's Violin Concerto, Max Bruch's *Scottish Fantasy,* and two violin concertos by Saint-Saëns. His own compositions were all for violin or violin combined with other instruments.

RECORDINGS: Caprice *Basque; Carmen* Fantasy; Introduction and Tarantella; *Navarra* for two violins; *Spanish Dances; Zigeunerweisen.*

Sargent, (Harold) Malcolm (Watts) (April 29, 1895–October 3, 1967) An English conductor of both orchestral and choral music, Malcolm Sargent began his career as an organist. His work as a conductor began in 1921 with a performance of his own composition, *Impressions of a Windy Day,* at the London Promenade Concerts (of which he later became principal conductor). In 1923 he taught conducting at the Royal College of Music and from 1928 was chief conductor of the Royal Choral Society. He was associated with the British National Opera and conducted several English choral and orchestral organizations, including the Hallé Orchestra (1939–43), Liverpool Welsh Choral Union (from 1941), Liverpool Philharmonic (1942–48), and Leeds Philharmonic Society (from 1947), and was chief conductor of the BBC Symphony from 1950 to 1957 and chief guest conductor thereafter. In 1926 he conducted a season at D'Oyly Carte, and his recordings of nearly all the Gilbert and Sullivan operettas are well reputed. He conducted at numerous summer festivals in the British Isles and premiered a number of English operas (Vaughan Williams' *Hugh the Drover,* 1924; Gustav Holst's *At the Boar's Head,* 1924; William Walton's *Troilus and Cressida,* 1954). Also an arranger of English folk music, he revived Arne's melody of the British hymn *Rule, Britannia.* He was knighted in 1947. His many recordings range from Handel's *Messiah* through the Romantic repertoire to Prokofiev.

713

Ali Akbar Khan playing sarod

courtesy, American Society for Eastern Arts

sarod A northern Indian instrument of the lute family, played, either by plucking or bowing, in classical dance orchestras and solo with *tablah* (drums) and tambura (drone-lute). It has a deep body with a skin belly, a broad neck with an unfretted metal fingerboard, four melody strings, and several sympathetically vibrating strings. The melody strings are tuned c'–f'–g'–c″, beginning with middle C.

Sarti, Giuseppe (baptized December 1, 1729–July 28, 1802) An Italian opera composer, Giuseppe Sarti studied with Francesco Antonio Vallotti in Padua and Giovanni Battista Martini in Bologna, becoming organist at the cathedral of Faenza (1748–50) and of the theater there (from 1752). His first two operas were successfully produced in Faenza (1752) and Venice (1753). He served the Danish court at Copenhagen intermittently (1754–75) and became director of the Ospedaletto Conservatory in Venice (1775) and maestro di cappella of the Milan Cathedral (1779), where Cherubini was among his pupils and served as his assistant. His most successful operas were written during this Italian period: *Farnace* and *Le gelosie villane* (Venice, 1776), *Achille in*

Sciro (Florence, 1779), *Giulio Sabino* (Venice, 1781), and *Fra i due litiganti* (Milan, 1782). In 1784 he was invited by Catherine II to St. Petersburg as director of court music. On his way he stopped at Vienna, where he met Mozart, who used an aria from *Fra i due litiganti* as a theme for a set of variations (K.460) and in *Don Giovanni*. Sarti greatly improved the standard of Italian opera in St. Petersburg and wrote both sacred and operatic works, including a Te Deum that used fireworks and the firing of real cannon and a Russian opera *Nakalnoy upravlenye Olega* ("The Early Reign of Oleg") with a libretto by the empress. Sarti fell out of favor at court and while temporarily exiled founded a school of singing in the Ukraine. He returned to St. Petersburg in 1793 and was restored to his position as court composer and became director of the St. Petersburg Conservatory. After the death of Catherine and the murder of her successor Paul I, Sarti left Russia (1802) and returned to Berlin. Although the melodic and harmonic aspects of Sarti's serious operas are not always distinguished, his accompanied recitatives have much character, and his comic operas are remarkable for their ensembles.

Satie, Erik (Alfred Leslie) (May 17, 1866–July 1, 1925) A French composer whose highly individual style gives him a unique place in modern music, Erik Satie studied at the Paris Conservatoire from 1879 and later worked as a café pianist. About 1890 he became associated with the Rosicrucian movement and wrote several works under its influence, notably the *Messe des pauvres* (1895). In his 40th year he began study at the Schola Cantorum with d'Indy and Albert Roussel. Satie made a deliberate cult of eccentricity by giving his works grotesque titles and sprinkling their pages with comical annotations, but his genuine originality won the admiration of major composers, including Debussy (who orchestrated two of the *Gymnopédies* for piano) and Ravel. His Sarabandes (1887) and *Gymnopédies* (1888) revealed him as a pioneer in harmony. In his ballets, *Parade* (1916) and *Mercure* and *Relâche* (both 1924), he created a new style of choreographic music. He wrote little for voice, but *Socrate* (1918) for four sopranos and chamber orchestra on extracts from the *Dialogues* of Plato is his master work.

BIBLIOGRAPHY: Rollo H. Myers, *Erik Satie* (1948; reprint, 1968); Pierre-Daniel Templier, ed., *Erik Satie* (1969).

RECORDINGS: Numerous recordings of many works.

Sauer, Emil von (October 8, 1862–April 28, 1942) A pupil of Nicholas Rubinstein at the Moscow Conservatory and briefly of Liszt, the German pianist Emil von Sauer was known as an immaculate player with taste and style. He taught in Vienna and in Dresden and composed numerous works for the piano.

Sax, Adolphe, real name, Antoine Joseph Sax (November 6, 1814–February 7, 1894) A maker of instruments and the inventor of the saxophone, Adolphe Sax was born at Dinant, Belgium, the son of Charles Joseph Sax, a maker of wind instruments—especially brass, pianos, harps, and guitars. Adolphe Sax studied flute and clarinet at the Brussels Conservatoire and in 1842 went to Paris, where he exhibited the saxophone, a single-reed instrument made of metal with a conical bore, overblowing at the octave, the result of his efforts to improve the tone of the bass clarinet.

It was patented in 1846. With his father he evolved the saxhorn (patented in 1845), an improvement on the bugle horn; the saxotromba, producing a tone between that of the bugle and the trumpet; and the saxtuba. In 1857 Sax was appointed instructor of saxophone at the Paris Conservatoire. In the latter part of his life Sax improved several instruments and invented others without, however, establishing a basis for their commercial exploitation. In his 80th year he was living in abject poverty; Chabrier, Massenet, and Saint-Saëns petitioned the minister of fine arts to come to his aid.

saxophone A family of reed wind instruments patented by Adolphe Sax in Paris in 1846. A saxophone has a conical brass tube with about 24 openings controlled by padded key mechanisms. A single-reed mouthpiece akin to that of the clarinet is placed over the narrow end. The instrument overblows at the octave by means of two octave-key vents operated by a thumb key. The normal compass is written from B-flat below the treble staff to F three lines above the staff sounding differently with each member of the family. The B-flat soprano saxophone, sounding a tone lower than written pitch, is built straight like a clarinet. The other members of the family have the lower end upturned and the upper end made as a detachable crook. They are the E-flat alto sounding a sixth lower than written; the B-flat tenor, with undulating crook, sounding a ninth lower; the E-flat baritone, with looped crook, an octave below the alto; and the rarer B-flat bass, similar in shape to the baritone but larger, an octave below the tenor. Little-used sizes include the C melody saxophone, a tenor in C for playing from vocal music without transposition. Originally the whole family of saxophones was pitched in C and F alternately.

Sax left no historical account of his invention, intended for military bands, which he may have discovered through experiments with reed mouthpieces on brass instruments such as ophicleides. He quickly procured its official adoption by the French army, and saxophones from alto to baritone are regularly included in bands constituted on French mod-

alto saxophone
courtesy, Henri Selmer & Cie., Paris

els. In the United States they have been used in bands from Patrick Sarsfield Gilmore's time. In British military bands only an alto and a tenor are obligatory. The saxophone was a popular solo instrument in the United States about the time of World War I and was then adopted by dance bands in which the standard team remains two altos and a tenor. Larger bands use more than four saxophones and include the baritone. The use of saxophones in dance bands brought mechanical improvements and changes in mouthpiece design to produce brighter, more penetrating sounds.

As a serious concert instrument the saxophone was cultivated by virtuosi, notably Sigurd Rascher in the United States and Marcel Mule, founder both of the Paris Saxophone Quartet (soprano, alto, tenor, baritone) and of the class at the Paris Conservatoire. Debussy, Glazunov, and Ibert are among earlier composers who wrote solo works for saxophone, all for the alto instrument. From Bi-

zet's *L'Arlésienne* (1872) until the 1920s, orchestral works using the saxophone were few, though Richard Strauss wrote for a quartet of saxophones in his *Symphonia domestica* (1904). Paul Creston has written both a sonata (1939) and a concerto (1941), Milhaud *Scaramouche* (1942) for saxophone and piano, and Heitor Villa-Lobos a fantasia (1948) for saxophone and orchestra.

Sayão, Bidù, real name, Balduína de Oliveira Sayão (b. May 11, 1902) A student of Jean De Reszke, the Brazilian soprano Bidù Sayão made her operatic debut in Rome (1926) as Rosina in Rossini's *Il barbiere di Siviglia* and then sang with the Opéra-Comique. Her U.S. recital debut was in New York City in 1935, and she first sang at the Metropolitan Opera in 1937 as Massenet's Manon, appearing there until 1952. Her last operatic appearance was in Rio de Janeiro in 1958. Her repertoire included the roles of Mimi (Puccini's *La Bohème*), Violetta (Verdi's *La Traviata*), and Gilda (Verdi's *Rigoletto*).

scale Any selected sequence of notes or intervals dividing the octave. This is a theoretical conception by which the material of an existing or a historical practice can be systematized for readier understanding and explanation. Theoretically the octave can be divided into a number of microtones; *i.e.,* tones smaller than a semitone. In antiquity, and currently in the Orient but not to any marked extent in the West, intervals smaller than a semitone were in regular use. Such a practice yields a scale that is unfamiliar to the modern Western listener.

pentatonic Many historical and some existing traditions of music make use of five notes only (with their octave transpositions), and such a practice yields a pentatonic scale. This is a gapped scale; *i.e.,* a scale containing intervals of more than a tone. One of the more familiar pentatonic scales is the equivalent of the black notes of the keyboard.

diatonic The division of the octave into seven notes appears very early in Western music. Medieval musicians employed a variety of seven-note scales known as modes (*see* MODE). These contained two semitone intervals that occurred in a different relation to the *final* in each mode. Two modes, the Ionian and the Aeolian (in a slightly modified form), remain in general use as the diatonic major and minor scales (*see* GREEK MUSIC, ANCIENT). In each major and each minor scale the semitone intervals occur in the same relation to the key note (or tonic). In the major scale the semitones occur between notes 3–4 and 7–8:

Semitone   Semitone

The minor scale has two forms, the melodic minor and the harmonic minor. In the melodic minor the semitones occur between notes 2–3 and 7–8 ascending and between notes 6–5 and 3–2 descending:

Semitone   Semitone

Semitone   Semitone

In the harmonic minor the semitones occur between 2–3, 5–6, and 7–8, with the interval of an augmented second (a tone plus a semitone) between notes 6–7:

Semitone   Semitone   Semitone
                              Augmented

In all forms of the diatonic scale the names given to the degrees of the ascending scale are: tonic, supertonic, mediant, subdominant, dominant, submediant, and leading tone.

chromatic A scale that comprises all the 12 semitones in the octave, the chromatic scale can be considered as a coloring of the diatonic scale. The medieval musician regarded the notes C and C-sharp, for example, not as separate notes but as two aspects of one note. This could be written as C and altered in performance "by reason of necessity or of beauty."

At a later date, because of equal temperament, diatonic scales were built on any of the 12 notes of the octave. In the late 19th century the extreme use of CHROMATICISM caused the partial destruction of diatonic tonality.

The scale of 12-tone, or dodecaphonic, music (*see* SERIALISM) uses the notes of the chromatic scale but does not permit the establishment of any tonal center.

whole-tone The whole-tone scale is often associated with Debussy, although it had been used as early as the 18th century by Mozart (in a sextet called "A Musical Joke"). As its name implies, it is a scale without semitones and therefore consists of only six notes.

19th and 20th-century composers created other experimental scales.

Scarlatti, (Pietro) Alessandro (Gaspare) (May 2, 1660–October 24, 1725) An Italian composer of operas and religious works and one of the most important figures in the development of classical harmony, Alessandro Scarlatti was sent at about age 12 to Rome, where he may have studied with Carissimi. The first of his 115 operas, *Gli equivoci nel sembriante* (1679), written for a religious fraternity in Rome, won him the protection of Queen Christina of Sweden, for whom he wrote *L'onestà negli amori* (1680) and in whose service he remained until 1683. These works brought commissions for operas from Naples, where in 1684 he became maestro di cappella in the royal service. He remained there until 1702, writing more than 40 operas and musical entertainments for the court and its circle. *Gli equivoci in amore* (1690) is a typical example of that period.

In 1702 Scarlatti went to Pratolino near Florence, where over the next two years he wrote four operas for the theater of Prince Ferdinando de' Medici; the scores of these works have disappeared. In 1703 he was appointed assistant to Antonio Foggia at Sta. Maria Maggiore in Rome, succeeding him as

maestro di cappella in 1707. That year Scarlatti wrote two larger-scale operas, *Il trionfo
della libertà* and *Mitridate Eupatore,* for the
carnival in Venice. He returned to his old post
at Naples in 1709, and a period of intense
activity produced serenades and masses as well
as operas such as *La principessa fedele* (1710),
Scipione nelle Spagne (1714), and *Tigrane*
(1715). The ternary aria form was developed
in these works, which are also remarkable for
a bolder use of the orchestral stringed instruments. In 1716 he wrote a mass for Pope
Clement XI and completed his first opera
buffa, *Il trionfo dell'onore* (Naples, 1718).

Scarlatti uses thematic development and
chromatic harmony with great mastery that
anticipates such composers as Mozart and
Schubert. Though he is chiefly remembered
for his operas, in which he established the
form of the "Italian" overture, his chamber
music is equally characteristic and shows him
to have had a commanding conception of
form. More than 500 chamber cantatas from
all periods of his life are extant. His church
music is of unequal value, though the second
of his two masses with orchestra (1720) marks
a new development, anticipating the masses
of Bach and Beethoven. He wrote little orchestral music, but he contributed to the development of the opera orchestra.

BIBLIOGRAPHY: Edward J. Dent,
Alessandro Scarlatti: His Life and Works, 2nd
ed. (1960).

RECORDINGS: Cantatas; Concerti grossi
(12); Madrigals (complete); Motets—*Domine,
refugium; O magnum mysterium; Stabat Mater.*

Scarlatti, (Giuseppe) Domenico (October 26,
1685–July 23, 1757)   An Italian harpsichord
composer and virtuoso in an age that was principally interested in the voice, opera, orchestra, and violin, Domenico Scarlatti was born
in Naples, the son of the opera composer Alessandro Scarlatti. At the age of 15 he was appointed organist and composer to the royal
chapel in Naples, leaving in 1705 to travel
through Florence to Venice, where he met
Handel and Thomas Roseingrave. Roseingrave did much to spread Scarlatti's fame in

Domenico Scarlatti
engraving by an unknown artist
G. Handel—Ziolo

England and described his playing as though
"ten hundred devils had been at the instrument." Early in 1709 in Rome Scarlatti succeeded his father as composer to the former
Queen Maria Casimira of Poland. In 1713 he
was appointed assistant and in 1714 maestro
di cappella at St. Peter's, but he left Rome
in 1719 "for England," and by 1720 he appears
to have been in Lisbon, where he became master of the royal chapel and harpsichord teacher
to Princess Maria Barbara. He followed the
future queen to Spain when she married in
1729 and served her in Madrid until her death.

Scarlatti composed wholly or in part at least
12 operas between 1703 and 1715; two operatic intermedi; a number of oratorios, serenades, cantatas, and arias, and some church
music. Much of this music is lost, but a fine
ten-part *Stabat Mater* and a serenata, *Contesa
delle Stagioni,* with prominent parts for trumpets and horns, were published in modern
times. His most distinctive production by far,
however, is his series of at least 555 sonatas:
about 10 are for violin and continuo, three
are specifically for organ, and the remainder

for harpsichord. In 1738 he published 30 harpsichord sonatas as *Essercizi per gravicembalo,* followed quickly by a number of English and French publications of other relatively early sonatas. His most mature period and largest output (350 sonatas) was concentrated in the years between 1753, when he was 67, and his death four years later. Most of the sonatas survived in two dated manuscript collections now in Venice and Parma, one of which was copied for Queen Maria Barbara herself.

Although a few of the early sonatas, such as those for violin, consist of up to four movements, the bulk are single movements, normally in two sections. At least 388, however, were composed as pairs in the same or related keys and represent in effect 194 two-movement sonatas; at least a dozen more are in triptychs. In style the earliest are not unlike Handel's keyboard music. The middle-period sonatas exhibit technical brilliance—including hand crossing—and display a pronounced individuality. The late sonatas show a maturing of these tendencies and span an endless range of moods and emotions that frequently recall the everyday life of his adopted Spain.

BIBLIOGRAPHY: Ralph Kirkpatrick, *Domenico Scarlatti,* rev. ed. (1955; reprint, 1968).

RECORDINGS: Sinfonias (3) for flute, oboe, and strings; Sonatas; *Stabat Mater.*

Schaeffer, Pierre (b. August 14, 1910) A French composer, acoustician, and electronics engineer, Pierre Schaeffer and his staff at Radiodiffusion et Télévision Française introduced in 1948 MUSIQUE CONCRÈTE. Schaeffer's 10-movement *Symphonie pour un homme seul* (1949–50), produced in collaboration with Pierre Henry, was the first major concrete piece. This and other works of *musique concrète* had an important influence on composers of aleatory, or chance, music. Schaeffer wrote the experimental opera *Orphée 53* (1951–53, with Henry) and music for piano. Schaeffer's books *À la recherche d'une musique concrète* (1952) and *Solfège de l'objet sonore* (1967) give an account of his work. Under the auspices of the French Radio, he developed the first studio devoted to electronic music.

Scheherazade: *see* SHEHERAZADE.

Scheidt, Samuel (1587–March 30, 1654) A German composer best known for his works for organ, Samuel Scheidt went to Amsterdam in about 1605 and studied with Jan Pieterszoon Sweelinck. In 1609 he returned to his native Halle, where he was first appointed organist at the Moritzkirche and about 1619 organist and later Kapellmeister to the Margrave of Brandenburg. Scheidt remained in Halle and established a reputation as a teacher; his most famous pupil was Adam Krieger.

Scheidt's first published works contain sacred vocal music; they include *Cantiones sacrae* (1620) for eight voices, and four books of *Geistliche Concerten* (1631–40) for two to four voices and continuo. The publication of his *Tabulatura nova* (three parts, 1624) was an important event in the history of organ music, "new" in the use of Italian staff notation in place of the traditional German organ tablature. The work contains fantasias, toccatas, echo pieces, sets of variations, and organ responses for liturgical use. Although the influence of Sweelinck is noticeable, Scheidt's work displays a technical skill and feeling for the organ with well-developed counterpoint and carefully indicated directions for registration. By contrast, his *Tabulatur-Buch* (1650), containing harmonized accompaniments for 100 "sacred songs and psalms," is indicative of the growing practice of congregational chorale singing that was to become customary in the Lutheran Church.

RECORDINGS: Organ pieces.

Scherchen, Hermann (June 21, 1891–June 12, 1966) Associated with performances of 20th-century music, the German conductor Hermann Scherchen played viola in the Berlin Philharmonic (1907–10) and then studied for two years with Schoenberg. In 1912 he was Schoenberg's associate in the premiere of *Pierrot Lunaire.* From 1914 he conducted in Russia and Germany, where he founded the Neue Musikgesellschaft in 1918 and became general director of music at Königsberg (1928–31). After leaving Germany in 1932 he worked in Vienna and Switzerland, conducting and teaching at festivals of modern music. He was a prominent member of the International Society for Contemporary Music and in 1964 made his U.S. debut with the Philadelphia Orchestra. He edited several periodicals on modern music (*Melos,* 1919–21; *Musica Viva,* 1933–36) and founded the magazine *Gravesaner Blätter,* devoted to electronic music, in 1954; the same year he inaugurated an electro-acoustical studio in Gravesano, Switzerland. In 1950 he founded the publishing house Ars Viva in Zürich, later taken over by B. Schott's Söhne. Scherchen also encouraged performances of the music of Schoenberg, Webern, Luigi Dallapiccola, and Luigi Nono. He wrote a *Handbook of Conducting* (1933; in German, 1929) and *The Nature of Music* (1950; in German, 1946). Interested in the technical side of recordings, he made many acoustical experiments. His own recordings, not limited to contemporary music, included much standard repertoire (*e.g.,* symphonies of Haydn, Beethoven, and Mahler).

scherzo   A form whose Italian name means "jest" or "caprice." Humor is, however, not always a characteristic of the form. The *Scherzi musicali* (1607) of Monteverdi are canzonets that are bright rather than humorous, and in 1614 religious pieces were published in Rome under the title *Scherzi sacri.* The term acquired a new meaning in the sonatas, quartets, and symphonies of the 19th century, principally those of Beethoven. In these works the scherzo was a development of the 18th-century minuet, which in fact had already acquired some of the characteristics of the scherzo. Several of the minuets of Haydn, in both his quartets and his symphonies, use reiterated or abrupt rhythms that are foreign to the stately nature of the minuet and that anticipate the gruesome humor of the Beethoven type of scherzo. In his Opus 33, known as *Gli scherzi,* Haydn actually uses the term scherzo in place of minuet.

The distinguishing feature of the 19th-century symphonic scherzo is that it is in rapid $\frac{3}{4}$ time with elements of surprise in dynamics and orchestration. The solo drumbeats in the scherzo of Beethoven's Ninth Symphony form one of the most dramatic effects in this form. Frequently the playfulness of the Beethoven scherzo is designed to conceal an underlying dramatic tension. In the Fifth Symphony the theme of the jubilant scherzo is used as a bridge passage expressing a mood of terror. Other composers who developed the symphonic scherzo were Schubert and Bruckner. In sonatas and symphonies the scherzo is usually followed by a trio, a piece in a slower tempo, with a repeat of the opening scherzo according to the scheme ABA.

In the 19th century the scherzo was also an independent instrumental or orchestral movement in a vivacious, airy style. The masters of this animated type of scherzo were Weber, Berlioz, and Mendelssohn. Brilliant effects of orchestration and exhilarating, pointed rhythms in a swift tempo mark such virtuoso works of this kind as Berlioz' *Queen Mab* scherzo and Mendelssohn's scherzo from his *Midsummer Night's Dream* music. Mendelssohn's chamber works, particularly the octet, the two piano trios, and the two quintets, contain remarkable examples of the light, swift-moving scherzo.

In the symphonies and instrumental works of Schumann the scherzos have a lyrical or a nostalgic nature, and they are frequently combined with two trios. Brahms in his symphonies and chamber music similarly conceived the scherzo as a movement with dark undertones. The four scherzos of Chopin are in a class by themselves. His use of the term appears to be purely arbitrary, unless it was meant to convey an element of ironic humor at the core of such highly Romantic works. In later Romantic music one of the most successful examples of the form is Paul Dukas' *Sorcerer's Apprentice,* described as a "scherzo based on a ballad of Goethe." The scherzo or scherzando movements in the symphonies of Mahler combine humor with lugubrious or even diabolic elements. In the scherzo of Mahler's Tenth Symphony these darker elements are so boldly exteriorized as to determine the essential character of the movement. The score of this scherzo bears the inscription, "The devil dances with me. Madness seizes me. . . annihilates me."

Schikaneder, Emanuel: *see* MOZART (later life).

Schippers, Thomas (March 9, 1930–December 16, 1977)   The principal interpreter of Menotti, with whom he founded the Spoleto (Italy) Festival of Two Worlds in 1958, the U.S. conductor Thomas Schippers studied at the Curtis Institute and privately (piano) with Olga Samaroff. He made his living as a church organist until his debut as a conductor in 1948 with the Lemonade Opera Company in New York City. In 1950 he conducted the premiere of Menotti's opera *The Consul,* the following year becoming resident conductor of the New York City Opera (until 1954). He first conducted at La Scala and at the Metropolitan Opera in 1955, conducting the premiere of Copland's *The Tender Land.* He became the first U.S. conductor to be assigned an opening night performance at the Metropolitan and ultimately conducted more opening nights than any conductor in the preceding 40 years, including the opening of the new opera house at Lincoln Center in 1966 with Samuel Barber's *Antony and Cleopatra.* He was the only U.S. conductor to hold three major Italian posts: music director at Spoleto (resigned 1975), director of special projects for RAI (Italian Radio, 1970–74), and music director of the Santa Cecilia Academy orchestra in Rome. In 1959 and 1976 he toured the Soviet Union with the New York Philharmonic. In 1970 he was appointed music director of the Cincinnati (Ohio) Symphony, where he remained until his death.

Schmelzer, Johann Heinrich (*c.* 1623–February/March 1680)   Associated with the Court Chapel at Vienna from 1649, the Austrian violinist and composer Johann Heinrich Schmelzer became Kapellmeister there in 1679. He wrote numerous vocal and instrumental works, ballet music for the operas given at court, violin sonatas (mostly written between 1659 and 1664), a *missa nuptialis,* and trumpet fanfares for a festival play by Antonio Bertali (1667). Much of his music remains in manuscript.

RECORDINGS: *Sacro-profanus concentus musicus.*

Schmidt-Isserstedt, Hans (May 5, 1900–May 28, 1973)   After study in his native Germany the conductor Hans Schmidt-Isserstedt conducted opera at Wuppertal (1925–28), Rostock (1931–33), and Darmstadt (1931–33) before becoming principal conductor at the Hamburg State Opera (1935–42). In 1943 he became director of the Deutsches Opernhaus in Berlin, remaining until 1945. In that year he founded the North German Radio Symphony in Hamburg and served as conductor. He was also principal conductor of the Stockholm Philharmonic (1955–64). Schmidt-Isserstedt was especially interested in the early Italian operas of Mozart and composed a comic opera (*Hassan gewinnt,* 1928) as well as chamber and orchestral music and songs.

Schmitt, Florent (September 28, 1870–August 17, 1958)   A French composer known for his orchestral works, Florent Schmitt studied at Nancy and in 1889 entered the Paris Conservatoire, where he was a pupil of Massenet and Fauré. In 1900 he won the Prix de Rome with his lyric scene *Sémiramis* and later traveled throughout Europe. He gained fame with the *Psaume XLVI* (1906) for chorus and orchestra, the ballet *La Tragédie de Salomé* (1907), and a piano quintet (1908). He wrote many orchestral works that showed a bold sense of orchestral color, including *Antoine et Cléopâtre* (1920), *Mirages* (1924), and *Salammbô* (1927). Among his piano pieces, several of which he orchestrated, are the *Reflets d'Allemagne* (1905). He wrote unaccompanied choral works and chamber music, including *Suite en rocaille* (1935), *A tour d'anches* (1947), woodwind and brass quartets, and a sextet for clarinets.

RECORDINGS: *Psaume XLVI; Quatre Poèmes de Ronsard; La Tragédie de Salomé; Trois Chants.*

Schnabel, Artur (April 17, 1882–August 15, 1951)   To many in the first half of the 20th century, the Austrian pianist Artur Schnabel was "Mr. Beethoven," although he played Mozart, Schubert, Schumann, and Brahms as well. The first to record (1931–35) all of Beethoven's piano sonatas, he also published a

Artur Schnabel, 1950   *Camera Press photograph, Jack Greenstone*

widely-used practical edition (1935). A pupil of Annette Essipoff and of Leschetizky, he was not at all typical of the Leschetizky school. His interests were intellectual and musical—not technical. Though a classical player, he composed in an advanced, atonal idiom, and his works were not very popular. Schnabel taught in Berlin (1925–33) and attracted pianists from all parts of the world to his summer master classes in Switzerland.

BIBLIOGRAPHY: César Saerchinger, *Artur Schnabel* (1957; reprint, 1973); Konrad Wolff, *The Teaching of Artur Schnabel* (1972).

Schneider, Alexander (b. December 21, 1908) An organizer and promoter of festivals and opportunities for young people, the Lithuanian-born U.S. violinist and conductor Alexander Schneider studied at the Frankfurt Conservatory and with Carl Flesch in Berlin. After playing with the Budapest Quartet (1933–44; 1957–62), he founded his own ensemble. In 1956 he established the New School Concerts and in the 1970s the Brandenburg Ensemble. His innovations include the Bach-at-Midnight concerts, the 1973 Weekend of Brahms, outdoor concerts in Washington Square, and the Mostly Mozart Festival (since 1966) in New York City. He was assistant musical director of the Casals Festival (1957–75) and has been associated with the Marlboro (Vermont) Festival both as violinist and conductor.

Schnorr von Carolsfeld, Ludwig (July 2, 1836–July 21, 1865) The German Wagnerian tenor Ludwig Schnorr von Carolsfeld studied at the Leipzig Conservatory. He appeared in Karlsruhe and then at the Dresden Court Opera (1860–65), where his wife Malwina Garrigues was the dramatic soprano. Together they created the roles of Wagner's Tristan and Isolde (1865) in Munich. They also wrote poetry, a book of which was published posthumously (1867).

Schoeck, Othmar (September 1, 1886–March 8, 1957) A Swiss composer of lieder, Othmar Schoeck studied first at Zürich and in 1907 with Max Reger in Leipzig. His first songs appeared the following year on his return to Zürich, where until 1917 he conducted choral societies. From 1917 to 1944 he was conductor of the symphony concerts at Sankt Gallen. His principal song cycles for voice and small ensemble include *Elegie* (1915–22) on poems on Nikolaus Lenau and Jospeh von Eichendorff, *Gaselen* (1923) on poems of Gottfried Keller, and *Wandersprüche* (1928) on poems of Eichendorff. He also wrote eight stage works, including *Penthesilea* (1927) and *Massimilla Doni* (1937), and orchestral and chamber works.

RECORDINGS: Horn Concerto; *Notturno* for baritone and quartet; *Sommernacht* for strings.

Schoeffler, Paul (b. September 15, 1897) After study in Dresden and Milan, the German baritone Paul Schoeffler sang in Dresden (1925–37) and then at the Vienna State Opera. His U.S. debut was at the Metropolitan Opera in 1950 as Jokanaan in Richard Strauss's *Salome,* and he continued to sing roles there of Strauss and Wagner, especially that of Hans Sachs *(Die Meistersinger).*

Schoenberg, Arnold (September 13, 1874– July 13, 1951)   The Austrian-U.S. composer whose innovations were among the most powerful influences in 20th-century music, Arnold Schoenberg was born in Vienna and lived there, apart from two short periods in Berlin (1901–03 and 1911–15), until he was over 50. He learned to play the violin as a child and later taught himself the cello, but he was not originally destined for a musical career. He worked in a bank for several years before finally devoting himself to music (1895). As a composer he was almost entirely self-taught, though he received some help from his friend Alexander von Zemlinsky, whose sister he married in 1901. Schoenberg's first model was Brahms, but the earliest works he published, the string sextet *Verklärte Nacht* and the choral work *Gurrelieder,* are indebted to Wagner. These two influences are reconciled in the First and Second Quartets (1905 and 1908) and the First Chamber Symphony (1906), all of which show Schoenberg's lifelong concern with structural unity and at the same time an advanced form of chromaticism that threatened to undermine the traditional major-minor tonal system.

About 1909 Schoenberg began to write music that could no longer be related to a single tonal center; hence the term atonality, or as he preferred, pantonality. Dissonances are no longer felt to need resolution, and the recapitulations and symmetrical melodic paragraphs belonging to tonality disappear. Three Pieces,

Arnold Schoenberg   *Pictorial Parade*

Op. 11, for piano and Five Pieces, Op. 16, for orchestra (both 1909) opened unexplored fields of expression and soon became internationally famous. They were followed by two one-act operas, *Erwartung* (1909; performed 1924) and *Die glückliche Hand* (1908–13; performed 1924); the chamber work *Pierrot Lunaire* (1912); and the oratorio *Die Jakobsleiter* (1913; unfinished).

From 1907 onward Schoenberg was also painting pictures. He became friends with Wassily Kandinsky and in 1912 exhibited with the Blue Rider group. Through this association the term expressionist was applied to Schoenberg's music and to that of his two most gifted pupils, Webern and Berg. These composers were to remain his close friends, adapting his successive technical discoveries to their own needs. A by-product of his work as a teacher, which continued throughout his life, was a series of important theoretical works on music, the first of which was the *Harmonielehre* (1911; *Theory of Harmony,* 1947).

From 1920 Schoenberg became preoccupied with a group of works embodying a new prin-

723

ciple of composition. Since abandoning tonality he had confined his instrumental music to short pieces built of contrasting lyrical or dramatic elements. His longer works had been vocal, the text providing the basis for the form. Large-scale instrumental composition had formerly depended on two elements, the tonal and the thematic. Schoenberg realized that the loss of the one could be offset by strengthening the other. He gradually evolved the technique of SERIALISM, through which a whole composition could be derived from a series of notes, usually the 12 notes of the chromatic scale, disposed in an order specially chosen for the particular work. He called it a "method of composing with twelve notes related only to one another." In the works of the 1920s, which are all serial, Schoenberg's profound sympathy with the Viennese Classical tradition reasserts itself in his adaptation of his new language to symphonic forms. He wrote four important chamber works, including the Third Quartet, Variations for orchestra, a short comic opera, *Von Heute auf Morgen* (produced 1930), and the first two acts of *Moses und Aron* (1930–32; produced 1957). This opera is concerned with the nature of divine revelation and the problem of its communication, and it embodies Schoenberg's deepest beliefs.

In 1923 Schoenberg's first wife died, and the following year he married Gertrud Kolisch, the sister of the violinist Rudolf Kolisch. In 1926 he went to Berlin as director of a master class in composition at the Prussian Academy of Arts but in 1933 was dismissed from this post because he was a Jew. He moved to Paris for a few months and returned to the Jewish faith, which as a young man he had left for the Lutheran Church. In the autumn of the same year, he went to Boston and spent a year teaching there and in New York City. From 1936 to 1944 he taught at the University of California, Los Angeles, becoming a U.S. citizen in 1941.

During his last months in Europe Schoenberg wrote concertos for cello and for string quartet, based on material from concertos by Georg Matthias Monn and Handel respectively, and in 1934 a Suite in G for string orchestra. After these tonal works, his first

in more than 20 years, Schoenberg completed two major serial works in 1936, the Violin Concerto and the Fourth Quartet. In the last 15 years of his life he composed less, overcome at first by the political situation in Europe and later because of failing health. Some of the works of this period are serial, among them such masterpieces as the Piano Concerto (1942), String Trio (1946), and the unfinished *Moderner Psalm* (1950) on his own text; others are based on tonality in one form or another. All show the composer's extraordinary mastery in developing a whole work within the terms of the opening idea. His strong personality is similarly felt through every phase of his output; the revolutionary, who strongly influenced the course of musical history both in his break with tonality and his formulation of serialism, was also a traditionalist for whom innovation was never experiment but simply the most direct means to an end.

BIBLIOGRAPHY: Egon Wellesz, *Arnold Schönberg* (1925; reprint, 1969); Merle Armitage, ed., *Schoenberg: Articles by Arnold Schoenberg, Erwin Stein & Others, 1929–1937* (1937; reprint, 1977); Dika Newlin, *Bruckner-Mahler-Schoenberg* (1947); René Leibowitz, *Schoenberg and His School* (1949; reprint, 1970); Arnold Schoenberg, *Letters* (1964) and *Style and Idea* (1975); Anthony Payne, *Schoenberg* (1968); Willi Reich, *Schoenberg: a Critical Biography* (1971); Arnold Whittall, *Schoenberg Chamber Music* (1972); Charles Rosen, *Arnold Schoenberg* (1975); Malcolm MacDonald, *Schoenberg* (1976); H.H. Stuckenschmidt, *Schoenberg* (1977).

RECORDINGS: Numerous recordings of many works.

schöne Müllerin, Die: *see* SCHUBERT (maturity) and (final years).

Schreiner, Alexander (b. July 31, 1901) The German-born U.S. organist Alexander Schreiner is known to millions through network broadcasts of the Mormon Tabernacle Choir in Salt Lake City, beginning in 1929. Educated at the University of Utah, he studied organ with Charles-Marie Widor and Louis Vierne in Paris. He was organist of the tabernacle (1924–78) and served on the faculty of the University of California at Los Angeles (1930–39).

Schröder, Jaap (b. December 31, 1925) Educated at the Amsterdam Conservatory and later a professor there, the Dutch violinist and conductor Jaap Schröder won the Jacques Thibaud Competition in 1948. He led the Radio Chamber Orchestra (1950–63), played in the Netherlands String Quartet (1952–69), and founded the Quadro Amsterdam (1960–66) and Concerto Amsterdam in 1962. His recordings range from Telemann to Hindemith.

Schröder-Devrient, Wilhelmine (December 6, 1804–January 26, 1860) The daughter of a singer and an actress, German dramatic soprano Wilhelmine Schröder-Devrient appeared as a child actress until her successful singing debut in Vienna in 1821 as Pamina (Mozart's *Die Zauberflöte*). The following year she was acclaimed there as Leonore (Beethoven's *Fidelio*), which did much to assure the success of the work (it was first heard there in its final form in 1814). She sang in Dresden, Paris, and London, where she was popular at Covent Garden. She created the Wagnerian roles of Adriano (*Rienzi,* 1842), Senta (*Der fliegende Holländer,* 1843), and Venus (*Tannhäuser,* 1845). Her sympathy with the 1848 revolution forced her exile, but she later sang in Berlin until the early decline of her voice.

Schubert, Franz (Peter) (January 31, 1797–November 19, 1828) One of the originators of the Romantic style and yet one of the greatest of the post-Classicists, the Viennese composer Franz Schubert was the fourth surviving son of a schoolmaster. The family was musical and cultivated quartet playing, the boy Schubert playing the viola. He received the foundations of his musical education from his father and his brother Ignaz, continuing later with organ and theory with the parish church organist. In 1808 he won a scholarship that earned him a place in the imperial court chapel choir (now known as the Vienna Choir Boys) and education at the Stadtkonvikt, the principal boarding school for commoners in Vienna, where his tutors were Wenzel Ruzicka and later Antonio Salieri, then at the height of

his fame. Schubert played violin in the student orchestra, was quickly promoted to leader, and in Ruzicka's absence conducted. With his fellow pupils Josef von Spaun, Albert Stadler, and Anton Holzapfel, he cultivated chamber music and piano playing.

From the evidence of his school friends, Schubert was inclined to be shy and was reluctant to show his first compositions. His earliest works included a long fantasia for piano duet, written in 1810, D.1 (*i.e.,* No. 1 in Otto Erich Deutsch's *Schubert: Thematic Catalogue of All His Works in Chronological Order,* 1951); his first song, "Hagars Klage," D.5 (1811); several orchestral overtures; various pieces of chamber music, and in 1811 three quartets. An unfinished operetta on a text by August von Kotzebue, *Der Spiegelritter,* D.11, belongs to that year also. The interest and encouragement of his friends overcame his shyness and eventually brought his work to the notice of Salieri.

In 1813 Schubert's voice broke; he left the college but continued his studies privately with Salieri for at least another three years. During this time he entered a teachers' training college in Vienna and in the autumn of 1814 became assistant in his father's school. Rejected for military service because of his short stature, he continued as a schoolmaster until 1818.

years of promise The numerous compositions written between 1813 and 1815 are remarkable for their variety and intrinsic worth. They are the products of young genius still short of maturity but displaying style, originality, and imagination. In addition to five quartets, including those in E-flat, D.87, and g minor, D.173, there were three full-scale masses and three symphonies. The Third Symphony in D Major, a charming example of Schubert's youthful lyricism and high spirits, was finished in 1815. His first full-length opera, *Des Teufels Lustschloss,* was finished in 1814 while he was at the training college. But at this period song composition was his chief, all-absorbing interest. On October 19, 1814, he set his first poem by Goethe, "Gretchen am Spinnrade" from *Faust;* it was his 30th song, and in this masterpiece he created at one stroke the 19th-century German lied. The following year he composed more than 140

Franz Schubert
watercolor by W. A. Rieder, 1825
courtesy, Historisches Museum der Stadt Wien

songs, including many of the first order such as "Rastlose Liebe," "Meerestille," and "Erlkönig" and such exquisite specimens of his lyrical art as "Heidenröslein" and "Erster Verlust." The author of the texts of all these was Goethe, whose poems always inspired Schubert.

The many unfinished fragments and sketches of songs left by Schubert provide some insight into the working of his creative mind. Clearly the primary stimulus was melodic. The words of a poem engendered a tune; harmony and modulation were then suggested by the contours of the melody, but the external details of the poet's scene—natural, domestic, or mythical—prompted such graphic images in the equally important piano parts as the spinning wheel, the ripple of water, or the "shimmering robe" of spring. These features were fully present in the songs of 1815. The years that followed deepened and enriched but did not revolutionize these novel departures in song. In 1815 also Schubert continued to be preoccupied with his ill-fated operas: between May and December he wrote *Der vierjährige Posten, Fernando, Claudine von Villa Bella,* and *Die Freunde von Salamanka.*

At this time Schubert's outward life was uneventful. Friends of his college days were faithful, particularly Spaun, who in 1814 introduced him to the poet Johann Mayrhofer. He also induced the young and brilliant Franz von Schober to visit Schubert. Late in 1815 Schober went to the schoolhouse in the Säulengasse, found Schubert in front of a class with his manuscripts piled about him, and inflamed the young composer—a willing listener—with a desire to break free from his duties. In the spring of 1816 Schubert applied for the post of music director in a college at Laibach (now Ljubljana, Yugoslavia) but was unsuccessful. His friends tried to interest Goethe in the songs and in April 1816 sent a volume of 16 settings to the poet at Weimar. It produced no result. Despite his father's reluctance he obtained a leave of absence in December 1816 and spent eight months with Schober, living in the home of his friend's widowed mother and paying for his keep whenever he could.

Early in 1817 Schober brought the baritone Johann Michael Vogl to meet Schubert. As a result of this meeting Vogl's singing of Schubert's songs became the rage of the Viennese drawing rooms. His friendships with the Hüttenbrenner brothers Anselm and Josef and with Josef von Gahy, a pianist with whom he played duets, date from these days. But this period of freedom did not last, and in the autumn of 1817 Schubert returned to his teaching duties. He wrote to his friends of himself as a *verdorbener* ("frustrated") musician. The two earlier years had been particularly fruitful. Songs of this period include "Litanei auf das Fest aller Seelen," "An Schwager Kronos," "Ganymed" (the song that had captivated Vogl at their first meeting), "Der Wanderer," and the *Harper's* Songs from Goethe's novel *Wilhelm Meister*. Smaller but equally remarkable are "An die Musik," "Der Tod und das Mädchen," and "Die Forelle." There were two more symphonies: the Fourth in c minor, which Schubert himself named the *Tragic* (1816), and the popular Fifth in B-flat (1816). The Fourth Mass in C Major was composed in 1816. The year 1817 is notable for the beginning of his masterly series of piano sonatas. Six were composed at Schober's home, the finest being the Eighth in E-flat, D.568, and the Tenth in B Major, D.575; both were published posthumously.

Schubert's years of uncongenial schoolmastering ended in the summer of 1818. His frustrated period in the spring had produced only one substantial work, the Sixth Symphony in C Major. But in the meantime his reputation was growing, and the first public performance of one of his works, the *Italian* Overture in C Major, took place on March 1, 1818, in Vienna. In June he left the city to take up the post of music master to the two daughters, Marie and Karoline, of Johann, Count Esterházy, in the family's summer residence at Zseliz, Hungary. Letters to his friends show him in exuberant spirits, and the summer months were marked by a fresh creative outburst. The Variations for piano duet in e minor, D.624, the piano duet Sonata in B-flat, D.617, sets of dances, songs, and a German Requiem were all composed at Zseliz.

maturity On his return to Vienna he shared lodgings with Mayrhofer and during the winter months composed the operetta *Die Zwillingsbrüder*. Although sponsored by Vogl the production of the work was postponed, and in June 1819 Schubert and Vogl set off for a protracted holiday in the singer's native district of Steyr in upper Austria. The composer delighted in the beauty of the countryside and was touched by the enthusiastic reception given everywhere to his music. At Steyr he composed the first of his widely known instrumental compositions, the Piano Sonata in A Major, D.664, and the celebrated *Trout* Quintet for piano and strings, D.667. The close of 1819 saw him engrossed in songs to poems by his friend Mayrhofer and by Goethe, who inspired the masterly *Prometheus*. The Fifth Mass in A-flat was started but laid aside. Another sacred work, begun in 1820 but left unfinished, was the cantata *Lazarus,* anticipating Wagner in its fusion of lyrical and declamatory styles.

In June 1820 *Die Zwillingsbrüder* was performed with moderate success at the Kärntnerthor Theater in Vienna, Vogl doubling the parts of the twin brothers. It was followed by the performance of incidental music for the play *Die Zauberharfe,* given at the Theater an der Wien in August of the same year. The lovely, melodious overture became famous as the *Rosamunde* Overture. Schubert was achieving renown in wider social circles than the restricted spheres of friend and patron. The Sonnleithner family was interested in his development; their son Leopold became a great friend and supporter. At the close of the year 1820 Schubert composed the *Quartettsatz* in c minor, heralding the great quartets of the middle 1820s, and another popular piece, the motet for female voices on the text of Psalm XXIII. In December 1820 he began the choral setting of Goethe's "Gesang der Geister über den Wassern" for male octet, D.714, completed in February 1821.

All Schubert's efforts to publish his own work were fruitless. Early in 1821, however, a few friends, including Leopold von Sonnleithner and Josef Hüttenbrenner, offered the "Erlkönig" on a subscription basis. The response was so successful that enough money was raised for the printing of "Gretchen am Spinnrade." "Erlkönig" appeared as Schubert's Opus 1 on April 2, 1821, and "Gretchen" as Opus 2 on April 30, 1821. From then on songs, part songs, dances, and piano duets were published. Eighteen months later Opus 12 had been reached.

In Vienna the popularity of Schubert's songs and dance music became so great that concert parties were entirely devoted to them. These parties, called *Schubertiade,* were frequently given in the homes of wealthy merchants and civil servants. But the wider worlds of opera and public concerts still eluded him. He worked during August 1821 on the Seventh Symphony in e minor and major, but this too was put aside along with many other unfinished works of the period. His determination to establish himself in opera led him in September and October to spend a short holiday with Schober at St. Polten, where the friends devoted their energies to the production of a 3-act opera *Alfonso und Estrella.* It was completed in February 1822 but was never performed. While spending a few days at Atzenbrugg in July 1822 with Schober and other friends, he produced the document called *Mein Traum* ("My Dream"), describing a quarrel between a music-loving youth and his father. Fanciful biographical interpretations of this document have little, if any, factual foundation. The autumn of 1822 saw the beginning of yet another unfinished composition—but this time not destined to obscurity: the *Unfinished* Symphony No. 8 in b minor, which speaks from Schubert's very heart. Two movements were completed in October and November 1822, the abandoned work including also a half-finished scherzo. In November of the same year Schubert composed a piano fantasia in which the variations are on a theme from his song "Der Wanderer." The Mass in A-flat was also completed in this month.

At the close of 1822 Schubert contracted a venereal disease, probably syphilis, and the following year was one of illness and retirement. He continued to write almost incessantly. In February he wrote the Piano Sonata in a minor, D.784, and in April he made another attempt to gain success in the Viennese theaters with the one-act operetta *Die Verschworenen* ("The Conspirators"), the title changed later (because of political censorship) to *Der häusliche Krieg* ("War in the Home"). The famous work of the year, however, was the song-cycle *Die schöne Müllerin,* representing the epitome of Schubert's lyrical art. Other songs of this period are "Auf dem Wasser zu singen" and "Du bist die Ruh'." Schubert spent part of the summer in the hospital and probably started work while a patient on his most ambitious opera *Fierrabras.* The

work was rejected by the directorate of the Kärntnerthor Theater. The year 1823 closed with Schubert's composition of the music for the play *Rosamunde,* performed at the Theater an der Wien in December. This production failed; the text of the play is lost, and the music was subsequently heard only in the concert hall.

The early months of 1824 were again unhappy. Schubert was ill, penniless, and plagued by a sense of failure. Yet during these months he composed three masterly chamber works: Quartet in a minor, Quartet in d minor containing variations on his song "Der Tod und das Mädchen," and Octet in F Major for strings and wind instruments. His dejection transpires in a letter of March 31, 1824, to his friend Leopold Kupelwieser, the painter, in which he speaks of himself as "the most unfortunate, the most miserable being in the world." In desperate need of money he returned in the summer to his teaching post with the Esterházy family and in May 1824 went again to Zseliz. Once more his health and spirits revived. The period was marked by some magnificent piano duets, the *Grand Duo* Sonata in C Major, D.812, the Variations on an original theme in A-flat, D.813, and the *Hungarian* Divertissement, D.818. The first work was published posthumously; the other two in Schubert's lifetime, in 1825 and 1826.

Although his operas remained unperformed there were frequent public performances of his songs and part songs in Vienna in these and the following years. Publication proceeded rapidly, and his financial position, though still strained, was eased. In 1825 he spent another holiday in upper Austria with Vogl, visiting Linz, Gmunden, and Gastein and finding a warm welcome for himself and his music wherever he went. This is the period of the *Lady of the Lake* songs (to words of Sir Walter Scott, translated by P. Adam Storck), including the popular "Ave Maria," and the Sonatas in a minor, D.845, and in D Major, D.850, the latter composed at Gastein. He sketched a symphony during the summer holiday (in all probability the beginnings of the *Great* C Major Symphony completed in 1826). The spring of 1825 had seen the composition of two well-known songs, "Im Abendrot" and "Die junge Nonne," followed in the late summer by "Die Allmacht" and "Das Heimweh," two of his greatest songs inspired by nature. New friends, Moritz von Schwind, a young painter, and Eduard Bauernfeld, a dramatist, were almost continuously in his company during this period. Schwind left pictorial records of Schubert; Bauernfeld, reminiscences.

final years The resignation of Salieri as imperial Kapellmeister in 1824 had led to the promotion of his deputy Josef Eybler. In 1826 Schubert applied for the vacant post of deputy Kapellmeister, but in spite of strong support by several influential people he was unsuccessful. From then on until his death two years later he seems to have let matters drift. Neither by application for professional posts nor submission of operatic work did he seek to establish himself. It can hardly be believed that Schubert was unaware of his exceptional powers; yet together with an awareness of genius and the realization that it opened doors into cultivated society went the knowledge of his humble birth and upbringing and of his somewhat uncouth bearing. This self-consciousness made him diffident, reserved, and hesitant. His life was almost entirely devoted to composition, and he derived his livelihood from publishers' fees and occasional teaching. The songs of 1826 include the settings of Shakespeare's "Hark! Hark! the lark!" and "Who is Silvia?" written during a brief stay in the village of Währing. Three fine instrumental works of this summer and autumn are the last Quartet in G Major, the Sonata in G Major, D.894, and the start of the Piano Trio in B-flat, D.898.

In 1827 he composed the first 12 songs of *Winterreise,* a return to the poems of Wilhelm Müller, author of *Die schöne Müllerin.* Beethoven's death in 1827 undoubtedly had a profound effect on Schubert. It is perhaps going too far to imagine that he considered himself Beethoven's heir and that henceforth he deliberately attempted to reproduce Beethoven's manner in his work. But there is no denying that a more profound and intellectual quality appears in his last instrumental works. Some of them, especially the Piano Trio in

E-flat (1827) and the c minor Sonata (1828), suggest the authority of Beethoven, but his own strong individuality is never submerged.

In September 1827 Schubert spent a short holiday in Graz as a guest of Karl and Marie Pachler. On his return he composed the Piano Trio in E-flat and resumed work on the second part of the *Winterreise;* the 13th song, "Die Post," was written in October 1827. This is the period of his piano solos, the Impromptus and *Moments musicaux.*

A succession of masterpieces marks the last year of his life. Early in the year he composed the greatest of his piano duets, the Fantasia in f minor, D.940. The *Great* C Major Symphony was concluded in March as was the cantata *Miriams Siegesgesang.* In June he worked at his Sixth Mass in E-flat. A return to songwriting in August produced the series published together as the *Schwanengesang.* In September and early October the succession was concluded by the last three sonatas, in c minor, A major, and B-flat (D.958, 959, and 960), and the great String Quintet in C Major—the swan song of the Classical era in music.

The only public concert Schubert gave took place on March 26, 1828. It was both artistically and financially a success, and the impecunious composer, it is recorded, was at last able to buy himself a piano. At the end of August he moved into lodgings with his brother Ferdinand, then living in a suburb of Vienna. Schubert's health, broken by the illness of 1823, had deteriorated, and his ceaseless work had exhausted him. In October he developed typhoid fever as a result of drinking tainted water. His last days were spent in the company of his brother and several close friends. He died in Vienna, and on his tomb in the Währingerstrasse Cemetery was engraved the epitaph of Grillparzer: "The Art of Music has here entombed a rich treasure, but yet far fairer hopes."

Schubert's place in the history of music is equivocal: he stands between the worlds of Classical and Romantic music. His music—subjectively emotional in the Romantic manner, poetically conceived, and revolutionary in language—is nevertheless cast in the formal molds of the Classical school—with the result that in the 20th century it is increasingly apparent that Schubert belongs more to the age of Haydn, Beethoven, and Mozart than to that of Schumann, Chopin, and Wagner.

BIBLIOGRAPHY: Oskar Bie, *Schubert, the Man* (1928; reprint, 1970); Otto E. Deutsch, *Schubert: A Documentary Biography* (1946; reprint, 1977) and *Schubert: Memoirs by His Friends* (1958); Maurice J. E. Brown, *Schubert: A Critical Biography* (1958; reprint, 1977), *Essays on Schubert* (1966; reprint, 1977), *Schubert Songs* (1969), and *Schubert Symphonies* (1971); Marcel Schneider, *Schubert* (1959; reprint, 1976); Jack A. Westrup, *Schubert Chamber Music* (1969); Franz Schubert, *Franz Schubert's Letters and Other Writings* (1970); Philip Radcliffe, *Schubert Piano Sonatas* (1971); John Reed, *Schubert: The Final Years* (1972); Arthur Hutchings, *Schubert*, rev. ed. (1973); Hans Gal, *Franz Schubert and the Essence of Melody* (1974); C. Whitaker-Wilson, *Franz Schubert, Man and Composer* (1976); Dietrich Fischer-Dieskau, *Schubert's Songs: A Biographical Study* (1977); Joseph Wechsberg, *Schubert: His Life, His Work, His Time* (1977); Peggy Woodford, *Schubert* (1978).

RECORDINGS: Numerous recordings of many works.

Schuller, Gunther (b. November 22, 1925) The U.S. composer, conductor, jazz scholar, and educator Gunther Schuller is the son of a New York Philharmonic violinist and received his early musical training at the St. Thomas Choir School. From that time he was largely self-taught, but he played principal horn with the Cincinnati Symphony (1943–45) and in the Metropolitan Opera orchestra (1945–59), teaching horn at the Manhattan School (1951–59). He taught at Yale University (1964–67), served as president of the New England Conservatory (1967–77), and supervised contemporary music activities at Tanglewood from 1965.

Schuller's early works were influenced by Mahler and Schoenberg and include Horn and Cello Concertos (both 1945) and Symphony for brass and percussion (1950). His chamber music is notable for unusual instrumental combinations such as the Fantasia Concer-

tante (1947) for three oboes or trombones and piano, Quartet (1947) for four double basses, Fantasy Quartet (1959) for four cellos, and *Tre invenzione* (1972) for harpsichord, piano, winds, and percussion. By 1955 Schuller was combining elements from disparate styles in works such as his *12 by 11* for chamber orchestra and jazz improvisation. His larger-scale works continued the trend and include the serial Seven Studies on Themes of Paul Klee (1959); *Spectra* (1960); the ballet *Variants* (1961); Piano Concerto (1962); Symphony (1965); *American Triptych* (1965) after Alexander Calder, Jackson Pollock, and Stuart Davis; *Shapes and Designs* (1968); and *Museum Piece* (1970) for Renaissance instruments and orchestra. The abstract titles indicate Schuller's fascination with color and pictorial allusions. Choral works include Psalm 98 (1966) and an oratorio, *The Power Within Us* (1972).

Schuller coined the term "third stream" to denote the amalgamation of jazz with classical contemporary music. It is well illustrated in his *Conversations* (1959) for jazz and string quartets and ultimately in Concerto for orchestra and his opera *The Visitation* (both 1966).

Schuller is the author of *Horn Technique* (1962) and *Early Jazz: Its Roots and Musical Development* (1968).

RECORDINGS: *Contours* for chamber orchestra; *Dramatic* Overture; Five Bagatelles; *Five Moods* for tuba quartet; *Lines and Contrasts* for 16 horns; Oboe Sonata; Quartet No. 1; Symphony for brass and percussion; *Tre invenzione;* Woodwind Quintet.

Schuman, William (Howard) (b. August 4, 1910) One of the major 20th-century exponents of the mainstream of Western symphonic music, the U.S. composer William Schuman was educated at Columbia University and studied with Charles Haubiel, Bernard Wagenaar, and Roy Harris. Schuman taught at Sarah Lawrence College, Bronxville, New York (1935–45), and was president of the Juilliard School (1945–62). There he effected academic reforms and innovations in teaching methods and curriculum. He was president of the Lincoln Center for the Performing Arts (1962–69) and since 1970 has been chairman of the board of the Videorecord Corporation of America.

Schuman's music is influenced by the possibilities of orchestral sound and by U.S. popular music and jazz. Two early symphonies and a quartet were performed and later withdrawn. The *American Festival* Overture and the Third Quartet (both 1939), the Third Symphony (1941), and the cantata *A Free Song* (1942; on poems by Walt Whitman) established his reputation and won numerous awards. The Third and Fourth Symphonies utilize established formal procedures as the basis for dissonances. Textures are polyphonic; old forms such as passacaglia, fugue, and chorale are invested with new sonorities. Of the Fifth through Eighth Symphonies (1943–62), the last, composed for the opening of Philharmonic Hall (now Avery Fisher Hall) at Lincoln Center, is the most successful. The Ninth Symphony (subtitled *Le Fosse ardeatine*), premiered in Philadelphia in 1969, is dedicated to Italian civilians murdered by the Nazis in World War II.

The ballet *Undertow* (1945; choreographed by Antony Tudor) has traces of expressionism. *Night Journey* (1947) and *Judith* (1950) were choreographed by Martha Graham. *New England Triptych* (Three Pieces after William Billings, 1956) borrowed themes from Billings' psalms and fuguing tunes. *A Song of Orpheus* (1962) for cello and orchestra is a fantasy based on Schuman's song "Orpheus with His Lute" (1944).

Schuman has written four quartets; a violin concerto (1947), an opera, *The Mighty Casey* (1953); *Credendum* (1955) and *In Praise of Shahn* (1970) for orchestra; and various choral works. His music has influenced that of William Bergsma, Vincent Persichetti, and Robert Ward.

BIBLIOGRAPHY: Flora Rheta Schreiber and Vincent Persichetti, *William Schuman* (1954).

RECORDINGS: *Carols of Death; Chester Overture; Credendum; In Praise of Shahn; New England Triptych; Prayer in Time of War;* Quartet No. 3; *A Song of Orpheus;* Symphonies Nos. 3, 4, 5, 7, and 8; Variations on *America* (after Charles Ives); Violin Concerto; *When Jesus Wept.*

Schumann, Clara (Josephine), before her marriage, Clara Josephine Wieck (September 13, 1819–May 20, 1896) The leading classical pianist of the 19th century, Clara Schumann studied with her father Friedrich Wieck, who was a successful pedagogue in Leipzig. Well established by the time of her marriage (1840) to the composer Robert Schumann, much of her life was thereafter devoted to him and their eight children. She found some time to concertize, however, and to promote her husband's compositions. Her playing and her musical standards were the antithesis to those of Liszt and his followers, and her opposition to him was almost pathological. After her husband's death in 1856 she lived in Berlin and at Baden-Baden until her appointment to the Frankfurt Conservatory (1878–92). She again toured extensively, playing the works of her close friend Brahms and as the great authority on Robert Schumann.

Schumann, Elisabeth (June 13, 1885–April 23, 1952) Known for her operatic roles of Mozart and songs of Richard Strauss, the German soprano Elisabeth Schumann made her debut in Hamburg in 1910 after studying there with Alma Schadow. For 20 years she was associated with the Vienna State Opera, also singing at festivals in Berlin, Munich, and London. Her Metropolitan Opera debut was in 1914 as Sophie in Richard Strauss's *Der Rosenkavalier.* In 1921 she toured the United States with Strauss, and she created the role of Ilia in his revision of Mozart's *Idomeneo.* Following her retirement from opera she taught (from 1938) at the Curtis Institute. She took part in the first Edinburgh Festival (1947) and published *German Song* (1948).

Schumann, Robert (Alexander) (June 8, 1810–July 29, 1856) One of the leading early Romantic German composers, Robert Schumann is known particularly for his nearly 250 songs and his major contribution to the literature for the piano. He was born at Zwickau, Saxony, the son of a bookseller and publisher. After four years at a private school, he entered the Zwickau Gymnasium in 1820 and remained there for eight years. He began his musical education at the age of six and in 1822 produced his earliest known compo-

Robert and Clara Schumann
lithograph by J. Hofelich
The Bettmann Archive, Inc.

sition, a setting of Psalm 150. Young Schumann also began to show literary ability, embarking on plays (a comedy and two "horror dramas") and poems, including some translations of Horatian odes. In 1827 he came under the musical influence of Schubert and the literary influence of Jean Paul Richter; both proved deep and enduring.

early career In 1828 Schumann left school, and under pressure from his mother and his guardian (his father having died) he entered Leipzig University as a law student; but his time was devoted not to the law but to song composition, improvisation at the piano, and attempts to write autobiographical novels in the manner of Jean Paul. For a few months he studied the piano seriously with a celebrated teacher, Friedrich Wieck, and thus became acquainted with Wieck's nine-year-old daughter Clara, a brilliant pianist who was beginning a successful concert career.

In the summer of 1829 he left Leipzig for Heidelberg, where one of the law professors, Justus Thibaut, was known as a writer on musical aesthetics. Under Thibaut's influence he made the acquaintance of a great deal of cho-

ral music, from Palestrina to Bach. He composed Schubertian waltzes (later used in the piano cycle *Papillons*) and practiced industriously with the intention of abandoning law and becoming a virtuoso pianist. His mother allowed him to return to Leipzig in October 1830 to study for a trial period with Wieck, who thought highly of his talent but doubted his stability and capacity for hard work.

Schumann's relations with Wieck were never happy, nor were they with the conductor Heinrich Dorn with whom he worked for a year at harmony and counterpoint. He always found it difficult to concentrate, and he was distracted from his musical studies by the writing of yet another autobiographical novel, *Die Davidsbündler,* in which two self-projections, Florestan and Eusebius, were created. These two characters also appeared in Schumann's first published critical essay on Chopin's *Là ci darem* variations (*Allgemeine musikalische Zeitung,* December 7, 1831) and often later in critical writings, as reviewers of new music, and even as the composers of his own works. His Opus 1, a set of variations originally conceived—like Chopin's—for piano and orchestra, had been published just two months before the Chopin article. An accident to one of the fingers of his right hand put an end to his hopes of a career as a virtuoso but was perhaps not an unmitigated misfortune, as it confined him to composition. This was a period prolific in piano pieces, which were published either at once or later in revised forms. In October 1832 Schumann embarked on a Symphony in g minor; the first movement was played three times in public, the third time in Clara Wieck's concert at the Leipzig Gewandhaus, but the symphony was never completed.

Two important piano works of 1834 resulted from a love affair with another of Wieck's pupils, Ernestine von Fricken: the cycle *Carnaval,* based on the letters A, S (Es, *i.e.,* E-flat), C, H (B-natural in German), which spelled the town Asch where she lived and were also in his own name; and the Études *symphoniques,* variations on a theme by her father. The affair lasted for more than a year, but long before the engagement was formally broken off (January 1, 1836), Schumann had fallen in love with the now 15-year-old Clara Wieck. Clara returned his affection but obeyed her father when he ordered her to break off the relationship. Schumann found himself abandoned for 16 months, during which he expressed his alternate despair and resignation in the great Fantasy in C Major for piano, drank wildly, sought consolation with other girls, and even published a bitter, veiled lampoon on Clara in the *Neue Zeitschrift für Musik* (a periodical he had helped to found in 1834 and of which he had been editor and principal proprietor since the beginning of 1835). Clara herself made the first move toward a reconciliation, and on September 13, 1837—her 18th birthday—Schumann formally asked her father's permission to marry her; the request was at first evaded rather than refused.

Schumann now entered on one of his most fertile creative periods, producing the *Davidsbündlertänze, Novelletten, Kinderscenen, Arabeske, Blumenstück, Humoreske,* and *Faschingsschwank aus Wien,* among other well-known piano works. (Most of the *Faschingsschwank* was actually written in Vienna during a visit in which Schumann unearthed a number of Schubert manuscripts, including that of the *Great* Symphony in C Major.) Even this was not a time of unalloyed happiness, for Clara refused to marry without financial security, and her father still withheld his consent. A formal statement by Clara on June 15, 1839, initiated legal proceedings for the setting aside of that condition. The affair dragged on for more than a year; it was taken to a court of appeal, which upheld Wieck's objection that Schumann was a heavy drinker, and to a yet higher one, which ruled that Wieck must produce proof of habitual drunkenness. This he failed to do, and on September 12, 1840, the marriage took place. Early that year Schumann returned to a field he had neglected for nearly 12 years, that of the solo song; in 11 months (February–December 1840) he composed nearly all the songs on which so much of his reputation rests: the cycles *Myrthen,* the Heine and Chamisso *Liederkreis, Dichterliebe, Frauenliebe und -leben,* and many separate songs.

larger works   Clara had been pressing him to widen his scope, to launch out in other media—above all, the orchestra. He had in earlier days made at least five unsuccessful attempts at works for piano and orchestra; even the g minor Symphony was never finished. Now in January–February 1841 he composed his First Symphony in B-flat *(Spring),* which was performed under Mendelssohn at the Leipzig Gewandhaus on March 31; an Overture, Scherzo, and Finale (April–May); Fantasy for piano and orchestra (May), which was expanded into the famous Piano Concerto in a minor by the addition of two more movements in 1845; Symphony in d minor (June–September; revised in 1851 as the Fourth); and the sketches for yet another symphony (in c minor) of which only the scherzo survives as the piano piece Opus 99, No. 13. The orchestral impulse was temporarily spent. Schumann was much occupied with his *Neue Zeitschrift;* he wanted to write an opera; and his first experience of a concert tour with Clara showed that the public regarded him only as "the great pianist's husband." He returned to Leipzig alone and drowned his melancholy in "beer and champagne."

On Clara's return he essayed another new medium—new except for a youthful Piano Quartet in c minor (1829)—chamber music. Between June 1842 and January 1843 he wrote Three Quartets, the Piano Quintet, the Piano Quartet in E-flat, a piano trio in a minor (recast in 1850 as the *Fantasiestücke,* Op. 88), and Andante and Variations for two pianos, two cellos, and horn that has become better known in a later version for pianos only. The year 1843 was marked by Schumann's most ambitious work to date, a secular oratorio (originally conceived as an opera) on Thomas Moore's *Paradise and the Peri.* He made his debut as a conductor—a role in which he was invariably ineffective—with its first performance.

During his work on *The Peri* the Leipzig Conservatory had been opened with Mendelssohn as director and Schumann as professor of "piano playing, composition, and playing from score"; again he had embarked on activities for which he was unsuited. The period February–May 1844 was spent on a concert tour of Russia with Clara, which again depressed Schumann by the consciousness of his inferior role. On returning to Leipzig he resigned the editorship of the *Neue Zeitschrift*. In August he composed some numbers for an opera on Goethe's *Faust,* but work was interrupted by a serious nervous collapse that led to the Schumanns' leaving Leipzig. From December 1844 to September 1850 they lived in Dresden, where his health was gradually restored. He began to teach Clara counterpoint, a preoccupation that led to an outburst of contrapuntal composition, including the organ Fugues on B-A-C-H. Next he completed the Piano Concerto and in December 1845 began the Second Symphony in C Major; because of aural nerve trouble nearly ten months passed before the score was finished. Other outstanding works of the Dresden period were two Piano Trios (Op. 63 and Op. 80 [1847]); the opera *Genoveva,* based on a conflation of the dramas by Tieck and Hebbel (1847–50; produced at Leipzig, June 25, 1850); a fine overture and incidental music to Byron's *Manfred* (1848–49); the piano *Album für die Jugend* (1848); the *Spanisches Liederspiel* (1849), a cycle for four voices and piano; and the *Requiem für Mignon* (1849) for solo voices, chorus, and orchestra. There were also other instrumental pieces, a host of part songs, a renewal of solo song composition, and from time to time additions to the *Szenen aus Goethe's "Faust"* (to which the overture was written last—in 1853).

last years   The insurrection of May 1849 terminated Schumann's never very close friendship with Wagner; indeed he had failed either to make close friends or to obtain any official position in Dresden. Attempts to get posts in Leipzig and Vienna had also been abortive. For want of anything better he finally accepted the appointment of municipal director of music at Düsseldorf. At first things went tolerably well; in 1850–51 Schumann composed a Cello Concerto, the Third Symphony in E-flat *(Rhenish);* overtures to Schiller's *Die Braut von Messina* and Shakespeare's *Julius Caesar;* the cantata *Der Rose Pilgerfahrt* and other choral works; the third Piano Trio and the first two Violin Sonatas; and he drastically

rewrote the ten-year-old d minor Symphony ultimately published as the Fourth. He also conducted eight subscription concerts, but temperamental differences soon showed themselves, and Schumann's shortcomings as a conductor became obvious. There were painful scenes and chaotic rehearsals; in December 1852 he was asked to resign but declined, and in October 1853 the refusal of the choir to sing Mendelssohn's *Walpurgisnacht* under his direction brought the final break. He conducted for the last time on October 27, when the young Joseph Joachim played the Fantasy for violin and orchestra Schumann had just written for him. The day after the concert appeared Schumann's last contribution to the *Neue Zeitschrift,* an enthusiastic article in praise of Joachim's still younger friend Brahms. Two other works written for Joachim in October–November 1853 (but published only many years later) were the Violin Concerto and the Third Violin Sonata.

On February 10, 1854, Schumann complained of a "very strong and painful" attack of the ear malady that had troubled him before; this was followed by aural illusions such as the dictation by angels of a theme (actually a reminiscence of the Violin Concerto) on which he proceeded to write some variations for piano. On February 26 he asked to be taken to an asylum, and the next day he attempted suicide by drowning. (He had contemplated suicide on at least three occasions in the 1830s.) On March 4 he was removed to a private asylum at Endenich near Bonn, where he lived for nearly two and one-half years, able to correspond for a time with Clara and his friends. One or two visits by Brahms or Joachim agitated him terribly, and Clara was kept from him until July 27, 1856, just two days before his death. He seemed to recognize her but was unable to speak intelligibly.

assessment   As a composer Schumann was first and most naturally a miniaturist. Until after his marriage the great bulk of his work—including much of his best and that by which he is best known—consisted of short piano pieces and songs, two genres so closely related in his case as to be hardly more than two facets of the same. The song accompaniments are often almost self-sufficient piano pieces, and the piano pieces often seem to have been melodically inspired by lyrical poems; indeed the slow movements of the g minor and f-sharp minor Piano Sonatas have also survived in their original forms as songs. Even when the musical idea did not originate in literature but as a waltz, polonaise, or some striking harmonic progression found at the piano by his improvising fingers, it was usually given a quasi-literary title or brought into relationship with some literary idea—whether openly revealed or not. All his most characteristic work is introverted, a selection of pages from a secret diary; his notebooks show how he cherished musical ideas not only for their own sake but because they recorded precise moments and their moods. The carnival and the masked ball appealed to him *(Papillons, Carnaval, Faschingsschwank aus Wien);* all his early music—and much of the later—is full of enigmas, musical quotations (usually in subtle disguises), and veiled allusions. In the field of the piano miniature and the pianistic song, Schumann is a supreme master; in the simpler kind of lyrical inspiration and in the invention of aphorisms he has seldom been surpassed.

When he embarked on more ambitious composition under Clara's influence, he was often less happy. He was unsure in writing for the orchestra and relied too often on safe routine procedures; his string writing was pianistic; and his most characteristic musical ideas, which he had hitherto been content to fit together in mosaics or remold plastically by variation, were seldom suited for development on a big scale. Nor in sustained thought did he find a satisfaction comparable with the creations of his private dreamworld. It is astonishing that Schumann was able to overcome these natural limitations as well and as often as he did; that he was able to construct a symphony as firmly welded as the d minor or a symphonic first movement as organic as that of the E-flat; that he could conceive orchestral music of such gloomy power as the *Manfred* Overture or the penultimate movement of the E-flat Symphony, or as light-handed and imaginative as the "Witch of the Alps" scene in the incidental music to *Man-*

fred. Some of the large-scale works, such as the Piano Concerto and the Piano Quintet, depend overmuch on the piano for their salvation, but the piano certainly saved them. Drama was beyond him—though there are fine passages in the *Faust* music—and *Genoveva* is a failure; yet even *Genoveva* is a fascinating failure, abreast—sometimes even ahead—of the Wagner of the same period in its harmonic idiom and in its use of thematic reminiscence not only to make dramatic points but to build up a character.

It was long customary to detect in the works of Schumann's last years evidence of his approaching collapse. But he had been mentally unstable all his life, haunted by fears of insanity since the age of 18, and the change of style noticeable in the music of the 1850s— the increasing angularity of his themes and complication of his harmony—may be attributed to other causes, including the influence of Bach. He was rightly considered an advanced composer in his day, and his influence on later 19th-century composers as different as Brahms and Tchaikovsky, to say nothing of a host of lesser figures, was considerable. He stands in the front rank of German Romantic artists. Even his critical writing, as fantastic, subjective, and lyrical as his early music, constitutes a valuable document of the trend and period.

BIBLIOGRAPHY: Robert Schumann, *Early Letters of Robert Schumann* (1888; reprint, 1970) and *Life of Robert Schumann Told in His Letters,* 2 vols. (1890); John A. Fuller-Maitland, *Robert Schumann, 1810–1856* (1913; reprint, 1970) and *Schumann's Pianoforte Works* (1927); Victor Basch, *Schumann, a Life of Suffering* (1931; reprint, 1970); Herbert Bedford, *Robert Schumann, His Life and His Work* (1933; reprint, 1971); Gerald E. H. Abraham, ed., *Schumann: A Symposium* (1952; reprint, 1977); André Boucourechliev, *Schumann* (1959; reprint, 1976); Joan Chissell, *Schumann,* rev. ed. (1967), and *Schumann's Piano Music* (1972); Leon Plantinga, *Schumann as Critic* (1967; reprint, 1976); Astra Desmond, *Schumann Songs* (1972); Alan Walker, ed., *Robert Schumann: The Man and His Music* (1974).

RECORDINGS: Numerous recordings of many works.

Schumann-Heink, Ernestine, before her marriages, Ernestine Rössler (June 15, 1861–November 17, 1936)   Renowned for an opulent voice, dramatic interpretive power, and a divergent repertoire, the Czech-Austrian contralto Ernestine Schumann-Heink studied in Graz, Austria, and made her first appearance there at age 15 in the Ninth Symphony of Beethoven. Her operatic debut came in 1878 in Dresden as Azucena in Verdi's *Il Trovatore.* After singing in Hamburg and Berlin she made her U.S. debut in Chicago (1898) as Ortrud (Wagner's *Lohengrin*). She sang the same role the following year for her Metropolitan Opera debut, singing there regularly until 1904. From 1896 to 1906 she sang at Bayreuth, and she created the role of Klytemnestra in Richard Strauss's *Elektra* in Dresden (1909). After numerous recitals to benefit U.S. servicemen and the Red Cross and a 20,000-mile farewell tour, she sang a final operatic appearance as Wagner's Erda (*Siegfried,* one of her best-loved roles) at the Metropolitan in 1932. In 1935 she appeared in the motion picture

Ernestine Schumann-Heink as Fidès
*in Meyerbeer's Le Prophète, c. 1901
courtesy, Metropolitan Opera Association*

Here's to Romance. She knew 150 operatic roles (including Bizet's Carmen, Meyerbeer's Fidès [*Le Prophète*], and Orlovsky from Johann Strauss the Younger's *Die Fledermaus*) and a great number of songs; she was often heard in recital and on radio broadcasts and made a few early recordings (1906–07).

Schütz, Heinrich (October 8, 1585–November 6, 1672)   The greatest German composer before Bach, Heinrich Schütz was born at Köstritz. In 1599 he became a chorister at Kassel, where the Landgrave of Hesse-Kassel provided him with a wide general education. In 1608 Schütz entered the University of Marburg to study law, but in 1609 he went to Venice, where he studied with Giovanni Gabrieli. In Venice Schütz wrote his first known works, a set of Italian madrigals for five voices (1611). In 1613 he returned to Germany to resume his legal studies at Leipzig, but the landgrave offered him the post of second organist at the court in Kassel. He went to Dresden in 1614 to supervise the music for the christening of the son of the Elector of Saxony, and eventually the landgrave was persuaded to allow him to take a permanent post in the electoral chapel. In 1628 Schütz again visited Venice, where Monteverdi was now the chief musical figure, and it is possible that Schütz studied with him. Three years after his return to Dresden, Schütz left the elector's court and from 1633 to 1635 was Kapellmeister to the court of Copenhagen. Apart from further visits to the Danish court, he then remained in the elector's service at Dresden in spite of frequent pleas for dismissal.

After the early set of madrigals most of Schütz's known works are vocal settings of sacred texts with or without instruments. Of his known secular works *Daphne* (1627), the first German opera, and compositions for the marriage of Johann Georg II of Saxony in 1638 were lost. Schütz's special achievement was to introduce into German music the new style of the Italian monodists (as typified in Monteverdi's work) without creating an unsatisfactory hybrid; his music remains extremely individual and German in feeling. After the Latin of *Symphoniae sacrae I* (1629), he used the vernacular. The first German re-

Heinrich Schütz
*detail of a portrait by an unknown artist
courtesy, Universitatsbibliothek,
Karl Marx Universitat, Leipzig, DDR*

quiem was his *Musikalische Exequien* (1636) for soloists and choir in which the writing for solo voice or duet is often florid in the Italian manner, while the choral sections are firmly based on German chorale tradition. The final section is for double choir, a form that recalls Schütz's studies with the earlier Venetian composers. Other principal works from the middle of his life are two sets of *Kleine geistliche Konzerte* (1636, 1639) for solo voice and continuo, *Geistliche Chormusik* (1648), and *Symphoniae sacrae II* and *III* (1647, 1650) for various combinations of voices and instruments. In all these Schütz's dramatic sense is strong. The *Christmas* Oratorio of 1664 for soloists, choir, and instruments foreshadows his austere last works, the a cappella Passions according to Matthew, Luke, and John. In these works even the sparing vocal figuration of the *Christmas* Oratorio is absent; the plain scriptural text is delivered by the appropriate soloist in a kind of recitative against the brief polyphonic *turba* choruses.

BIBLIOGRAPHY: Hans J. Moser, *Heinrich Schütz: His Life and Work* (1959); Richard Petzoldt, *Heinrich Schütz and His Times in Pictures* (1972).

RECORDINGS: *Cantiones sacrae; Christmas* Oratorio; *Deutsches* Magnificat; *Easter* Oratorio; Italian Madrigals; *Kleine geistliche Konzerte a 1–5; Musikalische Exequien;* Passions (3); *Seven Words from the Cross; Symphoniae sacrae;* motets; psalms.

Schwarz, Gerard (b. August 19, 1947) The son of Viennese parents, the U.S. trumpeter and conductor Gerard Schwarz was educated at the Juilliard School and studied composition with Paul Creston. He played first trumpet with the American Symphony under Stokowski (1965–72) and the New York Philharmonic (1973–77) and was a member of the American Brass Quintet (1965–73). Active in chamber music ensembles, he conducted the premiere of Peter Mennin's *Voices* for the Chamber Music Society of Lincoln Center and has served as music director of the Montclair College chamber orchestra and conductor for the Eliot Feld Ballet. Schwarz was named music director of the Los Angeles Chamber Orchestra in 1978. His trumpet recordings feature 20th-century music, and he is also involved in computer music projects.

Schwarzkopf, Elisabeth (b. December 9, 1915) The Polish-born German soprano Elisabeth Schwarzkopf studied at the Hoch-

Elisabeth Schwarzkopf
courtesy, Angel Records

737

schule für Musik in Berlin and made her debut at the German Opera House there in 1938 as a flower maiden in Wagner's *Parsifal.* In 1943 she became a member of the Vienna State Opera and has also concertized in Europe and the United States, where she is esteemed in both opera and lieder. In 1951 she created the role of Ann Truelove in Stravinsky's *The Rake's Progress.* In 1964 she first sang at the Metropolitan Opera as the Marschallin in Richard Strauss's *Der Rosenkavalier,* a role with which she became associated. Notable among her recordings are the four major Mozart operas, operas and songs of Strauss, and music of Bach, Brahms, Mahler, and Hugo Wolf.

Schweitzer, Albert (January 14, 1875–September 4, 1965)   The Alsatian organist and Bach authority Albert Schweitzer was known to the world as humanitarian, theologian, and physician. He studied philosophy and theology at the universities of Strasbourg, Paris, and Berlin and organ at Strasbourg and with Charles-Marie Widor in Paris. He joined the faculty at Strasbourg in 1902 and while teaching there studied medicine in order to become a medical missionary in Africa (1913). Schweitzer's booklet *Deutsche und französische Orgelbaukunst und Orgelkunst* (1906; "The Art of German and French Organ Builders and Players") marked the beginning of the classical organ revival that got underway 20 years later. His *Jean Sébastien Bach, le musicien-poète* (1905; expanded German edition, 1908; Eng. trans., 1911) was an influential, though highly subjective, study of the master. With Widor he edited a critico-practical edition of Bach's organ works (completed in collaboration with Édouard Nies-Berger). He was awarded the Nobel Peace Prize in 1952.

scordatura   An alteration of the normal tuning of stringed instruments to extend the range, increase the brilliance, or facilitate the playing of certain passages. In the 16th and 17th centuries it was common practice in lute music, especially, to lower the bottom string. By the 17th century no normal tuning existed, resulting in a frequent accordatura at the beginning of a piece to indicate the necessary

tuning. Scordatura carried over to the violin and was used especially by Heinrich von Biber. Paganini often tuned all four of his strings as much as a third higher for greater brilliance, and Mozart specified the solo viola in his Sinfonia concertante in E-flat, K.364, to be tuned a half tone higher so that the instrument would stand out more from the orchestra, more evenly matching the companion violin. Since the late 19th century scordatura has been used chiefly for special effects.

Scott, Cyril (Meir) (September 27, 1879–December 31, 1970)   An English composer and poet, Cyril Scott began in 1891 to study piano at Frankfurt am Main, returning in 1895 for three years' training in composition with Ivan Knorr. During this period he became a friend of the writers Stefan George and Charles Bonnier and began to write poetry about 1900. He published translations of Baudelaire and two volumes of poems in 1910 and 1912. His early musical compositions, which he later destroyed, were performed at Liverpool, Manchester, and Darmstadt; his reputation was established with a Piano Quartet (1901) and Second Symphony (1903). Under the influence of Debussy and of Oriental music, he developed a freer harmonic and rhythmic style, notably in his sonatas for piano and for violin and piano. In 1913 *La Princesse Maleine,* the third of his overtures on plays of Maeterlinck, was performed in Vienna. Between 1915 and 1948 he wrote several orchestral and choral works, including concertos for piano, harpsichord, violin, and cello, a symphony, and a setting of Keats's *La Belle Dame sans merci.* His opera *The Alchemist* was given at Essen in 1925. Chamber works include trios, quartets, quintets, and numerous short pieces for the piano. His songs, written between 1903 and 1939, include settings of his own poems and those of Ernest Dowson, Christina Rossetti, R. M. Watson, and Walt Whitman. His critical works include *The Philosophy of Modernism in Its Connection with Music* (1926) and *The Influence of Music on History and Morals* (1929). His memoirs, *My Years of Indiscretion,* were published in 1924.

RECORDINGS: Piano Concerto; Piano Sonata No. 3; piano pieces.

Scott, Tom (May 28, 1912–August 12, 1961) The U.S. composer and folk singer Tom Scott gained his first professional experience playing violin in dance bands and then studied composition with George Antheil and Wallingford Riegger. He made collections and arrangements of folk songs and wrote articles on folk music. Original compositions include two quartets (1944; 1956), a symphony (1946), *The Ballad of the Harp Weaver* (1947) for chorus on a text from Edna St. Vincent Millay, an opera, *The Fisherman* (1956), and miscellaneous orchestral works.

Scottish Symphony (Third): *see* MEN-DELSSOHN; PROGRAM MUSIC (program symphony).

Scriabin, Aleksandr (Nikolayevich) (January 6 [December 25, 1871, old style], 1872–April 27 [April 14, old style], 1915) A Russian composer of piano and orchestral music who explored musical symbolism through unusual timbres, Aleksandr Scriabin was trained as a soldier at the Moscow cadet school from 1882 to 1889. But in 1888 he entered the Moscow Conservatory, where he studied piano with Vassily Safonov and composition with Sergey Taneyev and Anton Arensky. When he graduated in 1892, he had composed the piano pieces that constitute his first seven opus numbers. His first recital in St. Petersburg in 1894 led to a friendship with Mitrofan Belyayev, who not only published nearly all his later works but acted as his concert agent for recital tours in western Europe. In 1897 he married the pianist Vera Isakovich and from 1898 until 1903 taught at the Moscow Conservatory. He then devoted himself entirely to composition, and in 1904 settled in Switzerland.

After 1900 he was much preoccupied with mystical philosophy, and his First Symphony of that year has a choral finale to his own words glorifying art as a form of religion. In Switzerland he completed his Third Symphony, *Le Divin Poème,* first given under Arthur Nikisch in Paris in 1905. The literary program of this work, devised by Tatiana Schloezer with whom he had formed a relationship after abandoning his wife, was said to represent "the evolution of the human spirit from pantheism to unity with the universe ('The divine Ego')." Theosophical ideas similarly provided the basis of the orchestral *Poème de l'extase* (New York City, 1908) and *Prometheus,* which included a part for an instrument to project colors onto a screen during the performance, though it was not used at the first performance (Moscow, 1911).

From 1906 to 1907 Scriabin toured the United States, where he gave concerts with Safonov and Modest Altschuler, and in 1908 he frequented theosophical circles in Brussels. In 1909 he was encouraged by the conductor Serge Koussevitzky, who both performed and published his works, to return to Russia. He was no longer thinking in terms of music alone but was looking forward to an all-embracing mystery that was planned to open with a "liturgical act" in which music, poetry, dancing, colors, and scents were to unite to induce in worshipers a "supreme, final ecstasy." He even went so far as to proclaim himself a sort of messiah whose function it was to "sound the final chord of our race, reuniting it with the Spirit." He continued to give concerts, however, both in Russia and abroad and in 1914 played under Henry Wood in London. He wrote the poem of the "Preliminary Action" of the mystery but left only sketches for the music.

Scriabin was a composer of the most sensitive, exquisitely polished piano music. His piano works include ten sonatas (1892–1913), an early concerto, and many preludes and other short pieces. Even his orchestral works create the impression of orchestrated piano music. An idolater of Chopin in his youth, he early developed a personal style. As his thought became more and more mystical, egocentric, and ingrown, his harmonic style—based on chords of fourths built up from the higher partials of the harmonic series—became ever less generally intelligible, and he failed to carry with him, as other harmonic innovators have done, enough admirers to establish his new idiom as a permanent, accepted contribution to the language of music. Yet the synthesis he effected of Chopin, French Impressionism, Richard Strauss, and undercurrents of Russian musical styles gave him a place in the development of modern Russian music. A few works (*e.g.,* the Piano Concerto and the Preludes for piano) brought him an enduring international following.

BIBLIOGRAPHY: Alfred J. Swan, *Scriabin* (1923; reprint, 1970); Michel D. Calvocoressi and Gerald E. H. Abraham, *Masters of Russian Music* (1936; reprint, 1971); Donald Brook, *Six Great Russian Composers* (1946); Faubion Bowers, *Scriabin,* 2 vols. (1969), and *The New Scriabin: Enigma and Answers* (1973).

RECORDINGS: Piano Concerto; Piano Études (23); Piano Preludes (29); Piano Sonatas (10); *Poème de l'extase; Prometheus;* Symphonies (3); piano pieces.

Scribe, Eugène: *see* AUBER; BOIELDIEU; HALÉVY; LIBRETTO (19th-century influences); MEYERBEER; VERDI.

Seasons, The: *see* CLASSICAL PERIOD (vocal music, 1750–1800); HAYDN (late oratorios); ORATORIO (late 18th century).

Seefried, Irmgard (b. October 9, 1919) Known for her operatic roles of Mozart, the Bavarian soprano Irmgard Seefried studied at the conservatory at Augsburg and made her debut in 1939 at Aachen as the Priestess in Verdi's *Aida.* After further study with Herbert von Karajan, she sang with the Vienna State Opera from 1943 and three years later first sang at Salzburg. She made her Metropolitan Opera debut in 1953 as Susanna in Mozart's *Le nozze di Figaro.* In addition to opera she is known for her recitals of lieder and is heard on recordings of the Bach *St. Matthew* Passion, Brahms lieder, and the Mozart Requiem. She has sung many "trouser" roles and is especially notable as the Composer in Richard Strauss's *Ariadne auf Naxos.*

Seeger, Ruth (Porter) Crawford (July 3, 1901–November 18, 1953) A student at the American Conservatory in Chicago and later a teacher there and at Elmhurst (Illinois) College (1925–29), the U.S. composer Ruth Crawford Seeger transcribed U.S. folk music from recordings at the Library of Congress and composed piano accompaniments for hundreds of them. She developed teaching methods for children using folk music and edited *American Folksongs and Ballads* by John and Alan Lomax. Her original compositions include the quasi-serial Quartet (1931), Three Songs (1932) for contralto, oboe, piano, and

percussion, with orchestral ostinato, and Suite (1952) for wind quintet.

RECORDINGS: Piano Preludes (9); Quartet; *Study in Mixed Accents* for piano; Suite for wind quintet; Two Movements for chamber orchestra.

Segovia, Andrés (b. February 17, 1893) Educated at the music institute in Granada and influenced by de Falla, the Spanish guitarist Andrés Segovia made his debut in Granada in 1909. He toured in Europe and South America for six years before making his U.S. debut in 1928. He created a new technique of guitar playing that broke from much of the classical Spanish tradition, and he was instrumental in establishing the guitar as a medium for art music. To that end he has continued to give recitals throughout the world. He also developed the contrapuntal capabilities of the guitar and has transcribed much Baroque music. Many works have been written for him, including a concerto by Mario Castelnuovo-Tedesco. His extensive recordings cover guitar music from the 18th to the 20th century.

Andrés Segovia
courtesy, ICM Artists, Ltd.

Seidl, Anton (May 7, 1850–March 28, 1898)
A champion of the music of Wagner, the Hungarian-born conductor Anton Seidl was educated at the Leipzig Conservatory. He assisted at the first Bayreuth Festival (1876) and made the first copy of the score for Wagner's *Der Ring des Nibelungen*. In 1879 he became conductor at the Leipzig Opera, where he remained until 1882; he then undertook a tour of Wagner operas that were cut and edited drastically for facility of performance. In 1885 he succeeded Walter Damrosch as conductor of German opera at the Metropolitan Opera, making his debut in Wagner's *Lohengrin*. There he conducted the first U.S. performances of most of the Wagnerian canon, including the *Ring* (1889). In 1891 he succeeded Theodore Thomas as conductor of the New York Philharmonic Society, a post he held simultaneously with the Metropolitan position until his death. He also introduced new European symphonic works to the United States including the *New World* Symphony of Dvořák.

Sembrich, Marcella, originally Praxede Marcelline Kochanska (February 15, 1858–January 11, 1935)   The daughter of violinist Kasimir Kochanski, Polish soprano Marcella Sembrich played violin and piano as a child. In 1874 she played and sang for Liszt, who encouraged her to develop her voice. She studied in Vienna and Milan and made her operatic debut in 1877 in Athens as Elvira (Bellini's *I Puritani*). Her German debut the following year as Lucia (Donizetti) began a two-year engagement with the Dresden Court Opera, and her London debut (1880) in the same role led to four seasons with the Royal Italian Opera there. She made her U.S. debut at the Metropolitan Opera in 1883, also as Lucia, and sang there from 1898 to 1909, continuing to give concerts until 1917. Her roles spanned the coloratura and lyric repertoire, including Rosina (Rossini's *Il barbiere di Siviglia*), Gilda (Verdi's *Rigoletto*), Susanna (Mozart's *Le nozze di Figaro*), Mimi (Puccini's *La Bohème*), and Eva (Wagner's *Die Meistersinger*); in concert she sang in Italian, French, German, Polish, Russian, Spanish, and English. After 1917 she taught at the Curtis Institute and the Juilliard School.

Semele: *see* HANDEL (life) and (works); ORATORIO (Handel).

Semiramide: *see* GLUCK.

sequence   A melodic or chordal figure repeated at a new pitch, thus unifying and developing material. Real sequences are exact repetitions; tonal sequences are modified to conform to the key of the composition.

In the Middle Ages the sequence was a Latin text sung to plainchant at mass between the Alleluia and the Gospel. It developed about the 8th century from the TROPE to the jubilus, the florid ending of the last syllable of the Alleluia. Sequences became highly popular throughout Europe, and thousands of examples survive appropriate to different liturgical feasts. Secular musical forms influenced by the sequence include the estampie and the lai.

The melodic tropes originally added to the jubilus were normally broken into phrases that were repeated in performance (as *aa, bb, cc,. . .*) by alternating choirs. Texts set to these and to Alleluia melodies were originally prose, hence the medieval name *prosa*. By the 9th century the sequence developed a common poetic form that reflected the musical structure: typically introductory and closing lines enclosed a series of rhymed, metrical couplets of varying lengths *(x-aa-bb-cc. . .y)*. Each syllable was set to a single note of music. Eventually texts were set to newly composed melodies, and the lengths of the couplets were equalized.

In the 16th century the Council of Trent removed all but four sequences from the liturgy: *Victimae Paschali laudes, Veni Sancte Spiritus, Lauda Sion,* and *Dies irae.* The *Stabat Mater* was reinstated in 1727.

BIBLIOGRAPHY: Richard L. Crocker, *The Early Medieval Sequence* (1977).

Serafin, Tullio (December 8, 1878–February 2, 1968)   Educated in Milan, the Italian opera conductor Tullio Serafin began his career at the Teatro Communale in Ferrara in 1900. Nine years later he became conductor at La Scala, where he later made many acclaimed recordings. His Metropolitan Opera conducting debut was in Verdi's *Aida* in 1924, and he remained until 1935. There he conducted many U.S. premieres (Italo Montemezzi's

Giovanni Gallurese, 1925; de Falla's *La Vida Breve,* 1926; Mussorgsky's *Sorochinsky Fair,* 1930; Verdi's *Simon Boccanegra,* 1932) and world premieres (*The King's Henchman,* 1927, and *Peter Ibbetson,* 1931, both by Deems Taylor; Howard Hanson's *Merry Mount,* 1934). After positions in London, Paris, and Buenos Aires, he returned to New York City and after 1952 conducted at the New York City Opera. In his early career he conducted Wagner's *Parsifal* in Italy, but he was remembered for Italian opera. His recordings include the major operas of Verdi, Puccini, Bellini, and Donizetti.

serenade   A composition that was originally a song of courtship. The word is French for "evening music" as opposed to AUBADE, "morning music." The serenade to Zerlina, "Deh! vieni alla finestra," in Mozart's *Don Giovanni* is an outstanding example in opera. Losing its association of courtship, the term serenade was applied about 1770 to instrumental works for a small ensemble in several movements, similar to works of the same period entitled cassation, divertimento, and notturno. The indefinite sequence of movements included marches, minuets, and sonata movements and resembled that of the suite. Mozart's *Haffner* Serenade and *Eine kleine Nachtmusick* are two of the best known examples. Later in works by many composers from Beethoven to Elgar, Richard Strauss, and Schoenberg, the term was applied to works in several movements for small orchestra, a solo instrument, or winds or strings.

serialism or **12-tone music**   A 20th-century technique of composition; its invention is credited to Schoenberg, though he was anticipated in its use by such composers as Ives and Josef Hauer. More strictly a serial pattern is one that repeats. In this sense medieval composers wrote serial music using ISORHYTHM, a distinct rhythmic pattern that repeats regardless of the melodic element. Another pre-20th-century example of serialism is the GROUND bass, a pattern of harmony or melody that repeats, most often in the lower parts. Countless composers have written music on a ground.

Between 1912 and 1922 Schoenberg searched for a method of composition that would provide a new basis for musical structure to replace tonality, which he felt was being stretched and distorted too much to remain a unifying structural principle. Instead of using one or two tones as main points of focus, or key centers, Schoenberg suggested using the 12 tones of the chromatic scale "related only to one another." In such a system, unlike tonality, no notes predominate as focal points, nor is any hierarchy of importance assigned to the individual tones. The new unifying principle arises from the order given a collection of the 12 tones, an order different for each composition. The basic order came to be known as its basic set, its 12-tone row, or its 12-tone series—all of which are synonymous. The basic set for Schoenberg's Wind Quintet (1924) is E♭–G–A–B–C♯–C–B♭–D–E–F♯–A♭–F; for his Fourth String Quartet (1936) it is D–C♯–A–B♭–F–E♭–E–C–A♭–G–F♯–B.

The 12-tone row is not a theme, for it has no specific shape, rhythm, or dynamic level. It is a backbone, a musical idea that permeates the composition in which it is used. Because of various principles of composing and of manipulation of the tone row, it is not often possible nor even desirable to hear the row when the composition is performed. This has led many to attack Schoenberg's method as unmusical and as mathematical madness; but as Schoenberg pointed out, his method specifies only a fraction of the total nature of a finished composition—no more than composing with tonality.

Schoenberg's best known pupils were Webern and Berg, each of whom wrote 12-tone music. Neither used the idea of the basic row in the same manner as Schoenberg, and the music of all three differs greatly. Other important composers who have worked with 12-tone music include Stravinsky (who earlier criticized the approach severely), Roger Sessions, Ernst Krenek, Luigi Dallapiccola, and Hans Werner Henze.

Some composers have serialized other elements. In *Structures* for two pianos (I, 1952; II, 1961) by Pierre Boulez, serial elements include pitch, rhythm, dynamics, and attack; in *Simon Says* (1972) by Beauregard Forth, serial elements include specific harmonies, melodies, meters, and key centers. Additional composers who have written music that serializes more than pitch include Roberto Gerhard, Ernst Krenek, and Stockhausen.

BIBLIOGRAPHY: Rene Leibowitz, *Schoenberg and His School* (1949; reprint, 1970); Reginald S. Brindle, *Serial Composition* (1966); Robert Kelly, *Theme and Variations: A Study of Linear Twelve Tone Composition* (1969); Arnold Schoenberg, *Style and Idea* (1975); George Perle, *Serial Composition and Atonality: An Introduction to the Music of Schoenberg, Berg, and Webern,* 4th ed. (1978).

Serkin, Peter (b. July 24, 1947) The son of pianist Rudolf Serkin, U.S. pianist Peter Serkin studied with his father at the Curtis Institute. He made his debut at age 12 (1959) at the Marlboro (Vermont) Festival, playing a Haydn concerto; the same year he made his New York City debut. He has performed with orchestras and as a recitalist and recorded concertos of Mozart, Beethoven, and Bartók as well as music of Schubert, Berg, and Messiaen. He also tours with his chamber music ensemble Tashi, which performs much 20th-century music of the avant-garde.

Serkin, Rudolf (b. March 28, 1903) Educated in Vienna, including composition with Schoenberg, the Bohemian pianist Rudolf Serkin is a noted interpreter of the Viennese Classical school. Early in his career he joined the violinist Adolf Busch (whose daughter he married) in a duo; they performed all of the Beethoven piano and violin sonatas in a series of recitals in New York City (1938). Serkin was appointed to the faculty of the Curtis Institute (1939) and later as director (1968) and was one of the founders of the Marlboro Festival in rural Vermont (1951).

serpent A bass wind instrument sounded by the vibration of the lips against a cup mouthpiece. Invented probably in 1590 by Edme Guillaume of Auxerre as an improvement on bass versions of the closely related cornett, it is made of wood in a serpentine curve with a seven- or eight-foot (two- or two-and-one-half-meter) conical bore and six finger holes. Originally it accompanied plainchant in churches; from the 18th century until superseded by brass basses in the 19th century, it was a standard wind bass in military bands. Possessing a rich tone and wide dynamic

Rudolf Serkin
courtesy, Judd Concert Bureau

soldier blowing serpent
from Filippo Bonanni's Gabinetto armonico,
18th century courtesy, Dover Publications, Inc.

743

range, it was the instrument of several early 19th-century virtuosos and was sometimes used in orchestras. Around 1800 keys were added, extending the player's reach and allowing higher notes to be produced. Metal serpents also appeared, as did bassoon-shaped versions. Serpents were played in a few rural French churches early in the 20th century and in some Spanish bands as late as 1884.

serva padrona, La: *see* CLASSICAL PERIOD (vocal music, 1720–50); GALLANT STYLE; INTERMEZZO; OPERA (developments in the 18th century); OPERA BUFFA; PERGOLESI.

Sessions, Roger (Huntington) (b. December 28, 1896) A U.S. composer of symphonic and instrumental music, Roger Sessions was important in educating his contemporaries to an appreciation of modern music. He studied at Harvard and Yale Universities and later with Ernest Bloch. Between 1928 and 1931 he and Copland presented a series of concerts of modern music, the Copland–Sessions Concerts in New York City. He taught composition at Princeton University (1935–45), at the University of California at Berkeley (1945–52), and again at Princeton from 1953. In 1965 he was appointed to the faculty of the Juilliard School. Among his pupils are Milton Babbitt, David Diamond, and Andrew W. Imbrie.

His first important work, an orchestral suite from the incidental music for Leonid Andreyev's play *The Black Maskers* (1923), has remained his most popular score. His eight symphonies (1927–68) are severe in idiom, using a polyphonic technique and asymmetrical rhythms. Similar qualities mark his two quartets (1936 and 1951), string quintet (1958), three piano sonatas (1930, 1946, and 1965), and chorale preludes for organ (1925). Sessions considers his Violin Concerto (1935) to be one of the earliest of his mature works. His one-act opera *The Trial of Lucullus* (1947) and his *Idyll of Theocritus* (1954) for soprano and orchestra have affinities with the central European expressionist style. The Violin Sonata (1953) is dodecaphonic. His opera *Montezuma* (1941–62) was produced in West Berlin in 1964. Later works are Rhapsody

(1970) for orchestra and the cantata *When Lilacs Last in the Dooryard Bloom'd* (1971). His critical works include *The Musical Experience of Composer, Performer, and Listener* (1950), *Harmonic Practice* (1951), *Questions about Music* (1970), and *Roger Sessions on Music* (1979), which deal with the artistic and socio-cultural concerns of musical life.

RECORDINGS: *Black Maskers* Suite; Concertino for chamber orchestra; *From My Diary* for piano; Quartet No. 2; Rhapsody; Symphony No. 8; Violin Concerto; Violin Sonata; *When Lilacs Last in the Dooryard Bloom'd.*

Seven Last Words, The: *see* HAYDN (late oratorios) and (achievement); ORATORIO (Schütz); PASSION (Schütz) and (later passion music).

Shankar, Ravi (b. April 7, 1920) Important for his role in popularizing Indian music in the Western world, the Indian sitar virtuoso and composer Ravi Shankar began his career as a member of a troupe of Indian musicians and dancers. He later became director of music for the All-India Radio and in 1962 founded the Kinnara School of Music in Bombay. He has recorded some of his compositions, including a sitar concerto and works based on the Indian ragas, and has composed a ballet (*Samanya Kshati,* 1961) and the film score for *Pather Panchali.*

BIBLIOGRAPHY: Ravi Shankar, *My Music, My Life* (1968).

Shapey, Ralph (b. March 12, 1921) A pupil of Stefan Wolpe, the U.S. composer, conductor, and violinist Ralph Shapey conducted the Philadelphia National Youth Administration Orchestra (1938–42) and then conducted concerts of contemporary music throughout the United States. He taught at the University of Pennsylvania in 1963 and the next year joined the faculty of the University of Chicago, where he directs the Contemporary Chamber Players, with whom he has recorded some of his music. Much of his music consists of overlapping blocks of sound. Representative works include seven quartets (1957–58; No. 5 with female voice); *Incantations* for soprano and 10 instruments (1961); *Configurations* for flute and piano (1965); *Songs of Ecstasy* for soprano, piano, percussion, and tape (1967); and the oratorio *Praise* (1971).

RECORDINGS: *Incantations; Praise; Quartet No. 6; Rituals* for orchestra; *Songs of Ecstasy.*

sharp The sign ♯ placed immediately to the left of a note that raises its pitch a semitone (half step). The word is also used to denote incorrect intonation (above the correct pitch).

Sharp, Cecil (James) (November 22, 1859–June 23, 1924) An English musician whose work as a collector of English folk song and dance had an important influence on 20th-century British music (especially on Gustav Holst and Vaughan Williams) was Cecil Sharp. Educated at Uppingham and Cambridge University, he was self-taught as a musician. In 1882 he emigrated to Australia, where after some false starts he became assistant organist of the Adelaide Cathedral and co-director of the Adelaide College of Music. In 1892 he returned to England and obtained posts as music master at Ludgrove School (1893–1910) and principal of the Hampstead Conservatoire (1896–1905).

In 1903 Sharp discovered that an unsuspected wealth of native folk song survived in England. Although work in this field had already begun, the publication of Sharp's collection *Folk Songs from Somerset* (1904–09) and of his study *English Folk Song: Some Conclusions* (1907) led to a new and widespread interest in English folk music. In 1911 he founded the English Folk Dance Society (later to be amalgamated with the Folk Song Society); he demonstrated and taught annually at the Vacation School of Folk Song and Dance at Stratford-upon-Avon; and he initiated the teaching of folk song and dance in English schools. Between 1916 and 1918 Sharp visited the United States three times to teach and to collect songs of English origin. With Olive Dame Campbell he published *English Folk Songs from the Southern Appalachians* (1917). In 1923 he received the honorary degree of Mus.M. at Cambridge. Sharp's other published works include *English Folk Songs* (1921) and teaching handbooks of morris, sword, and country dances.

BIBLIOGRAPHY: Maud Karpeles, *Cecil Sharp: His Life and Work* (1967); Cecil Sharp, *Cecil Sharp's Collections of English Folk Songs,* 2 vols. (1974).

Shaw, Robert (b. April 30, 1916) Educated at Pomona College (California), the U.S. conductor Robert Shaw founded (1941) the Collegiate Chorale in New York City and revolutionized American choral singing with a vitality and rhythmic precision it had not previously known. In 1948 he founded the Robert Shaw Chorale, whose recordings embrace Handel, Beethoven, Stravinsky, Poulenc, Britten, Negro spirituals, and sea chanteys. He directed choral music at the Berkshire Music Center and was on the faculty of the Juilliard School (1946–50). He was associate conductor of the Cleveland Orchestra from 1956 to 1967, when he became conductor of the Atlanta Symphony.

shawm A wind instrument of Near-Eastern origin that was a precursor of the OBOE. Like the oboe the shawm is conically bored and sounds with a double reed of cane. Bore, bell, and fingerholes are, however, wider than the oboe's, and the tone, intended for the open air, is of great power.

The shawm first appeared in the Near East about the beginning of the Christian era. It was later widely disseminated by Islamic influence, and numerous Oriental varieties are still played in many countries from Morocco to China. At the time of the Crusades the shawm was introduced into Europe and became widely used for dance and ceremonial music. In the 16th century shawms were constructed in various pitches from treble to great bass, the larger sizes known in French as *bombardes* and in German as *Pommern.* The shawm was rarely used in Europe after the 17th century, but in Spain it survived as the *tiple* (treble) and *tenora* (tenor), which—modernized with complete keywork—still lead the bands for the sardana, the national dance of Catalonia. See illustrations on following page.

Sheherazade: *see* BALLET (Diaghilev Ballet); PROGRAM MUSIC (problem of form); RAVEL; RIMSKY-KORSAKOV; SYMPHONIC POEM.

sheng: *see* CHINESE MUSIC (musical practice) and (history).

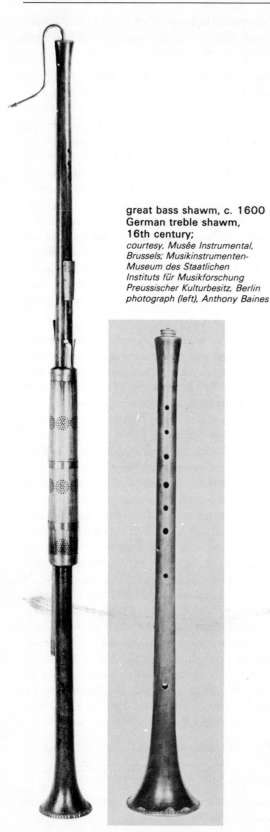

great bass shawm, c. 1600
German treble shawm,
16th century;
*courtesy, Musée Instrumental,
Brussels; Musikinstrumenten-
Museum des Staatlichen
Instituts für Musikforschung
Preussischer Kulturbesitz, Berlin
photograph (left), Anthony Baines*

Sherman, Russell (b. March 25, 1930)   Educated at Columbia University, the U.S. pianist Russell Sherman was a pupil of Eduard Steuermann. His debut with orchestra (1959) was in the Brahms d minor Concerto with the New York Philharmonic. Sherman taught at Pomona College and at the Claremont Graduate School (California) from 1959 to 1963, and at the University of Arizona until 1967, when he was appointed chairman of the piano department at the New England Conservatory. His recital (1975) of Liszt's *Transcendental* Études at Alice Tully Hall in Lincoln Center received critical acclaim; his recordings include the Liszt and Beethoven.

Shifrin, Seymour (b. February 28, 1926)   A student of William Schuman, Otto Luening, and Milhaud, the U.S. composer Seymour Shifrin taught at the University of California at Berkeley from 1952 to 1966, when he became a professor at Brandeis University (Massachusetts). The formal outlines of his music are neoclassical, onto which he juxtaposes conflicting tonalities and thematic materials. He writes mainly chamber music but also for voice, chorus, and orchestra. Important works include four quartets (1949; 1961–62; 1965–66; 1967), Chamber Symphony (1952–53), *Hear, O Ye Heavens* (1959) for chorus and organ, *Satires of Circumstance* (1966) for soprano and six instruments, and *The Nick of Time* (1978) for flute, clarinet, piano, violin, cello, bass, and percussion after Thoreau's *Walden.*

RECORDINGS: *The Odes of Shang* for chorus, piano, and percussion; Quartet No. 4; *Satires of Circumstance;* Serenade for five instruments; Three Pieces for orchestra.

Shostakovich, Dmitri (Dmitriyevich) (September 25 [September 12, old style], 1906–August 9, 1975)   The most important Soviet composer, Dmitri Shostakovich was primarily a symphonist (15 symphonies) and composer of chamber music (13 quartets), though his output includes two operas, three ballets, seven concertos, and important piano pieces, film music, and choral works.

Shostakovich was born in St. Petersburg, the son of an engineer. He entered the Petrograd Conservatory in 1919, where he studied

Dmitri Shostakovich   *EB Inc.*

piano with Leonid Nikolayev and composition with Glazunov and Maximilian Steinberg. He participated in the Chopin International Competition for pianists in Warsaw in 1927 and received an honorable mention but made no subsequent attempt to pursue the career of a virtuoso, confining his public appearances as a pianist to performances of his own works.

Even before his keyboard success in Warsaw, he had made an impact as a composer with the precocious First Symphony (1926), which quickly achieved worldwide currency. The symphony's stylistic roots were as diverse as Tchaikovsky, Hindemith, and Prokofiev, and in the next few years he submitted to an even wider range of influences. The cultural climate in the Soviet Union was remarkably free at that time, permitting even the music of Stravinsky and Berg. Bartók and Hindemith visited to perform their own works, and Shostakovich himself openly experimented with avant-garde trends. His satiric opera *The Nose* (1930), based on Gogol's story, displayed a comprehensive awareness of what was new in Western music, although the satire seems to be extended to the styles themselves. Not surprisingly his much finer second opera, *Lady Macbeth of the Mtsensk District* (1934; later

revived as *Katerina Izmaylova*), marked a stylistic retreat. Yet even this more accessible musical language was now too radical for the authorities.

From 1928, when Stalin inaugurated his first five-year plan, an iron hand fastened on Soviet culture, and in music a direct and popular style was demanded. Avant-garde music and jazz were banished, and for a while even the unproblematic Tchaikovsky was out of favor. Shostakovich did not experience immediate official displeasure, but when it came it was devastating. It is said that it was Stalin's attendance at a performance of *Lady Macbeth* in 1936 that precipitated the official condemnation of the opera and of its creator. Shostakovich was bitterly attacked in the official press, and both the opera and the still unperformed Fourth Symphony (eventually performed 1962) were withdrawn. The composer's next major work was his Fifth Symphony (1937), which he described as "A Soviet artist's reply to just criticism." A trivial, dutifully optimistic work might have been expected; but what emerged was largely serious, even somber and elegiac music presented with a compelling directness that scored an immediate success with the public and the authorities.

With the Fifth Symphony Shostakovich escaped from the stylistic instability of his earlier works, finally forging the personal style of his subsequent compositions. Mahler was a clear progenitor of both the Fourth and Fifth Symphonies, but the latter represented a drastic shift in technique. Whereas the earlier symphony had been a sprawling work founded on a free proliferation of melodic ideas, the first movement of the Fifth was marked by melodic concentration—certain particles provide the main basis that grows organically to a relentless climax. This singlemindedness is reflected elsewhere in Shostakovich's work in his liking for the Baroque structures of the fugue and chaconne.

In 1937 Shostakovich was appointed a teacher of composition in the Leningrad Conservatory, and the German attack on the Soviet Union in 1941 found him still in that city. He composed his Seventh (Leningrad) Symphony in beleaguered Leningrad during the latter part of that year, and the work achieved a quick fame, though this sprang more from the quasi-romantic circumstances of its composition than from its musical quality, which is often banal. Indeed Shostakovich was always an unequal composer. When some extramusical force conditioned the music, empty rhetoric and impoverished invention all too often resulted. After evacuation to Kuybyshev in 1942 Shostakovich settled in Moscow in 1943 as a teacher of composition at the conservatory, and from 1945 he also taught at the Leningrad Conservatory.

Shostakovich's works written in the mid-1940s contain some of his best music, especially the Eighth Symphony (1943), Piano Trio (1944), and First Violin Concerto (1955). Their prevailing seriousness—even grimness—was to contribute to Shostakovich's second fall from official grace. Under the gathering clouds of the cold war, the Soviet authorities sought to impose a firmer ideological control, demanding a more accessible musical language than some composers were then using. In Moscow in 1948 at a now notorious conference presided over by Andrey Zhdanov, a prominent Soviet theoretician, the leading figures of Soviet music, including Shostakovich, were attacked and disgraced. As a result the quality of Soviet composition slumped in the next few years, and Shostakovich produced a number of poor pieces. His personal influence was reduced by the termination of his teaching activities at both conservatories. Yet Shostakovich was not completely intimidated, and in his Fourth (1949) and especially Fifth (1951) Quartets he offered a splendid rejoinder to those who would have had him renounce completely his style and musical integrity. His Tenth Symphony (1953), composed the year of Stalin's death, flew in the face of Zhdanovism; yet like his Fifth Symphony of 16 years earlier, it compelled acceptance by sheer quality and directness. His Eleventh Symphony (1957), inspired by the Russian Revolution of 1905, was awarded the Lenin Prize in 1958.

Shostakovich was then left to pursue his creative career largely unhampered by official interference. He did, however, experience some difficulty over the texts by the poet Yevgeny Yevtushenko on which he based his Thirteenth Symphony (1962), and the work was suppressed after its first performance. Yet he was clearly undeterred, and his deeply impressive Fourteenth Symphony (1970), cast as a cycle of 11 songs on the subject of death, was not the sort of work to appeal to official circles. His last symphony, the Fifteenth (1972), was considered autobiographical with allusions to Rossini's *William Tell,* Debussy's *Jeux,* and Wagner's *Ring* and showing the influence of Mahler.

The composer visited the United States in 1949, and in 1958 he made an extended tour of western Europe, including Italy where he had been elected an honorary member of the Accademia Nazionale di Sta. Cecilia in Rome, and Britain where he received an honorary doctorate at Oxford University.

Despite the brooding typical of so much of his music, which might suggest an introverted personality, Shostakovich was noted for his apparent gregariousness. After Prokofiev's death in 1953 he was the undisputed head of Russian music. There is no reason to doubt that he was a sincere Communist, and he even participated in political conferences; yet as a composer he always refused to be a mere cipher of official politics. Indeed he appears to have flourished in the tension between his own creative drives and the demands of authority, writing much of his best music when his fiercely independent creative thought was—under the pressure from his masters for comprehensible expression—channelled into a musical language of the utmost directness.

BIBLIOGRAPHY: Gerald E. H. Abraham, *Eight Soviet Composers* (1943); Victor I. Seroff, *Dmitri Shostakovich: The Life and Background of a Soviet Composer* (1943; reprint, 1970); Ivan I. Martynov, *Dmitri Shostakovich, the Man and His Work* (1947; reprint, 1969); Norman Kay, *Shostakovich* (1971).

RECORDINGS: Numerous recordings of most works.

Sibelius, Jean (Johan Julius Christian) (December 8, 1865–September 20, 1957) The most significant Scandinavian composer, Jean Sibelius contributed to the development of the symphony in his seven works in that form and also the symphonic poem. Two themes

Jean Sibelius
photograph by Karsh, 1949; © *Karsh*

run through his art: a love of nature and of the northern landscape and a preoccupation with myth, in particular the mythology enshrined in the Finnish national epic, the *Kalevala.*

Born in Hämeenlinna, Finland, Sibelius early showed a talent both for the violin and for composition. After studying in Helsinki he went to Berlin in 1889 and to Vienna the following year. The first performance of his *Kullervo* Symphony (1892) established him as the leading Finnish composer of his generation, a position consolidated by the *Four Legends* (one of which is the famous "Swan of Tuonela") and by patriotic works such as *Karelia* and *Finlandia,* all written in the 1890s. A measure of his success is the fact that the Finnish Senate voted him a small life pension in 1897 before he had composed his First Symphony (1899). The 1890s show his developing as a nationalist composer, working within the Romantic tradition and responding positively to the influence of Tchaikovsky. After the Second Symphony (1901) and the Violin Concerto in d minor (1903, revised 1905), there

is a change in his style prompted by discontent with the musical language of post-Romanticism and the development of a stronger sense of classical discipline. The year 1900 marked the beginning of his international career. Championed by conductors such as his countryman Robert Kajanus, as well as by several noted European musicians of the day and such important critics as Rosa Newmarch and Ernest Newman, Sibelius' music gradually won acceptance abroad.

He made numerous visits to the rest of Europe before World War I and also went in 1914 to the United States, for which country he had written the tone poem *The Oceanides* (1914). In 1909 he had been operated on for throat cancer, and this may account for the greater austerity and depth of the Fourth Symphony (1911) and the seriousness and concentration of his other music of this period, *The Bard* and *Luonnotar* (both 1913). During World War I he wrote many lighter instrumental pieces in the hope of repeating the enormous success of *Valse triste* (1903), the rights to which he had sold outright, making a fortune for his publishers.

His career before 1926 is a record of ceaseless creative activity, but after the Seventh Symphony (1924), *Tapiola* (1925), and *The Tempest* (1926), he virtually ceased composing, though promises of an eighth symphony were made to Serge Koussevitzky, Thomas Beecham, and other major conductors. In the 1930s Sibelius' popularity soared to unprecedented heights in England, and the great claims made on his behalf by the British musicologist Cecil Gray and other critics doubtless had an inhibiting effect on a composer who was highly self-critical and given to self-doubt. He lived in quiet retirement until his death from a cerebral hemorrhage at the age of 91 at his home in Järvenpää.

As a man Sibelius was far more complex than has been generally supposed; although his life was outwardly uneventful, he lived it to the full. He was sensitive to criticism, and his keen self-criticism was responsible for the suppression of the early quartet and the *Kullervo* Symphony as well as the destruction of his Eighth Symphony, which he had certainly completed by 1929. He was generous by nature and scarcely recorded an unkind word about his contemporaries. His practical circumstances were not comfortable until the 1920s, although he loved travel almost as much as he did his native Finland and had a love of good wine and cigars.

Each of his symphonies is totally fresh in its approach to structure: one cannot distill from the earlier symphonies any set of rules that can be applied to his later works. It was equally difficult to foresee from one symphony the character of the next. The heroism of the Fifth Symphony (1915, revised 1916, 1919) is far removed from the quietism of the Sixth (1923), while the Seventh, a one-movement structure of remarkable unity, seems to explore the epic world of man pitting himself against nature. All show a seemingly infinite capacity for evolving new material from simple germinal ideas.

Sibelius' contributions to the development of the symphonic poem are no less significant. They reveal a power to encompass the imaginative world of Finnish mythology within the strongest formal framework. *Pohjola's Daughter* (1906) is as perfect an example of the narrative tone poem as any of those written by his German contemporary Richard Strauss; yet it is totally satisfying as pure music to the listener ignorant of its program. *Tapiola* is, however, his most original and awe-inspiring tone poem, for it is here that his vision is most intense. Sibelius, like Berlioz in 19th-century France or Mahler somewhat later in Austria, was one of the great masters of the orchestra: each line seems conceived directly in terms of the instrumental timbre in which it is cast. So personal is his idiom in *Tapiola* that it is not susceptible of imitation. Sibelius composed prolifically in the smaller orchestral forms, though with varying degrees of success. His incidental music to his contemporary Maurice Maeterlinck's Symbolist drama *Pelléas et Mélisande* or to Shakespeare's *The Tempest* shows with what skill he could communicate atmosphere with so few strokes and the minimum of orchestral means. He composed about 100 songs, mostly to Swedish texts, some of great lyrical power. Though he wrote a great deal of chamber music in his youth, he composed only one quartet in

maturity, *Voces intimae* (1909), a work that reaffirms the depth of his classical sympathies as much as it demonstrates his mastery of the medium.

BIBLIOGRAPHY: Karl Ekman, *Jean Sibelius: His Life and Personality* (1938; reprint, 1972); Gerald E. H. Abraham, ed., *The Music of Sibelius* (1947; reprint, 1975); Fred Blum, *Jean Sibelius: An International Bibliography* (1965); Cecil Gray, *Sibelius: The Symphonies* (1970); Robert Layton, *Sibelius and His World* (1970); Santeri Levas, *Sibelius: A Personal Portrait* (1972); Erik Tawaststjerna, *Sibelius,* Vol. 1 (1976).

side drum: *see* SNARE DRUM.

Siegfried: *see* COUNTERPOINT (Romantic period); LEITMOTIV; WAGNER (life).

Siegmeister, Elie (b. January 15, 1909)   The U.S. composer, conductor, pianist, author, and teacher Elie Siegmeister studied with Wallingford Riegger and Boulanger. He taught at Brooklyn College and since 1949 at Hofstra (New York) College (now Hofstra University; composer in residence since 1966). He organized the American Ballad Singers in 1939 to promote understanding of U.S. folk music, elements of which are seminal to his own composition (*Ozark Set,* 1943; *Wilderness Road,* 1945). With Olin Downes he compiled *A Treasury of American Song* (1943). He was one of the founders of the American Composers' Alliance (1937) and in 1978 was composer in residence at the Brevard (North Carolina) Music Center. He composes in many forms, often combining traditional with contemporary elements, including jazz (Sextet for brass, 1965) and blues (Clarinet Concerto, 1956). He wrote four operas (including *The Plough and the Stars* after Sean O'Casey, 1963), five symphonies, two quartets, four violin sonatas, a flute concerto (1960), musicals, and film music. Works of Americana include *Songs of Early America* (1940), *Prairie Legend* (1947), and *I Have a Dream* (1967). His writings include *Invitation to Music* (1959), *Harmony and Melody,* 2 vols. (1965), and *The New Music Lover's Handbook* (1971).

RECORDINGS: Clarinet Concerto; *Fantasy and Soliloquy* for solo cello; Flute Concerto; Piano Sonata No. 2; Sextet for brass and percussion; Symphony No. 3; Violin Sonatas (Nos. 2, 3, and 4); *Western* Suite; songs.

Siepi, Cesare (b. February 10, 1923) Acclaimed in the role of Mozart's Don Giovanni, the Italian bass-baritone Cesare Siepi made his debut in 1941 as Sparafucile (Verdi's *Rigoletto*) in Florence. He joined the company of La Scala in 1946. His U.S. debut was at the Metropolitan Opera in 1951 as Philip II in Verdi's *Don Carlos,* and his subsequent roles there included Mussorgsky's Boris Godunov. He returned to the Metropolitan in 1962 after a season in a Broadway musical. He has recorded operas of Mozart, Rossini, Puccini, and Verdi.

Sills, Beverly, originally Belle Miriam Silverman (b. May 26, 1929) A pupil of Estelle Liebling, the U.S. lyric coloratura soprano Beverly Sills began her career as a radio performer (at age three) and while in her teens sang light opera and Gilbert and Sullivan operettas with the Charles Wagner Opera Company. Her operatic debut in the 1953 season in San Francisco was in several roles, including Donna Elvira (Mozart's *Don Giovanni*), although she was later better known for her Donna Anna. In 1955 she first sang with the New York City Opera (as Rosalinda in Johann Strauss the Younger's *Die Fledermaus*), and

Beverly Sills
courtesy, Edgar Vincent Associates
photograph, Christian Steiner

she has remained affiliated with that company, being named director effective in 1979. She was especially acclaimed in 1966 for her Cleopatra in Handel's *Giulio Cesare*. She had successful first appearances at La Scala (1969) and the Metropolitan Opera (1975) in Rossini's *Assedio di Corinto* and as Donizetti's Lucia at Covent Garden (1970). She is noted for her roles of Baby Doe (Douglas Moore, *The Ballad of Baby Doe*) and Donizetti's Tudor queens (Elizabeth in *Roberto Devereaux,* Maria Stuarda, and Anna Bolena), for which she made extensive historical research of costuming and makeup. A volume of memoirs, *Bubbles; a Self-Portrait,* was published in 1976.

Silverman, Stanley (b. July 5, 1938) After study at Boston and Columbia Universities, the U.S. composer Stanley Silverman worked at Mills (California) College with Milhaud, Leon Kirchner, and Henry Cowell. He received grants from the Rockefeller Foundation (1964, 1970), the Fromm Foundation (1968, 1971), and the Koussevitzky Foundation (1972). He was on the faculty of the Berkshire Music Center (1962–68) and in 1969 was music consultant for the Stratford National Theatre of Canada. Until 1973 he was music director for the Repertory Theater of Lincoln Center in New York City. His compositions include two operas (*Elephant Steps,* 1968; *Dr. Selavy's Magic Theatre,* 1972), 20 theater scores, and works for chorus and instruments such as *Oedipus* (1972).

RECORDING: *Planh* (chamber concerto for guitar).

Simionato, Giulietta (b. December 15, 1910) Educated in Florence, the Italian mezzo-soprano Giulietta Simionato made her debut there in 1938 in Ildebrando Pizzetti's *L'Orsèolo.* The following year she sang at La Scala, where she remained for some 20 years, acclaimed as both a singer and an actress. She sang at the Chicago Lyric Opera before making her Metropolitan Opera debut in 1959 as Azucena in Verdi's *Il Trovatore.* The same year she sang there the role of Santuzza (Mascagni's *Cavalleria rusticana*), which was to become one of her greatest roles. She has recorded much of the Italian operatic repertoire.

Simon Boccanegra: *see* BOITO; VERDI.

Simpson or **Sympson, Christopher** (*c.* 1610–1669) The English gambist Christopher Simpson was a music tutor to the son of Sir Robert Bolles and was known as a composer, pedagogue, and theorist. His contemporaries attested to his skill on his instrument, and many of his works demonstrate the evolution of the variation form. His works that were most influential for theory and practice are *The Division Violist, or an Introduction to Playing upon a Ground* (1659) and *The Principles of Practicle Musick. . .either in Singing or Playing upon an Instrument* (1665).

sinfonia A name given to several forms. In the Baroque era (*c.* 1600–*c.* 1750) sinfonia usually referred to an orchestral introduction to an opera or opera scene, a cantata, or a suite. In the 17th century it was also used interchangeably with sonata and canzona for independent instrumental compositions. Around 1690 the Italian opera overture, or sinfonia, became standardized in a three-section pattern, allegro–adagio–allegro, and was one of the precursors of the Classical symphony. Sinfonia also occasionally refers to a symphony or other instrumental piece; *e.g.,* Bach's three-part Inventions.

sinfonia concertante: *see* CONCERTANTE.

singspiel German 18th-century opera that contains spoken dialogue and is usually comic. The earliest singspiele were light plays interspersed with popular songs. Resembling the contemporary English BALLAD OPERA and the French OPÉRA COMIQUE (both of which stim-

ulated its development), the singspiel rose to great popularity in the late 18th century. Its success was caused partly by a reaction of composers and audiences against the artificial conventions of the then dominant Italian opera.

Leading composers of the singspiel included Johann Adam Hiller, Georg Benda, and Karl Ditters von Dittersdorf. In the hands of Mozart (*Die Entführung aus dem Serail,* 1782; *The Abduction from the Seraglio*) it evolved into a serious, many-faceted art form. Ultimately it gave rise both to German Romantic opera of the 19th century and to popular Viennese operetta.

sitar A northern Indian stringed instrument of the lute family used as a solo instrument with tambura (drone-lute) and *tablah* (drums) and in ensembles, as for Northern Indian *kathak* dances. It developed under medieval Muslim influence from the tanbur, a Near Eastern long-necked lute, and from the vina, or *bīn*, a narrow, elaborate Indian zither. Like the tanbur it has a deep, pear-shaped body, metal strings strung with the treble away from the player, and both front and side tuning pegs. Its neck, however, is wider than the tanbur's, and its frets are movable.

The sitar normally has five melody strings, two drones, and beneath the convex frets in the hollow neck nine to 13 sympathetic strings. The range extends upward from about the F below middle C. The convex frets facilitate pulling the string to the side to play ornaments. There is often a gourd under the peg-

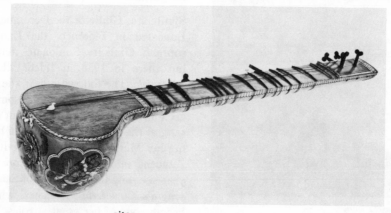

sitar
courtesy, Victoria and Albert Museum

box end of the neck reminiscent of the vina. The sitar is plucked with a wire plectrum worn on the right forefinger.

Sivori, (Ernesto) Camillo (October 25, 1815–February 19, 1894) A student of Paganini and of Paganini's teacher Giacomo Costa, the Italian violinist Camillo Sivori toured Germany, Austria, and Russia at age 16. He wrote two concertos and numerous pieces for violin, including fantasias on arias from the operas of Verdi and Donizetti. He perpetuated the virtuoso style of Paganini.

Six, Les A group of early 20th-century French composers whose music represents a strong reaction against the German Romanticism of Wagner and Richard Strauss and the Impressionism of Debussy. Members were Milhaud, Poulenc, Honegger, Georges Auric, Louis Durey, and Germaine Tailleferre. The term was originated by the French critic Henri Collet in his article "The Russian Five, the French Six, and M. Erik Satie" (1920) to draw a parallel between the well-known nationalistic group of five late-19th-century Russian composers (Rimsky-Korsakov, Mussorgsky, Borodin, Balakirev, and César Cui) and the later group of French composers who drew inspiration from the music of Satie and the poetry of Jean Cocteau. The artificiality of Collet's assemblage has often been cited, and certainly each of the six composers developed along lines best suited to his own tastes and abilities. Yet it is impossible to ignore such distinctive elements as dry sonorities, sophisticated moods, and jazz rhythms that tend to bind the music of these composers into a discrete school.

Skalkottas, Nikos (March 8, 1904–September 19, 1949) A prolific composer whose achievement was recognized posthumously, Greek-born Nikos Skalkottas studied at the Athens Conservatory and then in Berlin with Kurt Weill and Schoenberg. He played violin in chamber orchestras, conducted, and worked on a recording project for the Athenian Folk Music Archives, but his compositions were mainly collected and performed by a Skalkottas society after 1961. Much of his work is dense and long (the Symphonic Suite, No. 2, 1942–44, lasts an hour and a

quarter), and some uses multiple tone rows. Representative works include concertos for piano (1933; 1938), cello (1937), violin (1938), and double bass (1940); 36 Greek Dances (1936) for orchestra; and more than 50 pieces of chamber music.

RECORDINGS: 36 Greek Dances; piano pieces.

Skrowaczewski, Stanislaw (b. October 3, 1923) A student of Boulanger, the Polish conductor and composer Stanislaw Skrowaczewski first had his music performed in public when he was eight. He has written four symphonies, film scores and incidental music for stage plays, songs, and a violin concerto (1978) for the 75th anniversary of the Minnesota Orchestra. Better known as a conductor, he was permanent conductor of the Wrocław (Poland) Philharmonic (1946–47) and held similar positions in Katowice (1949–54), Kraców (1955–56), Warsaw (1957–59), and Minneapolis (1960–79). Noted recordings include the two suites from Prokofiev's *Romeo and Juliet* and a four-disk set of the orchestral music of Ravel.

Sleeping Beauty, The: *see* BALLET (Russia before 1900); TCHAIKOVSKY (later life and works).

sléndro: *see* GAMELAN.

Slezak, Leo (August 18, 1873–June 1, 1946) The Czech Wagnerian tenor Leo Slezak made his debut at Brno in 1896 as Wagner's Lohengrin. He sang at the Berlin Royal Opera and at Breslau before beginning his long association with the Vienna Court Opera (from 1901). He repeated his Lohengrin success at a Covent Garden debut in 1900. After a year of study with Jean De Reszke, he sang Otello (Verdi) in 1909 at Covent Garden and at his Metropolitan Opera debut. He was popular as a comedian in Austrian motion pictures after his retirement from the operatic stage, and his son Walter Slezak has appeared in musical comedy in Europe and the United States. Leo Slezak wrote four volumes of memoirs, of which *Der Wortbruch* (1927) has been translated as *Songs of Motley: Being the Reminiscences of a Hungry Tenor* (1938). He made many 78-rpm recordings of arias from Italian, French, and German operas.

Smetana, Bedřich (March 2, 1824–May 12, 1884) A Bohemian nationalist composer of operas and symphonic poems, Bedřich Smetana studied piano in his youth with Josef Proksch and later became music teacher to the family of Count Leopold Thun. Encouraged by Liszt, he opened a piano school in Prague in 1848 and the following year married the pianist Katharina Kolař. In 1856 he wrote his first symphonic poems and in the same year was appointed conductor of the philharmonic society of Göteborg (Sweden), where he remained until 1861. He then returned to Prague, where he played the leading part in the establishment of the national opera.

Smetana's first opera, *Braniboři v Čechách* ("The Brandenburgers in Bohemia"), was produced in Prague in 1866, followed the same year by *Prodaná nevěsta (The Bartered Bride),* which later established Smetana's reputation. His later operas were less successful: *Dalibor* (1868) was influenced by Wagner; *Libuše,* named after a legendary figure of Prague and intended to celebrate the projected coronation of Emperor Francis Joseph I as King of Bohemia, was not given until 1881, when its production marked the opening of a new opera house. In 1874 Smetana resigned his conductorship of the Prague Opera and by later that year was totally deaf. Between 1874 and 1879, however, he wrote some of his finest works, notably the cycle of six symphonic poems bearing the collective title *Má vlast (My Fatherland)* and the quartet entitled *Z mého života (From My Life). Hubička* ("The Kiss") was successfully produced in 1876, but *Čertova stěna* (1882; "The Devil's Wall") shows signs of declining powers. Following attacks of depression and symptoms of mental instability, Smetana entered an asylum at Prague.

BIBLIOGRAPHY: Bedřich Smetana, *Bedřich Smetana: Letters and Reminiscences* (1955); Brian Large, *Smetana* (1970); John Clapham, *Smetana* (1972).

RECORDINGS: *The Bartered Bride* (overture; dances); *Dalibor; My Fatherland; Quartet From My Life;* Symphonic Poems; piano pieces.

Smith, Gregg (b. August 21, 1931) Best known as the founder of the Gregg Smith Singers, the U.S. conductor Gregg Smith was educated at the University of California, Los Angeles. The Gregg Smith Singers have performed most of the choral music of Stravinsky, Ives, and William Billings, and additional recordings include works by Giovanni Gabrieli, Heinrich Schütz, Schoenberg, and Copland.

snare drum or **side drum** An orchestral and military drum with gut, nylon, wire, or wire-covered silk strings (snares) stretched across the lower, or snare, head; the snares vibrate sympathetically with the lower head (to which vibration is transmitted from the upper, or batter, head by air vibrations inside the drum), causing a snappy, penetrating, relatively high-pitched sound.

The modern snare drum has a cylindrical shell of wood or metal 5–12 inches (13–30 centimeters) high and 14–16 inches (35–40 centimeters) in diameter; deeper models, called field or guard's pattern drums, are used in many military bands. The heads, beaten with two tapered wooden sticks ending in a small knob, are of calfskin or plastic. They are held in place by a flesh hoop (around which the membrane is lapped) and a counter-hoop. Membrane tensioning is by screws that act independently on each head, metal rods, or, chiefly in military bands, on rope lacings.

Snares were known in ancient Egypt and occur on many modern Near Eastern tambourines. In medieval Europe they appeared on the upper head or sometimes both heads of the tabor (*see* DRUM). Large versions of the tabor developed into the snare drum when two sticks rather than one were adopted, and the snares were transferred to the lower head. Suspended at the left side by a belt or a shoulder strap, it was paired with the fife in Swiss infantry *(lansquenet)* regiments from the 14th century, subsequently spreading throughout Europe. The military role of the *lansquenet's* drum was crucial: it kept the marching pace and beat signals to action.

Early forms of the snare drum were equal to or slightly greater in height than diameter. They utilized thicker membranes and sticks than modern instruments, producing a heavier, less brilliant sound. The drum changed most drastically in the 19th century,

snare drum
courtesy, Ludwig Industries

becoming shallow and often gaining a brass shell and rod or screw tensioning. Although the tension of the snares has been adjustable by a screw or lever since early in the 17th century, only in the 20th was a mechanism developed to release them instantaneously (for special effects or to avoid unwanted sympathetic vibrations caused by other instruments). Before the 20th century snares were usually of gut.

Military playing of the snare drum was learned by rote and oral tradition into the 19th century, and only with the drum's eventual orchestral use did players need musical notation. Certain drummers in Basel, Switzerland, maintain a particularly difficult traditional playing technique. Modern compositions and jazz playing may require special effects, such as those obtained by releasing the snares, striking the rim, or using fingers, non-standard sticks, or wire brushes. The first conclusively documented orchestral use of the snare drum was by the French composer–viol virtuoso Marin Marais in a storm scene in his opera *Alcyone* (1706). It reappeared in Rossini's opera *La gazza ladra (The Thieving Magpie*, 1817) with a solo part but did not become a standard orchestral instrument until its use by Rimsky-Korsakov and other Russian composers of the late 19th century. A concerto, the *Geigy Festival* Concerto for Basel drum and orchestra (1958), was written by the Swiss composer Rolf Liebermann.

Soldier's Tale, The: *see* STRAVINSKY.

Soler, Antonio (December 3, 1729–December 20, 1783) The most important Spanish instrumental and church music composer of the later 18th century, Antonio Soler was educated in the choir school of Montserrat and at an early age was appointed maestro de capilla at Lérida Cathedral. In 1752 he joined the order of St. Jerome (Hieronymites) and in the same year became organist at the Escorial monastery near Madrid. Later he was a pupil of Domenico Scarlatti, then in residence at the Spanish court, and he himself taught members of the royal family. Scarlatti's influence may be perceived in the lively keyboard technique, the form, and the often unexpected harmonic progressions of his numerous harpsichord sonatas. He also wrote much church music in which he indulged a taste for intricate canons, incidental music for plays by Calderón and others, Six Quintets for organ and strings, and Six Concertos for two organs. He was the author of a theoretical treatise, much discussed by his contemporaries, entitled *Llave de la modulación* (Madrid, 1762) and experimented in microtones, inventing for the purpose a keyboard instrument called the *afinador.*

RECORDINGS: Concertos (6) for two organs; Fandango; Harpsichord Sonatas.

solfeggio (French form, solfège) Vocal exercises sung to the SOLMIZATION syllables (do, re, mi, etc.) and by extension vocalises, or exercises sung to a single vowel, often florid and difficult to master. Solfeggio collections survive from the 17th century onward with examples by such composers as Nicola Antonio Porpora (also a singer and famed singing teacher), Alessandro Scarlatti, and Cherubini. Later composers of such exercises include Ravel, Fauré, and d'Indy.

The term also refers to the study of intervals and their notation and other rudiments of music.

solmization A system of designating musical notes by syllable names; the term is derived from two of the syllables used in the Western system, "sol–mi." A well-developed system also exists in the music of India, using the syllables *sa, ri, ga, ma, pa, dha, ni;* and similar systems occur, for example, in Chinese, Southeast Asian, and ancient Greek music.

The system that predominates in European

music was introduced by an 11th-century Italian monk, Guido of Arezzo, who derived it from the Latin hymn *Ut queant laxis,* the first six lines of which begin on successively higher notes. Taking the syllables sung on the first note of each line, he arrived at the series ut, re, mi, fa, sol, la. This six-note series, or hexachord, facilitated the reading of music at sight by giving the singer a musical interval with any two syllables. For example, mi–fa was always a semitone, no matter how high or low the two pitches were sung. By mutating, or moving from one hexachord (say, beginning on C) to an overlapping one (say, beginning on F), the singer could always place the syllables mi–fa on any half step in the music.

Changing musical styles at the end of the 16th century made mutation necessary too often to be practical. In the 17th century an adaptation of the system to the seven-note major and minor scales was introduced in France, the syllable si (later ti in some countries) added for the seventh note. The syllable ut was replaced by the more singable do.

Two modern uses of the solmization syllables subsequently developed. In France, Italy, and Spain the syllables became attached to fixed pitches (fixed-do system): do meaning C; re, D; mi, E; fa, F; sol, G; la, A; and si, B. Elsewhere a movable-do system prevailed in which do always represented the first pitch of the major scale (thus allowing the singer to associate syllable names with given intervals as in the old hexachord system).

Various systems of teaching singing and sight-reading based on the movable-do system were devised, the most prominent being tonic sol–fa, developed about 1850 in England by John Curwen. Tonic sol–fa emphasizes the relation of the notes to one another and to the tonic, or key note (do in major scales, la in minor scales). If the key changes, do (or la) shifts to a new pitch (similar to the old practice of mutation). A special notation using the initial letters of each syllable is utilized.

In England and America in the 18th century, a four-syllable system was common in which the major scale was sung fa–sol–la–fa–sol–la–mi–(fa). Often called fasola, it survives in the shape-note hymnal found in some areas of the United States.

Solomon, real name, Solomon Cutner (b. August 9, 1902) A pupil of Mathilde Verne, the English pianist Solomon was a child prodigy who interrupted his career for further study in Paris and reappeared as an adult in 1923. Although his professional life was cut short by serious illness, he was highly regarded as a player of extreme clarity and musical intelligence. His recordings of 18 of the Beethoven Piano Sonatas and the concertos of Beethoven and Brahms were reissued in the late 1970s.

Solti, Georg (b. October 21, 1912) An outstanding interpreter of Wagner and Mahler, the Hungarian conductor Georg Solti studied with Bartók, Ernst von Dohnányi, and Kodály. He became affiliated with the Budapest Opera in 1930, was conductor there (1934–39), and assisted Toscanini at Salzburg (1936–37). He fled to Switzerland in 1939 for political reasons and worked as a pianist; in 1942 he won first prize for piano at the Concours Internationale in Geneva. He conducted the Munich Opera from 1945, Frankfurt State Opera from 1952, and Covent Garden (1961–71). Solti became musical director of the Chicago

Georg Solti conducting the Chicago Symphony Orchestra
courtesy, Edgar Vincent Associates

Symphony (1969) and while retaining the Chicago position was named head of the Orchestre de Paris (1971) and the London Philharmonic (1979). He has conducted the San Francisco Opera (U.S. debut, 1953) and the Metropolitan Opera. His most successful recordings are of opera and large-scale choral and orchestral works. He conducted the first integral recording of Wagner's *Der Ring des Nibelungen* and has recorded all the Wagner operas, except for a projected *Lohengrin,* as well as the symphonies of Beethoven and of Mahler. He was knighted in 1971.

BIBLIOGRAPHY: Paul Robinson, *Solti: The Art of the Conductor* (1978).

Sombrero de tres picos, El: *see* THREE-CORNERED HAT, THE.

sonata An instrumental work (from the Italian for "sounded" as opposed to *cantata,* "sung"). Since the late 18th century the term has usually meant a composition in three or four movements for one or two instruments. A similar form is used in the symphony (a sonata for orchestra), in chamber music (a sonata for trio, quartet, quintet, etc.), and in the concerto (a sonata for solo instrument and orchestra). Thus the difference in terms is primarily the difference in performing mediums.

Baroque sonata In Italy at the beginning of the 17th century the FANTASIA developed a tendency to be built up in brief sections, and it was these sections that were made slightly longer and more distinct to form sonatas of several movements. Some of these sonata movements continued to be given the loosely fugal texture characteristic of the fantasia; others were in the form of dances such as the saraband or the coranto. Such dances were familiar in the court balls and other fashionable entertainments of the period to which the newly developed family of violins was regarded as a particularly suitable accompaniment because of their brilliant tone and assertive articulation. The sonata, like the violin family itself, was first cultivated by the Italian musicians, and developments both of the form and of the instruments were interdependent.

The old equal-voiced polyphony of the 16th-century fantasia continued to be developed by English composers of the early 17th century, whose idiom was thoroughly instrumental, into a magnificent school of contrapuntal chamber music for viols; their lighter tone and more transparent coloring enabled them to perform their own elaborate counterpoint with impressive clarity. Elsewhere—and above all in Italy—the trend in music passed from equal-voiced polyphony to solo melody for which the viols were less suited than the violins. Here is one of the distinguishing characteristics of the sonata as opposed to the fantasia. Although the texture of the Baroque sonata remained essentially contrapuntal, and although some of its movements (especially the second) tended to be fugal, there is no equal-voiced polyphony in the 16th-century sense; the emphasis is on solo melody.

This solo melody is ordinarily supported by a bass line that is almost as melodic in quality as the main melody itself. A further development consisted of writing two main melodies at about the same level of pitch that continually cross and recross in the treble register until more or less equal. It is as if the solo melody had divided into a pair of copartners, still supported at some distance below by the strongly melodic bass line. The harmony in between is not filled out with independent parts as it is in the fantasia. On the contrary, it is left to the continuo player to improvise on the bass line with a few figures for assistance. There could be no clearer indication of the new inclination to exploit melody at the expense of equal-voiced polyphony.

This dual-melody sonata became known as the TRIO SONATA. Two treble melodies and one bass melody add up to three; and though a keyboard, lute, or other continuo accompaniment was also normally used, the work was regarded as complete without this fourth instrument. The music can be performed without continuo, though this leaves it less rich and brilliant. When a continuo instrument was used it was possible to dispense with a melody instrument playing the bass, but this too was felt to be an undesirable impoverishment. Solo sonatas for violin or other instruments were also developed through the 17th century, but the trio sonata became the standard form of serious chamber music and held a position corresponding to that of the quartet from the time of Haydn onward. Keyboard sonatas appeared intermittently in the 17th century, notably those of Johann Kuhnau.

The sonata as understood in the Baroque era owes most to the famous violinist-composers of the Italian school. These were successfully active very early in the 17th century, but the school reached a peak in the solo and trio sonatas of Corelli. In the same generation Purcell, who had already composed the last great English fantasias, became acquainted with the Italian idiom and produced the first English sonatas of enduring significance. These, for two violins and continuo and for three violins and continuo, have not the classic perfection of form of the Corelli sonatas; but the harmonic interest is greater in Purcell's music, and the feeling is warmer and more heart-searching. These features are due partly to Purcell's individual genius and partly to the singular intensity of the English tradition that he inherited.

The Italian sonata as perfected by Corelli took two slightly different forms: one designed for performance in church; the other for secular occasions. The former variety was the *sonata da chiesa,* the latter the *sonata da camera.* Dance movements were favored in chamber sonatas but less in church sonatas whose style might be somewhat more solemn; in other respects there is no difference that strikes the modern ear.

A further distinction—stressed at the time but less noticeable to modern ears—is that between Italian and French styles. This distinction provoked much controversy in the second half of the 17th century and most of the 18th. The Italian style brought the melody into prominence and employed rich harmonies characterized by suspensions. A flowing tempo was desirable, the parts quiet-moving, and the movements—normally without descriptive title—designed to follow each other in an established order. The French instrumental style was notable for precise, clearly marked rhythms, short phrases, and in the slow movements elegant ornamentation and poignant sentiment. The movements, often with literary or pictorial associations, were assembled in many different ways. The Italian style was regarded as brilliant by its admirers

but as intemperate by its detractors; the French style was regarded as tenderly expressive by its admirers but as stiff and insipid by its detractors. The genius of François Couperin rose above this embittered quarrel; he not only composed in both national styles but combined them in a series of splendid trio sonatas that are to the French tradition what Purcell's are to the English.

The Germans were early followers of the Italians and produced solo violin sonatas and trio sonatas in the 17th century as well as sonatas in which the viola da gamba takes a middle part. Telemann, Handel, and others composed many sonatas of value, but the greatest Baroque sonatas come from Bach, particularly those for unaccompanied violin (for which there are German precedents) or cello and for violin with harpsichord obbligato or viola da gamba with harpsichord obbligato; he also wrote a small number of trio sonatas. His writing for the violin owed something to Vivaldi, the greatest of all the 18th-century Italian violinist-composers, whom he greatly admired.

Though these Baroque works were called sonatas and are still rightly known by this name, they can be more accurately described as suites rather than as sonatas in the later sense of the term. Moreover there is no essential difference between the Baroque sonata and the Baroque suite; they are basically the same form for which other names, such as partita or *ordre,* were also freely in use.

The principle is to contrast a succession of movements—each more or less homogeneous in itself. The contrast may be of tempo, rhythm, major or minor mode, or general style; an underlying unity is provided by a single key, occasionally varied by its near relatives. The degree of internal contrast within the movement varies, but it was never the determining element in the construction of the sonata as it became from the time of Haydn onward.

transition The transition from the Baroque sonata, which is in effect a suite, to the Classical sonata, which is in true sonata form, occupied the middle of the 18th century. An outstanding pioneer was Domenico Scarlatti. His father Alessandro was in the front rank of Italian opera composers in his day; the son Domenico was in advance of his. Though born in the same year as Handel and Bach, Domenico Scarlatti did much to prepare the change of style that was to follow those two last geniuses of the Baroque era. Most of his sonatas for harpsichord are untypical in one respect: they are essentially single-movement works, two of which may have been paired in performance. Within the single movement they make a deliberate and effective use of internal contrast, and it is this feature that became decisive in sonata form as understood from Haydn onward. Domenico Scarlatti combined astonishing brilliance with a remarkable depth of poetry, and his sonatas, though best classified as transitional from the formal viewpoint, are masterpieces in their own right.

Bach's sons continued the development away from the Baroque toward the subsequent conception of the sonata. In particular Carl Philipp Emanuel Bach and Johann Christian Bach contributed to the use of contrasted keys—not only between movements but more significantly within the movement. It is here that the history of true sonata form begins.

sonata form The term sonata form in its stricter modern use denotes both the organization of tonal material within the movement and the relationship between movements. The main divisions within a movement in sonata form are the exposition, the development, and the recapitulation.

In the exposition the tonal material is dual with an inherent element of contrast. Its themes, though not necessarily two in number, present a conflict of mood that tends to divide the material into two fields of force. The tension between these two fields is heightened by a conflict of key: the opening material is· in the tonic key; the contrasting material is in a contrasting key, normally in a close relationship to the tonic key but sufficiently distinct to mark a certain distance from the starting point. The listener feels a sense of opposites: very often the familiar human opposition of a masculine with a feminine mood, or of an energetic with a reflective temperament, or of strength with tenderness. All of this may be preceded by an introduction. The

exposition is commonly marked with repeat signs, but these are optional. Some expositions seem to gain from being heard twice, others not; the modern tendency is to omit the repeat.

In the development any portion of the preceding material and in many cases new, or seemingly new, material may appear in any order and in any combination. Frequently the material is broken down into its constituent fragments, and these fragments are themselves combined and developed. Opposing moods are illustrated and made to interact. Tonality becomes as fluctuating as the argument. The key is in constant modulation; if it settles it is likely to be in a tonality remote from either of those established in the exposition. Toward the end of the development section a sense of premonition is introduced that is fulfilled by a return of the tonic key and with it the original opening material.

What follows is the recapitulation. Both opposites that set up their contrasting tonalities and their contrasting fields of force in the exposition are heard again and in the same order. They may show considerable differences on this second appearance; there may be felicitous new touches showing how little a second appearance need be mechanical; but the opposites are still recognizably and often literally the same. Their effect on the listener, however, is not the same. They are heard anew because they have gone through the revealing experience of the development. The listener is prepared in consequence to find their initial opposition reconciled; this sense of inner reconciliation is confirmed, like the initial opposition, by the tonality. Instead of appearing in a key or keys contrasted with the tonic key, the opposing material now appears in the same, or mainly in the same, key as the opening material. What began as a conflict in the exposition proceeds as dialectic in the development and ends as synthesis in the recapitulation. The tension of the opposites is not so much relaxed as brought into balance. A coda may then follow, sometimes of such elaborate proportions as to simulate further development; but a sonata-form movement is complete only if it ends with reconciliation.

A form is not a mold to be filled by a composer pouring suitable material into it; a vital form is based on the principle of organic growth. This principle is illustrated in many different ways. Mozart's sonata-form movements show different inclinations from Haydn's, and Beethoven's from Mozart's. But they all show the same principle based primarily on a conflict of mood and tonality that leads through development and interplay to reconciliation. It is a drama so fundamental to human experience that it may be readily seen why the expression of it in music produced a form of such enduring conviction. This reached its perfection in the three Classical masters just mentioned, but it served some of the Romantics of the later 19th century equally well.

The unified contrasts in the first aspect of sonata form (the organized exposition, development, and recapitulation of tonal material within the movement) continue into its second aspect (the organized relationship between movements). The sonata-form movement as described above is the first movement of the sonata at its most characteristic—so much so that it is alternatively described as first-movement form. This, however, is not a desirable alternative, as the first movement is not invariably in sonata form, and later movements often are. These normally comprise a slow movement in the middle and a quick movement at the end with the optional insertion of a lighter movement either before or after the slow movement. In the sonata as developed by Haydn, the keys of the separate movements are contrasted with the same attention to dramatic effect as the key sequences within the movement.

This was not a new principle, but it was pressed to new lengths. Whereas a Baroque suite (even when passing under the name of sonata)—or indeed a late Baroque opera with its suites of arias—is a series of arresting scenes, a sonata by Beethoven or an opera by Wagner is in the form of a dramatically developed plot. The dramatic element is greater in 19th-century music than in Baroque music, and the sonata is the chief instrumental form that gave strength and coherence to this new sense of drama.

In the Classical sonata there is not usually a conscious thematic connection between the material of one movement and another, but some Romantic composers from Schumann onward experimented extensively in the use of transformed material. Liszt transformed his material in such a way that he was able to maintain the original elements of his themes throughout all movements of his sonata forms; but, though his poetic intentions were undeniable, his inspiration did not always sustain his preconceived plan. Deliberate use of the same material to fill out the different movements is alien to the spirit of sonata form, though fleeting references from one movement to another can add to the sense of coherence and are often moving. In sonata form unity is achieved within a movement by relating the tonalities of the contrasting sections to an underlying key. The tonalities of the different movements are also related. The slow movement and the trio are normally contrasted in key with the other movements.

The slow movement does not usually follow the plan of the first-movement sonata form, as its slow-moving tempo would not allow an expanded development without unreasonably prolonging the length. A common form for the slow movement is the aria or lied form—ABA, often called song form. This consists of a section complete in itself, a section contrasting both in mood and tonality, and the first section repeated—often with substantial variation. An alternative, which can be elaborate, is variation form: a melody complete in itself, variations on it, and sometimes the plain melody again. Some of Beethoven's slow movements are in variation form (*e.g.,* the *Appassionata* and the Quartet, Op. 135).

The slow movement may be preceded or followed by a movement whose purpose is to lighten the mood and relax the tension. In the 18th century the minuet was used for this purpose. This was often followed in suites and divertimenti by a second minuet (perhaps in the minor if the first was in the major), the first minuet then returning without its repeats. As the Classical sonata developed a trio became usual in place of the second minuet (the name probably deriving from the convention of four-part writing being replaced by three-part writing). The convention was not obligatory and later declined. Many trios have an elegiac charm, almost a naiveté, providing relief in an otherwise tense composition. Later the SCHERZO supplanted the minuet; the scherzo was sometimes divided by a trio, elements of which could be repeated. In all these schemes the function of this movement remains the same: to provide either light relief or at least relief in the sense of some decisive change of mood (some of Beethoven's scherzos are notoriously ferocious).

The function of the last movement in a sonata is variable. Some works begin with a first movement so powerful that the entire sequel becomes a prolonged commentary on it without detracting from its prominence. This is more commonly found in the works of Haydn or Mozart than in those of Beethoven. Another pattern is to set the main weight in the slow movement followed by a slighter but brilliant finale. It is also possible to lead up to a massive last movement to which the others seem no more than an elaborate preparation. But a quiet and contemplative ending can sometimes carry profound conviction. RONDO form and variation form (see VARIATIONS) are common choices; they are sometimes so handled (especially rondo form) as to contain elements of sonata form, while true sonata form (perhaps somewhat modified) is a further possibility for the last movement of a sonata, particularly if the first movement has been in some other form.

Symphonies, quartets, and to some extent concertos of the 18th and 19th centuries are commonly, in effect, sonatas. At the beginning of the 20th century, the concept that reached maturity with Haydn became transfigured by Sibelius, whose symphonies, though consistent with sonata principles, often grow from small germs instead of developing self-sufficient material. But there are still contrasting elements ultimately reconciled.

The drama of key and modulation is at the basis of sonata form. If it is found to be of less value to 20th-century composers, this is not because they do not wish music to express such fundamental ideas as conflict, growth, and reconciliation but because—key-tonality having lost much of its significance—other technical means must be found to express these perennial concepts.

BIBLIOGRAPHY: Charles Rosen, *The Classical Style* (1971); William S. Newman, *The Sonata in the Baroque Era, The Sonata in the Classic Era,* and *The Sonata Since Beethoven,* rev. eds. (1972).

sonata da camera: *see* TRIO SONATA.

sonata da chiesa: *see* TRIO SONATA.

sonatina A modified variety of the SONATA usually in three relatively short movements. The first movement is normally in sonata form; *i.e.,* with exposition, development, and recapitulation. But the development section of a sonatina is characteristically much shorter than in a sonata or is omitted altogether. The sonatina form is common in slow movements of 18th-century sonatas and also appears in some early 19th-century opera overtures. Many piano sonatinas, such as those of Clementi and Friedrich Kuhlau (1786–1832), were written for instruction. In contrast the piano sonatinas of such composers as Ravel and Busoni require considerable technical proficiency. Less common are sonatinas for instruments other than piano, as that for violin, viola, and cello by Milhaud.

Sondheim, Stephen: *see* MUSICAL COMEDY.

song A piece performed by a single voice, with or without instrumental accompaniment; songs for two or more voices are more accurately described as duets, trios, quartets, etc. The music of a song is normally a setting of intelligible words; examples of wordless songs (vocalises) occur in the works of 20th-century composers, but they are exceptional. Such a conception of song is possible only in a civilized society. To primitive man words and tune were inseparable, and this is largely true of European and American folk song. Primitive songs are also closely associated with nature and with the supernatural inherent in nature; hence they always have a definite purpose. In European and American folk songs purpose survives in the shape of lullabies, work songs, sea chanteys, and the like; but a great many songs do no more than tell a story or sing of the joys and disappointments of love (see FOLK MUSIC).

early European song The records of European song, as distinct from folk song, are scanty before the 12th century. For recreation monks and students sang songs in Latin, as this was the language of their education. The words of many have been preserved, but the tunes were rarely written down because they were well known, or the skill to record them was lacking, or possibly composers wanted to preserve them for themselves. It is to the 12th-century TROUBADOUR in the south of France that we owe not only what appears to be a new art of lyrical poetry in the vernacular but also a large number of melodies wedded to the poems. This art was imitated by the TROUVÈRE of northern France; here a considerably larger corpus of songs with music survived as well as in Spain, Italy, and what is now Germany and Austria. Whether the melodies were written by the poets themselves or by musicians associated with them is a matter of dispute; but they are all highly organized—in most cases with an exact or modified repetition of the first section—and many of them reveal a subtlety of expression not surpassed by later composers. Songs of this kind could have been composed only in an aristocratic society where there was sufficient leisure for invention and where expert scribes were available to copy them into the beautiful manuscripts that have survived. No accompaniment is indicated in the manuscripts; if any was used it was presumably improvised.

polyphony It was inevitable that this flood of melody should have influenced the composers of polyphonic music. The 13th-century motet, even though founded on a fragment of plainchant, shows this influence very clearly; it becomes even more marked in settings of French words intended for secular use. Furthermore, delight in the sound of the solo voice encouraged 14th-century French and Italian composers to assign all but one of the parts in a polyphonic composition to instruments. In this way a new art of solo song with accompaniment arose and continued to be practiced throughout the 15th century. This art was inevitably more elaborate than the melodies of the trouvères and in some cases became highly mannered, creating a problem that has faced all songwriters—how to do justice to the words while allowing the music to develop to its fullest capacity.

Though there was often considerable elabo-

ration in the instrumental parts of these compositions, on the whole they were dominated by the vocal line. But in the course of the 15th century, composers of polyphonic music for voices came more and more to integrate their works by the use of imitation. This practice spread to the composition of solo songs, with the tune sung either by an inner voice (particularly popular in Germany) or by the soprano, accompanied by instrumental parts based on fragments of the melody. At the same time, about the end of the 15th century, there was a reaction against elaborate polyphony in songs with the simplest possible accompaniment, a large number of which were composed in Italy (under the name FROTTOLA) and also in Spain. In songs of this kind accompaniment by an instrumental ensemble was hardly necessary, and it was often replaced by a single part for the lute. No doubt it was the popularity of these arrangements, many of which were published, that encouraged Spanish composers in the 1530s to write original songs with an accompaniment for the vihuela (a flat-backed instrument, tuned and played in the same way as the lute). This accompaniment could be quite simple, but the virtuosity of performers was an inducement to write varied accompaniments that offered a challenge to the accompanist without interfering with the simplicity of the vocal line.

French composers of the 16th century remained faithful to the CHANSON for several voices, though many of these were also published in transcriptions for voice or lute. In England the old tradition of solo song with imitative accompaniment for an instrumental ensemble survives in Byrd's *Psalmes, Sonets, and songs of Sadnes and pietie* (1588), though these were published with words added to the instrumental parts. Other English composers at the end of the 16th century wrote original songs with lute accompaniment, some of which were also made available for singing by four voices.

recitative and aria By this time the Italians had developed a different manner of setting and accompanying words. This arose from the fact that composers of the MADRIGAL in Italy, unlike their English imitators, had generally set distinguished poetry. The impor-

762

tance of the words in singing is suggested by Baldassare Castiglione's reference in 1528 to "cantare alla viola per recitare"; *i.e.,* singing a solo song with instrumental accompaniment. In the course of the 16th century there was a growing feeling that the intricacy of the madrigal did less than justice to the words, though composers often avoided complication for short periods by making all the voices sing the same words at the same time. But homophonic writing, as opposed to polyphonic elaboration, did not solve the problem of allowing the words to be recited as if they were spoken. Hence toward the end of the 16th century, a new style of word setting developed in which a single voice had complete freedom of time and expression, and the accompaniment—the simplest possible—was provided by a continuo instrument on which the accompanist improvised chords indicated by a FIGURED BASS. This style was known as stile recitativo and subsequently simply as RECITATIVE.

This manner of singing was ideal for dramatic performance, and it was adopted in the first operas at the end of the 16th century. It was not intended to be simply a translation of speech into song; composers were too near the madrigal, which continued to be written in the early 17th century, to ignore the possibilities of expression in vocal music. But it was realized that occasional lyrical pieces were appropriate in the pastoral setting of these early operas, and when recitative was employed in the concert room it became obvious that the variety achieved by alternating recitative with song, or ARIA, was indispensable. Though recitative could be intensely moving when performed by a first-rate actor, the purely musical pleasure afforded by the aria was obviously more attractive to the average members of an audience, and it also offered more opportunities to a singer. Hence the aria came more and more to dominate opera and also oratorio; it also became very much extended by the use of instruments other than the continuo to alternate with the voice or to work in close association with it. The need for a significant musical structure on a large scale led to the da capo aria in three sections, the third a repetition of the first apart from ornamentation of the vocal melody, which was left to the singer. The fact that this repetition sometimes made nonsense of the words does not seem to have unduly disturbed either composers or audiences, though protests against it were heard from time to time in the 18th century. The da capo aria, however, was not universal; there are many examples of shorter arias without this repetition.

strophic settings   Outside the world of opera the simple strophic song with keyboard accompaniment continued to thrive—notably in England, France, and Germany. In England it earned renewed interest through the popularity of *The Beggar's Opera* (1728) and its successors, and in France its introduction into popular comedies in the early 18th century led to the creation of OPÉRA COMIQUE, which—unlike Italian opera buffa—remained faithful to spoken dialogue. The idea that such songs, as opposed to the operatic style of the solo cantata, could be a medium for artistic expression was hardly realized in the 18th century. The songs of Haydn and Mozart are for the most part little more than simple ditties, though Mozart's "Das Veilchen" and "Abendempfindung an Laura" pointed to the possibilities of a deeper art of expression. Schubert, who began by imitating the narrative ballads of his immediate predecessors, showed what could be done to turn even the simplest strophic song into something more than an agreeable entertainment; the songs of his last year, such as "Der Doppelgänger," outstripped all his contemporaries in the power of dramatic realization. His example was not lost on the Romantic composers of the 19th century—among them Mendelssohn, Schumann, Liszt, and Brahms—who learned from him not only the art of varying a strophic melody but also the significance that could be given to the accompaniment. For Hugo Wolf the accompaniment often became a piece of music in its own right, allowing the voice to follow rhythm dictated by the words and to achieve its own expressive melody without being fettered to the piano. *See* LIED.

challenge of songwriting   Since that time there have been few composers who have not felt impelled to face the challenge of songwriting. The nature of the challenge is obvious enough. Inspired music, as Schubert showed, can often redeem inferior words; but fine poetry may appear so self-sufficient that to add music to it is to spoil it. There is also the problem that the rhythm of spoken verse is normally more subtle than that of music, however ingeniously the composer may try to match it; and the more ingenious the attempt, the greater the danger of music's becoming merely a vehicle for the poem. Italian recitative of the early 17th century solved the problem by allowing the singer complete freedom with only the simplest accompaniment. But however effective this may be in an opera, it risks undermining the musical structure of an independent piece.

There is no ideal solution. A continuous texture in the accompaniment may serve to unify the music, but it may also deny the singer the opportunity to make the words sound convincing as music. At first sight a strophic setting seems almost like an avoidance of the problem and may easily be regarded as much the easiest way of writing a song. In fact it is one of the most difficult forms of songwriting if it is to achieve anything like fidelity to the words. There are, however, ways of modifying a simple strophic scheme by varying the melody or the key or both; in exploring these possibilities Schubert showed incomparable skill.

The influence of language on song is not unimportant, particularly as songwriting in its turn often influences instrumental composition. The da capo aria grew out of the Italian language, for which it was the ideal medium. When the same style was borrowed by German composers the result was likely to be less successful. All French songwriting has a character of its own, as the language—unlike Italian, German, and English—has no regular tonic accent. This means that syllables can be set equally well on accented or unaccented beats; it also results in a peculiar fluidity that is absent from the regular accents of German song. It would seem likely that this fluidity is at least partly responsible for the shifting, kaleidoscopic harmonies that are one of the features of Fauré's songwriting. In the same way the dramatic realism of Mussorgsky's songs is not merely an expression of his own temperament but also a consequence of the actual sounds of the Russian language. Some-

thing similar is to be found in Czech songwriting, where the lightweight syllables of the language suggest a similar treatment in the music.

Whatever the origins of song may be in remote antiquity—as a means of attracting attention, or telling a story, or providing encouragement in war or the chase—in civilized society it has developed as a natural response to the beauty of the human voice. Hence the melodic style of a song is likely to sound distorted if the capacity of the voice for phrasing and for blending syllables is ignored. Wide leaps are within the capacity of any trained singer and have often been used by composers of many different periods in the interests of dramatic intensity. But a vocal line that consists almost entirely of leaps can hardly be described as vocal and is certainly not a line. There is a tendency among some mid-20th-century composers to treat the voice instrumentally rather than vocally.

Sonnambula, Il: *see* BELLINI.

Sontag, Henriette, originally Gertrud Walburga Sonntag (January 3, 1806–June 17, 1854)   A student at the Prague Conservatory, the German soprano Henriette Sontag made her operatic debut at age 15 as a replacement for an ailing soprano. While singing in Vienna she attracted the attention of Weber, who requested her to create the title role of *Euryanthe* (1823). She also sang the first pre-publication performance (1824) of the Beethoven Ninth Symphony. After appearing in Leipzig and Berlin she made her Paris (1826) and London (1828) debuts as Rosina (Rossini's *Il barbiere di Siviglia*)—all with great success. Secretly married to Sardinian Count Carlo Rossi in 1827, she was forced to retire from the stage in 1830, singing only privately until her return in 1849. Her last appearance was in Mexico City in Donizetti's *Lucrezia Borgia*. Some of her best roles were Mozart's Susanna *(Le nozze di Figaro)* and Zerlina *(Don Giovanni)* and Marie (Donizetti's *La Fille du régiment*).

soprano   The highest human voice. The term is generally applied only to the highest of the three types of voice of female singers (and of the 17th- and 18th-century male CAS-

TRATO). The boy's unchanged voice is usually called boy soprano or treble. Soprano also refers to the highest member of certain families of instruments, such as a soprano recorder, and to the written part sung or played by soprano voices or instruments.

Sor, Fernando, real name, Fernando Sors (February 13, 1780–July 8, 1839) The Spanish guitarist and composer Fernando Sor increased the popularity of the guitar in Paris and especially in London, where he performed as soloist with the Philharmonic Society. He wrote pieces and études for the guitar that are still regularly studied and an opera and two ballets.

RECORDINGS: Guitar pieces—*L'Encouragement;* Études; Introduction and Allegro; Sonata in C; Variations on a Theme of Mozart.

Sorcerer's Apprentice, The: *see* DUKAS; PROGRAM MUSIC (problem of form); SCHERZO; SYMPHONIC POEM.

Sousa, John Philip: *see* BAND; MARCH.

Sowerby, Leo (May 1, 1895–July 7, 1968) The U.S. composer, teacher, and organist Leo Sowerby studied in Chicago, where in 1917 he presented a program of his orchestral works and songs and in 1921 was named the first recipient of the American Grand Prix de Rome. He taught composition and theory at the American Conservatory in Chicago (1925–62) and was organist and choirmaster at St. James's Church (now the Cathedral of St. James) from 1927. He was director of the College of Church Musicians at the Washington Cathedral from 1962. Sowerby's early works were influenced by Max Reger and Grieg. His numerous vocal works include cantatas (*Forsaken of Man,* 1939; and *Canticle of the Sun,* 1945, which won a Pulitzer Prize), services, anthems, and songs. Other works include five symphonies; concertos for piano, cello, and organ (*Classic* Concerto, 1944); chamber works; and pieces for piano and for organ (Symphony in G).

RECORDING: Organ Symphony in G.

Spalding, Albert (August 15, 1888–May 26, 1953) The only U.S. violinist to be invited as a soloist (1922) at the Paris Société des Concerts du Conservatoire, Albert Spalding graduated with highest honors at age 14 from the Bologna Conservatory. He made his Paris debut in 1905 and his U.S. debut three years later. A soloist with the New York Symphony on its first European tour (1920), he subsequently made repeated tours of the United States and Europe. He composed two violin concertos, pieces for piano and violin, and songs. To commemorate his bravery in World War I, he was named a chevalier of the Legion of Honor. He wrote an autobiography, *Rise to Follow* (1943), and a fictionalized biography of Giuseppe Tartini, *A Fiddle, a Sword, and a Lady* (1953).

spinet A small, compact form of HARPSICHORD. It is often wing shaped and has only one set of strings placed at an oblique angle to the keyboard. The spinet appeared about 1660 and became popular as a substitute for the larger harpsichord, especially for small rooms. Large numbers were made in the late 17th and 18th centuries, particularly in England.

In modern usage spinet commonly refers to a small form of upright piano. *See illustration on following page.*

Spitta, (Julius August) Philipp (December 7, 1841–April 13, 1894) One of the principal figures in 19th-century musicology, the German writer and teacher Philipp Spitta studied at Göttingen and later formed a friendship with Brahms. In 1874 he helped found the Bachverein in Leipzig, and the following year he became professor of musical history at the University of Berlin. His *Johann Sebastian Bach* (1873–80), dealing with Bach's life and the religious and technical aspects of his work, was the first comprehensive work on this composer. His editions of the works of Heinrich Schütz and Dietrich Buxtehude established a high standard of scholarship. With Brahms, Karl Franz Friedrich Chrysander, and others, he was one of the chief founders in 1892 of the great edition of the works of German composers, *Denkmäler deutscher Tonkunst.*

Spohr, Louis (April 5, 1784–October 22, 1859) The German composer, conductor, and violinist Louis Spohr had great influence as a violin teacher, and his compositions mark the beginning of the Romantic period in German music.

wing-shaped spinet by John Crang, London, 18th century
courtesy, Metropolitan Museum of Art
Rogers fund and funds from various donors, 1976

He was largely self-taught, acquiring his knowledge of composition from studying the scores of Mozart. He took violin lessons from the director of the orchestra in his native Brunswick and was appointed chamber musician there in 1799. In 1802 he studied with a pupil of Johann Stamitz, Franz Eck, who took him on a tour to Russia. While Kapellmeister in Vienna (Theater an der Wien, 1812–15), be came under the influence of the French violinist Pierre Rode, a pupil of Giovanni Battista Viotti, and later he toured Italy with Paganini. In 1817 he was appointed conductor at Frankfurt am Main and in 1822 at the court at Kassel, where he remained until he was pensioned in 1857. Shortly afterward he broke his left arm and was no longer able to play.

As a teacher of violin Spohr carried the traditions of Stamitz and Viotti into the 19th century. His method was set out in his *Violinschule* (1831). Though opposed to the forward-looking composers of his time—he failed to appreciate the works of Weber and of Beethoven's last period—he nonetheless conducted two works of Wagner, *The Flying Dutchman* and *Tannhäuser,* at Kassel despite

great opposition. He was a prolific composer; the style of his works, predominantly in the minor key, have kinship with that of Schubert and Mendelssohn. Of his 10 operas *Faust* (Prague, 1816), together with E. T. A. Hoffmann's *Undine,* was the first of the German Romantic operas; his *Jessonda* (Kassel, 1823) held the stage throughout the 19th century. Of his nine symphonies the fourth, *Die Weihe der Töne* ("The Consecration of Sound"), was the most successful and was revived in the 20th century. The best known of his 15 violin concertos is the eighth, in a minor, written for his Italian tour. His chamber works include 34 quartets, four double quartets, and the well-known nonet.

RECORDINGS: Clarinet Concertos (2); Double Quartets (4); *Duos concertants* (3) for two violins; German Songs, Op. 103 (6); Harp Fantasy; Nonet; *Notturno* for winds and Turkish band; Quintet for piano and woodwinds; *Sonates concertantes* (3) for harp and violin; Violin Concerto No. 8.

Spontini, Gasparo (Luigi Pacifico) (November 14, 1774–January 24, 1851)   An Italian opera composer whose German operas had some influence on Wagner, Gasparo Spontini studied singing and composition at Naples. His first opera *I Puntigli delle donne* was produced in Rome in 1796, followed by others at Venice, Florence, Naples, and Palermo. In 1803 he went to Paris; after writing unsuccessful works in the light French style, he collaborated with the writer Étienne de Jouy in dramatic operas, producing *Milton* (1804) and his masterpiece, *La Vestale* (1807). The success of the latter, given at the Opéra under the patronage of Empress Josephine, led to the award of a prize from Napoleon. *Fernand Cortez* (1809) was similarly successful, and the following year Spontini was appointed director of the Italian Opera in Paris. As a conductor Spontini introduced works of Haydn and Mozart to Paris. In 1814 he was appointed court composer by Louis XVIII and wrote stage works that glorified the Restoration, among them *Pélage, ou le roi de la paix* (1814). Later he held a similar appointment at the court of Frederick William III in Berlin, where between 1821 and 1829 he produced *Olympia* (earlier given in Paris as *Olympie;* on Voltaire, translated into German by E. T. A. Hoffmann); *Nurmahal* (based on Thomas Moore's *Lalla Rookh*); *Alcidor;* and *Agnes von Hohenstaufen.* Spontini spent his later years in France and Germany and eventually returned to his birthplace Majolati.

Sprechstimme A cross between speaking and singing (German for "speech-voice") in which the speech is heightened and lowered in pitch along melodic contours indicated in the musical notation. *Sprechstimme* is frequently used in 20th-century music. Its introduction is especially associated with Schoenberg, who first used it in his *Pierrot Lunaire* (1912). It had been used earlier, however, in the melodrama *Königskinder* (1897) by Engelbert Humperdinck.

Spring Symphony: *see* BRITTEN; SCHUMANN, ROBERT (larger works).

square piano: *see* PIANO (early development).

Stadler, Anton (1753–June 15, 1812) A member of the Viennese court orchestra from 1787 to 1799, the Austrian clarinetist Anton Stadler was a friend of Mozart, who composed for him the Trio, K.498; Quintet, K.581; and Clarinet Concerto, K.622.

staff or **stave** Five parallel horizontal lines that, with a clef, indicate the pitch of notes placed on its lines and in the spaces between those lines (*see* NOTATION [definitions]). The invention of the staff is traditionally ascribed to Guido of Arezzo around the year 1000, although there are earlier manuscripts in which neumes are arranged around one or two lines in order to orient the singer. Guido used three or four lines of different colors. A four-line staff is still used to notate plainchant. The standard five-line staff appeared about 1200 in polyphonic music. Some 16th-century keyboard music used a staff of more lines. A precise staff notation made possible the composition of complex works that characterize Western art music.

Stainer, John (June 6, 1840–March 31, 1901) An English organist, composer of church music, and early musicologist, John Stainer sang in the choir of St. Paul's Cathedral (1847–56) and at the age of 16 was appointed organist at the newly opened St. Michael's College, Tenbury, a school for church musicians. Named organist at St. Paul's in 1872, Stainer served in that position until 1888, when he resigned because of failing eyesight. He was a founder of the Musical Association (now Royal) in 1874 and taught at the National Training School for Music (opened 1876). Knighted in 1888, Stainer was professor of music at Oxford from 1889 to his death.

Stainer's Romantic church music is now mainly performed in England, although his oratorio *The Crucifixion* (1887) and *Sevenfold Amen* are also performed in other English-speaking countries. His compositions include songs, cantatas, services, anthems, and other church music. He also published treatises on the organ and theory and collaborated on a dictionary of musical terms. Stainer's most lasting contribution is his compilation *Early Bodleian Music. . . ,* 3 vols. (1901), with musical examples from the 12th to the 16th century, and *Dufay and His Contemporaries* (publication begun in 1898), an edition of 15th-century music prepared with the help of his children, Cecilia and J. F. R. Stainer. Both publications helped open the way to the study of medieval and Renaissance music, which during Stainer's time was almost unknown.

Stamitz, Carl (Philipp), original name, Karel Stamic (May 7, 1745–November 9, 1801) The son of Johann Stamitz, Carl Stamitz was a leading composer of the second generation of the Mannheim school. He played second violin in the Mannheim orchestra (1762–70), going to Strasbourg, Paris, London, and St. Petersburg as a virtuoso player of the viola and viola d'amore. He eventually settled in Jena (1794). His works include about 70 symphonies, including one for double orchestra and 26 sinfonias concertantes; concertos for violin, viola, viola d'amore, cello, flute, oboe, clarinet, bassoon, horn, and keyboard; chamber music; and operas.

RECORDINGS: Concertos for bassoon, clarinet, flute, viola; Quartets for winds and strings; Sinfonias concertantes (2).

Stamitz, Johann (Wenzel Anton), original name, Jan Václav Antonín Stamic (June 19, 1717–March 27, 1757)   Usually regarded as the founder of the Mannheim school, the Bohemian-born composer, violinist, and conductor Johann Stamitz received his first musical tuition from his father before going to a Jesuit school. He appeared as a violinist at the coronation of Emperor Charles VII in Frankfurt am Main in 1742, but it appears likely that he was already in the musical establishment of the elector palatine at Mannheim, where he was later made director of the court chamber music. Stamitz brought the Mannheim court orchestra to a standard unrivaled both for precision and scope of expression. Although he did not invent the crescendo and diminuendo effects in orchestral playing, he developed them as a feature of his style, which was then imitated by other Mannheim and later by other European musicians. Another characteristic of his style was the use of sighing suspensions, especially at cadences. These became incorporated in gallant style music throughout Europe. His use of the minuet and trio as the third movement of a four-movement symphony was similarly adopted by Classical composers. His orchestral trios, a gallant version of the Baroque sonata, were perhaps more influential in the development of sonata form than were his symphonies, since they were more regular in design. It is

difficult to overestimate Stamitz' influence in these various fields. Although contemporary composers in Berlin, Vienna, and in Italy also developed some of these features, it was the first generation of Mannheimers (Stamitz and his associates Franz Xaver Richter, Anton Filtz, Ignaz Holzbauer, and Franz Beck) who were most influential in establishing the mid-18th-century style of orchestral writing. His sons Carl and Anton were important members of the second Mannheim generation.

RECORDINGS: Clarinet Concerto in B-flat; Symphonies (74); Trios (10) for orchestra.

Stanford, Charles Villiers (September 30, 1852–March 29, 1924)   An Irish composer, conductor, and teacher who had a wide influence on the younger British composers of his time, Charles Villiers Stanford studied organ at Trinity College, Dublin, and from 1870 at Queen's College, Cambridge. Between 1874 and 1877 he studied with Carl Reinecke in Leipzig and with Friedrich Kiel in Berlin. In 1883 he was appointed professor of composition at the Royal College of Music, London, and in 1887 professor of music at Cambridge. Vaughan Williams, Arthur Bliss, and Gustav Holst were among his pupils. Between 1885 and 1902 he was conductor of the London Bach Choir and from 1901 to 1910 of the Leeds Triennial Festival. He was knighted in 1901.

Stanford was a prolific composer in all spheres but was especially known during his lifetime for his orchestral works, his songs, and his operas; but his church music has survived the longest. He adopted the broad features of the late 19th-century Romantic style into which he introduced Irish folk-song elements. His first opera, *The Veiled Prophet of Khorassan,* was given in German as *Der verschleierte Prophet* at Hanover in 1881, followed by *Savonarola* (Hamburg, 1884). He developed his Irish manner in *Shamus O'Brien* (London, 1896). *Much Ado about Nothing* (1901), based on Shakespeare, and *The Critic* (1916), based on Sheridan, were given in London, but *The Travelling Companion,* based on a story of Hans Christian Andersen, was not performed until 1925 at Liverpool. Stanford's orchestral works include seven symphonies and five *Irish Rhapsodies.* Among his choral works are *Songs of the Sea* and *Songs of the Fleet,* both on poems of Henry Newbolt. Church music includes services, anthems, and canticles. Stanford's lyrical style is best seen in his songs, which include settings of Keats, Shelley, Tennyson, and Heine. His pedagogical works are *Musical Composition* (1911) and, with Cecil Forsyth, *A History of Music* (1916).

Starker, Janos (b. July 5, 1924)   The Hungarian-born cellist Janos Starker began a professional career at the age of 10 and played in a quartet at the Budapest Conservatory the following year. After playing as solo cellist in the Budapest Philharmonic, he moved in 1948 to the United States, where he joined the Dallas Symphony and later the Metropolitan Opera orchestra under Fritz Reiner. When Reiner became conductor of the Chicago Symphony, he invited Starker to be his principal cellist. A recitalist as well as an orchestral musician, Starker's repertoire spans Baroque to modern literature, and he specializes in the unaccompanied music of Bach. In 1948 he won the Grand Prix du Disque for his recording of the unaccompanied Cello Sonata by Kodály. He tours annually and in 1958 became a professor at Indiana University.

Stavenhagen, Bernhard (November 24, 1862–December 26, 1914)   One of the last pupils of Liszt, the German pianist and conductor Bernhard Stavenhagen held various posts in Weimar, Munich, and Geneva. He was also known for his teaching and as a composer.

Steber, Eleanor (b. July 17, 1916)   Educated at the New England Conservatory, the U.S. soprano Eleanor Steber sang opera and recitals in Boston before winning the Metropolitan Opera auditions of the air in 1940 and subsequently making her debut as Sophie in Richard Strauss's *Der Rosenkavalier.* She sang there until 1962, returning in 1965 to cover a last-minute performance as Minnie in Puccini's *La fanciulla del West.* She created the title role in Samuel Barber's *Vanessa* (1958) and commissioned from Barber his *Knoxville: Summer of 1915.* She had a broad range of repertoire but was at her best in the music of Mozart and Richard Strauss; her recordings span Bach, Berlioz, and Wagner (a *Lohengrin*

from Bayreuth). Active as a teacher, she has been on the faculties of the Cleveland Institute (from 1962), New England Conservatory, and Juilliard School.

Steffani, Agostino (July 25, 1654–February 12, 1728)   An Italian composer, singer, cleric, and diplomat, Agostino Steffani was celebrated in his own time for his cantatas for two voices. He studied music in Venice, Rome, and Munich, where he served the Elector of Bavaria (1674–88), becoming by 1681 director of chamber music and the object of great favors. In spite of this he left Munich and entered the service of the Duke of Brunswick, later Elector of Hanover, remaining until his death. After some years he ceased to be musical director and entered upon a new career: while continuing to practice music be became a diplomat, going on several missions and acting for a short time as ambassador in Brussels. It was he who induced Handel to settle in Hanover and hence indirectly in London, when the new elector became King George I. Steffani was ordained in 1680 and later became papal protonotary for northern Germany with the status of bishop. He composed about 20 operas, most of them before 1700. It was his numerous chamber duets in cantata form—following models of Carissimi and Alessandro Stradella—that won for Steffani a European reputation; more than 100 of these are known. His *Stabat Mater* for six voices, strings, and continuo was one of the finest works of the period.

RECORDING: *Stabat Mater.*

Steinberg, William, originally Hans Wilhelm Steinberg (August 1, 1899–May 16, 1978)   Known as an interpreter of Wagner, Mahler, and Elgar, the German conductor William Steinberg began his career as an apprentice to Otto Klemperer at the Cologne Opera (1920), becoming principal conductor there in 1924. He conducted opera in Prague (1925–29) and Frankfurt (1929–33). In 1936 he went to Israel and cofounded with Bronislaw Huberman the Palestine Symphony, later the Israel Philharmonic. In 1938 Toscanini invited Steinberg to the United States to assist in the creation and training of the NBC Symphony. He then conducted the San Francisco Opera

(1944–47) and the Buffalo Philharmonic for five seasons. In 1952 he began his 24-year term as music director of the Pittsburgh Symphony, also conducting the London Philharmonic (1958–60), New York Philharmonic (as principal guest conductor), and the Boston Symphony (1969–72).

Stern, Isaac (b. July 21, 1920) A pupil of Louis Persinger, the Soviet-born U.S. violinist Isaac Stern made his debut at age 11 with the San Francisco Symphony and played in New York City six years later. Popular in the U.S.S.R. and in Israel, he was the first U.S. musician to perform on Soviet television. He has played the Mozart Concertos Nos. 1, 3, and 5 on U.S. television and is heard in the sound track of many films, including *Fiddler on the Roof.* He has performed and recorded with Eugene Istomin and Leonard Rose and is acclaimed as a chamber music player. After heading a campaign to save Carnegie Hall from demolition, Stern served as president of the hall's board of directors. Performing a broad repertoire, he has introduced many new works and often gives up to 150 concerts in a year. He received the first Albert Schweitzer Music Award for service to music and humanity.

Steuermann, Eduard (June 18, 1892–November 11, 1964) A pupil of Schoenberg and Busoni, the Polish-U.S. pianist Eduard Steuermann taught in Poland at the Paderewski School and at the Jewish Conservatory. He went to the United States in 1937 and taught at the Philadelphia Conservatory from 1948 to 1952. In that year he joined the faculty of the Juilliard School, where he remained until his death. He specialized in the Viennese school of atonal and 12-tone composers and arranged Schoenberg's *Kammersymphonie* for piano. He recorded music of Busoni and the complete piano music of Schoenberg.

Stevens, Risë (b. June 11, 1913) Long associated with the Metropolitan Opera, the U.S. mezzo-soprano Risë Stevens made her debut there in 1938 as Octavian in Richard Strauss's *Der Rosenkavalier.* She was educated at the Juilliard School and made her European debut in Prague as Ambroise Thomas's *Mignon*, singing there for the two seasons prior to her

appearance at the Metropolitan. She subsequently sang at Glyndebourne, La Scala, Vienna State Opera, and San Francisco Opera. Her best roles at the Metropolitan were Octavian, Fricka (Wagner's *Die Walküre*), Bizet's Carmen, Saint-Saëns' Dalila, and Gluck's Orfeo. Her final stage appearance there was in 1962, after which she became co-manager (with Michael Manuel) of the Metropolitan Opera National Company inaugurated in 1964 and president of the Mannes College in 1975. A popular and glamorous singer-actress, she appeared in the motion pictures *The Chocolate Soldier* (1941), *Going My Way* (1944), and *Carnegie Hall* (1947).

Stignani, Ebe (July 10, 1907–October 5, 1974) Educated in Naples, the Italian contralto Ebe Stignani made her debut at the San Carlo Opera in 1925 as Amneris in Verdi's *Aida* and was engaged by Toscanini at La Scala (debut as Princess Eboli in Verdi's *Don Carlos*), where she was a principal from 1925 to 1956. She sang intermittently at Covent Garden (1937–57) and in the United States, where she sang Santuzza (Mascagni's *Cavalleria rusticana*) at the San Francisco Opera (1938) and at the Chicago Lyric Opera. Her recordings include operas of Verdi and Bellini.

Still, William Grant (May 11, 1895–December 3, 1978) The first notable U.S. black composer and conductor, William Grant Still studied medicine at Wilberforce (Ohio) University before turning to music. He studied composition at the Oberlin Conservatory and then with George Whitefield Chadwick at the New England Conservatory and later with Edgard Varèse during the latter's most radical avant-garde period. The diversity of Still's musical education was increased when in the 1920s he worked as an arranger for Paul Whiteman, W. C. Handy, and other prominent band leaders. In 1939 he married the white pianist and journalist Verna Arvey, author of many of his librettos, and settled in Los Angeles.

Still's concern with the position of the Negro in U.S. society is reflected in many of his works: *Afro-American* Symphony (1931), his best-known piece; ballets *Sahdji* (1931), set in Africa and composed after extensive study of African music, and *Lenox Avenue* (1937); and the opera *The Troubled Island* (1949), libretto by the poet Langston Hughes. Still's compositions from the mid-1930s show the jazz band as a major influence on his eclectic style. He was a prolific composer with a large number of operas, ballets, symphonies, and other large- and small-scale works to his credit.

RECORDINGS: *Afro-American* Symphony; *Danzas de Panama* for strings; *Darker America* for orchestra; *Ennanga* for harp, strings, and piano; *Festive* Overture; *From the Black Belt* for orchestra; *Pastorela* for violin and piano; *Sahdji; Song for Lonely; Songs of Separation* (5); Suite for violin and piano; *Three Visions* for piano.

stochastic music A composition produced by probability systems with the aid of a computer. The term stochastic is derived from the Greek, meaning "target," and was first used by the 18th-century Swiss mathematician Jacques Bernoulli in his Law of Large Numbers. It was applied to music by the Greek composer Iannis Xenakis in experiments beginning in 1954, a chance system of composition in which the overall scheme of the composer is programmed into the computer with the details to be determined by the laws of probability. The result is notated, leaving the element of chance out of the actual performance.

Stock, Frederick (August) (November 11, 1872–October 20, 1942) Educated at the Cologne Conservatory, the German conductor and composer Frederick Stock played violin in the Cologne orchestra and in 1895 went to the United States to play in the Chicago Symphony. In 1899 he became Theodore Thomas' assistant conductor, succeeding him in 1905. He also directed the Musical Art Club (1907–09) and the Civic Music Student Orchestra (after 1920). He gave numerous premieres and programmed many works by U.S. composers. His own compositions include two symphonies, symphonic sketches, a violin concerto (1915), *Festival Prologue* (1915) for the 25th anniversary of the Chicago Symphony, violin pieces, and songs.

Stockhausen, Karlheinz (b. August 22, 1928) Highly influential on younger avant-garde composers and theoreticians of electronic and serial music, the German composer Karlheinz Stockhausen studied with Frank Martin in Cologne and then in Paris with Messiaen and Milhaud. Returning to Cologne in 1953, he co-founded (with Herbert Eimert) the electronic music studio there, becoming its director in 1963. He studied phonetics, acoustics, and information theory at the University of Bonn (1954–56), and since 1957 he has lectured at contemporary music seminars at Darmstadt and in North America. From 1955 he was coeditor (again with Eimert) of the theoretical musical journal *Die Reihe.*

Stockhausen explored fundamental psychological and acoustical aspects of music and has been relatively unconcerned with those aspects that stem from any particular historical tradition. "He who does not recreate traditions anew every day is three times dead," he has said. These preoccupations were intensified by the development of electronic music; but as a counterbalance to the increasing mechanization of music, Stockhausen endeavored to give performers an additional role in creating a composition afresh, even to the extent of determining the form of a piece, reflecting the influence of John Cage's chance, or aleatory, operations.

In each work certain elements, or parameters, are played against one another simultaneously and successively. In *Kontra-Punkte* (1952) pairs of instruments and extremes of note values confront one another in a series of dramatic cadenzas and pedal points; in *Gruppen* (1957–59) fanfares and passages of varying speed are flung among the three orchestras; in *Zeitmasse* (1955–56) for five woodwinds various rates of accelerando and *decelerando* oppose one another. In *Kontakte* (1960) there is contact between the instruments and the electronic sounds they respond to, and there are points of contact between the different electronic sounds themselves: one pitch (frequency) is set in motion and reiterated at a certain rate. If this reaches a certain frequency a new pitch is created.

Other major compositions include: *Refrain* (1959) for three players; *Zyklus* (1959) for one

Karlheinz Stockhausen, 1964–65
Universal Edition, Ltd., London

percussion player; *Carré* (1959–60) for four orchestras and four choruses; *Momente* (1962–64) for soprano, four choruses, and 13 players; *Trans* (1971) for orchestra; *Alphabet für Liège* (1972); and *Am Himmel Wandre ich* (1972; 12 Indian songs). His electronic works include: *Elektronische Studien I* and *II* (1953); *Gesang der Jünglinge* (1956; "Song of the Three Children") with text from the *Benedicite* for five-track electronic tape incorporating a prerecorded human voice; *Teletape* (1966) for electronic tape incorporating prerecorded excerpts from Oriental, African, and Western music; and *Pole* and *Mantra* (both 1970) for two pianos and electronics. He has also written a group of piano pieces, *Klavierstücke XI* (1956), in which the music consists of separate fragments, and the performer is given a certain freedom in regard to dynamics, attack, and even the order or number of fragments played.

BIBLIOGRAPHY: Jonathan Cott, *Stockhausen; Conversations with the Composer* (1973); Karl H. Worner, *Stockhausen: Life and Work*, rev. ed. (1973); Robin Maconie, *The Works of Karlheinz Stockhausen* (1976).

RECORDINGS: *Bird of Passage; Ceylon; Gesang der Jünglinge; Hymnen; Kontakte; Kurzwellen* for piano, tamtam, and electronics; *3 Lieder* for alto and chamber orchestra; *Mikrophonie I* and *II; Momente; Refrain; Schlagtrio* for piano and timpani; *Setzt die Segel zur Sonne;* Sonatine for violin and piano; *Spiel* for orchestra; *Stop; Ylem; Zeitmasse; Zyklus.*

Stokowski, Leopold (April 18, 1882–September 13, 1977) Known for his flamboyant showmanship and the rich sonorities he evoked from an orchestra, the English-born conductor Leopold Stokowski may well have set a record in a profession known for longevity when he signed a recording contract at age 94 (his final recording session was on June 4, just three months before he died).

Educated at the Royal College of Music, London, and Queen's College, Oxford, Stokowski also studied in Paris and in Munich, moving to the United States in 1905 as organist and choirmaster at St. Bartholomew's Church in New York City. His first conducting post (and very nearly his first orchestral conducting) was with the Cincinnati Symphony (1909–12). He gained an international reputation as musical director of the Philadelphia Orchestra (1912–38), making it one of the great ensembles of the world.

Perhaps more than any other conductor, Stokowski was dedicated to sound for its own sake. To that end he experimented with orchestral seating arrangements and, to the despair of his colleagues, with rearranging and reorchestrating the music at will. He championed contemporary music, including premieres of works by Rachmaninoff, Schoenberg, and Edgar Varèse, the first complete performance of Ives's Fourth Symphony (1965; though composed 1910–16), and first U.S. performances of Mahler, Stravinsky, and Berg. After Philadelphia he formed the All-American Youth Orchestra (1940–42) and subsequently conducted the NBC Symphony, the New York Philharmonic, the Houston Symphony (1955–62), and founded (1962) the American Symphony.

Leopold Stokowski   *EB Inc.*

Stokowski made three films with the Philadelphia Orchestra, including Walt Disney's *Fantasia* (1940), and was both famous and infamous for his symphonic transcriptions of Bach works.

BIBLIOGRAPHY: Paul Robinson, *Stokowski: The Art of the Conductor* (1978); Abram Chasins, *Leopold Stokowski: A Profile* (1979).

stop: *see* HARPSICHORD; ORGAN.

Stradella, Alessandro (*c.* 1645–February 28, 1682) An Italian composer, singer, and violinist, Alessandro Stradella was surrounded by mystery and much legend. He apparently lived for periods in Modena, Venice, Rome, and Florence. In Turin in 1677 an attempt was made to murder him for reasons that are not definitely known, though it was believed to be at the instigation of a Venetian senator with whose fiancée Stradella had eloped. His death was the result of a similar incident. Stradella was one of the finest composers of chamber cantatas, of which he wrote more than 200; his fresh, mellifluous melodies are frequently supported by harmonies bolder than usual in music of the period. His instrumental music, both chamber and orchestral, is also worthwhile; particularly interesting is his novel application of concerto grosso texture to accompaniments of arias in some of his stage works and oratorios. But on the whole his dramatic works are not distinctive. Stradella's legendary life, embroidered from suspicion and exiguous facts, was the subject of eight 19th-century operas and of at least one novel.

RECORDING: Cantatas.

Stradivari, Antonio (?1644–December 18, 1737) The Italian violin maker Antonio Stradivari was associated throughout his life

Violins			
Name	Date	Name	Date
Hellier	1679	Alard*	1715
Sellière	before 1680	Cessot	1716
		Messiah	1716
Tuscan	1690	Sasserno	1717
Betts	1704	Maurin	1718
Ernst	1709	Lauterbach	1719
La Pucelle	1709	Blunt	1721
Viotti	1709	Rode	1722
Vieuxtemps	1710	Sarasate	1724
Parke	1711	Deurbroucq	1727
Boissier	1713	Kiesewetter	1731
Dolphin	1714	Habeneck	1736
Gillot	1715	Muntz	1736
Violas		Cellos	
Name	Date	Name	Date
Tuscan	1690	Archinto	1689
†		Tuscan	1690
Archinto	1696	Aylesford	1696
Macdonald	1701	Cristiani	1700
Paganini	1731	Servais	1701
		Gore-Booth	1710
		Duport	1711
		Adam	1713
		Batta	1714
		Piatti‡	1720
		Baudiot	1725
		Gallay	1725

*The finest violin. †Two unnamed violas of 1696 formerly belonging to Philip IV of Spain. ‡The finest cello.

Famous instruments of Antonio Stradivari

with the city of Cremona, where he brought the craft of violin making to its highest perfection. He was still a pupil of Nicolo Amati in 1666 when he began to insert his own label on violins. These at first followed the smaller Amati model, solidly constructed with a thick yellow varnish. In 1684 he began to produce larger models, using a deeper-colored varnish and improving the craftsmanship. His long models, dating from 1690, represent an innovation in the proportions of the instrument; from 1700, after returning for a few years to an earlier style, he again broadened and otherwise improved his model. He also made some fine cellos and violas. The Stradivari method of violin making created a standard for subsequent times, but the secret of his varnish— soft in texture and shading from orange to red—has never been discovered.

BIBLIOGRAPHY: F. J. Fétis, *Anthony Stradivari* (1864; reprint, 1976); William H. Hill *et al, Antonio Stradivari: His Life and Work 1644–1737*, 2nd ed. (1909); William D. Orcutt, *The Stradivari Memorial* (1938; reprint, 1977); Dirk J. Balfoort, *Antonius Stradivarius* (1945?); William Henley, *Antonio Stradivari, Master Luthier* (1961); Herbert K. Goodkind, *Violin Iconography of Antonio Stradivari* (1972).

Straube, Karl (January 6, 1873–April 27, 1950)   The German organist and conductor Karl Straube was one of the most important players in the early 20th century, and his conversion in 1926 to the classical revival in organ building and in performance practices was one of the major forces in the movement. Straube studied organ with Heinrich Reimann in Berlin and was appointed organist of the Thomaskirche in Leipzig in 1902, conductor of the Leipzig Bach Society in 1903, professor of organ at the Leipzig Conservatory in 1907, and cantor of St. Thomas' in 1918. He was a close friend of Max Reger, and it was for Straube that Reger composed most of his major organ works. He edited several collections of organ pieces by old masters as well as choral compositions by Bach and Handel. He conducted the second German Bach Festival in 1904 (and many later ones) and introduced to Germany many choral works both old and new.

Strauss, Franz (February 26, 1822–May 31, 1905)   Father of composer Richard Strauss, the German horn virtuoso and composer Franz Strauss played at the Munich Hofoper (until 1889) and taught at the music academy there (until 1896). During those years he also conducted an amateur orchestra. Though an anti-Wagnerian, he played in several Wagner premieres. His compositions include Horn Concerto in c minor and pieces for horn and piano.

RECORDING: Horn Concerto.

Strauss, Johann the Elder (March 14, 1804– September 25, 1849)   One of the principal composers of Viennese waltzes, Johann Strauss became a viola player in the dance orchestra of Michael Pamer, a composer of light music. Later he conducted the orchestra of Josef Lanner and in 1826 performed at the gardens of the Zwei Tauben the *Täuberlwalzer,* the first of many sets of Viennese waltzes named after the places where they were heard. He established his reputation as a composer of Viennese waltzes in 1830 by conducting at the Sperl, a popular dance hall in the Leopoldstadt. There he was idolized to the extent of becoming known in the musical world as "the Austrian Napoleon." In 1834 he was appointed bandmaster to the 1st Vienna militia regiment and the following year was made director of the imperial court balls. He embarked in 1833 on the first of his many tours throughout Europe, visiting London in 1838. Strauss's complete works, including—in addition to waltzes—galops, polkas, quadrilles, and other dances, were published by his son Johann in 1889. Remarkable for their rhythmic verve and charm of melodic design, they represent the style of Viennese dance music at its best.

BIBLIOGRAPHY: Heinrich E. Jacob, *Johann Strauss, Father and Son: A Century of Light Music* (1939; reprint, 1971); Hans Fantel, *The Waltz Kings; Johann Strauss, Father and Son, and Their Romantic Age* (1972).

RECORDINGS: *Radetzky* March; galops, marches, polkas, waltzes.

Strauss, Johann the Younger (October 25, 1825–June 3, 1899)   The second Johann Strauss developed the style of the Viennese waltz and became known for his operettas. He started his career as a bank clerk, as his father wished him to follow a profession other than music. He studied violin without his father's knowledge, however, and in 1844 conducted a dance band he formed at a Viennese restaurant. In 1849, when the elder Strauss died, Johann combined his orchestra with his father's and with it traveled through Europe, including Russia (1865–66) and England (1869), winning great popularity. In 1872 he visited the United States and conducted concerts in New York City and Boston. He had married Henrietta (Jetty) Treffz, a popular singer, in 1870 and the same year relinquished leadership of his orchestra to his brother Eduard to spend his time writing music.

Strauss's most famous single composition is "The Blue Danube" (1867), the main theme of which became one of the best-known tunes in 19th-century music. His many other melodious and successful waltzes include "Morgenblätter" (1864), "Künstlerleben" (1867), "Geschichten aus dem Wienerwald" (1868), "Wein, Weib und Gesang" (1869), "Wiener Blut" (1871), and "Kaiserwalzer" (1888). His waltzes number more than 150, their popularity earning him the name "the Waltz King." Like his father he also wrote dances of several other kinds. Among his stage works, *Die Fledermaus* (1874) became the classical example of Viennese operetta. Other successful operettas were *Der Karneval in Rom* (1873), *Cagliostro in Wien* (1875), *Das Spitzentuch der Königin* (1880), *Der lustige Krieg* (1881), *Eine Nacht in Venedig* (1883), *Der Zigeunerbaron* (1885), and *Waldmeister* (1895).

BIBLIOGRAPHY: Heinrich E. Jacob, *Johann Strauss, Father and Son: A Century of Light Music* (1939; reprint, 1971); Hans Fantel, *The Waltz Kings; Johann Strauss, Father and Son, and Their Romantic Age* (1972); Egon Gartenberg, *Johann Strauss: The End of an Era* (1974).

RECORDINGS: *Die Fledermaus; The Gypsy Baron (Der Zigeunerbaron)*; waltzes.

Strauss, Richard (Georg) (June 11, 1864–September 8, 1949) The last of the great German Romantic composers, Richard Strauss was also an eminent conductor who developed

Richard Strauss
*portrait by Max Liebermann, 1918
courtesy, Staatliche Museen zu Berlin*

into an anti-Romantic on the podium. He was born in Munich; his mother belonged to the Pschorr brewing family, and his father, Franz Strauss (1822–1905), played principal horn in the court orchestra and was the finest horn soloist in Germany. Strauss had his first piano lessons when he was four and wrote his first composition, a Christmas carol, when he was six. He studied violin from 1871 and theory from 1875, but his formal education was a normal academic one, carried to university level with the study of philosophy, history, and aesthetics. He wrote music abundantly throughout his school years; the earliest of his works to be acknowledged was the orchestral *Festmarsch* (performed 1876). By 1880 his works were being performed in public, and before he graduated from Munich University eight songs (Opus 10) were published, including three—"Zueignung," "Die Nacht," "Allerseelen"—that became perennial favorites.

After graduation Strauss spent some time

in Berlin, where he met Hans von Bülow. Having conducted Strauss's Wind Serenade (1881), Bülow asked him to compose a longer suite for the woodwinds of the Meiningen Court Orchestra. This was included on a tour by the orchestra, and Bülow invited Strauss to conduct the premiere of the work in Munich on November 18, 1884. As a result of this debut Bülow obtained for Strauss the post of assistant conductor at Meiningen. Here were laid the foundations of Strauss's secondary career as an outstanding conductor; and at Meiningen too he was converted as a composer to the forward-looking ideals of Liszt and Wagner. When his stay at Meiningen ended in 1886, Strauss was appointed third conductor at the Munich Opera; his subordinate status irked him, but during this time he composed the symphonic poems *Aus Italien, Macbeth* (first version), and *Don Juan* and began his first opera *Guntram*. He also met the singer Pauline de Ahna, whom he later married and with whom he often appeared in song recitals.

From 1889 to 1894 he held the directorship of the Weimar Court Orchestra; the great success of *Don Juan* in 1889 was followed by *Death and Transfiguration* (1890), a revised *Macbeth* (1890), and the Wagnerian *Guntram* (Weimar, 1894). Strauss then returned to a more senior post in Munich. The brilliant, uproarious *Till Eulenspiegel* (1895), *Also sprach Zarathustra* (1896) based on Nietzsche, and *Don Quixote* (1898), the finest and most elaborate of all these tone poems, were all produced during this period. Strauss was now frustrated in Munich, and the fiasco of *Guntram* there turned him against his native city. As a result he wrote the satirical comic opera *Feuersnot* on a libretto by Ernst von Wolzogen, mocking small-town prudery and hypocrisy; its premiere (1901) was the first of many of his works introduced at Dresden. Fortunately Strauss, at the climax of his disenchantment with Munich, was appointed first conductor of the Prussian Royal Orchestra, and in 1898 he moved to Berlin. There he spent fruitful years conducting concerts and opera, completing the autobiographical tone poems *Ein Heldenleben* (1899) and *Symphonia Domestica* (1904; a New York City premiere dur-

ing Strauss's tour of the United States), undertaking guest appearances in Germany and abroad, and establishing himself as Germany's foremost composer. The orchestral symphonic poems, completed with the *Alpine* Symphony (1915), proclaim an extraordinary mastery of the big post-Romantic symphony orchestra, an unrivaled descriptive power, and a remarkable ability to convey psychological detail. This last quality was particularly developed in his operas from *Salome* (Dresden, 1905; on the play by Oscar Wilde) onward.

Elektra (composed 1906–08) marked the beginning of a collaboration with Hugo von Hofmannsthal that lasted until the poet's death in 1929 and produced many of Strauss's finest works. *Der Rosenkavalier* (Dresden, 1911), the second of their joint works, was the most successful of all Strauss's operas. *Ariadne auf Naxos,* at first designed to include a German adaptation of Molière's play *Le Bourgeois gentilhomme,* was produced in this form by Max Reinhardt (Stuttgart, 1912) and later revised as a self-sufficient opera with an explanatory prologue (Vienna, 1916). *Die Frau ohne Schatten* (Vienna, 1919), a symbolic fantasy on the relationship between the individual and society, is sometimes held to be their greatest joint work. *Die ägyptische Helena* (Dresden, 1928) is a fanciful drama on the subject of Menelaus and Helen on their return journey from Troy. Finally *Arabella* (Dresden, 1933), a Romantic comedy, was set in the Vienna of 1860. The libretto was completed shortly before Hofmannsthal's sudden death.

In 1908 Strauss settled at Garmisch-Partenkirchen in the Bavarian Alps and devoted most of his time to composition. His other major works during the period of collaboration with Hofmannsthal are the ballet *Josephslegende* (scenario by Hofmannsthal and Harry Kessler) for Sergey Diaghilev's Ballets Russes (Paris, 1914), the autobiographical comic opera *Intermezzo* to his own libretto (Dresden, 1924), the entertaining ballet *Schlagobers* (Vienna, 1924), and a performing version of Mozart's *Idomeneo* (Vienna, 1930). In 1919 he accepted the post of musical director to the Vienna Opera, in collaboration with Franz Schalk, which he held until 1924, when difficulties caused by his frequent tours abroad forced his resignation. In recognition of his 60th birthday he was granted the freedom of the cities of Vienna and Munich and was given a villa in Vienna.

Hofmannsthal's death left Strauss in search of a librettist. Stefan Zweig provided him with an adaptation of Ben Jonson's *Epicœne*, produced at Dresden as *Die schweigsame Frau* (1935). But in Nazi Germany Zweig, a Jew, was unacceptable, and despite Strauss's protests of loyalty Zweig retired in favor of Joseph Gregor, who wrote (with much assistance from Zweig and later from Clemens Krauss and others) the texts of three operas, *Friedenstag* (Munich, 1938), *Daphne* (Dresden, 1938), and *Die Liebe der Danae* (Salzburg, 1952).

Strauss's position in Nazi Germany was ambivalent. He lacked political affiliations and interests to a point of naiveté. He disliked the philistine characteristics of Nazi officials and made himself unpopular by his objections to government interference in artistic matters, especially when these concerned his own music. Not wishing to leave home, he accepted Hitler's regime more or less passively. He served as president of the state music council (1933–35) and replaced Toscanini and Bruno Walter as conductor when they refused to work in Nazi Germany.

After completing *Die Liebe der Danae* in 1940, he intended to retire from composition. But he wrote one more opera, *Capriccio* (Munich, 1942), based on an elegant Romantic discussion on the relationship between words and music in opera, the protagonists being Parisian characters of the period of Gluck. He wrote the libretto with Krauss and others. During his last years he found creative energy to return to orchestral music and to compose a series of cool, neoclassical works: Second Horn Concerto (1943), two works for wind band (1944, 1946), the somber, meditative *Metamorphosen* for 23 solo strings (1946), Oboe Concerto (1946), and Duet Concertino (1948) for clarinet and bassoon with strings. His life's work was completed with the richly scored, poignantly retrospective *Vier letzte Lieder* (1950; *Four Last Songs*) for soprano and orchestra.

During World War II Strauss had lived at home at Garmisch, and after the war he lived in Switzerland. His health deteriorated, but he was able to attend a Strauss festival in London in 1947. He returned to Germany for his 85th birthday celebrations, and in July 1949 he conducted an orchestra for the last time.

Strauss was reared on the musical classics and on the early Romantic composers up to the period of Schumann; so much may be gathered from his youthful works, including the Violin Concerto (1883), the f minor Symphony (1884), the First Horn Concerto (1885), and the Violin Sonata (1887). He came under the influence of Berlioz, Liszt, and Wagner just when his technique and imagination were sharpened to make the most of their impact. From *Aus Italien* onward his style becomes recognizable as the big, bravura, flexible, post-Romantic panoply that dominated audiences and influenced composers as different as Bartók and Karol Szymanowski. In *Elektra* Strauss occasionally broke the bounds of tonality, but this was to achieve special effects and not to establish a nontonal technique.

In *Der Rosenkavalier*, reflecting the outlook and the temper of 18th-century Vienna, Strauss regained his authentic manner. Thereafter he spent 38 years refining and polishing his style, writing often for small orchestras, partly out of practical considerations (to ensure, for instance, the audibility of sung words in the theater), partly because large-scale Romantic textures were becoming less and less significant. In later years Strauss's style became more Classical in the Mozartian sense. In *Capriccio, Metamorphosen,* and the *Four Last Songs,* he may be said to have achieved a perfect fusion of the Romantic German and the neoclassical manner. After *Elektra* his evolution as a composer was pursued in isolation and was barely influenced by the course of music outside his own country.

BIBLIOGRAPHY: Ernest Newman, *Richard Strauss* (1908; reprint, 1970); Norman R. Del Mar, *Richard Strauss: A Critical Commentary on His Life and Works,* 3 vols. (1962–72); William S. Mann, *Richard Strauss: A Critical Study of the Operas* (1964); Romain Rolland, *Richard Strauss and Romain Rolland; Correspondence, Diary, and Essays*

(1968); Ernst Krause, *Richard Strauss: The Man and His Work* (1969); Alan Jefferson, *The Lieder of Richard Strauss* (1971) and *The Life of Richard Strauss* (1973); Michael Kennedy, *Richard Strauss* (1976).

RECORDINGS: Numerous recordings of most works.

Stravinsky, Igor (Fedorovich) (June 17, 1882–April 6, 1971)   One of the most original, fertile, and influential figures in 20th-century music, the Russian-born composer Igor Stravinsky was the son of the leading bass singer at the Russian Imperial Opera. Although he was not intended for a musical career, as a boy he was taught piano, harmony, and counterpoint, and he frequented opera and ballet performances at the Maryinsky Theater. As a university student he read law but showed no special aptitude for his studies, having apparently made up his mind to devote himself to composition. In the summer of 1902 he obtained an introduction to Rimsky-Korsakov through one of the latter's sons, who was also a student at the university. Rimsky-Korsakov was sufficiently interested in the young man's early composition (of which a piano Scherzo dated 1902 has survived in manuscript) to advise him not to enter the conservatory for conventional academic training but to pursue his studies privately. This advice was followed. A year later Rimsky-Korsakov agreed to tutor him privately, mainly in instrumentation and analysis. The arrangement continued until 1906. Stravinsky would discuss his compositions with his mentor as they were planned and written, and Rimsky-Korsakov arranged for several of these, including the Symphony in E-flat Major (1905–07), to be performed at private or public concerts in St. Petersburg. The last composition to be presented in this way was *Fireworks* (1908), a brief symphonic poem that Stravinsky intended as a wedding present for Rimsky-Korsakov's daughter. After Rimsky-Korsakov's death (1908) Stravinsky wrote a funeral dirge in memory of his master. It was performed in St. Petersburg the following season, but the score is lost.

When *Fireworks* and an earlier orchestral piece, Scherzo *Fantastique* (1907–08), were performed in St. Petersburg on February 6,

Igor Stravinsky
drawing by Pablo Picasso, 1920
Giraudon
© SPADEM, 1979

1909, they were heard by the impresario Sergey Diaghilev, who was then making preliminary arrangements for the summer season of his Ballets Russes to be held in Paris. He was so favorably impressed by Stravinsky's promise as a composer that he invited him to orchestrate various pieces of ballet music for the 1909 season, including two piano numbers by Chopin for *Les Sylphides.* For the 1910 season Diaghilev commissioned a completely new ballet score. This was *The Firebird* (Paris Opéra, 1910) in which Stravinsky showed how fully he had assimilated the Romantic idiom and orchestral palette of his master as well as echoes of Debussy. The success of *The Firebird* was so complete that Stravinsky became known overnight as one of the most gifted of the younger composers, and Diaghilev was eager to secure his continued cooperation. Stravinsky started to write a *Konzertstück* for piano and orchestra; but, yielding to Diaghilev's arguments, he agreed to adapt the music to fit a new ballet scenario, and this work, *Petrushka,* received its first performance during the Ballets Russes 1911 season in Paris.

Before this Stravinsky had had the idea of writing a kind of primitive spring symphony to be called *Great Sacrifice;* here too Diaghilev persuaded him that it should be cast in the form of a ballet. After two years of composition (1911–13), *The Rite of Spring* (as it was finally called) created a major scandal at its first performance at the Théâtre des Champs Élysées, Paris (May 29, 1913), because of its elemental, primitive rhythms and dissonances. Stravinsky then reverted to the task of finishing a short opera based on the Danish writer Hans Christian Andersen's tale "The Nightingale," which he had started in 1908–09 but which had been interrupted by the commission to write *The Firebird.* This opera was now requested by the Moscow Free Theater; but when that new venture suddenly collapsed, Diaghilev arranged for the work to be produced as part of the Ballets Russes seasons in Paris and London in the summer of 1914.

That summer also marked the conception of a new ballet cantata, *Les Noces (The Wedding),* based on Russian peasant themes and customs. The vocal score was completed by 1917, although the final form of the instrumentation was not decided until 1923.

World War I seriously disrupted the Ballets Russes's activities, and Stravinsky could no longer rely on it as a regular outlet for his new compositions. During these years of enforced exile in Switzerland he concentrated on chamber music and produced two strikingly original stage works, *Renard* (1915–16) and *The Soldier's Tale* (1918). His first exposure in 1912 to Wagner's *Parsifal* at Bayreuth and to Schoenberg's *Pierrot Lunaire* in Berlin was influential in his rejection of standard music drama. In *Renard* the action is performed by acrobats on stage, and the text is sung by a male quartet in the orchestra. *The Soldier's Tale,* in collaboration with the Swiss novelist Charles Ferdinand Ramuz, was an entertainment "to be read, played, and danced," intended to be played on tour by a small traveling theater; it shows Stravinsky's first contact with U.S. jazz. The project collapsed after a successful first performance in Lausanne because of a sudden epidemic of Spanish influenza.

As soon as the war was over, Stravinsky moved to France and from 1920 to 1939 lived in Biarritz, Nice, Voreppe, and Paris. His ties with Diaghilev and the Ballets Russes were renewed, though on a much looser basis, for he saw that in the case of an itinerant company without a firm base there could be no guarantee of permanence. The only new ballet commissioned by Diaghilev from Stravinsky was *Pulcinella* (1920), whose score was arranged from music by Pergolesi and adapted to a Neapolitan commedia dell'arte scenario. *Apollo Musagetes* (1928) was the last new ballet of his to be mounted by the Ballets Russes. The following year Diaghilev died, and his ballet company disbanded.

Financial necessity had forced him to develop subsidiary careers as concert pianist and conductor. He performed as soloist in some of his new works, such as the Concerto for piano and wind instruments (1923–24), Piano Sonata (1924), Serenade in A Major for piano (1925), Capriccio for piano and orchestra (1929), and Concerto for two solo pianos (1935). A considerable part of each year was devoted to touring in Europe and the Americas.

These Paris years were marked by an important change in Stravinsky's music. The compositions of his first maturity—from *The Rite of Spring* to the Symphonies of wind instruments (1920; dedicated to the memory of Debussy)—make use of a modal idiom based on Russian sources and are characterized by a highly sophisticated feeling for irregular meters and syncopation and by brilliant orchestral mastery. The work on *Pulcinella* helped him to review his attitude to the main European musical tradition, and the result was a series of works that adopted a neoclassical idiom and abandoned the Russian features. The two peaks of this period are the opera *Oedipus Rex* (1926–27) on a libretto by Jean Cocteau based on Sophocles and translated into Latin by Jean Daniélou, and the *Symphony of Psalms* (1930) on extracts from the Vulgate.

Stravinsky's composition of ballet scores did not end with Diaghilev's death. In the late 1920s the Russian dancer Ida Rubinstein assembled a company and commissioned two ballet scores—*The Fairy's Kiss* (1928) and *Persephone* (1934). The former was based on a selection of piano and vocal music of Tchaikovsky. The latter was a setting of a poem by the 20th-century French writer André Gide as a melodrama with song and speech and dance and mime. For the then recently founded American Ballet he wrote *The Card Party* (1937).

The years 1938 and 1939 were marked by a succession of family bereavements. In the autumn of 1938 his elder daughter died of tuberculosis. The deaths of his wife and mother followed in March and June 1939.

The outbreak of World War II in 1939 led to a completely new orientation of his life. An invitation from Harvard University to deliver the Charles Eliot Norton Lectures on the poetics of music during the 1939–40 academic year gave him the opportunity to leave Europe and settle in the United States. Early in 1940 he remarried. His second wife was the artist Vera de Bosset, with whom he remained in the United States for more than a quarter of a century.

The immediate postwar years were devoted to an attempt to regain the copyright on his early scores, which, having been originally published while he was a Russian citizen, were unprotected outside Russia because his native country had not adopted the Berne Convention. He issued revised versions of the scores, amounting to little more than corrections except in the cases of *Petrushka* (revised 1947) and the Symphonies of wind instruments (revised 1947), each of which was given a completely new instrumentation.

The appearance of two important symphonies coincided with the beginning and end of World War II: the Symphony in C (1938–40; a summation of neoclassical symphonic form) and the Symphony in Three Movements (1942–45; combining features of concerto and symphony). To the immediate postwar years belong the ballet *Orpheus* (1947), written for the Ballet Society of New York; the Mass (1944–48); *Ebony* Concerto (1945) for clarinet and orchestra; and his only full-length opera, *The Rake's Progess* (1948–51) on a libretto by W. H. Auden and Chester Kallman.

Although the success of these works was not in dispute, Stravinsky seemed to feel that he had outgrown the particular neoclassical conventions in which he had been working

for 30 years. He had recently met Robert Craft, a young conductor in New York City who later became invaluable to him as a musical assistant. Stravinsky welcomed the opportunity afforded by Craft's interest in serial music to familiarize himself with the compositions of Webern and Schoenberg, and he became so interested in serialism that he gradually adopted it for his own purposes. His earliest serial essays, such as *In Memoriam Dylan Thomas* (1954), *Canticum Sacrum* (1955), and the ballet *Agon* (1953–57), all retained some kind of tonal framework; not until *Threni* (1957–58; a cantata on the Old Testament) and *Movements* (1958–59) did he become the complete serialist. The most ambitious work of this period is *The Flood* (1961–62; dance–drama to a medieval text); but this was written for television and makes a somewhat diffuse and patchy effect in the theater or concert hall. More concentrated and more moving are the *Requiem Canticles* (1965–66), where each of the brief nine movements is carefully characterized and sharply differentiated. The music composed between 1963 and 1966, beginning with the sacred ballad *Abraham and Isaac,* is characterized by continued dodecaphony, formal symmetry, brevity, concentration, and detachment. After the *Requiem Canticles* ill health caused a slowing down of Stravinsky's compositional activity, but even as late as 1970 he was working on instrumental transcriptions of some of Bach's preludes and fugues.

Stravinsky's special contribution to music in the 20th century was wide and varied. He explored the asymmetrical patterns of compound meters and, by using devices of prolongation and elision, broke down the tradition of symmetrical phrasing. He was meticulous about degrees of articulation and emphasis. He restored to music the sense of a healthy, unwavering pulse that is essential in dance compositions. His music made a "clean" sound—there was no filling in merely for the sake of filling in—and after his symphonic poem *The Song of the Nightingale* (1917), his orchestral practice became mainly a question of using concertante groups of instruments with much breathing space around them. He never worked to an instrumental formula, but every work, regardless of idiom, had a different instrumental specification and a different sound.

Stravinsky also pioneered in the revival of musical forms from the past, which influenced such works as the Harpsichord Concerto (1927–28) of Poulenc and the First Symphony of Roger Sessions (1927). His exploration of jazz and pop idioms was continued by Copland and Milhaud; and although he wrote no electronic music, the principles of ostinato and of sectional stratification were used in such music by Henri Pousseur, Morton Subotnick, and Mario Davidovsky.

BIBLIOGRAPHY: Edwin Corle, ed., *Igor Stravinsky* (1949); Minna Lederman, ed., *Stravinsky in the Theatre* (1949; reprint, 1975); Heinrich Strobel, *Stravinsky: Classic Humanist* (1955; reprint, 1973); Selma J. Cohen, *Stravinsky and the Dance* (1962); Igor Stravinsky, *Igor Stravinsky: An Autobiography* (1966); Eric Walter White, *Stravinsky: The Composer and His Works* (1966); Roman Vlad, *Stravinsky,* 2nd ed. (1967); Robert Siohan, *Stravinsky* (1970); Robert Craft, *Stravinsky: Chronicle of a Friendship, 1948–1971* (1972), and with Vera Stravinsky, *Stravinsky in Pictures and Documents* (1979); Paul Horgan, *Encounters with Stravinsky* (1972); Lillian Libman, *And Music at the Close: Stravinsky's Last Years* (1972); Nancy Goldner, *The Stravinsky Festival* (1973); Francis Routh, *Stravinsky* (1975).

RECORDINGS: Numerous recordings of many works.

Striggio, Alessandro (*c.* 1535–*c.* 1595) An Italian composer and instrumentalist, Alessandro Striggio was one of those who carried the Italian madrigal to its final perfection. Apart from a stay in Florence (*c.* 1560–70) and a journey to England (1567), he spent his life in his native Mantua. Striggio's fame lies in his seven collections of madrigals (1560–97) and his quasi-dramatic pieces, one of which depicts women chattering on washday. He was a brilliant violist, lutenist, and organist, and some of his *intermedi* and one of his few motets are early examples of Renaissance instrumentation.

stringed instruments Instruments that owe their existence to the musical properties inher-

ent in an elastic filament made to vibrate regularly when energized while stretched between two fixed points. They are called chordophones in an acoustical classification. The tension, length, thickness, and mass of the filament, or string, all affect the rate of vibration and consequently the pitch it will produce. The shorter or tenser the string, the higher the note; a heavy string produces a lower note than a lighter one of the same length and tension.

resonators For musical purposes the stretched string is not enough; if the result is to be musically acceptable, it must be in contact with a resonator capable of radiating vibrations. All stringed instruments therefore possess a resonant body, usually of wood, whose essential feature is always the soundboard or belly, which lies directly under the strings and receives their vibrations through the bridge over which they are stretched. The form of the belly varies with the instrument, but it is in effect a thin diaphragm capable of responding to the vibrations transmitted by the bridge and of propagating them freely and instantaneously over all its area and made as large as practical considerations allow. Straight-grained pine is the favored material for the bellies of the majority of European instruments because of its excellent resonating properties and its ability to distribute musical vibrations rapidly and evenly both along and across the grain. A stretched skin membrane has been used, notably in the European banjo, the Indian *sarinda* and sarangi and the Arab *kamanga* and *rabab*. The wooden bellies of all developed instruments are reinforced in a variety of ways by crossbars glued to the underside; these bars serve as girder stiffeners and prevent the belly from sinking under pressure of the strings while preserving its general flexibility and response. Such bars also assist in the propagation of transverse vibrations across the pine belly. The bowed stringed instruments, whose string tensions and bridge load are relatively high, employ a distinctive vertical strut, the soundpost, which not only gives greater support to the belly but also is a vital agent in the tonal adjustment of the instrument, as in the VIOLIN family.

With only a few primitive exceptions, the belly forms the lid of a box that is in fact the body of the instrument. If the air space thus enclosed is to resonate freely, it must be in contact with the surrounding atmosphere, and it is usual to cut soundholes through the belly to ensure this. The form of the soundholes varies enormously, but to some extent their shape, position, and area are functional, serving to regulate both the stresses to which the belly is subject and the effect of the resonant air space. In the violin family especially they have a marked influence on the overall tone quality.

string supports There must of course be two limiting supports between which a string is made to vibrate. The bridge has already been described. In practice the second bridge, called the nut, is usually fixed rigidly to the fabric of the instrument beyond the area of the belly. Exceptions to this are the VIRGINAL and instruments of the DULCIMER family, where both bridges stand on the belly and share the function of transmitting vibrations thereto. The upper extremity of the string is carried over and beyond the nut and wound on a peg for tuning. At the other end it is hitched to a string holder or a fixed pin attached to the instrument. Both these terminals are arranged below the level of the bridge and nut to secure a firm down-beating upon them when the string is tightened to its working tension. The bridge, and through it the belly, are then subject to a vertical pressure from the string that ensures sensitivity of response to its vibrations. This pressure bridge is the same type as used on the violin and other bowed instruments, on all keyboard instruments, and on certain plucked instruments (MANDOLIN, banjo, CITTERN, etc.).

In keyboard instruments, with their many, carefully graded strings, the bridge is necessarily fixed to the belly, usually by glue. But bridges of the violin type are held in position only by the pull of the strings, thus allowing some latitude for adjusting their position to get the best result.

A contrast to the pressure bridge is the tension bridge. In this type the strings are attached directly to the bridge unit, which is glued to the belly. The pull of the strings is sustained by the bridge alone instead of by a separate anchorage beyond the bridge. Such bridges are found on instruments of the GUITAR and LUTE families, which are characterized by low-lying, rather slack strings and very thin, light bellies. In the HARP the strings pull upward away from the plane of the belly, the bridge being a central rail to which they are pinned.

producing scales The scale of notes that a stringed instrument will give is produced in one of two different ways: either by providing separate strings for every note or by "stopping" a given string somewhere along its working length, thus temporarily shortening the portion left free to vibrate and raising the pitch of the resulting note. Keyboard instruments, dulcimers, and zithers belong to the first class, as also do harps, although for some centuries European harps have employed a limited form of stopping device for the chromatic alteration of some or all of the notes of the scale.

In the majority of cases stopping is accomplished by the player's fingers; the string is pressed against a fingerboard that is either raised above the belly as in some forms of ZITHER or, more characteristically, carried on a handle or neck extending beyond the belly to give the hand easier access to the strings. These necked instruments, which always carry the nut and tuning pegs in a head at the upper end of the fingerboard, exhibit a greater variety of form and size than any other type.

In many instances the fingerboard is fretted; that is, set with a number of raised markers, usually spaced at semitone intervals along the string so that each marker acts as an auxiliary nut when the string is pressed against it. Fretting is not merely a guide to correct intonation in the early stages of learning to play the instrument; rather it is an integral part of the tone and technique of those instruments that use it. Among the common Western instruments only the members of the violin family are not fretted; in that family the pressure of the fleshy part of the fingertip on a plain fingerboard seems to provide exactly the right kind of stop for a bowed string.

In instruments of the harp kind the many strings must be graded in length and thickness from the lowest to the highest. None of the developed necked instruments derives the whole of its scale merely from stopping a single string all the way up. All employ several strings of the same length, laid close to each other on the fingerboard so that the same stopping technique may be used on all; but they are graded in thickness and tension in such a way that they may be tuned to widely spaced intervals. The number of strings and their tuning varies with particular instruments, but all have a common purpose: to produce the scale, or large parts of it, by a combination of finger-stopping and crossing from one string to the next above or below, the fingered notes bridging the gap, or interval, between a string and its nieghbors. It is also possible to produce chordal effects on such an instrument by stopping and sounding selected notes on different strings simultaneously. Normally the lowest-tuned string lies to the left of the neck, viewed from the front, and the highest to the right, those between being arranged in order of pitch. It is customary to refer to the highest-pitched string as number one and to number the others in descending order.

inducing vibration   Musical strings may be set in vibration by applying energy in various ways, and it is of course the precise method employed that determines the character of the instrument and the kind of sound it produces. Energy may be applied either by plucking or striking or by subjecting the string to continuous friction or wind pressure.

The first method of inducing vibrations is at once the most primitive and universal. If the string is pulled aside and suddenly released, it will continue vibrating until the initial energy stored by its elasticity is dissipated and it comes to rest. Such a note, consisting of a sharp ictus followed by a more or less rapid decay of loudness, does not really sing, although the ear readily accepts the convention that it does; both the performer's skill and the maker's craft are directed to sustain the illusion.

Moreover a wide variety of tone color can be obtained even from a single string by altering the plucking point, the nature of the material that does the plucking, or the string itself. The player's own fingertips pluck the strings directly in the lute, guitar, and harp and their

derivatives, where the strings are mainly of highly elastic catgut and the playing of chords is an everyday occurrence involving the plucking of several strings at once with different fingers. For many wire-strung instruments such as the mandolin, a plectrum is used. This is a small lozenge-shaped spatula of hard, flexible material such as tortoise shell held in the player's hand and struck across the strings. (For a description of the keyboard plucking mechanism of the harpsichord *see* HARPSICHORD.)

Striking with some form of hammer presupposes that the string shall offer rather more resistance to the blow than strings intended for plucking. Metal strings at comparatively high tension behave best under these conditions and afford the least latitude in the point of striking. What has been said about regarding the ictus and decay of the note applies equally here. This system of tone production is not adaptable to instruments with fingerboards, although for completeness it should be said that it has been so applied in one solitary instance, the short-lived English keyed guitar of Christian Clauss (1783). The basic type is rather the dulcimer, a struck version of the older plucked PSALTERY. The dulcimer has separate strings (usually duplicated) for every note; the strings are stretched over a flat body or soundboard and are played with hand beaters. This ancient instrument survives in central and eastern Europe; the Hungarian CIMBALOM and Swiss *hackbrett* are best known. The classic example, however, is of course the PIANO with its elaborate keyboard hammer mechanism.

The application of continuous friction to the string in order to obtain sustained sound is the principle of the violin bow. The BOW, which also is used with such other instruments as the Oriental rebab and the European REBEC, consists of a flat ribbon of resined horsehair that is kept under tension by a light, specially curved stick. The bow is drawn across the string at right angles to the string and rather near the bridge. The bow will naturally be designed to suit the weight and size of the instrument, and it is of course used in both directions of travel: downstroke when the hand is moving away from the strings and upstroke when moving toward them. Because of the nature of this technique, the player has absolute control over the pressure of the bow on the string, its velocity in traveling across it, and of the exact point at which it is applied to the string. All of these factors are employed to vary not only the attack or articulation by which the note is started but also the volume and actual quality of the tone produced; these varieties can, if necessary, be introduced within the duration of a single stroke. In its higher flights the bowed technique is probably capable of a wider range of musical effect than any other form of tone production.

A more mechanical application of the friction principle is that of the medieval *organistrum* and *symphony,* later to become known as the HURDY-GURDY, in which a resined wheel turned by a handle passes over the strings. Nearly all such instruments, which have never died out at the folk level, have a system of touchpieces for stopping the strings—as opposed to the direct contact with the player's fingers—and are equipped with drones that form a single and continuous accompaniment to the tune in bagpipe fashion. The hurdy-gurdy principle has been applied to keyboard instruments many times during the past four centuries but has met no general acceptance.

The final method of eliciting tone from strings is by wind pressure. This is the principle of the AEOLIAN HARP and of one or two abortive keyboard instruments where a wind jet directed at the string sets it vibrating. Attractive though the resulting sound is, it is too uncontrollable in attack and duration to have any practical application. *See also:* BALALAIKA; BARYTON; CELLO; CEMBALO; CLAVICHORD; CRWTH; DOUBLE BASS; FIDDLE; KOTO; LIRA; LYRE; MARINE TRUMPET; SITAR; SPINET; VIHUELA; VIOL; VIOLA; VIOLA D'AMORE; VIOLA DA GAMBA.

Structures: *see* BOULEZ; MODERN PERIOD (rediscovery of serialism); NOTATION (20th-century notation); SERIALISM.

style galant: *see* GALLANT STYLE.

subdominant   The fourth tone of the diatonic scale, so named because it is a fifth below the tonic as the dominant is the fifth above the tonic.

subject: *see* THEME.

submediant   The sixth tone of the diatonic scale, halfway between the subdominant and the tonic. It is also called superdominant.

Subotnick, Morton (b. April 14, 1933)   Associated with Mills College in California first as a student (with Milhaud and Leon Kirchner) and then as a faculty member, the U.S. composer Morton Subotnick co-founded the Mills Performing Group and the San Francisco Tape Music Center. He played clarinet in the Denver and San Francisco symphonies and was involved in many performances of new music. In 1967 he became music director of the Repertory Theater at Lincoln Center in New York City. He taught at New York University and the University of Maryland and inaugurated the electronic music studio at the University of Pittsburgh. Since 1969 he has taught at the California Institute of the Arts in Valencia, where he has been director of electronic music. Concerned with mixed-media and created environments, much of his music requires audience participation to determine the structure of the piece (*Play!4,* 1967; *A Ritual Game Room,* 1970, includes game players but no audience). He has created electronic environments in New York offices and stores, where elevator buttons and a panel of buttons pushed by shoppers enable instant creation of electronic music through activation of tape loops. Other works of interest include *Misfortunes of the Immortals: A Concert* (1968) for wind quintet, lights, two films, tape, and conventional quintet repertoire; and *Lamination 1* (1969) for orchestra and tape. *Silver Apples for the Moon* (1967) was the first electronic work composed for records.

RECORDINGS: *4 Butterflies;* Prelude No. 4 for piano and tape; *Sidewinder; Silver Apples for the Moon; Until Spring; The Wild Bull.*

suite   A group of self-contained instrumental movements of varying character, usually in the same key. The term is from the French *suite de pièces.* In the 17th and early 18th centuries, the period of its greatest importance, the suite was comprised principally of dance movements. In the 19th and 20th centuries, however, the term was used in a more general sense to cover almost all sets of instrumental pieces, mainly in forms smaller than those of the sonata, including selections for concert performance of music from ballets or from incidental music to plays.

The principle of related dance movements may be said to have its origins in the paired dances of the 14th century; *e.g.,* the estampie and saltarello. The practice of grouping dances of related key but contrasting tempo and meter continued, but by the 16th century the order of the dances had begun to be dictated more by considerations of music than of dance. By the middle of the 17th century, French composers had established the principal features of the suite. This essentially French form of the genre was to remain the model for composers of all countries for 100 years.

The classical suite of the time of Bach and Handel consists essentially of four principal dance movements, with one to three lighter movements inserted before the final principal one:

allemande   The first movement of the classical suite, it is a staid dance in $\frac{4}{4}$ time with a characteristically rich, flowing rhythm; it frequently begins with either one or three short notes before the first full measure.

courante   The second movement is of two kinds, the French and the Italian. The French courante begins with either one or three short notes before the first full measure. It is a dignified dance in an ambiguous rhythm that alternates between $\frac{3}{2}$ and $\frac{6}{4}$.

saraband   The slow third movement is in triple time, traditionally beginning on the full measure. The Italian type (the corrente) is a brilliant, continuously running piece in a quick $\frac{3}{4}$ or $\frac{3}{8}$.

gigue   The concluding movement is an animated dance in a triplet rhythm ($\frac{12}{8}$, $\frac{6}{8}$, or $\frac{3}{8}$), lightly fugal in style.

Bach's *French* Suites may be said to mark the end of the classical suite in the French style. His *English* Suites and Partitas (*German* suites) are on a larger scale and show a tendency toward a symphonic conception. This is apparent in the scope of the long and characteristic first movement, the prelude. Some of Bach's large-scale suites end with a finale after the gigue.

Sullivan, Arthur (Seymour) (May 13, 1842–November 22, 1900)   The English composer Arthur Sullivan with W. S. Gilbert established the distinctive national form of the operetta. Born in London, Sullivan was the son of an Irish bandmaster at the Royal Military College; his mother was of Italian descent. He joined the choir of the Chapel Royal and later held the Mendelssohn scholarship at the Royal Academy of Music, where he studied with William Sterndale Bennett and John Goss. His studies were continued at the Leipzig Conservatory. In 1862 his music to *The Tempest* achieved great success at the Crystal Palace, followed by his *Kenilworth* cantata (1864), the ballet *L'Île Enchantée* (Covent Garden, 1864), a symphony, a cello concerto, the *In Memoriam* and the *Di Ballo* Overtures, and numerous songs, including "Orpheus with His Lute."

Sullivan's first comic opera was his setting of Francis Cowley Burnand's *Cox and Box* (1867). An operetta, *The Contrabandista,* also on a libretto by Burnand, was produced in the same year. *Thespis* (1871), the first work in which Sullivan collaborated with W. S. Gilbert, met with little success when produced at the Gaiety Theatre. It was Richard D'Oyly Carte, then manager of the Royalty Theatre, who brought the two men together again in 1875; the result was *Trial by Jury,* originally performed as an afterpiece to an Offenbach operetta. It won instant popularity and ran for more than a year. Carte thereupon formed the Comedy Opera Company to present full-length operettas by Gilbert and Sullivan. The first of these, *The Sorcerer* (1877), was succeeded by *H.M.S. Pinafore* (1878), whose eventual success was phenomenal. It was pirated in the United States, where Carte, the author, and composer produced an official version in 1879. The U.S. rights for their next operetta, *The Pirates of Penzance,* were secured by a production of this work in New York City shortly before the London production in 1880. During the run of *Patience*

(1881) Carte transferred the production to his newly-built Savoy Theatre, where the later operettas were presented. These were *Iolanthe* (1882), *Princess Ida* (1884), *The Mikado* (1885), *Ruddigore* (1887), *The Yeomen of the Guard* (1888), and *The Gondoliers* (1889). In all these Gilbert's satire and verbal ingenuity were matched by Sullivan's unfailing melodiousness, resourceful musicianship, and sense of parody.

From time to time, however, Sullivan protested against the artificial nature of Gilbert's plots; this led to a disagreement between them that climaxed when Sullivan supported Carte in a minor business dispute. Sullivan's next opera, *Haddon Hall* (1892), had a libretto by Sydney Grundy, and subsequent collaboration with Gilbert, in *Utopia Limited* (1893) and *The Grand Duke* (1896), did not reach their former standard. Three other operettas were completed by Sullivan: *The Chieftain* (1894), largely an adaptation of *The Contrabandista;* the *Beauty Stone* (1898) with a libretto by Arthur Pinero and Comyns Carr; and *The Rose of Persia* (1899) with Basil Hood, who also wrote the libretto for *The Emerald Isle,* left unfinished by Sullivan and completed by Edward German.

Sullivan's more serious and ambitious compositions, such as *The Prodigal Son* (1869), *The Light of the World* (1873), *The Martyr of Antioch* (1880), *The Golden Legend* (1886), and the romantic opera *Ivanhoe,* written for the opening of the Royal English Opera House (now the Palace Theatre), built by Carte in 1891, were not maintained in the repertoire, though they were acclaimed in their day. He also wrote much church music, including the well-known hymn tune for "Onward, Christian Soldiers"; and his song "The Lost Chord" attained great popularity. In 1876 he accepted the principalship of the National Training School for Music (later the Royal College of Music), which he held for five years; he was active as a conductor, particularly at the Leeds festivals (1880–98). He was knighted in 1883.

BIBLIOGRAPHY: Arthur Lawrence, *Sir Arthur Sullivan* (1899; reprint, 1972); Herbert Sullivan and Newman Flower, *Sir Arthur Sullivan, His Life, Letters and Diaries,* 2nd ed. (1950); Leslie Baily, *The Gilbert and Sullivan Book,* rev. ed. (1956); Gervase Hughes, *The Music of Arthur Sullivan* (1960; reprint, 1973); Reginald Allen, *Sir Arthur Sullivan: Composer and Personage* (1975); Benjamin W. Findon, *Sir Arthur Sullivan: His Life and Music* (1976).

RECORDINGS: *Cox and Box; The Gondoliers; The Grand Duke; H.M.S. Pinafore; In Memoriam* Overture; *Iolanthe;* Suite from *The Merchant of Venice; The Mikado; Patience; The Pirates of Penzance; Princess Ida; Ruddigore; The Sorcerer;* Incidental music for *The Tempest; Trial by Jury; Utopia Limited; The Yeoman of the Guard.*

Suor Angelica: *see* OPERA (the 19th century); PUCCINI.

supertonic   The second tone of the diatonic scale, so named because it is the note next above the tonic.

Suppé, Franz von, real name, Francesco Ezechiele Ermenegildo Suppé Demelli (April 18, 1819–May 21, 1895)   An Austrian composer of light operas in the style of Offenbach, Franz von Suppé influenced the development of Austrian and German light music. He came from a family of Belgian origin that had lived in Italy for two generations. In his youth he went to Vienna, where he studied composition with Simon Sechter and Ignaz Xaver Seyfried and was advised by Donizetti. Later Suppé conducted at the Theater an der Wien, the Josephstadt, and other theaters in Vienna. In 1841 he wrote the incidental music for a play at the Josephstadt and thereafter wrote numerous comic operas, operettas, and incidental music, including the overture for the play *Dichter und Bauer* (*Poet and Peasant,* Vienna, 1846). His most successful comic operas were produced in Vienna and include *Leichte Kavallerie* (1866), *Fatinitza* (1876), and *Boccaccio* (1879). He also wrote choral works, a symphony, and string quartets.

RECORDINGS: Overtures.

Surprise Symphony (Haydn No. 94): *see* PROGRAM MUSIC (program symphony).

Susanna: *see* HANDEL (life) and (works).

Susannah: *see* FLOYD; OPERA (the 20th century).

suspension   A note that is prolonged while the harmony around it changes and makes that note dissonant, or discordant; the suspended note then resolves into the new harmony, becoming consonant, or concordant, with it. A suspension is a means of creating musical tension that is then resolved; the change in harmony making it dissonant normally occurs on a strong beat, increasing the tension. In the example the top note is suspended, then resolved.

Sutherland, Joan (b. November 7, 1926)   A pioneer in reviving the early 19th-century bel canto repertoire and the art of improvisatory embellishment, the Australian soprano Joan Sutherland made her debut in Sydney in 1947 in Purcell's *Dido and Aeneas.* She sang in Australia until 1952, when she joined the company at Covent Garden in roles by Mozart, Verdi, and Wagner. In 1955 she created the role of Jennifer in Michael Tippett's *The Midsummer Marriage.* Her Metropolitan Opera debut was in 1961 as Donizetti's Lucia, a role for which she became celebrated. In her later career she developed a coloratura that was most impressive in the music of Bellini, Donizetti, and

Joan Sutherland
(courtesy, Colbert Artists Management, Inc. photograph, Christian Steiner

Handel. This quality was developed by her coach and later husband, the Australian conductor and pianist Richard Bonynge (b. 1930), who specializes in 18th- and 19th-century bel canto opera. In 1975 Bonynge was appointed artistic director of the Vancouver (Canada) Opera, and he revived several operas for Sutherland, the most recent being Massenet's *Le Roi de Lahore.* In most of Sutherland's many recordings (including operas of Handel, Donizetti, Bellini, Verdi, and Gounod) Bonynge appears as conductor or accompanist.

Swan Lake: *see* BALLET (Russia before 1900); TCHAIKOVSKY.

Swan of Tuonela: *see* PROGRAM MUSIC (problem of form); SIBELIUS; SYMPHONIC POEM.

Sweelinck, Jan Pieterszoon (April 1562–October 16, 1621)   One of the principal figures in the development of organ music before Bach, the Dutch organist and composer Jan Pieterszoon Sweelinck succeeded his father as organist of the Oude Kerk, Amsterdam, about 1580 and remained in this post until his death. He seems never to have left the Low Countries and to have traveled only to Rotterdam and Antwerp. Although he composed much sacred and secular vocal music—including the Chansons *à* 5, *Cantiones sacrae,* and settings of the Psalms—in the polyphonic traditions of France and The Netherlands, Sweelinck was chiefly known as an organist and keyboard composer. His keyboard music includes chorale variations that are remarkable for their double and triple counterpoint, toccatas and fantasias showing the influence of the Venetian organ school, and sets of variations on secular tunes. The set of variations on *Mein junges Leben hat ein End'* is perhaps his best-known work.

It is possible that Sweelinck met the English composers John Bull and Peter Philips during their visits to the Low Countries; Bull's Fantasia on a Theme of Sweelinck was the tribute of one keyboard virtuoso to another. Sweelinck's keyboard playing was widely known, and his organ pupils included the German composers Samuel Scheidt and Heinrich Scheidemann. Scheidemann's pupil Jan Adams Reinken was to hand on this tradition of organ playing to Dietrich Buxtehude.

BIBLIOGRAPHY: Robert L. Tusler, *The Organ Music of Jan Pieterszoon Sweelinck* (1958).

RECORDINGS: Organ and clavier pieces.

symphonic poem or **tone poem** A composition for orchestra, usually in one movement, that expresses a program; *i.e.*, a story or idea (*see* PROGRAM MUSIC). Typically one or more themes are assigned a nonmusical significance and are transformed in various ways to express the underlying program. The program thus helps to shape the musical form; hence the symphonic poem differs from its precursor, the program symphony, which, although supplemented by a program, usually gains musical coherence from the manipulation of an abstract musical form.

Both the symphonic poem and the term itself were invented by Liszt, who in works such as *Les Préludes* (1848; after Alphonse de Lamartine's *Méditations poétiques*) used thematic transformation to parallel poetic emotions. His musical form is free although somewhat following sonata form used in the first movements of symphonies.

The specific handling of a symphonic poem differs among composers and according to the subject matter. When Richard Strauss portrays erotic adventures in *Don Juan* (1889) or chivalric adventures in *Don Quixote* (1897) or a day in his family life in the one-movement *Symphonia Domestica* (1903), he freely modifies episodic forms, such as the rondo or variation; or he writes in the form of a loose rhapsody held together only by key and the recurrence of themes symbolizing the persons and events of the story. In contrast to the parallel of poem and musical evocation found in Liszt's *Les Préludes,* Strauss created music for living incidents such as a baby's bath, the disturbance of a flock of sheep, and the hanging of a rogue.

A different handling of the form occurs in Tchaikovsky's *Hamlet* in which the story is told in a kind of sonata form. The musical recurrences demanded by such a form are made possible by dissolving the chronological element in Shakespeare's play.

The symphonic poem proved particularly amenable to musical Romanticism, and its range of subjects was greatly expanded. Literature was well to the fore in works such as Tchaikovsky's *Francesca da Rimini* (1876), Liszt's *Mazeppa* (1851), and Franck's choral-orchestral *Psyché* (1888), as was legend in Rimsky-Korsakov's *Sheherazade* (1888). Nationalism also found expression in legend, as in Sibelius' "Swan of Tuonela" from *Four Legends* (1893), and in the evocation of landscapes—*e.g.,* Sibelius' *Finlandia* (1900) and Smetana's *Mé vlasti* (*My Country;* 1874–79). Philosophical themes underlie Strauss's *Also sprach Zarathustra* (1896, after Nietzsche) and *Death and Transfiguration* (1889). Paintings formed the inspiration for Rachmaninoff's *Isle of the Dead* (1907; after Arnold Böcklin) and Liszt's *Hunnenschlacht* (*The Battle of the Huns;* 1857, after Wilhelm von Kaulbach).

With the passing of Romanticism the symphonic poem reflected such differing musical styles as those of Debussy in his *Prélude à l'après-midi d'un faune* (1894), Paul Dukas in his scherzo *The Sorcerer's Apprentice* (1897), Stravinsky in *Feu d'artifice* (*Fireworks;* 1908), and Honegger in *Pacific 231* (1923). But the increasing 20th-century emphasis on abstract music, coupled with the almost over-refinement of the symphonic poem, led to a decline in its prominence as a musical form.

Symphonic Variations: *see* CONCERTO (Classical concerto); VARIATIONS; *see also* VARIATIONS SYMPHONIQUES.

Symphonie fantastique: *see* BERLIOZ; COUNTERPOINT (Romantic period); CYCLIC FORM; LEITMOTIV; LISZT; PROGRAM MUSIC (program symphony); SYMPHONY (the 20th century).

Symphonie pour un homme seul: *see* ELECTRONIC MUSIC (tape music); MUSIQUE CONCRÈTE; SCHAEFFER.

symphony A term that since the middle of the 18th century has denoted a type of composition for orchestra; the classical symphony is in sonata form. The word is derived from the Greek *symphonia,* "concord." In Luke 15:25 *symphonia* is distinguished from *choroi,* and the two are translated as "music and dancing." The word has also been applied to two musical instruments, the sistrum in ancient times and the hurdy-gurdy in the Middle Ages. In the 17th century the term was used for certain vocal compositions accompanied by instruments; *e.g.,* the *Symphoniae sacrae* of Heinrich Schütz. The term is also found in Schütz's *Kleine geistliche Concerte,* but applied to the instrumental ritornello of a song.

origins Since the middle of the 18th century the interpretation of the term symphony has become freer, but any work bearing this name requires close scrutiny. Preoccupation with vocal counterpoint until the 17th century ensured that musical designs remained essentially static. Tonality was a kind of anchor, and the music consisted of simply related harmonies. As instrumental techniques developed, greater freedom of line, harmony, and to some extent tonality became possible, though for a long time composers tended to regard instruments as if they were more agile and brilliant voices. This applies to Bach in the first half of the 18th century; Handel shows more sense of adventure in this respect, but his work is still basically polyphonic. In a prelude of Bach or a movement of a concerto grosso by Handel the treatment of key (tonality) is totally undramatic; the music swings from harmony to related harmony without more than a hint that it is ever likely to move out of an orbit centered on its original key. The harmonic scheme in fact is as calm and relaxed as that of a simple hymn tune whose successive chords are now spun out to accommodate elaborations of the texture, mainly of a contrapuntal nature. At the end of such a piece, no impression of movement is created. Violent changes of mood or texture are rare and real changes in tonality almost impossible. When Bach in the b minor Mass passes through mysteriously foreign harmony at the words "et expecto resurrectionem mortuorum," his purpose is expressive rather than structural; it is a way of drawing attention to the nature of the text at this point and of making a convincing transition between the f-sharp minor of the "Confiteor" and the brilliant D major of the exultant movement, separately designed, which follows it. This is the process of modulation, and real modulation in music before the early 18th century is usual only in such transitions between otherwise independent designs. It is scarcely ever found within the course of a homogeneous move-

ment, where it would be disrupting to the calmly proportioned architecture.

The concept of modulation, however, is at the root of the SONATA principle. While Bach was perfecting his polyphonic art, other composers (including his sons) were creating a kind of music that was entirely based on instrumental as opposed to vocal technique. Counterpoint is almost entirely dispensed with in these early examples, which aim at achieving maximum mobility in terms of simple chordal harmonies and rhythms. Their straightforward themes, often founded on triads, would have been utterly unsuitable as contrapuntal subjects. The use of simple harmony made it imperative to find a new means of contrast, and it was found that an increase of tension resulted from the music moving from one tonal region to another. The rhythmic impulse was at the same time sustained, or even intensified, so that there was no sense of discontinuity but a sweeping momentum hitherto unknown. When the new tonal region was reached, some kind of momentary relaxation was provided, leading perhaps to a new theme, possibly more ingratiating than the first. The so-called first and second subjects referred to in textbook analyses of sonata forms thus arose from a new attitude to tonality. To regard them merely as conveniently contrasting themes is to divest them of their underlying dynamic purpose. The second subject is not necessarily a tune at all; it begins at the moment when modulatory tension relaxes into a new channel—a new theme may or may not emerge. The essence of sonata music lies in its newfound ability in the 18th century to thrust a key over the tonal horizon so that a new vista is created. This was the nature of the new dynamism in music. Composers of this new kind of music, if it was written for orchestra, called it symphony, and it originated in the theatrical or operatic OVERTURE, often termed sinfonia. The fresh sense of movement permeated all kinds of music, but the word symphony thereafter was almost exclusively applied to orchestral works.

Haydn, Mozart, and Beethoven At first there was little to distinguish the early symphony from the divertimento or cassation or even from the quartet. The orchestra itself became more stabilized with the strings as its basis, at first with the keyboard continuo to keep a middle going, but gradually doing away with this device as wind instruments were more extensively and skillfully used. Oboes and horns in pairs were used in many symphonies of the 1750s and 1760s. Flutes and bassoons were added and trumpets and drums for special ceremonial occasions. The orchestra thus developed into a standardized unit as homogeneous as the keyboard. As soon as the orchestral tutti became a norm, composers were free to explore its depths. Haydn, even in his earliest symphonies, thus had a ready-made instrument allowing him to compose unselfconsciously; and he owed this fact to Georg Matthias Monn, Giovanni Battista Sammartini, and Georg Christoph Wagenseil even more than to Johann Stamitz, the founder of the Mannheim orchestra and the school of composers it inspired. Haydn was not the father of the symphony—he was its progeny. Nevertheless it was due to him that the title symphony came to denote an orchestral work of the highest concentration, organization, and comprehensiveness.

The early operatic overture was often in three movements—an allegro, a slow movement, and a lively finale (that was often in fast triple or sextuple time) at which the curtain rose. It is often supposed that the succession of movements in a Classical symphony originated here, but contrasting movements became more necessary than ever when the explosive tensions of tonality were released. Everything that happens in such music is born of tonal tension, even the division into separate movements that had previously been no more than decorative. To the three movements a minuet was added. This served two purposes: to increase the sense of comprehensiveness by including a dance element and to complement the brevity of the finale. So the four-movement symphony became a normal format that persisted almost unchallenged for 100 years and is still not discarded. Haydn and Mozart are the first complete masters of the symphony who were concerned with the felicitous interpenetration of certain prime elements—pure formal balance, concentration, variety of expression within the same work, and what may

be called athleticism. With them the symphony became a complete kind of orchestral music, and the term symphony has ever since been used to arouse the listener's highest musical faculties.

The greatest intensification of this challenge was made by Beethoven. He did not surpass Haydn or Mozart in perfection of design or even in sheer athleticism; in concentrated depth and variety of expression, however, mastered within the physically limited yet imaginatively vast confines of single works, no composer before or since has approached him. It was this attribute that made Brahms—one of his most masterly successors—fearful of composing symphonies at all. Beethoven, moreover, widened the scope of the orchestra itself by increasing the number of instruments, adding an extra horn in the *Eroica* and trombones in the Fifth, Sixth, and Ninth, sometimes also using piccolo, contrabassoon, and (in the Ninth) extra percussion. He also tended to place more weight on the finale of a symphony than did his precursors, especially in the Fifth, Seventh, Eighth, and Ninth; in the latter, the last and greatest of the series, he took the unprecedented step of adding a chorus and vocal soloists to the finale.

later developments After Beethoven the Romantic movement of the 19th century was inclined to inflate the idea of symphony, expressive intensity arising from a high degree of subjectivity often being allowed to oust the more rigorous formal considerations. Beethoven's music cannot be held responsible for this, since no other composer, except possibly Bach, was so aware of structure, no matter how fierce or dramatic the expression. This gave his work an objectivity that is the reverse of Romantic. Some loosening of the discipline may be noticed in Schubert, though one should be careful not to confuse this element with positive new discoveries made by Schubert involving a more deliberate pace of thought. Nineteenth-century composers who showed resistance to the tendency to inflation and loose discipline—clearly followers of Beethoven and Schubert—are Schumann (whose great economy is often overlooked), Brahms, and Dvořák; they maintained Classical traditions and Classical energy while achieving complete individuality. Two early-19th-century symphonists of essentially 18th-century makeup were Mendelssohn and the Swedish composer Franz Berwald, both of whom show less concern with the heroic than with elegance and balance.

The composers just mentioned may be said to represent one trend, perhaps the most faithful to the essential nature of the symphony as it had so far developed, not because of adherence to any rule book but because they strove to achieve a fine balance between the complexities of form and the more importunate demands of expression on a scale comparable with that of the Classical symphony. But the Romantic preoccupation with the emotional moment was inevitably slowing down the pace of music; it was becoming increasingly difficult to write a true allegro. Schubert's retardation of pace was a beginning, and Wagner's discovery of how to make musical structures large enough to encompass a whole act of a stage drama (and large enough means slow enough) had an overwhelming effect upon other composers whose aims were unconnected with the theater. The most notable of these was Bruckner; while creating music with an individual grandeur—in spirit perhaps closer to Giovanni Gabrieli than to Wagner —he constructed vast symphonies whose motion is for the most part of huge slowness, impossible without Wagner's influence. Wagner's sense of movement also had a deep effect on Mahler, who also wrote symphonies on an enormous scale for enormous orchestras; here, however, subjective Romanticism sometimes intervenes at moments when structural demands might have been better met.

the 20th century Mahler brings the history of the symphony to the beginning of the 20th century. Parallel with German Romanticism the Russian nationalists—particularly Borodin, Balakirev, and Tchaikovsky—were also producing an individual conception of the symphony. Tchaikovsky, however, proved to be less a nationalist than a subjective Romantic, whose violent emotional impulses frequently broke down discipline in a formal method derived largely from Schumann. Tchaikovsky's symphonies, like Mahler's, are basically programmatic in character (and to

that extent only sporadically symphonic), for the expressive-illustrative elements sometimes ignore structural necessities.

A movement such as the first of Tchaikovsky's Fourth Symphony, however, achieves a just balance such as Berlioz (who greatly influenced him) more often found. The structural concentration of true symphony has not attracted French composers, and Berlioz (nearest in time to the Classical symphonists—he began his *Symphonie fantastique* while Schubert was writing his great C Major Symphony) is still the finest French symphonic composer; his best work is purer and more controlled than his reputation for Romantic illustrative extravagance would lead the casual listener to believe.

While German Romanticism was reaching the limits of inflation at the end of the 19th century, two Scandinavian masters were renewing the Classical symphony by making fresh discoveries—Sibelius with the concept of movement and Carl Nielsen with that of tonality. Their reactions against the indiscipline of Romanticism are essentially complementary. The slowing down of musical movement mastered by Wagner had two serious effects on his successors: many composers lost the power of Classical movement, the ability to write the kind of allegro whose impetus is exemplified in Haydn and Beethoven; and tonality was no longer used coherently, for the slowness meant that the conception of key as an anchor could no longer easily be sustained in such a time scale. Sibelius, for the first time, found a way to combine the vast slowness of the Wagnerian world with the athleticism of Beethoven; his series of seven symphonies is a progressive mastering of this problem, culminating in the one-movement Seventh in which transitions from one extreme to the other are made with astonishing skill and imaginative power. Sonata form no longer applies, but the disciplines are all derived from the phenomena that sonata music made possible, and the range of expression is comparable with that of the fully developed four-movement Classical symphony.

This is true also of Nielsen's six symphonies, but here the discovery is tonal. The originality of this Danish composer lay in his clear understanding of the problem that was baffling the Romantics, whose dilemma was the result of a single great assumption—that tonality must be an anchor. Schoenberg, who plunged into atonality and devised new serial disciplines to compensate for the loss, did so because he also shared this assumption as shown by his remark that "there is still a lot of good music to be written in C major." The operative phrase here is "in C major," with its suggestion of fixity. Nielsen discovered a structural way of making a symphony travel from one tonality—or sometimes a complex of warring tonalities—to another. The phenomenon is sometimes called progressive tonality, though emergent tonality would be a more accurate description. From it Nielsen was able to produce a new dynamism and music of great strength as well as variety of character.

The reaction to the general slowing down of musical processes that came with the twilight of Romanticism has in the 20th century been more often negative than positive, and compositional methods have tended to produce totally static rather than dynamic results. Therefore valid symphonic music is rarer than in the past. Composers of the mid-20th century who have used the title have often done so loosely. It is no longer indicative of any particular method or format. But as the term symphony has been the highest challenge in the field of orchestral music for many of the greatest composers of the last 200 years, it will no doubt continue to be applied to works in which the composer has essayed the widest range of expression and movement within the scope of a single work. The essence of symphony is disciplined inclusiveness; the comprehensiveness of symphony will not exclude any natural resources of music—harmony, melody, rhythm, tonality, etc. Any avoidance of one such element, however concentrated, must necessarily bring about a sense of exclusiveness that will inevitably limit the music to less than the widest powers of the imagination. A symphony must be genuinely and consistently active if it is to rise to its proper level; it is by this standard, by which the greatest symphonists have survived, that it must stand or fall. Its actual form is no longer definable or predictable.

BIBLIOGRAPHY: Ernest M. Lee, *The Story of Symphony* (1916; reprint, 1968); H. C. Robbins Landon, *Haydn Symphonies* (1966); Robert Simpson, *Symphony,* 2 vols. (1967); Paul Henry Lang, *Symphony, 1800–1900* (1969); Louise Cuyler, *The Symphony* (1973); Roland Nadeau, *The Symphony: Structure and Style* (1974).

Symphony of a Thousand: *see* MAHLER (middle period).

Symphony of Psalms: *see* COUNTERPOINT (modern period); FUGUE (after Bach and Handel); STRAVINSKY.

syncopation A device used to disturb the listener's expectation of regular metric groups by accenting normally weak beats in a measure, by resting on a normally accented beat, or by tying over a note to obscure the strong beat. The effect of syncopation can also be obtained by frequent changes of meter. Syncopation appears in music as early as the 14th century, and it is common in jazz and in 20th-century music.

synthesizer A complex and flexible computerized instrument used specifically for the composition of ELECTRONIC MUSIC. The synthesizer, like the digital computer, accepts coded data from the composer, processes it, and translates the data into sound. The information fed to the synthesizer is coded on a punched paper tape, which is then subjected to the functions of thousands of sound-generating devices, such as oscillators, circuits, and vacuum filters, that are capable of producing effects far beyond the range and versatility of conventional musical instruments.

The intricate apparatus of the synthesizer generates simple wave forms and then subjects them to alteration in intensity, duration, frequency, and timbre, as programmed by the composer. The aural product is usually recorded on magnetic tape to be played back, edited, or modified as desired.

The first electronic sound synthesizer was developed by the U.S. acoustical engineers Harry Olson and Herbert Belar in 1955 at the Radio Corporation of America (RCA) laboratories at Princeton, New Jersey. Designed for research into the properties of sound, it attracted composers seeking to extend the

Moog synthesizer   *Allen H. Kelson*

range of available sound or to achieve total control of their music (because no performer is necessary).

The earliest synthesizer was an instrument of awesome dimensions. During the 1960s synthesizers of more compact design were produced: first the Moog and soon after others, including the Buchla and Syn-Ket, the last approximately the size of an upright piano. Many newer synthesizers have keyboards or some modification of traditional performing mechanisms. The Syn-Ket has two three-octave keyboards. Compositions for it include the *Microtonal* Fantasy recorded in 1968 by composer-pianist John Eaton.

The Moog III, developed by the U.S. physicist Robert Moog, has two five-octave keyboards that control voltage changes (and thus pitch, timbre, attack, decay, and other aspects of sound), allowing the composer an almost infinite variety of tonal control. A notable use of the Moog is in Alwin Nikolais' television ballet *The Relay.*

The Buchla synthesizer, developed by the U.S. scientist Donald Buchla, is activated by a "keyboard" that is a touch-sensitive metal plate without movable keys, comparable to a violin fingerboard. It has been used in such works as Morton Subotnick's *Silver Apples of the Moon* (1967) and *The Wild Bull* (1968).

The above small synthesizers use subtractive synthesis—removing unwanted components from a signal containing a fundamental tone and all related overtones (sawtooth-wave signals). The harmonic tone generator developed by James Beauchamp at the University of Illinois, in contrast, uses additive synthesis—building tones from signals for pure tones; *i.e.,* without overtones (sine-wave signals)—and offers certain advantages in the nuances of tone colors produced.

Szell, George (June 7, 1897–July 30, 1970) The conductor who made the Cleveland Orchestra into one of the major ensembles of the world, the Hungarian George Szell was educated in Vienna but had appeared as a child prodigy on the piano. He made his debut as a conductor at age 16 and, at the recommendation of Richard Strauss, was appointed to the Municipal Theater in Strasbourg (1917) and subsequently to the opera houses at Darmstadt, Düsseldorf, Berlin, and Prague. In the United States at the outbreak of World War II, Szell taught in New York City, con-

George Szell   *courtesy, Cleveland Orchestra*

ducted at the Metropolitan Opera (1942–46), and was in Cleveland from 1946. A specialist in the Viennese school, he was known as a master technician who had an almost chamber music-like approach and achieved elegance and clarity.

Szeryng, Henryk (b. November 22, 1918)   A five-time winner of the Grand Prix du Disque, the Polish-born Mexican violinist Henryk Szeryng studied with Carl Flesch in Berlin and Jacques Thibaud in Paris and made his debut in 1933. In 1946 he became a Mexican citizen and two years later joined the faculty of the conservatory in Mexico City. He has performed many works by modern Mexican composers as well as the standard repertoire. In 1971 he rediscovered and recorded the Third Concerto in E Major of Paganini. His style is a unique combination of the rugged and the refined.

Szigeti, Joseph (September 5, 1892–February 19, 1973)   A student of Jenö Hubay in Budapest, the Hungarian violinist Joseph Szigeti

made his debut at age 13. He taught at the Geneva Conservatory (1917–24) and then made his reputation in England. In 1925 he made his U.S. debut, becoming a U.S. citizen in 1951. He played and promoted new music, especially that of Bartók with whom he toured, and Prokofiev. Busoni, Hamilton Harty, and Alfredo Casella dedicated concertos to him. He was noted for his understanding of the interpretive problems inherent in different musical styles. He was named a commander of the French Legion of Honor and the Belgian Order of Leopold. His autobiography, *With Strings Attached,* was published in 1947.

Szymanowski, Karol (Maciej) (October 6 [September 24, old style], 1882–March 29, 1937)   The Polish nationalist composer Karol Szymanowski was born in the Ukraine, the son of a cultured landowner. In 1901 he entered the Warsaw Conservatory and studied with Sigismund Noskowski. His early piano works include Nine Preludes (composed 1900, published 1905). He lived in Berlin (1906–08), Vienna (1912–14), and eventually in Warsaw (from 1919). Successive influences on his work were German post-Romanticism, especially Mahler and Richard Strauss (First Symphony, later withdrawn), Aleksandr Scriabin (Second Symphony, 1909; Second Piano Sonata, 1910), Oriental mysticism (*Love Songs of Hafiz,* 1914; the opera *Hagith,* 1912–13, produced in Warsaw, 1922), and eventually (after 1921) Polish folklore (the ballet *Harnasie,* 1926, produced in Prague, 1935). One of his closest friends was the violinist Paul Kochanski, and for him he wrote two violin concertos (1917; 1933) and a triptych, *Mythes* (1915), which includes the well-known "Fountain of Arethusa." Piano cycles include *Métopes* (1915), *Masques* (1916), 12 Études (1917), and 20 Mazurkas (1924–26). Szymanowski became director of the Warsaw Conservatory in 1926, but failing health forced his resignation three years later. However, he was piano soloist in one of his last works, Symphonie Concertante, at its first performance in 1932.

RECORDINGS: *Masques;* Mazurkas; *Métopes; Mythes; Notturno e Tarantella* for violin and piano; Piano Études; Piano Sonata No. 2.

T

tabarro, Il: *see* OPERA (the 19th century); PUC-CINI.

tablature A notation that shows playing positions. Hence a tablature for a plucked stringed instrument guides the player's fingers to the string to be plucked and to the fret at which the string is stopped. Similarly a tablature for a wind instrument guides a player's fingers to cover certain holes, and a tablature for percussion directs a player as to which drum to strike, which hand and stick to use, and what type of stroke to execute. Each single instruction in a tablature corresponds to one action by the performer. The order of action is automatically prescribed, and more precise rhythmic indication can be given quite easily as the length of time between successive actions—rests are unnecessary. Thus a tablature for a plucked instrument (for example, a lute, guitar, or zither) requires signs for each string, each fret, and possibly also each right-hand plucking finger, direction of stroke, and ancillary techniques such as harmonics, vibrato, and left-hand plucking. To indicate these the tablature may use letters, numbers, and graphic signs.

French lute tablature
from Willi Apel, The Notation of Polyphonic Music 900–1600, *5th ed. (1961); reproduced by permission of the Mediaeval Academy of America, Cambridge, Massachusetts*

Lute tablatures had three main varieties, French, Italian (used also in Spain), and German. The French variety (*c.* 1500–*c.* 1800) eventually proved to be the most practical and contained an important repertoire of lute music. It used a staff of five (after the late 16th century, six) horizontal lines, each of which represented a course of strings. In five-line tablature, the sixth course was printed below the staff. Stylized letters, from *b* to *i* or *k,* indicated which fret the player was to stop to produce the proper note; the letter *a* indicated plucking an open string. Rhythms were indicated by placing note stems above the staff. The lowest line of tablature represented the lowest pitched string on the lute. Signs such as dots and slurs indicated right-hand fingerings, ornaments, and special effects. For the theorbo, a 17th-century variety of lute, special signs indicated the instrument's off-the-fingerboard bass strings.

Italian or Spanish tablature (flourished 1500–1650) resembled the French system, using six lines to represent the six courses of strings. Except in the lute book of Luis Milán, the lowest line represented the highest pitched string. Numbers, rather than letters, indicated which fret was to be stopped. Rhythms were shown by note stems above the diagram.

Unlike these systems German lute tablature (flourished 1511–1620) did not provide a diagram of the strings. Instead it used 54 or more symbols for as many possible junctions of fret and string. The symbols were aligned vertically if more than one fret should be stopped. Note stems above the symbols showed the rhythm.

Keyboard tablatures flourished in Germany *c.* 1450–*c.* 1750 and in Spain *c.* 1550–*c.* 1680. The German system was a hybrid—the top voice part was shown in ordinary musical notation, the lower parts by the letters of the musical scale (A, B, etc.). Special signs indicated when a note should be sharped (D-sharp usually indicating E-flat, etc., but signs for flat notes appeared occasionally) and ornamented. Small note stems, typically joined together to resemble fences, showed rhythm. After *c.* 1570 the top line also was printed in tablature; this was called the new German tablature as opposed to the old German tablature, the hybrid system. Even in the mid-18th century Bach used tablature in his *Orgelbüchlein* when it saved space.

In Spanish keyboard tablature (called *cifras,* "numbers") each line of the staff represented a different voice part of the music. In the most commonly used system numbers from one to seven indicated the notes of the musical scale. Sharps and flats were printed above the number when necessary, and signs showed the octave in which the note occurred. Note stems above the diagram showed rhythm. Other systems numbered all notes from one to 42, and all white notes from one to 23, sharps and flats showing the black notes.

Other tablatures have been used for bowed instruments, such as the viol, and for plucked instruments, such as the cittern, guitar, and zither. Guitar music once employed lute tablature or a simpler notation showing chords; later it used ordinary musical notation. In the 20th century guitar and ukulele popular music used a tablature in which a grid represented string and fret intersections, and dots showed proper finger placement.

The tablature for the Japanese koto zither is simpler in that its 13 strings are not stopped. The pitch of each string is indicated at the beginning of a tablature, and thereafter the strings are represented by numbers combined with graphic signs for special technical effects. The tablature for the Chinese ch'in, a zither whose strings are stopped, uses a combination of numbers (for strings and for stopping points) and ideograms (for other technical details). These are grouped together in composite symbols. One composite symbol may contain an ideogram for the left-hand finger, a number for the stopping point, another number for the string itself, an ideogram for the right-hand finger, and possibly an ideogram indicating loudness, legato, glissando, etc.

Tabuteau, Marcel (July 2, 1887–January 4, 1966)   The French-born oboist Marcel Tabuteau studied with Georges Gillet at the Paris Conservatoire, winning a first prize in 1904. At the invitation of Walter Damrosch he moved to the United States to play in the New York Symphony. He was a member of the Metropolitan Opera orchestra (1908–15) under Toscanini before joining the Philadelphia Orchestra as principal oboist (until 1954), appearing as soloist some 50 times. Tabuteau also taught at the Curtis Institute for nearly 25 years, training a generation of oboists who were to hold principal positions in most of the major U.S. orchestras. He was made a chevalier of the Legion of Honor by the French government in 1937.

Taffanel, (Claude-) Paul (September 16, 1844–November 22, 1908)   The French flutist and conductor Paul Taffanel studied at the Paris Conservatoire. After more than 20 years as solo flutist with the Paris Opéra orchestra and the orchestra of the Société des Concerts du Conservatoire, he was appointed conductor of both organizations. In 1893 he succeeded Joseph-Henri Altès as professor of flute at the Conservatoire. With his pupil Philippe Gaubert he wrote a *Méthode complète de flûte, en 8 parties* (published 1923), which is still studied by flutists.

Takemitsu, Toru (b. October 8, 1930)   Concerned with timbres, textures, and the relationship between sound and silence, the Japanese composer Toru Takemitsu is primarily self-taught except for two years of study with Yasuji Kiyose. In 1951 he collaborated with artists and composers in organizing an experimental workshop in Tokyo (Jikken Kobo). He became associated with the Institute for 20th Century Music in 1958. In 1966, with Seiji Ozawa and others, he founded Orchestral Space, a biennial contemporary music festival. He conceived the idea for a space theater, a concert hall equipped with laser beams and 800 loudspeakers, which was built for the 1970 World Exposition in Osaka, Takemitsu becoming artistic director. In the 1950s he wrote primarily for tape *(Vocalism A-1)*, showing the influence of the *musique concrète* of Pierre Schaeffer, an aesthetic of sound effects captured on tape. Later works include film scores (*Harakiri,* 1962; *Woman in the Dunes* and *Kwaidan,* both 1964); works for indigenous Japanese instruments (*November Steps* No. 1, 1967, for *shakuhachi, biwa,* and orchestra); *Asterism* (1968) for piano and orchestra, showing how the linguistic connotations of a title can influence the structure of the music; *Quatrain* (1975) for large orchestra and percussion (also a chamber version); and *A Flock Descends into the Pentagonal Garden* (1977; commissioned for the San Francisco Symphony), a dissonant quasi Wagner–Debussy work in five pentatonic modes.

RECORDINGS: *November Steps* No. 1; *Textures.*

Tailleferre, Germaine: *see* SIX, LES.

Tales of Hoffmann: *see* HOFFMANN; OFFENBACH.

Tallis, Thomas (*c.* 1505–November 23, 1585) The most important English composer of sacred music of the generation preceding Byrd, Thomas Tallis held posts at Dover Priory (1532) and St. Mary-at-Hill, London (1537), and his name appears in a list of persons who in 1540 received wages and rewards for services at the dissolution of Waltham Abbey in Essex. From Waltham he appears to have gone briefly to Canterbury and then to the Chapel Royal. In a petition to Queen Elizabeth I made jointly with Byrd in 1577, he refers to having "served your Majestie and your Royall ancestors these fortie years," but his appointment as a gentleman of the Chapel Royal can hardly have been before 1542. The same document refers to only one previous instance of preferment and that from the hand of "your Majestie's late deare syster quene Marie." This was a 21-year lease of the manor of Minster in the Isle of Thanet (Kent) granted in 1557 to Tallis and Richard Bowyer, Master of the Children.

On January 22, 1575, Queen Elizabeth granted Tallis and Byrd the monopoly for printing music and music paper in England. This gesture of royal favor to the two musicians, who were joint organists of the Chapel Royal, did not at first operate to their advantage. The above-mentioned petition of 1577 seeks relief in the form of an additional lease for the loss of 200 marks incurred during the first two years. The lease was granted. The first publication under their license was a collection of 34 motets, 17 by Tallis and 17 by Byrd, entitled *Cantiones sacrae* (1575). These Latin pieces, together with five anthems to English texts printed by John Day in his *Certaine Notes* . . . (1560–65), comprise all of his music that Tallis saw in print during his lifetime. His last years were spent in Greenwich. According to his epitaph Tallis was married "ful thre and thirty Yeres" (*i.e.,* in 1552) but had no children.

Tallis' long life spans a period of important changes of style between the generations of John Taverner and Byrd, changes necessitated by the introduction of an English liturgy and the development of an impressive school of keyboard composition. His Latin works include a mass each of four, five, and seven voices; two settings of the Magnificat; two settings of the *Lamentations of Jeremiah;* responsory settings and office hymns; a seven-part *Miserere nostri,* an extraordinary feat of canonic writing involving retrograde movement with several degrees of augmentation; and the famous 40-part *Spem in alium,* a unique monument in British music for eight five-part choirs in a remarkable example of imitative writing seemingly not at all limited by the scale of the work. Tallis was one of the first composers to provide settings of the English liturgy, including settings of the *preces* and responses, the litany, and a complete service "in the Dorian mode." There are also three sets of psalms, several psalm tunes for Archbishop Matthew Parker's Psalter (printed in 1567 or 1568 but withheld from sale), and a number of anthems. Tallis' secular vocal music is negligible and his music for instrumental ensemble virtually so, but his keyboard music is substantial and significant. This includes both sacred and secular pieces, extended cantus firmus compositions, and arrangements of vocal works. Of his 23 extant keyboard pieces 18 occur in the mid-16th-century manuscript known as the Mulliner Book.

BIBLIOGRAPHY: Paul Doe, *Tallis,* 2nd ed. (1976).

RECORDINGS: *Lamentations of Jeremiah;* collections of church music.

Tamagno, Francesco (December 28, 1850–August 31, 1905) The creator of Verdi's Otello, the Italian dramatic tenor Francesco Tamagno studied in Turin and Palermo, where he made his operatic debut in Verdi's *Un ballo in maschera* in 1873. Success as Verdi's Ernani at La Scala in 1880 led to a South American tour, after which he sang in Lisbon and Madrid. After the premiere of *Otello* (1887) at La Scala, he sang the role for his debuts in London (1889, Lyceum Theatre) and the United States (1891, Metropolitan Opera).

While engaged at the Metropolitan (1894–95) he sang Saint-Saëns' Samson, Verdi's Manrico *(Il trovatore),* and Rossini's William Tell, but he failed to achieve the success of his Otello.

Tamberlik, Enrico (March 16, 1820–March 13, 1889)   After a debut in Naples in 1840/41 in Bellini's *I Capuletti ed i Montecchi,* the Italian dramatic tenor Enrico Tamberlik sang in Spain, Portugal, and London, where he was with the Royal Italian Opera (1850–64). He sang in Berlioz' *Benvenuto Cellini* (in English) at Covent Garden in 1853 and also appeared in Russia and the Americas. Among his roles were Manrico (Verdi's *Il trovatore*), Don Ottavio (Mozart's *Don Giovanni*), and Florestan (Beethoven's *Fidelio*).

tambourine   A small frame drum (one whose shell is too narrow to resonate the sound) having one or two skins nailed or glued to a shallow circular or polygonal frame; it is normally played with the bare hands and often has attached jingles, pellet bells, or snares. European tambourines typically have one skin and jingling disks set into the sides of the frame. Tambourine refers specifically to the European frame drum, but the term is often extended to include all related frame drums, such as those of the Arabic countries, and sometimes those probably unrelated—the shaman's drums of Central Asia, North America, and the Arctic.

In ancient Sumer large frame drums were used in temple rituals. Small tambourines were played in Mesopotamia, Egypt, and Israel (the Hebrew *tof*) and in Greece and Rome (the *tympanon* or *tympanum*) and were used in the cults of the mother goddesses Astarte, Isis, and Cybele. Today they are prominent in Near

and Middle Eastern folk music and are also used to accompany recitations of the Koran. As in ancient times they are largely played by women.

Crusaders brought the instrument to Europe in the 13th century. Called timbrel or tabret, it continued to be played mainly by women and as accompaniment to song and dance. The modern tambourine reentered Europe as part of the Turkish Janissary music in vogue in the 18th century. It appeared occasionally in 18th-century opera scores (*e.g.,* by Gluck and André Modeste Grétry), coming into general orchestral use in the 19th century with composers such as Berlioz and Rimsky-Korsakov.

Tamburini, Antonio (March 28, 1800–November 9, 1876)   Originally a student of the French horn, the Italian dramatic baritone Antonio Tamburini sang opera first at Bologna (1818) and then throughout Italy. In 1832 he appeared in London and continued there, alternating with appearances in Paris, until 1841. He then sang in Italy and Russia, where he stayed until 1852; although his voice was nearly gone, he returned to concertize in Holland and Paris.

Taming of the Shrew, The: *see* GÖTZ.

tam-tam: *see* GONG.

Taneyev, Sergey (Ivanovich) (November 25 [November 13, old style], 1856–June 19 [June 6, old style], 1915)   The Russian composer and theorist Sergey Taneyev was the principal practitioner of counterpoint and an influential figure in 19th-century Russian music. He studied composition with Tchaikovsky and piano with Nicholas Rubinstein in Moscow. In 1878 he interrupted his career as a pianist in order to succeed Tchaikovsky at the Moscow Conservatory, where he served as director (1885–89), subsequently holding the post of professor of counterpoint and fugue. His operatic trilogy *Oresteia* was produced in St. Petersburg in 1895. He resigned his professorship in 1905 in protest to measures against the threatened revolution and resumed his career as pianist and composer. In 1909 he completed his two-volume work on counterpoint in the strict style on which he had worked for 20 years. His masterpiece, the cantata *At the Reading*

tambourine
courtesy, Ludwig Industries

of the Psalm (1914; text by Aleksey Khomyakov), appeared shortly before his death in Moscow.

Taneyev's compositions are relatively few but finely wrought. They are more romantically beautiful than might have been expected of a composer who disliked all 19th-century music except that of Tchaikovsky (some of whose works he completed). Taneyev regarded counterpoint as a branch of mathematics, reserving his highest admiration for Renaissance composers Jean d'Ockeghem, Josquin des Prés, Orlando di Lasso, and Palestrina. Taneyev was a great teacher, a popular eccentric, and a lifelong bachelor who for many years attracted without reciprocating the passionate love of the Countess Tolstoy.

BIBLIOGRAPHY: Gerald E. H. Abraham and Michel D. Calvocoressi, *Masters of Russian Music* (1936; reprint, 1971).

tango   A ballroom dance of Argentine origin that evolved about 1880 in lower class districts of Buenos Aires from the *milonga,* a fast, sensual, and disreputable Argentine dance; it shows possible influences also from the Cuban habanera. In the early 1900s the tango became socially acceptable and by 1915 was a craze in fashionable European circles. The first tango music, in $\frac{4}{4}$ time, by known composers was published around 1910. In ballet it is featured prominently in *Façade* (1931; choreography by Frederick Ashton, music by William Walton).

Tannhäuser: *see* CYMBALS; ROMANTIC PERIOD (Wagnerian development); SPOHR; WAGNER (life) and (development).

Tapiola: *see* SIBELIUS.

tarantella   A south Italian folk dance in rapid $\frac{6}{8}$ time, danced in couples and characterized by light quick hops and tapping foot movements. Its origin is connected with tarantism, a disease or form of hysteria that appeared in Italy in the 15th to the 17th century and was obscurely associated with the bite of the tarantula spider: victims seemingly were cured by frenzied dancing. The name tarantella may be more directly derived from Taranto, a town located in the region where tarantism was especially prevalent. The tarantella appears in many ballets, the most famous in the third act of *Swan Lake.* Chopin, Liszt, and Weber wrote tarantellas for piano.

Tárrega, Francisco (November 21, 1852–December 15, 1909)   Called the creator of the modern school of guitar playing, the Spanish guitarist and composer Francisco Tárrega taught at the Madrid Conservatory. He revolutionized technique with his way of plucking and placement of the hands, especially concerning the use of the right hand. He expanded the guitar repertoire by original compositions and by transcriptions of music by Bach, Beethoven, Mozart, Haydn, and Albéniz. He inspired de Falla, Heitor Villa-Lobos, and Joaquín Turina to compose for the guitar.

Tartini, Giuseppe (April 8, 1692–February 26, 1770)   The Italian violinist, composer, and theorist Giuseppe Tartini helped establish the modern style of violin bowing and formulated principles of ornamentation and harmony. He studied divinity and law at Padua and at the same time established a reputation in fencing. Before the age of 20 he secretly married a protégée of the Archbishop of Padua, resulting eventually in his arrest. Disguised as a monk, he fled from Padua and took refuge in a monastery at Assisi. There his violin playing attracted attention and ultimately influenced the archbishop to allow Tartini to return to his wife at Padua. In 1716 he went to Venice, later to Ancona, and eventually returned to Padua, where he was appointed principal violinist at the Church of S. Antonio in 1721. He directed the orchestra (1723–25) of the chancellor of Bohemia in Prague, returning once again to Padua, where he founded (1728) a school of violin playing and composition. He made only one concert tour of Italy, in 1740.

Tartini's playing was said to be remarkable for its combination of technical and poetic qualities, and his bowing became a model for later schools of violinists. Pietro Nardini and Gaetano Pugnani were among his pupils. His works include more than 100 violin concertos; numerous sonatas, including the "Trillo del Diavolo" (Devil's Trill), written after 1735; quartets; trios; symphonies; and religious works, including a five-part *Miserere* and a four-part *Salve Regina.*

He contributed to the science of acoustics by his discovery of the difference tone (*see* COMBINATION TONE), also called the Tartini tone. Tartini held that double stopping on the violin was not in tune unless the player could hear this difference tone. He also devised a theory of harmony based on affinities with algebra and geometry, set forth in his *Trattato di musica* (1754) and expanded into *Dissertazione dei principi dell'armonia musicale* (1767). His theoretical works also include *Trattato delle appogiature,* a treatise on ornamentation.

RECORDINGS: *L'Arte dell' arco;* Sonata *a quattro* in D; Violin Concertos in A, B-flat, G, and d minor; Violin Sonatas (12) with continuo.

Tauber, Richard, originally Ernst Seiffert (May 16, 1892–January 8, 1948) Known for opera (especially Mozart) and even more for operetta (especially Franz Lehár), the versatile Austrian tenor Richard Tauber studied at the Hoch Conservatory in Frankfurt and made his debut as Tamino (Mozart's *Die Zauberflöte*) at Chemnitz. In 1913 he joined the Dresden Hofoper and subsequently sang in Berlin, Vienna, London, and North America. He composed operettas and film music and appeared in a number of British films (*Blossom Time,* 1932; *Pagliacci,* 1937; *The Lisbon Story,* 1945). He recorded recitals of operatic and operetta arias.

Tausig, Carl (November 4, 1841–July 17, 1871) Probably Liszt's greatest piano pupil and—except for his early death—his logical heir, the Polish-born Carl Tausig was described by Anton Rubinstein as "the infallible." As a technician he was considered Liszt's equal, but in contrast to his master he was extremely quiet at the piano—almost motionless. He hated to teach, and before his final illness he lived as a recluse. Tausig played the entire repertoire of his day and was a composer and arranger. His transcription of Bach's organ Toccata and Fugue in d minor was for many years a standard recital piece.

BIBLIOGRAPHY: Wilhelm von Lenz, *The Great Piano Virtuosos of Our Time* (1971).

Taverner, John (*c.* 1495–October 25, 1545) A composer whose work represents the culmination of early 16th-century English polyphony, John Taverner first appears (1525) in a visitation record as a clerk-fellow of the collegiate church of Tattershall in Lincolnshire. In October 1526 a letter from Bishop Longland of Lincoln to Cardinal Wolsey represents Taverner as being reluctant to give up his living at Tattershall "and the prospect of a good marriage which he would lose by removal"; nevertheless a month later he took up his duties as *informator* or master of the choir in the chapel of Wolsey's Cardinal College (later Christ Church), Oxford. In 1528 Taverner was accused of heresy and imprisoned on the charge that he had concealed heretical books. John Foxe records that "the Cardinal for his musick excused him, saying, that he was but a musitian, and so he escaped." In 1530 he left Oxford, at which time his musical career may be considered to have terminated. He appears to have been an agent of Thomas Cromwell in the suppression of monastic establishments. He lived out his life in Boston, Lincolnshire, where in 1537 he was elected a member, and in 1541 a steward, of the Guild of Corpus Christi.

Taverner's Latin church music, which includes eight masses, demonstrates a variety and skill, a range and a power that comes as the climax of pre-Reformation English music. In the field of instrumental music an adaptation of the words "in nomine Domine" in the Benedictus of his Mass *Gloria tibi Trinitas* became the prototype of a large number of instrumental compositions known as IN NOMINE in the succeeding century and a half.

RECORDINGS: Kyrie *Le Roy;* Mass *The Western Wynde.*

Tchaikovsky, Peter Ilich (May 7 [April 25, old style], 1840–November 6 [October 25, old style], 1893) A major Russian Romantic composer, Peter Ilich Tchaikovsky demonstrated a wealth of melodic inspiration and imagination and a flair for orchestration. Highly subjective, he showed lapses of taste that were partly redeemed by his enormous technical efficiency. Though his work may be said to illustrate the cosmopolitan tendencies of Russian music, its underlying sentiment and character are as distinctively Russian as that

Peter Ilich Tchaikovsky, 1888
Novosti Press Agency

of the Russian nationalists. His success in bridging the gulf between the musician and the general public partly accounts for the exalted position he enjoys.

Tchaikovsky was born at Votkinsk in Vyatka Province. After an early emotional attachment both to his mother and to a French governess, the tender feminine atmosphere of his childhood was rudely broken when he was sent to school in St. Petersburg at the age of eight. In 1852 he entered the School of Jurisprudence, which he left in 1859 to join the Ministry of Justice as a senior clerk. But he had become an amateur musician and made some attempts at composition. In 1861 he began to study harmony, and the following year he entered the St. Petersburg Conservatory. At the end of his course he was appointed professor of harmony at the newly opened Moscow Conservatory. The composition of his First Symphony in 1866 produced acute nervous disorders that, together with hallucinations, were to affect him throughout his life.

In 1868 he visited St. Petersburg, where he met Aleksandr Dargomyzhsky, Balakirev, Rimsky-Korsakov, and others. Surprisingly

he was received with more understanding by these nationalists than by the conservatory-trained Moscow composers, and Balakirev in particular gave him invaluable help and advice. In 1869 his first opera, *The Voyevoda,* was produced in Moscow with mixed success, and later that year he composed the first version of his masterpiece, the *Romeo and Juliet* Overture, whose subject had been suggested to him by Balakirev. The main compositions of the next few years were the First Quartet (containing the well-known andante cantabile movement), the Second Symphony, and the First Piano Concerto and the Third Symphony (both 1875). The concerto was written for his friend Nicholas Rubinstein, but he refused to play it and criticized it so mercilessly that Tchaikovsky rededicated it to Hans von Bülow. In 1876 he wrote *Francesca da Rimini* and his first ballet, *Swan Lake;* his fourth opera, *Vakula the Smith,* was produced that year.

later life and works The year 1877 was one of critical importance. It marked the beginning of his extraordinary association with his benefactress, Nadezhda von Meck, a wealthy widow who provided him with financial independence for 13 years in the form of a generous annual allowance. By mutual agreement they never met, a fact that resulted in a voluminous intimate correspondence, throwing much light on Tchaikovsky's character. Another significant event was his disastrous marriage in July of the same year with Antonina Milyukova, a former music student. She had become infatuated with him in much the same way as Tatyana was infatuated with Eugene Onegin in the Pushkin opera on which Tchaikovsky was working at the time. Not able to behave with Onegin's heartlessness and perhaps hoping that marriage would conceal his homosexual inclinations, Tchaikovsky married her on the understanding that, though physical love with a woman was denied to him, he would remain her friend. The resulting tension drove him to an attempt at suicide, and they were legally separated in October 1877.

Yet during this period he wrote some of his finest works. While working on *Eugene Onegin* he also wrote the Fourth Symphony, both completed abroad while he was recovering from his state of nervous depression. This rest did indeed help him forget the horrors of the past months, but both his compositions and his letters show that whatever happiness he was to enjoy during the remainder of his life would be increasingly modified by a tendency to melancholy and morbid introspection, which had always been ingrained in his nature. Soon after returning to Russia Tchaikovsky abandoned his irksome conservatory duties and in 1881 declined the directorship of the conservatory. Between 1878 and 1881 he produced the Violin Concerto, Second Piano Concerto, Capriccio *italien, 1812* Overture, and Serenade for strings. Of his operas the *Maid of Orleans* was a failure in 1881, but in 1884 *Onegin,* which had hitherto achieved only a *succès d'estime* in Moscow, enjoyed great popularity in St. Petersburg due largely to the tsar's personal admiration for it. The third and best of his four orchestral suites also dates from 1884, and the following year he wrote his *Manfred* Symphony, again to a plan suggested by Balakirev. He began to spend more and more time traveling in Russia and abroad, and in 1888 he successfully undertook his first international tour as a conductor, visiting Leipzig, Berlin, Prague, Hamburg, Paris, and London. On his return to Russia he moved to Frolovskoye, where in 1888 he wrote his Fifth Symphony and the *Hamlet* Overture. After a second tour the following year, he composed *The Sleeping Beauty* ballet, and in 1890 his second Pushkin opera, the *Queen of Spades.* An event embittering the remaining years of his life occurred in the autumn of 1890 when Mme von Meck discontinued her allowance under the false impression that she was near bankruptcy. Their epistolary friendship was thus brought to an end. In 1891 Tchaikovsky visited the United States, where he conducted concerts in New York City, Baltimore, and Philadelphia. His two last works for the stage, the one-act opera *Iolantha* (1891) and the *Nutcracker* ballet (1892), were first performed together in December 1892 with only moderate success, although the famous ballet suite had already won favor. In 1892 Tchaikovsky moved to a house at Klin (later established as the Tchai-

kovsky Museum), where he wrote his Sixth Symphony (*Pathétique,* 1893), which he rightly believed to be a masterpiece. He lived only to hear the first performance, indifferently received; ten days later he died suddenly in St. Petersburg from cholera caused by drinking unboiled water. Whether this action entailed an element of suicide—which he had often contemplated and once attempted—has never been established.

evaluation Since Tchaikovsky's death no composer has suffered more from changes of fashion or from the extremes of over- and undervaluation. On the one hand he achieved an enormous popularity with a wide audience largely through his more emotional works; on the other the almost hypnotic effect that he was able to induce led to serious questioning of his true musical quality. It seems probable that time will add to, rather than diminish, his stature if only because performances, recordings, and publications have disclosed that there are fine works of Tchaikovsky still to be discovered. He is certainly the greatest master of the classical ballet, demonstrated by *Swan Lake* and the symphonically conceived *Sleeping Beauty.* The six symphonies may lack formal unity, but all contain delightful music. The last three are deservedly famous, though to these should be added the neglected *Manfred* Symphony. The First Piano Concerto and the Violin Concerto deserve a higher reputation than just vehicles for virtuosity. Notable among his other orchestral works are the early *Romeo and Juliet* Overture and the exquisite Serenade for strings. Although his operas contain many fine pages, Tchaikovsky was never a true operatic composer. *Eugene Onegin* is, however, a masterpiece, and the *Queen of Spades* is dramatically effective. The chamber and piano music is largely undistinguished, but his numerous songs include several fine examples.

BIBLIOGRAPHY: Rosa H. Newmarch, *Tchaikovsky: His Life and Works* (1900; reprint, 1970); Modeste Tchaikovsky, *The Life and Letters of Peter Ilich Tchaikovsky* (1906; reprint, 1973); Eric Blom, *Tchaikovsky Orchestral Works* (1927; reprint, 1970); Gerald E. H. Abraham, *Studies in Russian Music* (1935; reprint, 1976), *On Russian Music* (1939;

reprint, 1976), ed., *The Music of Tchaikovsky* (1946; reprint, 1974), and with Michel D. Calvocoressi, *Masters of Russian Music* (1936; reprint, 1971); Herbert Weinstock, *Tchaikovsky* (1943); Peter Ilich Tchaikovsky, *The Diaries of Tchaikovsky* (1945; reprint, 1973); Donald Brook, *Six Great Russian Composers* (1946); John Warrack, *Tchaikovsky Symphonies and Concertos* (1971) and *Tchaikovsky* (1973); Edward Garden, *Tchaikovsky* (1973); Vladimir Volkoff, *Tchaikovsky* (1975); Wilson Strutte, *Tchaikovsky* (1978); David Brown, *Tchaikovsky: The Early Years, 1840–1874* (1979).

RECORDINGS: Numerous recordings of many works.

Tcherepnin, Alexander (January 21 [January 9, old style], 1899–September 30, 1977)   The son of Nikolay Tcherepnin, the Russian-born pianist and composer Alexander Tcherepnin studied piano with Annette Essipoff at the St. Petersburg Conservatory, then at the Tiflis (Tbilisi) Conservatory where his father was director, and eventually at the Paris Conservatoire with Isidore Philipp. His early compositions show a strong influence of Prokofiev, who was a conducting pupil of the elder Tcherepnin and a frequent guest of the family. Alexander Tcherepnin made his debut as a pianist in Paris in 1922 and made his first recital tour of the United States in 1926. Between 1934 and 1937 he visited China and Japan and established a firm in Tokyo for the publication of works by Japanese and Chinese composers. He married the Chinese pianist Ming Lee in 1937. He taught piano and composition (1949–64) at DePaul University in Chicago, becoming a U.S. citizen in 1958.

As a composer Tcherepnin experimented with a nine-note scale and a system of polyphony he called "interpoint." Some of his music shows the influence of Georgian and Oriental folklore. His output included three operas, more than a dozen ballets (*Ajantas Frescoes* was commissioned by Anna Pavlova and premiered by her in 1923), four symphonies (he was writing another for the Chicago Symphony at the time of his death), six piano concertos, a harmonica concerto, chamber music, choral works, and piano pieces.

RECORDING: Symphony No. 2.

Tcherepnin, Nikolay (Nikolayevich) (May 14 [May 2, old style], 1873–June 26, 1945)   A Russian composer of ballets, songs, and piano music, Nikolay Tcherepnin was born in St. Petersburg. After studying law at the university, he entered the St. Petersburg Conservatory as Rimsky-Korsakov's pupil for composition (1895–98). He became conductor of the Belyaev Symphony concerts and of the imperial opera and conducted Sergey Diaghilev's opera and ballet productions in western Europe (1908–14). From 1918 to 1921 he was director of the Tiflis (Tbilisi) Conservatory. He then settled in Paris, where he directed a Russian conservatory. Tcherepnin was a gifted but not strikingly individual composer. The best of his ballet scores was the first, *Le Pavillon d'Armide* (1907). The most successful of the others were *Narcisse et Echo* (1911), *The Masque of the Red Death* (1916), and *Romance of a Mummy* (1925). Among his other works are symphonic poems, piano pieces (including *Esquisses sur les images d'un alphabet russe*), and songs. His son Alexander Tcherepnin was also a composer and a pianist.

Tebaldi, Renata (b. February 1, 1922)   Celebrated throughout Europe and the Americas for her interpretation of Verdi's Desdemona *(Otello)*, the Italian soprano Renata Tebaldi studied with her compatriot Carmen Melis. Her debut in Rovigo, Italy, in 1943 was as Elena in Arrigo Boito's *Mefistofele*. She sang Desdemona for her first appearances in Trieste (1946), Covent Garden (1950), and Metropolitan Opera (1955). She has recorded all the major operas of Verdi and Puccini and is also reputed for her Violetta (Verdi's *La traviata*).

BIBLIOGRAPHY: Victor I. Seroff, *Renata Tebaldi, the Woman and the Diva* (1961; reprint, 1970).

Te Deum or **Te Deum laudamus** ("Thee, God, we praise")   Perhaps the most famous of all hymns of the plainchant repertoire, the Te Deum was, according to legend, improvised antiphonally by St. Ambrose and St. Augustine at the latter's baptism. It has been attributed, however, to Nicetas (flourished early 5th century), Bishop of Remesiana, and its present form—equal sections devoted to the first and second persons of the Trinity, a half-clause to the third person, followed by a litany—fits historically with the 4th-century Arian controversy over the nature of Christ. Much of the text comprises traditional statements of belief; unlike most hymns, it is prose. The melody derives from various archaic and plainchant melodic styles.

It was composed in part settings as early as the 15th century. Prominent composers who have set the text include Palestrina, Purcell, Handel, Berlioz, Bruckner, Dvořák, Verdi, Kodály, Vaughan Williams, and Britten.

Te Kanawa, Kiri (b. March 6, 1944) Educated in her native New Zealand, soprano Kiri Te Kanawa made her debut (1971) at Covent Garden as a flower maiden in Wagner's *Parsifal* and remained as a resident member there. She has sung at the Metropolitan Opera and Chicago's Lyric Opera and is best known for the Italian roles of Mozart, Puccini, and Verdi and the French roles of Marguérite (Gounod's *Faust*) and Bizet's Carmen. She made her Houston Opera debut in the 1977–78 season in the title role of Richard Strauss's *Arabella*.

Telemann, Georg Philipp (March 14, 1681–June 25, 1767) The most highly regarded German composer of his time, Georg Philipp Telemann entered the University of Leipzig in 1701 to study law, but he soon abandoned his studies for a musical career. He founded the Collegium Musicum, undertook the direction of the Leipzig Opera, and in 1704 was appointed organist at the Neue Kirche. The following year he left Leipzig, and after some years as court composer at Sorau and Eisenach and as musical director at Frankfurt-am-Main, he settled in Hamburg in 1721. When he declined the post of organist at Leipzig's Thomaskirche in 1722, it was given to Bach. In 1737–38 he traveled for eight months in France.

As a composer Telemann was amazingly productive. In Hamburg he provided five churches with music, conducted the opera, and gave frequent concerts with the Hamburg Collegium Musicum that he had formed. In addition he regularly supplied music for several courts and for the city of Frankfurt.

Georg Philipp Telemann
*engraving by Georg Lichtensteger (1700–81)
courtesy, Kunsthalle, Hamburg*

Within 15 years no fewer than 44 of his works were published—some engraved by himself—among them several complete sets of cantatas for the church year, the large instrumental collection *Musique de Table* (1733), and the first music periodical, *Der Getreue Music-Meister,* which alone contains 70 of his compositions.

Telemann was on friendly terms with Bach, for whose son Carl Philipp Emanuel he became godfather; Handel sent him rare plants for his garden; and Johann Mattheson was enthusiastic in his praise. Both Bach and Handel copied and arranged several of his works for their own use. He was twice married and had eight sons and two daughters, but of his family only one grandson, Georg Michael Telemann, became a musician.

In his lifetime Telemann was most admired for his church compositions, but his secular vocal music also has a wide range—from simple strophic songs to the dramatic cantata *Ino,* written at the age of 84. Of his more than 50 operas the comic ones were the most successful, especially *Pimpinone* (1725), based on the same plot as Pergolesi's *La serva padrona,* which it preceded by eight years. His orchestral works consist of suites (called *ouvertures*), concerti grossi, and concertos. His chamber works are remarkable not only for their quantity but for the great variety of instrumental combinations and the expert writing for each instrument.

BIBLIOGRAPHY: Romain Rolland, *A Musical Tour through the Land of the Past* (1922); Richard Petzoldt, *Georg Philipp Telemann* (1974).

RECORDINGS: Numerous recordings of many works.

Telephone, The: *see* MENOTTI.

temperament: *see* TUNING AND TEMPERAMENT.

Tempesta, La: *see* HALÉVY.

tenor   The highest male vocal range, normally extending from about the second B below middle C to the A above; an extremely high voice, extending into the alto range, is usually termed a COUNTERTENOR. In families of instruments tenor refers to the instrument of more or less comparable range (*e.g.,* tenor horn). The word is from the Latin *tenere,* "to have, to hold."

In polyphonic music of the 13th–16th century, tenor referred to the part "holding" the cantus firmus, the plainchant or other melody on which a composition was usually built. The line above was termed *superius* (the modern soprano), and the third added voice was termed *contratenor.* In the mid-15th century writing in four parts became common, and the *contratenor* part gave rise to the *contratenor altus* (the modern alto) and *contratenor bassus* (the modern bass). The term tenor gradually lost its association with a cantus firmus and began to refer to the part between the alto and bass and to the corresponding vocal range.

In plainchant psalm singing tenor refers to the reciting note on which most of the syllables fall.

tenor drum   A cylindrical drum larger and deeper toned than the closely related snare drum but lacking snares. Usually about 18 inches (45 centimeters) in diameter and 14 inches (35 centimeters) in height, it is normally beaten with two soft-headed sticks. The heads are tensioned by rope lacings (military)

tenor drum
courtesy, Ludwig Industries

or metal rods (orchestral). Like the snare drum the tenor drum descended from the medieval tabor. Associated with military bands, especially since the early 19th century, it occasionally appears in orchestral scores; a notable example is Britten's opera *The Rape of Lucretia* (1946).

ternary form   A form consisting of three sections, the last of which is a repeat of the first. The symmetrical construction of this scheme (ABA) provides one of the basic shapes in music and may be found as a guiding principle in music from the Middle Ages (in plainchant, for instance, the arrangement antiphon–verse–antiphon is common) to the 20th century (a well-known example being the Minuet and Trio from Schoenberg's Piano Suite, Op. 25).

Although any kind of ABA pattern may correctly be defined as ternary, it is most proper to speak of ternary as a definite formal type when each of its sections forms an intelligible musical entity that is relatively complete within itself. Thus section A forms a logical whole, which is harmonically closed. It is most often in BINARY FORM, a variety of two-section form. The same may be said about section B, which is placed in a key different from—though closely related to—that of section A. Ternary form may be found in the Baroque instrumental suite in which two dances (most often a minuet and trio) are performed in the standard ABA pattern. It survived into the Classical era as the combination of minuet (or scherzo) and trio that serves as the third movement of the typical Classical symphony.

In his Fourth and Seventh Symphonies and Quartet in e minor (Op. 59, No. 2), Beethoven modified the form by giving both the A and B sections an extra repeat, thus producing a five-part (ABABA) form. The even more striking phenomenon of a second trio (AB-ACA) may be seen in the First and Second Symphonies of Schumann and in Bruckner's Seventh.

Tertis, Lionel (December 29, 1876–February 22, 1975)   Most influential in establishing the viola as an instrument in its own right, the English violist Lionel Tertis studied viola at the Royal Academy of Music and violin at the Leipzig Conservatory. He played viola in Henry Wood's Queen's Hall Orchestra (1897–1904) and toured as a soloist and ensemble player. Among the composers who wrote for him were Vaughan Williams, Cyril Scott, Arnold Bax, and William Walton. Tertis retired from performing in 1936 to design the now-standard viola. He also designed a less universally used violin and cello. His arrangements for viola of music originally composed for other instruments expanded the repertoire of the viola enough to make recitals and solo appearances more interesting and diversified.

Tetrazzini, Luisa (June 29, 1871–April 28, 1940)   One of the best-known coloratura sopranos of her time, Luisa Tetrazzini studied in her native Florence, making her debut there in 1895 as Inez in Meyerbeer's *L'Africaine.* Success in Italy led to tours of Europe, Russia, and South America. Her Covent Garden debut in 1907 was as Verdi's Violetta *(La traviata),* the same role she sang for her New York City debut with Oscar Hammerstein's Manhattan Opera in 1908. She made her Metropolitan Opera debut as Lucia (Donizetti) in 1911 and sang with the Chicago Opera for the 1913–14 season. After World War I she appeared in recitals and taught in Milan. She wrote an autobiography, *My Life of Song* (1921), and *How to Sing* (1923). The spaghetti dish chicken Tetrazzini is named after her.

Teyte, Maggie, originally Maggie Tate (April 17, 1888–May 26, 1976)   Chosen by Debussy to sing the lead role in his *Pelléas et Mélisande* (succeeding Mary Garden in 1908), the En-

glish soprano Maggie Teyte was educated at the Royal College of Music and studied with Jean De Reszke in Paris from 1903 to 1907, the year of her debut at Monte Carlo (as Zerlina in Mozart's *Die Zauberflöte*). She sang at the Opéra-Comique (1908–10), Covent Garden (from 1910), Chicago Opera (1911–14), and Boston Opera (1915–17). She created the role of Suzanne in Ermanno Wolf-Ferrari's *The Secret of Suzanne* (Munich, 1909), but she is remembered primarily for her singing of French art songs on extensive recitals (some with Debussy at the piano) and in recordings. She made her final stage appearance in London in 1951 as Belinda in Purcell's *Dido and Aeneas* and final recital tours of England and the United States in 1954. Teyte was made a chevalier of the Legion of Honor (1957) and a dame of the Order of the British Empire (1958). Her book of memoirs, *Star on the Door,* was published in 1958.

BIBLIOGRAPHY: Garry O'Conor, *The Pursuit of Perfection: A Life of Maggie Teyte* (1979).

Thaïs: *see* MASSENET.

Luisa Tetrazzini
courtesy, Metropolitan Opera Archives

Thalberg, Sigismond (January 8, 1812–April 27, 1871)   The leading rival of Liszt as a great pianist, the Swiss-born Austrian Sigismond Thalberg was of noble blood and studied with Johann Nepomuk Hummel and Ignaz Moscheles. Called "Old Arpeggio" from his innovative stunt of thumbing a melody in the middle register while surrounding it in both treble and bass with arpeggios, he was a sensation. Unlike Liszt, however, he was nearly motionless at the keyboard—pressing the keys rather than striking them. Admired by his contemporaries Clara and Robert Schumann, Hans von Bülow, Mendelssohn, Chopin, and even Liszt, his playing was described by Charles Hallé as beautiful but cold. He was one of the first of the great pianists to tour the United States, and, although he could and did program serious literature, he played mostly his own arpeggiated operatic fantasies with great success. Some of his compositions, consisting of piano works, a piano trio, a violin and piano duet, and 54 German songs, have had a late 20th-century revival.

RECORDINGS: Fantasy on Meyerbeer's *Robert le Diable;* Piano Concerto in f minor; Piano Sonata in c minor; Piano Trio; piano pieces.

theme or **subject**   A musical idea in melodic form used as a basis for a composition or movement. It normally appears at the beginning of a piece or section and is made up of several figures or motifs. A theme may be a point of departure for development (*i.e.,* the subject of a fugue or a movement in a sonata, symphony, quartet, etc.) or a set of variations.

theorbo: *see* LUTE.

theory   Musical theory in the late 20th century includes all the technical aspects of composition, including COUNTERPOINT, HARMONY, MELODY, NOTATION, RHYTHM, SERIALISM, etc. Before about 1800 theory was primarily involved with the scientific and philosophical aspects of music (*see* INTERVAL; MODE; OVERTONE; SCALE; TUNING AND TEMPERAMENT). The subject is often considered to cover musical forms (*see* such major forms as FUGUE; SONATA; VARIATIONS; and innumerable minor forms) and such subjects as MUSICOLOGY; PERFORMANCE PRACTICE; SOLFEGGIO.

theremin   An electronic instrument invented in the early 1920s by the Soviet scientist Leon Theremin that produces sound by two oscillators—one at a fixed frequency, the other with variable frequencies. The pitch is determined by the difference between the two and is controlled by moving the hand or a baton toward or away from an antenna, thus altering one of the inaudible frequencies. Harmonics, or component tones, of the sound can be filtered out, allowing production of several tone colors over a range of six octaves. Henry Cowell and Edgard Varèse have written for the theremin, and it is often used in motion picture scores.

Thibaud, Jacques (September 27, 1880–September 1, 1953)   A pupil of Martin Pierre Joseph Marsick at the Paris Conservatoire, the French violinist Jacques Thibaud was a leading exponent of the French classic school of violin playing. He began his career with the Colonne Concerts and in 1898 appeared 54 times as soloist. On the faculty of the École Normale de Musique in Paris, he toured throughout the world (in the United States after 1903). He played chamber music with Casals and Alfred Cortot and was best known for his interpretation of Mozart, Beethoven, and French music. The biennial Marguerite Long-Jacques Thibaud competition (established 1943) for pianists and violinists is named for him. He played a Stradivari violin once owned by the French violinist Pierre Baillot.

Thomas, (Charles Louis) Ambroise (August 5, 1811–February 12, 1896)   Remembered as a composer of operas, the French composer and pianist Ambroise Thomas studied at the Paris Conservatoire and won the Prix de Rome in 1832; in Rome he wrote primarily chamber music and choral works. After his return to Paris he wrote ballets for the Opéra but then composed nearly exclusively for the Opéra-Comique. Best received was the opera *Mignon* (1866), the only one of his works regularly performed in the 20th century. In 1852 he became professor at the Conservatoire and director in 1871. Between 1837 and 1889 he composed 20 operas and three ballets, all of which were immediately popular.

RECORDINGS: *Mignon* (Overture and selections).

Thomas, Michael Tilson (b. December 21, 1944) Proficient in a wide repertoire, the U.S. conductor and pianist Michael Tilson Thomas studied with Ingolf Dahl at the University of Southern California and then at the Berkshire Music Center, where he won the Koussevitzky Prize for conducting. By age 21 he had become assistant to Pierre Boulez at the Ojai Festival in California and at Bayreuth. In 1969 he was appointed assistant conductor of the Boston Symphony, associate conductor (1970), and principal guest conductor (1971). In that year he also became music director of the Buffalo Philharmonic (until 1979) and of the New York Philharmonic Young People's Concerts. He drew public attention when, in 1969, he finished a concert of the Boston Symphony in New York for William Steinberg, who had become ill during the performance. He has been a guest conductor throughout the United States and in Europe, Japan, and Israel, and also performs as a pianist in chamber music. Notable recordings include Carl Orff's *Carmina Burana* and music of Walter Piston and Ives.

Thomas, Theodore (October 11, 1835–January 4, 1905) Though born in Germany, Theodore Thomas was brought to New York City as a child of 10 and can be considered the first great U.S. conductor. He was taught by his violinist father, and, until the founding of his own orchestra in 1864, he earned his living as a violinist. Though his orchestral repertoire was based on the trivia then in fashion, Thomas increasingly included major works, soon devoting one program a week to a symphonic night. The new and old works he introduced to America were numerous, and he toured extensively "spreading the gospel." He also was conductor of the Brooklyn Philharmonic and the New York Philharmonic before assuming the leadership of the Chicago Symphony at its founding in 1891. Although autocratic, uncompromising, and frequently at the center of controversy, he built ensembles that may have been unequalled in their day; his contribution to the musical education of the United States is inestimable.

Thompson, Randall (b. April 21, 1899) Especially notable for his choral music, the U.S. composer Randall Thompson studied at Harvard University and later with Bloch. He was director of the Curtis Institute (1939–41) before joining the faculties at the University of Virginia (1941–46), Princeton (1946–48), and Harvard (1948–66). His music is conservative and neoclassical, combining traditional forms with 20th-century styles and exhibiting a highly developed sense of form and counterpoint. Of his three symphonies the second (1932) was especially successful. Notable among his vocal works are *The Peaceable Kingdom* (1936), the popular *Alleluia* (1940), and Mass *of the Holy Spirit* (1955) for unaccompanied voices and *The Testament of Freedom* (1943) for men's voices and orchestra to words by Thomas Jefferson. Other works include a one-act opera, *Solomon and Balkis* (1942); an oratorio, *The Nativity according to St. Luke* (1965); incidental music for the theater; two quartets (1924, 1941); and songs.

RECORDINGS: *Americana* for chorus and orchestra; *The Peaceable Kingdom; The Testament of Freedom.*

Thomson, Virgil (b. November 25, 1896) The U.S. composer, conductor, and critic Virgil Thomson studied at Harvard University and

Theodore Thomas
courtesy, Chicago Symphony Orchestra

later with Boulanger in Paris. There he came under the strong influence of French composers (especially Debussy, Satie, and the group known as Les Six) and of Gertrude Stein. His musical style is basically neoclassical, combining traditional forms with contemporary techniques such as atonality and polytonality, and is marked by careful craftsmanship and frequently humor.

His operas are among his best-known works; *Four Saints in Three Acts* (1928) and *The Mother of Us All* (1947) boast libretti by Gertrude Stein. A later opera was *Lord Byron* (1968). His instrumental music includes two symphonies, several symphonic poems, and concertos for cello and for flute (composed 1950; 1954). He also composed songs, choral works, chamber music, piano pieces, and film music (*The Plough that Broke the Plains,* 1936; *The River,* 1942; and *Louisiana Story,* 1948). He was music critic for the New York *Herald Tribune* (1940–54) and published his autobiography, *Virgil Thomson* (1966), *Music Revisited, 1940–54* (1967), and *American Music since 1910* (1971) among a number of books.

RECORDINGS: *Autumn* (Concertino for harp, strings, and percussion); *The Feast of Love* for baritone and orchestra; Flute Concerto; *Louisiana Story* (suite); *The Mother of Us All;* Piano Sonata No. 3; *The Plough that Broke the Plains;* Quartet No. 2; *The River* (suite); Symphony on a Hymn Tune.

thoroughbass: *see* FIGURED BASS.

Three-Cornered Hat, The: *see* BALLET (Diaghilev Ballet); FALLA.

Threepenny Opera, The: *see* WEILL.

Threni: *see* MODERN PERIOD (rediscovery of serialism); STRAVINSKY.

Thus Spake Zarathustra: *see* ALSO SPRACH ZARATHUSTRA.

Tibbett, Lawrence (November 16, 1896–July 15, 1960)   A popular U.S. opera, recital, and radio singer, Lawrence Tibbett initially trained as an actor. He then sang with a light opera company in works by Victor Herbert and Gilbert and Sullivan. He first sang at the Metropolitan Opera in 1923 as a monk in Mussorgsky's *Boris Godunov* and sang minor French, German, and Italian roles there until

1925, when he sang Ford on short notice in Verdi's *Falstaff,* creating a sensation. Subsequently he was a leading baritone at the Metropolitan for the next 25 years. Tibbett created several roles, among them Louis Theodore Gruenberg's Emperor Jones (1933). A memorable Iago (Verdi's *Otello*), he sang the role at the Metropolitan in 1937–38 after singing it in London, Paris, and Vienna. In 1937 he also made his Covent Garden debut as Scarpia in Puccini's *Tosca.* He appeared in several musical films, including *The Rogue Song* and *The New Moon* (both 1930) and *Metropolitan* (1936).

Tichatschek, Joseph Alois (July 11, 1807–January 18, 1886)   The Bohemian Wagnerian tenor who created the roles of Rienzi (1842) and Tannhäuser (1845), Joseph Alois Tichatschek first studied medicine but in 1827 began to study music in Vienna. For two years he was a leading tenor at the opera houses of Graz and Vienna, and in 1837 he made his debut as Daniel François Esprit Auber's Gustave III at the Dresden Opera, where he sang until 1870. He coached with Wilhelmine Schröder-Devrient, with whom he sang several Wagner premieres.

Till Eulenspiegel: *see* BALLET (Diaghilev Ballet); CYCLIC FORM; STRAUSS, RICHARD.

time signature   A sign indicating the meter of a composition. Most time signatures consist of two vertically aligned numbers such as $\frac{2}{2}$, $\frac{3}{4}$, $\frac{6}{8}$, $\frac{11}{16}$. The upper figure shows the number of beats in each measure, or metrical unit; the lower figure indicates the note value receiving one beat (here half note, quarter note, eighth note, sixteenth note). When measures contain an uneven number of beats falling regularly into two subgroups, the division may be indicated, $\frac{3+4}{4}$ instead of $\frac{7}{4}$.

Two other time signatures are common: c (common time, or $\frac{4}{4}$) and ¢ (cut time, or alla breve, $\frac{2}{2}$). Both are derived from symbols of mensural notation (*c.* 1250–*c.* 1600), the system preceding the modern one. The mensural time signature indicated a basic unit *(tempus)* of two notes and the subdivision *(prolatio)* of these notes into two parts (modern equivalent $\frac{2}{4}$ time, ♩ ♩ and ♫ ♫). But c was a proportion sign indicating that the breve (▬; modern double whole note) should take the time formerly occupied by the semibreve (◇; modern whole note), hence the name alla breve.

Other time signatures of mensural notation (and their modern equivalents) were ○ ($\frac{3}{4}$), ₵ ($\frac{6}{8}$), and ⊙ ($\frac{9}{8}$).

timpani The kettledrums in the orchestra (plural of Italian *timpano*). Introduced in the orchestra in the second half of the 17th century, they first appear in scores of Matthew Locke (*Psyche,* 1673), Lully (*Thésée,* 1675), and Purcell (*Fairy Queen,* 1692), where they were used in pairs—one small and one large— each pair tuned to the tonic and dominant.

Each kettledrum consists of a bowl-shaped shell of copper, brass, or other metal over which is stretched a head of calfskin secured by a metal hoop. A hole is pierced at the bottom of the shell to avoid air concussion and the splitting of the head in fortissimo passages. The tension of the skin, and accordingly the pitch of the drum, is varied either by means of hand screws fixed to the shell or by a number of mechanical devices. These devices include a pedal or a hand mechanism that varies the tension of the head by means of rods connected to the hoop. The skin vibrates when struck with the drumsticks, the tone produced depending on the texture of the hard or soft felt or other substance forming the head of the stick. The tone also varies according to whether the drum is struck nearer the rim of the shell or the center of the head. Occasionally the head is made to vibrate by the fingers.

The orchestral kettledrum has a practical compass of five full tones. The compass covered by a pair of timpani is normally an octave from F below middle C downward. The tuning of an orchestral set of three instruments generally covers the following ranges:

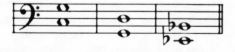

In certain cases this compass has been extended upward as far as B (in Stravinsky's *Le Sacre du printemps,* 1913) and downward to D-flat (in the symphonies of Mahler).

Although similar in many respects to the earlier nakers (*see* DRUM), the kettledrum has

a completely separate history. In the mid-15th century pairs of large kettledrums of the Ottoman Turks were brought to Europe by way of Hungary and Germany. They were military and ceremonial instruments and formed an important part of the retinue of emperors, kings, and noblemen. From the time of their introduction to Europe, kettledrums were associated with trumpets; the players of both instruments belonged to the same exclusive guild. By the beginning of the 16th century, trumpet and kettledrum players were established in most important noble households in Europe, and the word "dromme" (having the same derivation as "trumpet") first appears in the English language. Kettledrums were often played on horseback, one drum on either side of the horse, as the Turkish armies used kettledrums on camelback.

Although no written drum parts survive from the 16th century, such works as the chanson *La Bataille de Marignon* by Clément Janequin, in which the voices imitate the calls of the trumpets and drums, give a reasonably clear picture of a technique based on a tonic and dominant tuning of the kettledrums that was not to be substantially altered for more than two centuries. An early example of trumpet and drum music is the toccata, or fanfare (the contemporary English word was "tucket"), at the beginning of Monteverdi's opera *Orfeo* (1607). In the 17th and 18th centuries kettledrumming developed into an elaborate ceremonial and ostentatious art that used complicated drum patterns based on the multiple tonguing technique of the trumpeters. The orchestral use of the instrument was confined to passages that expressed rejoicing, as in Bach's cantata *Tönet, ihr Pauken! erschallet Trompeten,* or supported the brass in loud passages.

The expressive use of the kettledrum in the 19th-century orchestra (played softly, crescendo, and with the drums not necessarily tuned to the tonic and dominant) was largely due to the innovations of Beethoven. Later Berlioz, who in his Requiem (1837) used the formidable number of 16 kettledrums, discussed in his book on orchestration (1843) the use of drumsticks with wooden ends or ends covered with leather or sponge. Special

orchestral timpani with pedal-controlled tension
courtesy, Ludwig Industries

effects include damped or muffled notes, as in Liszt's *Faust* Symphony (1857), the striking of a note with two sticks, as in Berg's *Wozzeck* (1925), and a pedal glissando on a roll used by Bartók. Occasionally muted timpani are used, as in Mahler's First Symphony (1888), a strip of cloth being placed over the drumhead.

BIBLIOGRAPHY: J. Ernst Altenburg, *Trumpeters' and Kettledrummers' Art* (1795; reprint, 1974).

Tinctoris, Johannes (*c.* 1436–October 1511) A Flemish theorist and composer, Johannes Tinctoris was the author of the earliest dictionary of musical terms. He studied law and theology at the University of Louvain, which he left before 1476 in order to take up the position of chaplain to Ferdinand I, King of Naples. He had much to do with the music of the king's chapel, and to Beatrice of Aragon, Ferdinand's daughter, he dedicated his dictionary, *Terminorum musicae diffinitorium* (*c.* 1476; printed *c.* 1495). His other theoretical works include *Proportionale musices,* dealing with musical notation, and *Liber de arte contrapuncti,* a survey of the art of composition as practiced in the late 15th century. The *Missa l'homme armé* is his best-known composition.

RECORDING: *Missa trium vocum.*

Tippett, Michael (Kemp) (b. January 2, 1905) Although largely self-taught, the En-glish composer and conductor Michael Tippett studied at the Royal College of Music with Charles Wood and Malcolm Sargent. His early compositions were withdrawn prior to publication. He was director of music at Morley College in London (1940–51), after which he devoted himself to composing and conducting his own works. His first significant work was an oratorio on his own libretto, *A Child of Our Time* (1941), and it is in his large works that he is most successful: four operas on his own librettos (*The Midsummer Marriage,* 1955; *King Priam,* 1962; *The Knot Garden,* 1970; and *The Ice Break,* 1977); four symphonies (1945, 1958, 1972, 1977); *The Vision of St. Augustine* (1966) for baritone, chorus, and orchestra; and three concertos (for double string orchestra, 1939; piano, 1955; and orchestra, 1963). Other works include three early quartets, three piano sonatas, song cycles, and other orchestral pieces. His early works often join sonata form with Elizabethan polyphony and intricate counterpoint; his middle style shows influences of Bartók, Hindemith, and the blues; and his later compositions have affinities with Beethoven. The literary ideas behind the opera librettos are explored in his prose essays *Moving into Aquarius* (1959). He was knighted in 1966.

BIBLIOGRAPHY: Ian Kemp, ed., *Michael Tippett: A Symposium on His 60th Birthday* (1965).

RECORDINGS: *A Child of Our Time;*

Concerto for double string orchestra; Concerto for orchestra; *The Knot Garden; Little Music* for strings; Magnificat and Nunc dimittis; *The Midsummer Marriage;* Quartets (3); Sonata for four horns; *Songs for Dov;* Suite for the Birthday of Prince Charles; Symphonies (3); Variations on a Theme by Corelli; *Weeping Babe* for soprano and chorus.

toccata A form for keyboard instruments in which the stylistic elements idiomatic to the instrument are exploited to create an effect of improvisation (from the Italian *toccare,* "to touch"). In the late 16th century in Venice such composers as Giovanni Gabrieli and Claudio Merulo wrote organ toccatas (many with such titles as fantasia or *intonazione*), often achieving a majestic virtuosity by means of florid scale passages, embellishments, unsteady rhythms and harmonies, changes of mood, and freedom of tempo. Merulo initiated the later common practice of alternating fugal sections with rapid toccata passages. In Rome Frescobaldi (died 1643) composed toccatas consisting of improvisatory sections loosely strung together and marked by sudden changes in harmonies and figuration. Frescobaldi's German pupil Johann Jakob Froberger was an important transmitter of the style to Germany. Like his teacher he delighted in the use of chromatic harmonies, and like Merulo he characteristically placed a contrasting fugal section between introductory and closing passages in toccata style.

The juxtaposition of improvisatory and fugal passages—which appealed to the Baroque fascination with the union of opposites—became a prominent feature of the toccatas of the organist-composers of north Germany, culminating in the works of Dietrich Buxtehude and later Bach. Buxtehude's toccatas, in contrast to Frescobaldi's, for example, are shaped by an underlying formal structure. Two, even three, fugal sections often alternate with toccata passages, and the fugue subjects are frequently variations of a basic motif. In the late Baroque era, as in many works of Bach, the association of the two opposite styles' often took the form of an improvisatory first movement (termed prelude, toccata, fantasia, etc.) followed by a fugue, as in Bach's Toccata and Fugue in F Major, BWV 540, for organ.

In the late 19th century the toccata became popular as a showpiece for the organ, especially in the French school. The best-known example is in Charles-Marie Widor's Fifth Symphony, and an outstanding 20th-century one is in Maurice Duruflé's Suite (1934). Similar *moto perpetuo* types were also written for the piano, such as in Debussy's suite *Pour le piano* (1901) and Prokofiev's Toccata (1912).

Toch, Ernst (December 7, 1887–October 1, 1964) The Austrian-born U.S. composer Ernst Toch is known for his orchestral and piano works. He studied piano with Walter Rehberg at Frankfurt am Main but was otherwise self-taught. His operas and instrumental works were widely performed in Germany between 1925 and 1930, and he taught piano and composition in Berlin (1929–33). He moved to New York City in 1935 and to California two years later, teaching at the University of California at Los Angeles from 1940 and becoming a U.S. citizen. Some of his best works are his smaller pieces for piano. His orchestral works were written with humor, notably the *Bunte* Suite (1929), and though his style is largely traditional he experimented with new devices as in his *Gesprochene Musik* for speaking voices (1930). He also wrote six symphonies (1950–64); two piano concertos (1927, 1932); *Big Ben* (1934), variations for orchestra; *Pinocchio* Overture (1936); *Peter Pan* (1956), a fairy tale for orchestra; 13 quartets; a piano sonata; chamber operas; and music for films. In 1956 Toch won the Pulitzer Prize for his Third Symphony. He published two theoretical works, *Melodielehre* (1923) and *The Shaping Forces in Music* (1948).

RECORDINGS: Divertimenti (2); *Geographical* Fugue and *Valse* for speaking chorus; *Miniature* Overture; Piano Quintet; *Poems to Martha* for voice and strings; Quartets (4); Serenade in G; String Trio; Symphony No. 5; Violin Sonata No. 1.

Tod und Verklärung: *see* DEATH AND TRANSFIGURATION.

Tomkins, Thomas (1572–buried June 9, 1656) One of the most inspired of the English madrigalists, Thomas Tomkins came from a family of musicians and was a pupil of Byrd. He was organist of the Worcester Cathedral (*c.* 1596–1646), marrying the widow of his predecessor. He received his Mus. B. degree at Oxford (1607) and was appointed one of the organists of the Chapel Royal (1621). He composed music for the coronation of Charles I in 1625. Tomkins' *Songs of 3, 4, 5 and 6 parts* was published in 1622 and contains mostly madrigals and ballets. Five services and 95 anthems, including a 12-part "O praise the Lord, all ye heathen," make up *Musica Deo sacra,* published in 1668, 12 years after his death. Other church music was left in manuscript, and he also wrote a good deal of instrumental music for virginal and for viols.

BIBLIOGRAPHY: Denis W. Stevens, *Thomas Tomkins, 1572–1656* (1957).

tom-tom A high-pitched snareless drum, often two-headed, and usually used in pairs or larger groups (sets of seven are common). Dating from the 1920s in jazz bands in imitation of African drums, it may be pitchless or tuned. When tuned it is sometimes used as an upward extension of the timpani as in Stravinsky's *Agon* (1957).

tonadilla A short, satirical comic opera that was highly popular in 18th-century Spain, originating as a short scenic interlude between acts of other short theatrical pieces. The term is a diminutive of the Spanish *tonada,* a lyric folk song. The leading exponents of the form were Luis Mison (d. 1766), Pablo Esteve (b. *c.* 1730), and Blas Laserna (1751–1816). It replaced the ZARZUELA in a battle that was similar to the War of the Buffoons in Paris.

BIBLIOGRAPHY: Mary Neal Hamilton, *Music in Eighteenth Century Spain* (1937).

tonality The principle of organizing music around a central note, the tonic; a system of relationships between notes, chords, and keys that dominated most Western music from *c.* 1650 to *c.* 1900 and that continues to regulate much music.

Sometimes called major–minor tonality, the system uses the notes of the major and minor diatonic scales plus optional auxiliary, or chromatic, notes as the raw material with which to build melodies and chords. Within each key there is a specific hierarchy of strong and weak relationships both to the keynote, or tonic note, and to the chord built on that note, the tonic chord. Different keys are also strongly or weakly related to the principal, or tonic, key.

In this system of tonal relations the notes and chords within a given key can create tension or resolve it as they move away from or toward the tonic. Likewise any modulation or movement away from the tonic key creates tensions that may then be resolved by modulation back to it. The potential for contrast and tension inherent in the chord and key relationships of tonality became the basis for 18th-century musical forms such as the sonata.

Tonality is sometimes used as a synonym for the closely related concept of key. *Compare* ATONALITY.

tone poem: *see* SYMPHONIC POEM.

tonic The first tone of the diatonic scale; also called the keynote. It is the most important degree of the scale and dominates both melody and harmony. *See* TONALITY.

Torelli, Giuseppe (April 22, 1658–February 8, 1709) An Italian violinist and composer who helped to establish the form of the violin concerto, Giuseppe Torelli studied with Giacomo Antonio Perti in Bologna and in 1686 played viola in the orchestra at the church of S. Petronio there. In 1695 he went to Vienna and about 1696 was appointed Kapellmeister at Ansbach. His oratorio *Adam* was given in Vienna in 1700, and the following year he returned to Bologna, where he played violin in the orchestra.

Torelli wrote many concertos for stringed instruments and was one of the first to write concertos for the solo violin. He also produced sonatas and concertos for brass instruments and strings. Many of his works were published in Bologna between 1686 and 1692; others survive in manuscript collections at Bologna and Modena.

RECORDINGS: Concerti grossi (12), Op. 8; Sinfonie *a 2–4 stromenti,* Op. 3; various concertos and sinfonias with trumpets, oboes, and strings.

Tosca: *see* LIBRETTO (modern status); OPERA (the 19th century); PUCCINI; VERISMO.

Toscanini, Arturo (March 25, 1867–January 16, 1957)   Though established as an operatic conductor in his native Italy before 1900, Arturo Toscanini was the founder of a new school of conducting that is associated with the 20th century. In his own words, "The tradition is to be found only in one place—in the music." His younger contemporary George Szell described his tremendous influence thus: "that he changed the whole concept of conducting and that he rectified many, many arbitrary procedures of a generation of conductors before him, is now authentic history."

Toscanini graduated from the Parma Conservatory (1885) as a cellist and while playing in a performance of *Aida* in Rio de Janeiro (1886) was unexpectedly called upon to conduct. His phenomenal ability was recognized immediately, and his reputation was soon established. Though he proceeded to conduct in all major music centers, his work was primarily in Milan (La Scala, 1898–1908 and 1921–29) and in New York City (Metropolitan Opera, 1908–15; New York Philharmonic,

Arturo Toscanini   *EB Inc.*

1928–36; NBC Symphony, founded expressly for him, 1937–54). His repertoire was all encompassing; among world premieres he conducted were Leoncavallo's *Pagliacci* (1892) and Puccini's *La Bohème* (1896) and *The Girl of the Golden West* (1910); he introduced to Italian audiences Wagner's *Götterdämmerung* (1895) and *Siegfried* (1899) and to U.S. audiences Gluck's *Armide* (1910) and Mussorgsky's *Boris Godunov* (1913); but he was probably best known for his interpretations of Verdi operas and Beethoven symphonies.

BIBLIOGRAPHY: Robert C. Marsh, *Toscanini and the Art of Orchestral Performance* (1956; reprint, 1973); Spike Hughes, *The Toscanini Legacy,* rev. ed. (1969); George Marek, *Toscanini* (1975); Samuel Chotzinoff, *Toscanini: An Intimate Portrait* (1976); Harvey Sachs, *Toscanini* (1978).

Totentanz: *see* LISZT.

Tourel, Jennie, real name, Jennie Davidson (June 22, 1900–November 23, 1973)   Known as an interpreter of contemporary music, the Russian-born U.S. mezzo-soprano Jennie Tourel studied in Paris; her professional name was taken as an anagram of that of her teacher, Anna El-Tour. She made her debut in Paris at the Opéra-Comique as Bizet's Carmen in 1933. In 1937 she first sang at the Metropolitan Opera as Ambroise Thomas's Mignon and was a member of the company (1943–47). She sang the role of Lisa in Tchaikovsky's *Pique Dame* in the initial season (1941–42) of the New Opera Company of New York. In 1951 she created the role of Baba the Turk in Stravinsky's *The Rake's Progress* in Venice. She recorded several recital programs and music of Mahler, Lukas Foss, and Bernstein and was at home in Italian, German, French, and Russian repertoire. She taught at the Juilliard School from 1963 until her death.

Tournemire, Charles (Arnould) (January 22, 1870–November 3, 1939)   A pupil of Franck and Charles-Marie Widor at the Paris Conservatoire where he later became professor of chamber music, the French organist and composer Charles Tournemire later studied composition with d'Indy. In 1898 he succeeded Gabriel Pierné as organist of the church of

Sainte-Clothilde (Paris), where his improvisations became almost legendary. Compositions include an opera (*Les Dieux sont morts,* 1924), eight symphonies, chamber music, choral works (*Le Sang de la sirène,* 1904) and a trilogy *(Faust, Don Quichotte, St.-François d'Assise),* and an important collection of 255 pieces for organ, *L'Orgue mystique (51 Offices de l'année liturgique).* He wrote a treatise on organ playing, an organ method, and a biography of Franck.

Tovey, Donald Francis (July 17, 1875–July 10, 1940)   An English pianist and composer, Donald Francis Tovey is known for his works of musical scholarship. He studied piano with Sophie Weisse and counterpoint with Walter Parratt, graduating from Oxford in 1898. He gave recitals of his works in London, Berlin, and Vienna (1900–02), played his Piano Concerto in London (1903), and organized concerts of chamber music at Chelsea (1906–12). His compositions include two quartets, the opera *The Bride of Dionysus* (1929), and Cello Concerto (1934). In 1914 he was appointed Reid professor of music at Edinburgh and in 1917 founded there the Reid Symphony. For the concerts given by this orchestra Tovey wrote analytical notes dealing with problems of composition in a perspicacious and lively manner; these notes were published as *Essays in Musical Analysis,* six volumes (1935–39). Among other historical studies were his articles on music written for *Encyclopædia Britannica* (reprinted as *Musical Articles from the Encyclopædia Britannica,* 1944) and his *Essays and Lectures on Music* (1949). The elegance and wit of his style broadened the appeal of music criticism and helped to establish it as a literary genre.

   BIBLIOGRAPHY: Mary Grierson, *Donald Francis Tovey* 1952; reprint, 1970).

tracker action: *see* ORGAN (mechanism).

Tragic Overture: *see* BRAHMS (works).

Tragic Symphony: *see* MAHLER (middle period); SCHUBERT (years of promise).

Trampler, Walter (b. August 25, 1915)   Educated at the State Academy in Munich, the German violist Walter Trampler played in Berlin (1934–37) and went to the United States in 1939. He was a member of the Boston

Symphony (1942–44) and became a naturalized U.S. citizen. He founded the New Music Quartet and played with it (1947–56). A featured artist at the Casals Festival in Puerto Rico, he has been on the faculties of the Berkshire Music Center, Aspen Festival, Juilliard School (1962–72), Boston University (from 1972), and Yale University. He has appeared as guest artist with the Budapest String Quartet (with whom he recorded the Mozart string quintets), the Juilliard Quartet (with whom he recorded music of Berio), and the Beaux Arts Trio. He frequently performs on the viola d'amore, playing one made by Carcassi in 1743. Hindemith (Sonata), Stravinsky (*Elegy,* 1944), and Max Reger (solo suites) wrote music for him. He plays a 1620 Amati viola.

Transcendental Études: *see* LISZT.

transcription: *see* ARRANGEMENT.

transposing instruments   Instruments that produce pitches different from the notation indicated. Most are wind instruments, such as the B-flat clarinet and B-flat trumpet, whose natural key involves numerous accidentals or that are pitched so high (piccolo) or low (double bassoon) that many ledger lines would be required to notate the actual pitch. In a B-flat instrument, for example, the easiest key to play is B-flat, but the easiest key to read is C; so the notation is a whole tone higher than the actual sound.

   The practice dates from the time before the introduction of valves and keys, when only natural tones were available from most wind instruments. The need no longer exists, but the custom prevails, and 20th-century attempts to change the system by publishing untransposed scores (Schoenberg, Berg, and Webern, for instance) have not met with success. Except for the trombone, almost all wind instruments not pitched in C are transposing instruments or, more accurately, use transposing notation. In the orchestra these include the English horn and French horn, clarinets and trumpets. The double bass is the only string considered a transposing instrument, playing an octave lower than written.

transposition   Writing or performing a composition in a key other than the original. The purpose is almost always to accommodate the range of singers or in the substitution of instruments different from what the composer specified. Transposition is also used, especially in an a cappella chorus, to obtain a brighter or darker sound. Keyboard accompanists often become very adept at transposing at sight.

Traubel, Helen (June 20, 1899–July 28, 1972) A noted U.S. Wagnerian soprano, Helen Traubel made her debut as soloist with the St. Louis Symphony in 1925. In the spring season of the Metropolitan Opera in 1937 she created the role of Mary Rutledge in Walter Damrosch's *The Man Without a Country* and in 1939 made her debut in the regular season as Sieglinde (Wagner's *Die Walküre*). For two years she alternated in Wagnerian roles with Kirsten Flagstad, succeeding her in 1941 as the leading Wagnerian soprano of the company; she was especially acclaimed as Isolde *(Tristan und Isolde)*. In 1953 she resigned from the Metropolitan over a dispute with general manager Rudolf Bing over her appearances in night clubs. She continued to sing in clubs and motion pictures and on radio, television, and Broadway (Rodgers' and Hammerstein's *Pipe Dream,* 1955). She wrote two mystery novels and an autobiography.

Trauersymphonie: (No. 44): *see* CLASSICAL PERIOD (instrumental music, 1750–1800); HAYDN (Esterházy service).

traviata, La: *see* BAND; ROMANTIC PERIOD (non-German music of the 19th century); VERDI.

triad: *see* CHORD.

triangle A percussion instrument consisting of a steel rod bent into a triangular shape, one corner being left open. It is suspended by a loop of gut or nylon and is struck with a beater of the same material and thickness as the instrument itself. As the overtones are inharmonic, the sound produced is theoretically of no definite pitch; in practice, however, players find that some suggestion of pitch is discernible. As a single stroke on the instrument is clearly audible through the full force of the modern symphony orchestra, the triangle is perhaps most effective when used sparingly.

trio Any music in three parts. It originally referred to contrapuntal writing in three parts as in the Baroque TRIO SONATA. The term is also used to refer to a performing group of three voices or instruments.

In the Classical sonata the trio is performed between the minuet or scherzo and its repetition. It evolved from the 17th-century practice of writing minuets and other dances in three parts. Lully, for example, often wrote a second minuet for two oboes and bassoon to be played between the first minuet and its repetition. Bach followed the practice in his First *Brandenburg* Concerto, and the same type of writing for harpsichord is found in his Sixth *French* Suite. In the sonata its purpose was to provide a light relief or change of mood.

In chamber music for three players the most important is the piano trio—piano, violin, and cello. Haydn composed 31 piano trios, and the form developed through Mozart, climaxing in Beethoven and Schubert. The string trio is usually for violin, viola, and cello, though Haydn's 20 string trios are for two violins and cello. Other combinations usually include one or more wind instruments such as Brahms's Opus 40 for horn, violin, and piano and his Opus 114 for clarinet, cello, and piano.

trio sonata A Baroque form of chamber music written for two high melody instruments, typically violins, and continuo (a bass melody

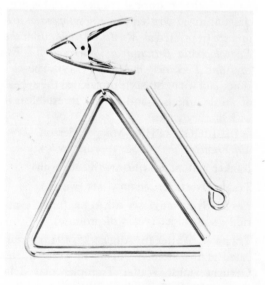

triangle and striking rod
courtesy, Ludwig Industries

instrument such as a viola da gamba, plus a harmony instrument such as the harpsichord). In performance the instrumentation of a given piece might vary, flutes or oboes replacing violins, and bassoon or cello substituting for viola da gamba. Occasionally trio sonatas were performed orchestrally. The genre's texture of one low and two high melody instruments (hence the name trio sonata) plus a harmony instrument was highly favored in the Baroque era not only for the trio sonata but for other forms of orchestral and chamber music.

The trio sonata was the most common variety of Baroque sonata, which developed from the late Renaissance CANZONA, an instrumental piece of several sections in contrapuntal style. In the late 17th and early 18th centuries, there were two types of trio sonata. The *sonata da camera,* or chamber sonata, intended for secular performance, consisted of several movements in dance forms. The *sonata da chiesa,* or church sonata, often more serious in style, normally used an organ as the harmony instrument; the number of its movements varied, but four movements (slow–fast–slow–fast) was a common pattern. There was give-and-take between the two types. The church sonata might contain dance movements, usually not labeled as such, and the chamber sonata often adopted the fugal style typical of the church sonata's opening movement.

Notable composers of trio sonatas include Corelli, Handel, Purcell, François Couperin, and Vivaldi. The trio sonatas for organ or pedal harpsichord of Bach represent an adaptation of the trio sonata format for a solo instrument.

Tristan und Isolde: *see* COUNTERPOINT (Romantic period); HARMONY (Wagnerian harmony); LEITMOTIV; MODERN PERIOD (disintegration of tonality); WAGNER (life), (development), and (influence).

Trittico, Il: *see* PUCCINI.

tromba marina: *see* MARINE TRUMPET.

trombone   A brass wind instrument sounded by lip vibration across a cup mouthpiece. Known in its original form as the SACKBUT, it has an extendable slide whose function is to extend the length of the instrument's tub-

ing. The slide thus performs the function of the valves in other brass instruments. Some trombones are made with valves instead of the slide, but their use was never universal, and in the 20th century they became less common.

The trombone is a 15th-century development of the TRUMPET, with a similar cylindrical bore flared to a bell. The mouthpiece, however, is larger, suited to its deeper musical register, and is parabolic in section like that of a cornet. The slide comprises two parallel and stationary inner tubes, thickened at their lower ends, and two movable outer tubes. The two sets of tubes are moved together by means of a cross-stay manipulated by the player's right hand. The other half of the trombone, the bell joint, passes over the player's left shoulder, counterbalancing the weight of the slide, its bend usually incorporating a tuning slide.

The most common form of the instrument is the tenor trombone, built in B-flat and sounding an octave below the B-flat trumpet. With the slide drawn in (first position), the notes of the harmonic series of the B-flat below the bass staff are available. Shifting the slide a few inches to the second position allows the harmonic series of A, a semitone lower, to be sounded. Further chromatic extensions of the slide progressively lower the key of the instrument to E (seventh position). A chromatic scale is thus available from E below the bass staff. The highest note of the range is determined by the player's ability.

Many orchestral instruments are Bb–F trombones. These have an F attachment consisting of a coil of extra tubing placed in the loop of the bell. A rotary valve actuated by the left thumb connects this attachment to the main tube, thus lowering the pitch of the instrument by a fourth. The scale can then be extended below low E down to C, the additional low notes known as fundamentals, or pedals. Trombones vary in bore. The older narrow bore, no wider than that of a trumpet, was largely superseded by medium and large bores, with wider bells reaching nine and one-half inches (24 centimeters) in diameter. The widest bores are made for playing bass trombone parts. The mid-20th-century vogue of

modern B♭-F trombone   courtesy, C. G. Conn Corporation, Ltd.

the trombone as a virtuoso instrument in dance music is mainly associated with a B-flat tenor instrument of medium-large bore.

Trombones of the 16th century differ from 20th-century models in little but narrow bells and details of craftsmanship. Extensively used in polyphonic part music, they were built in alto, tenor, and bass sizes, the treble part having been supplied by the cornett. This arrangement survives in the trombone trio of classical orchestration, the parts being respectively written in the old vocal clefs—alto, tenor, and bass. Orchestral trombonists normally read in these three clefs. (In brass bands the tenor trombone is written in the treble clef to sound a ninth lower.) In the 19th century pitches of orchestral trombones varied: the alto trombone was in E-flat or F, the tenor in B-flat or C, the bass in low F or G. Some orchestral players use an E-flat alto trombone for its good effect in the higher register prescribed by Schumann and others. A bass trombone in G in used in many British bands and orchestras, often with a D attachment corresponding to the F attachment on the B-flat instrument. Some Italian bands use a bass trombone in F with valves. But in the main the old bass trombones were superseded by the B♭–F designs. The contrabass trombone, demanded by Wagner in *The Ring* and later by Stravinsky, is in C or B-flat an octave below the tenor and has either a double slide (to keep the shifts within the reach of the arm) or valves.

Though specified occasionally by composers as early as Bach and Handel (for reinforcing voice parts) and used by Mozart and Beethoven, it was not until after 1850 with Berlioz and Wagner that the trombone was an estab-lished member of the orchestra. Solo literature includes a Concerto (1878) by Rimsky-Korsakov, Ballade (1940) by Frank Martin, and Sonata (1942) by Hindemith. In the 20th century it has been used in chamber music by such composers as Stravinsky, Poulenc, Hindemith, and Henry Cowell.

BIBLIOGRAPHY: Robin Gregory, *The Trombone: The Instrument and Its Music* (1973); Philip Bate, *The Trumpet and Trombone,* rev. ed. (1978); C. Robert Wigness, *The Soloistic Use of the Trombone in Eighteenth-Century Vienna* (1978).

trope   In medieval church music, a melody, explicatory text, or both added to a plainchant melody. Tropes are of two general types: those adding a new text to a melisma (section of music having one syllable extended over many notes) and those inserting new music, usually with words, between existing sections of melody and text.

Troping was rooted in similar practices in the ancient Byzantine liturgy and arose in the West by the 8th century, probably in France. The custom reached the musically important Swiss monastery of Saint Gall by the 9th century and soon became widespread throughout Europe. It was abolished in the 16th century by the Council of Trent.

Two important medieval musical-literary forms developed from the trope: the LITURGI-CAL DRAMA and the SEQUENCE. A troped chant is sometimes called a farced (*i.e.,* interpolated) chant.

troubadour or **troubador**   The lyric poet-musician of southern France, northern Spain, and northern Italy who wrote in the langue d'oc of Provence from the late 11th to the late 13th century.

Troubadours' social influence was unprecedented in the history of medieval poetry. Favored at court, they had great freedom of speech, occasionally intervening even in the political arena, but their great achievement was to create around the ladies of the court an aura of cultivation and amenity that nothing had hitherto approached. Troubadour poetry formed one of the most brilliant schools that ever flourished, and it was to influence all later European lyrical poetry.

The word troubadour is a French form derived ultimately from the Occitanian *trobar*, "to find," "to invent." A troubadour was thus one who invented new poems, finding new verse for elaborate love lyrics. Much of the troubadours' work has survived, preserved in manuscripts known as *chansonniers* ("songbooks"), and the rules by which their art was governed are set out in a work called *Leys d'amors* (1340). The verse form they used most frequently was the canso, consisting of five or six stanzas with an envoi. They also used the *dansa,* or *balada,* a dance song with a refrain; the *pastorela,* telling the tale of the love request by a knight to a shepherdess; the *jeu parti,* or *débat,* a debate on love between two poets; the alba, or morning song, in which lovers are warned by a nightwatchman that day approaches and that the jealous husband may at any time surprise them. Other forms were frameworks for a lyrical conversation between two or more persons discussing, as a rule, some point of amorous casuistry or matters of a religious, metaphysical, or satirical character.

Troubadour songs are monophonic and comprise a major extant body of medieval secular music. Somewhat fewer than 300 melodies survive; they display a certain consistency of style but are far more varied than was once suspected.

Some of the melodies were composed by the poets themselves. The Provençal "life" of the troubadour Jaufré Rudel states that he wrote many songs "with fine melodies but poor texts." Evidently the writer thought the melodies were by Jaufré and that his distinction lay therein.

Many of the melodies, however, were not by the poet. According to a contemporary account, Raimbaut de Vaqueyras wrote his famous poem "Kalenda maya" to a dance tune played by some fiddle players at Montferrat. At least four troubadour songs are based directly on Latin sacred melodies. Several troubadour melodies are slightly different in form from the poem to which they are attached, and it must be assumed that these were originally composed for another poem, perhaps in another language. Conversely many troubadour melodies were appropriated from songs in French and German. Even when a melody was written expressly for its poem, it is possible that the poet devised it with the help of a more experienced musician. Most of the poems have attributions, for the poets valued their originality. For the music, however, anonymity was the rule; authorship was a subsidiary consideration.

In their poems the troubadours avoided copying stanza patterns from others. The melodies, however, show an increasing use of an *a a b* form, repeated identically for each stanza, with the *b* section repeated at the end of the song for the *tornada* (short final stanza). The pattern is rarely more complicated. Dante, in his description of troubadour songs, gave pride of place to the *oda continua,* a melody without any repetitions within the stanza. This is the form for some of the finest songs in the tradition, such as Bernard de Ventadour's "Quan vei l'aloete mover" ("When I see the lark rise") and Arnaut Daniel's comic sestina "Lo ferm voler."

The earliest melodies show many connections with Latin church music. Similar influences are dominant in the 19 surviving melodies for songs by Bernard de Ventadour and even in the 48 very late melodies for poems of Guiraut Riquier, among the finest of the repertoire.

An entirely different style is found in some music for songs by Peire Vidal, Folquet de Marseille, and Gaucelm Faidit. The tonal center seems to shift with an abandon foreign to the known European chant of the time. If the hotly disputed Arabic influence on troubadour poetry is also to be found in the music, perhaps it is in these strange songs, although there survives no early Arabic music to prove it.

From the later 12th century folk song elements occasionally appear, probably under the influence of the TROUVÈRE, the troubadour's French-language counterpart to the north. Thus Guiraut de Borneilh stated that he started by writing in the fashionably complex style of the *trobar clus* (a verse form) and then cultivated a simpler manner so that anyone could sing his work.

The performance and notation of the troubadour music had much in common with that of the trouvères. Because the notation in which the music survives does not indicate rhythm, the edition for modern performance is a subject of lively dispute. Many of the songs in popular style should possibly be interpreted with a regular meter. Some scholars propose, others strongly oppose, the use of the medieval rhythmic modes (short triple-rhythm patterns based on poetic meters). Troubadour poetry was apparently constructed not accentually but on a syllable count. Further, many songs show a strongly melismatic style rooted in the Roman-Frankish chant traditions, and their qualities are seriously obscured by the superimposition of rhythmic patterns. The wide range of styles among the melodies makes it unlikely that one solution is uniformly appropriate.

BIBLIOGRAPHY: Henry John Chaytor, *The Troubadours* (1912; reprint, 1970); Pierre Aubry, *Trouvères and Troubadours: A Popular Treatise* (1914); John Arnold Fleming, *The Troubadours of Provence* (1952; reprint, 1977); Robert Briffault, *The Troubadours* (1965); Hendrik van der Werf, *The Chansons of the Troubadours and Trouvères* (1972); Linda M. Paterson, *Troubadours and Eloquence* (1975); Jack Lindsay, *The Troubadours and Their World* (1976).

Trout Quintet: *see* CHAMBER MUSIC; QUINTET; SCHUBERT (maturity).

trouvère The 12th- and 13th-century lyric poet-musician of northern France, the counterpart of the Provençal TROUBADOUR from whom was derived highly stylized themes and metrical forms. The essence of trouvère rhetoric lies in the combination of traditional themes and the use of established forms in which to express them. The audience gained pleasure from familiarity with these clichés rather than from the poet's originality. It is thus perhaps the least characteristic trouvères, such as Rutebeuf (flourished 1250–80), generally considered the last and greatest of the trouvères, who are most appreciated today.

Communication between northern and southern France was facilitated and encouraged by the Crusades, and a number of trouvères, such as the Châtelaine de Coucy and Conon de Béthune, took part in them. However, the trouvères developed a lyric poetry distinct from that of the troubadours, and unlike the latter they did not prize obscurity of metaphor for its own sake. Their poetry is sometimes satirical and sometimes (as in the case of Colin Muset) concerned with the pleasures of the good life, but the basic theme remains that of courtly love in which the poet describes his unrequited (and adulterous) passion for an inaccessible lady.

Although originally connected with feudal courts, around which the trouvères traveled looking for patronage, their poetry was not only popular with aristocratic circles, and they tended increasingly to find their patrons in the middle classes. Half the extant trouvère lyrics are the work of a guild of citizen poets of Arras. Many of the trouvères, such as Gace Brûlé (late 12th century), were of aristocratic birth; Thibaut de Champagne (1201–53) was King of Navarre. But others, including Rutebeuf, were of humble origin.

The texts of about 4,000 trouvère poems survive along with the music for about 1,400 of them. The songs were monophonic. Their exact mode of performance is not known. Probably they were sometimes sung with instrumental accompaniment provided by a hired musician, or minstrel; or possibly both singing and accompaniment were performed by minstrels. The form of the accompaniment is unknown, but it almost certainly included instrumental preludes, postludes, and interludes.

The trouvères used a variety of musical forms, some for any of several of the various poetic categories and some linked to the type of the verse. Four broad categories can be discerned: forms based on multiple repetitions of a short phrase, as in a litany; dance songs with refrains; songs based on pairs of repeated lines; and through-composed songs.

Perhaps the oldest structure in trouvère music is the litany associated with epic verse such as the chansons de geste. Well suited to the performance of a long, sectional, but non-strophic poem, it comprised in its simplest form a repeated phrase sung for all but the last line of a section, and a final phrase for the last line *(a a a. . .b)*. A common elaboration of the form is the pattern *ab ab ab. . .c,* found in the *chantefable Aucassin et Nicolette* and also used for settings of strophic verse.

In the dance songs with refrain the term refrain has a special meaning, referring to the recurrence of a line of text not merely at the end of each stanza but also—in whole or in part—within the stanza. It is believed that the refrains, at least at first, were sung chorally in response to the solo lines sung by the dance leader. The dance songs consisted of two or more musical phrases repeated in given patterns, sometimes with the text of the verse, sometimes with that of the refrain; the refrain pattern was an important clue to the musical form of the piece. All of the refrain forms were subject to variation, and they did not always fall into the formal patterns of the later polyphonic songs in those forms: BALLADE, RONDEAU, and VIRELAI.

Songs in which the musical form is based on pairs of repeated lines derive from the sequence, basically a series of repeated sections, often with an unrepeated prelude and unrepeated postlude. This form or one of its variants was used in secular songs of the lai type (basically long poems with irregular stanzas). Short songs with repeated sections are also classifiable here. Compositions with no repetition within the stanza include the *vers* and the chanson. In the chanson, however, a short initial section is repeated, and a piece of the opening section may recur at the end.

Most surviving trouvère music is written in a notation that indicates the pitch of the notes but not their relative duration or accentuation, an omission that has given rise to much debate as to rhythmic interpretation in editions for modern performance.

BIBLIOGRAPHY: Pierre Aubry, *Trouvères and Troubadours: A Popular Treatise* (1914); Hendrik van der Werf, *The Chansons of the Troubadours and Trouvères* (1972).

trovatore, Il: *see* ROMANTIC PERIOD (non-German music of the 19th century); VERDI.

Troyens, Les: *see* BERLIOZ; LIBRETTO (19th-century influences) and (modern status); OPERA (the 19th century).

trumpet A brass wind instrument sounded by lip vibration across a cup-mouthpiece. Its history dates from about 1500 B.C. in Egypt, when it was a small ritual or military instrument producing only one or two sounds. It came into prominence as a musical instrument in the late Middle Ages, later forms being the natural trumpet of the 16th to the 18th century and the valve trumpet from 1813. This is ordinarily built in B-flat. It maintains the traditional trumpet bore, cylindrical with a terminal bell flare, though usually the bore tapers toward the mouthpiece to provide additional flexibility of tone. The bend near the bell incorporates a tuning slide. The compass ranges from F-sharp below the treble staff to well above the staff, and the music is notated a tone higher than the sounded notes. As with most brass instruments, the highest note is determined by the player's ability; G, four lines above the staff, is employed by some dance band players.

In addition to the B-flat trumpet, instruments in several other keys are frequently used. Some players, especially in France, use a higher trumpet in C. Higher still is the piccolo trumpet in D, invented by Victor Charles Mahillon about 1890, for the high obbligati parts in the music of Bach and Handel. Continental bands sometimes still include the older type of trumpet in E-flat, a fifth lower than the B-flat trumpet. The bass trumpet demanded by Wagner in *The Ring* is in B-flat or C, an octave lower than the ordinary B-flat trumpet.

In order to play notes outside the natural series, various trumpets with a sliding section of the tube were devised from the Renaissance onward, the most important being the TROMBONE. A German trumpet with sliding mouthpipe, the *tromba da tirarsi,* was some-

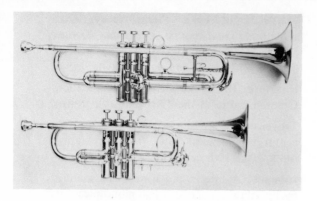

modern trumpets in (right) Bb and (left) D
courtesy, Boosey & Hawkes, Ltd.

times used for chorale melodies in the music of Bach. The English flat trumpet (*c.* 1695) had a sliding upper bend near the mouthpiece; it later reappeared as the slide trumpet much used in 19th-century English orchestras. In Austria and Italy after 1798 a vogue for the keyed trumpet, with side holes covered by padded keys and a full chromatic scale, followed Anton Weidinger's performances of the concertos for this instrument by Haydn and others.

The valved trumpet appeared in Germany about 1818 and was introduced into France about 1820. It was usually pitched in F. Its adoption in the United States and Britain was delayed in the course of the 19th century by the preference of most players for the cornet in orchestral trumpet parts. By the time the valved trumpet in F was accepted in Britain (*c.* 1890), Germany and France had already favored the smaller B-flat trumpet.

Solo repertoire includes concertos by Haydn, Johann Nepomuk Hummel, and Leopold Mozart, sonatas by Purcell (with strings), Hindemith (piano), and Alan Hovhaness (organ), and such works as Vincent Persichetti's *Hollow Men* (1946) for trumpet and strings and Copland's *Quiet City* (1940) for trumpet, English horn, and orchestra.

BIBLIOGRAPHY: Johann Ernst Altenburg, *Trumpeters' and Kettledrummers' Art* (1795; reprint, 1974); Werner Menke, *History of the Trumpet of Bach and Handel* (1960; reprint, 1972); J. Murray Barbour, *Trumpets, Horns, and Music* (1964); Don Smithers; *The Music and History of the Baroque Trumpet*

before 1721 (1973); Reine Dahlquist, *The Keyed Trumpet and Its Greatest Virtuoso: Anton Weidinger,* rev. ed. (1975); Philip Bate, *The Trumpet and Trombone,* rev. ed. (1978).

tuba Originally a Roman trumpet, straight-built and from three to four feet long. The term now refers to a deep-pitched brass instrument with valves and of wide conical bore. Fourteen years after the invention of the valve mechanism in Berlin about 1815, bass valved instruments for bands are mentioned, but little is now known about them. In 1835, again in Berlin, Wilhelm Wieprecht and Johann Gottfried Moritz patented the bass tuba in F with five valves. Subsequent designs were considerably influenced by the French saxhorn contrebasse.

Modern military and brass band tubas, known as basses, are of two sizes, used together. They are the E-flat bass (or bombardon) and BB-flat bass, a fourth lower. With three valves their lowest notes are respectively A below the bass staff and the E below that. The E-flat bass generally has a fourth valve that lowers the pitch by a fourth, giving the low E below which the compass can be continued downward in fundamentals, E-flat, D, etc. These basses are held aslant the body with the bell pointing to the right. In the United States the bell may be turned forward. Alternative designs, likewise in E-flat and BB-flat

military brass band tuba
courtesy, Boosey & Hawkes, Ltd.

but encircling the body, include circular basses, or helicons, with the bell resting across one shoulder, and the U.S. sousaphone, with a very wide bell raised above the player's head.

Orchestral tubas vary in different countries. Large instruments in BB-flat, or a note higher in C, are used in the United States and some European countries. The original pitch of F is preferred in Great Britain and (with rotary valves) in Germany. All have the fourth valve and often a fifth valve tuned to a wide semitone for facilitating good intonation in certain fingerings. Some English tubas incorporated D. J. Blaikley's compensating valves. French orchestras use a small C tuba pitched a fifth above the F tuba. This is a six-valved development of the earlier saxhorn basse. Tuba parts are written at actual pitch (except in brass bands where transposed notation in treble clef allows the parts to be read with cornet fingering). The tenor tuba is normally the military band EUPHONIUM. Vaughan Williams wrote a Concerto (1954) and Gunther Schuller a Capriccio (1960) for tuba and orchestra and *Five Moods* (1972) for tuba quartet.

The Wagner tuba, or Bayreuth tuba, was designed for Wagner's *Ring*. Four are required: two tenor tubas in B-flat (the same pitch as the euphonium) and two bass tubas in F, a fourth lower. They are four-valved small-bored tubas to be played by French horn players with horn mouthpieces, and they were also used by Bruckner and Richard Strauss.

Tucker, Richard (August 28, 1914–January 8, 1975) A student of Paul Althouse, the U.S. tenor Richard Tucker sang in synagogues from his youth. He made his Metropolitan Opera debut in 1945 as Enzo in *La Gioconda* (Amilcare Ponchielli). He remained a leading tenor at the Metropolitan and sang in Europe between seasons. His recordings encompass much of the standard Italian repertoire, especially the operas of Verdi and Puccini. A popular recitalist throughout North America, he continued to be heard as a synagogue cantor. He was brother-in-law to the tenor Jan Peerce.

Tuckwell, Barry (b. March 5, 1931) One of the few horn players to make a career as a touring soloist, the Australian Barry Tuckwell began playing the horn when he was 13 and studied at the Sydney Conservatory. At 15 he joined the Melbourne Symphony and six months later the Sydney Symphony, moving to England in 1950. He was a member of the Hallé Orchestra and the Scottish National Orchestra before playing first horn for the London Symphony (1955–68). Tuckwell did not take formal lessons after his youth, but he credits Dennis Brain, Gottfried von Freiburg, and Tommy Dorsey as major influences on his playing.

tune: *see* AIR; MELODY.

tuning and temperament Musical temperament refers to the exact details of the placement of notes in a scale or the precise tuning or choice of the frequency ratios of the tones. Well-known temperaments are named and include equal, just, Pythagorean, and Werckmeister III and other meantone temperaments. There are two bodies of natural law that form the bases for scales and their tuning. These have to do with the physical nature of musical sound and the psychoacoustic phenomena of human hearing. These will be discussed briefly, and a scale will be formed to illustrate the problems involved. Conscious compromises in temperament must be made to build workable musical scales and instru-

Richard Tucker as Rodolfo in La Bohème
courtesy, Metropolitan Opera Archives

ments. Some of the problems in this area will be discussed along with their attempted solutions. Finally, a few comments on the lore of temperaments will be made.

physical and psychoacoustic bases for temperament A musical tone produced by a real instrument is made up of a collection of different frequencies, or partials, sounding together. In a sustained tone, such as that produced by an organ pipe, the partials are harmonic; *i.e.*, they are integral (1, 2, 3 . . .) multiples of the lowest partial, called the fundamental. In a percussive stringed instrument such as the piano, the higher partials depart progressively from the integer-multiple relationship and become more and more sharp because of string stiffness. Brasses, woodwinds, and bowed strings produce more or less harmonic partials except for the modifications produced by the normal playing transients. Percussives such as bells and drums have essentially nonharmonic partials except that considerable tuning of partials is possible. When two tones are sounded together all the partials interact and all the strong ones influence the exact choice of tuning. It can be imagined that problems arise in trying to choose exact tunings to allow these diverse instruments to play together acceptably.

The cochlea of the inner ear analyzes sound according to frequency, with high frequencies causing most stimulation of the entry region and low frequencies penetrating to the innermost region. Each pure tone (only one frequency, or partial) has its own region of maximum stimulation. When a second tone is within that region (within the critical bandwidth), the two interact and produce beats and dissonance. When the second is outside the critical bandwidth of the first, we hear two separate tones. When the two tones have nearly the same frequency, we hear beats— the familiar *wah-wah-wah* sound as two instruments are tuned together. The beat occurs at a frequency that is the difference between the two frequencies. Our ears readily perceive beats of a few cycles per second, but at rates of around 10 Hz. (abbreviation for hertz, a unit of frequency for cycle[s] per second) the individual beats are lost, and we perceive a roughness, or dissonance. Finding note pairs

that avoid beating and dissonance in their adjacent and interacting partials has been the basis of the formation and tuning of scales. For example, if two musical tones with many harmonic partials have a frequency ratio of 3 to 2 (the upper note has a frequency of 1.5 times the lower one), even-numbered partials of the upper note coincide exactly with odd partials of the lower note and produce no beats. At the same time the alternate partials are far from each other and produce no dissonant interaction. This interval is the very consonant musical fifth (for example C–G). This interval, and others like it, are fundamental to the musical scales of all cultures. The use, avoidance, and abuse of these anchor notes in the scale vary, but all music recognizes them, and all temperament schemes hinge on them.

interaction of partials Before discussing the building of a scale, an overview picture of an entire scale, showing the partials of all the notes, is instructive to help visualize the interactions of the partials. Figure 1 shows the notes and partials of a chromatic just-tempered scale with marks to allow comparison with an equal-tempered scale.

The tonic note, to which all others are related, appears at the bottom left and is labeled "C" (by custom). The harmonic partials of C are numbered up the left ordinate, and horizontal lines are drawn from each to facilitate comparison with the partials of the other notes. The vertical lines represent each note of the scale, and the diagonal lines show the position of each partial of each note. If a note is made flat all the partials of that note slide down the diagonal lines to the left; if it is made sharp they slide up to the right. Thus tuning brings them into and out of coincidence with other partials. The labeling under each note gives the name of the interval and the ratio of the frequency of that note to that of the tonic.

technical digression on frequency and cents The actual frequency of any note or any partial is not necessary in discussing temperament, but it can be found by multiplying together the frequency ratio of that note to the tonic, the number of the partial of interest, and the frequency of the tonic. Thus to com-

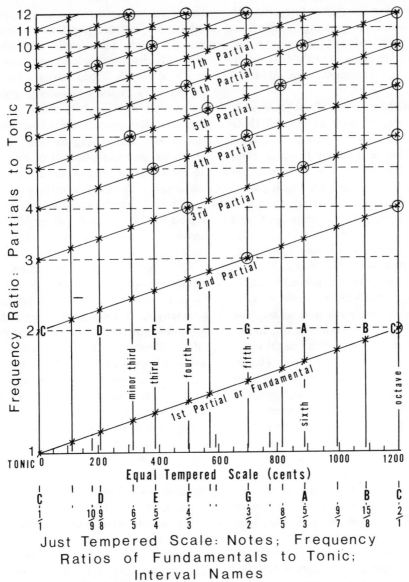

Figure 1
Relationships among frequencies of partials of the notes of a just scale. Unequal spacing of the notes is clearly seen. An equal-tempered scale is marked for comparison.
drawing by E. Paul Palmer

pute the frequency of the fourth partial of G, multiply ³⁄₂ (the ratio of G to C) by 4 (the partial of interest) and by 261.63 Hz. (the frequency of middle C, the tonic). The result is 1569.78 Hz., which is exactly equal to the frequency of the sixth partial of C, or 6 × 261.63, so that these two partials produce no beating.

The cent is a logarithmic measure of the frequency ratio of two notes and is designed to correspond to the logarithmic (octave) nature of musical scales and keyboards. Cents can be added and subtracted to study ratios rather than the awkward multiplying and dividing necessary with ratios. The cent value of a ratio is defined by: (cents) = 3986 log(R), where R is the fractional ratio of the two notes. The 3986 is 1200/log2. The cent value of an equal-tempered half step is 100, and of an octave is 1200. A frequency ratio of 4 or 5 cents begins to be discernible. A just-tempered fifth is 702 cents, which is not distinguishable from the equal-tempered value of 700 cents. A just minor third of 316 cents is easily distinguishable from the equal-tempered interval of 300 cents.

In Figure 1 the position of each partial of each note is marked with an X, and those that coincide exactly with a partial of the tonic are circled. Observe the building-block notes of the scale; first, the octave C, with a frequency twice that of the tonic: each partial coincides perfectly with one from the tonic. The two notes are perfectly consonant, and octaves are the natural basis of all scales. The fifth, C–G, has been mentioned. The important musical interval of the fourth, C–F, is similar except that two partials miss coincidence by an appreciable distance, the next coincides, the next two miss, and so on. The sixth, C–A, follows the same pattern. In the case of the third, C–E, the third and fifth partials are impinging well into the critical bandwidths associated with the fourth and sixth partials of the tonic. This gives roughness, but the partials are not close enough together to give beats. This interval was considered dissonant and was avoided by many early composers. Contrast these building-block notes with the dissonant seventh, C–B. Here the first, second, sixth, and seventh partials interact roughly, and the first coincidence occurs with the eighth partial. Then the ninth and 10th are dissonant and so on.

Figure 1 is designed to show the relationships with the tonic. The relationships between other notes can be found by drawing horizontal lines through the partials of the desired note and comparing them with the others. For example, comparing E with G we find an interval of a minor third with the same partial pattern as the minor third from C to E-flat.

building a scale Scales are built by filling in the gaps between the basic beat-free notes and trying to adjust or temper the exact frequencies for the best results. The building-block notes—customarily called C, E, F, G, and A—are easy to find because slight mistuning gives strong beating between the partials that should be exactly coincident. This cannot

be done using electronic, pure-tone, sine-wave oscillators without partials; it requires real musical tones. Historically this theory was first fully developed using organ pipes sounding loudly with strong partials. These basic notes form a five-note pentatonic scale, which was widely used in early music. The second step is to start from these five basic notes (plus the octave) and—using the same procedure involving beat-free intervals of third, fourth, and fifth—fill in the gaps of the 12-note chromatic scale. The total procedure is illustrated in Figure 2, which could actually be used as a plan for tuning an organ by following the arrows. This is one version of a just-tempered scale.

Some problems are immediately obvious: There are two Ds, two notes between F and G, and two between G and A! Actually there are many more notes, well recognized, arising from different versions of just intonation. The intervals between these near-neighbor notes are well known and named; for example, the 22 cents between the two Ds is a syntonic comma, and the 42 cents between G-sharp and A-flat is the diesis.

As a first approach to solving the problem, choose one of the Ds and live with it. The upper D might be more useful (in major scales) because the D–G relationship is possibly used more than D–A. Similar choices can be made for the other notes. This works fairly well when the music is restricted to key signatures involving only one or two sharps or flats.

Another approach is to try another procedure for arriving at the tones. One can use only intervals of fourths and fifths (plus octaves). This produces the Pythagorean scale. It has a new set of problems in that the major and minor thirds are out of tune. As another approach a circle of fifths (plus octaves)—C, G, D, A, E, B, F♯, C♯, G♯, D♯, A♯, F, and back to C—gives all the notes; but if each interval is tuned beat free, the octave comes out wrong, and that is unacceptable. Various meantone tunings have been developed to divide the differences between the two Ds (and the others) in equal or unequal parts. The Werkmeister III scale, for example, makes a few adjustments to the just scale to bring it more in tune in keys using more than two

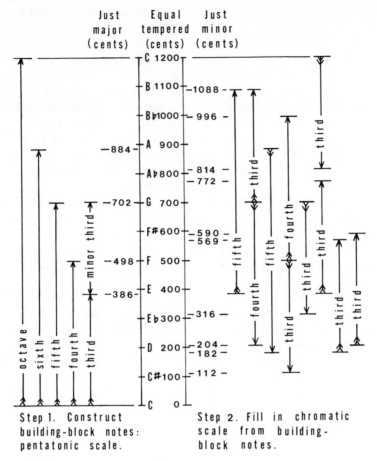

Step 1. Construct building-block notes: pentatonic scale.

Step 2. Fill in chromatic scale from building-block notes.

Figure 2
Building a pentatonic scale and filling in the gaps to form a 12-note chromatic scale. Only consonant, beat-free intervals are used. The origins of double notes D-D, F♯-G♭, and G♯-A♭ are shown. *drawing by E. Paul Palmer*

flats or sharps without compromising the key of C too much.

A completely different approach, which has actually been tried, is to use separate keyboard keys (and separate organ pipes) for each of the Ds and other required multiple notes. This has been rejected by players as too cumbersome and of little ultimate value.

central problem of temperament The major problem with all these scales has been hinted at. It is that the harmonious beat-free relations upon which the scale was built disappear when modulating to keys containing sharps and flats; the scales and chords are out of tune. For example, the beat-free major triad (plus octave) C, E, G, (C) has the follow-

ing ratios expressed in cents in just temperament.

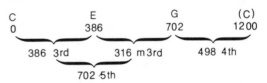

The major triad E♭, G, B♭, (E♭), which uses none of the double notes we have mentioned, is out of tune.

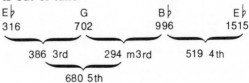

827

The fifth is too narrow, the minor third is too narrow, and the fourth is too wide—all by the ubiquitous 22-cent syntonic comma that originally appeared elsewhere. All this is cured by raising B-flat by 22 cents to 1018 cents, but now the chord B♭, D, F, (B♭) beginning on the new B-flat is out of tune. The F must be moved up just as the B-flat was previously, but this leads to worse problems in other chords using the F. Leaving the B-flat where it was makes the third wide and leaves the minor third narrow. There is no solution to this problem of changing keys if beat-free just tuning is desired!

The practical approach has been equal temperament, or making each half step exactly the same frequency ratio above its predecessor. Since the octave is divided into 12 parts, each ratio is $2^{\frac{1}{12}} = 1.05946$. Expressed in cents this is 100 cents. As a percentage each half step is 5.946% above its predecessor. This compromise makes all scales equally bad or equally good, depending on one's point of view.

The table compares the just major and minor and the equal-tempered scales in frequency ratios and in cents. The equal-tempered scale has good (beat-free) fourths and fifths in all keys and somewhat dissonant major and minor thirds.

comments on tempering With modern music's use of many keys and key changes, and with musical instrument standardization, equal tempering dominates. Some historic organs still use other tunings. Bach was a great proponent of the equal-tempered scale, and much of his music avoids dwelling on the harsh, out-of-tune major and minor thirds. Other music of his and earlier eras was composed for just-tuned organs and made extensive use of thirds. It is uncomfortable on modern organs.

There is a residual musical mysticism surrounding the just-tempered scale as if it were a goal to be sought or a standard by which to measure all temperaments. Although its beat-free intervals formed the basis of all scales, many problems have led to its virtual abandonment. Studies have indicated that string ensembles and a cappella choruses, which are free to choose the best-sounding temperament, actually choose something closer to the discredited Pythagorean temperament than the just. Excessive preoccupation with a few nonbeating partials overlooks the total effect of the interaction of many partials of many notes.

The piano presents special problems. It is tuned to some nominal equal temperament.

Note	Interval Name	Just Major		Just Minor		Equal Temperament		
C	Octave	2/1	1200¢	2/1	1200¢	$2^{12/12}$	= 2.0000	1200¢
B	major 7th	15/8	1088			$2^{11/12}$	= 1.8877	1100
B♭	minor 7th			9/5	1018	$2^{10/12}$	= 1.7818	1000
A	major 6th	5/3	884			$2^{9/12}$	= 1.6818	900
A♭	minor 6th			8/5	814	$2^{8/12}$	= 1.5874	800
G	perfect 5th	3/2	702	3/2	702	$2^{7/12}$	= 1.4983	700
F#	—					$2^{6/12}$	= 1.4142	600
F	perfect 4th	4/3	498	4/3	498	$2^{5/12}$	= 1.3348	500
E	major 3rd	5/4	386			$2^{4/12}$	= 1.2599	400
E♭	minor 3rd			6/5	316	$2^{3/12}$	= 1.1892	300
D	major 2nd	9/8	204			$2^{2/12}$	= 1.1225	200
D	minor 2nd			10/9	182			
C#	—					$2^{1/12}$	= 1.0595	100
C	unison	1/1	0	1/1	0	2^{0}	= 1.0000	0

Comparison of frequency ratios in fractions and cents for just major and minor and equal-tempered scales. Both Ds are used—one major and one minor. A♭ is the upper one of Figure 2. B♭ is new, fitting the minor scale.

However, the partials of any single note are progressively sharp so that it must be tuned with slightly stretched octaves to make it sound good with itself. It ends up about 30 cents or one-third semitone sharp at the top and one-third semitone flat at the low end when compared with strict equal-tempered tuning. When the piano is used to accompany other instruments, musicians can usually make slight adjustments while playing to maintain satisfactory intonation. These adjustments are not possible with an organ, and the strict equal temperament of the organ (resulting from its strictly harmonic partials) will make it out of tune with a piano at both ends of its range.

summary As music lovers we seem to have only a few choices left. We can listen to music too fast to allow tuning to be considered, or to inherently dissonant music, or to music so soft that no higher partials are excited to interact, or to electronic oscillators with no high partials; or we can try to enjoy what the composer and performers are doing with only a few backward glances at the fine points of temperament.

BIBLIOGRAPHY: Arthur H. Benade, *Fundamentals of Musical Acoustics* (1976); John Backus, *The Acoustical Foundations of Music,* rev. ed. (1977).

E. Paul Palmer

tuning fork A narrow, two-pronged steel bar that when tuned to a specific pitch retains its tuning almost indefinitely. It was apparently invented by Handel's trumpeter John Shore (d. 1752). Because it produces a nearly pure tone (without overtones), it is useful in experimental study of the physics of sound. It has also been used in musical instruments—*e.g.,* the dulcitone, or typophone, a set of graduated tuning forks struck by felt hammers by means of a keyboard mechanism.

Turandot: *see* GONG; OPERA (the 19th century); PUCCINI.

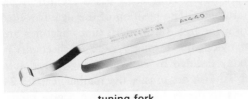

tuning fork

Turangalîla-Symphonie: *see* MESSIAEN; MODERN PERIOD (rediscovery of serialism); RONDO.

Tureck, Rosalyn (b. December 14, 1914) A student of Olga Samaroff at the Juilliard School, the U.S. pianist and harpsichordist Rosalyn Tureck is known primarily for her playing of Bach. She first performed Bach's complete 48 preludes and fugues of the *Well-Tempered Clavier* and the *Goldberg* Variations in a series of six recitals in New York City's Town Hall in 1937. She has taught in Philadelphia, New York City, and San Diego and published *An Introduction to the Performance of Bach* (1960).

Turina (y Pérez), Joaquín (December 9, 1882–January 14, 1949) A Spanish composer who helped to promote the national character of 20th-century Spanish music, Joaquín Turina studied at Seville and Madrid and in 1905 went to Paris, where he was a pupil of Moritz Moszkowski in piano and d'Indy in composition. Though he absorbed elements of the French style, he was inspired in Paris by Albéniz to establish a distinctively Spanish style. He wrote Sonata *española* for violin and piano and the symphonic poem *La Procesión del Rocío* (1912) and in 1913 returned to Spain, where he quickly made his reputation. His native city of Seville figures largely in his predominantly picturesque works, notably in the *Sinfonía sevillana* (1920), *Canto a Sevilla* (1927) for voice and orchestra, and in his albums of piano miniatures, among them *Rincones sevillanos* and *La leyenda de la Giralda.* He was most successful in his many songs. He also wrote two operas, *Margot* (Madrid, 1914) and *Jardín de oriente* (Madrid, 1923), incidental music, and chamber works. He taught composition at the Madrid Conservatory from 1931, headed the music division of the National Education Ministry from 1941, was critic of the Madrid newspaper *El debate,* and wrote a short musical encyclopedia.

RECORDINGS: *Danzas fantásticas; Danzas gitanas;* Piano Trio No. 1.

Turkish music In classical Western music Turkish music denotes music influenced by 18th-century Janissary bands of wind and percussion instruments attached to the imperial Ottoman court and to the households of its envoys in the capitals of Europe. These bands contributed bass drum, kettledrum, cymbals, and triangle to the orchestra, and their influence led to the modern military band. *See* JANISSARY MUSIC.

types of music (1) Traditional folk music has been the least influenced by high Turkish culture and survives among remnants of the nomadic Turks of Anatolia, who are culturally close to the Turkmens of Soviet Turkmenistan and of Afghanistan. The repertoire includes vocal and instrumental genres—epics, ballads, dance songs, dance tunes, laments, etc. (2) Traditional art music (classical Turkish music) ranges from survivals of late medieval song traditions to music of the 17th to the 19th century. (3) Religious music overlaps the preceding, but certain styles of solo chanting are used exclusively in a religious context: the call to prayer *(ezan);* the reading of the Koran *(Koran okumak);* the singing of *na'at* (in glorification of the Prophet); *kaside,* eulogistic or commemorative verses; and *Mevlût* (Arabic, *Mavlid*), chanted in celebration of the Prophet's birthday. Chanting is improvised within the tradition for each genre. Measured religious songs include hymns *(ilâhi)* and canticles *(temcid).* The most highly organized compositions are suitelike sequences of instrumental and vocal compositions, the rites *(âyin)* of the Mevlevî dervishes. (4) Urban popular music includes the simple, short form of art song, the *şarki*—a song of unrequited passion, and survivals from an earlier era of cafe music and transient hits. Notwithstanding the presence of radio, the influence of Western music has been minimal. (5) Modern Western art music was introduced to Turkey by Joseph Marx and Hindemith, who were engaged by the Turkish government for the purpose in the 1930s. The best-known native composers are Ahmed Adnan Saygun, who wrote an oratorio *Yunus Emre* (1942) and an opera *Kerem* (1953), and Ulvi Cemal Erkin.

history The development of Turkish art music owed much to the musical culture of the Islamic world between the 8th and the 13th century. The music of the Arab conquerors was transformed in contact with Persian

culture; some of the most influential musical theorists of the Arabic world were wholly or partly of Turkish stock though of Islamic culture—men such as al-Farabi, born of a Turkish family in Transoxiana. The instrument historically associated with the Turks is the ancient, long-necked type of lute *(saz* or *bağlama)* by which Turks of Thrace and Anatolia are linked with Turkic peoples of central Asia. In their fretting Turkish rural lutes are more like those of central Asia and Afghanistan than those of Iran.

Turkey is unique among Muslim countries in possessing a highly developed religious music, which includes instrumental music. This development seems to have occurred in the first half of the 13th century, when music and sacred dance were introduced into religious ceremony in eastern Turkey. The ceremonies of the Mevlevî, the dancing dervishes, were shaped by Jalal-ud-din Rumi some 50 years later.

note system Islamic music inherited from older cultures knowledge of the relationship between different pitches and simple fractions of the length of a stretched string. If, for example, a stretched string yields a given note, say C, its half (at the same tension) will yield the octave above, C'; two-thirds, the fifth above, G; three-quarters, the fourth, F; four-fifths, the just major third, E. Frets placed on the neck of a lute at distances between the nut and the bridge corresponding to these fractions would thus yield the notes C E F G C'. By extending the series, gaps may be filled. In addition to such rational frets other frets came to be interpolated in accordance with local or individual taste for a particular shade of intonation. It was Safi ud-Din in the 13th century who substituted an extended rational system for empirical interpolation. Shades of intonation were identified with higher members of the harmonic series. The resulting note system—still in use in modified form in Iran, Turkey, and Arabia—is based exclusively on harmonics. The position of the ligatures that form the frets (in modern times ligatures are of nylon, but formerly were of sheepgut) is today decided by ear. The long-necked lute of Turkish art music, the tambur, carries 24 frets to the octave over a two-octave range.

The frets distinguish between major and minor tones and larger and smaller semitones. By contrast the urban-made *saz* or *bağlama* for amateur use has 13 frets to the octave and the rural *saz* even fewer.

The note series of some of the 12 or 13 simple modes can be approximately equated with those of certain diatonic modes, but the effect of the Turkish *makam* (mode) is subtly different in each case. Half the *makam* described as simple *(basit)* are chromatic; they include a group of four notes with a gap of almost a minor third (a so-called augmented second) between the second and third notes: A Bb C♯ D (approximately). Such a group may start or end the octave series, or it may occur in both of these positions. There are also many compound *makam* in which the note series extends over an octave and a fifth. These begin in one mode and change to another as the series is descended.

rhythm and rhythmic cycles Art music and folk music make use both of regular rhythms—equivalent to $\frac{4}{4}, \frac{2}{4}, \frac{3}{4}, \frac{6}{8}$—and irregular rhythms of the kind referred to by Bartók as "Bulgarian." They are known to the Turks as *aksak* ("limping"). The most common irregular rhythm is 2+2+2+3, where the value of the unit may range from a fast thirty-second note to a half note. In art music rhythmic organization is specified not by a time signature but by the name of a rhythmic cycle *(usul)*. Sometimes cycles are no longer than a measure in the Western sense; for example, *sofyan* equals a pattern of a half and two quarter notes as compared with an extended pattern such as *devri-kebir* of seven units. A cycle is repeated an integral number of times and should be executed on the *kudüm*—a pair of small kettledrums about a fifth apart in pitch. Today the *kudüm* is banished from most performances, and the rhythmic framework is no longer perceptible.

melody Turkish melody characteristically moves conjunctly and often includes short phrases in sequential repetition. Melodic rhythmic patterns vary and sometimes move against the primary rhythmic cycle. The patterns are not related to word stress, and syllables typically are sung to several notes, making the melodies melismatic, not syllabic.

forms Improvisation plays a major role in art music but not a dominant role as in Indian art music. The chief vehicle for extended improvisation is the rhythmically free *taksim*. Its pace is faster than *alapa* in Hindustani music, and modulation is frequent. The note series of the mode is explored segment by segment, and related modes are systematically exhibited as the exposition proceeds. By contrast a major fixed instrumental form is the *peşrev;* the simplest type consists of a sequence of four differing sections—all in the same mode and all consisting of the same number of measures. In performance the melodic instruments play in unison (or at the octave) but with minor variation suited to each instrument.

folk music Turkish folk melody is regarded as basically pentatonic, and Turkish musicologists have demonstrated that a majority of tunes can be referred to a skeleton of the type A G E D C A'. Tunes tend to begin on a high note and descend. Their compass ranges from a minor or major third to a ninth or more; many do not exceed the range of a fourth or a fifth. Songs may be both unmeasured (*uzun hava*, "long song") and measured (*kırık*, "broken").

singing voice Between the voice of the singer of art songs and that of the folk singer there are great differences, and in different regions different singing styles are to be heard among folk singers. The style of singing also differs between men and women. On the whole males sing in a more relaxed way than do women, among whom the voice is forced and shrill. The voice of the finest woman singers of art songs, however, is full and penetrating without shrillness, and their use of vibrato as an ornament has no parallel in the technique of modern Western singers.

instruments The instrumentarium of religious and art music includes: hand cymbals *(zil);* small, paired copper kettledrums *(kudüm);* frame drums with or without jingles *(mazhar);* half-trapezoidal psaltery *(kanun);* long-necked, hemispherical, fretted lute (tambur); pear-shaped, bent-necked, unfretted lute *(ud);* fiddle *(kemençe);* and end-blown, vertical, open-ended flute *(ney)*. Some of these instruments may be heard in ensemble. Folk instruments include: spoons *(kaşik);* finger cymbals *(parmak zili);* tongs with cymbals *(zilli maşa);* bass drum *(davul);* single-headed, open-ended, pottery drum *(dümbelek, deblek);* single-headed frame drum with or without jingles *(def);* long-necked, pear-shaped, fretted lutes *(saz, bağlama, cura,* etc.); fiddles *(kabak, kemençe);* end-blown, vertical, open-ended flutes *(kaval);* whistle flutes *(düdük);* cylindrical, double-reed pipe (*mey* or *nay*); conical, double-reed shawm *(zurna);* single- and double-clarinets *(sipsi, çijte);* Thracian bagpipe with single chanter and single drone *(gayda);* and northeastern Turkish bagpipe with double chanter and no drone *(tulum).* The best-known folk ensemble is the loud combination of bass drum and shawm *(davul-zurna).* The shepherd's flute may be introduced into an indoor chamber music group together with the lute and frame drum but is usually confined to the pastures. In the village home a single, long-necked lute may be joined by finger cymbals, frame drum, and/or pottery drum. Since the folk lutes (and the classical tambur also) are strung with brass and steel strings, their sound is rich in higher partials; the tone of the classical unfretted, short, bent-necked lute with silk, gut, or nylon strings resembles that of 16th-century Western lutes.

Turn of the Screw, The: *see* BRITTEN; OPERA (the 20th century).

twelve-tone: *see* SERIALISM.

Tye, Christopher (*c.* 1500–1573?) The English composer Christopher Tye was an innovator of the style of cathedral music (particularly the anthem) perfected by Tallis, Byrd, and Gibbons. His early history is not known, but he may have been a chorister at King's College, Cambridge, as early as 1511. In 1536 he received a Mus.B. degree at Cambridge and in 1545 a Mus.D.; in 1548 he was incorporated a D.Mus. of Oxford. In 1541 or 1542 he was appointed choirmaster at Ely Cathedral. He seems to have continued there until 1561, when he resigned, having been ordained deacon and priest and presented to the living of Doddington-cum-Marche on the Isle of Ely. He was succeeded at Doddington on March 15, 1573. It is probable that Tye was music

tutor to Prince Edward, later Edward VI, as the references to Tye in Samuel Rowley's play *When You See Me You Know Me* (1605) would suggest. The title page of his four-part setting of his own versification of *The Acts of the Apostles* (the first 14 chapters), which appeared in 1553, claims him as one of the gentlemen of the Chapel Royal, though this is otherwise undocumented.

Tye, like Tallis, bridged the mid-century change of musical style and liturgy in England. Much of his Latin church music is incomplete; two masses survive, one a most attractive and fluent four-part setting based on the English secular song *Western Wynde* used also by John Taverner and John Shepherd. Fourteen English anthems remain and a quantity of music for instrumental ensemble, including 19 in nomines.

RECORDINGS: Mass *Euge bone;* Mass *Western Wynde.*

U

Undine: *see* HENZE; HOFFMANN; OPERA (the 19th century); SPOHR.

Unfinished Symphony (Eighth): *see* SCHUBERT (maturity).

V

Vanessa: *see* BARBER, SAMUEL; MENOTTI; OPERA (the 20th century).

Varèse, Edgard, originally Edgar Varèse (December 22, 1883–November 8, 1965) An innovator in 20th-century techniques of sound production, the French composer and conductor Edgard Varèse spent his boyhood in France and Italy. After composing as a youth without formal instruction, he later studied with d'Indy, Albert Roussel, and Charles-Marie Widor and was strongly encouraged by Romain Rolland and by Debussy. In 1907 he went to Berlin, where he was influenced by Richard Strauss and Busoni, and in 1915 he emigrated to the United States.

Varèse's music is dissonant, nonthematic, and rhythmically asymmetric; he conceived of it as bodies of sound in space. He was one of the first composers to employ recorded sounds and electronic music.

Varèse actively promoted performances of works by other 20th-century composers and was one of the founders of the International Composers' Guild (1921) and the Pan-American Association of Composers (1926); these organizations were responsible for performances and premieres of works by Bartók, Berg, Carlos Chávez, Henry Cowell, Ives, Ravel, Wallingford Riegger, Poulenc, Webern, and others. He also founded the Schola Cantorum of Santa Fe (1937) and the New Chorus (1941, later the Greater New York Chorus) to perform music of past eras, including works of Pérotin, Heinrich Schütz, Monteverdi, and Marc-Antoine Charpentier.

Varèse's works include *Hyperprism* (1923) for wind instruments and percussion; *Ionisation* (1931) for percussion, piano, and two sirens; and *Density 21.5* (1935) for unaccompanied flute, composed to demonstrate the sonority of the platinum flute. His *Déserts* (1954) employs tape-recorded sound. In *Poème électronique* (1958), written for the Philips Pavilion at the Brussels Exposition, the sound was distributed by 400 loudspeakers. Two of his last works were *Nocturnal* (1961) for soprano, men's chorus, and orchestra and *Nuit* (1965) for soprano, woodwinds, brass, double bass, and percussion.

BIBLIOGRAPHY: Louise Varèse, *Varèse: A Looking-Glass Diary* (1972).

RECORDINGS: *Amériques* and *Arcana* for orchestra; *Density 21.5; Déserts; Ecuatorial* for bass voice, brass, piano, organ, two theremins, and percussion; *Hyperprism; Intégrales* for woodwinds, brass, and percussion; *Ionisation; Nocturnal; Octandre* for seven winds and double bass; *Offrandes* for soprano and orchestra; *Poème électronique.*

variations   The term given to groups of progressively developed versions of a complete self-contained theme, retaining the form of that theme though not necessarily its melody. This is the classical sense of the term, but there are modern developments of the variation form to which this definition is both too broad and too precise.

Edgard Varèse
The Bettmann Archive, Inc.

The aesthetic principle of variations appeared at very early stages of music. During the 16th century an artistically mature variation form automatically arose in the polyphonic treatment of Gregorian hymns verse by verse. Accordingly the hymns and Magnificats of Palestrina might be described as contrapuntal sets of variations on ecclesiastical tunes, like rich and free examples on the simple plan shown later by Haydn's variations on his Austrian national anthem in the *Emperor* Quartet. Already in the 16th century instrumental music was climbing up the trellis of a primitive variation form. A favorite plan was to put together several popular or original tunes with an ornamental variation sandwiched between. Sometimes sets of variations on a single tune were produced with excellent effect, as in Byrd's variations on "The Carman's Whistle." Such variations were natu-

833

rally grouped in order of increasing brilliance, and they often included passages that would catch the greatest pianists.

In the 17th century a highly artistic form of variation solved with great simplicity the problem of expanding instrumental pieces to a length that permitted growth to a big climax. This was the GROUND BASS, a single phrase placed in the bass and repeating itself ad infinitum. It originated in the dance forms of the PASSACAGLIA and the CHACONNE. Both were in slow triple time, the chaconne having a strong accent on the second beat, while the passacaglia developed the liberty to transfer its theme to parts other than the bass. The genius of Purcell was cruelly hampered by the absence of large musical forms in his time, and he seized upon the ground bass with avidity. By the time of Bach and Handel, lighter sets of variations that consisted essentially of embroidery on a melody had come into vogue. Bach's *Aria variata alla maniera Italiana* shows where this fashion began, and in France that *air et doubles* was taken over from early English virginal music. In *doubles* each variation divides the rhythm into quicker notes than the preceding one. The most familiar example is "The Harmonious Blacksmith" in Handel's E Major Suite. Sometimes the air itself was stated in a tangle of ornamentation, while the *doubles* simplified the melody and varied the accompaniment. But Bach applied the principle of the ground bass to variations on a complete symmetrical movement in bi-

nary form. His aria with 30 variations, commonly known as the *Goldberg* Variations, is (with the exception of Beethoven's 33 *Veränderungen* on a waltz by Anton Diabelli) the most gigantic set of variations. A melodically interesting ground bass could not be maintained on so large a scale, but the 32 measures of Bach's theme are so many clear harmonic steps that can be represented by many analogous progressions without loss of identity. There is no question of retaining or varying the melody of the aria, which is a tissue of ornaments that will bear neither development nor simplification. See below.

The rise of the sonata style again brought the melodic-embroidery variation into prominence, for in sonata form themes are identified entirely by their melodies. With not more than three or four exceptions, the best sets of variations by Mozart and Haydn are movements in their sonata works, and their independent sets are either early or perfunctory exercises and encore pieces. Two common errors of professional and amateur criticism are the judging of Haydn's and Mozart's variations by these embellishments and the much graver mistake of despising the embroidery variation on principle. It is either vulgar or sublime. And it is handled lovingly by precisely the greatest masters of deep harmonic and rhythmic variation, Beethoven and Brahms. Haydn is fond of a special form first known in Carl Philipp Emanuel Bach. It consists of alternating variations on two themes, alternately ma-

a

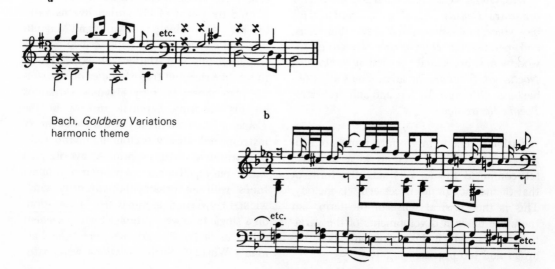

Bach, *Goldberg* Variations
harmonic theme

b

jor and minor, the first a rich and complete binary melody and the other a shorter binary melody often beginning with the same figure as the first. The first theme usually returns as if it were going to be unvaried, but its first repeat is an ornamental variation. The form is rarely worked out far enough to include more than one variation of the second theme, and sometimes (as in the famous "Gypsy" Trio) there are new episodes instead of variations of the second theme so that the form becomes a sectional rondo. The only strict example of Haydn's type of alternating variations in later music is the first allegretto of Beethoven's Piano Trio in E-flat (Op. 70, No. 2); but a magnificent application of it, without change of mode though with a wide range of key, is shown in the slow movement of his c minor Symphony.

Beethoven in his last works invented another variation form on two themes, of which the second is in a different key and time. The examples of this are the slow movement of the Ninth Symphony and the Lydian figured chorale in the a minor Quartet. In the slow movement of Brahms's F Major Quintet (Op. 88), the alternation of the two keys gives rise in the last line of the movement to one of the most astonishing dramatic strokes in all music. Beethoven uses embroidery variations as means of obtaining extraordinary repose in slow movements. The extreme case of this is the slow movement of the *Appassionata*. In this and in many other instances his method is that of the *air et doubles,* which grows to a natural climax that can subside into the rhythm of the plain theme. Until his latest works such sets of variations are never finished. Their dramatic intent is that of a repose that is too unearthly to last; and at the first sign of dramatic motion or change of key the sublime vision "fades into the light of common day," a light that Beethoven is far too great an idealist to despise (the Andante of the B-flat Trio, Op. 97, and the slow movement of the Violin Concerto, which contains two episodic themes in the same key). In his later works Beethoven, by striking out into foreign keys, found the means of organizing a coda that finally spins down in fragmentary new variations or even returns to the plain theme.

Thus he was able to end his Sonatas, Opp. 109 and 111, with solemn slow movements.

Beethoven also found other applications of the variation forms. Thus the finale of the *Eroica* Symphony has not only the theme but many other ideas in common with the brilliant set of Variations and Fugue for piano on a theme from *Prometheus;* and the Fantasia for piano, chorus, and orchestra and the choral finale of the Ninth Symphony are sets of melodic variations with freely-developed connecting links and episodes. In the Ninth Symphony a second thematic idea eventually combines with the figures of the first theme in double fugue.

But Beethoven's highest art in variation form is independent of the sonata. From his earliest display of piano playing, the wonderful 24 Variations on a Theme by Righini, to his supreme variation work, the 33 on Diabelli's waltz, he uses and transcends every older means of variation and adds his own discoveries. Before Beethoven the basis of variations might be a ground bass, a melody, or a harmonic scheme. Beethoven discovered that rhythm and form can, with a suitable theme, be a solid basis for variations. The aria of Bach's *Goldberg* Variations is in its phrasing as uniform as a chessboard, and if its harmonies had not a one-to-one correspondence with each variation the form would be lost. But there are themes, such as Haydn's "Corale St. Antonii" that Brahms varied, where the phrasing is interesting in itself. A similar example is the theme by Paganini that inspired Brahms to compose two complete sets on it. See figures a and b on following page.

The climax in the history of variations dates from the moment when Beethoven was about to begin his Ninth Symphony and received from Anton Diabelli a waltz that the publisher was sending to all the musicians in Austria so that each might contribute a variation to be published for the benefit of the sufferers in the late Napoleonic wars. Diabelli's theme was absurdly prosaic, but it happened to be perhaps the sturdiest piece of musical anatomy that Beethoven (or any composer since) ever saw; and it moved Beethoven to defer his work on the Ninth Symphony! The shape of Diabelli's waltz may be illustrated by a diagram that

a

theme by Paganini

b

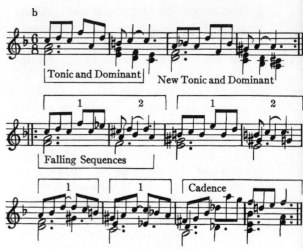

outline of variation by Brahms

represents its first 16 measures; the upright strokes signify the measures, and the brackets and dots indicate the rhythmic groups.

tonic   dominant   rising sequence   close in dominant

The second part also consists of 16 measures, moving harmonically back from the dominant to the tonic and rhythmically the same as the first part. This plan is astonishingly elastic. The alternation of tonic and dominant in the first eight measures may be represented by another familiar form in which three measures of tonic and a fourth of dominant are answered by three measures of dominant and a fourth of tonic, as in Variation 14 (which must be reckoned in half-measures). Again, when the theme answers the tonic by the dominant, it raises the first melodic figure by one step, and this may be translated by the answer on the supertonic harmony. In the course of 50 minutes a few of these 33 variations become vague as to more than the beginnings and cadences of the theme, and there are three simple variations in which one would like to ask Beethoven whether he had not inadvertently omitted a measure; but the momentum of the theme is never lost, and after a group of three slow and rather free variations this momentum breaks into an entirely free fugue (Variation 32) on a salient feature of what must by cour-

tesy be called Diabelli's melody. A free fugue is a favorite solution to the problem of the coda in a set of variations. The momentum produced by the revolution of true variations in the orbit of the theme gives the key to the whole problem. A fugue solves it by flying off at a tangent. Very sublime is the way in which Beethoven, after letting his fugue run its torrential course, returns to the orbit of his theme in an ethereal little minuet with a short coda of its own, which—16 measures before the end—shows signs of beginning to revolve again.

Again let us regard the period of the theme not as an orbit but as diurnal rotation. We can then describe the codas of Brahms's *Paganini* Variations as produced by accelerating the spin until it breaks away and then resumes for a few final catastrophic whirls—exactly like a dying top (though this, of course, does not accelerate its spin). Without acceleration Beethoven ended his wonderful c minor Variations (most perfect of passacaglias) in this way. Brahms found in Haydn's "Corale St. Antonii" the opportunity for another method. He took the first five measures as a ground bass within which narrow orbit the finale moves until its climax broadens into the rest of the glorious theme and so rounds off the whole work.

Bach poised the contrasts and climaxes of the *Goldberg* Variations so accurately that the ending of the whole by a simple da capo of the theme is astonishingly effective. It is as if a charming old ancestress of a great family were to step from the frame of her Holbein portrait and bow to her assembled posterity.

To speak of the progress in variation form since Beethoven is like speaking of the progress in reinforced concrete since the Parthenon. The classical variation form is limited only by the composer's imagination and technique, and the removal of its foundations does not enlarge it at all. There is no reason to condemn other kinds of variation; many great and beautiful works in non-classical variation form exist, from Schumann's Études *Symphoniques* (first version, 1834) to Elgar's *Enigma* Variations (1899) and Ernst von Dohnányi's Variations on a Nursery Song (1916). But no free variation that breaks down the phrasing of its theme and follows its own discursive ways will ever achieve anything externally so unlike the theme as a strict harmonic and rhythmic variation on classical lines. (See Example 2b.) Nor will a series of such variations acquire anything like the classical momentum. On the contrary, in clumsy hands the free variation becomes apologetic in the way in which it offers raw chunks of the original melody as evidence that it has not forgotten its duty, like Lewis Carroll's poetic *Tema con Variazioni,* the preface to which is an unconscious epitome of modern misunderstandings of the form.

Variation writers may be scientifically classified into those who know their theme and those who do not. There is no reasonable doubt that many very clever composers, from Mendelssohn onward, have completely misunderstood the nature of the deeper classical variations and have thought that anything so unlike the original tune must be quite independent of it. Mendelssohn's Variations *sérieuses* (1841) have a beautiful theme with a structure that might have given rise to splendid features, but Mendelssohn simply ignores this structure and replaces it by weaker things in almost every variation. Schumann shows more insight. He has no great grip of his theme, but he tries to distinguish by titles those variations that are true from those that are episodic; thus in the Études *Symphoniques*

the études are numbered separately from the variations; the Andante of the F Major Quartet is called *quasi variazioni;* and the strictest set he ever wrote (on a theme by Clara Wieck) is called Impromptus.

Brahms stands alone in his grip of his theme. Max Reger is no nearer the classical form in his variations than in his other works. The present state of the form seems to indicate that if the composer does not aim at strict variations, the most vital results will be on the line of melodic development, as in the above-mentioned works of Elgar and Dohnányi, the *Symphonic* Variations (1877) of Dvořák, and those variations of Reger that are closest to this type. A number of 20th-century composers have returned to Baroque forms of variations, especially the chaconne and passacaglia, including Webern, Busoni, Ernst Krenek, Berg, and Walter Piston. The variations form has also been combined with serialism by such composers as Schoenberg and Webern. Hindemith used three themes in *The Four Temperaments* (1943), and Elliott Carter described his Variations for orchestra (1956) as a "unified musical action of gesture. . . . Form, rhythmic and development processes as well as texture and thematic material differ in each. . ."

BIBLIOGRAPHY: Robert U. Nelson, *The Technique of Variation* (1948; reprint, 1973).

Variations symphoniques: *see* DIÉMER; FRANCK.

Varnay, (Ibolyka) Astrid (Maria) (b. April 25, 1918)   The daughter of singers, Swedish-U.S. soprano Astrid Varnay went to the United States as a child and made her debut at the Metropolitan Opera in 1941 as Sieglinde (Wagner's *Die Walküre*). She excelled there in German opera, singing Wagner and Richard Strauss (especially *Elektra*). In 1947 she sang in the first complete performance of Wagner's *Der Ring des Nibelungen* in Buenos Aires, and she was the first U.S. singer to sing Brunnhilde at Bayreuth. Varnay sang there from 1951 to 1967 and recorded Wagner's *Der fligende Holländer* and *Lohengrin*. She was chosen by the U.S. State Department to perform at the Berlin Opera in the Allied Festival of the Arts in 1951.

Vaughan Williams, Ralph (October 12, 1872–August 26, 1958) The dominant English composer of the first half of the 20th century and founder of the English nationalist movement, Ralph Vaughan Williams studied at Trinity College, Cambridge, and in London at the Royal College of Music under two principal figures of the late 19th-century renascence of English music, Charles Villiers Stanford and Hubert Parry. He studied in Berlin with Max Bruch and in Paris with Ravel. About 1903 Vaughan Williams began to collect folk songs, and in 1904–06 he was musical editor of *The English Hymnal,* for which he wrote his celebrated tune "Sine Nomine" for the hymn "For All the Saints." After artillery service in World War I he became professor of composition at the Royal College of Music.

English folk song and music of the Tudor period fertilized his talent, contributing modal elements and rhythmic freedom to a style both highly personal and deeply English. His compositions include orchestral, stage, chamber, and vocal works. Three *Norfolk* Rhapsodies (the second and third were later withdrawn), notably the first in e minor (1906), were the first works to show his assimilation of folk song contours into a distinctive melodic and harmonic style. His symphonies cover a vast expressive range: the First *Sea* Symphony (1910) for voices and orchestra is based on poems of Walt Whitman; the Second *London* Symphony (1914; rewritten 1915; revised 1918, 1920, 1934) suggests moods and scenes of London; the Third *Pastoral* Symphony (1922) has no detailed extramusical references; the Fourth (1935) ventures into harsh dissonances and complex rhythms; the Fifth (1943) returns to a more modal, serene style, based on sketches for his opera *The Pilgrim's Progress* (1951); the Sixth Symphony (1948) is in many ways expressive of the tensions and tragedy of World War II; the Seventh, Sinfonia *Antarctica* (1953), is an adaptation of his music for the film *Scott of the Antarctic* (1949); the Eighth Symphony (1956) is noted for its lyricism and dramatic impact, and the Ninth (1958) for its strong note of pessimism and despair. Other orchestral works include Fantasia on a Theme by Tallis (1910), concertos for piano (later arranged for two pianos and orchestra), oboe, and tuba, and Romance (1952) for harmonica and orchestra.

Of his stage works *The Pilgrim's Progress* (1951) and *Job* (1931; after William Blake), a masque for dancing, reflect his serious, mystical side. *Hugh the Drover* (1924), a ballad opera, stems from his folk song interest. *Riders to the Sea* (1937) is a poignant setting of John Millington Synge's play.

Vaughan Williams wrote many songs of great beauty, including *On Wenlock Edge* (1909; to poems of A. E. Housman), a cycle for tenor, string quartet, and piano later arranged for tenor and orchestra, and Five *Mystical* Songs (1911; optional version with chorus) to poems of George Herbert. His *Flos Campi* (1925) for small chorus, viola, and chamber orchestra draws its inspiration from the Song of Solomon and utilizes polytonality and wordless vocalises. Also notable among his choral works are the cantatas *Toward the Unknown Region* (1907; after Whitman), *Dona nobis pacem* (1936), and *Hodie* (1954); Mass in g minor (1923); the oratorio *Sancta Civitas* (1926); and Te Deum in G Major (1928). He also wrote church music (his setting of "Old 100th" and the motet *O Clap Your Hands* are performed in churches whenever brass players can be assembled), many part songs, and hymn and folk song settings.

Vaughan Williams was the English composer who broke the ties with continental Europe, which for two centuries through Handel, Mendelssohn, and lesser German composers had made Britain virtually a musical province of Germany. Like many nationalist composers, Vaughan Williams turned to folk song as a wellspring of native musical style. After World War I his idiom became established and unmistakable. He wrote in every form and in particular served the English choral tradition generously.

BIBLIOGRAPHY: Hubert Foss, *Ralph Vaughan Williams* (1950; reprint, 1974); Frank Howes, *The Music of Ralph Vaughan Williams* (1954); James Day, *Vaughan Williams* (1961); Alan E. F. Dickinson, *Vaughan Williams* (1963); Michael Kennedy, *The Works of Ralph Vaughan Williams* (1964); Elliott S. Schwartz, *The Symphonies of Ralph Vaughan Williams* (1964); Ursula Vaughan

Williams, *R.V.W.; A Biography of Ralph Vaughan Williams* (1964); John E. Lunn *et al, Ralph Vaughan Williams: A Pictorial Biography* (1971); Roy Douglas, *Working with Vaughan Williams* (1972).

RECORDINGS: Numerous recordings of many works.

Vecchi, Orazio (baptized December 6, 1550–February 19, 1605)   An Italian poet and composer known for his canzonets and madrigal-comedies, Orazio Vecchi was born at Modena. He was musical director at Reggio Emilia in 1586 and the same year became a canon at the cathedral of Correggio. From 1596 to 1604 he was musical director at the cathedral of Modena. Vecchi is best known for his *L'Amfiparnaso* (performed at Modena, 1594; printed in Venice, 1597), a series of four- and five-part madrigals with texts based on the commedia dell'arte, conceived in a quasidramatic form (prologue and three acts). Though the work is not intended for stage presentation, Vecchi's deft mingling of humor, caricature, and gravity achieves by musical means a vivid, almost theatrical effect. *Le veglie di Siena* (1604) was another collection of the kind. Vecchi wrote the texts of his four books of canzonets and two books of madrigals; his compositions also include lamentations, motets, and masses.

RECORDING: *L'Amfiparnaso.*

Verdi, Giuseppe (Fortunino Francesco) (October 10, 1813–January 27, 1901)   The leading Italian composer of the 19th century, Giuseppe Verdi changed the whole face of Italian opera. Beginning his career after the death of Bellini, after Rossini's retirement, and near the end of Donizetti's creative life, Verdi transformed opera into music drama as his contemporary Wagner was doing in Germany.

Verdi was born at Le Roncole in the duchy of Parma. He showed his musical gift at an early age and received some lessons from the village organist. His father, a tavern keeper and grocer, was too poor to give him a thorough education; but the boy attracted the notice of Antonio Barezzi, a merchant and musical amateur in the neighboring town of Busseto, who encouraged and assisted him in his musical education. In addition to copying

Giuseppe Verdi
portrait by Giovanni Boldini, 1886
SCALA, Firenze

parts and deputizing for the town organist, Verdi began to compose pieces for the local philharmonic society and the church. At age 18 he was sent to Milan on a scholarship secured for him by Barezzi to enter the conservatory. But he was rejected because he was over the age limit. He remained in Milan for three years, studying with Vincenzo Lavigna, a musician on the staff of La Scala.

In 1834 Verdi returned to Busseto to claim, with Barezzi's support, the vacant office of maestro di cappella. The clerical party, however, had secured the post for a candidate of its own, and a factional dispute followed. This experience fostered Verdi's anticlericalism, though he always remained a Catholic. He was appointed master of music to the commune and played a busy part in the life of the town. In 1836 he married Margherita Barezzi, his patron's daughter.

An opportunity of composing an opera, *Oberto,* took Verdi to Milan in 1836 for its production at the Teatro Filodrammatico, but the project was abandoned. This first opera of Verdi was produced instead at La Scala on November 17, 1839, and was sufficiently successful to secure him a commission to write three more operas for La Scala. The first of these, *Un giorno di regno* (September 1840), an opera buffa, was so ill received that it was withdrawn after one performance. Verdi, who had recently lost his wife and infant son— and another child had died before he left Busseto—was overcome with despair and vowed he would never write another opera. Bartolomeo Merelli, the director of La Scala, released him from his contract but later pressed on the young composer a libretto based on the story of Nebuchadrezzar. Verdi read it reluctantly, but coming upon the words of a chorus of Jews in captivity he was suddenly released from his inhibitions. On this libretto he composed *Nabucco;* its production in 1842 established his reputation in Italy. Among the singers in the cast was Giuseppina Strepponi, at this time Merelli's mistress, who had been instrumental in the acceptance of *Oberto* by La Scala. After a scandal-ridden interlude she was to become Verdi's second wife.

Verdi had been born in a divided Italy. He was a citizen of France at the time of his birth and now felt himself to be a foreigner in Austrian-dominated Milan. It may be that the chorus in *Nabucco* set a spark to his patriotism, which in succeeding years made him a spokesman of Italian aspirations and led to conflicts with Austrian censorship. The Italian public certainly applied the prayer of the Jews for delivery from captivity to their own condition as subjects of the Austrian Empire. The succeeding operas—*I Lombardi* (1843), a tale of the Crusades; *Ernani* (1844), based on Hugo's *Hernani; I due Foscari* (1844), based on Byron's *The Two Foscari;* and *Giovanna d'Arco* (1845)—all provided opportunities for the expression of patriotic sentiments in spite of the censorship under the guise of dramatic propriety. Until Cavour and Garibaldi succeeded in establishing a united and independent Italy under the king of Sardinia and first king of Italy, Victor Emmanuel II, Verdi— whose very name was taken to stand for *V*ittorio *E*mmanuele *R*e d'*I*talia—remained the unofficial musician laureate of the popular cause to the detriment for a while of his development as a musician.

In *Macbeth* (1847) Verdi took a definite step forward. Just as the biblical theme had contributed to the grandeur of *Nabucco,* un-matched in the romantic melodramas that followed it, so the tragic theme of Shakespeare's drama was bound to call forth the best in a composer of his stature. Much that is trite and crude as well as immensely forceful remains in *Macbeth,* but there are also intimations of the genius that was to produce *Don Carlos, Aida,* and *Otello.*

Verdi's popularity in Italy attracted attention abroad. In 1846 he went to Paris for a production of *Ernani* and in the following year to London, where *I masnadieri* (based on Schiller's *Die Räuber*) was performed for the first time. He returned to Paris and revised *I Lombardi* for performance in French as *Jérusalem* and remained in Paris for some months. There he renewed his friendship with Giuseppina Strepponi, who had retired from the stage to teach singing. An intimate relationship developed, but though there was no impediment to their marriage neither was willing to go through the formality. Strepponi apparently felt herself unworthy to be Verdi's wife. Verdi aggravated the scandal and brought upon himself the rebuke of his first wife's father by installing Strepponi at Sant' Agata, a property he had purchased near Busseto. Verdi seems to have been quite unconscious of the social enormity of his conduct. He responded to local censure by refusing to have anything to do with Busseto and its musical activities, having first repaid with interest the contribution made by the town to his musical education. In 1859, seven years after their arrival in Busseto, he and Strepponi—destined to live in happy union for the remainder of their lives—went off to a village in Savoy and legalized their relationship in the eyes of church and state.

In the meantime he had composed the three operas that have done most to familiarize his name: *Rigoletto* (1851), *Il trovatore* (1853), and *La traviata* (1853). In *Rigoletto* he made an important advance toward a coherent presentation of the dramatic action in music. There is less distinction between the recitatives, which tend toward melodic arioso, and the arias, which (with the obvious exception of the Duke's strophic song in the last act) have lost some of their formality and are skillfully dovetailed into what precedes and follows.

Moreover the musical interest is concentrated mainly in the series of duets culminating in the famous quartet, which is in effect a double duet for Gilda and Rigoletto on one side of a wall and Maddalena and the Duke on the other.

Il trovatore, with its violent heroic action and melodramatic horrors, evoked a different kind of music—powerful and impassioned in its outpouring of splendid melody. An even greater contrast is afforded by *La traviata* with its more intimate mood and lyrical pathos, a vein that Verdi had previously attempted in *Luisa Miller* (1849).

These three great successes of Verdi's middle years were not achieved without tribulation. The composer was by now strongly suspect to the censors, and Hugo's *Le Roi s'amuse* (on which *Rigoletto* was based) contained an attempted assassination of a king, which was politically taboo, and a curse, which was blasphemous. Only after numerous concessions to the authorities was the libretto sanctioned. With *La traviata* it was a different matter. Alexander Dumas's *La Dame aux camélias* had just caused a considerable scandal in Paris, and Verdi's operatic version of it, though at first performed in late 17th-century costume, too obviously broke away from the type of remote subject considered proper in opera. For this reason and because a stout prima donna was cast in the role of the frail heroine, the first performance was a fiasco. "Is it my fault or the singers'? Time will show," was Verdi's laconic comment.

Verdi had now become an international figure, and the change in his status was reflected in the development of his art. From 1855 to 1870 he was mainly occupied in producing works for the Paris Opéra and other theaters conforming to Parisian operatic standards, which demanded spectacular dramas in five acts with a ballet. Verdi, always a conscientious craftsman willing to provide whatever his patrons demanded, set himself to compose grand operas on the Meyerbeerian scale, though he groaned at the Opéra's lavish demands. His first essay in the new manner, *Les Vêpres siciliennes* (1855), represents a sad falling-off from the standards of *Rigoletto* and its two successors. The fault lay partly with

the libretto by Eugène Scribe, who simply transferred the action of a book he had written for Donizetti *(Il Duca d'Alba)* from the Netherlands in the 16th century to Sicily in the 13th, where it was considerably less appropriate. As Donizetti's opera had not been performed, Verdi was unaware of the deception.

Two operas for Italian theaters, *Simon Boccanegra* (Venice, 1857) and *Un ballo in maschera* (Rome, 1859), show in a lesser degree the impact of the grand operatic style and the enrichment of Verdi's powers as an interpreter of human character in music. *Boccanegra,* despite a gloomy and excessively complex story, holds the attention by the subtle presentation of character and not, as in most of the earlier operas, simply by means of melodious music and the effective *coups de théâtre. Un ballo in maschera,* a romantic version of the assassination of Gustavus Adolphus III of Sweden, was potentially a more satisfactory drama. But the ferment of Italian nationalism was at this time powerful, and because of the attempt in 1858 on the life of Napoleon III by Felice Orsini the censorship was particularly severe upon the subject of assassination. After a long wrangle it was agreed that the scene should be set in Boston in the 17th century instead of Stockholm in the 18th. This was the last occasion on which Verdi had to endure interference from a foreign censorship. In 1861 Italy was united as a kingdom. Cavour, the political architect of the new state, was eager to obtain the services in Parliament of distinguished Italians outside the world of politics. Verdi reluctantly agreed to stand for election to the Chamber of Deputies, which he dutifully attended in Turin; but he took no active part in politics. He resigned his seat in the Senate, and in his last years he declined a marquisate.

In 1862 Verdi represented the musicians of his country at the Great Exhibition in London, for which he composed a cantata to words by Arrigo Boito. In the same year his next grand opera, *La forza del destino,* was produced in St. Petersburg. This was followed in 1867 by *Don Carlos,* based on Schiller's drama, for the Paris Opéra (the Italian version *Don Carlo* dates from 1884 at La Scala). Again there is an evident advance in subtlety of characterization and in the handling of the orchestra. These qualities were brought to the highest pitch in *Aida,* commissioned by the khedive to celebrate the opening of the Suez Canal and produced in Cairo in 1871. For this masterpiece, as for *Macbeth,* Verdi wrote a detailed scenario; Antonio Ghislanzoni was commissioned to turn this into verse, whose form was in many instances stipulated by Verdi.

Verdi had reached the summit of his career, and, apart from supervising Italian productions of the operas earlier produced abroad, he retired to his estate at Busseto, whose cultivation he superintended with no less care than he applied to operatic rehearsal. In 1873, while awaiting the production of *Aida* at Naples, he wrote a string quartet, the only instrumental work of his maturity. In the same year he was moved by the death of the Italian patriot and poet Alessandro Manzoni to compose a requiem in his honor; in it he incorporated the final movement of an abandoned mass for Rossini that was to have been written by a number of Italian composers.

Tito Ricordi, Verdi's publisher, was reluctant to allow his most profitable composer to rest on his laurels. He contrived a reconciliation with Boito, who had offended Verdi by some youthful criticism. A proposal that Boito should write a libretto based on Shakespeare's *Othello* attracted Verdi, but the poet was first asked to revise the unsatisfactory libretto of *Simon Boccanegra,* which he greatly improved. The project then took shape, and the opera *Otello* was presented at La Scala in 1887. In his 74th year Verdi, stimulated by a libretto incomparably superior to anything he had previously set, had produced his tragic masterpiece. The drama is completely absorbed into a continuous and flexible musical score that reflects every aspect of the characters and every movement of the action.

After an enormously successful tour with *Otello* throughout Europe, Verdi once more retired to Sant' Agata, declaring that he had produced his last work. But one more Shakespearean opera was to come. With infinite skill, Boito converted Shakespeare's *The Merry Wives of Windsor,* strengthened with passages adapted from the Henry IV plays,

into the perfect comic libretto *Falstaff,* which Verdi set to miraculously mercurial music. This, his last dramatic work, was produced at La Scala in 1893, avenging the cruel failure of his only other comedy in the same theater 53 years before.

After *Falstaff* Verdi turned to choral composition, producing experimental settings of *Ave Maria* and of *Laudi alla Vergine Maria,* the words from Dante's *Paradiso.* These, together with the more substantial *Stabat Mater* and Te Deum, were published in 1898 under the title *Quattro pezzi sacri.* He wrote nothing more. In 1897 Giuseppina's death had broken the long partnership, and Verdi himself grew gradually weaker in health. While staying in Milan he suffered a stroke and died six days later.

BIBLIOGRAPHY: Frederick J. Crowest, *Verdi: Man and Musician* (1897; reprint, 1978); Giuseppe Verdi, *Verdi: The Man in His Letters* (1942; reprint, 1973); Francis Toye, *Giuseppe Verdi: His Life and Works* (1946; reprint, 1972); Vincent Sheean, *Orpheus at Eighty* (1958; reprint, 1975); Frank Walker, *The Man Verdi* (1962); Dyneley Hussey, *Verdi,* 3rd ed. (1963); Charles Osborne, *The Complete Operas of Verdi* (1970); Julian Budden, *The Operas of Verdi* (1973–); Joseph Wechsberg, *Verdi* (1974); Vincent Godefroy, *The Dramatic Genius of Verdi: Studies of Selected Operas,* Vol. 1 (1976), Vol. 2 (1978); William Weaver, ed., *Verdi, a Documentary Study* (1977), and with Paul Hume, *Verdi: The Man and His Music* (1977); William Weaver and Martin Chusid, eds., *The Verdi Companion* (1979).

RECORDINGS: Numerous recordings of most works.

verismo A school of Italian opera writing in the last decade of the 19th century. The leading exponents were Mascagni (*Cavalleria rusticana,* 1890) and Leoncavallo (*Pagliacci,* 1892). Another example is Umberto Giordano's *Andrea Chénier* (1896). Puccini was influenced by verismo, particularly in *Tosca* (1900), and occasional veristic operas were written in the 20th century; *e.g.,* Ermanno Wolf-Ferrari's *I gioielli della Madonna* (1911; *The Jewels of the Madonna*).

Verismo, Italian for "realism," was marked by melodramatic, often violent plots with characters drawn from everyday life. Musical devices included passionate declamation by solo voices and emotionally charged harmonies and melodies.

Verrett, Shirley (b. May 31, 1931?) Educated at the Juilliard School, the U.S. mezzo-soprano Shirley Verrett made her New York City debut (1958) in Kurt Weill's musical *Lost in the Stars* and her European debut (1959) at Cologne in Nicolas Nabakov's *The Death of Rasputin.* A noted Carmen, she first sang the role at Spoleto (1962), then in the Soviet Union (1963), the United States (1964), La Scala (1966), and for her Metropolitan debut (1968). There she also sang the Verdi roles of Eboli *(Don Carlo),* Amneris *(Aida),* and Azucena *(Il trovatore).* In 1969 she sang Elisabetta (Donizetti's *Maria Stuarda*) at Edinburgh and in 1973 the two roles of Cassandra and Dido in Berlioz' *Les Troyens* at the Metropolitan. She has also sung soprano roles (Verdi's Lady Macbeth, Bellini's Norma, and Leonora in Donizetti's *La Favorita*). Her recordings include complete operas by Gluck *(Orfeo ed Euridice),* Rossini *(Siege of Corinth),* Donizetti *(Anna Bolena* and *Lucrezia Borgia),* and Verdi *(Don Carlo* and *Luisa Miller)* and such works as the Beethoven Ninth Symphony, Mendelssohn's *Elijah,* and Stravinsky's *Oedipus Rex* and *A Sermon, a Narrative, and a Prayer.*

Viardot, Pauline, originally Michelle Ferdinande Pauline García (July 18, 1821–May 18, 1910) Daughter of the Spanish tenor and vocal teacher Manuel García and sister of Maria Malibran, the French-born mezzo-soprano Pauline Viardot studied voice with her father, piano with Liszt, and composition with Anton Reicha. A successful debut in Brussels in 1837 led to European tours, where she was acclaimed for her singing and her acting. She sang at the Théâtre des Italiens in Paris in 1839 and two years later married the manager of the theater, Louis Viardot. She sang regularly in London (1848–58) and at the Paris Opéra created the roles of Fidès (Meyerbeer's *Le Prophète,* 1849) and Sapho in Gounod's opera (1851). Saint-Saëns wrote his *Samson*

et Dalila for her, and she is credited with establishing the mezzo-soprano as a leading role. Brahms's Alto Rhapsody (1870) was also written for her. She taught at the Paris Conservatoire (1871–75), and she composed operettas on texts by her companion, the Russian novelist Turgenev, songs, and pieces for violin and piano. She was the subject of George Sand's novel *Consuelo.*

vibraphone or **vibraharp** A percussion instrument much like the xylophone but with metal rather than wooden keys. It is classified as a metallophone. Each key has a tubular, tuned resonator with a mechanically operated fan that causes a vibrato by repeatedly closing and opening the resonator. Felt or wool beaters are used, giving a soft, mellow tone quality. A damper pedal permits playing short notes and unblurred series of chords. Cutting off the fans, changing their speed, or using hard mallets alters the normal tone quality.

Invented about 1920 in the United States, the vibraphone was soon common in dance bands and became a prominent jazz instrument. It was first used in the orchestra in Berg's opera *Lulu* (1937) and later in Messiaen's *Trois Petites Liturgies* (1944). The compass varies; three octaves upward from the F below middle C is common.

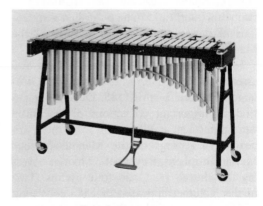

vibraphone
courtesy, Ludwig Industries

Vickers, Jon (b. October 29, 1926) Best known in the role of Britten's Peter Grimes and that of Aeneas (Berlioz' *Les Troyens*), the Canadian tenor Jon Vickers studied at the Royal Conservatory in Toronto. He made his Covent Garden debut in 1956 and in 1958 sang Siegmund (Wagner's *Die Walküre*) in Bayreuth. He has sung at the Vienna Staatsoper (1958–59), the San Francisco Opera (1959), and La Scala (1961). His Metropolitan Opera debut was in 1960 as Canio in Leoncavallo's *Pagliacci,* and his subsequent roles there included Florestan (Beethoven's *Fidelio*) and Siegmund. His recordings of complete operas include *Fidelio* (two), *Les Troyens,* Bizet's *Carmen,* Saint-Saëns' *Samson et Dalila,* Verdi's *Aida* and *Otello,* and a complete *Ring* of Wagner (and a second *Die Walküre*).

Victoria, Tomás Luis de (*c.* 1548–August 27, 1611)   The greatest Spanish composer of his time, Tomás Luis de Victoria was born near Avila between 1544 and 1550 and was sent by Philip II in 1565 to prepare for holy orders at the German College in Rome. Soon he was serving as a singer in addition to his chaplaincy, and he probably studied composition with Palestrina, then director of music at the Roman Seminary. In 1569 he renounced the priesthood to become maestro di cappella at S. Maria di Monserrato. In 1571 he was again assisting with the music at his old college, and in the same year he succeeded Palestrina at the Roman Seminary. A book of his motets was published in Venice in 1572. The following year he was appointed musical director at the German College and was ordained there two years later. In 1576 he published a miscellany of masses, motets, and settings of the Magnificat.

In 1578 he left the German College and assisted St. Philip Neri as chaplain of S. Girolamo della Carità until 1585. During this period six important collections of his music were published in Rome. In 1581 there appeared 16 settings of the Magnificat, four Marian antiphons, a cycle of 32 hymns covering the church year, and four psalms. Two further volumes appeared in 1583 consisting of 53 motets and psalms (largely reprints) and a set of nine masses, four of them new. Another pair of publications followed in 1585: music for Holy Week, including two passions, Improperia, and Lamentations of Jeremiah, and a set of motets for the whole year, of which 10 were new.

In 1578 he had met the pious dowager empress Maria, widow of Maximilian II, and later became her chaplain. In 1584 she entered the convent of the Descalzas Reales in Madrid, where Victoria became priest and organist. He settled in Madrid in 1594 and remained there until his death. His last Roman publication was a second book of seven masses (1592). A miscellany published in Madrid in 1600 contains masses, motets, psalms, hymns, and two Magnificat settings. His last work was the Requiem (1605), written in memory of the empress Maria.

Victoria's 21 masses and 44 motets are among the finest of the period, though his most characteristic manner more often found expression in the hymns, the Marian works, and—above all—in the music for Holy Week and the four offices for the dead. His duties as a Jesuit priest no doubt prevented him from composing more than he did, though the practice of his vocation gave his music a depth of purpose.

His technique belongs partly to an earlier period and reflects his training in the school of Morales. He was fond of reusing his own and other music through the technique of parody and was a master of canonic devices. His use of plainchant canti firmi was surprisingly rare. He nevertheless made use of more modern devices. The portrayal of the fury of wild beasts in *Cum beatus Ignatius* surpasses the pictorialism of the madrigalists. His use of repeated notes for emphasis reflects the growing Florentine interest in recitative. In his polychoral works he exploited the contemporary Venetian manner, and his provision of written organ parts anticipates the age of the continuo. From the harmonic viewpoint his music shows a remarkable sense of tonal contrast, foreshadowing the major–minor concept of tonality characteristic of the Baroque era.

RECORDINGS: *Missa O quam gloriosum; O magnum mysterium; O vos omnes;* Psalms for 8, 9, and 12 voices; Requiem; Tenebrae Responsories; various motets.

vielle: *see* FIDDLE.

Vierne, Louis (October 8, 1870–June 2, 1937)   A pupil of Franck and Charles-Marie Widor at the Paris Conservatoire, the blind French organist and composer Louis Vierne served as Widor's assistant at Saint-Sulpice from 1892 until his appointment in 1900 to Notre-Dame, where he served for the remainder of his life. He taught organ at the Schola Cantorum from 1912; among his many pupils were Joseph Bonnet, Marcel Dupré, Maurice Duruflé, and Boulanger. Though he composed a symphony, vocal works, and chamber music, his most important output was for organ, including six symphonies (1898–1930); *24 Pièces en style libre* (1913), and four suites of *Pièces de fantaisie* (1927).

RECORDINGS: *Pièces de fantaisie* (24); movements of organ symphonies in various collections.

Vieuxtemps, Henri (February 17, 1820–June 6, 1881)   A student of Charles de Bériot, the Belgian violinist and composer Henri Vieuxtemps concertized in Paris with his teacher at the age of eight. After further European tours he played in Russia (1838) and then in the United States (1844). From 1846 to 1852 he was in St. Petersburg as soloist at the court and professor at the conservatory; he did much to influence Russian concert life and violin composition. He taught at the Brussels Conservatory (1871–73) and with de Bériot was a leader of the contemporary Franco-Belgian school of violin playing. Two of his most prominent pupils were Jenö Hubay and Eugène Ysaÿe. Vieuxtemps's compositions, which are still standard in the violin repertoire, include six concertos, a sonata, numerous pieces, and three cadenzas for the Beethoven Concerto in D.

RECORDINGS: *Ballade et polonaise;* Fantasia *appassionata;* Violin Concerto No. 5 in a minor.

vihuela or **vihuela de mano**   A 16th-century Spanish stringed instrument that held the popularity accorded the lute elsewhere in Europe. Built like a large guitar, it had six, sometimes seven, double courses of strings tuned like the lute: G–c–f–a–d'–g', beginning with the second G below middle C. (The guitar then had four double courses.) The *vihuela* was played by the aristocracy, the guitar by the people. By the 18th century both instruments had given rise to the six-stringed guitar. The *vihuela de arco* was a viola da gamba, or viol.

Villa-Lobos, Heitor (March 5, 1887–November 17, 1959)   The foremost Latin-American composer of the 20th century, Brazilian Heitor Villa-Lobos was a cellist in his youth and began to investigate Brazilian folk and popular music in 1905. Leaving home because his widowed mother opposed a musical career, he became a musical vagabond at the age of 18 and played popular music engagements on the cello and guitar while absorbing Brazilian folk music and incorporating it into his own compositions.

On his return to Rio de Janeiro he enrolled at the Instituto Nacional de Música but soon was off on another journey, this time to northern Brazil (Bahia), where he remained for three years.

Back in Rio with a large group of manuscripts and an intimate knowledge of Afro-Brazilian music of the districts, he studied Bach, Wagner, Puccini, and other composers whose influence his music was to absorb. A vital boost to his career occurred in 1915, when his music began to be published by the firm of Artur Napoleão. Music poured out ceaselessly (more than 2,000 works are credited to him), and by the time of his first trip to Europe in 1923, he had compiled a long list of compositions in every form.

In 1919 he met the pianist Artur Rubinstein, whose playing of his music throughout the world brought Villa-Lobos increasing recognition. Villa-Lobos was appointed director of musical education at São Paulo in 1930, and in 1932 he took charge of musical education throughout Brazil. He established a conservatory for popular singing (1942) and founded the Brazilian Academy of Music (1945). He traveled widely in the United States and Europe (1944–49), where he received many honors and was much in demand as a conductor.

Villa-Lobos wrote operas, ballets, symphonies, concertos, symphonic suites, and solo pieces in a style that was influenced by Bach, French composers, and Wagner. His style was also suffused with an original use of Brazilian percussion instruments and Brazilian rhythms. One of his most characteristic works is *Bachianas brasileiras* (1930–44), a set of nine pieces for various instrumental and vocal groups in which a contrapuntal technique in the manner of Bach is applied to themes of Brazilian origin. A similar series of 14 works bears the generic title *Chôros* (1920–29), a Brazilian country dance. His 12 symphonies (1920–58) are mostly associated with historic events or places. Other works include the symphonic poems *Uirapuru* (1917), *Amazonas* (1929), and *Dawn in a Tropical Forest* (1954); concertos for cello (two), harp, harmonica, and guitar; *Rudepoema* for piano (1926; orchestrated 1932); *Momoprecoce* (1929) for piano and orchestra; and 16 quartets (1915–55).

BIBLIOGRAPHY: Nicolas Slonimsky, *Music of Latin America* (1945; reprint, 1972).

RECORDINGS: Numerous recordings of many works.

villancico A genre of Spanish song that was most prevalent in the Renaissance but found also in earlier and later periods. It is a poetic and musical form and was sung with or without accompanying instruments. Originally a folk song, frequently with a devotional song or love poem as text, it developed into an art music genre.

The *villancico* consisted of two parts, beginning with the refrain, or *estribillo*, which alternates with the stanza, or *copla*. The *copla* has two parts, the *mudanza* and the *vuelta*. The *vuelta* rhymes with the last line of the *mudanza* but is sung to the melody of the *estribillo*. This overlap of poetic and musical form is a characteristic trait of the *villancico*.

The late 15th–early 16th-century repertoire is found in several *cancioneros* (song collections). Pieces were in three or four voice parts and were either homophonic or contrapuntal. An important composer was Juan del Encina. About 1500 settings of *villancicos* as solo songs accompanied by *vihuela* appeared, some in Portuguese as well as Spanish. Composers included some of the great masters of the *vihuela* such as Luis Milán and Miguel de Fuenllana.

The *villancico* of the 17th century had a sacred text, often for Christmas. The *estribillo*, elaborately written in four-part polyphony, alternated with *coplas*, short, simple, four-line songs with organ accompaniment and other instruments frequently included. In the 18th century this form expanded into a dramatic cantata with arias and choruses, but by the 20th century the term was confined to the Spanish Christmas carol.

villanella A secular Italian composition of the Renaissance, usually for three voices with no characteristic poetic form other than a refrain. The villanella was most often written in chordal style with clear, simple rhythm. Traditional rules of composition were sometimes broken; for instance, the normally forbidden movement of voices in parallel fifths was common. The villanella was not a folk form but a reaction against the more refined madrigal, often parodying well-known madrigal texts and music.

Originating in Naples as the *villanesca*, the first known collection was an anonymous group in 1537. The greatest early master of the form was Giovan Domenico da Nola, whose *Canzoni Villanesche* (1541) became famous and gave considerable impetus to the development of the form. By *c.* 1570 the term villanella (also known as *villanella alla napoletana*) had superseded the earlier *villanesca*, and such major composers of madrigals as Adriaan Willaert, Orlando di Lasso, and Luca Marenzio contributed to the genre.

The villanella was closely related to several other light vocal forms, including the *mascherata*, the *moresca*, and the *giustiniana*.

Vinci, Leonardo (1690–May 27, 1730) A prominent member of the Neapolitan school of opera composers (which included Pergolesi and Leonardo Leo), Leonardo Vinci was born at Strongoli, Calabria, and was a pupil of Gaetano Greco at the Conservatorio dei Poveri in Naples. His first known work was a comic opera in the Neapolitan dialect, *Lo cecato fauzo* (*Il falso cieco*, 1719). Vinci was then maestro di cappella to the Prince of Sansevero. His earliest extant serious opera, *Silla dittatore* (1723), inaugurated a series of about 40 operas of which 25 were written for Naples and 11 for Rome. In 1725 he was appointed to a conductorship of the royal chapel at Naples. Vinci's operas led to the formation of the classical style, while his overtures (sinfonie) play a part in the history of the symphony. He also wrote oratorios, masses, and motets.

viol A family of bowed stringed instruments used principally from the 16th to the 18th century. The family replaced the various medieval fiddles (*see* REBEC) and was gradually superseded by members of the VIOLIN family. The Renaissance viol shared with the contemporary lute the tuning of its six strings (two fourths, a major third, two fourths) and the gut frets on its neck. It was then made in three sizes as a self-contained family: treble, tenor, and bass, with their bottom strings tuned respectively to d, G (or A), and D. To these three there was later added the violone, a double bass viol often tuned an octave below the bass.

It was the larger (tenor and bass) viols of the early 16th century that fixed the characteristics of the family: sloping shoulders; deep ribs; thin, flat backs; and above all the vertical playing position with the bottom of the instrument resting on the knee or held between the legs—hence the term viola da gamba (*gamba,* Italian for "leg"). The breadth of the bridge, which was arched to give the bow separate access to each string, made forceful playing impossible. The instrument could be only lightly bowed, and the supine position of the bow hand, palm uppermost, encouraged this. The frets gave to each note the clarity of an open string—a clear, ringing, penetrating tone for which the viols were much prized when used in their characteristically polyphonic chamber music.

treble viol by Henry Jay, early 17th century
Behr Photography

By the second half of the 16th century, the viol had acquired a significant repertoire for ensemble; for solo bass; and for the lyra viol, a small bass viol, or *viola bastarda,* and also a quasi-polyphonic style of viol playing in which two- to six-part chords were stopped with the player's left hand. Lyra viol music often used special tunings and included solo and ensemble music and song accompaniments. The lyra viol was particularly popular in England from *c.* 1600 to about the middle of the century.

As the style of instrumental composition changed during the 17th century, with more and more emphasis given to an expressive, vocal-like sound in the soprano register, the use of the smaller viols gradually declined in favor of the violin; viols were unable to compete because their deep bodies created a hollow nasal timbre. The most successful member of the group, the bass viol, had already in the mid-16th century developed a repertoire of complex solo divisions; when that fashion eventually died out toward the end of the 17th century, the solo bass viol, or viola da gamba (this term came to be synonymous with bass viol as the other sizes of viols fell into disuse), took its place in the newer instrumental forms of the Baroque period.

In Germany and France solo playing continued into the 18th century, as the various elaborate obbligati in Bach's passion music and elsewhere show; and—especially in France—the instrument even acquired a seventh string, tuned to A'. Elsewhere the viola da gamba survived chiefly because its sustained tone was a pleasing support to the harpsichord in continuo playing, the core of the instrumental ensemble throughout the Baroque period. When composers in the newer Classical style began to write complete harmonies in the upper instrumental parts, the viol—deprived of its last useful function—dropped out of use altogether.

In the 20th century viols have been successfully revived for the performance of Renaissance and Baroque music.

viola (German, *Bratsche;* French, *alto*) The tenor of the VIOLIN family, pitched a fifth lower than the violin and similar to it in every

essential. Because of its larger size, it has never
been completely standardized in its main dimensions, since—whatever they are—they tax
the human frame and fingers when the instrument is played. A compromise must be effected between ideal size for the best tonal
results and what is practicable to the player
in handling. Too large an instrument is simply
unplayable; too small an instrument is weakest
where it is most wanted—on the lower strings.
The problem has never been solved to everyone's satisfaction, but it has produced a viola
tone that is darker, more weighty, and more
somber than the violin and without which the
string ensemble cannot now be imagined. Violas have been made at various times with a
body length of $14\frac{1}{2}$ to 17 inches (37 to 43
centimeters), about two inches longer than a
violin. Its four strings are tuned c–g–d'–a',
beginning with the C below middle C. The
modern symphony orchestra contains from six
to 10 violas.

viola, front view and side view
EB Inc.

In the 18th-century orchestra the viola usually doubled cello parts. Gluck, Mozart, and
Haydn gave it distinctive treatment, and it
gradually assumed an independent orchestral
role and its place in the string quartet. Berlioz
included a long viola solo in his *Harold in
Italy;* in Richard Strauss's *Don Quixote* the
viola carries the theme of Sancho. The viola
also gained in prominence through the viola
sonatas of Hindemith (himself a violist), Bartók's and William Walton's viola concertos,
and violists such as Lionel Tertis, William

Primrose, and Walter Trampler. It has been
frequently used in 20th-century chamber-music ensembles; *e.g.,* by Schoenberg and Pierre
Boulez.

BIBLIOGRAPHY: Sheila M. Nelson, *The
Violin and the Viola* (1972).

viola da gamba   Originally the name for the
VIOL family because the instruments rested
on the knee or were held between the legs
(*da gamba,* Italian for "of the leg"). By the
end of the 17th century, it applied to the bass
viol, the only remaining member of the family
in general use.

It has six strings that are usually tuned D–
G–C–e–a–d'. Its solo literature includes ricercari in Silvestro Ganassi's *Regola Rubertina*
(1542) that involved double stops, fourth and

man playing bass viol
from Christopher Simpson, The Division Violist,
*1659 courtesy, trustees of the British Museum
photograph, J. R. Freeman & Co., Ltd.*

fifth positions, and other virtuoso techniques. Outstanding 17th- and 18th-century players of the instrument include Christopher Simpson (*The Division Violist,* 1659) and Marin Marais, who wrote five volumes of pieces for one to three viola da gambas. The last of the great gambists was Karl Friedrich Abel. Both Bach and Handel wrote sonatas for viola da gamba. It continued as a continuo instrument through the Baroque era and has been revived in the 20th century for similar use.

BIBLIOGRAPHY: Edmund van der Straeten, *History of the Violoncello, the Viol da Gamba, Their Precursors and Collateral Instruments* (1915; reprint, 1977).

viola d'amore A viol–violin hybrid played like a violin. Of 18th-century origin, it has six or seven melody strings and several sympathetic strings and is unfretted.

viola d'amore by J. U. Eberle, Prague, 1740?
courtesy, Royal College of Music, London

It was popular with such composers as Vivaldi, Bach, and Carl Stamitz, but its use died out about 1800. Among later revivals are those by Meyerbeer *(Les Huguenots),* Gustave Charpentier *(Louise),* Puccini *(Madama Butterfly),* Richard Strauss *(Symphonia domestica),* and Hindemith (a sonata and a concerto).

A 17th-century violin with five wire strings was also called viola d'amore.

violin A bowed stringed instrument that evolved during the Renaissance from earlier bowed instruments: the medieval fiddle; its 16th-century Italian offshoot, the *lira da braccio;* and the rebec. Like its predecessors, but unlike its cousin the VIOL, the violin has a fretless fingerboard. Its strings are hitched to tuning pegs and to a tailpiece, passing over a bridge held in place by the pressure of the strings. The bridge transmits the strings' vibrations to the violin belly, or soundboard, which amplifies the sound. Inside the instrument, beneath the treble foot of the bridge and wedged between the violin belly and back, is the sound post, a thin stick of pine that transmits the string vibrations to the instrument's back, contributing to the characteristic violin tone. The belly is supported from beneath by the bass bar, a narrow wood bar running lengthwise and tapering into the belly. It also contributes to the resonance of the instrument.

violin, front view and side view
EB Inc.

The violin was early recognized for its singing tone, especially in Italy, its birthplace, where the earliest makers, Gasparo da Salò, Andrea Amati, and Giovanni Paolo Maggini, had settled its average proportions before the end of the 16th century. During its history the violin has been subject to modifications that have progressively adapted it to its evolving musical functions. In general the earlier violins are more deeply arched in the belly and back; the more modern, following the innovations of Antonio Stradivari (1644–1737), are shallower, yielding a more virile tone. In the 19th century, with the advent of large auditoriums and the violin virtuoso, the violin

849

underwent its last changes in design. The bridge was heightened, the sound post and bass bar were thickened, and the body became flatter. The neck was angled back, giving greater pressure of the strings on the bridge. The result was a stronger, more brilliant tone in place of the delicate, intimate tone of the violin of the 18th century.

interior of violin, showing corner and end blocks and linings; underside of table with bass bar and internal modeling, or curvature
EB Inc.

The earliest violins were used for popular and dance music. In the 17th century it replaced the viol as the primary stringed instrument in chamber music. The Italian composer Monteverdi included violins in the orchestra of his opera *Orfeo* (1607). In France the king's orchestra, *les 24 violons du roi,* was organized in 1626. Corelli, a virtuoso violinist, was among the earliest composers to contribute to the new music for the violin, as did Vivaldi, Bach, and Giuseppe Tartini. Most major composers from the 18th century on wrote solo music for the violin, among them Haydn, Mozart, Beethoven, Mendelssohn, Schumann, Brahms, Tchaikovsky, Sibelius, Berg, Prokofiev, Schoenberg, Bartók, Hindemith, Wil-

liam Walton, and Shostakovich. Such virtuosos as Francesco Geminiani, Paganini, Joachim, Leopold Auer, Eugène Ysaÿe, Fritz Kreisler, Heifetz, Yehudi Menuhin, and David Oistrakh stimulated the composition of fine violin music.

The violin was assimilated into the art music of the Near East and South India and, as the fiddle, is played in the folk music of many countries.

BIBLIOGRAPHY: George Hart, *The Violin and Its Music* (1881; reprint, 1976) and *The Violin: Its Famous Makers and Their Imitators* (1885; reprint, 1977); Paul Stoeving, *The Violin: Its Famous Makers and Players* (1928; reprint, 1970); Edmund van der Straeten, *The History of the Violin,* 2 vols. (1933; reprint, 1968); Hyacinth Abele and Friedrich Niederheitman, *The Violin: Its History and Construction* (1952; reprint, 1977); David D. Boyden, *The History of Violin Playing from Its Origins to 1761 and Its Relationship to the Violin and Violin Music* (1965); Alberto Bachmann, *An Encyclopedia of the Violin,* 2nd ed. (1966); Franz Farga, *Violins and Violinists,* rev. ed. (1969); Sheila M. Nelson, *The Violin and the Viola* (1972); William Henley, *Universal Dictionary of Violin and Bow Makers,* 2nd ed. (1973).

violoncello: *see* CELLO.

Viotti, Giovanni Battista (May 12, 1755–March 3, 1824) The Italian violinist and composer Giovanni Battista Viotti was a founder of the 19th-century school of violin playing. In 1768 he went to Turin, where he studied with the virtuoso Gaetano Pugnani. After traveling with Pugnani in Germany, Poland, and Russia, he made his Paris debut as a violinist in 1782. He became court musician to Marie Antoinette and established himself as a teacher and opera impresario. In 1792 he went to London, where he conducted Italian operas and appeared as soloist in his own violin concertos at the Salomon Concerts. Viotti went to Germany in 1798 but returned to London three years later to enter the wine business. He was director of the Italian opera in Paris (1819–22) and died in London. Viotti greatly developed the violin concerto, using sonata form and a rich sense of the orchestra.

He wrote 29 violin concertos, of which No. 22 in a minor is the best known; 10 piano concertos, some of them transcriptions of the violin concertos; and chamber music.

RECORDINGS: Violin Concerto No. 22.

virelai One of the *formes fixes* in French lyric poetry and song of the 14th and 15th centuries (*compare* BALLADE; RONDEAU). It probably did not originate in France, and it takes on several different forms even within the French tradition. Similar forms can be found in most of the literatures of medieval and early Renaissance Europe: in the Galician *cantiga,* the Arabic *zajal* and *muwashshah,* the Italian *lauda,* ballata, and frottola, the Spanish *villancico,* and the English carol.

The standard virelai form has three stanzas, each preceded and followed by a refrain. Each stanza is in three sections, the first two having the same rhyme scheme and the last having the rhyme scheme of the refrain. In a musical setting the third section of each stanza therefore takes the same music as the refrain, while the first two sections have different music. In the following diagram uppercase letters represent a repeat of the same music with the same text, lowercase the same music with different text; R means refrain and Roman numerals refer to stanzas:

R	I	R	II	R	III	R
A	b b a	A	b b a	A	b b a	A

In the Italian ballata (14th century) and the Spanish *villancico* (late 15th century), as also in several of the 13th-century forms, the final "a" section of the stanza begins with the rhyme scheme of the two "b" sections and ends with the rhyme of the refrain; this gradual return is called a *vuelta* (Spanish, "turn").

The musical history of the virelai in France has three distinct stages. First came the monophonic settings of simply rhythmized and syllabic melodies. Guillaume de Machaut (*c.* 1300–1377) wrote most of his virelais in this monophonic style, though he preferred to call them *chansons balladées.*

The next stage, in the second half of the 14th century, was one of large polyphonic settings. Their tremendous length was made acceptable by the often lighthearted nature of virelai texts. Jean Vaillant, Solage, Jacob de Senleches, and other composers included imitations of bird calls and the sounds of nature in their virelais; and to judge from the number of surviving sources, the songs achieved exceptional popularity.

The virelai fell out of favor in the first half of the 15th century but returned in a curtailed form with just one stanza, thereby providing the form for some of the most attractive songs of the later 15th century. Though in the 14th century the virelai, like each of the other *formes fixes,* had a distinct musical and poetic style, none is apparent in the 15th-century revival. For the later composers, especially Antoine Busnois and Jean d'Ockeghem, the main attraction of the virelai seems to have been that the music for the first two sections of the stanza could be entirely different from that for the refrain, and it was usually in a different meter. The form thus allowed more musical variety than did the rondeau. These later virelais with only one stanza are often called *bergerettes.*

virginal (French, *épinette, virginale;* Italian, *spinetta*) A stringed instrument of the harpsichord family that differs from the HARPSICHORD chiefly in that the strings are parallel, or nearly so, to the keyboard. The bass strings are nearest to the player; consequently the length of the keys increases from bass to treble. The jacks form a diagonal line across the strings and protrude through slots cut directly in the soundboard. This allows both the bridges to be in optimum positions on the soundboard. By placing the keyboard slightly to the left or to the right, a great variety of tone color can be obtained.

The virginal and the harpsichord always shared the same repertoire, and in England in the 16th and 17th centuries the term virginal was used for both instruments. Many polygonal virginals were made in Italy during this period. The Italian virginal had a fairly centrally placed keyboard, and the strings were plucked at the 30 percent position over the central part of the compass, giving a fuller and more colorful tone than the harpsichord. The Flemish virginal was rectangular and had the keyboard placed either to the right (plucking point 40 percent, giving a very colorful

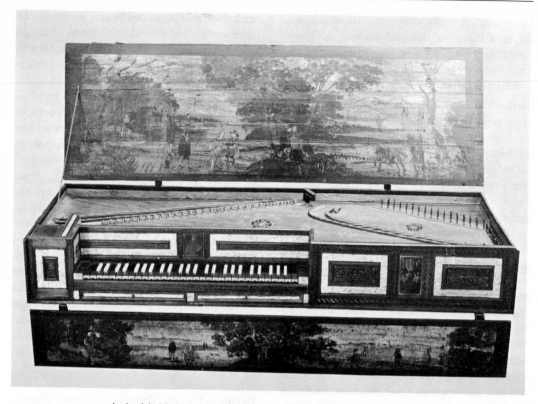

virginal (with jack rail removed) by Robert Hatley, London, 1664
courtesy, Benton-Fletcher Collection at the National Trust property,
Fenton House, Hampstead

and hollow tone but making the instrument difficult to control in the bass) or, less often, to the left (plucking point 10 percent, rising to 30 percent toward the top, giving a tone even brighter than the harpsichord). Surviving English instruments belong to the short period 1640–80 and are similar to the second Flemish style; their brilliant tone makes them particularly suitable for the elaborately ornamented compositions of the English virginalists (Byrd, Gibbons, and others).

The double virginal, of Flemish origin, consisted of two virginals built together, a small one fitting like a drawer into the case of the larger. The smaller, at 4-ft. pitch, could be placed on top of the 8-ft. virginal and the two played as a single instrument. There were even a few triple virginals.

The manufacture of virginals suddenly ceased about the end of the 17th century, and the instrument was not revived until the early 20th century.

Vishnevskaya, Galina (b. October 25, 1926) The Soviet soprano Galina Vishnevskaya sang at the Leningrad Operetta Theater and made her operatic debut in 1952 at the Bolshoi Theater in Moscow. After appearances in Europe and England she made her New York City debut in 1960 as soloist with the Moscow State Symphony. Her debuts at the Metropolitan Opera (1961) and Covent Garden (1962) were as Verdi's Aida. She is acclaimed in Russian music, especially that of Mussorgsky. She is married to the Soviet cellist and conductor Mstislav Rostropovich (also her accompanist), with whom she was prevented from performing in the Soviet Union while also being forbidden to leave the country. With him she went to the United States to live in 1974, and they were stripped of Soviet citizenship in 1978. In addition to the Russian repertoire (including complete operas *Boris Godunov* by Mussorgsky, *The Tsar's Bride* by Rimsky-Korsakov, and *Eugene Onegin* by Tchaikovsky), she has recorded music of Britten and the Verdi Requiem.

Vitry, Philippe de (October 31, 1291–June 9, 1361) The French composer, theorist, and poet Philippe de Vitry is known primarily for his treatise *Ars nova* (*c.* 1320), whose title was used by historians for the music of the 14th century (particularly France) as opposed to the ars antiqua of the late 13th century. He was in the service of the French court and in 1351 was appointed Bishop of Meaux. His few surviving compositions show him to be a master of the isorhythmic motet, and his treatise expounds a new theory of mensural notation, particularly the uses of red coloration, the classification of meter, and the recognition of duple time.

Vivaldi, Antonio (March 4, 1678–buried July 28, 1741) The violin virtuoso Antonio Vivaldi was one of the principal Italian composers of instrumental music in the first half of the 18th century. The son of Giovanni Battista Vivaldi, a violinist at St. Mark's, Venice, he studied with his father and Giovanni Legrenzi. He took holy orders in March 1703 and was known as *il prete rosso* ("the red priest") because of his auburn hair. From 1703 to 1740 he was associated with the Ospedale della Pietà in Venice, a home for girl foundlings. The girls studied music in all its branches, both vocal and instrumental, and under Vivaldi's guidance they produced one of the best-disciplined orchestras in Italy. For this institution Vivaldi composed hundreds of concertos, not only for stringed instruments but also for wind instruments, including the then novel clarinets, in combination with strings. He also composed many operas, most of which were produced in Venice. Although he was engaged at the Pietà, he made several journeys in Italy, Germany, to Vienna (1719–22), and to Amsterdam (1737–38). For three years (probably 1720–23) he was in the service of the Landgrave of Hesse-Darmstadt at Mantua. After 1725 he seems to have lived a wandering life as virtuoso and conductor but frequently returned to Venice to produce his operas. In 1735 he was reappointed *maestro di concerti* at the Pietà, the post he originally held at

Antonio Vivaldi
drawing by Pier Leone Ghezzi, 1723
courtesy, Biblioteca Apostolica Vaticana

least as early as 1709. In 1737 he was in Verona and in 1738 had returned to Venice. Throughout his life Vivaldi had to contend with a severe asthmatic condition. He died in Vienna.

Vivaldi was one of the greatest violinists of his era. He was a remarkable composer, abundant in inspiration and with a fine feeling for instrumental effect. He published 14 sets of works, mostly with the firm of Roger and Le Cene of Amsterdam, but he composed at least 450 concertos for many different instruments as well as sonatas for violin and continuo, trio sonatas, operas, oratorios, and cantatas. Much of this music shows signs of haste, but the finer examples—particularly the concertos published in his lifetime—are not only valuable in themselves but are remarkable for the influence they exerted. Vivaldi's ritornello–rondo form for concerto movements became a favorite with the late Baroque composers, including Bach, who transcribed several of Vivaldi's concertos; and it led to the concerto forms of the gallant and Classical composers. Vivaldi was also an accomplished composer of program music, as is evident from his Opus 8 set of concertos, *Il cimento dell'armonia e dell'invenzione,* which includes the concertos called *The Four Seasons*—musical illustrations of four sonnets that are printed with the music. Vivaldi's music, neglected after his death, became reestablished in the repertoire in the 20th century largely as a result of the Bach revival.

BIBLIOGRAPHY: Marc Pincherle, *Vivaldi: Genius of the Baroque* (1957); Walter Kolneder, *Antonio Vivaldi; His Life and Work* (1970); Arlan S. Martin, *Vivaldi Violin Concertos; a Handbook* (1972).

RECORDINGS: Numerous recordings of many works.

Vivier, Eugène (Léon) (December 4, 1817– February 24, 1900)   Socially popular as a humorist, the self-taught French horn player Eugène Vivier played in Paris at the Théâtre des Italiens and at the Opéra. He could play the equivalent of double and triple stops on his instrument, which delighted his audiences but was frowned on by other horn players. A favorite of Louis-Philippe of France and then of Napoleon III, he played with great success until the fall of the latter.

Voice of Ariadne, The: *see* OPERA (the 20th century); MUSGRAVE.

Von Stade, Frederica (b. June 1, 1945)   A specialist in the roles of Mozart and Rossini, the U.S. mezzo-soprano Frederica Von Stade studied at the Mannes College of Music in New York City, where she was selected by Rudolf Bing to sing *comprimario* roles at the Metropolitan Opera (Mozart's *Die Zauberflöte,* 1970); her first starring role there was Rosina (Rossini's *Il barbiere di Siviglia*), the role in which she made her Covent Garden debut in 1975. Her Paris Opéra debut in 1973 was as Cherubino, and in 1974 she premiered the role of Nina in Thomas Pasatieri's *The Seagull* with the Houston Opera. Other roles include Theobald in Verdi's *Don Carlo,* Stephano in Gounod's *Roméo et Juliette,* and Hansel in Engelbert Humperdinck's *Hänsel und Gretel.* Her recordings include Haydn's *Harmoniemesse.*

Voříšek, Jan Hugo (Václav) (May 11, 1791– November 19, 1825)   Educated in Prague as organist, pianist, and violinist, the Bohemian composer Jan Hugo Voříšek went to Vienna in 1813 expressly to meet Beethoven. While there he also became the intimate of Meyerbeer, Johann Nepomuk Hummel, and Ignaz Moscheles. In 1818 he became conductor of the Gesellschaft der Musikfreunde, and in 1822 he was appointed organist of the Viennese imperial chapel. His music typifies the transition from Beethoven to Schubert; his Impromptus, Op. 7 (1822), influenced those of Schubert. He also wrote a piano sonata, a symphony, and chamber music. Much sacred music and instrumental pieces remain in manuscript.

RECORDINGS: Impromptu No. 4; Piano Sonata in b-flat minor; Sinfonia in D.

Wagner, (Wilhelm) Richard (May 22, 1813– February 13, 1883)   The leading German composer of the late 19th century, Richard Wagner was considerably more. He maintained that he was not simply a composer but a musical dramatist. Alone among the great theater composers he created his dramas single-handed—plot, characters, text, and symbolism as well as music. His work had a revolutionary impact on the whole course of Western music.

life   Wagner was born at Leipzig the year his father, a minor civil servant, died, and in 1814 his mother married Ludwig Geyer, a painter and singer–actor. The artistic and theatrical background of Wagner's early years (several elder sisters became opera singers or actresses) was a formative influence. Impulsive and self-willed, he was a negligent scholar at the Kreuzschule at Dresden and the Nicolaischule at Leipzig; but under the inspiration of Beethoven, Mozart, Weber, Shakespeare, Goethe, and Schiller, he taught himself the piano and composition and wrote a five-act verse-tragedy. At 17 he had a crude overture performed at the Leipzig Theater.

A Hoffmannesque romantic youth, he was attracted by the glamour of German student life. Not having matriculated, he enrolled at

Richard Wagner
drawing by Franz Lenbach, c. 1870
courtesy, Richard Wagner Gedenkstatte,
Bayreuth, West Germany

Leipzig University as a second-class student; although he lived wildly, he applied himself earnestly to composition. Because he was impatient with all academic techniques, he spent a mere six months acquiring a groundwork with Theodore Weinlig, cantor of the Thomasschule; his real schooling was a close personal study of the scores of the masters, notably the quartets and symphonies of Beethoven. His own Symphony in C was performed at the Leipzig Gewandhaus concerts in 1833. On leaving the university that year, he spent the summer as operatic coach at Würzburg, where he composed his first opera, *Die Feen (The Fairies)*. As with all his subsequent works the libretto, after a fantastic tale by Carlo Gozzi, was his own. The opera was refused at Leipzig, so he became conductor for a provincial theatrical troupe from Magdeburg, impelled by having fallen in love with one of the actresses, Wilhelmine (Minna) Planer.

The next six years he spent struggling as a provincial conductor of third-rate opera companies in Magdeburg, Königsberg, and Riga, striving idealistically to raise standards and incurring enormous debts from his care-

less expenditures and poor pay. At Königsberg in 1836 he directed a single disastrous performance of his second opera, *Das Liebesverbot (The Ban on Love* after Shakespeare's *Measure for Measure)*. Later in the same year and in the same city he married Minna Planer. In 1839, fleeing from his creditors in Riga, he assayed his long-cherished plan to conquer Paris. German opera composers were without honor in their native country, which preferred French and Italian models; Wagner, precociously convinced of his coming greatness, thought a dazzling success in Paris would win him recognition at home.

His three years in Paris were disastrous. Despite Meyerbeer's recommendation he could not break into the closed circle at the Opéra. Living with the colony of poor German artists, he staved off starvation by means of musical journalism and hack work. But in 1840 he completed *Rienzi* (after Bulwer-Lytton's novel), and in 1841—his technique having profited from his hearing music of Berlioz—he composed his first representative opera, *Der fliegende Holländer (The Flying Dutchman)*, based on the old legend. He offered *Rienzi* to Dresden, where it was accepted.

He gladly returned to Dresden, where *Rienzi* was triumphantly performed on October 20, 1842. *The Flying Dutchman* (produced at Dresden, January 2, 1843) was less successful because of its innovative style and method. But he was appointed Hofkapellmeister at the court opera, a post he held until 1849. *Tannhäuser* (October 19, 1845; based, like all his future works, on Germanic legends) was coolly received but soon proved a steady attraction; each succeeding new work achieved popularity with the public despite persistent hostility from many critics. For the next 20 years, however, Wagner was not to present any further new works. He completed *Lohengrin* in 1848, but his projected administrative and artistic reforms alienated the court opera authorities. His mind having turned to ideas of social regeneration, he became embroiled in the German revolution. He wrote inflammatory articles and took an active part in the Dresden uprising of 1849. When this failed he fled from Germany with a price on his head, unable to attend the first performance of *Lohengrin* at Weimar by his friend Liszt on August 28, 1850.

Until 1858 Wagner lived in Zürich, composing, writing treatises, and conducting (he directed the London Philharmonic concerts in 1855). Having studied the Siegfried legend and the Norse myths as a possible basis for an opera and having written an operatic poem, *Siegfrieds Tod (Siegfried's Death)*, in which Siegfried was conceived as the new type of man who would emerge after the successful revolution he had hoped for, Wagner now thought intensely concerning revolution—social and artistic. From 1849 to 1852 he wrote his basic prose works: *Die Kunst und die Revolution (Art and Revolution), Das Kunstwerk der Zukunft (The Art Work of the Future), Eine Mitteilung an meine Freunde (A Communication to My Friends),* and *Oper und Drama (Opera and Drama).* The latter foreshadowed a new, revolutionary type of musical stage work—the vast work in fact on which he was engaged. By 1852 he had added to the poem of *Siegfrieds Tod* three others to precede it, the whole being called *Der Ring des Nibelungen* and providing the basis for a tetralogy of musical dramas: *Das Rheingold; Die Walküre; Der junge Siegfried,* later called simply *Siegfried;* and *Siegfrieds Tod,* later called *Götterdämmerung (Twilight of the Gods).*

By 1857 Wagner's style had been enriched by the stimulus of Liszt's discoveries, and he had composed *Das Rheingold, Die Walküre,* and two acts of *Siegfried.* But he now suspended work on *The Ring;* the impossibility of mounting this colossus within the foreseeable future was enforcing a stalemate on his career and led him to project a more normal work capable of immediate production. Also his optimistic social philosophy had yielded to a metaphysical, world-renouncing pessimism, nurtured by his discovery of Schopenhauer's philosophy. The outcome was *Tristan und Isolde* (1857–59), of which the crystallizing agent was his hopeless love for Mathilde Wesendonk (the wife of a wealthy friend and patron), which led to separation from his wife Minna.

Life in Zürich had become too embarrassing, and Wagner completed *Tristan* in Venice

and Lucerne. In 1859 he went to Paris, where two years later sumptuous productions of a revised version of *Tannhäuser* were a fiasco, resulting in scandalous riots by a powerful clique. But in 1861 an amnesty allowed him to return to Germany; from there he went to Vienna, where he heard *Lohengrin* for the first time. He was in and out of Vienna for three years, enjoying enthusiastic recognition, traveling widely as a conductor, and awaiting a projected production of *Tristan.* As this failed to materialize from the artists' bewilderment over its revolutionary style, Wagner began a second normal work, the comedy–opera *Die Meistersinger von Nürnberg.* But by 1864 his lavish expenditure and inveterate habits of borrowing and living on others had brought him to financial disaster; he had to flee from Vienna to avoid imprisonment for debt. *The Ring* was still incomplete and *Tristan* apparently unperformable. He had powerful enemies largely because of his own bad dealings, which arose from blind artistic self-centeredness and a sense of persecution. Without a penny he arrived in Stuttgart, a man of 51 without a future.

A miracle saved him. He had always made loyal friends because of his fascinating personality, his towering genius, and his artistic integrity. A new friend of the highest influence now came to his rescue. In 1864 Louis II, a youth of 18, ascended the throne of Bavaria. He was a fanatical admirer of Wagner's art; having read the poem of *The Ring* (published the year before with a plea for financial support), he invited Wagner to Munich to complete the work there.

The king set him up in a villa, and during the next six years there were successful Munich productions of all of Wagner's representative works to date, including the first performances of *Tristan* (1865) and *Die Meistersinger* (1868), conducted by Hans von Bülow, and *Das Rheingold* (1869) and *Die Walküre* (1870). At first a new theater at Munich was projected for this purpose with a music school attached, but this came to nothing because Wagner raised a storm by his way of living. Not only did he constantly run into debt despite his princely salary, but he also attempted to interfere in the government of the kingdom. He also entered into a relationship with von Bülow's wife Cosima, the daughter of Liszt. She bore him three children before her divorce in 1870 and her marriage to Wagner the same year (his first wife Minna died in 1866). In the summer of 1865 he began dictating to her his autobiography, *Mein Leben* (*My Life;* printed privately, 1870; first official publication, 1911). Wagner ceased to live in Munich as early as 1865, but he never forfeited the friendship of the king, who set him up at Triebschen on the Lake of Lucerne. From there he paid lengthy visits to Munich to supervise the productions of his works. His profound essay *Beethoven* appeared in 1870.

In 1869 Wagner had resumed work on *The Ring*, which, in keeping with his later views, he now brought to its world-renouncing conclusion. It had been agreed with the king that the first performance of the entire tetralogy should be at Munich, but Wagner broke the agreement, convinced that a new type of theater must be built for the purpose. Having discovered a suitable site at Bayreuth, he toured Germany, conducting concerts to raise funds and encouraging the formation of societies to support the plan. In 1872 the foundation stone was laid. In 1874 Wagner moved into a house at Bayreuth that he called Wahnfried ("peace from madness"), and that year he completed *The Ring*. The vast project was eventually realized in spite of enormous difficulties—artistic, administrative, and financial. The king, who had provided Wahnfried for Wagner, gave him 100,000 talers, and loans were obtained to be paid off by future royalties on Wagner's works. *The Ring* received its triumphant first performance in the new Festspielhaus at Bayreuth on August 13, 14, 16, and 17, 1876.

Wagner spent the remainder of his life at Wahnfried, making several visits to Italy and one to London in 1877 to give a successful series of concerts. During these years he composed his last work, the sacred festival drama *Parsifal*, begun in 1877 and completed and produced at Bayreuth in 1882. He died of heart failure at the height of his fame in Venice, and he was buried in the grounds of Wahnfried in the tomb he had himself prepared. A few days later King Louis rode to Bayreuth

alone at night to pay his personal tribute. Except for interruptions occasioned by the two world wars, the Festspielhaus has staged yearly festivals of Wagner's works; he had intended that it also present works of any outstanding German composers who might follow him.

Wagner's life was crammed with intense and variegated activity. His inexhaustible energy went not only into his work but also into innumerable friendships, enmities, and love affairs; into various far-reaching projects that he abandoned; and into sporadic political activity—and most of the countless separate happenings of his life were surrounded by tortuous intrigue.

development His development, achievement, and influence can only be understood by accepting his view that he was not simply a composer but a musical dramatist. Music never interested him for its own sake but as emotional and psychological expression. It is significant that he first taught himself composition to provide music for his boyhood verse-tragedy and that the conception that eventually materialized as *The Ring* originally presented itself as an alternative between a poetic drama concerned with Frederick I Barbarossa and a musical drama on the Siegfried legend. He composed few purely formal instrumental works; his whole significant *oeuvre* is musicodramatic. Nevertheless his search for the utmost depth, subtlety, and precision in the musicodramatic expression of feeling resulted in a radical revolution of compositional technique that crucially affected the development of music as an art.

Wagner's slow and erratic development, from the crudest beginner to a supremely original master creator, is unique. Beginning with the poorest technical equipment, he achieved greatness by sheer persistent force of artistic imagination and hard-won experience. However, his early incapacity should not be exaggerated. He made a considerable step forward from the gauche Symphony in C of his 20th year to the opera *Die Feen* of his 21st; the latter is a really professional work. In using the fantastic–legendary atmosphere and style of the new Romantic German opera so newly founded by Weber and continued by Heinrich

August Marschner, Wagner was already following his ordained path; his primary achievement was to bring this tradition to a magnificent climax and thus to set Germany on the operatic map once and for all. The crucial deficiency of *Die Feen* is its lack of any personal musical style. But an additional section for an aria in Marschner's *Der Vampyr,* written the same year, reveals Wagner's individuality clearly; it develops a vivid thematic complex that later became a main element in *The Ring.*

His two subsequent operas were not an advance but a diversion along a false path. Acutely aware of the provincialism of German opera (and with one eye on Paris), he wrote *Das Liebesverbot,* a clumsy plagiarism of Bellini and Donizetti, and *Rienzi,* a grandiose attempt at opera in the manner of Meyerbeer and Spontini. The former was so much wasted energy, but in the latter he learned something about constructing a musical stage work on the vast scale he was to adopt later. But it was in his comparatively compact next opera that his personality was first defined. Homesick in Paris and disillusioned with his false gods, he composed *The Flying Dutchman* in which his mature Romantic German style clearly emerged. If the subsidiary parts of the work followed conventional models, the main dramatic situations showed a Wagner who had hitherto appeared only in the music added to the *Vampyr* aria. The essence of this new style was the symphonic expression of aspects of the unconscious linked with the characters portrayed symbolically on the stage.

In *Tannhäuser* and *Lohengrin* Wagner developed this style on the large scale he had broached in *Rienzi.* The sheer scope of these works—the building of musicodramatic climax on climax—is masterly. But as before Wagner was only his true self in the symphonic handling of the main situations. In the subsidiary parts he was now worse off than before; having abandoned conventional models he handled the supporting action in an amateurish, four-square, semirecitative style that would later amuse him. And even at the great climaxes he sometimes used vulgar material, which is recognizable early Wagner but bears little relation to his definitive style. He wanted to reject as mere artifice all conventional methods of operatic construction and to extend dramatic and psychological development over a whole work by means of a continuous symphonic web, but he had not yet discovered a way to do this. The three early operas contain much deadwood of his own or others' devising.

It was during his period of concern with social theory that he found the way at last. Theoretically, in *The Art Work of the Future,* and autobiographically, in *A Communication to My Friends,* he projected a revolutionary type of musical stage work that he specified in full in *Opera and Drama.* This treatise analyzed intellectually the art form toward which he was moving creatively in building *The Ring.* Basing himself on the romantic–socialistic doctrine of the natural man and looking forward to the imminent creation of a socialist state in which this concept would flourish, he prophesied the disappearance of opera as artificial entertainment for an elite and the emergence of a new kind of musical stage work for the people, expressing the self-realization of free humanity. This new type of work was later to be called music drama, though Wagner preferred simply drama. It was intended as a return to the Greek drama as Wagner understood it—the public expression of national and human aspirations in symbolic form by enacting racial myths and using music for the full expression of the dramatic action.

Wagner's emphasis on opera as drama merely resumed and developed the ideas of Monteverdi and Gluck, but in propounding the revolutionary conception he had been striving for in his three previous works he went much further. He envisaged the disappearance of the old operatic type, with its libretto provided by a hack versifier as an opportunity for the composer to make a set-piece opera out of purely musical forms separated by recitative. The new art form would be created by a single artist, who would write a poetic drama that should find full expression as a musical drama when set to a continuous vocal-symphonic texture. This texture would be woven from basic thematic ideas called leitmotive (singular, LEITMOTIV), or "leading motifs"; these would arise naturally as expressive vocal phrases sung by characters at crucial emotional points of the drama and would then be developed by the orchestra as reminiscences in accordance with the expressive need of the dramatic and psychological development of the action.

This conception found full embodiment in *The Ring,* except that the leading motifs did not always arise as vocal utterances but were often introduced by the orchestra to portray characters, emotions, or events in the drama. With his use of this method he rose immediately to his amazing full stature; his style became unified and deepened immeasurably, and he was able now to fill his works from end to end with intensely characteristic music. Except for moments in *Das Rheingold* the old weaknesses—formal and stylistic—vanished altogether, and with them disappeared the last vestiges of the old opera. Wagner's works now fulfilled his new conception literally except in two respects: (1) Whereas in *Das Rheingold* and *Die Walküre* the symphonic development of the motifs was largely explanatory of the drama, Wagner used it with much greater subtlety from *Tristan* onward. The impact of Schopenhauer's theory of the supremacy of music among the arts (brilliantly developed in Wagner's own essay *Beethoven*) led him to tilt the expressive balance of musical drama more toward music; the motifs ceased to remain neatly identifiable with their dramatic source but worked with greater psychological complexity in the manner of free association. (2) For the comedy of *Die Meistersinger* Wagner incorporated into his new conception certain of the old operatic elements (aria, quintet, etc.).

achievement Wagner's creation of his own type of musical drama was a fantastic single-handed achievement, considering the scale and scope of his art. His method was to condense the confused mass of material at his disposal—the innumerable conflicting versions of the legend chosen as a basis—into a taut dramatic scheme; and in this scheme, as in his model, the *Oresteia* of Aeschylus, the stage events are few but crucial, the main part of the action devoted to the working out of the characters' psychological motivations. The poem—the verbal drama—he laid out with

musical structure in mind so that it formed a natural basis for large-scale musical forms comprising detailed musical–emotional development.

In setting the poem he used his mastery of large-scale construction, which he had learned from studying Beethoven, to keep the broad outlines clear while he consistently developed the leading motifs to mirror every shifting nuance of the psychological situation. Criticism of these motifs as arbitrary, factual labels shows a complete misunderstanding of Wagner; he called them "carriers of the feeling," and—because of their essentially emotional character, their pliability, and Wagner's resource in alternating, transforming, combining, and intermingling them—they function as the subtle expression of the changing feelings, conscious or unconscious, behind the dramatic symbols.

The result of these methods was a new art form of which the distinguishing feature was a profound and complex symbolism working on three indivisible planes—dramatic, verbal, and musical. The vital significance of this symbolism is more and more realized, though its involution of layer beneath layer of meaning has hardly been explored exhaustively. Through all the various stages of Wagner criticism—the opposition to him as a modernist in his lifetime, the heavy-handed exegesis of his philosophy during the high Wagnerian period (1880–1914), and the ill-informed abuse of his art when reaction set in between the two world wars—Wagner's complex interrelation of dramatic, verbal, and musical symbolism has not been approached with anything like the thoroughness it deserves.

Wagner's symbolic art was a fundamental contribution to the stream of thought and feeling passing from Ludwig Feuerbach, through Schopenhauer and Nietzsche, to modern depth psychology. The common theme of all his mature works, except *Die Meistersinger,* is the romantic concept of "redemption through love"; but this element, used rather naively in the three early operas, became in the later musical dramas a mere catalyst for much deeper complexes of ideas on various levels. In *The Ring* there are at least five interwoven strands of overt meaning concerned with German nationalism, international socialism, and the philosophies of Schopenhauer, Buddhism, and Christianity. (Wagner sketched a dramatic scheme for a Buddhist musical drama, *Die Sieger* [*The Victors*], and for a *Jesus von Nazareth,* neither of which he completed.) On another level there is a prophetic treatment of some of the dominant themes of depth psychology: power complex arising from sexual inhibition, incest, mother-fixation, and Oedipus complex.

Tristan stands in a line of symbolism extending from the themes of night and death explored by such German Romantic poets as Novalis, through the Schopenhauerian indictment of life as an evil illusion and the renunciation of the will to live, to the modern psychological insight into the relationship between eroticism and the death wish. *Die Meistersinger* stands apart as a work in which certain familiar themes are treated on a purely conscious plane with mellow wisdom and humor: the impulsiveness of youth and the resignation of age, the ecstacy of youthful love, the value of music as an art. But in Wagner's last work, *Parsifal,* the symbolism returns on a deeper level. He has been much criticized for this strongly personal treatment of a religious subject, which mingles the concepts of sacred and profane love; but in the light of modern knowledge, his insight into the relationship between religious and sexual experience can only seem much in advance of his time. The themes of innocence and purity, sexual indulgence and suffering, remorse and sexual renunciation are treated with a subtle intensity and depth of compassion that explore deeply into the unconscious and make *Parsifal* in some ways the most visionary of all Wagner's works.

influence Wagner's influence as musical dramatist and composer was powerful. Later operatic composers were greatly indebted to him—not only the many who adopted his methods more or less implicitly, like Richard Strauss, or the few who turned them to entirely personal account, like Debussy, but even those who rejected his conception and continued the older type of set-piece opera. Although few have been able to follow him in providing their own verbal basis, all significant opera composers have profited from his reform in

the matter of giving dramatic depth, continuity, and cohesion to their works. Music drama is dead, but musical drama is still fully alive.

In the purely musical field Wagner's influence was even more far-reaching. He developed such a wide expressive range that he made each of his works inhabit a unique emotional world of its own, and in doing so he raised the melodic and harmonic style of German music to its highest emotional and sensuous intensity. It was this intensity that caused him to bestride the late 19th century like a Colossus; the subsequent history of music, apart from the nationalist schools and the development of the traditional symphony by composers like Sibelius and Shostakovich, stems entirely from him either by extension of his discoveries or reaction against them. There was, of course, his immediate effect on late Romantics like Richard Strauss and like Bruckner and Mahler, both of whom exploited his gains in the field of the gigantic Austrian symphony; but his influence was far more widespread than this. The sensuous and symbolic content of his works profoundly affected artists of all kinds in France and impelled Debussy, partly by subtilization and partly by rejection, to evolve his own elusive, sensuous, symbolic, and epoch-making art. Moreover Wagner's persistent modulation without perfect cadences and his intensive development of German chromaticism, notably in *Tristan,* was later carried further by Schoenberg to the point where it led to the crucial breakthrough into atonality. On the negative side the psychological intensity of his music caused a violent reaction that resulted in the fierce abstract intellectualism of the theory and practice of the neoclassical school headed by Stravinsky. Wagner was the great turning point of Western music, representing at once the final Romantic culmination of the old tonal system and the source of the new music of the 20th century.

BIBLIOGRAPHY: George Bernard Shaw, *The Perfect Wagnerite,* 4th ed. (1923; reprint, 1967), and *Major Critical Essays* (1932; reprint, 1971); Richard Wagner, *Letters of Richard Wagner to Anton Pusinelli* (1932; reprint, 1972) and *Letters of Richard Wagner: The Burrell Collection* (1950; reprint, 1972); Ernest

Newman, *The Life of Richard Wagner*, 4 vols. (1933–46; reprint, 1976); Edward M. Terry, *A Richard Wagner Dictionary* (1939; reprint, 1971); Jack M. Stein, *Richard Wagner and the Synthesis of the Arts* (1960; reprint, 1973); Robert Donington, *Wagner's Ring and Its Symbols: Music and Myth*, rev. ed. (1974); Robert W. Gutman, *Richard Wagner: The Man, His Mind, and His Music* (1974); Herbert Barth *et al*, eds., *Wagner: A Documentary Study* (1975); John Culshaw, *Reflections on Wagner's Ring*, rev. ed. (1976); Dietrich Fischer-Dieskau, *Wagner and Nietzsche* (1976); Hans Gal, *Richard Wagner* (1976); Charles Osborne, *Richard Wagner and His World* (1977); John Chancellor, *Wagner* (1978); Cosima Wagner, *Cosima Wagner's Diaries 1869–1877* (1978).

RECORDINGS: Numerous recordings of most works.

Wagner, Roger (b. January 16, 1914) The French-born U.S. choral conductor Roger Wagner sang as a boy soprano and at age 12 became organist and choirmaster at the Church of St. Ambrose in Los Angeles. After studying organ (with Marcel Dupré), voice, and church music in France, he returned in 1937 to Los Angeles, where he studied with Bruno Walter and became musical director of St. Joseph's Church. The choral concert series he established there led to his appointment (1945) as supervisor of youth choruses for the City of Los Angeles Bureau of Music. In 1948 he founded the Roger Wagner Chorale, with which he has toured and recorded works from Palestrina and Monteverdi to Carl Orff and Lukas Foss. Since 1965 he has also been conductor of the Los Angeles Master Chorale. He is director of choral music at the University of California, Los Angeles, and at Marymount College in Palos Verdes. He has published many choral arrangements.

Wagner tuba: *see* TUBA.

Walcha, Helmut (b. October 27, 1907) Noted as an interpreter of Bach on Baroque instruments, the blind German organist Helmut Walcha studied in Leipzig with Günther Ramin, serving as his assistant at the Thomaskirche. In 1929 Walcha became organist at the Friedenskirche in Frankfurt-am-Main. He joined the faculty of the Hoch Conservatory in 1933 and five years later became professor at the State Music Academy in Frankfurt. He has edited the organ concertos of Handel, has composed sets of organ chorale preludes, and has written about the organ and on the organ music of Max Reger. He concertizes widely and has made numerous recordings of the music of Bach.

Waldstein Sonata (Beethoven, No. 21): *see* MELODY.

Waldteufel, Émile (December 9, 1837–February 16, 1915) Educated at the Paris Conservatoire, the Alsatian pianist and composer Émile Waldteufel was pianist to the Empress Eugénie and director of the balls at court, for which he wrote much music. Of his 250 dances for orchestra, many are arranged for piano; the most popular were *Skaters' Waltz* and *Les Sirènes*. His *España* waltz was based on themes by Emmanuel Chabrier. In his day he was considered to be as important an exponent of the French waltz as Johann Strauss the Younger was to the Viennese waltz.

RECORDINGS: Waltzes and polkas.

Walküre, Die: *see* GLOCKENSPIEL; LEITMOTIV; WAGNER (life) and (development).

Walter, Bruno, real name, Bruno Walter Schlesinger (September 15, 1876–February 17, 1962) A German conductor of the romantic tradition, Bruno Walter was known for his spiritual approach to music. Though out of step with 20th-century trends, he was so well equipped musically that he became a major figure—filling the wide gulf between the extremes of his day, Toscanini and Wilhelm Furtwängler.

Educated in his native Berlin (Stern Conservatory), he began as a pianist but made his debut as a conductor at the Cologne Opera in 1894. By 1900 he was at the State Opera in Berlin, and the following year he became Mahler's associate in Vienna—the beginning of what was to be a lifetime in the promotion of the master's music (he conducted the premieres of *Das Lied von der Erde* [1911] and the Ninth Symphony [1912]). Walter moved to the Munich Opera (1914–22) and from 1922 conducted at Salzburg, where his interest in Mozart developed. Appointments followed at

Bruno Walter   *EB Inc.*

the Berlin Municipal Opera (1925–29) and as Furtwängler's successor in Leipzig with the Gewandhaus Orchestra (1929–33). The advent of the Nazi regime in Germany forced him to leave Leipzig and his Berlin concerts; he moved first to Vienna (1936–38), then Paris, and finally the United States (1939). He conducted frequently at the Metropolitan Opera and the New York Philharmonic (musical adviser, 1947–49). Known primarily for his interpretations of the Viennese school, he was generally considered to have no equal in the works of Mahler and of Bruckner.

Walther, Johann Gottfried (September 18, 1684–March 23, 1748)   The German organist and composer Johann Gottfried Walther was a pioneer of musical lexicography. Born at Erfurt, he was a pupil there of Johann Bernhard Bach. In 1702 he was organist at the Thomaskirche at Erfurt, in 1707 organist at Weimar, and from 1721 court musician there. Between 1708 and 1714 he formed a friendship at Weimar with Johann Sebastian Bach, of whom he was a second cousin. His compositions include chorale preludes and variations for the organ and organ arrangements of con-

certos by Tommaso Albinoni, Giuseppe Torelli, and other Italian composers. His *Musicalisches Lexikon* (1728–32) was the first music encyclopedia of biography, bibliography, and musical terms and has remained an invaluable work.

RECORDINGS: Chorale-Variations (4); Concertos (7); Partita, "Jesu meine Freude."

Walton, William (Turner) (b. March 29, 1902) An English composer whose works illustrate one of the main trends in the development of English music in the second half of the 20th century, William Walton went to Oxford in 1912, where he was a chorister at Christ Church. In composition he was self-taught, though he received advice from Ernest Ansermet and Busoni.

Most of Walton's early compositions were destroyed. His First Quartet was performed at Salzburg in 1923, and in the same year *Façade,* a set of pieces for chamber ensemble written to accompany a recitation of poems by Edith Sitwell, was given in London. The overture *Portsmouth Point* (Zürich, 1926), inspired by a print of Thomas Rowlandson, established Walton's reputation as a composer for orchestra, and in 1927 a selection of pieces from *Façade,* reorchestrated, was performed as an orchestral suite (*Façade* was used in Frederick Ashton's ballet by that name in 1931, which has become a repertoire standard). The Sinfonia Concertante for piano and orchestra (first performed 1928; revised 1943) was followed by the Viola Concerto, one of Walton's finest works, first given in London in 1929 with Hindemith as soloist. The oratorio *Belshazzar's Feast* (Leeds, 1931) on texts from the Book of Psalms showed Walton's gift as a composer of choral music, and though his First Symphony (1935) was influenced by Sibelius, it proclaimed his originality. His Violin Concerto (Cleveland, 1939, with Heifetz) showed a romantic tendency, but the overture *Scapino* (1941) developed the style of his earlier works. A series of scores for motion pictures, begun in 1934 with *Escape Me Never,* continued with scores for George Bernard Shaw's *Major Barbara* (1941) and Shakespeare's *Henry V* (1944), *Hamlet* (1947), and *Richard III* (1954). In 1948 he collaborated with the poet Christopher Hassall in the opera *Troilus and Cressida* (Covent Garden, 1954) after the tale of Chaucer, and a one-act opera, *The Bear* (1967), was composed for the Aldeburgh Festival. Other later works include *Johannesburg Festival* Overture (1955), Cello Concerto (1956), Partita for orchestra (1958), Second Symphony (1960), Variations on a Theme of Hindemith (1963); Missa brevis (1966); Improvisations on an Impromptu of Benjamin Britten (1970); and Five Bagatelles for guitar (1972).

Walton excels in the larger musical forms. Though his work incorporates elements of the styles of his older contemporaries, notably Elgar, Hindemith, and Stravinsky, it nevertheless possesses a distinctive melodic and harmonic character. Walton was knighted in 1951.

BIBLIOGRAPHY: Frank Stewart Howes, *The Music of William Walton* (1965).

RECORDINGS: *Belshazzar's Feast; Coronation* Te Deum; *Crown Imperial* March; *Façade;* Improvisations on an Impromptu of Benjamin Britten; *Orb and Sceptre* March; Partita for orchestra; Sonata for strings; Suites from *Hamlet, Henry V,* and *Richard III;* Symphony No. 2; Variations on a Theme of Hindemith; Viola Concerto; Violin Concerto; Violin Sonata.

waltz A dance in $\frac{3}{4}$ time evolved from the LÄNDLER in the 18th century (from the German *walzen*, "to revolve"). Danced in couples and characterized by a step, slide, and step, it enjoyed widespread popularity as a ballroom dance throughout the 19th century and into the 20th. Its variations include the rapid, whirling Viennese waltz and the gliding, dipping Boston. Since its introduction in Pierre Gardel's *La Dansomanie* (1800), the waltz has appeared in many ballets, including *The Sleeping Beauty* (Tchaikovsky), *Gaîté Parisienne* (Offenbach), and *Façade* (William Walton). It was Weber who established the waltz as a concert form with his *Invitation to the Dance* (1819) for piano. Beethoven soon followed with his monumental 33 Variations on a Waltz by Diabelli, and notable examples for piano were written by Chopin, Liszt, Brahms (Brahms also composed two sets of

Liebeslieder waltzes for piano duet and vocal quartet), and Ravel. The concert waltz for orchestra was used by Berlioz *(Symphonie fantastique),* Liszt *(Mephisto* Waltzes), Saint-Saëns *(Danse macabre),* and Sibelius *(Valse triste).* Parallel to the development of the concert waltz was that of the dance waltz, especially in Vienna and most notably by Johann Strauss the Younger.

Wanderer, Der: *see* CYCLIC FORM; FANTASIA; ROMANTIC PERIOD (Wagnerian development); SCHUBERT (years of promise) and (maturity).

War and Peace: *see* OPERA (the 20th century); PROKOFIEV.

Ward, Robert (Eugene) (b. September 13, 1917) Educated at the Eastman School (Howard Hanson and Bernard Rogers), Juilliard School (Frederick Jacobi), and Berkshire Music Center (Copland), the U.S. composer and conductor Robert Ward taught at Juilliard and at Columbia University. He was director of the Third Street Settlement Music School (1952–55) in New York City and in the latter year became president of the American Composers' Alliance. He has served on many advisory boards for music and since 1967 has been president of the North Carolina School of the Arts in Winston-Salem. He has also conducted orchestras in the United States and Europe. His opera *The Crucible* (1961) after Arthur Miller won the 1962 Pulitzer Prize. He has written two other operas *(Pantaloon,* 1956, later titled *He Who Gets Slapped; The Lady from Colorado,* 1964); four symphonies (1941–58); Piano Concerto (1968); and choral music, organ pieces, and chamber music.

RECORDINGS: *The Crucible;* Piano Concerto.

Warfield, William (b. January 20, 1920) Educated at the Eastman School, the U.S. baritone William Warfield worked with the professional training program of the American Theater Wing and made his recital debut in New York City's Town Hall in 1950. In 1955 he toured Europe as soloist with the Philadelphia Orchestra. He sang in Marc Blitzstein's *Regina,* as Porgy in the touring company of Gershwin's *Porgy and Bess,* and as Joe in *Show*

Boat (Jerome Kern and Oscar Hammerstein II) both in Vienna and in the 1951 film version. He was married for a time to soprano Leontyne Price.

Warlock, Peter, real name, Philip Heseltine (October 30, 1894–December 17, 1930) An English composer, critic, and editor known for his songs and for his exemplary editions of Elizabethan music, Peter Warlock was largely self-taught, though he received encouragement from Frederick Delius and Bernard van Dieren. In 1920 he founded the musical journal *The Sackbut* and in 1923 published a book on Delius. With Cecil Gray he wrote a study of Carlo Gesualdo (1926) and also published monographs on Thomas Whythorne and the English ayre. He transcribed and edited works of John Dowland, Thomas Ravenscroft, Purcell, and others. He composed many songs, including the cycles *Lilligay* (1923), *The Curlew* (1924), and *Candlelight* (1924); choral works; and *Capriol* Suite (1927) for strings.

RECORDINGS: *Capriol* Suite; Serenade for strings.

Warren, Leonard (April 21, 1911–March 4, 1960) Educated at the Greenwich House Music School in New York City and in Milan, the U.S. baritone Leonard Warren won a Metropolitan Opera audition in 1938 and made his debut the following year as Paolo Albiani in Verdi's *Simon Boccanegra.* A mainstay of the company, he sang primarily roles of Verdi, although he was heard as Mussorgsky's Rangoni *(Boris Godunov)* and Puccini's Scarpia *(Tosca);* he was unsurpassed as Iago *(Otello)* and Rigoletto. Warren toured Europe, South America, and Russia (1958), the homeland of his father (the name Warren was an Americanization of Varenov). He died on the Metropolitan stage in the middle of a performance of Verdi's *La forza del destino.*

War Requiem: *see* BRITTEN; MASS (requiem).

Water Music: *see* HANDEL (life) and (works); ROREM.

Watts, André (b. June 20, 1946) A product of the Philadelphia Musical Academy and of Leon Fleisher at the Peabody Conservatory in Baltimore, the U.S. pianist André Watts was catapulted into stardom as a last-minute

replacement in Liszt's Piano Concerto in E-flat Major with the New York Philharmonic (1963). He has had a continuing success as a bravura pianist in the romantic tradition. His recordings range from Haydn to Franck.

Watts, Helen (Josephine) (b. December 7, 1927) Educated at the Royal Academy of Music in London, the Welsh soprano Helen Watts sang with the chorus of the BBC until 1953, when she sang a leading role in Gluck's *Orphée et Eurydice.* A noted singer of Bach and Handel, she made her stage debut in 1958 singing *Theodora* with the Handel Opera Society of London. Recordings, in addition to much Bach and Handel, include Purcell's *Dido and Aeneas,* four Haydn masses, Mahler symphonies, Brahms, Frederick Delius, Vaughan Williams, and Britten.

Weber, Ben (Brian) (b. July 23, 1916) One of the first U.S. composers to use the dodecaphonic idiom, Ben Weber was principally self-taught, although he was encouraged by Artur Schnabel and Schoenberg. Since 1945 he has taught composition and orchestration privately and has served on executive boards of the International Society for Contemporary Music, Composers Recordings, Inc., and the American Composers Alliance. His music is contrapuntal, and his forms are generally those associated with diatonic music. Later works increase length, density, and number of players. He has written more than 30 pieces of chamber music and some 15 works for orchestra; important representative works include Five Pieces (1941) for cello and piano, Symphony on Poems of William Blake (1952), Violin Concerto (1954), Piano Concerto (1961), *Concert Poem* (1970) for violin and orchestra, *Consort of Winds* (1974), sonatas for violin and cello, quartets, song cycles, and choruses.

RECORDINGS: *Bagatelles* (5) for piano; *Consort of Winds; Dolmen, An Elegy;* Fantasia for piano; Piano Concerto; Quartet No. 2; Three Pieces for piano.

Weber, Carl Maria (Friedrich Ernst) von (November 18, 1786–June 5, 1826) The German composer Carl Maria von Weber was also celebrated in his lifetime as pianist, conductor, critic, and opera director. His most important work was in the field of opera, and his *Der Freischütz* (1821) was not only the most immediately and widely popular German opera that had then been written but remains his most famous and in many ways most characteristic composition. It is the keystone of Romantic opera, and all Weber's music and his energetic work as a practicing musician were devoted to the Romantic movement of which he is the most typical representative.

Weber was born at Eutin, Holstein, into a musical and theatrical family. His father, Franz Anton von Webern, was a musician and soldier of fortune who formed a small traveling theater company; his mother was a singer; and his uncles, aunts, and brothers were mostly involved to some degree in music and the stage. Franz Anton seems to have wished upon the family the baronial "von" to which it had in fact no title. When Carl Maria, from his birth a sickly child, began to show signs of talent, he was set to work under various teachers in towns visited by the family troupe in the hope that he might prove a Mozartian *Wunderkind*. These included Michael Haydn, under whose eye Weber wrote and published his Six Fughettas.

Pausing briefly in Munich on their wanderings, Weber learned the craft of lithography from its inventor, Aloys Senefelder, and moving on to Freiberg the Webers planned to set up a lithographic works that would help to propagate the young composer's music. The scheme fell through, but meanwhile Weber had composed the first of his operas to survive in part, *Das Waldmädchen* (an earlier piece is lost). It was a failure, but on a return visit to Salzburg Weber completed his first wholly surviving opera, *Peter Schmoll,* an agreeable work that can still make an effect on the stage. But it failed on its production in Augsburg, and Weber renewed his studies under the charlatanesque but influential Abbé Vogler. Through Vogler he was appointed Kapellmeister at Breslau (now Wrocław, Poland) in 1804. After many troubles occasioned by the difficulty of so young a director in putting through reforms and a near-fatal accident when he ruined his voice by swallowing some engraving acid, Weber was forced to resign. He was rescued with an appointment by Duke

Eugen of Württemberg, for whose private orchestra he wrote two symphonies. They are attractive, inventive works; but symphony, with its dependence on established forms, was not the natural medium of a composer who was to lead his fellow Romantics into experiments based on freer forms derived from literary, poetic, or pictorial ideas.

From here Weber passed to a secretarial post at the corrupt court of King Friedrich of Württemberg. In this feudal backwater of Germany he lived so carelessly and ran up so many debts that, after a brief imprisonment, he was banished. The fruit of these years (1807–10) was the Romantic opera *Silvana* (which in some ways foreshadows *Der Freischütz*), songs, piano pieces, chamber music, and other works. Weber and his father fled to Mannheim, and it was here that he was, in his own words, "born for the second time." He made friends with an influential circle of artists, from whom he stood out not only by his talent as a singer, pianist, and guitarist but for his considerable personal charm and Romantic theories. Moving on to Darmstadt he met Vogler again and came to know Meyerbeer as a fellow pupil. From this period date

Carl Maria von Weber
drawing by Christian Hornemann, 1820
courtesy, Deutsche Staatsbibliothek,
Musikabteilung, DDR Berlin

principally an excellent piano concerto and the delightful little opera *Abu Hassan.*

Disappointed in not obtaining a post in Darmstadt, Weber traveled to Munich, where his friendship with the clarinet virtuoso Heinrich Bärmann led to the writing of a concertino and two brilliant clarinet concertos. In all he was to write six clarinet works for Bärmann, with whom he also toured. The clarinet remained, with the horn, one of the favorite instruments of a composer whose ear for new sounds was to make him one of the greatest orchestrators in the history of music. He was also a great piano virtuoso; his music reflects something of the brilliance and melancholy and somewhat exhibitionist charm that is described by his contemporaries. Touring through Germany in the years before Waterloo, with the country still disunited and at war, he exemplified the artist as representative of a new age—no longer servant but a free spirit. All his work—both his music and his critical writings—is in furtherance of the ideals of Romanticism as an art in which feeling now took pride of place over form, and heart over head.

After a period in Berlin when he caught the patriotic fervor of the day in some stirring choruses and songs, Weber was appointed to the opera in Prague (1813) and was able at last to put his theories into full practice. His choice of works showed his care for Romantic ideals, his choice of artists his concern for a balanced ensemble rather than a group of virtuosos; and by publishing introductory articles he saw to it that his audiences were carefully prepared. His path was not easy; a stormy love affair left him disconsolate, and opposition to his work forced him to resign in 1816. Such by now was his reputation that he was able to secure an appointment as director of the German opera at Dresden.

In a city more backward than most in Germany and one with a flourishing rival Italian opera, Weber as the prophet of a German national opera was faced with even greater difficulties. Happily married to one of his former singers, Caroline Brandt, he applied himself energetically to the foundation of a new style. No detail escaped him; he supervised repertoire, recruitment, casting, scenery, lighting,

and production as well as the orchestra and the singing, taking care to see that every performer fully understood the words and plot of each opera. It left him little time for writing operas himself, especially with the inexorable advance of his tuberculosis, though his many other works of the period include the last of his four piano sonatas, many songs, smaller piano pieces such as the famous *Invitation to the Dance,* and the *Konzertstück* for piano and orchestra. But in 1821 all Germany rang with the success of *Der Freischütz* in Berlin. Here for the first time was an opera of genius about things familiar to every German: the simple village life with its rough humor and sentimental affections, the surrounding forest with its smiling aspect concealing a supernatural horror in the famous Wolf's Glen scene of the midnight casting of the magic bullets, and above all the characters—from the cheerful huntsmen and village girls to the simple, valiant hero and the prince who rules over them—were all expressed in music of sunny, Germanic tunefulness and eeriness, a mirror in which every German could find a reflection.

Der Freischütz made Weber a national hero; though his next opera *Euryanthe* (1823) is a more ambitious work and a larger achievement—anticipating Wagner as his piano music does Chopin and Liszt—it foundered on the clumsy though not intolerable libretto. Commissioned by Covent Garden for a new opera, Weber took on the task of learning English and working with the librettist James Robinson Planché by correspondence; his motive was to earn enough money to support his family after his death, which he knew to be not far off. In form *Oberon* was little to his taste, having too many spoken scenes and elaborate stage devices for a composer who had always worked for the unification of the theatrical arts in opera. But into it he poured some of his most exquisite music, and to London he traveled for the premiere in 1826. Barely able to walk, he was sustained by the kindness of his host, Sir George Smart, and by the longing to get home again to his family. *Oberon* was a success and Weber was feted; but he was sinking fast, and shortly before he was to start the journey back to Germany, he was found dead in his room.

866

BIBLIOGRAPHY: Max Maria von Weber, *Carl Maria von Weber: The Life of an Artist,* 2 vols. (1865; reprint, 1969); Hector Berlioz, *Mozart, Weber, and Wagner* (1918; reprint, 1976); William Saunders, *Weber* (1940; reprint, 1970); John Warrack, *Carl Maria von Weber,* 2nd ed. (1976); Carl Maria von Weber et al, *Weber in London, 1826* (1976).

RECORDINGS: Numerous recordings of many works.

Webern, Anton (December 3, 1883–September 15, 1945)   The Austrian composer, conductor, and musicologist Anton Webern was a pupil and lifelong disciple of Schoenberg. He refined and crystallized 12-tone serial technique and composed music whose brevity and asceticism made him one of the most important influences on composers of the post-World War II generation.

Born in Vienna, Webern received his first musical training from his mother, who was an amateur pianist. The family moved to Klagenfurt in 1894, and there he studied piano and theory with Edwin Komauer. He also learned to play the cello, and his first known compositions were two pieces for cello and piano and some songs dating from 1899. Before entering the University of Vienna in 1902, he attended performances of Wagner operas at Bayreuth that made deep impressions on the young musician. At Vienna he studied musicology with Guido Adler and received his Ph.D. in 1906 for a dissertation on Heinrich Isaac's *Choralis Constantinus II,* of which he published an edition in 1909. Webern said that the complex procedures of canonic writing and inversion employed by Isaac had an enormous influence on his own compositions.

In 1904 Webern had begun to study composition with Schoenberg, who was almost unknown and whose principle of "composition with twelve notes related only to one another" was not to be evolved for another 13 years. Webern and Berg were to become Schoenberg's greatest pupils and perhaps the only ones to add anything significant to Schoenberg's techniques. Both younger composers remained strongly under Schoenberg's influence to the ends of their lives.

The year 1908 marked the completion of

Anton Webern
Bild-Archiv der Oesterreichischen Nationalbibliothek, Wien

Webern's Passacaglia for orchestra and the choral canon *Entflieht auf leichten Kähnen* and the beginning of a successful conducting career that was to be his main livelihood until 1934. Posts he occupied during this career included that of Kapellmeister in Prague, Danzig, and Stettin as well as the distinguished positions of conductor of the Vienna Arbeiter-Symphoniekonzerte (from 1921) and of the Arbeiter-Singverein (from 1923). In the years of Schoenberg's Society for Private Musical Performances Webern conducted many premieres and later became director of the society. In 1927 he was appointed conductor for the Austrian radio. This career came to an end for political reasons in 1934, and the final years of his life were spent in poverty, with only a small amount of teaching and spasmodic work for Universal Edition to support him. He published two theoretical works: *Der Weg zur Komposition mit 12 Tönen* (1932; "The Path to 12-tone Composition") and *Der Weg zur neuen Musik* (1933; Eng. trans., *The Path to the New Music,* 1963). After spending World War II at Mödling near Vienna, he went to Mittersill near Salzburg, where he was accidentally shot by a soldier in the U.S. occupation forces.

Webern's compositions show how early was the split with traditional musical conceptions, subsequently causing the disapproval of the Nazi regime. The Passacaglia is lushly scored, very much after the style of Richard Strauss or of Max Reger, but the succeeding works show a rapid development to the Six Pieces for orchestra and the Four Pieces for violin and piano (both 1910). These show an extraordinary sparseness of texture and compactness of design that perhaps reached its extreme manifestation in the Three Little Pieces (1914) for cello and piano.

From this point Webern's music was to become simpler, as the various elements were rationalized in a new way. The Five Canons (1924) for soprano and two clarinets are absolutely strict in following their canonic design, and *Kinderstück* (1924) for piano is the first to use Schoenberg's serial technique, which Webern was to employ in all succeeding works.

The 14 works of the final 20 years of his life, culminating in the two cantatas and the Variations for orchestra (1940), show a more lyrical approach to composition and a richer texture, despite the ever increasing internal organization and the serialization—not only of pitch but also of rhythm—of instrumental timbre and even of dynamics.

It was this total serialization that first appealed to the early post-World War II composers, especially to Stockhausen and Pierre Boulez and later to Stravinsky. Within 10 years of his death Webern was rediscovered and widely studied, analyzed, and idolized. Perhaps the most important factors in the rediscovery were the publication of all his works with opus numbers (concluded in 1956), the recording of the complete works under Robert Craft, and the foundation by Hans Moldenhauer of an archive of Webern documents (now at Northwestern University, Evanston, Illinois).

BIBLIOGRAPHY: René Leibowitz, *Schoenberg and His School* (1949; reprint, 1970); Hans Moldenhauer, *The Death of Anton Webern: A Drama in Documents* (1961), *Anton von Webern Perspectives* (1966; reprint,

1978), and with Rosaleen Moldenhauer, *Anton von Webern: Chronicle of His Life and Work* (1978); Friedrich Wildgans, *Anton Webern* (1966); Anton Webern, *Letters to Hildegard Jone and Josef Humplik* (1967); Walter Kolneder, *Anton Webern: An Introduction to His Works* (1968).

RECORDINGS: Cantatas (2); Cello Sonata; Five Movements for quartet; Five Pieces for orchestra; Four Pieces for violin and piano; Passacaglia for orchestra; Quartets (2); Six Bagatelles for quartet; Six Pieces for orchestra; Symphony for chamber orchestra; Three Little Pieces for cello and piano; Variations for piano.

Weelkes, Thomas (c. 1570?–November 30, 1623) One of the most important English madrigal composers, Thomas Weelkes was also an organist. Nothing definite is known of his early life, but his later career suggests that he came from southern England. He may have been the Thomas Wikes who was a chorister at Winchester College (1583–84), as he was organist there from about 1598 to 1601. The dedications of his first two sets of madrigals (1597–98) refer to his youthfulness at that time. His finest work is in the two books of madrigals, of five and six parts respectively, that appeared in 1600. He was appointed organist of Chichester Cathedral probably late in 1601. In 1602 he received the degree of bachelor of music at Oxford, and the following year he married. From the time of his appointment at Chichester, he composed chiefly sacred works. In his last volume of madrigals (1608) he claims the title "Gentleman of the Chapel Royal." From 1609 he was frequently reprimanded at Chichester for bad language and drunkenness. He died in London.

Nearly 100 of his madrigals survive. They combine the elegance of Luca Marenzio and the firm sense of tonality characteristic of Morley with the verbal sensitivity of Byrd. Weelkes is remarkable for his word painting, his lively rhythms, and his highly developed sense of form and structure. He also wrote music for virginal, viols, and organ. His sacred compositions, largely unpublished, suffered much loss and destruction. Of Weelkes's 10 Anglican services not one survives complete;

three that have been reconstructed are the work of an original mind that could blend the solo writing of the English verse anthem with the massive antiphonal style of the Venetian school. Twenty of Weelkes's 48 anthems are either complete or restorable; the full anthems (with no solo verses) show that he was at his best when deploying large numbers of voices. His range of expression is wide. In the light style it is illustrated by the airy ballett "On the Plains Fairy Trains"; examples of the graver manner include the madrigal "O Care, Thou Wilt Despatch Me," remarkable for its chromaticism, and the massive "O Lord, Arise."

BIBLIOGRAPHY: Edmund H. Fellowes, *The English Madrigal Composers,* 2nd ed. (1948), and *English Cathedral Music,* rev. ed. (1973); David Brown, *Thomas Weelkes* (1969).

RECORDINGS: Madrigals; church music.

Weidinger, Anton (1767–September 20, 1852) Long considered the inventor of the keyed trumpet, the Viennese trumpet virtuoso Anton Weidinger was instead its foremost performer. He studied trumpet with the chief court trumpeter Peter Neuhold and completed (1785) his apprenticeship in less than the usual two years. He served as field trumpeter in military regiments, including that of Archduke Joseph, until 1792, when he was engaged by the Royal Imperial Theater in Vienna. The earliest known concerto for a chromatic trumpet was Haydn's (1796), and it is quite likely that it was composed for Weidinger; Haydn was one of the witnesses at Weidinger's wedding (1797), so it is presumed that they were friends. By 1800 Weidinger was a leading musical figure in Vienna, and in 1803 he toured Germany, England, and France as a soloist. He appeared with his trumpeter son Joseph in 1817, but by 1819 interest in solo trumpet had waned. He continued playing in orchestras until his retirement in 1850.

Weill, Kurt (March 2, 1900–April 3, 1950) The German-born U.S. composer Kurt Weill was the creator of a revolutionary kind of satirical opera. He studied first with Albert Bing at Dessau and briefly with Engelbert Humperdinck and gained experience as

an opera coach and conductor in the 1919–20 season at Dessau and Ludenscheid. Settling in Berlin, he studied with Busoni (1921–24) and began as a composer with instrumental works.

Weill's early music was expressionist, experimental, and abstract. His first three operas, *Der Protagonist* (1926; one act with libretto by Georg Kaiser), *Na und?* (1926), and *Royal Palace* (1927), established his position, together with Ernst Krenek and Hindemith, as one of Germany's most promising young opera composers. His first collaboration with Bertolt Brecht was the singspiel *Mahagonny,* which was a *succès de scandale* at the Baden-Baden Festival in 1927. *Die Dreigroschenoper* (1928; "The Threepenny Opera," also with Brecht), a transposition of John Gay's *Beggar's Opera* with 18th-century thieves, highwaymen, jailers, and their doxies turned into typical characters in the Berlin underworld of the 1920s, established both the topical opera and the reputations of composer and librettist. Weill's music was in turn harsh and hauntingly melancholy. The libretto was soon translated into 11 languages, and with this success *Mahagonny* was expanded into a full-length opera under the title *Aufstieg und Fall der Stadt Mahagonny* ("The Rise and Fall of the City Mahagonny") and produced in Dresden in 1930. The music for it showed a remarkably skillful synthesis of U.S. popular–ragtime–jazz idioms, and it sharply satirized modern life in an imaginary southern U.S. town. Weill's wife, the actress Lotte Lenya, had sung for the first time in *Mahagonny* (1927) and was a great success in it and in *Dreigroschenoper.* These works, the cantata *Der Lindberghflug* (1929), in which Hindemith collaborated, and a children's opera *Der Jasager* (1930; "The Yea-sayer") aroused much controversy. Weill's political and musical ideas and his Jewish birth made him *persona non grata* to the Nazis, and after the production of the opera *Die Burgschaft* (1932; "The Surety" with libretto by Caspar Neher) he left Berlin. His music was banned in Germany until after World War II.

Weill spent time in Paris and London and in 1935 went to New York City, where he became highly successful as a composer of

Broadway musicals. He wrote incidental music for Paul Green's *Johnny Johnson* (1936) and Franz Werfel's *The Eternal Road* (1937), the score for Maxwell Anderson's *Knickerbocker Holiday* (1938), followed by *Lady in the Dark* (1941; libretto and lyrics by Moss Hart and Ira Gershwin), *One Touch of Venus* (1943; libretto and lyrics by S. J. Perelman and Ogden Nash), the musical version of Elmer Rice's *Street Scene* (1947), and *Lost in the Stars* (1949; libretto by Maxwell Anderson). Weill's folk opera *Down in the Valley* (1948) was much performed, and two years after his death *Dreigroschenoper* was adapted with new lyrics by Marc Blitzstein under the title *Threepenny* Opera and produced at Brandeis University (Massachusetts), the first of many successful performances off Broadway and on tour. Its song "Mack the Knife" and "September Song" from *Knickerbocker Holiday* both became popular hits.

RECORDINGS: *Berlin* Requiem; Concerto for violin and winds; *Happy End; Mahagonny;* Quodlibet for orchestra; *Seven Deadly Sins* for soprano, men's chorus, and orchestra; Symphonies (2); *Threepenny* Opera.

Weinberger, Jaromir (January 8, 1896–August 8, 1967) A student of Max Reger, the Czech composer Jaromir Weinberger established his reputation with the folk opera *Schwanda the Bagpiper* (1927). In 1922 he taught at the Ithaca (New York) Conservatory and then returned to Czechoslovakia, living mostly in Prague. He moved to London in 1937 and finally to St. Petersburg, Florida, in 1939. Weinberger wrote four other operas (one based on Bret Harte's story, *The Outcasts of Poker Flat,* 1932), orchestral works (Variations on "The Chestnut Tree," 1938; *Lincoln* Symphony, 1941), Five Songs from *Des Knaben Wunderhorn* (1962), piano music, and sacred music for voice and organ and for chorus and orchestra. The orchestral Polka and Fugue from *Schwanda* have become popular favorites.

RECORDINGS: Polka and Fugue *(Schwanda).*

Weingartner, (Paul) Felix (June 2, 1863–May 7, 1942) One of the giants of his day, the Austrian conductor Felix Weingartner was educated at the Leipzig Conservatory, and he studied piano with Liszt at Weimar. Though associated primarily with Vienna, he served appointments in various European cities and as guest conductor with most of the major orchestras on both sides of the Atlantic. He spent many years conducting opera, but he is most remembered as a great symphonic conductor and especially as an interpreter of Beethoven and Wagner. Weingartner was one of the first of the Romantic conductors to return to a classic approach, and he was known for his taste and generally faithful dedication to

Felix Weingartner
Bild-Archiv der Oesterreichischen Nationalbibliothek, Wien

the score. He wanted to be thought of as a composer and produced abundant works—all of them promptly forgotten. His writings on musical subjects were also profuse.

Weisgall, Hugo (b. October 13, 1912) Concerned with musical theater, the Czech-born U.S. composer Hugo Weisgall studied at the Curtis Institute, Peabody Conservatory, and privately with Roger Sessions. He was head of the music faculty at the Jewish Theological Seminary (1952–62) in New York City and on the faculty of the Juilliard School (1957–69) and Queens College (from 1960).

His music joins the chromaticism of the second Viennese school with neoclassical clarity; it is sometimes serial with intricate orchestration. Vocal lines are governed by natural declamation without *Sprechstimme* or pointillism. Leitmotivs are recognizable, and rhythms are defined and reiterated with echoes of Berg, Schoenberg, and Hindemith. Weisgall's major works include three ballets, seven operas (*The Tenor*, 1952, after Frank Wedekind; *The Stronger*, 1952, after August Strindberg; *Six Characters in Search of an Author*, 1959, after Luigi Pirandello; *Purgatory*, 1961, William Butler Yeats; *Athalia*, 1964, after Jean Racine; *Nine Rivers from Jordan*, 1968, after Denis Johnston; and *The Hundred Nights*, 1976, with libretto by John Hollander on a Nō play by Mishima Yukio); cantatas (*A Garden Eastward*, 1952; *Song of Celebration*, 1976); and song cycles (*Fancies and Inventions*, 1970, after Robert Herrick; *Translations*, 1972; *End of Summer*, 1974).

RECORDINGS: *End of Summer; Fancies and Inventions; The Stronger.*

Weissenberg, Alexis (b. 1929) A student of Olga Samaroff at the Juilliard School in New York City (1946), the Bulgarian pianist Alexis Weissenberg won the Leventritt Award (1946). The Weissenberg repertoire ranges from Bach to Prokofiev.

Wellesz, Egon (Joseph) (October 21, 1885–November 9, 1974) Educated at the University of Vienna (with Guido Adler) and the New Vienna Conservatory, the Austrian musicologist Egon Wellesz also studied with Schoenberg. He taught music history at the University of Vienna from 1913 to 1938 and the following year joined the faculty at Oxford University. A specialist in Byzantine music and opera and Western plainchant, his principal writings in English include *Eastern Elements in Western Chant* (1947) and *A History of Byzantine Music and Hymnography* (1949; 4th ed., 1971). He edited the first volume (1957) of the *New Oxford History of Music*, two volumes of *Studies in Eastern Chant* (1966, 1970), and an important study on Schoenberg (1921; English translation, 1925). He has written six operas, including *Die Bakchantinnen* (1931; after Euripides) and *Incognita* (1951; after William Congreve); sev-

eral ballets (*Das Wunder der Diana*, 1924; *Achilles auf Skyros*, 1927); nine symphonies (1945–71), concertos, nine quartets (1912–66), a Magnificat (1967), songs, and masses. He was created a commander in the Order of the British Empire in 1957.

RECORDINGS: Cello Sonata; Octet for winds and strings.

Well-Tempered Clavier: *see* BACH, JOHANN SEBASTIAN (Köthen); BAROQUE ERA (Handel and Bach); CLASSICAL PERIOD (instrumental music, 1750–1800); COUNTERPOINT (Baroque era); FUGUE (Bach); HARMONY (temperament and just intonation).

Werther: *see* MASSENET.

Wesley, Samuel (February 24, 1766–October 11, 1837) An English composer and organist who helped introduce the music of Bach in England, Samuel Wesley was the son of Charles Wesley, the hymn writer, and a nephew of the religious reformer John Wesley. Like his brother Charles (1757–1834) he showed musical gifts in his infancy and at the age of six began to write an oratorio, *Ruth*. Though he suffered from 1787 onward from an injury to his skull, he became one of the finest organists and extemporizers of his time. With Karl Friedrich Horn he published an English edition (1813) of Bach's *Well-Tempered Clavier*. A man of wide culture, he won renown as a conductor and lecturer. His many compositions include symphonies, concertos, services, anthems, and motets, of which *Exultate Deo* and the eight-part *In exitu Israel* are outstanding. His son Samuel Sebastian Wesley (1810–76) was also a composer and organist of prominence.

white noise Sound produced by all audible sound-wave frequencies sounding together. It is analogous to white light, which contains all the frequencies of the light spectrum. The sound of cymbals and snare drums is largely white noise. When it is produced by a synthesizer, white noise can be filtered to obtain combinations of frequencies not obtainable from traditional musical instruments; or the white noise itself may be used as an element of music.

White noise is aperiodic sound (that is, its wave pattern is not uniform); the different frequencies that compose it are of random amplitude and occur at random intervals.

Widor, Charles-Marie (-Jean-Albert) (February 24, 1844–March 12, 1937) The French organist, teacher, and composer Charles-Marie Widor was a pupil of his father, organist of Saint-François in Lyon, and later of Nicolas Jacques Lemmens (organ) and François-Joseph Fétis (composition) in Brussels. He succeeded his father in Lyon in 1860, was organist of Saint-Sulpice in Paris (1870–1934), succeeded Franck (1890) as professor of organ at the Paris Conservatoire, and Théodore Dubois as professor of composition (1896–1905). He taught a whole generation of organists, including Charles Tournemire, Louis Vierne, Marcel Dupré, and Albert Schweitzer. With Schweitzer he edited the first five volumes of a definitive edition of Bach's organ works. As a composer he wrote in all forms but is remembered for his organ works, especially his 10 Symphonies that perhaps should be called suites. Various movements have become standard repertoire but especially the Toccata from the Fifth Symphony.

RECORDINGS: *Conte d'avril:* Romance for flute; Introduction and Rondo for clarinet; Organ Symphonies (No. 5 complete; movements from No. 6).

Wieniawski, Henryk (July 10, 1835–March 31, 1880) One of the finest violin virtuosos of his day, the Polish-born Henryk Wieniawski entered the Paris Conservatoire at the age of 8 and studied with Lambert Joseph Massart, graduating with first prize in violin at the unprecedented age of 11. He toured Europe with his brother Joseph, a pianist. In 1860 he became soloist at the court of the Tsar of Russia and from 1862 to 1869 taught at the St. Petersburg Conservatory. In 1872 he toured the United States with Anton Rubinstein, and in 1877 he was on the faculty of the Brussels Conservatory. He was equally distinguished as a soloist and a chamber musician. He composed two concertos, études, and various pieces for violin; still often played as encores are his *Souvenir de Moscou* and *Légende.*

RECORDINGS: Polonaises (2); Scherzo-Tarantelle; Violin Concertos (2).

Wilbye, John (baptized March 7, 1574–November? 1638) One of the finest English madrigalists of his time, John Wilbye was the son of a successful farmer and landowner of Diss, Norfolk. His musical abilities early attracted the notice of the local gentry; when one of them married Sir Thomas Kytson of nearby Hengrave Hall, Bury St. Edmunds, Wilbye became (*c.* 1595) resident musician there. The Kytsons treated him handsomely, leasing him a prosperous sheep farm in 1613. In time he came to own lands in Diss, Bury, and elsewhere. When the household broke up at the death of Sir Thomas' widow in 1628, Wilbye was employed by Kytsons' younger daughter in Colchester.

Wilbye's fame rests on 66 madrigals, all except two published in his volumes of 1598 and 1609. Very little of his instrumental music survives, and that is fragmentary; there are only two unimportant sacred works. The madrigals include none of the dancelike balletts for which Thomas Weelkes was famous, though some are light-textured and others recall the solo air of the lutenists. Wilbye's real achievement lies in the grave music of his serious madrigals—a style familiar from Luca Marenzio and Italian music generally but then largely unpracticed in England. The new poetry of the Italianizing Sir Philip Sidney and Edmund Spenser, which flourished from 1580 to 1600, found in Wilbye's settings its perfect musical equivalent. He was far more careful of literary excellence in choosing texts for his music than most of his fellow madrigalists and must often have met Sidney, who was a frequent visitor to Hengrave Hall. He set to music many translations of Italian verse previously used by Marenzio. Wilbye was a master of rhythm, and his alert ear for prosody fills his music with passages where the verbal accent is counterpointed against the musical meter. Like Weelkes he exploited musical form, experimenting with sequence, recurring refrains, and thematic development in such works as "Adieu, sweet Amaryllis" and the more complex "Draw on, sweet night." The latter, his masterpiece, and the well-known "Flora gave me fairest flowers" and "Sweet honey-sucking bees" display his skill in vocal orchestration; all voices are not kept in constant play, but for much of the time he writes for ever-changing smaller groups within the ensemble.

BIBLIOGRAPHY: Edmund H. Fellowes, *The English Madrigal Composers,* 2nd ed. (1948).

RECORDINGS: Madrigals.

Wilhelmj, August (Daniel Ferdinand Victor) (September 21, 1845–January 22, 1908) The German violinist August Wilhelmj studied with Ferdinand David in Leipzig on the recommendation of Liszt. His debut in London (1866), arranged through the influence of soprano Jenny Lind, presaged the ovations he always received from English audiences. In 1876 he was concertmaster at Bayreuth, where he participated in the premiere of Wagner's *Der Ring des Nibelungen.* He helped establish a school for violin playing (1882) at Wiesbaden and in 1894 became professor at the Guildhall School of Music in London. His world tours embraced Europe, the Americas, and Asia. Known for his transcriptions of Wagner's music and his cadenzas for the Beethoven Violin Concerto, he made the original arrangement for violin of the Air from the Third Suite by Bach. With James Brown he wrote a violin method (first part published in 1903), and he was interested in the craft of violin making.

Willaert, Adriaan (*c.* 1490–December 8, 1562) The Flemish composer Adriaan Willaert was an important figure in the development of the Italian madrigal and established Venice as one of the most influential musical centers of the 16th century. He began to study law at the University of Paris but abandoned this in favor of music, becoming a pupil of Jean Mouton. He later traveled to Italy. He was employed (1522–25) at the court of the Este family at Ferrara and served (1525–27) Ippolito (II) d'Este, Archbishop of Milan. In 1527 he was elected music director of St. Mark's, Venice, where he created a school that was to attract musicians from all over Europe.

Willaert's early chansons reflect the influence of Mouton; his later chansons are richer and more Italianate. His madrigals show a gradual synthesis of Franco-Netherland polyphony, of which he was a master, and Italian

emphasis on harmonic color. As a composer of sacred music Willaert is primarily known for his motets. Probably inspired by the two opposing choir lofts at St. Mark's, he developed a style of polyphony in which two four-part choirs are heard alternately but occasionally combine in an eight-part section. This was to lead directly to the polychoral writing that became a characteristic feature of Venetian music in the latter half of the 16th century. Willaert's many published works include five masses (1536); three collections of motets (1539–61); *Canzone villanesche* (1545); two sets of madrigals (1546, 1563); and a collection of psalms (1555).

RECORDING: Motets.

Willcocks, David (Valentine) (b. December 30, 1919) The choral conductor and organist David Willcocks studied at the Royal School of Church Music in his native England and then at Cambridge University. From 1947 to 1950 he was organist at Salisbury Cathedral and conductor of the Salisbury Musical Society. For the next seven years he was organist at Worcester Cathedral and conducted the City of Birmingham Choir and the Worcester Three Choirs Festival. He was director of music at King's College, Cambridge (1957–73), during which time he made numerous recordings with the King's College choir in works ranging from Palestrina to Britten. In 1974 he became director of the Royal College of Music. Since 1960 he has directed the London Bach Choir, with whom he recorded music of Britten and Vaughan Williams. He has been coeditor of several volumes of anthems and since 1960 has been general editor for Oxford church music.

William Tell: *see* GUILLAUME TELL.

Williams, John (b. April 24, 1941) A prodigy virtuoso on the guitar, the Australian-born John Williams studied at the Royal College of Music in London and later with Andrés Segovia. He has concertized in Europe, North America, and Japan and has recorded music ranging from the Baroque to Spanish moderns, including music for two guitars with Julian Bream.

Winterreise: *see* SCHUBERT (final years).

Wolf, Hugo (Philipp Jakob) (March 13, 1860–February 22, 1903)   The Austrian composer who brought the 19th-century German lied to its highest point of development, Hugo Wolf began in 1875 to study at the Vienna Conservatory, where his teachers were Robert Fuchs (harmony) and Franz Krenn (composition). Wolf had a rebellious temperament and was expelled in 1877 following his outspoken criticism of his masters. In 1875 he had met Wagner, from whom he had received encouragement, and he was also supported by well-known amateurs in Vienna, among them Freud's collaborator Josef Breuer. Wolf's literary tastes were distinguished, and among his early songs are settings of Goethe, Lenau, Heine, and Eichendorff. In 1883 he began his symphonic poem *Penthesilea,* based on the tragedy by Heinrich von Kleist; and in the same year he became music critic of the *Wiener Salonblatt.* His weekly reviews provide a valuable insight into the contemporary Viennese musical world. From 1888 onward a vein of abundant inspiration enabled him to compose a vast number of songs on poems of Goethe, Mörike, and others. The *Spanisches Liederbuch,* on poems of Paul Heyse and Emanuel Geibel, appeared in 1891, followed by the *Italienisches Liederbuch* (1892, 1896). Other song cycles were on poems of Ibsen and Michelangelo. In 1895 he wrote the opera *Der Corregidor,* based on a story of Pedro de Alarcón, but it was a failure when it was produced at Mannheim the following year. A revised version was produced at Strasbourg in 1898. His second opera, *Manuel Venegas,* also after Alarcón, remained unfinished.

Wolf's reputation as a song composer resulted in the formation in his lifetime of Wolf societies in Berlin and Vienna. Yet the meager income he derived from his work compelled him to rely on the generosity of friends. He was stricken with severe mental disorders, and in 1897—ostensibly following a rebuke from Mahler but actually from growing signs of insanity and general paresis—he was confined to a mental home. He was temporarily discharged in 1898 but later attempted suicide, and in October 1898 he requested to be placed in an asylum in Vienna, where he remained until his death.

Wolf wrote about 300 songs, many of which were published posthumously. Belonging to the finest tradition of the German lied, they are unique in their poetic insight and in the richness of their evocative accompaniments. His instrumental works include the *Italienische Serenade* for orchestra (1892; a transcription of the Serenade for quartet of 1887). His collected writings, *Hugo Wolfs Musikalische Kritiken,* appeared in 1911.

BIBLIOGRAPHY: Ernest Newman, *Hugo Wolf* (1907); Frank Walker, *Hugo Wolf* (1951); Eric Sams, *The Songs of Hugo Wolf* (1961); Henry Pleasants, ed., *The Music Criticism of Hugo Wolf* (1977).

RECORDINGS: *Italienisches Liederbuch; Italienische* Serenade; *Mörike* Lieder; Quartet in d minor; *Spanisches Liederbuch* (selections); miscellaneous songs.

Wolf-Ferrari, Ermanno (January 12, 1876–January 21, 1948)   An Italian composer of operas who followed both the comic and the realistic traditions, Ermanno Wolf-Ferrari was born at Venice of a German father and an Italian mother. He studied music in Munich but later returned to Venice, where he was director of the Liceo Benedetto Marcello from 1902. Both his career and his musical style reflect his dual nationality. He wrote Italian operas, of which five are based on the comedies of Goldoni, but his humor was Germanic rather than Italian, and most of them were produced in Germany. His most successful comic operas, *I quattro rusteghi* (Munich, 1906; later produced in English as *The School for Fathers*) and *Il segreto di Susanna* (Munich, 1909), presented 18th-century styles orchestrated in the manner of the 20th century. Comic points in these operas are delicately underlined. In his tragic operas, *I gioielli della Madonna* (Berlin, 1911) and *Sly* (Milan, 1927; based on the opening scenes of *The Taming of the Shrew*), he was influenced by the realistic style of Mascagni. He also composed chamber, instrumental, and orchestral works and a violin concerto.

RECORDINGS: *Idillio-concertino* for oboe, two horns, and strings; *Il segreto di Susanna.*

Wölffl, Josef, also spelled Woelfl and other variants (December 24, 1773–May 21, 1812) A rival of Beethoven as a pianist, the Austrian Josef Wölffl was also known as a composer, though his works seem trivial today. A pupil of Leopold Mozart and of Michael Haydn, he was considered to be a bravura pianist of some elegance and an exacting teacher.

Wolkenstein, Oswald von (*c.* 1377–August 2, 1445)   Leading the colorful and lawless life typical of knights of the time, the Austrian minnesinger Oswald von Wolkenstein traveled throughout Europe and from 1415 was in the service of King Sigismund of Germany. Much of his poetry was written in praise of Margaret, Queen of Aragon. The music to which he set these poems were actual songs rather than the recitative forms of his predecessors. He was concerned with mensural notation, and some of the songs show conscious two- and three-part counterpoint.
RECORDING: Songs.

Wolpe, Stefan (August 25, 1902–April 4, 1972)   A pupil of Busoni, Webern, and Hermann Scherchen and influenced by Paul Klee and the Bauhaus school of artists, the German-born, U.S.-naturalized composer Stefan Wolpe wrote music in many forms and styles, from tonal to atonal. He wrote theater music for Bertolt Brecht in the 1920s and taught at the Palestine Conservatory from 1934 to 1938. Arriving in the United States in that year, he became a prominent composition teacher, holding several posts that included the Settlement Music School (Philadelphia; 1939–42), the Philadelphia Academy of Music (1949–52), Black Mountain College (North Carolina; 1952–56), C. W. Post College (of Long Island University; 1957–68), and Mannes College of Music in New York City (from 1968). His music was always contrapuntal and asymmetrical with many contrasts, such as sound blocks against linear motion and short notes against sustained passages. Early works included an opera (*Zeus and Elida,* 1929), cantatas (*On the Education of Man,* 1930; *Israel and His Land,* 1939), the ballet *The Man from Midian* (1942), and chamber music. His mature period began with *Enactments* (1950–53)

for three pianos and includes chamber music for diverse instruments (Piece for piano and 16 players, 1961; Piece in two parts for six players, 1962; Piece for two instrumental units, 1962; Quartet in two parts, 1969; Piece for trumpet and seven instruments, 1971). He wrote a symphony (1956; revised 1964) and a number of compositional exercises.
RECORDINGS: Chamber Piece No. 1; *Form* for piano; Piece for two instrumental units; Piece in two parts for flute; Piece in two parts for six players; Quartet for tenor saxophone, trumpet, piano, and percussion; Quartet in two parts; Solo Pieces for trumpet; Trio in two parts for flute, cello, and piano.

Wood, Henry J(oseph) (March 3, 1869–August 19, 1944)   Paramount in popularizing classical orchestral music in his native England, conductor Henry J. Wood studied at the Royal Academy of Music in London. He toured as an opera conductor with the Arthur Rousbey Company in 1889, and in 1894 he helped establish a series of Wagner concerts in London. The following year he organized a nightly season of Promenade Concerts that became a major part of English musical life. These concerts were a forum for 18th- and 19th-century orchestral music and for introducing works by contemporary composers (Debussy, Schoenberg, Richard Strauss). After 1927 the concerts were managed by the BBC. Wood composed songs and published arrangements of music of Bach, Handel, and Purcell. He conducted numerous English music festivals and established the Nottingham City Orchestra in 1899. For the 1925–26 season he was guest conductor of the Los Angeles Philharmonic and after 1923 taught at the Royal Academy. He premiered Vaughan Williams' *Serenade to Music* (1938), which was written as a tribute to him, and recorded it 10 days after the premiere. His books include *The Gentle Art of Singing,* four volumes (1927–28), *My Life of Music* (1938), and *About Conducting* (1945). He was knighted in 1911.

wood block   A percussion instrument made from a hollow brick-shaped block of wood with slits in the side and played with a drumstick. It may have developed from the Cuban *cajita china* (Spanish for "small Chinese box"). It is used in Western rhythm bands and produces a dry, hollow sound; it is also known as a Chinese block, or Korean temple block.

woodwind instruments Wind instruments, classified as aerophones, in which tone is generated by a column of air set in motion by a vibrating reed or by air blown on the sharp edge of an aperture. The name comes from the fact that originally woodwinds were made of wood, though this is no longer true. The standard woodwind instruments of the orchestra are: FLUTE and PICCOLO; OBOE, ENGLISH HORN, BASSOON, and contrabassoon; CLARINET and bass clarinet. Occasional use is also made of the SAXOPHONE, BASSET HORN, HECKELPHONE, and bass flute. *See also* REED INSTRUMENTS.

BIBLIOGRAPHY: Roy Houser, *Catalogue of Chamber Music for Woodwinds,* rev. ed. (1960; reprint, 1973); Anthony Baines, *Woodwind Instruments and Their History,* rev. ed. (1963).

Work, John Wesley, Jr. (June 15, 1901–May 18, 1967)   The son of a Fisk University (Tennessee) music faculty member, the U.S. composer John Wesley Work, Jr., was educated at Fisk and later at Columbia and Yale Universities and the Juilliard School. He returned to Fisk in 1927 to direct the men's chorus and remained as a professor, conductor of the Fisk Jubilee Singers (1948–57), and department chairman until his retirement in 1965. In addition to chamber music and songs, he composed a cantata, *The Singers* (1946); *Yenvalou* (1955), a suite for strings; *Picture of the South* for orchestra; and the well-known "Go Tell It on the Mountain."

Wozzeck: *see* ATONALITY; BERG; LIBRETTO (modern status); MODERN PERIOD (disintegration of tonality); OPERA (the 20th century).

Wright, Harold (b. December 4, 1927)   A graduate of the Curtis Institute, the U.S. clarinetist Harold Wright was associated with the Marlboro Festival (1958–76) and the Casals festivals in Prades and Puerto Rico. He has taught at Boston University since 1973 and at the Berkshire Music Center since 1976. Wright played with the National Symphony

in Washington, D.C., and the Houston and Dallas Symphonies before becoming principal clarinetist of the Boston Symphony in 1970. He has performed as guest artist with the Galimir, Guarneri, Budapest, and Juilliard quartets and has recorded the Mozart Clarinet quintet and Copland's Sextet for clarinet, piano, and string quartet.

Wuorinen, Charles (b. June 9, 1938)   Active in the production and presentation of new music, the U.S. pianist, composer, and teacher Charles Wuorinen studied with Vladimir Ussachevsky, Jack Beeson, and Otto Luening. A graduate of Columbia University, he joined the faculty there in 1964, remaining until he began teaching in 1972 at the Manhattan School of Music. In 1962 he and flutist Harvey Sollberger founded the Group for Contemporary Music at Columbia, which was the prototype for many subsequent university-affiliated contemporary music ensembles. His music exhibits great complexity and is primarily for solo instruments or small ensembles. His idiom to 1960 was primarily an extension of that of Schoenberg and Stravinsky with nondiatonic harmony and symmetrical rhythms (Three Symphonies). A further attempt to integrate pitch and rhythm occurred in works from 1961 to 1963 (*Evolutio transcripta* and Chamber Concerto for cello and 10 players). After 1963 he used the 12-tone system, and his models were Milton Babbitt, Stefan Wolpe, and Elliott Carter. Representative works include Chamber Concerto for flute and 10 players (1964), Piano Concerto (1966), *Making Ends Meet* (1966) for piano four hands, *Ringing Changes* (1970) for percussion ensemble, and Variations for bassoon, harp, and timpani (1972). *Time's Encomium* (1969) was the first all-electronic work to receive a Pulitzer Prize (1970).

RECORDINGS: Chamber Concerto for cello and 10 players; Chamber Concerto for flute and 10 players; Composition for oboe and piano; *Janissary Music* for one percussion; *Making Ends Meet;* Piano Concerto; Piano Sonata; *Ringing Changes;* String Trio; *Time's Encomium;* Variations for bassoon, harp, and timpani.

Wyner, Yehudi (b. June 1, 1929)   Composer,

pianist, conductor, and educator, the U.S. musician Yehudi Wyner studied at the Juilliard School and at Harvard and Yale Universities. He has been on the composition faculty of the latter since 1964. He was music director of the Turnau Opera Company in Woodstock, New York (1962–64), and since 1968 music director of the New Haven (Connecticut) Opera Society and pianist for the Bach Aria Group. His composition teachers include Walter Piston, Randall Thompson, and Hindemith, and much of his music is written for the synagogue, based on Jewish chant traditions (*Passover Offering,* 1959, for flute, clarinet, trombone, cello; *Friday Evening Service,* 1963, for cantor, organ, chorus; *Liturgy for the High Holidays,* 1970). His harmonic language is chromatic and improvisatory but always tonal. His piano works show the influence of jazz (Partita, 1952), as does *Intermedio* (1977), a textless three-movement work for soprano and strings. Chamber works include Serenade (1958) for seven instruments and *De novo* (1971) for cello and small ensemble.

RECORDINGS: *Intermedio;* Three Short Fantasies for piano.

X

Xenakis, Iannis (b. May 29, 1922)   The Romanian-born Greek composer, architect, and mathematician Iannis Xenakis is best known as the originator of STOCHASTIC MUSIC, music composed with the aid of electronic computers and based on mathematical probability systems. He graduated from the Athens Institute of Technology, worked with the architect Le Corbusier for 12 years, was exiled from Greece for political activities, and at age 30 turned seriously to musical composition. After study in Paris with Honegger, Milhaud, and Messiaen, he began in 1954 his experiments in stochastic music with the composition *Métastasis.* His article "La Crise de la musique sérielle" (1955; "The Crisis of Serial Music") attacked the strict determinism of neoserial composition and elucidated rigorously logical techinques wherein the performers, mostly on standard instruments, are directed by a spe-

cially devised notation to produce sounds specified by a computer programmed by the composer.

His work *Achorripsis* (1958) for 21 instruments led Xenakis to formulate his minimal rules of composition. These rules were expanded in the program for *ST/10-1,080262;* the symbols of the title indicate that this is a stochastic work, his first for 10 instruments, computed on February 8, 1962. Several other compositions, including *ST/4-1,080262* for string quartet, *Atrées (Hommage à Blaise Pascal)* for 10 instruments, and *Morisma-Amorisma* for four instruments, were based on the same program; Xenakis' goal was that each program should engender a family of related compositions. For this series of works he used an IBM 7090 computer to control note sequence, instrumentation, pitch, duration, and dynamics. The resulting sounds, relying on massed sonorities and glissandos, influenced Krzysztof Penderecki and Witold Lutoslawski.

Xenakis has written few works for solo instruments, but his association with the Paris Instrumental Ensemble for Contemporary Music has led to frequent performances and recordings for chamber ensemble. Two works, *Terrêtektorh* (1966) and *Nomos gamma* (1969), are for orchestra that is scattered among the audience. He established the School of Mathematical and Automatic Music in 1966.

Xenakis' *Polla ta dhina* for children's chorus and orchestra was commissioned in 1962 by the Stuttgart Festival for Light Music and is dedicated to Hermann Scherchen, with whom Xenakis had studied. *Akrata* (1966) for 16 wind instruments, dedicated to the memory of Serge Koussevitzky and his wife, was commissioned by the Library of Congress. *Hibiki-Hana-Ma* (1970) is for 12 tapes played over 800 loudspeakers.

A collection of his writings was published as *Formalized Music; Thought and Method in Composition* (1971).

RECORDINGS: *Achorripsis; Akrata; Bohor I; Concret P-H II; Diamorphoses II; Eonta* for piano and brass; *Herma; Métastasis* for orchestra; *Orient-Occident III; Pithoprakta* for strings.

xylophone   A percussion instrument consisting of a series of tuned wooden plates graded in size and struck with padded hammers or mallets held in the player's hands. The instrument originated in Indonesia, and in the more primitive forms the plates were sometimes made from sections of bamboo. In these forms the plates were placed over a resonating chamber, such as a pit in the ground, or across the legs of a seated player.

The oldest forms of the xylophone are those in the Malayan Peninsula and in Madagascar. The instrument was found in Java between the 8th and 14th century and later was widely played in Africa. It became known toward the end of the 18th century in China, introduced there from Burma.

The xylophone was not known before the 16th century in Europe and may be seen in the series of woodcuts, *Dance of Death* (1538), by Hans Holbein the Younger. Later it was introduced in Flanders, Poland, and southern Russia. At the beginning of the 19th century it became known in Europe as a solo instrument. A Polish virtuoso, Michal Jozef Guzikov (1806–37), toured Europe playing pieces of his own and arrangements of well-known works, among them Paganini's *La Campanella*. Later the instrument was used in café orchestras, and in 1874 Saint-Saëns introduced it into the symphony orchestra in his *Danse macabre*. In the 20th century it has been effectively used in orchestral works by Mahler, Debussy, Stravinsky, and others; it also has enjoyed a vogue in popular music, where emphasis is placed on its agile character. It is at the same time widely used in the indigenous music of the Far East, where it plays a prominent part in the gamelan.

An improvement in the tone of the xylophone, introduced by Hermann E. Winterhoff in 1927, resulted from a hollow groove cut along the underside of each plate. A resonator was also attached to each of the plates. The 20th-century instrument has a compass of four octaves from middle C upward. A similar instrument, the MARIMBA, is pitched an octave lower with a range of three octaves. Associated instruments are the GLOCKENSPIEL, with metal plates producing a bell-like tone, and the VIBRAPHONE, a larger instrument with metal plates and resonators.

Y

Yepes, Narciso (b. November 14, 1927)   The Spanish guitarist Narciso Yepes was educated at the Valencia Conservatory and made his debut in 1947 with the Madrid Chamber Orchestra. He first performed in Paris in 1950 and studied there with Georges Enesco and Walter Gieseking. In 1952 he composed and played the music for the award-winning French film *Forbidden Games*. He tours regularly throughout the world, and his recordings range from the Baroque to Joaquín Rodrigo. He plays a 10-string guitar built for him by Ignacio Fleta in Barcelona. Yepes was made a commander of the Order of Isabella of Castile in 1961. *See* photograph at GUITAR.

Young Lord, The: *see* JUNGE LORD, THE.

Young Person's Guide to the Orchestra, The: *see* BRITTEN.

Ysaÿe, Eugène (July 16, 1858–May 12, 1931)   Considered the best interpreter in his day of French and Belgian music, the Belgian violinist Eugène Ysaÿe was also a conductor and composer. He was a pupil of Lambert Joseph Massart, Henri Vieuxtemps, and briefly of Henryk Wieniawski. In 1894, while

xylophone   *courtesy, Ludwig Industries*

a professor at the conservatory at Brussels, he conducted and managed a series of orchestral concerts to introduce new music to a wide audience. That same year he organized the Ysaÿe Quartet, to which Debussy dedicated his Quartet. From 1918 to 1922 he was conductor of the Cincinnati (Ohio) Symphony. His violin playing was notable for virtuosity and expressiveness, and he played with an intense vibrato. Saint-Saëns, d'Indy, Fauré, and Franck all wrote for him. Ysaÿe composed an opera in the Walloon dialect.

Yun, Isang (b. September 17, 1917) Educated in Korea, Japan, and Europe, where his teachers included Boris Blacher, the Korean composer Isang Yun writes in a style combining Oriental and 12-tone procedures. Since 1969, when he was released by the South Korean government on a charge of spying, he has taught at the Hochschule für Musik in Berlin, where he was formerly a student. He withdrew his compositions prior to 1969, but in that year appeared two serial works, Piano Pieces and Music for Seven Instru-Korean court music. Eastern influences in the Third Quartet (1959–60) include the use of pizzicatos and glissandos. Characteristic devices are tone clusters and lack of metrical patterns. Other important works include *Bara* (1960) for orchestra, *Colloides sonores* (1961) for strings, *Loyang* (1962) for nine instruments, *Fluctuations* (1964) for orchestra, and two two-act operas (*Geisterliebe,* 1970; and *Sim Tjong,* 1972).

RECORDING: Music for Seven Instruments.

Z

Zabaleta, Nicanor (b. January 7, 1907) Educated in Madrid and Paris, the Basque harpist Nicanor Zabaleta has expanded the repertoire for the harp through his editing of forgotten works and commissions for contemporary music, including works by Milhaud, Joaquín Rodrigo, Alberto Ginastera, and Germaine Tailleferre. He has toured Europe and the Americas. His recordings include standard concertos and Spanish and Baroque harp music.

Zacconi, Lodovico (June 11, 1555–March 23, 1627) The Italian music theorist Lodovico Zacconi was, with Domenico Pietro Cerone, the last of a distinguished line of Renaissance writers on music. He became a priest, later an Augustinian, and studied music with Andrea Gabrieli in Venice, where he was musical director for his order. He went to Vienna in 1585 at the invitation of Archduke Charles. In 1592 he published the first part of his *Prattica di musica,* dedicated to William V, Duke of Bavaria, whose service he had entered three years earlier. In 1596 he returned to Italy and in 1622 published the second part of his treatise in Venice.

Zacconi's lucidly written compendium is an authoritative and encyclopedic summary of the theory and practice of Renaissance music. His handling of theoretical matters is strikingly illuminated by the practical nature of the book. His descriptions of contemporary instruments, their construction, compass, and use and his discussion of improvised ornamentation are particularly valuable to the modern scholar and performer. Zacconi's compositions include a set of ricercari for organ and four books of canons. His autobiography (1626), in which he describes himself as a musician, painter, and poet, is in the Liceo Musicale, Bologna.

Zarlino, Gioseffo (March 22, 1517–February 14, 1590) An Italian composer and writer, Gioseffo Zarlino was the most learned and celebrated music theorist of the mid-16th century. He entered the church, taking deacon's orders in 1541. Already a prodigy of learning, he then moved to Venice to study music with Adriaan Willaert. In 1565 he became music director of St. Mark's. Few of the works he composed during his duties have survived, but he seems to have been an estimable composer, and Jan Pieterszoon Sweelinck was among his pupils. In 1583 he was offered the bishopric of Chioggia, but the Venetian Senate persuaded him to remain in Venice, and he retained his post at St. Mark's until his death.

Zarlino's first and greatest treatise, *Istitutioni harmoniche* (1558), brought him rapid fame. It gives a shrewd account of the musical thinking of the first half of the 16th century with some conventional repetition of outmoded formulas and some remarkable anticipations of the future. Zarlino adopts the Ptolemaic tetrachord and stresses the importance of the major and minor third. He continues this striking prophecy of modern thought by renumbering the modes, placing the Ionian pair first and the Aeolian last; these modes later became the major and minor scales of classical tonality. He also gives one of the two earliest accounts of double counterpoint and detailed advice on the underlay of words. *Dimostrationi harmoniche* (1571) consists of five dialogues between Willaert and four friends, who supposedly met at the master's house in 1562; the discussion amplifies much of the material of the *Istitutioni*.

In 1581 Zarlino's former pupil Vincenzo Galilei, the theorist of the Florentine camerata, violently attacked his teacher in the *Dialogo della musica antica et della moderna,* wrongly proposing the Pythagorean tetrachord and setting out the monodic doctrines of his circle. Zarlino replied with *Sopplimenti musicali* (1588), and he collected his works into a complete edition in 1589. The *Sopplimenti* reinforces and develops his previous theories. One passage prophetically suggests equal temperament (for the lute); another gives valuable descriptions of early organs. He strongly decries the recitative of the camerata, insisting that music has its own laws and should not abandon them in order to imitate the spoken word. Galilei and later Giovanni Maria Artusi continued to attack Zarlino's ideas long after his death.

BIBLIOGRAPHY: Oliver Strunk, ed., *Source Readings in Music History* (1950).

zarzuela A Spanish musical play with spoken passages, songs, choruses, and dances. It originated in the 17th century as an aristocratic entertainment (with mythological or heroic subject matter) at the royal residence of La Zarzuela near Madrid. Writers of zarzuelas included the playwrights Lope de Vega (1562–1635) and Pedro Calderón de la Barca (1600–81) and the composer Juan Hidalgo (c. 1600–85). The form declined in the late 17th and 18th centuries as Italian opera increased in popularity and the TONADILLA replaced it in a rivalry that corresponded to the parallel War of the Buffoons in Paris.

In the mid-19th century the zarzuela was revived. Witty and satirical, it dealt with characters from everyday life and included folk music, dance, and improvisation. Two definite varieties evolved: the *género chico,* a one-act comic zarzuela, and the *grande,* a serious musical play in two to four acts, similar to opera but with spoken dialogue.

BIBLIOGRAPHY: Gilbert Chase, *The Music of Spain,* rev. ed. (1959).

Zauberflöte, Die: *see* MAGIC FLUTE, THE.

Zeisler, Fanny Bloomfield: *see* BLOOMFIELD ZEISLER, FANNY.

Zeno, Apostolo: *see* LIBRETTO (emergence of historical subjects); OPERA SERIA; ORATORIO (beginnings).

zither An instrument consisting of a flat, shallow soundbox with gut or metal strings stretched across from side to side. The zither is placed across the knees of the player or on a table. The strings nearest the player run above a fretted fingerboard against which they are stopped by the left hand to provide the notes of the melody; they are plucked by a plectrum worn in a ring on the right thumb. Fingers of the right hand pluck an accompaniment on the farther strings, which remain unstopped.

In the late 18th century two principal varieties developed: the Salzburg zither with a rounded side away from the player and the Mittenwald zither with both sides rounded. Tunings vary; a common tuning for the

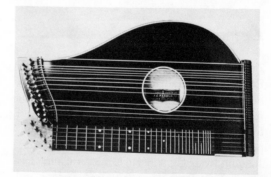

European folk zither, 19th century
courtesy, Pitt Rivers Museum, Oxford

Salzburg zither is five melody strings tuned a', d', g', g, and c and 29 accompanying strings tuned in a cycle of fifths through the 12 notes of the chromatic scale.

Older zithers, such as the alpine *Scheitholt,* have narrow rectangular soundboxes and fewer melody strings, and the three or more bass strings provide merely a drone-like accompaniment on tonic and dominant. Their age is unknown. They are found from Romania to Scandinavia and Iceland (*e.g.,* the Swedish *hummel*), later influenced by the Austrian zither and the Norwegian *langleik.* A French form that disappeared in the 19th century was the miniature *épinette des Vosges.* With some of these instruments the melody strings are stopped by pressing them against the frets with a short metal bar, a method preserved in the U.S. variety, the Appalachian, or mountain, dulcimer. Both in Europe and the United States there are zithers that are sounded with a bow.

Zither is also a generic term for stringed instruments with a soundbox lacking projecting neck or arms. This class includes—in addition to true zithers—the PSALTERY and DULCIMER as well as numerous Oriental and primitive forms.

Zukerman, Pinchas (b. July 16, 1948) The Israeli violinist Pinchas Zukerman studied with Ivan Galamian at the Juilliard School on the recommendation of Casals and Isaac Stern, who had heard him in Israel. He has toured the United States and Europe and has recorded much of the standard repertoire. He has performed chamber music with Daniel Barenboim and Jacqueline du Pré and tours with his wife, flutist Eugenia Zukerman, and guitarist Carlos Bonell. Pinchas Zukerman has been appearing with increasing frequency as a conductor in Los Angeles, New York City, Toronto, and London and has made a number of recordings in that capacity with the English Chamber Orchestra.